DISTRICT OF COLUMBIA MARRIAGE LICENSES

Register 1: 1811-1858

Wesley E. Pippenger

HERITAGE BOOKS
2007

HERITAGE BOOKS
AN IMPRINT OF HERITAGE BOOKS, INC.

Books, CDs, and more—Worldwide

For our listing of thousands of titles see our website
at
www.HeritageBooks.com

Published 2007 by
HERITAGE BOOKS, INC.
Publishing Division
65 East Main Street
Westminster, Maryland 21157-5026

Copyright © 1994 Wesley E. Pippenger

All rights reserved. No part of this book may be reproduced or transmitted in any form or by any means, electronic or mechanical, including photocopying, recording or by any information storage and retrieval system without written permission from the author, except for the inclusion of brief quotations in a review.

International Standard Book Number: 978-1-58549-354-8

DEDICATED

TO

DOROTHY S. PROVINE

INTRODUCTION

The provision for keeping a public record of marriages is not widely documented during the 1790's while the District of Columbia was being developed. Basic powers which were exercised by similar courts in Maryland were used as the basis for establishing a system in the District of Columbia. In 1812, the terms of an act to amend the charter for the City of Washington outlined that the duties of the court were to provide for recording births, deaths and marriages.

In March 1993, the earliest extant marriage records were moved from the Marriage Bureau of the District of Columbia's Superior Court to the Archives. In effect, the transfer rescued the surviving documents from further destruction by careless users. Some of the older pages are brittle, and others are now without portions which once contained information.

This volume contains over 18,850 marriage records which were kept in the District of Columbia from December 1811 through August 1858. What is presented here is all information found in "Marriage Register 1," for this period: name of groom, name of bride, and date. It was not until 1870 that the format of information found in District of Columbia marriage records was changed.

Some uncertainty exists as to how and for what purpose the extant register was created. It occasionally contains records of seemingly duplicate events but with dates which differ from several days to many months. Based on data from outside sources, we know that the register is comprised of entries of *when a marriage license was issued*. Overall, one can expect that the actual date of marriage occurred several days after the license date given here. Several notations throughout indicate particular licenses were not issued as recorded in the register. A scrap pasted to one page of the register confirms that marriage licenses were issued in the District of Columbia during this period. Just what happened to these licenses cannot be determined, as they are not known to exist today.

Beyond the register itself, the only other record of marriages which can now be found is an index. This index completely duplicates the register, and it is sorted alphabetically by the name of both the groom and bride. It appears all in the same handwriting, and contains over 1,000 pages to cross-reference nearly 18,850 marriages. Because the index was done in a legible and consistent hand, the compiler chose to begin work on this volume by typing each of the approximately 37,700 alphabetical index entries. This data was sorted chronologically for proofing against the register, then reformatted as presented here.

One might characterize the register as being a jumble of phonetic puzzles. It contains many names which are seemingly impossible or poorly spelled, e.g. Mary A. Fullalove, Mary One-days Work, or Daniel Shitpoel. To preserve the integrity of the original record, the spelling presented in this volume is as close to the original as can be interpreted by the compiler. Therefore, users are cautioned to consider and search for any and every possible spelling of a surname.

Spelling in the register was compared with marriage notices which appeared in the <u>National Intelligencer</u> newspaper that was published in Washington, D.C. from October 1800 to early 1863. Vital statistics from the Intelligencer were abstracted, chiefly by Frank Johnson Metcalf and George A. Martin, and published in the <u>National Genealogical Society Quarterly</u>, beginning in June 1938. Though a large number of marriage announcements can be found in the Intelligencer, it only reflects a small portion of the total licenses issued. Of course, the announcements typically provide a marriage date which follows the date of license given in this volume. It is indeed worthwhile to consult the Intelligencer, as it often contains valuable genealogical information. Some notations have been made in brackets "[ ]" by the compiler, and these typically involve personal titles of the bride or groom, e.g., Capt., Col., Dr., Hon., Lieut, Maj., Mrs., Sen. , or insertion of missing information.

Where damage to the register has occurred, the term [torn out] is used in this volume as it impacts a record entry. No explanation is made in the register for marriage records where the name of the groom or bride is either incomplete or missing. The lack of this type of information is noted by the term [blank]. Questionable characters are underscored in the text. The register's references to race, and notes black persons (blk) or colored persons (col'd) has been preserved here.

I am indebted to archivist Dorothy S. Provine whose generosity in providing photocopies of the register and index has literally made this work possible.

Wesley E. Pippenger
Arlington, Virginia

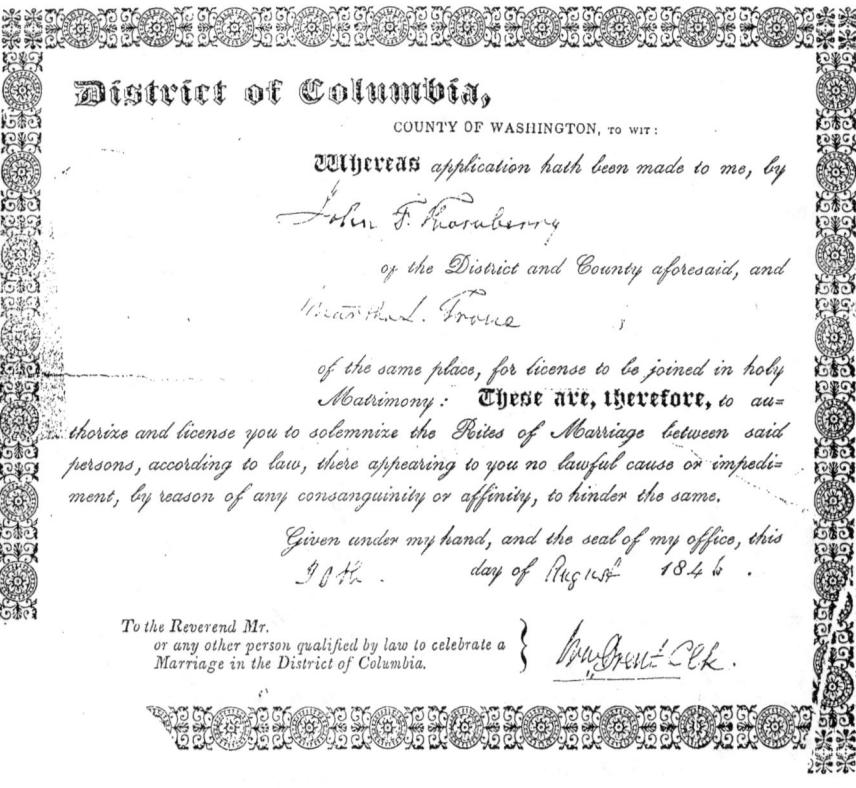

Figure 1 - Sample Marriage License

1842		
Oct. 11	De Vere Burse	Sarah McDaniels
✓ "	Capt. Wm H. Gardner US Navy	Frances E. Selden
✓ 12	Jeremiah West	Elizabeth Foskee
✓ 15	James T. Moran	Mary Fletcher
✓ "	William Henry Talburt	Margaret Ann Arnold
✓ 17	William I. Lenoir	Elizabeth T. Garner
✓ 22	Peter A. Hutchins	Catherine Jane Wood
✓ 24	Owen Murray	Mary Murray
✓ "	William Stafford	Mary ann Huster
✓ "	John Berry	Ann V. Piper
✓ 25	Addison Jackson	Jane Cole
✓ 27	Aquila F. Summers	Rebecca Cross
✓ "	Benedict Magill	Barbara Miller
✓ 29	William Smith	Mary Ann Jones
✓ "	Columbus Harrison	Eleanor Ann Ferguson
✓ 31	Owen Leddy	Malinda Crupper
✓ "	William Kay	Jane Loveless
Nov 1	Basock B. Ellman	Helen Parris
✓ "	Thomas W. O'Neal	Ann E. Carter
✓ "	William D. Beall	Martha Louisa Marbury
✓ 3	Peter Barnes	Fanny Sprigg
✓ 5	Thomas Berry	Mary Kelly
✓ 7	Hillary C. Spalding	Margaret A. Cassin
✓ 8	Hector Sears	Lucy Ann Rumage
✓ 9	Francis Morrow	Mary Hilton
"	Thomas H. Langley	Mary Ellen Simpson
✓ 10	Josias Pickrell	Sally Coombs
✓ "	James Rodier	Susanna Clements
✓ "	Thomas Challen	Amanda Pegg
✓ 11	James Lauder	Margaret Hunter
✓ "	George W. Graham	Eliza Gaston
✓ "	Edward Grew	Jane Davis (BLKS)
12	John Erring	Elizabeth Hasting
✓ 13	Francis A. Sutt	Mary A. Skellalove
"	Charles L. Telford	Susan M. Totten

Figure 2 - Sample Page From Marriage Register

DISTRICT OF COLUMBIA
MARRIAGE LICENSES
1811-1858

A

ABBEGIL, Ellen	JOHNSON, Silas	AUG 22 1857
ABBERNATHY, Thomas	AUERAN, Charlotte	JUL 25 1835
ABBETT, Thomas M.	APPLER, Mary Ann	JAN 17 1831
ABBOT, Elizth. C.	BUTLER, Ferdinand	DEC 03 1853
ABBOT, George D.	MOULDER, Mary D.	MAR 26 1833
ABBOT, Richard	WILLIAMSON, Dinah	FEB 25 1843
ABBOTT, Benjamin	WEST, Matilda	APR 25 1848
ABBOTT, Bryan	MADDEN, Bridget	JUL 22 1829
ABBOTT, Charles	DIGGES, Mary Jane	JUN 16 1841
ABBOTT, Charles	AUSTIN, Sarah Ann	FEB 18 1845
ABBOTT, Elizabeth (blk)	CHINN, John F.	OCT 02 1854
ABBOTT, James W.	BRIGGS, Jane Rebecca	JAN 15 1852
ABBOTT, John	GOULD, Laura A.	MAR 13 1855
ABBOTT, Joseph	PHILIPS, Elizabeth	APR 27 1825
ABBOTT, Mary Anna R.	PAYNE, Pearson F.	DEC 23 1854
ABBOTT, Richard H.	HARRIS, Rebecca J.	JAN 14 1852
ABBY, Henrietta	WADDEY, Benjamin F.	SEP 01 1849
ABEL, Elizabet	JOHNSON, John	MAY 22 1855
ABELL, Alexander G.	AUSTIN, Sarah J.	FEB 03 1845
ABENDSHINE, Sophia	AIGLOR, James	APR 17 1841
ABERCOMBIE, Sophia Douglass	HARRIS, Joseph Francis Wood	AUG 11 1815
ABERCROMBIE, Agnes O.	EDELIN, Joseph B.	JAN 20 1848
ABERCROMBIE, Mary H.	SAXTON, Joseph	APR 15 1850
ABERCROMBIE, Nannie B.	BERRET, Joseph H.	JUN 29 1846
ABERT, Catherine M.	HERSTEL, William	AUG 15 1853
ABERT, Charles	BACHE, Henrietta C.	APR 16 1845
ABERT, James M.	STONE, Jane L.	OCT 21 1844
ABERT, John J.	STRETCH, Ellen	JAN 24 1812
ABERT, Louisa	BYRNE, Bernard M.	NOV 17 1851
ABERT, Mary	JOHNSON, Henry D.	FEB 14 1854
ABIGAIL, Elizabeth	MORTIMER, George S.	SEP 25 1854
ABIGINN, Sally	HARTLY, John	FEB 08 1825
ABLE, Clara	HARDING, Levy	MAR 16 1832
ABLE, Hetty	DUNSEATH, Andrew	MAY 28 1817
ABLE, John B.	CLEMENTS, Susan	JAN 13 1813
ABLE, Sarah M.	HENSEY, Henry	MAR 19 1853
ACHLESS, Rachel Ann	HANY, William	MAR 20 1829
ACKER, Jacob	SCHNEIDER, Caroline	APR 10 1840
ACKER, John F.	ROAN, Mary M.B.	MAR 12 1856
ACORS, Richard	HARRIS, Sarah	JAN 18 1849
ACRES, Lucy Ann	RACE, Andrew J.	FEB 25 1853
ACTON, Ann M.	COOKSEY, George R.	JUN 02 1855
ACTON, Aquilla	MADDOX, Elizabeth	OCT 18 1825
ACTON, Christian	BEARY, John H.	JAN 01 1840
ACTON, Elizabeth	ROBEY, Thomas	JAN 26 1826
ACTON, Elizabeth Jane	GUINAND, William	JAN 05 1852
ACTON, Jane C.	KIRBY, Francis S.	JUN 07 1853
ACTON, Mary Louisa	EDELIN, Chas. C.	OCT 13 1849
ADAM, Mary Ann	MILLS, John S.	SEP 12 1826
ADAMS, Abraham	BROWN, Queen Ann (blk)	DEC 07 1853
ADAMS, Alexander	BROWN, Mary Jane	JUN 17 1856

District of Columbia Marriage Licenses, 1811-1858

ADAMS, Ann	SHUE, George E.	MAY 09 1853
ADAMS, Ann Elizabeth	HARDIN, William	DEC 20 1822
ADAMS, Ann Elizabeth	ADDISON, Edward	JAN 20 1849
ADAMS, Ann J.	CRAVER, Henry P.	DEC 27 1851
ADAMS, Ann Maria	TUNNELL, Rezin	OCT 19 1833
ADAMS, Anne H.	WHEAT, Samuel C.	JAN 27 1847
ADAMS, Austin L.	HARVEY, Harriet Eliza	DEC 25 1823
ADAMS, Austin L.	HARVEY, Harriet Eliza	DEC 25 1825
ADAMS, Barbara Ellen	KORFF, Harman George	AUG 29 1840
ADAMS, Benedict L.	GLENN, Elizth. Ann	NOV 16 1824
ADAMS, Benjamin	SIMS, Nancy (blk)	FEB 24 1827
ADAMS, Caleb	WATERS, Martha (blk)	DEC 27 1843
ADAMS, Catharine	BERRIAN, Hobart	SEP 08 1841
ADAMS, Catharine J.	CLARK, Gustavus A.	AUG 02 1837
ADAMS, Catharine R.	WINDSOR, Wm. L.	SEP 08 1853
ADAMS, Catherine	SUTER, Richard	SEP 02 1834
ADAMS, Catherine	LADEN, Benjamin	JUL 12 1838
ADAMS, Charles	LONG, Elizabeth	AUG 17 1813
ADAMS, Charles	BURROWS, Henny	JAN 26 1819
ADAMS, Chloe Ann	MAGAR, Benjamin C.	FEB 09 1839
ADAMS, Christopher	BOYD, Martha Jane	FEB 15 1856
ADAMS, Delia Ann	BARRY, David	OCT 22 1833
ADAMS, Delilah (blk)	YOUNGER, Edward C.	NOV 05 1844
ADAMS, Eliza	BOHLAYER, John C.	OCT 26 1836
ADAMS, Eliza	WHITMORE, James L.	NOV 02 1848
ADAMS, Eliza (blk)	JACKSON, George	MAY 09 1848
ADAMS, Eliza Ann	LEWIS, Thomas S.	JAN 15 1829
ADAMS, Eliza Peyton	JONES, James H.	NOV 26 1845
ADAMS, Elizabeth	HURDLE, William	MAR 21 1826
ADAMS, Elizabeth	CECIL, Washington	SEP 27 1841
ADAMS, Elizabeth (col'd)	FRANCIS, Henry	MAY 06 1828
ADAMS, Elizabeth A.	SEWALL, William	AUG 09 1821
ADAMS, Elizabeth Ann	DOVE, John	NOV 30 1838
ADAMS, Ellen E.	COX, George F.	JAN 07 1856
ADAMS, Ellen E.	COX, George F.	JUN 21 1856
ADAMS, Ellen V.	WILSON, Geo. H.	SEP 25 1850
ADAMS, Emily	BRUCE, Henry M.	JUL 21 1833
ADAMS, Fanny	LOGAN, Elijah	JUL 08 1835
ADAMS, Frances A.	WILLEY, John	JUN 30 1841
ADAMS, Frances Catherine	RYON, Alfred	AUG 18 1853
ADAMS, George	COLLARD, Jamima	FEB 13 1816
ADAMS, George	EDINBOROUGH, Sophia (blk)	APR 20 1840
ADAMS, George	VIGAL, Ann	FEB 19 1857
ADAMS, George A.	WATERS, Deborah	MAY 19 1825
ADAMS, George F.	CLEMENTS, Rosanna	MAY 17 1856
ADAMS, George P.	COLCLASER, Martha E.	FEB 03 1845
ADAMS, Henrietta A.	PADGETT, William Henry	JUL 24 1845
ADAMS, Henry	SHERTER, Betsey (blk)	NOV 07 1814
ADAMS, Herman C.	BURR, Frances	SEP 06 1850
ADAMS, Hester R.	NEWELL, Thomas M.	MAY 27 1830
ADAMS, Hugh	YOUNG, Caroline	DEC 13 1825
ADAMS, Isaac	STEPHENSON, Ann	NOV 26 1816
ADAMS, James	LONGDON, Alice	MAR 26 1833
ADAMS, Jane	SPRIGG, Thomas B.	JUN 08 1820
ADAMS, Jane (blk)	BECKETT, William	DEC 13 1847
ADAMS, John	MITCHELL, Matilda	FEB 12 1824
ADAMS, John	HELLEN, Mary Catharine	FEB 19 1828
ADAMS, John	YOUNG, Catharine	DEC 21 1829

District of Columbia Marriage Licenses, 1811-1858

ADAMS, John	DODSON, Mary	AUG 13 1834
ADAMS, John	SILENCE, Margaret Catherine	NOV 14 1835
ADAMS, John	PEAKE, Eliza Ann	DEC 21 1850
ADAMS, John Henry	DICKSON, Mary A.M.	APR 23 1829
ADAMS, John N.	JONES, Elizabeth	APR 29 1856
ADAMS, John Q.	RAGON, Louisa	MAR 13 1856
ADAMS, John Quincy	SIMMS, Mary Ann	JAN 27 1846
ADAMS, Joseph H., Jr.	DeLEON, Adelina M.	SEP 27 1852
ADAMS, Josiah	MARTIN, Catherine R.	AUG 19 1857
ADAMS, Julia Ann	HARVEY, Thomas L.	DEC 25 1849
ADAMS, Juliana A.	MOORE, Thomas	JUN 11 1821
ADAMS, Leona	BUCKINGHAM, Franklin L.	OCT 10 1849
ADAMS, Leonard	SPUNOGLE, Catherine	JUN 26 1812
ADAMS, Lucinda (blk)	BROWN, Solomon G.	JUN 05 1854
ADAMS, Malinda	BECKET, John	NOV 12 1857
ADAMS, Margaret A.	KING, Joseph W.	NOV 10 1849
ADAMS, Mariah R.	WATSON, Allison	OCT 06 1832
ADAMS, Martha	BAUMBACH, Amandus	NOV 15 1856
ADAMS, Martha (blk)	CLARK, Cornelius	APR 14 1842
ADAMS, Martha Jane	ATTICK, John	JUN 24 1853
ADAMS, Mary	WILLIAMS, William	JUL 01 1830
ADAMS, Mary	NICHOLSON, Henry	AUG 16 1839
ADAMS, Mary Ann	CARTER, James	OCT 27 1814
ADAMS, Mary Ann	LAZINBY, Elisha	DEC 09 1852
ADAMS, Mary E.	KING, Thomas A.	MAY 10 1849
ADAMS, Mary E.	OFFUT, John R.	DEC 15 1857
ADAMS, Mary Jane	JENKINS, George F.	FEB 18 1843
ADAMS, Mary Jane	CLEMANS, Josias	DEC 20 1852
ADAMS, Mary Louisa	JOHNSON, William C.	JUN 27 1853
ADAMS, Mary R.	RICHARDS, William G.	APR 16 1853
ADAMS, Milly	SMITH, Samuel	OCT 12 1812
ADAMS, Mima (blk)	BROWN, Charles	MAR 24 1853
ADAMS, Nancy	TINSEY, William	MAR 12 1816
ADAMS, Notley L.	DAVIDSON, Eliza A.H.	APR 26 1821
ADAMS, Rachel	LEWIS, Thomas S.	SEP 30 1829
ADAMS, Rebecca	CADY, Daniel H.	OCT 23 1845
ADAMS, Richard	MARTIN, Louisa Virginia	DEC 22 1852
ADAMS, Richard H.	CROWN, Mary Ann	DEC 22 1848
ADAMS, Samuel	UNCLEMAN, Elizabeth	JUL 09 1832
ADAMS, Samuel	MORRISON, Margaret	SEP 07 1842
ADAMS, Samuel	CARTEO, Catherine (blk)	SEP 03 1857
ADAMS, Sandy	BELL, Mary	JUN 10 1835
ADAMS, Sarah Ann	WARFIELD, Able	JUN 28 1838
ADAMS, Sarah E.	ROLLIN, Daniel G.	MAR 05 1849
ADAMS, Sarah E.	ARNOLD, James	JUL 09 1849
ADAMS, Sarah Shaw	PULLIN, Hanson	MAY 24 1849
ADAMS, Susan	SHELTON, Samuel	SEP 17 1835
ADAMS, Susannah	ROLLINS, Robert	DEC 04 1824
ADAMS, Sylvester	RADCLIFF, Margt. Ann	OCT 19 1853
ADAMS, Thomas J.	WRIGHT, Annie	NOV 30 1854
ADAMS, Virginia	SOTHORON, John	MAR 30 1858
ADAMS, West	TRAMMEL, Margaret	MAR 14 1816
ADAMS, West	DUHA, Mary	MAR 14 1846
ADAMS, William	SHORTER, Verlinda	OCT 08 1818
ADAMS, William	SIMMS, Margt.	DEC 22 1825
ADAMS, William	HUNT, Caroline	MAY 10 1828
ADAMS, William	DAVIS, Rachael	AUG 12 1830
ADAMS, William	SERRA, Mary Ann	APR 21 1831

District of Columbia Marriage Licenses, 1811-1858

ADAMSON, Mary Ellen	WELLS, Nathaniel	MAR 14 1850
ADAMSON, Roger	QUEST, Jane	MAR 19 1844
ADAMSON, Roger	COTTRELL, Margaret	FEB 22 1851
ADAMSON, Walter H.	ALBY, Ruth	FEB 08 1854
ADAMSON, Washington	SUMMERS, Sophia	NOV 10 1835
ADDAMS, William	MADDOX, Margaret	JUL 27 1836
ADDINGTON, Wm. X.	LLOYD, Susan A.	DEC 26 1849
ADDISON, Ann Elizabeth, Mrs.	POTTS, David	AUG 27 1858
ADDISON, Daniel Dulany	GORDON, Maria Louisa	JUL 05 1831
ADDISON, Edward	ADAMS, Ann Elizabeth	JAN 20 1849
ADDISON, Eliza R.	HESTER, James W.	JUN 12 1855
ADDISON, Elizabeth C.	BERRY, Zachariah, of Washn.	JAN 16 1854
ADDISON, Henrietta Maria	ASH, Rev. Robert	JUN 19 1830
ADDISON, Henry	CLAGETT, Martha E.	JAN 04 1821
ADDISON, John, Jr.	SMALLWOOD, Mary E.	OCT 15 1834
ADDISON, Lucy E.	SPRIGG, James C.	JUL 15 1850
ADDISON, Maria E.	ADDISON, Thomas G.	APR 15 1856
ADDISON, Maria L.	PRATT, Henry D.J.	SEP 23 1857
ADDISON, Martha E.	BEALL, Zachariah B.	JAN 09 1856
ADDISON, Mary	MURRAY, Alexander J.	DEC 15 1828
ADDISON, Mary E.	PERKINS, Edmund T.	MAY 13 1848
ADDISON, Rebecca (blk)	MITCHELL, James Henry	AUG 14 1845
ADDISON, Samuel	BIGGES, Eliza	AUG 06 1839
ADDISON, Thomas B.	ELIASON, Eliza	MAY 11 1818
ADDISON, Thomas G.	ADDISON, Maria E.	APR 15 1856
ADDWORTH, Bernard	BRANNAN, Margaret	DEC 26 1841
ADERTEN, Sarah E.	EASTON, Thomas S.	DEC 11 1832
ADGATE, Sally	COLLINS, Joseph S. [Rev.]	FEB 05 1829
ADLER, Mary Virginia	DOUGAL, William H.	JUN 02 1851
ADLER, Morris	LUTZ, Melvina	OCT 03 1827
ADLER, Morris	KURTZ, Mary C.	DEC 21 1854
ADLUM, Anna Maria	DENT, Henry H.	SEP 14 1841
ADLUM, Margaret	BARBER, Cornelius	JAN 31 1833
ADMONSON, David	HICKS, Elizabeth	JUN 26 1849
ADREAN, George W.	BRISCOE, Ruth A.	OCT 23 1844
ADREON, Susannah	BENSON, Thomas J.	NOV 30 1843
ADSIT, Clara E.	HATCH, Loranzo	AUG 19 1846
AFFLEY, John Holmes	HEATON, Catharine VanRanselor	SEP 21 1825
AGATE, Alfred T.	KENNEDY, Elizabeth Hill	SEP 09 1845
AGATE, Elizabeth H.	DuHAMEL, Wm. J.C.	APR 30 1853
AGER, James B.	DRAKE, Susan E.	DEC 29 1847
AGER, John E.	HERO__, Mary A.	JAN 21 1847
AGER, John H.	BURRS, Jane E.	FEB 04 1858
AGER, Jones	FISHER, Lydia	JUL 19 1819
AGER, Laura V.	LEISHEAR, William W.	JUL 22 1857
AGER, Marcelia	KNOWLES, John Thomas	OCT 25 1843
AGER, Margaret Ann	CHILDS, Lewis H.	JUN 11 1832
AGER, Mary Ann	BALL, Issac S.	NOV 05 1839
AGER, Mary F.	BURDETT, James H.	NOV 25 1856
AGER, Sarah	FRANKLAND, George W.	DEC 09 1856
AGER, Sarah Frances	DONALDSON, James W.	AUG 18 1836
AGER, Uriah H.	CHILDS, Melvina	NOV 14 1832
AGER, Uriah H.	BLAKE, Emily	DEC 13 1842
AGETT, Mary	MAHONEY, Samuel	JUN 12 1856
AGINTON, Henry	GALITZEN, Eliza	OCT 06 1813
AGLETON, Richard	MOORE, Susan	JUL 01 1826
AGNUE, Martha	WARD, Charles	OCT 07 1827
AHEARN, Catherine	KENNEDY, Samuel J.A.	JUL 01 1857

District of Columbia Marriage Licenses, 1811-1858

AHEREN, Bartholomew	HAYS, Ellen	JUN 01 1854
AHERN, Julia	SULLIVAN, Patrick	APR 11 1853
AHMA, Frederick	KELLION, Helen Margaretta	SEP 19 1843
AHRENS, Adolph F.	TOWNLEY, Maria Virginia Antoinetta	AUG 05 1846
AHUMADA, Soledod Jeulet	MaTULET, Antonio Ma	JUL 14 1849
AIGEN, John	O'BRIEN, Catherine	JUN 17 1854
AIGLER, Barbara	LENZE, Noah	APR 01 1852
AIGLER, Christopher	KINSBY, Eva	NOV 10 1849
AIGLOR, James	ABENDSHINE, Sophia	APR 17 1841
AIKEN, Adelaid	COLEMAN, William H.	FEB 27 1855
AIKEN, Mary Ellen	CLARKE, Parker P.	DEC 09 1844
AIKEN, Mathew	WILKINSON, Mary	OCT 04 1852
AIKEN, William John	MORGAN, Eliza	JUL 28 1848
AIKIN, Jane	WILKINSON, James	MAR 10 1853
AIRHART, Julia	KEARNEY, Frederick	OCT 16 1835
AIRINGTON, John	HALL, Catharine	FEB 20 1841
AIRS, Anna (blk)	REYNOLDS, Samuel	JUN 09 1848
AIRY, Samuel	TURNER, Margaret	AUG 06 1846
AKERS, Mary Ann	MANDERS, Levin H.	JAN 16 1845
AKINS, William	BRADLEY, Julia	DEC 18 1830
ALBACH, Mary	RIEHTMÜLLER, Eknaz	OCT 13 1853
ALBAUGH, Ann V.	ALBAUGH, James A.	OCT 28 1854
ALBAUGH, James A.	ALBAUGH, Ann V.	OCT 28 1854
ALBER, William	RITTER, Catharine	OCT 23 1852
ALBERS, Henry	BROOKES, Rebecca	FEB 01 1820
ALBERT, Rudolph	SMITH, Kate	AUG 05 1856
ALBEY, Elizabeth	STEWART, William	SEP 16 1848
ALBEY, John	MAYHEW, Rebecca	JUN 15 1835
ALBINGER, Emily	REDSTRAKE, William J.	NOV 19 1849
ALBRETON, James	BURNETT, Ann	AUG 01 1818
ALBRIGHT, Frederick	McKENNEY, Mary F.	NOV 17 1857
ALBRIGHT, Leonard	HIGHLAND, Magdalina	JUN 14 1853
ALBRIGHT, Thomas J.	BEEDLE, Ann Maria	AUG 29 1857
ALBURGER, Emily	REDSTRAKE, Wm. J.	NOV 01 1849
ALBUS, Marie Anne	ROYER, Lewis August Francois	MAY 28 1839
ALBY, Henrietta	SAMUEL, William	MAR 29 1823
ALBY, Mary M.	KING, Charles	JUN 09 1829
ALBY, Ruth	ADAMSON, Walter H.	FEB 08 1854
ALCOTT, Charles W.	COCHRAN, Adelaid J.	JAN 13 1854
ALDEN, Mary L.	TUCKER, James M.	MAR 09 1858
ALDERIDGE, Alethia	HURLEY, William	FEB 01 1817
ALDRIDGE, Margaret	MURPHY, Alexander	FEB 20 1821
ALDRIDGE, Martha	ROBEY, Edgar	DEC 24 1840
ALDRIDGE, Washington	MILLER, Margaret Ann	AUG 03 1839
ALEXANDER, Amanda	BRAWNER, James L.	SEP 27 1836
ALEXANDER, Caroline	JOHNSON, Reubin C.	NOV 04 1851
ALEXANDER, Charles	BERTEAND, Mary	DEC 02 1818
ALEXANDER, Clarrissa (blk)	ROBINSON, John	NOV 12 1850
ALEXANDER, Columbus	HAY, Rebecca	JAN 21 1840
ALEXANDER, Elimira E.E.	BEALE, John S.H.H.E.	FEB 26 1829
ALEXANDER, Jane	DEFALCO, Pasquale	MAR 24 1835
ALEXANDER, John	PERRY, Emily	JAN 13 1817
ALEXANDER, John	PETTIT, Sallie E.	JAN 03 1850
ALEXANDER, John	DUNAWAY, Mary Ann	APR 18 1857
ALEXANDER, John R.	HODGKIN, Lizzie S.	JUL 01 1858
ALEXANDER, Lewis	CONNOWAY, Louisa (blk)	NOV 05 1855
ALEXANDER, Margaret	DOBSON, Alfred	JAN 27 1853
ALEXANDER, Margt. M.	NEVINS, Archibald A.	APR 04 1850

District of Columbia Marriage Licenses, 1811-1858

ALEXANDER, Maria McCoy	CARLISLE, James B.	APR 26 1834
ALEXANDER, Mary	DURHAM, Lemuel J.	JUN 23 1841
ALEXANDER, Mary	McCORMICK, Hugh	JUL 13 1842
ALEXANDER, Mary Ann	BOHRER, Abraham	JUL 01 1814
ALEXANDER, Oscar	BRAWNER, Ellen	OCT 04 1834
ALEXANDER, Rebecca	LANE, George A.	FEB 27 1852
ALEXANDER, Sandy N.	FLETCHER, Margaret	MAY 24 1838
ALEXANDER, Walter B.	POTTER, Eliza	FEB 07 1844
ALFORD, Henry	THOMAS, Ann	SEP 22 1826
ALFRED, Ann	WILLIAMS, John	JUL 10 1841
ALFRED, Elizabeth	WALKER, William	MAR 22 1843
ALGER, Francis	JONES, Mary Louisa	MAY 09 1835
ALISON, John H.	MAY, Anna	MAY 29 1854
ALKARD, A.B.	STYLES, Ann	FEB 03 1842
ALLAN, Kesiah L.	WOOD, Thomas	JUL 23 1855
ALLBUS, Elizabeth	SCHIHOLM, Frederick	JAN 30 1841
ALLDRIDGE, Darcus	VALDENIER, James	FEB 08 1812
ALLDRIDGE, Leucresa	JIRDINSTON, William	DEC 08 1819
ALLEN, Ann [Mrs.]	McGUIRE, George	MAR 02 1827
ALLEN, Ann	POPKINS, John	FEB 11 1836
ALLEN, Ann	DUCKETT, Basil	MAY 26 1848
ALLEN, Ann L.	KEYS, Andrew J.	JAN 05 1846
ALLEN, Anthony	KELLY, Vincentia	OCT 30 1856
ALLEN, Aquilla R.	JOHNSON, Mary Ann	JAN 01 1848
ALLEN, Benjamin	SANSBERY, Eliza	MAR 05 1849
ALLEN, Betsey	GUSTY, John	DEC 11 1817
ALLEN, Bridget	LISTON, James	FEB 05 1855
ALLEN, Caroline F.	SELECMAN, Thomas L.	SEP 02 1841
ALLEN, Catherine (blk)	GRANTAM, Peter	DEC 04 1849
ALLEN, Charity Ann	MANKINS, Thomas Edwin	JAN 21 1834
ALLEN, Charity Ann	PIERCE, Thomas	OCT 02 1854
ALLEN, Charles	BAGGETT, Mary Ellen	MAR 24 1851
ALLEN, Dennis	PAYNE, Charity	MAR 20 1817
ALLEN, Edmund M.	STONE, Harriet A.	JUN 09 1856
ALLEN, Edward S.	CAMMACK, Martha	APR 14 1851
ALLEN, Edwin O.	SLY, Eliza Jane	NOV 06 1855
ALLEN, Elijah	BERRY, Harriet	FEB 19 1828
ALLEN, Elijah	DAVIS, Anna M. (blk)	AUG 17 1854
ALLEN, Elizabeth	SPINKS, William	NOV 23 1826
ALLEN, Elizabeth	DELANY, John	OCT 04 1827
ALLEN, Ely	McKENSEY, Sarah	JAN 06 1814
ALLEN, Emily	BARRON, Daniel	FEB 12 1850
ALLEN, Emly Ann	ELLIS, George Thomas	APR 01 1837
ALLEN, Francis	BARKER, Anna	MAY 03 1853
ALLEN, George	SMITH, Letha	JAN 04 1858
ALLEN, George T.	BROWN, Mary	OCT 10 1850
ALLEN, George William	JACOBS, Mary M.R.B.	MAR 06 1847
ALLEN, Hannah	HAMLIN, William	MAY 15 1812
ALLEN, Harriet	BURRISS, Hezekiah	FEB 28 1843
ALLEN, Henry J.	OWNER, Hannah	OCT 28 1813
ALLEN, Hiram	HENSON, Mary	JUL 30 1853
ALLEN, Ignatius	ATWELL, Louisa C.	OCT 12 1840
ALLEN, Isabella D.	OGDEN, John W.	JUL 13 1848
ALLEN, James	KIRBY, Rachel	SEP 03 1827
ALLEN, James	SUMMELL, Lucinda (blk)	MAY 08 1837
ALLEN, James	DINES, Catharine Ann (blk)	FEB 22 1843
ALLEN, James A.	HARDT, Juliet A.	DEC 24 1850
ALLEN, James W.	SMITH, Matilda E.	JAN 27 1848

District of Columbia Marriage Licenses, 1811-1858

ALLEN, Jane Catherine	BEACH, Ferdinand	NOV 18 1852
ALLEN, John	HARVEY, Tilley	OCT 07 1813
ALLEN, John	DEERY, Bridget [Mrs.]	JUN 10 1816
ALLEN, John	BLUNDON, Mary	DEC 31 1816
ALLEN, John	MEASLEY, Mary	OCT 04 1826
ALLEN, John	BALL, Elizabeth	NOV 02 1833
ALLEN, John	HUGHES, Eleanor A.	FEB 19 1840
ALLEN, John C.	PATTERSON, Sarah A.	JUN 23 1854
ALLEN, Joseph Enoch	ALLEN, Sarah Ellingdes	DEC 30 1844
ALLEN, Joseph H.	BLADES, Mary A.	MAY 08 1856
ALLEN, Joseph R.	DAYTON, Margaret	MAR 14 1849
ALLEN, Josephine	SUMMERS, James H.	NOV 01 1853
ALLEN, Julia	WALKER, David T.	MAR 06 1855
ALLEN, Linney	HUTCHINSON, Thomas	MAY 30 1839
ALLEN, Louisa C.	LOWE, Warren	SEP 26 1854
ALLEN, Louisa M.	WOOD, George K.	MAY 19 1857
ALLEN, Lucinda	COCKRELL, Henry W.	APR 10 1855
ALLEN, Margaretta	WALKER, Samuel T.	JAN 16 1846
ALLEN, Martha	PAYNE, Henry Fairfax	DEC 27 1855
ALLEN, Martha L.	SMITH, John	NOV 14 1855
ALLEN, Martin	WESTIRMAN, Andrew	SEP 27 1837
ALLEN, Mary	MILES, Benjamin	NOV 04 1819
ALLEN, Mary	MOOR, Joseph W.	SEP 30 1850
ALLEN, Mary	SHERWOOD, James	OCT 06 1851
ALLEN, Mary Ann	LONG, John	JUL 11 1825
ALLEN, Mary G.	CHAMBERS, London G.	APR 06 1820
ALLEN, Mary Jane	BALL, John Henry	OCT 13 1847
ALLEN, Massa	PETERS, William	MAR 04 1823
ALLEN, Matilda	HOFFMAN, John P.	JAN 27 1814
ALLEN, Mira Ann	BRIGHT, John W.	JAN 13 1853
ALLEN, Nathan	PAYNE, Susan Britania	JAN 06 1853
ALLEN, Oliver	BOWLIN, Nancy Ann	DEC 16 1829
ALLEN, Patrick	BARRON, Maria	APR 05 1858
ALLEN, Philip H.	SWEENY, Maria E.	OCT 02 1851
ALLEN, Priscilla H.	SMITH, Bernard	APR 29 1812
ALLEN, Rachael	BARRETT, James	JAN 13 1847
ALLEN, Rachel E.	PILES, Thomas E.	JUL 28 1842
ALLEN, Rebecca	BARRETT, William H.	JAN 05 1857
ALLEN, Richard	KNOX, Susan	NOV 13 1832
ALLEN, Richard	BRADLEY, Jane	NOV 06 1854
ALLEN, Robert	DOVE, Ann	FEB 09 1821
ALLEN, Robert	VanHORN, Alethia	MAR 03 1825
ALLEN, Robert	ANDERSON, Catherine M.	JUL 16 1840
ALLEN, Ruth	ROANE, Archibald	JAN 09 1851
ALLEN, Saml.	BREWER, Elizabeth	OCT 30 1828
ALLEN, Samuel E.	THOMPSON, Susannah	APR 21 1849
ALLEN, Samuel Thomas	BIGGS, Mary Ann	JAN 28 1845
ALLEN, Sarah E.	BLUNDEN, John A.	JAN 13 1842
ALLEN, Sarah Ellingdes	ALLEN, Joseph Enoch	DEC 30 1844
ALLEN, Thomas	ROBINSON, Peggy	JUN 27 1815
ALLEN, Thomas	JONES, Mary	JAN 06 1820
ALLEN, Thomas	RISEN, Louisa	NOV 07 1844
ALLEN, Thomas	KELLY, Mary M.	JUL 24 1854
ALLEN, Thomas D.	WILLIAM, Mary E.	MAY 06 1857
ALLEN, Thomas T.	PERKINS, Mary E.	NOV 18 1856
ALLEN, Timothy	NUGENT, Johanna	JUN 30 1855
ALLEN, William	BELL, Letty	OCT 26 1819
ALLEN, William	COOK, Eleanor	NOV 08 1821

District of Columbia Marriage Licenses, 1811-1858

ALLEN, William	TURNER, Letetia	APR 08 1839
ALLEN, William	PILES, Charlotte M.	FEB 24 1846
ALLEN, William	SEBASTIAN, Leanna	APR 20 1850
ALLEN, William	TUTTLE, Delia Ann	MAY 03 1852
ALLEN, William H.	SKIDMORE, Mary D.	OCT 01 1850
ALLEN, William H.	GALE, Clara A.	JUL 13 1858
ALLEN, William T.	PRITCHET, Susan	JAN 03 1828
ALLESON, Robert	CARNEY, Bridget	MAY 30 1821
ALLEY, Alethea	OWENS, James	JAN 28 1830
ALLHOUSEN, Dorothy	RITER, Peter	FEB 02 1825
ALLIN, Jemima	SHEENWOOD, Hezekiah	JUN 11 1821
ALLING, Hellen Maria	NOYES, Joseph C.	JUL 09 1838
ALLIS, Martha Ann	MERIVEN, Henry B.	NOV 29 1847
ALLISON, Almay	MIFFLETON, Henry	MAY 13 1840
ALLISON, Conry	DONALDSON, Sandford	OCT 16 1820
ALLISON, Elizabeth	POTTER, James	MAY 20 1824
ALLISON, Elizabeth	PETTIT, George	JUL 04 1836
ALLISON, Elizabeth (blk)	COAKLEY, George	JUL 16 1853
ALLISON, Elizabeth Ann [Mrs.]	LATRUITE, John P.	MAR 24 1829
ALLISON, Emeline (blk)	BARKER, Andrew	APR 19 1849
ALLISON, John	MITCHELL, Eliza	OCT 31 1832
ALLISON, John W.	HASLUP, Susan	JAN 24 1839
ALLISON, Mary	WALLS, James F.	MAY 17 1856
ALLISON, Robert	WEST, Mary	MAY 07 1836
ALLISON, Robert	CUSHLY, Mary	JUN 06 1850
ALLISON, Sarah	WESTON, Lewis	FEB 23 1832
ALLISON, Thomas	SHREAVE, Ann	DEC 28 1820
ALLISON, Virginia S.	HATTON, Benjamin	APR 17 1851
ALLOWAY, John	THOMAS, Sidney	MAY 16 1844
ALLOWAY, John	THOMAS, Sidney	JUN 15 1844
ALLRIDGE, Rebecca	BURNS, Alexander	JUN 06 1812
ALLROY, Sarah	GIBSON, Joshua	JUL 28 1831
ALLSOP, Samuel	STREET, Catharine E.	MAY 06 1852
ALLYN, Rufus B.	UPTON, Rebecca P.	OCT 17 1840
ALMIN, Daniel	O'BRIEN, Julia	NOV 06 1855
ALMOND, Barnett B.	COOPER, Ann S.	APR 07 1840
ALMY, John J.	GARDNER, Sarah A. McL.	JAN 30 1854
ALNUTT, William P.	JEWELL, Catharine	OCT 23 1839
ALOISI, Salvatore	TALBOT, Frances	JUN 10 1853
ALPHIN, Walter	WEBSTER, Susan	JUN 18 1822
ALRICK, Ann P.	FROST, John E.	AUG 01 1820
ALRICKS, Marguerite P.	JAUDON, Samuel	AUG 04 1823
ALSOC, Robert	CASH, Ann C.	MAY 27 1854
ALSOP, Samuel	HAYDEN, Mary S.	APR 09 1832
ALTDORFER, Philip Jacob	WINGLERIN, Mary Barbara	SEP 04 1852
ALTDORFER, Philip Jacob	MILLER, Margaret	APR 07 1853
ALTEMUS, Thomas	FORREST, Mary	MAR 07 1838
ALTER, Amelia	SEITZ, John	NOV 25 1846
ALTMANN, Charles	GROS, Wielhilmine	NOV 11 1854
ALTOERFER, Ludwig	MULLIKIN, Caroline	JUL 06 1849
ALTON, Elizabeth	BURCH, William	FEB 11 1812
ALTVETER, August	KRUG, Lehna	AUG 31 1857
ALVERS, Marion Virginia	BRONSON, Simon D.	JAN 05 1847
ALVEY, Christana	HANDLEY, James	MAY 08 1827
ALVEY, John	FUTTERER, Mary	JAN 02 1838
ALVEY, William	GOLDSMITH, Martha Ann	JUL 12 1844
ALWINE, Jacob	WATHEN, Catherine	OCT 06 1857
AMAN, Frederick	SCHEEP, Maria	OCT 05 1854

District of Columbia Marriage Licenses, 1811-1858

AMAN, Jos. Andrew	FLENINGER, Catharine	FEB 11 1854
AMANDA, Caroline	JORDON, John	NOV 25 1828
AMANT, Theresa	MUTH, Andrew	FEB 20 1857
AMATT, George	BEST, Susanna	JUL 31 1830
AMBER, Julia	MERCER, James	OCT 17 1844
AMBER, Louisa (blk)	BELL, Daniel	OCT 04 1852
AMBLER, F.E.	WILLIS, A. Murat	DEC 20 1847
AMBLER, John Jaquilin	BARBOUR, Elizth.	FEB 12 1828
AMBROSE, Elizabeth	HILL, William	MAY 03 1831
AMBROSE, Robert	JONES, Sally Ann	FEB 13 1821
AMBROSE, Verlinda	BUTLER, William	FEB 06 1827
AMBUSH, Calvert	CRYDE, Patsey	MAR 22 1834
AMBUSH, Edward	DOGINS, Maria	DEC 06 1854
AMBUSH, Edward	RICHARDSON, Frances (blk)	JUL 29 1858
AMBUSH, Elizabeth	SCHUREMAN, William	MAY 23 1844
AMBUSH, Enoch	HALL, Laura (blk)	AUG 20 1855
AMBUSH, Patience	CAREY, John	JUN 06 1812
AMBUSH, Patsey (blk)	SMALLWOOD, Abraham	OCT 05 1825
AMBUSH, Rebecca	LONDON, James	FEB 24 1857
AMBUSH, Sally	YOUNGER, Richard	AUG 24 1820
AMERICA, John	CARRINGTON, Jane	MAR 08 1823
AMERICA, William	GLOVER, Susannah	NOV 05 1844
AMERIGE, George	STEDMAN, Mary	NOV 20 1839
AMERY, Joseph W.	BUNNELL, Alba	OCT 11 1842
AMES, Elizabeth M.	HALL, Rev. Charles H.	SEP 09 1857
AMES, John	BOSTON, Virginia	JAN 12 1854
AMES, Sarah E.	MATLOCK, Jeremiah G.	JAN 26 1843
AMES, Thomas	HARVEY, Eleanor	JAN 14 1822
AMESWORTH, Elizabeth	DUTCH, James	MAY 07 1819
AMIS, Mary S.	PATTERSON, Fielder S.	MAR 31 1858
AMISS, Martha E.W.	COX, James Newton	DEC 22 1857
AMISS, Richard L.	HENRY, Mary C.	DEC 27 1854
AMOS, Caroline	RANDALL, Augustus	SEP 09 1836
ANCHERS, Nancy	POOLE, Jesse	OCT 09 1833
ANCHOES, Susan	FOLLIN, George	DEC 09 1839
ANCHORS, John	HESS, Harriet Ann	MAR 30 1825
ANDERS, Elizabeth	HENTON, Robert	NOV 06 1813
ANDERSON, Absolum A.	GOODALL, Harriott S.	MAY 04 1846
ANDERSON, Adna	VanWYCK, Juliet C.	OCT 15 1856
ANDERSON, Alexander	HAMILTON, Louisa	APR 03 1815
ANDERSON, Alexander	WHITTAKER, Margaret	DEC 31 1852
ANDERSON, Allen	BROWN, Laura	APR 06 1854
ANDERSON, Amanda	VIOLETT, Robert G.	AUG 23 1849
ANDERSON, Ann	WELSH, Joseph	OCT 28 1817
ANDERSON, Ann	MANN, Jesse F.	APR 30 1846
ANDERSON, Ann	KING, Charles	APR 15 1847
ANDERSON, Ann Maria	PEGG, William	JUN 04 1839
ANDERSON, Ann Maria	BOPP, Peter	DEC 06 1851
ANDERSON, Anna	KEYWORTH, Robert W.	OCT 30 1850
ANDERSON, Anthony L.	WESTERFIELD, Rebecca	MAY 27 1852
ANDERSON, Caroline	WEBSTER, Zachariah	DEC 30 1845
ANDERSON, Catherine M.	ALLEN, Robert	JUL 16 1840
ANDERSON, Charles	JENKINS, Ellen	NOV 19 1853
ANDERSON, Charles	BOND, Rachel (blk)	JAN 17 1855
ANDERSON, Charles A.	SANDISON, Eliza	DEC 24 1846
ANDERSON, Charles D.	HAZARD, Lucy A.	AUG 18 1856
ANDERSON, Charles H.	BEARDSLY, Josephine	JUL 16 1856
ANDERSON, Charlotte E.W.	BENTHALL, W.C.	JUL 12 1837

District of Columbia Marriage Licenses, 1811-1858

ANDERSON, Cinderella J.	HERSHLEY, Clement	JUN 08 1852
ANDERSON, Dorcas Ann	GRAY, Joseph B.	JAN 01 1853
ANDERSON, Easter (blk)	BOND, Levi	JUL 23 1850
ANDERSON, Elijah	SHACKLEFORD, Eliza	DEC 19 1829
ANDERSON, Eliza	WALTON, James Henry	JAN 03 1852
ANDERSON, Eliza Jane (blk)	JOHNSON, Joseph	DEC 12 1855
ANDERSON, Elizabeth	WALKER, Samuel	AUG 05 1817
ANDERSON, Elizabeth	DAY, James	JAN 05 1822
ANDERSON, Elizabeth	SMALLWOOD, Thomas	FEB 24 1836
ANDERSON, Elizabeth Ann	HAVENER, Benedict	AUG 06 1849
ANDERSON, Elizabeth Ellen	SWAIN, John	AUG 01 1847
ANDERSON, Elizah M.	MURRAY, Elizabeth A.	JAN 29 1839
ANDERSON, Ellen Jane	PRIEST, John	OCT 15 1855
ANDERSON, Ellen Ora	McDANIEL, James W.	MAR 10 1853
ANDERSON, Emma F.	DAVIS, William	OCT 20 1853
ANDERSON, Fanny	WEST, Thomas	DEC 03 1829
ANDERSON, Fanny	MORRISETT, Thomas	FEB 23 1853
ANDERSON, Frederick	GRAY, Mary	OCT 03 1837
ANDERSON, Frederick	GRYMES, Elizabeth	JUL 12 1845
ANDERSON, Garret	SAWKINS, Eliza	DEC 21 1833
ANDERSON, George	SULLIVAN, Elizabeth	MAR 05 1817
ANDERSON, George W.	HORN, Margaret L.	APR 24 1847
ANDERSON, George W.	VERMILLION, Julia Ann	SEP 20 1855
ANDERSON, Gertrude	RANKEN, John W.	MAY 31 1852
ANDERSON, Hervey	CUSHAW, Charlotte	JUN 09 1853
ANDERSON, Hezekiah	OSBOURNE, Elizth. Ellen	MAY 22 1858
ANDERSON, James	EDELEN, Rosanna B.	SEP 18 1824
ANDERSON, James	KING, Martha E.	NOV 30 1835
ANDERSON, James F.	PRIOR, Mary Jane (blk)	MAY 02 1849
ANDERSON, Jane	GRIFFIN, Dennis	OCT 27 1853
ANDERSON, Jane C.	JOHNSON, Daniel T.	AUG 17 1850
ANDERSON, Jane I.	WINGARD, Jacob B.	APR 06 1835
ANDERSON, Jefferson	PENNY, Lucinda E. (blk)	NOV 11 1841
ANDERSON, Jesse	TUCKER, Sarah	FEB 22 1827
ANDERSON, Joeanas	TIMBERLAKE, John	APR 04 1839
ANDERSON, John	TAYLOR, Julia Ann	MAY 04 1818
ANDERSON, John	MATHERS, Catharine	FEB 05 1821
ANDERSON, John	MILLS, Mary	FEB 12 1822
ANDERSON, John	THOMPSON, Ann	JUL 07 1829
ANDERSON, John	CARMON, Elsey	DEC 23 1829
ANDERSON, John S.	COSTIGAN, Martha R.	APR 20 1843
ANDERSON, John W.	COFFER, Ann Elizabeth	APR 04 1853
ANDERSON, John W.	KNIGHT, Charlotte L.	FEB 08 1858
ANDERSON, John Wm.	SPILMAN, Elizabeth	JUL 25 1835
ANDERSON, Joseph	MITCHELL, Harriot	AUG 03 1816
ANDERSON, Joseph	OLDHAM, Elizabeth	MAY 21 1825
ANDERSON, Josephine L.	EVANS, William T.	OCT 27 1853
ANDERSON, Joshua	THOMPSON, Ann Grezela	JUN 27 1853
ANDERSON, Levinia	HARVEY, James O.	DEC 12 1857
ANDERSON, Librun	WILSON, Barbary	AUG 13 1857
ANDERSON, Ligon	GRIFFITH, Susan	JUL 18 1850
ANDERSON, Louisa (blk)	PLUMMER, Richard	SEP 08 1846
ANDERSON, Luke	CLARKE, Fanny	AUG 03 1854
ANDERSON, Margaret	GUILDER, Joseph W.	DEC 10 1856
ANDERSON, Maria	TALBERT, Overton	MAY 12 1832
ANDERSON, Marshal R.	EMBRY, Sarah	JUL 17 1852
ANDERSON, Martha D.	TILSON, Rev. Jonathan	DEC 23 1851
ANDERSON, Martha R.	YOUNG, George A.	MAR 19 1853

District of Columbia Marriage Licenses, 1811-1858

ANDERSON, Mary	STARLING, Thomas	AUG 20 1833
ANDERSON, Mary	DENHAM, Zebulon W.	NOV 01 1837
ANDERSON, Mary (blk)	JACKSON, Thomas	MAR 26 1840
ANDERSON, Mary Ann Hines Montgomery	DEAN, Samuel	MAR 20 1821
ANDERSON, Mary A.	BERAULT, Charles	MAR 26 1849
ANDERSON, Mary Ann Trecy	CARRICO, Wm. Bartholomew	SEP 29 1821
ANDERSON, Mary Ann	HAYES, John	JAN 31 1850
ANDERSON, Mary Elizth.	BROWN, Rezin H.	NOV 11 1856
ANDERSON, Mary O.	WALKER, George H.	NOV 30 1854
ANDERSON, Matilda	COX, Fredk.	OCT 16 1838
ANDERSON, Meda A.	BLANCHARD, Claude D.	SEP 18 1848
ANDERSON, N.D.	MILLER, Catharine B.	FEB 21 1853
ANDERSON, Neley	McCLUN, A.B.	OCT 20 1818
ANDERSON, Noble	ARNOLD, Mary Ellen	JUN 21 1836
ANDERSON, Noble	WEAVER, Ann	AUG 25 1853
ANDERSON, Only P.	BURGER, William B.	JUN 16 1834
ANDERSON, Patsey	WALKER, Sandford	SEP 14 1818
ANDERSON, Rezin	KING, Mary Ann Maria	DEC 12 1829
ANDERSON, Rhoda Ann	DIDSHER, Andrew	SEP 12 1839
ANDERSON, Richard	LLEWLYN, Ellen Jane	OCT 04 1852
ANDERSON, Robert	HOWARD, Mary Jane (blk)	APR 20 1854
ANDERSON, Saml.	WHEATON, Susan D.	MAY 13 1817
ANDERSON, Sarah	BANNISTER, John	DEC 02 1844
ANDERSON, Sarah A.	BRANDENBURG, George	NOV 17 1855
ANDERSON, Sarah E.	BEALL, James E.	MAY 03 1858
ANDERSON, Sarah Ellen	HILTON, Alphonsus L.R.	JUL 12 1850
ANDERSON, Sarah Jane	KING, William	APR 20 1853
ANDERSON, Thomas	DIXON, Eliza Ann	MAY 13 1826
ANDERSON, Thomas	SCHIDMORE, Mahala	JAN 07 1847
ANDERSON, Thomas	THOMPSON, Maria	DEC 20 1853
ANDERSON, Thomas	JOHNSON, Anna Maria	MAY 31 1854
ANDERSON, Thomas F.	BOWLING, Eliza Maria	OCT 04 1820
ANDERSON, Thomas H.	MITCHELL, Martha Ann	OCT 25 1852
ANDERSON, Thomas Wm.	BURTON, Sarah	AUG 23 1850
ANDERSON, W. George	COLSTON, Nannie	SEP 05 1855
ANDERSON, William	MAHEW, Elizabeth	MAR 18 1815
ANDERSON, William	TRUX, Ann	DEC 24 1823
ANDERSON, William	DETRO, Ellen	AUG 24 1848
ANDERSON, William	SCOTT, Mary Ann (blk)	DEC 15 1857
ANDERSON, William H.	SHADRACH, Catharine	NOV 23 1852
ANDERSON, Wm.	JEFFERSON, Euphemia	AUG 12 1815
ANDERSON, Wm.	ANDREWS, Mary Ann Hines Montgomery	NOV 20 1820
ANDISON, John P.	DOOLY, Elizabeth	JUL 19 1847
ANDISON, Sanford	TROUP, Margaret Ann	JUN 28 1821
ANDRE, William E.	SUTTON, Emily J.	APR 15 1852
ANDREA, Christina	WATT, James	AUG 12 1845
ANDREW, Charles	RAMSDALL, Caroline	SEP 29 1846
ANDREW, Margaret	SPENCE, Edward B.	SEP 07 1850
ANDREW, William H.	NASH, Sarah A.	JUL 03 1854
ANDREWS, Alfred W.	MOORE, Ann Virginia	SEP 21 1854
ANDREWS, Ann	CAMMACK, Edmund	MAR 29 1821
ANDREWS, Charles	BLAKE, Susan	JAN 23 1854
ANDREWS, Christina V.	CALLAN, Nicholas, Jr.	NOV 15 1841
ANDREWS, Elizabeth	HANES, Stacy	FEB 14 1823
ANDREWS, Ellen	CAMP, Joseph W.	MAR 27 1834
ANDREWS, James G.	LANDON, Christina VanNess	JUL 31 1838
ANDREWS, Julia Ann	PIC, John	DEC 06 1824
ANDREWS, Mary Ann Hines Montgomery	ANDERSON, Wm.	NOV 21 1820

District of Columbia Marriage Licenses, 1811-1858

ANDREWS, Sebastian	KRAFT, Louisa	APR 25 1854
ANDREWS, Susan	WILLIAMS, William W.	NOV 25 1824
ANDREWS, William	VERMILLION, Lucinda	SEP 29 1818
ANDREWS, William Henry	GOFF, Elizabeth	JUN 16 1832
ANDREWS, William W.	WATSON, Elizabeth	JAN 06 1821
ANEBEY, William	DAVIS, Elizabeth	NOV 24 1814
ANELUG, Christian	HOBERT, Mary	JUN 05 1844
ANESTEAD, Sarah J.	O'BRIEN, Jos. H.	MAR 06 1850
ANGEL, Catherine A.	CRAMPTON, Job Edwin	DEC 30 1857
ANGEL, Henry	COLE, Maria	SEP 16 1837
ANGEL, John	JONES, Mary	SEP 02 1828
ANGEL, John T.	STILLINGS, Elizabeth E.	JUL 12 1851
ANGEL, Mary Ellen	TRUE, Edwin E.	OCT 01 1851
ANGEL, Sarah Jane	MATHENY, William H.	SEP 11 1854
ANGELL, Thomas	MILLS, Hannah Matilda	MAY 17 1827
ANGIL, Jane E.	FOSTER, William J.	NOV 22 1853
ANGNEY, Isaac	CLARK, Matilda D.	MAY 02 1856
ANN, Piscilla	BARON, Jerome	JUL 11 1812
ANNADEL, Robert	MILES, Margaret	MAY 18 1829
ANNADEL, William	TENLEY, Mary	SEP 29 1827
ANNAM, Mary	BURK, John	MAY 20 1846
ANNASON, Ratio	WALKER, Matilda Ann	JAN 12 1837
ANNIN, Roberdeau	McCORMICK, Helen Custis	JAN 03 1828
ANNIS, Mary V.	STONNELL, John A.	FEB 14 1855
ANSY, Sarah Ann	KELLERBY, Joseph	SEP 19 1827
ANTHONY, Joseph	ROGERS, Rachel	NOV 21 1820
ANTHONY, Joseph	THOMPSON, Elizabeth	MAY 20 1848
ANTHONY, Michael	NEWELL, Justa Mary	DEC 07 1818
ANTREO, Albert	HARTMAN, Torronneger	APR 06 1854
APPICH, David	BRODBACK, Barbara Ann	JUL 23 1828
APPLEBY, Bignal	BLAND, Sarah Ann	JAN 22 1839
APPLEBY, Franklin E.	SWEET, Sarah M.	JUN 24 1858
APPLEBY, Horatio G.	PAYNE, Clarissa Ellen	DEC 04 1855
APPLEGATE, John C.	PHILLIPS, Eliza	NOV 22 1841
APPLER, Jonathan	MADDOX, Nancy	SEP 29 1812
APPLER, Mary Ann	ABBETT, Thomas M.	JAN 17 1831
APPLETON, Margaret	FOWLER, James H.	SEP 22 1838
APPLETON, Thomas	SIBLEY, Amelia	APR 29 1812
ARANGO, Antonio	GOTHIER, Caroline	DEC 30 1828
ARARD, Mary F.	BROWN, James B.	OCT 11 1832
ARCELL, Barbara	PEASNER, John	FEB 26 1852
ARCHER, Amelia J.	PURRINGTON, Tablas	JAN 20 1848
ARCHER, Andrew J.	SMITH, Ellen V.	JUL 05 1854
ARCHER, William	WILSON, Eliza	SEP 14 1826
ARCHFIELD, Isabella	DUGAN, John	JUL 08 1839
ARCHIBALD, James	BALEY, Maria	DEC 27 1843
ARDERRY, Angelica Elizabeth	JOHNSON, Henry	NOV 04 1820
ARDIESER, Christian	BRADEKAM, Catherine	JUN 28 1851
ARDIESER, Mary M.	LECHALKER, Charles	APR 18 1857
ARDREY, Rachel	DISPAUX, John	NOV 28 1812
ARGILL, Lewis	TURNER, Mary Ann	JUN 19 1826
ARINGTON, Cintha E.	DONALDSON, John E.	JAN 16 1858
ARLETT, Constantine	WARFIELD, Mary Elizabeth	JAN 31 1839
ARLETT, Mary Elizabeth	GIBBINS, Matthew	MAY 01 1843
ARMAN, David	CASSELLS, Ann	AUG 13 1852
ARMAR, David	RILEY, Julia	JUN 20 1855
ARMBRUSTER, Ernst	KRAFFT, Rosina	NOV 14 1855
ARMISTEAD, Cecelia L.	GREAVES, Matthew	MAY 28 1855

District of Columbia Marriage Licenses, 1811-1858

ARMOUR, James W.	MAGRAW, Juliana	NOV 14 1820
ARMSTEAD, Samuel	POPE, Mary	NOV 26 1842
ARMSTEAD, Wm. C.	SIMPSON, Sarah Ann	NOV 05 1852
ARMSTRONG, Caroll	COOMBS, Mary	JUN 19 1858
ARMSTRONG, Cordelia S.	POWELL, Edward B.	NOV 04 1850
ARMSTRONG, Elizabeth	HICKS, John T.	NOV 03 1852
ARMSTRONG, Francis	CARROLL, Mary	OCT 14 1851
ARMSTRONG, Francis W. [Col.]	MILLARD, Ann M.	APR 05 1831
ARMSTRONG, Henrietta R.	WELCH, Aristides	MAR 01 1856
ARMSTRONG, Hulday	WILSON, William	MAR 31 1832
ARMSTRONG, James	CLEMENTS, Mary	JUN 22 1821
ARMSTRONG, James	WEAVER, Ann M.	NOV 05 1835
ARMSTRONG, Jefferson	BUTLER, Amelia (blk)	SEP 07 1850
ARMSTRONG, John T.	LYNCH, Lucy Ann	JUN 13 1835
ARMSTRONG, Peter	GOODRICT, Mary	JUL 10 1813
ARMSTRONG, Samuel	PORTER, Margaret	JUL 17 1817
ARMSTRONG, Sarah	WHITE, Levi	MAY 31 1825
ARMSTRONG, Susan (blk)	GREEN, Alfred	JUL 16 1857
ARMSTRONG, Virginia	SIMMONS, Thomas J.	SEP 14 1847
ARMSWAY, Wm.	SHERMINTINE, Ann	SEP 09 1826
ARNEY, Caroline H. [Mrs.]	EMMERT, William	OCT 01 1833
ARNOLD, Ann	PEARSON, Bernard	DEC 16 1834
ARNOLD, Aquila	BRINE, Sophia	JUN 01 1816
ARNOLD, Benedict	BLAND, Mary Jane	AUG 11 1831
ARNOLD, Charles W.	TALBUTT, Elizabeth A.	MAR 27 1844
ARNOLD, Drasey	RUPPERD, Casper	JUN 17 1852
ARNOLD, Eleanor	SHERIFF, John	APR 18 1820
ARNOLD, Eliza	GREEN, James	JUN 02 1842
ARNOLD, Elizabeth	SOMMERS, Judson	DEC 21 1816
ARNOLD, Elizabeth	TALBURT, George M.	JUL 15 1845
ARNOLD, Elizth. Ann	REID, James	AUG 30 1845
ARNOLD, George	TILLEY, Elizabeth M.	MAY 09 1854
ARNOLD, George L.	CHAMPION, Lydia	JAN 22 1855
ARNOLD, Harriot	McNEAR, Daniel	OCT 29 1825
ARNOLD, James	VERMILLION, Sarah	FEB 21 1816
ARNOLD, James	TIMS, Sarah	JUL 17 1830
ARNOLD, James	FOSTER, Mary Ann	APR 29 1840
ARNOLD, James	ADAMS, Sarah E.	JUL 09 1849
ARNOLD, James	FOSTER, Elizabeth	MAR 02 1852
ARNOLD, James	CARRICO, Amelia	JUL 24 1856
ARNOLD, John H.	GREEN, Lucinda A.	NOV 09 1825
ARNOLD, John Hy.	DAVIS, Elizabeth	JAN 02 1843
ARNOLD, John W.	PADGETT, Jane V.	APR 20 1852
ARNOLD, Joseph	GRAY, Ann	MAR 31 1812
ARNOLD, Joseph W.	BERRET, Eliza U. O'D.	APR 22 1846
ARNOLD, Lemuel H.	SHONNARD, Catharine	JUN 21 1847
ARNOLD, Margaret	NEFF, Francis	JUL 27 1839
ARNOLD, Margaret	BARNES, Henry	DEC 17 1839
ARNOLD, Margaret Ann	TALBURT, William Henry	OCT 15 1842
ARNOLD, Margretha	HOHMANN, Carl	DEC 07 1852
ARNOLD, Martha E.	PAGE, Yelverton P.	SEP 21 1847
ARNOLD, Mary Ellen	ANDERSON, Noble	JUN 21 1836
ARNOLD, Matilda	RADCLIFF, William, Junr.	AUG 04 1831
ARNOLD, Rachel M.A.	TURTON, William H.	FEB 04 1850
ARNOLD, Rezin	WILSON, Mary Ellen [Mrs.]	DEC 21 1827
ARNOLD, Rezin	TALBERT, Amelia	JAN 02 1835
ARNOLD, Robert	LEEKE, Julia Ann	JUL 15 1826
ARNOLD, Samuel	SHRIEVE, Elizabeth	DEC 29 1814

District of Columbia Marriage Licenses, 1811-1858

ARNOLD, Samuel E.	CHAMPION, Sarah Ann	DEC 10 1851
ARNOLD, Sophia	ORNTINE, Charles	SEP 23 1835
ARNOLD, Sophia Alexander	CARPENTER, Whittington	NOV 06 1850
ARNOLD, Susan	WILLIAMS, James	JUN 18 1824
ARNOLD, Thomas	VERMILLION, Mary	FEB 01 1815
ARNOLD, Thomas	SUMMERS, Sarah Phelps	MAY 13 1817
ARNOLD, Thomas	ROBEY, Ann	APR 01 1820
ARNOLD, Thomas	ROBINSON, Mary	JUN 28 1831
ARNOLD, Thomas B.	MAUD, Margaret	NOV 07 1854
ARNOLD, Thomas O.	HENNON, Julia Ann	OCT 25 1847
ARNOLD, William	BERRY, Eliza	JUN 11 1828
ARNOLD, William H.	BAYNE, Mary A.	OCT 13 1852
ARNY, Caroline Christiana	HERBST, Francis Theodore	JAN 25 1851
ARP, James	BROWN, Ann	JAN 24 1825
ARP, Susan	MORGAN, Aquilla R.L.	FEB 01 1826
ARRINGTON, Alcinda	HALL, Isaac	OCT 22 1853
ARRINGTON, Catharine E.	BEACH, William A.	AUG 04 1856
ARRINGTON, Emma	DONNELSON, Sanford A.	JAN 24 1857
ARRINGTON, Gayton	DUVALL, Sarah A.	AUG 31 1818
ARRINGTON, Margaret	GARDNER, William	MAY 31 1827
ARRINGTON, Margt. M.	DELLS, John Thos.	OCT 23 1856
ARRINGTON, Maria	BEVER, Alexander	OCT 01 1834
ARRINGTON, Mary	MOUNTJOY, Lemuel	JUN 13 1829
ARRINGTON, Mary E.	McKERVAN, Albert A.	AUG 03 1858
ARRINGTON, Matilda	WALKER, Lemuel	JUL 04 1846
ARRINGTON, Sarah	TURRELL, David	OCT 30 1856
ARTES, Daniel	GRAMMER, Sophia	SEP 05 1854
ARTH, Elizabeth	KOONS, Henry	APR 16 1853
ARTH, Klara	LEYNS, Bertram	JUL 05 1853
ARTH, Mary Louisa	MARYMAN, Horatio R.	JAN 01 1853
ARTHUR, James	GAITHER, Elizabeth	JUN 28 1855
ARTIS, Jane	HURLY, Obid	JAN 31 1826
ARTLEY, George	BRADY, Sarah	APR 21 1852
ARTRIDGE, Ann	JOYCE, Richard	SEP 09 1824
ARUNDELL, John	BURCH, Julia Ann	MAR 23 1847
ARUNDELL, Mary	MAYHEW, Edward	JAN 25 1834
ARVENGINE, Caroline	WEIGLE, John	JUL 19 1854
ARVIN, Mary Ann	WINDSOR, Benjamin	JUN 09 1840
ARYES, Daniel	DAVIS, Amanda M.	DEC 08 1840
ASCUE, Susan	LEE, John	OCT 21 1835
ASEL, John	MILLER, Barbara	JUL 31 1851
ASEL, Mary	NEIMAN, John A.	AUG 14 1849
ASH, Mary	BROWN, Wesley	JAN 24 1833
ASH, Michael	CASSIDY, Mary	OCT 19 1850
ASH, Robert, Rev.	ADDISON, Henrietta Maria	JUN 19 1830
ASHBURY, Prudence	BENTZ, Ezra	MAY 26 1834
ASHBURY, Sarah	DEMENT, Richard	MAY 13 1828
ASHBY, Francis W.	GREGORY, Margaret D.	OCT 12 1854
ASHBY, John	PICKETT, Mary	JAN 30 1827
ASHBY, John R.	TODD, Ellen G.	OCT 04 1848
ASHBY, Maria Louisa	BEACH, Nathaniel	AUG 23 1852
ASHCRAFT, Louisa	GASZ, Charles J.	SEP 20 1853
ASHDOWN, Elizabeth E.	CUSTIS, Lemuel W.	FEB 11 1858
ASHDOWN, Sarah J.	DULIN, Joshua V.	FEB 21 1855
ASHFERD, Thos.	HODGSKIN, Elizth.	JAN 25 1823
ASHFORD, Ann	MOORE, Alexander C.	AUG 26 1824
ASHFORD, Craven	DARNE, Emerella	MAR 05 1839
ASHFORD, Henry	WILLIAMS, Ann	APR 27 1829

District of Columbia Marriage Licenses, 1811-1858

ASHFORD, Michael	HUSTER, Mary Ann	OCT 24 1842
ASHFORD, Rachel	CASSIN, Francis	OCT 01 1851
ASHLEY, Elizabeth	CRITTENDEN, J.J.	FEB 26 1853
ASHMORE, Joseph	GREEN, Mary	DEC 05 1820
ASHTON, Ann Sophia	DENT, George	OCT 21 1833
ASHTON, Caroline H.	RAMSAY, Charles R.	MAY 30 1833
ASHTON, Charles	CARPENTER, Jane E.	JUN 10 1852
ASHTON, Eleanor E.	MILES, James	FEB 15 1827
ASHTON, Gurden C.	HARRISON, Helen A.	JAN 20 1853
ASHTON, James	SLY, Mary	MAY 15 1817
ASHTON, Jane C.	WALKER, Dudley	JAN 16 1832
ASHTON, Jeremiah	JOHNSON, Mary Ann (blk)	DEC 05 1823
ASHTON, John N.	STEUART, Margaret M.	NOV 01 1847
ASHTON, Leonard	CURRIN, Eveline	SEP 11 1819
ASHTON, Louisa	HASEW, William	JAN 24 1828
ASHTON, Louisa A.	ROBINS, Joseph H.	APR 10 1847
ASHTON, Margaret	PAWLEY, Andrew	DEC 15 1835
ASHTON, Martha J.	DISHMAN, James V.	AUG 17 1857
ASHTON, Mary B.	TAYLOR, George	AUG 05 1847
ASHTON, Mary D.	STEWART, Joseph N. [Dr.]	MAR 31 1829
ASHTON, Mary D.	WASHINGTON, John Tayloe	JUN 10 1850
ASHTON, Rebecca	DYER, Alexander	OCT 19 1822
ASHTON, Rebecca (blk)	NUJAN, Shedrach	MAY 13 1829
ASHTON, Rosetta	JOHNSON, Samuel	SEP 21 1838
ASHTON, Sarah	MITCHELL, Charles W.	OCT 17 1855
ASHTON, William	EVANS, Rebecca	JUL 21 1856
ASHWORTH, Charles S.	McKIM, Lois	DEC 31 1814
ASKEW, Eleanor	WINDSOR, Henry	AUG 12 1817
ASKINS, Ann Rebecca	DAVIS, Augustus	JAN 01 1829
ASKINS, Catharine Ann	THOMPSON, Charles	APR 03 1828
ASKINS, Erasmus	HUTCHINSON, Jemima	SEP 01 1812
ASKINS, Jos.	WILSON, Harriot	FEB 13 1823
ASTHMUS, Mary	SCHEIDA, Henry	JUN 02 1848
ATCHERSON, Eliza Ann	MAGNUS, Frederick	AUG 15 1843
ATCHERSON, John F.	SWANN, Mary	DEC 20 1838
ATCHISON, George H.	DICKSON, Ann B.	JUN 21 1838
ATCHISON, James E.	BROWN, Sarah Ann C.	NOV 08 1838
ATCHISON, Mary E.	HILTON, Saml. N.	SEP 25 1855
ATCRISON, John	LINDSAY, Sarah L.	JUN 30 1836
ATES, C.	THOMAS, Elizabeth	JUN 29 1843
ATHEY, Catharine	DISNEY, John B.	JUN 22 1826
ATHEY, Elijah L.	STERLING, Mary	MAY 16 1839
ATHEY, Eliza	McCUEN, Richard	MAR 14 1843
ATHEY, Elizabeth	HAMMEL, Hugh	DEC 30 1830
ATHEY, Elizabeth	PAYNE, Lewis	OCT 09 1833
ATHEY, Elizabeth	WOODYARD, George	SEP 03 1836
ATHEY, George	MASSEY, Leanna	OCT 07 1813
ATHEY, George W.	REEVES, Catharine E.	FEB 18 1845
ATHEY, Georginna	WADE, John W.	MAR 05 1842
ATHEY, John M.	BIRCH, Mary Ellen	MAR 07 1849
ATHEY, Leanor	HEDGES, Nicholas	JAN 03 1828
ATHEY, Mary Ann	GRAY, George	APR 12 1834
ATHEY, Susannah	CRAWFORD, James	JUN 21 1826
ATHEY, Thomas	BROWN, Elizabeth	JUN 16 1842
ATHY, Juliana	McCARTHY, Carahin	JUL 07 1825
ATKINS, Margaret (blk)	SIMS, George	NOV 26 1851
ATKINS, Samuel G.	PARROTT, Sarah C.	MAY 05 1849
ATKINS, William	SPARROW, Mary	JUL 15 1837

District of Columbia Marriage Licenses, 1811-1858

ATKINSON, George	BOGUS, Elizabeth	MAY 29 1812
ATKINSON, Guy C.	TRUMP, Mary	MAY 18 1844
ATKINSON, James	BAUGESS, Lydia	JAN 14 1817
ATKINSON, Mary B.	STEWART, Adam D.	MAR 04 1844
ATKISON, Elea	BROWN, William	JUL 03 1829
ATRIDGE, John	MORAN, Elizabeth	OCT 01 1839
ATRIDGE, Mary	RUTHERFORD, Alexander	SEP 20 1838
ATTER, James	BACON, Ann Elizabeth	DEC 24 1849
ATTICK, John	ADAMS, Martha Jane	JUN 24 1853
ATTRIDGE, Elizabeth	HINANT, Garvy	JUL 02 1842
ATTWOOD, Eleanor	LAKE, George	JUN 23 1815
ATWELL, Ann Amanda	SPENCER, Thomas H.	JAN 31 1856
ATWELL, Ann Julia	ROCKWELL, Seth	OCT 29 1828
ATWELL, James R.	BULLARD, Lucy E.	NOV 05 1856
ATWELL, John	SIMPSON, Lucinda C.	NOV 29 1855
ATWELL, Louisa C.	ALLEN, Ignatius	OCT 12 1840
ATWELL, Virginia	KING, John T.	DEC 23 1845
ATWOOD, James	HILL, Nancy	FEB 06 1817
ATWOOD, Mary S.	TATE, William R.	MAY 23 1839
ATWOOD, William	HURLEY, Cornelia	FEB 19 1852
ATWOOD, William	GREENFIELD, Arianna	NOV 23 1853
ATZ, Christopher	ROBINSON, Ellen Ann	JAN 10 1843
ATZS, Charles C.	CUNNINGHAM, Rebecca	AUG 02 1852
AUD, James	HICKEY, Ann	FEB 09 1822
AUDREY, Elizabeth	STATFORD, Robert	MAY 09 1817
AUERAN, Charlotte	ABBERNATHY, Thomas	JUL 25 1835
AUGUST, Philip	BEARSON, Catherine	MAY 03 1824
AUGUST, Samuel	LOWMAN, Mary Ann	JUL 23 1850
AUKWARD, Francis	RUSTAGE, Elizabeth	APR 10 1824
AUKWARD, Harry	McCLOSKEY, Margaret	APR 20 1815
AUKWARD, Margaret	BENNETT, John	SEP 09 1819
AULD, Grace	MORRISON, Alexander	MAY 03 1838
AULD, James	RILEY, Mariah	DEC 16 1830
AULD, Jennette	DELLETT, James C.	MAR 14 1853
AULFEET, Elizabeth	McKENNEY, John	JUL 19 1858
AULICK, Julia	STOUT, Edward C.	FEB 01 1847
AUSBURN, Sarah Ann	CHURCH, William	JUN 09 1835
AUSPIN, Chloe Ann	SPARKS, William	AUG 09 1853
AUSTIN, Anna	WORTHMILLER, John	JUL 31 1855
AUSTIN, Anna	KING, James B.	DEC 02 1856
AUSTIN, David	NOSE, Martha	JUN 29 1816
AUSTIN, Eliza	RENNER, John	JAN 14 1817
AUSTIN, Francis L.	SIMMS, Elizabeth T.	NOV 20 1849
AUSTIN, Hester A.	MERRIWEATHER, Reubin H.	NOV 03 1846
AUSTIN, Martha A.	HOLT, William	FEB 02 1855
AUSTIN, Mary Ann P.	LINDSAY, Robert G.	SEP 14 1841
AUSTIN, Mary E.	MARCELLUS, Henry E.	MAY 11 1846
AUSTIN, Mary Elizabeth	MARCELLUS, Edson	MAY 06 1846
AUSTIN, Matilda [Mrs.]	GARDNER, William	DEC 01 1829
AUSTIN, Sarah Ann	ABBOTT, Charles	FEB 18 1845
AUSTIN, Sarah J.	ABELL, Alexander G.	FEB 03 1845
AUSTIN, Thomas A.	HAYNES, Mary Ann	JAN 01 1818
AUSTIN, William	WARRENSFORD, Matilda	DEC 26 1818
AUSTIN, William	BROWN, Sarah	APR 19 1852
AUSTIN, William G.	GRAHAM, Elizabeth	FEB 22 1845
AUSTINGS, Elizabeth	WALTER, John	APR 05 1843
AUTH, Anton	MITZ, Catherine	JUN 20 1854
AUTH, Mary M.	LITTLE, Joseph T.	MAY 06 1847

District of Columbia Marriage Licenses, 1811-1858

AVART, Sampson	BALL, Eliza H.	SEP 14 1828
AVERETT, Elizabeth Ann	McGLUE, Edward Skyloe	FEB 15 1832
AVERSON, Catherine (blk)	WEEB, Samuel	MAY 14 1833
AVERY, James	PEARSON, Elizabeth	JUL 11 1837
AVERY, John	STATFORD, Susan	MAY 14 1815
AVERY, Margaret	LIMMY, William	APR 14 1834
AVERY, Susan	GLEER, L.B.	MAY 13 1856
AVERY, Thornton	GATES, Eliza	OCT 16 1854
AVERY, Westley	CROSS, Mary	NOV 07 1838
AVERY, William B.	SMITH, Margaret	APR 22 1848
AVIS, Mary	SHARPLESS, Wm.	JUN 26 1813
AVORY, Elizabeth	BENTOR, William	FEB 14 1826
AVREY, George Wm.	GOODGER, Eliza	JUN 29 1835
AYLOR, Sarah F.	ROMINE, Thomas	JUL 13 1857
AYRES, Dorcas	GREEN, Joseph J.	MAR 06 1829
AYRES, Mary	TAGGART, Saml. [Hon.]	MAR 14 1816
AYTON, Mary Cornelia	COOK, Abram	SEP 25 1845

District of Columbia Marriage Licenses, 1811-1858

B

BAARE, Ferdinand Rudolph	FISHER, Eliza	FEB 24 1847
BABBINGTON, William	FOLEY, Bridget	MAY 08 1852
BACH, Barbara	PLFAEGER, Jacob	NOV 13 1854
BACH, Ernst	KLEMKE, Elizabeth	JUL 24 1857
BACHE, George M.	PATTERSON, Eliza C.	MAY 23 1837
BACHE, Hartman	MEADE, Maria del Carmel	FEB 28 1829
BACHE, Henrietta C.	ABERT, Charles	APR 16 1845
BACHE, Maria C.	McLANE, Allen	DEC 17 1850
BACHE, Matilda W.	EMORY, William H.	MAY 26 1838
BACHE, Sally Franklin	WAINWRIGHT, Richard	FEB 28 1849
BACHE, Sophia A.	IRVIN, William W.	FEB 28 1839
BACHENHEIMER, Herz	WALLACH, Rosa	MAY 30 1856
BACKETT, Anna Maria	BURTO, Nicholas	OCT 07 1815
BACON, Alice (blk)	HULL, George	MAY 19 1857
BACON, Ann	McCUTCHEN, John	JUL 01 1824
BACON, Ann E.	LOCKE, John B.	APR 15 1820
BACON, Ann Elizabeth	ATTER, James	DEC 24 1849
BACON, Caroline	SPENCER, George D.	AUG 10 1830
BACON, Ebenezer	GREENLEAF, Susan	JAN 24 1828
BACON, Elizabeth	HAZLE, Zachariah	FEB 15 1817
BACON, Ida	LATHAM, Richd. P.	DEC 23 1854
BACON, Jane	SPEAKS, John	APR 06 1822
BACON, Peter	CLARKE, Elizabeth C.	JAN 25 1838
BACON, Samuel	McCUTCHEN, Elizabeth	OCT 20 1817
BACON, Samuel	HOWARD, Mary Ann	OCT 09 1838
BACON, Samuel P.	SMITH, Caroline	MAY 18 1836
BACON, Washington	LOCKE, Prudence D.	NOV 21 1829
BADDEN, Elizabeth	CARROLL, John B.	APR 23 1828
BADDEN, Mary	RAWLINS, William C.	MAY 29 1830
BADDEN, Matilda	DAVIS, James D.	FEB 10 1823
BADEN, John H.	WRIGHT, Elizabeth	AUG 26 1857
BADEN, John W.	WALLACE, Mary Ann K.	MAR 03 1851
BADEN, Margaret A.	GARDINER, Leonard A.	MAR 26 1838
BADEN, Mary	POWERS, Thomas	SEP 08 1840
BADEN, Thomas E.	HENSHAW, Frances L.	OCT 23 1856
BADEN, William	BURGESS, Eliz. Ann	FEB 17 1815
BADGER, Alfred N.	GALPIN, Gracy Ann	JUN 23 1831
BADGER, Harriet M.	HOBSON, Owen H.	SEP 01 1849
BADGET, William B.	HUTCHINS, Margaret Ann	NOV 12 1822
BADING, Mary Ann	DAY, Fielder	JAN 15 1827
BAEBEL, Christopher Adam	EICHELE, Catharine	JUL 18 1854
BAECHE, Catherine	KLINE, Valentine	OCT 10 1857
BAESCHLIN, Fredk.	RULE, Mary Elizth.	JUN 21 1855
BAGBY, Robert B.	KEECH, Evelina	DEC 08 1856
BAGE, William	FOXTON, Mary	DEC 05 1818
BAGGET, Ignatius	BAGGETT, Julia	APR 20 1819
BAGGETT, Celia Ann	COOKE, William H.	NOV 02 1847
BAGGETT, Elizabeth	CLUTE, Henry D.	MAY 31 1841
BAGGETT, John	PETITT, Sarah	OCT 12 1852
BAGGETT, John C.	BURRIS, Eliza Ann	JUN 16 1845
BAGGETT, Julia	BAGGET, Ignatius	APR 20 1819
BAGGETT, Margaret L.	BEALL, Samuel	NOV 06 1856
BAGGETT, Mary Ellen	ALLEN, Charles	MAR 24 1851
BAGGETT, Samuel	HUNTER, Mary	JAN 05 1837
BAGGETT, Susan	PADGETT, John G.	MAY 03 1832
BAGGETT, Susannah H.	CALDERWAY, John G.	AUG 07 1837

District of Columbia Marriage Licenses, 1811-1858

BAGGITT, Ann E.A.	FIROE, Ephraim A.	SEP 14 1852
BAGGOT, Susan	VARDIN, Joseph	MAY 25 1839
BAGGOTT, Hester A.	PRICE, Geo. E.	JUL 06 1858
BAGGOTT, James W.	HOWARD, Lucy Ann	SEP 25 1845
BAGGOTT, James W.	HOWARD, Lucy N.	DEC 16 1847
BAGGS, Elizabeth	SMETHER, Robert	FEB 28 1826
BAGLEY, Daniel	CONNER, Margaret	JUL 18 1851
BAGY, Michael	GALLOWAY, Catherine	FEB 04 1853
BAHM, Valintine	SMYTH, Elizabeth	FEB 17 1846
BAIGLEY, Ellen	LONG, Michael	MAY 03 1851
BAILESS, Edward	DANIEL, Linny Ann	JAN 18 1830
BAILESS, Sarah Ann	WHEATLEY, Andrew J.	JUN 28 1852
BAILEY, Adam	SNOWDEN, Caroline (blk)	SEP 30 1839
BAILEY, Anna E.	SAVOY, Samuel W.	JUN 11 1856
BAILEY, Catherine	FURGESON, Andrew	JUN 06 1849
BAILEY, Elizabeth	WELLS, Richard	NOV 22 1814
BAILEY, Elizabeth	FRANCIS, George W.	APR 22 1845
BAILEY, Elizth. M. (blk)	GILBERT, Thomas	MAY 22 1851
BAILEY, George K.	NORTON, Eliza E.	DEC 19 1837
BAILEY, Hannah	KANE, Patrick	OCT 16 1856
BAILEY, Hannah Johnson	BARGY, Peter, Jr.	OCT 11 1832
BAILEY, Hanson	WELCH, Sarah E.	MAR 23 1857
BAILEY, Harriet	WOOD, Henry	JAN 08 1853
BAILEY, Harvey	JENKS, Sarah E.	NOV 04 1853
BAILEY, Ignatius	WATERS, Mary V.	AUG 02 1858
BAILEY, John	BORROWS, Catherine	SEP 08 1813
BAILEY, John	YOUNG, Ann	NOV 14 1822
BAILEY, John E.	YOUNG, Rebecca	OCT 17 1844
BAILEY, John P.	EMBREY, Esther A.	JAN 08 1857
BAILEY, John R.	HOOKER, Margaret	JUN 25 1858
BAILEY, John Richard	SEWALL, Maria (blk)	MAY 25 1847
BAILEY, Joseph F.	BRADLEY, Mary C.	JAN 06 1857
BAILEY, Josiah R.	LAPORTE, Ann Elizth.	DEC 13 1849
BAILEY, Julia A.	MEADE, James H.	MAY 08 1849
BAILEY, Juliet	UTTERBACK, Westward	AUG 14 1838
BAILEY, Martha Jane	BRISCOE, John A.	MAY 12 1858
BAILEY, Mary	HALL, Wm. C.	MAY 07 1853
BAILEY, Rebecca	BEAKER, Jacob	JUL 24 1841
BAILEY, Rebecca	SHELTON, James	JUL 21 1856
BAILEY, Rebecca	TEELIN, Charles	MAR 02 1857
BAILEY, Sabina	LLOYD, Samuel	JUN 04 1846
BAILEY, Sampson P.	SMITH, Francis C.	DEC 09 1846
BAILEY, Sarah	LOWE, William M.	NOV 10 1857
BAILEY, Sarah Jane	SMALLWOOD, George F.	AUG 02 1855
BAILEY, Susan Burrows	TOWERS, John	DEC 11 1834
BAILEY, William	CROWLEY, Ann	APR 12 1825
BAILEY, William L.	MOLDEN, Jane Eliza	SEP 25 1830
BAILEY, Wm.	JOHNSON, Lucinda	NOV 21 1844
BAILISS, Collin	SKIDMORE, Sarah	AUG 06 1833
BAILLIO, Emily A.	CHICHESTER, William D.	NOV 11 1856
BAILY, Albert	HOBSON, Sally	NOV 04 1817
BAILY, Ann Eliza	CLOUD, George	MAY 12 1814
BAILY, Elizabeth	WILLIAMS, Zadock	NOV 17 1823
BAILY, Lydia	WHELAN, John	FEB 09 1839
BAILY, Margaret	JOHNSON, Robert	NOV 08 1832
BAILY, Mary	RAY, Paul	FEB 22 1836
BAILY, Sandy	DAVIS, Nelly (blk)	MAY 13 1835
BAILY, Solomon	DEMENT, Mrs.	MAY 19 1835

District of Columbia Marriage Licenses, 1811-1858

BAINBRIDGE, John	SPEAKE, Henrietta Maria	JUL 12 1838
BAINE, Andrew	WHE, Martha Rebecca	DEC 23 1856
BAIRD, Mathew	CAUTHORN, Ophela	FEB 14 1832
BAIRD, Samuel	LOWRIE, Mary	FEB 26 1834
BAIRD, Sarah	MUNRO, David	MAR 14 1827
BAIRD, William A.	DALE, Catherine B.	MAR 28 1853
BAKER, Alfred	LANPHIER, Eliza	NOV 17 1827
BAKER, Arthur	BROWN, Mary	NOV 29 1841
BAKER, Atha Ann	DEAN, John A.	OCT 09 1856
BAKER, Augusti	HEINZERLING, Phillip	APR 29 1858
BAKER, Benjamin F.	HOWARD, Mary Ellen	AUG 21 1852
BAKER, Catharine	DETRO, Thomas	DEC 16 1847
BAKER, Charles	SHIELDS, Ann Selena	MAY 12 1841
BAKER, Charles M.	SULLIVAN, Elizabeth F.	JAN 10 1833
BAKER, Charles T.M.	NEWTON, Virginia	JUL 14 1851
BAKER, Edmund	O'NEALE, Christi Ann	DEC 31 1833
BAKER, Eliza Ann	HOOKER, Jesse	JUL 28 1858
BAKER, Eliza B.	INGLE, John P.	AUG 06 1855
BAKER, Eliza Jane	TENLY, John T.	OCT 21 1851
BAKER, Elizabeth	MORAN, William	JUL 24 1816
BAKER, Elizabeth	MOREHOUSE, Isaac	OCT 30 1816
BAKER, Elizabeth	DOVE, John	SEP 11 1832
BAKER, Elizabeth	SMITH, Joseph	MAY 31 1837
BAKER, Elizabeth A.	CHEW, Samuel B.	FEB 22 1823
BAKER, Elizabeth A.	OFFUTT, Artaperxes F.	JAN 31 1837
BAKER, Ellenora	CUSTIS, George	AUG 12 1858
BAKER, Emily	KNOTT, James	MAY 30 1834
BAKER, Emily	DAYTON, Albert	AUG 27 1850
BAKER, Flora [Mrs.]	SMITH, Jacob	APR 06 1827
BAKER, George	BROWN, Elizabeth	AUG 29 1842
BAKER, George	CORBIT, Mary	OCT 13 1853
BAKER, George L.	BRYAN, Ellen V.	JUN 26 1857
BAKER, Hannah	HURLEY, Fendell	DEC 17 1822
BAKER, Harriet	MULLER, James	MAY 22 1821
BAKER, Harriet Jane	WELLS, George Anthony	JUL 26 1858
BAKER, Hattie R.	WINDSOR, Henry C.	JUN 27 1856
BAKER, Henry	DEMOORE, Sarah L.	AUG 20 1844
BAKER, Henry	WEAVER, Catharine	JUL 08 1845
BAKER, James	HIGDON, Polly	OCT 21 1812
BAKER, James	TAYLOE, Catherine C.	MAY 20 1824
BAKER, James H.	BURL, Rebecca (blk)	AUG 13 1850
BAKER, Jane	STEPHENS, James	APR 28 1819
BAKER, John	WATHEN, Jane	FEB 23 1816
BAKER, John	EVANS, Martha	MAY 06 1847
BAKER, John C.	PERRIE, Sophia A.	JUN 15 1847
BAKER, John H.	SPRIGG, Eliza B.	NOV 21 1826
BAKER, John T.	BRYAN, Elizabeth	MAY 25 1829
BAKER, Julia Ann	KING, Zachariah	JUL 14 1830
BAKER, Lawrence	STREIDENBERGER, Catherine	SEP 05 1854
BAKER, Levi T.	BLUMER, Amelia	JUN 16 1857
BAKER, Louisa A.M.	BOONE, John F.	JUN 05 1832
BAKER, Lucinda	GIBSON, Robert	DEC 22 1857
BAKER, Margaret	BLEW, Chs. W.	DEC 06 1822
BAKER, Margaret	BONTZ, George	SEP 01 1840
BAKER, Maria	HEYDER, John Frederick	MAR 24 1845
BAKER, Mary Ann	BURK, Thomas	AUG 23 1823
BAKER, Mary Ann	BROWNING, Jeremiah	APR 24 1830
BAKER, Mary Ann	BARNES, Horatio	JUL 12 1834

District of Columbia Marriage Licenses, 1811-1858

BAKER, Matthias	McALLISTER, Elizabeth	JUN 05 1817
BAKER, Mildred H.	INGLE, John P.	DEC 19 1846
BAKER, Rachael	HERBERT, Nathan	MAY 24 1822
BAKER, Rosetta	GROSS, Joseph H.	DEC 02 1854
BAKER, Sarah A.F.	HACKNEY, William	MAY 26 1838
BAKER, Sarah Catharine	THOMAS, James D.	APR 15 1847
BAKER, Stephen M.	LANGFITT, Sibby	SEP 08 1846
BAKER, Susan H.	INGLE, John P.	AUG 29 1825
BAKER, Thomas	BEARDSLEY, Eliza	DEC 07 1832
BAKER, Thomas E.	GODFREY, Eliza	JUN 16 1827
BAKER, Troless	STEVENSON, Abgail	AUG 24 1826
BAKER, Virginia C.	OFFUTT, Henry L.	MAY 24 1847
BAKER, William	HOWES, Sarah Ann	MAY 15 1837
BAKER, William	HOG, Sophia	JUN 20 1857
BAKER, William E.	HOPKINS, Mary C.	MAY 28 1855
BAKER, William M.	COOPER, Martha A.	JUL 21 1857
BAKER, Zachariah	[blank]	JUL 15 1817
BAKER, Zachariah	BAYLISS, Margaret A.	JUL 07 1851
BALCH, Eliza M.	TUSTON, Septimus	JAN 31 1825
BALCH, George Beall	VINSON, Julia Grace	DEC 24 1844
BALCH, Jane Whann	WILLIAMSON, Wm.	SEP 23 1823
BALCH, Stephen B. [Rev.]	KING, Elizabeth	NOV 04 1828
BALD, Hannah	CAIN, James	OCT 17 1820
BALDIN, Elizabeth	RIGHTER, Anthony	MAY 24 1836
BALDIN, George	PILLING, Caroline	JUN 30 1842
BALDIN, Sarah Ann	OSBOURN, John	FEB 07 1831
BALDING, Theopolis	LOWE, Elizabeth	DEC 24 1818
BALDING, William	GOLDSMITH, Elizabeth	MAR 09 1826
BALDSWELL, Caroline	MATTINGLY, William	NOV 10 1849
BALDWIN, Anna Maria	CAMERON, William	JAN 07 1850
BALDWIN, Caroline	SELVEY, Henry E.	SEP 15 1831
BALDWIN, Clara	BOMFORD, George	APR 20 1816
BALDWIN, Edward	BIRTH, Lizzie T.	MAY 06 1856
BALDWIN, Elizabeth Ann	HOLTZCLAW, George W.	JAN 19 1843
BALDWIN, Elizabeth L.	THOMPSON, Charles B.	JUN 29 1842
BALDWIN, Frances Ann	MACE, Thomas	DEC 23 1852
BALDWIN, Gabriel L.	LOCKE, Elizabeth A.	FEB 27 1851
BALDWIN, Henry Clay	MOORE, Virginia B.	JUN 01 1853
BALDWIN, Henry, Jr.	O'HAMMOND, Elizabeth	MAY 25 1858
BALDWIN, Isaac P.	SEXSMITH, Harriet	JAN 31 1848
BALDWIN, Jamima	TIPPETT, Maxwell	AUG 21 1823
BALDWIN, John S.	DEWEY, Ann E.	JUN 29 1853
BALDWIN, Martha Elizabeth	PAYNE, Robert	FEB 17 1854
BALDWIN, Mary	KAVENAUGH, Thomas	SEP 03 1835
BALDWIN, Nelly	MacCAULY, Carlton	JAN 19 1816
BALDWIN, Sarah	CALBERT, Bartholomew	APR 12 1851
BALDWIN, Sarah Jane	WILSON, John Henry	AUG 03 1843
BALDWIN, Selina	BESTOR, Whitman C.	OCT 13 1849
BALDWIN, Thomas J.	MATHIS, Cornelia A.	MAR 05 1855
BALDWIN, Verlinda	STONE, John	AUG 07 1813
BALDWIN, William	SIBLEY, Mary	SEP 14 1840
BALDWIN, William H.	GILMAN, Cornelia A.	MAR 09 1853
BALDWIN, William T.	LOWE, Mary Ann	JAN 15 1825
BALEY, John	PARKER, Elizabeth (blk)	FEB 18 1839
BALEY, Maria	ARCHIBALD, James	DEC 27 1843
BALEY, Mary Ann	BARNES, Alexander	JUN 13 1837
BALIS, Alfred	DANIEL, Senior	DEC 24 1835
BALIS, Geo.	ROBERSON, Eleanor	OCT 18 1823

District of Columbia Marriage Licenses, 1811-1858

BALISS, Thomas	SWALLER, Margaret	FEB 07 1828
BALL, Alice C.	DUVALL, Eli, Junr.	AUG 12 1857
BALL, Amelia	REINTZEL, Samuel	DEC 25 1813
BALL, Andrew A.	MARLOW, Mary Elizabeth	MAY 09 1853
BALL, Ann Virginia	GARRETT, Simon	MAY 30 1850
BALL, Aquilla	FOX, Susan	JUL 10 1817
BALL, Caroline E.	ENGLEBRECHT, John C.	FEB 19 1850
BALL, Charles G.	HAY, Mary Virginia	DEC 31 1851
BALL, Cornelia (blk)	CRYER, Henry	APR 23 1857
BALL, Daniel	EDMONSTON, Sarah R.	JUN 10 1843
BALL, Eliza H.	AVART, Sampson	SEP 14 1828
BALL, Eliza M. (blk)	MUSE, Lindsay	APR 04 1825
BALL, Elizabeth	ALLEN, John	NOV 02 1833
BALL, Elizabeth	DILLINGER, Henry M.	FEB 21 1843
BALL, Ellen Nora	DYER, William B.	DEC 12 1842
BALL, George W.	LEONARD, Eve	JAN 06 1832
BALL, George W.	MYERS, Sarah Ann	FEB 22 1834
BALL, George W.	MARLOW, Sarah Ann	MAY 11 1843
BALL, Griffin	CHEW, Diana (blk)	APR 01 1840
BALL, Henrietta D.	HANDY, Levin	SEP 06 1834
BALL, Henry M., Jr.	STONE, Frances H.	JAN 06 1844
BALL, Horatio	MARCEY, Catherine	OCT 10 1815
BALL, Horatio	MARSEY, Elizabeth	DEC 07 1831
BALL, Horatio	RICKETS, Mary Jane	APR 14 1853
BALL, Isaac, Jr.	SWAIN, Dorcas Ann	SEP 02 1834
BALL, Issac S.	AGER, Mary Ann	NOV 05 1839
BALL, James P.	SMITH, Margt. P.	NOV 14 1831
BALL, James T.	SEWALL, Mary	FEB 11 1835
BALL, John	SHREVE, Margaret Ann	OCT 01 1834
BALL, John Dent	BRYAN, Chloe Ann	DEC 16 1823
BALL, John Henry	ALLEN, Mary Jane	OCT 13 1847
BALL, John T.	TYLER, Mary Scott	JAN 23 1834
BALL, John W.	SANSBURY, Sarah Ann R.	FEB 20 1849
BALL, Joseph P.	LAWRENCE, Mrs. Phillippi E.W.	MAY 26 1829
BALL, Linah	THRIFT, James	MAY 22 1813
BALL, Louisa	DAY, William	JUN 10 1833
BALL, Louisa	DAILEY, Hiram B.	AUG 28 1835
BALL, Lucy (blk)	LEE, Jesse	MAR 28 1840
BALL, Margaret	WHITNEY, Joseph	DEC 02 1824
BALL, Martha	TREXLER, Peter	MAR 05 1853
BALL, Mary Ann	DONALDSON, James W.	AUG 21 1844
BALL, Mary F.	FEBREY, John E.	DEC 30 1854
BALL, Mary M.	REED, Richard S.	MAR 13 1833
BALL, Nancy	SWAIN, Thomas	JAN 28 1826
BALL, Nancy	WAUGH, William	JUN 16 1834
BALL, Richard D.	MURPHY, Ann A.	NOV 28 1849
BALL, Robert	McELWEE, Elizabeth	SEP 18 1848
BALL, Samuel	BLUNDIN, Jane Ann	DEC 29 1846
BALL, Sarah	WINEKLER, Benjamin	NOV 26 1835
BALL, Sarah Ann	ROLLINS, John W.	JAN 17 1824
BALL, Sarah Ann	SHERMAN, Daniel	JUL 01 1831
BALL, Sheldon H.	LEE, Emma	APR 24 1847
BALL, Siby	MARKWOOD, Charles	JAN 13 1819
BALL, Stephen	WOODWARD, Mary	JUL 26 1815
BALL, Susan	BEVERS, John A.	SEP 28 1854
BALL, Thomas	MAYHEW, Ann	JAN 09 1834
BALL, Verlinder	FEVER, Nicholas	JAN 25 1827
BALLANGER, John	WELLS, Anne	DEC 22 1814

District of Columbia Marriage Licenses, 1811-1858

BALLANGER, Susan	SHAFER, Christian	MAY 01 1834
BALLANTYNE, Margaret	JAMES, William	OCT 14 1854
BALLARD, Ann	THOMPSON, Nicholas	SEP 19 1850
BALLARD, Charles	DOUGHERTY, Eleanor	MAY 05 1831
BALLARD, Clara	GODDARD, Samuel B.	JAN 18 1843
BALLARD, Julia (blk)	HENSON, Andrew	JUN 17 1839
BALLARD, Margaret R.	NORVILL, William H.	SEP 17 1846
BALLARD, Richard	WHITE, Terese Ann	SEP 17 1814
BALLARD, Richard	WALKER, Louisa	DEC 10 1822
BALLAUFF, Mary	WURDEMAN, Herman	DEC 21 1852
BALLAUFF, William	WALDSCHMIDT, Elizabeth	MAY 25 1853
BALLENGER, George William	SEBASTIAN, Mary Virginia	MAY 13 1858
BALLENGER, Henry W.	KING, Susan Ann	DEC 28 1852
BALLENGER, John T.	TENNISEN, Charlotte E.	OCT 10 1835
BALLENGER, Mary V.	MILSTEAD, George E.	DEC 18 1856
BALLENGER, Peyton	WROE, Jane	OCT 24 1833
BALLENGER, Richard	BOUCHER, Ann	FEB 22 1831
BALLENGER, Spencer	WADE, Ann Maria	FEB 19 1857
BALLENGER, Wesley	DOVE, Ann	FEB 03 1825
BALLER, Mary E.	SUIT, John L.	APR 02 1821
BALLINGER, Francis	CLEMENS, Martha A.	OCT 31 1850
BALLINGER, George W.	NICHOLSON, Mary A.	DEC 12 1839
BALLINGER, Joseph	O'NEALE, Sarah	OCT 06 1840
BALLINGER, Lydia	WILLIAMS, John	AUG 13 1827
BALLINGER, Milly Maria	REN, Sabret	FEB 18 1836
BALLINGER, Nancy Ann	DORSEY, Benjamin Warren	DEC 19 1844
BALLINGER, Solomon	DOVE, Velinda	JAN 11 1827
BALLMAN, John H.	HOFFMEISTER, Mary	MAY 17 1855
BALLSEL, Margaret	KNOWLES, Hamilton	FEB 06 1857
BALMAIN, Louisa C.	JOHNSON, Richmond [Dr.]	MAR 31 1819
BALMAIN, Margaret T.	JOHNSON, Richmond	JAN 04 1823
BALSTER, John	GODRON, Fredericka Wilhelmina	APR 04 1846
BALTIMORE, Elizth. (blk)	TRIVIS, Augustus	MAY 20 1852
BALTIMORE, Joseph	WILSON, Sarah (blk)	OCT 31 1833
BALTIMORE, Kitty (blk)	BRADLEY, Henry	NOV 03 1836
BALTIMORE, Thomas	MARBURY, Marbury (blk)	MAY 08 1834
BALTZELL, Priscilla	MATTINGLY, Reubin	APR 29 1852
BALTZER, Catherine	KROUSE, Everard	MAR 24 1846
BALTZER, Eliza Jane	ELLISS, James A.	JAN 30 1845
BALTZER, Elizabeth	THOMPSON, William, Jr.	MAY 19 1814
BALTZER, Jacob	QUADE, Ruthia	MAY 06 1816
BALTZER, John	CROWLEY, Catharine	MAR 01 1831
BALTZER, Margaret	THOMAS, James	FEB 01 1825
BALTZER, Sarah	KURTZ, John	MAY 25 1831
BAMBERGER, George U.	INGERSOLL, Elizabeth Ann	JAN 06 1853
BAMBERGER, Henry C.	GRAVATT, Mary V.	OCT 05 1857
BANBERGER, William C.	STEPHENSON, Hannah	JUL 14 1840
BANDEN, Thomas	DAILEY, Maria	OCT 05 1822
BANERLE, Ann M.	HACKENIAS, Bartholemew	NOV 13 1854
BANF, Hugh	ENGEL, Catherine	FEB 06 1858
BANF, Margaret	DRUSHEIM, Eberhart	SEP 11 1852
BANGHARDT, Elizabeth	DECK, Martin	APR 11 1857
BANGS, Cassandra V.	JOHNSON, James A.	JUN 25 1851
BANGS, Charles	McCANN, Rebecca	JAN 06 1858
BANGS, David	BOON, Elizabeth	OCT 19 1820
BANGS, Henrietta	COX, John E.	OCT 11 1851
BANGS, James C.	GOMLEY, Mary	NOV 21 1845
BANGS, John T.	McCANN, Amanda	APR 18 1846

District of Columbia Marriage Licenses, 1811-1858

BANGS, John W.	JENKINS, Adelphia	DEC 14 1850
BANGS, Samuel	PAYNE, Susan	OCT 16 1824
BANGS, Thomas	GRIFFINS, Chloe Ann	JUL 31 1833
BANGS, William H.	WOODWARD, Nancy	APR 09 1833
BANGS, William H.	DRAKE, Elizabeth G.	JUN 06 1849
BANISTER, Aquila	WILLIAMS, Susan	APR 28 1829
BANISTER, Charlotte	DAVIS, David	DEC 27 1831
BANISTER, Mary C.	CUMBERLAND, Wm.	AUG 15 1854
BANKHEAD, Ellen M.	CARTER, John C.	JUL 06 1832
BANKS, Delia	SIMMS, William	APR 08 1822
BANKS, John	SIMS, Catharine (blk)	MAY 10 1856
BANKS, Mary Elizth.	STEWART, Wm. Edward	MAY 31 1853
BANKS, Richard	SERRATT, Sarah	MAR 30 1812
BANKS, Saml. N.	WEAVER, Ann E.	FEB 26 1857
BANKS, Susan A.	BOSS, Joseph S.	APR 30 1856
BANNERMAN, Rosina E.	HARTWELL, George	OCT 27 1854
BANNISTER, Caroline	KNIGHT, William	JUN 26 1849
BANNISTER, John	ANDERSON, Sarah	DEC 02 1844
BANNISTER, Mary Ann	EASTON, Levin	AUG 08 1836
BANSWELL, Sarah	WATSON, John	FEB 11 1819
BANY, James	FOY, Elizabeth	APR 25 1836
BAR, Mary	TURNER, William	FEB 10 1848
BARBARIN, Fras. S.	HYDE, Rebecca	APR 08 1856
BARBER, Almira D.	LAYTON, John L.	MAR 05 1857
BARBER, Ann Maria	CLAPHAM, John	FEB 10 1851
BARBER, Caroline (blk)	COLE, Francis	DEC 08 1853
BARBER, Catharine	HUTCHINSON, William	JAN 29 1857
BARBER, Catherine (blk)	SHORTER, William H.	SEP 10 1849
BARBER, Clement	PILES, Eleanor	OCT 03 1816
BARBER, Cornelius	ADLUM, Margaret	JAN 31 1833
BARBER, Delilah Ann Mary	GOULDING, George	JAN 13 1848
BARBER, George	MILBURN, Jane Lucinda	MAR 30 1842
BARBER, George	OSBORNE, Elizabeth	NOV 20 1849
BARBER, George	BUTLER, Elizabeth	NOV 25 1853
BARBER, Ida	GEIER, Bernard	JUL 31 1854
BARBER, John	IDEAN, Catherine	NOV 20 1815
BARBER, Jonathan [Dr.]	DUNKIN, Martha [Mrs.]	APR 01 1824
BARBER, Lizetta	GUEMANN, George	SEP 27 1848
BARBER, Mary Ann	HARP, Caleb	DEC 09 1812
BARBER, Nancy	COLLINS, Zachariah	SEP 21 1854
BARBER, Sophia	BERGLING, George	FEB 04 1850
BARBER, William	BEACH, Mary	SEP 27 1856
BARBOUR, Andrew	HUTCHINS, Susan	OCT 02 1841
BARBOUR, Elizth.	AMBLER, John Jaquilin	FEB 12 1828
BARBOUR, James L.	MOORE, Anne E.	FEB 16 1857
BARBOUR, Mary R.	BARKER, Robert H.	DEC 26 1854
BARBOUR, Thomas	BROWN, Susan	JAN 21 1840
BARBOUR, William H.	MARKS, Eleanor N.	OCT 25 1855
BARCLAY, Annie	CATHCART, Thomas J.	MAY 22 1855
BARCLAY, Eliza Jane	CATHCART, James Leander	AUG 14 1845
BARCLAY, James	FAGAN, Mary	OCT 30 1849
BARCLAY, Jane	McCATHARIN, James	JUL 11 1822
BARCLAY, John D.	WOODSIDE, Ann A.	NOV 08 1814
BARCLAY, Mary M.	SIMMONS, James	MAY 20 1813
BARCROFT, Henrietta P.	LEE, Alexander	APR 21 1840
BARGELY, Joseph	PEDEGREE, Catharine	APR 08 1825
BARGEVIN, Mary A.	WATSON, Thomas P.	MAY 19 1854
BARGY, Peter, Jr.	BAILEY, Hannah Johnson	OCT 11 1832

District of Columbia Marriage Licenses, 1811-1858

BARKER, Adolphus	THOMPSON, Alice	JUL 01 1857
BARKER, Andrew	LEE, Rebecca	JUL 16 1814
BARKER, Andrew	ALLISON, Emeline (blk)	APR 19 1849
BARKER, Anna	ALLEN, Francis	MAY 03 1853
BARKER, Atheriah	WEST, Covington O.	JAN 02 1851
BARKER, Edward	SWANN, Jane Ann	SEP 10 1832
BARKER, Eleanor (blk)	HOWARD, Jeffry	SEP 07 1826
BARKER, Eliza Jane	GRAY, John William D.	JUL 01 1846
BARKER, Elizabeth S.	STEUART, H. Clay	MAY 17 1858
BARKER, George	SIMMONS, Catherine	JAN 09 1850
BARKER, Irwin S.	TUCKER, Jeannette	MAY 08 1851
BARKER, Isaac	DENT, Caroline	OCT 11 1830
BARKER, James	FOOT, Frances	FEB 17 1845
BARKER, James	VENABLE, Anne V.	MAY 17 1855
BARKER, James W.	HINES, Sarah A.N.	AUG 22 1843
BARKER, John B.	GARDINER, Eliza A.	OCT 25 1832
BARKER, John H.	RHINE, Margaret	AUG 21 1852
BARKER, Lucinda	DODSON, Ignatius	NOV 01 1832
BARKER, Martha Ann	GIBSON, William H.	FEB 10 1855
BARKER, Mary	TRAVERS, John	NOV 22 1849
BARKER, Mary R.	KEYS, Richard B.	DEC 17 1850
BARKER, Murray	CAMPBELL, Matilda (blk)	APR 10 1841
BARKER, Presley	CONNER, Charlotte	APR 08 1823
BARKER, Rebecca	HOEFLICH, Isaac C.	DEC 30 1856
BARKER, Robert H.	BARBOUR, Mary R.	DEC 26 1854
BARKER, Sarah J.	GARRETT, James	DEC 23 1856
BARKER, Thomas	KING, Barbara Ann	OCT 12 1830
BARKER, William	THOMAS, Emily	APR 26 1834
BARKER, William H.	GRAY, Minia (blk)	OCT 27 1847
BARKER, William N.	HANSON, Rebecca D.	JUN 17 1856
BARKLEY, Eliza	BURY, William	SEP 30 1824
BARKLEY, Elizth.	MADDOX, John	FEB 09 1828
BARKLEY, John	FOWLER, Mary	JUL 22 1831
BARKLEY, Mary Henrietta	JAMESON, Thomas A.	AUG 07 1845
BARKLEY, Samuel	JAMESON, Teresa Celestia	JUL 30 1817
BARKMAN, George	JAVINS, Margaret	SEP 15 1836
BARKMAN, Martha	SHINN, John R.	OCT 29 1855
BARLOW, John	MILES, Catharine (blk)	JUN 06 1832
BARLOW, Marthena	SAUNDERS, Alvin	MAR 11 1856
BARN, Wm. Thomas	ROBERTSON, Jane	DEC 22 1842
BARNACLO, Richard W.	TURNER, Catharine P.	FEB 21 1854
BARNACLO, Virginia	RIDDLEMOSER, Geo. W.	NOV 09 1857
BARNACLOE, John M.	WALL, Rachel R.	JUN 03 1840
BARNARD, Caroline M.	FLEURY, Lewis Augustus	OCT 03 1835
BARNARD, Charles C.P.	BOWEN, Eliza Ann [Mrs.]	SEP 13 1836
BARNARD, Harriet R.	CAPRON, Erastus A.	MAY 28 1836
BARNARD, Mary C.	CISSEL, Richard S.T.	DEC 26 1850
BARNARD, Robert	CROPLEY, Sophia	APR 20 1821
BARNARD, Samuel J.	CROPLEY, Amelia P.	SEP 02 1833
BARNARD, Sophia Dorothy	HIGGINS, John Hamilton	MAY 06 1848
BARNARD, Theodore	BERRY, Matilda R.	AUG 05 1844
BARNECLO, Ann H.	EDMONSTON, Charles	OCT 29 1840
BARNECLOE, Julia Ann	HOOVER, Andrew P.	MAY 03 1847
BARNES, Alexander	BALEY, Mary Ann	JUN 13 1837
BARNES, Ann	PIERCE, Ivan	OCT 07 1820
BARNES, Charlotte	STEWART, John	AUG 13 1812
BARNES, Chas. W.	PAINE, Margaret A.	JUL 09 1856
BARNES, Eleanor	LIGHTFOOT, George W.	DEC 18 1827

District of Columbia Marriage Licenses, 1811-1858

BARNES, Elias	JOHNSON, Harriett	JAN 15 1828
BARNES, Eliza Ann	DAVIS, Solomon	NOV 16 1850
BARNES, Elizabeth	NASH, Patrick F.	JUN 17 1830
BARNES, Elizabeth	HUNT, Noah	JUN 28 1838
BARNES, Elizabeth	RUNDELL, Addison	JUL 07 1841
BARNES, Elizabeth	HAMILTON, William H.	SEP 16 1845
BARNES, Elizabeth	DOONE, John Francis	MAR 12 1858
BARNES, Elizabeth L.	THOMAS, Addison Newton	SEP 20 1823
BARNES, Elizth. E.	MARCERON, Joseph F.	OCT 27 1855
BARNES, Ellen (blk)	WATTS, Augustus	OCT 14 1839
BARNES, Ellen C.	SANDERSON, James Overton	JUL 24 1855
BARNES, Ephraim	MILLER, Ellen	APR 13 1852
BARNES, Eveline	LYON, Evan	NOV 29 1831
BARNES, George	HUNTER, Mary	SEP 03 1828
BARNES, George	BROWN, Rachel	APR 16 1833
BARNES, Georgiana	VARNALL, Thomas L.	DEC 01 1856
BARNES, Harriet Ann	POOR, John F.	APR 05 1853
BARNES, Henry	GRAVES, Mary	DEC 22 1814
BARNES, Henry	ARNOLD, Margaret	DEC 17 1839
BARNES, Henry L.	LONGSTON, Mary E.	SEP 23 1857
BARNES, Horatio	BAKER, Mary Ann	JUL 12 1834
BARNES, James	McATEE, Elizabeth	MAY 11 1813
BARNES, James	BEANS, Elizabeth	SEP 02 1836
BARNES, James T.	KING, Harriet	JAN 27 1852
BARNES, James Wm.	HAWKINS, Frances Louisa (col'd)	NOV 14 1855
BARNES, John	CONNELL, Catherine	NOV 12 1813
BARNES, John	GRAY, Polly	NOV 27 1828
BARNES, John	LANE, Sarah	MAR 26 1831
BARNES, John H.	FOX, Mary Isabella	NOV 04 1851
BARNES, Jonathan	BERRY, Ancaret	APR 24 1821
BARNES, Joseph	COLLINS, Elizabeth M.	MAR 20 1837
BARNES, Marietta	FEARSON, John W.	JUN 17 1840
BARNES, Mary	GRANGER, Clement	MAR 06 1821
BARNES, Mary	PEARCE, Valentine	DEC 18 1832
BARNES, Mary	DOWNEY, Michael	NOV 12 1840
BARNES, Mary	MORAN, Wm. M.	MAY 10 1856
BARNES, Mary A.	MORTIMER, William Henry	AUG 27 1846
BARNES, Mary Ann	FEDLINE, James A.	SEP 01 1831
BARNES, Mary Ann	EVANS, James	OCT 26 1835
BARNES, Mary Ann	WEAVER, Henry	JAN 01 1848
BARNES, Mary Cecelia	McDONALD, Thomas	JUN 11 1839
BARNES, Mary E.	BOSSE, William	OCT 17 1854
BARNES, Mary Jane	MILLER, John Francis	JUN 28 1853
BARNES, Miranda Ann	HESHLEY, Conrad	NOV 05 1851
BARNES, Overton	SMALLWOOD, Mary Jane (blk)	NOV 30 1852
BARNES, Peter	SPRIGG, Fanny (blk)	NOV 03 1842
BARNES, Richard	WILSON, Eliza	APR 15 1845
BARNES, Robert	TUCKER, Mary	JUN 05 1817
BARNES, Samuel	O'LEARY, Lucy	OCT 15 1817
BARNES, Thomas J.	JOHNSON, Sarah Ann	JAN 01 1839
BARNES, Thomas T.	ORME, Lucy Ann	JAN 05 1832
BARNES, Trueman	LOKER, Mary Ann	JUL 27 1815
BARNES, William	COOKE, Mary E.	JUN 04 1835
BARNES, William	McCOY, Elizabeth	DEC 21 1844
BARNES, William A.	BERRY, Ann Amelia	FEB 25 1854
BARNES, William H.	McMURRAY, Margaret	MAR 28 1826
BARNET, Charles	MORGAN, Ann	DEC 12 1826
BARNET, Elizabeth	CLARKE, Joseph	JUL 15 1815

District of Columbia Marriage Licenses, 1811-1858

BARNET, Mary	HANSON, Thomas S.	OCT 31 1823
BARNETT, Catharine	CONNOR, John	MAR 28 1845
BARNETT, Lucy	TALBOTT, J.P.	APR 01 1845
BARNETT, Margaret	COLLINS, Dennis	AUG 07 1849
BARNETT, Rebecca	TOUPET, Francis	MAR 31 1812
BARNEY, Samuel C.	DeKRAFFT, Mary Eleanor	JUN 14 1847
BARNEY, Solomon P.	HACK, Frances A.	SEP 30 1833
BARNHILL, Gabriel	HART, Abegail	JAN 27 1814
BARNHILL, Louisa M.	BARTLETT, John H.	OCT 20 1857
BARNHISEL, Elizabeth	SPILMAN, Thomas K.	SEP 22 1831
BARNHOUSE, Alcuszera	FOWLER, Joseph	SEP 08 1851
BARNHOUSE, Caleb	LANE, Mary	SEP 12 1819
BARNHOUSE, Caleb	DARLEY, Lavinia	SEP 04 1847
BARNHOUSE, Jane	BAUM, William	FEB 11 1845
BARNHOUSE, Mary A.	DOOLING, William	AUG 27 1842
BARNHOUSE, Richard	DEVLEN, Frances Ann	OCT 29 1840
BARNISH, Barbara	SULLIVIN, Jeremiah	MAR 13 1822
BARNS, Christian	KNOTHE, Elizabeth	AUG 06 1855
BARNS, James	GOODIN, Martha Ellen	DEC 05 1837
BARNS, Mary	BIVINS, William W.	JUL 10 1852
BARNS, Mary Ellen	FASNAUGHT, George	DEC 11 1849
BARON, Ellen	HODGSON, John W.	DEC 14 1840
BARON, Jerome	ANN, Piscilla	JUL 11 1812
BARON, Josiah	BLOWERS, Lucretia A.	AUG 14 1855
BARON, William H.	MASON, Leeanah	APR 05 1817
BARR, James R.	McCLELLAND, Rosina	MAY 03 1839
BARR, John	SULLIVAN, Catharine	FEB 04 1854
BARR, John H.	BRIN, Francis A.	NOV 07 1849
BARR, Mary Jane	BROWN, Robert F.	MAR 06 1851
BARR, Robert	DAY, Mary	DEC 12 1844
BARR, Thomas	JENKINS, Chloe M.	JUN 21 1819
BARRACKE, Margaret A.	DRAKE, William H.	JUN 08 1858
BARREL, Robert	DUNNIGAN, Johanna	MAR 28 1856
BARREMANS, Charles	HURDLE, A.	MAY 02 1829
BARRESFORD, John	YOUNG, Charlot	MAY 03 1820
BARRET, Ellen	FLORVIN, Timothy	FEB 07 1853
BARRET, John	CALUNE, Mary	SEP 20 1851
BARRET, Michael	PRINDERVILL, Mary	FEB 20 1855
BARRET, Thomas J.	[RUSTREGE], Susan Ann	DEC 18 1832
BARRETT, Augustus	CONNOLLY, Elizabeth	AUG 03 1858
BARRETT, Catherine	RIGGLES, John	NOV 06 1834
BARRETT, Daniel	BRANDON, Mary	JUL 10 1855
BARRETT, Dennis	CRAIGHEN, Ellen	NOV 22 1851
BARRETT, Dennis	HALORAN, Mary	AUG 19 1854
BARRETT, Eleanor	EATON, Alexander	JUL 12 1817
BARRETT, Eliza	HADLEY, Job	APR 09 1818
BARRETT, Elizabeth	GRIMES, Alfred	JUL 25 1836
BARRETT, Ellen	LEVY, Thomas	NOV 23 1852
BARRETT, Ellen Ann	FISHER, Henry	JUL 02 1851
BARRETT, Emily E.	PRIOR, Thomas O.	DEC 11 1851
BARRETT, Erastus B.	HASTINGS, Julia	DEC 31 1855
BARRETT, Henrietta	MACKEY, Thomas	FEB 10 1838
BARRETT, Henrietta	TERLY, George L.	SEP 04 1856
BARRETT, Isaac	SHECKELLS, Elizabeth	NOV 15 1831
BARRETT, James	ALLEN, Rachael	JAN 13 1847
BARRETT, James J.	PAINE, Roberta	DEC 10 1850
BARRETT, Johanna	FITZGERALD, David	JUN 02 1855
BARRETT, John F.	GALER, Mary Louisa	DEC 27 1825

District of Columbia Marriage Licenses, 1811-1858

BARRETT, Levi G.	TARMAN, Ann	AUG 31 1835
BARRETT, Louisa	REYNOLDS, Samuel L.	OCT 07 1829
BARRETT, Margaret	RATCLIFFE, Lewis	JUN 15 1830
BARRETT, Mary	DELLAMAN, Harmon	JUN 13 1836
BARRETT, Mary	CALLAGHAN, Daniel	JUL 06 1857
BARRETT, Mary A.	CLARKE, Richard W.	FEB 21 1852
BARRETT, Mary A.	WOOD, William W.	NOV 23 1857
BARRETT, Mary Ann	RATCLIFF, John U.	JAN 15 1853
BARRETT, Michael	LANDRICHIN, Catherine	SEP 16 1853
BARRETT, Michael	POLLEY, Bridget	JUN 12 1858
BARRETT, Nancy	SAUNDERS, B.J.	FEB 04 1851
BARRETT, Rheuhama	PERRY, David	NOV 15 1827
BARRETT, Rosetta	McPHERSON, Samuel	FEB 12 1831
BARRETT, Thomas J.	RATCLIFF, Catherine	FEB 28 1854
BARRETT, William D.	MEEM, Ann E.	MAY 03 1825
BARRETT, William H.	ALLEN, Rebecca	JAN 05 1857
BARRETT, [blank]	SMITH, [blank]	OCT 04 1834
BARRINGER, Mary	ROGERS, John	APR 04 1826
BARRITT, Ann E.	THOMAS, Jenkin	JUN 17 1848
BARRON, Alethia	DIX, John	OCT 04 1828
BARRON, Alexander	GOODS, Ellen	APR 30 1838
BARRON, Annie E.	JOHNSON, George J.	FEB 07 1856
BARRON, Augustin	THOMPSON, Jane	SEP 23 1837
BARRON, Bridget	MORIARTY, William	OCT 02 1851
BARRON, Catharine	GRAHAM, Guy	FEB 25 1851
BARRON, Cornelius	MARSHALL, Mary	DEC 31 1838
BARRON, Daniel	ALLEN, Emily	FEB 12 1850
BARRON, Eliza	WHITE, Enoch	DEC 27 1827
BARRON, George O.	WILLIAMSON, Harriet	MAY 08 1845
BARRON, George O.	CRAGE, Mary A.	NOV 07 1850
BARRON, Hannah	PAXTON, John	SEP 18 1837
BARRON, Henry	HARKNESS, Mary S.	NOV 28 1826
BARRON, Henry	DEAN, Mary Ellen	JUN 02 1835
BARRON, Henry	DAVIS, Elizabeth A.	MAY 13 1850
BARRON, Henry	HOOTEE, Sarah Eliza	NOV 14 1855
BARRON, Henry A.	LATIMORE, Rebecca Ann	FEB 23 1825
BARRON, Henry L.	DYSON, Mary Ann	MAR 15 1853
BARRON, James	STEWART, Elizabeth	OCT 17 1826
BARRON, James W.	DYER, Jusia	MAY 20 1829
BARRON, Janet	KNOWLES, William	APR 24 1817
BARRON, Maria	ALLEN, Patrick	APR 05 1858
BARRON, Mary	LANGLEY, Francis	NOV 17 1849
BARRON, Mary Ann	BOSWORTH, Eliphalet [Rev.]	JUN 02 1835
BARRON, Michael	MATTHEWS, Bridget	MAY 07 1838
BARRON, Samuel	WILLIAMSON, Mary Ann	JAN 29 1850
BARRON, Thomas H.	DONIPHAN, Catherine	DEC 29 1846
BARRON, Virginia E.M.	PARDOW, Henry F.B.	APR 30 1851
BARRON, Wm. H.	DUGANS, Elizabeth	OCT 05 1818
BARROTT, Eliza	GODDARD, Benjamin	MAR 28 1815
BARROTT, Sabriet Cissel	TIMS, Ann	DEC 13 1814
BARROWS, Winny	HALL, Hezekiah	FEB 01 1814
BARRS, Ruth Ann	DARMHARDT, John	DEC 21 1857
BARRY, Ann Margaret	MOHUN, Francis	JAN 29 1835
BARRY, Anna	JOSETTY, Martin L.B.	JUL 05 1851
BARRY, Bridget	NOLAND, John	MAY 06 1851
BARRY, Bridget	LYNCH, Michael	JAN 14 1858
BARRY, Catherine	LYNCH, John	JUN 25 1853
BARRY, David	ADAMS, Delia Ann	OCT 22 1833

District of Columbia Marriage Licenses, 1811-1858

BARRY, David	BERLIN, Mary S.	MAY 12 1853
BARRY, Edward	BUTLER, Julianna	JUL 25 1850
BARRY, Edward	DOOLEY, Catherine	SEP 23 1852
BARRY, Eliza G.	HOLTZMAN, Wm. F.	MAY 20 1816
BARRY, Eliza R.	BRODHEAD, Thomas W.	JAN 04 1854
BARRY, Ellen	MEGHEGAN, David	JUN 06 1857
BARRY, Francis, Jr.	LOWE, Mary Jane	FEB 03 1845
BARRY, James	COOTE, Ann	MAY 02 1838
BARRY, Jane	WILKINSON, John	NOV 05 1840
BARRY, John	FARLAND, Harriott	JUL 15 1827
BARRY, John	HOGAN, Mary	JUL 24 1858
BARRY, John W.	HUTCHINSON, Martha B.	OCT 01 1834
BARRY, Joseph O.	FIELDS, Mary	JUL 20 1815
BARRY, Kurdelin, Mrs.	TUTTLE, John Thomas	DEC 21 1839
BARRY, Lucy C.	MARSHALL, John J.	APR 20 1858
BARRY, Maria	BROOKS, Peter	FEB 16 1836
BARRY, Mary	TRIMBLE, Jacob B.	JUN 22 1848
BARRY, Mary P.	HANSON, Thomas M.	MAY 17 1853
BARRY, Michael	CALAHAN, Catherine	DEC 27 1843
BARRY, Michael	SULLIVAN, Ann	NOV 11 1854
BARRY, Richard	TOWNSEND, Eliza	SEP 06 1828
BARRY, Richard	DAWSON, Margaret	MAY 14 1840
BARRY, Richard N.	SIMPSON, Elizabeth	DEC 14 1833
BARRY, Teresa	SMITH, James	JUN 02 1849
BARSICK, Lucretia	JONES, William P.	MAR 06 1841
BARTELMISS, Katharina	DUBEL, Henry	JUN 13 1857
BARTH, Henry	BEELER, Frances	NOV 11 1856
BARTHCOLON, J. Presley	PHILIPS, Isabella	FEB 13 1856
BARTHEL, Edward	CONRAD, Wilhelmine	SEP 02 1856
BARTHEL, John	POEHLMANN, Margaretha	MAY 26 1857
BARTHEL, Mary	OSTHAUS, Hermin	AUG 07 1855
BARTHOLIC, Jonathan W.	HAGAN, Cena R.	DEC 08 1855
BARTHOLOMEW, Isabella	GEIGER, John Jacob	JUN 19 1851
BARTLE, Cordelia	DANKWORTH, Frederick	DEC 07 1841
BARTLE, Ellen Francis	MUSE, Walker I.	OCT 27 1853
BARTLE, George	ELLIS, Miranda	OCT 11 1849
BARTLE, Mary Ann	DOUGHERTY, William	MAY 12 1838
BARTLES, Maria	MASON, George	FEB 16 1853
BARTLETT, Burgiss D.	TEMMS, Armenia	MAR 23 1846
BARTLETT, Elizth. B.	GLYNN, Anthony Greville	JUL 24 1826
BARTLETT, Fitz James	BEALL, Martha S.	NOV 07 1849
BARTLETT, Frances V.	BOSWELL, Ignatius M.	SEP 23 1856
BARTLETT, Isaac	FITZ, Elizabeth	OCT 17 1818
BARTLETT, Isaac C.	BEAN, Mary A.	MAR 10 1842
BARTLETT, John	FRAZIER, Jane	DEC 20 1816
BARTLETT, John H., Jr.	FOOG, Dolly	APR 26 1834
BARTLETT, John H.	BARNHILL, Louisa M.	OCT 20 1857
BARTLETT, Walter	BEACH, Catherine	JUL 10 1851
BARTLETT, William	JOHNSON, Mary Ellen	FEB 08 1848
BARTLEY, Fielder	SIMPSON, Chloe	OCT 16 1823
BARTLEY, Isiah	BLAIR, Ann C.	OCT 27 1843
BARTLEY, James T.	TURNER, Elizabeth	FEB 22 1842
BARTLEY, Walter	TUCKER, Margaret	JUN 12 1838
BARTLY, James	HIGDON, Eleanor	OCT 25 1815
BARTON, Adeline (col'd)	THOMAS, Henry (col'd)	JUN 28 1852
BARTON, Benjamin	KENNEDY, Eliza Douglass	APR 13 1846
BARTON, Demarines H.	BENSON, Thomas J.	AUG 30 1856
BARTON, Elizabeth (blk)	HICKS, Henry	AUG 13 1841

District of Columbia Marriage Licenses, 1811-1858

BARTON, Green H.	WARING, Rachel E.	MAY 12 1847
BARTON, Henry	TIPPETT, Julia Ann	OCT 11 1832
BARTON, James	JOHNSON, Harriet	MAR 07 1837
BARTON, James	WOODWARD, Mary (blk)	MAY 13 1848
BARTON, James	FARRAL, Mary	FEB 02 1856
BARTON, Levi Ann (blk)	PROCTOR, John Henry	JAN 08 1852
BARTON, Mary Ann	LOUNDS, Richard (blk)	OCT 09 1845
BARTON, Richard C.	FLEMMING, Alice	FEB 24 1849
BARTON, Sarah Jane (blk)	ORR, William Henry	MAY 15 1843
BARTON, Sarah Jane (blk)	BECKET, William H.	AUG 15 1850
BARTON, Thomas Pennant	LIVINGSTON, Sophie Cora	APR 24 1833
BARTON, Thomas [Rev.]	SAMPLE, Margaret	NOV 04 1824
BARTON, Thos. B. [Lieut.]	KING, Louisa	AUG 17 1819
BARTON, William	LEE, Nelly (blk)	APR 18 1843
BARTON, William	BERK, Harriat (blk)	MAR 04 1858
BARTRUFF, Adeline V.	DARNOLD, Thomas L.	MAR 28 1848
BARTZ, Lanehard	KNATZ, Katherine	NOV 02 1855
BARXTALL, Ann E.	VYER, Bernard A.	MAY 21 1853
BASAEBASE, Elizabeth	HEISLAND, Michael	OCT 05 1846
BASELER, Mary	KEYSER, Robert	APR 17 1857
BASFORD, Mary Jane	PRICE, George C.	JUN 04 1842
BASHAW, Daniel	MITCHELL, Pleasant	NOV 26 1828
BASHAW, Rawleigh	WIRT, Hannah Sophia	APR 01 1834
BASHELBRIDGE, Joseph	RATCLIFF, Margaret R.	MAY 21 1853
BASSAN, Emelie	MARKS, Harvey R.	JUN 08 1849
BASSET, Assel	HOLBERT, Rachael	MAR 18 1819
BASSET, Simion	TWEDY, Uphemy	MAR 06 1819
BASSETT, Catharine	BROWN, Benedict P.	DEC 22 1842
BASSETT, David	DUNCANSON, Catherine M.	APR 18 1845
BASSETT, George A.	WILLIAMS, Clorinda M.	NOV 05 1856
BASSETT, Isaac	HURDLE, Adaline	DEC 26 1838
BASSETT, Marinda	LEYDANE, Patrick	FEB 26 1844
BASSETT, Mary J.	KERR, William W.S.	NOV 05 1851
BASSETT, Rachael	TENLEY, Theodore	NOV 06 1828
BASSETT, Robert Tweedy	DEMAREST, Susan	JUN 03 1847
BASSETT, Sydney D.	FERGUSON, Mary	JUL 27 1850
BASSFORD, Sarah	CROSS, Reed	JAN 23 1821
BASSFORD, William T.	BURCH, Mary Priscilla	MAY 06 1852
BASSON, Mary Ann	BELT, James	JUN 16 1828
BASTABLE, Charles	McGINN, Mary	DEC 30 1852
BASTABLE, Rebecca	McGINN, James	NOV 23 1855
BASTEANELLI, Titus	TRUITTE, Mary DeLa	NOV 13 1846
BASTOW, John	MARKS, Arabella	DEC 08 1853
BATCHELOR, William Anglis	GIBBS, Lucretia Ann	APR 10 1843
BATEMAN, Abraham	BROWN, Sarah (blk)	MAY 22 1823
BATEMAN, Catharine Ann	FORREST, Edward	APR 29 1837
BATEMAN, Ellen	WILKINSON, George	NOV 22 1855
BATEMAN, Emeline (blk)	CLARKE, Stephen	APR 22 1856
BATEMAN, Isaiah	PARKER, Priscilla (blk)	AUG 29 1849
BATEMAN, Jemima C.	SLEIGH, Charles	NOV 11 1857
BATEMAN, Joshua	DEAKINS, Jane	JUN 20 1828
BATEMAN, Mahlon	BROOKS, Emeline (blk)	NOV 13 1856
BATEMEN, Hannah J.	WAYSON, Nicholas	FEB 11 1858
BATES, Catharine	BUTLER, Edward	MAR 19 1853
BATES, David	VENABLE, Ann	FEB 13 1817
BATES, Eliza	SEARLES, Isaac	JUL 15 1854
BATES, Fanny	WEBSTER, Stephen	MAY 24 1832
BATES, Frederick	DAWES, Sarah Taylor	APR 26 1842

District of Columbia Marriage Licenses, 1811-1858

BATES, Jane L.	CADLE, John	MAY 21 1825
BATES, John	SAVAGE, Mary Elizabeth	OCT 09 1847
BATES, John E.	LITTLE, Julia A.	JUN 04 1849
BATES, John E.	WILLIAMS, Charlotte J.	JAN 06 1852
BATES, Julia A.	KESLEY, William	MAR 03 1835
BATES, Lydia	WILLIAMS, Lemuel	OCT 06 1830
BATES, Mary	LUNDY, Emmer K.	OCT 10 1848
BATES, Mary Elizabeth	WOODWARD, James M.	AUG 24 1854
BATES, Robert	BIENDER, Bertha (blk)	JUN 15 1858
BATES, Robert W.	DYER, Sarah Rebecca	JUN 03 1835
BATES, William	TONGE, Mary	MAY 11 1843
BATHAN, John	SKINNER, Jane Charlotte	DEC 09 1837
BATMAN, Elizabeth	BURROWS, John	OCT 30 1824
BATSON, Daniel	BROOKS, Mary M. (blk)	MAY 08 1856
BATSON, Selin	MURPHEY, Mary (blk)	AUG 12 1840
BATT, Catherine	LAMAN, John H.	JAN 10 1842
BATT, Lavinia	GERMAN, George	MAR 02 1854
BATT, Lavinia	MacDANIEL, George	JUN 18 1857
BATT, Thomas Henry	GENTLE, Rebecca	JUN 30 1835
BATT, Wm.	DENNISON, Sarah Ann	MAY 24 1825
BATTER, Mary M.	THOMAS, Gwynneir	DEC 16 1850
BATTHROPE, Ann Maria	KERCHEVAL, William	MAR 10 1836
BATTLE, John	CALVERT, Betsey	JAN 29 1831
BATTLE, Sally (blk)	DEAN, William	AUG 14 1851
BATTON, Priscilla	THOMAS, William	APR 13 1843
BATTS, Thomas	FYE, Bridget	AUG 24 1851
BATZOLD, Frederick	DAW, Eliza	JUN 11 1821
BAUCHE, John Frederick	HAGER, Henrietta	NOV 26 1853
BAUER, Andon	WEIGHORN, Amalia	NOV 12 1855
BAUER, Fanny	VOGEL, Jacob	MAY 16 1854
BAUFRE, Anna M.	RICHARDSON, Thomas S.	APR 14 1857
BAUGESS, Lydia	ATKINSON, James	JAN 14 1817
BAULWIN, Rebecca	PRIME, William J.	FEB 23 1826
BAUM, Charles	HILL, Elizabeth	JUN 12 1832
BAUM, Elizabeth V.	WINN, James T.	MAR 10 1842
BAUM, John C.	LARCOMB, Emily	JAN 12 1847
BAUM, Susan D.	BOWEN, James	JUL 23 1835
BAUM, William	BARNHOUSE, Jane	FEB 11 1845
BAUMBACH, Amandus	ADAMS, Martha	NOV 15 1856
BAWLDING, Judson	TIPPETT, Mary	OCT 02 1823
BAWLDING, Thomas	SUIT, Susannah	OCT 23 1818
BAWLING, Emily	McDANIEL, Michael	JAN 07 1822
BAXTER, James	CLOAKEY, Mary	OCT 08 1828
BAXTER, Jane Ellen W.	CHAPPELARE, Wm. H.	MAY 28 1855
BAXTER, Samuel	McNEALE, Frances	NOV 18 1857
BAXTER, Woolsey	DODD, Elizabeth	JAN 08 1857
BAYER, Ferdinand	IMES, Mary	JUN 20 1817
BAYERS, Mary	PETIT, John	MAY 30 1823
BAYLEY, Elizabeth	THOMPSON, William	NOV 16 1844
BAYLEY, Elizabeth (blk)	SAMSON, Thos. Hamilton	OCT 07 1856
BAYLEY, Jane	BRIGHT, John	OCT 18 1823
BAYLISS, Augustin	DANIELL, Susan A.	OCT 06 1834
BAYLISS, Buckner	COYLE, Catherine B.	JUN 28 1834
BAYLISS, George R.	CLEVELAND, Louisa	JUL 21 1848
BAYLISS, Lucinda	DESHAZO, James E.	DEC 22 1857
BAYLISS, Margaret A.	BAKER, Zachariah	JUL 07 1851
BAYLISS, Margaret J.	TIPIT, John T.	APR 14 1857
BAYLISS, Martha A.	DANIELS, William T.	JUL 05 1849

District of Columbia Marriage Licenses, 1811-1858

BAYLISS, May	WILLIAMS, James	DEC 05 1821
BAYLISS, Nancy	SAULS, Edward	SEP 14 1848
BAYLISS, Payne	BIGGS, Telley	FEB 27 1812
BAYLISS, Rebecca	GRISLEY, John	SEP 06 1834
BAYLISS, Robert	DRISCOE, Fanny W.	MAR 06 1854
BAYLISS, Sanford	SKIDMORE, Rebecca	FEB 23 1830
BAYLISS, Thomas	SUIT, Mary Ann	OCT 27 1840
BAYLISS, William	BURCH, Rebecca	APR 12 1827
BAYLISS, William	DEVERS, Elizabeth	FEB 15 1831
BAYLISS, William	WISE, Elizth.	MAY 13 1837
BAYLISS, William P.	EVANS, Susan Ann	JUN 14 1827
BAYLISS, William P.	DANIEL, Julia	JAN 02 1845
BAYLOR, Chas. G.	WADSWORTH, Louisa D.	JAN 05 1853
BAYLOR, Gwynnetta W.	DADE, Charles E.	MAY 18 1832
BAYLY, Edward	KING, Rosanna	MAR 26 1835
BAYLY, Eleanor	HANSON, Samuel, of Ths.	MAR 13 1817
BAYLY, George N.	POTTER, Susan	JAN 26 1818
BAYLY, Mary R.	SMITH, John [Lieut.]	NOV 14 1821
BAYLY, Sarah	DYER, Philip	MAR 06 1815
BAYLY, Thomas L.	BEAN, Julia	DEC 24 1855
BAYLY, William	MASON, Mary Ann H.	SEP 21 1824
BAYLY, William Cole	MURRAY, Anna	MAY 28 1850
BAYLY, William E.	BRITTENHAM, Elizabeth	OCT 30 1833
BAYLYS, Pain	EVANS, Susan Ann	SEP 08 1825
BAYN, Horatio	GRAY, Elizabeth	SEP 21 1815
BAYNE, Elizabeth	KITLEN, William	OCT 20 1825
BAYNE, George H.	SPEEDIN, Marion E.	NOV 02 1853
BAYNE, James	CLEMENTS, Matilda	NOV 18 1824
BAYNE, Jno. H., Dr.	McDANIEL, Mary Frances	JAN 10 1827
BAYNE, Joseph	BOSTON, Ellen (blk)	MAY 13 1856
BAYNE, Martha	HUSSEY, Jeremiah	NOV 03 1856
BAYNE, Mary	McGOLDRICK, Charles	JUL 07 1835
BAYNE, Mary A.	ARNOLD, William H.	OCT 13 1852
BAYNE, Sallie A.	KING, Venerando E.	NOV 20 1847
BAYNE, Sallie A.	KING, Venerando E.	NOV 20 1849
BAYNE, Sarah Ann	DAWSON, Samuel	MAR 20 1834
BAYNE, Susan	GREENLIEF, Thomas	MAY 31 1821
BAYNE, William H.	TAYLOR, Elizabeth A.	JUL 17 1838
BAYSE, Polly (blk)	BURGESS, Cyrus	FEB 13 1836
BAZELL, John	HEARTLOVE, Mary Ann	APR 20 1820
BAZIN, Alfred Auguste	McLAUGHLIN, Mary	OCT 31 1844
BEACH, Albert H.	THORP, Evelina B.	NOV 24 1847
BEACH, Amelia Maria	MEDFORD, Charles Franklin	APR 08 1854
BEACH, Annette R.	SIMPSON, James E.	MAY 20 1856
BEACH, Catharine	SIMPSON, Bernard	SEP 15 1831
BEACH, Catherine	BARTLETT, Walter	JUL 10 1851
BEACH, Cinderella	BEACH, Thomas J.	JAN 08 1824
BEACH, Columbus	HARR, Caroline V.	AUG 24 1858
BEACH, Elizabeth	FUNSON, James	OCT 05 1822
BEACH, Elizabeth	DAVIS, John	MAR 09 1852
BEACH, Emily J.	CANNON, Joseph	NOV 29 1855
BEACH, Ferdinand	ALLEN, Jane Catherine	NOV 18 1852
BEACH, Headley	TAYLOR, Mildred L.	DEC 04 1856
BEACH, Henry	PETTIT, Mary C.	FEB 18 1858
BEACH, James Henry	CHESER, Adeline	JUN 22 1854
BEACH, James T.	COOK, Jane	JAN 01 1852
BEACH, Jane	FINNIGAN, Charles	NOV 02 1839
BEACH, Jane Elizabeth	HALL, Tempel	JAN 20 1848

District of Columbia Marriage Licenses, 1811-1858

BEACH, Jeremiah	BEACH, Penelope	JUN 05 1828
BEACH, Lucinda	COOK, James G.	SEP 21 1848
BEACH, Margaret	GRANGER, William H.	FEB 14 1817
BEACH, Mary	BARBER, William	SEP 27 1856
BEACH, Mary Ann	LANE, Francis W.	JUN 11 1846
BEACH, Mary Ann	COLEMAN, Francis	OCT 02 1855
BEACH, Mary Eliza	RAGAN, William	DEC 26 1850
BEACH, Nancy	FRAZIER, Horace	DEC 07 1815
BEACH, Nathaniel	ASHBY, Maria Louisa	AUG 23 1852
BEACH, Penelope	BEACH, Jeremiah	JUN 05 1828
BEACH, Robert	MURRAY, Lucinda	FEB 17 1852
BEACH, Samuel	CRAWFORD, Sarah	APR 02 1835
BEACH, Sarah A.	McDANIEL, Calvin S.	MAR 14 1850
BEACH, Susan	PHILIPS, Isaac	FEB 01 1818
BEACH, Susan	NORRIS, Daniel	JUN 17 1826
BEACH, Theodocia	BOND, Joseph	AUG 26 1851
BEACH, Thomas J.	BEACH, Cinderella	JAN 08 1824
BEACH, Virginia	HALL, Daniel	APR 28 1851
BEACH, William	PRICE, Mary Ann	JUL 13 1815
BEACH, William A.	ARRINGTON, Catharine E.	AUG 04 1856
BEACH, William E.	DeVAUGHAN, Susan H.	NOV 01 1847
BEACH, William H.	HALL, Elizabeth J.	AUG 16 1849
BEACH, Wm.	BOYCE, Catharine	AUG 02 1842
BEACH, Zachariah	PRICE, Elizabeth	JUL 10 1851
BEACHUM, Fenton Sarah	TUCKER, William N.	AUG 04 1858
BEAGLE, Ann	MILSTEAD, Judson	OCT 13 1824
BEAGLE, Ann	WHITMORE, Edward	JUL 02 1825
BEAGLE, Eliza	LACEY, John	NOV 20 1851
BEAGLE, Mary Frances	HEISE, Joseph Lewis	NOV 26 1853
BEAGLE, William	BYERS, Henrietta	SEP 28 1854
BEAKE, Jacob	BAILEY, Rebecca	JUL 24 1841
BEAKE, William	HAMILTON, Jane	AUG 27 1851
BEAKLEY, Kage	FREE, Margaret	SEP 01 1829
BEALE, Andrew	SANDERS, Mahala Ann	FEB 02 1843
BEALE, Catharine A.	CROSBY, John	OCT 26 1820
BEALE, Cyrus	HOPKINS, Nancy	APR 08 1841
BEALE, Elizabeth	PORTER, William D.	FEB 27 1839
BEALE, Elizabeth K.	McREA, James M.	SEP 01 1820
BEALE, Emily T.	WHEELER, Junius B.	SEP 18 1855
BEALE, Eugenia D.	DAVIS, James W.	DEC 31 1855
BEALE, George N.	WHEELER, Elizth. B.	JUN 02 1851
BEALE, John S.H.H.E.	ALEXANDER, Elmira E.E.	FEB 26 1829
BEALE, Margaret	BROWN, Jacob J.	AUG 31 1813
BEALE, Matilda	MULLIKIN, Basil	JAN 27 1815
BEALL, Agnes	ERSKIN, John	DEC 27 1819
BEALL, Alfred	RIDGWAY, Harriet	SEP 17 1826
BEALL, Amelia T.	DORSETT, Fielder [Col.]	FEB 02 1813
BEALL, Andrew	TURNER, Mary	OCT 18 1817
BEALL, Andrew	BECKET, Barbara	DEC 30 1823
BEALL, Andrew	BEALL, Eleanor	JAN 06 1830
BEALL, Ann	TURNER, John W.	DEC 08 1831
BEALL, Ann Eliza	PARALTA, Manuel	SEP 17 1849
BEALL, Ann Elizabeth	FORD, George	DEC 31 1844
BEALL, Ann Emma Beall	WILSON, James Campbell	JAN 18 1816
BEALL, Annie E.T.	WALLACH, Cuthbert P.	OCT 21 1847
BEALL, Benjamin	MIDDLETON, Caroline	FEB 13 1838
BEALL, Beverly W.	PLOWMAN, Catherine	JAN 18 1844
BEALL, Charles	LEWIS, Sarah Jane	MAY 14 1846

District of Columbia Marriage Licenses, 1811-1858

BEALL, Charles	PUMPHREY, Rachel A.	JUL 31 1856
BEALL, Charles R.	BUTT, Rebecca R.	JAN 28 1840
BEALL, Deborah B.	DASHIELL, George W.	JUN 03 1817
BEALL, Edmund	RALY, Maria	NOV 30 1825
BEALL, Eleanor	BEALL, Andrew	JAN 06 1830
BEALL, Eleanor L.	WILSON, James S.	JAN 23 1834
BEALL, Elijah	SELBY, Eleanor	NOV 26 1818
BEALL, Elijah	PARSONS, S. Smith	JAN 04 1854
BEALL, Eliza J.	HOPKINS, George W.	OCT 06 1846
BEALL, Elizth. [Mrs.]	McDANIEL, John, Sr.	OCT 20 1812
BEALL, Elizabeth	BURCH, Joseph Alexander	MAY 12 1817
BEALL, Elizabeth	HANSON, Thomas	FEB 10 1820
BEALL, Elizabeth	SIMMS, Basil	OCT 10 1822
BEALL, Elizabeth	LEE, Alfred	DEC 14 1825
BEALL, Elizabeth Ann	HAGERTY, John	JUL 07 1831
BEALL, Elizabeth T.	YOUNG, Manduit	DEC 09 1813
BEALL, Ellen	BEALL, Theophilus	JAN 16 1817
BEALL, Emily Orman	WATSON, Isaac	MAY 27 1830
BEALL, George A.	YERBY, Lucretia V.	MAY 07 1856
BEALL, George Ingham	WALKER, Mary	NOV 24 1831
BEALL, George W.	DAVIS, Mary Ann	DEC 24 1841
BEALL, Grandison	LANHAM, Margaret	DEC 09 1852
BEALL, Harriet	BEANS, Scipio	OCT 18 1819
BEALL, Harriet	PARSON, Joseph B.	MAY 13 1831
BEALL, Henrietta	PHILLIPS, Johnathan	APR 29 1823
BEALL, Henry	BELT, Martha	APR 22 1844
BEALL, Hezekiah	LLOYD, Jane	MAR 05 1833
BEALL, Horatio	SIMS; Elizabeth Ann	DEC 02 1843
BEALL, Indiana M.	FOSTER, William C.	MAY 18 1857
BEALL, Jackson	HILL, Georgie	OCT 01 1855
BEALL, James E.	ANDERSON, Sarah E.	MAY 03 1858
BEALL, James F.	OWEN, Julia Ann	OCT 26 1837
BEALL, James H.	MORGAN, Elizabeth A.R.	DEC 29 1856
BEALL, John	WALKER, Catherine	JUL 29 1834
BEALL, John	DODSON, Lavinia	JUN 29 1841
BEALL, John	McCURDYS, Mary	NOV 02 1848
BEALL, John A.	WILSON, Narcissa	JUL 26 1825
BEALL, John R.	LUCKETT, Martha	MAY 12 1831
BEALL, Joseph	SIMMS, Julia (blk)	NOV 22 1849
BEALL, Laura Lee	BUTLER, David, Jr. [Capt.]	FEB 07 1828
BEALL, Lawson	WEBB, Rachel	JUL 12 1823
BEALL, Levin Covington	FENWICK, Elizabeth E.	APR 06 1858
BEALL, Louisa	FRENCH, Edmund [Lt.]	DEC 21 1831
BEALL, Maria	BRADLEY, Charles	MAY 24 1825
BEALL, Maria	McFARLAND, William	DEC 10 1831
BEALL, Martha Ann (blk)	BREWER, Joseph W.	NOV 02 1853
BEALL, Martha S.	BARTLETT, Fitz James	NOV 07 1849
BEALL, Mary Ann	REMICK, Timothy	APR 20 1843
BEALL, Mary B.	COOKE, William	MAY 06 1817
BEALL, Mary Eliza	READ, William	MAY 27 1848
BEALL, Mary Ellen	DAWES, Harrison J.	DEC 26 1856
BEALL, Othy	BUTLER, Elizabeth	DEC 27 1825
BEALL, Peter	HAMILTON, Kitty (col'd)	MAY 17 1832
BEALL, Phineas B.	BOYD, Ann C.	MAY 03 1833
BEALL, Rachel Ann (blk)	YOUNG, Edmund	JUN 23 1831
BEALL, Richard J.	EDMONSTON, Cornelia	MAY 30 1853
BEALL, Richard M.	TILLEY, Eliza	FEB 19 1827
BEALL, Richd. B.W.	SAVAGE, Ann	APR 11 1834

District of Columbia Marriage Licenses, 1811-1858

BEALL, Robert	FORBES, Elizth. Jane	JUN 02 1829
BEALL, Robert A.	NORTON, Ann M.	FEB 19 1827
BEALL, Rufus	WHITE, Caroline	NOV 08 1837
BEALL, Sallie F.	MILSTEAD, Henry	MAY 24 1849
BEALL, Samuel	BAGGETT, Margaret L.	NOV 06 1856
BEALL, Sarah	TURNER, Richard	MAR 28 1833
BEALL, Sarah (blk)	LOMACK, Dennis	OCT 01 1838
BEALL, Sarah A.B.	JOHNSON, William S.	OCT 26 1853
BEALL, Susan	McDONALD, Patrick	MAY 08 1822
BEALL, Susan	KUHN, Joseph L.	AUG 07 1834
BEALL, Susan C.	KNOTT, Ignatius M.	NOV 12 1846
BEALL, Susan Virlinda	WARD, Ulyssus	SEP 26 1816
BEALL, Theophilus	BEALL, Ellen	JAN 16 1817
BEALL, Thomas	LONG, Mary	SEP 23 1823
BEALL, Thomas	OWENS, Mary	DEC 08 1830
BEALL, Thomas D.	MIDDLETON, Marcaline	JUN 19 1839
BEALL, Tobertha	PUMPHREY, Dennis	SEP 28 1835
BEALL, William D.	ELLIS, Mary	NOV 12 1841
BEALL, William D.	MARBURY, Martha Louisa	NOV 01 1842
BEALL, Wm.	WHEAT, Rebecca	DEC 13 1814
BEALL, Zachariah B.	ADDISON, Martha E.	JAN 09 1856
BEALS, Orpheus W.	KINGMAN, Mary E.	OCT 23 1855
BEAMS, Mary Jane (blk)	SIMMES, John Thomas	JUN 16 1851
BEAN, Alexander H.	MILBURN, Ann	MAY 30 1850
BEAN, Amos W.	COLE, Mary Ann	JUN 10 1851
BEAN, Ann	ROACH, Gustavus	OCT 29 1815
BEAN, Ann Olivia	VanRESWICK, William	MAY 05 1846
BEAN, Benjamin	WILLCOXON, Margaret	MAR 04 1822
BEAN, Colley W.	FUSS, Elizabeth	JAN 29 1857
BEAN, Colley Williams	WILKISON, Emeline	MAY 24 1845
BEAN, Colmore	MURRAY, Winefred	NOV 28 1812
BEAN, Eleanor	PAYNE, Andrew	DEC 29 1825
BEAN, Elizabeth	KESSLER, John	MAY 16 1853
BEAN, Elizabeth Ann S. [Mrs.]	BRYAN, Enoch	AUG 05 1824
BEAN, Elizabeth Olivia	GOODRICH, Henry	JUL 08 1847
BEAN, George	MILSTEAD, Ann	MAY 01 1842
BEAN, George	WHEELER, Caroline C.	NOV 24 1852
BEAN, Harriet (blk)	CORNISH, William A.	JUL 30 1839
BEAN, James	McCOY, Eliza	DEC 19 1844
BEAN, James W.	WARE, Martha E.	DEC 22 1855
BEAN, Jane	CASTELL, Edward O.	JAN 29 1841
BEAN, John	WILLIAMS, Elizabeth Ann Sabrina	DEC 23 1820
BEAN, John	NORTON, Catharine	OCT 01 1840
BEAN, Julia	BAYLY, Thomas L.	DEC 24 1855
BEAN, Lancelot	HARROD, Betsey	DEC 09 1817
BEAN, Margaret E.	SKELLY, William E.	MAR 29 1847
BEAN, Margarett	REED, William	FEB 05 1848
BEAN, Martha Ann	BOMAN, Allen	JAN 02 1851
BEAN, Mary	GATES, Richard L.	MAR 07 1848
BEAN, Mary A.	BARTLETT, Isaac C.	MAR 10 1842
BEAN, Mary Ann	JORDAN, Richard L.	OCT 21 1840
BEAN, Mary Ann	RICKETTS, Anthony	MAR 23 1852
BEAN, Noble	LEE, Elizabeth	DEC 21 1815
BEAN, Richard	YOUNG, Eleanor	OCT 09 1817
BEAN, Sarah	WILKINSON, Newman B.	MAY 02 1844
BEAN, Sarah Ann	DOVE, George M.	OCT 12 1840
BEAN, Silas	GITTINGS, Margaret Ann	JUN 29 1847
BEAN, Sophia W.	JONES, Thomas W.	MAY 19 1841

District of Columbia Marriage Licenses, 1811-1858

BEAN, Thomas	JOHNSON, Mary	OCT 11 1830
BEAN, Thomas	CECIL, Jane	JUL 26 1851
BEAN, William R.	LUXTON, Mary Ann	JUN 23 1840
BEAN, William W.	OLLIVER, Sophia	NOV 28 1853
BEAND, George	BENING, Elizabeth	SEP 12 1818
BEANES, Colmore	HILLARY, Ary Ann	DEC 01 1815
BEANES, Eliza S.	CROSS, Trueman [Maj.]	SEP 25 1821
BEANES, Mary B.	THOMAS, Frederick [Lt.]	MAY 01 1828
BEANS, Charlotte A. (blk)	BOOKER, Robert H.	OCT 27 1851
BEANS, Dawson	GRAY, Elizabeth	DEC 23 1817
BEANS, Eleanor	MORAN, John	FEB 08 1814
BEANS, Elizabeth	DAWNY, William	JUN 02 1827
BEANS, Elizabeth	BARNES, James	SEP 02 1836
BEANS, Francis	SMITH, Ann	SEP 21 1824
BEANS, Harrietta (blk)	SIMPSON, Tobias	JUN 19 1851
BEANS, Scipio	BEALL, Harriet	OCT 18 1819
BEAR, Robert	CARVER, Elizth.	AUG 18 1828
BEARD, Angeroner	COOPER, George	JAN 11 1858
BEARD, Catharine	BURROUGHS, James	MAY 31 1855
BEARD, George	DYE, Mary Elizabeth	AUG 05 1827
BEARD, John James	CREAMER, Emma Rebecca	AUG 16 1852
BEARD, William	HAMPTON, Mary	DEC 09 1824
BEARD, William H.	BESTOR, Harriott W.	OCT 22 1814
BEARD, Wm. W.	HOPKINS, Ann Janetta	DEC 04 1855
BEARDLY, George	LOURST, Lidian	APR 06 1822
BEARDS, John	TRICE, Delelah	JUN 01 1826
BEARDSLEY, Catharine	PURDEU, John	SEP 07 1839
BEARDSLEY, Eliza	GLEASON, Charles	DEC 29 1829
BEARDSLEY, Eliza	BAKER, Thomas	DEC 07 1832
BEARDSLEY, George	MOORE, Elizabeth	OCT 20 1821
BEARDSLEY, Joseph	TYSER, Susannah	DEC 18 1832
BEARDSLEY, Mary A.	CLARKE, James A.	SEP 12 1844
BEARDSLEY, Sarah J.	DANT, William E.	DEC 04 1851
BEARDSLEY, Susanna	CLARKE, Melton	FEB 08 1851
BEARDSLEY, William H.	SCHIEBLER, Maria S.O.	SEP 18 1855
BEARDSLY, Josephine	ANDERSON, Charles H.	JUL 16 1856
BEARSON, Catherine	AUGUST, Philip	MAY 03 1824
BEARY, John H.	ACTON, Christian	JAN 01 1840
BEASLEY, F.A.	MORRISON, A.J.	OCT 27 1852
BEASLEY, Fanny A.	HOBBS, Edward	APR 07 1858
BEASLEY, George	SMITH, America M.	MAY 24 1849
BEATLEY, Eliza J.	WILLIAMS, John A.	OCT 15 1857
BEATLEY, Joseph L.	NORRIS, Margaret H.	FEB 03 1855
BEATLEY, Kadge B.	SIMMONS, Ruth Ann	OCT 08 1851
BEATON, Farquharson	UNGERA, Lydia H.	SEP 10 1856
BEATTY, Ann	SEMMES, Joseph	SEP 10 1816
BEATTY, Archibald	McCAFFERY, Margaret	OCT 30 1832
BEATTY, Charles F.	ELLIOTT, Isabella Jane	JUN 08 1842
BEATTY, Charles F.	PAYNE, Eliza	MAR 25 1845
BEATTY, Charles U.	SCHWARTZE, Augusta M.	JAN 03 1854
BEATTY, Eleanor	SEMMES, Alexander	SEP 26 1820
BEATTY, Francis D.	BRADY, Catharine	FEB 02 1839
BEATTY, George W.	HECTER, Mary George	MAY 31 1856
BEATTY, Jane Court F. Harrison	SCOTT, John D.	MAR 14 1820
BEATTY, Robert H.	OTT, Mary C.	MAR 06 1826
BEATTY, Robert M.	REYNOLDS, Mary Ann	MAY 27 1839
BEATTY, Robert M.	HODGES, Catherine N.	FEB 07 1854
BEATTY, Rosannah A.	RITCHIE, John T. [Lieut.]	AUG 23 1820

District of Columbia Marriage Licenses, 1811-1858

BEATTY, Theophilus	WHITE, Elizabeth A.	FEB 23 1842
BEATY, Amanda M.F.	HURDLE, Henry M.	MAR 22 1841
BEAUCHAMP, Harriett	HINTON, John	JAN 29 1829
BEAUGRAND, Peter	REDING, Jane	JUL 06 1827
BEAVEN, Julia C.	MILLER, George W.	FEB 02 1856
BEAVENS, Francis W.	LANGLEY, Catharine C.	MAR 21 1856
BEAVER, John W.C.	HARRISON, Martha A.	NOV 21 1849
BEAVERS, Andrew	ROBEY, Sarah B.	SEP 09 1818
BEAVERS, Delilah	ROWLES, Thomas	AUG 07 1844
BEAVERS, Elizabeth	RUPHERT, Joseph	JAN 04 1858
BEAVERS, James	LAWSON, Jane Francis	FEB 14 1848
BEAVERS, James S.	WILKERSON, Sarah	SEP 08 1851
BEAVERS, Lydia	BROOKBANK, Thomas	JUL 06 1858
BEAVERS, Sampson	LEWISON, Jane Frances	FEB 28 1848
BECHTEL, Ernst August	GILDEMEISTER, Mary Louise	JUL 18 1851
BECK, A.R.	PRINGLE, William P.	AUG 17 1839
BECK, Ann Maria	HALL, George L.	JUN 10 1848
BECK, Catharine	JORDON, William	OCT 24 1851
BECK, Frederick	WINTER, Wilhelmina C.	JUL 16 1855
BECK, Isabel Y.P.	HANDY, Edward G.	APR 05 1842
BECK, John	REIDMULLER, Christina	NOV 26 1855
BECK, Joseph W.	LAWRIE, Elizabeth O.	AUG 01 1815
BECK, Margaret	NOLTE, Ludwig	JAN 14 1846
BECK, Maria	MELINS, Conrad	NOV 15 1843
BECK, Marion L.	TATE, James A.	SEP 19 1838
BECK, Mary	PANCOAST, David	JUL 02 1823
BECK, Mary C.	McCALLUM, Archibald T.	JAN 30 1858
BECK, Nicholas	HARRISON, Matilda	JUL 12 1854
BECK, Rebecca	WILLIAMS, Brooke	SEP 04 1822
BECK, S. Zebulon	RAY, Mary Ellen	NOV 16 1854
BECK, Salome	RAINCISER, Lorenz	NOV 17 1832
BECK, Sarah	LANCASTER, Stephen	OCT 06 1817
BECK, Walters R.	DELPHY, Jane	JUL 19 1853
BECK, William	WATERS, Kavia M.	JAN 11 1819
BECKENBAUGH, William W.	STEWART, Margaret Ann	NOV 12 1846
BECKER, George	KEIMAN, Sarah Ann	OCT 20 1846
BECKER, Helena A.	WIENAND, George	DEC 03 1851
BECKER, Johanna S.	WINGENROTH, Frederick F.	NOV 20 1849
BECKER, John Henry	HARVEY, Mary Ann	SEP 18 1839
BECKER, William	STEINER, Mary Elizabeth	FEB 21 1843
BECKERT, Joseph	GALLANT, Rosine	JAN 22 1850
BECKET, Barbara	BEALL, Andrew	DEC 30 1823
BECKET, Ellenor Ann	DOWNER, Joel	NOV 11 1819
BECKET, John	MOCKEBEE, Maria	DEC 02 1820
BECKET, John	ADAMS, Malinda	NOV 12 1857
BECKET, Mary (blk)	DAY, Laurence	APR 04 1850
BECKET, Mary Ann	SPRAGUE, William	OCT 04 1854
BECKET, Matilda	HALL, John	AUG 09 1850
BECKET, Ruth Ann (blk)	BOSTON, Robert	FEB 25 1854
BECKET, Walter	FREE, Barbara	DEC 22 1815
BECKET, William H.	BARTON, Sarah Jane (blk)	AUG 15 1850
BECKETT, Alfred	SWAIN, Elizabeth Ann	NOV 28 1848
BECKETT, Eliza	TAYLER, John	JUN 21 1820
BECKETT, Elizabeth	MACKABEE, James R.	DEC 14 1843
BECKETT, Hannah (blk)	BRUCE, James	FEB 18 1832
BECKETT, Harriet F.	BELL, Joseph F.	JAN 17 1854
BECKETT, Matilda	KEITH, John Henry	MAR 26 1844
BECKETT, Theofolas	THORNTON, Sarah Jane (blk)	FEB 01 1853

District of Columbia Marriage Licenses, 1811-1858

BECKETT, William	SLATER, Caroline (blk)	DEC 08 1846
BECKETT, William	ADAMS, Jane (blk)	DEC 13 1847
BECKITT, Lemuel	BROOKS, Elizabeth (blk)	FEB 02 1843
BECKLEY, Amanda	BROWN, Abram	AUG 16 1827
BECKLEY, Joseph	COHEN, Sarah Ann	OCT 26 1841
BECKS, Elizabeth	BIRNSIDE, John Nelson	MAY 02 1835
BECKWITH, Mary	CROWN, James	FEB 10 1836
BECKWITH, Singleton	BROWN, Mary A.	SEP 07 1839
BECKWORTH, Ann	RUFFEL, Jacob	APR 09 1825
BECRAFT, Sarah E.	BOUDIN, Alexander	OCT 10 1855
BEDDING, Joseph	BOYLE, Mary	AUG 19 1852
BEDDO, Ann	LOVEJOY, John N.	JUL 01 1819
BEDDO, Henry	MOORE, Jane	SEP 28 1841
BEDDO, James	BETTY, Violetta	OCT 08 1817
BEDE, George	OWEN, Ann	APR 03 1820
BEDE, Georgea Emma	ROBEY, John H.	APR 02 1857
BEECH, Allen	GENTLE, Mary Ann	FEB 17 1837
BEECH, Delilah	COGWILL, John S.	MAR 19 1855
BEECH, Ephraim Mc.	STEEL, Sarah Jane	MAR 10 1840
BEECH, Garrison	HARRISON, Harriet	JUN 11 1829
BEECH, Hidley	GODFRY, Elizabeth	SEP 21 1838
BEECH, Levi	BRADLEY, Eliza	JUL 15 1838
BEECH, Mariah	MUSGROVE, Aaron R.	NOV 15 1825
BEECH, Martha	MARZLIN, Frederick	AUG 09 1848
BEECH, Mary	BEECH, Solomon	JUL 22 1824
BEECH, Nathaniel	LILES, Elizabeth	MAY 10 1827
BEECH, Solomon	BEECH, Mary	JUL 22 1824
BEECHEM, Mary	RIGSBY, James	JUN 23 1836
BEECHER, Alice	HEDLEY, Wm. W.	FEB 03 1855
BEECK, Susanna	BROTZEN, John	JUN 07 1856
BEEDING, Mary	LAKE, George	JAN 12 1818
BEEDING, Susan	LAWRENCE, Joseph	MAY 03 1817
BEEDLE, Alexander B.	ROBERTSON, Leanna	AUG 16 1825
BEEDLE, Alfred	DOVE, Matilda	FEB 28 1832
BEEDLE, Andrew F.	HODGE, Emma	FEB 06 1851
BEEDLE, Ann Maria	ALBRIGHT, Thomas J.	AUG 29 1857
BEEK, Elizabeth S.	HESTON, Rev. Newton	JAN 06 1847
BEEK, William	YOUNG, Rachael	SEP 08 1831
BEEKE, Jane	KISENTUFER, Christopher	MAY 14 1857
BEEL, Mary	MORGAN, Richard	JAN 12 1848
BEELER, Frances	BARTH, Henry	NOV 11 1856
BEELER, Louis F.	FILINS, Amanda	FEB 01 1851
BEELER, Rosa Louisia	JENKINS, Loline	DEC 08 1848
BEERS, Benjamin F.	DUVALL, Susan	JUL 26 1849
BEERS, C. Isaac	DUVALL, Ann E.	NOV 12 1857
BEERS, James	WEBSTER, Lucinda	AUG 25 1846
BEERS, Mary Ann	CHARLES, Samuel M.	NOV 08 1838
BEERS, Virginia	KIRBY, Wallace	DEC 01 1852
BEETSTONE, Mary	STAFFAN, Christian	JAN 13 1836
BEEVERS, Catharine	HARRISON, Alfred L.	AUG 23 1849
BEEVES, Jane A.L.	LAMBRECHT, Reinard	MAY 23 1831
BEEWER, Eliza	BENDY, Anthony	JAN 28 1813
BEGGANE, Jeremiah	DAILEY, Bridget	MAY 19 1853
BEGLE, William	JOURDAN, Jane	JUL 29 1833
BEHERNS, Sophia	OBERHEIN, John	MAY 04 1858
BEHLE, Babetta	ERB, Henry	OCT 28 1856
BEHLEN, Elizabeth	SEITZ, Henry	DEC 24 1853
BEHLEN, Frederika	BOERNSTEIN, August S.	JAN 11 1854

District of Columbia Marriage Licenses, 1811-1858

BEHRENS, Caroline	VOIGT, Fredk.	OCT 02 1855
BEIGLER, Philip	TYLER, Elizabeth	JUL 10 1841
BEIGLER, Philip	SCHNEIDER, Catherine	DEC 28 1844
BEILER, Elizabeth	GARDINER, Aaron	FEB 16 1831
BEINKERT, Barbara	HORNBACH, Valentine	MAY 12 1858
BEKER, Antoinette	BERG, Frederick	MAR 18 1854
BeKROFFT, Julia Ann (blk)	FERRIS, Plato	OCT 16 1832
BELDRECH, Mary	WAGNER, George	FEB 17 1849
BELER, Lewis	KNELLER, Mary	OCT 10 1825
BELFILS, Eugene	NOLLAND, Sarah	NOV 03 1848
BELKNAP, Edward	SORAN, Ellen C.	OCT 19 1857
BELL, Amelia (blk)	JONES, Washington	MAY 20 1841
BELL, Ann	COOPER, Wm., Jr.	AUG 13 1822
BELL, Ann	WHITE, John W.	JUN 15 1844
BELL, Anne	HERBERT, George	AUG 05 1815
BELL, Arthur W.	BURY, Mary Ann	NOV 16 1826
BELL, Benjamin	SILENCE, Chloe Ann	DEC 22 1823
BELL, Benjamin H.	WILLIAMS, Orellar	OCT 21 1837
BELL, Caroline (blk)	SHORTER, Isaac	MAR 17 1832
BELL, Caroline (blk)	LEE, Henry	DEC 08 1846
BELL, Catharine (blk)	HALL, Joseph	JUL 24 1851
BELL, Charlotte (blk)	SIMMS, George	NOV 28 1844
BELL, Chloe Ann	BRANNAN, Wilson	NOV 06 1819
BELL, Daniel	AMBER, Louisa (blk)	OCT 04 1852
BELL, David	TALBOTT, Elizabeth (blk)	MAR 06 1858
BELL, Dory	FREE, Kitty	JAN 04 1813
BELL, Elizabeth (blk)	STANFORD, James	APR 18 1827
BELL, Elizth. Rebecca	SANFORD, Linas	SEP 12 1848
BELL, Emily M.	LYNN, John W.	DEC 14 1854
BELL, George	BROWN, Henny (blk)	JUL 06 1826
BELL, George	HARVEY, Margaret	SEP 01 1852
BELL, George	CUNNINGHAM, Emeline	NOV 24 1852
BELL, George J.	HUGHES, Mary	JAN 17 1818
BELL, George J.	MADDOX, Martha E.	DEC 08 1855
BELL, George W.	DAVIS, Susanna	JAN 23 1837
BELL, Hanson	HILL, Jane	DEC 16 1847
BELL, Harriet	COOPER, William, Jr.	MAY 04 1826
BELL, Harriet (blk)	WATKINS, Peyton	DEC 10 1834
BELL, Henry	WINDSOR, Martha	JUN 10 1847
BELL, Henry	FORD, Henrietta (blk)	SEP 27 1849
BELL, Henry C.	BULLOCK, Sophia	OCT 04 1849
BELL, Ignatius	HANSON, Caroline (blk)	FEB 08 1849
BELL, James	WILLIAMS, Betsey	JUL 08 1813
BELL, James	JOHNSON, Susan (blk)	AUG 28 1834
BELL, James W.	BURNS, Mary	MAR 23 1840
BELL, John	CLARKE, Eliza	OCT 07 1819
BELL, John	HINES, Rachel (blk)	NOV 02 1854
BELL, John A.	COLLINS, Sarah Eliza	DEC 28 1847
BELL, John Thomas	WANSFOOT, Eliza	DEC 10 1846
BELL, Joseph	QUEEN, Ann (blk)	OCT 05 1848
BELL, Joseph F.	BECKETT, Harriet F.	JAN 17 1854
BELL, L.A.W.	COURTNEY, Joseph C.	FEB 14 1842
BELL, Letty	ALLEN, William	OCT 26 1819
BELL, Letty	STEWART, William	OCT 17 1853
BELL, Littleton A.	IRONTON, Martha	SEP 15 1847
BELL, Loyd	DAY, Ellen (blk)	NOV 26 1841
BELL, Lucy	BROWN, William	MAY 14 1825
BELL, Margt. R.	BROWN, John R.	JUN 30 1851

District of Columbia Marriage Licenses, 1811-1858

BELL, Martha	WHALEN, John W.	JAN 26 1854
BELL, Mary	FARLAND, William M.	MAR 11 1825
BELL, Mary	ADAMS, Sandy	JUN 10 1835
BELL, Mary	JACKSON, Francis	FEB 13 1851
BELL, Mary	BUCK, John, Jr.	APR 04 1854
BELL, Mary Ann	NALLEY, Henry	JAN 05 1831
BELL, Mary Ann	FLANAGAN, Francis	MAY 14 1835
BELL, Mary Ann	FOWLER, William H.	NOV 11 1856
BELL, Mary Jane	WASHBURN, Sylvanus N.	MAY 08 1843
BELL, Mary Jane	SNYDER, John Adam	JAN 16 1855
BELL, Matilda	GODDARD, Thomas	JAN 09 1828
BELL, Matilda E.	HARSHMAN, Jesse W.	JAN 24 1856
BELL, Moses	GEORGE, Eliza (blk)	SEP 25 1856
BELL, Nace	WALTERS, Maria (blk)	AUG 02 1858
BELL, P.H.	EATON, Ella	OCT 22 1856
BELL, Richard	VERMILLION, Christina	MAY 06 1856
BELL, Robert	GREENHALGH, Mary	DEC 08 1830
BELL, Robert	BOLAND, Mary	JUL 15 1856
BELL, Sarah	TURNER, Henry	DEC 21 1824
BELL, Sarah	RAWLINGS, William	JAN 08 1846
BELL, Sarah	McGOWAN, James	FEB 02 1857
BELL, Sarah F.	HALL, Allen F.	DEC 16 1857
BELL, Solomon	SNAUBER, Catherine	SEP 10 1846
BELL, Susan Clarinda	ROBINSON, Charles	NOV 13 1856
BELL, Thomas	WARD, Christiana (blk)	APR 01 1840
BELL, Thomas	WARNER, Maria (blk)	NOV 07 1854
BELL, Tracey (blk)	HALL, Horatio	JUL 16 1851
BELL, Washington	GATES, Mary	SEP 24 1855
BELL, William	COULSON, Jane	APR 08 1833
BELL, William	RAWLINGS, Susana	JUL 18 1837
BELL, William	GINK, Eleanor	JAN 24 1848
BELL, William	ROBERTSON, Catharine	DEC 03 1850
BELL, William	THORN, Elizabeth	JAN 03 1855
BELL, Winifred Connor	MAGAR, John	DEC 21 1854
BELLAND, Louis	BLOCK, Henrietta	MAY 04 1857
BELLARD, John	HAROLD, Elizabeth	NOV 10 1851
BELLIER, Mary Ann	FRESCH, Charles	MAR 06 1843
BELLING, Caroline C.	REED, Josiah F.	DEC 28 1826
BELLOWS, Alfred	GASSAWAY, Margaret Ann (blk)	JUN 03 1852
BELMIRE, Eliza C.	PETTIT, Charles	SEP 04 1819
BELT, Alfred	WHITEMORE, Mary Ellen	MAY 22 1854
BELT, Alfred C.	McGILL, Agnes	OCT 07 1845
BELT, Amanda Melvina	FERGUSON, Worden H.	SEP 05 1839
BELT, Ann Rosina	TRENHOHN, John Howard	SEP 21 1842
BELT, Anne C.	MACKALL, Richard L.	DEC 12 1839
BELT, Caroline	ERKLINE, John	JAN 21 1812
BELT, Catherine P.	WINDSOR, Lemuel H.	DEC 29 1853
BELT, Eliza (blk)	THOMAS, James H.	SEP 21 1857
BELT, Elizabeth	BUCHANAN, Henry	MAR 21 1837
BELT, Elizabeth (blk)	WILLIAMS, Tobias	DEC 31 1852
BELT, Elizabeth E.	DYER, Edward C.	JUL 14 1851
BELT, Henrietta (blk)	ROSS, Benjamin	SEP 10 1850
BELT, Ignatius	RIDGLEY, Martha (blk)	AUG 06 1856
BELT, James	HEDGES, Sarah Ann	NOV 23 1820
BELT, James	BASSON, Mary Ann	JUN 19 1828
BELT, James M.	GRADY, Bridget	DEC 03 1855
BELT, Martha	BEALL, Henry	APR 22 1844
BELT, Martha	PRATHER, Joseph	FEB 01 1848

District of Columbia Marriage Licenses, 1811-1858

BELT, Martha A.C.	NELSON, John S.	AUG 02 1852
BELT, Mary Ann	HALL, George R.	JUL 17 1851
BELT, Mary E.	STEELE, James R.	JUL 16 1849
BELT, Mary Levina	REYNOLDS, Joseph	DEC 19 1837
BELT, Paul	ROI, Seraphine	AUG 06 1850
BELT, Stattire	PLUMMER, Robert	JUN 11 1829
BELT, Thomas	BROWN, Elizabeth	JAN 31 1839
BELT, Thomas	SEWALL, Sarah (blk)	MAR 28 1848
BELT, Thomas J.	WATKINS, Ann E.	SEP 29 1820
BELT, Thomas W.	BRADFORD, Mary C.	SEP 04 1852
BELZAROS, Adam	HADT, Christina	JAN 29 1844
BENDER, Anna Lucinda	TANSILL, Robert	OCT 17 1849
BENDER, George [Capt.]	BRISCOE, Mary	DEC 21 1816
BENDER, Jacob A.	PHEBIAN, Harriot	FEB 25 1819
BENDER, Josephine	McDERMOTT, William	OCT 11 1845
BENDER, Julianna M.	WILSON, Thomas L.	MAY 06 1824
BENDER, Maria	HINEZEL, George	NOV 20 1838
BENDER, Mary E.	FISK, C.B.	OCT 25 1837
BENDER, Mary E.	BUTT, George J.	APR 08 1847
BENDY, Anthony	BEEWER, Eliza	JAN 28 1813
BENEZETT, Hazael	CARLIN, Ann E.	NOV 25 1834
BENEZETTE, Hazael	DECOVER, Lana Mari	MAR 19 1850
BENEZETTE, Laura Ann	MOORE, James H.	APR 04 1854
BENGHN, Betty T.	NAPIER, Richard K.	DEC 23 1854
BENGURL, Alene	McDONNELL, Daniel	AUG 03 1853
BENHAM, Spencer C.	WHITE, Sallie E.	FEB 14 1855
BENIDICK, Frederick W.	LAUSON, Mary E.	AUG 25 1842
BENING, Elizabeth	BEAND, George	SEP 12 1818
BENJAMIN, John	THOMPSON, Ruth	NOV 08 1841
BENJAMIN, John R.	JOHNSON, Marcelina (blk)	OCT 06 1857
BENJAMIN, Mary E.	WIGGIN, Benjamin F.	DEC 28 1854
BENNARD, Ann	COOKE, Jacob	FEB 10 1857
BENNER, Anne L.	GAWLER, Joseph	DEC 18 1850
BENNET, Johanna	RYAN, Thomas	JUL 20 1850
BENNET, Margaret	TUCKER, Levi	MAR 08 1831
BENNET, Maria (blk)	CROCKET, David	OCT 26 1833
BENNETT, Andrew	PURSILL, George Anna	JUN 20 1849
BENNETT, Betsey	HARMAN, James	NOV 11 1813
BENNETT, Daniel	BROOKS, Ann Eliza (blk)	AUG 16 1854
BENNETT, Eli	SAVOY, Elizabeth (blk)	JUN 13 1849
BENNETT, Elizabeth	JONES, Hugh	FEB 03 1852
BENNETT, Elizabeth E.	HOUGHTON, Ceylon S.	NOV 01 1843
BENNETT, Geo.	McFARLIN, Nancy	DEC 12 1821
BENNETT, Hiram	WINDHAM, Caroline	DEC 27 1827
BENNETT, John	AUKWARD, Margaret	SEP 09 1819
BENNETT, John	JENKINS, Catherine	MAR 28 1850
BENNETT, John	SAUNTRY, Ellen	MAY 30 1856
BENNETT, Joseph	HALL, Catharine	MAR 05 1822
BENNETT, Margaret	HILL, Francis	NOV 18 1815
BENNETT, Martha A.	DUVAL, George W.	MAR 31 1856
BENNETT, Mary	CLAGETT, Benjamin D.	JUN 08 1819
BENNETT, Mary Ann	DAVIS, James B.	APR 23 1840
BENNETT, Mary Ann	LESTER, John G.	AUG 01 1843
BENNETT, Mary Ann	MORTIMER, John Thos.	JUN 17 1856
BENNETT, Michael	COLLINS, Ellen	MAR 18 1854
BENNETT, Nicholas	LEE, Sarah Jane	APR 17 1855
BENNETT, Rezin	HOBBS, Eleanor	NOV 07 1846
BENNETT, Sarah B.	WARING, Basil H.	OCT 27 1829

District of Columbia Marriage Licenses, 1811-1858

BENNETT, Susan G.	CHOATE, Warren C.	AUG 14 1839
BENNETT, Thomas S.	EVANS, Margaretta L.	MAY 19 1813
BENNETT, Thompson N.	DREW, Susan G.	FEB 06 1829
BENNETT, William	EVANS, Susan	JUN 27 1854
BENNETT, William T.	KILLDEFF, Catherine	SEP 12 1855
BENRISER, Jacob J.	KING, Sarah A.	AUG 24 1848
BENSEL, George	KING, Reke	OCT 12 1848
BENSLEY, John	ROBERTSON, Martha	AUG 28 1841
BENSON, Amelia Jane	WALKER, Jonathan Thomas	OCT 12 1833
BENSON, Elizabeth	MILES, Edward	OCT 17 1833
BENSON, Elizabeth	YOAST, Benedict	OCT 09 1834
BENSON, Elizth. H.	JOHNSON, Albert E.H.	JAN 09 1851
BENSON, Hester Ann	KELLY, Nathaniel	MAY 05 1835
BENSON, John	FARR, Alzira	JUN 29 1840
BENSON, Jonathan B.	TALBERT, Mary Ann	FEB 20 1816
BENSON, Leonora	GODMAN, Elijah	JUN 12 1834
BENSON, Margaret E.	MOCKBEE, Richard	JUN 14 1837
BENSON, Mary	McDONALD, Charles	AUG 12 1829
BENSON, Mary Maria	BING, John	SEP 23 1836
BENSON, Patrick	OHAGAN, Sarah	JAN 14 1823
BENSON, Susan H.	WINDSOR, Henry J.	APR 16 1851
BENSON, Thomas J.	ADREON, Susannah	NOV 30 1843
BENSON, Thomas J.	BARTON, Demarines H.	AUG 30 1856
BENSON, Thomas N.	BENTON, Julia Ann	OCT 23 1849
BENSON, [blank]	DONN, George W.	APR 03 1837
BENSTON, Kesiah (blk)	WARD, Henry	JUL 01 1829
BENTEN, Mary Ann	HUBBARD, Jeremiah	SEP 29 1836
BENTER, Henry	KAHL, Elizabeth	OCT 24 1853
BENTHALL, W.C.	ANDERSON, Charlotte E.W.	JUL 12 1837
BENTIN, Elizabeth	BRIGHT, James	JAN 09 1823
BENTLEY, Charles	GENTRY, Sarah (blk)	JUN 20 1857
BENTLEY, Thomas	SMITH, Elizabeth Ann	FEB 23 1850
BENTLY, Sophia M.	CASSIN, Stephen	APR 27 1838
BENTON, Catherine	DISHER, Lewis	APR 20 1842
BENTON, Eliza C.P.	JONES, William Carey	MAR 18 1847
BENTON, Jessie Ann	FREEMOUNT, John Charles	OCT 19 1841
BENTON, Julia Ann	BENSON, Thomas N.	OCT 23 1849
BENTON, Juliet	WHEATLEY, Benedict	MAY 11 1826
BENTON, Samuel	COAX, Mary Ellen	JUL 03 1840
BENTON, Samuel	CURRAY, Ann Eliza	OCT 05 1842
BENTON, Susan M.	BOILLEAU, Charles	JUN 04 1855
BENTON, William	COCKE, Catherine W.	MAY 22 1855
BENTOR, William	AVORY, Elizabeth	FEB 14 1826
BENTZ, Charles	SMITH, Christina	JAN 26 1856
BENTZ, Ezra	ASHBURY, Prudence	MAY 26 1834
BENVANIDA, Louisa C.	WILSON, William T.	JUL 01 1844
BENZETTE, Brittania	PORES, Antonio	MAY 11 1858
BEOG, John	JONES, Anna	MAR 19 1857
BERAULT, Charles	ANDERSON, Mary A.	MAR 26 1849
BERCKMANN, John H.	WILSON, Mary Ann	OCT 09 1850
BERDINE, Hannah	ROBEY, John	NOV 23 1816
BERG, Frederick	BEKER, Antoinette	MAR 18 1854
BERGAN, Vilette	LARKIN, John F.	JUL 18 1855
BERGER, Charlotte	HASELBUSCH, Hermann	OCT 27 1855
BERGER, Christiana S.	BROWN, Henry	AUG 03 1857
BERGER, John Thomas	BERON, Mary Ann C.	OCT 01 1840
BERGER, William	HEITMÜLLER, Charlotte	DEC 07 1855
BERGES, Charlotte	LAVENDER, James	APR 04 1857

District of Columbia Marriage Licenses, 1811-1858

BERGLING, George	BARBER, Sophia	FEB 04 1850
BERGLING, Henrich	SCHLETTMANN, Maria Louise	FEB 12 1855
BERGMAN, Charles William	MULLER, Dougherty Augusta	DEC 22 1853
BERGMAN, William	SCHLIEVER, Wilhelmina L.C.P.	NOV 07 1854
BERGMANN, Heinrich	VonBEHREN, Marie	JUL 24 1845
BERGUMOT, Jane	NUGENT, John	NOV 09 1840
BERK, Harriat (blk)	BARTON, William	MAR 04 1858
BERKELEY, George N.	MUNROE, Eliza	DEC 08 1813
BERKELEY, [blank]	SHELTON, Sarah	FEB 19 1837
BERKHART, Mary	BUCHER, Bernhard H.	AUG 10 1857
BERKLEY, Ann	DANFERD, James	NOV 22 1824
BERKLEY, Ann E.	LUSBY, James H.	FEB 20 1838
BERKLEY, Benjamin	DRURY, Martha A.	SEP 15 1849
BERKLEY, Deby	VERMILLION, Otha F.	DEC 17 1822
BERKLEY, Edmund	COLBERT, Joanna	SEP 07 1852
BERKLEY, Enos E.	McCATHRAN, Sarah M.	DEC 03 1855
BERKLEY, Harriet	CLARKE, Richard	DEC 02 1846
BERKLEY, John D.	SIMS, Rachael Ann	OCT 20 1823
BERKLEY, John T.	HAYDEN, Mary H.	MAR 06 1839
BERKLEY, Maria	BLAND, John D.	SEP 24 1841
BERKLEY, Mary Ellen	PADGETT, Robert T.	OCT 27 1856
BERKLEY, Rebecca	RAWLINGS, David	SEP 19 1833
BERKLEY, Susan H.	SHACKLETT, Robert	DEC 02 1828
BERLE, Rebecca	FERGUSON, Benjamin	MAR 25 1851
BERLIN, Mary S.	BARRY, David	MAY 12 1853
BERLIN, Samuel	MARSHALL, Louisa V.	NOV 19 1853
BERMANN, Catherine	HUHN, Jacob Karl	NOV 11 1857
BERNARD, Hezekiah	CRANDLE, Matilda	JUN 22 1824
BERNARD, Peter	NARDEN, Harriet	OCT 02 1819
BERNARD, William	MOORE, Elizth.	SEP 23 1822
BERNARD, William	LEWIS, Mary Ann Elizabeth	DEC 09 1828
BERNASON, Sarah	VENABLE, William	FEB 19 1833
BERNEY, Auguste	SESSFORD, Martha	JUN 11 1825
BERNHARD, John	SUTTON, Juliet	MAY 28 1849
BERON, Jeroma	ROBEY, Henry	DEC 26 1843
BERON, Mary Ann C.	BERGER, John Thomas	OCT 01 1840
BERON, William	BRIGHT, Elizabeth Ann	JAN 06 1846
BERRAMANS, Mary A.	HOPKINS, George W.	MAY 19 1857
BERRET, Eliza U. O'D.	ARNOLD, Joseph W.	APR 22 1846
BERRET, Joseph H.	ABERCROMBIE, Nannie B.	JUN 29 1846
BERRIAN, Hobart	ADAMS, Catharine	SEP 08 1841
BERRIEN, Margaret L.M.	ECHOLS, Philip Henry	JUL 12 1831
BERRON, Eliza F.	MECHAM, Gaylord	FEB 14 1843
BERRY, Albert M.	HOLLAND, Angelina B.	JUL 20 1843
BERRY, Alfred	PARSONS, Ann C.	JUL 14 1827
BERRY, Alfred M.	BERRY, Martha E.	AUG 04 1840
BERRY, Ancaret	BARNES, Jonathan	APR 24 1821
BERRY, Ann	HAGAN, Judson	SEP 09 1817
BERRY, Ann	HOWELL, John	AUG 24 1822
BERRY, Ann Amelia	BARNES, William A.	FEB 25 1854
BERRY, Anna K.	COLUMBUS, Albert G.	MAR 21 1853
BERRY, Annie Maria	MIDDLETON, John A.	JUN 14 1854
BERRY, Barbara	HUME, E.J.	FEB 25 1833
BERRY, Benjamin, Jr.	FORBES, Eleanor B.E.	MAY 15 1817
BERRY, Catherine	SIOUSSA, Augustus	NOV 30 1852
BERRY, Cecelia (blk)	PAYNE, Oscar	APR 04 1850
BERRY, Charles M.	BROOKE, Maria Ann	DEC 16 1824
BERRY, Charles M.	WOLFORD, Susan E.	APR 03 1852

District of Columbia Marriage Licenses, 1811-1858

BERRY, Christopher C.	BUTT, Ann Rebecca	DEC 08 1840
BERRY, Elisha D.	GODY, Mary A.	DEC 15 1818
BERRY, Eliza	ARNOLD, William	JUN 11 1828
BERRY, Eliza Henrietta	COOK, Joseph	NOV 02 1852
BERRY, Elizabeth	TALTON, James	MAY 08 1817
BERRY, Elizabeth	BOOTHE, James	OCT 22 1839
BERRY, Elizabeth	HICKS, John	MAY 22 1844
BERRY, Elizabeth A.	GOODMAN, Charles A.	NOV 19 1856
BERRY, Elizabeth A.W.	TSCHIFFILY, Frederick A.	JUL 20 1840
BERRY, Elizabeth E.	BROOKE, Robert W.	JUL 30 1849
BERRY, Ellen	OWEN, Thomas	MAY 16 1830
BERRY, Ellen	FERGUSON, Enos D.	OCT 01 1842
BERRY, Frances	MERRYMAN, Benjamin	DEC 06 1843
BERRY, George F.	KAIN, Mary Ann D.	APR 14 1829
BERRY, Harriet	ALLEN, Elijah	FEB 19 1828
BERRY, Horatio Edwin	MANNING, Martha Louise	OCT 20 1845
BERRY, Jane	TYLER, Dennis	JUL 31 1852
BERRY, Jane (blk)	MASON, Enoch G.	JUL 12 1843
BERRY, Jerome C.	CLOUD, Susan	JAN 16 1854
BERRY, John	BOSTICK, Susan	OCT 09 1816
BERRY, John	FISTER, Ann	OCT 24 1842
BERRY, John	HILL, Martha A.	OCT 19 1857
BERRY, John K.	SACREY, Elizabeth C.	SEP 21 1853
BERRY, Lethe Ann	BROWNING, John N.	AUG 15 1845
BERRY, Louisa E.	STANLEY, Henry E.	JUN 25 1846
BERRY, Louisa L.	MORRISON, William M.	OCT 26 1826
BERRY, Lucy B.	COX, Walter	AUG 04 1818
BERRY, Martha E.	BERRY, Alfred M.	AUG 04 1840
BERRY, Mary	DUNMORE, Solomon	APR 05 1843
BERRY, Mary	WAIDER, Barney	OCT 31 1853
BERRY, Mary	DONALDSON, Saml. H.	NOV 15 1853
BERRY, Mary A.	CRAVER, Philip	DEC 14 1843
BERRY, Mary E.	STEADMAN, Marshall B.	JUL 02 1852
BERRY, Mary Ellen	DODGE, Allen	JUN 11 1849
BERRY, Mary Maria	PRATHER, Overton J.	OCT 24 1834
BERRY, Massaliner	MIDDLETON, Samuel	APR 17 1825
BERRY, Matilda	OFFERTT, Zepheniah K.	APR 10 1822
BERRY, Matilda R.	BARNARD, Theodore	AUG 05 1844
BERRY, Nathaniel	DEMENT, Mary	JAN 11 1851
BERRY, Nicholas T.	BOUCHER, Josephine	SEP 05 1855
BERRY, Noble	HAYWARD, Sarah R.	JUL 07 1828
BERRY, Noble	MALDER, Catherine	JUN 06 1833
BERRY, Nora Ann	McINTOSH, John	SEP 07 1852
BERRY, Peter	SMART, Mary Ann	MAR 10 1832
BERRY, Philip T.	HAW, Mary Ann	FEB 10 1825
BERRY, Philip T.	McKENNERY, Sarah	MAY 14 1839
BERRY, Robert	DONOHO, Margaret	SEP 08 1832
BERRY, Samuel	YEATS, Mary E.	APR 04 1850
BERRY, Sarah	HILLER, John	OCT 12 1829
BERRY, Sarah	DIX, Thomas	DEC 07 1844
BERRY, Sarah Catharine	MAGEE, Robert F.	OCT 17 1843
BERRY, Sarah G.	JOHNSON, John H.	JUL 01 1848
BERRY, Susan	PHILLIPS, Samuel	FEB 21 1831
BERRY, Thomas	KELLY, Mary	NOV 05 1842
BERRY, Thomas C.	HUME, Ellen A.	NOV 17 1856
BERRY, Virginia (blk)	BUCKINGHAM, Charles	MAY 27 1852
BERRY, Walter Q.	EDMONSTON, Virginia R.	SEP 09 1856
BERRY, Washington	SKIDMORE, Columbia	DEC 07 1854

District of Columbia Marriage Licenses, 1811-1858

BERRY, Washington O.	HART, Amy	JUL 28 1851
BERRY, William	MOORE, Eliza	NOV 18 1823
BERRY, William	RIGSBY, Rachael	JUN 19 1845
BERRY, Wyatt S.	MOORE, Mary E.	OCT 31 1854
BERRY, Zachariah, of Washn.	ADDISON, Elizabeth C.	JAN 16 1854
BERRYMAN, C.N.	PAYNE, W.S.	NOV 23 1857
BERRYMAN, Eliza R.	RENNOLDS, Abert	MAY 20 1823
BERRYMAN, George	FUGATE, Henrietta	JAN 11 1828
BERRYMAN, Leroy H.	MOORE, Mary	SEP 13 1842
BERRYMAN, Louisa Hipkins	BUCKNER, Richard Bernard	FEB 25 1828
BERRYMAN, Maria N.	COOLIDGE, John H.	JUN 11 1832
BERRYMAN, Wm. B.	LAUB, Elizabeth	FEB 23 1832
BERST, Anthony	McDONALD, Rosetta	MAY 29 1841
BERTEAND, Mary	ALEXANDER, Charles	DEC 02 1818
BEST, Susanna	AMATT, George	JUL 31 1830
BESTOLD, Nealy	FRAILING, Lena	JAN 22 1855
BESTOR, Chauncey	McCLEOD, Mary	OCT 19 1819
BESTOR, Harriott W.	BEARD, William H.	OCT 22 1814
BESTOR, Owen H.	BRIGHTWELL, Eliza	SEP 20 1836
BESTOR, Whitman C.	BALDWIN, Selina	OCT 13 1849
BETKER, Emile F.	MELSON, John, Jr.	DEC 16 1856
BETOUT, Eugene J.	DUFLOS, Alphosina	MAY 01 1858
BETTER, Alavegius	HAWKINS, Diana (blk)	JUL 27 1854
BETTINGER, Benjamin F.	LIBBEY, C. Malvina	MAY 13 1850
BETTINGER, Margaret A.E.	JACOBS, Henry	JAN 21 1852
BETTNER, Robert	HAAG, Mary	NOV 17 1851
BETTNER, Robert	KNELLER, Dorothy	NOV 27 1851
BETTO, Catharine (blk)	DOUGLASS, William	SEP 04 1828
BETTON, Turbutt R.	LANE, Eliza	SEP 02 1816
BETTS, Catharine	CRIDDLE, Jonathan	MAR 26 1824
BETTS, Eleanor	HARRINGTON, Patrick	OCT 04 1852
BETTS, Elizabeth	SMITHLY, Theodore	APR 15 1839
BETTS, Henrietta T.	BROWN, John S.	JUL 31 1852
BETTSWITH, John	CAROLAN, Catherine	MAR 18 1817
BETTY, Lewis A.	JEWELL, Catharine	JAN 14 1826
BETTY, Violetta	BEDDO, James	OCT 08 1817
BETZ, Christian	MILLER, Caroline	MAY 31 1856
BETZ, William	GORDON, Matilda	MAR 24 1830
BETZINGER, Margaret	HARMANN, George	OCT 31 1854
BETZOLD, David	WERNER, Dorothy	JUL 02 1818
BEULTO, William	SMITH, Henrietta	OCT 04 1842
BEUR, Josephine	WAIZENEGGER, Norbert	APR 17 1855
BEUROU, Sophia	GILBERT, Louis Momus	SEP 25 1839
BEVANS, David H.	HUNTER, Ellen B.	AUG 15 1850
BEVANS, Elizabeth	HAMMER, John Gutleib	JUN 16 1827
BEVANS, John	YOUNG, Marion	FEB 03 1834
BEVELY, William	HOLTZMAN, Mary	AUG 13 1818
BEVENS, Mary Ann	CLARKE, William	JUN 01 1833
BEVER, Alexander	ARRINGTON, Maria	OCT 01 1834
BEVEREDGE, Francis	TALMIE, Margaret	SEP 21 1812
BEVERIDGE, Benjamin F.	GOLDSMITH, Mary E.	AUG 22 1856
BEVERIDGE, H.M.	RIDDLEMOSER, J.D.	OCT 14 1851
BEVERIDGE, Margaret Ann	CAMPBELL, Robert G.	JUL 18 1835
BEVERLEY, James B.	PETER, Jane	MAY 04 1819
BEVERLY, Roberta	LIGHTFOOT, William B.	FEB 06 1832
BEVERS, John A.	BALL, Susan	SEP 28 1854
BEVIES, Catherine	SWORD, Charles	MAR 28 1853
BEVIN, James C.	RICHARDS, Sarah Ann	SEP 07 1847

District of Columbia Marriage Licenses, 1811-1858

BEVOISE, Charles De	HAIGHT, Mary C.	JAN 25 1855
BEVONS, Martha	KEECE, John Henry Lewis	OCT 12 1846
BEYER, Mary E.	EVANS, Benjamin	JAN 16 1844
BEYER, Rosella	CLARVOE, John A.W.	SEP 25 1856
BIAR, Margaretta	NESENSOHN, Jos.	AUG 31 1855
BIAS, Mary	WEST, Guslie	DEC 16 1851
BIAS, Matilda (blk)	SCOTT, Henry	AUG 20 1845
BIASDERFER, Frances	BOWMAN, Joseph	DEC 03 1832
BIBB, Fillipa Estelle	CAULFIELD, John P.	JUL 21 1856
BIBB, George M.	DYER, Mary R.	MAY 22 1832
BIBB, Henry F.	HARPER, Martha A.	MAR 31 1857
BIBB, J.J.C.	CARUSI, Estelle	SEP 03 1850
BIBB, Virginia	WALLER, Edward	JUL 07 1853
BIBB, Virginia Frances	DAVIES, Cumming	JAN 28 1851
BICK, Fidel	FUHRER, Catharine	APR 13 1833
BICKLEY, William	JONES, Amelia (blk)	MAY 23 1835
BICKSLER, Ann V.	HURST, John H.	DEC 11 1854
BICKSLER, Jane E.	FARR, James W.	MAY 30 1856
BICKSLER, John	STONE, Mary Ann	MAR 30 1840
BICKSLER, Samuel	FRAZIER, Sarah L.	MAR 18 1830
BICVERS, Anna	CANDY, John	JUL 18 1854
BIDDLE, James	DAVIS, Pricy	JUN 18 1818
BIDDLE, William	RICHARDSON, Rebecca J.	OCT 13 1857
BIDDLEMAN, Daniel	SCHLEY, Emeline	AUG 31 1835
BIEDINGER, Margaretha	NEITER, Peter	JUL 21 1856
BIEGEL, Caroline	KING, Samuel	MAR 26 1857
BIENDER, Bertha (blk)	BATES, Robert	JUN 15 1858
BIENVENIDA, Lazaro	COULSTON, Susan	OCT 30 1840
BIEWEND, Adolph	MARTIN, Sophie	AUG 01 1844
BIGGES, Eliza	ADDISON, Samuel	AUG 06 1839
BIGGES, Jane	COOK, Peter Zeddick	JUL 17 1845
BIGGES, Perry	MASSIE, Elizabeth Frankey	JAN 06 1848
BIGGES, Thomas	COOK, Mary	JUL 17 1845
BIGGINS, James	MORGAN, Susan	NOV 08 1855
BIGGINS, Martha A.E.	FORD, James	JUL 20 1838
BIGGINS, Mary F.	CHAMBERS, Robert H.	JUN 05 1854
BIGGS, Alfred	LIZOR, Elizabeth	MAR 19 1835
BIGGS, Chloe Ann	GOODGER, Peter	MAY 10 1853
BIGGS, Edward	BROOKS, Anna	NOV 05 1850
BIGGS, Eliza	ROBINSON, John M.	NOV 15 1851
BIGGS, George	GUN, Mary	JUL 07 1826
BIGGS, Harriet	COOKE, John	FEB 25 1834
BIGGS, Henry D.	BREWER, Elizabeth D.	JAN 17 1843
BIGGS, James E.	MAGILL, Elizth. C.	MAY 13 1846
BIGGS, James Henry	BRADBURN, Mary Elizabeth	JUN 08 1840
BIGGS, Jane	WEST, John	AUG 09 1855
BIGGS, Levy	SMALLWOOD, Maria	AUG 30 1821
BIGGS, Lottee	GRAY, Hezekiah	OCT 29 1823
BIGGS, Mahaly	COHENS, William	DEC 05 1823
BIGGS, Mary Ann	ALLEN, Samuel Thomas	JAN 28 1845
BIGGS, Sarah	WASHINGTON, Lund	JUN 11 1819
BIGGS, Sarah	HOW, John	AUG 27 1834
BIGGS, Telley	BAYLISS, Payne	FEB 27 1812
BIGLE, Serile	SEQUIN, Jacqous	JUN 01 1846
BIGLER, John	ESTREI, Catherine	FEB 14 1856
BIGLER, Philip	HERBERT, Franciska	NOV 17 1856
BIGLEY, Julia	HORAN, Richard	APR 17 1858
BIGLEY, Lawrence	POTTERS, Mary	MAY 06 1830

District of Columbia Marriage Licenses, 1811-1858

BIGS, Catharine	COOK, Benjamin	MAY 28 1816
BIGWOOD, Anna	CREAGER, Michael	JAN 04 1817
BIHLER, Charles F.	LOSSER, Rosalia	NOV 04 1833
BIHLER, Gottlieb	TROUTMANN, Anna Barbara	OCT 26 1846
BIHLER, Rosalie	CLAVADETSCHER, Lucien	SEP 23 1845
BILD, Rudolph	GOAB, Margaret	DEC 23 1852
BILL, Milley	PARKER, Thomas	AUG 12 1818
BILLING, Augusta M.	COX, Samuel K.	DEC 23 1847
BILLING, Frederick S.	MOUNTZER, Mary M.	NOV 11 1856
BILLING, William W.	WALKER, Rebecca K.	MAR 07 1827
BILLINGS, Augusta M.	McNEER, Wm.	FEB 28 1818
BILLIPS, Eliza	HUTCHINS, Hillery	OCT 06 1855
BILLMYER, Thomas	DIXON, Cecilia	MAR 10 1816
BIND, Sarah	WILSON, Zachariah	SEP 18 1818
BING, Geo. W.	HOLTZMAN, Celinda J. Cook	AUG 24 1833
BING, John	BENSON, Mary Maria	SEP 23 1836
BINGHAM, Allen W.	HUDSON, Eliza Ann	NOV 23 1857
BINGHAM, Thomas	CADLE, Elizabeth	OCT 05 1816
BINGUY, Thomas	FORD, Sarah	MAY 03 1814
BINGY, Catherine	SCOTT, John	OCT 29 1850
BINGY, Mary H.	CROWLEY, William F.	JUN 28 1845
BINGY, Rutha Ann	SIMMONS, John	JAN 15 1834
BINKS, Eliza (blk)	HACKETT, Dennis	OCT 11 1843
BINKS, Mary (blk)	FORD, Herbert	MAY 14 1846
BINNE, Charlott	PRINZHORN, Henry	MAR 09 1855
BINNS, Frederick E.	WARREN, Martha Jane (blk)	FEB 15 1849
BINS, Charles	SHORTER, Mary Ann (blk)	NOV 23 1826
BIRAM, Edward J.	KING, Margaret A.	JAN 01 1855
BIRCH, Angeline	BIRCH, Elwin	JUN 09 1842
BIRCH, Edward	COURTNEY, Ellen	JAN 14 1858
BIRCH, Elizabeth Jane	DEEBLE, Edward K.J.	MAY 31 1838
BIRCH, Elwin	BIRCH, Angeline	JUN 09 1842
BIRCH, George Azariah	HODGSON, Susan	MAY 08 1838
BIRCH, Henry	JONES, Pamelia A.	JUL 18 1855
BIRCH, James H.	CORNWALL, Jane C.	JUL 02 1857
BIRCH, John Douglass	BIRCH, Mary F.	DEC 27 1856
BIRCH, Joseph	THOMPSON, Nancy V.	JUN 10 1856
BIRCH, Joseph E.	SPEAR, Mary E.	APR 28 1855
BIRCH, Joseph F.	DURHAM, Anne E.	JUN 15 1840
BIRCH, Margaret Ann	MacNEER, Joseph E.	FEB 01 1843
BIRCH, Mary Elizabeth	MASSEY, James	FEB 08 1855
BIRCH, Mary Ellen	ATHEY, John M.	MAR 07 1849
BIRCH, Mary F.	BIRCH, John Douglass	DEC 27 1856
BIRCH, Randolph	ELLIS, Mary Frances	APR 06 1854
BIRCH, Thomas	HODGSON, Franzoni	NOV 05 1834
BIRCH, William	REDMAN, Virginia	SEP 04 1856
BIRCH, William H.	COOK, Sophia	JUL 23 1845
BIRCHEAD, Mary Elizth.	MIDDLETON, Samuel C.	APR 16 1855
BIRCKHEAD, Edward	CLARK, Ann P.	DEC 22 1818
BIRCKHEAD, Mary Jane	COOPER, Samuel Barron	JAN 15 1857
BIRD, Ann E.	WEST, John P.	SEP 24 1835
BIRD, Benjamin	HILL, Mary	DEC 13 1827
BIRD, John H.	POLKINHORN, Georgiana C.	SEP 24 1855
BIRD, Spencer	CLINKSCALES, Delila	JAN 20 1827
BIRD, William	SULLIVAN, Margaret Virginia	NOV 20 1829
BIRD, William	DAWS, Mary	NOV 09 1846
BIRD, William	BUTLER, Rebecca (blk)	FEB 05 1849
BIRGE, Annie E.	SMITH, Francis H.	APR 12 1858

District of Columbia Marriage Licenses, 1811-1858

BIRGE, Mary H.	RANKIN, James	NOV 29 1854
BIRK, Annica	CORRIGAN, Hugh	FEB 22 1825
BIRNEY, Eliza Jane	PAYNE, George W.	AUG 17 1853
BIRNSIDE, John Nelson	BECKS, Elizabeth	MAY 02 1835
BIRTH, James	LEFEVER, Ann	MAY 02 1821
BIRTH, Lizzie T.	BALDWIN, Edward	MAY 06 1856
BIRTH, Lydia Ann	DUVALL, Benjamin H.	SEP 24 1840
BIRTH, William W.	TAYLOR, Elizabeth	MAY 05 1834
BISBIN, John	MILLER, Mary	AUG 09 1823
BISHOP, Daniel H.	CORLISS, Charlotte Ann	APR 25 1856
BISHOP, Henry	MOUNTZ, Maria Louisa	DEC 15 1847
BISHOP, Joseph	HERBERT, Gertrude	NOV 17 1851
BISHOP, Mary F.	GOODWIN, James R.	MAY 03 1842
BISHOP, Phebe	HOPKINS, Jason R.	JUL 30 1858
BISHOP, William G.	PIERCE, Emeline	JAN 03 1851
BISSELL, S.B.	LUFBOROUGH, S.M.	MAY 13 1840
BITNER, Ann Elizth.	BOYD, Robert	OCT 04 1854
BITNER, Henry	BRECHT, Katherina	MAR 02 1857
BITZ, Mary Dorothea	FRIESS, Christopher F.	NOV 12 1852
BIVINS, William W.	BARNS, Mary	JUL 10 1852
BIXBY, Nathaniel B.	SINCLAIR, Margaret	SEP 22 1813
BIXLER, Rachel	DYER, William	JAN 09 1856
BIXTER, Julia Elizabeth	POOLE, Hanson	SEP 30 1836
BIZET, Charles	SEMPET, Mary Ann	SEP 25 1824
BLACK, Abraham	COLE, Henrietta (blk)	JUN 11 1851
BLACK, Barbara	VERMILLION, Lewin	FEB 25 1836
BLACK, Betsey (blk)	WALLACE, Israel	AUG 15 1828
BLACK, Delie M.	ROGERS, Gilbert, Jr.	OCT 06 1845
BLACK, Gusty	CARNES, Charlotte (blk)	DEC 15 1842
BLACK, James A.	FREE, Martha	JUN 05 1855
BLACK, John M.	MARKS, Ellen Handy Wilson	AUG 20 1844
BLACK, Margaret (blk)	BUTLER, Columbus	AUG 08 1849
BLACK, Mary Ann	WILSON, David	MAR 18 1829
BLACK, Mary Ann	HAMILTON, Francis	JUN 28 1852
BLACK, Polly	HIGBY, John W.	APR 29 1813
BLACK, Rebecca	SHUNK, James F.	MAR 10 1858
BLACK, Samuel	JONES, Barbara	JUL 14 1813
BLACK, Sarah C.	PARISH, Henry A.	JAN 17 1845
BLACK, Susan Taylor	FULLER, William	APR 22 1843
BLACK, Tobias	WILLIS, Elizabeth (blk)	MAY 10 1822
BLACKBURN, John	BRIGHT, Ann	AUG 21 1827
BLACKBURN, Mary E.	MAINE, R.S.	JUN 16 1854
BLACKBURN, Nancy	LAIHAN, Michael	JUL 06 1839
BLACKBURN, William	PERRY, Elizabeth	MAY 19 1831
BLACKFAN, Ogden W.	WATKINS, Mary Agnes	SEP 16 1854
BLACKISTON, Lewis	DASHIELDS, Mary Caroline	NOV 30 1844
BLACKLEY, John W.	TIMBERLAKE, Sarah J.F.	MAR 26 1856
BLACKLOCK, Elizabeth C.	MARBURY, Francis F.	NOV 23 1816
BLACKMAN, Mary J.	WEEMS, William M.	JUN 29 1855
BLACKMAN, William	CLARK, Elizabeth	JUL 26 1830
BLACKMAN, William	SUTTON, Mary Ann	NOV 15 1847
BLACKSON, Henry	DAVIS, Sarah	JUN 01 1841
BLACKSTOCK, George C.	CLEMENTS, Mary C.	JUL 17 1854
BLACKSTONE, Catherine (blk)	HOMANS, Daniel	JUL 26 1848
BLACKSTONE, Hamilton	BURROWS, Ann	JAN 02 1856
BLACKWELL, Ann	O'BRIAN, James B.	AUG 31 1835
BLACKWELL, Oliver C.	FOLEY, Caroline	MAY 30 1836
BLACKWELL, William	SEMMES, Ann	SEP 30 1826

District of Columbia Marriage Licenses, 1811-1858

BLACKWELL, William	BROWN, Nancy	SEP 04 1844
BLADEN, Charles	HACKNEY, Ann	JAN 08 1846
BLADEN, John	GATES, Sarah	AUG 08 1843
BLADEN, John	FINESY, Sarah	JUN 22 1844
BLADEN, John	CRAFT, Mary	DEC 23 1846
BLADEN, Joseph	IVERY, Polly	AUG 24 1815
BLADEN, Julian	RANDALL, Joseph	JAN 18 1838
BLADEN, Lucinda	DOVE, Henry	MAY 15 1830
BLADEN, Mary Jane	SLACK, James	MAY 27 1858
BLADEN, Matilda E.	SIMPSON, Lewis F.	SEP 15 1857
BLADEN, Westley	REYNOLDS, Elizabeth	DEC 19 1839
BLADEN, William	MURRAY, Jane	DEC 31 1827
BLADEN, William	FRYE, Elizabeth	JUL 21 1842
BLADEN, William	MURRAY, Elizabeth	SEP 26 1844
BLADES, Mary A.	ALLEN, Joseph H.	MAY 08 1856
BLAGBURN, Emeline (blk)	THOMAS, Edward	JUN 09 1852
BLAGDEN, Emily W.	PHILLIPS, George W.	MAY 07 1836
BLAGDEN, Mary Anne	PHILLIPS, George William	JUN 12 1845
BLAGROVE, Henry B.	RATCLIFF, Gracy Ann	JUN 04 1817
BLAGROVE, Henry B.	DUVALL, Lorane	JUN 02 1825
BLAGROVE, Mary Ann	McKELDEN, William P.	JUN 24 1834
BLAIDEN, Augustus	TAYLOR, Mary	NOV 18 1840
BLAIR, Ann C.	BARTLEY, Isiah	OCT 27 1843
BLAIR, Elizabeth	LEE, S. Phillips	APR 27 1843
BLAIR, James	JESUP, Mary E.	JAN 12 1846
BLAIR, Louisa	PRENOT, Charles	SEP 21 1840
BLAKE, Emily	AGER, Uriah H.	DEC 13 1842
BLAKE, George W.	HURDLE, Sarah O.	MAY 19 1857
BLAKE, Glorvina	GORDON, Wm. A.	NOV 04 1830
BLAKE, Jane	WILLIAMS, William	OCT 15 1835
BLAKE, Jenny M.	WALBRIDGE, Hiram	AUG 31 1857
BLAKE, John	NICHOLSON, Bridget	DEC 08 1857
BLAKE, John A.	NEVITT, Ellen	MAY 20 1834
BLAKE, Julia Ann	SMITH, Washington	AUG 24 1835
BLAKE, Margaret	GRANT, Richard	NOV 24 1854
BLAKE, Mary Atawa	BURNS, James Alfred	SEP 05 1837
BLAKE, Parmelia J.	PARKS, John A.	DEC 03 1853
BLAKE, Royal	SWEENEY, Jane	APR 21 1831
BLAKE, Samuel	FRISBY, Mary E.	DEC 21 1855
BLAKE, Sarah J.	PADDY, John Henry	NOV 06 1854
BLAKE, Susan	ANDREWS, Charles	JAN 23 1854
BLAKE, William	COOPER, Elizabeth	MAR 14 1821
BLAKE, William H.	COOK, Jane	JUL 09 1827
BLAKE, William J.	SCOTT, Mary Ann	DEC 18 1852
BLAKENEY, John	REED, Catharine	MAY 29 1827
BLAKEY, Mary	NEWMAN, Thomas	NOV 19 1845
BLAKSLEE, George	MARKS, Catherine	SEP 04 1824
BLAN, Ellen	KING, Hiram	OCT 01 1838
BLAN, Joseph A.	FREEMAN, Laura V.	AUG 14 1851
BLANCHARD, Caroline Sarah	PEUGH, Samuel A.	DEC 27 1849
BLANCHARD, Claude D.	ANDERSON, Meda A.	SEP 18 1848
BLANCHARD, Constantine Andw.	LOWE, Teresa Ann	AUG 12 1851
BLANCHARD, Jane	FARNHAM, R. [Robert]	NOV 21 1836
BLANCHARD, Lucy Ann	O'BRYON, William	JAN 15 1825
BLANCHARD, Valentine	THOMPSON, Frances	MAR 23 1841
BLAND, Charlotte Maria	MILSTEAD, Ignatius	SEP 30 1826
BLAND, Cornelia Lee	McCREA, James W.F. [Dr.]	APR 08 1833
BLAND, Jane Maria	CLARK, T. Edward	MAY 11 1857

District of Columbia Marriage Licenses, 1811-1858

BLAND, John D.	BERKLEY, Maria	SEP 24 1841
BLAND, Mary Jane	ARNOLD, Benedict	AUG 11 1831
BLAND, Sarah Ann	APPLEBY, Bignal	JAN 22 1839
BLAND, Susan	ROLLS, Gustavus	JUL 02 1846
BLAND, William H.	BUREY, Margaret	JAN 08 1838
BLAND, William S.	DAVIS, Mary E.	JAN 02 1840
BLANDFORD, Mary Elizth. Cecelia	GOULD, John Alfred	JAN 20 1845
BLANEY, Bridget	LYNCH, Patrick	DEC 10 1856
BLANEY, Dennis	[blank], Johanna	FEB 08 1853
BLANEY, James	TARLTON, N.	APR 08 1826
BLANEY, Mary	LYNCH, Timothy	APR 20 1854
BLANFORD, Mary	REID, Benjamin	JUL 07 1824
BLANK, John	SHAEFFER, Ellen	APR 03 1851
BLANN, Laura	CURTIS, Mason	JUN 23 1858
BLANSDELL, Harriot	SMITH, Henry	JUL 05 1820
BLANY, Mary	HIGGINS, John	FEB 05 1856
BLASSINGER, Peter	BRIAN, Catharine	FEB 18 1840
BLAUIS, Rebecca	WARREN, Robert	MAY 07 1829
BLAW, Herman	LUTTGENZ, Frances	FEB 16 1852
BLEDNER, Wilhelmine	SCHOENEBERGER, George	JAN 02 1857
BLEDSOE, Susan	LLOYD, George	JAN 18 1834
BLEIGHT, Samuel R.	CHAPMAN, Georgeanna A.	FEB 12 1846
BLEW, Chs. W.	BAKER, Margaret	DEC 06 1822
BLEXLEY, Catharine	MOODY, William	DEC 23 1830
BLICK, Louisa Elizabeth	McMAHON, Philip	AUG 19 1848
BLIGH, James J.	CONNOR, Elizabeth	NOV 05 1853
BLINCOE, Albert T.	BURCH, Mary E.	JAN 16 1832
BLINKHORN, Mary	SAVAGE, James	NOV 22 1818
BLISCH, George	SCHRINKEL, Teresa	JAN 15 1846
BLISCH, Mary Elizth.	SCHNABEN, Leopold Joseph	SEP 05 1854
BLISH, Mary	PLANT, Pascal	JUL 08 1858
BLOCH, Dassiar	JOSEFF, Yetta	MAY 15 1854
BLOCK, Henrietta	BELLAND, Louis	MAY 04 1857
BLOCK, Moses	EDINBORO, Amelia (blk)	DEC 11 1856
BLOCKMAN, Wiley	DUVALL, Mary (blk)	FEB 21 1832
BLOCKSON, Jane Eliza	WHALEY, William H.	DEC 14 1837
BLOGET, Lorin	GIBBS, Mary E.	DEC 11 1856
BLOICE, Mary	STEWART, Charles	MAR 02 1841
BLOIS, Francoise	GAUDEMAR, Jean Baptiste	MAR 18 1819
BLOIS, Zachariah	CRAIN, Elizabeth	JUL 02 1812
BLOOD, Olympha	KING, George	JAN 29 1846
BLOODGOOD, Delavan	RUGER, Jennie	MAY 05 1857
BLOOMER, Mary A.	WOOD, Elexius A.	FEB 15 1855
BLOSCH, George	BRAITHAUPT, Margaret	JUL 23 1828
BLOSSOM, Electa J.	WILLIAMS, John H.	JUN 12 1856
BLOUNT, Annie Isabella	STORES, Amariah	NOV 26 1853
BLOWERS, Lucretia A.	BARON, Josiah	AUG 14 1855
BLOXHAM, Mary T.	WILSON, Charles	APR 10 1850
BLOXOM, Levi	WEST, Frances	AUG 07 1852
BLOXTON, Charles	CRAIG, Susan C.	JAN 04 1832
BLOXTON, Thomas	SEYMORE, Mary [Mrs.]	AUG 10 1816
BLOY, Rosanna	RADY, James	APR 10 1857
BLOYES, Annie	ROBY, Luther S.	AUG 11 1853
BLOYES, James H.	FORBES, Lucretia D.	MAR 28 1853
BLOYS, Nancy	DOTEN, Isaac	OCT 30 1817
BLOYSE, John	STEWARD, Ann Elizabeth	MAY 29 1834
BLUAHER, John T.	SCHUTZ, Malvina	APR 13 1857
BLUME, Catherine Ann	BUSHBY, James H.	MAR 07 1844

District of Columbia Marriage Licenses, 1811-1858

BLUMER, Amelia	BAKER, Levi T.	JUN 16 1857
BLUNDEN, Andrew	WELCH, Catharine	MAR 30 1847
BLUNDEN, Daniel W.	JONES, Mary Elizth.	MAR 03 1849
BLUNDEN, George	MUDD, Harriott	NOV 18 1828
BLUNDEN, Jane	SHEARWOOD, William	JAN 12 1818
BLUNDEN, Jane	TRACEY, Noland	NOV 10 1843
BLUNDEN, John A.	ALLEN, Sarah E.	JAN 13 1842
BLUNDEN, Owen Thomas	SCOTT, Mary Lavinia	JAN 03 1852
BLUNDER, Elizabeth	MURPHEY, John	SEP 15 1819
BLUNDER, James A.	WILSON, Ann	NOV 27 1854
BLUNDIN, Jane Ann	BALL, Samuel	DEC 29 1846
BLUNDON, Mary	ALLEN, John	DEC 31 1816
BLUNT, Harry W.D.	COOLIDGE, Marion A.	NOV 13 1854
BLUNT, Mary Ann B.	JOHNSTON, James	DEC 07 1830
BLUNT, Simon F.	KEY, Ellen L.	JAN 27 1846
BOAMAR, Marcellina	KIRBY, James P.	NOV 20 1840
BOARDMAN, William C.	COX, Rosina L.	APR 30 1838
BOARDMAN, Winfield Scott	DODDRIGE, Martha Ann	APR 11 1844
BOARMAN, Eleanor	PARKER, George	DEC 21 1815
BOARMAN, Elizabeth A.	YOUNG, Wilfred	FEB 02 1847
BOARMAN, Ellen	RICHARDSON, Judson, Junr.	JUN 14 1842
BOARMAN, Francis L.	PETERS, Cecelia Frances	JAN 24 1854
BOARMAN, Joseph B.	NORRISS, Margaret	DEC 09 1823
BOARMAN, Richard A.	SULLIVAN, Charlotte	AUG 21 1847
BOARMAN, Richard A.	FOWLER, Eliza	MAR 06 1858
BOARMAN, Sylvester B.	MORGAN, Maria L.	NOV 21 1844
BOASMAN, John	MERCER, Elizabeth	JAN 21 1857
BOATMAN, Ann B.	SMITH, Henry T.	OCT 03 1839
BOCKMAN, Eleanor	PARDINGTON, James	JUN 20 1816
BOCKMAN, William	PAYNE, Margaret	JUL 18 1827
BODE, George Wm.	HASSELHOFF, Ann	JUN 27 1843
BODE, Lewis	BUEHRE, Caroline	NOV 27 1852
BODEMAN, Sophia	SCHNEIDER, William	JUN 02 1855
BODENMÜLLER, Eliese	STEFFNER, Carl	AUG 22 1854
BODIEN, Henry A.	HOGG, Eliza J.	MAR 22 1856
BODINE, John	TILLET, Margarett	MAR 15 1815
BODINE, Malvina	ROSE, George W.	OCT 04 1854
BODISCO, Alexander	WILLIAMS, Harriet	APR 07 1840
BODMAN, George W.	WIDDICOMBE, Harriet	AUG 08 1854
BOERNSTEIN, August S.	BEHLEN, Frederika	JAN 11 1854
BOGAN, Ann R.	BUTT, Samuel	MAY 30 1844
BOGAN, John	McCARTY, Mary	JAN 26 1858
BOGAN, Martin V.B.	THOMPSON, Noemi	JUN 29 1853
BOGAN, Susan S.	VARNELL, George H.	NOV 18 1852
BOGARDUS, Peter E.	NEWMAN, Susan Ann	AUG 12 1850
BOGGESS, Thomas	SEDDON, Joanah	MAR 07 1838
BOGGS, W. Brenton	CARTER, Ellen Williams	OCT 10 1842
BOGLE, James	RICHARDS, Ann	JUL 14 1812
BOGLE, Julia Ann	HANEY, Joseph	NOV 24 1852
BOGS, John W.	WILSON, Hester A.	MAY 02 1854
BOGUE, Charlotte E.	WALL, Thomas	DEC 09 1844
BOGUE, Eliza M.L.	BOUCHER, Theodore F.	APR 02 1849
BOGUS, Elizabeth	ATKINSON, George	MAY 29 1812
BOGUSCH, Sophia Mary	WERNER, Charles	MAY 10 1854
BOHAIMAN, Ann	PENDRELL, Saml.	APR 14 1813
BOHANAN, Nancy	DUVALL, Henry A.	JUL 25 1850
BOHANEN, Ellen	PENDRED, Samuel	MAY 29 1815
BOHANNER, Levenia	MANLEY, Harrison	OCT 12 1818

District of Columbia Marriage Licenses, 1811-1858

BOHLAYER, John C.	ADAMS, Eliza	OCT 26 1836
BOHLAYER, Mary C.	SNIFFEN, Theodore	JUN 07 1852
BOHN, John	MARTELL, Elizabeth	APR 24 1851
BOHN, Mary	RAAB, Michael	MAR 04 1848
BOHRER, Abraham	ALEXANDER, Mary Ann	JUL 01 1814
BOHRER, Augusta M.	HINES, Christian M.	JUL 11 1854
BOHRER, Benj. S.	LUFBOROUGH, Eliza	OCT 03 1820
BOHRER, Benjamin	FENDLEY, Matilda	MAY 22 1826
BOHRER, Benjamin R.	SULLIVAN, Margaret L.	JAN 03 1848
BOHRER, Benjamin S. [Dr.]	TAYLOE, Maria [Mrs.]	JUN 09 1834
BOHRER, Elizabeth	WALKER, Richard H.	NOV 10 1849
BOHRER, George A.	OTTERBACK, Catherine	APR 02 1839
BOHRER, Harriet A.	SHEKELL, Richd. R.	OCT 28 1823
BOHRER, Jacob	WILMS, Mrs. Elizabeth	AUG 12 1815
BOHRER, Mary L.	CLITZ, John M.B.	SEP 20 1842
BOHRER, Sarah	WILLET, Marinus	OCT 02 1838
BOILLEAU, Charles	BENTON, Susan M.	JUN 04 1855
BOISEAU, James T.	MEAD, Deborah	SEP 02 1841
BOLAND, Daniel	SIMPSON, Ann Sophia	APR 05 1842
BOLAND, Mary	BELL, Robert	JUL 15 1856
BOLAND, Tobias	McCAULEY, Ellen	MAY 28 1831
BOLAYER, John	KEITHLEY, Sarah Ann	MAR 30 1844
BOLDEN, Rebecca	MARR, James D.	JAN 27 1844
BOLDER, Matilda	YATES, Alexander	SEP 19 1825
BOLDT, August	INDERIDEN, Maria	MAY 08 1835
BOLEAR, John	MEHONE, Nancy	JUL 02 1823
BOLER, Alice	PURSLEY, Felin	MAY 21 1855
BOLER, James	HADY, Mary Ellen	APR 23 1853
BOLER, Martha (blk)	BURKE, James	JUL 12 1855
BOLES, James T.	BRISCOE, Louisa (blk)	AUG 10 1854
BOLEY, Sarah Ann	CARRICO, Robert L.	JUN 20 1853
BOLIND, Thomas	MORSELL, Margaret	JUL 03 1852
BOLLING, George Washington	NICHOLLS, Martha Smith	NOV 19 1827
BOLLING, Robert B.	DOUGHTY, Margaret	NOV 11 1856
BOLLINGER, Margaretta	INDERMAUER, Jeremiah	MAY 01 1828
BOLLISON, Elizabeth	PORTER, John	AUG 06 1822
BOLLISTON, Timothy	GOLDING, Bridget	JAN 10 1856
BOLYE, Susanna	JUPE, George W.	APR 23 1814
BOMAN, Allen	BEAN, Martha Ann	JAN 02 1851
BOMAN, Susan	NICHOLSON, Peter	AUG 06 1819
BOMBAUGH, Harman	WEBER, Margaret	OCT 28 1845
BOMBGARDNER, George	OWENSTEIN, Sarah	JUL 30 1853
BOMFORD, George	BALDWIN, Clara	APR 20 1816
BOMFORD, Louisa S.	LEAR, Benjamin Lincoln	AUG 08 1831
BOMFORD, Ruth Theodora	PAINE, John Stone	OCT 28 1845
BOMKER, Catherine	WEIKER, Casper	MAY 14 1835
BONARD, Frederick	KANSLEY, Barbara	MAY 06 1834
BOND, Ann	HURLEY, Theodore	SEP 14 1852
BOND, Charles	HENDERSON, Ann (blk)	SEP 09 1845
BOND, Daniel	GOINGS, Laura (blk)	APR 21 1842
BOND, David	SHIVERIN, Mary (blk)	MAY 08 1856
BOND, Elizabeth	HAYNE, Lewis	JAN 15 1844
BOND, Harriet E. (blk)	McCOY, Martin	JUN 03 1851
BOND, James L.	ISRAEL, Mary E.	OCT 25 1847
BOND, John	WALLACE, Mary Jane (blk)	DEC 05 1855
BOND, Joseph	BEACH, Theodocia	AUG 26 1851
BOND, Levi	ANDERSON, Easter (blk)	JUL 23 1850
BOND, Levi	CARROLL, Sarah (blk)	APR 01 1857

District of Columbia Marriage Licenses, 1811-1858

BOND, Mary A.	FOWLER, William	JAN 21 1845
BOND, Rachel (blk)	ANDERSON, Charles	JAN 17 1855
BOND, Rebecca Ann	MITCHELL, Dennis	AUG 24 1840
BOND, Ridgly Alex	PADGETT, Keziah	DEC 12 1813
BOND, Samuel	HENLY, Ann	DEC 19 1844
BOND, William S.	GOINGS, Mary C. (blk)	APR 30 1851
BONDS, Columbia (blk)	SHEPHERD, Elias	DEC 29 1856
BONDS, Tholand, Miss	JENKINS, Edward	DEC 23 1825
BONIFER, Elizabeth	CONLY, John	JUN 15 1816
BONINI, John	THOMPSON, Mary	APR 27 1853
BONN, Ignatius	THRUSTON, Caroline (blk)	APR 30 1842
BONNYCASTLE, Ann M.	ROBINSON, William M.	OCT 22 1849
BONNYCASTLE, Mary	SHAW, James B.	JAN 15 1857
BONTZ, George	BAKER, Margaret	SEP 01 1840
BONTZ, Henry	SCARCE, Harriet	JUN 01 1840
BONTZ, John	HILL, Ann Elizabeth	JUN 13 1849
BONTZ, William C.	POWELL, Ruth Armer	MAY 17 1858
BONTZE, Elizabeth C.	COWLING, Thomas C.	JAN 03 1857
BOOCOCK, William	DIXON, Maria	MAR 24 1830
BOOKER, Robert H.	BEANS, Charlotte A. (blk)	OCT 27 1851
BOOKMAN, Joseph	DOUGLASS, Sarah	DEC 31 1839
BOON, Abraham	BROOKS, Julia	FEB 15 1838
BOON, Elizabeth	BANGS, David	OCT 19 1820
BOONE, Alexius	CLOUD, Naomi	DEC 20 1831
BOONE, David	WILLIAMS, Ann (blk)	OCT 04 1855
BOONE, Eleanor	MITCHELL, George	MAR 17 1831
BOONE, Elizabeth Emily	HICKS, Thomas	SEP 21 1844
BOONE, Henrietta	REDMOND, Benjamin P.	MAY 09 1833
BOONE, Jane M.	DYER, John R.	MAY 23 1826
BOONE, John B.	ORME, Jane Elizabeth	JUN 02 1829
BOONE, John F.	BAKER, Louisa A.M.	JUN 05 1832
BOONE, John F.	DYER, Henrietta H.	APR 28 1851
BOONE, John Lewis	HARROD, Ann Rebecca (blk)	AUG 11 1853
BOONE, Mary Matilda	SUMMERS, Judson	JUL 04 1827
BOONE, Priscilla A.	GRAHAM, John F.	FEB 02 1837
BOONE, Rachel	CLARKE, Walter	SEP 20 1814
BOONE, Robert	QUEEN, Catharine J.	APR 14 1817
BOONE, Robert	WEAVER, Rachael Ann	AUG 23 1831
BOONE, William	EVANS, Ann	JAN 30 1851
BOOSE, John	REA, Martha	JUL 29 1822
BOOSE, John	OSBORN, Sarah	JUN 01 1825
BOOSE, William Henry	DETERMAN, Margaret Ann	MAY 20 1858
BOOTES, Elizabeth	CLARK, Cantwell	DEC 12 1837
BOOTES, Samuel Massey	SMITH, Elizabeth	SEP 29 1828
BOOTH, Ann	GOURLEY, Thomas	JAN 21 1851
BOOTH, Edward	HOWE, Mary Ann	MAY 19 1814
BOOTH, Elizabeth	CROSS, Thomas	AUG 04 1832
BOOTH, Ellen Jane	FRANKS, Jacob	DEC 22 1834
BOOTH, Harriet F.	BOWEN, John	APR 21 1836
BOOTH, Henry Mansfield	CONLY, Mary	JUN 18 1853
BOOTH, Henry P.	BORDERMAN, Louisa	MAR 22 1856
BOOTH, Jane	NELSON, Levi	JAN 29 1825
BOOTH, Margaret	COVILLIER, Theodore	JAN 20 1836
BOOTH, Mary	WASON, Israel	AUG 06 1836
BOOTH, Mary (blk)	SHORTER, Charles	AUG 16 1832
BOOTH, Mary Ellen	QUIGLY, Daniel	FEB 12 1839
BOOTH, Nathaniel	LIPSCOMB, Eleanor H.	OCT 24 1844
BOOTH, Richard E.	CUNNINGHAM, Elizabeth	JAN 12 1847

District of Columbia Marriage Licenses, 1811-1858

BOOTH, Sarah E.	STACKS, Joseph E.	OCT 31 1854
BOOTHE, Ann	BOWLING, Ignatius	OCT 25 1826
BOOTHE, Catharine Ann	McALWEE, Aaron	OCT 12 1829
BOOTHE, George	SCOTT, Mary	AUG 13 1812
BOOTHE, Henry	JOHNSON, Ann	JUN 26 1821
BOOTHE, James	BERRY, Elizabeth	OCT 22 1839
BOOTHE, James	CRAMPTON, Catherine Virginia	JUN 09 1857
BOOTHE, John	DICKSON, Mary	MAR 15 1833
BOOTHE, John	JORDAN, Elizabeth (blk)	SEP 06 1837
BOOTHE, Mary Matilda	PALLY, James H.	APR 27 1842
BOOTHE, Sarah	POOR, John	FEB 10 1836
BOOTS, Matilda	EDMONSON, Thomas	JUN 25 1818
BOOZE, Erasmus	HILL, Margaret	MAR 01 1851
BOPP, James	TAYLOR, Ann L.	JUL 26 1856
BOPP, Louisa A.	DRURY, William C.	JUL 08 1856
BOPP, Peter	ANDERSON, Ann Maria	DEC 06 1851
BORDERMAN, Louisa	BOOTH, Henry P.	MAR 22 1856
BORDING, Mrs.	WIEDERMAN, Augustus	JUL 02 1845
BORELAND, Jane	McDOWALL, Washington	MAY 16 1836
BORELAND, John	MILLER, Ellen S.	FEB 06 1855
BORELAND, Samuel	WALKER, Catharine	SEP 21 1835
BORGESS, Susannah	RYAN, John	DEC 20 1814
BORLAND, Alexander	McKIB, Mary	JAN 12 1818
BORLAND, Alexander C.	BORLAND, Mary C.	JAN 17 1855
BORLAND, Catherine	RIGGLES, Thomas	MAY 10 1842
BORLAND, John A.	CONNELL, Mary Jane	OCT 29 1857
BORLAND, Maria E.	HARVEY, James F.	DEC 09 1850
BORLAND, Mary C.	BORLAND, Alexander C.	JAN 17 1855
BORLAND, Mary E.	WILSON, Frederick T.	DEC 24 1853
BORLAND, Thomas	FLETCHER, Ellen (blk)	DEC 23 1851
BORLAND, Thomas	KING, Mary	OCT 02 1852
BORMAN, Charles	SEBASTIAN, Mary	AUG 16 1842
BORNE, Elizabeth	DAY, Charles	AUG 19 1858
BORREMANS, Louis	YATES, Anna Catharine	AUG 18 1831
BORROWS, Catherine	BAILEY, John	SEP 08 1813
BORROWS, Laura Matilda	FREE, Lambert	FEB 12 1823
BORROWS, Mary Ann	ROTHWELL, Andrew	APR 17 1824
BORTLE, Mary E.	SARGENT, James	JUL 27 1852
BORZEL, Gertrude	KOSTNER, Joseph	JAN 25 1849
BOSCEDO, Lewis [Capt.]	GUMEAR, Martha	OCT 15 1834
BOSCHKE, Mary	KAYSER, Alexander	FEB 21 1854
BOSLEY, Laura J.	HOBSON, Richard V.	FEB 24 1857
BOSNELL, William	CLARKE, Ann	DEC 29 1854
BOSOMWORTH, Mary Jane	FUSS, William H.	FEB 09 1853
BOSS, James H.	VEN___, Ann Sophia	JUN 15 1840
BOSS, John P.	PETTIT, Caroline S.E.	NOV 28 1848
BOSS, Joseph S.	BANKS, Susan A.	APR 30 1856
BOSS, Matilda	REEVES, Hezekiah James	OCT 11 1815
BOSS, William A.	LEWIS, Eliza A.	AUG 29 1846
BOSSE, Dora	WETHEFT, William	JUL 17 1851
BOSSE, William	BARNES, Mary E.	OCT 17 1854
BOSSEL, Mary	SUMMERS, Edward	DEC 29 1851
BOSSERT, Christina	SHUSTER, Christopher	JUL 25 1842
BOSTIC, Jane	ROBERTSON, James	FEB 01 1816
BOSTICK, Edward	MARTIN, Sally Maria	SEP 23 1850
BOSTICK, Susan	BERRY, John	OCT 09 1816
BOSTON, Alexander	NORRIS, Elizabeth	OCT 21 1837
BOSTON, Charles	DAVIS, Martha Ann	DEC 20 1827

District of Columbia Marriage Licenses, 1811-1858

BOSTON, Daniel	DOUGLASS, Mary Ann M. (blk)	MAY 29 1854
BOSTON, Edward	TUT, Eliza (blk)	OCT 19 1854
BOSTON, Ellen (blk)	BAYNE, Joseph	MAY 13 1856
BOSTON, George	FITZHUE, Elizabeth (blk)	JAN 24 1854
BOSTON, George	FITZHUGH, Elizabeth (blk)	AUG 08 1854
BOSTON, Isabella (blk)	BULGER, John	JAN 24 1856
BOSTON, Julia Ann J.	HENION, John	JUN 25 1838
BOSTON, Louisa (blk)	MINOR, James	SEP 24 1851
BOSTON, Robert	BECKET, Ruth Ann (blk)	FEB 25 1854
BOSTON, Thomas	LAWN, Annie (blk)	JAN 22 1852
BOSTON, Virginia	AMES, John	JAN 12 1854
BOSWELL, A.V.	SUMMERS, Nathan	JAN 26 1858
BOSWELL, Allen T.	COLLIER, Ellen	APR 02 1855
BOSWELL, Amanda M.	WALKER, Peyton B.	DEC 22 1845
BOSWELL, Amanuel H.	SKIDMORE, Octaver	JUL 02 1858
BOSWELL, Ann M.	CLARKE, John M.	SEP 01 1849
BOSWELL, Barbara E.	KIDWELL, Samuel	JUN 25 1850
BOSWELL, Benjn.	THOMPSON, Eleanor	NOV 18 1822
BOSWELL, Charlotte	KIDWELL, William	JUL 15 1845
BOSWELL, Eliza	JEFFERSON, Thomas	APR 02 1840
BOSWELL, Eliza Ann	COLLARD, James Irvin	DEC 25 1830
BOSWELL, Elizabeth	REEDER, William	SEP 18 1816
BOSWELL, Elizabeth	WISE, Elisha	OCT 13 1836
BOSWELL, Elizabeth	CURTIN, James R.N.	FEB 16 1843
BOSWELL, Ellen	COATNEY, John	APR 02 1829
BOSWELL, Ellen	JOHNSON, John	OCT 12 1843
BOSWELL, George	WILLIAMS, Jane	APR 13 1816
BOSWELL, George	FLETCHER, Martha	MAY 22 1816
BOSWELL, Ignatius M.	BARTLETT, Frances V.	SEP 23 1856
BOSWELL, J.J.W.	JONES, Mary E.	MAY 27 1858
BOSWELL, Jacob	RUSSELL, Rebecca	APR 26 1817
BOSWELL, James	DILLARD, Eliza Catherine	NOV 28 1842
BOSWELL, James	BROWN, Catharine	MAY 12 1846
BOSWELL, James B.	JONES, Flavilla	JUN 10 1833
BOSWELL, James H.	PAINE, Ellen	JUN 29 1858
BOSWELL, James J.	KING, Mary Ann	DEC 27 1853
BOSWELL, Johanna	WALLS, John N.	MAY 11 1857
BOSWELL, John W.	HALEY, Sarah Jane	FEB 21 1853
BOSWELL, Margaret H.	THOMPSON, John	AUG 26 1846
BOSWELL, Martha Ann	SCOTT, Thomas	JAN 21 1833
BOSWELL, Mary Ann	SHADE, Thompson	APR 09 1818
BOSWELL, Mary Ann	GRINDER, William	AUG 06 1842
BOSWELL, Mary Ann	GARRETT, Henry Ashton	APR 27 1843
BOSWELL, Mary C.	GEE, Samuel P.	AUG 03 1858
BOSWELL, Mary Louisa	COXEN, Robert	OCT 24 1854
BOSWELL, Phelly D.	GARDINER, Wm. T.	FEB 15 1847
BOSWELL, Robert	GOODRICH, Anna	NOV 05 1853
BOSWELL, Sarah	SINCOX, Alexander	JUN 09 1821
BOSWELL, Sarah Ellen	SMALLWOOD, Richard T.	FEB 21 1850
BOSWELL, Sophronia	THOMAS, Moses W.	SEP 07 1853
BOSWELL, Susan E.	TUCKER, James F.	AUG 08 1849
BOSWELL, Susan E.	LYONS, Daniel R.E.	SEP 04 1850
BOSWELL, Thomas P.	LEMON, Lucy A.	NOV 22 1849
BOSWELL, Uriah	CLARK, William	AUG 14 1829
BOSWELL, Washington G.	GLASCOW, Mary M.	JUN 28 1853
BOSWELL, Wm. H.	FLETCHER, Elizabeth	JUL 05 1821
BOSWELL, Wm. R.	FAFF, Mary	JUL 19 1846
BOSWORTH, Eliphalet [Rev.]	BARRON, Mary Ann	JUN 02 1835

District of Columbia Marriage Licenses, 1811-1858

BOTELER, B.W.	PHILLIPS, Ellen Amelia	OCT 17 1846
BOTELER, Caroline	DONN, John M.	MAY 05 1831
BOTELER, Charles W.	MORIARTY, Mary	AUG 04 1818
BOTELER, Charles W.	LUPTON, Mary Ann	OCT 09 1839
BOTELER, Eliza	LOMAX, Thomas M.	JUL 06 1858
BOTELER, Elizabeth	VARDEN, Edmund	JAN 21 1841
BOTELER, Ellen	WILSON, John Q.	APR 29 1847
BOTELER, John D.	MILLS, Eliza	OCT 12 1820
BOTELER, Joseph Isaac	IRWIN, Ellen Williams	NOV 07 1833
BOTELER, Mary (blk)	HILL, Charles	JUL 20 1848
BOTELER, Mary A.J.	FALCONER, Wm. H.	JAN 07 1856
BOTELER, Mary Ann	PRATHER, Henry A.	APR 27 1826
BOTELER, Sarah A.P.	MAGRUDER, Thomas J.	MAR 27 1844
BOTELER, Susana W.	BOYD, John D.	OCT 26 1853
BOTELER, Thomas	FAGAN, Matilda	OCT 06 1818
BOTHE, William M.	VIEBUCKEN, John Peter	MAY 15 1857
BOTLER, Margaret (blk)	WOODLAND, Joseph	NOV 10 1840
BOTSFORD, Eliza	MYERS, John H.	JUN 08 1833
BOTSFORD, William	McCANN, Elizabeth	JUN 22 1816
BOTT, James	CULLISON, Mary	JUN 01 1843
BOTT, Margaret	MARTIN, John	SEP 09 1851
BOTTIN, James	LOMAX, Frances	AUG 04 1855
BOTTOMLY, John	KNOTT, Rosanna	SEP 04 1821
BOTTS, Mary V.	GAINES, Edwin	DEC 29 1845
BOUCHER, Ann	BALLENGER, Richard	FEB 22 1831
BOUCHER, Chloe	CROW, John	FEB 01 1845
BOUCHER, Joseph W.	SPALDING, Kate V.	JAN 16 1852
BOUCHER, Josephine	BERRY, Nicholas T.	SEP 05 1855
BOUCHER, Offert	MADDOX, Mary Ann	NOV 12 1838
BOUCHER, Oxford	SKIDMORE, Margaretta	JUL 26 1851
BOUCHER, Sarah E.	THORN, Judson H.	SEP 27 1850
BOUCHER, Theodore F.	BOGUE, Eliza M.L.	APR 02 1849
BOUCK, Nicholas	WORCESTER, Sarah B.	MAY 20 1839
BOUCK, William	DIEDERICK, Catharine	AUG 19 1856
BOUDET, Maria	MAY, James	APR 15 1812
BOUDIN, Addison	DOUGLASS, Mary Ellen	JUL 03 1856
BOUDIN, Alexander	BECRAFT, Sarah E.	OCT 10 1855
BOUDINOT, Henry Clay	PRICE, Mary Elizth. H.	FEB 28 1854
BOUGHIN, Edward	COLBERT, Eliza	FEB 07 1853
BOUGLEY, John	O'NEALE, Mary	JAN 13 1830
BOULDEN, Mary (blk)	JOHNSON, Collins	JUN 04 1847
BOULER, Emelie	FAVIER, Aezricol	OCT 21 1828
BOULTON, Rebecca	EDMONSTON, Thomas	NOV 24 1836
BOUNDS, Joseph	SAKER, Elizabeth A.	MAY 10 1856
BOURGUENOT, Ferdinand	HEWIT, Fanny	AUG 14 1854
BOURNE, Mary Jane	FITZPATRICK, James	MAY 27 1857
BOUS, Frederick	ZIMMERMAN, Helena	NOV 13 1855
BOUTCHER, Alfred	MacETEE, Sarah	JUN 26 1818
BOUTWELL, Martha S.	SMITH, James M.	MAY 22 1845
BOUTZ, Henry	MORRISON, Elizabeth M.K.	OCT 28 1843
BOUVET, Sophie C.	HARRISON, Uriah B.	NOV 06 1856
BOWAN, Hannah	MORAN, Dicen	JAN 05 1846
BOWDEN, Mary Ann	BURKE, Thomas E.	JUL 15 1844
BOWEN, Abram O.	SMITH, Frances S.	AUG 05 1841
BOWEN, Anthony	COLLINS, Mary (blk)	SEP 19 1839
BOWEN, Artemus	PLANT, Gracey	SEP 23 1817
BOWEN, B.F.	VESSEY, Mary A.	AUG 14 1855
BOWEN, Benjamin	SEAVER, Mrs. Martha	SEP 20 1825

District of Columbia Marriage Licenses, 1811-1858

BOWEN, Eleanor	HINES, Abraham	DEC 19 1815
BOWEN, Eliza Ann [Mrs.]	BARNARD, Charles C.P.	SEP 13 1836
BOWEN, Elizabeth T.	DUVALL, William T.	JUN 25 1833
BOWEN, Fielder	HOGANS, Rachel (blk)	APR 11 1837
BOWEN, George	SUMBY, Lucy Ann (blk)	MAR 19 1852
BOWEN, George W.	LEWIS, Eliza A.	JUN 10 1824
BOWEN, Harriett M.	MARBURY, Wm.	SEP 05 1822
BOWEN, Harriot	SMITH, John	JAN 01 1818
BOWEN, James	COOKE, Anne	SEP 06 1813
BOWEN, James	BAUM, Susan D.	JUL 23 1835
BOWEN, James A.	TURNER, Elizabeth	JUL 19 1843
BOWEN, Jane Eliza	EDMONSON, Jackson	FEB 25 1841
BOWEN, Janie (blk)	SMITH, Amos	MAY 16 1833
BOWEN, John	SLOAN, Anna Rebecca	DEC 22 1832
BOWEN, John	BOOTH, Harriet F.	APR 21 1836
BOWEN, John G.	McPHERSON, Ann	OCT 21 1813
BOWEN, John Thomas	HURLEY, Jane Rebecca	MAR 16 1850
BOWEN, Joseph O.D.	REED, Elizabeth	JUN 28 1836
BOWEN, Leonidas	LARCOMBE, Mary Ann	SEP 18 1845
BOWEN, Martha	TURNER, Goalin	JAN 19 1847
BOWEN, Mary Ann	EDMONSTON, Elijah	NOV 06 1839
BOWEN, Mary E.	STEWART, George W.	JUN 05 1840
BOWEN, Mary E.	CRIDLING, Henry N.	AUG 05 1856
BOWEN, Rebecca	DAVIS, Hezekiah	AUG 24 1816
BOWEN, Rosina	BROWN, Reuben R.	MAY 28 1849
BOWEN, Sarah	STEPHENSON, Alfred	OCT 29 1835
BOWEN, Silas T.	KIBLER, Susanah	NOV 04 1853
BOWEN, Uriah R.	DEMAR, Elizth. A.M.	MAR 12 1852
BOWEN, Virginia	REESE, John	JUN 26 1854
BOWENS, Martha Ann	HARRIS, George P.	JAN 03 1856
BOWER, George	KEESIEKIN, Sophia	OCT 25 1851
BOWER, Harriett	JONES, James	MAY 28 1845
BOWER, Mary	WEBER, John	OCT 25 1851
BOWERS, Bennionuel B.	KELLEY, Maria Catharine	SEP 30 1833
BOWERS, Richard S.	GAINES, Louisa J.	JUN 29 1853
BOWERS, Samuel	NOLAND, Winney E.	APR 12 1855
BOWIE, Aquilla	HAUS, Margaret Ann	JUN 11 1840
BOWIE, Catharine	BRADY, Andrew	AUG 30 1819
BOWIE, Catherine	GRANT, John	JAN 01 1816
BOWIE, Charles	SUITER, Sarah Maria	FEB 14 1838
BOWIE, Charles	SIMMS, [blank]	FEB 15 1848
BOWIE, Elizabeth (blk)	FITZHUGH, Clem	JAN 06 1844
BOWIE, George Washington	RAPINE, Mary	MAY 22 1828
BOWIE, James W.	HORNSBURY, Ann (blk)	APR 28 1858
BOWIE, John E.	MORSELL, Jane S.	OCT 13 1856
BOWIE, Julian	COAX, William	SEP 29 1823
BOWIE, Lucinda	PARRY, Cyrus B.	AUG 05 1822
BOWIE, Lucinda	EVANS, John Thomas	SEP 29 1823
BOWIE, Mary M.	WEEMS, Franklin	JUN 06 1854
BOWIE, Mary S.	McCALLEY, Henry	SEP 28 1842
BOWIE, Matilda	TINCY, Donotius	SEP 09 1820
BOWIE, Richard	THOMAS, Ann (blk)	APR 21 1838
BOWIE, Richard C.	RAPINE, Martha M.	NOV 24 1829
BOWIE, William F.	WARDER, Mary V.	JAN 21 1851
BOWIER, Mary Ann	CARTER, William	JUN 15 1832
BOWLER, Fanny	BROOKES, Henry	DEC 31 1829
BOWLES, Charles	JACKSON, Eleanor	NOV 27 1841
BOWLES, Martin	LAMPKIN, Jane	APR 04 1829

District of Columbia Marriage Licenses, 1811-1858

BOWLIN, Mary A. (blk)	MATTHEWS, John A.	NOV 23 1853
BOWLIN, Nancy Ann	ALLEN, Oliver	DEC 16 1829
BOWLING, Ann	MARCEY, William	OCT 01 1829
BOWLING, Ann W.	SMITH, Saml. Owen	OCT 22 1816
BOWLING, Edward M.	MATTINGLY, Mary Martina	MAY 27 1858
BOWLING, Eliza Maria	ANDERSON, Thomas F.	OCT 04 1820
BOWLING, Ignatius	BOOTH, Ann	OCT 25 1826
BOWLING, Jane S.	COOK, Peter	JAN 07 1817
BOWLING, Joseph	BROWN, Sarah	DEC 05 1821
BOWLING, Mary	MARCEY, James	JUN 09 1829
BOWLING, Sarah P.	TASTET, Nicholas	NOV 28 1825
BOWMAN, Catherine	KRIMMELLY, John G.	DEC 13 1854
BOWMAN, Henry D.	MAGRATH, Henrietta	OCT 06 1844
BOWMAN, James	SHELTON, Elizabeth (blk)	SEP 16 1857
BOWMAN, Jane	GOLDSBOROUGH, Richard T.	MAR 23 1829
BOWMAN, John D.	BUTLER, Elizabeth (blk)	MAR 09 1848
BOWMAN, John M.	CRATTY, Ellen	DEC 26 1855
BOWMAN, Joseph	BIASDERFER, Frances	DEC 03 1832
BOWMAN, Leonard	FRYE, Caroline V.B.	MAY 13 1846
BOWMAN, Mary Ann	GREENWOOD, Benjamin	MAY 14 1845
BOWMAN, Miss (blk)	DICK, John H.	MAY 02 1851
BOWMAN, Raphael H.	O'BRIEN, Ellen Maria	SEP 15 1857
BOWMAN, Sarah	DEAVER, Stephen	FEB 27 1817
BOWMAN, Sophia N.	PAYNE, John H.	JAN 14 1836
BOWMAN, William	MENIFE, Catharine (blk)	DEC 27 1824
BOWMANN, Charles	WALLS, Maria E.	JAN 01 1855
BOWSER, Thomas	JOHNSON, Elizabeth (blk)	DEC 02 1833
BOWSHER, Susan	BROADWELL, Josiah	APR 14 1813
BOWYER, Elizabeth	HEAP, David Porter	SEP 28 1854
BOWYER, James H.	McDONALD, Aurelia	JAN 13 1848
BOXLEY, Jane E.	NUCKOLS, George B.	JUN 11 1835
BOYCE, Abraham	PRESTON, Adaline	JUL 27 1829
BOYCE, Ann	COLLARD, George	OCT 04 1821
BOYCE, Catharine	BEACH, Wm.	AUG 02 1842
BOYCE, James	COLLISON, Julia Ann	SEP 24 1844
BOYCE, James	MADIGAN, Mary	DEC 27 1855
BOYCE, Jane	PETER, George W.	FEB 04 1840
BOYCE, Margaret	CROW, Martin	JUL 17 1852
BOYCE, Mary	COLE, Samuel	JUN 06 1857
BOYD, Adaline	MAGRUDER, Haswell	JUL 04 1832
BOYD, Amanda	GREEVES, John	FEB 11 1840
BOYD, Ann (blk)	ROBINSON, Fielding	NOV 07 1839
BOYD, Ann C.	BEALL, Phineas B.	MAY 03 1833
BOYD, Constantine	HYDE, Thomas V.	OCT 10 1839
BOYD, Eliza	HOOE, Howson L.	OCT 06 1825
BOYD, Elizabeth R. (blk)	SMITH, Robert	JAN 06 1858
BOYD, George K.	MANN, Virginia P.	JUN 19 1845
BOYD, Jacob	HERN, Mary	APR 15 1856
BOYD, James J.	DEMPSEY, Anne	AUG 27 1852
BOYD, James L.	PEERCE, Helen C.	FEB 01 1837
BOYD, Jane C.	LEWIS, Edward W.	APR 20 1824
BOYD, John D.	PADGETT, Ann	DEC 28 1843
BOYD, John D.	BOTELER, Susana W.	OCT 26 1853
BOYD, John G.	EASLEY, Sally N.	MAY 31 1853
BOYD, Lucy	WILLIAMS, John	MAY 25 1836
BOYD, Margaret	DAWSON, Thomas H.	DEC 22 1856
BOYD, Maria (blk)	TOY, Reuben	NOV 25 1845
BOYD, Martha Jane	ADAMS, Christopher	FEB 15 1856

District of Columbia Marriage Licenses, 1811-1858

BOYD, Mary	ORR, John	NOV 03 1812
BOYD, Mary Ann	ROBBINS, Isaac H.	JUL 07 1827
BOYD, Mary Jane	JONES, Dangerfield	DEC 14 1847
BOYD, Robert	KELLY, Jane	FEB 28 1828
BOYD, Robert	BITNER, Ann Elizth.	OCT 04 1854
BOYD, Rosanna	McLANE, George W.	AUG 14 1849
BOYD, Sarah	STINCHCOMB, Noah	OCT 13 1832
BOYD, Thomas	BRUCE, Sarah J.	JUN 11 1858
BOYD, William	WILSON, Jane	APR 18 1850
BOYDE, George	O'HAGAN, Mary	AUG 15 1850
BOYED, Ann	GREEN, Patrick	JAN 22 1824
BOYER, Caroline	GREENWELL, James	JUN 20 1839
BOYER, Frederick	DAVIS, Elizabeth	JUN 08 1826
BOYER, George	GRAY, Elizabeth	AUG 16 1858
BOYER, Henry	HERBET, Mary Jane	MAR 08 1854
BOYER, Peter D.	SHIPLEY, Susanna	JAN 04 1813
BOYER, Susan	JOURNEY, John A.	JAN 10 1819
BOYL, Mary	REDDING, Joseph	APR 28 1853
BOYLAN, Andrew	McCARTY, Mary	NOV 09 1853
BOYLE, Alice	GAUTIER, Pierre Charles	NOV 08 1839
BOYLE, Ann	CAMPBELL, Bartley	JUN 02 1852
BOYLE, Catharine Ann	STUBBS, William E.	APR 18 1843
BOYLE, David	DOLAN, Mary	JUL 03 1858
BOYER, Frederick	FARRELL, Caroline	AUG 01 1836
BOYLE, Isabella M.	CLEMENTS, Stephen C.	NOV 19 1857
BOYLE, James	RYLEY, Alice	APR 18 1857
BOYLE, Jane	DONOVAN, Randall	OCT 28 1854
BOYLE, John	SULLIVAN, Mary Ann	SEP 03 1849
BOYLE, John	SHAY, Catharine	FEB 08 1853
BOYLE, John F.	COLLINS, Harriet Maria	FEB 23 1841
BOYLE, Junius J. [Lt.]	McLEOD, Ann Eliza	JUL 18 1832
BOYLE, Mary	KRAFT, Christopher	OCT 05 1850
BOYLE, Mary	BEDDING, Joseph	AUG 19 1852
BOYLE, Patrick	DELANEY, Bridget	JAN 06 1854
BOYLE, Robert	SULLIVAN, Ann	FEB 02 1853
BOYLE, Thomas	HILLORIN, Catharine	FEB 05 1856
BOYLE, Uys	WALKER, Malinda	AUG 01 1844
BOZELL, Jane	WISE, Uriah	FEB 27 1850
BOZZEL, Robert L.	FOXWELL, Isabel A.	JUL 14 1853
BRACK, Morris	CUNNINGHAM, Mary	FEB 02 1856
BRACKENRIDGE, Attelia A.	HANDY, Edward G.	NOV 21 1827
BRACKENRIDGE, James W.	CLARKE, Eliza [Mrs.]	JAN 04 1820
BRADBURN, John D.	CAMMACK, Elizabeth Ann	FEB 15 1844
BRADBURN, Mary Elizabeth	BIGGS, James Henry	JUN 08 1840
BRADBURN, Peter	DERRET, Catharine	MAR 05 1822
BRADBURY, John W.	FRENCH, Martha E.	SEP 24 1857
BRADDOCK, Amelia	HIPBURN, Moses	MAY 26 1827
BRADDOCK, William	PORTER, Robert V.	FEB 28 1843
BRADEKAM, Catherine	ARDIESER, Christian	JUN 28 1851
BRADEN, Elizabeth	RIDGEWAY, Eden	AUG 10 1813
BRADFORD, Caroline A.	ROBINSON, Samuel	OCT 13 1836
BRADFORD, Catharine A.	MASI, Seraphin	NOV 08 1825
BRADFORD, Elizabeth	BROWN, William	MAR 24 1835
BRADFORD, Mary C.	BELT, Thomas W.	SEP 04 1852
BRADFORD, Sarah Elizabeth	COALE, William	SEP 23 1848
BRADFORD, William	BUTLER, Eleanor	FEB 15 1813
BRADLEY, Abraham, 3d	HALL, Mary G.	MAY 30 1822
BRADLEY, Abrahamie	WHITE, Ashton S.H.	OCT 16 1843

District of Columbia Marriage Licenses, 1811-1858

BRADLEY, Alexander	RAY, Elila	FEB 04 1822
BRADLEY, Ambrose	PHELAN, Ellen T.	MAY 02 1857
BRADLEY, Ann	HARMAN, William	JAN 31 1813
BRADLEY, Ann	MARTIN, Archibald	JUN 22 1835
BRADLEY, Ann E.	MAYHEW, Coffet	AUG 07 1855
BRADLEY, Anne M.	GRAHAM, John W.	JUN 01 1842
BRADLEY, Catharine	LEE, Samuel	JAN 03 1833
BRADLEY, Catherine	WHITNEY, Ebenezer	NOV 21 1847
BRADLEY, Charles	BEALL, Maria	MAY 24 1825
BRADLEY, Charles	COYLE, Catharine A.	JUL 10 1841
BRADLEY, Eliza	BEECH, Levi	JUL 15 1838
BRADLEY, Elizabeth	CARRICO, Peter G.	JAN 15 1844
BRADLEY, Elizabeth (blk)	KELLY, Silas	JAN 09 1845
BRADLEY, George	BUCKLEY, Mary	DEC 23 1852
BRADLEY, Hannah	GAITHER, George R.	MAR 12 1822
BRADLEY, Hannah S.	SAUNDERS, William H.	DEC 24 1851
BRADLEY, Henry	BALTIMORE, Kitty (blk)	NOV 03 1836
BRADLEY, Henry	PROUT, Mary	OCT 12 1837
BRADLEY, Henry	EVANS, Elizabeth	AUG 25 1845
BRADLEY, Isaac	RIDGLEY, Elizabeth (blk)	DEC 11 1850
BRADLEY, Isaac	BROADHEAD, Frances	JAN 22 1855
BRADLEY, Jane	ALLEN, Richard	NOV 06 1854
BRADLEY, Jane Eliza	HARBIN, James H.	DEC 24 1842
BRADLEY, Jane M.	CROWN, George W.	JAN 08 1857
BRADLEY, Jeannette	LINTON, John A.	JUL 12 1855
BRADLEY, John	NEWMAN, Maria	FEB 23 1850
BRADLEY, Julia	AKINS, William	DEC 18 1830
BRADLEY, Julia	GALLAGHER, Hugh	JUN 11 1842
BRADLEY, Maria T.	GILLISS, Levin I. [Rev.]	APR 13 1819
BRADLEY, Mary	LIPPOT, John Henry	MAY 03 1834
BRADLEY, Mary (blk)	BURLEY, Thomas	SEP 07 1836
BRADLEY, Mary (blk)	WILSON, Robert	FEB 19 1840
BRADLEY, Mary Ann (blk)	DICK, Robert S.	AUG 01 1845
BRADLEY, Mary C.	BAILEY, Joseph F.	JAN 06 1857
BRADLEY, Mary E.	FALES, William R.	JAN 03 1856
BRADLEY, Mary V.	McCATHRAN, Wm. W.	JUN 29 1854
BRADLEY, Robert	REPROGLE, Catharine	FEB 08 1812
BRADLEY, Rosetta	ROUSE, Thomas	JUN 07 1855
BRADLEY, Sarah	JEWELL, Fielder	NOV 13 1828
BRADLEY, Sarah D.	SHERMAN, Charles A.	NOV 21 1855
BRADLEY, Sarah R.	KIDWELL, John H.	DEC 05 1848
BRADLEY, Susan	WOODWARD, William	MAY 22 1833
BRADLEY, William	HARRIS, Sarah Ann	APR 07 1840
BRADLEY, William A.	THRUSTON, Sidney Ann	AUG 03 1820
BRADLEY, Wm. W.	SIMMONS, Sarah	JAN 12 1854
BRADLY, Jos. S.	WARD, Martha W.	JUN 20 1855
BRADMAN, Sally	HOOPER, Thomas	APR 21 1814
BRADSHAW, Ann	WISE, John	SEP 16 1819
BRADSHAW, Britania	TYLER, Josiah	DEC 05 1836
BRADSHAW, Elizabeth	EVANS, Johnson	MAY 19 1837
BRADSHAW, Liton	EVANS, Tillitha	SEP 30 1837
BRADSHAW, Nathan	CROCKETT, Sippora	MAY 15 1849
BRADT, Albert H.	HUNTT, Susan C.	OCT 01 1843
BRADY, Abigail I.	THECKER, James A.	JAN 03 1848
BRADY, Andrew	BOWIE, Catharine	AUG 30 1819
BRADY, Ann	KIDWELL, Martin VanBuren	DEC 24 1857
BRADY, Basil	FARR, Louisa	MAY 09 1842
BRADY, Catharine	BEATTY, Francis D.	FEB 02 1839

District of Columbia Marriage Licenses, 1811-1858

BRADY, Edwin	FORSYTH, Mary	JUL 15 1833
BRADY, Felix	DOUGHERTY, Susanna	JUN 07 1817
BRADY, Helen Ann	ESTESS, Alexander	MAY 18 1839
BRADY, Henry	COOK, Mary Jane	MAR 25 1837
BRADY, Henry B.	HALL, Elizabeth	DEC 23 1830
BRADY, James S.	VENABLE, Teresa Ann	NOV 27 1846
BRADY, John	BRYAN, Sarah	JUN 03 1824
BRADY, Juliana	DEENE, Jacob	MAR 25 1826
BRADY, Margaret	KERR, Michael	FEB 01 1858
BRADY, Margaret A.	FRENCH, Edmund F.	JUL 01 1848
BRADY, Owen	BUCKLER, Mary	APR 26 1823
BRADY, Peter	RAINSFORD, Ann	NOV 20 1821
BRADY, Purmelia	FULLER, Enos	FEB 08 1831
BRADY, Sarah	ARTLEY, George	APR 21 1852
BRADY, Sarah E.	DAVIS, Samuel S.	MAR 09 1857
BRADY, Silas S.	KING, Margaret	APR 17 1855
BRADY, Stephen	HAYS, Ellen	FEB 08 1838
BRADY, Susan	WALLACE, Hanson	JAN 23 1827
BRADY, Terance	TEARNEY, Polly	JAN 24 1822
BRAFIELD, Marth A.	MITCHELL, George W.	OCT 12 1854
BRAGDON, Sarah Ann	SCHUREMAN, Peter D.	JUL 29 1823
BRAITHAUPT, Margaret	BLOSCH, George	JUL 23 1828
BRAITHWAIT, Caroline	McCLOSKEY, Bernard	JAN 06 1840
BRAMELL, James W.	LOVELESS, Elizabeth	JUN 22 1852
BRAMELL, Sarah F.	HARRISON, Elias	JUN 08 1854
BRAN, Maria	GROSS, John	MAY 21 1816
BRANCH, Margaret	DONELSON, Daniel S.	OCT 17 1830
BRANCH, Rebecca B.	WILLIAMS, Robert W. [Col.]	APR 19 1831
BRANCH, Wm. B.	MAGRUDER, Ann M.L.	JAN 12 1814
BRAND, Dorothy	HEINZERLING, John P.	MAR 16 1858
BRANDELL, Phillipe	CRONES, John	SEP 16 1843
BRANDENBERG, F. Wm.	SIMS, Martha S.	NOV 04 1853
BRANDENBURG, George	ANDERSON, Sarah A.	NOV 17 1855
BRANDON, Mary	BARRETT, Daniel	JUL 10 1855
BRANDSELL, Mary	YOUNGER, John	OCT 07 1839
BRANDSWELL, James	HENNING, Margaret Ann	SEP 18 1844
BRANDT, Gerard W.	PALMER, Jane V.	MAR 23 1853
BRANDT, John D.	COLE, Rosanna E.	JUN 12 1849
BRANDT, Logan	SELDEN, Bettie	MAY 23 1853
BRANE, Jane	WOOD, Joseph	MAY 13 1833
BRANGAN, Nancy (blk)	HANNON, Nathan	APR 04 1849
BRANGEL, George	ROSE, Martha Ann	OCT 09 1845
BRANHAM, Elizabeth	HARRINGTON, Patrick	APR 20 1821
BRANICAN, George	CANNADY, Caroline	NOV 16 1849
BRANIGAN, Henry	KINDEL, Mary	SEP 25 1816
BRANN, Frederick	WIESSNER, Christianna	NOV 21 1854
BRANNAGAN, Mary	DONALLY, Patrick	MAR 26 1852
BRANNAN, Arthur	HICKSON, Rusia	JAN 09 1840
BRANNAN, Eliza	KELLY, William	SEP 21 1850
BRANNAN, John	MYER, Sarah Salome	OCT 21 1816
BRANNAN, John	KELLY, Eliza	JUL 26 1836
BRANNAN, John	FAGAN, Catharine	MAY 26 1853
BRANNAN, Louisa F.	MATLACK, Armistead G.	AUG 03 1846
BRANNAN, Margaret	ADDWORTH, Bernard	DEC 26 1841
BRANNAN, Mariana	GINNETY, James	OCT 09 1854
BRANNAN, Mary	KEARRON, Robert	AUG 13 1846
BRANNAN, Mary E.	MIDDLETON, John H.	SEP 29 1855
BRANNAN, Sarah Ann	ERVIN, James	JUN 05 1819

District of Columbia Marriage Licenses, 1811-1858

BRANNAN, Sarah S. [Mrs.]	KING, John	MAR 04 1833
BRANNAN, Wilson	BELL, Chloe Ann	NOV 06 1819
BRANNAN, Wilson	HILL, Charity	MAR 25 1823
BRANNEN, Lucinda	BROWN, Bernard	SEP 26 1854
BRANNEN, William	SULLIVAN, Elizabeth	AUG 26 1819
BRANNER, Margt.	SHAW, Stephen	OCT 01 1855
BRANNER, Peter	WARD, Julia Ann	NOV 17 1825
BRANNON, Mary Ann	CROWLEY, Edward	JUL 09 1824
BRANNSTEIN, Jacob	MITCHELL, Mary J.	DEC 27 1856
BRANSON, Mary L.	TIPPETT, William H.	DEC 03 1857
BRANSTON, William Henry	GATTIN, Mary Eliza	MAY 27 1858
BRANSUM, Mary Frances	POSEY, Francis	JUN 26 1850
BRANTNER, Francis	RAINEY, Eliza	JUL 24 1855
BRANUM, John W.	JACKSON, Elizabeth (blk)	OCT 26 1843
BRANUM, Rachael (blk)	LANCASTER, Isiaih	NOV 28 1854
BRARDON, Patrick	CRAVEN, Johanna	MAY 18 1857
BRASCHEARS, Christopher H.	GILLER, Jane	FEB 02 1843
BRASE, Sophia Elnore	KUBLOMANN, Charles F.A.	OCT 14 1841
BRASHEARS, Amelia	FIELDS, Edward	APR 15 1813
BRASHEARS, Eleanor	PATTERSON, James	NOV 07 1822
BRASHEARS, John W.	JOLLY, Elizabeth	AUG 19 1819
BRASHEARS, Mary	WARRING, Erasmus G.	DEC 28 1833
BRASHEARS, Mary Ann	STEVENSON, Jacob Wesley	MAR 06 1849
BRASHEARS, Mary Elizth.	JIRDINSTON, James A.N.	SEP 26 1853
BRASHEARS, Robert	BROWN, Eliza	JUN 12 1821
BRASHEARS, Sarah F.	HOLT, William O.	JUN 27 1853
BRASHEARS, Thomas	HULL, Jane	APR 20 1831
BRASHEARS, Thomas	HOOD, Rebecca	SEP 01 1849
BRASHEARS, William B.	MAZINE, Adaline	JUN 19 1845
BRATCHER, Keziah	MARSHALL, John	MAR 01 1848
BRATCHER, Litleton	EVANS, Lidie	JUN 01 1839
BRATCHER, Severn	TODD, Mary	MAR 02 1830
BRATCHER, Thomas	TYLER, Eliza Ann	MAY 31 1839
BRAUER, M.	KRAFFT, J.	JUN 24 1826
BRAUMAN, Hanche	STRASBURGER, Isaac	MAY 03 1855
BRAUNER, Elizabeth	KNOWLES, Robert	JUL 19 1834
BRAUNER, Elizabeth	LYON, William H.	OCT 08 1849
BRAWNER, Basil	SEMMES, Eleanor H.	JUN 17 1830
BRAWNER, Catharine S.	BRAWNER, John W.	DEC 02 1843
BRAWNER, Charlotte	JACKSON, William	MAY 01 1855
BRAWNER, Eleanor	PENNINGTON, Joseph W.	MAR 13 1837
BRAWNER, Elizabeth	GROVES, Henley	NOV 25 1816
BRAWNER, Elizabeth	KEYS, Andrew J.	MAR 19 1850
BRAWNER, Ellen	ALEXANDER, Oscar	OCT 04 1834
BRAWNER, Hezekiah	DIMENT, Ellen	APR 27 1847
BRAWNER, James L.	ALEXANDER, Amanda	SEP 27 1836
BRAWNER, John W.	BRAWNER, Catharine S.	DEC 02 1843
BRAWNER, Laura	BURDINE, Charles	AUG 30 1852
BRAWNER, Robert	McPHERSON, Harriet	MAY 20 1834
BRAWNER, Rosella A.	MOLUM, Michael P.	DEC 31 1850
BRAWNER, Susan V.	UNDERWOOD, William	MAR 26 1846
BRAWNER, Thornton	PARSONS, Lucretia	JUN 13 1826
BRAWNER, William H.	ORMS, Emily B.	SEP 13 1856
BRAWZELL, Mary Ann	TAIT, Robert C.	JUN 09 1849
BRAXTON, John T.	TUCKER, Mary J.	OCT 25 1854
BRAY, James L.	NANCE, Mary E.	SEP 11 1850
BRAYFIELD, Cath. Sophia	HARRISON, Williamson	MAR 18 1852
BRAYS, Rebecca T.	VEIRS, William A.	MAY 02 1853

District of Columbia Marriage Licenses, 1811-1858

BREARLEY, Mary Bernard	SMALLWOOD, William A.	MAR 29 1825
BREAST, George Alonzo	HARRINGTON, Selina	JUN 16 1834
BREAST, Henrietta	PARKS, James	OCT 09 1813
BREAST, James A.	RILEY, Jane	DEC 08 1853
BREAST, Rosina	HART, Hezekiah	JUN 05 1827
BREAST, Walter W.	VAINE, Eleanora	DEC 04 1854
BRECHT, Katherina	BITNER, Henry	MAR 02 1857
BRECK, John	RUPLY, Anna Barbara	MAR 24 1856
BREEDING, Mason P.	CURFMAN, Harriet M.	DEC 10 1816
BREENCHN, Marie	DEMONOT, Peter	MAY 30 1825
BREESE, Saml. L.	LOVETT, Emma	JUN 20 1855
BREGAN, James	SHEAHAN, Ann	FEB 25 1856
BREIGENSEE, Maria T.	ROTH, Julius	FEB 21 1852
BRENAN, Patrick	LYONS, Catharine	DEC 03 1851
BRENARD, Maria	MOORE, John L.	NOV 18 1832
BRENGLE, Henry	CLARKE, Emeline	JUN 29 1847
BRENNAN, Catherine E.	BRENNER, John A.	MAY 30 1850
BRENNAN, Ellen	LAMB, Patrick	FEB 05 1851
BRENNAN, John	MAHER, Mary	FEB 13 1852
BRENNER, Catherine	RICHARDS, John H.D.	APR 11 1850
BRENNER, John A.	BRENNAN, Catherine E.	MAY 30 1850
BRENNIN, John	DANTE, Mary	JAN 15 1838
BRENNIN, Patrick	BURKE, Catharine	MAY 12 1855
BRENON, Ellen	GUILD, James	DEC 12 1853
BRENT, Catharine	ELLIOT, George	JUL 19 1834
BRENT, Clarissa	THOMAS, Edwd. M. (blk)	OCT 23 1846
BRENT, Henry J.	CARROLL, Elizabeth	JAN 07 1834
BRENT, Henry W.	CADEN, Lavinia T.	JUN 21 1858
BRENT, James R.	BROOK, Susannah	FEB 13 1827
BRENT, James R.	WARING, Eleanor	MAY 17 1831
BRENT, James R.	LIDENBERGER, Anne E.	MAR 01 1851
BRENT, Jane	SWEENY, George	DEC 28 1835
BRENT, John Carroll	YOUNG, Sarah	NOV 11 1851
BRENT, Mary Virginia	CHILTON, Robert S.	MAY 12 1852
BRENT, Rachel	BROOKS, Edward (col)	MAR 12 1851
BRENT, Robert Y.	COTTRINGER, Harriet	JAN 06 1824
BRENTON, Sarah	JACOB, Richard F.	JAN 15 1848
BRERETON, John	STEWART, Eliza Ann	APR 28 1842
BRERETON, John A.	LOVERING, Amelia	DEC 13 1815
BRERETON, Martha A.E.	SHARRETTS, John F.	NOV 30 1841
BRERETON, Mary Ann	LAMBERT, Francis	OCT 15 1835
BRERETON, Samuel	GOODMAN, Sarah Ann	MAY 12 1858
BRERETON, Sarah	DOVE, William	NOV 10 1836
BRERETON, Wm. Henry	TAYLOR, Georgiana	SEP 06 1848
BRESCHARD, Cleophila	BURR, Henry A.	AUG 01 1842
BRESLYN, George W.	CORNWELL, Sarah J.	JUN 18 1856
BRESNER, Hugh	ROCHE, Margaret	NOV 25 1857
BRESSNAHAN, Margaret	GLARSON, James	JAN 12 1852
BRESSNAHAN, Margaret	GLARSON, James	JUN 12 1852
BREST, Henrietta	WILLIAMS, Pius	NOV 03 1851
BREST, Lucretia	GEE, Thomas	SEP 16 1818
BREUN, Michael	SCHNEIDER, Rosina	JAN 21 1841
BREVITT, Edwin W.	WARD, Caroline	JUL 13 1842
BREW, Elizabeth	SCHWITZER, Peter	NOV 11 1850
BREWER, Albert	WELLS, Harriet E.	SEP 17 1857
BREWER, Edward [Dr.]	BROOKE, Susannah	MAR 10 1829
BREWER, Eliza Ann	JETT, William Henry	JUN 09 1858
BREWER, Elizabeth	ALLEN, Saml.	OCT 30 1828

District of Columbia Marriage Licenses, 1811-1858

BREWER, Elizabeth D.	BIGGS, Henry D.	JAN 17 1843
BREWER, George	MARBURY, Matilda	JUL 28 1846
BREWER, George G.	HARWOOD, Susan Ann	NOV 01 1825
BREWER, H. Elizabeth	GETTY, Gardner T.	OCT 27 1852
BREWER, Henry	JONES, Susan	OCT 06 1842
BREWER, John M.	VanLEAR, Mary A.	JAN 17 1849
BREWER, Joseph W.	BEALL, Martha Ann (blk)	NOV 02 1853
BREWER, Lucinda J.	JOLLY, Bushrod	MAY 15 1851
BREWER, Mary Ann	READ, Joshua	JUL 22 1858
BREWER, Mason	KIRKPATRICK, Hannah	JAN 08 1856
BREWER, Rebecca	KIRBY, John	MAR 17 1836
BREWER, Susan	MORELAND, Paul H.	MAR 01 1837
BREWER, Thomas	HOBBS, Ann	SEP 06 1838
BREWER, Zachariah J.	SHERWOOD, Mary Ellen	JAN 10 1849
BREZO, Ann	MITCHELL, Richard	FEB 14 1822
BRIAN, Catharine	BLASSINGER, Peter	FEB 18 1840
BRIAN, Mary A.	McINTOSH, Joseph	JUL 14 1857
BRICELAND, Isaac N.	WALKER, Emily M.	OCT 22 1856
BRICK, Michael	CRAY, Margaret	APR 23 1851
BRICKLEY, John T.	MARTIN, Rebecca	OCT 27 1852
BRICKLEY, Mary	SALOON, Daniel	APR 19 1853
BRIDEWELL, Moses Thomas	NELSON, Martha	JUL 22 1843
BRIDEWELL, William	CROSS, Mary Ann	AUG 03 1841
BRIDGE, Margaret	SMITH, John	SEP 29 1825
BRIDGE, Sarah Ann	HANSEY, John	JAN 30 1826
BRIDGEMAN, Mary	WOHLFERTH, George	OCT 14 1857
BRIDGES, Dennis	MURRAY, Sarah	OCT 31 1816
BRIDGES, James	McKIM, Mary	APR 22 1817
BRIDGET, James Arthur	SANNER, Ann Elizabeth	APR 27 1843
BRIDGET, John F.	JAMISON, Mary E.	APR 15 1844
BRIDGET, Mary Ann	WHARTON, Charles	DEC 24 1839
BRIDGETT, Christina	FIERBRON, Frederick	JUL 01 1856
BRIDGMAN, Samuel	THOMPSON, Mary	AUG 29 1848
BRIDICOMB, Herman	DIPPLE, Elizabeth	MAR 02 1855
BRIDON, Pauline	VIEL, Victor Just	NOV 14 1825
BRIDON, Virginia	GREIRHN, Frederick	NOV 19 1819
BRIDWELL, Catharine P.	EADER, Jonathan	MAY 04 1852
BRIDWELL, Virginia	FRANKLIN, Henry T.	SEP 18 1851
BRIDY, George	MINDENDORF, Sophia	FEB 27 1857
BRIEM, Barbara	COPP, George	NOV 29 1852
BRIEN, Bernard	O'BRIEN, Eliza	MAR 13 1821
BRIEN, Burnard	MASSI, Mary	AUG 29 1846
BRIEN, Francis	BUTLER, Sarah	JUL 09 1818
BRIEN, Hanora	DACEY, Patrick	AUG 03 1852
BRIEN, Maria	SHEA, Michael	MAR 30 1858
BRIEN, Mary	HOLLOHAN, Jno.	MAR 22 1856
BRIENER, Catharine	REINHARD, Carl	SEP 21 1853
BRIGEMAN, Zachariah	HENDERSON, Elizabeth	NOV 18 1826
BRIGGES, Sarah Ann	HARFORD, William	SEP 16 1836
BRIGGS, Andrew	HOFFMAN, Matilda	JAN 09 1819
BRIGGS, James Marion	SMITH, Mary Ellen	MAY 25 1853
BRIGGS, Jane Rebecca	ABBOTT, James W.	JAN 15 1852
BRIGGS, Robert	GILLUM, Mary Ann	NOV 04 1829
BRIGGS, Virginia P.	TRAYLOR, Richard	NOV 08 1836
BRIGHT, Amelia	YOUNG, Thomas	FEB 15 1812
BRIGHT, Ann	BLACKBURN, John	AUG 21 1827
BRIGHT, Anna B.	WENZELL, Adam	MAR 26 1856
BRIGHT, Apolonia	HUTCHINGSON, Thomas	JAN 19 1853

District of Columbia Marriage Licenses, 1811-1858

BRIGHT, Betsey	KENDALL, George W.	SEP 03 1853
BRIGHT, Catharine	RING, William	JUL 17 1837
BRIGHT, Elizabeth Ann	BERON, William	JAN 06 1846
BRIGHT, Elizabeth Ann	SHORT, William E.	SEP 27 1848
BRIGHT, Jacob	SANSBURY, Rebecca	MAY 07 1822
BRIGHT, James	BENTIN, Elizabeth	JAN 09 1823
BRIGHT, John	BAYLEY, Jane	OCT 18 1823
BRIGHT, John	O'NEAL, Araminta	MAR 14 1854
BRIGHT, John W.	ALLEN, Mira Ann	JAN 13 1853
BRIGHT, Margaret	WENTHAL, George	OCT 05 1854
BRIGHT, Maria	TURNER, Chs.	FEB 27 1821
BRIGHT, Mary Ann	HANDY, Samuel	JUN 01 1849
BRIGHT, Mary E.	LUSBY, Lemuel L.	OCT 23 1849
BRIGHT, Mary Jane	MARTIN, Andrew	MAY 01 1848
BRIGHT, Michael E.	GRAINGER, Malinda A.	SEP 21 1847
BRIGHT, Rachel	LEWIS, Daniel W.	APR 19 1848
BRIGHT, Washington	CROSS, Eliza	SEP 18 1827
BRIGHTMAN, Mary	WESTCOTT, John	MAY 29 1813
BRIGHTWELL, Ann E.	NAYLOR, Francis Y.	DEC 04 1837
BRIGHTWELL, Eliza	BESTOR, Owen H.	SEP 20 1836
BRIGHTWELL, Joshua	JONES, Malvina	NOV 22 1855
BRIGHTWELL, Mary	GREENLEAF, Wm. C.	JAN 02 1847
BRIGHTWELL, Thomas	VENABLE, Sarah E.	SEP 13 1841
BRIGHTWELL, Thomas R.	MOORE, Mary L.	NOV 15 1852
BRILL, Louisa	PAFF, Frederick	OCT 01 1857
BRIN, Francis A.	BARR, John H.	NOV 07 1849
BRINE, Sophia	ARNOLD, Aquila	JUN 01 1816
BRINKLEY, Saml.	JOHNSON, Jane C.	OCT 22 1857
BRINKMANN, Caroline	PLUGGE, Frederick	JUN 02 1857
BRINN, William	LEWIS, Jane	JUN 07 1828
BRINNELL, Charles H.	MURPHY, Mary A.	MAR 06 1850
BRINTNALL, Charlotte S.	BURROUGHS, Hon. Silas M.	MAY 11 1858
BRINTNALL, Malvina	MOORE, Festus H.	JAN 19 1853
BRISCOE, Caroline	GRIFFIN, Peter	JUN 05 1823
BRISCOE, Charlotte	SULLIVAN, J. [Edward]	JUL 04 1836
BRISCOE, G.B.	SASSCER, Elizth. A.	FEB 18 1857
BRISCOE, George	COOPER, Ceily	SEP 30 1820
BRISCOE, George	HERBERT, Susan	NOV 08 1855
BRISCOE, Henry	WOOD, Anne (blk)	NOV 28 1833
BRISCOE, Henry	WALLACE, Linda (blk)	OCT 02 1837
BRISCOE, Henry	HANSON, Betsy (blk)	JUN 27 1850
BRISCOE, Henry	COGY, Charlotte (blk)	OCT 07 1852
BRISCOE, Henry	WALLACE, Eliza (blk)	APR 21 1858
BRISCOE, Isabella (blk)	DOVE, Henry	JUN 28 1855
BRISCOE, Jane Love	GRIFFIN, Peter	APR 04 1816
BRISCOE, Jarrard	DEMENT, Mary E.	APR 16 1833
BRISCOE, John A.	BAILEY, Martha Jane	MAY 12 1858
BRISCOE, Louisa (blk)	BOLES, James T.	AUG 10 1854
BRISCOE, Lucinda M.	FLETCHER, Geo. [Capt.]	SEP 17 1822
BRISCOE, Mary	BENDER, George [Capt.]	DEC 21 1816
BRISCOE, Michael	CROSS, Dianna	APR 28 1836
BRISCOE, Philip T.	DELOIZIER, Anne	FEB 13 1816
BRISCOE, Richard G.	CLARKE, Ann Maria	NOV 21 1831
BRISCOE, Ruth A.	ADREAN, George W.	OCT 23 1844
BRISCOE, William	CROWLEY, Eliza (blk)	MAY 30 1844
BRISON, James	HOBBS, Kitty	AUG 09 1821
BRISSY, Elizabeth	DAVIS, William	JUL 31 1856
BRITINGHAM, Mary Ann	DUNCAN, Hiram	MAR 30 1825

District of Columbia Marriage Licenses, 1811-1858

BRITTENHAM, Elizabeth	BAYLY, William E.	OCT 30 1833
BRITTNER, Daniel	YOASTE, Ann Elizth.	DEC 09 1852
BRITTON, Geo.	BRUER, Rebecca	FEB 04 1818
BRITTON, James H.	WHITE, Martha Ann	NOV 17 1855
BROADBECK, Henry	LUCAS, Ann	SEP 12 1832
BROADBECK, Henry	TATTERSON, Sarah	OCT 11 1838
BROADHEAD, Frances	BRADLEY, Isaac	JAN 22 1855
BROADLUP, Salina	FRASER, James	DEC 09 1847
BROADWELL, Josiah	BOWSHER, Susan	APR 14 1813
BROCCHUS, Thomas W.	STANTON, Mary	JUL 09 1831
BROCK, Perry B.	CHEW, Charlotte (blk)	NOV 04 1852
BROCK, William G.	JAMES, Mary F.	NOV 11 1851
BROCKENBROUGH, Austin	BROWN, Mary H.	DEC 18 1826
BROCKET, Annabella	FRANCE, Thomas E.	APR 09 1844
BROCKET, Eliza (blk)	SHADD, Absalom	MAR 28 1843
BROCKET, Elizabeth	CUNNINGHAM, John Scott	OCT 27 1845
BROCKETT, Amelia (blk)	COSTIN, William G.	MAY 12 1847
BROCKETT, Ann	THOMP<u>SO</u>N, Lewis	DEC 05 1839
BROCKETT, Nancy (negro)	SIMMS, Richard	JUL 07 1834
BROCKWAY, Charles	REMINGTON, Mary Ann	OCT 06 1832
BRODBACK, Barbara Ann	APPICH, David	JUL 23 1828
BRODDUS, Andrew	BRODDUS, Jane C.	MAR 08 1816
BRODDUS, Jane C.	BRODDUS, Andrew	MAR 08 1816
BRODEN, Patrick	HARTIGAN, Bridget	APR 09 1858
BRODER, Michl.	CONELL, Ellen	DEC 26 1855
BRODERICK, Ann	CARROLL, Thomas	MAY 31 1852
BRODERICK, Hanora	LARKIN, Daniel	SEP 09 1854
BRODERICK, Thomas	COLBERT, Hanora	NOV 26 1817
BRODERS, Jane Eliza	REILY, John M.	OCT 22 1849
BRODHEAD, John George	STEPPER, Barbara Gaitrut	SEP 01 1837
BRODHEAD, Thomas W.	BARRY, Eliza R.	JAN 04 1854
BRODTBECK, Ursala	MOLLER, Frederick	APR 13 1826
BROGDEN, Jeffrey	ORM, Susan (blk)	SEP 24 1827
BROKER, Margaret	YOUNG, John	JUN 16 1830
BROME, Jane Joannah	HOLTZMAN, John	MAY 30 1827
BROMELL, John	WARFIELD, Sarah	FEB 09 1822
BRONAUGH, E. Louisa	CARTER, George F.	SEP 05 1850
BRONAUGH, Elizabeth H.	SHANKLAND, Robert H.	FEB 07 1856
BRONAUGH, Frances P.T.	BRONAUGH, John W.	SEP 01 1841
BRONAUGH, Jeremiah W.	WILCOX, Elizabeth C.	DEC 09 1839
BRONAUGH, John	HUGHES, Fanny M.	DEC 27 1824
BRONAUGH, John W.	BRONAUGH, Frances P.T.	SEP 01 1841
BRONAUGH, Mary Ann	HOOK, Col. James H.	DEC 30 1840
BRONAUGH, Mary Elizabeth	FIELDING, John	DEC 22 1841
BRONAUGH, Mary Jane	MAGILL, William B.	SEP 04 1850
BRONAUGH, Nancy M.	TAYLOR, Alfred	JUL 18 1842
BRONAUGH, Virginia M.	DUCKWELL, Joseph S.	AUG 30 1851
BRONAUGH, William John	MITCHELL, Mary Chesley	JAN 07 1817
BRONEL, Lorieno	LIPPHARD, Adolph	JAN 21 1839
BRONN, Bernard	BRANNEN, Lucinda	SEP 26 1854
BRONNER, Eleanor	CAPRON, Henry A.	JUL 01 1835
BRONOUGH, Frances [Mrs.]	KING, John A.	APR 28 1830
BRONOUGH, Jane (blk)	POWEL, Granvill	JAN 04 1854
BRONSON, Simeon D.	THOMAS, Julia	FEB 11 1843
BRONSON, Simeon D.	FARRELL, Ann	JAN 20 1853
BRONSON, Simon D.	ALVERS, Marion Virginia	JAN 05 1847
BROOK, Elizabeth W.	MATTHEWS, Joseph	JAN 30 1840
BROOK, Robert W.	FRENCH, Sarah Jane	APR 09 1855

District of Columbia Marriage Licenses, 1811-1858

BROOK, Susannah	BRENT, James R.	FEB 13 1827
BROOKBANK, Ann Maria	JOHNSON, Wm. J.A.	SEP 07 1848
BROOKBANK, Thomas	BEAVERS, Lydia	JUL 06 1858
BROOKBANK, Thos.	DEEVER, Letty	AUG 23 1858
BROOKE, Ann	LYONS, John	APR 23 1839
BROOKE, Betsey (blk)	CHISLEY, Richard	JAN 10 1815
BROOKE, Clement H.	CARROLL, Anne	MAY 08 1817
BROOKE, Edmund	QUEEN, Eugenea	APR 09 1844
BROOKE, Edmund H.	GETTY, Emily	JUL 06 1840
BROOKE, Henrietta T.	JORDAN, John R.	JUL 03 1855
BROOKE, James C.	PERKINS, Mary Catherine	JAN 09 1855
BROOKE, Lawrence	CLIFFORD, Ann Lucretia	JUL 02 1831
BROOKE, Margaret Ellen	STOOPS, Walter	APR 25 1842
BROOKE, Maria Ann	BERRY, Charles M.	DEC 16 1824
BROOKE, Mary Ann	WATERS, Franklin	JUN 05 1855
BROOKE, Mary Virginia	TENNISON, William A.	FEB 09 1847
BROOKE, Nicholas	WARING, Mary	JAN 12 1836
BROOKE, Philip L.	LEWIS, Elizabeth	JAN 29 1842
BROOKE, Robert W.	BERRY, Elizabeth E.	JUL 30 1849
BROOKE, Sarah Virginia	DARRELL, William S.	AUG 31 1835
BROOKE, Susan E.	NAYLOR, Henry	JAN 18 1853
BROOKE, Susannah	BREWER, Edward [Dr.]	MAR 10 1829
BROOKE, Thomas A.	DAVIS, Mary Kervand	APR 16 1855
BROOKE, Walter B.	SPRIGG, Mary	SEP 07 1824
BROOKES, Biddy	LARNER, Mathew	JUN 30 1815
BROOKES, Bradley	KAHSE, Chloe Ann	AUG 10 1827
BROOKES, Chloe	GRAY, Hezekiah	APR 01 1837
BROOKES, Eliza	MOORE, David	JAN 09 1830
BROOKES, Elizabeth (blk)	SHORTER, Charles	NOV 24 1835
BROOKES, Elizth.	PALMER, Otha	JUN 27 1822
BROOKES, Henry	BOWLER, Fanny	DEC 31 1829
BROOKES, Mary (blk)	BRUCE, William	JUN 11 1829
BROOKES, Nathaniel	SHORTER, Priscilla	AUG 20 1840
BROOKES, Rebecca	ALBERS, Henry	FEB 01 1820
BROOKES, Richard	SMALLWOOD, Harriet E.	APR 13 1857
BROOKES, Sophia	FROST, John T.	JUN 02 1829
BROOKES, Theodore	WOODLEY, Jane (blk)	JAN 03 1839
BROOKMEYER, Johanna	LEDRER, John	OCT 07 1856
BROOKS, Adaline (blk)	WILLIAMS, Henry	OCT 12 1830
BROOKS, Adeline	DUTTON, Thomas	DEC 02 1845
BROOKS, Albert	FLETCHER, Henrietta (blk)	DEC 05 1853
BROOKS, Alfred	PAYNE, Hester (blk)	DEC 09 1847
BROOKS, Ann Eliza (blk)	BENNETT, Daniel	AUG 16 1854
BROOKS, Ann Maria (blk)	GREEN, Mantray	NOV 30 1837
BROOKS, Anna	BIGGS, Edward	NOV 05 1850
BROOKS, Bazil	FORREST, Mary Jane (blk)	OCT 17 1843
BROOKS, Catharine	KIERMAN, Patrick	AUG 04 1818
BROOKS, Catharine Ann	NASH, Robert James	MAY 25 1830
BROOKS, Catherine (blk)	BROOKS, Samuel	JUN 11 1846
BROOKS, Cecelia (blk)	GIPSON, James V.	SEP 24 1852
BROOKS, Charles	SMITH, Jane (blk)	JUL 05 1836
BROOKS, Christiana	ROBINSON, Thomas H.	JAN 21 1852
BROOKS, Clement	HICKS, Ann (blk)	MAR 04 1844
BROOKS, Daniel M.	GASSAWAY, Emily M. (blk)	NOV 25 1851
BROOKS, David	DYER, Eliza (blk)	MAY 26 1842
BROOKS, Edward	BRENT, Rachel (col)	MAR 12 1851
BROOKS, Elizabeth	SHERWOOD, John	NOV 12 1845
BROOKS, Elizabeth (blk)	LEE, Thomas	APR 19 1815

District of Columbia Marriage Licenses, 1811-1858

BROOKS, Elizabeth (blk)	BECKITT, Lemuel	FEB 02 1843
BROOKS, Elizthn Ann	LAUB, William B.	SEP 01 1834
BROOKS, Emeline (blk)	BATEMAN, Mahlon	NOV 13 1856
BROOKS, Erastus	CRANCH, Margaret D.	JAN 12 1844
BROOKS, Fanny (blk)	JONES, Joseph	JUN 30 1852
BROOKS, George Washington	BURGESS, Catherine (blk)	MAY 04 1854
BROOKS, Gracy	FORD, Charles	AUG 29 1831
BROOKS, Henry	FORD, Lucinda (blk)	APR 28 1852
BROOKS, Howard	CLEMENTS, Dorcas A.	JUL 13 1842
BROOKS, Ignatius	MADDOX, Rebecca	MAY 27 1819
BROOKS, James	BURRIS, Rebecca	SEP 05 1850
BROOKS, Jehiel	QUEEN, Ann Margaret	MAY 19 1830
BROOKS, John C.	PARRIS, Caroline W.	MAY 10 1847
BROOKS, John H.	PHELPS, Margt. Ann	SEP 24 1855
BROOKS, John H.	HALL, Susan	OCT 21 1856
BROOKS, John T.	TSCHISFFELY, Elizabeth A.	AUG 25 1852
BROOKS, Joseph	EASTON, Annette (blk)	NOV 08 1854
BROOKS, Joseph C.	HAWKE, Laura F.	SEP 02 1856
BROOKS, Julia	BOON, Abraham	FEB 15 1838
BROOKS, Lawson	HORTON, Sarah Ann Frances	NOV 14 1844
BROOKS, Louisa (blk)	HICKS, William	JUN 07 1855
BROOKS, Lucinda	HAMMON, August	JAN 13 1840
BROOKS, Malinda V.	CRAWFORD, Saml. T.	NOV 24 1856
BROOKS, Malvina	DIFFNER, George	MAR 19 1840
BROOKS, Margaret Ann (blk)	DAVIS, John	MAY 26 1835
BROOKS, Mary Ann	WILLIS, Henry	MAR 30 1847
BROOKS, Mary Ellen	MAHORNEY, Robert	JUL 12 1843
BROOKS, Mary M. (blk)	BATSON, Daniel	MAY 08 1856
BROOKS, Matilda (blk)	FREEMAN, John W.	OCT 18 1853
BROOKS, Peter	BARRY, Maria	FEB 16 1836
BROOKS, Priscilla	NICHOLSON, John	DEC 20 1837
BROOKS, Rebecca Ann	JOHNSON, Albert	JUN 09 1856
BROOKS, Richard	JONES, Mary	MAR 18 1830
BROOKS, Samuel	BROOKS, Catherine (blk)	JUN 11 1846
BROOKS, Samuel D.	TRACY, Jane	JUN 25 1850
BROOKS, Samuel M.	KING, Laura V.	SEP 28 1857
BROOKS, Susan (blk)	WATTS, William	MAY 05 1831
BROOKS, Susannah (blk)	COLLINS, William H.	DEC 01 1853
BROOKS, Virginia	GALLAHER, Marcellus	SEP 06 1853
BROOM, Helen T.	HACKER, W.T.	JAN 14 1856
BROOM, James	GUTTSLICK, Elizabeth H.	OCT 09 1843
BROOM, Mary Ann	MICKUM, Samuel	OCT 28 1819
BROOM, Mary E.	EDWARDS, Lewis	OCT 14 1840
BROOM, Robert H.	MEEHAN, Maria	JAN 23 1851
BROOM, Susana	WALKER, John	JUN 15 1837
BROOME, John	PROCTOR, Mary J. (blk)	APR 27 1857
BROSNAHAM, Julia	FITZGERALD, Thomas	JAN 27 1854
BROSNAHAN, Jeremiah	HANDRAHAN, Johnie	FEB 02 1856
BROSNAHAN, Jeremiah	SHAY, Bridget	FEB 16 1858
BROSNAN, John	WILLIAMS, Joanna	JUL 27 1852
BROSNEHAN, John	TUSH, Catherine	JUN 16 1857
BROTSCAMP, Catherine Margt.	LINDMAN, Philip	AUG 20 1838
BROTT, Mary A.	REICHERT, Francis L.	AUG 04 1857
BROTZEN, John	BEECK, Susanna	JUN 07 1856
BROWER, Hannah Christiana	KRAFFT, George	OCT 07 1828
BROWERS, John	DELANEY, Bridget	AUG 18 1849
BROWERS, John	WRIGHT, Jane Eliza	FEB 11 1854
BROWERS, Maria	WILEY, John	MAY 18 1833

District of Columbia Marriage Licenses, 1811-1858

BROWERS, Mary Ann	DUBANT, Peter M.	OCT 12 1854
BROWN, A.G.	YOUNG, Roberta E.	JAN 09 1841
BROWN, Abigail B.	DODGE, Henry W.	OCT 10 1839
BROWN, Abraham	MORRISON, Sarah Ann	APR 29 1837
BROWN, Abraham	HODGE, Betsey	APR 13 1844
BROWN, Abram	BECKLEY, Amanda	AUG 16 1827
BROWN, Absolam	THOMPSON, Eliza Ann	DEC 30 1845
BROWN, Adam Crawford	TALBERT, Rachael	MAR 07 1820
BROWN, Addison	WHITTLE, Rachel	SEP 06 1826
BROWN, Addison	MATLEY, Elizabeth	JUL 23 1842
BROWN, Addison	TRUNNELL, Ann C.	DEC 11 1850
BROWN, Albertius E.	QEWELLE, P. Felicia	MAY 20 1852
BROWN, Alex. H.	MURRAY, Mary J.	FEB 05 1851
BROWN, Alexander	SAYERS, Elizabeth	MAY 23 1855
BROWN, Alfred	SILENCE, Mary L.	DEC 30 1857
BROWN, Amelia	CODRICK, John	OCT 14 1854
BROWN, Amelia F. (blk)	BROWN, Lewis A.	MAY 17 1858
BROWN, Andrew	GRIFFITH, Maria	AUG 17 1850
BROWN, Anjelica	FRENCH, Benjamin F.	JUN 07 1821
BROWN, Ann	WESTON, John	APR 06 1825
BROWN, Ann	ARP, James	JAN 24 1825
BROWN, Ann	LONG, Madison	DEC 24 1829
BROWN, Ann	WALL, Robert	APR 27 1830
BROWN, Ann	CLEMENTS, William	JAN 04 1833
BROWN, Ann	CISSELL, Salene E.	FEB 05 1843
BROWN, Ann (blk)	HACKLEY, Philip	APR 19 1823
BROWN, Ann (blk)	JONES, William H.	MAY 23 1853
BROWN, Ann A.	CHANEY, Peter	NOV 02 1841
BROWN, Ann E.	SMITH, James H.	JAN 08 1852
BROWN, Anne (blk)	LOWNDES, Thomas	SEP 10 1850
BROWN, Anne E.	RAULINGS, Wm. A.	MAY 24 1847
BROWN, Arch	WATERS, Emily	JUL 07 1857
BROWN, Archibald	KIRBY, Ann	APR 17 1824
BROWN, Archibald	CLARK, Sarah	NOV 23 1830
BROWN, Archibald	LUXON, Mary Ann	MAR 20 1837
BROWN, Augustus	KELLY, Elizabeth	AUG 04 1855
BROWN, Bedford, Jr., Dr.	SIMPSON, Mary E.	JUN 30 1852
BROWN, Benedict P.	BASSETT, Catharine	DEC 22 1842
BROWN, Benjamin	BUTLER, Elizabeth	NOV 09 1818
BROWN, Benjamin Franklin	WAUGH, Susan J.	OCT 19 1839
BROWN, Benjamin G.	O'BRYON, Margaret Ann	FEB 14 1848
BROWN, Bridget	MYRTHY, Macheol	JAN 13 1853
BROWN, Bridget	GRIFFIN, Thomas	OCT 31 1857
BROWN, Calvin	FISHER, Roselie	MAR 13 1848
BROWN, Caroline	KRAFFT, Lawrinc	JUN 09 1834
BROWN, Caroline	BROWN, John	JUN 04 1842
BROWN, Caroline	GAINES, Edward	JUN 14 1843
BROWN, Caroline (blk)	MASON, Jas. F.	NOV 01 1855
BROWN, Catharine	FLOTHERON, Lewis	APR 12 1836
BROWN, Catharine	BOSWELL, James	MAY 12 1846
BROWN, Catharine J.	FLETCHER, William H.	MAY 07 1852
BROWN, Catharine J.	NEWELL, John	MAY 20 1853
BROWN, Catharine N.	FOSSETT, James	MAY 03 1837
BROWN, Catharine S.	MAYNADIER, William M.	MAR 02 1830
BROWN, Catharine W.	KURTZ, John	DEC 10 1818
BROWN, Catherine	WATERS, Samuel	JUN 03 1845
BROWN, Catherine R.	CONDRY, Dennis	FEB 07 1848
BROWN, Charles	GREEN, Matilda	APR 02 1823

District of Columbia Marriage Licenses, 1811-1858

BROWN, Charles	THOMAS, Elizth. (blk)	AUG 17 1829
BROWN, Charles	FLINN, Elizabeth	SEP 01 1842
BROWN, Charles	POOL, Ann Jane	JUN 22 1847
BROWN, Charles	STEWART, Catherine	MAY 11 1848
BROWN, Charles	HANSON, Ann Amelia (blk)	JUN 05 1850
BROWN, Charles	ADAMS, Mima (blk)	MAR 24 1853
BROWN, Charles B.	THOMPSON, Mary Ann E.	JUN 01 1826
BROWN, Charles E.	WINFIELD, Susan	APR 04 1848
BROWN, Charlotte L.	MAYFIELD, Benja. R.	SEP 01 1851
BROWN, Christiana	ISHERWOOD, Robert	MAR 21 1825
BROWN, Christopher	EVANS, Rebecca	MAY 09 1825
BROWN, Clarissa	SIMPSON, Nathan	AUG 22 1820
BROWN, Clary (blk)	SMITH, John A.	AUG 10 1826
BROWN, Commodore Perry	EARPE, Mary Ellen	APR 28 1849
BROWN, Cora L. (blk)	PETERS, Charles H.	DEC 26 1855
BROWN, Cumberland G.	TOPHAN, Phobe E.	JAN 16 1856
BROWN, Daniel	CLOON, Honora	APR 19 1851
BROWN, Daniel	MURPHY, Catharine	SEP 01 1852
BROWN, Daniel	WHITE, Ellen	JUN 16 1855
BROWN, Daniel	MASON, Sarah (blk)	FEB 28 1856
BROWN, David	FARREE, Lydia	MAR 06 1828
BROWN, David	JONES, Virginia	OCT 30 1851
BROWN, Delah	CARTER, James	OCT 20 1821
BROWN, Ebon G.	MOORE, Mary B.	JUL 27 1840
BROWN, Edmund	DAVIS, Martha Ann (blk)	SEP 11 1848
BROWN, Edmund F.	OWEN, Isabella	OCT 03 1828
BROWN, Edmund F.	McDANIEL, Elizabeth	APR 29 1833
BROWN, Edward	GRAY, Mary Ann	APR 21 1829
BROWN, Edward	TUTTLE, Jannette	DEC 31 1849
BROWN, Edward	KING, Johanna	AUG 04 1854
BROWN, Edward	DISHER, Mary	MAY 29 1858
BROWN, Edward H.	RICE, Ellen	DEC 17 1851
BROWN, Eleanor	KING, William	MAY 13 1823
BROWN, Eleanor	NALLEY, William	DEC 13 1830
BROWN, Eleazer	MURRAY, Margaret C.	SEP 20 1838
BROWN, Eli	ROLLINS, Mary	DEC 29 1853
BROWN, Elias E.	MOORE, Mary Ann	DEC 25 1844
BROWN, Eliza	BRASHEARS, Robert	JUN 12 1821
BROWN, Eliza	DUVALL, Alfred J.	APR 25 1843
BROWN, Eliza (blk)	LEAPER, Hanson	JUN 25 1829
BROWN, Eliza (blk)	RICHARDS, Isaac	MAY 23 1831
BROWN, Eliza A.	KIRBY, Edmund	FEB 12 1825
BROWN, Eliza Ann	COOPER, S.B.B.	JAN 26 1839
BROWN, Eliza E.	WOLFENDEN, James T.	SEP 04 1846
BROWN, Eliza F.	HAW, Henry [Dr.]	OCT 27 1829
BROWN, Elizabeth	McDADE, Daniel	JAN 08 1824
BROWN, Elizabeth	DELANY, Matthias	APR 25 1826
BROWN, Elizabeth	HERBERT, William	FEB 23 1838
BROWN, Elizabeth	BELT, Thomas	JAN 31 1839
BROWN, Elizabeth	ATHEY, Thomas	JUN 16 1842
BROWN, Elizabeth	BAKER, George	AUG 29 1842
BROWN, Elizabeth	MURRAY, Elijah	JUL 01 1844
BROWN, Elizabeth	MULLINS, John H.	NOV 23 1844
BROWN, Elizabeth (blk)	WHITE, Edward	MAY 26 1858
BROWN, Elizabeth E.	GORDON, Charles	AUG 05 1839
BROWN, Ella S.	BROWN, Joel Y.	DEC 26 1849
BROWN, Ellen	BURNS, George	NOV 04 1846
BROWN, Ellen	COLLINS, James	FEB 01 1856

District of Columbia Marriage Licenses, 1811-1858

BROWN, Emeline	BUCKLY, Thomas	OCT 26 1837
BROWN, Emily S.	HOOVER, John W.	FEB 16 1852
BROWN, Emma	MYERS, Benjamin S.	AUG 29 1851
BROWN, Emma	EVANS, Paul R.	JAN 22 1855
BROWN, Emma J.	OGGELVIE, Walter	DEC 08 1856
BROWN, Esther	FERREE, Abraham	NOV 24 1829
BROWN, Frances	WILEY, John	APR 24 1851
BROWN, Frances	SWANN, Zachariah	NOV 22 1855
BROWN, Francis	CRANDLE, Polly	JAN 06 1831
BROWN, Francis	FOWLER, Dradey	JAN 03 1832
BROWN, Francis	WASHINGTON, Mary J. (blk)	APR 16 1850
BROWN, Francis C.	RUDD, Almira	APR 20 1858
BROWN, George	BURCH, Mary	APR 27 1815
BROWN, George	JOICE, Sarah (blk)	JUN 19 1839
BROWN, George	GLASCOE, Priscilla (blk)	JUL 29 1854
BROWN, Hannah	LEWIS, James	OCT 12 1821
BROWN, Hanson	DAY, Ann Elizth.	FEB 21 1844
BROWN, Harriet (blk)	FOGG, Martin	MAR 18 1842
BROWN, Hellen	THOMPSON, Richard H.	FEB 05 1850
BROWN, Henny (blk)	BELL, George	JUL 06 1826
BROWN, Henrietta (blk)	FERGUSON, John H.	JUL 07 1851
BROWN, Henry	WHITEFORD, Sarah	DEC 27 1819
BROWN, Henry	JULIUS, Julia (blk)	JUN 27 1833
BROWN, Henry	BERGER, Christiana S.	AUG 03 1857
BROWN, Henry J.	PETERS, Polena	DEC 02 1854
BROWN, Henson	CAMPBELL, Mary	JUN 19 1832
BROWN, Hester G.	NALLY, James S.	FEB 01 1858
BROWN, Isaac	MYERS, Victoria	FEB 09 1856
BROWN, Isabella C.	LONGDON, Charles	DEC 02 1847
BROWN, J. Frank	DAVIS, Francis M.	MAR 31 1856
BROWN, Jacob J.	BEALE, Margaret	AUG 31 1813
BROWN, James	RICE, Nancy	MAR 25 1819
BROWN, James	FISHER, Letty	AUG 16 1821
BROWN, James	KING, Elizabeth	NOV 16 1822
BROWN, James	STINGER, Sarah Jane [Mrs.]	NOV 23 1835
BROWN, James	GIDDINGS, Eliza Ann	DEC 19 1842
BROWN, James	PRICE, Mary Ann	AUG 08 1846
BROWN, James	GILL, Mary A.	JUN 07 1848
BROWN, James	TUCKER, Mary	OCT 05 1850
BROWN, James	KIRBY, Mary	SEP 03 1857
BROWN, James A.	WRIGHT, Mary A.	JAN 19 1854
BROWN, James B.	ARARD, Mary F.	OCT 11 1832
BROWN, James W.	STRETCH, Susan Ann	FEB 15 1844
BROWN, Jane	HUNTER, William J.	JUL 01 1839
BROWN, Jane (blk)	HARRIS, Alonzo	DEC 13 1849
BROWN, Jane Eliza	MATTINGLY, Zachariah	OCT 10 1843
BROWN, Jefferson	JOHNSON, Caroline (blk)	OCT 31 1853
BROWN, Jeffry	HAWKINS, Mary (blk)	JUL 29 1857
BROWN, Jerdina	GOODE, John	MAY 08 1854
BROWN, Jerome, Jr.	PADGETT, Mary Ann Elizabeth	JAN 03 1846
BROWN, Joanna	COLLINS, James	MAY 25 1853
BROWN, Joel Y.	BROWN, Ella S.	DEC 26 1849
BROWN, John	MYERS, Elizabeth	DEC 17 1813
BROWN, John	TEWELL, Rebecca	JUN 21 1819
BROWN, John	FAGAN, Ann	SEP 09 1820
BROWN, John	COOPER, Mary (blk)	SEP 13 1821
BROWN, John	OLIVER, Elizabeth	JAN 30 1823
BROWN, John	GLENN, Ann	JUN 07 1828

District of Columbia Marriage Licenses, 1811-1858

BROWN, John	BROWN, Rebecca (blk)	SEP 01 1829
BROWN, John	WORMLEY, Elizabeth	JAN 05 1831
BROWN, John	WHITE, Henrietta	FEB 28 1831
BROWN, John	JONES, Mary Ann	MAY 04 1837
BROWN, John	BUTLER, Maria (blk)	JUN 28 1840
BROWN, John	MANNING, Sarah Ann	DEC 02 1840
BROWN, John	FRERE, Elizabeth Eleanor	MAY 28 1842
BROWN, John	BROWN, Caroline	JUN 04 1842
BROWN, John	OLIVE, Sarah Ann	JUN 14 1843
BROWN, John	FRAZIER, Catherine (blk)	MAY 24 1844
BROWN, John	GRAVES, Susanna Eliza	JUN 20 1847
BROWN, John	OLLUFF, Mary	DEC 13 1849
BROWN, John	HAMILTON, Mary A.V.	AUG 28 1852
BROWN, John	HOGAN, Eliza	JUL 17 1855
BROWN, John	JONES, Mary	JUL 09 1856
BROWN, John B.	WILLIAMS, Rachael	MAY 29 1830
BROWN, John F.	HASKINS, Margt. (blk)	MAY 31 1856
BROWN, John H.	FISHER, Sarah A. (blk)	DEC 23 1852
BROWN, John P.	RODIER, Mary Jane	JUL 08 1840
BROWN, John P.	McBAIN, Mary E.	SEP 30 1851
BROWN, John R.	BELL, Margt. R.	JUN 30 1851
BROWN, John S.	BETTS, Henrietta T.	JUL 31 1852
BROWN, Jno. T.	SHORTER, Catharine E. (blk)	OCT 23 1855
BROWN, John T.	COHEN, Rachael W.	DEC 23 1851
BROWN, Joseph	TENNY, Elizabeth Ann	FEB 14 1835
BROWN, Julia	ROGAN, Hugh	FEB 05 1855
BROWN, Lafayette J.	CARUSI, Julia	AUG 12 1857
BROWN, Laura	ANDERSON, Allen	APR 06 1854
BROWN, Lettis (blk)	BROWN, Tarlton	SEP 03 1825
BROWN, Lewis A.	BROWN, Amelia F. (blk)	MAY 17 1858
BROWN, Lewis S.	TOLES, Ann Maria	MAR 26 1832
BROWN, Lloyd	SCOTT, Mary (blk)	MAY 29 1834
BROWN, Lloyd	CARTWRIGHT, Norah (blk)	DEC 15 1849
BROWN, Louisa	HINES, Edward	AUG 16 1828
BROWN, Louisa	CHAMBERLING, James	JUL 28 1830
BROWN, Louisa	LUFBOROUGH, John	JAN 26 1850
BROWN, Louisa (blk)	CURTIS, James	NOV 01 1849
BROWN, Louisa W. (blk)	MARTIN, Thomas	DEC 14 1857
BROWN, Louise G.	SIMMONS, Washington	OCT 15 1840
BROWN, Lucy Ann	CAULK, Phillip R.	JAN 16 1858
BROWN, Mandley	HARTMAN, Lucy E.	SEP 26 1850
BROWN, Margaret	CLEMENTS, Francis	OCT 07 1823
BROWN, Margaret	FOULKE, Grafton	MAR 27 1835
BROWN, Margaret	LEWIS, Edward	OCT 20 1841
BROWN, Margaret A.	SUIT, Edward, Jr.	MAY 11 1852
BROWN, Margaret A.H.	DONELSON, Wm. Henry	MAY 19 1855
BROWN, Margt. A.	LINKINS, Louis F.	JUN 18 1851
BROWN, Maria	PRENTISS, William	JUN 18 1829
BROWN, Marshal	SMITH, Charlotte (blk)	APR 22 1846
BROWN, Marshall	STITH, Louisa Stuart	NOV 16 1837
BROWN, Martha	CRUCKSHANK, Charles	FEB 04 1817
BROWN, Martha (blk)	CURTIS, James	APR 29 1852
BROWN, Martha A.	JANNEY, Lewis	AUG 03 1837
BROWN, Martha Ann	WOOD, Robert	DEC 24 1846
BROWN, Mary	VAUGHN, Martin	AUG 28 1819
BROWN, Mary	WHEELER, John H.	APR 19 1830
BROWN, Mary	SCOTT, James	NOV 21 1839
BROWN, Mary	RYALE, George C.	FEB 03 1841

District of Columbia Marriage Licenses, 1811-1858

BROWN, Mary	BAKER, Arthur	NOV 29 1841
BROWN, Mary	HALE, Bland	OCT 05 1843
BROWN, Mary	CLARK, Cornelius	APR 24 1847
BROWN, Mary	ALLEN, George T.	OCT 10 1850
BROWN, Mary	McCORMICK, Patrick	DEC 28 1852
BROWN, Mary	SLATTERY, James	APR 09 1855
BROWN, Mary	SLATTERY, James	APR 07 1855
BROWN, Mary (blk)	LIVERPOOL, Sylvester	JUL 09 1853
BROWN, Mary A.	BECKWITH, Singleton	SEP 07 1839
BROWN, Mary Ann	OWENS, Isaac, Jr.	APR 15 1823
BROWN, Mary Ann	POLKINHORN, Henry	JAN 27 1839
BROWN, Mary Ann Dolly	DOWNING, William	MAR 09 1843
BROWN, Mary Ann	VANE, Samuel	DEC 21 1849
BROWN, Mary Ann Virginia	FOWLER, Joseph	JUL 02 1851
BROWN, Mary Ann	HUNTER, James W.	JAN 24 1853
BROWN, Mary E.	HATTON, Henry D., Jr.	SEP 29 1838
BROWN, Mary E.	PINKERTON, Hugh	OCT 01 1857
BROWN, Mary E.	KRAFT, Paul	JAN 19 1858
BROWN, Mary Ellen	TILLEY, Henry	MAY 02 1838
BROWN, Mary F.	NORTON, A.S.	AUG 30 1843
BROWN, Mary H.	BROCKENBROUGH, Austin	DEC 18 1826
BROWN, Mary H.	MILLARD, Robert F.	FEB 07 1832
BROWN, Mary J. (blk)	DELANEY, Levi	AUG 21 1850
BROWN, Mary Jane	GATEWOOD, William H.	MAR 21 1850
BROWN, Mary Jane	ADAMS, Alexander	JUN 17 1856
BROWN, Mary V.	McCONCHIE, John W.	AUG 18 1857
BROWN, Matilda	JARBOE, William J.	JAN 31 1826
BROWN, Matilda	SMITH, Andrew	FEB 21 1843
BROWN, Matilda Ann	LUTRELL, James	DEC 27 1828
BROWN, Michael	CAMPBELL, Kitty (blk)	MAY 21 1823
BROWN, Moses	BUCHANAN, Mary A.	OCT 13 1853
BROWN, Nancy	MORTIMER, James	OCT 03 1812
BROWN, Nancy	BLACKWELL, William	SEP 04 1844
BROWN, Nehemiah	CLAIR, Ann	FEB 28 1838
BROWN, Owen W.	IRELAND, Anna M. (blk)	OCT 30 1855
BROWN, Patience	GILL, John	MAY 03 1839
BROWN, Patience E.	GILL, John F.	MAY 22 1839
BROWN, Patrick	HOLLOHAN, Mary	JUN 28 1856
BROWN, Paul	SIMMS, Virginia (blk)	FEB 23 1852
BROWN, Peter	FOOT, Catharine	NOV 06 1830
BROWN, Phillis (blk)	REEDE, Jacob	DEC 14 1848
BROWN, Queen Ann (blk)	ADAMS, Abraham	DEC 07 1853
BROWN, Rachael	KING, William	FEB 10 1817
BROWN, Rachel	BARNES, George	APR 16 1833
BROWN, Ransdale	HALL, Frances A.	MAY 29 1855
BROWN, Rebecca	DAY, William	NOV 04 1817
BROWN, Rebecca (blk)	BROWN, John	SEP 01 1829
BROWN, Rebecca (blk)	SLATER, James	FEB 27 1838
BROWN, Rebecca (blk)	WILKINSON, James	NOV 23 1843
BROWN, Rebecca (blk)	LEWIS, David	APR 05 1849
BROWN, Reuben R.	BOWEN, Rosina	MAY 28 1849
BROWN, Rezin H.	ANDERSON, Mary Elizth.	NOV 11 1856
BROWN, Rhoda S.	WATSON, Edward B.	APR 01 1824
BROWN, Richard	ROBEY, Matilda	OCT 20 1827
BROWN, Richard	TALBERT, Mary	JAN 13 1831
BROWN, Richard	MERCHANT, Elizabeth J.	JAN 08 1838
BROWN, Richard	DEAKINS, Ann Maria	FEB 12 1839
BROWN, Richard	NALLEY, Elizabeth	APR 17 1849

District of Columbia Marriage Licenses, 1811-1858

BROWN, Richard H.	KEYS, Nancy	APR 30 1855
BROWN, Richard J.	HAMPTMERE, Johanna	NOV 16 1842
BROWN, Robert	STEWARD, Magdelina	JUL 13 1821
BROWN, Robert	SARDO, Fortunate Mary	FEB 08 1825
BROWN, Robert	ROYED, Maria (blk)	JUL 21 1829
BROWN, Robert	CAMPBELL, Elizabeth (blk)	NOV 14 1837
BROWN, Robert	JONES, Louisa	SEP 24 1845
BROWN, Robert F.	BARR, Mary Jane	MAR 06 1851
BROWN, Rolley	HARRISS, Emily	NOV 17 1831
BROWN, Rosa	WALLACH, Richard	APR 03 1856
BROWN, Rosa C.	DOWDEN, William L.	DEC 24 1855
BROWN, Rosamond	LOW, Abner W.	JAN 16 1856
BROWN, Sally	PRYOR, Ralph	FEB 15 1838
BROWN, Samuel	ALBERTINE, Davis (blk)	NOV 27 1855
BROWN, Samuel	DAVIS, Albertine (blk)	NOV 27 1855
BROWN, Samuel L.	HARBOUGH, Ellen A.	NOV 19 1857
BROWN, Sarah	BOWLING, Joseph	DEC 05 1821
BROWN, Sarah	KING, Ignatius	MAR 25 1825
BROWN, Sarah	KING, Ignatus	MAR 25 1826
BROWN, Sarah	EARL, Richard W.	MAR 14 1835
BROWN, Sarah	SUTER, William	DEC 07 1837
BROWN, Sarah	AUSTIN, William	APR 19 1852
BROWN, Sarah (blk)	HENRY, William	DEC 18 1812
BROWN, Sarah (blk)	BATEMAN, Abraham	MAY 22 1823
BROWN, Sarah Ann C.	ATCHISON, James E.	NOV 08 1838
BROWN, Sarah G.	HUTCHINS, Samuel A.	NOV 28 1829
BROWN, Septimus L.	CAUSIN, Amanda	FEB 09 1844
BROWN, Signet A.	WILSON, George W.	OCT 20 1856
BROWN, Solomon G.	ADAMS, Lucinda (blk)	JUN 05 1854
BROWN, Sophiah (blk)	CUSTUS, Charles	DEC 20 1825
BROWN, Stephen T.	CISSEL, Virginia	JAN 25 1855
BROWN, Susan	BARBOUR, Thomas	JAN 21 1840
BROWN, Susan (blk)	SMITH, John T.	MAR 08 1852
BROWN, Susan A.	GRIMES, Geo. E.	APR 03 1854
BROWN, Tarlton	BROWN, Lettis (blk)	SEP 03 1825
BROWN, Teresa (blk)	SIMPSON, John	DEC 23 1854
BROWN, Thomas	MAYO, Ruth	JUN 24 1815
BROWN, Thomas	SMALLWOOD, Mary Ann (blk)	JUL 27 1831
BROWN, Thomas	WATERS, Elizabeth (blk)	JUN 21 1832
BROWN, Thomas	PIERVILL, Elizabeth	APR 21 1836
BROWN, Thomas	WYMAN, Nancy	SEP 26 1854
BROWN, Thomas	WALKER, Emma	MAR 25 1856
BROWN, Thomas B.	ROTHWELL, Laura E.	OCT 02 1845
BROWN, Thomas B.	HOMANS, Roddy Caroline Harris	AUG 19 1846
BROWN, Thomas B.	PERRY, Mary A.	FEB 04 1858
BROWN, Thomas Charles	CUNNINGHAM, Margaret E. (blk)	JUL 07 1858
BROWN, Thomas H.	EMACK, Mary Ann C.	DEC 21 1819
BROWN, Thos.	JOHNSON, Mary (blk)	SEP 11 1845
BROWN, W.H.	HULL, Rebecca	NOV 21 1849
BROWN, Wesley	ASH, Mary	JAN 24 1833
BROWN, William	McINTIRE, Sarah Justice	JUN 13 1816
BROWN, William	KNIGHT, Mary	SEP 25 1817
BROWN, William	COOKE, Johannna	MAR 20 1819
BROWN, William	WARD, Eliza	APR 16 1822
BROWN, William	BELL, Lucy	MAY 14 1825
BROWN, William	ROUCKENDORFF, Maria	OCT 26 1826
BROWN, William	CARROLL, Peggy (blk)	SEP 19 1828
BROWN, William	VENABLE, Ann	DEC 17 1829

District of Columbia Marriage Licenses, 1811-1858

BROWN, William	ATKISON, Elea	JUL 03 1829
BROWN, William	WHITING, Eliza (blk)	DEC 21 1830
BROWN, William	GILLUM, Cordelia (blk)	APR 23 1831
BROWN, William	CANTON, Jane	AUG 05 1834
BROWN, William	HUSTLER, Eleanor	MAR 05 1835
BROWN, William	BRADFORD, Elizabeth	MAR 24 1835
BROWN, William	MAHANY, Anna (blk)	JUN 09 1840
BROWN, William	SMITH, Laurena (blk)	OCT 26 1843
BROWN, William	LUCAS, Sarah Agatha	JAN 09 1844
BROWN, William	NETH, M. Elizabeth	NOV 16 1844
BROWN, William	MARSHALL, Rebecca (blk)	JUN 24 1845
BROWN, William	DOVE, Mary Jane	SEP 18 1845
BROWN, William	COFFEE, Mary (blk)	SEP 27 1849
BROWN, William	WARD, Mary Ann (blk)	FEB 21 1850
BROWN, William	HENDERSON, Eliza	OCT 07 1852
BROWN, William	DAVIS, Lutecia (blk)	MAR 14 1854
BROWN, William Edward	MATTINGLY, Barbara Ellen	DEC 17 1842
BROWN, William H.	SULLIVAN, Ann Maria	DEC 26 1857
BROWN, William I.	GRIFFIS, Verlinda	FEB 28 1844
BROWN, William M.	TIPPETT, Mary Ellen	OCT 20 1853
BROWN, William P.	MITCHELL, Amanda H.	APR 09 1853
BROWN, William R.	MOORE, Mary M.	JUN 21 1848
BROWN, William T.	LANHAM, Elizabeth	AUG 09 1847
BROWN, William W.	ROBINSON, Ellen J.	FEB 14 1849
BROWN, Winna Ann (blk)	COOPER, Samuel	SEP 06 1855
BROWN, Zedekiah	COLLINS, Ann Maria	NOV 04 1833
BROWNE, Ann Eilbeck	SMITH, William S.	FEB 25 1858
BROWNE, Causten	MAYNADIER, Kate Eveleth	MAY 31 1852
BROWNE, John M.	LITLE, Mary E.	JAN 06 1830
BROWNE, John Ross	MITCHELL, Lucy Anna	NOV 13 1844
BROWNE, Lucien C.	MATTINGLY, Clara V.	APR 19 1847
BROWNE, William H.	WISHART, Ann S.	JUL 15 1842
BROWNE, William Henry	WISHART, Letitia S.	SEP 23 1837
BROWNE, William J.	McCULLOH, Annie L.	JUN 06 1853
BROWNELL, Charles H.	SMITH, Mary C.	NOV 03 1851
BROWNER, Abner	HAGER, Sarah	AUG 24 1813
BROWNING, Eliza H.	KELLY, Arthur	JUN 22 1854
BROWNING, Ellen	PERKINS, Hector	NOV 16 1823
BROWNING, George G.	GRIFFIN, Catherine Virga.	NOV 07 1855
BROWNING, Harriet	WRIGHT, Benjamin	JUL 03 1858
BROWNING, Horatio	MILLER, Catharine Virginia	MAY 20 1858
BROWNING, Jeremiah	BAKER, Mary Ann	APR 24 1830
BROWNING, John Henry	HOFFMAN, Magdalen Eva	NOV 16 1843
BROWNING, John N.	BERRY, Lethe Ann	AUG 15 1845
BROWNING, Martha R.	McCAUSLEN, William C.	JUN 07 1855
BROWNING, Mary Ellen	STEWART, Richard	MAY 15 1838
BROWNING, Peregrine Warfield	WOOD, Margaret Ann	JAN 17 1833
BRUCE, Agnes	HOUSTON, Andrew	SEP 12 1853
BRUCE, Catharine Ann	FOX, Henry	OCT 01 1840
BRUCE, Charles	HARRIS, Martha	OCT 09 1851
BRUCE, Charles	CARROLL, Hannah (blk)	MAR 29 1854
BRUCE, Clarissa Ann	GILES, John A.	DEC 28 1848
BRUCE, George N.	SRYOCK, Virginia L.	MAR 28 1843
BRUCE, Hannah A. (blk)	ROZIER, John W.	NOV 15 1848
BRUCE, Harriet E. (blk)	PARK, Montgomery	JUN 27 1850
BRUCE, Henry M.	ADAMS, Emily	JUL 21 1833
BRUCE, James	BECKETT, Hannah (blk)	FEB 18 1832
BRUCE, Mary	McKECHNIE, Neil	SEP 08 1854

District of Columbia Marriage Licenses, 1811-1858

BRUCE, Mary A.	FORTUNE, Thomas L.	APR 18 1846
BRUCE, Nancy	CHEW, Phillip	JUN 14 1827
BRUCE, Philip	MARSHAL, Mary (blk)	MAR 12 1840
BRUCE, Robert J.	FINNEY, Mary Ann	MAR 18 1856
BRUCE, Rutha (blk)	SMITH, George	MAY 08 1834
BRUCE, Sarah J.	BOYD, Thomas	JUN 11 1858
BRUCE, William	BROOKES, Mary (blk)	JUN 11 1829
BRUCE, William C.	JOHNSTON, Julia Ann	FEB 05 1844
BRUDEROFKI, Elizabeth	WILLIAMS, Lewis	MAY 08 1854
BRUER, Rebecca	BRITTON, Geo.	FEB 04 1818
BRUEST, Robert	VanHORN, Adda Eliza	NOV 17 1827
BRUEST, Robert	VanHORN, Adda E.	NOV 17 1829
BRUFF, Mary Augusta	GADSBY, William	JUN 28 1843
BRUFF, Richard W.	FOY, Jane C.	MAY 30 1853
BRUFF, Susan M.	RIND, William A.	NOV 16 1818
BRUGGY, Jeremiah	MALONE, Ann	MAY 11 1853
BRUGGY, Mary	CONROY, Thomas	APR 02 1853
BRUHL, August	MELLER, Margaret	MAY 31 1853
BRUMBACK, Catherine	GROVES, Daniel	SEP 18 1857
BRUMER, Theodore	STOUT, Caroline	MAY 08 1855
BRUMFIELD, Nathan	MILES, Rosetta	FEB 23 1838
BRUMLEY, Hannah	GIBSON, Joseph	APR 14 1818
BRUMLEY, Margaret	GAITHER, Greenbury	MAY 18 1824
BRUMLEY, Sarah E.	JOHNSON, Albert	NOV 13 1836
BRUMNER, Catharine	SIMINGTON, Peter	JUL 14 1821
BRUNET, John Baptist	LABILLE, Eliza	SEP 16 1818
BRUNETTE, Louis A.	KING, Mary Jane	DEC 23 1847
BRUNNER, Laurence	STUMP, Celia	SEP 17 1855
BRUNNER, Washington	CAMMICK, Frances C.	MAY 20 1846
BRUNNOR, Jacob	GUILDA, Eleanor	MAR 06 1816
BRUSH, John C.	DOYNE, Mary [Mrs.]	MAR 26 1813
BRUSH, Mary Ann	EVANS, John K.	MAY 04 1818
BRUSH, Mary S.	CLEMENTS, John T., Jr.	MAR 02 1857
BRUSH, Truman M.	DeNEALE, Mary J.	NOV 28 1846
BRUSNAR, John	KALAHAR, Catherine	JUN 10 1843
BRYAN, Ann J.	GRIFFIN, Jesse	JUN 18 1827
BRYAN, Benjamin	FREE, Elizth.	NOV 08 1821
BRYAN, Benjamin	LEMMON, Emily (blk)	AUG 21 1845
BRYAN, Bernard M.	HOWE, Sarah V.	APR 16 1857
BRYAN, Caroline C.	VILLARD, Thomas J.	OCT 25 1848
BRYAN, Charity A.	LOCKER, Henley	JAN 21 1836
BRYAN, Chloe Ann	BALL, John Dent	DEC 16 1823
BRYAN, Dorothy Ann	RUFF, John A.	OCT 10 1848
BRYAN, Eleanor	CONNELL, John	DEC 24 1811
BRYAN, Eleanor	MILLER, Charles	NOV 29 1820
BRYAN, Elizabeth	HUCHERSON, William	JUN 28 1815
BRYAN, Elizabeth	BAKER, John T.	MAY 25 1829
BRYAN, Ellen V.	BAKER, George L.	JUN 26 1857
BRYAN, Enoch	WILSON, Susanah M.	JUN 15 1819
BRYAN, Enoch	BEAN, Elizabeth Ann S. [Mrs.]	AUG 05 1824
BRYAN, Hannah	HUDSON, Richard	SEP 25 1817
BRYAN, James D.	WHITING, Elizabeth	MAY 29 1816
BRYAN, James M.	EWING, Caroline	DEC 12 1848
BRYAN, John	KILLIGAN, Ellen	JUL 02 1857
BRYAN, John L.	DONIPHAN, Ann Elizabeth	SEP 19 1832
BRYAN, Joseph	EDMONSTON, Octabia	APR 06 1822
BRYAN, Kate	DOWELL, William	JUN 30 1858
BRYAN, Lavinia	FRANCIS, Thomas	NOV 18 1856

District of Columbia Marriage Licenses, 1811-1858

BRYAN, Lee	WILLIAMS, Josephine (blk)	JUN 25 1846
BRYAN, Lucy Ann	LOWE, Lloyd M.	MAY 01 1833
BRYAN, Mary	CLARKE, William	MAR 13 1817
BRYAN, Mary	JONES, James	MAY 18 1820
BRYAN, Mary	PROBY, Thomas	FEB 19 1831
BRYAN, Mary Elizth.	FALCUNER, William K.	MAY 04 1846
BRYAN, Mary Ellen	SPICER, John Frederick	FEB 07 1850
BRYAN, Priscilla	GORDON, Worthington	APR 01 1824
BRYAN, Rebecca Jane	NELSON, Charles Edward	DEC 24 1852
BRYAN, Sallie Ann	SWART, Bernard T.	MAY 01 1855
BRYAN, Sally	SPALDING, Thomas F.P.	NOV 17 1835
BRYAN, Samuel	WILLIAMS, Catharine	FEB 11 1820
BRYAN, Samuel L.	HOWE, Margaret Ann	JUN 26 1850
BRYAN, Sarah	BRADY, John	JUN 03 1824
BRYAN, Sarah	MUDD, William	DEC 24 1844
BRYAN, Thomas	ESSEX, Susannah	SEP 16 1815
BRYAN, William	SWAN, Maria H.	MAY 21 1812
BRYAN, William	KINGSBURY, Sarah	JUN 23 1829
BRYAN, William	DIX, Sophia Ann	MAR 21 1829
BRYANT, Ann	FOXVILL, Charles	MAR 12 1823
BRYANT, Benj.	DAVIS, Eliza	OCT 18 1852
BRYANT, Deborah F.	WRIGHT, Joseph S.	SEP 30 1857
BRYANT, Enoch	SMITH, Kitty	FEB 06 1828
BRYANT, James R.M.	ELLIS, Dorcas Gardner	JUL 22 1822
BRYANT, John Y.	MOULDER, Anna Jane	DEC 24 1834
BRYANT, Samuel Drake	FISHER, Anna Palmer	APR 10 1824
BRYANT, William	RUSSELL, Geniza E.	FEB 27 1850
BRYANT, William	PAYNE, Sarah	FEB 24 1858
BRYDON, John	SMITH, Rachel Ann	MAR 20 1841
BRYNE, Patrick	HOGAN, Catherine	MAR 07 1848
BRYON, John	SCOTT, Ellen	NOV 06 1840
BRYON, Zechiel Orick	GEESTER, Rebecca	DEC 30 1845
BRYSON, Hester	CRAGGS, Thomas	JUL 12 1855
BRYSON, Sarah	SPRATT, James	AUG 05 1816
BUCHANAN, Caroline V.M.	FRYE, Nathl., Jr.	JUL 03 1817
BUCHANAN, Henry	BUSH, Mary	OCT 30 1832
BUCHANAN, Henry	BELT, Elizabeth	MAR 21 1837
BUCHANAN, John	REED, Sarah	NOV 18 1850
BUCHANAN, Mary A.	BROWN, Moses	OCT 13 1853
BUCHER, Bernhard H.	BERKART, Mary	AUG 10 1857
BUCHLY, Christian	MACKALL, Harriot	SEP 23 1818
BUCK, John, Jr.	BELL, Mary	APR 04 1854
BUCK, Louisa	JOACHIM, John	MAY 15 1844
BUCK, Sophia	SCUFFARLAIN, John	NOV 19 1847
BUCKANAN, Elizabeth (blk)	LANDICK, Isaac	MAY 14 1840
BUCKEY, Ann M.	ISAAC, Charles A.	AUG 28 1833
BUCKEY, Chas. A.	SHOEMAKER, Elizabeth L.	NOV 19 1856
BUCKEY, Mathias V.	PARSONS, Jane	FEB 18 1835
BUCKEYE, John	RABBIT, Mary	AUG 14 1851
BUCKINGHAM, Caleb	FARRELL, Liddia	AUG 08 1820
BUCKINGHAM, Charles	BERRY, Virginia (blk)	MAY 27 1852
BUCKINGHAM, Eleanor	GIDLOW, William	JAN 13 1826
BUCKINGHAM, Franklin L.	ADAMS, Leona	OCT 10 1849
BUCKINGHAM, Virginia (blk)	HILL, Richard	JAN 30 1854
BUCKINGHAM, William	WEAST, Eleanor	NOV 25 1817
BUCKLEE, Benedict	UNDERWOOD, Rebecca	MAY 22 1826
BUCKLER, Margaret	CONNER, Robert	NOV 03 1845
BUCKLER, Mary	BRADY, Owen	APR 26 1823

District of Columbia Marriage Licenses, 1811-1858

BUCKLEY, Albert	SMITH, Britania A.	NOV 27 1850
BUCKLEY, Alexander W.	POLAND, Mary Ann	JAN 12 1849
BUCKLEY, Ann Louisa	SHEKELL, George A.	SEP 20 1856
BUCKLEY, Bridget	TWOOMEY, Cornelius	SEP 05 1857
BUCKLEY, Catherine	McCARTY, Charles	JUN 03 1846
BUCKLEY, Dennis	DAIDY, Mary	JUL 13 1839
BUCKLEY, Eliza	CAMPBELL, John A.	SEP 13 1852
BUCKLEY, Eliza	COLINS, Patrick	FEB 02 1853
BUCKLEY, Ellen	FRYE, Robert	JUL 19 1823
BUCKLEY, James	PERCEL, Hannah	DEC 29 1820
BUCKLEY, James	SIMONS, Louisa	JUN 21 1831
BUCKLEY, James S.	FENWICK, Elizabeth O.	JAN 13 1857
BUCKLEY, James W.	SHECKELLS, Sarah	AUG 09 1855
BUCKLEY, Jerry	McVARRY, Bridget	JUL 09 1852
BUCKLEY, Johanna	FITZGERALD, Edward	MAY 07 1853
BUCKLEY, John	CONDON, Ellen	APR 05 1852
BUCKLEY, John	FLYNN, Bridget	JUN 03 1854
BUCKLEY, Margaret	KENNEDY, William	MAY 14 1855
BUCKLEY, Mary	BRADLEY, George	DEC 23 1852
BUCKLEY, Mary	CRONIN, Patrick	MAY 26 1853
BUCKLEY, Posey	SINCLAIR, Thomas B.	MAR 29 1823
BUCKLEY, Susan	WINDSOR, John A[lexan]der	FEB 27 1812
BUCKLEY, Thomas	LATKIN, Margaret	JAN 23 1858
BUCKLEY, Thomas A.	GARDNER, Sarah H.	JUL 11 1857
BUCKLEY, Timothy	HOGAN, Margaret	DEC 09 1844
BUCKLEY, Timothy	RING, Mary	JUN 07 1856
BUCKLY, Anthony	MARTIN, Elizabeth Jane	MAY 30 1854
BUCKLY, Catherine	KELLY, Patrick	FEB 04 1854
BUCKLY, Thomas	BROWN, Emeline	OCT 26 1837
BUCKMINSTER, Jacob	YOUNG, Ann Maria	SEP 18 1851
BUCKNER, Eliza A.	GALLAHER, B. Franklin	MAY 12 1857
BUCKNER, Elizabeth M.	WAYLAND, Benjamin C.	SEP 27 1847
BUCKNER, Ella Alice	SMITH, Edward Jaquelin	OCT 23 1848
BUCKNER, Mary F.	PRALL, Wm. Livingston	JUN 12 1828
BUCKNER, Richard Bernard	BERRYMAN, Louisa Hipkins	FEB 25 1828
BUCLE, Elizabeth D.	SMITH, Abner C.	APR 23 1839
BUDD, Daniel	WATERS, Catharine (blk)	AUG 28 1849
BUDD, John L.	CARPENTER, Mary E.	JUN 07 1853
BUDD, William	TURNER, Jane (blk)	JUN 03 1851
BUDE, Christina	YOUNG, William	FEB 21 1851
BUDINGTON, William Ives	GUNTON, Elizabeth Livingston	JAN 04 1841
BUEDE, Henry	LINGEBACK, Henrietta	DEC 30 1843
BUEHRE, Caroline	BODE, Lewis	NOV 27 1852
BUELL, Martin	O'BRYEN, Lucy Ann	DEC 30 1837
BUERY, Catharine	KNOTT, George A.	OCT 20 1841
BUGBEE, Jane L.	NOYES, Thomas L.	MAY 14 1834
BUGGY, Patrick	FENTON, Catharine	OCT 23 1844
BUGH, James L.	GRANT, Ann	SEP 04 1820
BUGH, Margaret Jane	DOWNER, Richard M.	SEP 07 1847
BUGH, Richard	PRYSE, Elizabeth	OCT 29 1818
BUHLER, John	SURRY, Margaret	JAN 21 1836
BULER, Mary Ann	MAULEY, Thomas C.	APR 13 1844
BULFINCH, Susan A.	HALL, David A.	SEP 27 1821
BULGER, John	BOSTON, Isabella (blk)	JAN 24 1856
BULGER, Margaret A.	JARDELLA, John A.C.	DEC 31 1850
BULGER, Mary T.R.	McDONALD, James M.	FEB 21 1852
BULL, Ann Maria (blk)	RUSTIN, Basil	OCT 11 1823
BULL, Daniel M.	McCAULLY, Martha Jane	JUN 20 1844

District of Columbia Marriage Licenses, 1811-1858

BULL, Enoch	CANNON, Ann Eliza	JUN 02 1834
BULLARD, Lucy E.	ATWELL, James R.	NOV 05 1856
BULLER, Mary	PRICE, Samuel	AUG 24 1847
BULLEY, Michael	FORREST, Eleanor C.	NOV 26 1821
BULLIT, Martha A.	STEWART, John	DEC 03 1856
BULLOCH, John	GREEN, Eliza	MAR 19 1835
BULLOCK, Oscar F.	KYLE, Catharine E.	OCT 22 1857
BULLOCK, Richard	DENNIS, Margaret	OCT 03 1812
BULLOCK, Sophia	BELL, Henry C.	OCT 04 1849
BULLUS, John N.	HATTON, [blank]	APR 06 1822
BULLY, Mary Jane	MITCHELL, Charles	AUG 04 1840
BULSEN, Mary	KING, Zachariah	MAR 08 1828
BUMERY, Mary (blk)	NOKES, Edward	MAR 02 1858
BUMLEY, Harriet	CRITTENDEN, Robert H.	MAY 17 1853
BUMPASS, Ann N.	PHILLIPS, Lancelot	NOV 07 1833
BUNGER, Charles	HERTELL, Amelia Ernstina	APR 14 1835
BUNNEL, Eliab	ROBERTSON, Jane M.	NOV 09 1812
BUNNELL, Alba	AMERY, Joseph W.	OCT 11 1842
BUNTHRON, John	HARPER, Grace	MAR 02 1822
BUNTHRON, Mary Ann	LANGFITT, William J.	SEP 29 1843
BUNTON, Amelia	CONNER, Mitchell	JUN 23 1831
BUNTON, Eleanor	RICHARDS, Thomas	JUL 21 1823
BURAGE, Thomas	CAMELL, Eleanor	APR 11 1833
BURCH, Amanda	KNIGHT, John	JAN 27 1849
BURCH, Ann Virginia	HARRIS, James	JUL 06 1852
BURCH, Balum	NOWLAN, Elizabeth	OCT 15 1822
BURCH, Caleb	SHERMAN, Sarah	NOV 24 1845
BURCH, Catharine	STEPHENSON, John	SEP 24 1822
BURCH, Catherine	HARE, Francis	JAN 09 1844
BURCH, Charles J.	GILL, Margaret E.	JAN 12 1849
BURCH, Columbia	HARRISON, Robert	MAY 27 1833
BURCH, Elizabeth	KURTZ, David	APR 17 1816
BURCH, Elizabeth	WRIGHT, William	JUN 26 1822
BURCH, Elizabeth Ann	JONES, Richard J.	AUG 27 1840
BURCH, Elizabeth Jane	HAWKINS, Reuben A.	SEP 12 1836
BURCH, Elizabeth V.	RIDGEWAY, James F.	NOV 01 1853
BURCH, Emily	TAYLOR, William H.	JAN 03 1854
BURCH, Emily Ann	ESPEY, Samuel C.	OCT 04 1845
BURCH, Eugenia E.	SNYDER, Luther L.	SEP 03 1857
BURCH, Frances O.	CLARK, Lemuel F.	MAY 09 1848
BURCH, George H.	SEBASTIAN, Ann	NOV 07 1837
BURCH, James Albert	KING, Margaret	APR 08 1837
BURCH, Jane	LIGHTFOOT, George	APR 12 1827
BURCH, Jane H.	GATTON, Elisha A.	MAY 06 1816
BURCH, Jesse	ELLIS, Sarah	JUL 15 1830
BURCH, John	PENNINGTON, Mary	DEC 29 1835
BURCH, John	THOMPSON, Susannah	JAN 14 1836
BURCH, John T.	HATTON, Mary G.	APR 18 1854
BURCH, John Wesley	COX, Eliza	MAY 26 1842
BURCH, Joseph	FRIDLEY, Jane	FEB 13 1850
BURCH, Joseph Alexander	BEALL, Elizabeth	MAY 12 1817
BURCH, Julia	LaBILLE, Louis	JUN 01 1857
BURCH, Julia Ann	ARUNDELL, John	MAR 23 1847
BURCH, Martha A.	LINTON, Philip H.	SEP 08 1857
BURCH, Martha Ann	EDMONSTON, John C.	OCT 29 1833
BURCH, Martha M.	CAIN, [George] J.	MAY 29 1828
BURCH, Mary	BROWN, George	APR 27 1815
BURCH, Mary	HARDY, Henry	AUG 06 1836

District of Columbia Marriage Licenses, 1811-1858

BURCH, Mary Ann	GROVES, William H.	MAY 04 1838
BURCH, Mary Ann	SHAW, Richard	DEC 13 1838
BURCH, Mary Ann	LANGTON, James W.	JUL 19 1843
BURCH, Mary Ann	MARSY, Samuel	DEC 23 1854
BURCH, Mary E.	BLINCOE, Albert T.	JAN 16 1832
BURCH, Mary Priscilla	BASSFORD, William T.	MAY 06 1852
BURCH, Melinda	RHODES, Williams	OCT 19 1814
BURCH, Nancy	LOWMAN, Edward	JUL 24 1817
BURCH, Rebecca	BAYLISS, William	APR 12 1827
BURCH, Rebecca	MOORE, John	SEP 23 1850
BURCH, Remigins	PICKERELL, Eleanor	FEB 14 1816
BURCH, Richard H.	MYERS, Georgeanna	NOV 26 1849
BURCH, Robert	HARRISON, Mary Ann	FEB 16 1833
BURCH, Samuel	SIMMONS, Rachael	FEB 05 1834
BURCH, Samuel	MORRIS, Thursday	JUN 12 1849
BURCH, Sarah [Mrs.]	HUGGINS, Joseph	JUN 07 1834
BURCH, Sarah Ann	HITCHCOCK, Thomas	NOV 16 1847
BURCH, Sarah Jane	FOSTER, Adams	MAY 29 1849
BURCH, Susan Ann	EFFLINE, David James	JAN 30 1845
BURCH, Susan L.	HEWITT, Wm.	DEC 29 1812
BURCH, Thomas	NEWMAN, Deborah	FEB 19 1828
BURCH, Thomas	FARRELL, Lucinda Ann	MAY 12 1835
BURCH, Thomas	HUMES, Martha	MAY 20 1841
BURCH, Verlinda Mary	WILTBERGER, Charles H.	JUL 09 1821
BURCH, Virginia	COOK, John	DEC 03 1845
BURCH, William	ALTON, Elizabeth	FEB 11 1812
BURCH, William	DOUGHERTY, Susan	NOV 02 1824
BURCH, William	SHRIEVE, Julia Ann	DEC 28 1838
BURCH, William S.	COCK, Frances E.	OCT 16 1840
BURCH, William S.	HURDLE, Mary	SEP 16 1846
BURCHARD, J.	WOODWORTH, H.E.	MAR 18 1830
BURCHE, America G.E.	FATIO, Lewis Charles Francis	JUN 26 1841
BURCHE, Ellen M.	McCONVEY, Henry	SEP 20 1856
BURCHE, Mary E.	ST. CLAIR, James W.	DEC 04 1854
BURCHE, Raymond Wison	HEWITT, Catherine	JAN 19 1848
BURCHELL, Elizabeth	SISSON, George	DEC 21 1846
BURCHELL, Norval B.	LANDON, Sarah F.	OCT 19 1854
BURCKHARTT, Lenne	RICK, John	OCT 18 1855
BURCKHEAD, Edward	DONN, Mary Ann	JUL 01 1832
BURCKHER, Joseph	ROSS, Elizabeth	DEC 28 1824
BURD, Thomas	OGDEN, Matilda	DEC 07 1815
BURDEET, Eliza	HERRELL, George M.	NOV 13 1851
BURDETT, Francis	CHAMBERLIN, Angemima	OCT 19 1857
BURDETT, Hilleary	SHOEMAKER, Mary Ann	MAY 05 1853
BURDETT, James H.	AGER, Mary F.	NOV 25 1856
BURDETT, Matilda J.	JONES, James W.	NOV 02 1850
BURDETT, Wm. Thomas	WALL, Mary Elizth.	AUG 16 1852
BURDETTE, Ellen	DEEBLE, Wm. H.	JUL 03 1855
BURDINE, Alfred	LEFEVER, Ann Maria	NOV 03 1841
BURDINE, Alfred	BYER, Lucy Ann	OCT 17 1850
BURDINE, Caroline	OBER, Henry N.	JAN 15 1852
BURDINE, Charles	BRAWNER, Laura	AUG 30 1852
BURDINE, James	SHECKELLS, Emma Frances	MAR 04 1846
BURDINE, Margaret E.	MORGAN, William	JUN 30 1842
BURDITT, Mary A.	PORTER, Richard M.	AUG 10 1857
BUREY, Margaret	BLAND, William H.	JAN 08 1838
BURFORD, John A.	SELBY, Sarah	SEP 23 1813
BURFORD, Maria	SPICER, Frederick	JUL 03 1830

District of Columbia Marriage Licenses, 1811-1858

BURFORD, Sarah	OTTERBACK, Philip	JAN 31 1821
BURFORD, William B.	THOMPSON, Elizabeth A.	JAN 10 1854
BURGAMAL, Joseph	SCHAMDTS, Jane	DEC 03 1834
BURGAMORE, Sophia C.	McDONALD, Alexander	SEP 01 1848
BURGAMY, Joseph	CAMBERS, Elizabeth	OCT 30 1828
BURGDORPF, Louis	SMITH, Louise	DEC 30 1851
BURGEE, Emma R.	WEBB, Edward	OCT 11 1853
BURGER, Christiana	MASON, William H.	AUG 25 1853
BURGER, Mary	HEINE, Wm.	OCT 31 1855
BURGER, Mary A.	PERREGORY, Joseph C.	MAY 30 1850
BURGER, William B.	ANDERSON, Only P.	JUN 16 1834
BURGES, Cirus	PATERSON, Margaret	APR 22 1813
BURGES, John	WHITE, Susan	JAN 30 1812
BURGESS, Addison	UTTERBACK, Olivia	AUG 08 1853
BURGESS, Andrew	FROST, Elizabeth	MAR 31 1849
BURGESS, Ann	HALBERT, Philip	MAY 06 1819
BURGESS, Catherine (blk)	BROOKS, George Washington	MAY 04 1854
BURGESS, Cecelia Ann (blk)	SIMES, Joseph	APR 20 1840
BURGESS, Charles	BUTLER, Emily	SEP 12 1837
BURGESS, Charles	HADLEY, Mary Jane	MAY 31 1856
BURGESS, Cornelius N.	MILES, Emily	OCT 16 1834
BURGESS, Cyrus	BAYSE, Polly (blk)	FEB 13 1836
BURGESS, Dawson P.	CRAIG, Henrietta	MAY 25 1815
BURGESS, Delpha Ann	READ, George	JUL 07 1836
BURGESS, Eliz. Ann	BADEN, William	FEB 17 1815
BURGESS, Eliza	WHITE, Lloyd	MAR 06 1821
BURGESS, Eliza	PARKER, John	OCT 25 1831
BURGESS, Eliza A.	STILLWELL, Tobias H.	SEP 19 1855
BURGESS, Elizabeth	DANDERSON, William	DEC 22 1812
BURGESS, Francis B.F.	YOUNG, Elizabeth	MAY 31 1858
BURGESS, George	BUTLER, Jane	JUN 13 1846
BURGESS, Harriet	SWEENY, George	FEB 03 1830
BURGESS, James	CANNEN, Sarah J.	JUL 29 1851
BURGESS, John	DIGGES, Rachel Ann	JUN 17 1843
BURGESS, John	DIGGES, Rachel Ann	JUL 17 1843
BURGESS, John T.	JONES, Ellen	APR 01 1857
BURGESS, Josaph	SHELTON, Eliza	AUG 05 1837
BURGESS, Mary	TAYLOR, Edward, Jr.	JUN 09 1852
BURGESS, Mary (blk)	MORLEN, Rubin	NOV 26 1839
BURGESS, Mary Ann	NEWTON, Clement	AUG 23 1815
BURGESS, Mary Ann	SMITSON, Alcana	NOV 03 1835
BURGESS, Mary Ann	HULBERT, Joseph P.	OCT 10 1846
BURGESS, Mordica	McDANIEL, Ellen	NOV 05 1838
BURGESS, Rachel	NOKES, Francis	JUL 18 1827
BURGESS, Richard	CRAWFORD, Ann	MAY 16 1816
BURGESS, Samuel	OLIVER, Mary	APR 29 1812
BURGESS, Samuel	DELLINGER, Elizabeth	JUL 14 1815
BURGESS, Sarah	SMITH, Thomas A.	FEB 15 1847
BURGESS, Sarah A.	WILSON, James W.	AUG 09 1843
BURGESS, Sarah Ann	LUSBY, Noah	DEC 25 1820
BURGESS, Sophia	GODDARD, Lawson F.	APR 04 1826
BURGESS, Thomas	JONES, Elizabeth	JAN 25 1816
BURGESS, Verlinda A.	DAVIS, John S.	JUN 08 1837
BURGESS, Washington	LANE, Susan	MAR 27 1834
BURGESS, Washington	HUTCHINSON, Mary	MAR 29 1836
BURGESS, William	MILLARD, Patsey	DEC 30 1828
BURGESS, William B.	HUNT, Susan	DEC 13 1838
BURGESS, William F.	WEAVER, Charity	APR 05 1849

District of Columbia Marriage Licenses, 1811-1858

BURGIN, John F.	McHUGH, Catharine	MAR 25 1854
BURK, John	ANNAM, Mary	MAY 20 1846
BURK, John L.	CROSSEN, Mary Ann	AUG 30 1826
BURK, Maria	FIFE, William	APR 05 1820
BURK, Redmond	QUINLIN, Julian	SEP 01 1852
BURK, Thomas	BAKER, Mary Ann	AUG 23 1823
BURK, William	JARRETT, Eliza	MAR 17 1819
BURKE, Albert	SOLOMON, Sarah Ann (blk)	MAR 20 1850
BURKE, Belle	SHAW, William B.	AUG 30 1856
BURKE, Bridget	SHAUSNESY, John	DEC 02 1854
BURKE, Catharine	BRENNIN, Patrick	MAY 12 1855
BURKE, Catharine	CHAMBERS, Wm.	SEP 14 1855
BURKE, Catherine	MORSE, Julius	DEC 31 1855
BURKE, David	CALLAHAN, Ellen	JAN 03 1831
BURKE, Eleanor	FOYE, Barney	FEB 26 1829
BURKE, Elizabeth	CRIDDLE, Jonathan	NOV 21 1836
BURKE, Ellen	BURKE, Michel	FEB 02 1853
BURKE, Ellen	O'GRADY, Dennis	FEB 06 1855
BURKE, Ellen (blk)	JACKSON, Jacob	MAY 11 1840
BURKE, James	SHIELDS, Sarah	APR 15 1828
BURKE, James	JACKSON, Tracy	NOV 07 1844
BURKE, James	BOLER, Martha (blk)	JUL 12 1855
BURKE, John	WHEATON, Mary W.P.	JAN 04 1812
BURKE, John	McDONOUGH, Mary	DEC 03 1852
BURKE, John	SULLIVAN, Catharine	APR 02 1853
BURKE, John	LYCETT, Catharine	JAN 03 1855
BURKE, John	GORMAN, Catharine	AUG 23 1856
BURKE, John	SPALDING, Mary	JUL 19 1856
BURKE, John T.	SKINNER, Virginia F.	DEC 16 1856
BURKE, Margaretta	ENST, Charles	MAY 07 1853
BURKE, Mary	MARSHAL, Isaac	JAN 01 1821
BURKE, Mary	QUINLAN, Lawrence	JUN 15 1854
BURKE, Mary W.J.	HANDY, Samuel	JAN 27 1835
BURKE, Michel	BURKE, Ellen	FEB 02 1853
BURKE, Rebecca	O'DONNOGHUE, Peter, Jr.	JAN 27 1852
BURKE, Richard	McCORMICK, Mary	MAY 06 1844
BURKE, Richard	MANNS, Rebecca (col'd)	JUN 25 1857
BURKE, Sarah	HOPKINS, Thomas B.	MAY 29 1833
BURKE, Thomas	GRADY, Catherine	MAY 01 1852
BURKE, Thomas E.	BOWDEN, Mary Ann	JUL 15 1844
BURKE, Timothy	MADIGAN, Elizabeth	AUG 12 1854
BURKE, Wesley	GANT, Sarah (blk)	FEB 23 1854
BURKE, William	CODMAR, Julia	JUL 15 1853
BURKE, William	DARITY, Eliza	FEB 09 1855
BURKE, William	SUTTON, Maria Terese	JUN 30 1855
BURKE, [blank]	LYNCH, Dorothy	JAN 30 1843
BURKENNE, George	SCHREIBER, Emilie A.	JUN 18 1853
BURKETT, Eliza Ann	GIRDIN, George	OCT 11 1834
BURKHARDT, Mary A.	LaBARRE, Francis	AUG 20 1853
BURKHART, Lewis I.	PARSON, Mary Ann	OCT 03 1846
BURKHEAD, Ann	VanCOBLE, Aaron	DEC 30 1821
BURKLEY, Catharine	TAYLOR, Sanford	MAR 20 1832
BURL, John McLane	ROEMMELÉ, Mary Ellen	SEP 16 1851
BURL, Rebecca (blk)	BAKER, James H.	AUG 13 1850
BURLEY, Clarisa (blk)	TOPMAN, Alfred	DEC 12 1839
BURLEY, Elizabeth	DULANEY, William H.	OCT 28 1856
BURLEY, Thomas	BRADLEY, Mary (blk)	SEP 07 1836
BURLEY, Thomas	LUCAS, Ann	JAN 13 1857

District of Columbia Marriage Licenses, 1811-1858

BURMAN, Anna A.	MOFFITT, Alexander M.	FEB 04 1847
BURMAN, Martha E.	CAMPBELL, John J.C.	FEB 22 1849
BURMESTER, Sophie	CLAUSS, F.C.	MAY 29 1852
BURN, Mathias	McDONALD, Jane	OCT 27 1817
BURNAY, Caroline A.	DENHAM, Louis R.	APR 21 1852
BURNES, Alice	KELLY, Michael	OCT 25 1856
BURNES, Betsey	DOVE, Hanson	FEB 07 1833
BURNES, Charles	RICE, Mary	FEB 23 1819
BURNES, Elizabeth	HOLTZMAN, Elie	OCT 10 1818
BURNES, Elizabeth	FORTUNE, James	APR 23 1830
BURNES, Henry	WARD, Sarah	APR 06 1858
BURNES, Lucinda	MITCHELL, John	AUG 10 1848
BURNES, Marcia E.	WILLIAMS, William Hy.	APR 25 1844
BURNES, Patrick	KING, Elizabeth	APR 25 1822
BURNES, Rebecca A.W.	RADCLIFF, Wm. S.	OCT 05 1816
BURNES, Samuel	TUCKER, Frances	AUG 22 1854
BURNES, Sarah E.	COCHRAN, George W.	OCT 13 1847
BURNET, William	CLARK, Susan M.	JAN 30 1841
BURNETT, Ann	ALBRETON, James	AUG 01 1818
BURNETT, Barbar	WARE, Thomas	SEP 30 1839
BURNETT, Caroline	KRZYRANOWSKI, Waldimir	DEC 27 1853
BURNETT, Clark	PADGETT, Sarah Ann	SEP 07 1816
BURNETT, Elizabeth	FRERE, Richard	NOV 22 1853
BURNETT, Ellen Louisa	MURDOCK, William D.C.	OCT 26 1833
BURNETT, Henry	WINGETT, Mary Ann	DEC 11 1821
BURNETT, Jane R.	LEVERING, Clinton	JUN 24 1839
BURNETT, Richard	WADE, Mary Ann	FEB 10 1830
BURNETT, Richard	ROTH, Mary	AUG 01 1844
BURNETT, Richard	HILL, Mary Ann	JUN 03 1844
BURNETT, Sarah	WATSON, John R.	APR 13 1820
BURNETT, Sophia	KEALEY, James	SEP 24 1840
BURNETT, William T.	LUXEN, Emma F.	APR 03 1852
BURNETT, Wm.	REDFERN, Mary M.	SEP 22 1838
BURNETTE, Lewis L.	JOHNSON, Mary J.	NOV 03 1857
BURNHAM, Nathan	MUDD, Catherine	JUN 01 1858
BURNS, Benjamin	CROSS, Ann	JUL 28 1836
BURNS, Bridget	CARMAN, Morris	DEC 04 1829
BURNS, Eliza	STEWART, David	MAR 12 1816
BURNS, Eliza	DRISCOLL, Timothy	DEC 15 1852
BURNS, George	BROWN, Ellen	NOV 04 1846
BURNS, George	HAMMOND, Sallie H.	AUG 20 1856
BURNS, Harman	DeSAULES, Julia Louisa	FEB 26 1852
BURNS, Harry	GRAY, Eleanor	MAR 30 1820
BURNS, James	DEAKINS, Elizabeth	APR 06 1813
BURNS, James	WATKINS, Catherine	APR 29 1823
BURNS, James Alfred	BLAKE, Mary Atawa	SEP 05 1837
BURNS, John	DWYER, Margaret	JAN 31 1857
BURNS, John	DUFFEY, Mary	APR 15 1858
BURNS, Kennedy	ROWE, Charlotte Creusa	MAR 22 1813
BURNS, Laurence	TURNER, Louisa	DEC 12 1857
BURNS, Lucinda (blk)	EVANS, David	SEP 29 1830
BURNS, Margaret	HUGHES, Andrew	MAY 07 1857
BURNS, Mary	BELL, James W.	MAR 23 1840
BURNS, Mary	MANNING, Francis A.	JAN 29 1857
BURNS, Mary Ann	FERGUSON, John W.	OCT 30 1847
BURNS, Mary Ann	QUINN, Patrick	JAN 11 1856
BURNS, Mary C.	WELLS, Nathaniel	JAN 23 1856
BURNS, Mary E.	MORAN, Samuel C.	JAN 14 1829

District of Columbia Marriage Licenses, 1811-1858

BURNS, Patrick	KELLY, Mary	JUN 09 1858
BURNS, Robert	YOUNG, Margaret (blk)	MAY 27 1852
BURNS, Samuel F.	SHECKELLS, Harriet A.	JUN 11 1850
BURNS, Thomas	RING, Margaret	JAN 26 1854
BURON, James	MONEY, Jane	JUL 12 1855
BURR, Charles	TIPPETT, Mary Ann	MAR 26 1814
BURR, Cinrod	SGRAN, Henrietta	OCT 26 1835
BURR, David H.	HOWELL, Sophia Augustine	AUG 03 1835
BURR, Elizabeth C.	UPTON, Edward P.	JAN 22 1838
BURR, Frances	ADAMS, Herman C.	SEP 06 1850
BURR, Henry A.	BRESCHARD, Cleophila	AUG 01 1842
BURR, James	DAVIS, Sarah Ann	FEB 04 1846
BURR, John	MULLEN, Sarah	JUN 15 1854
BURR, John R.	FARR, Jane E.	OCT 26 1841
BURR, Rd. R.	THOMPSON, Mary	MAR 14 1823
BURR, Richard W.	RATCLIFF, Fanny A.	JUN 01 1852
BURR, Sarah B.	PEACOCK, John	MAY 05 1842
BURR, Thomas S.	ROBINSON, Elizabeth	SEP 07 1847
BURRE, DeVere	McDANIEL, Sarah	OCT 11 1842
BURRELL, Harry	DAWSEY, Elizabeth	DEC 12 1848
BURRELL, John	GETTYS, Elizabeth (blk)	APR 06 1839
BURRESS, John F.	LEIZEAR, Comfort W.	OCT 04 1838
BURRIS, Alexander	ALLRIDGE, Rebecca	JUN 06 1812
BURRIS, Eliza Ann	BAGGETT, John C.	JUN 16 1845
BURRIS, John	NEVITT, Mary	JUN 25 1812
BURRIS, Nicholas	HOWSER, Sarah	FEB 19 1822
BURRIS, Rebecca	BROOKS, James	SEP 05 1850
BURRIS, Rutha E.	KROUSE, George	APR 03 1856
BURRISS, Benjamin	WALLACE, Clarinda	MAY 05 1828
BURRISS, Hezekiah	ALLEN, Harriet	FEB 28 1843
BURRISS, Margaret Ann	WOOD, Andrew Jackson	AUG 05 1847
BURRISS, Obadiah	PUPO, Harriet	JUL 18 1853
BURRISS, Thomas	TURNER, Mary Ann Davis	JUL 07 1828
BURRISS, William A.	HURLEY, Cornelia	FEB 27 1858
BURROUGH, Mary	SOTHORON, John	APR 05 1856
BURROUGHS, Amanda E.	GORDON, Daniel S.	AUG 29 1853
BURROUGHS, Elizth.	MURRAY, James	DEC 29 1852
BURROUGHS, Hezekiah	McCLARING, E. Ann	DEC 17 1834
BURROUGHS, James	BEARD, Catharine	MAY 31 1855
BURROUGHS, Mary Ann	GROSS, Jacob E.	MAY 14 1851
BURROUGHS, P.B.	QUEEN, Mary Emily	JUN 29 1852
BURROUGHS, Silas M., Hon.	BRINTNALL, Charlotte S.	MAY 11 1858
BURROUGHS, Zedekiah	CONNELL, Rachael Ann E.	DEC 15 1857
BURROWS, Ann	HENDLEY, Michael	AUG 16 1832
BURROWS, Ann	BLACKSTONE, Hamilton	JAN 02 1856
BURROWS, Basil M.	CALHOUN, Elizabeth	MAR 20 1847
BURROWS, Caroline	GATES, James W.	JUL 13 1854
BURROWS, Eliza (blk)	MAHOENEY, Warren	NOV 16 1847
BURROWS, Elizabeth	LEIZEAR, Robert	JUL 16 1839
BURROWS, Emeline	HARRISON, John Thomas	NOV 07 1845
BURROWS, Francis Harriett, Miss	NELSON, John	NOV 18 1816
BURROWS, Hanson Gassaway	BURROWS, Sarah Ann	MAR 04 1844
BURROWS, Henny	ADAMS, Charles	JAN 26 1819
BURROWS, Hezekiah	SHOEMAKER, Mary	JUN 30 1846
BURROWS, John	HOOVER, Elizabeth	DEC 03 1812
BURROWS, John	BATMAN, Elizabeth	OCT 30 1824
BURROWS, John	PHELAN, Elizabeth	JUL 15 1843
BURROWS, Margaret	PHILLIPS, Samuel	SEP 14 1847

84

District of Columbia Marriage Licenses, 1811-1858

BURROWS, Mary A.E.	WARD, Thomas	APR 04 1844
BURROWS, Mary Elizth.	GATES, Charles L.	AUG 29 1848
BURROWS, Mary Virginia	BURROWS, Samuel	APR 01 1845
BURROWS, Obadiah	PAXTON, Cassandria	SEP 28 1840
BURROWS, Rebecca	WILLIAMS, Robert	MAR 08 1852
BURROWS, Samuel	BURROWS, Mary Virginia	APR 01 1845
BURROWS, Samuel	GENTLE, Sarah Ann	JUN 20 1850
BURROWS, Sarah	TATE, Andrew	JUN 07 1813
BURROWS, Sarah Ann	BURROWS, Hanson Gassaway	MAR 04 1844
BURROWS, Thomas H.	DYER, Susan	JAN 17 1842
BURROWS, William	WILKINS, Henrietta	JAN 17 1846
BURRS, Jane E.	AGER, John H.	FEB 04 1858
BURRUSS, Amanda	GATEWOOD, Jackson D.	DEC 28 1854
BURRUSS, Harris D.	DAVIS, Mary E.	DEC 14 1839
BURSON, Tacy	SHOEMAKER, David	OCT 09 1817
BURT, Edmund B.	TENCH, Julia	FEB 21 1852
BURTO, Nicholas	BACKETT, Anna Maria	OCT 07 1815
BURTON, Caroline	STRINGASSER, Joseph	OCT 30 1825
BURTON, Eleanor	NOLAND, Edward	SEP 13 1827
BURTON, John	COLLINS, Mary (blk)	SEP 27 1826
BURTON, Joseph	McDONALD, Eleanor	FEB 14 1830
BURTON, Richard	LATHAM, Mary	NOV 15 1849
BURTON, Sarah	ANDERSON, Thomas Wm.	AUG 23 1850
BURWELL, Elizabeth A.	McCARGO, William T.F.	MAR 09 1850
BURY, Adelaide	WILSON, John H.A.	DEC 12 1846
BURY, Elizabeth A.	BYINGTON, Samuel L.	DEC 03 1828
BURY, John	CALVERT, Anne M.	JAN 03 1852
BURY, Margaret	GALLIVAN, Dennis	NOV 20 1832
BURY, Mary Ann	BALL, Arthur W.	NOV 16 1826
BURY, William	BARKLEY, Eliza	SEP 30 1824
BUSCHER, Henry	WEICHAND, Matilda	OCT 27 1857
BÜSCHING, Henry	HEITMÜLLER, Dorethea	DEC 06 1855
BUSEY, Hezekiah	HITMAN, Elsey	OCT 16 1822
BUSH, Clora Ann (blk)	GRAY, Charles	JUN 16 1853
BUSH, Frances (blk)	SCOTT, Henry	OCT 05 1846
BUSH, Frederick	REED, Margaret	AUG 03 1841
BUSH, Ignatius	MIDDLETON, Chloe Ann	NOV 04 1845
BUSH, John H.	GRAY, Hannah Elizabeth	MAR 25 1837
BUSH, Julia (blk)	CASSELL, William	NOV 11 1845
BUSH, Mary	BUCHANAN, Henry	OCT 30 1832
BUSH, Mary (blk)	FLETCHER, Richard	JUN 07 1849
BUSH, Thomas	WASHINGTON, Cassilla	JUN 21 1854
BUSH, William	CLARK, Lucy	SEP 14 1820
BUSH, William	PAGE, Rebecca	JAN 31 1837
BUSH, William	KERNAN, Mary Ann	MAY 07 1851
BUSHBY, Elizabeth H.	ROBERTS, Jonathan [Hon.]	APR 21 1814
BUSHBY, James H.	BLUME, Catherine Ann	MAR 07 1844
BUSHLEY, Cathn. B.	WAUGH, Beverly	APR 21 1812
BUSK, Thos. Murphy	KING, Caroline	JUL 10 1851
BUSSELL, Jane	MEDCALF, John	SEP 11 1852
BUSTLE, Maria	SMITH, Samuel	SEP 22 1854
BUTCHER, Maria	MATTINGLY, William	DEC 06 1816
BUTHMANN, John H.	DeSAULES, Adile Emile	FEB 14 1849
BUTLER, Abraham	TAYLOR, Eliza Ann (blk)	JUL 19 1837
BUTLER, Abraham	OTRIDGE, Sarah	FEB 07 1839
BUTLER, Alectius	SHORTER, Charity	JAN 31 1818
BUTLER, Amelia (blk)	ARMSTRONG, Jefferson	SEP 07 1850
BUTLER, Ann Maria T.	WARREN, George H.	MAR 23 1847

District of Columbia Marriage Licenses, 1811-1858

BUTLER, Anna	DIGGES, Ignatius	MAY 22 1815
BUTLER, Anne (blk)	PLUMMER, Richard	DEC 20 1841
BUTLER, Augustus	MORGAN, Isabella (blk)	AUG 03 1840
BUTLER, Barbara	HARBERT, John	MAY 18 1815
BUTLER, Benjamin	COOPER, Louisa	JUL 13 1841
BUTLER, Benjamin	PAYNE, Eliza (blk)	APR 10 1850
BUTLER, Betsey (blk)	WARE, George	JUL 28 1831
BUTLER, Bridget	CLARKE, Patrick	JUL 29 1853
BUTLER, Caroline	JONES, William	MAR 19 1832
BUTLER, Caroline	GRAY, Hiram	MAY 31 1847
BUTLER, Cassy	JACKSON, Joseph	DEC 18 1817
BUTLER, Catharine	DETTON, Levin	MAY 15 1821
BUTLER, Catharine A. (blk)	SMITH, Geo. R.	JAN 03 1853
BUTLER, Catherine	MASON, James	APR 13 1838
BUTLER, Cecelia (blk)	LAWRENCE, James H.	DEC 23 1852
BUTLER, Cecelia (blk)	ROBINSON, William	NOV 10 1853
BUTLER, Charity (blk)	MORRIS, Mason	MAR 31 1818
BUTLER, Charles	LUTTLES, Pheba	AUG 07 1828
BUTLER, Charles	JEFFERSON, Cassa Ann (blk)	MAY 10 1845
BUTLER, Charles	GOINGS, Emily (blk)	JUL 31 1854
BUTLER, Chloe	HARRIS, John	JAN 23 1818
BUTLER, Columbus	BLACK, Margaret (blk)	AUG 08 1849
BUTLER, David	SELBY, Frances	NOV 15 1849
BUTLER, David	WATTS, Rebecca (blk)	DEC 05 1850
BUTLER, David, Jr.	COOMBE, Mary	SEP 06 1821
BUTLER, David, Jr. [Capt.]	BEALL, Laura Lee	FEB 07 1828
BUTLER, Edward	BATES, Catharine	MAR 19 1853
BUTLER, Eleanor	BRADFORD, William	FEB 15 1813
BUTLER, Elijah	WALLACE, Susan	FEB 01 1827
BUTLER, Eliza	WHEELER, George	JUN 26 1845
BUTLER, Eliza	LANG, Robert	JAN 13 1847
BUTLER, Eliza J. (blk)	GREEN, George W.	NOV 24 1851
BUTLER, Elizabeth	BROWN, Benjamin	NOV 09 1818
BUTLER, Elizabeth	BEALL, Othy	DEC 27 1825
BUTLER, Elizabeth	DOWLING, William	SEP 02 1851
BUTLER, Elizabeth	BARBER, George	NOV 25 1853
BUTLER, Elizabeth	HOOPER, Thomas	NOV 19 1856
BUTLER, Elizabeth (blk)	DYSON, Charles	APR 12 1831
BUTLER, Elizabeth (blk)	COLE, Raphael	NOV 12 1844
BUTLER, Elizabeth (blk)	BOWMAN, John D.	MAR 09 1848
BUTLER, Elizabeth B.	KITCHEN, Wm.	MAY 11 1818
BUTLER, Elizabeth C.	EARHART, Thomas J.	MAY 06 1837
BUTLER, Emily	BURGESS, Charles	SEP 12 1837
BUTLER, Ferdinand	ABBOTT, Elizth. C.	DEC 03 1853
BUTLER, Flavillar	TORRENS, Manuel	JUL 07 1827
BUTLER, Geneva	THOMPSON, Anthony	JUL 08 1858
BUTLER, George	SAVOY, Jane (blk)	MAR 13 1834
BUTLER, George	HAMILTON, Catharine Ann (blk)	SEP 17 1840
BUTLER, George G.	INGLE, Adeline	JUL 03 1854
BUTLER, Gertrude	MURRAY, Thomas S.	DEC 07 1846
BUTLER, Hannah	KEANE, Stephen	MAY 26 1824
BUTLER, Hannah E.	CURRELL, William	APR 17 1833
BUTLER, Harriet S. (blk)	JACKSON, Louis B.	APR 12 1852
BUTLER, Hellen M.	ROCHE, Francis N.	NOV 22 1854
BUTLER, Henny	RIGHTER, James	MAY 12 1812
BUTLER, Henrietta (blk)	KING, Elisha	NOV 21 1850
BUTLER, Henry	MAHEW, Mary	MAY 18 1815
BUTLER, Henry	WOODLAND, Eleanor	MAY 30 1817

District of Columbia Marriage Licenses, 1811-1858

BUTLER, Henry	JOHNS, Sarah Ann	MAR 15 1831
BUTLER, Henry	CHAMBERS, Ellen (blk)	OCT 31 1833
BUTLER, Henry	HANDY, Sarah	AUG 27 1838
BUTLER, Henry	PRIOR, Sarah Ann (blk)	DEC 13 1839
BUTLER, Henry	HODSON, Mary	NOV 01 1845
BUTLER, Hope Ann	COOK, Alfred	MAY 04 1830
BUTLER, Ignatius	JACOBS, Elizabeth	JUL 08 1818
BUTLER, Jacob	[blank], Casander	JUN 01 1819
BUTLER, James	ROLLINS, Sarah Ann	OCT 15 1829
BUTLER, James	SIMS, Verlinda (blk)	JAN 16 1839
BUTLER, James	DINES, Sarah (blk)	AUG 03 1852
BUTLER, James E.	LAWSON, Henrietta A.	OCT 25 1855
BUTLER, Jane	WATSON, Benjamin	APR 08 1833
BUTLER, Jane	BURGESS, George	JUN 13 1846
BUTLER, Jeason	GAINER, Mary	JUN 26 1854
BUTLER, John	TAYLOR, Catharine	MAR 22 1815
BUTLER, John	CARTER, Elizabeth J.	FEB 26 1820
BUTLER, John	LEWIS, Nancy (blk)	NOV 01 1826
BUTLER, John	SHADDOWS, Louisa	APR 10 1833
BUTLER, John	HOOE, Mary	MAY 03 1842
BUTLER, John	CUSTARD, Mary (blk)	DEC 17 1849
BUTLER, John	COKE, Mary (blk)	SEP 16 1852
BUTLER, John	HARRIS, Agnes B.	MAY 17 1853
BUTLER, John B.	CALDERBAUGH, Francis	NOV 06 1817
BUTLER, John D.	CATLETT, Jane (blk)	NOV 06 1839
BUTLER, Jno. George, Rev.	SMITH, Clara E.	OCT 15 1851
BUTLER, John Lewis	STEVENS, Elizabeth (blk)	DEC 27 1849
BUTLER, Joseph	THOMAS, Matilda	JUL 19 1813
BUTLER, Joseph	HUDSON, Martha F.	DEC 31 1832
BUTLER, Julianna	BARRY, Edward	JUL 25 1850
BUTLER, Kitty	CROKER, Samuel	AUG 04 1821
BUTLER, Letty	WINTERS, Charles	OCT 21 1822
BUTLER, Louisa (blk)	QUALLS, Benjamin	JUL 13 1854
BUTLER, Louisa (col'd)	RANDOLPH, Francis	MAY 30 1844
BUTLER, Lucinda (blk)	DIGGS, Levi	DEC 12 1839
BUTLER, Mahlon	EDWARDS, Harriet	APR 18 1820
BUTLER, Malon	HOLBROOKS, Nancy	AUG 04 1835
BUTLER, Margaret	WILLIAMS, Caesar	JUN 09 1835
BUTLER, Margt. Ellen	TONGE, John	SEP 17 1846
BUTLER, Maria (blk)	BROWN, John	JUN 28 1840
BUTLER, Marian (blk)	TENNY, Andrew	OCT 15 1844
BUTLER, Martha A. (blk)	PARMER, Chas. W.	FEB 06 1854
BUTLER, Mary	WARE, McKimsey	JUN 17 1813
BUTLER, Mary	CRAIG, George	JUN 25 1838
BUTLER, Mary (blk)	BUTTS, Harrison	OCT 17 1850
BUTLER, Mary (blk)	CURTIS, Charles	MAY 02 1853
BUTLER, Mary (blk)	HAWKINS, Henry	JUN 22 1853
BUTLER, Mary C.	OLLIFF, Robert H.	JAN 07 1854
BUTLER, Mary V.	WILSON, Charles E.	JUN 30 1858
BUTLER, Mathias	GANTT, Julia (col'd)	AUG 29 1851
BUTLER, Matilda (blk)	SPRIGGS, Horace	JUL 13 1847
BUTLER, Morgan E.	DAVIS, Mary Jane	FEB 12 1850
BUTLER, Otelia	MAHONE, William	FEB 07 1855
BUTLER, Philip	WILSON, Ann	JUL 12 1828
BUTLER, Rebecca	GRANTON, Michael	FEB 17 1845
BUTLER, Rebecca (blk)	BIRD, William	FEB 05 1849
BUTLER, Rebecca (blk)	JONES, Henry	APR 13 1857
BUTLER, Richard	HATTON, Jane	MAR 18 1841

District of Columbia Marriage Licenses, 1811-1858

BUTLER, Richard C.	PERSLEY, Doretha Ann	APR 17 1856
BUTLER, Robert	DUCHER, Evelina	AUG 14 1818
BUTLER, Robert	BUTLER, Sarah (blk)	MAR 29 1856
BUTLER, Samuel H.	HUTT, Mary R. (blk)	MAR 04 1856
BUTLER, Sanford	TYLER, Serina (blk)	AUG 14 1851
BUTLER, Sarah	BRIEN, Francis	JUL 09 1818
BUTLER, Sarah (blk)	BUTLER, Robert	MAR 29 1856
BUTLER, Susan (blk)	THOMAS, James H.	JUL 15 1829
BUTLER, Thomas	HUTCHINSON, Elizabeth	NOV 14 1838
BUTLER, Thomas	HASLUP, Emily (blk)	DEC 27 1855
BUTLER, Thomas	RIXGLEY, Ellen (blk)	JAN 07 1858
BUTLER, Thomas Henson	MASSEY, Rachel A.	NOV 24 1857
BUTLER, Walter	FLETCHER, Ann (blk)	NOV 29 1841
BUTLER, William	DIX, Hannah	APR 13 1820
BUTLER, William	AMBROSE, Verlinda	FEB 06 1827
BUTLER, William	CALVERT, Louisa	JAN 19 1837
BUTLER, William	SMITH, Clara (col'd)	NOV 07 1837
BUTLER, William	WEBSTER, Cassy Ann (blk)	DEC 07 1843
BUTLER, William	MATTINGLY, Anna Elizth.	APR 20 1848
BUTLER, William	GATES, Martha (blk)	MAR 15 1855
BUTLER, William	LITTLE, Catherine (blk)	MAR 18 1856
BUTLER, William Alexander	WEBSTER, Mary Ann	SEP 11 1852
BUTLER, William H.B.	THOMAS, Mary A.	MAY 24 1854
BUTLER, William Judson	POSTON, Jane	OCT 12 1833
BUTT, Ann Rebecca	BERRY, Christopher C.	DEC 08 1840
BUTT, Easther Ann	WILLIAMS, Benjamin	MAY 01 1834
BUTT, Emeline	OFFUTT, Thomas H.	MAY 20 1857
BUTT, George J.	BENDER, Mary E.	APR 08 1847
BUTT, Jonathan	GENTLE, Emily	SEP 20 1832
BUTT, Matilda	JONES, Nathan	MAY 08 1828
BUTT, Rebecca R.	BEALL, Charles R.	JAN 28 1840
BUTT, Richard	DOUGLASS, Rebecca	DEC 23 1834
BUTT, Samuel	BOGAN, Ann R.	MAY 30 1844
BUTT, Solomon	STEWART, Rebecca M.	APR 06 1844
BUTTCHER, Frederick	YOUNK, Elizabeth	NOV 12 1853
BUTTERFIELD, Franklin	WAILES, Mary N.H.	MAR 15 1853
BUTTLER, Lydia	THOMAS, George	NOV 07 1818
BUTTNER, William G.	HINES, Elizabeth	JUL 15 1835
BUTTS, Harrison	BUTLER, Mary (blk)	OCT 17 1850
BUTTS, Jane (blk)	JOHNSON, Archy	JUN 06 1833
BUTTS, Laffayette W.	WELLS, Mary E.	DEC 18 1843
BUYSEY, John H.	DELAVAN, Jane P.	DEC 28 1854
BYER, James	SHECKELLS, Mary Ann	AUG 30 1852
BYER, Lucy Ann	BURDINE, Alfred	OCT 17 1850
BYERS, Henrietta	BEAGLE, William	SEP 28 1854
BYERS, James F.	ROBINSON, Ellen	AUG 28 1852
BYINGTON, Mary F.	EAKLE, Elias H.	JAN 29 1855
BYINGTON, Samuel L.	BURY, Elizabeth A.	DEC 03 1828
BYNUM, Jesse A.	FUNSTEN, Maria	MAR 19 1835
BYRAM, James H.	REED, Elizabeth	MAY 26 1858
BYRAM, John W.	JUDINGTON, Caroline	JUN 17 1842
BYRAN, John W.	ROBERTSON, Eliza C.	JAN 13 1857
BYRN, Mary	HUNTER, William C.	JUL 22 1851
BYRNE, Bernard M.	ABERT, Louisa	NOV 17 1851
BYRNE, Catharine	PACK, Enos	DEC 30 1818
BYRNE, Catharine	McCARTHY, Charles	FEB 02 1856
BYRNE, Christopher	FARRELL, Maria	JUL 01 1816
BYRNE, Christopher R.	MIDDLETON, Fanny V.	NOV 13 1852

District of Columbia Marriage Licenses, 1811-1858

BYRNE, Frances V.	COLE, Richard F.	OCT 11 1855
BYRNE, James	MAHONY, Catherine	JUN 17 1813
BYRNE, Julia	CASSEY, Patrick	SEP 02 1853
BYRNE, Julia M.	ZELL, Bernard A.	MAY 22 1849
BYRNE, Margaret	MURPHEY, William	NOV 25 1843
BYRNE, Mary	LINNY, Edward	FEB 24 1851
BYRNE, Patrick	PATTERSON, Sarah Ann	OCT 29 1840
BYRNE, Patrick A.	GROSS, Mary Jane	OCT 14 1841
BYRNE, Thomas	HERBERT, M. Josephine	MAY 20 1846
BYRNE, Wm.	REED, Margaret	NOV 09 1821
BYRNES, Dennis	HARDY, Mary	MAY 24 1858
BYRNES, Eliza Ann	STREAKES, Richard W.J.T.	OCT 08 1835
BYRNES, James	KARNEY, Margaret	MAY 01 1858
BYRNES, Margaret	REYNOLDS, John	SEP 19 1857
BYRNS, Michael	WOODS, Sarah	DEC 17 1845
BYRON, Jesse	CLEMENTS, Angeline	OCT 16 1851
BYUS, Matilda (blk)	MINOR, Francis	MAR 27 1858

District of Columbia Marriage Licenses, 1811-1858

C

CABEL, James H.M.	VanZANDT, Nicholas H.	OCT 17 1853
CABEL, Stephen	HAMMOND, Mary	NOV 30 1837
CADDINGTON, Sophia	TAYLOR, John F.	JUN 23 1857
CADEN, Lavinia T.	BRENT, Henry W.	JUN 21 1858
CADEN, Mary Elizth.	McLAUGHLIN, James Alexander	JUN 30 1846
CADLE, Elizabeth	BINGHAM, Thomas	OCT 05 1816
CADLE, Georgiana	PARCELLS, William	DEC 18 1856
CADLE, James Gibson	ROBERTSON, Elizabeth Maria	NOV 23 1835
CADLE, John	BATES, Jane L.	MAY 21 1825
CADLE, Mary	DOWNES, William	MAY 06 1837
CADLE, William	LOWE, Mary Ann	DEC 24 1842
CADMAN, Walter	LEONARD, Mary Ann	JAN 07 1854
CADY, Daniel H.	ADAMS, Rebecca	OCT 23 1845
CADY, William A.	THOMPSON, Nancy	SEP 15 1849
CAGE, William	DEVALL, Mary	JAN 22 1841
CAHIL, Catherine	LEARY, Jeremiah	FEB 13 1852
CAHIL, Ellen	CULINANA, Patrick	FEB 14 1857
CAHIL, Honora	TIERNEY, Michael	NOV 11 1850
CAHILL, Ann	DONN, John	NOV 27 1852
CAHILL, John	SHECKLES, Emily	SEP 17 1825
CAHILL, Margaret	O'CONNER, Francis D.	FEB 09 1852
CAHILL, Mary Ann	CUNNINGHAM, Matthew	SEP 01 1854
CAHILL, William	CAWOOD, Elizabeth	OCT 02 1834
CAHO, Eliza E.W.	DICK, John W.	APR 02 1849
CAHO, Joseph M.	THOMAS, Martha Virginia	MAY 20 1843
CAHO, Mary Elizabeth	LEAK, John H.	OCT 15 1825
CAHO, Susan W.	MORAN, Joseph C.	MAY 08 1848
CAHOE, Mary	O'LEARY, Timothy	JUL 10 1854
CAIN, [George] J.	BURCH, Martha M.	MAY 29 1828
CAIN, James	BALD, Hannah	OCT 17 1820
CAIN, John	CREMIN, Johanna	MAY 24 1858
CALAHAN, Catherine	BARRY, Michael	DEC 27 1843
CALAHAN, Jeremiah	O'MARA, Sarah	JUL 17 1847
CALAHAN, Jerome	DUDLEY, Mary	MAY 05 1855
CALAHAN, Mary Ann	O'BRIEN, William	JUL 13 1833
CALBERT, Bartholomew	BALDWIN, Sarah	APR 12 1851
CALBERT, George	LANCASTER, Christina (blk)	APR 12 1852
CALBERT, Georgeanna (blk)	SALMOND, Francis	MAY 04 1840
CALBERT, John	NELLEGAN, Ellen	FEB 22 1851
CALBERT, Mathew	MOUNT, Joanna	JUN 15 1852
CALBERT, William	JOHNSTON, Sarah	MAY 29 1844
CALBERT, William S.	MORGAN, Sarah T.	JUN 13 1835
CALBOT, Margaret A. (blk)	PARKER, Philip	MAY 11 1853
CALBURT, John	SEDWICK, Susan	SEP 17 1831
CALCUTT, Charles	LAURENCE, Anne E.	AUG 03 1850
CALDER, Hellen M.	SMOOT, J.G.	JAN 20 1841
CALDERBAUGH, Francis	BUTLER, John B.	NOV 06 1817
CALDERWAY, John G.	BAGGETT, Susannah H.	AUG 07 1837
CALDWELL, Armstead M.	HUGHES, Mary Frances	OCT 10 1855
CALDWELL, Hannah	JENKINS, Elisha	JUN 05 1837
CALDWELL, Harriet Maria	SAMMONS, Stephen	JUL 18 1844
CALDWELL, James	McCORMICK, Catherine	NOV 24 1856
CALDWELL, John H.	ROCKET, Mary C.	AUG 14 1855
CALDWELL, John M.	TYLER, Augusta	NOV 01 1853
CALDWELL, Margaret	RODGERS, Thomas Robinson	JUL 11 1855
CALDWELL, Perry	JEFFERSON, Ann Wale	JUL 05 1821

District of Columbia Marriage Licenses, 1811-1858

CALDWELL, Rosa	HARRIS, Michael	DEC 13 1851
CALDWELL, Sarah V.	ZIMMERMAN, Henry F.	AUG 06 1855
CALDWELL, William A.	DUVALL, Margaret M.	AUG 31 1858
CALDWELL, William Mackey	TOWSON, Caroline Evaline Archer	NOV 21 1846
CALERN, Mary	SCHLAB, Christian	JUN 26 1845
CALES, Thomas	JAMES, Sarah Ann	JAN 13 1825
CALHOUN, Amanda M.	POWER, John T.	MAR 07 1855
CALHOUN, Amanda M.	POWER, John F.	FEB 22 1855
CALHOUN, Andrew P.	GREEN, Margaret M.	MAY 05 1836
CALHOUN, Elizabeth	BURROWS, Basil M.	MAR 20 1847
CALHOUN, J. Edward	SIMKINS, Maria E.	FEB 03 1839
CALHOUN, Wm. H.	THOMAS, Cornelia P.	JAN 30 1847
CALHOUND, William	TOWNSAND, Heneretta	FEB 10 1820
CALLAGHAN, Bridget	HANLON, Timothy	FEB 05 1856
CALLAGHAN, Daniel	BARRETT, Mary	JUL 06 1857
CALLAGHAN, David	CALLAGHAN, Mary E.A.	DEC 03 1850
CALLAGHAN, Francis	HERRON, Eleanor	MAY 11 1858
CALLAGHAN, Mary E.A.	CALLAGHAN, David	DEC 03 1850
CALLAGHAN, Mary M.	HARRINGTON, George W.	APR 25 1853
CALLAGHAN, Patrick	DELANEY, Johanna	JUL 06 1852
CALLAGHAN, Patrick	HAGERTY, Mary E.	JAN 26 1856
CALLAHAN, Allen T.	EMNIS, Sarah M.	AUG 28 1852
CALLAHAN, Bridget	SHAAHY, James	DEC 30 1854
CALLAHAN, Dennis	LINDSAY, Mary Ann	DEC 17 1839
CALLAHAN, Ellen	BURKE, David	JAN 03 1831
CALLAHAN, Julia	TAYLOR, William	JUL 12 1848
CALLAHAN, Margaret	HOWSER, Jas.	DEC 10 1822
CALLAHAN, Mary	LEARY, John	AUG 22 1851
CALLAHAN, Michael	O'DONNELL, Mary	DEC 29 1821
CALLAHAN, Richd.	COALE, Jane	MAY 01 1817
CALLAHAN, Thomas	ROWARK, Ann	JUN 23 1830
CALLAHER, Ellen	DURNIAN, Edward	DEC 26 1854
CALLAHER, James	TRUNNELL, Henrietta	AUG 19 1837
CALLAHER, Mary	McINTYRE, Patrick	NOV 24 1857
CALLAN, Alice Elizth.	GRAY, Anthony	MAY 06 1851
CALLAN, Ann	NIXTAIR, Love	DEC 03 1841
CALLAN, Christopher C.	HOLMEAD, Susanna J.M.	FEB 10 1858
CALLAN, Elizabeth	THOMAS, Charles	MAY 10 1845
CALLAN, James	HIGDON, Margaret	NOV 22 1851
CALLAN, Margaret S.	DUFFY, Owen E.	APR 09 1857
CALLAN, Mary Ann	McQUILLIN, Patrick	JUN 03 1824
CALLAN, Nicholas, Jr.	ANDREWS, Christina V.	NOV 15 1841
CALLAN, Peter	DOWNER, Rowine	APR 30 1829
CALLANAN, Ellen	COLLINS, Thomas	FEB 03 1836
CALLENBURG, Francis	HILLEARY, Mary Ann	OCT 17 1837
CALLENDER, Catharine O.	RISTON, Benjamin	NOV 25 1844
CALLENDER, Rebecca	FORSYTH, Joseph W.	MAR 07 1846
CALLENDER, William	MEADE, Octavia	SEP 28 1839
CALLIGAN, Rose	SIMMES, John	AUG 22 1857
CALLIGHAN, Nancy	McGUIRE, Bryan	AUG 16 1855
CALLIHAN, Jeremiah	CLANSEY, Bridget	JUL 04 1853
CALLIN, Monica	WOGAN, John	APR 27 1853
CALLOW, William	ROBERTSON, Jessie	APR 09 1858
CALUNE, Mary	BARRET, John	SEP 20 1851
CALVERT, Anne M.	BURY, John	JAN 03 1852
CALVERT, Betsey	BATTLE, John	JAN 29 1831
CALVERT, Cidney	FARR, William	OCT 07 1834
CALVERT, Elizabeth	CLARKE, Thomas	AUG 12 1851

District of Columbia Marriage Licenses, 1811-1858

CALVERT, George W.	OSBORN, Helen B.	NOV 29 1854
CALVERT, Grace M.	HURDLE, Samuel V.	JUN 17 1850
CALVERT, Harriet A.	WESTCOTT, James	FEB 13 1845
CALVERT, Henrietta (blk)	MAHORNEY, Peyton	OCT 04 1854
CALVERT, John	RODEN, Jane (blk)	AUG 22 1839
CALVERT, John	REED, Susan (blk)	JAN 23 1850
CALVERT, John	REED, Susan (blk)	FEB 20 1850
CALVERT, John James	HURDLE, Frances Marion	NOV 08 1854
CALVERT, Louisa	BUTLER, William	JAN 19 1837
CALVERT, Lydia	ROBERTSON, Chas. F.	JUN 19 1856
CALVERT, Margaret	PALMER, William	OCT 11 1850
CALVERT, Mary Jane	LOWRY, Henry M.	JUN 04 1847
CALVERT, Rebecca (blk)	JACKSON, Henry	FEB 22 1848
CALVERT, Rebecca (col'd)	PETERS, John	SEP 07 1830
CALVERT, Sarah (blk)	JOHNSON, Henry	JUL 08 1854
CALVERT, Susan	JONES, Mark	MAY 21 1840
CALVERT, Thomas	QUEEN, Ann	DEC 27 1821
CALVERT, William	CATTISIES, Susan	OCT 04 1837
CALVERT, William Henry	JAMES, Frances Anna	JUN 08 1854
CALVI, Maria	RAPETTI, Gaetano	APR 28 1847
CALWHITE, Cassy	HINTON, William	MAR 01 1838
CAMACK, Sarah	GIBSON, Richard	FEB 07 1828
CAMALIER, Vincent	KAIL, Catharine	DEC 19 1820
CAMBELL, James	WILBERN, Elizabeth	NOV 11 1829
CAMBELL, John	REYNOLDS, Mary	SEP 16 1813
CAMBERS, Elizabeth	BURGAMY, Joseph	OCT 30 1828
CAMDEN, William	OLIVER, Rebecca	DEC 23 1819
CAMEL, George	HOPKINS, Elizabeth	NOV 27 1832
CAMELL, Eleanor	BURAGE, Thomas	APR 11 1833
CAMERON, Charles E.	SEBASTIAN, Sarah F.	MAR 19 1856
CAMERON, John	EASBURN, Elizabeth Jane	MAY 06 1831
CAMERON, John	WHITE, Mary J.	NOV 06 1856
CAMERON, John A.	MORSE, Susan E.	JAN 16 1854
CAMERON, Joseph	DAVIS, Sarah	MAY 04 1840
CAMERON, Laurentia	CAMERON, Mark L.	OCT 20 1853
CAMERON, Mark L.	CAMERON, Laurentia	OCT 20 1853
CAMERON, Sarah	DUNLOP, Robert	SEP 06 1854
CAMERON, William	BALDWIN, Anna Maria	JAN 07 1850
CAMERON, Wm. H.	WILLIAMS, Susan	OCT 02 1854
CAMFIELD, Charles	PRENTISS, Margaret I.	OCT 10 1844
CAMMACK, Catherine	KING, Henry	AUG 17 1848
CAMMACK, Christopher	CHELL, Elizabeth	MAR 12 1829
CAMMACK, Edmund	ANDREWS, Ann	MAR 29 1821
CAMMACK, Elizabeth	SKIPPEN, John	FEB 09 1818
CAMMACK, Elizabeth Ann	BRADBURN, John D.	FEB 15 1844
CAMMACK, Elizabeth E.	MERROLL, Charles H.	SEP 02 1852
CAMMACK, Hannah	DEWDENEY, John	MAY 10 1827
CAMMACK, Jane	TAVENER, James M.	OCT 06 1852
CAMMACK, Martha	ALLEN, Edward S.	APR 14 1851
CAMMACK, Martha	KIRBY, Henry	MAY 31 1851
CAMMACK, Mary	WILLIAMS, John W.	NOV 14 1846
CAMMACK, Mary	SOUISSA, John, Junr.	MAY 22 1848
CAMMACK, Mary E.	EDMONSTON, Charles	MAR 29 1858
CAMMACK, Rebecca	CORNWALL, Joseph W.	SEP 11 1849
CAMMACK, Thomas	GRAVES, Mary Elizth.	APR 29 1844
CAMMACK, William	CONNELL, Eleanor	AUG 03 1820
CAMMACK, William	TAYLOR, Margaret E.	JAN 13 1851
CAMMEL, Jane	MURPHY, Peter	MAR 26 1830

District of Columbia Marriage Licenses, 1811-1858

CAMMEL, Marlborough	FLETCHER, Jane (blk)	MAY 21 1827
CAMMELL, William	HURBERT, Ugean	JAN 16 1836
CAMMELL, William	HURBERT, Ugean	JAN 16 1837
CAMMICK, Francis C.	BRUNNER, Washington	MAY 20 1846
CAMMICK, William	MOFFIT, Ann	JAN 24 1823
CAMP, Eben	WALLER, Frances E.	SEP 15 1852
CAMP, John W.	COOPER, Harriet E.	FEB 27 1851
CAMP, Joseph W.	ANDREWS, Ellen	MAR 27 1834
CAMPBALL, Ann	KELLEY, Martin	AUG 21 1852
CAMPBELL, Adelia	WHITTLE, John	MAR 10 1828
CAMPBELL, Ann	GRIFFITH, Richard	DEC 28 1812
CAMPBELL, Ann	POTTER, John	SEP 07 1815
CAMPBELL, Ann	MACKAY, William	NOV 30 1817
CAMPBELL, Bartley	BOYLE, Ann	JUN 02 1852
CAMPBELL, Bernard Moore	MOORE, Emily Jane	NOV 15 1854
CAMPBELL, C.M.	WHITNEY, Asa	OCT 01 1852
CAMPBELL, Catharine	WILSON, Isaac	NOV 13 1856
CAMPBELL, Charlotte Q.	SMOOT, John H.	MAY 07 1856
CAMPBELL, Christine V.	MOORE, Fredk. L.	SEP 06 1855
CAMPBELL, Daniel	RODBURD, Jane	OCT 25 1831
CAMPBELL, Draden	CRAVER, Philip	NOV 14 1833
CAMPBELL, Elizabeth	RUSTRIDGE, James	MAY 19 1836
CAMPBELL, Elizabeth (blk)	BROWN, Robert	NOV 14 1837
CAMPBELL, Ellen (blk)	LAWRENCE, James	JUN 26 1855
CAMPBELL, Enoch	DeQUIT, Margaret	DEC 26 1831
CAMPBELL, Enoch Henry	KIDWELL, Rosetta	DEC 03 1849
CAMPBELL, George	WHITTLE, Maria	DEC 27 1828
CAMPBELL, George	JEFFRIES, Jane	MAY 08 1839
CAMPBELL, George W.	WINGARD, Marcaline A.	MAR 24 1835
CAMPBELL, Henrietta	LAY, George W.	JUL 14 1855
CAMPBELL, James	TAYLOR, Eleanor	JAN 19 1825
CAMPBELL, James	SIMMES, Rebecca	AUG 20 1833
CAMPBELL, James	RILEY, Margaret	SEP 26 1853
CAMPBELL, James Mason	TANEY, Anne Arnold	MAY 27 1834
CAMPBELL, James Washington	SHAKES, Selestia Maria Veronaci	SEP 04 1832
CAMPBELL, Jane	GETCHENDENER, Henry	JAN 25 1845
CAMPBELL, Jane E.	McKENZIE, James W.	JUN 02 1858
CAMPBELL, Jean	LEPREUX, Lewis	MAR 19 1822
CAMPBELL, John	MOCLA, Bridget	FEB 19 1852
CAMPBELL, John	MOCKLER, Bridget	OCT 18 1852
CAMPBELL, John A.	BUCKLEY, Eliza	SEP 13 1852
CAMPBELL, John G.	COLFAR, Catharine A.	NOV 25 1853
CAMPBELL, John J.C.	BURMAN, Martha E.	FEB 22 1849
CAMPBELL, John W.	DYER, Mary A.	MAY 02 1840
CAMPBELL, John W.	MOSS, Alcinda	OCT 05 1854
CAMPBELL, Julia	LINKINS, George	MAR 21 1835
CAMPBELL, Julia	MURPHEY, John	APR 01 1837
CAMPBELL, Julia A.	RUSSELL, A.W.	APR 26 1855
CAMPBELL, Julia Ann	SMITH, Jacob A.	DEC 19 1835
CAMPBELL, Kitty (blk)	BROWN, Michael	MAY 21 1823
CAMPBELL, Leonidas C.	KENNEDY, Mary E.	OCT 02 1856
CAMPBELL, Mahaly	PADGETT, John	APR 26 1852
CAMPBELL, Margaret	WILSON, Thomas C.	DEC 16 1835
CAMPBELL, Margaret	GAU, Alexander	FEB 19 1856
CAMPBELL, Margaret	CARROLL, Andrew R.	MAY 12 1857
CAMPBELL, Margaret M.	McLEAN, Charles [Dr.]	APR 16 1832
CAMPBELL, Mary	BROWN, Henson	JUN 19 1832
CAMPBELL, Mary	FRENCH, Thomas	MAY 14 1835

District of Columbia Marriage Licenses, 1811-1858

CAMPBELL, Mary	GOUVERNEUR, Saml. L.	MAR 02 1855
CAMPBELL, Mary Ann	MARTIN, William N.	MAY 18 1814
CAMPBELL, Matilda (blk)	BARKER, Murray	APR 10 1841
CAMPBELL, Patrick	SMITH, Elizabeth	OCT 07 1852
CAMPBELL, Peter	TIMON, Margaret	FEB 05 1856
CAMPBELL, Rebecca	POOR, John	APR 24 1855
CAMPBELL, Rebecca H.	GRAHAM, J. Thompson	FEB 02 1852
CAMPBELL, Rebecca W.	SMITH, John W.	NOV 23 1829
CAMPBELL, Robert	WHITMORE, Betsey	FEB 20 1814
CAMPBELL, Robert G.	BEVERIDGE, Margaret Ann	JUL 18 1835
CAMPBELL, Saml. [Hon.]	QUEEN, Maria Regina	FEB 11 1823
CAMPBELL, Samuel	PAYNE, Martha	JUL 13 1858
CAMPBELL, Statia	MORAN, Peregrine	DEC 09 1812
CAMPBELL, William	GRAHAM, Rachel (blk)	JUN 12 1854
CAMPBELL, William Henry	DeSAULES, Louisa Frazer	OCT 18 1845
CAMPBELL, Wm. H.	INGLE, Mary	MAR 22 1825
CAMPBELL, [torn out]	JARDINE, Lucy Virginia	JUL 02 1847
CAMPITT, Maria	COOMBS, Henry	AUG 26 1822
CANA, Frederick	STATINIUS, Mary	DEC 07 1816
CANADY, Philenia	EATON, Nathan	SEP 19 1816
CANAVAN, Mary	McVARY, Peter	SEP 12 1856
CANDY, John	BICVERS, Anna	JUL 18 1854
CANE, Daniel	HAGERTY, Catharine	FEB 08 1858
CANFIELD, James	RYAN, Ann	OCT 18 1856
CANLER, Levinia (blk)	DICKSON, Thomas	JUN 20 1839
CANN, Catherine	REILY, John	FEB 23 1846
CANNA, John	ROE, Sally McDermot	OCT 18 1814
CANNADY, Caroline	BRANICAN, George	NOV 16 1849
CANNARD, Jaqueline Jamie	JERRIOT, Noel	SEP 10 1825
CANNAVAN, Ann	CRAVEN, Roger	FEB 08 1853
CANNEN, Boil	PETERS, Margaret	APR 18 1820
CANNEN, Sarah Jane	BURGESS, James	JUL 29 1851
CANNIGAN, Daniel	PRATT, Elmira	SEP 10 1818
CANNON, Alice M.	ROSS, Charles A.	SEP 28 1853
CANNON, Ann Eliza	BULL, Enoch	JUN 02 1834
CANNON, Daniel	McCARTY, Mary Jane	FEB 03 1843
CANNON, Jane	McCABA, Andrew	JAN 01 1850
CANNON, John	SHERMAN, Mary	NOV 12 1843
CANNON, Joseph	BEACH, Emily J.	NOV 29 1855
CANNON, Mary	SHEPHARD, William J.	AUG 22 1843
CANNON, Patrick	LLOYD, Catherin	JUL 01 1833
CANNON, Sarah	McDONALD, Walter	FEB 06 1817
CANNON, William H.	CROSS, Sarah	AUG 29 1844
CANNON, William P.	EVANS, Julia A.	NOV 06 1846
CANTATORE, John B.	WAGGAMAN, Sallie	SEP 02 1857
CANTER, Andrew E.	LARNED, Jane	JUL 04 1853
CANTER, Jemima	FORD, Telamanchus	NOV 02 1853
CANTER, Mary	PIERCE, Richard	AUG 31 1841
CANTER, Priscilla	WALKER, Samuel	MAY 07 1814
CANTON, Jane	BROWN, William	AUG 05 1834
CANTWELL, Michael	SHANAHAN, Margaret	APR 19 1856
CAPELL, John A.	MILLER, Ellen E.	JUL 10 1834
CAPERTON, Hugh	MOSHER, Eliza	DEC 27 1842
CAPERTON, John	COKE, Mary E.	APR 03 1856
CAPLAIN, Sosthene Eugene	GARDINER, Josephine Alice	JAN 04 1858
CAPLES, Sarah E.	TANSLEY, Thomas	MAY 03 1851
CAPRETS, Jeremias	HITZ, Anna Magdalena	OCT 28 1846
CAPRON, Erastus A.	BARNARD, Harriet R.	MAY 28 1836

District of Columbia Marriage Licenses, 1811-1858

CAPRON, Harriet R.F.	VINSON, Charles	JUN 03 1851
CAPRON, Henry A.	BRONNER, Eleanor	JUL 01 1835
CAPRON, Rachael	STEEL, Peter	JUL 20 1814
CARAHAN, Sarah	MAHONEY, Dennis	AUG 23 1858
CARAWAY, James	CROWN, Betsey	JUL 19 1816
CARAY, Thomas	MOORE, Annah M.	DEC 10 1835
CARBERRY, Henry	THOMPSON, Maria	APR 15 1817
CARBERY, Catharine	SMITH, Robert E.	OCT 02 1850
CARBERY, Christopher	RILEY, Margaret	NOV 14 1853
CARBERY, Hellen Mary	McSHERRY, James	APR 21 1852
CARBERY, James	CLOUD, Emza	MAY 01 1820
CARBERY, John	KANE, Catherine	FEB 09 1852
CARBERY, Lewis	CLOUD, Artimesia	SEP 09 1817
CARBERY, Martha	CATALANO, Salvadore	JUN 22 1813
CARBERY, Martha L.	SHOEMAKER, Pierce	JUL 17 1855
CARBERY, Mary S.	RITCHIE, Joshua A.	DEC 16 1839
CARBERY, Mrs.	SMITH, Thomas	MAY 27 1856
CARBERY, Thomas	MANNING, Mary H.	NOV 02 1826
CARDEN, Susanna G.	PULLIN, John	JAN 12 1854
CARDEN, Thomas	MOTHERSHEAD, Margaret	JAN 02 1852
CARDENAS, Vincent	GRAY, Elizabeth	FEB 18 1857
CAREW, Rosanna Eliza	WALKER, Singleton S.	OCT 11 1825
CAREY, Bridget	FLYNN, Patrick	APR 28 1852
CAREY, John	AMBUSH, Patience	JUN 06 1812
CAREY, Mary	SULLIVAN, Thomas	APR 09 1853
CAREY, Mary Alice (blk)	JOHNSON, John	JUN 19 1851
CAREY, Verlinda	STEVENSON, Robert	SEP 07 1819
CAREY, William	KERR, Elizabeth	JUL 07 1851
CARL, Margaret	FRANKINBERGER, Charles	MAY 03 1852
CARL, Margaret	HOLSCHUH, John	SEP 16 1852
CARLIN, Ann E.	BENEZETT, Hazael	NOV 25 1834
CARLIN, Anne	HOFFMAN, Frederick	AUG 16 1815
CARLISLE, James B.	ALEXANDER, Maria McCoy	APR 26 1834
CARLISLE, Michael H.	ODEN, Louisa	APR 29 1854
CARLISLE, Rachel N.	TRAMMELL, George W.	APR 23 1857
CARLISLE, Samuel H.	GRIGGS, Mary Virginia	JAN 12 1855
CARLISS, Margaret	O'BRIEN, Michael	MAR 09 1850
CARLON, James	FOYLES, Elizh.	AUG 19 1814
CARLON, Robert	MUNROE, Hannah [Mrs.]	JUN 03 1820
CARLTON, Henry L.	WATKINS, Mary	JAN 29 1833
CARLTON, Henry L.	CLARKE, Ann W.	NOV 07 1843
CARMAN, Margaret	REYNOLDS, Enos	JUN 15 1839
CARMAN, Morriss	BURNS, Bridget	DEC 04 1829
CARMAN, Sarah Ann	SMITH, Thomas	FEB 23 1819
CARMICHAEL, Alexander	PIERCE, Susannah	MAY 02 1826
CARMICHAEL, Edward	PHILIPS, Betsey	MAY 01 1817
CARMICHAEL, Emily	PAGE, Charles	MAY 26 1852
CARMIKLE, Sarah	CUMMERFORD, John	AUG 31 1820
CARMINE, Mary	RICAND, John	APR 03 1816
CARMODY, Avus	HILL, Joseph H.	MAY 11 1858
CARMON, Elsey	ANDERSON, John	DEC 23 1829
CARNES, Charlotte (blk)	BLACK, Gusty	DEC 15 1842
CARNES, Ellen J.	DOLEY, Wilmot W.	JUL 13 1856
CARNES, Isabella	PEARCE, John	JUN 17 1841
CARNES, John	RAY, Mariah	FEB 09 1814
CARNES, Maria	CRAIG, Robert	JAN 04 1821
CARNEY, Alexander	COLLINS, Susan	JAN 08 1820
CARNEY, Bridget	ALLESON, Robert	MAY 30 1821

District of Columbia Marriage Licenses, 1811-1858

CARNEY, Delphia	HICKEY, John W.	JAN 05 1854
CARNEY, Eliza	MURPHY, Benjamin	NOV 03 1817
CARNEY, Julia	O'TOOLE, John	JUL 05 1858
CARNEY, Mary	NOLAN, Thomas	JUN 10 1852
CARNEY, Valentine P.	RISON, Margaret R.	AUG 20 1824
CAROLAN, Catherine	BETTSWITH, John	MAR 18 1817
CAROTHERS, Andrew	GIVEN, Mary Ann	FEB 01 1827
CAROTHERS, Andrew	HOLLAND, Eleanor Ann	SEP 07 1842
CARPENTER, Ann	DEAN, Samuel	FEB 11 1843
CARPENTER, Betsey	PARSONS, John	DEC 03 1829
CARPENTER, Catharine	PETTY, Beverly	FEB 23 1832
CARPENTER, Hamilton A.	MAFITT, Margaret Davidson	APR 25 1839
CARPENTER, Jane E.	ASHTON, Charles	JUN 10 1852
CARPENTER, John A.	PAYNE, Elizabeth	OCT 31 1856
CARPENTER, Lucinda (blk)	HUNTER, George	FEB 18 1857
CARPENTER, Mary	RAGAN, John	JUL 02 1844
CARPENTER, Mary E.	BUDD, John L.	JUN 07 1853
CARPENTER, Mary Jane	WILLIAMS, Samuel	SEP 21 1852
CARPENTER, Patrick	MARTIN, Catherine	MAR 25 1853
CARPENTER, Tamandra	JOHNSON, James H.	JUL 24 1855
CARPENTER, Whittington	ARNOLD, Sophia Alexander	NOV 06 1850
CARPENTER, William	TRAVERS, Eliza (blk)	MAY 24 1853
CARPER, Thomas J.	SLACK, Lydia L.	OCT 10 1856
CARR, Ann R.	MASTIN, William E.	MAY 16 1850
CARR, Artemesia	PETIT, John	FEB 16 1837
CARR, Benjamin	PAUL, Elizabeth	FEB 05 1840
CARR, Caldwell	REYNOLDS, Cornelia	JAN 13 1829
CARR, Edmund	WATERS, Ann Eliza	MAY 16 1848
CARR, Elizabeth	MONDOWNEY, Thomas	JUN 25 1828
CARR, Emily E.	MUDGE, Daniel C.	APR 12 1847
CARR, George	YEOCUM, Louisa	JUL 17 1856
CARR, John	ROGAN, Mary Ann	SEP 18 1852
CARR, John W.	NEWTON, Francis B.	JAN 09 1854
CARR, Julia A.	ETTER, Joseph H.	MAY 20 1844
CARR, Julia A.	HILTON, Joseph H.	MAY 14 1844
CARR, Julia Ann	HILTON, Joseph H.	NOV 30 1843
CARR, Louisa C.	TAYLOE, E. Poinsett	APR 23 1857
CARR, Mary	EDMONSTON, Brooke	JUL 22 1814
CARR, Mary C.	GREER, Chauncey F.	OCT 30 1848
CARR, Mary C.	LEVY, Wesley W.	FEB 14 1857
CARR, Nancy	EDELIN, James	JUL 31 1844
CARR, Nimrod	HAMPTON, Penny	AUG 07 1817
CARR, Susannah C.	COLLINS, Joseph H.	NOV 01 1852
CARR, William E.	McFARLAND, Eliza	JUN 03 1851
CARRAHER, Thomas	FARRALL, Ellen	JUL 26 1858
CARRELL, Michael	CLEAVER, Ellen	DEC 07 1819
CARRICO, Amelia	ARNOLD, James	JUL 24 1856
CARRICO, Ann E.	PRATHER, Overton J.	FEB 05 1830
CARRICO, Dorothy	O'BRIAN, Josephus	JUN 06 1822
CARRICO, Eliza A.	EDELIN, Francis S.	SEP 17 1853
CARRICO, Eliza J.	STIDER, Samuel	MAR 17 1858
CARRICO, James	OWENS, Mary	MAY 17 1815
CARRICO, James	MERILIOR, Susan	MAR 18 1833
CARRICO, Jane R.	SMITH, James F.	AUG 28 1847
CARRICO, John	GIBBONS, Rebecca	MAY 03 1827
CARRICO, Lucretia	PEAKE, James	MAY 01 1841
CARRICO, Mary	GRIFFIN, John	FEB 25 1827
CARRICO, Peter B.	JOHNSON, Mary	FEB 17 1813

District of Columbia Marriage Licenses, 1811-1858

CARRICO, Peter G.	BRADLEY, Elizabeth	JAN 15 1844
CARRICO, Robert L.	BOLEY, Sarah Ann	JUN 20 1853
CARRICO, William	DOWNS, Sophenia	AUG 04 1836
CARRICO, William H.	MOHUM, Rosella Ann	OCT 25 1856
CARRICO, Winny Ann	SMITH, Abijah	AUG 13 1816
CARRICO, Wm. Bartholomew	ANDERSON, Mary Ann Trecy	SEP 29 1821
CARRICOE, John	O'BRIEN, Jane	NOV 16 1815
CARRIGAN, John	FLEMING, Catharan	AUG 28 1855
CARRIGAN, Mary	SMITH, Hugh	APR 25 1856
CARRIGON, Lawrence	CRAILY, Catharine	JAN 23 1852
CARRINGTON, Jane	AMERICA, John	MAR 08 1823
CARRINGTON, William	WATSON, Sophia E.	SEP 26 1854
CARRO, Barny	WILSON, Eliza	AUG 11 1841
CARROLL, Agatha (blk)	WILSON, William	JUN 06 1850
CARROLL, Andrew	THOMAS, Sophia (blk)	JUL 31 1851
CARROLL, Andrew R.	CAMPBELL, Margaret	MAY 12 1857
CARROLL, Ann	HALL, Elexius	JUL 12 1851
CARROLL, Ann	REYNOLDS, Michael	JUN 07 1851
CARROLL, Anne	BROOKE, Clement H.	MAY 08 1817
CARROLL, Bennett	WILBERM, Mary	MAY 01 1826
CARROLL, Charles	DOYNE, Ellen	MAY 19 1836
CARROLL, Charles	MILLSON, Susanna P.	MAY 16 1854
CARROLL, Charles H.	VERMILLION, Susan	APR 17 1827
CARROLL, Daniel	TALBERT, Maria E.	JAN 14 1823
CARROLL, Daniel	LOWE, Darkey	DEC 28 1825
CARROLL, Daniel	MULLEN, Margaret M.	NOV 17 1851
CARROLL, Elizabeth	MAGRUDER, Fielder	MAY 01 1826
CARROLL, Elizabeth	BRENT, Henry J.	JAN 07 1834
CARROLL, Elizabeth	HURDLE, Robert	AUG 15 1848
CARROLL, Elizabeth	CROOK, John Henry	NOV 06 1854
CARROLL, Fanny K.	RAWLINGS, David	OCT 01 1855
CARROLL, Fielder	LEE, Mary (blk)	AUG 22 1855
CARROLL, George W.	SEABORN, Susan I.	JAN 03 1854
CARROLL, Hannah (blk)	BRUCE, Charles	MAR 29 1854
CARROLL, Henry	WINTERS, Margaret (blk)	AUG 24 1826
CARROLL, Horatio	FRYE, Rebecca	JUN 16 1818
CARROLL, Jas.	WALL, Catherine	APR 18 1855
CARROLL, James	LAHEY, Elizabeth	JUN 03 1824
CARROLL, James	NEWGENT, Bessie	MAY 02 1854
CARROLL, James J.	FONES, Frances Ann	MAY 11 1846
CARROLL, James J.	FONES, Frances Ann	MAR 11 1846
CARROLL, Jane	SOPER, George F.D.	FEB 22 1853
CARROLL, John	RICHEY, Margaret	JUL 05 1833
CARROLL, John	DARWIN, Mary	FEB 02 1836
CARROLL, John	MARTIN, Eliza C.	MAR 26 1856
CARROLL, John	MULREIA, Bridget	MAY 10 1856
CARROLL, John B.	BADDEN, Elizabeth	APR 23 1828
CARROLL, John B.	ROSS, Sarah	NOV 19 1833
CARROLL, John Linkins	DIXON, Harriet	OCT 13 1831
CARROLL, John T.	WALKER, Maria C.	OCT 12 1853
CARROLL, Joseph G.	SIMMS, Mary E.	NOV 09 1854
CARROLL, Julia	PHELPS, George	MAY 17 1849
CARROLL, Julia A.	WHITE, Cary W.	NOV 30 1846
CARROLL, Julia Ann	SELF, Bradley	MAY 02 1849
CARROLL, Laurence	WHELAN, Catherine	NOV 11 1856
CARROLL, Margaret	CORRIGAN, Bernard	JUL 17 1848
CARROLL, Maria	FITZHUGH, Robert	FEB 05 1833
CARROLL, Maria	MUNTZ, James	NOV 14 1850

District of Columbia Marriage Licenses, 1811-1858

CARROLL, Martha A.	LANDERL, Louis A.	AUG 13 1850
CARROLL, Mary	ARMSTRONG, Francis	OCT 14 1851
CARROLL, Mary	WARWICK, William D.	NOV 04 1856
CARROLL, Mary Ann (blk)	MINER, James	JUL 31 1832
CARROLL, Mary Ellen	FOGLE, Zachariah	SEP 07 1837
CARROLL, Mary Jane	DEEBLE, John George	JAN 03 1853
CARROLL, Michael	GAEER, Jane	DEC 20 1820
CARROLL, Patrick	CRAIGHEN, Margaret	JAN 27 1853
CARROLL, Peggy (blk)	BROWN, William	SEP 19 1828
CARROLL, Procilla J.	SHIPMAN, John James	DEC 22 1856
CARROLL, Robert T.	CLARKE, Susan C. (blk)	APR 07 1858
CARROLL, Sally	NICHOLSON, Augustus A.	FEB 01 1847
CARROLL, Sarah (blk)	JASPER, Henry	JAN 15 1834
CARROLL, Sarah (blk)	BOND, Levi	APR 01 1857
CARROLL, Sarah Ann	PILES, Charles	DEC 12 1820
CARROLL, Sarah Ann	PRICE, Augustus	APR 08 1837
CARROLL, Sarah Ann	LANDRICK, Edward	JAN 11 1838
CARROLL, Sarah Jane	LONG, Joseph	OCT 04 1854
CARROLL, Susan	FORD, Charles F.	SEP 12 1854
CARROLL, Sylvester	DIAMOND, Mary	SEP 14 1854
CARROLL, Thomas	GOODRICH, Mary	JUN 01 1816
CARROLL, Thomas	O'DONNELL, Mary	AUG 09 1851
CARROLL, Thomas	BRODERICK, Ann	MAY 31 1852
CARROLL, Thomas	FLINN, Margaret	AUG 30 1855
CARROLL, Violetta L.	MERCER, Thomas S.	OCT 01 1856
CARROLL, Virginia	MIDDLETON, Samuel S.N.	MAY 16 1855
CARROLL, Virginia Elizth.	TEMPS, William Henry	NOV 08 1851
CARROLL, Walter	COOK, Susanna H.	FEB 12 1828
CARROLL, Washington	WHITING, Artridge	JUN 04 1829
CARROLL, William	DAY, Elizabeth (blk)	SEP 09 1840
CARROLL, William	GLEASON, Mary	APR 14 1855
CARROLL, William O.	CLIFT, Mary M.	JUN 22 1858
CARSON, Emma F.	SIMPSON, William G.	AUG 23 1856
CARSON, Sarah Ann	QUEEN, Julius B.A.	JAN 18 1856
CART, Sarah	SIMONS, Daniel	OCT 02 1817
CARTEO, Catherine (blk)	ADAMS, Samuel	SEP 03 1857
CARTER, Alice	O'RILEY, Lawrence	AUG 12 1842
CARTER, Ann E.	O'NEAL, Thomas W.	NOV 01 1842
CARTER, Ann Maria A.	GODDARD, [torn out]	JUL 02 1847
CARTER, Anne	LAMB, James	DEC 24 1852
CARTER, Anne (blk)	DATCHER, Galan	AUG 25 1857
CARTER, Catharine	GIBSON, Woolman	SEP 17 1828
CARTER, Catherine	MILLS, William McC.	NOV 10 1857
CARTER, Charlotte (blk)	HUTCHINSON, Jeremiah	JUN 23 1857
CARTER, Edward A.	PETIT, Elizabeth	AUG 18 1841
CARTER, Elizabeth	TUCKER, Francis Asbury	SEP 27 1837
CARTER, Elizabeth	WATSON, Robert	OCT 23 1851
CARTER, Elizabeth	DIXON, William E.	JUN 14 1852
CARTER, Elizabeth	WINFIELD, Richard	SEP 16 1854
CARTER, Elizabeth J.	BUTLER, John	FEB 26 1820
CARTER, Ellen Williams	BOGGS, W. Brenton	OCT 10 1842
CARTER, Emilie P.	MARTIN, Henry C.	NOV 06 1849
CARTER, Frances	MADDOX, William C.	SEP 28 1827
CARTER, Frances A.	GREY, Stephen W.	NOV 19 1829
CARTER, Frances Ann	LAW, John	MAR 18 1815
CARTER, George F.	BRONAUGH, E. Louisa	SEP 05 1850
CARTER, Griffin	JOHNSON, Barbara Ann	SEP 13 1836
CARTER, Gustavus Q.	REDD, Edmonia B.	JUN 02 1857

District of Columbia Marriage Licenses, 1811-1858

CARTER, Henry	LANG, Mary	JAN 17 1833
CARTER, Henry	DALE, Eliza (blk)	MAY 11 1854
CARTER, Jacob, Jr.	SMITH, Mariah A.	OCT 03 1827
CARTER, James	ADAMS, Mary Ann	OCT 27 1814
CARTER, James	BROWN, Delah	OCT 20 1821
CARTER, James	COCKRELL, Elizabeth	FEB 12 1838
CARTER, James	SMITH, Sarah (blk)	AUG 16 1848
CARTER, Jeremiah	CLEMENTS, Etheldra	SEP 10 1857
CARTER, John [Hon.]	MARBURY, Eleanor	FEB 06 1829
CARTER, John	SMALLWOOD, Mary Ann (blk)	JUL 29 1835
CARTER, John C.	BANKHEAD, Ellen M.	JUL 06 1832
CARTER, John E.	WEBSTER, Emeline	AUG 18 1847
CARTER, John H.	GURGUSON, Mary Ann (blk)	JAN 26 1843
CARTER, John Hill, Jr.	LOUGHBOROUGH, Jane	MAY 07 1833
CARTER, John W.	SHACKLETT, Sally T.	OCT 02 1834
CARTER, Joseph	TAYLOR, Fanny	FEB 09 1815
CARTER, Laura Ann (blk)	SHARPER, Samuel	FEB 09 1854
CARTER, Letitia (blk)	WISE, Arthur	JUN 23 1849
CARTER, Libern	LANG, Elizabeth	AUG 24 1833
CARTER, Lucinda (blk)	NASH, Thomas	AUG 24 1840
CARTER, Luke	WILLIAMS, Elizabeth	FEB 15 1821
CARTER, Maria (blk)	SHORTER, James	NOV 04 1851
CARTER, Maria Jane Molin	CLARKE, John James	NOV 12 1853
CARTER, Marion Stewart	RHODES, Hilry H. [Lt.]	MAY 21 1834
CARTER, Martha R.	CROSS, Robert H.	MAY 13 1858
CARTER, Mary	MURPHY, William	NOV 18 1819
CARTER, Mary Ann	QUINN, Bernard	AUG 18 1845
CARTER, Mary L.	THOMPSON, Gillies	JUN 01 1816
CARTER, Rachel	PEARSON, John	JUN 01 1835
CARTER, Richard W.	NORRIS, Sarah	APR 21 1836
CARTER, Robert	MORRIS, Caroline	APR 07 1845
CARTER, Robert	SMITH, Eliza (blk)	MAY 07 1850
CARTER, Robert W.	TAYLOE, Elizabeth M.	MAY 11 1829
CARTER, Samuel P.	POTTS, Caroline C.	JUL 16 1851
CARTER, Sarah	FRAZIER, John	JUN 19 1819
CARTER, Sarah Ann	WHITE, William W.	SEP 27 1825
CARTER, Sarah Maria	STEWART, Townshend	OCT 06 1836
CARTER, Sophia	CLARK, John	FEB 19 1851
CARTER, Susan Sophia	WHITE, William G.W.	JUL 02 1835
CARTER, William	BOWIER, Mary Ann	JUN 15 1832
CARTER, William	GIBSON, Elizabeth	JUL 18 1849
CARTER, Willoby N.	MILSTED, Harriet	DEC 14 1848
CARTER, Wormly	SHACKLETT, Ann	MAR 06 1832
CARTWRIGHT, Alfred G.	SCOTT, Jane	OCT 23 1839
CARTWRIGHT, Joseph W.	PETERS, Adelaid (blk)	FEB 03 1858
CARTWRIGHT, Levin	SOUTHERN, Elizabeth	DEC 30 1826
CARTWRIGHT, Levin T.	KURTZ, Elizabeth E.	JUN 03 1856
CARTWRIGHT, Lewis	DUCKETT, Louisa (blk)	MAY 19 1841
CARTWRIGHT, Mary E.	GODY, William H.	DEC 20 1842
CARTWRIGHT, Norah (blk)	BROWN, Lloyd	DEC 15 1849
CARTWRIGHT, Seth	SINCLAIR, Sarah	AUG 23 1830
CARTWRIGHT, Susan (blk)	JOHNSON, Lewis	NOV 27 1850
CARTWRIGHT, Susan R.	KURTZ, William H.	NOV 28 1849
CARTWRIGHT, William F.	GODEY, Rebecca	AUG 08 1844
CARUSI, Estelle	BIBB, J.J.C.	SEP 03 1850
CARUSI, Jane D.	PETERSON, August Fredk.	JAN 13 1858
CARUSI, Julia	BROWN, Lafayette J.	AUG 12 1857
CARUSI, Philippa	DOVILLIER, Victor Leopold	SEP 12 1851

District of Columbia Marriage Licenses, 1811-1858

CARVELLO, Emanuel	CAUSTEN, Mary Elizabeth	NOV 01 1834
CARVER, B. Franklin	MORSE, Leonora	FEB 04 1857
CARVER, Charles	CRUMP, Frances	AUG 28 1855
CARVER, Elizth.	BEAR, Robert	AUG 18 1828
CARVER, Hiram	MYER, Hannah Zenobia	OCT 19 1815
CARY, Isaa N.	FLEET, Serana	APR 28 1830
CARY, William	DOOLY, Bridget	OCT 20 1852
CASANAVE, Joannah	HOWLE, Park G.	MAY 07 1821
CASE, Martha Ann	GIDINGS, Josias Richard	MAR 26 1850
CASE, Shedrick B.	MYERS, Eliza Ann C.	DEC 20 1837
CASEY, Bridget	MADIGAN, John	DEC 20 1856
CASEY, Ellen	GRANT, Michael	APR 02 1853
CASEY, Francis W.	GIBBS, Margaret V.	MAY 26 1855
CASEY, James	McCARTHY, Catharine	MAY 03 1856
CASEY, Johanna	McCUTE, Richard	AUG 13 1858
CASEY, John	TIERNEY, Catherine	SEP 06 1848
CASEY, John	FLANNIGAN, Mary	SEP 13 1851
CASEY, John	FLAHERTY, Ellen	MAR 23 1852
CASEY, John	SULLIVAN, Catherine	NOV 15 1852
CASEY, Patrick	RONAN, Catherine	JAN 18 1853
CASH, Ann C.	ALSOC, Robert	MAY 27 1854
CASH, Eliza	CASSIDAY, Wm.	JAN 24 1816
CASH, John C.	INGLE, Mary	NOV 23 1852
CASH, Leonard	HALL, Maria (blk)	OCT 03 1855
CASH, Levoy	TYLER, Mary Maria	AUG 13 1816
CASH, London	DORSEY, Mary (blk)	JUL 09 1841
CASH, Mary	SUMMERS, William	MAY 06 1819
CASH, Stacia	SIMMES, George	MAY 29 1834
CASHELL, Samuel S.	GROOMES, Christiana	OCT 22 1839
CASHMAN, Catharine	WELSH, Daniel	DEC 20 1856
CASHMAN, Catherine	CROTTY, Patrick	JAN 12 1853
CASICK, Catharine	SHAAHY, John	JAN 10 1852
CASICK, Patrick	KELLY, Ann	JAN 24 1852
CASPARIS, James F.	HITZ, Christina	DEC 11 1845
CASS, Mary	GITTINGS, George	APR 10 1852
CASSADAY, Susan	WHALAND, William	JUN 09 1852
CASSADAY, Susan	WHALAND, William	MAY 09 1852
CASSADY, Lola Montez A.	MADERIA, W.J.	MAY 26 1853
CASSADY, Margaret	TENNANT, John	FEB 15 1833
CASSEDY, John G.	FOWLER, Sarah D.	JAN 16 1834
CASSEDY, Margaret Ann	DAVIS, John B.	MAY 14 1833
CASSELL, Charles	MURRAY, Sarah	MAY 22 1822
CASSELL, John	MILLER, Mary	SEP 19 1831
CASSELL, John A.	HANEY, Sarah Ann	FEB 23 1832
CASSELL, Sarah E.	DAVIS, William S.	JAN 09 1854
CASSELL, Thomas M.	DANT, Virginia C.	JAN 08 1856
CASSELL, William	STRAIGHT, Mary A.	NOV 04 1839
CASSELL, William	BUSH, Julia (blk)	NOV 11 1845
CASSELLS, Ann	ARMAN, David	AUG 13 1852
CASSEY, Patrick	BYRNE, Julia	SEP 02 1853
CASSIDAY, Wm.	CASH, Eliza	JAN 24 1816
CASSIDY, Eleanor	O'DONNELL, Bernard	NOV 03 1829
CASSIDY, Mary	ASH, Michael	OCT 19 1850
CASSIDY, Rebecca Ann	HAYS, Patrick	NOV 07 1834
CASSIN, Francis	ASHFORD, Rachel	OCT 01 1851
CASSIN, L.M.	COOLIDGE, James	AUG 12 1841
CASSIN, Margaret A.	SPALDING, Hilleary C.	NOV 07 1842
CASSIN, Mary Eliza	DYER, Robert W.	JAN 11 1841

District of Columbia Marriage Licenses, 1811-1858

CASSIN, Stephen	BENTLY, Sophia M.	APR 27 1838
CASSIN, Virginia Jane	SMITH, John Johnson	NOV 04 1857
CASTEEL, John	HUDSON, Martha	FEB 23 1831
CASTEL, Elizabeth	McCAULEY, John	MAR 21 1840
CASTEL, Harriet	CROMWELL, John	DEC 31 1828
CASTEL, Julia A.	JACOBS, Thomas E.	MAR 07 1837
CASTEL, Margaret E.	NOKES, George W.	APR 11 1857
CASTEL, Mary	HIXON, Jonathan W.	AUG 23 1830
CASTELL, Edward O.	BEAN, Jane	JAN 29 1841
CASTELL, Marion	DOBSON, Walter B.	DEC 24 1857
CASTERTINE, Charlotte	MILLER, Adam	MAR 15 1834
CASTLEMAN, Stephen D.	COOKENDORFER, Jane	DEC 13 1843
CASTLEMAN, Thomas	ROE, Norah McDermott	NOV 03 1814
CASTOR, Henry	DOLAN, Ellise	SEP 10 1856
CASWELL, John A.	MINNEITT, Mary	FEB 23 1846
CATALANO, Antonio	OBRIAN, Julia	MAR 27 1820
CATALANO, Salvadore	CARBERY, Martha	JUN 22 1813
CATER, Benjamin	WINKLER, Eleanor	MAY 06 1819
CATER, Ruth Ann	HAVERSTACK, Matthew	OCT 07 1847
CATHCART, Amelia H.	PEABODY, John [Capt.]	JUN 13 1828
CATHCART, Elizth. W.	HUTTON, James	JUL 16 1821
CATHCART, James Leander	BARCLAY, Eliza Jane	AUG 14 1845
CATHCART, Robt.	FRYER, Susan	MAR 30 1822
CATHCART, Thomas J.	BARCLAY, Annie	MAY 22 1855
CATING, Catherine T.	SMITH, John Francis	AUG 03 1857
CATITTON, James W.	McEWING, Mary	SEP 13 1852
CATLETT, George	WASHINGTON, Jane (col'd)	SEP 18 1830
CATLETT, Jane (blk)	BUTLER, John D.	NOV 06 1839
CATO, Elizabeth	FORD, John A.	JUN 06 1829
CATON, Ann	DONN, John	MAY 22 1858
CATON, Eliza J.	FAHERTY, John P.	JAN 20 1852
CATON, Ellen	KENNEDY, Patrick	NOV 29 1843
CATON, George	MOORE, Sarah Haus	MAY 10 1822
CATON, George W.	WOOD, Mary E.	JUL 24 1827
CATON, George W.	JOHNSON, Ruth	JUN 03 1854
CATON, Judith	KELLY, Edward	MAR 30 1815
CATON, Maria	EARL, John	SEP 07 1852
CATON, Mary	KING, James	JUN 27 1828
CATON, Mary	GERNER, Patrick	FEB 01 1838
CATON, Michael	KING, Sally	OCT 16 1819
CATON, Michael	CURRAN, Rosanna	JUL 17 1857
CATON, Patrick	FOOBLE, Sarah Ann	MAY 01 1833
CATON, Patrick	WALLS, Mary Ann	NOV 07 1855
CATON, Patrick	SHURTS, Sarah	JUN 08 1857
CATON, Thomas	HURLEY, Martha Ann	NOV 20 1844
CATON, Thomas	DALE, Ariana	DEC 21 1848
CATOR, George	HUTCHINSON, Matilda	JAN 15 1857
CATOR, John	MARSHALL, Nancy Ann	AUG 20 1838
CATOR, Joseph	DAILEY, Isabella	JAN 05 1852
CATOR, Nancy	RANDALL, Edward	DEC 29 1812
CATTISIES, Susan	CALVERT, William	OCT 04 1837
CATTON, Elizabeth	GILL, Theophilus Anthony	OCT 18 1820
CAUCHLIN, Mary	RAIDY, Maurice	APR 19 1851
CAUFIN, Mary Ann	RAWLINGS, Benjamin	APR 03 1843
CAUGHLIN, Dennis	NOLAND, Margaret	JUL 28 1853
CAUGHMAN, Amelia	PRESTON, Wainwright	NOV 20 1846
CAULBOT, John	CHATMAN, Lutecia (blk)	FEB 07 1854
CAULFIELD, Bernard	McVAY, Bridget	JUN 06 1822

District of Columbia Marriage Licenses, 1811-1858

CAULFIELD, John P.	BIBB, Fillipa Estelle	JUL 21 1856
CAULK, Mary Ann	SKIDMORE, Raymond	MAR 22 1855
CAULK, Phillip R.	BROWN, Lucy Ann	JAN 16 1858
CAUSIN, Amanda	BROWN, Septimus L.	FEB 09 1844
CAUSIN, Amanda	ELLIOTT, William	FEB 09 1844
CAUSIN, Ann M.	WEEDEN, Henry A.	MAR 10 1836
CAUSIN, Elizabeth	TRAVERS, John	APR 22 1824
CAUSIN, Elizabeth	GLOVER, Thomas N.	JUL 09 1852
CAUSIN, Jane Adelaide	CONDICT, Henry	MAR 27 1832
CAUSIN, Julia Ann	SKIDMORE, Samuel	AUG 14 1822
CAUSIN, Mary Jane	WEEDEN, Benjamin F.	APR 13 1843
CAUSSEEN, Samuel	HUGHES, Maria	SEP 26 1820
CAUSTEN, Henrietta J.	SHRIVER, Joseph	DEC 03 1834
CAUSTEN, James H., Dr.	PAYNE, Anna	APR 09 1850
CAUSTEN, Josephine C.	YOUNG, McClintock	NOV 09 1841
CAUSTEN, Mary Elizabeth	CARVELLO, Emanuel	NOV 01 1834
CAUSTIN, Augustus	WARREN, Lucinda (blk)	JUN 20 1844
CAUTHORN, Ophela	BAIRD, Mathew	FEB 14 1832
CAVALCANTI, Anna Maria Francisca deP.	VILLENEUVE, Julius Constantius	MAY 23 1857
CAVANAGH, Arthur	WELSH, Catharine	JUN 29 1857
CAVANAUGH, Michael	REED, Emeline	JUN 06 1839
CAVENAUGH, Ellen C.	DAVIS, George O.	DEC 18 1857
CAVENAUGH, Emily	MURPHEY, Daniel	JAN 02 1858
CAVENAUGH, Margaret	WILSON, Thomas	SEP 09 1840
CAVENAUGH, Mary A.	RAY, William A.	JAN 19 1858
CAVENER, Thomas	RILEY, Mary	MAY 19 1854
CAVENOR, Jane	GOODEN, John	MAR 10 1828
CAVILIER, Josephine	STEWART, Caleb	MAY 26 1853
CAVNAGH, Emily	MURPHY, Daniel	OCT 14 1856
CAVNAUGH, John	HOGAN, Catharine	AUG 11 1836
CAWOOD, Benjn. F.	KENDRICK, Jane	NOV 19 1855
CAWOOD, Elizabeth	CAHILL, William	OCT 02 1834
CAWOOD, John B.	COHILL, Elizth. A.F.	NOV 18 1853
CAYNOR, Nancy	RECTOR, Thompson	JUN 06 1834
CEALIX, Alice	COULTER, Peter	MAR 11 1831
CECIL, Jane	BEAN, Thomas	JUL 26 1851
CECIL, Washington	ADAMS, Elizabeth	SEP 27 1841
CECILL, Thomas	GLOYD, Catherine	AUG 12 1815
CEDERQUIST, Amalie Constanzie	HASSELBACH, Wm. Rudolph	JUL 08 1857
CEPHAS, Sophia	LEE, Sylvester	JUN 10 1850
CEPHAS, Thomas	PENNY, Catharine	MAY 06 1835
CERRICK, John	MADIGAN, Eliza	SEP 27 1855
CESSYL, Thomas	GREENWELL, Monica	AUG 12 1820
CHA__, Elizabeth Jane	WISE, John H.	MAY 23 1845
CHADWELL, Priscilla	HARRISON, John	JUN 27 1844
CHAFEE, William E.	WOOD, Lydia Ann	AUG 03 1850
CHAFFILD, Margaret	ESCH, Michael	JUL 03 1858
CHAFFINCH, Sally	POLKINHORN, Charles	DEC 07 1826
CHAGROO, John	CONNELL, Johanna	AUG 23 1856
CHAILLE, Maria	WALLER, James D.	DEC 29 1830
CHAKE, Henry H.	PENIFILL, Martha A.	FEB 26 1857
CHALMERS, Ann [Mrs.]	WILSON, Offa	SEP 22 1825
CHALMERS, Anthony	FITZSIMMONS, Sarah	MAR 12 1818
CHALMERS, Charles [Lt.]	WATKINS, Anna	JUL 01 1834
CHALMERS, Dorothy Ann	EVANS, Thomas [Dr.]	JAN 10 1828
CHALMERS, John	STONE, Mary	DEC 09 1815
CHALMERS, John, Senr.	WILSON, Ann	JUN 18 1812
CHALMERS, Laura Rebecca Isadore	WATKINS, Octavus	DEC 11 1833

District of Columbia Marriage Licenses, 1811-1858

CHALMERS, Mary Jane	ROSZEL, Stephen C.	JUL 09 1830
CHAMBERLAIN, Amy	PAYNE, Henry	MAR 25 1837
CHAMBERLAIN, Ann	TIPPETT, Thomas J.N.	AUG 09 1830
CHAMBERLAIN, Barbara	REARDON, Daniel	JUN 02 1831
CHAMBERLAIN, Chloe	LEMP, Francis	OCT 20 1817
CHAMBERLAIN, Edward	PRICE, Julianna J.	SEP 22 1828
CHAMBERLAIN, Eliza	MOXLEY, William	AUG 25 1836
CHAMBERLAIN, Elizabeth	STACKS, Joseph	AUG 19 1830
CHAMBERLAIN, George W.	EARP, Ann	JUL 12 1830
CHAMBERLAIN, John U.	WEAVER, Elizabeth	SEP 20 1856
CHAMBERLAIN, Luther	TATTERSON, Martha E.	SEP 24 1849
CHAMBERLAIN, Margaret	POOLEY, Thomas	JUN 21 1828
CHAMBERLAIN, Mary	HOUSTON, Abraham [Dr.]	JAN 13 1835
CHAMBERLEN, Barbara	NICHOLSON, George	JAN 01 1825
CHAMBERLEN, David	GOODRICK, Catherine	OCT 13 1833
CHAMBERLIN, Angemima	BURDETT, Francis	OCT 19 1857
CHAMBERLIN, Mary Elizth.	DRUDGE, William	DEC 20 1856
CHAMBERLIN, Mary L.	THOMAS, Columbus	APR 07 1858
CHAMBERLIN, William	GOWN, Martha	JUN 10 1837
CHAMBERLING, James	BROWN, Louisa	JUL 28 1830
CHAMBERS, Ann Eliza	LUSBY, James H.	SEP 29 1840
CHAMBERS, Benjamin B.	SUIT, Mary F.	MAY 26 1849
CHAMBERS, Charles	COLE, Eleanor (blk)	JAN 07 1829
CHAMBERS, Elenda	HILL, William	NOV 17 1838
CHAMBERS, Ellen (blk)	BUTLER, Henry	OCT 31 1833
CHAMBERS, John	ROLLINS, Eliza	NOV 04 1819
CHAMBERS, John	JEFFERS, Ann	APR 21 1823
CHAMBERS, London G.	ALLEN, Mary G.	APR 04 1820
CHAMBERS, Martha Ellen	KING, Daniel	AUG 08 1839
CHAMBERS, Patrick	NAGLE, Ann	JAN 11 1853
CHAMBERS, Robert H.	BIGGINS, Mary F.	JUN 05 1854
CHAMBERS, William	SHIRLOCK, Catharine M.	APR 14 1846
CHAMBERS, Wm.	BURKE, Catharine	SEP 14 1855
CHAMBLAIN, John	HICKMAN, Catharine	JAN 08 1833
CHAMILLON, Mary A.	O'NEALE, John	DEC 23 1839
CHAMLYN, Elizabeth R.	HUTCHINS, Wm. H.	DEC 25 1850
CHAMNEY, Virginia	SWEENY, Robert	MAY 26 1849
CHAMPION, Lydia	ARNOLD, George L.	JAN 22 1855
CHAMPION, Martha	WEEDON, William C.	JUL 21 1856
CHAMPION, Sarah Ann	ARNOLD, Samuel E.	DEC 10 1851
CHAMPION, William H.	HART, Elizabeth J.	SEP 11 1854
CHANCELLOR, Joshua	KELLEY, Sarah E.	AUG 21 1855
CHANCELLOR, Melzie S.	FRAZER, Lucy F.	NOV 23 1837
CHANCEY, Elizabeth	JOHNSON, Joseph	SEP 25 1851
CHANCEY, John T.	KEENE, Emily Jane	JUL 25 1855
CHANCEY, Lydia A.	HOLBROOK, Charles F.	AUG 01 1857
CHANCEY, Mary Ann	COOK, William H.	MAY 04 1839
CHANDLER, Fanny	PRIOR, George	JUN 26 1819
CHANDLER, James T.L.	KEELING, Mary F.	JUN 15 1839
CHANDLER, Jane	GANTT, Benjn. E.	NOV 02 1826
CHANDLER, Kitty	THOMPSON, John	JUN 26 1824
CHANDLER, Lucy	HAY, Charles	APR 20 1824
CHANDLER, Margaret	HUMPHREYS, Joshua	NOV 28 1842
CHANDLER, Mary Ann	PHEASTER, Obadiah	FEB 06 1845
CHANDLER, Mary Ann	PHEASTER, Obadiah	FEB 04 1845
CHANEY, Annie Maria	STOCKETT, Charles	SEP 09 1854
CHANEY, Christopher C.	FISHER, Rachel Ann	JAN 21 1847
CHANEY, Christopher C.	SHOPE, Laura	AUG 25 1851

District of Columbia Marriage Licenses, 1811-1858

CHANEY, Elijah, Jr.	CORBETT, Mary	OCT 07 1824
CHANEY, Harriet (blk)	DORSEY, Isaac	JAN 08 1835
CHANEY, Levi	MITCHELL, Viletta S.	DEC 12 1839
CHANEY, Lewis	CLARKE, Julia	MAR 25 1845
CHANEY, Mary Ann	GIDDINGS, Joseph	JUL 27 1846
CHANEY, Peter	BROWN, Ann A.	NOV 02 1841
CHANEY, Rignel G.	COALE, Sarah A.L.	APR 07 1831
CHANEY, Samuel	GOLDSMITH, Susannah [Mrs.]	DEC 20 1827
CHANEY, Sarah	WRIGHT, Addison	DEC 28 1812
CHANEY, Thomas	HIDE, Ann P.R.	JUL 11 1842
CHANEY, Thomas S.	MITCHEL, Eliza	APR 22 1819
CHANEY, William	JACKSON, Hannah (blk)	MAY 08 1850
CHANEY, Zachariah	DAVIS, Margaretta	DEC 11 1847
CHAPIN, Erastus M.	WEAVER, Helen M.	MAR 28 1854
CHAPIN, Nathan C.	FOUNTAIN, Mary A.	SEP 28 1854
CHAPIN, Sarah L.M.	LYDNOR, Thomas W.	OCT 15 1840
CHAPMAN, Ann	WILLIAMS, John	JUL 01 1833
CHAPMAN, Bridget	FRANK, Lewis E.	NOV 05 1855
CHAPMAN, Cela	McCALLUM, Andrew C.	MAY 09 1814
CHAPMAN, Charles L.	MILLER, Anne E.	FEB 29 1848
CHAPMAN, Eleanor	YATES, John	JUL 04 1819
CHAPMAN, Emily	FEATHERSTONBAUGH, James D.	JAN 17 1844
CHAPMAN, Fanny J.	DODGE, Francis	JAN 22 1852
CHAPMAN, Georgeanna A.	BLEIGHT, Samuel R.	FEB 12 1846
CHAPMAN, Jane E.	DODGE, Francis, Jr.	OCT 23 1833
CHAPMAN, John	O'BRIEN, Mary Ann	AUG 12 1858
CHAPMAN, Mary	MAGRUDER, Hezekiah	JUN 30 1841
CHAPMAN, Selena Ann	PATTERSON, William G.	APR 29 1835
CHAPMAN, Virginia Clay	NEALE, Christopher	SEP 08 1847
CHAPMAN, Washington	LUCAS, Ann (blk)	MAY 28 1833
CHAPMAN, William	LENMAN, Mary Ann	AUG 26 1839
CHAPPELARE, Wm. H.	BAXTER, Jane Ellen W.	MAY 28 1855
CHAPPELL, Amelia	GRAYHAM, William	JAN 29 1849
CHAPPELL, Clara C.	HURT, Floyd B.	MAY 05 1854
CHAPPELL, Emmert T.	PLANT, Hannah Ann	MAR 13 1851
CHAPPELL, Irene Ann E.	HANES, John W.	AUG 05 1846
CHAPPELL, John E.	WOLFORD, Sara	OCT 30 1849
CHAPPELL, MIranda	NEWCOME, Henry C.	OCT 19 1854
CHAPPULL, Seraphina E.	SMITH, Hilleary M.	APR 03 1848
CHAPTMON, Virginia E.	DUNNINGTON, John F.	OCT 04 1848
CHARLES, Albert	FAY, Ann	NOV 04 1851
CHARLES, Catharine	WHALEN, Stephen P.	DEC 23 1834
CHARLES, Eliza	ROBINSON, John G.	OCT 15 1822
CHARLES, Maria	SMITH, William	MAR 24 1835
CHARLES, Mary Ann	HARWOOD, Samuel	JUN 21 1821
CHARLES, Mary Ann	FLOYD, John Brintnall	OCT 25 1848
CHARLES, Samuel M.	BEERS, Mary Ann	NOV 08 1838
CHARLES, Wm. B.	SMALLWOOD, Jane K.	APR 18 1822
CHARLTON, Henry	LACEY, Agnes	NOV 19 1853
CHARLTON, Secelem	SCOTT, James	JUL 23 1829
CHARLTON, Thomas	GATCHELL, Mary Jane	MAR 28 1837
CHARLTON, Thomas	PEGG, Amanda	NOV 10 1842
CHASE, Anna (blk)	POWELL, John	AUG 24 1840
CHASE, Chloe Ann (blk)	YOUNG, William	AUG 18 1840
CHASE, Daniel	CHASE, Sarah	MAR 26 1851
CHASE, Daniel	FRASIER, Sarah A. (blk)	APR 28 1857
CHASE, Elizabeth (blk)	FRISBY, William	FEB 26 1844
CHASE, Hamilton	MARTIN, Elizabeth	NOV 04 1854

District of Columbia Marriage Licenses, 1811-1858

CHASE, Harriet (blk)	PARKER, Joseph	JUL 09 1855
CHASE, Henrietta	DOWNS, Solomon	JUN 01 1837
CHASE, Maria (blk)	WATTS, Lewis	MAY 06 1858
CHASE, Patsy	LOGGINS, LEvi	MAY 27 1840
CHASE, Saml.	McCOY, Ann Eliza	JUL 12 1854
CHASE, Samuel [Hon.]	WHETCROFT, Mary Frances	JUN 24 1828
CHASE, Sarah	CHASE, Daniel	MAR 26 1851
CHASE, William	DADE, Margt. (blk)	JUL 10 1855
CHASE, William	LINKINS, Margt. E.	DEC 30 1856
CHATMAN, Lutecia (blk)	CAULBOT, John	FEB 07 1854
CHAUNCEY, James W.	HUNTER, Virginia E.	AUG 28 1856
CHAUNCEY, Jane Eliza	KEITHLEY, Francis	NOV 03 1846
CHEATHAM, Thomas M.	HALL, Sopha L.	JUL 11 1855
CHEDAL, James D.	NALLY, Martha Ann	APR 27 1836
CHEEK, Nancy	FRIZELL, Robert	SEP 26 1837
CHEEVER, Benjamin H.	HUGHES, Anna Maria	SEP 08 1842
CHELL, Elizabeth	CAMMACK, Christopher	MAR 12 1829
CHELL, Mary	McKELDEN, John C.	APR 28 1831
CHENEY, Joseph Warren	MAGEE, Mary A.F.	JUN 14 1849
CHEROKEE, Elizabeth (blk)	GREENS, Jacob	SEP 14 1839
CHERRY, Dominick	HURDLE, Ann	FEB 08 1813
CHERY, Clayton	KNOWLES, Lethe A.	SEP 05 1849
CHESELDINE, Geo. W.	COMPTON, Rosa L.	NOV 22 1855
CHESER, Adeline	BEACH, James Henry	JUN 22 1854
CHESER, Elizabeth	PARKS, Ruebin	JAN 07 1831
CHESHIRE, Ann Louisa	FORD, Stephen Calvert	SEP 03 1833
CHESHIRE, Archibald	SHANKS, Rosanna	MAY 11 1813
CHESHIRE, Jane Allen	DAVIS, Jeremiah	JUN 06 1849
CHESHIRE, Mary	PIPER, John R., M.D.	NOV 06 1845
CHESHIRE, Rosina	INGLE, Henry	MAY 02 1843
CHESHIRE, Samuel J.	CLIFFORD, Jane	FEB 21 1856
CHESHIRE, Shadrach	SIMPKINS, Mary Jane	MAY 11 1844
CHESLEY, Elizabeth (blk)	DICK, Robert	FEB 18 1851
CHESLEY, Nathaniel D. [Dr.]	HARRY, Mary Ann	OCT 30 1844
CHESLEY, Robert	TALBERT, Maria	OCT 28 1828
CHESLEY, Zadock C.	THORNTON, Jane E.B.	OCT 30 1817
CHESSER, Ephraim	HALL, Adeline	JUN 12 1850
CHESTER, Eliza L.	DUNCANSON, John A.M.	JUN 17 1828
CHESTER, Emeline M.	REYNOLDS, Richard	AUG 29 1829
CHEW, Adeline (blk)	DARE, Henry	MAR 12 1838
CHEW, Arthur	CHISLEY, Terry (blk)	JUN 25 1840
CHEW, Charlotte (blk)	BROCK, Perry B.	NOV 04 1852
CHEW, Daniel	CRYER, Mary Jane (blk)	JUL 25 1843
CHEW, Diana (blk)	BALL, Griffin	APR 01 1840
CHEW, Edward B.	FERRELL, Frances M.D.	OCT 31 1845
CHEW, Ellen (blk)	CRUISER, William	FEB 14 1843
CHEW, Henry M.	HAW, Elizabeth Ann	JAN 14 1833
CHEW, John	MOGGEY, Matilda	MAY 17 1835
CHEW, John	RILLEN, Mary	DEC 06 1842
CHEW, Mary E.	LANGLEY, Gabriel	JUL 18 1846
CHEW, Phillip	BRUCE, Nancy	JUN 14 1827
CHEW, Robert Smith	SMITH, Elizabeth R.	JAN 26 1842
CHEW, Rosina	MILLER, George	FEB 23 1854
CHEW, Samuel B.	BAKER, Elizabeth A.	FEB 22 1823
CHEW, Thomas R.	GRAYSON, Mary C.	NOV 07 1854
CHEW, Walter B.	SCOTT, Mary C.	APR 28 1828
CHEWNING, Mary E.	CURTIS, Wm. A.	MAR 17 1849
CHEZLEY, William	COAL, Ann	OCT 19 1820

District of Columbia Marriage Licenses, 1811-1858

CHICHESTER, Elizabeth	JEWELL, Smallwood R.	SEP 09 1834
CHICHESTER, Savannah	HATERWAY, Nancy	OCT 04 1822
CHICHESTER, William D.	BAILLIO, Emily A.	NOV 11 1856
CHICHESTER, William S.	TALIFFERO, Jane E.	NOV 06 1834
CHICK, Eliza	REINTZEL, John	OCT 05 1837
CHICK, Joseph	ROBEY, Chloe	MAR 10 1812
CHICK, Richard T.	STICKLE, Mary Ann	OCT 21 1845
CHIDRESS, Lavenia	PUMPHREY, Arthur G.	MAY 11 1854
CHIELER, George	CLINE, Catherine	OCT 04 1856
CHILD, Mary A.	HALL, Alexander C.	JUL 20 1857
CHILDRESS, Mary A.	MAY, James R.	SEP 18 1854
CHILDS, Asaph K.	INGLE, Susan B.	JAN 17 1856
CHILDS, Elizabeth A.	SULLIVAN, William J.	SEP 29 1849
CHILDS, Henry	KENNEDY, Jane H.	JUN 23 1824
CHILDS, Lewis H.	AGER, Margaret Ann	JUN 11 1832
CHILDS, Margaret Ann	DONALDSON, John Thomas	MAY 12 1836
CHILDS, Mary Y.	WREN, John R.	SEP 01 1827
CHILDS, Melvina	AGER, Uriah H.	NOV 14 1832
CHILDS, Robert	DAVIS, Jane E.	MAR 05 1855
CHILDS, S.D.	EVANS, Cora C.	AUG 28 1858
CHILDS, Theresa A.	ROGERS, John T.	AUG 12 1851
CHILDS, Wentworth L.	MURDOCK, Louise	NOV 12 1855
CHILES, Elizabeth	GLOVER, William	DEC 06 1816
CHILES, Samuel A.	RATCLIFF, Mary	APR 23 1818
CHILTON, Robert S.	BRENT, Mary Virginia	MAY 12 1852
CHINGE, Lucinda	GOLDIN, John	FEB 22 1842
CHINK, Jesse	PRATHER, Sarah E.	JAN 16 1856
CHINN, Georgiana (blk)	SIMS, Thomas	JAN 26 1858
CHINN, John F.	ABBOTT, Elizabeth (blk)	OCT 02 1854
CHIPLEY, Sarah E.	WHITMORE, Jno. F.W.	JUN 11 1851
CHISIM, Jane V.	NASH, William	APR 26 1854
CHISLEDINE, Elizabeth	THOMPSON, John T.	MAY 16 1845
CHISLEY, Richard	BROOKE, Betsey (blk)	JAN 10 1815
CHISLEY, Terry (blk)	CHEW, Arthur	JUN 26 1840
CHISM, Elizabeth	GROVER, Charles	APR 01 1839
CHISM, John	WILLIAMS, Catharine Ann	NOV 03 1836
CHISM, Lewis	RHAY, Sarah Ann	APR 01 1830
CHISM, Lewis	PARKER, Elizabeth	DEC 27 1832
CHISM, Mary	JOHNSTON, Thomas	FEB 11 1834
CHISM, Wm. L.	REMINGTON, Ruth A.	SEP 13 1853
CHISOM, George	MOHLDER, Elizth.	APR 13 1848
CHIZEM, Catharine	NICHOLS, George M.	FEB 07 1853
CHOATE, Warren C.	BENNETT, Susan G.	AUG 14 1839
CHOCHRAN, Thos. L.	DORSEY, Mary E.	AUG 09 1853
CHOPPER, William	LUTREL, Matilda	JUL 19 1841
CHOPPIN, Mary E.	HARRY, Joseph U.	MAY 10 1854
CHOTARD, Henry	MINOR, Stephania	OCT 14 1851
CHOUTEAU, Charles P.	GRATIOT, Julia A.	NOV 24 1845
CHRISMOND, Oscar B.	SCANLON, Jane	OCT 12 1857
CHRISMOND, Sarah Jane	INSCOW, Uriah	FEB 26 1849
CHRISTELL, Mary Ann	CONNER, Thomas	FEB 06 1850
CHRISTIA, Agness	ROBERTSON, Thomas	JUL 21 1817
CHRISTIAN, Caroline C.	WALKER, James C.	APR 15 1851
CHRISTIAN, Laura N.	PATE, Robert W.	MAY 07 1849
CHRISTIAN, Maisa	PAPAN, Christina	JAN 21 1833
CHRISTIE, Francis C.	GARNER, Mary Kate	JUN 16 1857
CHRISTINE, Henry A.	NOTT, Josephine B.	NOV 04 1854
CHRISTOPHER, Andw.	GALLAGHER, Elizabeth	AUG 04 1855

District of Columbia Marriage Licenses, 1811-1858

CHRISTOPHER, Mary Ann	FITZGERALD, Edmund	APR 29 1825
CHRONYAN, Philip	REED, Sarah	JAN 09 1819
CHUB, Henry	MARTHA, Ann	FEB 01 1816
CHUBB, Charles St. John	WARRINGTON, Eliza Crane	APR 03 1850
CHUBB, Mary Virginia	WARNER, George, Jr.	OCT 27 1856
CHURCH, Alfred	SLATER, Ellen (blk)	OCT 20 1845
CHURCH, Ammasa F.	MANSFIELD, Sarah	OCT 07 1836
CHURCH, Catherine	GETTINGS, Alexander	DEC 13 1815
CHURCH, Charles B.	HARRIS, Matilda S.	MAR 04 1847
CHURCH, Comfort	TUNEY, William	JUL 17 1844
CHURCH, Eleanor	HUTCHINSON, James	JUL 30 1850
CHURCH, George C.	WALL, Catharine E.	OCT 16 1852
CHURCH, Joseph	PEARSON, Linny	JUL 10 1832
CHURCH, Mary (blk)	CURTIS, John	JUN 05 1849
CHURCH, Richard	FUGETT, Sarah Jane	NOV 29 1833
CHURCH, Sally	HYATT, Samuel	MAR 24 1814
CHURCH, Sally	HOOPER, Sandy	SEP 20 1815
CHURCH, Sally	VanRESWICK, Wilford	MAY 18 1826
CHURCH, Samuel	STEPHENSON, Amelia	MAY 15 1827
CHURCH, William	AUSBURN, Sarah Ann	JUN 09 1835
CHURCH, William E.	SCARCE, Eleanor A.	JAN 01 1840
CHURCH, William J.	TEASDALE, Emma H.	JAN 22 1857
CHURCHILL, Lewis F.	DREW, Harriet A.	DEC 30 1849
CHURCHMAN, Elizabeth	HILTON, Thomas	JAN 17 1844
CHURN, James	GRAY, Emeline	MAY 21 1840
CHURN, James	OSBORN, Jane	MAY 20 1848
CHURNE, James	McDONALD, Priscilla	SEP 18 1852
CIDER, Mary	COOMBES, Ignatius	NOV 21 1818
CIPPERLY, Clara M.	HALLEY, Richard T.	NOV 07 1855
CISSEL, Elizabeth Rebecca	CLABAUGH, William	JAN 15 1851
CISSEL, George W.	GATRELL, Ellenora	NOV 23 1857
CISSEL, Mary C.	CLARK, Lemuel F.	DEC 30 1851
CISSEL, Richard S.T.	BARNARD, Mary C.	DEC 26 1850
CISSEL, Sarah Ann	TAYLOR, Thomas	DEC 09 1847
CISSEL, Thomas	LAMBERT, Eliza	MAR 16 1826
CISSEL, Virginia	BROWN, Stephen T.	JAN 25 1855
CISSELL, Ann	CRAWFORD, Samuel	FEB 25 1837
CISSELL, Catharine	HALL, Benedict	JAN 04 1844
CISSELL, Elizabeth	NAUGHTON, Leonard	NOV 30 1831
CISSELL, Jackson	MAGRUDER, Eliza J. (blk)	DEC 03 1853
CISSELL, John Granison	STROTHERD, Anne Elizth. (blk)	AUG 23 1856
CISSELL, Maria	SCRIVNER, John	JUL 31 1823
CISSELL, Richard	WHITE, Olivia	JAN 07 1858
CISSELL, Salene E.	BROWN, Ann	FEB 05 1843
CISSELL, Sarah C.	WOOD, Benja. P.B.	JUN 30 1855
CISSELL, Thos.	WILSON, Mary L.	OCT 22 1857
CISSELL, William	GROVES, Sarah	MAY 10 1841
CISSELL, William	GITTINGS, Christia	DEC 21 1841
CISSILL, George	GRIFFIN, Ann	DEC 24 1832
CLABAUGH, William	CISSEL, Elizabeth Rebecca	JAN 15 1851
CLACK, Mary L.	WHEELOCK, Edward W.	DEC 19 1854
CLAGETT, Benjamin D.	BENNETT, Mary	JUN 08 1819
CLAGETT, David	COLLINS, Ann (blk)	OCT 03 1832
CLAGETT, Henry B.	FULLER, Elizabeth D.	APR 01 1845
CLAGETT, Jane H.	COMPTON, John S.	APR 13 1818
CLAGETT, John B.	GUNNELL, Margaret	NOV 14 1848
CLAGETT, Martha E.	ADDISON, Henry	JAN 04 1821
CLAGETT, Mary Ann	THOMPSON, Smith	APR 23 1846

District of Columbia Marriage Licenses, 1811-1858

CLAGETT, Mary F.	WOODS, James S.	DEC 08 1852
CLAGETT, Sarah Ann	WILEY, John	JUN 20 1816
CLAGETT, Thomas	OFFUTT, Jane Maria	MAR 11 1834
CLAGETT, William	TUTOR, Elizabeth	DEC 26 1855
CLAGETT, William D.	YOUNG, Sarah	APR 20 1819
CLAGETT, William H.	CLARE, Mary Adele	SEP 01 1857
CLAHERTY, Anthony	SHERIDAN, Catharine	JAN 25 1858
CLAIR, Ann	BROWN, Nehemiah	FEB 28 1838
CLAIR, Peter	WEST, Catharine	DEC 31 1833
CLAMPETT, William Henry	COOK, Eliza Margaret	MAY 04 1847
CLAMPIT, Maria	SINCLAIR, John	MAR 29 1832
CLAMPITT, Annie	STEWART, Leo P.	SEP 01 1857
CLAMPITT, William H.	HILLEARY, Catherine	JAN 28 1836
CLANCEY, Margaret	MARONEY, Michael	NOV 22 1851
CLANCEY, Mary	GEERHAGAN, James	AUG 13 1857
CLANCY, Honora	NEENAN, Thomas	AUG 30 1856
CLANCY, Mary	GREEN, Henry T.	JAN 10 1853
CLANSEY, Bridget	CALLIHAN, Jeremiah	JUL 04 1853
CLANSEY, Margaret	GRANT, Michael	JAN 02 1855
CLANSEY, Michael	FLEMING, Bridget	AUG 04 1853
CLANSEY, Peter	FEENEY, Sarah	SEP 14 1853
CLANSEY, Susan	HOLOHAN, Simon	JUN 15 1854
CLANSY, Bridget	MORAN, Patrick	OCT 19 1854
CLANSY, Catharine	FLANY, John	OCT 04 1854
CLANSY, Margaret	MAGUIRE, Martin	APR 18 1853
CLANTICE, William R.	PUTTS, Mary M.	MAR 28 1855
CLAPDORE, Amelia	GALDNER, William F.	MAR 16 1853
CLAPDORE, Jacob H.	TAYLOR, Ann V.	APR 26 1855
CLAPHAM, John	BARBER, Ann Maria	FEB 10 1851
CLAPON, John	HOWARD, Elizth.	NOV 13 1855
CLARE, Araminta	LITTLE, James	JUL 20 1841
CLARE, Mary Adele	CLAGETT, William H.	SEP 01 1857
CLAREY, Roger	YOUNG, Elizabeth	SEP 12 1843
CLARK, Ann	DYKES, William	JAN 11 1827
CLARK, Ann P.	BIRCHHEAD, Edward	DEC 22 1818
CLARK, Bainbridge S.	SNYDER, Armedia	DEC 17 1855
CLARK, Cantwell	BOOTES, Elizabeth	DEC 12 1837
CLARK, Caroline [Mrs.]	TAYLOR, Garrett	JUN 11 1829
CLARK, Catharine	HARVEY, James	FEB 11 1817
CLARK, Christine	CLEMENTSON, Edward	DEC 30 1829
CLARK, Christopher	PARISH, Mary Ann	DEC 27 1827
CLARK, Cornelius	ADAMS, Martha (blk)	APR 14 1842
CLARK, Cornelius	BROWN, Mary	APR 24 1847
CLARK, Edward W.	FOYLES, Ann	JAN 26 1813
CLARK, Eliza	McCUBBIN, Nicholas	OCT 01 1839
CLARK, Elizabeth	BLACKMAN, William	JUL 26 1830
CLARK, Elizabeth A.	WARING, Thomas B.	FEB 27 1855
CLARK, Emma	ELLIOTT, Lynde	DEC 24 1828
CLARK, Frances M.	SMITH, John P.	JUN 22 1853
CLARK, Gustavus A.	ADAMS, Catharine J.	AUG 02 1837
CLARK, Henry	DAVIS, Eliza	DEC 26 1837
CLARK, Isaac	WHITE, Eleanor	OCT 13 1831
CLARK, J. Thomas	COCKRELL, Cornelia J.	JAN 16 1849
CLARK, James [Hon.]	THORNTON, Margaret E. [Mrs.]	MAR 03 1829
CLARK, John	GODFREY, Matilda	AUG 27 1838
CLARK, John	HAMILL, Margaret Ann	APR 22 1842
CLARK, John	CARTER, Sophia	FEB 19 1851
CLARK, John	CLAVALOUX, Mary	SEP 15 1855

District of Columbia Marriage Licenses, 1811-1858

CLARK, John F.	STETTINIUS, Julia	JUN 07 1831
CLARK, John M.	EMERSON, Alethea	JUN 11 1829
CLARK, Lawson A.	KNOTT, Catherine	JUN 06 1815
CLARK, Lemuel F.	BURCH, Frances O.	MAY 09 1848
CLARK, Lemuel F.	CISSEL, Mary C.	DEC 30 1851
CLARK, Lucy	BUSH, William	SEP 14 1820
CLARK, Maria	MULLER, Frederick	OCT 01 1839
CLARK, Mary	DEAN, Charles	JUN 19 1828
CLARK, Mary Ann	McMILLAN, John	SEP 07 1838
CLARK, Mary Ellen	LOVELESS, John W.	FEB 15 1854
CLARK, Mason E.	FULLER, Ruth	JUN 06 1831
CLARK, Matilda	HAWKINS, Saullimon	APR 28 1819
CLARK, Matilda D.	ANGNEY, Isaac	MAY 02 1856
CLARK, Otho	CULP, Susan (blk)	JAN 29 1840
CLARK, Priscilla	PORTER, Normand M.	OCT 24 1840
CLARK, Robert C.	GIBSON, Hester Ellen	AUG 30 1844
CLARK, Ruth	SCAGGS, George B.	NOV 09 1857
CLARK, Samuel	HAGERTY, Ann	JUN 30 1827
CLARK, Samuel	TURNER, Mariam	FEB 04 1845
CLARK, Samuel C.	HOLTZMAN, Eliza Ann	SEP 18 1839
CLARK, Sarah	BROWN, Archibald	NOV 23 1830
CLARK, Shelby	WOODWARD, Lizzie A.	JUN 20 1855
CLARK, Stephen	SAVOY, Elizabeth A. (blk)	MAY 04 1850
CLARK, Susan M.	BURNET, William	JAN 30 1841
CLARK, T. Edward	BLAND, Jane Maria	MAY 11 1857
CLARK, Teresa (blk)	JONES, Aaron	MAY 18 1857
CLARK, Thomas	WALKER, Fanney	JUN 19 1822
CLARK, W.S.	MILLSTEAD, M.E. (blk)	SEP 25 1855
CLARK, Wesley	YATES, Elizabeth (blk)	APR 22 1858
CLARK, William	KIRBY, Delia	APR 14 1823
CLARK, William	BOSWELL, Uriah	AUG 14 1829
CLARK, Wm. H.	SERGSTACK, Margaret E.	DEC 19 1843
CLARKE, Alexander	FARR, Rebecca	OCT 24 1814
CLARKE, Alice	WINTERS, William	FEB 12 1813
CLARKE, Anastasia	DAY, Edward William	APR 18 1854
CLARKE, Ann	HENNING, John	DEC 02 1813
CLARKE, Ann	GORDEN, William	JAN 21 1828
CLARKE, Ann	TRUXEL, William	JUN 08 1830
CLARKE, Ann	TILLEY, John	JUN 17 1835
CLARKE, Ann	BOSNELL, William	DEC 29 1854
CLARKE, Ann (blk)	DIGGS, George	SEP 19 1833
CLARKE, Ann M.	NASH, Michael	JUN 20 1850
CLARKE, Ann Maria	BRISCOE, Richard G.	NOV 21 1831
CLARKE, Ann Octavia (blk)	GANTT, Benjamin	JUL 20 1853
CLARKE, Ann W.	CARLTON, Henry L.	NOV 07 1843
CLARKE, Anna M.	HOWARD, William T.R.	JAN 11 1858
CLARKE, Arthur T.	SEARS, Charlotte	NOV 09 1847
CLARKE, Benjamin	HARRIS, Eleanor	DEC 20 1823
CLARKE, Bernard	TYLER, Henrietta (blk)	JUL 10 1856
CLARKE, Catharine C.	FURGUSON, Henry W.	OCT 18 1848
CLARKE, Catherine (blk)	LEMMON, Dennis	JUL 17 1845
CLARKE, Charles	MURRAY, Ann	MAY 10 1856
CLARKE, Charles G.	ELSEY, Christiana	JUN 22 1820
CLARKE, Charlotte	WATSON, Alexander R.	APR 20 1822
CLARKE, Christine	TURNER, William	JAN 15 1833
CLARKE, Christopher C.	WHITAKER, Maria C.	DEC 19 1850
CLARKE, Daniel B.	CRIPPS, Ann Maria	JAN 14 1847
CLARKE, Daniel D.	JARBOE, Mary L.	JAN 29 1856

District of Columbia Marriage Licenses, 1811-1858

CLARKE, Drady Ann	COLEMAN, Andrew S.	JUN 08 1833
CLARKE, Edward	PIERCE, Valinda	JAN 15 1839
CLARKE, Eleanor	RAY, Josiah	MAY 12 1831
CLARKE, Eliza	BELL, John	OCT 07 1819
CLARKE, Eliza [Mrs.]	BRACKENRIDGE, James W.	JAN 04 1820
CLARKE, Elizabeth	COLE, Richard	AUG 25 1830
CLARKE, Elizabeth	MARKWARD, George W.	SEP 01 1846
CLARKE, Elizabeth (blk)	DORSEY, Hamilton	MAY 16 1844
CLARKE, Elizabeth C.	BACON, Peter	JAN 25 1838
CLARKE, Ellen	TONGE, Richard	MAR 04 1851
CLARKE, Ellen E.	NOYES, George S.	JUN 18 1833
CLARKE, Ellen Marian	SMITH, Richard S.	FEB 02 1837
CLARKE, Emeline	BRENGLE, Henry	JUN 29 1847
CLARKE, Fanny	ANDERSON, Luke	AUG 03 1854
CLARKE, Frances L.	OBER, John	JUN 19 1851
CLARKE, George W.	MILLER, Eliza W.	SEP 16 1841
CLARKE, George W.	HUTCHISON, Huldah C.	NOV 01 1855
CLARKE, George W.	TROTER, Charlotte Maria	APR 29 1858
CLARKE, Harriet A.	FUGETT, Benjamin	JUL 30 1855
CLARKE, Henrietta	RICHARDSON, John	APR 29 1837
CLARKE, Henrietta E.	GLOVER, William	MAR 23 1846
CLARKE, Henry	DIX, Matilda	FEB 16 1828
CLARKE, Henry A.	RUMPFF, Mary Emily	NOV 20 1845
CLARKE, Isaac	GODDARD, Ann [Mrs.]	OCT 07 1819
CLARKE, Isaac	FRANKLIN, Elizabeth (blk)	SEP 07 1848
CLARKE, James	OSBORNE, Lucinda	JUN 02 1818
CLARKE, James	JACKSON, Eliza A.	FEB 08 1848
CLARKE, James A.	BEARDSLEY, Mary A.	SEP 12 1844
CLARKE, James A.	LACKEY, Jane E.	OCT 29 1856
CLARKE, James B.	YOUNG, Elizabeth W.	NOV 22 1844
CLARKE, Jane	POOR, John	DEC 18 1817
CLARKE, Jane	DAVIS, John	JUL 17 1834
CLARKE, Jane	FAIRBANKS, George M.	FEB 26 1852
CLARKE, Jane Eliza	GODY, Walter	APR 29 1840
CLARKE, Jane Elizabeth	SOLLERS, William	SEP 30 1837
CLARKE, Jane Elizabeth	PATTEN, Larkin	OCT 25 1848
CLARKE, Jane [Mrs.]	MEIGS, Samuel	NOV 23 1815
CLARKE, John	GOODRICK, Ann	NOV 24 1836
CLARKE, John	JORDAN, Elizabeth	NOV 14 1840
CLARKE, John	LEE, Adeline M.	MAR 06 1849
CLARKE, John D.	JAMESON, Terese C.	JUN 14 1814
CLARKE, John F.	EVERETT, Rebecca	OCT 05 1835
CLARKE, John George	MECKLIN, Bertha Maria	OCT 03 1854
CLARKE, John James	CARTER, Maria Jane Molin	NOV 12 1853
CLARKE, John M.	BOSWELL, Ann M.	SEP 01 1849
CLARKE, John P.	SHINN, Mary V.	AUG 14 1851
CLARKE, John T.C.	DORSETT, Jane E.	MAY 31 1842
CLARKE, John W.	YOUNG, Kate	NOV 07 1853
CLARKE, Jos. H.	MUDD, Jane	AUG 30 1821
CLARKE, Joseph	BARNET, Elizabeth	JUL 15 1815
CLARKE, Joseph C.R.	DAWES, Julia	JUN 08 1857
CLARKE, Joshua	NAYLOR, Ann Maria	NOV 04 1856
CLARKE, Julia	CHANEY, Lewis	MAR 25 1845
CLARKE, Laura O.	RHEES, William J.	NOV 12 1856
CLARKE, Louisa	KIDWELL, James	OCT 29 1838
CLARKE, Lucinda J.	WILLIAMS, Thomas W.	JUN 23 1858
CLARKE, Lucy	HUGHES, John	OCT 02 1828
CLARKE, Lucy	FRY, Henry B.	APR 09 1831

District of Columbia Marriage Licenses, 1811-1858

CLARKE, Margaret	JOHNSON, Albert W.	NOV 02 1857
CLARKE, Marsaline	HOLTZMAN, Christopher C.	AUG 18 1842
CLARKE, Martha	MOORE, Robert	MAR 29 1855
CLARKE, Martha Ann	PHELAN, Nicholas	APR 14 1853
CLARKE, Mary	O'NEAL, Paul	MAY 09 1822
CLARKE, Mary (blk)	JOHNSON, Abraham	APR 05 1850
CLARKE, Mary A.	TUNE, Steptoe T.	SEP 29 1846
CLARKE, Mary A.	McPHERSON, Henry H., Jr.	OCT 08 1850
CLARKE, Mary Ann	SANFORD, Bushrod	MAY 04 1849
CLARKE, Mary Matilda	REMINGTON, James	MAY 05 1834
CLARKE, Melton	BEARDSLEY, Susanna	FEB 08 1851
CLARKE, Owen	ORR, Sarah (blk)	SEP 23 1840
CLARKE, Parker P.	AIKEN, Mary Ellen	DEC 09 1844
CLARKE, Patrick	BUTLER, Bridget	JUL 29 1853
CLARKE, Rachel	THOMAS, John	APR 08 1829
CLARKE, Reubin B.	THOMAS, Margaret E.	DEC 26 1848
CLARKE, Richard	BERKLEY, Harriet	DEC 02 1846
CLARKE, Richard W.	BARRETT, Mary A.	FEB 21 1852
CLARKE, Robert	MOORE, Louisa	DEC 12 1815
CLARKE, Robert	McGRATH, Jane	NOV 04 1819
CLARKE, Robert	TALBURT, Martha A.	APR 11 1837
CLARKE, Robert C.	[torn out]	JUN 03 1847
CLARKE, Robert T.	CLARKE, Sarah A.	JUN 16 1857
CLARKE, Ruth Ann	HARKNESS, George W.	SEP 06 1836
CLARKE, Samuel T.	MARYMAN, Josephine	DEC 12 1850
CLARKE, Sarah (blk)	PARKER, Philip	JAN 02 1840
CLARKE, Sarah A.	CLARKE, Robert T.	JUN 16 1857
CLARKE, Stephen	BATEMAN, Emeline (blk)	APR 22 1856
CLARKE, Susan	O'NEALE, Thos.	MAR 05 1821
CLARKE, Susan C. (blk)	CARROLL, Robert T.	APR 07 1858
CLARKE, Susannah	HARLEY, Wesley	MAY 09 1833
CLARKE, Thomas	NEVIT, Harriet	JAN 04 1821
CLARKE, Thomas	CALVERT, Elizabeth	AUG 12 1851
CLARKE, Thomas	FRENCH, Elizabeth	FEB 25 1854
CLARKE, Thomas	CLUTZ, Lucretia	MAR 17 1856
CLARKE, Thomas E.	LEE, Sarah Jane	JUN 25 1846
CLARKE, Thompson	SMITH, Dolly	DEC 26 1833
CLARKE, Timothy	WEST, Eleanor	SEP 30 1848
CLARKE, Virginia	LEWIS, Joseph Knowles	OCT 16 1854
CLARKE, Walter	BOONE, Rachel	SEP 20 1814
CLARKE, Wesley	HAWKINS, Ellen (blk)	JUN 12 1854
CLARKE, Willbur	FERRIS, Elizabeth N.	APR 12 1856
CLARKE, William	LAUVALL, Catherine	DEC 07 1815
CLARKE, William	BRYAN, Mary	MAR 13 1817
CLARKE, William	BEVENS, Mary Ann	JUN 01 1833
CLARKE, William	KELLEY, Elizabeth	MAY 20 1839
CLARKE, William D.	LYONS, Amanda	AUG 30 1852
CLARKE, William H.	DRAKE, Elizabeth	NOV 20 1849
CLARKE, William T.	TALBOT, Lucinda	JAN 29 1835
CLARKE, William T.	HUNT, Amelia	MAY 07 1840
CLARKE, Winifred	KELLY, Thomas	JAN 12 1852
CLARKSON, Jacob	COLLEY, Eliza An	FEB 15 1817
CLARKSON, Joseph	TYREL, Mary A.E.	JUN 15 1844
CLARKSON, Robert	SEIFERT, Caroline	JUL 28 1853
CLARKSTON, Harriet	YOUNG, Owen	JAN 30 1827
CLARNCEY, Michael	MANAY, Ann	AUG 02 1856
CLARVOE, John A.W.	BEYER, Rosella	SEP 25 1856
CLARVOE, John H.	SOMMERS, Mary Elizabeth	JUN 19 1844

District of Columbia Marriage Licenses, 1811-1858

CLARVOE, Mary Ann H.	JACKSON, George C.	SEP 30 1844
CLARY, Amanda J.	RAY, Albert	APR 21 1851
CLARY, Catharine	COLLITA, Thomas	OCT 25 1856
CLARY, James	DORON, Hannah	FEB 15 1858
CLARY, Mary	COSGERY, James	APR 12 1853
CLASHEM, Bridget	DONLEVY, John	JUL 05 1853
CLAUSS, F.C.	BURMESTER, Sophie	MAY 29 1852
CLAVADETSCHER, Lucien	BIHLER, Rosalie	SEP 23 1845
CLAVALOUX, Mary	CLARK, John	SEP 15 1855
CLAVELEUX, J. Marc	MURRAY, Mary	DEC 22 1849
CLAXTON, A.B.	FISHER, E.J.	JAN 05 1854
CLAXTON, Amelia A.	DAVIS, Richard	FEB 02 1858
CLAXTON, C.F.	PALMER, Wm. Henry	JUN 25 1833
CLAXTON, Catharine A.	LUCKETT, Robert P.	MAR 01 1858
CLAXTON, Martha	COLLINS, Edward W.	AUG 16 1830
CLAXTON, Richard W.	LUCKETT, Catharine Ann	OCT 27 1829
CLAY, Amanda M.	KEESE, Geo. P.	NOV 26 1822
CLAY, Edward	COST, Mary	SEP 16 1823
CLAY, Joseph A.	FLETCHER, Cornelia	MAR 12 1835
CLAYTON, Elizabeth A.	TRAINER, William W.	NOV 24 1850
CLAYTON, James R.	WILLIAMSON, Virginia E.	APR 12 1852
CLEARY, Bridget	FITZGERALD, Patrick	JAN 29 1855
CLEARY, Catharine	McKENNA, Phelix	AUG 13 1850
CLEARY, Catherine	GALLAGHER, Michael	OCT 09 1857
CLEARY, James	HARRIS, Caroline	JUN 22 1852
CLEARY, Mary	MENGIN, Morris	MAR 31 1857
CLEARY, Maurice	SHERHEN, Margaret	OCT 18 1856
CLEARY, Patrick	LYCETT, Johanna	JAN 04 1856
CLEAVER, Ellen	CARRELL, Michael	DEC 07 1819
CLEAVER, William Evans	WEST, Sarah	JAN 17 1852
CLEMANS, Josias	ADAMS, Mary Jane	DEC 20 1852
CLEMENS, Joseph M.	DEVERS, Amarion	JUL 08 1852
CLEMENS, Martha A.	BALLINGER, Francis	OCT 31 1850
CLEMENS, William	STUART, Sarah Ann	MAY 12 1851
CLEMENSON, Ellen	HOWELL, Thomas	JAN 15 1849
CLEMENSON, William Henry	SCHADD, Henrietta	FEB 07 1854
CLEMENTS, Alban	PEAK, Eliza	SEP 12 1823
CLEMENTS, Alexander	MARTIN, Eliza	JUN 14 1853
CLEMENTS, Aloysius N.	VONDALIER, Elizabeth	NOV 09 1843
CLEMENTS, Andrew J.	HERD, Ann E.	FEB 17 1855
CLEMENTS, Angeline	BYRON, Jesse	OCT 16 1851
CLEMENTS, Ann	VERMILION, John	AUG 17 1815
CLEMENTS, Ann	GIDDINGS, John	JAN 18 1819
CLEMENTS, Ann Matilda	MARTIN, Robert	JUN 13 1854
CLEMENTS, Benjamin	SANNER, Rebecca	APR 15 1843
CLEMENTS, Ben<u>nett</u>	HYDE, Eliza	AUG 05 1817
CLEMENTS, Caroline Virginia	WOOD, Samuel M.	MAY 19 1856
CLEMENTS, Catherine S.	HILGARD, Jules E.	AUG 28 1848
CLEMENTS, Charles	LUCKETT, Ellen	JUN 19 1851
CLEMENTS, Dorcas A.	BROOKS, Howard	JUL 13 1842
CLEMENTS, Dorothy	WAGNER, Henry C.H.	FEB 05 1851
CLEMENTS, Edmund	DAWNING, Hester Ann	FEB 01 1849
CLEMENTS, Eleanora C.	DANT, Thomas E.	JAN 27 1835
CLEMENTS, Elizabeth	RIDGEWAY, John	NOV 30 1820
CLEMENTS, Elizabeth	GOLDSMITH, William	JUN 02 1851
CLEMENTS, Elizabeth	RODIER, Charles H.	NOV 17 1853
CLEMENTS, Ellen Virginia	McLEAN, Thomas	APR 22 1852
CLEMENTS, Emeline	LAMBERT, Isaac	AUG 14 1855

District of Columbia Marriage Licenses, 1811-1858

CLEMENTS, Etheldra	CARTER, Jeremiah	SEP 10 1857
CLEMENTS, Francis	BROWN, Margaret	OCT 07 1823
CLEMENTS, Francis	HANSON, Mary Ann	NOV 10 1832
CLEMENTS, Francis H.	HIGDON, Ellen	JUN 11 1838
CLEMENTS, Harriet	MOORE, Alexander	MAY 25 1815
CLEMENTS, Ignatius	CUNNINGHAM, Jane	JAN 27 1857
CLEMENTS, Ignatius N.	STODDARD, Mary Ann	SEP 14 1844
CLEMENTS, Johanna	HILL, Isaac	AUG 22 1831
CLEMENTS, John	GLOSTER, Susanna	AUG 30 1816
CLEMENTS, John F.	McCLEARY, Marion J.	MAR 18 1856
CLEMENTS, John Francis	OGLE, Rebecca Ann	OCT 21 1833
CLEMENTS, John T., Jr.	BRUSH, Mary S.	MAR 02 1857
CLEMENTS, John Thomas	LARNER, Eliza [Mrs.]	JAN 08 1830
CLEMENTS, John W.	HURLEY, Elizabeth R.	FEB 28 1848
CLEMENTS, John W.	COGSWELL, Sophia Jane	OCT 18 1848
CLEMENTS, Joseph E.	HILL, Mary E.	DEC 24 1850
CLEMENTS, Josephine E.	O'BYRNE, Dominick A.	APR 16 1855
CLEMENTS, Margaret	HURLEY, John W.	AUG 29 1853
CLEMENTS, Martha	THOMPSON, John W.	JAN 09 1821
CLEMENTS, Mary	ARMSTRONG, James	JUN 22 1821
CLEMENTS, Mary A.	COOK, John F.P.	APR 20 1835
CLEMENTS, Mary Ann	DALY, James	APR 20 1846
CLEMENTS, Mary C.	BLACKSTOCK, George C.	JUL 17 1854
CLEMENTS, Mary E.	ELLIOTT, Richard G.	AUG 07 1844
CLEMENTS, Mary E.	JEWELL, William	AUG 06 1858
CLEMENTS, Mary Elizabeth	SHAFFER, John	AUG 06 1845
CLEMENTS, Mary Ellen	LEISHEAR, Francis	MAY 23 1856
CLEMENTS, Matilda	BAYNE, James	NOV 18 1824
CLEMENTS, Oswald	DOBYN, Petronelia	NOV 26 1834
CLEMENTS, Rachel Amelia	HENRY, James	MAR 03 1852
CLEMENTS, Rebecca	FORD, John G.	JAN 27 1818
CLEMENTS, Rebecca	STEVENS, Henry	SEP 22 1857
CLEMENTS, Richard J.	FAVIER, Malvina R.L.	JAN 31 1856
CLEMENTS, Robert	ECTOR, Mary	OCT 16 1851
CLEMENTS, Robert S.	NOKES, Mary	APR 27 1820
CLEMENTS, Rosanna	ADAMS, George F.	MAY 17 1856
CLEMENTS, Sarah A.	DOVE, Robert W.	NOV 07 1853
CLEMENTS, Stephen C.	BOYLE, Isabella M.	NOV 19 1857
CLEMENTS, Susan	ABLE, John B.	JAN 13 1813
CLEMENTS, Susanna	RODIER, James	NOV 10 1842
CLEMENTS, Terese	COX, Francis	FEB 20 1821
CLEMENTS, Thomas	JAMESON, Charlotte	JAN 27 1812
CLEMENTS, Thomas	SUMMERS, Dorcas	JUL 26 1821
CLEMENTS, Thomas	HAWKINS, Mary	APR 13 1847
CLEMENTS, Thomas	PUMPHREY, Sarah	NOV 25 1857
CLEMENTS, William	MANKINS, Ellen	JAN 10 1832
CLEMENTS, William	BROWN, Ann	JAN 04 1833
CLEMENTS, William	WEBSTER, Ann Maria	JUN 24 1847
CLEMENTSON, Ann H.	LAUCK, Robert M.	OCT 13 1847
CLEMENTSON, Edward	CLARK, Christine	DEC 30 1829
CLEMENTSON, Eleanor	YOUNG, Robert	NOV 07 1827
CLEMENTSON, Jane C.	LOWE, Thomas	JAN 18 1858
CLEMENTSON, John	McKIM, Sarah	MAY 22 1818
CLEMENTSON, Sarah	GRAHAM, Alexr.	OCT 07 1815
CLEMENTSON, Sarah A.	PENDEL, S.F.	DEC 01 1852
CLEMENTSON, William H.	HUSLER, Caroline	NOV 29 1823
CLEMENTSTON, Edward	POWER, Jane	JUN 17 1844
CLEMMONS, John	SHIPLEY, Catharine	JAN 06 1823

District of Columbia Marriage Licenses, 1811-1858

CLEMSON, John, Jr.	CROSS, Louisa	MAY 15 1855
CLEPHANE, Catherine	GRAY, James L.	JAN 18 1858
CLEPHANE, James	OGILVIE, Ann	OCT 10 1819
CLEVELAND, Caleb	ELLIS, Minty	JAN 01 1829
CLEVELAND, John	WALKER, Nancy	APR 02 1839
CLEVELAND, Louisa	BAYLISS, George R.	JUL 21 1848
CLEVELAND, Maranda M.	LACY, Beverly J.	AUG 17 1847
CLEVELAND, Sarah E.	OWENS, Elias	FEB 03 1858
CLIBER, Jacob	HEPBURN, Ann	MAY 26 1832
CLICK, John H.	YOKUM, Josephine C.	DEC 31 1849
CLIENT, Agnes	PUMPHREY, James B.	MAR 08 1856
CLIFF, Ephelinda	KENNEDY, Younger	SEP 11 1849
CLIFFORD, Ann Lucretia	BROOKE, Lawrence	JUL 02 1831
CLIFFORD, James	MULHOLLOM, Sarah	FEB 12 1853
CLIFFORD, Jane	CHESHIRE, Samuel J.	FEB 21 1856
CLIFFORD, Margaret	KING, Shirley	APR 17 1858
CLIFT, Mary M.	CARROLL, William O.	JUN 22 1858
CLINCY, Patrick	GRANT, Margaret	SEP 09 1851
CLINE, Catharine	HILDNER, Jacob	JUL 18 1855
CLINE, Catherine	CHIELER, George	OCT 04 1856
CLINE, Mary Elizabeth	PUMPHREY, Benjamin F.	JUL 28 1858
CLINKSCALES, Delila	BIRD, Spencer	JAN 20 1827
CLINTON, Mary Ann	WILSON, William F.	MAY 29 1846
CLINTON, Thomas G.	JOHNS, L. Rebecca	MAY 22 1854
CLIPT, James C.	FOWKE, Eliza R.	JUN 18 1849
CLITZ, John M.B.	BOHRER, Mary L.	SEP 20 1842
CLOAK, Caroline	EMMETT, Henry	NOV 26 1829
CLOAKEY, Jane	WIGFIELD, James	MAY 09 1814
CLOAKEY, John	STANDAGE, Marcia	NOV 08 1830
CLOAKEY, Mary	BAXTER, James	OCT 08 1828
CLOAKLEY, Richard	SIMMS, Betsey (blk)	JUL 12 1828
CLOAKLY, Philip H.	FREEMAN, Eleanor F.	APR 08 1824
CLOCK, Frances Ann	ROBEY, Tobias	MAY 06 1858
CLOCK, Fredericke	HAGER, Christopher	DEC 16 1837
CLOKEY, John	DARNES, Susan A.	JUL 02 1851
CLOKEY, Robert B.	DYER, Emeline	JUL 13 1824
CLOON, Honora	BROWN, Daniel	APR 19 1851
CLOONAN, Ann	WELSH, James	JUN 08 1851
CLOONAN, Ann	WELSH, James	JUN 08 1854
CLOTWORTHY, William P.	MATTINGLY, Kate	MAY 22 1858
CLOUD, Artimesia	CARBERY, Lewis	SEP 09 1817
CLOUD, Elizabeth	TAYLOR, G.W.	JAN 27 1857
CLOUD, Emza	CARBERY, James	MAY 01 1820
CLOUD, George	BAILY, Ann Eliza	MAY 12 1814
CLOUD, Naomi	BOONE, Alexius	DEC 20 1831
CLOUD, Susan	BERRY, Jerome C.	JAN 16 1854
CLOXTON, Ann B.	SHAW, Lemuel D.	APR 17 1829
CLUB, Benjamin	LITTLEFORD, Mary	NOV 07 1831
CLUB, Drury Ann	SANFORD, Robert	JAN 14 1813
CLUB, Elizabeth	MAHONY, Thomas	JAN 23 1823
CLUB, Jane	GALLAHAM, Samuel	DEC 23 1824
CLUB, Rodey A.D.	WHITMORE, George	DEC 27 1825
CLUBB, Eliza A.M.	OWENS, Richard B.	SEP 05 1836
CLUBB, George	LANGLEY, Martha	APR 20 1854
CLUBB, John Lewis	PAGE, Miranda	JUN 06 1833
CLUBB, Levin	LOVELACE, Alethia	FEB 15 1825
CLUBB, Sarah	SANDERS, Joseph	APR 14 1812
CLUIN, Ann	COSTIN, Thomas	FEB 16 1854

District of Columbia Marriage Licenses, 1811-1858

CLUNE, Ann	FLANNIGAN, Thomas	NOV 23 1853
CLUSKEY, Mary E.	CROMWELL, Stephen A.	MAY 14 1857
CLUTE, Henry D.	BAGGETT, Elizabeth	MAY 31 1841
CLUTZ, Lucretia	CLARKE, Thomas	MAR 17 1856
CLYMER, George	SHUBIRCK, Mary	MAY 08 1845
CLYNE, John W., Jr.	HARRIS, Mary Elizth.	FEB 21 1849
COAD, Jane	SMITH, John W.	DEC 11 1826
COAD, John	DAW, Mary Ann	JAN 01 1820
COADY, Michael	STONE, John	JUN 21 1855
COAKLEY, George	ALLISON, Elizabeth (blk)	JUL 16 1853
COAKLEY, John	WINGFIELD, Josephine	SEP 26 1857
COAL, Ann	CHEZLEY, William	OCT 19 1820
COAL, John	GOLDING, Elizabeth	OCT 10 1829
COAL, Sarah	CROSS, Lloyd	JAN 12 1830
COAL, William	PICKRELL, Elizabeth	APR 24 1832
COALE, Charles B.	SANFORD, Julia	JUL 13 1831
COALE, Jane	CALLAHAN, Richd.	MAY 01 1817
COALE, Mary Ann	TAUNSAND, James	OCT 26 1818
COALE, Sarah A.L.	CHANEY, Rignel G.	APR 07 1831
COALE, William	PARADISE, Margaret	JUN 20 1833
COALE, William	BRADFORD, Sarah Elizabeth	SEP 23 1848
COALKEY, George W.	PETTERS, Anna (blk)	AUG 18 1845
COALMAN, Charlotte [Mrs.]	HARVEY, John	JUN 05 1820
COATES, Wm. Henry	DAVIS, Sarah (blk)	NOV 11 1852
COATNEY, John	BOSWELL, Ellen	APR 02 1829
COATRIGHT, William	ROBEY, Sarah Ellen	JUL 16 1856
COATS, Albin	REEDER, Cadah	DEC 26 1817
COATS, William	FRAZIER, Elizabeth	JUL 07 1814
COAX, Mary Ellen	BENTON, Samuel	JUL 03 1840
COAX, William	BOWIE, Julian	SEP 29 1823
COBB, Sarah Ann	McDUELL, George	FEB 01 1820
COBB, Susan	KENNEDY, James A.	MAY 29 1824
COBB, William D.	LANG, Angelina	OCT 03 1838
COBBS, Elizabeth M.	HARDGROVE, Samuel	JUN 09 1829
COBIE, William	GLASCO, Elizth.	OCT 10 1826
COBURN, Eliza Maria	WILLIAMS, John James	JUN 19 1845
COBURN, Joannah	MILLER, James	AUG 03 1833
COBURN, John D.	GALLAWAY, Martha	MAR 10 1824
COBURN, William A.	ELLIOTT, Annie R.	MAR 24 1857
COBY, Mary Amelia	WILKINSON, Alfred Berry	OCT 09 1852
COCHRAN, Adelaid J.	ALCOTT, Charles W.	JAN 13 1854
COCHRAN, Eglantine	COKE, Richard	JAN 06 1848
COCHRAN, Emily V.	DAVIS, John T.	JAN 18 1856
COCHRAN, George W.	BURNES, Sarah E.	OCT 13 1847
COCHRAN, James	SMARR, Elizabeth	SEP 08 1829
COCHRAN, James	COOLEY, Martha	SEP 08 1849
COCHRAN, John	SMITH, Elizabeth	JAN 12 1818
COCHRAN, John	O'BRIEN, Mary	APR 20 1853
COCHRAN, Kate Pleasants	REYNOLDS, E.K.	JUN 18 1856
COCHRAN, Louisa	LANSING, Arthur Breese	JUL 02 1849
COCHRAN, Timothy	LACKEY, Margaret	APR 17 1857
COCHRAN, Virginia A.	HAVENER, Peter	NOV 11 1847
COCHRAN, William	PEARSON, Sarah Ann	AUG 18 1834
COCHRANE, John T.	MANNING, Ellen	OCT 31 1849
COCK, Frances E.	BURCH, William S.	OCT 16 1840
COCKE, Anna	WHEELER, Simeon	MAY 17 1854
COCKE, Catherine W.	BENTON, William	MAY 22 1855
COCKE, James H.	NORFOLK, Elizabeth	SEP 13 1825

District of Columbia Marriage Licenses, 1811-1858

COCKE, Sarah E.	TAYLOR, Rufus	DEC 23 1856
COCKER, Elizabeth	HERLEHY, Michael	MAY 12 1856
COCKERILL, Bushrod E.	ELGIN, Eliza F.	JAN 14 1850
COCKERILL, Harriet	ESKRIDGE, Hatley A.	NOV 10 1831
COCKERILLE, Mary Ellen	SEXTON, John	NOV 01 1849
COCKING, Jane	GLOVER, Charles	AUG 19 1813
COCKREILL, Jane E.	LLOYD, Spencer	DEC 13 1832
COCKREL, Susanna	CRUMP, Edward W.	DEC 16 1851
COCKRELL, Ann	DAVIS, Charles	MAR 03 1840
COCKRELL, Catharine	HARVEY, William C.	AUG 25 1853
COCKRELL, Cornelia J.	CLARK, J. Thomas	JAN 16 1849
COCKRELL, Elizabeth	CARTER, James	FEB 12 1838
COCKRELL, Henry W.	ALLEN, Lucinda	APR 10 1855
COCKRELL, Patsey	WINE, William T.	NOV 03 1835
COCKRILL, Benjamin D.	THOMAS, Emily	DEC 09 1839
COCRELL, Elizabeth Ann	ELLIS, John B.	JUN 08 1844
CODEY, Bridget	O'BRIEN, John	AUG 11 1858
CODLIN, James	O'DONNELL, Biddy	AUG 04 1818
CODMAR, Julia	BURKE, William	JUL 15 1853
CODMORE, Bridget	KLOONE, Patrick	FEB 12 1855
CODMORE, John	MAACK, Bridget	JUL 17 1855
CODRICK, Elizabeth	MULLIN, William S.	MAR 23 1844
CODRICK, James F.	DENNISON, Ann Virginia	OCT 16 1845
CODRICK, John	HASLIP, Lucy	JUN 23 1841
CODRICK, John	BROWN, Amelia	OCT 14 1854
CODRICK, Joseph	HUTCHINSON, Elizabeth	MAY 13 1856
CODWISE, Charles Ferdinand	RANDOLPH, Martha Jane	JUN 23 1840
COE, Benjamin E.	DIGGS, Mary E.	FEB 05 1835
COE, Guinnetta (blk)	DAILEY, Uriah	MAY 20 1856
COE, Willie Ann (blk)	TRIPLETT, Ross	MAY 16 1856
COEN, Margaret	SUTER, Nicholas	JUN 30 1827
COFFEE, Francis	JONES, Mary	JUL 29 1835
COFFEE, Mary	SULLIVAN, Daniel	MAY 01 1854
COFFEE, Mary	QUINN, Edward	AUG 07 1856
COFFEE, Mary (blk)	BROWN, William	SEP 27 1849
COFFER, Ann Elizabeth	ANDERSON, John W.	APR 04 1853
COFFER, Jane M.	SMITH, Charles B.	AUG 18 1846
COFFER, Joseph	TOWNSEND, Bridget Ann	NOV 29 1838
COFFIN, John H.C.	HARRISON, Louisa	APR 09 1845
COFFY, Patrick	McMANN, Bridget	SEP 25 1850
COGAN, Thomas	MURRAY, Mary	NOV 04 1850
COGAY, Henrietta (blk)	DOUGLASS, William	DEC 12 1848
COGEE, Matilda (blk)	GRAHAM, Hannible	MAR 20 1851
COGER, John	QUEEN, Maria (blk)	JUN 14 1848
COGEY, Benjamin	FORD, Ann (blk)	OCT 25 1852
COGIN, Hanorah	DAILY, William T.	DEC 03 1857
COGSWELL, Aaron	STIMMEL, Sophia	OCT 08 1831
COGSWELL, Albert G.	UMBERFIELD, Elizabeth C.	OCT 05 1846
COGSWELL, Eveline	WHITNEY, William	AUG 30 1842
COGSWELL, Joseph	STIMMELL, Lydia	JAN 04 1825
COGSWELL, Joseph P.	MURPHY, Lucy D.	MAY 06 1856
COGSWELL, Sophia Jane	CLEMENTS, John W.	OCT 18 1848
COGSWELL, William	USHER, Martha	MAY 19 1858
COGWILL, John S.	BEECH, Delilah	MAR 19 1855
COGY, Charlotte (blk)	BRISCOE, Henry	OCT 07 1852
COHEN, Abram	REISS, Caroline	JUN 03 1856
COHEN, James H.	FRANCIS, Agnes	MAY 24 1855
COHEN, Rachael W.	BROWN, John T.	DEC 23 1851

District of Columbia Marriage Licenses, 1811-1858

COHEN, Sarah Ann	BECKLEY, Joseph	OCT 26 1841
COHENS, William	BIGGS, Mahaly	DEC 05 1823
COHICK, James	LOWE, Margaret	JUL 25 1812
COHILL, Elizth. A.F.	CAWOOD, John B.	NOV 18 1853
COHILL, Henry R.	GRIMES, Mary S.	AUG 26 1858
COHLMAN, Henry	FUCHS, Caroline	OCT 11 1855
COIN, Margaret	CURREN, Morgan	FEB 24 1825
COINER, Susanna M.	WILEY, Lewis B.	FEB 14 1855
COINER, William	STIFLE, Nancy	SEP 08 1819
COKE, Mary (blk)	BUTLER, John	SEP 16 1852
COKE, Mary E.	CAPERTON, John	APR 03 1856
COKE, Richard	COCHRAN, Eglantine	JAN 06 1848
COKE, William, Rev.	SIMPSON, Elizabeth (blk)	APR 08 1856
COKELEY, Gabriel	GALLOWAY, Mary (blk)	AUG 14 1850
COKLEY, George W.	WEBSTER, Martha Ann (blk)	JUL 10 1832
COKLEY, Jane	WHARTON, Augustus	JUL 10 1856
COLBAT, Eliza	SKAHAN, John	FEB 09 1858
COLBERT, David	O'LEARY, Margaret	MAR 31 1853
COLBERT, Eliza	BOUGHIN, Edward	FEB 07 1853
COLBERT, Ellen	WELCH, John	JAN 02 1847
COLBERT, Hanora	BRODERICK, Thomas	NOV 26 1817
COLBERT, Joanna	BERKLEY, Edmund	SEP 07 1852
COLBERT, Lloyd	MASON, Mary Jane (blk)	DEC 20 1855
COLBERT, Malind	FREEMAN, John	MAR 24 1818
COLBERT, Michael	QUEEN, Johanna	APR 19 1852
COLBERT, Thomas	O'CONNOR, Hannah	JUL 21 1855
COLBURN, Elizabeth (blk)	HAMANDS, Dennis	JUL 27 1858
COLBURN, James	NEWTON, Susanna	SEP 22 1825
COLBURN, Theadocia A.	DUVAL, Joseph	OCT 10 1848
COLBY, Ann Catherine	GOLDIN, R.R.	JUL 24 1845
COLCLASER, Martha E.	ADAMS, George P.	FEB 03 1845
COLCLAZER, Mary Ann	FARSON, William	DEC 29 1818
COLCLAZIER, Daniel V.	CRAWFORD, Mary A.	NOV 26 1841
COLCLAZIER, Jacob	CRAWFORD, Elizabeth	DEC 21 1840
COLCLAZIER, John	POWELLS, Mary J.	OCT 31 1850
COLCUER, Joseph J.	POWERS, Hester L.	MAY 20 1856
COLDEN, James	TIE, Julia	AUG 07 1855
COLDERSTROTH, George	SCHRAMM, Lene	APR 06 1853
COLDWELL, Joseph T.	WILLIAMS, Virginia J.	JUL 31 1854
COLE, Barbara A. (blk)	WILLIAMS, William	NOV 17 1856
COLE, Charles	ROSIER, Susan	DEC 24 1817
COLE, Charles	TOLSON, Maria	SEP 18 1832
COLE, Delila	MILLS, John L.	SEP 09 1840
COLE, Eleanor (blk)	CHAMBERS, Charles	JAN 07 1829
COLE, Elias	HOLLEY, Mary	MAY 09 1818
COLE, Elizabeth	PHILLIPS, William Henry	JUN 20 1848
COLE, Elizabeth	SHERWOOD, Zachariah	SEP 01 1856
COLE, Ellen	PARKER, David (blk)	NOV 30 1848
COLE, Francis	BARBER, Caroline (blk)	DEC 08 1853
COLE, Georgiana	FEDDON, Andrew F.	AUG 24 1855
COLE, Georgiana	JAVINS, Randolph	JUL 17 1858
COLE, Harriet	WASHINGTON, James	SEP 15 1847
COLE, Henrietta (blk)	BLACK, Abraham	JUN 11 1851
COLE, James	EVANS, Mary Ann	SEP 05 1821
COLE, James	WALKER, Mary	NOV 19 1835
COLE, Jane	JACKSON, Addison	OCT 25 1842
COLE, Jane F.	KLOFFER, Edwin J.	NOV 27 1847
COLE, Jeremiah M.	MASON, Elizabeth (blk)	JAN 05 1825

District of Columbia Marriage Licenses, 1811-1858

COLE, John T.	STONE, Elizabeth A.	NOV 22 1848
COLE, Levi P.	EVISON, Lydia	SEP 30 1815
COLE, Lydia	MACE, William	SEP 11 1845
COLE, Maria	ANGEL, Henry	SEP 16 1837
COLE, Martin	SMITH, Mary (blk)	NOV 13 1828
COLE, Mary Ann	WHITE, William W.	SEP 24 1839
COLE, Mary Ann	BEAN, Amos W.	JUN 10 1851
COLE, Matilda	WEADON, Richard W.	MAR 14 1821
COLE, Raphael	BUTLER, Elizabeth (blk)	NOV 12 1844
COLE, Raphael	DODSON, Margaret (blk)	OCT 16 1848
COLE, Richard	CLARKE, Elizabeth	AUG 25 1830
COLE, Richard F.	BYRNE, Frances V.	OCT 11 1855
COLE, Robert	SHERBERTT, Martha	SEP 12 1854
COLE, Robert	WILSON, Barbara E. (blk)	JUN 28 1856
COLE, Rosanna E.	BRANDT, John D.	JUN 12 1849
COLE, Samuel	ROSS, Elizabeth (blk)	OCT 28 1841
COLE, Samuel	BOYCE, Mary	JUN 06 1857
COLE, Samuel L.	ENGLISH, Adelia A.	DEC 17 1845
COLE, Sarah B.	WOOD, George E.	OCT 12 1848
COLE, Thomas W.	WILSON, Sarah Ann	MAY 06 1853
COLE, Vanilla (blk)	SMITH, Richard	APR 14 1852
COLE, William	THOMAS, Mary Elizth. (blk)	NOV 30 1848
COLEBURT, Edward	HARRIGAN, Margaret	MAR 12 1858
COLEGATE, James	LAURIE, Elizabeth W.	JUN 13 1842
COLEGATE, Nancey	PARKER, William	APR 06 1820
COLEMAN, Andrew S.	CLARKE, Drady Ann	JUN 08 1833
COLEMAN, Ann Elizth.	LEE, Henry	JAN 22 1836
COLEMAN, Ann M.	GOSZLER, Thomas D.	DEC 03 1842
COLEMAN, Catharine C.	MITCHELL, Thomas	APR 29 1848
COLEMAN, Charles W.	FARR, Lavinia V.	OCT 03 1853
COLEMAN, Edmond W.	WILSON, Caroline	MAR 19 1828
COLEMAN, Francis	BEACH, Mary Ann	OCT 02 1855
COLEMAN, George G.	RUSH, Mary J.	JUL 18 1854
COLEMAN, Hawes N.	TINSLEY, Sallie A.E.	OCT 20 1856
COLEMAN, Huldah	DeJARNATT, Daniel	DEC 21 1817
COLEMAN, James	DELANEY, Mary	FEB 08 1853
COLEMAN, Jeremiah	MURPHEY, Mary Ann	AUG 23 1823
COLEMAN, Louisa	SIPE, Hezekiah	OCT 18 1832
COLEMAN, Lucy Ann	CONNER, Henry W.	MAR 09 1839
COLEMAN, Martha Ann	RAYHILL, Dominick	JUN 10 1837
COLEMAN, Mary	McCALLA, John	JUN 06 1857
COLEMAN, Mary Susan	MONTAGUE, Philip H.L.	MAY 28 1846
COLEMAN, Patrick	NIECEY, Catherine	NOV 29 1855
COLEMAN, Randle	DAVIS, Sarah Ann	JUL 11 1842
COLEMAN, Sarah J.	WATHEN, Wlias	NOV 23 1818
COLEMAN, V.A.	TALLIAFERRO, Wm. W.	SEP 27 1847
COLEMAN, William	EMORE, Azeno	APR 14 1832
COLEMAN, William H.	AIKEN, Adelaid	FEB 27 1855
COLES, Charles	MASON, Delia A.	NOV 07 1853
COLES, Charles	O'ROARK, Sarah Ann	MAR 11 1858
COLEY, Henry	GOUGH, Sarah	MAR 04 1834
COLFAR, Catharine A.	CAMPBELL, John G.	NOV 25 1853
COLGLAZIER, Jacob	HIGDON, Eleanor	MAR 31 1812
COLGRIFF, James	MOLQUEEN, Ellen	AUG 01 1853
COLIER, Peyton	KING, Martha Ann	JUN 18 1845
COLINBAUGH, Catherine	DYER, John F.	NOV 28 1837
COLINS, Patrick	BUCKLEY, Eliza	FEB 02 1853
COLISON, James R.	SAUNER, Mary M.	NOV 21 1843

District of Columbia Marriage Licenses, 1811-1858

COLISON, Peter	KIRSEY, Hellen P.	FEB 21 1855
COLLAMER, Ellen	RICE, Thomas	JUL 29 1850
COLLARD, Augustine	LIEPPE, Francois	MAR 17 1825
COLLARD, Eliza	MOBRAY, James	JUN 18 1834
COLLARD, Eliza S.	WHITNEY, Phineas S.	DEC 31 1836
COLLARD, Ellen	TALBERT, John	JUN 08 1835
COLLARD, George	BOYCE, Ann	OCT 04 1821
COLLARD, James Irvin	BOSWELL, Eliza Ann	DEC 25 1830
COLLARD, Jemima	ADAMS, George	FEB 13 1816
COLLEY, Eliza An	CLARKSON, Jacob	FEB 15 1817
COLLIER, Ellen	BOSWELL, Allen T.	APR 02 1855
COLLIER, Frederick H.	KING, Catharine	JUL 18 1849
COLLIER, Jane	GERMAN, Francis	DEC 24 1851
COLLIER, John N.	HUFF, Mary E.	JAN 15 1849
COLLIER, Joseph	SHANE, Ann	SEP 01 1825
COLLIER, Mary	TOLTY, Thomas H.	MAY 12 1855
COLLIER, Mary A.	THOMPSON, James R.	DEC 18 1852
COLLIER, Richard H.	DAILEY, Mary Frances	JAN 05 1849
COLLIER, Thomas T.	IRVING, Mary E.	AUG 03 1839
COLLIER, William	KNIGHT, Milly	JAN 18 1819
COLLIN, Henry	REYNOLDS, Maria	AUG 04 1855
COLLIN, Susan	POOL, Levi	MAR 07 1823
COLLINGS, Bridget	GALVIN, Henry	FEB 20 1854
COLLINGS, George	SOPER, Maria	JUN 10 1815
COLLINGSWORTH, Arivuel D.	DIXON, Rebecca	APR 20 1840
COLLINGWOOD, Andrew	PIERCE, Rachel	MAY 06 1822
COLLINGWOOD, Elizth.	MULLIKIN, James	APR 20 1829
COLLINGWOOD, John	POWER, Elizabeth	MAY 30 1822
COLLINS, Alfred	COURTNEY, Amelia	FEB 02 1839
COLLINS, Alice	LYNCH, John	JUL 31 1852
COLLINS, Ann	HUGHES, Ansburn	DEC 24 1818
COLLINS, Ann	COLLINS, Morris	OCT 04 1856
COLLINS, Ann (blk)	CLAGETT, David	OCT 03 1832
COLLINS, Ann C.	HARRY, Alonzo W.	JAN 16 1854
COLLINS, Ann C.	RATCLIFF, Alexander	JUL 12 1855
COLLINS, Ann Catherine	HARRY, Alonzo W.	APR 30 1853
COLLINS, Ann Maria	BROWN, Zedekiah	NOV 04 1833
COLLINS, Anna Julia	PARIS, Albert Joseph	SEP 03 1831
COLLINS, Bernard	O'RILEY, Rose Ann	MAY 28 1828
COLLINS, Catharine	HOMILLER, Charles	NOV 15 1832
COLLINS, Catharine	HAVENNER, William H.	NOV 25 1850
COLLINS, Charles	HURLEY, Margaret	JUL 02 1836
COLLINS, Daniel	RING, Norah	SEP 05 1857
COLLINS, Dennis	BARNETT, Margaret	AUG 07 1849
COLLINS, Dennis	SCANLON, Honora	JUL 29 1852
COLLINS, Dorcas E.	SMITH, John W.	MAY 21 1850
COLLINS, Edward W.	CLAXTON, Martha	AUG 16 1830
COLLINS, Eliza	JONES, William	MAR 06 1843
COLLINS, Eliza	MILLS, Thomas A.	NOV 11 1856
COLLINS, Eliza Ann	PAROTT, Abner	JUN 26 1854
COLLINS, Eliza S.	MORROW, William	MAY 12 1824
COLLINS, Elizabeth (blk)	PETERS, James	NOV 30 1844
COLLINS, Elizabeth M.	BARNES, Joseph	MAR 20 1837
COLLINS, Ellen	BENNETT, Michael	MAR 18 1854
COLLINS, Ellin	FITZGERALD, Patrick	JAN 01 1851
COLLINS, Emily	COLLINS, James E.	MAY 28 1855
COLLINS, Fanney	HARPER, Nicholas	DEC 09 1812
COLLINS, Frances M.	PALMER, John	JUN 25 1838

District of Columbia Marriage Licenses, 1811-1858

COLLINS, Frederick	TILGHMAN, Sharlotte (blk)	DEC 21 1826
COLLINS, Geo.	WOOD, Maria	DEC 23 1823
COLLINS, George	SMITH, Elizabeth	DEC 23 1843
COLLINS, George	POORE, Mary	FEB 01 1845
COLLINS, George	MATNEY, Maria	MAR 01 1851
COLLINS, George	MARION, Selina	JUL 15 1852
COLLINS, George T.	ESHBACH, Elizabeth	AUG 23 1852
COLLINS, Harriet Maria	BOYLE, John F.	FEB 23 1841
COLLINS, Henrietta	WARTHEN, Charles	JUL 02 1816
COLLINS, Henrietta	NORTON, Robert	MAY 01 1832
COLLINS, Hester Ann	KING, John J.	JAN 15 1812
COLLINS, James	PAYNE, Mary C.	DEC 12 1836
COLLINS, James	CREAMER, Susan	SEP 07 1844
COLLINS, James	BROWN, Joanna	MAY 25 1853
COLLINS, James	WHITE, Mary	FEB 19 1855
COLLINS, James	BROWN, Ellen	FEB 01 1856
COLLINS, James A.	LEACH, Mary E.	MAY 02 1843
COLLINS, James E.	COLLINS, Emily	MAY 28 1855
COLLINS, James H.	NEVITT, Henrietta	OCT 19 1839
COLLINS, James H.	DEEVERS, Harriet	OCT 05 1850
COLLINS, James L.	PADGETT, Mary Emily	OCT 04 1856
COLLINS, Jane	USHER, John	DEC 21 1825
COLLINS, Jane	MANGUM, George T.	NOV 06 1855
COLLINS, Jeremiah	COUNOL, Johana	FEB 16 1858
COLLINS, John	COLLINS, Milley	JUN 06 1813
COLLINS, John	GLADMAN, Ann	JAN 13 1819
COLLINS, John	DUMPHREY, Ellen	JUN 23 1858
COLLINS, Joseph	WOODWARD, Susannah	APR 18 1846
COLLINS, Joseph	HAZLE, Charlotte	DEC 31 1846
COLLINS, Joseph	HURDLE, Mary A.	DEC 22 1851
COLLINS, Joseph H.	CARR, Susannah C.	NOV 01 1852
COLLINS, Joseph S. [Rev.]	ADGATE, Sally	FEB 05 1829
COLLINS, Joshua	LONG, Attaway	OCT 20 1812
COLLINS, Julia	RIELY, William	MAY 22 1843
COLLINS, L.B.	SANFORD, Jemima	JUL 08 1845
COLLINS, Lemuel Everett	WHITE, Catharine	JAN 10 1846
COLLINS, Leonard	KING, Valinda	APR 08 1834
COLLINS, Levi	JENNIFER, Mary Ann	NOV 06 1834
COLLINS, Levi	LEE, Susan	NOV 23 1837
COLLINS, Louisa	DRURY, James	JAN 28 1822
COLLINS, Margaret	PAYNE, Joseph	MAR 30 1833
COLLINS, Margaret	FITZGERALD, Michael	SEP 22 1854
COLLINS, Margaret	GUBERNATOR, Jacob	NOV 02 1857
COLLINS, Margaret	HARRINGTON, John	FEB 06 1858
COLLINS, Maria	MATTINGLY, Thomas	MAR 08 1855
COLLINS, Martha E.	TUCKER, Samuel W.	JUN 28 1839
COLLINS, Martin	O'DONNELL, Susannah	NOV 13 1821
COLLINS, Mary	SMALLWOOD, George	AUG 01 1817
COLLINS, Mary	McCUE, Owen	MAY 24 1819
COLLINS, Mary	EWING, James	APR 08 1820
COLLINS, Mary	WILSON, John	NOV 16 1833
COLLINS, Mary	HURLEY, William	JAN 07 1836
COLLINS, Mary	TALTY, Stephen	APR 04 1850
COLLINS, Mary	JOHNSON, James	DEC 31 1856
COLLINS, Mary	CURTING, John	JAN 12 1858
COLLINS, Mary (blk)	BURTON, John	SEP 27 1826
COLLINS, Mary (blk)	BOWEN, Anthony	SEP 19 1839
COLLINS, Mary A.	WHITE, Thomas P.	MAY 17 1855

District of Columbia Marriage Licenses, 1811-1858

COLLINS, Mary Ann	CONNOLLY, John C.	DEC 27 1851
COLLINS, Mary E. (blk)	HALL, Henry W.	MAR 26 1856
COLLINS, Mary Elizabeth	SHOEMAKER, Charles	SEP 02 1843
COLLINS, Maurice	O'RIELLY, Margaret	JUN 07 1853
COLLINS, Milley	COLLINS, John	JUN 06 1813
COLLINS, Morris	COLLINS, Ann	OCT 04 1856
COLLINS, Owen J.	STEPHENSON, Catharine	JUN 10 1843
COLLINS, Owen J.	RATCLIFF, Mary E.	NOV 26 1851
COLLINS, Patrick	RING, Johanna	JAN 31 1853
COLLINS, Patrick	RAGAN, Mary	JUN 07 1856
COLLINS, Rebecca	SUITT, Samuel	NOV 05 1844
COLLINS, Reubin	McLAUGHLIN, Margaret E.	APR 28 1840
COLLINS, Richard	POLLE, Sarah	AUG 12 1853
COLLINS, Richard	POOLE, Sarah	AUG 12 1858
COLLINS, Richard John	McLAUGHLIN, Elizabeth	APR 01 1826
COLLINS, Robert	GLADMEN, Rebecca	APR 04 1816
COLLINS, Rose	McGUIRE, Terence	JUN 06 1838
COLLINS, Rosetta	LAMBERT, Thomas	APR 19 1856
COLLINS, Samuel	DIMOND, Maria	MAR 29 1833
COLLINS, Sarah	JOHNSON, William	APR 18 1840
COLLINS, Sarah	MASON, Thomas	JUN 22 1853
COLLINS, Sarah	HURDLE, George W.	DEC 14 1854
COLLINS, Sarah Ann	KURTS, Peter	OCT 07 1817
COLLINS, Sarah Eliza	BELL, John A.	DEC 28 1847
COLLINS, Susan	O'BRYAN, John	OCT 14 1817
COLLINS, Susan	CARNEY, Alexander	JAN 08 1820
COLLINS, Susan	MANGUM, John G.F.	MAR 13 1856
COLLINS, Susan E.	DALTON, William	OCT 07 1824
COLLINS, Teresa	HOWARD, George W.	DEC 29 1831
COLLINS, Theodore B.	MULLIN, Susan	OCT 04 1855
COLLINS, Thomas	MARTIN, Susan	JUN 17 1828
COLLINS, Thomas	DASHIELDS, Mary	JUN 27 1830
COLLINS, Thomas	CALLANAN, Ellen	FEB 03 1836
COLLINS, Virginia Rosella	HAZLE, William Conway	AUG 06 1846
COLLINS, William	SLATFORD, Louisa	DEC 22 1825
COLLINS, William	MOREHOUSE, Elizabeth	FEB 20 1830
COLLINS, William	SPILMAN, Nancy	SEP 02 1844
COLLINS, William	INGALL, Izabella	DEC 23 1845
COLLINS, William	GLADMAN, Amelia	OCT 23 1851
COLLINS, William	CONNOR, Mary	APR 05 1853
COLLINS, William	GREEN, Mary Lou	OCT 31 1853
COLLINS, William H.	BROOKS, Susannah (blk)	DEC 01 1853
COLLINS, William T.	ROBINSON, Martha M.	MAY 16 1850
COLLINS, Zachariah	BARBER, Nancy	SEP 21 1854
COLLISON, Catharine C.	WHITMORE, William	DEC 12 1844
COLLISON, Eliza	LUCAS, John	FEB 16 1828
COLLISON, Elizth. J.	WIMER, James	MAY 09 1844
COLLISON, Emily L.	NOYES, Henry O.	JAN 05 1857
COLLISON, Joseph	DREW, Elizabeth	DEC 04 1824
COLLISON, Julia Ann	BOYCE, James	SEP 24 1844
COLLISON, Lucinda	GRANT, William M.	OCT 20 1847
COLLISON, S.G.	HALL, R.B.	DEC 20 1847
COLLISON, Susen E.	GARST, David	NOV 01 1855
COLLISSON, Mary E.	MORSELL, J. William	SEP 18 1857
COLLITA, Thomas	CLARY, Catharine	OCT 25 1856
COLSON, Joseph	SHORTER, Tresy	NOV 04 1819
COLSTON, Elizabeth E. (blk)	JAMISON, Elias	OCT 06 1842
COLSTON, Mary	CUNNINGHAM, Thomas	AUG 02 1830

District of Columbia Marriage Licenses, 1811-1858

COLSTON, Nannie	ANDERSON, W. George	SEP 05 1855
COLSTON, Octavia	GRIMES, Leonard	MAY 27 1833
COLT, Chester A.	MANNING, Frances M.	MAY 12 1841
COLT, Sylvia	LARNED, Charles	MAR 26 1816
COLTER, Lydia Ann	GREENWELL, Joseph W.	NOV 15 1825
COLTER, Margaret	SHEELE, Augustus Danl.	MAY 01 1828
COLTER, Thomas	REVES, Ann Maria	JUL 29 1851
COLTMAN, Charles L.	DRUMMOND, Mary Ann	JUL 02 1829
COLTMAN, Charles L.	McCLELLAND, Rebecca	DEC 27 1848
COLTMAN, Mary F.	JONES, William H.	AUG 21 1851
COLUMBUS, Albert G.	BERRY, Anna K.	MAR 21 1853
COLUMBUS, Anna M.	SAFFELL, Charles	JUN 08 1857
COLUMBUS, Anna N.	SAFFELL, Chas. H.	JAN 21 1858
COLUMBUS, Chas. J.	SHEID, Martha R.	DEC 29 1847
COLUMBUS, Josephine	KING, Francis	FEB 05 1842
COLUMBUS, Mary L.	HITAFFER, James R.	APR 27 1853
COLUMBUS, William Francis	PADGET, Julia Amanda	APR 30 1849
COLVIN, James	LACKEY, Mary	OCT 23 1815
COLVIN, Lucy Ann	COLVIN, Wyatt Green	OCT 27 1855
COLVIN, Sarah Ann	MEREDITH, William	MAR 22 1853
COLVIN, Wyatt Green	COLVIN, Lucy Ann	OCT 27 1855
COMBES, George	WOODWARD, Mary	OCT 28 1824
COMBS, Ann	RAMSAY, Ezra J.	APR 04 1820
COMBS, Mary L.	PLUMMER, Fielder B.	OCT 14 1839
COMBS, Robert M.	FORREST, Catharine C.	OCT 08 1840
COME, Stephen	WHITE, Eliza	OCT 20 1824
COMER, Abraham	PARSONS, Mary Ann W.	FEB 03 1819
COMLY, Charles A.	TEMPLEMAN, Hetty B.	APR 12 1838
COMPTON, Frances	STEWART, Walter	NOV 27 1817
COMPTON, Frances Ann	MURRAY, Thomas I.	JUL 26 1834
COMPTON, Jane H.	DEMENT, Richard	MAY 01 1844
COMPTON, John J.	GETTINGS, Sarah Ann	OCT 25 1834
COMPTON, John S.	CLAGETT, Jane H.	APR 13 1818
COMPTON, Martha	HIPKINS, John L.	DEC 24 1849
COMPTON, Rosa	POLTON, William	JAN 01 1839
COMPTON, Rosa L.	CHESELDINE, Geo. W.	NOV 22 1855
COMPTON, Ruel K.	DEMENT, Rachel	APR 22 1850
COMPTON, Sarah Catharine	WOOD, Charles Frederick	OCT 30 1843
COMPTON, Wm. T.	FRENCH, Maria D.B.	MAY 17 1847
CONANT, James E.	RUTHERFORD, Susan A.	JUL 08 1854
CONCKLIN, William M.	JONES, Ann	APR 11 1812
CONCORAN, Harriett H.	MARBURY, John	JUN 01 1840
CONDICT, Henry	CAUSIN, Jane Adelaide	MAR 27 1832
CONDIRCH, Barbara A.	ELMORE, Jerome	NOV 05 1856
CONDON, Ellen	BUCKLEY, John	APR 05 1852
CONDRY, Dennis	BROWN, Catherine R.	FEB 07 1848
CONELL, Ellen	BRODER, Michl.	DEC 26 1855
CONELLY, Thomas	CRAWLEY, Ann	SEP 08 1818
CONGROSE, Eliza	WELCH, John	JAN 01 1826
CONINGTON, Rosina V.	DENT, Augustus S.	JUL 15 1858
CONINO, Michael	PORTER, Grace	AUG 25 1818
CONINX, Julia	HERRITY, James	JAN 10 1846
CONINX, Melchior	KAIN, Julianna	MAY 24 1815
CONKANNON, Margaret	CONKANNON, Patrick	DEC 14 1854
CONKANNON, Patrick	CONKANNON, Margaret	DEC 14 1854
CONKLIN, Latin	KALE, Mary	MAR 25 1820
CONKLIN, William	ECKTON, Christeen	JUN 06 1854
CONLAN, Ann Elizabeth	EICHHORN, Rudolph	JAN 06 1853

District of Columbia Marriage Licenses, 1811-1858

CONLAN, Maurice	REILEY, Ellen	NOV 12 1857
CONLAN, Michael	SKEAHAN, Bridget	JUL 10 1855
CONLEN, Winnie	HATCH, Charles	SEP 27 1852
CONLEY, Eliza	MACAVOY, Peter	JAN 26 1856
CONLEY, Francis	McCAFFREY, Mary	AUG 31 1822
CONLEY, Maria	DONOHOE, John	OCT 23 1854
CONLEY, Patrick	STREAKS, Ann	JAN 13 1824
CONLON, Charles	CONOLEY, Catharine	FEB 15 1820
CONLY, John	BONIFER, Elizabeth	JUN 15 1816
CONLY, Mary	BOOTH, Henry Mansfield	JUN 18 1853
CONN, Susan C.	TROOK, John N.	SEP 26 1833
CONNAL, Joanna	SHANAHAN, Timothy	MAY 28 1853
CONNALLY, John	HONDIRIN, Mary	APR 29 1854
CONNALLY, Thomas E.	FULLER, Hellen	FEB 13 1837
CONNARY, Edward	McDERMOTT, Eliza	APR 02 1839
CONNAUGHTON, Michael	DELANY, Elizabeth	SEP 23 1837
CONNEL, Mary	CURTA, Daniel	FEB 20 1855
CONNEL, Robert A.	WHITE, Ellen M.	OCT 15 1846
CONNELL, Bridget	CONNELLY, Patrick	JAN 27 1853
CONNELL, Catherine	BARNES, John	NOV 12 1813
CONNELL, Dennis	FLAHERTY, Ellen	FEB 07 1852
CONNELL, Eleanor	CAMMACK, William	AUG 03 1820
CONNELL, Elizabeth	ROBERTSON, John	APR 05 1827
CONNELL, Eudy	LOWRY, Allen	NOV 03 1814
CONNELL, Frances	CROUSE, Abraham	AUG 03 1841
CONNELL, James	TURNER, Ann P.	JAN 26 1833
CONNELL, Jeremiah	SWEENY, Margaret	OCT 24 1854
CONNELL, Johanna	FOLEY, Daniel	JAN 31 1852
CONNELL, Johanna	CHAGROO, John	AUG 23 1856
CONNELL, John	BRYAN, Eleanor	DEC 24 1811
CONNELL, John	PARROTT, Rebecca	DEC 24 1817
CONNELL, John	O'DAY, Mary	DEC 20 1853
CONNELL, John	O'BRIEN, Hanora	MAY 22 1856
CONNELL, John W.	DELANY, Elizabeth A.M.	OCT 08 1851
CONNELL, Julia	FITZGERALD, Thomas	NOV 13 1851
CONNELL, Mary	MURPHY, David	OCT 21 1854
CONNELL, Mary	HENLON, Edmund	NOV 13 1854
CONNELL, Mary C.	MARTIN, William M.	JUN 21 1853
CONNELL, Mary Jane	BORLAND, John A.	OCT 29 1857
CONNELL, Morris	LYNCH, Ellen	JUL 06 1858
CONNELL, Rachael Ann E.	BURROUGHS, Zedekiah	DEC 15 1857
CONNELL, Theophilus	WILLIAMS, Jane E.	APR 07 1858
CONNELL, Timothy	HOLOHAN, Margaret	JUL 11 1855
CONNELL, William F.	HOPKINS, Sarah A.D.	SEP 15 1849
CONNELLEN, Bridgett	WHEALAN, William	NOV 28 1834
CONNELLY, Charles	RICHARDSON, Eleanor	DEC 02 1816
CONNELLY, John	MUDD, Rebecca	DEC 27 1842
CONNELLY, Margaret	FARRIS, William	APR 19 1815
CONNELLY, Maria	McCONNELL, George	DEC 24 1836
CONNELLY, Michael	NICHOLLS, Drucilla	MAR 30 1826
CONNELLY, Patrick	CONNELL, Bridget	JAN 27 1853
CONNELLY, Thomas	THOMPSON, Sarah	AUG 14 1845
CONNER, Ann (blk)	WARNER, Nicholas	FEB 25 1826
CONNER, Anna	ROBERTSON, Nicholas	FEB 07 1853
CONNER, Bryan	HERLIHY, Julia	OCT 27 1852
CONNER, Catherine	McGAHAN, Bernard	JAN 31 1844
CONNER, Charlotte	BARKER, Presley	APR 08 1823
CONNER, Constantine O.	MILLER, Sarah C.	JUN 16 1858

District of Columbia Marriage Licenses, 1811-1858

CONNER, Cordelia (blk)	VODERY, Robert	SEP 10 1857
CONNER, Daniel	SUGRUA, Hannora	FEB 01 1853
CONNER, Dennis	CRONIN, Mary Ann	AUG 05 1838
CONNER, Dennis	COSTOLE, Ellen	MAY 08 1856
CONNER, Elizabeth	SEVERE, Frs.	MAR 08 1821
CONNER, Henry W.	COLEMAN, Lucy Ann	MAR 09 1839
CONNER, John	PRITCHETT, Mary	SEP 07 1837
CONNER, John	HORAN, Margaret	OCT 06 1852
CONNER, John	COX, Mary	MAY 23 1855
CONNER, John J.	MAUD, Martha A.	NOV 11 1857
CONNER, John L.	KINGSTON, Sarah E.	APR 22 1837
CONNER, Margaret	BAGLEY, Daniel	JUL 18 1851
CONNER, Margaret	HINES, James	AUG 24 1852
CONNER, Margaret	SHEA, Patrick	JAN 19 1858
CONNER, Martin	MILBURN, Mary Ann Elizabeth	MAY 25 1843
CONNER, Mary	WEBSTER, William	JUL 30 1840
CONNER, Mary	CONNER, Thomas	DEC 27 1852
CONNER, Mary	COSTELLO, Robert	JUL 08 1854
CONNER, Mary (blk)	FRANCIS, Richard	SEP 15 1854
CONNER, Mary Ann	REID, John	JUL 25 1825
CONNER, Mary Jane	FLETCHER, W.H.	SEP 22 1845
CONNER, Michael	WOODS, Mary	MAY 31 1839
CONNER, Michael	MUDD, Matilda A.	APR 13 1846
CONNER, Michael	FLETCHER, Catherine	DEC 27 1848
CONNER, Mitchell	BUNTON, Amelia	JUN 23 1831
CONNER, Patrick	SHEAHAN, Catherine	JUL 30 1852
CONNER, Robert	CROWN, Mary Ann	APR 12 1830
CONNER, Robert	BUCKLER, Margaret	NOV 03 1845
CONNER, Sarah	GORDON, Charles W.	JAN 04 1849
CONNER, Thomas	CHRISTELL, Mary Ann	FEB 06 1850
CONNER, Thomas	CONNER, Mary	DEC 27 1852
CONNER, Valentine	MILLS, Catharine	JAN 28 1822
CONNER, Virginia E.	CROSS, Joseph H.	DEC 01 1849
CONNER, William	WELLS, Jemima	MAY 09 1827
CONNER, William	GRAY, Jane	OCT 04 1831
CONNER, William	PRATHER, Ann Rebecca	OCT 28 1845
CONNERS, Hannah	CURRAN, Patrick	OCT 03 1856
CONNERS, Mary	STAPLETON, John	FEB 02 1833
CONNERS, Mary	McNAMARA, Thomas	OCT 10 1854
CONNERS, William	ROCHE, Margaret	JUL 13 1852
CONNEWAY, Joseph	HUGHES, Margaret (blk)	APR 04 1850
CONNIX, Grace [Mrs.]	HURST, Henry [Sgt.]	NOV 04 1828
CONNOLEY, Mary Ann	PETTIT, William	OCT 14 1819
CONNOLLY, Bridget	RIORDAN, Patrick	DEC 30 1854
CONNOLLY, Edmund	DONOVAN, Margaret	FEB 20 1849
CONNOLLY, Elizabeth	BARRETT, Augustus	AUG 03 1858
CONNOLLY, John C.	COLLINS, Mary Ann	DEC 27 1851
CONNOLLY, Owen	McCANDLESS, Elizabeth	MAY 05 1832
CONNOLLY, Robert J.J.	WILSON, Martha C.	JUN 22 1857
CONNOR, Ann W.	MOORE, John	JUN 04 1842
CONNOR, Bridget	CRAY, Peter	OCT 08 1853
CONNOR, Catherine	WALLIS, Henry	DEC 30 1850
CONNOR, Cornelius	McDONALD, Ann	NOV 27 1857
CONNOR, Daniel	HOGAN, Catharine	JUL 23 1853
CONNOR, Daniel	KALEHER, Ellen	MAR 29 1856
CONNOR, Elizabeth	ROONEY, Francis	NOV 22 1851
CONNOR, Elizabeth	BLIGH, James J.	NOV 05 1853
CONNOR, Emelina	HENDERSON, John	SEP 28 1833

District of Columbia Marriage Licenses, 1811-1858

CONNOR, Harriet L.	SHECKELL, Merrit A.	MAR 07 1855
CONNOR, Hugh	FREER, Ann	OCT 15 1850
CONNOR, James R.	CROSS, Louisa	AUG 13 1851
CONNOR, Jane	REEVES, Jno. U.	JUL 17 1855
CONNOR, Johanna	NEWMAN, John	JAN 18 1858
CONNOR, John	WEATHERALL, Ann	JUL 15 1817
CONNOR, John	SMITH, Ann	JUL 29 1824
CONNOR, John	DEVINE, Ann	SEP 09 1837
CONNOR, John	NARDEN, Josephine	OCT 07 1841
CONNOR, John	BARNETT, Catharine	MAR 28 1845
CONNOR, John	DRISCOLL, Mary	MAR 22 1858
CONNOR, John	DRISCOLL, Mary	MAY 22 1858
CONNOR, Lucinda L.	PHILLIPS, Edmund	JAN 30 1854
CONNOR, Margarett	CONNOR, Michael	APR 14 1856
CONNOR, Mary	WHALEY, Robert M.	DEC 16 1841
CONNOR, Mary	MOXLEY, Resin	JUN 08 1843
CONNOR, Mary	SUGRUE, John	APR 28 1853
CONNOR, Mary	COLLINS, William	APR 05 1853
CONNOR, Mary	McCABE, Daniel	NOV 10 1854
CONNOR, Mary	SHEA, Dennis	MAY 31 1856
CONNOR, Mary A.	MONMONIER, Francis	MAY 17 1841
CONNOR, Mary Ann	MAYSON, Israel	SEP 28 1842
CONNOR, Mary Ann	McLAUGHLIN, Thomas	JUL 13 1852
CONNOR, Michael	KIERMAN, Honora	NOV 12 1855
CONNOR, Michael	CONNOR, Margarett	APR 14 1856
CONNOR, Michl.	DONOHOE, Mary	JUL 29 1858
CONNOR, Patrick	O'BRIEN, Margaret	JUL 31 1858
CONNOR, Samuel W.	PRITCHARD, Virginia	MAY 25 1848
CONNOR, Sarah	PELKINTON, Michael	FEB 05 1852
CONNOR, Sarah C.	STATON, Benjamin S.	DEC 31 1857
CONNOR, William	DIGGINS, Eliza	MAY 21 1852
CONNORS, Bridget	CURTIN, Daniel	JAN 04 1851
CONNOWAY, Louisa (blk)	ALEXANDER, Lewis	NOV 05 1855
CONOLEY, Catharine	CONLON, Charles	FEB 15 1820
CONOLEY, Jane	COOGAN, John	NOV 19 1857
CONOWAY, Mary	TRUNNELL, Thomas	FEB 06 1851
CONRAD, Christian	LABOLD, Catharine	MAR 05 1846
CONRAD, Daniel	POWELL, Sarah J.	APR 05 1848
CONRAD, Mary Catherine	HOWARD, John Cornelius	JUL 07 1852
CONRAD, Michael H.	FRENCH, Mary Ellen	FEB 03 1858
CONRAD, Sarah E.	KEENE, Joseph R.	JUL 13 1857
CONRAD, Wilhelmine	BARTHEL, Edward	SEP 02 1856
CONROY, Ann	FINNELL, Simon	NOV 09 1844
CONROY, Bridget	WELSH, Bartholomew	JAN 29 1856
CONROY, Ellen T.	PHALEN, Patrick	JUL 11 1848
CONROY, Humphrey	SOTHORON, Elizabeth	APR 21 1837
CONROY, James	GREY, Mary	NOV 18 1852
CONROY, James	FENNEL, Eliza	OCT 30 1852
CONROY, Mary	MULLIGAN, Bernard	JUL 18 1851
CONROY, Thomas	BRUGGY, Mary	APR 02 1853
CONSERDINE, Eliza	MADIGAN, Luke	JUL 21 1853
CONSTABLE, Anna	HAIGHT, Charles W.	APR 14 1852
CONSTABLE, Anna	WEBSTER, William	JUL 17 1858
CONTEE, Jane (blk)	WEBSTER, William	JUN 17 1858
CONTEE, Kitty	MILES, Francis	MAR 28 1829
CONTEE, Mary Ann (blk)	GRANDISON, Benjamin	APR 09 1853
CONTNOR, Isaac	STEELE, Elizabeth	FEB 27 1838
CONVERSE, Freeman	McDONALD, Sarah	APR 08 1833

District of Columbia Marriage Licenses, 1811-1858

CONWAY, Harriet	NICOLL, William H.	MAY 07 1818
CONWAY, James	THOMAS, Eliza	JUN 18 1842
CONWAY, James	MULLOY, Elizabeth	JAN 27 1853
CONWAY, John B.	HORNER, Elizabeth	DEC 30 1847
CONWAY, Mary Ann	ROSEBERRY, John M.	JUL 25 1855
CONWAY, Michael	SHEPHERD, Francis	JAN 02 1839
CONWAY, William	KING, Martha (blk)	MAY 09 1833
CONWELL, Charles B.	HATCHER, Sarah M.	JAN 08 1857
COOGAN, John	CONOLEY, Jane	NOV 19 1857
COOK, Abitha	SOPER, Robert	FEB 17 1823
COOK, Abram	AYTON, Mary Cornelia	SEP 25 1845
COOK, Adeline	HILL, Washington	MAR 28 1839
COOK, Alfred	BUTLER, Hope Ann	MAY 04 1830
COOK, Alice	OWENS, David	DEC 03 1818
COOK, Angelina	ROACH, Andrew J.	FEB 10 1847
COOK, Ann	RICARD, Edward	FEB 02 1824
COOK, Annetty	SMITH, William	OCT 16 1820
COOK, Benjamin	BIGS, Catharine	MAY 28 1816
COOK, Benoni	SMITH, Emily	JUL 16 1846
COOK, Cecelia	DITTY, Samuel	APR 14 1825
COOK, Charles Jacob	FASTNACHT, Sophie	MAY 01 1849
COOK, Christiana S.	SMITH, John G.	SEP 08 1853
COOK, David	EDEN, Susan	MAY 06 1823
COOK, Edward	HARDESTY, Eliza Ann	MAR 05 1820
COOK, Eleanor	ALLEN, William	NOV 08 1821
COOK, Elisha J.	McKNEW, Minerva	JUL 17 1855
COOK, Eliza	YOUNG, William W.	NOV 27 1844
COOK, Eliza Margaret	CLAMPETT, William Henry	MAY 04 1847
COOK, Elizabeth	SMITH, Zachariah	JAN 04 1832
COOK, Elizabeth	GENAW, Daniel	APR 04 1853
COOK, Elizabeth A.	JOHNSON, William	FEB 07 1833
COOK, George	WASHINGTON, Marcelena	OCT 25 1837
COOK, George T.	WILLIAMS, Sarah D.	NOV 18 1852
COOK, H.A.	HUMPHREYS, Isabella A.	NOV 13 1856
COOK, Heny	WHITEHEAD, Richard	JUL 17 1813
COOK, James	TAYLOR, Virginia W.	FEB 22 1849
COOK, James E.	MITCHELL, Mary E.	OCT 29 1857
COOK, James G.	BEACH, Lucinda	SEP 21 1848
COOK, Jane	BLAKE, William H.	JUL 09 1827
COOK, Jane	BEACH, James T.	JAN 01 1852
COOK, Jane (blk)	PERKINS, Henry	FEB 08 1849
COOK, John	WALKER, Elizabeth	OCT 28 1824
COOK, John	BURCH, Virginia	DEC 03 1845
COOK, John	FRIEND, Henrietta	SEP 08 1852
COOK, John A.	WISEMAN, Ann Elizabeth	MAR 14 1820
COOK, John A. [Lt.]	OWNER, Frances	DEC 16 1828
COOK, John F.	HOOE, Elizabeth T.	JUN 08 1842
COOK, John F.P.	CLEMENTS, Mary A.	APR 20 1835
COOK, John Henry	NEILE, Louisa Ann	OCT 12 1843
COOK, John Henry	STEELE, Ann Rebecca	JAN 27 1853
COOK, Joseph	BERRY, Eliza Henrietta	NOV 02 1852
COOK, Laura B.	DENHAM, Thomas S.	SEP 22 1857
COOK, Louisa	FOOT, Fredk.	JUN 12 1855
COOK, Lucretia A.	GARNER, Charles N.	NOV 22 1849
COOK, Margaret	GOLDSMITH, William L.	NOV 09 1857
COOK, Martha	ROWLEY, John	MAY 21 1830
COOK, Martha	HEST, Jacob	DEC 24 1832
COOK, Martha	GRIFFITH, Thomas	JUL 24 1839

District of Columbia Marriage Licenses, 1811-1858

COOK, Martha E.	HOOPER, Jno. B.	MAR 06 1850
COOK, Martin	POWER, Sarah	NOV 30 1830
COOK, Mary	BIGGES, Thomas	JUL 17 1845
COOK, Mary	PRAKER, Bennart	MAR 28 1853
COOK, Mary Ann P.	SOPER, Basil	JUN 15 1833
COOK, Mary C.	HEARD, John F.	AUG 31 1858
COOK, Mary Drucilla	SMITHIA, William	JUL 23 1845
COOK, Mary E.	MARTIN, Albert W.	MAY 07 1849
COOK, Mary Ellen	PROSPERI, Frederick	MAY 09 1853
COOK, Mary Jane	BRADY, Henry	MAR 25 1837
COOK, Matthew	HUTTON, Sarah E.	JAN 25 1840
COOK, Milly Ann	HENNAND, Stephen	AUG 09 1820
COOK, Patrick	DIPPLEY, Margaret	JAN 11 1853
COOK, Peter	BOWLING, Jane S.	JAN 07 1817
COOK, Peter Zeddick	BIGGES, Jane	JUL 17 1845
COOK, Peter Zedick	METHINA, Jane	DEC 26 1833
COOK, Philip	ELIJA, Elizth. Ann	NOV 19 1831
COOK, Richard Henry	TALBERT, Margaret	JAN 16 1847
COOK, Richard W.	LANGLEY, Sarah	JUL 23 1835
COOK, Samuel	TOLBERT, Elizabeth	SEP 28 1813
COOK, Sarah	WILLIAMS, Elie	JUL 25 1829
COOK, Sarah Ann	ROGERS, Beverly	FEB 11 1826
COOK, Sarah Ann	GRISSET, Cyrus	JUL 27 1850
COOK, Sophia	BIRCH, William H.	JUL 23 1845
COOK, Susanna H.	CARROL, Walter	FEB 12 1828
COOK, Thomas	MacGLENON, Mary	AUG 15 1833
COOK, Thomas W.	GODDARD, Rosaline V.	JAN 08 1857
COOK, William	WEAVER, Elizabeth	FEB 03 1825
COOK, William	McKEE, Milly B.	DEC 07 1843
COOK, William H.	CHANCEY, Mary Ann	MAY 04 1839
COOK, WIlliam	GILL, Margaret	NOV 30 1852
COOKE, Anne	BOWEN, James	SEP 06 1813
COOKE, Catharine V.	DOWN, Orlando H.	MAY 08 1850
COOKE, Jacob	BENNARD, Ann	FEB 10 1857
COOKE, James Lewis	RIDGWAY, Christiana E.	DEC 19 1857
COOKE, Johanna	BROWN, William	MAR 20 1819
COOKE, John	LANG, Sarah	OCT 26 1828
COOKE, John	BIGGS, Harriet	FEB 25 1834
COOKE, John F.	MANN, Jane (blk)	DEC 13 1832
COOKE, Mary	WISEMAN, John	DEC 24 1817
COOKE, Mary E.	BARNES, William	JUN 04 1835
COOKE, Rebecca	DIXON, Tobias	SEP 18 1838
COOKE, Thomas	WILSON, Catharine [Mrs.]	OCT 18 1821
COOKE, Thomas	SLATFORD, Louisa	JUN 11 1849
COOKE, William	BEALL, Mary B.	MAY 06 1817
COOKE, William	SARCEVES, Rhodey	SEP 15 1831
COOKE, William H.	BAGGETT, Celia Ann	NOV 02 1847
COOKE, Zadack	TUCKER, Patsey	SEP 13 1836
COOKENDORFER, Jane	CASTLEMAN, Stephen D.	DEC 13 1843
COOKSEY, George R.	ACTON, Ann M.	JUN 02 1855
COOKSEY, Joshua J.	KIDWELL, Ellen S.	DEC 24 1850
COOKSEY, Mary Ann	HEPNER, Fred	FEB 25 1817
COOLAN, Nicholas	SIBLEY, Mary Ann	JUN 22 1838
COOLEY, Benjamin	GROOMS, Ann Elizabeth	DEC 01 1846
COOLEY, Jannett E.	WANNELL, Joseph F.	JAN 10 1846
COOLEY, Martha	COCHRAN, James	SEP 08 1849
COOLEY, Mary Ann	STICKELL, Joseph	MAY 31 1853
COOLEY, Susannah	LEPREUX, Louis	FEB 25 1847

District of Columbia Marriage Licenses, 1811-1858

COOLIDGE, Elizabeth A.	MARTINE, Andrew	APR 13 1854
COOLIDGE, James	CASSIN, L.M.	AUG 12 1841
COOLIDGE, John H.	BERRYMAN, Maria N.	JUN 11 1832
COOLIDGE, Leonora M.	WILLIAMS, John	MAR 18 1857
COOLIDGE, Marion A.	BLUNT, Harry W.D.	NOV 13 1854
COOLIDGE, Richard Hoffman	RINGGOLD, Harriet Bowen	FEB 22 1854
COOLIN, Catharine	SAUTER, Wendelin	OCT 21 1833
COOLY, Margaret Ann	HICKMAN, William T.	AUG 09 1855
COOMB, Catharine	KEYS, Fielding	NOV 15 1849
COOMBE, Ann	MOSELEY, Spencer	APR 28 1814
COOMBE, Eliza	GRISWOLD, George [Rev.]	MAY 27 1828
COOMBE, Mary	BUTLER, David, Jr.	SEP 06 1821
COOMBE, Ruhumah	HEWITT, Robert	DEC 06 1831
COOMBES, Charles	MURRAY, Mary M.	JUL 06 1858
COOMBES, Ignatius	CIDER, Mary	NOV 21 1818
COOMBES, John	MYERS, Anna	OCT 23 1834
COOMBES, Margaret	HARRISON, Wm.	NOV 04 1819
COOMBES, Mary Ann Elizabeth	HARVEY, Henry Thomas	MAR 24 1829
COOMBES, Thomas	MAYFIELD, Sarah Ann	DEC 12 1846
COOMBS, Henry	CAMPITT, Maria	AUG 26 1822
COOMBS, James W.	MICKUM, Mary E.	MAR 06 1850
COOMBS, John M.	PORTS, Anne E.	MAY 24 1856
COOMBS, Margaret L.	PASCHALL, Thomas	AUG 02 1852
COOMBS, Mary	LAWRENCE, John	OCT 18 1838
COOMBS, Mary	ARMSTRONG, Caroll	JUN 19 1858
COOMBS, Sally	PICKRELL, Josias	NOV 10 1842
COOMBS, Samuel	SWEENY, Ann	JUN 28 1828
COOMBS, Samuel	JARBOE, Mary Jane	OCT 01 1845
COOMBS, Samuel	CRAIG, Mary E.	NOV 02 1850
COOMBS, Sarah Ann	HUDSON, Samuel	SEP 22 1852
COOMBS, Wm. J.	EMERSON, Sarah A.	JAN 08 1856
COOMES, Sarah M.	JOHNSON, Alexander	JAN 28 1850
COOMS, Michael R.	KUNDELEHR, Catharine	APR 05 1842
COON, George G.	OSTRANDER, Mary Jane	MAR 14 1855
COONBECK, Catherine	JOHNSON, Henry	FEB 26 1849
COONES, Fredk.	THOMPSON, Dolly	FEB 07 1820
COONEY, James	NORWOOD, Samueletta	JUN 13 1853
COONEY, Maria	MORROW, William	AUG 31 1840
COONEY, Mary	HOOD, George	APR 17 1852
COONS, Juliana	CROWLEY, Patrick	JUN 27 1820
COONTES, Margaret	KLEIBER, Jacob	JUN 11 1818
COOPER, Amanda V.	SMITH, Joseph M.	NOV 16 1852
COOPER, Ann	HAVENER, John F.	DEC 10 1849
COOPER, Ann S.	ALMOND, Barnett B.	APR 07 1840
COOPER, Ceily	BRISCOE, George	SEP 30 1820
COOPER, Charles	SHORTER, [blank] (blk)	NOV 14 1844
COOPER, Edward	McDADE, Elizabeth	MAR 20 1820
COOPER, Edward	RAWLING, Mary	JAN 04 1826
COOPER, Edward	ROBINSON, Martha	JAN 21 1835
COOPER, Eleanor	HAMPTON, Thomas	JUL 25 1815
COOPER, Elizabeth	BLAKE, William	MAR 14 1821
COOPER, Ellen	TYLER, John	MAY 14 1842
COOPER, Ellen E.	DYER, Benjamin F.	NOV 15 1838
COOPER, Emma A.	WINCHELL, William R.	APR 06 1854
COOPER, Francis A.	RYAN, Mary E.	JUL 25 1850
COOPER, Franklin	STEIGER, Lavinia	MAY 10 1841
COOPER, George	THOMAS, Mary	MAR 06 1843
COOPER, George	BEARD, Angeroner	JAN 11 1858

District of Columbia Marriage Licenses, 1811-1858

COOPER, Grenville C.	SHEDDEN, Jane Agnes	JUN 13 1829
COOPER, Hannah	RANDOM, James M.	MAY 10 1832
COOPER, Harriet	HEPBURN, Henry C.	OCT 20 1856
COOPER, Harriet E.	CAMP, John W.	FEB 27 1851
COOPER, James A.	DOUGHERTY, Mary Ellen	SEP 15 1852
COOPER, Jane	STUCK, Ferdinand F.	DEC 31 1822
COOPER, John	SUMMERVILLE, Adeline (blk)	APR 28 1842
COOPER, Joseph	HUNT, Mary Elizabeth	FEB 19 1824
COOPER, Joseph	SANDIFORD, Phebe Ann [Mrs.]	JAN 03 1833
COOPER, Lewis	PAYNE, Rebecca (blk)	OCT 01 1844
COOPER, Louisa	BUTLER, Benjamin	JUL 13 1841
COOPER, Louisa (blk)	SELVEY, Patrick	MAY 11 1848
COOPER, Lucy Ann (blk)	DAVIS, James	MAR 18 1847
COOPER, Margaret	SINCLAIR, Robert	APR 18 1815
COOPER, Margaret	SLATER, William	APR 02 1829
COOPER, Margaret	DONN, John Y.	JUL 07 1853
COOPER, Maria Mason	WHEATON, Frank	FEB 04 1857
COOPER, Martha A.	BAKER, William M.	JUL 21 1857
COOPER, Mary (blk)	BROWN, John	SEP 13 1821
COOPER, Mary Elizth.	GOOD, William H.	JUL 18 1843
COOPER, Miles	EDELIN, Mary Matilda	JUL 25 1833
COOPER, Rebecca	KYLER, James W.	SEP 24 1836
COOPER, Rebecca (blk)	LUCAS, Rezin	APR 17 1857
COOPER, Rosanna	WAGGONER, John David	SEP 30 1853
COOPER, Rosetta	DULANY, Charles	APR 26 1827
COOPER, S.B.B.	BROWN, Eliza Ann	JAN 26 1839
COOPER, Samuel [Lieut.]	MASON, Sarah Maria	APR 04 1827
COOPER, Samuel	THOMPSON, Mary Ann	JUN 11 1846
COOPER, Samuel	BROWN, Winna Ann (blk)	SEP 06 1855
COOPER, Samuel Barron	BIRCKHEAD, Mary Jane	JAN 15 1857
COOPER, Sarah	MANNING, Ignatius F.	APR 21 1857
COOPER, Sarah (blk)	LANCASTER, Richard	APR 06 1844
COOPER, Sarah (blk)	GRIMES, Charles Wm.	FEB 14 1853
COOPER, Sarah Ann	PRENTISS, Wm. H.	SEP 29 1831
COOPER, Seth R.	GARRISON, Virginia A.	NOV 03 1857
COOPER, Tego	WILLIAMS, Mary Ann	JAN 14 1852
COOPER, Thomas	MIDDLETON, Sarah E.	NOV 10 1853
COOPER, William	HICKS, Elizabeth Ann (blk)	NOV 10 1841
COOPER, William B.	JOHNSTON, Julia	MAR 04 1856
COOPER, William H.	HELLEN, Frances (blk)	AUG 20 1850
COOPER, William, Jr.	BELL, Harriet	MAY 04 1826
COOPER, Wm., Jr.	BELL, Ann	AUG 13 1822
COOTE, Ann	BARRY, James	MAY 02 1838
COOTE, Margaret C.	MURRAY, Thomas, Jr.	MAY 08 1832
COOTE, Marian	SPEIDEN, William	OCT 07 1828
COOTE, Thomas	DAVIS, Caroline	NOV 19 1818
COOVER, George	STIMMELL, Anna Maria	JUN 17 1814
COPEN, Laura H.	KEYS, Peyton	FEB 02 1852
COPF, Minna	SHAFER, John	APR 10 1851
COPP, George	BRIEM, Barbara	NOV 29 1852
COPP, Moses	HUTCHINS, Margaretta A.	DEC 11 1850
COPPAGE, William	FOX, Mary	MAY 01 1854
COPPER, John	DORSER, Margaretta	OCT 11 1850
CORBATT, Ann	O'SHEA, William	JUL 14 1853
CORBETT, Mary	CHANEY, Elijah, Jr.	OCT 07 1824
CORBETT, Michael	GARDIVAN, Honora	APR 19 1856
CORBIN, Frances C.	THOMPSON, Thomas W.	JAN 24 1854
CORBIN, Spotswood Wellford	MAURY, Nannie Fontaine	APR 28 1858

District of Columbia Marriage Licenses, 1811-1858

CORBIT, Bridget	MALONEY, Michael	JAN 27 1858
CORBIT, Mary	BAKER, George	OCT 13 1853
CORBITT, Ann	SHANCKNESSY, Michael	AUG 07 1858
CORBOTT, John	HARRAHAN, Catherine	JUN 12 1847
CORCORAN, Henry W.	LINKIN, Margaret	JUN 21 1831
CORCORAN, James	REYNOLDS, Harriet	FEB 19 1819
CORCORAN, Jane	McATEE, Harrison	JUL 20 1815
CORCORAN, John	MOHLDER, Lucy	DEC 29 1851
CORCORAN, Martha Ellen	HILL, Stephen P. [Rev.]	DEC 08 1835
CORCORAN, Patrick	SHEA, Mary	JAN 11 1858
CORCORAN, Sarah	JONES, William [Dr.]	DEC 18 1821
CORCORAN, Sarah C.	THOM, Christopher N.	AUG 05 1856
CORCORAN, Walter Joseph	WILLIAMS, Ann	MAY 23 1818
CORD, William	SCHLETMAN, Mary T.	JUL 21 1851
CORDELL, Collin Mortimer	CRANDELL, Maranda, Miss	MAR 09 1835
CORE, John T.	DYER, Sarah Jane	JUL 26 1849
CORE, Mary L.	WADDEY, James E.	SEP 03 1856
CORIDON, Bridget	O'CONNOR, John	FEB 21 1857
CORIDON, Mary	DAILEY, Eugene	DEC 08 1854
CORIER, Abigal	LUCUS, Augustus	JUN 07 1834
CORLEY, Catherine	SPIES, James P.	APR 08 1858
CORLISS, Charlotte Ann	BISHOP, Daniel H.	APR 25 1856
CORMAN, William	DOWNES, Jane	JUN 04 1825
CORNELIUS, Samuel	WOODWARD, Virginia C.	DEC 24 1851
CORNELL, Robert	HALLER, Rebecca	DEC 10 1857
CORNISH, Harriet (blk)	DUNLAP, George W.	JAN 27 1853
CORNISH, William A.	BEAN, Harriet (blk)	JUL 30 1839
CORNOG, John	SHARPLESS, Sarah D.	JAN 07 1846
CORNWALL, Artemesia Griffin	TAYLOR, Joshua	OCT 30 1817
CORNWALL, Jane C.	BIRCH, James H.	JUL 02 1857
CORNWALL, John	DONALDSON, Susanna V.	FEB 28 1857
CORNWALL, John D.	ULMER, Mary E.	AUG 23 1858
CORNWALL, Joseph W.	CAMMACK, Rebecca	SEP 11 1849
CORNWATH, Mary F.	JOHNSON, James E.	NOV 20 1855
CORNWELL, Ann	LAWS, Newton	JAN 24 1833
CORNWELL, Sarah J.	BRESLYN, George W.	JUN 18 1856
CORNWILL, Lucinda	EVANS, Alexander	MAR 29 1830
CORRAN, Margarett	DONOHO, Michale	MAY 17 1854
CORRIDAN, Edward	LEIHY, Honora	NOV 27 1850
CORRIGAN, Bernard	CARROLL, Margaret	JUL 17 1848
CORRIGAN, Hugh	BIRK, Annica	FEB 22 1825
CORRIGAN, Owen	MILLY, Catharine	JUL 05 1853
CORRIGAN, Thomas M.	McLAUGHLIN, Celia	JUN 02 1851
CORRIGAN, Thomas M.	McLAUGHLIN, Celia	JUN 30 1851
CORRY, Ann	POSEY, Laurence	NOV 24 1856
CORSE, M. Percival	FITZHUGH, Margaretta	JAN 10 1849
CORSON, Hiram	ROLLIN, Caroline	SEP 12 1854
CORSON, Pierson	GEEN, Louisanna A.	SEP 05 1857
CORTER, Thomas	LANE, Martha Ann	MAY 22 1822
CORTIN, Ellen	DALY, Lawrence	OCT 22 1853
CORTNEY, Margaret	LONG, Bartholomew	AUG 25 1855
CORVIN, Julia	LONGDEN, Thomas	DEC 04 1815
COSBERRY, Phillis (blk)	LITTON, Samuel	SEP 22 1849
COSBY, Fortinnatus	MILLS, Ann S.	JUN 24 1854
COSGERY, James	CLARY, Mary	APR 12 1853
COSGROVE, Alice	SPELAUN, John	JUN 13 1854
COSGROVE, Bridget	DEVERUE, William P.	AUG 22 1857
COSLEY, Howard W.	WARREN, Harriet L.	JUN 02 1856

District of Columbia Marriage Licenses, 1811-1858

COSNAHAN, J.B.H.	WALLER, Louisa M.	AUG 05 1843
COST, John M.	FRANK, Sarah E.	JAN 09 1855
COST, Mary	CLAY, Edward	SEP 16 1823
COSTELLO, Catherine	LEARY, Arthur	SEP 30 1847
COSTELLO, Robert	CONNER, Mary	JUL 08 1854
COSTEN, Margaret	GRIMES, Craven F.	OCT 22 1838
COSTIGAN, James	TIPPETT, Caroline	SEP 27 1828
COSTIGAN, Joseph	EDELIN, Martha R.	DEC 22 1827
COSTIGAN, Martha R.	ANDERSON, John S.	APR 20 1843
COSTIN, Fanny Park	LEE, William W.	MAY 08 1851
COSTIN, George	HILLERY, Charlotte	MAR 24 1834
COSTIN, Harriet (blk)	FISKE, Richard H.	NOV 19 1849
COSTIN, James A.	SIMPSON, Adaline	DEC 24 1845
COSTIN, Martha P. (blk)	DAYS, Stephen W.	MAY 05 1845
COSTIN, Martha P.	DAYS, Woolberton	JUN 13 1848
COSTIN, Thomas	CLUIN, Ann	FEB 16 1854
COSTIN, William	MATTHEWS, Elizabeth (blk)	JUN 06 1838
COSTIN, William G.	BROCKETT, Amelia (blk)	MAY 12 1847
COSTOLE, Ellen	CONNER, Dennis	MAY 08 1856
COSWAY, John	SWEENY, Bridget	OCT 23 1854
COTES, John	SPALDING, Ann	JUL 02 1857
COTTER, James	SHERIDAN, Bridget	NOV 29 1852
COTTER, Richard	LANAGHAN, Mary	NOV 22 1851
COTTRELL, Margaret	ADAMSON, Roger	FEB 22 1851
COTTRINGER, Harriet	BRENT, Robert Y.	JAN 06 1824
COUFMAN, Elias	HIRCH, Beattie	SEP 10 1857
COUFMAN, Nehm	WOLF, Caroline	JUN 09 1854
COULSON, Jane	BELL, William	APR 08 1833
COULSTON Susan	BIENVENIDA, Lazaro	OCT 30 1840
COULTER, Peter	CEALIX, Alice	MAR 11 1831
COULTER, Sarah	STIVER, Henry	MAR 31 1821
COUMBE, Elizth. Jane	MILLER, Edward	AUG 31 1839
COUMBE, John T.	KENDRICK, Ann M.	FEB 18 1847
COUMBE, William	THOMPSON, Rachael	APR 06 1822
COUNAY, John	GRIFFITH, Susan	MAY 19 1854
COUNOL, Johana	COLLINS, Jeremiah	FEB 16 1858
COURAD, Godfred	TIMMS, Catherine	MAY 22 1822
COURSE, Margaretta	COURSE, Wilmer D.	APR 26 1852
COURSE, Wilmer D.	COURSE, Margaretta	APR 26 1852
COURTANEY, John	LOWE, Martha	AUG 15 1820
COURTNEY, Amanda	GRAHAM, French	AUG 24 1858
COURTNEY, Amelia	COLLINS, Alfred	FEB 02 1839
COURTNEY, Ann	MICHAELS, William S.	MAR 11 1847
COURTNEY, Ellen	BIRCH, Edward	JAN 14 1858
COURTNEY, Joseph C.	BELL, L.A.W.	FEB 14 1842
COURTNEY, Mary	HOGAN, Philip	MAY 02 1851
COURTNEY, Mary	ROSSITER, John	APR 16 1852
COURTNEY, Mary	LOYUNY, William	MAY 13 1852
COURTNEY, Sarah Ann	HUMPHRIES, John D.	SEP 09 1847
COUSINS, Harriet	MAGRUDER, Belford	FEB 06 1840
COVER, Ann Sophia	WALKER, James	JUL 22 1830
COVER, Daniel P.	THROOP, Kanarias	DEC 22 1848
COVER, Elizabeth B.	CURREN, Barney B.	MAR 21 1842
COVER, Jacob	OLIVER, Mary Ann	AUG 23 1823
COVER, Mary A.	SHIPMAN, John	JAN 22 1842
COVER, Philomon	OLIVER, Ann	JUN 14 1828
COVILLIER, Theodore	BOOTH, Margaret	JAN 20 1836
COVINGTON, Harry W.	GILHAM, Mary Ann	SEP 26 1828

District of Columbia Marriage Licenses, 1811-1858

COWAN, Edward	KING, Maria	DEC 09 1823
COWAN, James Edward	DOUGLASS, Ellen	DEC 20 1827
COWEN, David	ELLINGTON, Mary E.	JUL 12 1858
COWING, Granville	MORAN, Lucy	APR 17 1855
COWLEY, John	MORRIS, Elizabeth	FEB 04 1857
COWLING, Atwell	SANDS, Frances R.	NOV 27 1855
COWLING, Edward	WILSON, Mary	SEP 04 1855
COWLING, James	SKINNER, Mary	FEB 22 1855
COWLING, Thomas	SKINNER, Caroline	AUG 11 1853
COWLING, Thomas C.	BONTZE, Elizabeth C.	JAN 03 1857
COWPER, Virginia (blk)	WILLIAMS, John	DEC 18 1855
COX, Ann	TALBERT, Sydny G.	FEB 07 1831
COX, Ann [Mrs.]	ROSE, Charles S.	APR 24 1835
COX, Ann Lauretta	WILLS, John	MAY 21 1845
COX, Ann Maria H.	HORWELL, Edward C.	MAR 23 1829
COX, Anne	SULLIVAN, Jeremiah	MAY 17 1848
COX, Charles A.	GATES, Elizabeth E.	OCT 23 1846
COX, Charles F.	MEADE, Cecilia Ann	JUL 10 1847
COX, Clement	RINGGOLD, Mary	NOV 10 1825
COX, Clement	REGAN, Ellen	FEB 17 1849
COX, Eliza	BURCH, John Wesley	MAY 26 1842
COX, Eliza Jane	WEEKES, Joseph	AUG 14 1855
COX, Elizabeth	UNDERWOOD, Joseph R.	FEB 25 1839
COX, Ellen	HALIDAY, James F.	JUL 16 1838
COX, Ellen	MILLER, Isaac F.	DEC 02 1852
COX, Ellen May	McELDERRY, John P.	OCT 07 1852
COX, Fleet	SCOTT, Maria E.	JUL 12 1831
COX, Francis	CLEMENTS, Terese	FEB 20 1821
COX, Fredk.	ANDERSON, Matilda	OCT 16 1838
COX, Geo. C.	PURCELL, Sophia W.	DEC 29 1849
COX, George F.	ADAMS, Ellen E.	JAN 07 1856
COX, George F.	ADAMS, Ellen E.	JUN 21 1856
COX, George S.	TATSPAUGH, Mary Ann	APR 14 1841
COX, Henry N.	WORTHINGTON, Susan	APR 30 1845
COX, James	FENWICK, Mary	OCT 20 1832
COX, James	HOWARD, Elizabeth	MAY 23 1840
COX, James	LUCKETT, Julia Ann	JUN 05 1841
COX, James	SIMMS, Mary Ann	AUG 07 1845
COX, James Newton	AMISS, Martha E.W.	DEC 22 1857
COX, Jane Elizabeth	WILKINSON, Walter	DEC 18 1849
COX, John	KNIGHTON, Elizabeth E.	JUL 26 1853
COX, John E.	BANGS, Henrietta	OCT 11 1851
COX, John H.	JOHNSON, Anna T.	JAN 29 1850
COX, John Walter	SMITH, Ann Sophia	JUL 05 1842
COX, John [Col.]	THRELKELD, Jane	JAN 14 1818
COX, Julia Ann	PLANT, James W.	NOV 04 1847
COX, Lucy B.	WALKER, Zachariah	JAN 27 1825
COX, Margaret	LANEHART, John	SEP 18 1845
COX, Marion	HOFMAN, Wolfgan	NOV 18 1851
COX, Mary	TAYLOR, George	FEB 11 1823
COX, Mary	WILSON, Lewis C.	DEC 14 1835
COX, Mary	SPURLENS, James	DEC 10 1841
COX, Mary	CONNER, John	MAY 23 1855
COX, Mary Ann	WILLET, Daniel	AUG 20 1829
COX, Mary E.	COX, Peter F.	DEC 22 1856
COX, Mary J.	THOMPSON, Sammes H.	JAN 05 1857
COX, Mary Jane (blk)	MAGRUDER, Francis	JAN 29 1857
COX, Mary Jane	GROVES, Samuel	DEC 29 1857

District of Columbia Marriage Licenses, 1811-1858

COX, Matilda	PURCELL, Thomas Francis	NOV 05 1829
COX, Peter F.	COX, Mary E.	DEC 22 1856
COX, Philip Lansdale	ROY, Mary M.	MAY 18 1843
COX, Richard S.	WILLIAMS, Eliza	JAN 31 1849
COX, Rosina L.	BOARDMAN, William C.	APR 30 1838
COX, Sally	SMITH, John Addison	NOV 22 1825
COX, Samuel	COX, Walter Ann	DEC 06 1842
COX, Samuel A.	THORN, Catharine A.B.	MAY 26 1841
COX, Samuel G.	GARLAND, Ann Maria	DEC 23 1851
COX, Samuel K.	BILLING, Augusta M.	DEC 23 1847
COX, Sarah Ann	NOLER, William	JUL 17 1834
COX, Susan	EATON, Smauel	MAY 03 1841
COX, Susannah E.	MORAN, William M.	FEB 04 1850
COX, Walter	BERRY, Lucy B.	AUG 04 1818
COX, Walter Ann	COX, Samuel	DEC 06 1842
COX, Washington F.	FRYE, Sarah M.	DEC 23 1845
COX, William	WALCH, Bridget Ann	JUL 24 1830
COX, William	MITCHELL, Caroline	JAN 06 1846
COXE, Jane	O'DONNOGHUE, John	SEP 08 1837
COXE, Maria Matilda	EVANS, Alexander H.	FEB 08 1844
COXE, Mary	PENDLETON, William Armistead	FEB 07 1853
COXE, Mary G.	MAHON, Alexander M.	MAR 28 1846
COXE, Susan B.	WEIGHTMAN, Richard Hanson	MAR 29 1842
COXEN, Ann	HOAG, Sheldon J.	OCT 20 1853
COXEN, Henry	WHALEY, Martha	OCT 22 1853
COXEN, James	PADGETT, Lucretia	APR 01 1853
COXEN, John	TANEY, Sarah (blk)	APR 10 1851
COXEN, John Thomas	LANGLEY, Martha Ann	FEB 10 1848
COXEN, Martha	WELLS, Henry	DEC 10 1850
COXEN, Mary C.	MARTIN, William	MAR 18 1858
COXEN, Robert	BOSWELL, Mary Louisa	OCT 24 1854
COXEN, Susan	LINKINS, Joseph	MAY 01 1849
COXING, Ruth Ann	HOWLIN, Patrick	MAY 25 1848
COXON, Julia Ann	JONES, Augustus	OCT 16 1826
COXON, Rutha	WINKLER, William	JUN 14 1831
COYLE, Ann W.	WHITWELL, John Geo.	OCT 31 1822
COYLE, Catharine A.	BRADLEY, Charles	JUL 10 1841
COYLE, Catharine B.	BAYLISS, Buckner	JUN 28 1834
COYLE, James	TURNER, Susan	DEC 14 1839
COYLE, Leonidas	EDMUND, Harriet L.	APR 12 1836
COYLE, Maria H.	SPEER, Alexander	AUG 25 1846
COYLE, Terresa	VENABLE, Joseph	AUG 22 1812
COYNE, Margaret	DULANY, Thomas	FEB 03 1818
COZENS, Caroline	MELLINGTON, Thomas	MAY 18 1836
COZENS, Charlotte	STEELE, John A.	AUG 07 1847
COZENS, George W.	JETT, Margaret	SEP 07 1852
COZENS, Gustavus	LUCAS, Marian	APR 04 1857
COZENS, Lewis A.	WOODSIDE, Maria	MAR 04 1817
COZZINS, George	JETT, Margaret	DEC 02 1852
CRABB, Thomas [Lieut.]	CRAVEN, Jane Louisa	APR 19 1827
CRABBS, Ann M.	HEWITT, Robert C.C.	JUL 26 1858
CRACKLIN, Ann E.	HARRIS, Octavus C.	JUL 23 1853
CRAFT, Mary	BLADEN, John	DEC 23 1846
CRAFT, Samuel	HINEZ, Elizabeth	APR 06 1825
CRAGE, Mary A.	BARRON, George O.	NOV 07 1850
CRAGEAR, Mary Ann	CRUIT, Richard	JAN 24 1855
CRAGER, Eliza	POSTON, Fielder B.	APR 17 1817
CRAGGS, Thomas	BRYSON, Hester	JUL 12 1855

District of Columbia Marriage Licenses, 1811-1858

CRAGIN, Charles H.	McKENNEY, Mary	OCT 01 1845
CRAGIN, Charles H.	McKENNEY, Henrietta F.	APR 14 1857
CRAHAN, Thomas	McLEAN, Elizabeth	SEP 03 1853
CRAHEN, Thomas	GREEN, Bridget	APR 17 1851
CRAIG, Caroline	ROSE, Samuel	DEC 15 1829
CRAIG, Charles E.	RADCLIFF, Ann M.	SEP 05 1843
CRAIG, George	BUTLER, Mary	JUN 25 1838
CRAIG, Harriott E.	McCREERY, John	AUG 18 1815
CRAIG, Harrison	PARADISE, Mary Elizabeth	SEP 17 1838
CRAIG, Henrietta	BURGESS, Dawson P.	MAY 25 1815
CRAIG, Henry	REED, Shadey (blk)	JAN 23 1845
CRAIG, Josephine S.	TODD, John	APR 19 1852
CRAIG, Margaret	GIST, B.F.	FEB 13 1834
CRAIG, Margaret C.A.	DICKSON, Thomas H.	NOV 06 1832
CRAIG, Mary E.	COOMBS, Samuel	NOV 02 1850
CRAIG, Oliver	HALEY, Elizabeth	FEB 12 1848
CRAIG, Robert	CARNES, Maria	JAN 04 1821
CRAIG, Sarah Jane	WHITAKER, John T.	AUG 06 1855
CRAIG, Susan C.	BLOXTON, Charles	JAN 04 1832
CRAIG, Washington	PARKER, Eliza	MAR 04 1826
CRAIG, William H.	JONES, Caroline Amanda	FEB 01 1842
CRAIG, William T.	KELLY, Cassa Ann	JUL 09 1853
CRAIGHAN, Norah	McLEAN, John	JAN 08 1852
CRAIGHEN, Ellen	BARRETT, Dennis	NOV 22 1851
CRAIGHEN, Margaret	CARROLL, Patrick	JAN 27 1853
CRAIGHILL, Martha P.	MANNING, Nathaniel W.	JAN 31 1835
CRAIGHILL, Wm. P.	MORSELL, Mary Ann	OCT 09 1856
CRAIHEN, Maria	SULLIVAN, Daniel Eugene	NOV 19 1853
CRAILY, Catharine	CARRIGON, Lawrence	JAN 23 1852
CRAIN, Elizabeth	BLOIS, Zachariah	JUL 02 1812
CRAINER, Ellen	WELCH, Dennis	NOV 13 1851
CRAMER, Samuel J.	MOUNTZ, Elizabeth C.	SEP 15 1840
CRAMPSON, William D.	LEATHERBERRY, Eliza	MAY 15 1845
CRAMPSTIN, Caroline E.	SMITH, Joseph S.	JUN 30 1831
CRAMPTON, Catherine Virginia	BOOTHE, James	JUN 09 1857
CRAMPTON, Job Edwin	ANGEL, Catherine A.	DEC 30 1857
CRAMPTON, John F.	OFFUTT, Catherine V.	FEB 09 1850
CRANCH, Abby	ELIOT, Wm. G.	JUN 29 1837
CRANCH, Elizth. Eliot	DAWES, Rufus	MAY 18 1829
CRANCH, Margaret D.	BROOKS, Erastus	JAN 12 1844
CRANDALL, Mary Ann	LAMBRIGHT, George	JAN 19 1832
CRANDE, William	TRACY, Elizabeth	MAY 06 1818
CRANDELL, Catharine A.	HUNT, Robert Finley	NOV 25 1845
CRANDELL, Harriet Ann	THOMAS, John Dill	JUL 02 1853
CRANDELL, Maranda, Miss	CORDELL, Collin Mortimer	MAR 09 1835
CRANDELL, Mary	HALL, John	MAR 10 1842
CRANDELL, Rachel	LINDERWOOD, George	MAR 14 1837
CRANDELL, Sarah Jane	RUFF, George Ryland	AUG 31 1846
CRANDLE, Elizabeth	TALBERT, Adam	DEC 10 1844
CRANDLE, Joseph H.	GREAR, Martha L.	DEC 26 1854
CRANDLE, Matilda	BERNARD, Hezekiah	JUN 22 1824
CRANDLE, Polly	BROWN, Francis	JAN 06 1831
CRANE, Margaret	GOLDEN, John Aylmer	JUL 02 1845
CRANE, Patience	FLEMMON, Francis	JUN 27 1812
CRANFORD, Eliza	JOHNSON, Francis	JUN 22 1826
CRANSTON, Julia	YOUNG, John	JUN 22 1839
CRANSTON, Ophelia	NEWNAM, William	APR 02 1829
CRANSTON, Robert S.	WARD, May A.	JUN 16 1837

District of Columbia Marriage Licenses, 1811-1858

CRASK, Mary Ann	PERRY, Thomas J.	DEC 26 1855
CRATHY, Catharine	CRATHY, Patrick	MAR 31 1854
CRATHY, Patrick	CRATHY, Catharine	MAR 31 1854
CRATTEY, Mary	NASH, Henry	MAR 27 1849
CRATTY, Ellen	BOWMAN, John M.	DEC 26 1855
CRATTY, Michael	DUNN, Margaret	SEP 13 1851
CRATTY, Michael	GRAVIN, Norah	SEP 08 1853
CRAVEN, Ann	NEENIN, John	SEP 22 1854
CRAVEN, Eleanor	SCRIVNER, William	JUL 21 1836
CRAVEN, Elijah R. [Dr.]	LANDRITH, Sarah E.	JUN 05 1823
CRAVEN, Jane Louisa	CRABB, Thomas [Lieut.]	APR 19 1827
CRAVEN, Johanna	BRARDON, Patrick	MAY 18 1857
CRAVEN, John	GREEN, Sarah Rebecca	OCT 28 1848
CRAVEN, Philip	HIGGIN, Catharine (blk)	JUL 10 1849
CRAVEN, Roger	CANNAVAN, Ann	FEB 08 1853
CRAVEN, Sarah	PARISH, Levi H.	JUN 15 1841
CRAVER, Henry P.	ADAMS, Ann J.	DEC 27 1851
CRAVER, Isaac	MINCHER, Sarah	JUN 12 1830
CRAVER, Madelina	MENCH, John H.	JUN 02 1849
CRAVER, Philip	CAMPBELL, Draden	NOV 14 1833
CRAVER, Philip	BERRY, Mary A.	DEC 14 1843
CRAWFORD, Adam	GALES, Lucy Ann	JUL 08 1830
CRAWFORD, Adam	HOWARD, Mary Jane	JAN 13 1841
CRAWFORD, Ann	BURGESS, Richard	MAY 16 1816
CRAWFORD, Ann	DIGGINS, James	JAN 10 1832
CRAWFORD, Archibald	HUMPHREYS, Ann	AUG 31 1826
CRAWFORD, Ariana	WILSON, Benoni	FEB 01 1813
CRAWFORD, Caroline	FOWLER, Jesse	JUL 28 1827
CRAWFORD, Charles	MARKLAND, Mary Ann	JUN 08 1844
CRAWFORD, Clementina M.	DAVIDSON, Delozier	JUN 05 1844
CRAWFORD, Eleanor	STEUART, William	JUL 03 1812
CRAWFORD, Eleanor	ROBINSON, Joseph	MAY 20 1813
CRAWFORD, Eliza	DAVIDSON, Lewis Grant	JAN 20 1821
CRAWFORD, Elizabeth	MILLER, Archy	JUL 09 1817
CRAWFORD, Elizabeth	COLCLAZIER, Jacob	DEC 21 1840
CRAWFORD, Eulilia E.	EDWARDS, Louis A.	OCT 01 1850
CRAWFORD, Frances (blk)	CURTIS, John	SEP 21 1853
CRAWFORD, Frances (blk)	THOMAS, Robert	DEC 03 1855
CRAWFORD, Henrietta M.	DAVIDSON, Delozier	OCT 04 1848
CRAWFORD, James	ATHEY, Susannah	JUN 21 1826
CRAWFORD, James	THOMAS, Mary Ann	DEC 27 1845
CRAWFORD, James	TURNER, Mary Ann Amanda	MAR 10 1855
CRAWFORD, James T.	DAVIS, Eliza Ann	MAY 10 1853
CRAWFORD, Jane G.	POPE, Frederick	APR 04 1817
CRAWFORD, John	NEWMAN, Mahala (blk)	DEC 24 1850
CRAWFORD, John H.	LINDSEY, Catharine H.	MAR 20 1834
CRAWFORD, Julia	GORDON, Charles	NOV 27 1827
CRAWFORD, Mary	REEVES, Jas. W.	MAY 15 1855
CRAWFORD, Mary A.	COLCLAZIER, Daniel V.	NOV 26 1841
CRAWFORD, Mary Ann	SUIT, Josiah S.W.	NOV 04 1823
CRAWFORD, Saml. T.	BROOKS, Malinda V.	NOV 24 1856
CRAWFORD, Samuel	CISSELL, Ann	FEB 25 1837
CRAWFORD, Sarah	BEACH, Samuel	APR 02 1835
CRAWFORD, Sophia	SIMPSON, James	APR 18 1835
CRAWFORD, Sophia	O'NEALE, Charles	AUG 01 1835
CRAWFORD, William	TOWNSON, Sophia (blk)	OCT 14 1852
CRAWLEY, Ann	CONELLY, Thomas	SEP 08 1818
CRAWLEY, Eliza	TAYLOR, Allender	MAY 05 1837

District of Columbia Marriage Licenses, 1811-1858

CRAWLEY, Margaret	RADY, William	JUN 06 1817
CRAY, Margaret	BRICK, Michael	APR 23 1851
CRAY, Peter	CONNOR, Bridget	OCT 08 1853
CREAGER, Mary	THOMAS, Nathan	MAR 11 1816
CREAGER, Michael	BIGWOOD, Anna	JAN 04 1817
CREAGER, Michael	SIMS, Jane	APR 25 1820
CREAGH, Nancy	O'DONNELL, Thomas	FEB 02 1856
CREAGOR, Susan	RATRIE, William	DEC 23 1812
CREAMER, Charles	SPECHT, Jenivefer	MAR 19 1855
CREAMER, Elizabeth	STEWART, Charles	NOV 30 1841
CREAMER, Emma Rebecca	BEARD, John James	AUG 16 1852
CREAMER, James	HILL, Elizabeth	APR 07 1845
CREAMER, James	GAMBLE, Margaret	MAY 11 1854
CREAMER, Kate B.	FOWBLE, William A.	JAN 13 1857
CREAMER, Mary	SELBEY, James	DEC 13 1841
CREAMER, Mary	SUIT, James H.	SEP 26 1848
CREAMER, Sarah	SESSFORD, Joseph	JUL 05 1837
CREAMER, Susan	MARTIN, Tyrance	MAY 24 1838
CREAMER, Susan	COLLINS, James	SEP 07 1844
CREAMER, Susannah	MORGAN, George W.	APR 06 1846
CREASER, Thomas	MILLER, Sarah	NOV 27 1834
CREASY, Thomas	MITCHELL, Sarah E.	OCT 31 1837
CRECEY, Mary E. (blk)	GEORGE, W.M.	JUN 26 1856
CREED, Johanna	KELLY, Humphrey	JUL 03 1857
CREEK, Sophia	MORRIS, Gerrard	AUG 13 1824
CREGAR, Rebecca	FOWLER, John L.	APR 09 1823
CREGG, Nathaniel C.	REDMOND, Maria C.H.	NOV 04 1820
CREHEN, Eugene	SHEPHARD, Eliza	JAN 23 1854
CREIG, Lewis	STONE, Ann	AUG 14 1813
CREIG, Robert	STANSBERRY, Ann	JAN 09 1858
CREIK, Margaret (blk)	LEE, Alfred	SEP 06 1826
CREMANTE, John	HADEN, Susan	JUL 15 1815
CREMIN, Johanna	CAIN, John	MAY 24 1858
CREWS, Joseph	MARTIN, Hester Ann	FEB 17 1852
CRIDDLE, Jonathan	BETTS, Catharine	MAR 26 1824
CRIDDLE, Jonathan	BURKE, Elizabeth	NOV 21 1836
CRIDER, Michael	MARR, Elizabeth A.	APR 14 1834
CRIDLING, Henry N.	BOWEN, Mary C.	AUG 05 1856
CRIMM, Margaret	FOKLE, Adam	MAY 12 1835
CRIMMIN, Patrick	MURPHY, Ellen	APR 08 1852
CRIPPER, Miner A.	KNIGHT, Jane M.	NOV 11 1852
CRIPPS, Ann Maria	CLARKE, Daniel B.	JAN 14 1847
CRIPPS, William M.L.	SPALDING, Mary Ellen	SEP 14 1824
CRISMOND, James L.	EMMERSON, Rosabella	APR 02 1857
CRISS, Henry	TALBOT, Jane	DEC 29 1836
CRISSMAN, Mary	SULLIVAN, Edward	DEC 31 1857
CRISTOFF, Margaret	VARNEY, William	MAY 01 1813
CRITTENDEN, J.J.	ASHLEY, Elizabeth	FEB 26 1853
CRITTENDEN, Mary V.	SYPHAX, Charles, Jr.	NOV 10 1857
CRITTENDEN, Richard N.	JAMES, Lucy A.	OCT 11 1855
CRITTENDEN, Robert H.	BUMLEY, Harriet	MAY 17 1853
CROCKEN, James H.	MARKS, Julia	MAR 26 1844
CROCKER, Mary Ann	SWEENY, Thomas	APR 14 1834
CROCKET, David	BENNET, Maria (blk)	OCT 26 1833
CROCKET, Eliza Ann	DENNIS, John	MAY 16 1853
CROCKET, Risdon	FLUHART, Margaret	SEP 17 1852
CROCKETT, Ann	DISE, John	OCT 23 1851
CROCKETT, Elizabeth	LURTEN, James	JUN 18 1847

District of Columbia Marriage Licenses, 1811-1858

CROCKETT, Elizabeth E.	DWYER, Richard	MAY 14 1850
CROCKETT, Hugh G.	STIFFLER, Eliza	JUL 10 1850
CROCKETT, John	KIDWELL, Elizabeth M.	DEC 21 1854
CROCKETT, Sippora	BRADSHAW, Nathan	MAY 15 1849
CROCKING, James	TANNER, Ann	FEB 19 1816
CROFT, Arhot	SKIDMORE, Catharine	AUG 29 1839
CROFTON, Ragena	GOODIN, Henry	OCT 07 1830
CROGER, Francis	NORMAN, Drucilla (blk)	NOV 22 1841
CROGGAN, Isaac N.J.	OGLE, Louisa	JUL 02 1842
CROGGEN, Henry B.	ROLLINGS, Mary Ann	OCT 20 1834
CROGGIN, Mary	SHREEVE, John	AUG 07 1855
CROGGIN, Thomas	McCARTHEY, Jane	MAY 26 1849
CROGGINGS, James H.	WILLIAMS, Sarah Ann	APR 28 1846
CROGGINS, Charles	EDMONSEN, Matilda	DEC 04 1839
CROGGON, Emily	DALTON, William	MAR 16 1837
CROGGON, Gertrude	PETTIT, Charles W.	DEC 04 1843
CROGGON, Matilda B.	SMITH, Daniel	SEP 14 1840
CROGGON, William	SMITH, Jane Eliza	MAR 08 1833
CROGHAN, Francis	KERWIN, Catharine	FEB 15 1836
CROGHAN, Serena L.	RODGERS, Augustus F.	JUN 09 1858
CROKER, Samuel	BUTLER, Kitty	AUG 04 1821
CROMPTON, Rebecca	GALLAND, William	JUL 15 1813
CROMWELL, Harriett	JAMESON, John	MAR 12 1835
CROMWELL, Jesse	MOORE, Hetty	MAR 29 1823
CROMWELL, John	CASTEL, Harriet	DEC 31 1828
CROMWELL, Stephen A.	CLUSKEY, Mary E.	MAY 14 1857
CRONAN, James	WELSH, Ann	JUN 04 1853
CRONAN, Thomas	DOWNAY, Johanna	MAY 06 1854
CRONAY, Dabby	McCARTY, James	DEC 03 1853
CRONER, Michael	RUSS, Frances	NOV 16 1848
CRONES, John	BRANDELL, Phillipe	SEP 16 1843
CRONIAN, Ann	McCORD, Bernard	MAY 21 1846
CRONIN, Elizabeth	RENNEY, Patrick	OCT 17 1818
CRONIN, Ellen	DOWNEY, Patrick	JAN 31 1856
CRONIN, Francis	WEST, William	NOV 26 1850
CRONIN, James	KILLEFOIL, Winifred	FEB 10 1858
CRONIN, Johanna	REARDON, John	SEP 18 1851
CRONIN, John	DUNNINI, Johanna	MAY 12 1854
CRONIN, John	HILL, Margaret	MAY 21 1855
CRONIN, Margaret	THORNTON, Thomas	MAY 12 1857
CRONIN, Mary Ann	CONNER, Dennis	AUG 05 1838
CRONIN, Mathew	FLINN, Catharine	AUG 11 1851
CRONIN, Patrick	BUCKLEY, Mary	MAY 26 1853
CRONION, John	McCARTHEY, Mary	SEP 19 1844
CRONION, Mary Ann	LOWE, James W.	AUG 04 1858
CROOK, John Henry	CARROLL, Elizabeth	NOV 06 1854
CROOK, Joseph	GIBBONS, Emeline Jane	SEP 20 1830
CROOK, Richard	POWERS, Matilda	NOV 01 1825
CROOKS, Alexr. W.	ERSKINE, Sophia Elizabeth	JAN 11 1837
CROOKSHANK, Ann	OTT, John	OCT 08 1816
CROPLEY, Amelia P.	BARNARD, Samuel J.	SEP 02 1833
CROPLEY, Eliza	TENNY, William H.	APR 16 1842
CROPLEY, Esther	MOFFETT, Joseph F.	MAR 27 1847
CROPLEY, Horatio	MILLS, Nancy	SEP 01 1846
CROPLEY, Sophia	BARNARD, Robert	APR 20 1821
CROPLEY, Washington	JONES, Cath. Ann	DEC 01 1846
CROSAN, Samuel	RHODES, Cassindra	SEP 08 1817
CROSBY, John	BEALE, Catharine A.	OCT 26 1820

District of Columbia Marriage Licenses, 1811-1858

CROSBY, Mary E.	MOULDEN, William	MAR 22 1856
CROSBY, Sylvanus	SMITH, Patsey	MAY 14 1832
CROSBY, Therese N.	WATSON, James M.	JAN 23 1850
CROSEN, Mary	TAYLOR, Daniel	MAR 17 1832
CROSEN, Thomas	SOPER, Maranda E.	FEB 03 1839
CROSGROVE, Bridget	SHARKEY, Michl.	JUN 21 1852
CROSON, Armsted A.	RICHARDSON, Martha L.	AUG 03 1846
CROSON, Thomas S.	DOGAN, Mary A.	AUG 24 1858
CROSS, Abraham	LOVELISS, Rosanna	JUN 27 1836
CROSS, Alethia	HOOPER, John H.	MAR 02 1824
CROSS, Alexander	TRENNELL, Julia	APR 22 1837
CROSS, Andrew	JOY, Sarah	JUL 21 1858
CROSS, Ann	LOWE, Thomas	DEC 26 1816
CROSS, Ann	CROSS, Wm.	AUG 07 1821
CROSS, Ann	BURNS, Benjamin	JUL 28 1836
CROSS, Ann Elizabeth	WAGNER, John	APR 01 1846
CROSS, Ann Matilda	GREGG, Joseph	MAR 30 1837
CROSS, B.J.	HOMELLER, Lavinia	MAY 22 1855
CROSS, Benjamin	SAUNDERS, Elizabeth F.	MAY 19 1840
CROSS, Clara S.	HUBBARD, George W.	APR 07 1856
CROSS, Cordelia A.V.	KING, Stephen	DEC 20 1850
CROSS, Dianna	BRISCOE, Michael	APR 28 1836
CROSS, Eliza	BRIGHT, Washington	SEP 18 1827
CROSS, Eliza	MAGNIER, Thomas	OCT 20 1836
CROSS, Elizabeth	YERKEAS, Harman	NOV 11 1817
CROSS, Elizabeth	WALLS, William	DEC 26 1850
CROSS, Elizabeth Ann	HASLUP, Thomas M.	JUN 26 1845
CROSS, Elizabeth Marian	DEXTER, Thomas C.A.	SEP 25 1844
CROSS, Emma I.	NOKES, William	SEP 14 1853
CROSS, Fielder	DeVAUGHN, Susanna	OCT 01 1842
CROSS, Gabriel	LANGLEY, Margarett E.	MAY 16 1854
CROSS, George	JOHNSON, Minty A.	JAN 28 1823
CROSS, George	McCULLOGH, Isabella	NOV 17 1849
CROSS, Harriett	POLINS, John	DEC 19 1827
CROSS, Henry	STRONG, Julia	AUG 13 1828
CROSS, Indiana	SIMARKER, Leonard	FEB 15 1858
CROSS, James	WILSON, Mary Elizth.	NOV 14 1848
CROSS, Jane	HOWARD, William	FEB 14 1822
CROSS, Jeremiah	VERMILLION, Martha M.	NOV 19 1845
CROSS, Jesse	McDANIEL, Lethe	MAY 18 1817
CROSS, Joseph	PARSONS, MArtha A.	JAN 16 1845
CROSS, Joseph H.	CONNER, Virginia E.	DEC 01 1849
CROSS, Julia Ann	NOYES, Albert	JUN 03 1852
CROSS, Leo George	VASSEY, Elizabeth C.	OCT 23 1856
CROSS, Lloyd	COAL, Sarah	JAN 12 1830
CROSS, Louisa	CONNOR, James R.	AUG 13 1851
CROSS, Louisa	CLEMSON, John, Jr.	MAY 15 1855
CROSS, Lydia B.	WEBSTER, Daniel L.	MAY 02 1854
CROSS, Lydia R.	JONES, Jacob	OCT 11 1847
CROSS, Martha	LIZEAR, Richard	APR 05 1855
CROSS, Mary	HALL, William	NOV 04 1824
CROSS, Mary	HUNTT, Louis	APR 18 1835
CROSS, Mary	AVERY, Westley	NOV 07 1838
CROSS, Mary	RENO, Jesse L.	OCT 25 1853
CROSS, Mary	LAWLESS, Richard	MAR 17 1855
CROSS, Mary Ann	BRIDEWELL, William	AUG 03 1841
CROSS, Mary E.	McGURK, Owen	NOV 04 1843
CROSS, Mary Virginia	TUCKER, Charles C.	APR 20 1853

District of Columbia Marriage Licenses, 1811-1858

CROSS, Newman	PILES, Matilda	SEP 30 1834
CROSS, Nimrod J.	RAWLINGS, Octavia	MAR 30 1846
CROSS, Rebecca	SUMMERS, Aquila T.	OCT 27 1842
CROSS, Reed	BASSFORD, Sarah	JAN 23 1821
CROSS, Richard	SIMPSON, Elizabeth	APR 19 1831
CROSS, Robert H.	CARTER, Martha R.	MAY 13 1858
CROSS, Robert R.	SANFORD, Margaret R.	DEC 18 1852
CROSS, Rosanna	SIMONDS, E. Lewis	DEC 10 1855
CROSS, Rutha	SMITH, Samuel	JAN 26 1847
CROSS, Samuel	MILLER, Victoria Isabella	OCT 25 1854
CROSS, Sarah	CANNON, William H.	AUG 29 1844
CROSS, Sarah C.	TUCKER, John A.	OCT 21 1856
CROSS, Sarah Maria	HOWARD, Joseph	JUN 30 1840
CROSS, Thomas	WEBSTER, Rebecca	APR 09 1831
CROSS, Thomas	BOOTH, Elizabeth	AUG 04 1832
CROSS, Thomas	WILLIAMS, Anna (blk)	JAN 20 1853
CROSS, Thomas	DUVALL, Airy	APR 26 1853
CROSS, Trueman [Maj.]	VanKLEECK, Margt.	OCT 01 1835
CROSS, Trueman [Maj.]	BEANES, Eliza S.	SEP 25 1821
CROSS, Washington	WESTCOAT, Ann Maria	DEC 21 1833
CROSS, William	RAWLINGS, Eleanor	APR 13 1825
CROSS, William	LEWIS, Mary Ann	APR 15 1848
CROSS, Wm.	CROSS, Ann	AUG 07 1821
CROSS, Wm. B.B.	RITCHIE, Ann Eliza	OCT 25 1849
CROSSEN, Joanna	HARREN, Frederick	JUL 05 1838
CROSSEN, Mary Ann	BURK, John L.	AUG 30 1826
CROSSFIELD, George	FITZGERALD, Susan	DEC 12 1855
CROSSFIELD, James	HODGES, Catharine Jane	JUN 08 1836
CROSSFIELD, Jehiel	RICH, Ann Eliza	JUL 10 1830
CROSSFIELD, Josephine C.	HODGES, George W.	DEC 24 1850
CROSSFIELD, William E.	HODGES, Eliza M.	SEP 29 1834
CROSSON, H. Rosalie	DeRONCERAY, C.	FEB 10 1858
CROTTY, Patrick	CASHMAN, Catherine	JAN 12 1853
CROUL, Peter	OGLE, Mary Ellen	NOV 17 1836
CROUN, Ann Rebecca	SCHOLFIELD, John D.	SEP 09 1857
CROUSE, Abraham	CONNELL, Frances	AUG 03 1841
CROUSE, Evered	ROWLAND, Elizabeth	APR 22 1823
CROUSE, John Walter	SMITH, Mary Margaret	AUG 25 1825
CROUSE, Mary	MOORE, John	DEC 01 1821
CROUTHERS, Thomas	SHELTON, Pamelia	FEB 17 1844
CROW, Elizabeth	TALBERT, Mackenzie	OCT 06 1815
CROW, Emily	JOHNSON, French T.	DEC 19 1844
CROW, John	NEWTON, Ann Milched	JAN 05 1814
CROW, John	BOUCHER, Chloe	FEB 01 1845
CROW, Martin	BOYCE, Margaret	JUL 17 1852
CROW, Patrick	MALONEY, Mary	JAN 27 1852
CROW, Sarah	NEWTON, Charles A.	SEP 12 1844
CROWDER, Elizth. C.	STAMN, Christian	NOV 29 1842
CROWLEY, Ann	BAILEY, William	APR 12 1825
CROWLEY, Ann	MORAN, David	SEP 11 1852
CROWLEY, Ann	O'DAY, John	JAN 11 1853
CROWLEY, Cath.	GRIFFIN, William	NOV 22 1814
CROWLEY, Catharine	BALTZER, John	MAR 01 1831
CROWLEY, Catharine	MAGUIRE, Patrick	DEC 31 1851
CROWLEY, Christina	DUVALL, Samuel	MAY 05 1846
CROWLEY, Edward	BRANNON, Mary Ann	JUL 09 1824
CROWLEY, Eliza (blk)	BRISCOE, William	MAY 30 1844
CROWLEY, James	KEITH, Margaret	JUL 05 1851

District of Columbia Marriage Licenses, 1811-1858

CROWLEY, Jeremiah	SULLIVAN, Hanora	JAN 05 1853
CROWLEY, Joannah	O'CONNOR, Daniel	FEB 13 1855
CROWLEY, John	MURPHEY, Johanna	DEC 11 1857
CROWLEY, John	LISTON, Mary	JUN 12 1858
CROWLEY, Julia A.	FITTEN, Thomas	JUN 28 1820
CROWLEY, Julia A.	GARISON, Roy A.	NOV 30 1838
CROWLEY, Mary	MEDAN, Nicholas	FEB 11 1812
CROWLEY, Mary	WHELER, John	DEC 13 1815
CROWLEY, Mary Ann	HARRISON, James	JUN 19 1827
CROWLEY, Michael	HIGGINS, Bridget	JAN 04 1851
CROWLEY, Patrick	COONS, Juliana	JUN 27 1820
CROWLEY, Patrick	PHILLIPS, Elizabeth Ann	JUN 06 1833
CROWLEY, Patrick	MAHONEY, Ellen	JAN 29 1856
CROWLEY, Sally	KEEF, Patrick	MAY 16 1815
CROWLEY, Sarah	SHERWOOD, William	MAR 22 1838
CROWLEY, Thomas	GOODAN, Julia Ann	JUL 26 1825
CROWLEY, Thomas	SMITH, Susan	NOV 14 1837
CROWLEY, Timothy	MAHONEY, Nancy	FEB 07 1826
CROWLEY, William F.	BINGY, Mary H.	JUN 28 1845
CROWN, Anna R.	DIFFENDERFFER, Octavius	JUN 23 1857
CROWN, Betsey	CARAWAY, James	JUL 19 1816
CROWN, George W.	BRADLEY, Jane M.	JAN 08 1857
CROWN, James	GRAY, Caroline	JAN 27 1835
CROWN, James	BECKWITH, Mary	FEB 10 1836
CROWN, James F.	JOHNSON, Eliza D.	MAY 25 1858
CROWN, Jane	NESMITH, John	APR 15 1828
CROWN, Jeremiah	MULLIGAN, Ann	JAN 01 1824
CROWN, John	POOR, Margaret	JUN 04 1833
CROWN, John	SEMMES, Susanna	OCT 01 1845
CROWN, Joseph F.	WATERS, Priscilla Ann	JUL 29 1850
CROWN, Lucretia	PAYNE, James	JAN 02 1843
CROWN, Martha E.	TOLGLASE, Benjamin	FEB 26 1853
CROWN, Mary	HARKINS, John B.	MAY 05 1821
CROWN, Mary Ann	STINCHINCOE, Noah	JAN 06 1816
CROWN, Mary Ann	CONNER, Robert	APR 12 1830
CROWN, Mary Ann	WINSETT, Clinton	JUL 31 1834
CROWN, Mary Ann	ADAMS, Richard H.	DEC 22 1848
CROWN, Mary Elizth.	DUFFEY, John	NOV 13 1854
CROWN, Matilda	HUTCHINS, [blank]	JUL 18 1826
CROWN, Rebecca	SCHOFFIELD, John	MAY 16 1830
CROWN, Saml. T.	HUTCHINS, Mary E.	JAN 17 1856
CROWN, Samuel	TUCKER, Charlott	JUN 04 1829
CROWN, Samuel	SANDON, Mary	APR 02 1857
CROWN, William	RUNTZEL, Elizabeth	NOV 10 1843
CROWN, William	POPKINS, Mary Catherine	APR 10 1855
CROWNIN, Ellen	DUFFEY, Michael	APR 07 1849
CROXTON, Ann E.	CROXTON, Orville	APR 01 1848
CROXTON, Orville	CROXTON, Ann E.	APR 01 1848
CROZIER, Robert H.	SEARS, Virginia H.	MAR 01 1847
CRUCKSHANK, Charles	BROWN, Martha	FEB 04 1817
CRUIKSHANK, Richard	MACKEY, Ann Jane	APR 06 1830
CRUISER, William	CHEW, Ellen (blk)	FEB 14 1843
CRUIT, Richard	CRAGEAR, Mary Ann	JAN 24 1855
CRUITT, Catherine	EVANS, Evan	FEB 20 1847
CRUITT, James M.	LEACH, Martha	JUN 07 1845
CRUITT, Sarah	FOWLER, William R.	JUL 23 1839
CRUMP, Ann E.	LYLES, William H.	AUG 24 1848
CRUMP, Ann Eliza	DYER, Kinsey	SEP 23 1842

District of Columbia Marriage Licenses, 1811-1858

CRUMP, Carlisle F.	MILSTEAD, Maria E.	FEB 15 1855
CRUMP, Daniel F.	THOMPSON, Margaret	MAR 14 1842
CRUMP, Edward W.	COCKREL, Susanna	DEC 16 1851
CRUMP, Frances	CARVER, Charles	AUG 28 1855
CRUMP, George W.	GATES, Elizabeth	SEP 29 1840
CRUMP, John N.	PADGETT, Martha A.	NOV 03 1847
CRUMP, Lewis A.	IVES, Abagail	JAN 15 1851
CRUMP, Lydia	SCOTT, Thomas Edwin	JUL 08 1844
CRUMP, Margaret S.	TUNSTILL, George N.	FEB 11 1853
CRUMP, Susan	POTTER, John	MAR 01 1849
CRUMP, Susan	GUINN, Benjamin W.	SEP 29 1856
CRUMP, William	TYLER, Matilda	APR 01 1833
CRUPPE, A.B.	O'NEALE, Elizabeth	JUL 09 1840
CRUPPER, Benjamin	SKINNER, Penelope	NOV 16 1820
CRUPPER, Frances V.	MUNROE, James T.	SEP 02 1845
CRUPPER, Malinda	LEDDY, Owen	OCT 31 1842
CRUPSEY, James C.	MORTIMER, Susannah	MAY 05 1849
CRUSODOLPH, Wilhelmine	GEIGER, Adolph	JUN 30 1855
CRUSOE, Charlotte (blk)	WEBSTER, Alexander	APR 17 1832
CRUSOE, James C.	JONES, Charlotte (blk)	JUL 13 1849
CRUSOR, Edward	FLEET, Ann	SEP 25 1844
CRUSSELL, Mary E.	MORSE, John J.	OCT 19 1844
CRUTTENDEN, Harriet Lacy	MAGRUDER, Hezikiah	MAR 03 1830
CRUTTENDEN, Harvey	MURPHY, Catharine	NOV 24 1814
CRUTTENDEN, Harvey	FRANK, Mary	APR 14 1817
CRUTTENDEN, Mary Jane	WEBSTER, James [Dr.]	APR 28 1829
CRUTTENDEN, Sophia T.	RIGGS, Lawrenson	FEB 03 1840
CRUX, Thomas, Jr.	HALL, Hattie A.N.	NOV 13 1854
CRYDE, Patsey	AMBUSH, Calvert	MAR 22 1834
CRYER, Henry	BALL, Cornelia (blk)	APR 23 1857
CRYER, Margaret E.	FISHER, James H.	SEP 07 1850
CRYER, Mary	HAGERTY, Patrick	JUL 27 1850
CRYER, Mary Jane (blk)	CHEW, Daniel	JUL 25 1843
CRYER, Sarah Ann	O'NEALE, Hugh	DEC 26 1842
CUDIHAY, Julia	POWER, John	DEC 02 1854
CUDLIPP, Frederick	DRUMMOND, Eliza	NOV 14 1833
CUDLIPP, Isabel	WETZLEBON, L. Arthurvon	JAN 02 1858
CUDMORE, Paul	TIDINGS, Sophia	SEP 11 1813
CUDMORE, William	GANNON, Martha	APR 21 1830
CULBERSON, Virginia	MARTIN, John	NOV 15 1847
CULBERTSON, James F.	WHALEN, Biddy	JUN 12 1828
CULBRETH, Thomas	SLADE, Martha Morgan	DEC 04 1827
CULHAN, Michael	READY, Margaret	JAN 25 1855
CULHANEY, Patrick	SULLIVAN, Johanna	JAN 31 1857
CULIGAN, Timothy	MERIGAN, Fanny	JUN 14 1852
CULINANA, Patrick	CAHIL, Ellen	FEB 14 1857
CULL, James	FOSTER, Sarah L.	JUN 27 1831
CULL, John	RATCLIFFE, Elizabeth H.	FEB 19 1834
CULLAN, Margaret	MURPHEY, Patrick	APR 10 1858
CULLERTON, Thomas	FLENNERY, Annie	JUN 26 1852
CULLEY, James W.	PLUNKITT, Mary J.	NOV 19 1846
CULLEY, Mary	LITTLE, Peter, Junr.	JUN 16 1823
CULLIN, Mathew	DONALLY, Teresa	APR 14 1852
CULLINS, John	WICKLE, Mary	MAY 13 1822
CULLISON, Elizabeth	JOHNSON, Milton	APR 02 1841
CULLISON, Mary	BOTT, James	JUN 01 1843
CULLISON, Mary Ellen	JOHNSON, Alexander	DEC 05 1844
CULLISS, Jane M.	TOMBS, Henry M.	NOV 29 1822

District of Columbia Marriage Licenses, 1811-1858

CULLOTAN, Patrick	SULLIVAN, Catharine	JAN 10 1857
CULP, Susan (blk)	CLARK, Otho	JAN 29 1840
CULVER, Charles P.	MORRISON, Louisa E.	FEB 18 1858
CULVER, Frederick Burr	KENDALL, Adela	NOV 20 1839
CULVER, William	TILLY, Nancy	JAN 09 1819
CULVERWELL, Mary E.	TOPPING, Nathan H.	JUN 10 1848
CULVERWELL, Terese Ann	MORCOE, William E.	MAY 26 1849
CUMBERLAND, Ann	LUCAS, Ignatius	SEP 28 1819
CUMBERLAND, Charles	ROLAND, Elizabeth	OCT 05 1830
CUMBERLAND, Elizabeth E.	SERREN, Thomas	DEC 17 1857
CUMBERLAND, John	FREE, Harriot	JUL 24 1823
CUMBERLAND, John	WEASNER, Mary Ann	OCT 12 1835
CUMBERLAND, John	JOHNSON, Susan	MAY 25 1848
CUMBERLAND, John	McDERMOTT, Elizabeth	NOV 30 1854
CUMBERLAND, Mary Ellen	McDERMOTT, John	FEB 01 1848
CUMBERLAND, Sarah A.	SERRIN, William D.	NOV 06 1851
CUMBERLAND, Thomas	ROLLINS, Martha	MAY 14 1850
CUMBERLAND, Wm.	BANISTER, Mary C.	AUG 15 1854
CUMMERFORD, John	CARMIKLE, Sarah	AUG 31 1820
CUMMING, Charles F.P.	SIEBERT, Thora M.	JUN 24 1857
CUMMING, Robert	RUTMOND, Ellen	DEC 31 1855
CUMMINGS, King	HENDERSON, Sarah W.	DEC 28 1837
CUMMINGS, Mary Ann	MAGRUDER, Fielder M.	FEB 15 1853
CUMMINGS, Mary E.	McDOWELL, Robert	OCT 11 1838
CUMMINGS, Mary Jane	GERDES, Ferdinand H.	MAY 26 1842
CUMMINGS, Nancy Lavenia	GUNNELL, William H.	OCT 18 1847
CUMMINGS, Naomi F.	HITCHEN, John H.	APR 08 1856
CUMMINS, Edmund H.	HEATH, Josephine V.	NOV 14 1853
CUMMINS, James	THOMAS, Mary	MAR 15 1828
CUMMINS, Nathaniel	ROBERTSON, Minty	OCT 10 1815
CUMMYKEL, Elizabeth	LEWIS, James	APR 06 1824
CUMSTRONG, Thomas	MADDORE, Betsey	JUL 27 1816
CUNIC, David	HASTINGS, Nicholas	NOV 18 1849
CUNIO, Joanna	SCHIO, Peter	APR 16 1855
CUNLBERG, Clara	DOHNOR, Samuel	JAN 05 1858
CUNNINGHAM, Agness Ann	WEAVER, Samuel	NOV 09 1844
CUNNINGHAM, Anthony	GREEN, Jane	OCT 16 1822
CUNNINGHAM, Archibald	WILLSON, Janet	MAR 02 1825
CUNNINGHAM, Barbara	DAVIS, David	FEB 21 1840
CUNNINGHAM, Catharine	WILSON, William	DEC 05 1827
CUNNINGHAM, Catharine	SULLIVAN, John	JUL 08 1850
CUNNINGHAM, Charles W.	RABBITT, Mary Jane	OCT 15 1855
CUNNINGHAM, David	RIDGWAY, Barbara Ann	JAN 22 1828
CUNNINGHAM, Eliza	RHODES, George	MAR 06 1838
CUNNINGHAM, Elizabeth	BOOTH, Richard E.	JAN 12 1847
CUNNINGHAM, Elizabeth A.	ORTLY, Bartholomew	JUN 12 1854
CUNNINGHAM, Emeline	BELL, George	NOV 24 1852
CUNNINGHAM, Frederick A.	OAKLEY, Margaret J.	APR 03 1856
CUNNINGHAM, Hannah	O'FLAHERTY, Edmund	DEC 13 1855
CUNNINGHAM, James	JONES, Sarah Ann	JAN 11 1838
CUNNINGHAM, James H.	FORD, Louisa M.E.	JAN 01 1852
CUNNINGHAM, Jane	KNIGHT, Lewis J.	AUG 02 1845
CUNNINGHAM, Jane	CLEMENTS, Ignatius	JAN 27 1857
CUNNINGHAM, John Scott	BROCKET, Elizabeth	OCT 27 1845
CUNNINGHAM, Lydia A.	HINES, John B.	JUN 15 1853
CUNNINGHAM, Margaret	VENEBLE, Patrick	NOV 04 1847
CUNNINGHAM, Margaret	RIORDAN, John	JUL 30 1853
CUNNINGHAM, Margaret	McRAE, Daniel	JUN 22 1854

District of Columbia Marriage Licenses, 1811-1858

CUNNINGHAM, Margaret E. (blk)	BROWN, Thomas Charles	JUL 07 1858
CUNNINGHAM, Margaret P.	TRUNNELL, Richard H.	FEB 19 1852
CUNNINGHAM, Margt. E.	REED, Thomas E.	NOV 03 1851
CUNNINGHAM, Mary	DuVALL, Horace	MAY 27 1815
CUNNINGHAM, Mary	BRACK, Morris	FEB 02 1856
CUNNINGHAM, Mary Ann	SMALL, John H.	MAR 26 1850
CUNNINGHAM, Mary E.	FENDRICH, Xavier	JUN 14 1853
CUNNINGHAM, Mary Jane	DOUGLASS, William	MAY 09 1835
CUNNINGHAM, Matthew	CAHILL, Mary Ann	SEP 01 1854
CUNNINGHAM, Patk.	TALBOT, Ann	OCT 03 1854
CUNNINGHAM, Peter	CURLEY, Mary	DEC 27 1851
CUNNINGHAM, Rebecca	ATZS, Charles C.	AUG 02 1852
CUNNINGHAM, Sarah Ann	WRIGHT, George	MAY 29 1843
CUNNINGHAM, Susan	SAFFER, William	MAR 26 1812
CUNNINGHAM, Thomas	COLSTON, Mary	AUG 02 1830
CUNNINGHAM, William	WATERS, Jane	SEP 13 1845
CURAND, Christiana	HINES, Frederick	JAN 04 1817
CURFMAN, Harriet M.	BREEDING, Mason P.	DEC 10 1816
CURKWOOD, Elizabeth	RICHARDS, Jonathan	OCT 02 1816
CURLEY, Mary	CUNNINGHAM, Peter	DEC 27 1851
CURLEY, Warner	WINKFIELD, Mary	SEP 14 1843
CURLY, Borland	CURLY, Mary Jane	OCT 13 1856
CURLY, John	GARRITY, Margaret	AUG 11 1858
CURLY, Mary Jane	CURLY, Borland	OCT 13 1856
CURNEY, Alexander	TUCKER, Josephine	AUG 14 1855
CURRAN, Bartley	GREEN, Catharine	SEP 04 1856
CURRAN, Bridget Ellen	GRONARD, George Meservy	NOV 10 1844
CURRAN, Daniel	GRIFFIN, Catharine	APR 21 1832
CURRAN, Dennis	DAVIS, Sarah Rebecca	JAN 18 1855
CURRAN, Eleanor [Mrs.]	THOMPSON, John	MAY 15 1812
CURRAN, Eliz.	SHELL, Jacob	JUN 24 1815
CURRAN, Jane	RIDGEWAY, John	DEC 20 1824
CURRAN, John	LONG, Mary	NOV 28 1837
CURRAN, Mary	McCARTY, Thomas	APR 24 1843
CURRAN, Mary	McCARTY, Thomas	JAN 29 1844
CURRAN, Patrick	CONNERS, Hannah	OCT 03 1856
CURRAN, Rosanna	CATON, Michael	JUL 17 1857
CURRAN, Stephen M.	HARTNETT, Margaret T.	AUG 09 1858
CURRANS, Mary A.	MAGEE, James	JUN 05 1849
CURRAY, Ann Eliza	BENTON, Samuel	OCT 05 1842
CURRELL, Mary F.J.	LYNN, Luther L.	MAR 04 1839
CURRELL, William	BUTLER, Hannah E.	APR 17 1833
CURREN, Barney B.	COVER, Elizabeth B.	MAR 21 1842
CURREN, Lucretia	MOXLEY, Horatio	APR 21 1826
CURREN, Morgan	COIN, Margaret	FEB 24 1825
CURRHEY, William	LEWELLYN, Frances	JAN 22 1844
CURRIER, Jacob	DAMRON, Isabella	JUN 15 1858
CURRIN, Eveline	ASHTON, Leonard	SEP 11 1819
CURRY, Benjamin L.	HALSEY, Tarecy	AUG 18 1818
CURRY, Elizabeth	WOOD, Owen	DEC 10 1825
CURRY, John	MURPHY, Ellen	AUG 08 1850
CURRY, Mary	WAY, Thomas	NOV 30 1820
CURRY, Robert	WILSON, Elizabeth	AUG 10 1820
CURSEY, Sarah	PHIPPS, John	NOV 14 1843
CURSHAW, Matilda	DYER, James Henry	SEP 12 1854
CURTA, Daniel	CONNEL, Mary	FEB 20 1855
CURTAIN, Henry	GRIMES, Leonia	JUL 27 1839
CURTAIN, Kitty	TILLETT, Samuel	MAY 30 1812

District of Columbia Marriage Licenses, 1811-1858

CURTAIN, Mary	HERLEY, John	NOV 18 1845
CURTAIN, Mary Ellen	DUVALL, John L.	APR 13 1857
CURTEN, Kate	SULLIVAN, John	JAN 05 1857
CURTER, John F.	CURTER, Mary Ann	JUN 02 1856
CURTER, Mary Ann	CURTER, John F.	JUN 02 1856
CURTIN, Daniel	CONNORS, Bridget	JAN 04 1851
CURTIN, Eliza	WATSON, William	JUL 11 1853
CURTIN, Elizabeth	FENTON, Jeremiah	JUN 16 1824
CURTIN, James R.N.	BOSWELL, Elizabeth	FEB 16 1843
CURTIN, John A.	EDWARDS, Mary E.	JUL 07 1846
CURTIN, Julia Ann	VINSOR, William	JUN 26 1854
CURTIN, Mary	MANSIL, Peter	JUN 21 1858
CURTIN, Richard	WATSON, Mary Jane	AUG 19 1852
CURTIN, Thomas F.	HARRIS, Elizabeth C.	APR 09 1857
CURTIN, William A.	[torn out]	JUN 03 1847
CURTING, John	COLLINS, Mary	JAN 12 1858
CURTIS, Ann	ELLIS, Richd. Henry	DEC 29 1830
CURTIS, Armistead	WILLS, Geraldine	FEB 03 1857
CURTIS, Bridget	McBRIDE, Thomas	JAN 20 1849
CURTIS, Cecelia (blk)	EDINBOROUGH, William	APR 10 1851
CURTIS, Charles	BUTLER, Mary (blk)	MAY 02 1853
CURTIS, Eliza	SOMERVILLE, Arnold	DEC 22 1818
CURTIS, George	MILLS, Sarah Ann	MAR 13 1824
CURTIS, James	BROWN, Louisa (blk)	NOV 01 1849
CURTIS, James	BROWN, Martha (blk)	APR 29 1852
CURTIS, John	CHURCH, Mary (blk)	JUN 05 1849
CURTIS, John	CRAWFORD, Frances (blk)	SEP 21 1853
CURTIS, John	O'BRIEN, Mary Ann	AUG 12 1856
CURTIS, Lina	WILEY, Jeremiah	APR 15 1851
CURTIS, Mason	HAMMELL, Catharine	DEC 28 1837
CURTIS, Mason	BLANN, Laura	JUN 23 1858
CURTIS, Mildred M.	WALKER, Luther M.	OCT 13 1853
CURTIS, Peter	O'BRIEN, Sarah	NOV 23 1852
CURTIS, Rose	KNOX, James	SEP 04 1850
CURTIS, Sarah	FRENCH, James	AUG 26 1830
CURTIS, Thomas	TUCKER, Ann	NOV 10 1829
CURTIS, Thomas	JONES, Eliza (blk)	SEP 18 1834
CURTIS, Wm. A.	CHEWNING, Mary E.	MAR 17 1849
CURTISS, Charles	MANN, Rebecca	DEC 12 1825
CURTISS, Robert	PATTEN, Elizabeth	MAR 30 1858
CUSHAW, Charlotte	ANDERSON, Hervey	JUN 09 1853
CUSHING, Johanna	FLEMING, Michael	JAN 21 1853
CUSHING, Johanna	McCARTY, Dennis	AUG 09 1854
CUSHLY, Mary	ALLISON, Robert	JUN 06 1850
CUSICH, Mary J.	HURLEY, James W.	MAY 21 1857
CUSICK, Daniel	HENNESSEY, Ellen	APR 07 1855
CUSICK, Jane	STROTHER, Francis	MAY 29 1845
CUSICK, John	MAINY, Joanna	JAN 01 1853
CUSINS, Sarah	WILLIAMS, William H.	DEC 03 1845
CUSLEY, Margaret	MAZINE, John	JAN 07 1852
CUSTARD, Isabella	GOODRICK, Thomas	JUN 19 1856
CUSTARD, Jacob	RIFFEL, Mary	APR 13 1816
CUSTARD, Mary (blk)	BUTLER, John	DEC 17 1849
CUSTARD, Mary E.	WILSON, John F.	DEC 12 1857
CUSTARD, William H.	WILSON, Rebecca	DEC 02 1843
CUSTER, Ann Maria	ELLIS, John B.	JUL 04 1840
CUSTIS, George	HUTCHINS, Matilda	AUG 21 1856
CUSTIS, George	BAKER, Ellenora	AUG 12 1858

District of Columbia Marriage Licenses, 1811-1858

CUSTIS, Lemuel W.	ASHDOWN, Elizabeth E.	FEB 11 1858
CUSTUS, Charles	BROWN, Sophiah (blk)	DEC 20 1825
CUTHBERT, James	HINDS, Mary Ann	JAN 04 1830
CUTHBERT, Mary Ann	JOHNSON, James B.L.	SEP 13 1856
CUTTS, Adele	DOUGLASS, Stephen A.	NOV 20 1856
CUTTS, Charles	___UTHALL, Lucy Henry	JUL 07 1812
CUVILLIER, Joseph	LAURENCE, Eliza	JUN 02 1832
CUVILLIER, Joseph L.	OSBORNE, Mary E.	JAN 02 1857
CYER, Bennet	STEPPER, Mary	DEC 23 1843
CYLISS, Anne	DREEN, James M.	MAR 24 1856
CYPHER, Mary	UTTERMULE, Meney	MAY 08 1847

District of Columbia Marriage Licenses, 1811-1858

D

DABNEY, Clizwell	LEE, Elizabeth	OCT 23 1838
DACEY, Cornelius	MAHONEY, Ellen	MAY 16 1851
DACEY, Dennis	McNAMARA, Margaret	OCT 19 1852
DACEY, Ellen	LORDEN, Cornelius	AUG 31 1852
DACEY, Patrick	BRIEN, Honora	AUG 03 1852
DACEY, Roger	SIPPLE, Margaret	MAR 14 1853
DACY, Catharine	SULLIVAN, Jeremiah	FEB 14 1852
DACY, Elizabeth	WILLIAMS, Lawrence	JUL 02 1849
DADE, Adam	HAWKINS, Louisa (blk)	NOV 21 1855
DADE, Ann M.S.	DRANE, Washington	JUN 23 1816
DADE, Anna M. (blk)	GREY, John A.	MAY 04 1857
DADE, Charles E.	BAYLOR, Gwynnetta W.	MAY 18 1832
DADE, Margaret Ann	KEY, John	JUN 21 1847
DADE, Margt. (blk)	CHASE, William	JUL 10 1855
DADE, Sarah Ann (blk)	WINTERS, Richard	JAN 18 1845
DADE, Susan Ann (blk)	REED, Joseph H.	JAN 25 1849
DADE, Wesley	PATTERSON, Julia	JUN 02 1830
DADE, William Ball	MOOR, Mary	NOV 25 1828
DADISMAN, Harriet E.	VINSON, John J.	MAR 01 1842
DADLY, George William	FERREL, Caroline	DEC 22 1851
DAERY, John	LYONS, Mary	JAN 09 1840
DAFNEY, Marcus	HUTTON, Cecelia	APR 27 1821
DAGGES, Jacob	READ, Jane (blk)	SEP 21 1850
DAGGETT, Aaron W.	MARTIN, Jane	MAR 02 1824
DAGGS, Monteville	HERBERT, Martha (blk)	MAY 28 1850
DAGGS, Tamer	JOINER, James H.	JUL 13 1837
DAGGY, Peter	LUNT, Julia	DEC 04 1851
DAGS, Jane	JOHNSON, Jeremiah	AUG 05 1858
DAIDY, Mary	BUCKLEY, Dennis	JUL 13 1839
DAILEY, Ann	McGRANN, John	JUN 28 1855
DAILEY, Bridget	BEGGANE, Jeremiah	MAY 19 1853
DAILEY, Eliza	WALL, Michael	JUL 28 1856
DAILEY, Eugene	CORIDON, Mary	DEC 08 1854
DAILEY, Hiram B.	BALL, Louisa	AUG 28 1835
DAILEY, Isabella	CATOR, Joseph	JAN 05 1852
DAILEY, James	TAYLOR, Eliza	MAY 01 1821
DAILEY, Johanna	McGEORTY, James	MAY 17 1855
DAILEY, Julia A.	DORREL, John M.	APR 21 1824
DAILEY, Maria	BANDEN, Thomas	OCT 05 1822
DAILEY, Mary	WILSON, Thomas C.	JAN 19 1847
DAILEY, Mary Frances	COLLIER, Richard H.	JAN 05 1849
DAILEY, Peter	MANNEL, Bridget	OCT 30 1854
DAILEY, Rose	McDERMOTT, James	OCT 08 1856
DAILEY, Timothy	DRISCOLL, Mary Ellen	APR 17 1858
DAILEY, Uriah	COE, Guinnetta (blk)	MAY 20 1856
DAILY, Bytha	TRAMMELL, Jarrett B.	APR 13 1837
DAILY, John	JOICE, Mary Ann	FEB 11 1834
DAILY, Sophia	DORRELL, Thomas	NOV 28 1827
DAILY, Sophia	DORRELL, Thomas	DEC 01 1827
DAILY, William T.	COGIN, Hanorah	DEC 03 1857
DAIMOND, Catharine	LAFONG, Charles	FEB 07 1834
DAINGERFIELD, Henry	SEWALL, Susan J.B.	OCT 20 1823
DAINGERFIELD, William H.	DUNLAP, Mary L.	DEC 12 1848
DAINTY, Eliza	SHEPHARD, Samuel	JUL 31 1849
DALE, Ariana	CATON, Thomas	DEC 21 1848
DALE, Catherine B.	BAIRD, William A.	MAR 28 1853

District of Columbia Marriage Licenses, 1811-1858

DALE, Eliza (blk)	CARTER, Henry	MAY 11 1854
DALE, George M.	EVANS, Ellen L.	JUL 07 1853
DALE, John R.	MOUNDZ, Margaret	FEB 12 1846
DALE, Mary Jane	EVANS, Clifford	FEB 07 1854
DALEY, Ary	LANCASTER, Theophilus	JUN 12 1857
DALEY, Catharine	HILL, William	SEP 14 1832
DALEY, Edward	RILEY, Ann	JUL 07 1830
DALEY, Mary	SHEAHAN, John	JUL 14 1855
DALEY, Mary Ann	DORRELL, Thomas S.	MAY 25 1846
DALEY, Michael	REIDY, Hannora	FEB 01 1851
DALLAM, Josias W.	ENGLISH, Alice	NOV 07 1844
DALLAN, Benjamin R.	HEPBURN, Jane J.	OCT 18 1849
DALLAS, Alexander J.	MAIE, Frances V.	JAN 30 1855
DALLAS, Stephen J.	JOHNSON, Ann Elizabeth	JUN 10 1850
DALTON, D., Mrs.	PILLINGS, James	OCT 26 1839
DALTON, James	GRIMES, Jane	FEB 26 1821
DALTON, John	WYERS, Susan	APR 08 1842
DALTON, John	WYERS, Susan	NOV 02 1843
DALTON, Margaret	QUICK, Patrick	FEB 17 1857
DALTON, Mary	FARRAN, Terrence	MAY 06 1846
DALTON, William	COLLINS, Susan E.	OCT 07 1824
DALTON, William	CROGGON, Emily	MAR 16 1837
DALTY, Ann	SMITH, George	JUN 25 1858
DALY, James	CLEMENTS, Mary Ann	APR 20 1846
DALY, Julia	MATHIAS, Petro	NOV 18 1853
DALY, Lawrence	CORTIN, Ellen	OCT 22 1853
DALY, Michael	MORGAN, Winna	MAR 14 1857
DALY, William	KENNEDY, Fanny	MAR 01 1854
DAMMON, Anna	SMITH, John T.	JUN 02 1857
DAMRON, Isabella	CURRIER, Jacob	JUN 15 1858
DANAHY, Dennis	RYAN, Bridget	MAY 18 1855
DANAHY, Margaret	WELCH, William	JUL 30 1853
DANCE, Charles W.	DIMES, Mary R.	JUL 07 1857
DANCEY, Betsey (blk)	KENNEDY, Lewis James	JUN 22 1815
DANDERSON, Thomas	WHITE, Violetta	OCT 09 1832
DANDERSON, William	BURGESS, Elizabeth	DEC 22 1812
DANDRIDGE, Elizabeth (blk)	DULANEY, Adam	JUN 22 1854
DANDRIDGE, Sophia (blk)	POLLARD, Robert	OCT 02 1850
DANDRIDGE, Virginia (blk)	PIENE, William	SEP 26 1848
DANEHY, Hannah	LANE, Patrick	OCT 19 1855
DARRELL, William S.	BROOKE, Sarah Virginia	AUG 31 1835
DANEOLD, Francis Henry	TRAVERS, Mary	JUN 01 1836
DANFERD, James	BERKLEY, Ann	NOV 22 1824
DANFORD, Catherine	MINIX, John Newton	MAY 01 1849
DANFORD, James	WINDER, Sarah	DEC 02 1813
DANFORD, James H.	VERMILION, Eliza	FEB 09 1848
DANGEL, Valentine	KURTZ, Mary Ann	OCT 07 1847
DANIEL, Ann	DANIEL, James H.	OCT 02 1856
DANIEL, Annie W.	DeBELL, Jno. D.	AUG 21 1855
DANIEL, James	DENNISON, Wilhelmina	NOV 25 1824
DANIEL, James H.	DANIEL, Ann	OCT 02 1856
DANIEL, Jane P.	RATCLIFFE, Richard	JUN 10 1827
DANIEL, John	LLOYD, Julia Ann	JUN 20 1846
DANIEL, John T.	FAULKNER, Ophelia E.	OCT 05 1854
DANIEL, Joseph H.	TABLER, Ann	NOV 09 1837
DANIEL, Joseph H.	WHEELER, Mary L.	MAY 21 1855
DANIEL, Julia	BAYLISS, William P.	JAN 02 1845
DANIEL, Levinia	TAYLOR, Henry	JAN 31 1812

District of Columbia Marriage Licenses, 1811-1858

DANIEL, Linny Ann	BAILESS, Edward	JAN 18 1830
DANIEL, Mary E.	GRACE, Aaron B.	JUN 15 1854
DANIEL, Peter V.	HARRIS, Elizabeth	OCT 17 1853
DANIEL, Richard J.	HOOE, Lucinda James	SEP 16 1824
DANIEL, Senior	BALIS, Alfred	DEC 24 1835
DANIELL, Susan A.	BAYLISS, Augustin	OCT 06 1834
DANIELS, Francis	HOWARD, Maria	JAN 01 1830
DANIELS, William T.	BAYLISS, Martha A.	JUL 05 1849
DANIN, Sarah	LANHADY, Patrick	APR 26 1851
DANKWORTH, Frederick	BARTLE, Cordelia	DEC 07 1841
DANSKIN, Washington A.	RIDGWAY, Sarah Ann	OCT 02 1839
DANT, Amanda J.	FRENCH, James B.	NOV 18 1851
DANT, Francis X.	SEWALL, Mary	OCT 16 1838
DANT, George W.	YOUNG, Mary L.	OCT 25 1856
DANT, Jane	McKENNEY, Michael	DEC 28 1831
DANT, Jeremiah	DUCKET, Rachael (blk)	FEB 07 1826
DANT, Mary Ann	HURLEY, John F.	OCT 05 1841
DANT, Rosella	FITNAM, Thomas, Jr.	SEP 10 1849
DANT, Teresa	HEARD, Edmund	OCT 10 1826
DANT, Thomas E.	CLEMENTS, Eleanora C.	JAN 27 1835
DANT, Thomas E., Jr.	WALKER, Harriet	MAR 11 1858
DANT, Virginia C.	CASSELL, Thomas M.	JAN 08 1856
DANT, William	FENWICK, Susan	APR 05 1814
DANT, William E.	BEARDSLEY, Sarah J.	DEC 04 1851
DANT, William T.	WATSON, Sarah E.	MAR 13 1849
DANTE, Mary	BRENNIN, John	JAN 15 1838
DANTEY, Martha A.	GREMSLEY, Elias	AUG 18 1857
DARBY, Edward	PHILLIPS, Elizabeth	OCT 17 1833
DARCEY, Eliza Jane	SUMMERS, Warren	JUN 22 1844
DARE, Henry	CHEW, Adeline (blk)	MAR 12 1838
DARGNE, Joseph	MAGNESS, Elizabeth	JAN 31 1820
DARITY, Eliza	BURKE, William	FEB 09 1855
DARLEY, Frank	FENTON, Elizth. G.	AUG 23 1851
DARLEY, Lavinia	BARNHOUSE, Caleb	SEP 04 1847
DARLEY, Susan	WAYBORN, Horace	MAY 02 1830
DARMHARDT, John	BARRS, Ruth Ann	DEC 21 1857
DARMON, Albert	JONES, Sarah A.	NOV 06 1838
DARNALL, Eliza A.	SHEIRBURN, William L.	JUN 16 1856
DARNALL, Henry Washington	MOORE, Ann E.	OCT 30 1850
DARNALL, James M.	HUTCHINGS, Mary Ann	MAR 23 1843
DARNALL, Margaret	JEFFRYS, Harrison	DEC 16 1824
DARNALL, Richard B.	O'LEARY, Fanny M.	AUG 25 1858
DARNE, Emerella	ASHFORD, Craven	MAR 05 1839
DARNE, Sarah Frances	LLOYD, Lester	JAN 14 1856
DARNES, Mary Frances	LAZENBY, Amos A.	DEC 11 1849
DARNES, Richard H.	HASTINGS, Eliza L.	APR 04 1857
DARNES, Sarah Virginia	DOUGLASS, William J.	NOV 04 1845
DARNES, Simon	SMITH, Elizabeth Ann	OCT 03 1837
DARNES, Susan A.	CLOKEY, John	JUL 02 1851
DARNES, Washington F.	MAY, Columbia Ann	JUL 22 1851
DARNOLD, Thomas L.	BARTRUFF, Adeline V.	MAR 28 1848
DARNUM, George	GIBSON, Mary Ann	NOV 18 1830
DARRITY, Hariot	MITCHEL, Josias	OCT 20 1818
DARSER, Henrietta C.	FINLAY, Jonathan S.	AUG 02 1813
DARWIN, Mary	CARROLL, John	FEB 02 1836
DASHER, Virginia	DIAZ, Peter	JAN 22 1855
DASHIEL, Samuel K.	HAMILTON, Ellen M.	DEC 27 1848
DASHIELD, Sally	SMITH, Wm. H.	APR 08 1817

District of Columbia Marriage Licenses, 1811-1858

DASHIELDS, Mary	COLLINS, Thomas	JUN 27 1830
DASHIELDS, Mary Caroline	BLACKISTON, Lewis	NOV 30 1844
DASHIELL, George W.	BEALL, Deborah B.	JUN 03 1817
DASHIELL, Hester E.	HOPKINS, John S.	AUG 13 1851
DASHIELL, Robert L.	HANLY, Mary Jane	MAY 03 1854
DASHIELL, Sarah Ellen	WARNER, Edward	MAY 09 1842
DASSEY, Josephine H.	MORELAND, William A.	JUL 07 1851
DASSEY, Mary Ann	DAY, Fielder	APR 01 1852
DATCHER, Francis	LUCAS, Eleanor	MAY 08 1817
DATCHER, Galan	CARTER, Anne (blk)	AUG 25 1857
DATES, Philip	DITUS, Debror S.	OCT 16 1844
DAUGHERTY, Ann T.	MATHIEU, Joseph	JUN 29 1843
DAUGHERTY, James	MULLAN, Susan	OCT 15 1822
DAUGHERTY, Rebecca	McCANN, Arthen	SEP 16 1812
DAUGHTON, Darius D.	HUNTER, Catharine	MAY 22 1858
DAUM, John Andon	SCHNAPPAUF, Kanigunda	DEC 22 1851
DAUR, Mary	EARBACK, Charles	MAR 24 1857
DAURACEY, Rosanna J.	McKEON, Thomas	JUN 30 1854
DAUSEY, Lucretia Ann	SMOOT, Thomas Walter	JAN 11 1845
DAUSON, Robert G.	WALLACE, Emily Ann	DEC 01 1828
DAVENPORT, Ann	DAVENPORT, Joseph H.	MAY 28 1845
DAVENPORT, Henry K.	GRAHAM, Jeannie B.	DEC 07 1847
DAVENPORT, James	GRANDERSON, Catharine	JUN 05 1856
DAVENPORT, Joseph H.	DAVENPORT, Ann	MAY 28 1845
DAVID, Abram	GASSEMHEIMER, Sophia	FEB 10 1858
DAVIDGE, Joanna H.S.	DEAS, Charles	AUG 20 1849
DAVIDSON, Anna	WOODRUFF, A.D.	JUL 03 1845
DAVIDSON, Christopher P.	ROGERS, Mary E.	OCT 09 1846
DAVIDSON, Clementia	FARR, John B.	MAY 13 1856
DAVIDSON, Daniel D.	McINTYRE, Letitia M.	APR 04 1837
DAVIDSON, Delozier	CRAWFORD, Clementina M.	JUN 05 1844
DAVIDSON, Delozier	CRAWFORD, Henrietta M.	OCT 04 1848
DAVIDSON, Eliza A.H.	ADAMS, Notley L.	APR 26 1821
DAVIDSON, Elizabeth	WHITMORE, Zachariah H.	JUL 08 1833
DAVIDSON, Elizabeth G.	DODGE, Charles	JUN 11 1849
DAVIDSON, Henrietta Waring	RITTENHOUSE, Benjamin F.	OCT 15 1835
DAVIDSON, James	MULLOY, Mary Ann	JAN 16 1835
DAVIDSON, John	UPPERMAN, Mary Ann	SEP 04 1821
DAVIDSON, John	LANE, Maria	OCT 06 1852
DAVIDSON, John	POSTON, Eliza	FEB 23 1858
DAVIDSON, John B.	LAUB, Margaret W.	JUN 30 1857
DAVIDSON, Lewis Grant	CRAWFORD, Eliza	JAN 20 1821
DAVIDSON, Margaret	HALL, Basil D.	SEP 07 1836
DAVIDSON, Mary L.	FRYE, Hugh W., Jr.	JUN 14 1852
DAVIDSON, Minerva	SUTER, Henderson	JUN 06 1854
DAVIDSON, Nancy	TALBURT, McKINSEY	SEP 01 1826
DAVIDSON, Thomas	SHERLEY, Ann	JUN 01 1830
DAVIDSON, William H.	KING, Letitia H.	MAY 08 1828
DAVIES, Cumming	BIBB, Virginia Frances	JAN 28 1851
DAVIS, Abel G.	MARTIN, Mary	DEC 04 1837
DAVIS, Albertine (blk)	BROWN, Samuel	NOV 27 1855
DAVIS, Alethea Ann	ROBINSON, John P.	OCT 11 1832
DAVIS, Alexander	HOOPER, Elizabeth Jane	JAN 02 1841
DAVIS, Alice M.	FOXWELL, Gabriel J.L.	NOV 29 1855
DAVIS, Almond W.	WALTON, Cornelia H.	JUL 17 1854
DAVIS, Amanda M.	ARYES, Daniel	DEC 08 1840
DAVIS, Ann	THOMAS, James [Col.]	NOV 07 1818
DAVIS, Ann	HOUSE, Richard	MAR 25 1826

District of Columbia Marriage Licenses, 1811-1858

DAVIS, Ann	DUVALL, John	DEC 26 1839
DAVIS, Ann	ELKINS, John	JUL 14 1842
DAVIS, Ann	GRIPENSCHUTZ, Charles G.	JAN 04 1855
DAVIS, Ann C.	SAUNDERS, Thompson H.	AUG 10 1840
DAVIS, Ann E.	SANDS, Thomas F.	DEC 20 1855
DAVIS, Ann F.	PAGE, Frederick B.	JUN 03 1846
DAVIS, Ann Maria	McPHERSON, Robert M.	MAY 10 1834
DAVIS, Ann S.	SCOTT, George A.	AUG 04 1853
DAVIS, Anna M. (blk)	ALLEN, Elijah	AUG 17 1854
DAVIS, Asa	RIGHT, Kitty	JUL 10 1819
DAVIS, Asa	MILSTEND, Mary	DEC 18 1849
DAVIS, Augustus	ASKINS, Ann Rebecca	JAN 01 1829
DAVIS, Augustus	STANLEY, Mary	SEP 29 1850
DAVIS, Benjamin	SMITH, Justine	JAN 22 1852
DAVIS, Caroline	COOTE, Thomas	NOV 19 1818
DAVIS, Caroline (blk)	MITCHELL, John	MAY 12 1835
DAVIS, Caroline P.	WYNN, James Henry	APR 05 1855
DAVIS, Catherine	LUSE, Matthias, Jr.	APR 17 1823
DAVIS, Catherine	SIMMONS, Robert	JUL 07 1836
DAVIS, Catherine S.	WATERS, John	MAY 02 1848
DAVIS, Charles	COCKRELL, Ann	MAR 03 1840
DAVIS, Charles	HUTCHINSON, Amelia (blk)	JAN 28 1857
DAVIS, Charles Atkerson	WILLIAMS, Charlotte	MAY 27 1824
DAVIS, Charles E.	FINCKEL, Caroline A.	APR 05 1852
DAVIS, Charles M.	REED, Hester A.	OCT 22 1856
DAVIS, Charles W.	EWELL, Martha	SEP 04 1851
DAVIS, Charles W.	GLADMAN, Rutha R.	JUL 31 1855
DAVIS, Charlotte E.	MAURO, Charles G.	APR 03 1856
DAVIS, Charlotte P.	DAVIS, James W.	NOV 20 1848
DAVIS, Charlotte P.	JOHNSON, Thomas W.	DEC 13 1851
DAVIS, Clarissa (blk)	WATKINS, Adam	SEP 22 1847
DAVIS, David	FERGASON, Caroline	JUN 12 1821
DAVIS, David	BANISTER, Charlotte	DEC 27 1831
DAVIS, David	CUNNINGHAM, Barbara	FEB 21 1840
DAVIS, Dorcas	MADDOX, Thomas L.	JUN 01 1812
DAVIS, Edward	HURLEY, Sarah	OCT 30 1814
DAVIS, Edward	LIGHTFORD, Louisa	DEC 04 1834
DAVIS, Edward	LYNCH, Maria	JUL 29 1841
DAVIS, Eli	BURGIND, Catharine	SEP 22 1832
DAVIS, Eli	GIVINGS, Margaret	JUN 20 1834
DAVIS, Elie	LANHAM, Eliza	NOV 15 1825
DAVIS, Eliza	THOMPSON, Elzey	AUG 01 1815
DAVIS, Eliza	GRAVES, George	DEC 23 1826
DAVIS, Eliza	KEPNER, Henry	AUG 12 1834
DAVIS, Eliza	CLARK, Henry	DEC 26 1837
DAVIS, Eliza	BRYANT, Benj.	OCT 18 1852
DAVIS, Eliza A.	HAMACKER, Joseph	JUN 25 1857
DAVIS, Eliza Ann	CRAWFORD, James T.	MAY 10 1853
DAVIS, Elizabeth	ANEBEY, William	NOV 24 1814
DAVIS, Elizabeth	TOMPKINS, Caleb	JAN 01 1821
DAVIS, Elizabeth	HARRY, George	DEC 11 1823
DAVIS, Elizabeth	BOYER, Frederick	JUN 08 1826
DAVIS, Elizabeth	ARNOLD, John Hy.	JAN 02 1843
DAVIS, Elizabeth (blk)	MILLER, Charles	SEP 09 1852
DAVIS, Elizabeth A.	BARRON, Henry	MAY 13 1850
DAVIS, Elizabeth A.	SMITH, Edward A.	JUN 19 1851
DAVIS, Elizabeth H. [Mrs.]	THORN, Joseph O.	JUN 02 1834
DAVIS, Elizabeth S.	POWERS, James E.	FEB 24 1840

District of Columbia Marriage Licenses, 1811-1858

DAVIS, Elizabeth V.	DOVE, George Henry	DEC 27 1853
DAVIS, Emely (blk)	TOPPING, Elisha	FEB 22 1844
DAVIS, Ferdinand	KING, Julia	MAR 31 1852
DAVIS, Frances	DOBBYN, George W.	JAN 11 1844
DAVIS, Frances (blk)	LEE, William	APR 21 1840
DAVIS, Francis	McDONALD, Elizabeth (blk)	JUN 01 1848
DAVIS, Francis	MARSHALL, Nancy	JUN 19 1856
DAVIS, Francis M.	BROWN, J. Frank	MAR 31 1856
DAVIS, George	HILL, Elizabeth	JUL 22 1815
DAVIS, George	RUNNELS, Leathia Ann	DEC 21 1816
DAVIS, George	MARRICH, Margaret	JUL 14 1821
DAVIS, George	ROYALL, Mary (blk)	MAR 14 1855
DAVIS, George Augustus	SHEPPARD, Sarah Jane	FEB 05 1828
DAVIS, George M.	REINAGLE, Georgianna	JAN 25 1831
DAVIS, George O.	CAVENAUGH, Ellen C.	DEC 18 1857
DAVIS, George S.	WRIGHT, Mary A.	AUG 15 1834
DAVIS, George W.	NALLS, Rowena A.	AUG 18 1856
DAVIS, Georgianna	DEMSTER, Samuel W. Glenn	MAR 23 1850
DAVIS, Gusty	LANHON, Deborah	SEP 18 1819
DAVIS, Hanah	FRASER, Simon	DEC 12 1843
DAVIS, Hanson	LEE, Ann	JUL 01 1833
DAVIS, Harriet	KINCHELOE, John	APR 08 1830
DAVIS, Harriet Ann (blk)	FERGUSON, William J.	JUN 24 1850
DAVIS, Harriet M.	RUDD, John W.	MAY 11 1850
DAVIS, Henrietta	SMITH, Thomas	SEP 04 1838
DAVIS, Henry	SKIDMORE, Rebecca	APR 08 1815
DAVIS, Henry A.	GRENCHENER, Catharine	SEP 07 1836
DAVIS, Henry S.	GOLT, Mary E.	DEC 19 1850
DAVIS, Hezekiah	BOWEN, Rebecca	AUG 24 1816
DAVIS, Hezekiah	DRANE, Jane	FEB 22 1838
DAVIS, Isaac F.	WHYCOF, Margaret E.	MAR 13 1838
DAVIS, James	KNOTT, Harriot	JUL 24 1823
DAVIS, James	GOLDIN, Matilda	DEC 22 1826
DAVIS, James	NORRIS, Louisa	JAN 15 1829
DAVIS, James	JENIS, Charlotte (blk)	NOV 04 1829
DAVIS, James	SMITH, Sophia	SEP 23 1834
DAVIS, James	SEUFFERLE, Harriet	JAN 19 1841
DAVIS, James	EVANS, Josephine	MAY 15 1841
DAVIS, James	COOPER, Lucy Ann (blk)	MAR 18 1847
DAVIS, James	GODFREY, Martha E.	OCT 03 1854
DAVIS, James B.	BENNETT, Mary Ann	APR 23 1840
DAVIS, James B.	WALKER, Almea V.	NOV 04 1852
DAVIS, James D.	BADDEN, Matilda	FEB 10 1823
DAVIS, James N.	O'NEALE, Elizabeth	MAY 05 1840
DAVIS, James N.W.	SEWELL, Martha E.	MAY 29 1855
DAVIS, James T.	LANGLEY, Catharine S.	AUG 21 1833
DAVIS, James W.	DAVIS, Charlotte P.	NOV 20 1848
DAVIS, James W.	DELLS, Sarah C.	JAN 06 1853
DAVIS, James W.	BEALE, Eugenia D.	DEC 31 1855
DAVIS, Jane	WHITMORE, John P.	MAR 20 1830
DAVIS, Jane (blk)	GREEN, Edward	NOV 11 1842
DAVIS, Jane E.	CHILDS, Robert	MAR 05 1855
DAVIS, Jeremiah	CHESHIRE, Jane Allen	JUN 06 1849
DAVIS, Joanna	HUNT, Thomas	JUN 02 1848
DAVIS, John	WARFORD, Jane	JUL 27 1826
DAVIS, John	WEBSTER, Linda	DEC 25 1826
DAVIS, John	WEBSTER, Linda	DEC 25 1826
DAVIS, John	DAVIS, Mary A.	OCT 19 1829

District of Columbia Marriage Licenses, 1811-1858

DAVIS, John	CLARKE, Jane	JUL 17 1834
DAVIS, John	BROOKS, Margaret Ann (blk)	MAY 26 1835
DAVIS, John	SWANN, Elizabeth	JUN 29 1837
DAVIS, John	LOW, Mary	JUL 09 1839
DAVIS, John	HOWARD, Ann	OCT 07 1845
DAVIS, John	[torn out], Caroline	JUN 03 1847
DAVIS, John	BEACH, Elizabeth	MAR 09 1852
DAVIS, John A.	HUBBARD, Elizabeth	FEB 17 1830
DAVIS, John A.	FERGUSON, Elizabeth R.	JAN 14 1839
DAVIS, John B.	QUEEN, Mary H.	JUL 02 1831
DAVIS, John B.	CASSEDY, Margaret Ann	MAY 14 1833
DAVIS, John H.	WILLIAMS, Mary Elizth.	NOV 27 1832
DAVIS, John Henry	KIDWELL, Mary Elizth.	APR 09 1855
DAVIS, John L.	LYNN, Mary C.	JUN 01 1852
DAVIS, John S.	STEEL, Mary A.R.	SEP 12 1832
DAVIS, John S.	BURGESS, Verlinda A.	JUN 08 1837
DAVIS, John T.	MALONE, Sarah Elizth.	OCT 08 1850
DAVIS, John T.	COCHRAN, Emily V.	JAN 18 1856
DAVIS, John Truman	WHITEMAN, Elizabeth Ann	NOV 07 1850
DAVIS, John W.	DOVE, Sarah A.	SEP 13 1855
DAVIS, John W.	MACKBEE, Eliza V.	MAY 01 1856
DAVIS, John W.	DODSON, Linny Ann	JUL 10 1856
DAVIS, John W.	RICHARDSON, Sarah A.	JUN 28 1858
DAVIS, Jonas	MEEM, Elizabeth	MAR 16 1813
DAVIS, Joseph W.	EDWARDS, Sarah F.	APR 02 1857
DAVIS, Joshua	MacDANIEL, Lucy C.	NOV 20 1838
DAVIS, Josiah	SHERWOOD, Jane	NOV 16 1852
DAVIS, Julia Wingate	ELLERBY, Albert	FEB 14 1849
DAVIS, Laura Victoria	STICK, David Henry	FEB 21 1857
DAVIS, Levi	GUY, Sarah E.	APR 28 1841
DAVIS, Levia	JOHNSON, Archibald	MAY 05 1831
DAVIS, Levinia	MILLS, Sandford	NOV 20 1840
DAVIS, Lucy Ann	WROE, John	NOV 13 1844
DAVIS, Luke	GRIMES, Mary	DEC 16 1819
DAVIS, Lutecia (blk)	BROWN, William	MAR 14 1854
DAVIS, Malinda	MARCHE, Thomas	JUN 15 1826
DAVIS, Malinda	FORREST, Jonathan	FEB 24 1848
DAVIS, Margaret	SIMMS, George Washington	OCT 09 1856
DAVIS, Margaretta	CHANEY, Zachariah	DEC 11 1847
DAVIS, Maria	ROBERTSON, John	MAY 12 1825
DAVIS, Maria (blk)	SMILER, Henry	FEB 06 1834
DAVIS, Martha	SWANN, James	APR 19 1855
DAVIS, Martha Ann	BOSTON, Charles	DEC 20 1827
DAVIS, Martha Ann	BROWN, Edmund	SEP 11 1848
DAVIS, Mary	PEAT, John	APR 05 1819
DAVIS, Mary	HALL, Edward	JAN 28 1826
DAVIS, Mary	STEEL, Tapley	SEP 08 1829
DAVIS, Mary	THOMAS, John	AUG 03 1833
DAVIS, Mary	SCHAFER, Frederick	JUN 19 1851
DAVIS, Mary	RADY, John	OCT 11 1855
DAVIS, Mary (blk)	SCOTT, Levi	AUG 06 1840
DAVIS, Mary (blk)	LODGE, Henry	NOV 25 1841
DAVIS, Mary (blk)	LODGE, Edward	NOV 11 1841
DAVIS, Mary A.	DAVIS, John	OCT 19 1829
DAVIS, Mary A.	LEWIS, Charles	AUG 11 1854
DAVIS, Mary Ann	BEALL, George W.	DEC 24 1841
DAVIS, Mary Ann	GOODRICK, William	DEC 10 1844
DAVIS, Mary Ann	DAVIS, William	SEP 17 1850

District of Columbia Marriage Licenses, 1811-1858

DAVIS, Mary Ann	PARROTT, James	OCT 06 1855
DAVIS, Mary E.	BURRUSS, Harris D.	DEC 14 1839
DAVIS, Mary E.	BLAND, William S.	JAN 02 1840
DAVIS, Mary E.	MARTIN, Robert	JAN 18 1846
DAVIS, Mary E.	SUTER, George J.	JAN 20 1858
DAVIS, Mary E.	TRENT, Robert W.	AUG 13 1858
DAVIS, Mary Elizabeth	McCAUSLAND, James	JUN 21 1856
DAVIS, Mary Elizabeth	SUTER, George G.	FEB 10 1858
DAVIS, Mary Ellen	HOUGH, George Campbell	JUN 09 1849
DAVIS, Mary Ellen	GREEN, James	JUL 03 1851
DAVIS, Mary Frances	FORD, Joseph	APR 07 1849
DAVIS, Mary G.	HALE, William H.	JUN 01 1844
DAVIS, Mary H.	ORME, Rezin	NOV 07 1836
DAVIS, Mary J.	SPEER, George	JAN 31 1856
DAVIS, Mary J.	MERRILL, Saml.	JUL 15 1858
DAVIS, Mary Jane	GASSAWAY, Richard	NOV 05 1846
DAVIS, Mary Jane	BUTLER, Morgan E.	FEB 12 1850
DAVIS, Mary Jane	WARDER, Walter	DEC 02 1853
DAVIS, Mary Kervand	BROOKE, Thomas A.	APR 16 1855
DAVIS, Mary V.	FRANKLIN, Ben	AUG 30 1845
DAVIS, Matilda E.	SCOTT, William H.	DEC 01 1851
DAVIS, Nelly (blk)	BAILY, Sandy	MAY 13 1835
DAVIS, Patrick	FOLEN, Ellen	JUN 13 1856
DAVIS, Peter	GROSS, Matilda	AUG 15 1812
DAVIS, Peter L.	MILLER, Mary	JUN 05 1814
DAVIS, Philip	GODFREY, Caroline	MAY 03 1838
DAVIS, Presley	DAVIS, Sarah Ann	OCT 13 1814
DAVIS, Pricy	BIDDLE, James	JUN 18 1818
DAVIS, Priscilla	McEWING, Levi	JAN 23 1826
DAVIS, Rachael	ADAMS, William	AUG 12 1830
DAVIS, Rease	LYLAS, Henry	APR 24 1820
DAVIS, Richard	PAECHCOTT, Hannah	JUN 28 1837
DAVIS, Richard	SMITH, Sarah (blk)	NOV 07 1838
DAVIS, Richard	CLAXTON, Amelia A.	FEB 02 1858
DAVIS, Robert M.	JONES, Harriott B.	DEC 20 1834
DAVIS, Robert T.	WELCH, Maria J.	FEB 09 1852
DAVIS, Russel P.	DePUY, Martha E.B.	MAR 16 1852
DAVIS, Sabina (blk)	GREEN, John	AUG 19 1851
DAVIS, Samuel	HILTON, Mary Ann	SEP 08 1831
DAVIS, Samuel S.	BRADY, Sarah E.	MAR 09 1857
DAVIS, Sarah	OVERTON, John	NOV 21 1812
DAVIS, Sarah	McINTOSH, John	NOV 23 1815
DAVIS, Sarah	WOODYARD, Moses	JUL 14 1829
DAVIS, Sarah	CAMERON, Joseph	MAY 04 1840
DAVIS, Sarah	BLACKSON, Henry	JUN 01 1841
DAVIS, Sarah (blk)	COATES, Wm. Henry	NOV 11 1852
DAVIS, Sarah Ann	DAVIS, Presley	OCT 13 1814
DAVIS, Sarah Ann	COLEMAN, Randle	JUL 11 1842
DAVIS, Sarah Ann	BURR, James	FEB 04 1846
DAVIS, Sarah J.	HOLT, John R.	APR 07 1856
DAVIS, Sarah Olivia	MARSHALL, Armstead T.	AUG 07 1849
DAVIS, Sarah Rebecca	CURRAN, Dennis	JAN 18 1855
DAVIS, Solomon	BARNES, Eliza Ann	NOV 16 1850
DAVIS, Susan E.	KEEN, Nathaniel B.	NOV 27 1828
DAVIS, Susanna	BELL, George W.	JAN 23 1837
DAVIS, Susanna	DOVE, James	AUG 16 1842
DAVIS, Thomas	RILES, Sally	JUL 18 1814
DAVIS, Thomas	TURNER, Eliza	NOV 24 1819

District of Columbia Marriage Licenses, 1811-1858

DAVIS, Thomas	WHITE, Mary	MAY 12 1855
DAVIS, Thomas B.	HUDSON, Catherine A.S.	SEP 29 1847
DAVIS, Thomas Richard	IMERSON, Ede	JAN 21 1826
DAVIS, Thomas T.C.	ETCHISON, Elizabeth A.	DEC 30 1835
DAVIS, Virginia S.	PARKER, Moses T.	DEC 17 1839
DAVIS, Wesley	FENESEY, Sarah	AUG 31 1844
DAVIS, William	McCAHAN, Catherine	AUG 28 1812
DAVIS, William	MERCHANT, Martena	AUG 28 1826
DAVIS, William	JETT, Eliza	AUG 25 1831
DAVIS, William	DEAN, Elizabeth Ann	JUL 10 1834
DAVIS, William	KANKEY, Amelia Virginia	NOV 15 1834
DAVIS, William	SMOOT, Mary	OCT 07 1845
DAVIS, William	GRAY, Arenan (blk)	DEC 18 1849
DAVIS, William	DAVIS, Mary Ann	SEP 17 1850
DAVIS, William	ANDERSON, Emma F.	OCT 20 1853
DAVIS, William	BRISSY, Elizabeth	JUL 31 1856
DAVIS, William	EASTON, Mary F. (blk)	AUG 11 1856
DAVIS, William B.	TALIAFERO, Evelina O.	MAY 19 1848
DAVIS, William H.	FINNESY, Julia	FEB 07 1846
DAVIS, William, Jr.	WHEAT, Eleanor C.	JUN 26 1834
DAVIS, William L.	WHIPPLE, Ann	JUN 29 1848
DAVIS, William S.	CASSELL, Sarah E.	JAN 09 1854
DAVIS, William W.	WORTHINGTON, Catharine L.	FEB 17 1842
DAVIS, Wm. M.	LOWE, Eckstine M.	APR 04 1854
DAVISON, Emma	FORRESTER, Isaac N.	JUN 16 1856
DAVISON, Hannah	EARL, Richard	OCT 01 1851
DAVISON, Martha	STEAD, Samuel	JAN 31 1853
DAVISON, Mary Ann	PROCTOR, John C.	OCT 08 1856
DAVISON, Samuel	STRONG, Mary	MAY 28 1832
DAVISON, Sarah F.	ROGERSON, George T.	SEP 30 1854
DAW, Eliza	BATZOLD, Frederick	JUN 11 1821
DAW, John	KIDWELL, Martha	APR 02 1825
DAW, Marion J.	EDMONSTON, Decius W., Jr.	OCT 14 1854
DAW, Mary Ann	COAD, John	JAN 01 1820
DAW, Sarah V.	GRIFFIN, Henry C.	SEP 07 1857
DAW, William Henry	MILES, Mary Ann	DEC 05 1837
DAWES, Edward	PIERCE, Ann	JUL 22 1815
DAWES, Harrison J.	BEALL, Mary Ellen	DEC 26 1856
DAWES, Joseph	MOORE, Margaret	DEC 15 1829
DAWES, Julia	CLARKE, Joseph C.R.	JUN 08 1857
DAWES, Mary	KROWSE, John	JUL 17 1814
DAWES, Rufus	CRANCH, Elizth. Eliot	MAY 18 1829
DAWES, Sarah	WILSON, Levi E.	JUN 05 1850
DAWES, Sarah Taylor	BATES, Frederick	APR 26 1842
DAWNING, Hester Ann	CLEMENTS, Edmund	FEB 01 1849
DAWNY, William	BEANES, Elizabeth	JUN 02 1827
DAWS, Eliza	MOCKBEE, Joseph	DEC 17 1816
DAWS, Mary	BIRD, William	NOV 09 1846
DAWSEY, Elizabeth	BURRELL, Henry	DEC 12 1848
DAWSON, Aaron	GREEN, Sarah Ann	SEP 05 1825
DAWSON, Ann	MACUBBIN, Moses	AUG 11 1832
DAWSON, Ann R.	WICKLIFFE, Robert C.	FEB 28 1843
DAWSON, Dianna	SISSON, John B.	AUG 25 1836
DAWSON, Edward L.	HURLEY, Virginia A.	OCT 29 1850
DAWSON, George W., of Wm.	ISHERWOOD, Frances Ann	FEB 01 1855
DAWSON, Harriet	FRENCH, James W.	MAR 25 1850
DAWSON, Hugh	ROWLINGS, Ann	JUN 04 1818
DAWSON, James M.	GREENFIELD, Louisa V.	FEB 25 1856

District of Columbia Marriage Licenses, 1811-1858

DAWSON, John T.	LINDSEY, Ann M.	FEB 14 1850
DAWSON, Margaret	BARRY, Richard	MAY 14 1840
DAWSON, Margaret A.	ROWLES, William H.	NOV 05 1857
DAWSON, Maria Louisa	EDMONSTON, Edwin H.	MAR 29 1858
DAWSON, Mary Ann (blk)	HOGANS, John	JAN 05 1850
DAWSON, Rebecca A.	TODD, Samuel P.	JUN 24 1812
DAWSON, Sally	NEWHOUSE, Harvey M.	DEC 01 1851
DAWSON, Samuel	BAYNE, Sarah Anne	MAR 20 1834
DAWSON, Sarah (blk)	FISHER, Jacob	AUG 11 1828
DAWSON, Thomas	HALES, Mary	SEP 06 1826
DAWSON, Thomas B.	JEWELL, Elizabeth	OCT 23 1839
DAWSON, Thomas H.	BOYD, Margaret	DEC 22 1856
DAWSON, William	WHETZELL, Ann	JUN 30 1825
DAWSON, William	RIDGEWAY, Susan	FEB 26 1829
DAWSON, William P.	WHITE, Mary F.	FEB 20 1851
DAWSY, Susannah (blk)	ROBERTSON, Fortune	SEP 22 1815
DAY, Ann	WOOD, John W.	MAR 17 1837
DAY, Ann	GENTLE, Acquilla	SEP 26 1840
DAY, Ann Elizth.	BROWN, Hanson	FEB 21 1844
DAY, Bradley	WHITE, Amelia J.	MAR 28 1850
DAY, Catharine	MILES, Henry	AUG 25 1836
DAY, Charles	BORNE, Elizabeth	AUG 19 1858
DAY, Edward William	CLARKE, Anastasia	APR 18 1854
DAY, Elijah W.	LATIMER, Mary	MAY 05 1851
DAY, Eliza C.	SPILLMAN, Edward M.	SEP 04 1849
DAY, Elizabeth	MANKINS, William	DEC 24 1834
DAY, Elizabeth (blk)	SIMMS, Washington	FEB 03 1836
DAY, Elizabeth (blk)	CARROLL, William	SEP 09 1840
DAY, Elizabeth Martha	SWAIN, Stephen	MAY 04 1842
DAY, Ellen (blk)	BELL, Loyd	NOV 26 1841
DAY, Fielder	BADING, Mary Ann	JAN 15 1827
DAY, Fielder	DASSEY, Mary Ann	APR 01 1852
DAY, Hanora Ann	STALLINGS, Theodore P.	MAY 11 1849
DAY, James	ANDERSON, Elizabeth	JAN 05 1822
DAY, James	LIVINGTON, Sarah	APR 03 1823
DAY, Jane E.	FOWLER, Wm. W.	OCT 08 1853
DAY, John S.	FRIDLEY, Catherine V.	JUN 04 1850
DAY, Julia Ann	WINKLER, Benjamin	FEB 23 1832
DAY, Laurence	BECKET, Mary (blk)	APR 04 1850
DAY, Louisa	RIDDLE, Charles J.	JUN 23 1852
DAY, Loyd	WHITE, Sarah Ann	SEP 10 1840
DAY, Margaret Eleanor (blk)	THOMPSON, Joseph	MAY 29 1858
DAY, Mary	EDELIN, J.	APR 29 1817
DAY, Mary	BARR, Robert	DEC 12 1844
DAY, Peter	GARVEY, Bridget	NOV 13 1851
DAY, Rebecca	MITCHELL, John	JAN 29 1835
DAY, Roda	WATTS, Harriet Ann (blk)	DEC 05 1850
DAY, Samuel	MONN, Rosetta (blk)	JUN 10 1853
DAY, Susan	DOGAN, Andrew	NOV 25 1852
DAY, Susan Ellen	ROLLINS, John A.	FEB 01 1844
DAY, Thomas	MARR, Emeline	OCT 24 1845
DAY, Thomas	WASHINGTON, Mary V.	APR 21 1858
DAY, Trecinder	WILCOXEN, Washington	OCT 25 1824
DAY, William	BROWN, Rebecca	NOV 04 1817
DAY, William	BALL, Louisa	JUN 10 1833
DAY, Wm.	GRAY, Margaret	APR 18 1814
DAYS, Stephen W.	COSTIN, Martha P. (blk)	MAY 05 1845
DAYS, Woolberton	COSTIN, Martha P.	JUN 13 1848

District of Columbia Marriage Licenses, 1811-1858

DAYTON, Albert	BAKER, Emily	AUG 27 1850
DAYTON, Margaret	ALLEN, Joseph R.	MAR 14 1849
DEACANS, Ellen	POWERS, Jacob	MAR 19 1844
DEAKINS, Ann Maria	BROWN, Richard	FEB 12 1839
DEAKINS, Elizabeth	BURNS, James	APR 06 1813
DEAKINS, Jane	BATEMAN, Joshua	JUN 20 1828
DEAKINS, Jane P.	SERPELL, Richard	MAR 09 1836
DEAKINS, Philip	DOUGHERTY, Margaret	AUG 07 1813
DEAKINS, Philip	DRUMMOND, Jane	JUN 13 1839
DEAKON, John Archy	JARBER, Eleanor	JUN 03 1817
DEALE, Laura C.	GAULT, Matthew	MAR 05 1845
DEALE, Wm. G.	PHILLIPS, Emiline	JUN 20 1855
DEAN, Alexander	KING, Eliza	FEB 06 1840
DEAN, Ann	GIBSON, John	DEC 27 1827
DEAN, Catherine Ellen	SEBASTIAN, Nicholas	DEC 09 1845
DEAN, Charles	CLARK, Mary	JUN 19 1828
DEAN, Elizabeth	SCOTT, Hezekiah	MAR 22 1815
DEAN, Elizabeth Ann	DAVIS, William	JUL 10 1834
DEAN, ELizabeth	HENDLEY, William	OCT 30 1841
DEAN, Felix	NOWLAND, Mary Louisa	MAR 03 1846
DEAN, George	HUTCHINSON, Mary A.	OCT 16 1850
DEAN, Henry C.	ZEIGLER, Harriet V.	JUL 02 1851
DEAN, Hiram	WOOD, Mary	MAY 28 1844
DEAN, Isaiah	KREAMER, Margaret	APR 17 1852
DEAN, James William	SEBASTIAN, Jane Elizabeth	DEC 20 1845
DEAN, John A.	BAKER, Atha Ann	OCT 09 1856
DEAN, John E.	THOMPSON, Mary	DEC 10 1849
DEAN, John T.W.	SHERIFF, Mary Cornelia	SEP 04 1845
DEAN, Julia Ann	TRUNNELL, William J.	AUG 05 1847
DEAN, Leantha	JENNINGS, Horace	SEP 21 1836
DEAN, Lewis [Sergt.]	NICHOLSON, Eliza	DEC 14 1827
DEAN, Martha	KING, Henry	SEP 15 1838
DEAN, Mary Ann	HAWKINS, Phillip	FEB 20 1839
DEAN, Mary Ellen	BARRON, Henry	JUN 02 1835
DEAN, Rebecca	PAXTON, James	FEB 28 1840
DEAN, Samuel	KOONES, Catharine	AUG 23 1819
DEAN, Samuel	ANDERSON, Mary Ann H.M. Fisher	MAR 20 1821
DEAN, Samuel	WEBSTER, Ann	JUL 10 1824
DEAN, Samuel	CARPENTER, Ann	FEB 11 1843
DEAN, William	BATTLE, Sally (blk)	AUG 14 1851
DEANE, Nelly	KINDEL, Ensey	SEP 25 1816
DeANGLAS, Belinda	WATSON, David L.	APR 06 1857
DEANN, Harriet Ann	SHOEMAKER, Iziah	AUG 27 1844
DEARBORN, Christiana	WILEY, Parkerson R.	AUG 27 1849
DEARING, George T.	SMITH, Elizabeth C.	APR 09 1852
DEAS, Charles	DAVIDGE, Joanna H.S.	AUG 20 1849
DEAVER, Joshua	GARDINER, Ann	JAN 29 1823
DEAVER, Joshua	NORRIS, Ann	APR 11 1825
DEAVER, Stephen	BOWMAN, Sarah	FEB 27 1817
DEAVERS, John	RILEY, Margaret	APR 03 1826
DEAVERS, Julia A.	PARNELL, William B.	MAY 26 1854
DEAVERS, Julia Ann	GORUM, James Thos.	JAN 14 1858
DEAVERS, Launcelot	HALL, Eliza	JUN 14 1838
DEAVIS, Sarah	DOVE, Robert	NOV 13 1844
DeBELL, Fanny	WILCOXON, Rezin	JUN 18 1851
DeBELL, Jno. D.	DANIEL, Annie W.	AUG 21 1855
DEBELL, Nancy Ann	VanHORN, Benjamin	MAR 23 1841
DeBEVOISE, Charles	HAIGHT, Mary C.	JAN 25 1855

District of Columbia Marriage Licenses, 1811-1858

DeBODISCO, Caroline	WILLIAMS, Brooke B.	JAN 11 1848
DEBOIS, Jeremiah	JONES, Mary C.	FEB 26 1852
DeBOW, J.D.B.	POE, Caroline S.	AUG 05 1854
DeBREDA, Antoine Marie Francois Paul	DelaVERGA, Mlle. Rita Victoria	OCT 21 1856
DeBRISSON, Charles	THOMPSON, Catharine L.	JAN 23 1823
DeBUTTS, John H.	FORREST, Sophia	AUG 08 1818
DeBUTTS, Louisa [Mrs.]	HALL, Edward	OCT 24 1820
DeBUTTS, Richard E.	HALL, Sarah M.C.	JUL 17 1844
DeCARNEY, Caroline Charlotte	LOUIS, Henry Charles	NOV 16 1813
DECK, Martin	BANGHARDT, Elizabeth	APR 11 1857
DECKER, James	OLIVER, Mary	AUG 13 1833
DECKER, John, Jr.	PATTERSON, Hellen M.	MAR 24 1852
DECKER, Juliana	GERECKE, August	APR 26 1853
DECKER, Philip	RAPP, Mary	JUN 20 1857
DeCLUDE, Dorathy	KNOTT, Adam	APR 22 1815
DECOVER, Lana Mari	BENEZETTE, Hazael	MAR 19 1850
DEDERICH, Marietta	HAGER, John F.	JUN 16 1849
DEDMORTIA, Louisa	OLIVER, John	JUN 07 1852
DEEBLE, Ann Louisa	LOWRY, John	JAN 13 1848
DEEBLE, Edward K.J.	BIRCH, Elizabeth Jane	MAY 31 1838
DEEBLE, Edward K.S.	PAULEY, Elizabeth M.	OCT 14 1830
DEEBLE, John George	CARROLL, Mary Jane	JAN 03 1853
DEEBLE, Joseph A.	TSCHIFFELY, Elizabeth G.	AUG 15 1844
DEEBLE, Mary Jane	LOWRY, William H.	MAY 16 1843
DEEBLE, Wm. H.	BURDETTE, Ellen	JUL 03 1855
DEELY, Patrick	WELSH, Johanna	JUN 23 1852
DEENE, Jacob	BRADY, Juliana	MAR 25 1826
DEER, Patrick	MATTHEWS, Margaret	APR 15 1856
DEERY, Bridget [Mrs.]	ALLEN, John	JUN 10 1816
DEEVER, Letty	BROOKBANK, Thos.	AUG 23 1858
DEEVERS, Elizabeth	LACEY, Manuel	JUL 03 1849
DEEVERS, Harriet	COLLINS, James H.	OCT 05 1850
DEEVERS, Henry	WATSON, Mary	OCT 20 1852
DEFALCO, Pasquale	ALEXANDER, Jane	MAR 24 1835
DeFORD, Charles De.	NOYES, Maria V.	JUL 08 1844
DEGEN, Laura Louisa	SHANKLAND, Thomas	APR 11 1835
DEGGES, Laura V.	SULTON, Robert M.	DEC 13 1852
DEGGES, Robert Hamilton	SPALDING, Mary Ann	JAN 09 1844
DeGILSE, Dorothy	PASKINS, John	JAN 20 1824
DeGILSE, Godfrey	HARRISON, Mary E.	APR 23 1830
DeGILSE, Louisa	FADEWILKE, Wm.	AUG 19 1822
DEGNAN, Mary	MURPHY, Peter	JUL 08 1853
DEGNAN, Mary	MURPHY, Peter	JUL 18 1853
DEISCHER, Barbara	SEIFEL, Henry	DEC 26 1854
DEITER, Francis Joseph	SCHAENHERE, Carolina	MAR 12 1857
DEITZ, Joseph	NOETHLING, Eliza	NOV 23 1853
DeJARNATT, Daniel	COLEMAN, Huldah	DEC 21 1817
DeKRAFFT, Frederick W.	RITCHIE, Roseannah A., Mrs.	DEC 05 1833
DeKRAFFT, John W.	VanZANDT, Dolley Payne	JAN 17 1835
DeKRAFFT, Mary Eleanor	BARNEY, Samuel C.	JUN 14 1847
DeKRAFT, Edmund	DEWEES, Eleanor	JUN 05 1819
DeKRAFT, Edward	EVANS, Maria	MAY 10 1814
DeKRAFT, Hannah	GRIFFIN, Peter	DEC 20 1827
DELACEY, John	FARRELL, Ann	JUN 25 1858
DELAD, Margaret	KEEFE, Edmund	JUN 13 1853
DELAHAY, Mark W.	TURPIN, Ann Jane	JUL 16 1838
DELAHUNT, Eliza	SULLIVAN, Joseph	MAY 03 1855
DELAHUNT, John	McCOY, Bridget	NOV 28 1849

District of Columbia Marriage Licenses, 1811-1858

DELANEY, Ann E. (blk)	MASSEY, Robert	MAR 27 1852
DELANEY, Bridget	BROWERS, John	AUG 18 1849
DELANEY, Bridget	BOYLE, Patrick	JAN 06 1854
DELANEY, Catherine	WEST, Douglass	SEP 11 1850
DELANEY, Henry	EASTON, Catharine (blk)	MAY 05 1849
DELANEY, Johanna	CALLAGHAN, Patrick	JUL 06 1852
DELANEY, Levi	BROWN, Mary J. (blk)	AUG 21 1850
DELANEY, Levi	PARKER, Sarah Jane	SEP 20 1854
DELANEY, Lucy	McCAULEY, Richard	NOV 12 1856
DELANEY, Margaret	THOMPSON, William H.	AUG 17 1852
DELANEY, Mary	COLEMAN, James	FEB 08 1853
DELANEY, Mary	MAKIBBON, Charles	NOV 27 1855
DELANEY, Michael	NAUGHTEN, Bridget	SEP 01 1851
DELANEY, Sarah Ann (blk)	NEALE, Thomas	MAY 27 1847
DELANO, Mary Elizabeth	THOMPSON, William	APR 29 1843
DELANO, William Judah	GIVEN, Sarah Ann	DEC 22 1841
DELANY, Ann B.	TINGEY, Thomas [Capt.]	DEC 09 1812
DELANY, Catherine	HILAND, James	OCT 29 1832
DELANY, Elizabeth	CONNAUGHTON, Michael	SEP 23 1837
DELANY, Elizabeth A.M.	CONNELL, John W.	OCT 08 1851
DELANY, Jane (blk)	HALL, John	DEC 24 1840
DELANY, John	ALLEN, Elizabeth	OCT 04 1827
DELANY, Lewis	GRAHAM, Anne (blk)	FEB 10 1842
DELANY, Mary	MULROY, James	JAN 05 1857
DELANY, Matthias	BROWN, Elizabeth	APR 25 1826
DELANY, Michael	VILLARD, Sophia Louisa	DEC 28 1841
DELANY, Patrick	DRANE, Sarah	MAY 18 1829
DELARO, William H.	JOHNSON, Annie E.	JAN 08 1857
DeLAROCHE, Anna Jane Belt	PATTERSON, James Orvill	FEB 26 1852
DELAVAN, John P.	BUYSEY, John H.	DEC 28 1854
DelaVERGA, Mlle. Rita Victoria	DeBREDA, Antoine Marie Francois Paul	OCT 21 1856
DELAWAY, Adeline	MANKIN, John	DEC 24 1841
DELAY, Martha	VINCENT, William D.	JAN 06 1857
DELAY, Robert	FRIZZEL, Martha Jane	MAY 13 1844
DeLEON, Adeline M.	ADAMS, Joseph H., Jr.	SEP 27 1852
DELEWARE, Julia Ann	WALL, Benjamin M.	MAR 10 1842
DELIHINITY, Ann Maria	POWELL, James	MAY 31 1852
DELL, Thomas	KLEIBER, Laura Matilda	MAR 06 1841
DELLA, Andrew	TREAKLE, ELizabeth	AUG 10 1852
DELLAMAN, Harmon	BARRETT, Mary	JUN 13 1836
DELLAWAY, Virginia	EDMONSTON, Edwin H.	MAY 16 1850
DELLETT, James C.	AULD, Jannette	MAR 14 1853
DELLING, Dorothie Fredericke Wilhelmine	GRUPE, George Wm. Henry Louis	JAN 27 1845
DELLINGER, Elizabeth	BURGESS, Samuel	JUL 14 1815
DELLS, John Thos.	ARRINGTON, Margt. M.	OCT 23 1856
DELLS, Sarah C.	DAVIS, James W.	JAN 06 1853
DELLZELL, Alexander W.	WILSON, Laura V.	NOV 20 1854
DELMORE, Elonora	MILLER, John	JAN 23 1854
DELOIZIER, Anne	BRISCOE, Philip T.	FEB 13 1816
DELOZIER, Ann	THOMPSON, Wn. J.A.	NOV 13 1838
DELOZIER, Mary	RATCLIFF, Alexander	SEP 16 1837
DELPHEY, Bartholomew	REEVES, Sarah	NOV 07 1832
DELPHEY, Orlando	GROVES, Jane	NOV 13 1832
DELPHEY, Orlando R.	PRINGLE, Ann Rebecca	JAN 12 1847
DELPHY, Jane	BECK, Walters R.	JUL 19 1853
DELPHY, Matilda	TERRY, Brooklin	AUG 19 1819
DELPHY, Sarah Ellenor Mariana	FIELD, George W.	MAY 29 1858
DELZELL, Mary E.	KLEINDIENST, Joseph	NOV 18 1852

District of Columbia Marriage Licenses, 1811-1858

DELZELL, William	FOWLER, Mary E.	DEC 27 1848
DEMAINE, Jane	SWAIN, Julius Gabriael	SEP 10 1833
DEMAINE, Mary A.	FLETCHER, James A.	SEP 15 1857
DeMALTITZ, Baron Francis	LEE, Mary Elizabeth	JUN 06 1825
DEMAR, Elizth. A.M.	BOWEN, Uriah R.	MAR 12 1852
DeMARCOLETA, J.	KIECKHOEFOR, Julia Augusta	JUN 08 1853
DEMAREST, Susan	BASSETT, Robert Tweedy	JUN 03 1847
DEMARIST, Mary Ann	HUTCHISON, Archibald	OCT 26 1826
DeMARUEL, Henry Galway	FOLEY, Mary J.	FEB 22 1856
DEMENT, Caroline	McKEE, William	OCT 25 1856
DEMENT, Ellen	SYPE, John	JUN 09 1840
DEMENT, John D.	SMOOT, Mary Jane	OCT 29 1853
DEMENT, Laura	TUBMAN, George W.	DEC 07 1857
DEMENT, Mary	BERRY, Nathaniel	JAN 11 1851
DEMENT, Mary E.	BRISCOE, Jarrard	APR 16 1833
DEMENT, Mrs.	BAILY, Solomon	MAY 19 1835
DEMENT, Rachel	COMPTON, Ruel K.	APR 22 1850
DEMENT, Richard	ASHBURY, Sarah	MAY 13 1828
DEMENT, Richard	COMPTON, Jane H.	MAY 01 1844
DEMENT, Sue Ellen	LANE, Charles H.	OCT 05 1857
DEMENT, William	KENNEDY, Julia	FEB 22 1815
DEMENTSION, Francis	SHANNON, Catherine Ann	SEP 18 1841
DEMING, Jacob	SCOTT, Mary	OCT 28 1830
DEMONOT, Peter	BREENCHN, Marie	MAY 30 1825
DEMOORE, Sarah L.	BAKER, Henry	AUG 20 1844
DeMOUTHOLON, Charles Francois	GRATIOT, Mary Victoria	OCT 30 1837
DEMPF, Antoine	NOLTE, Anna	MAY 15 1858
DEMPHY, Julia	SULLIVAN, John	JUN 22 1850
DEMPHY, Martin	DIXON, Catharine	SEP 24 1824
DEMPSEY, Ann E.	MARMAN, Washington	AUG 07 1850
DEMPSEY, Anne	BOYD, James J.	AUG 27 1852
DEMPSEY, Catharine	MURPHY, John	JUN 01 1853
DEMPSEY, Fanny	NEIL, James	SEP 17 1839
DEMPSEY, Joseph	MASSY, Jane	SEP 27 1848
DEMPSEY, Mary	DROWNES, James	MAY 16 1853
DEMPSEY, Moses	HOLAN, Ann	MAY 15 1858
DEMPSEY, Owen	MANAHAN, Mary	JUL 23 1830
DEMPSEY, Rodey	SPELLING, Margaret	JUN 25 1858
DEMPSY, Mary A.	MURPHY, John W.	APR 22 1858
DEMPSY, Patrick	KENNY, Mary	AUG 30 1852
DEMSTER, Samuel W. Glenn	DAVIS, Georgianna	MAR 23 1850
DeMYERS, John	FLIN, Mary	JAN 18 1815
DENAHY, Jeremiah	SULLIVAN, Honora	MAY 13 1852
DENAHY, Mary	RIORDAN, Andrew	JUL 01 1852
DeNEALE, Jannet S.W.	SMITH, Richard H.	OCT 26 1853
DeNEALE, Mary J.	BRUSH, Truman M.	NOV 28 1846
DeNEALE, Ruth Ann	JENNERS, James S.	MAR 02 1853
DeNEALE, William Y.	PARKER, Ann E.	DEC 10 1857
DENEALE, Cleland K.	JARBOE, Sarah J.	MAY 06 1841
DENGAL, George	DEOG, Catherine	OCT 07 1854
DENGEL, Madalena	GRASER, Adam	OCT 01 1852
DENGLER, Ablona	WALTER, John	JUL 15 1842
DENHAM, A.W.	PRITCHET, Ellen	SEP 19 1835
DENHAM, Columbus	TABLER, Margaret E.	AUG 21 1843
DENHAM, David B.	FORREST, Josephine D.	JUN 05 1837
DENHAM, Louis R.	BURNAY, Caroline A.	APR 21 1852
DENHAM, Mary	KEITH, William	SEP 07 1827
DENHAM, Mary Ann	PIGOT, John	AUG 15 1842

District of Columbia Marriage Licenses, 1811-1858

DENHAM, Thomas S.	RAINBOW, Mary Ann	SEP 15 1835
DENHAM, Thomas S.	COOK, Laura B.	SEP 22 1857
DENHAM, Zebulon W.	ANDERSON, Mary	NOV 01 1837
DeNIEL, Susan S.	LATHAM, Robert W.	FEB 20 1855
DENIHER, Bridget	MITCHELL, John	NOV 10 1855
DeNIROTH, Charlotte	STETSON, John	JUL 13 1813
DENIS, L. Felix	SLOTT, Catharine	JUL 19 1853
DENISON, Eliza C.	MONTAGUE, Charles P.	JAN 16 1851
DENISON, John	MAHONY, Susan	APR 16 1831
DENISON, Lewis	GOLDSBOROUGH, Ann	JUN 06 1856
DENISON, Louisa I.	WADSWORTH, Alexander L. [Capt.]	NOV 08 1824
DENNEY, James M.	GOSLER, Jane	SEP 04 1854
DENNIS, Alcinda L.	McFARLAND, John F.	MAR 14 1842
DENNIS, Anderson T.	McCARTY, Harriet Ann	JAN 23 1835
DENNIS, John	CROCKET, Eliza Ann	MAY 16 1853
DENNIS, John P.	MELLINGTON, Jane E.	DEC 27 1851
DENNIS, Jonathan	PARSONS, Jane Elizabeth	DEC 01 1852
DENNIS, Margaret	BULLOCK, Richard	OCT 03 1812
DENNIS, Philip	MARTIN, Ann	OCT 09 1828
DENNISON, Ann	TAYLOR, John	JAN 14 1818
DENNISON, Ann Virginia	CODRICK, James F.	OCT 16 1845
DENNISON, Harvey A.	TANNER, Hester Jane	JUN 05 1843
DENNISON, John T.	HODGSON, Harriett H.	JAN 01 1850
DENNISON, Margaret	NICHOLSON, Walter	DEC 04 1834
DENNISON, Mary F.	ELLIS, Robert	AUG 04 1849
DENNISON, Myrna	HOWE, Thomas	JUL 04 1817
DENNISON, Sarah A.	BATT, Wm.	MAY 24 1825
DENNISON, Susan A.	SNIFFIN, Theodore	APR 26 1847
DENNISON, Thomas	WOOLARD, Julia	DEC 23 1854
DENNISON, Virginia	GOLDEN, George	MAY 02 1849
DENNISON, Wilhelmina	DANIEL, James	NOV 25 1824
DENNISON, William	ERSKINE, Elizabeth	DEC 29 1836
DENNY, Ann	HORSLEY, Doct. Saml.	JUL 05 1815
DENNY, William Henry	POE, Maria	JAN 13 1854
DENON, Mary	SUTTON, William	JUL 22 1848
DENOU, Edney Ann	WILLIAMS, Zadock	NOV 14 1828
DENSEHER, Mary	LIHALLENBERG, Christian	JAN 13 1857
DENT, Augustus S.	CONINGTON, Rosina V.	JUL 15 1858
DENT, Bruce	JOHNSON, Cassey (blk)	MAR 26 1840
DENT, Caroline	BARKER, Isaac	OCT 11 1830
DENT, Deborah	MANKIN, James	DEC 31 1838
DENT, Eliza (blk)	LEE, Washington	JUL 24 1854
DENT, George	ASHTON, Ann Sophia	OCT 21 1833
DENT, Henry H.	ADLUM, Anna Maria	SEP 14 1841
DENT, Jane S.	DENT, William H.	JAN 19 1842
DENT, Jarad	HACKLETT, Eliza (blk)	MAR 06 1838
DENT, Margaretta	MANKIN, James	FEB 13 1833
DENT, William H.	DENT, Jane S.	JAN 19 1842
DENT, Zachariah	REYNOLDSON, Catherine E.	SEP 27 1848
DENTON, William	VALENTINE, Jane	APR 29 1819
DENTY, Thomas	WILLIAMSON, Martha	APR 29 1856
DEOG, Catherine	DENGAL, George	OCT 07 1854
DEPUTY, Rachel Ella	MOORE, James A.	SEP 12 1854
DEPUY, Martha E.B.	DAVIS, Russel P.	MAR 16 1852
DeQUIT, Margaret	CAMPBELL, Enoch	DEC 26 1831
DERBY, Richard C.	LEAR, Louisa	SEP 07 1835
DEREAME, Eliza	FINAGAN, Philip	JUL 29 1845
DEREMEN, Jacob	MURPHY, Eliza	FEB 21 1824

District of Columbia Marriage Licenses, 1811-1858

DEREMER, Amanda M.F.	SCRIVENER, Lewis H.	APR 06 1841
DERGAN, Mary A.C.	ROLLAN, George W.	OCT 30 1827
DERICK, William S.	LYONS, Ann	AUG 08 1827
DeRIDGES, Ellen	TALBURT, Alfred	FEB 06 1845
DERMODY, Walter W.	LYDDAN, Nancy	FEB 15 1849
DERMOT, Charlotte Julia [Mrs.]	SIOUSSA, John	MAR 02 1820
DeRODIER, Phillebert	FARBER, Mary Ann	OCT 29 1816
DeRONCERAY, C.	CROSSON, H. Rosalie	FEB 10 1858
DERRET, Catharine	BRADBURN, Peter	MAR 05 1822
DERRICK, Alexander Hamilton	LYONS, Emma	MAY 31 1843
DERRICK, Estella	GILMORE, James H.	SEP 30 1857
DERRICK, Julia (blk)	YORK, John	MAY 22 1851
DERRICK, Lucretia H.	PITZER, Jeremiah K.	APR 21 1858
DERRIN, Charles	GARRISON, Charity Ann	SEP 13 1819
DeSAULES, Adele Emile	BUTHMANN, John H.	FEB 14 1849
DeSAULES, Julia Louisa	BURNS, Harman	FEB 26 1852
DeSAULES, Julius	SPEAKS, Sarah Susan	FEB 19 1852
DeSAULES, Louisa Frazer	CAMPBELL, William Henry	OCT 18 1845
DESHAZO, James E.	BAYLISS, Lucinda	DEC 22 1857
DeSHIELDS, Maria	WHITE, Richard H.	AUG 19 1841
DESLONDE, Adrien	WALKER, Mary	MAY 24 1858
DESMOND, Ellen	MALONEY, James	SEP 17 1853
DESMOND, Jane	KATELAY, Richard	FEB 08 1853
DESMOND, Timothy	McGANN, Catherine	JAN 06 1852
DESSAR, Leon	GEBHARDT, Minna	MAY 25 1857
DETERMAN, Margaret Ann	BOOSE, William Henry	MAY 20 1858
DETRO, Ellen	ANDERSON, William	AUG 24 1848
DETRO, Thomas	BAKER, Catharine	DEC 16 1847
DETTON, Levin	BUTLER, Catharine	MAY 15 1821
DETTRE, Thomas	ROBINSON, Eleanor (blk)	SEP 01 1836
DETTRO, Frederick	JOHNSON, Mary Ann (blk)	OCT 27 1840
DETWEILER, Frederick M.	TARLTON, Jane E.	FEB 16 1852
DEVALL, Louisa M.	SMITH, John W., Jr.	JUN 23 1857
DEVALL, Mary	CAGE, William	JAN 22 1841
DEVAN, Elizabeth Ann	SLYE, Henry	FEB 09 1827
DeVAUGHAN, John E.	MILLSON, Mary S.	JUL 03 1854
DeVAUGHAN, Susan H.	BEACH, William E.	NOV 01 1847
DeVAUGHAN, Thomas S.	SMITH, Caroline S.	AUG 12 1842
DeVAUGHAN, Thomas S.	MORELAND, Ann E.	FEB 04 1858
DeVAUGHN, Amanda	HENRY, Robert	MAY 18 1854
DeVAUGHN, Celia	GRAY, George W.	JAN 03 1831
DeVAUGHN, Columbia	WILSON, John	MAR 19 1845
DeVAUGHN, James	HIGDON, Harriet	MAR 14 1830
DeVAUGHN, John B.	PENN, Susannah	AUG 04 1853
DeVAUGHN, John T.	HURDLE, Martha E.	MAY 09 1842
DeVAUGHN, John T.	EVANS, Josephine	SEP 21 1846
DeVAUGHN, Mary E.	KELLY, William H.	JAN 09 1854
DeVAUGHN, Samuel H.	SMITH, Harriet Ann	MAY 07 1838
DeVAUGHN, Sarah Ann	GILL, John R.	NOV 09 1847
DeVAUGHN, Sarah E.	STANLEY, John T.	AUG 09 1847
DeVAUGHN, Sinah A.	MOODY, Geo. A.	OCT 04 1849
DeVAUGHN, Susanna	CROSS, Fielder	OCT 01 1842
DeVAUGHN, Walter	HACKETT, Helen Louisa	OCT 02 1832
DeVAUGHN, William H.	JOHNSON, Sarah Ann	JUL 11 1839
DeVAUGHN, Wm.	HOSKINS, Sarah	MAR 13 1821
DEVAUGHN, Mary	FLAHERTY, John	NOV 14 1855
DeVAUGN, Catharine E.	SPALDING, George S.	JAN 06 1852
DEVAUL, Elizabeth	HARMAN, Lawrance	JAN 03 1818

District of Columbia Marriage Licenses, 1811-1858

DEVAUN, Elizabeth A.	MANGUN, Robert H.	JUN 24 1856
DeVEAU, Andrew	SELBY, Catherine P.	SEP 25 1856
DEVEEN, Lemuel A.	DUNAWAY, Elizabeth	JUN 04 1823
DEVENY, Catharine	STODDART, James	JUN 27 1853
DEVENY, Charles	GANNON, Ann	OCT 19 1820
DEVERAUX, Catharine	TERRON, Victor	FEB 06 1826
DEVEREAUX, William	GREENE, Maria	AUG 31 1848
DEVERICKS, Susan	HARRIDAN, Nathaniel	DEC 24 1812
DEVERS, Alexander	WOOD, Sarah Ann	MAY 05 1849
DEVERS, Amarion	CLEMENS, Joseph M.	JUL 08 1852
DEVERS, Eliza Jane	DOVE, Andrew	SEP 26 1850
DEVERS, Elizabeth	BAYLISS, William	FEB 15 1831
DEVERS, Penney	LACY, Henry	DEC 26 1844
DEVERUE, William P.	COSGROVE, Bridget	AUG 22 1857
DEVILLEN, Henry	LUPTON, Mary	MAR 01 1837
DEVINE, Ann	CONNOR, John	SEP 09 1837
DEVINE, E.V.	DEVINE, T.D.	MAY 10 1856
DEVINE, Lewis McKendrie	SHAW, Emily Virginia	MAY 16 1848
DEVINE, Robert M.C.	PAXTON, Mary	NOV 18 1848
DEVINE, T.D.	DEVINE, E.V.	MAY 10 1856
DEVINEY, Edmond	MORAN, Bridget	DEC 31 1857
DEVIS, Craven	WHELAN, Mary	JUN 29 1852
DEVIS, Rebecca	JARBOE, Matthew	APR 09 1853
DEVITT, Edward	WOLSEY, Mary Jane	AUG 15 1850
DEVLEN, Frances Ann	BARNHOUSE, Richard	OCT 29 1840
DEVLIN, Charles Henry	DIAMOND, Sarah	JUL 09 1850
DEVLIN, John	KIERNAN, Catharine	MAR 02 1824
DEVLIN, John	FOY, Mary	AUG 25 1835
DEVLIN, John	SCHAHAN, Johanna	JAN 31 1856
DEVLIN, John S.	PULIZZI, Mary A.	NOV 20 1826
DEVOIN, Margaret	ROGERS, John	JAN 14 1854
DEVOLVE, Washington	GEE, Ann	MAR 30 1820
DEVON, Elizabeth	SANDFORD, Thomas E.	APR 04 1816
DeVOSS, Peter J.	NICHOLLS, Emily	NOV 19 1845
DEW, John W.	FARREYHOLD, Sarah S.	OCT 02 1846
DEWDENEY, John	CAMMACK, Hannah	MAY 10 1827
DEWDWEY, William T.	WEBSTER, Catherine E.	FEB 16 1858
DEWEES, Ann	ROTHWELL, Andrew	FEB 03 1831
DEWEES, Eleanor	DeKRAFT, Edmund	JUN 05 1819
DEWERS, Mary	SMITH, Archar B. [Rev.]	OCT 06 1829
DEWEY, Anne E.	BALDWIN, John S.	JUN 29 1853
DEXTER, Thomas C.A.	CROSS, Elizabeth Marian	SEP 25 1844
deYTURBIDE, Angel	GREEN, Alice	JUN 07 1855
DEZEL, Eliza Ann	PILES, William H.	SEP 24 1846
DeZEYK, Albert J.	WHITTLESEY, E.M.	MAR 10 1857
DIAL, Jane	SWANN, Nathaniel	FEB 21 1831
DIAMOND, Mary	CARROLL, Sylvester	SEP 14 1854
DIAMOND, Sarah	DEVLIN, Charles Henry	JUL 09 1850
DIAPER, James W.	FRANCIS, Mary Ann	DEC 16 1818
DIATT, Betsey	LINKINS, John	JUL 17 1817
DIAZ, Pater	DASHER, Virginia	JAN 22 1855
DIBBELL, Marian	RODSTEIN, Daniel	MAY 21 1857
DIBBLE, William H.	LONGDON, Jane Elizabeth	MAY 06 1847
DICE, Caroline M.	RENNIKER, George R.	MAR 26 1857
DICE, John	NACE, Duridy	FEB 28 1842
DICE, Margaret	SHILLING, Alexander	AUG 09 1856
DICINS, Caroline	RAMSEY, William	MAY 25 1831
DICK, Adaline	HARDY, Hezekiah	MAR 26 1845

District of Columbia Marriage Licenses, 1811-1858

DICK, Daniel	KEY, Lucy (blk)	SEP 04 1850
DICK, John H.	BOWMAN, Miss (blk)	MAY 02 1851
DICK, John W.	CAHO, Eliza E.W.	APR 02 1849
DICK, Juliet A.	HARDING, James	JUN 09 1857
DICK, Mary Ann	DIVINE, Aaron	MAY 11 1844
DICK, Robert	THOMAS, Caroline (blk)	MAY 26 1831
DICK, Robert	CHESLEY, Elizabeth (blk)	FEB 18 1851
DICK, Robert S.	BRADLEY, Mary Ann (blk)	AUG 01 1845
DICK, Sarah V.	PORTER, John E.	JAN 07 1852
DICKENS, Mary	WALKER, William	APR 20 1846
DICKENSON, John	SIDEBOTTOM, Sarah	MAY 28 1839
DICKENSON, Sarah	KEY, Wallace	AUG 20 1841
DICKERSON, Elizabeth	JONES, John	APR 02 1829
DICKERSON, James	POWERS, Elizabeth	JUL 16 1839
DICKERSON, Mary E.	TYLER, William	SEP 09 1857
DICKERSON, William	HARRAD, Charlotte	APR 12 1817
DICKEY, Ansey	FOLIN, Richard	JAN 26 1841
DICKEY, Benjamin	SWIGART, Hannah	DEC 14 1837
DICKEY, Catharine	RICE, Thomas	OCT 20 1818
DICKEY, Eleanor	DWYER, Thomas	JUN 07 1820
DICKEY, Elizabeth Uphema	MONEY, Elijah	JAN 07 1851
DICKEY, Julia Ann	YOUNG, Joshua	JAN 20 1848
DICKEY, Robert D.	FERTNER, Elizabeth	JAN 18 1853
DICKINS, James J.	THOMPSON, Augusta M.	OCT 05 1846
DICKINS, Lilia Elizth.	MACAULEY, Charles S. [Capt.]	OCT 20 1831
DICKINSON, Araminta Eliza	NOURSE, John	MAR 24 1835
DICKINSON, Townsend	RAMSDILL, Martha	NOV 10 1845
DICKSON, Ann B.	ATCHISON, George H.	JUN 21 1838
DICKSON, Elizabeth	FRANK, Luther M.	JUL 06 1824
DICKSON, Louisa	KLICKERMAN, Franklin William	DEC 23 1843
DICKSON, Margaret	VanALLEN, Douglass	AUG 13 1827
DICKSON, Mary	BOOTHE, John	MAR 15 1833
DICKSON, Mary A.M.	ADAMS, John Henry	APR 23 1829
DICKSON, Mary Louisa	EMMERSON, Edwin	JUL 02 1851
DICKSON, Thomas	CANLER, Levinia (blk)	JUN 20 1839
DICKSON, Thomas	MATTINGLY, Catharine S.	AUG 12 1843
DICKSON, Thomas H.	CRAIG, Margaret C.A.	NOV 06 1832
DIDENHOOVER, Mary C.	GARDINER, William	JAN 18 1831
DIDENHOVER, Ann	TORRENCE, James	DEC 05 1822
DIDENHOVER, William	S___ENER, Margaret	DEC 22 1832
DIDSHER, Andrew	ANDERSON, Rhoda Ann	SEP 12 1839
DIEDERICK, Catharine	BOUCK, William	AUG 19 1856
DIEDERIEN, Linner	HARTBOWER, Gottfrie	MAR 30 1833
DIES, Eliza	DIES, Peter	JAN 10 1845
DIES, Henry	EVANS, Charlotte	FEB 18 1835
DIES, Peter	DIES, Eliza	JAN 10 1845
DIETERICH, Caroline	DIETERICH, Lewis	JAN 24 1854
DIETERICH, Christian P.	ROWL, Sophia M.	APR 10 1856
DIETERICH, Lewis	DIETERICH, Caroline	JAN 24 1854
DIETRICH, Franc Lewis	SCHEERER, Katherine Marie	MAR 24 1854
DIFFENDERFFER, Octavius	CROWN, Anna R.	JUN 23 1857
DIFFNER, George	BROOKS, Malvina	MAR 19 1840
DIGGES, Ellen	MUNDOWNY, Thomas H.	APR 27 1836
DIGGES, Ellen M.	ELWOOD, Isaac T.	APR 25 1833
DIGGES, Ellen Maria	MINOR, John West	AUG 26 1835
DIGGES, George A.	WALKER, Sarah	OCT 29 1856
DIGGES, Henrietta (blk)	SIMLY, Samuel	DEC 12 1834
DIGGES, Ignatius	BUTLER, Anna	MAY 22 1815

District of Columbia Marriage Licenses, 1811-1858

DIGGES, Margaret Malvina	SCHEWOOD, Charles W.	JUN 07 1854
DIGGES, Mary Jane	ABBOTT, Charles	JUN 16 1841
DIGGES, Rachel Ann	BURGESS, John	JUN 17 1843
DIGGES, Samuel J.	SUTTON, Catherine Cecilia	APR 08 1837
DIGGES, Sarah	GEORGE, William	AUG 17 1843
DIGGES, Sophia (blk)	PARKER, James	SEP 16 1841
DIGGES, William	DIXON, Harriet	FEB 02 1833
DIGGIN, Patrick	McCULLOH, Ann	JUN 14 1852
DIGGINS, Eliza	CONNOR, William	MAY 21 1852
DIGGINS, James	CRAWFORD, Ann	JAN 10 1832
DIGGINS, Mary	McGUIRE, Michael	JUL 30 1853
DIGGS, Ann Maria (blk)	NORRIS, Henry	MAY 14 1834
DIGGS, Cordelia (blk)	EASTON, Sidney	DEC 08 1853
DIGGS, George	CLARKE, Ann (blk)	SEP 19 1833
DIGGS, James	WHITE, Ann Maria	OCT 03 1815
DIGGS, Jane C.	PETTIBONE, William	MAR 21 1841
DIGGS, Levi	BUTLER, Lucinda (blk)	DEC 12 1839
DIGGS, Mary	KLICH, Gunrod	APR 27 1844
DIGGS, Mary E.	COE, Benjamin E.	FEB 05 1835
DIGGS, Mathew	FORD, Jane (blk)	JAN 08 1838
DIGGS, Sothern	MAGRUDER, Louisa	APR 21 1845
DILE, Margaret	WEBSTER, William H.	JAN 23 1854
DILL, Peter	McDONALD, Ann	DEC 09 1852
DILLARD, Eliza Catherine	BOSWELL, James	NOV 28 1842
DILLEN, Mary Ann	WOODS, Charles P.	OCT 11 1849
DILLER, Louise	SCHLEGEL, Ferdinand John	FEB 20 1843
DILLI, George	METZ, Catharine	APR 05 1856
DILLINGER, Henry M.	BALL, Elizabeth	FEB 21 1843
DILLON, David	O'CONNOR, Honora	JAN 10 1853
DILLON, Mary Ann	LIPSICOMB, Overton	FEB 18 1817
DIMENT, Ellen	BRAWNER, Hezekiah	APR 27 1847
DIMES, Mary R.	DANCE, Charles W.	JUL 07 1857
DIMITRY, Alexander	MILLS, Mary Powell	APR 03 1835
DIMITRY, Eliza Virginia	RUTH, Enoch Fenwick	JAN 02 1857
DIMOND, Maria	COLLINS, Samuel	MAR 29 1833
DIMSEY, John	THOMPSON, Jane	SEP 02 1847
DINES, Catharine Ann (blk)	ALLEN, James	FEB 22 1843
DINES, Charity (blk)	THOMAS, Henry	SEP 27 1814
DINES, Eliza	GRANT, Westley	JUN 14 1848
DINES, Jane	SCOTT, Henry	NOV 19 1842
DINES, Martha (blk)	QUEEN, Thomas H.	DEC 23 1848
DINES, Sarah (blk)	BUTLER, James	AUG 03 1852
DINKLE, Magdalen	HERMANN, John	OCT 16 1856
DINNIGAN, Michael	SHEA, Ellen	JUL 15 1857
DINT, Catherine	HERBERT, Godlip	DEC 29 1854
DIPPEL, Louisa	FIERMANN, John Adam	JUN 21 1849
DIPPEL, William	UTTERMUHLE, Augusta	DEC 01 1840
DIPPLE, Agusta	FIEG, Jacob	JUL 05 1854
DIPPLE, Charles	WICHAND, Louisa	JAN 22 1847
DIPPLE, Elizabeth	BRIDICOMB, Herman	MAR 02 1855
DIPPLEY, Margaret	COOK, Patrick	JAN 11 1853
DISCALL, Daniel	DISCALL, Margaret	JUN 04 1853
DISCALL, Margaret	DISCALL, Daniel	JUN 04 1853
DISCHER, Henry	SMITH, Elizabeth	AUG 18 1833
DISE, George	POST, Christian	DEC 12 1832
DISE, John	CROCKETT, Ann	OCT 23 1851
DISHER, Lewis	BENTON, Catherine	APR 20 1842
DISHER, Lewis	HALL, Elizabeth	APR 10 1856

District of Columbia Marriage Licenses, 1811-1858

DISHER, Martha	HOFFMAN, John H.	AUG 31 1854
DISHER, Mary	BROWN, Canard	MAY 29 1858
DISHMAN, James V.	ASHTON, Martha J.	AUG 17 1857
DISKET, Richard	HERN, Mariah	JAN 22 1856
DISMOND, Margaret	RATCLIFFE, Thomas H.	OCT 15 1850
DISNEY, Elizabeth	HOLLAND, Isaac	JAN 02 1838
DISNEY, John B.	ATHEY, Catharine	JAN 22 1826
DISNEY, John B.	ATHEY, Catharine	JUN 22 1826
DISPAUX, John	ARDREY, Rachel	NOV 28 1812
DISTAR, Aloysius Peter	FISTER, Mary	OCT 08 1853
DITREH, Jacob	KEENAN, Elizabeth	JUL 05 1854
DITRICH, Dorothy	GENGENBACH, George Frederick	DEC 18 1832
DITTY, Samuel	COOK, Cecelia	APR 14 1825
DITTY, Samuel	LANPHIER, Martha R.	JUL 01 1834
DITTY, Thomas R.	GALLOWAY, Mary	MAY 28 1827
DITUS, Debror S.	DATES, Philip	OCT 16 1844
DIVINE, Aaron	DICK, Mary Ann	MAY 11 1844
DIVINE, Hugh G.	ROLLINGS, Mary E.	AUG 03 1841
DIVINE, Mary Ann	WILSON, Joseph	DEC 05 1842
DIVINE, Mary F.	FERGUSON, William	JAN 19 1858
DIX, Hannah	BUTLER, William	APR 13 1820
DIX, John	BARRON, Alethia	OCT 04 1828
DIX, Jonas	MARR, Sophia	MAY 15 1817
DIX, Martha Ellen	MORTIMER, John T.	JUL 12 1845
DIX, Matilda	CLARKE, Henry	FEB 16 1828
DIX, Sophia Ann	BRYAN, William	MAR 21 1829
DIX, Thomas	JOHNSON, Melvina	JUN 18 1835
DIX, Thomas	SARAH, Berry	DEC 07 1844
DIXON, Absalom	MILBURN, Joanna	DEC 04 1856
DIXON, Catharine	DEMPHY, Martin	SEP 24 1824
DIXON, Cecilia	BILLMYER, Thomas	MAR 10 1816
DIXON, Chloe Ann	KENDRICK, George	OCT 08 1835
DIXON, Daniel	ROSE, Sarah Eliza	MAY 15 1852
DIXON, David W.	LEE, Elizabeth (blk)	JAN 24 1839
DIXON, Eliza	JOHNSON, William T.	OCT 04 1844
DIXON, Eliza Ann	ANDERSON, Thomas	MAY 13 1826
DIXON, Elizabeth J.	SASSCER, William B.	SEP 04 1841
DIXON, Emilia	MYERS, Peter	APR 04 1837
DIXON, Francis	DIXON, John	SEP 21 1847
DIXON, Frank Wood	LYLES, Annie E.	NOV 22 1852
DIXON, George	GATES, Johanna	SEP 29 1857
DIXON, Harriet	CARROLL, John Linkins	OCT 13 1831
DIXON, Harriet	DIGGES, William	FEB 02 1833
DIXON, Jacob	HOLSIEN, Ruth	JUN 27 1815
DIXON, James A.	MURPHEY, Rebecca A.	JUN 12 1843
DIXON, John	LIPSCOMB, Ann	DEC 27 1824
DIXON, John	DIXON, Francis	SEP 21 1847
DIXON, John A.J.	ROSS, Salina	FEB 02 1843
DIXON, Lucretia	DOYLE, Robert E.	AUG 08 1839
DIXON, Maria	WOOD, Thomas	JUN 23 1823
DIXON, Maria	BOOCOCK, William	MAR 24 1830
DIXON, Mary J.	WARDELL, Samuel P.	NOV 22 1847
DIXON, Mary Jane	SCOTT, Alexr. B.	DEC 29 1821
DIXON, Matilda	HENDLEY, Richd.	APR 12 1814
DIXON, Priscilla	HODSON, Dillon	NOV 10 1812
DIXON, Prisey Ann	WISTER, Isaac	MAY 31 1845
DIXON, Rebecca	COLLINGSWORTH, Arivuel D.	APR 20 1840
DIXON, Rebecca A.	WETHERALL, James M.	DEC 10 1833

District of Columbia Marriage Licenses, 1811-1858

DIXON, Ruth	JOHNSON, John	JUN 25 1835
DIXON, Sophia	HENDLEY, Richard	FEB 15 1817
DIXON, Tobias	COOKE, Rebecca	SEP 18 1838
DIXON, William	GOLDEN, Lydia (blk)	MAR 23 1813
DIXON, William	KAIN, Hannah C.	JUN 01 1838
DIXON, William E.	CARTER, Elizabeth	JUN 14 1852
DIXON, William T.D.	WARDELL, Maria	JAN 08 1852
DOBBS, John H.	McGREEVY, Eliza Jane	APR 01 1857
DOBBYN, George W.	DAVIS, Frances	JAN 11 1844
DOBBYN, James	DOBBYN, Jane	AUG 02 1830
DOBBYN, Jane	DOBBYN, James	AUG 02 1830
DOBBYN, John F.	SMALLWOOD, Jane	SEP 25 1854
DOBLYN, Celestia	LEPPER, George A.	FEB 17 1837
DOBSON, Alfred	ALEXANDER, Margaret	JAN 27 1853
DOBSON, Walter B.	CASTELL, Marion	DEC 24 1857
DOBYN, Petronelia	CLEMENTS, Oswald	NOV 26 1834
DODD, Elizabeth	BAXTER, Woolsey	JAN 08 1857
DODD, Lucy Ann	DOWNES, Charles G.	MAY 12 1851
DODD, Margt. A.	HOWDERSHELL, Warner C.	OCT 06 1857
DODD, Mary Jane	McCOY, William	APR 23 1845
DODD, Sabra Ann	TREXLER, Samuel P.	FEB 03 1851
DODD, Thomas A.	NORRIS, Amanda A.	FEB 13 1851
DODDRIGE, Martha Ann	BOARDMAN, Winfield Scott	APR 11 1844
DODDS, Eliza P.	DUCKWORTH, John	SEP 27 1819
DODDS, James	FOWLER, Mary M.	APR 09 1851
DODEY, John	HORAN, Catherine	SEP 23 1854
DODGE, Adeline	LANMAN, Charles	JUN 11 1849
DODGE, Allen	BERRY, Mary Ellen	JUN 11 1849
DODGE, Charles	DAVIDSON, Elizabeth G.	JUN 11 1849
DODGE, Francis	CHAPMAN, Fanney J.	JAN 22 1852
DODGE, Francis, Jr.	CHAPMAN, Jane E.	OCT 23 1833
DODGE, Henry W.	BROWN, Abigail B.	OCT 10 1839
DODGE, Mary B.	MARBURY, Alexander H.	JUL 19 1836
DODGE, Virginia	POORE, Benjamin P.	JUN 11 1849
DODSON, Amelia	MIDDLETON, Theodore, Jr.	NOV 30 1830
DODSON, Ann	LATHAM, Jeremiah D.	AUG 19 1851
DODSON, Ann (blk)	REDDIN, Shedrick	JAN 30 1856
DODSON, Charles T.	KEENE, Ann	APR 04 1857
DODSON, Cynthia A.	HAMMACK, John D.	OCT 29 1849
DODSON, Ignatius	BARKER, Lucinda	NOV 01 1832
DODSON, James B.	WAUGH, Henrietta	SEP 28 1841
DODSON, John	GOODWYN, Mary Ann	JAN 11 1854
DODSON, Joseph	DOINS, Jane	MAY 09 1839
DODSON, Lavenia	BEALL, John	JUN 29 1841
DODSON, Linney Ann	DAVIS, John W.	JUL 10 1856
DODSON, Margaret (blk)	COLE, Raphael	OCT 16 1848
DODSON, Margaret V.	WROE, William A.	OCT 21 1847
DODSON, Martha Ann	HARPER, James	OCT 28 1837
DODSON, Mary	ADAMS, John	AUG 13 1834
DODSON, Robert Middleton	SHECKELLS, Julia Ann	MAY 21 1831
DODSON, Vanduden	WROE, Saml. C.	APR 11 1844
DOGAN, Andrew	DAY, Susan	NOV 25 1852
DOGAN, Mary A.	CROSON, Thomas S.	AUG 24 1858
DOGANS, Mary	MORGAN, Thomas	JUL 08 1818
DOGGETT, Martha A.	HUDSON, James A.	DEC 28 1855
DOGGETT, William O.	DUVALL, Lucy R.	NOV 04 1845
DOGGON, Ellen	O'CONNOR, Jeremiah	AUG 17 1858
DOGINS, Maria	AMBUSH, Edward	DEC 06 1854

District of Columbia Marriage Licenses, 1811-1858

DOHNOR, Samuel	CUNLBERG, Clara	JAN 05 1858
DOIG, Elizabeth	FERGUSON, William	APR 15 1844
DOINS, Jane	DODSON, Joseph	MAY 09 1839
DOLAN, Edward	MAHER, Mary Ann	SEP 28 1855
DOLAN, Ellise	CASTOR, Henry	SEP 10 1856
DOLAN, Mary	BOYLE, David	JUL 03 1858
DOLAN, Patrick	FANNING, Ann	FEB 26 1857
DOLEMAN, James	SANDFORD, Maria	DEC 07 1854
DOLEY, Wilmot W.	CARNES, Ellen J.	JUL 13 1856
DOLF, Susanna	HITZ, Florian	NOV 27 1857
DOLOHAN, Bridget	KEENAN, John	JUN 16 1851
DOMONET, Charles	MICHOT, Ida	DEC 05 1851
DONAHO, Honora	NOLEAN, Jeremiah	JUN 08 1855
DONAHO, Thomas	WHITE, Sarah F.	DEC 23 1818
DONALDSON, Ann	STODDARD, John M.	FEB 24 1852
DONALDSON, Anna Maria	SEBASTIAN, Richard	JUN 14 1836
DONALDSON, Benjamin	HAWIN, Ann	AUG 08 1816
DONALDSON, Benjamin S.	OLIVER, Miranda S.	DEC 04 1851
DONALDSON, Dorsey H.	DYE, Cornelia Ann	FEB 11 1852
DONALDSON, Edwin G.	HARRISON, Ann Rebecca (blk)	APR 21 1842
DONALDSON, Eliza	HARDING, William	JAN 07 1829
DONALDSON, Elizabeth	PAYNE, Charles W.	JUL 25 1844
DONALDSON, Elizabeth Jane	JOHNS, Francis A.	FEB 24 1843
DONALDSON, George T.	DUVALL, Catherine	AUG 27 1857
DONALDSON, George W.	WHITE, Sarah E.	NOV 05 1846
DONALDSON, Henry	MILES, Margaret J.	FEB 19 1850
DONALDSON, James W.	AGER, Sarah Frances	AUG 18 1836
DONALDSON, James W.	BALL, Mary Ann	AUG 21 1844
DONALDSON, John	MILLS, Rebecca	JUN 28 1814
DONALDSON, John A.	THOMPSON, Cassandray	OCT 22 1850
DONALDSON, John E.	ARINGTON, Cintha E.	JAN 16 1858
DONALDSON, John Thomas	CHILDS, Margaret Ann	MAY 12 1836
DONALDSON, John W.	MILLS, Margaret Ann	JUL 01 1847
DONALDSON, Josephine	KONNS, Joseph	JUL 14 1857
DONALDSON, Julia Ann	DYE, Henry	MAR 13 1852
DONALDSON, Lewis	HERVEY, Sarah	OCT 30 1816
DONALDSON, Margaret	THOMPSON, George	NOV 23 1836
DONALDSON, Mary	MATTINGLY, John	JAN 11 1843
DONALDSON, Mary Catherine	PAGGET, George H.	JAN 04 1849
DONALDSON, Richard F.	O'NIEL, Sarah B.	MAY 29 1855
DONALDSON, Robert B.	HALL, Anna M.	FEB 13 1854
DONALDSON, Robert H.	THOMPSON, Eleanor	FEB 07 1831
DONALDSON, Saml. H.	BERRY, Mary	NOV 15 1853
DONALDSON, Samuel	HOWARD, Mary Ann	MAR 13 1827
DONALDSON, Sandford	ALLISON, Conry	OCT 16 1820
DONALDSON, Sarah	GLOVER, William	NOV 14 1833
DONALDSON, Susanna V.	CORNWALL, John	FEB 28 1857
DONALDSON, Thomas	GASLER, Sarah	MAR 27 1813
DONALDSON, Thomas	LEE, Mary	JUL 30 1836
DONALDSON, Thomas A.	HOWARD, Sarah	SEP 06 1851
DONALDSON, Thomas G.	O'NEALE, Ann E.	SEP 29 1853
DONALDSON, William	HOWARD, Eliza	AUG 28 1827
DONALDSON, William	RUNDLE, Patsey	JUL 05 1834
DONALDSON, William H.	WELLS, Amanda M.	SEP 23 1843
DONALDSON, Wm. B.	WADE, Arabella	MAY 13 1856
DONALL, Mary (blk)	BLOCKMAN, Wiley	FEB 21 1832
DONALL, William	WALKER, Ann	JAN 10 1816
DONALLY, Patrick	BRANNAGAN, Mary	MAR 26 1852

District of Columbia Marriage Licenses, 1811-1858

DONALLY, Susan P.	FORBES, George C.	FEB 01 1851
DONALLY, Teresa	CULLIN, Mathew	APR 14 1852
DONALSON, Elizabeth (blk)	JOHNSON, Lloyd	DEC 24 1856
DONASON, Elizabeth	MOLLIN, Mordica	FEB 12 1835
DONAVAN, David	WELSH, Sarah	OCT 19 1825
DONE, Sarah Ann	GRIFFIN, Richard B.	OCT 28 1834
DONELAN, Mary	DRURY, John H.	APR 30 1845
DONELEY, Thomas	McCORMICK, Bridget	AUG 31 1857
DONELSON, Daniel S.	BRANCH, Margaret	OCT 17 1830
DONELSON, Elizabeth	DONELSON, James Z.	MAY 21 1857
DONELSON, James Z.	DONELSON, Elizabeth	MAY 21 1857
DONELSON, Mary E.	WILCOX, John A.	MAY 25 1852
DONELSON, Wm. Henry	BROWN, Margaret A.H.	MAY 19 1855
DONIGAN, Thomas	LYNCH, Mary	MAY 18 1854
DONIPHAN, Ann Elizabeth	BRYAN, John L.	SEP 19 1832
DONIPHAN, Catherine	BARRON, Thomas H.	DEC 29 1846
DONIPHAN, Thornton A.	FAITHFUL, Ann	DEC 19 1844
DONIPHAN, William T.	HEPBURN, Mary Ann	DEC 19 1839
DONLAY, Mary	WOOD, Joseph	OCT 04 1832
DONLEVY, John	CLASHEM, Bridget	JUL 05 1853
DONLEY, Mary L.	MURRAY, James A.	JUL 25 1855
DONN, George W.	BENSON, [blank]	APR 03 1837
DONN, John	CAHILL, Ann	NOV 27 1852
DONN, John	CATON, Ann	MAY 22 1858
DONN, John M.	BOTELER, Caroline	MAY 05 1831
DONN, John Y.	COOPER, Margaret	JUL 07 1853
DONN, Lavina D.	HOLLINGSWORTH, Wm. W.	OCT 02 1854
DONN, Mary Ann	BURCKHEAD, Edward	JUL 01 1832
DONN, Oliver P.	HIPKINS, Cecelia J.	JUL 04 1848
DONN, Orlando H.	COOKE, Catharine V.	MAY 08 1850
DONN, Richard	MILAN, Bridget	APR 12 1856
DONN, Sarah L.	MARTIN, Luther L.	AUG 14 1849
DONNEL, Ann	SMITH, James	SEP 01 1852
DONNEL, John	MARTIN, Ann	APR 04 1840
DONNELL, Jane	WILLIAMS, Henry	JUL 15 1833
DONNELLY, Ann	MAGUIRE, Edward	DEC 01 1837
DONNELLY, Bernard	FREEMAN, Catharine V.	FEB 19 1855
DONNELLY, Charles	JENNINGS, Ann	NOV 16 1850
DONNELLY, Elizabeth	MAGEE, Thomas	JAN 06 1855
DONNELLY, James	SULLIVAN, Joanna	JUL 03 1851
DONNELLY, Patrick	MORGAN, Susan	FEB 24 1857
DONNELLY, Robert	MAY, Marcellena	NOV 17 1851
DONNELSON, Sanford A.	ARRINGTON, Emma	JAN 24 1857
DONNOGHUE, Martin	NOCHTIN, Maria	OCT 24 1856
DONNOGHUE, Mary A.	ENNIS, Richard G.	OCT 17 1848
DONNOGHUE, Mary A.	HARPER, Francis	FEB 15 1854
DONNOGHUE, Patrick	WHELAND, Ann Elizabeth	MAY 28 1823
DONOGAN, Mary	WHITE, Thomas	JUN 10 1852
DONOHAN, Bridget	McCARTHY, Jeremiah	MAY 07 1857
DONOHO, Bridget	MURPHY, Michael	FEB 07 1857
DONOHO, Bridget	RAFFIGNON, Alphonse	JAN 22 1858
DONOHO, Catherine	HANNON, Thomas	JAN 14 1834
DONOHO, Elizabeth T.	KENNEDY, William T.	JAN 26 1836
DONOHO, Hannah	WHEATLY, Wm. J.	MAR 10 1835
DONOHO, Johanna	McNAMARA, Michael	JUL 19 1854
DONOHO, Joseph	KEMP, Margaret	FEB 08 1853
DONOHO, Margaret	BERRY, Robert	SEP 08 1832
DONOHO, Margaret	MURPHY, Timothy	AUG 22 1851

District of Columbia Marriage Licenses, 1811-1858

DONOHO, Michale	CORRAN, Margarett	MAY 17 1854
DONOHO, Thomas	MURTER, Jane	MAY 03 1851
DONOHO, Thomas S.	DUNN, Mary E.	OCT 01 1844
DONOHO, William H.	DUNN, Amelia C.	MAY 08 1852
DONOHOE, Ann Maria	HUME, Francis	JUN 04 1845
DONOHOE, Bridget	McGOWAN, Patrick	NOV 16 1818
DONOHOE, Dennis	LEONARD, Sarah	APR 25 1826
DONOHOE, John	CONLEY, Maria	OCT 23 1854
DONOHOE, Margaret	NOCTON, John	NOV 17 1814
DONOHOE, Margaret	KEYNE, John	JUN 20 1815
DONOHOE, Mary	CONNOR, Michl.	JUL 29 1858
DONOHOO, Bridget	SULLIVAN, Dennis	AUG 17 1858
DONOHOO, Daniel	ROURK, Mary	JUN 06 1857
DONOHOO, John A.	MINCHEN, Harriot	MAY 13 1823
DONOHOO, Sarah	MILES, Edward	FEB 12 1828
DONOHOUGH, Mary	HANNIFER, William	NOV 04 1851
DONOHUE, Jane	SHUEKHART, George	OCT 04 1856
DONOHUE, Thos. Henry	GASKINS, Alice Hester	SEP 13 1853
DONOHUGH, Mary	LARNER, Michael	JUN 02 1825
DONOLLE, Wille A.	GROVES, William G.	NOV 04 1848
DONOLSON, William	SANS, Elizabeth Jane	DEC 29 1848
DONOVAN, Catherine	KERR, Peter	JUN 22 1857
DONOVAN, Catherine	McCARTHY, Charles	NOV 16 1857
DONOVAN, Cornelius	KOHINE, Margaret	JAN 12 1852
DONOVAN, Corns.	SHEA, Julia	JUN 27 1857
DONOVAN, Daniel	DONOVAN, Honora	OCT 10 1848
DONOVAN, David	MILES, Elizabeth	DEC 04 1847
DONOVAN, Dennis	STANLEY, Elizabeth	FEB 02 1850
DONOVAN, Dennis	GILMURRAY, Catharine	FEB 09 1852
DONOVAN, Dennis	LYNCH, Johanna	FEB 20 1855
DONOVAN, Hanorah	LONG, Jeremiah	FEB 17 1855
DONOVAN, Honora	DONOVAN, Daniel	OCT 10 1848
DONOVAN, James	WILSON, Margaret	SEP 09 1850
DONOVAN, James	HODGKINSON, Mary T.	FEB 23 1855
DONOVAN, John	STANLEY, Ann	AUG 27 1847
DONOVAN, John	FLAHERTY, Mary	NOV 14 1850
DONOVAN, John	HODGES, Bridget	SEP 10 1856
DONOVAN, Margaret	CONNOLLY, Edmund	FEB 20 1849
DONOVAN, Margaret	SAUNTRY, Kennedy	JUN 16 1855
DONOVAN, Mary	MURPHY, Martin	APR 16 1836
DONOVAN, Mary	SULLIVAN, Patrick	JUL 31 1852
DONOVAN, Mary	LYNCH, Michael	JAN 14 1854
DONOVAN, Mary	DORRER, Patrick	MAR 10 1855
DONOVAN, Michael	HALLORAN, Margaret	MAY 01 1852
DONOVAN, Randall	BOYLE, Jane	OCT 28 1854
DONOVAN, Timothy	DOWNEY, Margaret	NOV 01 1856
DONOVAN, William	NARUTEN, Ellen	APR 22 1844
DOOD, James	OLIVER, Eliza	MAR 12 1818
DOODEY, Catherine	SEXTON, Patrick	JAN 01 1857
DOOLEY, Catherine	BARRY, Edward	SEP 23 1852
DOOLEY, Elizabeth	LANGTON, John	JUL 23 1813
DOOLEY, Louisa Virginia	SAUER, George Henry	MAY 25 1853
DOOLEY, Michael	HANNA, Ann	FEB 02 1837
DOOLEY, Michael	HOGAN, Honora	OCT 28 1850
DOOLIN, Mary Jane	MORRIS, William	SEP 05 1854
DOOLING, Ann Sally	THOMAS, Henry	JUN 10 1826
DOOLING, Armistead	KIRK, Sarah	MAY 16 1835
DOOLING, Sarah	JACKSON, Peter	JAN 16 1847

District of Columbia Marriage Licenses, 1811-1858

DOOLING, William	BARNHOUSE, Mary A.	AUG 27 1842
DOOLY, Bridget	CARY, William	OCT 20 1852
DOOLY, Elizabeth	ANDISON, John P.	JUL 19 1847
DOOLY, John	McKEOWIN, Ann	JUN 15 1857
DOOLY, Mary Ann	SHEPHERD, Henry	SEP 21 1833
DOONE, John F.	KING, Anna	MAY 09 1857
DOONE, John F.	BARNES, Elizabeth	MAR 12 1858
DORA, John	MURPHY, Margaret	AUG 13 1850
DORAN, James	THOMPSON, Sarah A.M.	JUN 03 1858
DORAN, Mary	McCOSKER, Hugh	DEC 05 1826
DORCY, Stephen	GARVEY, Anna	JAN 24 1857
DORETT, Mary Ann	PAUL, Alexander H.	AUG 20 1827
DORIN, Mary	RADY, Thomas	JAN 07 1857
DORITY, John	OWENS, Ann	JUL 25 1818
DORKINS, Henry	JACKSON, Mary Virginia	NOV 12 1857
DORMAN, Adele Albert	FRANCE, William C.	OCT 06 1847
DORMAN, Ann	GREEN, Edwd.	JAN 03 1854
DORMAN, Julia A.	WILKINSON, A. George	JUL 31 1857
DORN, Mary	TOMILTY, Hugh	NOV 10 1851
DORNEY, Edward	HARWOOD, Eleanor	JUN 18 1827
DORNEY, Sarah	KING, Charles	JUL 12 1820
DORNIN, Jane E.	KICKHAM, William	JUN 05 1849
DORNOLD, Parkerson	TURNER, Martha Jane	APR 03 1837
DORON, Hannah	CLARY, James	FEB 15 1858
DORR, Louis	MILLER, Elizabeth	DEC 11 1852
DORRANCE, George W.	McDUE, Eliza Bartella	DEC 02 1846
DORREL, John M.	DAILEY, Julia A.	APR 21 1824
DORRELL, Anna Louisa	WATERS, Robert	JUN 17 1849
DORRELL, Thomas	DAILY, Sophia	DEC 01 1827
DORRELL, Thomas	DAILY, Sophia	NOV 28 1827
DORRELL, Thomas S.	DALEY, Mary Ann	MAY 25 1846
DORRER, Patrick	DONOVAN, Mary	MAR 10 1855
DORRETT, Elizabeth	TONGE, Thomas	DEC 31 1844
DORRETT, Ellen	POLLARD, Edward J.	FEB 24 1840
DORRETT, Sarah	STECK, John	DEC 17 1824
DORSER, Margaretta	COPPER, John	OCT 11 1850
DORSET, Ann	TRAVASS, Mile	DEC 21 1827
DORSETT, Elizabeth	FRERE, James	MAY 29 1822
DORSETT, Fielder [Col.]	BEALL, Amelia T.	FEB 02 1813
DORSETT, Jane E.	CLARKE, John T.C.	MAY 31 1842
DORSETT, Sarah	NEWTON, William C.	FEB 22 1816
DORSEY, Allen	GAITHER, Elizabeth (blk)	DEC 06 1836
DORSEY, Allen S.	SHREEVE, Margaret N.	JUN 04 1851
DORSEY, Anna E.	PENNINGTON, Saml. C.	JAN 02 1854
DORSEY, Anne Priscilla	ROSEWAG, Godfrey	AUG 07 1851
DORSEY, Augustus	GATRELL, Frances E.	NOV 18 1857
DORSEY, Benjamin W.	JAMISON, Mary	DEC 08 1835
DORSEY, Benjamin Warren	BALLINGER, Nancy Ann	DEC 19 1844
DORSEY, Charlotte H.P.	MORAN, John Edward	JUL 03 1843
DORSEY, Elizabeth	GRIMES, George	MAR 06 1829
DORSEY, Elizabeth	PAYNE, Joseph	DEC 22 1853
DORSEY, Ephraim	LEE, Ann (blk)	DEC 29 1845
DORSEY, Ephraim	McCARTY, Maria (blk)	JUL 12 1856
DORSEY, Eudocia	GIRD, Joseph C.	JUL 22 1815
DORSEY, Francis	TUCKER, Christiana	JUN 03 1850
DORSEY, Hamilton	CLARKE, Elizabeth (blk)	MAY 16 1844
DORSEY, Hannah N.	MORRIS, Benja. F.	SEP 03 1857
DORSEY, Harriet	PETERS, John	SEP 21 1815

District of Columbia Marriage Licenses, 1811-1858

DORSEY, Harriet Ann	SIMMS, Henry	SEP 22 1852
DORSEY, Henry J.	LETT, Martha Ellen	FEB 26 1852
DORSEY, Isaac	CHANEY, Harriet (blk)	JAN 08 1835
DORSEY, John	JOHNSON, Harriet M.	JUN 24 1854
DORSEY, John Henry	TATE, Eliza (blk)	JAN 12 1852
DORSEY, John T.B.	HARRIS, Mary C.	JAN 11 1849
DORSEY, John Warfield	STEVENS, Amanda W.	JAN 14 1854
DORSEY, Lucinda	PILES, Philip S.	SEP 01 1853
DORSEY, Mary (blk)	CASH, London	JUL 09 1841
DORSEY, Mary Ann (blk)	HOGANS, John	NOV 02 1850
DORSEY, Mary E.	CHOCHRAN, Thos. L.	AUG 09 1853
DORSEY, Matilda	REINHART, Frederick	MAY 03 1844
DORSEY, Tobias	LAURY, Sally (blk)	APR 13 1825
DORSEY, Virginia	PARKER, Francis E.	AUG 19 1844
DORSEY, William B.	RYAN, Margaret Ann	NOV 21 1831
DORSEY, William E.	GOLDSMITH, Ann Maria	AUG 23 1853
DORSEY, William J.H.	FRANCE, Josephine A.	OCT 08 1850
DOTEN, Isaac	BLOYS, Nancy	OCT 30 1817
DOTY, Geo. W.	LYNCH, Julia	MAR 17 1854
DOTZLER, John	HOWARD, Susan	MAY 14 1845
DOUBLEDAY, Abner	HEWITT, Mary B.	JAN 27 1852
DOUGAL, William H.	ADLER, Mary Virginia	JUN 02 1851
DOUGERTY, Sarah	SAUNDERS, Thomas C.	AUG 26 1820
DOUGHERTY, Eleanor	BALLARD, Charles	MAY 05 1831
DOUGHERTY, Elizabeth	KING, Wm.	FEB 28 1821
DOUGHERTY, Ellen	O'LEARY, John	DEC 26 1855
DOUGHERTY, Hugh	EVANS, George Anna Jackson	AUG 22 1846
DOUGHERTY, James	WILSON, Priscilla	JUN 28 1832
DOUGHERTY, Margaret	DEAKINS, Philip	AUG 07 1813
DOUGHERTY, Mary	ELLIS, Edmund J.	JAN 05 1837
DOUGHERTY, Mary	FITZPATRICK, John	JUN 30 1853
DOUGHERTY, Mary Ellen	COOPER, James A.	SEP 15 1852
DOUGHERTY, Mrs.	SCOTT, Chas.	DEC 22 1825
DOUGHERTY, Nathaniel	POLENFORD, Eveline	MAR 25 1819
DOUGHERTY, Sarah Ann	EDMONDS, Charles	DEC 21 1854
DOUGHERTY, Sarah E.	LITTLE, David	JUN 12 1827
DOUGHERTY, Susan	BURCH, William	NOV 02 1824
DOUGHERTY, Susanna	BRADY, Felix	JUN 07 1817
DOUGHERTY, Thomas	SHALLOO, Eliza	FEB 24 1852
DOUGHERTY, Timothy	LEARY, Julia	AUG 27 1855
DOUGHERTY, William	BARTLE, Mary Ann	MAY 12 1838
DOUGHRITY, Fanny	TRETLER, John H.	JUL 10 1856
DOUGHTY, James W.	NICHOLLS, Margaret	FEB 13 1840
DOUGHTY, Margaret	BOLLING, Robert B.	NOV 11 1856
DOUGHTY, Mary Ann	YEAGER, Christian F.	MAY 08 1839
DOUGLAS, Sophia	EWELL, James B.	JAN 14 1813
DOUGLASS, Adaly	WHEELER, George W.	FEB 27 1838
DOUGLASS, Albert P.	PITCHER, Laura V.	FEB 04 1858
DOUGLASS, Ann E.	TUELL, Laurence A.	SEP 30 1841
DOUGLASS, Anne	ESLIN, George	JUN 25 1856
DOUGLASS, Balinda	LEECH, John	JUN 21 1821
DOUGLASS, Caroline	LASHLEY, Daniel L.	OCT 08 1837
DOUGLASS, Catharine (blk)	GANTT, Thomas	NOV 28 1839
DOUGLASS, Elizabeth	HOOVER, Andrew	DEC 20 1817
DOUGLASS, Elizabeth	MOORE, William	APR 28 1821
DOUGLASS, Elizabeth Ann	SANGER, George David	JUN 29 1858
DOUGLASS, Elizth.	FORD, William	DEC 08 1829
DOUGLASS, Ellen	COWAN, James Edward	DEC 20 1827

District of Columbia Marriage Licenses, 1811-1858

DOUGLASS, Helen	KALCLASER, John	MAY 16 1844
DOUGLASS, Jane	NEDAH, Parker	MAY 27 1857
DOUGLASS, John	KIRKPATRICK, Ann	MAY 12 1813
DOUGLASS, John	HOOPER, Elizabeth	JAN 20 1814
DOUGLASS, John	TAIT, Jane	JUN 29 1839
DOUGLASS, John V.	RAWLINS, Georgia M.	AUG 02 1855
DOUGLASS, Louis	McCOY, Martha (blk)	JUN 22 1850
DOUGLASS, Louis	ROBINSON, Jane (blk)	NOV 22 1851
DOUGLASS, Lucretia (blk)	HOWARD, Chas. A.	NOV 17 1856
DOUGLASS, Martha Ann (blk)	HOLLEY, Reuben	NOV 08 1853
DOUGLASS, Mary	McGILL, Thomas	MAY 29 1854
DOUGLASS, Mary (blk)	DYNES, Hanson	MAY 11 1840
DOUGLASS, Mary Ellen	BOUDIN, Addison	JUL 03 1856
DOUGLASS, Mary G.	THOMPSON, Michael	NOV 08 1855
DOUGLASS, Maryann M. (blk)	BOSTON, Daniel	MAY 29 1854
DOUGLASS, Matilda	LLOYD, William	OCT 07 1824
DOUGLASS, Rebecca	BUTT, Richard	DEC 23 1834
DOUGLASS, Samuel E.	HAUPTMAN, Elizabeth A.	DEC 08 1849
DOUGLASS, Sarah	GORSUCH, William G.	MAY 28 1829
DOUGLASS, Sarah	BOOKMAN, Joseph	DEC 31 1839
DOUGLASS, Stephen A.	CUTTS, Adele	NOV 20 1856
DOUGLASS, Thos.	DUCKET, Anney	NOV 07 1821
DOUGLASS, William	FORD, Ann	APR 02 1821
DOUGLASS, William	BETTS, Catharine (blk)	SEP 04 1828
DOUGLASS, William	CUNNINGHAM, Mary Jane	MAY 09 1835
DOUGLASS, William	HOWKE, Sophia E.	DEC 22 1838
DOUGLASS, William	COGAY, Henrietta (blk)	DEC 12 1848
DOUGLASS, William H.	MOATON, Nancy (blk)	DEC 10 1845
DOUGLASS, William Henry	MAHORNEY, Sally (blk)	JUN 16 1856
DOUGLASS, William J.	DARNES, Sarah Virginia	NOV 04 1845
DOUTSCH, Peter	WEAVER, Catherine	MAY 14 1840
DOVE, Andrew	WILLIAMSON, Mary A.	AUG 13 1846
DOVE, Andrew	DEVERS, Eliza Jane	SEP 26 1850
DOVE, Ann	ALLEN, Robert	FEB 09 1821
DOVE, Ann	BALLENGER, Wesley	FEB 03 1825
DOVE, Ann E.	YOUNG, William L.	AUG 10 1840
DOVE, Dorcas (blk)	WORMLEY, Ralph	JUN 09 1829
DOVE, Eleanor Jane	McCLOSKEY, Richard	DEC 19 1820
DOVE, Elizabeth	HARKNESS, Samuel, Jr.	SEP 24 1827
DOVE, Elizabeth	WOOD, Pliny	JUN 17 1845
DOVE, Elizabeth	WHALEY, John Thomas	OCT 09 1845
DOVE, George Henry	DAVIS, Elizabeth V.	DEC 27 1853
DOVE, George M.	BEAN, Sarah Ann	OCT 12 1840
DOVE, George W.	SIPES, Mary	JUN 16 1857
DOVE, Hanson	BURNES, Betsey	FEB 07 1833
DOVE, Harriet	NELSON, Edward	JUN 01 1837
DOVE, Henry	BLADEN, Lucinda	MAY 15 1830
DOVE, Henry	BRISCOE, Isabella (blk)	JUN 28 1855
DOVE, Hezekiah	ROWLES, Sarah	MAY 31 1843
DOVE, James	DAVIS, Susanna	AUG 16 1842
DOVE, James	KINNY, Harriet	JUN 03 1852
DOVE, Jane	LUCKETT, Francis	SEP 21 1850
DOVE, John	BAKER, Elizabeth	SEP 11 1832
DOVE, John	ADAMS, Elizabeth Ann	NOV 30 1838
DOVE, Joseph	TRIMMILL, Elizabeth	NOV 04 1824
DOVE, Liddy Ann	GORMAN, James	JAN 11 1855
DOVE, Margaret	SEISS, Samuel	JAN 10 1851
DOVE, Margaret Ann	SHERIFF, Dionysus	SEP 25 1845

District of Columbia Marriage Licenses, 1811-1858

DOVE, Mary Ann	LEWIS, Saml.	JAN 20 1820
DOVE, Mary Elizabeth	SEWALL, Charles Fenton	AUG 29 1853
DOVE, Mary Jane	BROWN, William	SEP 18 1845
DOVE, Mary M.	ENTWISTLE, Thomas	SEP 26 1843
DOVE, Matilda	BEEDLE, Alfred	FEB 28 1832
DOVE, Milton C.	LAWRENSON, Mary F.	JUN 16 1857
DOVE, Robert	DEAVIS, Sarah	NOV 13 1844
DOVE, Robert W.	CLEMENTS, Sarah A.	NOV 07 1853
DOVE, Samuel	McCLOSKEY, Ann	OCT 12 1815
DOVE, Sarah	FORD, James	APR 19 1851
DOVE, Sarah A.	DAVIS, John W.	SEP 13 1855
DOVE, Sarah Ann	TUCKER, Durbin	SEP 04 1854
DOVE, Serena	WILCOXIN, Nathan	OCT 19 1837
DOVE, Velinda	BALLINGER, Solomon	JAN 11 1827
DOVE, William	BRERETON, Sarah	NOV 10 1836
DOVE, William Thomas	PARKER, Ann Wright	JUN 26 1838
DOVE, Wm.	GOREM, Caroline	MAR 13 1856
DOVE, Zachariah	TARLTON, Eleanor	APR 28 1832
DOVER, George	WOOD, Nancy	MAR 28 1818
DOVER, Mary (blk)	GRAY, Richard	MAR 23 1846
DOVER, Sarah (blk)	PROCTER, John	OCT 24 1850
DOVILLIER, Victor Leopold	CARUSI, Philippa	SEP 12 1851
DOW, Sarah E.	HOGG, John W.	JAN 26 1852
DOWDEN, Julia Ann	MULLIKIN, James	OCT 14 1851
DOWDEN, Mary E.	FURTNEY, George H.	DEC 28 1843
DOWDEN, Sarah Emily	WILLIAMS, Lewis Western	NOV 06 1838
DOWDEN, William L.	BROWN, Rosa C.	DEC 24 1855
DOWDY, Mary Jane	HOLLAND, Thomas	JUN 20 1838
DOWELL, Emily	FISHER, Alexander	SEP 12 1827
DOWELL, Oliver W.	WADDLES, Mary	OCT 20 1857
DOWELL, Sarah	KIDWELL, George W.	FEB 10 1846
DOWELL, Thomas M.	KIDWELL, Jane E.	MAY 15 1858
DOWELL, William	BRYAN, Kate	JUN 30 1858
DOWING, Martha Jane	GREER, Henry T.	JAN 11 1841
DOWLER, Annie J.	SPRINGER, John	APR 14 1858
DOWLING, Burr P., Rev.	McCLEARY, Amanda W.	NOV 20 1847
DOWLING, Ellen (blk)	GRANTHAM, Henry	DEC 19 1839
DOWLING, James	NEWMAN, Ann	DEC 16 1844
DOWLING, John	POWELL, Mary D.	FEB 11 1834
DOWLING, Mary Ann	HEWITT, Charles	MAR 22 1856
DOWLING, Patrick	SIMMONS, Margaret	MAY 09 1839
DOWLING, Patrick	MARKS, Drucilla	OCT 02 1852
DOWLING, Thomas	SERRIN, Hetty Jane	MAR 08 1827
DOWLING, William	REEDER, Eliza	APR 17 1841
DOWLING, William	BUTLER, Elizabeth	SEP 02 1851
DOWNAY, Johanna	CRONAN, Thomas	MAY 06 1854
DOWNER, Joel	BECKET, Ellenor Ann	NOV 11 1819
DOWNER, Martha A.	WINTERS, William H.	JUL 02 1840
DOWNER, Minerva M.	LUCKETT, LeGian J.	OCT 22 1834
DOWNER, Richard M.	BUGH, Margaret Jane	SEP 07 1847
DOWNER, Rowine	CALLAN, Peter	APR 30 1829
DOWNES, Charles G.	DODD, Lucy Ann	MAY 12 1851
DOWNES, Elizabeth H.	PIERCE, John R.	SEP 12 1848
DOWNES, Jane	CORMAN, William	JUN 04 1825
DOWNES, John	GRAY, Anjamima	MAR 23 1840
DOWNES, Mary	HARRIS, William H.	AUG 09 1842
DOWNES, Mary R.	HENNING, Henry N.	JAN 30 1836
DOWNES, Patrick	RAGAN, Maria	SEP 28 1854

District of Columbia Marriage Licenses, 1811-1858

DOWNES, Robert F.	GIST, Salena	DEC 02 1856
DOWNES, Sarah	SHEKELL, B.O.	SEP 04 1828
DOWNES, William	CADLE, Mary	MAY 06 1837
DOWNEY, Bridget	TOUHY, Hugh	FEB 09 1848
DOWNEY, Bridget	O'CONNOR, Pierce	MAY 30 1853
DOWNEY, Johanna	KANE, Jeremiah	MAY 09 1853
DOWNEY, John	MASON, Mildred C.	FEB 23 1854
DOWNEY, Margaret	DONOVAN, Timothy	NOV 01 1856
DOWNEY, Mary	HUGHES, James	OCT 21 1851
DOWNEY, Mary	QUAID, Daniel	JUL 30 1858
DOWNEY, Michael	BARNES, Mary	NOV 12 1840
DOWNEY, Patrick	HINRAHAN, Honora	JAN 26 1855
DOWNEY, Patrick	CRONIN, Ellen	JAN 31 1856
DOWNING, E.H.	GIBSON, Catherine	JUL 11 1856
DOWNING, Joseph M.	LANGFITT, Maria Louisa	SEP 08 1846
DOWNING, Mary	FLYNN, John	NOV 15 1849
DOWNING, Robert	FOSTER, Molinda	APR 02 1855
DOWNING, William	BROWN, Mary Ann Dolly	MAR 09 1843
DOWNMAN, Rawleigh Wm.	MAGRUDER, Mary Alice	NOV 08 1854
DOWNS, Cornelius	WELLS, Malvinia	JUN 08 1858
DOWNS, Elizabeth Ellen	WHEELER, Grafton	APR 20 1857
DOWNS, Hillary	JEFFERS, Sarah	FEB 04 1817
DOWNS, James	POWELL, Marie	JUL 20 1839
DOWNS, Johanna	QUINN, William	NOV 03 1856
DOWNS, Solomon	CHASE, Henrietta	JUN 01 1837
DOWNS, Sophenia	CARRICO, William	AUG 04 1836
DOWNS, Steward D.	HUGGINS, Mary E.	MAY 21 1855
DOWRY, Alonzo	THROLS, Elizabeth	MAR 11 1820
DOYE, Garret	SULLIVAN, Ellen	JUL 31 1858
DOYES, Catharine Ann (blk)	HORLEY, Joseph	AUG 08 1846
DOYL, Johanna	FOY, Patrick	FEB 06 1854
DOYLE, Ann	PHELPS, Ezra	SEP 24 1828
DOYLE, Ellen	FLEMING, John	JAN 26 1856
DOYLE, Mary	WHALEN, Thomas R.	JUN 10 1854
DOYLE, Mary A.	WILLIAMS, William P.	SEP 25 1839
DOYLE, Mary A.	WILLIAMS, William P.	FEB 26 1840
DOYLE, Michael	WALL, Honnorah	APR 25 1856
DOYLE, Patrick	JONES, Sophia A.	OCT 16 1857
DOYLE, Philip	SULLIVAN, Barbara	DEC 30 1826
DOYLE, Robert E.	DIXON, Lucretia	AUG 08 1839
DOYLE, Thomas	MORGAN, Susan	SEP 14 1840
DOYLE, Thomas	GREEN, Sarah	SEP 13 1843
DOYLE, Thomas	POLLY, Margaret	MAR 19 1844
DOYNE, Eliza	GRAMMER, Gotlieb C.	APR 07 1813
DOYNE, Ellen	CARROLL, Charles	MAY 19 1836
DOYNE, Mary [Mrs.]	BRUSH, John C.	MAR 26 1813
DOZIER, Cader W.	SUIT, Emily	MAR 15 1855
DRAGA, Charles	PETERS, Caroline	OCT 12 1857
DRAIN, Henry	WARD, Rosena	DEC 30 1820
DRAIN, Mary	SINON, John	OCT 19 1827
DRAINE, Charles	McLEOD, Mary	NOV 20 1838
DRAKE, Catharine C.	GIDEON, George S.	OCT 08 1837
DRAKE, Elizabeth	CLARKE, William H.	NOV 20 1849
DRAKE, Elizabeth G.	BANGS, William H.	JUN 06 1849
DRAKE, Margaret B.	RIPLEY, Charles	AUG 12 1858
DRAKE, Maria Louisa	GODFREY, Chapman	NOV 25 1857
DRAKE, Martha Jane	SEAY, William P.	SEP 02 1837
DRAKE, Nathan B.	OVERMANN, E.L.	DEC 15 1855

District of Columbia Marriage Licenses, 1811-1858

DRAKE, Robert A.	MANN, Ellen	SEP 24 1847
DRAKE, Susan E.	AGER, James B.	DEC 29 1847
DRAKE, Wallard	WILSON, Margaret	OCT 10 1815
DRAKE, William E.	PATTERSON, Johannah	AUG 06 1828
DRAKE, William H.	BARRACKE, Margaret A.	JUN 08 1858
DRANE, Ann	OSBURN, Levi M.	APR 12 1838
DRANE, James W.	JONES, Elizth. A.	NOV 22 1851
DRANE, Jane	DAVIS, Hezekiah	FEB 22 1838
DRANE, Robert	ELGIN, Sally Ann	JAN 21 1853
DRANE, Sarah	DELANY, Patrick	MAY 18 1829
DRANE, Washington	DADE, Anne M.S.	JUN 23 1816
DRAPER, Frances	FOWLER, Alonzo	NOV 05 1851
DRAPER, Mary Ann	WORTH, Wm.	SEP 20 1836
DRAPER, Nathan C.	LANGFITT, Julia F.	JAN 06 1854
DREDGE, James W.	ELLIS, Susan M.M.	APR 24 1845
DREEN, James M.	CYLISS, Anne	MAR 24 1856
DREESE, Mary	GREEN, Robert	JUN 24 1840
DREISCH, Michael	FISCHER, Susanna	SEP 24 1842
DREW, Alice	HILL, William	SEP 05 1835
DREW, Columbus	ROBERTSON, Marietta H.	NOV 26 1840
DREW, Daniel	OWENS, Nancy	NOV 30 1820
DREW, Edward M.	WATERS, Mahala Ann	JAN 12 1832
DREW, Elizabeth	COLLISON, Joseph	DEC 04 1824
DREW, George W.	UMBERFIELD, Mary Ann	AUG 01 1843
DREW, Harriet A.	CHURCHILL, Lewis F.	DEC 30 1849
DREW, Jane	SMITH, Anderson	AUG 29 1826
DREW, John	FARRELL, Mary	OCT 15 1853
DREW, Margaret	LATCHFORD, John	JUN 12 1839
DREW, Susan G.	BENNETT, Thompson M.	FEB 06 1829
DREW, William O.	LUNSFORD, Mary E.	DEC 12 1850
DREWIT, James	MAUL, Susan	MAR 20 1817
DREWRY, Ann	STODDART, John	APR 21 1825
DRICKSEL, Elizabeth	GATTSCHLICK, Ernest	AUG 27 1819
DRIER, Mary	SHERPF, Eberhard	NOV 06 1843
DRINKARD, John Bragg	WINSTON, Louisa	JUN 19 1855
DRINKARD, Wm. F.	ELLYSON, Mary J.	JUN 07 1850
DRINKER, Elizabeth	KINSEY, Benjamin S.	JUL 28 1828
DRINKHOUSE, Catherine	LOHR, Charles	FEB 08 1856
DRISCOE, Fanny W.	BAYLISS, Robert	MAR 06 1854
DRISCOLL, Catharine	SULLIVAN, John	MAY 04 1852
DRISCOLL, Catherine	SHEAHAN, John	MAY 03 1858
DRISCOLL, Charles M.	POWELL, Alcinda J.	MAY 16 1853
DRISCOLL, Dennis	FITZGERALD, Mary	SEP 11 1855
DRISCOLL, Mary	CONNOR, John	MAY 22 1858
DRISCOLL, Mary Ellen	DAILEY, Timothy	APR 17 1858
DRISCOLL, Timothy	BURNS, Eliza	DEC 15 1852
DRISTALL, William	PHALAN, Julia	NOV 22 1852
DRISTHDEN, Margaret	HERLY, Cornelius	JUL 02 1856
DROWNES, James	DEMPSY, Mary	MAY 16 1853
DROWNS, Margaret	PADGETT, Wm. Henry	MAY 05 1853
DRUCE, Isaac W.	FERRIS, Susan	AUG 26 1858
DRUDGE, James	NEWTON, Harriet	DEC 24 1815
DRUDGE, Susan	FOWLER, William	JAN 06 1836
DRUDGE, William	CHAMBERLIN, Mary Elizth.	DEC 20 1856
DRUMMER, Mary	SULLIVAN, Charles O.	JUN 20 1854
DRUMMOND, Amelia	LOVE, Leonora	OCT 25 1849
DRUMMOND, Elicia C.	WILLIAMS, Richard	SEP 04 1856
DRUMMOND, Eliza	CUDLIPP, Frederick	NOV 14 1833

District of Columbia Marriage Licenses, 1811-1858

DRUMMOND, Jane	DEAKINS, Philip	JUN 13 1839
DRUMMOND, Jane	MURRAY, Thomas	JUL 10 1839
DRUMMOND, John W.	HARPER, Hester Ann	JUL 02 1840
DRUMMOND, Mary Ann	COLTMAN, Charles L.	JUL 02 1829
DRUMMONDS, Annetta	REYNOLDS, John	OCT 04 1849
DRURY, Ann M.	OWENS, Gassaway	MAR 29 1853
DRURY, Elizabeth	SMITH, John M.	AUG 24 1851
DRURY, James	COLLINS, Louisa	JAN 28 1822
DRURY, John H.	DONELAN, Mary	APR 30 1845
DRURY, Louisa	NORRIS, William	OCT 07 1824
DRURY, Martha A.	BERKLEY, Benjamin	SEP 15 1849
DRURY, Mary	PEAKE, John	NOV 26 1839
DRURY, Mary A.	GULICK, George F.	NOV 11 1856
DRURY, Mary Ann	NEDDY, Pierce	JAN 19 1831
DRURY, Mary Elizth.	SHEAHAN, James W.	MAY 25 1848
DRURY, Plummer J.	GANNON, Margaret	JAN 17 1814
DRURY, Samuel	NOWLAN, Mary	JUL 05 1815
DRURY, Samuel T.	GREER, Rachel	AUG 02 1848
DRURY, Samuel T.	SCOTT, Kate B.	MAR 06 1855
DRURY, Terence	O'NEAL, Louisa M.	OCT 14 1850
DRURY, William	THOMPSON, Aira	DEC 06 1821
DRURY, William	SIMS, Catharine	JUL 03 1841
DRURY, William C.	BOPP, Louisa A.	JUL 08 1856
DRURY, William P.	LENMAN, Mary E.	SEP 16 1845
DRUSHEIM, Eberhart	BANF, Margaret	SEP 11 1852
DRYDEN, Robert R.	ROGERS, Amelia	SEP 28 1839
DUBANT, Ellen E.	LEWIS, James	JUN 11 1851
DUBANT, Margaret	SHINCO, John	SEP 21 1844
DUBANT, Margaret Jane	FRENCH, Harrison Pirobie	MAY 11 1839
DUBANT, Mark	WEBSTER, Elizth. Eleanor	MAY 14 1821
DUBANT, Peter M.	MEADS, Delina	FEB 19 1850
DUBANT, Peter M.	BROWERS, Mary Ann	OCT 12 1854
DUBART, M.	McGEE, Sarah	MAY 01 1820
DUBEL, Henry	BARTELMISS, Katharina	JUN 13 1857
DUBLERVEY, Margaret	MADDOX, Huriah	JUN 19 1828
DUBOIS, Francois	JEANTET, Marie	FEB 28 1857
DUBOISE, Dudley McJ.	TOOMBS, Sallie	APR 15 1858
DUCHER, Evelina	BUTLER, Robert	AUG 14 1818
DUCKET, Anney	DOUGLASS, Thos.	NOV 07 1821
DUCKET, Basil W.	ECKTON, Caroline	DEC 06 1854
DUCKET, Edward	HARRIS, Virginia (blk)	JUL 16 1857
DUCKET, Lucinda (blk)	GALLOWAY, William	AUG 30 1845
DUCKET, Margaret	WILLET, John F.	NOV 01 1851
DUCKET, Rachael (blk)	DANT, Jeremiah	FEB 07 1826
DUCKETT, Ann Eliza	OGLETON, Caleb	DEC 15 1842
DUCKETT, Augustus	McCATHERAN, Sarah E.	SEP 29 1857
DUCKETT, Basil	ALLEN, Ann	MAY 26 1848
DUCKETT, Catherine	FRY, Edward	JAN 17 1853
DUCKETT, Ellen E.	RYAN, John W.	DEC 11 1844
DUCKETT, Jane	PERMILLION, John	SEP 30 1841
DUCKETT, Louisa (blk)	CARTWRIGHT, Lewis	MAY 19 1841
DUCKETT, Lucinda	FRYE, John H.	OCT 23 1844
DUCKETT, Richard	SIMPSON, Mary	MAR 21 1816
DUCKETT, Sophia	FRANKLIN, Nicholas	JUL 23 1825
DUCKWALL, Joseph S.	BRONAUGH, Virginia M.	AUG 30 1851
DUCKWORTH, Elizabeth	PICKERING, John	SEP 14 1837
DUCKWORTH, George	RING, Rebecca	MAR 22 1826
DUCKWORTH, John	DODDS, Eliza P.	SEP 27 1819

District of Columbia Marriage Licenses, 1811-1858

DUCKWORTH, Mary	ENTWISTLE, William B.	DEC 30 1844
DUCKWORTH, S. Cornelia	HEVENINGHAM, Charles S.	DEC 31 1849
DUCKWORTH, Sarah	GUNNELL, William H.	OCT 17 1822
DUCY, Catharine	LUDDY, Thomas	FEB 14 1833
DUDLEY, Charles E.	PETTIS, Charlott	SEP 01 1856
DUDLEY, Eliza Ann	McCOY, Benjamin M.	JAN 02 1851
DUDLEY, Henry	MACKNESS, Drucilla	AUG 10 1827
DUDLEY, Henry, Jr.	GILDER, Caroline C.	NOV 07 1854
DUDLEY, Mary	CALAHAN, Jerome	MAY 05 1855
DUDLEY, Mary D.	HANCOCK, John	AUG 24 1855
DUDLEY, William	GRIFFIN, Johanna	OCT 25 1849
DUDLY, John G.	JONES, Sarah M.	MAR 09 1854
DUEHAY, Alexander	HARLEY, Pauline	OCT 18 1855
DUEHAY, William	HOY, Marthan Ann	DEC 29 1830
DUELL, Susan Ann	SIMS, Benjamin	OCT 22 1855
DUESENBURY, Laura	SHITPOEL, Daniel	AUG 31 1858
DUFF, Ann Rose	LAWS, Adam J.	APR 20 1819
DUFF, James	FRANCIS, Adell	OCT 29 1839
DUFF, Mary Ellen	LEE, Jesse	MAR 07 1833
DUFF, Priscilla	WHITE, Rezen	OCT 14 1813
DUFF, Susan C.	RHODES, William	DEC 22 1856
DUFFEY, Ann	FLYNN, Patrick	SEP 06 1856
DUFFEY, Bridget	FARRELL, John	MAR 18 1853
DUFFEY, Bridget	QUIGLEY, John	NOV 23 1857
DUFFEY, Ellen	KELLY, Miles	DEC 31 1852
DUFFEY, John	CROWN, Mary Elizth.	NOV 13 1854
DUFFEY, John H.	MILLER, Mary	NOV 21 1826
DUFFEY, Louisa M.	EMERSON, John S.	SEP 01 1847
DUFFEY, Margaret	RICE, John	JUL 26 1851
DUFFEY, Martha	LECKIE, James	MAY 19 1834
DUFFEY, Mary	STEEL, John	JAN 04 1820
DUFFEY, Mary	KERR, Peter	OCT 01 1852
DUFFEY, Mary	BURNS, John	APR 15 1858
DUFFEY, Mary M.	MOORE, James	MAR 03 1831
DUFFEY, Michael	CROWNIN, Ellen	APR 07 1849
DUFFEY, William B.	McKENNEY, Francis A.	DEC 02 1852
DUFFIELD, Mary A.	PALMORE, John R.	AUG 01 1835
DUFFLEY, Christina	LANBINGER, John Michael	APR 29 1844
DUFFY, Ann	FLYNN, Patrick	JUN 26 1856
DUFFY, James	RABBITT, Rebecca J.	JUL 02 1856
DUFFY, Mary	McKAVICK, Thomas	JAN 02 1857
DUFFY, Owen E.	CALLAN, Margaret S.	APR 09 1857
DUFFY, Patrick	WELCH, Theresa	SEP 01 1851
DUFIEF, Jane S.	FOWLER, Samuel	JUL 23 1842
DUFIEF, Mary Margaret	FOWLER, William H.	APR 07 1835
DUFLOS, Alphosina	BETOUT, Engene J.	MAY 01 1858
DUGAN, John	ARCHFIELD, Isabella	JUL 08 1839
DUGAN, John E.	SULLIVAN, Abbie	MAR 16 1857
DUGAN, Julia Ann	STROUD, George W.	JUL 07 1842
DUGAN, Julia Ann	HOLT, John W.	MAY 02 1846
DUGAN, Susan	FARMER, Alfred D.	SEP 20 1855
DUGAN, Thomas	McNAUGHTEN, Mary	MAR 02 1857
DUGANS, Elizabeth	BARRON, Wm. H.	OCT 05 1818
DUGGAN, Marcella	MARCHOM, Daniel	APR 12 1856
DUGGIN, William	MANIKAN, Catharine	JUL 19 1853
DUGGINS, Eliza	ROLLINS, Joshua	JAN 12 1824
DUGINS, Lucinda	DUVALL, Benjn. F.	JUN 01 1835
DUGINS, Wesley	YOUNGER, Sarah (blk)	NOV 28 1849

District of Columbia Marriage Licenses, 1811-1858

DUGLASS, James	GOLDING, Mary	JAN 31 1820
DUHA, Mary	ADAMS, West	MAR 14 1846
DuHAMEL, Wm. J.C.	AGATE, Elizabeth H.	APR 30 1853
DUITY, Ann	TANER, Jesse	MAY 01 1824
DUITY, Leonard	PEEK, Mary	OCT 20 1818
DUKEHART, Mary	MILLER, Peter	MAR 25 1856
DULANEY, Adam	DANDRIDGE, Elizabeth (blk)	JUN 22 1854
DULANEY, Bladen	NOURSE, Caroline	JAN 31 1843
DULANEY, Caleb	FERGUSON, Ann (blk)	APR 10 1837
DULANEY, Thomas	SEMMES, Josephine (blk)	DEC 19 1844
DULANEY, William H.	BURLEY, Elizabeth	OCT 28 1856
DULANEY, William Lewis	MEEKS, Mary Ann	AUG 23 1852
DULANY, Charles	COOPER, Rosetta	APR 26 1827
DULANY, Daniel F., Jr.	GANTT, Margaret Ann	OCT 20 1832
DULANY, Eliza Virginia Clara	PADGET, Lewis William	JUN 10 1845
DULANY, George	WILSON, Margaret	JAN 09 1812
DULANY, Linney (blk)	LANDAY, Lewis	MAR 20 1837
DULANY, Rachel Ann (blk)	WOOD, Alfred	MAY 06 1831
DULANY, Sarah (blk)	SIMPSON, John	MAR 12 1840
DULANY, Thomas	COYNE, Margaret	FEB 03 1818
DULEY, Allen	LAZENBY, Ann	NOV 13 1823
DULEY, Anne	MILLER, Charles	MAY 02 1857
DULEY, Aquilla	STILES, Elizabeth	FEB 23 1826
DULEY, Elizabeth	MANGUM, Wm. James	APR 22 1847
DULEY, Elizabeth C.	FERGUSON, James B.	APR 29 1839
DULEY, Jonathan	ROBINSON, Isabella M.	OCT 11 1841
DULEY, Margaret R.	WIRT, John L.	JUL 06 1837
DULEY, Wm. W.	SANSBURY, Susan	MAY 08 1854
DULIN, Edward L.	STANLEY, Louisa E.	APR 09 1849
DULIN, Joshua V.	ASHDOWN, Sarah J.	FEB 21 1855
DULINHANTY, Patrick	MINOGUE, Eliza	APR 21 1854
DULL, Mary E.	HARRIS, Benjamin F.	MAR 11 1856
DULY, Sarah Jane	SANSBURY, James T.	FEB 17 1852
DUMBLETON, John	ROWLEY, Sarah	DEC 24 1819
DUMPHEY, Catharine E.	REYNOLDSON, Robert	SEP 04 1832
DUMPHREY, Ellen	COLLINS, John	JUN 23 1858
DUMPHY, John	WELLS, Catharine E.	JUN 04 1823
DUN, Mary	FREEZER, Jacob	NOV 14 1846
DUNAVAN, Catharine	O'HARN, David	APR 17 1858
DUNAVOUGHN, Jeremiah	LINGHAM, Mary	JAN 06 1831
DUNAWAY, Elizabeth	DEVEEN, Lemuel A.	JUN 04 1823
DUNAWAY, Mary Ann	ALEXANDER, John	APR 18 1857
DUNAWAY, Sarah H.	JOHNSON, George	NOV 22 1825
DUNAWIN, James E.F.	REGAN, Elen A.	APR 06 1848
DUNBAR, Eliza Jane	PAGE, William A.	JUN 03 1850
DUNBAR, George Anna	TALBERT, Isaac	MAY 26 1857
DUNBAR, Maria	KING, Edward	NOV 09 1820
DUNCAN, Ann R.	NELSON, William L.	JUN 20 1854
DUNCAN, Elizabeth C.	SHACKLEFORD, James	AUG 20 1831
DUNCAN, Francis	WHITE, Hester Ann	NOV 20 1841
DUNCAN, Hiram	BRITINGHAM, Mary Ann	MAR 30 1825
DUNCAN, James	WILKISON, Ann	JAN 22 1855
DUNCAN, John	HOWELL, Lucy Duncan	OCT 16 1856
DUNCAN, Joseph [Hon.]	SMITH, Elizabeth [Caldwell]	MAY 13 1828
DUNCAN, Sarah A.	MOORE, Risdon A.	MAR 16 1848
DUNCAN, Thomas	WILSON, Mary S.	AUG 25 1852
DUNCAN, Thomas	MORRIS, Maria L.	MAY 26 1857
DUNCAN, William	McEVOY, Sarah	AUG 01 1816

District of Columbia Marriage Licenses, 1811-1858

DUNCANSON, Catherine M.	BASSETT, David	APR 18 1845
DUNCANSON, John A.M.	CHESTER, Eliza L.	JUN 17 1828
DUNCANSON, John A.M.	MOULDER, Martha D.	DEC 08 1840
DUNDAS, Eliza	OLDHAM, James R.C.	JAN 07 1857
DUNDAS, Harriet H.	EVERETT, Charles, Jr.	MAR 13 1851
DUNFORD, James	MALVAHILL, Mary	JUN 14 1858
DUNGAN, Martha V.	MILLER, Henry V.	OCT 07 1856
DUNHAM, Francis S.	HANDY, Leah Ann	AUG 29 1843
DUNHAM, Freelove	UNDERHILL, Halbert	DEC 03 1853
DUNHAM, Mary W.	FOWLER, Joseph	FEB 08 1853
DUNHER, Thomas	McNAMARRAH, Ann	JAN 19 1856
DUNKBY, Martha Ann	HILL, Charles J.	OCT 13 1832
DUNKELL, Henry	HILL, Ann	FEB 27 1812
DUNKIN, Martha [Mrs.]	BARBER, Jonathan [Dr.]	APR 01 1824
DUNKINSON, Wm. H.	GRAMMER, Annie	DEC 09 1852
DUNKLEE, Jason	MATHEANEY, Jane Maria	JAN 30 1830
DUNKLER, Joanna Maria	THOMPSON, George	FEB 21 1835
DUNKLEY, Joseph	WROE, Mary Ann	MAR 02 1835
DUNLAP, Mary L.	DANGERFIELD, William H.	DEC 12 1848
DUNLAP, Patsey	LIVERPOOL, Moses	SEP 03 1827
DUNLAP, Sarah Ann	HITE, Jesse	MAY 07 1857
DUNLAP, Sarah S.	WALLACE, William H.	APR 22 1850
DUNLOP, George W.	CORNISH, Harriet (blk)	JAN 27 1853
DUNLOP, Harriet (blk)	SMITH, Joseph C.	SEP 29 1857
DUNLOP, James, Jr.	LAIRD, Barbara Lucinda	APR 07 1818
DUNLOP, Jane	DUNLOP, William H.	FEB 23 1846
DUNLOP, Julia (blk)	DUNLOP, Page Carter	DEC 18 1836
DUNLOP, Nathan	VINCENT, Mary Ann	NOV 17 1824
DUNLOP, Page Carter	DUNLOP, Julia (blk)	DEC 18 1836
DUNLOP, Richard G.	WINN, Mary Louisa	MAY 22 1840
DUNLOP, Robert	CAMERON, Sarah	SEP 06 1854
DUNLOP, William H.	DUNLOP, Jane	FEB 23 1846
DUNMORE, Solomon	BERRY, Mary	APR 05 1843
DUNN, Amanda	THOMPSON, William	MAY 10 1834
DUNN, Amelia C.	DONOHO, William H.	MAY 08 1852
DUNN, Ann	KEESE, John	JUL 03 1858
DUNN, Dennis	MULLIKIN, Mary	OCT 09 1852
DUNN, Edward	MARKS, Susanna S.C.	OCT 09 1857
DUNN, Francis A.	WOOD, Lydia Amanda	MAY 16 1842
DUNN, George	THOMPSON, Susanna E.	JUN 13 1853
DUNN, Isabella	GIVEN, James E.	JUN 04 1840
DUNN, James	HURLEY, Ellen	AUG 02 1851
DUNN, James C.	RATCLIFFE, Eliza	AUG 14 1822
DUNN, John	GILL, Ann	NOV 03 1829
DUNN, John O.	STANSBURY, Augusta	JUN 25 1828
DUNN, Margaret	CRATTY, Michael	SEP 13 1851
DUNN, Mary	KEYS, Nicholas	DEC 16 1851
DUNN, Mary E.	DONOHO, Thomas S.	OCT 01 1844
DUNN, S.J.	THORPE, C.J.R.	OCT 20 1840
DUNN, Samuel	LELAND, Rebecca	FEB 10 1819
DUNNAVANT, Wm. C.	MOODY, Georgiana	OCT 16 1851
DUNNIGAN, Hanora	ENRIGHT, Edward	OCT 19 1857
DUNNIGAN, Johanna	BARREL, Robert	MAR 28 1856
DUNNIGIN, John	KELLY, Mary E.	AUG 24 1858
DUNNIN, Mary A.	HIGGINS, Elijah H.	MAY 08 1855
DUNNING, Ann	ZEBOULD, Robert	NOV 20 1830
DUNNING, Margaret	TUCKER, Geo. H.	APR 12 1831
DUNNING, Mary M.	LEWIS, Thomas	FEB 01 1836

District of Columbia Marriage Licenses, 1811-1858

DUNNINGAN, John	O'DONNELL, Eleanor	DEC 28 1821
DUNNINGTON, Anna E.	WARD, Joseph D.	AUG 22 1849
DUNNINGTON, Jas. M.	LLOYD, Mary	AUG 17 1854
DUNNINGTON, John F.	CHAPTMON, Virginia E.	OCT 04 1848
DUNNINI, Johanna	CRONIN, John	MAY 12 1854
DUNNOGIIUE, Cornelius	SULLIVAN, Fanny	JAN 28 1856
DUNS__, Julia M.	[blank], William	JAN 14 1846
DUNSCOMB, Daniel E.	SIMMS, Jane E.	OCT 16 1848
DUNSEATH, Andrew	ABLE, Hetty	MAY 28 1817
DUNTY, George W.	WISE, Jane Elizth.	JAN 19 1854
DURAN, Francis	HARRIS, Ann (blk)	OCT 29 1833
DURELL, Nancy	GARVEY, Patrick	JAN 29 1851
DURGIND, Catharine	DAVIS, Eli	SEP 22 1832
DURHAM, Aaron	PRIME, Mary	JAN 19 1837
DURHAM, Anna E.	BIRCH, Joseph F.	JUN 15 1840
DURHAM, Catherine S.	STEVENS, Ezra L.	AUG 02 1848
DURHAM, Clayton	HICKS, Flora (blk)	DEC 10 1839
DURHAM, Lemuel J.	ALEXANDER, Mary	JUN 23 1841
DURITY, Elizabeth	PARKER, John	AUG 20 1816
DURITY, Jas. R.	FUGETT, Rebecca M.	SEP 28 1857
DURITY, Leonard	OSBERN, Ann	OCT 04 1821
DURLING, Jackson	McCOY, Margaret	APR 28 1857
DURN, John	WILHELM, Maria	NOV 30 1857
DURNIAN, Edward	CALLAHER, Ellen	DEC 26 1854
DURR, Christianna	SERRIN, William	JAN 25 1825
DURR, Elizabeth	THOMPSON, Wm.	OCT 21 1820
DURR, Mary C.	RUPLEY, Charles J.	JUL 17 1858
DUSAN, William	RICHARDS, Mary	OCT 13 1838
DUSENBERY, Constantine	WILSON, Virginia Hills	SEP 17 1856
DUTCH, Hillery	THOMAS, Jane (blk)	FEB 03 1858
DUTCH, James	AMESWORTH, Elizabeth	MAY 07 1819
DUTCHER, Jemima	HARRISS, Geo.	MAR 31 1820
DUTTON, George W.	HARRISON, Susan M.	JUN 03 1856
DUTTON, Thomas	BROOKS, Adeline	DEC 02 1845
DUTZLER, Susan	MATTINGLY, Jas. E.	AUG 03 1854
DUVAL, George W.	BENNETT, Martha A.	MAR 31 1856
DUVAL, Joseph	COLBURN, Theodocia A.	OCT 09 1848
DUVAL, Orilla	HYATT, Rezen	NOV 20 1819
DUVAL, Susa T.	NESBIT, Wilson	JUL 06 1819
DuVALL, Horace	CUNNINGHAM, Mary	MAY 27 1815
DUVALL, Airy	CROSS, Thomas	APR 26 1853
DUVALL, Alexander	TURNER, Jane	JUN 06 1834
DUVALL, Alfred J.	BROWN, Eliza	APR 25 1843
DUVALL, Amelia	KIDWELL, Elijah	FEB 13 1849
DUVALL, Ann A.	LEWIS, John W.	JAN 12 1830
DUVALL, Ann D.	KNOWLES, James J.	JUL 24 1843
DUVALL, Ann E.	BEERS, C. Isaac	NOV 12 1857
DUVALL, Ann M.	NEWELL, Harman	NOV 08 1855
DUVALL, Ann Maria	McDANIEL, Enoch T.	FEB 22 1858
DUVALL, Barton	MITCHELL, Ann Maria	NOV 30 1831
DUVALL, Benjamin H.	BIRTH, Lydia Ann	SEP 24 1840
DUVALL, Benjn. F.	DUGINS, Lucinda	JUN 01 1835
DUVALL, Caroline	MACNEW, Bazil	SEP 28 1831
DUVALL, Catherine	DONALDSON, George T.	AUG 27 1857
DUVALL, Clara V.	FITCH, George K.	APR 20 1857
DUVALL, Edmund B.	GATES, Mary N.	OCT 28 1840
DUVALL, Eli, Junr.	BALL, Alice C.	AUG 12 1857
DUVALL, Elisha	JOHNSON, Maria	AUG 18 1831

District of Columbia Marriage Licenses, 1811-1858

DUVALL, Elizabeth	HOOPER, George W.	MAY 21 1836
DUVALL, Ellen	VERMILLION, Fendall	NOV 10 1831
DUVALL, Ellen M.	JONES, Luther D.	FEB 28 1855
DUVALL, George W.	SIMMONS, Jane	NOV 14 1843
DUVALL, Henry A.	BOHANAN, Nancy	JUL 25 1850
DUVALL, Henry C.	FRY, Ann	JUN 12 1854
DUVALL, James M.	McFARLAND, Eliza Jane	AUG 02 1842
DUVALL, John	DAVIS, Ann	DEC 26 1839
DUVALL, John L.	CURTAIN, Mary Ellen	APR 13 1857
DUVALL, Lorane	BLAGROVE, Henry B.	JUN 02 1825
DUVALL, Lucy R.	DOGGETT, William O.	NOV 04 1845
DUVALL, Margaret E.	WROE, Everett	FEB 27 1851
DUVALL, Margaret M.	CALDWELL, William A.	AUG 31 1858
DUVALL, Martha Ann	INGLEHART, Edward	FEB 01 1840
DUVALL, Mary Emily	LEIZEAR, Robert	FEB 21 1850
DUVALL, Mary Jane	JACKSON, Andrew	AUG 19 1843
DUVALL, Milly	HART, Richard	SEP 16 1813
DUVALL, Orella	MORGAN, William	MAY 06 1831
DUVALL, Perry	THOMPSON, Sarah	SEP 15 1834
DUVALL, Priscilla W.	HUMES, George	NOV 04 1846
DUVALL, Rector	POOR, Tereaser	DEC 19 1820
DUVALL, Rhoda	HANEGAN, Thos.	AUG 24 1821
DUVALL, Rosella L.	ROLOSON, William H.	OCT 05 1836
DUVALL, Samuel	CROWLEY, Christina	MAY 05 1846
DUVALL, Sarah A.	ARRINGTON, Gayton	AUG 31 1818
DUVALL, Susan	BEERS, Benjamin F.	JUL 26 1849
DUVALL, Treacy	HOMILLER, William	JAN 24 1837
DUVALL, William H.	REEVES, Mary Ann	SEP 26 1844
DUVALL, William T.	BOWEN, Elizabeth T.	JUN 25 1833
DUVANN, Mary	EARHART, Jacob	AUG 22 1825
DWHEY, Timothy	WELSH, Bridget	MAY 13 1853
DWIGHT, Harrison	LANE, Mary	APR 15 1839
DWYER, Bridget	MacNAMARA, John	JAN 11 1851
DWYER, Edward	GRANT, Nora	MAY 10 1851
DWYER, Margaret	BURNS, John	JAN 31 1857
DWYER, Richard	CROCKETT, Elizabeth E.	MAY 14 1850
DWYER, Thomas	DICKEY, Eleanor	JUN 07 1820
DWYER, Thomas R.	ROBERTS, Margaret	MAR 13 1856
DWYRE, Edward	RAFFERTY, Mary	APR 13 1858
DWYRE, John	MORONEY, Mary	JUN 30 1851
DYE, Cornelia Ann	DONALDSON, Dorsey H.	FEB 11 1852
DYE, Elizabeth	EBERT, William	MAY 17 1847
DYE, Henry	TAYLER, Mary Ann	APR 13 1835
DYE, Henry	DONALDSON, Julia Ann	MAR 13 1852
DYE, Mary A.	VEITCH, John W.	DEC 03 1856
DYE, Mary Elizabeth	BEARD, George	AUG 05 1827
DYER, Aaron	FOWLER, Margaret	JUL 18 1812
DYER, Alexander	ASHTON, Rebecca	OCT 19 1822
DYER, Aloysius	LUCAS, Susan	MAY 10 1832
DYER, Amos	TAYLOR, Ellen	DEC 23 1834
DYER, Benjamin	KIRBY, Sarah C.	SEP 11 1844
DYER, Benjamin F.	COOPER, Ellen E.	NOV 15 1838
DYER, Catharine	KNOTT, William	APR 28 1836
DYER, Dianna	HUTCHINS, George W.	APR 24 1850
DYER, Edward	TARBELL, Henrietta	FEB 09 1833
DYER, Edward	JOHNSON, Emeline (blk)	JUN 23 1835
DYER, Edward C.	BELT, Elizabeth E.	JUL 14 1851
DYER, Elias	THOMPSON, Winney	SEP 17 1840

District of Columbia Marriage Licenses, 1811-1858

DYER, Elijah	DYER, Elizabeth Ann	FEB 08 1841
DYER, Eliza (blk)	BROOKS, David	MAY 26 1842
DYER, Eliza Ann	MARRON, John	FEB 23 1832
DYER, Eliza F.	DYER, John J.	MAY 17 1853
DYER, Elizabeth	TARMAN, Samuel	JAN 16 1812
DYER, Elizabeth Ann	DYER, Elijah	FEB 08 1841
DYER, Emeline	CLOKEY, Robert B.	JUL 13 1824
DYER, Harriet	EDELIN, Richard J. [Dr.]	JUN 16 1829
DYER, Henrietta H.	BOONE, John F.	APR 28 1851
DYER, James Henry	CURSHAW, Matilda	SEP 12 1854
DYER, John F.	COLINBAUGH, Catherine	NOV 28 1837
DYER, John J.	DYER, Eliza F.	MAY 17 1853
DYER, John R.	BOONE, Jane M.	MAY 23 1826
DYER, Joseph	HANY, Margaret S.	NOV 06 1841
DYER, Jusia	BARRON, James W.	MAY 20 1829
DYER, Kinsey	CRUMP, Ann Eliza	SEP 23 1842
DYER, Lethy	KENNEDY, Lewis James	APR 29 1841
DYER, Martha	JOHNSON, Charles E.	DEC 20 1849
DYER, Mary A.	CAMPBELL, John W.	MAY 02 1840
DYER, Mary R.	BIBB, George M.	MAY 22 1832
DYER, Matilda	FOWLER, Benjamin	NOV 10 1827
DYER, Peter	THOMPSON, Sarah Catharine	SEP 24 1840
DYER, Philip	BAYLY, Sarah	MAR 06 1815
DYER, Rachel	TRAVERS, John W.	FEB 26 1851
DYER, Robert	TRAVERS, Rebecca	OCT 08 1851
DYER, Robert W.	CASSIN, Mary Eliza	JAN 11 1841
DYER, Ruth	WHITE, William H.	JUL 10 1848
DYER, Sarah Jane	CORE, John T.	JUL 26 1849
DYER, Sarah Rebecca	BATES, Robert W.	JUN 03 1835
DYER, Susan	PERKINS, William H.	JUL 20 1830
DYER, Susan	BURROWS, Thomas H.	JAN 17 1842
DYER, Willia Ann	LINDSAY, Alfred	DEC 03 1840
DYER, William	BIXLER, Rachel	JAN 09 1856
DYER, William B.	BALL, Ellen Nora	DEC 12 1842
DYER, Wm. Ignatius	MAYFIELD, Emelia Ann	MAY 18 1840
DYKES, George T.	PATTERSON, Anne M.	AUG 23 1855
DYKES, William	CLARK, Ann	JAN 11 1827
DYLE, William	McNEMERA, Margaret	FEB 07 1853
DYNES, Hanson	DOUGLASS, Mary (blk)	MAY 11 1840
DYNES, Peter	SMITH, Nelly	FEB 23 1819
DYSON, Adeline R.L.	McBRIDE, Priestly H.	JUL 14 1857
DYSON, Charles	BUTLER, Elizabeth (blk)	APR 12 1831
DYSON, Geo. E.	ROWE, Adeline R.L.	OCT 24 1826
DYSON, Isabella (col'd)	PERRY, Danl.	MAY 11 1852
DYSON, Margaret C.	GILMAN, William H.	NOV 15 1848
DYSON, Mary Ann	BARRON, Henry L.	MAR 15 1853
DYSON, Robert H.	TUCKSON, Francis (blk)	JAN 31 1853

District of Columbia Marriage Licenses, 1811-1858

E

Name	Spouse	Date
EADER, Jonathan	BRIDWELL, Catharine P.	MAY 04 1852
EAGAN, Jane	FINN, Matthew	DEC 02 1852
EAGAN, Peter	RAY, Sarah J.	NOV 13 1856
EAGLIN, Lila Susan	WINDSOR, Sukey	DEC 13 1838
EAKEN, William D.	YOOLL, Juliana	MAR 09 1814
EAKLE, Elias H.	BYINGTON, Mary F.	JAN 29 1855
EAKLE, Mary	HACKENJOS, John	OCT 10 1857
EAPOWER, Margaret	STEPPER, Anthony	JUN 15 1833
EARBACK, Charles	DAUR, Mary	MAR 24 1857
EARHART, Ann Eliza	SARDO, Joseph	MAR 01 1826
EARHART, Jacob	DUVANN, Mary	AUG 22 1825
EARHART, Thomas J.	BUTLER, Elizabeth C.	MAY 06 1837
EARL, John	CATON, Maria	SEP 07 1852
EARL, Richard	DAVISON, Hannah	OCT 01 1851
EARL, Richard W.	BROWN, Sarah	MAR 14 1835
EARL, Robert	GLENN, Precilla	SEP 06 1825
EARL, Robert	HERMITAGE, Martha	DEC 18 1832
EARLE, Frances L.	JOHNSON, Thos. W.	MAR 22 1856
EARLE, Mary	HILBUS, George	MAY 26 1849
EARLY, Thomas R.	HOPKINS, Elizabeth A.	FEB 17 1853
EARNER, Bridget	NOONE, James	SEP 16 1851
EARNSHAW, Thomas T.	QUANTRILL, Cornelia J.	FEB 22 1847
EARP, Ann	CHAMBERLAIN, George W.	JUL 12 1830
EARP, James	MAY, Martha Ann	JUN 01 1812
EARP, Jno. Wm.	GARDNEIR, Matilda	JUL 22 1851
EARP, Susan	MORGAN, Aquilla R.	JAN 28 1826
EARPE, Mary Ellen	BROWN, Commodore Perry	APR 28 1849
EARSLING, Sarah	TANNER, Thomas	FEB 24 1820
EARTON, John W.	PAWLEY, Mary Ann	JUL 13 1831
EASBURN, Elizabeth Jane	CAMERON, John	MAY 06 1831
EASBY, Ellen	WHEELER, William	OCT 27 1852
EASBY, John W.	LOWRY, Rosina M.	JUL 29 1843
EASBY, Marian Eliza	KING, Henry [Dr.]	NOV 13 1833
EASBY, Wilhelmine M.	SMITH, William R.	JUN 13 1854
EASLEY, Sally N.	BOYD, John G.	MAY 31 1853
EASLY, Admonia (blk)	TASCOL, Thomas	NOV 19 1847
EASTEN, Mary	FILLEY, John	AUG 02 1822
EASTER, Ann, Mrs.	FINDLEY, Samuel	MAY 22 1828
EASTERDAY, Ann	ROBERTSON, Wm. B.	MAY 01 1820
EASTERLEIN, Mary M.	HAMMER, Michael	DEC 26 1856
EASTON, Anette (blk)	BROOKS, Joseph	NOV 08 1854
EASTON, Anne	MYERS, John T., Sr.	APR 17 1819
EASTON, Catharine (blk)	DELANEY, Henry	MAY 05 1849
EASTON, Deborah	HAMLEY, James	JUL 19 1832
EASTON, Hezekiah	TRACEY, Jane	JUL 05 1815
EASTON, James B.	REYNOLDS, Letitia	JUN 25 1839
EASTON, John T.	SIMMONS, Sarah E.	SEP 23 1856
EASTON, Levin	BANNISTER, Mary Ann	AUG 08 1836
EASTON, Mary	FIFE, William	MAY 11 1821
EASTON, Mary A.	POLK, Lucious J.	APR 10 1832
EASTON, Mary F. (blk)	DAVIS, William	AUG 11 1856
EASTON, Rhody	O'NEALE, Hugh	APR 17 1815
EASTON, Robert	GREEN, Charity	SEP 17 1835
EASTON, Sarah	RICKETTS, Abraham	JUL 05 1812
EASTON, Sarah A.	YONGE, Wm. P.	JUN 07 1820
EASTON, Sarah Ann	MEEKS, William A.	JUN 06 1821

District of Columbia Marriage Licenses, 1811-1858

EASTON, Sidney	DIGGS, Cordelia (blk)	DEC 08 1853
EASTON, Susanna	MATTINGLY, Lewis	DEC 04 1815
EASTON, Thomas S.	ADERTEN, Sarah E.	DEC 11 1832
EATON, Alexander	BARRETT, Eleanor	JUL 12 1817
EATON, Alexander W.	PEACHEM, Catharine V.	APR 26 1858
EATON, David	GWINN, Susan	OCT 27 1834
EATON, Edward H.	WATSON, Sarah E.	JUL 13 1848
EATON, Ella	BELL, P.H.	OCT 22 1856
EATON, John H.	TIMBERLAKE, Margaret	JAN 01 1829
EATON, Margaret Ann	MOORE, Thomas	OCT 11 1854
EATON, Mary Stanly	GRIFFITH, Daniel	APR 07 1853
EATON, Nathan	CANADY, Philenia	SEP 19 1816
EATON, Richard	SELBY, Mary Ann	NOV 29 1838
EATON, Samuel	COX, Susan	MAY 03 1841
EATOR, Catharine	SHECKELLS, Thomas	APR 18 1853
EBERBACH, Elizabeth Emilie	NOYES, Samuel V.	OCT 27 1857
EBERBACK, John H.	KUHL, Christena	FEB 18 1835
EBERHART, Elizth.	MIENDER, Jacob	APR 16 1858
EBERHART, John	GOULD, Masallina Lavinia	FEB 19 1849
EBERLE, A.W.	WILLIAMSON, James B.	AUG 13 1850
EBERLE, Caroline E.	MILLER, Benjamin A.	JAN 12 1846
EBERLEH, George	HACHMEYER, Wilhelmine	AUG 14 1836
EBERLI, Anton	KRESECKER, Margaretta	FEB 17 1849
EBERT, Isidor	ZELLER, Francisca	JAN 25 1857
EBERT, William	DYE, Elizabeth	MAY 17 1847
EBERY, George	HURDLE, Margaret	MAR 07 1848
ECCLESTON, Margaret	NEUMYER, Leopold	MAR 18 1851
ECHOLS, Philip Henry	BERRIEN, Margaret L.M.	JUL 12 1831
ECKARD, Rebecca	RIGGLES, Joseph	FEB 24 1858
ECKERT, Henry	FALCONER, Ellen	NOV 22 1852
ECKHARDT, Dorothy C.	MORRIS, George W.	APR 27 1853
ECKLOFF, Adolphus	RIDGEWAY, Sarah E.	JUN 14 1849
ECKLOFF, Ann Elizth.	GLOVER, William H.	JAN 19 1856
ECKLOFF, Caroline	LOMBARDI, Francis	NOV 25 1844
ECKLOFF, Charles G.	TWOMEY, Elizabeth	OCT 04 1850
ECKLOFF, Edward C.	ELLIS, Martha Jane	SEP 02 1844
ECKLOFF, Frederick W.	GODDARD, Margaret E.	JUN 02 1842
ECKLOFF, Henrietta F.	RIDGEWAY, Enoch	JUN 04 1850
ECKLOFF, Joseph W.	HELLFREY, Catharine	APR 10 1841
ECKLOFF, R.G.	SIMS, Josephine	AUG 03 1857
ECKLOFF, William C.F.	MYERS, Dulaney F.	DEC 15 1842
ECKTON, Caroline	DUCKET, Basil W.	DEC 06 1854
ECKTON, Christeen	CONKLIN, William	JUN 06 1854
ECKTON, Harriet	RICHARDS, William	JAN 12 1830
ECKTON, William	LYNCH, Elizabeth	SEP 22 1836
ECTON, John H.	McCHESNEY, Jane M.	APR 17 1851
ECTON, Julia Ann	GODDARD, James G.	NOV 28 1843
ECTON, Wallace M.	GATES, Emily Ann	AUG 04 1833
ECTOR, Mary	CLEMENTS, Robert	OCT 16 1851
EDD, John T.	HAMADINGER, Mary E.	MAR 01 1855
EDDIE, Edward C.	HAMMOND, Ellen	OCT 16 1857
EDDINS, Mary F.	NOEL, William F.	MAY 11 1854
EDDS, Caroline	HOWARD, Hiram	FEB 08 1834
EDDS, Ellen	HOWARD, Selre	DEC 10 1831
EDDS, James	SCHELL, Ann Maria	JAN 05 1843
EDDS, John	McDANIEL, Rebecca	JAN 01 1813
EDDUS, Sarah L.	REDFERN, Richard	SEP 22 1838
EDEDLIN, John Henry	EDELIN, Ann	SEP 13 1853

District of Columbia Marriage Licenses, 1811-1858

EDELEN, Joseph B.	ABERCROMBIE, Agnes O.	JAN 20 1848
EDELEN, Lucy Ann	GARNER, Hezekiah [Lieut.]	NOV 26 1827
EDELEN, Mary Dade	FERRIS, Henry	MAY 31 1838
EDELEN, Mary W.	JACKSON, John S. [Dr.]	MAY 04 1824
EDELEN, Raphael L.	LANHAM, Charlott A.	SEP 22 1832
EDELEN, Rosanna B.	ANDERSON, James	SEP 18 1824
EDELIN, Ann	EDELIN, John Henry	SEP 13 1853
EDELIN, Charles	WEBSTER, Caroline	FEB 22 1830
EDELIN, Chas. C.	ACTON, Mary L.	OCT 13 1849
EDELIN, Elizabeth Lucy Anna	OSBORNE, Walter	DEC 25 1838
EDELIN, Francis S.	CARRICO, Eliza A.	SEP 17 1853
EDELIN, George T.	HARVEY, Sarah M.	DEC 25 1838
EDELIN, Henrietta Mary	KIRK, Andrew M.	DEC 17 1818
EDELIN, J.	DAY, Mary	APR 29 1817
EDELIN, James	CARR, Nancy	JUL 31 1844
EDELIN, James	LANGLEY, Elizabeth	JUL 27 1852
EDELIN, Joseph	HICKS, Sarah	MAY 14 1845
EDELIN, Joshua Thomas	LANGLEY, Caroline	APR 17 1843
EDELIN, Martha R.	COSTIGAN, Joseph	DEC 22 1827
EDELIN, Mary	SMOOT, George C.	JAN 15 1828
EDELIN, Mary	VENABLE, William	FEB 08 1851
EDELIN, Mary E.	WOOD, Richard J.	DEC 23 1848
EDELIN, Mary Matilda	COOPER, Miles	JUL 25 1833
EDELIN, Matilda Jane	EVANS, Walter	AUG 13 1845
EDELIN, Richard J. [Dr.]	DYER, Harriet	JUN 16 1829
EDELIN, Susannah	JACK, James, Junr.	NOV 16 1847
EDELINE, Cecelia Jane	NAILOR, William	JUN 04 1839
EDELMANN, Charles	SCHLAYER, Wilhelmina	MAR 19 1857
EDEN, Susan	COOK, David	MAY 06 1823
EDENBOROUGH, Henry	SNOWDEN, Eliza (blk)	APR 17 1827
EDENBURGH, Mary Ann	HUTTON, John B.	APR 07 1825
EDENBURR, Edward	GRAY, Harriet (blk)	DEC 07 1826
EDES, William H.	RATCLIFF, Martha	OCT 20 1829
EDGCOMB, William	THOMAS, Mary Elizabeth	NOV 10 1828
EDINBORO, Amelia (blk)	BLOCK, Moses	DEC 11 1856
EDINBOROUGH, Sophia (blk)	ADAMS, George	APR 20 1840
EDINBOROUGH, William	CURTIS, Cecelia (blk)	APR 10 1851
EDLE, Maria	HIRD, Fidel	NOV 28 1853
EDMONDS, Charles	DOUGHERTY, Sarah Ann	DEC 21 1854
EDMONDS, Cordelia	FLOWERS, Richard	MAR 14 1833
EDMONDS, Thornton	ROSE, Ailsa	SEP 13 1824
EDMONDSON, B.B.	WILLIS, Martha Ann	DEC 12 1848
EDMONDSON, James	LYONS, Emly	AUG 26 1841
EDMONSEN, Matilda	CROGGINS, Charles	DEC 04 1839
EDMONSEN, Eliza	GERMON, Vincent D.	SEP 26 1821
EDMONSON, Jackson	BOWEN, Jane Eliza	FEB 25 1841
EDMONSON, John	TANNER, Sarah A.	MAY 22 1834
EDMONSON, Thomas	BOOTS, Matilda	JUN 25 1818
EDMONSTON, Ann	MORAN, Dyson	MAR 20 1819
EDMONSTON, Ann Maria	MYERS, Benjamin B.	JAN 26 1825
EDMONSTON, Brooke	CARR, Mary	JUL 22 1814
EDMONSTON, Catharine	STUART, Charles	OCT 18 1849
EDMONSTON, Catherine Ann	FOWLES, James	NOV 16 1831
EDMONSTON, Charles	BARNECLO, Ann H.	OCT 29 1840
EDMONSTON, Charles	CAMMACK, Mary E.	MAR 29 1858
EDMONSTON, Chas. T.	TRUNNELL, Mary Ann	FEB 27 1850
EDMONSTON, Cornelia	BEALL, Richard J.	MAY 30 1853
EDMONSTON, Decius W.	GRIFFITH, Charlotte	AUG 31 1815

District of Columbia Marriage Licenses, 1811-1858

EDMONSTON, Decius W., Jr.	DAW, Marion J.	OCT 14 1854
EDMONSTON, Dorithy	MOORE, Silas	MAY 24 1828
EDMONSTON, Dorothy S.	KILLMAN, Samuel	FEB 16 1820
EDMONSTON, Edwin H.	DELLAWAY, Virginia	MAY 16 1850
EDMONSTON, Edwin H.	DAWSON, Maria Louisa	MAR 29 1858
EDMONSTON, Elijah	BOWEN, Mary Ann	NOV 06 1839
EDMONSTON, Elizabeth B.	GIVEN, Thomas	DEC 07 1815
EDMONSTON, Ethan A.	SHERWOOD, Mary Virginia	AUG 05 1850
EDMONSTON, Franklin	GATEWOOD, Eliza T.	DEC 23 1848
EDMONSTON, Grafton	HARDING, Elizabeth Ann	MAY 23 1826
EDMONSTON, John C.	BURCH, Martha Ann	OCT 29 1833
EDMONSTON, Leonidas A.	WELLS, Elizabeth	JAN 16 1849
EDMONSTON, Marcelia	WATERS, Dwight R.	APR 05 1852
EDMONSTON, Martha Ellen (blk)	YOUNG, Forrester	APR 26 1841
EDMONSTON, Mary	MYERS, Benjamin	SEP 18 1813
EDMONSTON, Mary Jane	McHENRY, Hamilton	OCT 07 1843
EDMONSTON, Octabia	BRYAN, Joseph	APR 06 1822
EDMONSTON, Sarah R.	BALL, Daniel	JUN 10 1843
EDMONSTON, Thomas	SELBY, Amelia	NOV 09 1816
EDMONSTON, Thomas	BOULTON, Rebecca	NOV 24 1836
EDMONSTON, Thomas J.	SHERLOCK, Victoria A.	MAY 13 1852
EDMONSTON, Virginia R.	BERRY, Walter O.	SEP 09 1856
EDMONSTON, William A.	STEVENS, Matilda	NOV 25 1850
EDMUND, Harriet L.	COYLE, Leonidas	APR 12 1836
EDMUNDS, Frances M.	KENDRICK, John	MAR 19 1844
EDMUNDS, Julia	HUNTER, Zachariah	FEB 24 1834
EDMUNSTON, Ann	TURNER, Elbert	JAN 30 1839
EDSON, Silas D.	SAUNDERS, Sarah P.	NOV 27 1833
EDWARD, Rowles	RICE, Mary E.	OCT 19 1838
EDWARDS, Anne	LUCAS, James	JUL 05 1815
EDWARDS, Catharine	KELL, John	MAY 03 1837
EDWARDS, Catherine	WHITMORE, William	DEC 08 1855
EDWARDS, Charles	FINNEGAN, Martha Jane	MAY 03 1851
EDWARDS, Edward	THOMPSON, Eleanor	DEC 24 1844
EDWARDS, Eliza	FERRY, James Thomas	JAN 21 1845
EDWARDS, Frances	SOPER, Bazil	FEB 04 1817
EDWARDS, Harriet	BUTLER, Mahlon	APR 18 1820
EDWARDS, Henry C.	HENSLEY, Mary	MAR 03 1855
EDWARDS, Isabella	KEILER, John	SEP 12 1855
EDWARDS, Issadore	KEMBLE, Mary Ann	NOV 17 1821
EDWARDS, James	RAMSAY, Eliza	SEP 18 1824
EDWARDS, James	SANDIFORD, Elizabeth	JUN 29 1842
EDWARDS, James	PROSPERI, Aspasia	APR 15 1850
EDWARDS, James	RIGGLES, Eliza	SEP 15 1854
EDWARDS, James A.	WILLIAMS, Ann	OCT 19 1829
EDWARDS, John S.	MacPHERSON, Susan W.	MAY 08 1838
EDWARDS, Levi	FRANK, Mary Ellen	JUN 05 1852
EDWARDS, Lewis	PERRY, Sarah	OCT 30 1816
EDWARDS, Lewis	BROOM, Mary E.	OCT 14 1840
EDWARDS, Louis A.	CRAWFORD, Eulilia E.	OCT 01 1850
EDWARDS, Louisa	STEVENS, Henry	FEB 13 1821
EDWARDS, Mary (blk)	LANSDALE, Thomas	NOV 24 1856
EDWARDS, Mary Ann	LANGLEY, George Thos.	MAR 27 1843
EDWARDS, Mary E.	CURTIN, John A.	JUL 07 1846
EDWARDS, Mary E.	LIPSCOMB, James L.	AUG 21 1855
EDWARDS, Ogden J.	LOYED, Louisa A.	APR 22 1856
EDWARDS, Robert	PACKER, Caroline (blk)	FEB 22 1838
EDWARDS, Rosina (blk)	POWELL, Granville	APR 15 1840

District of Columbia Marriage Licenses, 1811-1858

EDWARDS, Sarah	FERRY, Hugh	JUL 30 1840
EDWARDS, Sarah A.H.	MICKUM, William P.	JAN 11 1820
EDWARDS, Sarah E.	HAYRE, John F.	DEC 26 1848
EDWARDS, Sarah F.	DAVIS, Joseph W.	APR 02 1857
EDWARDS, Washington	WILLIAMS, Catharine	APR 17 1828
EDWARDS, Wm. W.	FISHER, Ellen Rebecca	AUG 22 1843
EFFLINE, David James	BURCH, Susan Ann	JAN 30 1845
EGGLESTON, Laura R.	JOHNSON, Robert	FEB 02 1857
EGLOFF, Godfried	HEERE, Catharine	JUL 17 1818
EHARDT, Jacob	FREE, Mary	SEP 19 1822
EHERN, Margaret	O'LEARY, John	MAY 24 1853
EHMORE, Hulkey	STARR, George	FEB 23 1836
EHRAN, Margaret	O'LEARY, John	OCT 14 1854
EHRLICH, Sophia	HANLEIN, Feist	DEC 31 1851
EHRMANTRAUT, Joseph	FOWLER, Christy	FEB 02 1848
EICHELE, Catherine	BAEBEL, Christoph Adam	JUL 18 1854
EICHHORN, Elizabeth	MULLER, John C.	MAY 01 1848
EICHHORN, Elizabeth	MENKE, Meinard	OCT 06 1851
EICHHORN, Rudolph	CONLAN, Ann Elizabeth	JAN 06 1853
EICHHORN, Theressa	LOCHBOEHLER, Frank	JAN 03 1857
EICHLER, William	LETMATE, Fredericka W.	OCT 13 1855
EIGENBRODT, George	GROSS, Magdalena	JUN 10 1850
EIGHLER, Henry	KAISER, Sophia	JAN 05 1847
EIGHSTADT, Adolph	SCHWARZKOPF, Metta	JUL 25 1853
EIKHORN, George	KLEINDENST, Mary	APR 13 1858
EISENRING, Mary	NICHOLS, Jacob	JUN 03 1850
ELBERT, John	KINSLAR, Margaret	MAY 11 1833
ELBERT, John L.	WATTS, Martha B.	APR 26 1815
ELD, Aquila	PAYNE, Laura	AUG 11 1843
ELD, Henry A.	RUMMAGE, Mary	DEC 02 1847
ELD, Henry Albert	LOVELESS, Mary Elizabeth	NOV 30 1843
ELDER, Mary Agnes	RAGAN, Michael	SEP 16 1851
ELDER, Matilda C.	ROBERTS, John H.	OCT 16 1838
ELDER, William	STAMP, Matilda	NOV 26 1818
ELDRIDGE, Marinda	REED, Francis A.	AUG 11 1857
ELGIN, Eliza F.	COCKERILL, Bushrod E.	JAN 14 1850
ELGIN, Mary J.	KEYS, James	SEP 05 1854
ELGIN, Sally Ann	DRANE, Robert	JAN 21 1853
ELI, Agnes	KAYSER, John Christof.	JUN 30 1845
ELI, Sarah	McLILLEY, Samuel	MAY 07 1850
ELIASON, Elias A.	LYON, Mary	APR 17 1832
ELIASON, Eliza	ADDISON, Thomas B.	MAY 11 1818
ELIASON, James M.	FREEBERGER, Rachel Ann	JUL 18 1853
ELIJA, Elizth. Ann	COOK, Philip	NOV 19 1831
ELIOT, Caroline	KASSON, John A.	APR 30 1850
ELIOT, Catharine Mary	MIDDLETON, Lemuel J.	SEP 16 1830
ELIOT, Elizabeth Margaret	FURNESS, James Thiring	OCT 25 1838
ELIOT, Frank Andrew	WHIPPLE, Mary J.	SEP 11 1854
ELIOT, Hannah D.	LAMB, Thomas	OCT 25 1828
ELIOT, Johnson	LLEWELLYN, Mary J.	NOV 29 1850
ELIOT, Wm. G.	CRANCH, Abby	JUN 29 1837
ELIS, Verlinda	HOLLAND, Elias	SEP 28 1826
ELKINS, Allen N.	HALLEY, Margaret P.	MAR 18 1828
ELKINS, John	DAVIS, Ann	JUL 14 1842
ELKINS, Nathaniel	GRAVATE, Catherine W.	JUN 08 1852
ELKY, Elizabeth	ROBBINS, Patrick	JUN 29 1835
ELLERBY, Albert	DAVIS, Julia Wingate	FEB 14 1849
ELLETT, Catharine	O'REILY, Wm. H.	JUN 18 1855

District of Columbia Marriage Licenses, 1811-1858

ELLICOTT, John, Junr.	GORDON, Jennie	NOV 05 1856
ELLIN, Benjamin	RIGGLES, Mary Ann	OCT 27 1841
ELLIN, Mary Ann	MILLER, John C.	JAN 27 1858
ELLINGTON, Mary E.	COWEN, David	JUL 12 1858
ELLIOT, Caroline	FLINN, William	AUG 14 1848
ELLIOT, Elizabeth	RITTER, John E.	DEC 04 1855
ELLIOT, Ellen	REEVEL, Randolph C.	NOV 17 1829
ELLIOT, George	BRENT, Catharine	JUL 19 1834
ELLIOT, Henry	LOVE, Elizabeth S.	OCT 14 1847
ELLIOT, James B.	MOULTON, Hannah M.	JUL 18 1857
ELLIOT, Jonathan	KING, Elizabeth	APR 06 1845
ELLIOT, William	LITTLE, Elizabeth E.	DEC 30 1822
ELLIOT, William P.	FRISELL, Margaret A.	MAR 02 1858
ELLIOTT, Annie R.	COBURN, William A.	MAR 24 1857
ELLIOTT, Catharine	O'REILY, William H.	JUL 11 1854
ELLIOTT, E.G., U.S.A.	MILLER, Asinath M.	AUG 28 1848
ELLIOTT, Ellen U.	HOUSE, George E.	MAR 20 1854
ELLIOTT, Ellender	WHITE, Fielder L.	JUL 30 1825
ELLIOTT, Harriet	GOODRICH, Josiah	AUG 10 1840
ELLIOTT, Isabella Jane	BEATTY, Charles F.	JUN 08 1842
ELLIOTT, John T.	LANKFORD, Ann R.	MAR 05 1858
ELLIOTT, John Washington	JOHNSON, Mary	SEP 08 1843
ELLIOTT, Jonathan	EVANS, Sarah	MAY 03 1813
ELLIOTT, Lynde	CLARK, Emma	DEC 24 1828
ELLIOTT, Martha Ann	TRUEMAN, William	APR 02 1856
ELLIOTT, Mary Ann	RIVES, John C.	JAN 11 1836
ELLIOTT, Perry	HENLY, Catharine	JAN 31 1856
ELLIOTT, Richard G.	CLEMENTS, Mary E.	AUG 07 1844
ELLIOTT, Samuel B.	RANDALL, Juliana M.	NOV 23 1847
ELLIOTT, Sarah E.	STONELL, Jno. Worton	JUL 14 1855
ELLIOTT, Susan L.	SHIVELY, John M.	MAR 27 1847
ELLIOTT, William	CAUSIN, Amanda	FEB 09 1844
ELLIOTT, William A.S.	VanRISWICK, Phebe E.	AUG 05 1844
ELLIS, Alexander	WILLIAMS, Eliza	JAN 01 1842
ELLIS, Amelia (col'd)	ROBINSON, David	AUG 17 1853
ELLIS, Ariann	WOOD, Charles	AUG 03 1829
ELLIS, Dorcas Gardner	BRYANT, James R.M.	JUL 22 1822
ELLIS, Edmund	RODBIRD, Eliza	SEP 05 1856
ELLIS, Edmund J.	DOUGHERTY, Mary	JAN 05 1837
ELLIS, Eliza	STEWART, John	OCT 23 1852
ELLIS, Elizabeth	MADDISON, Austin	JUL 27 1848
ELLIS, Elizabeth Jane	THECKER, William H.	OCT 17 1848
ELLIS, Frances	ROBERTSON, James	MAY 17 1851
ELLIS, Francis	HUTCHINS, Lavinia	JUN 11 1851
ELLIS, George Thomas	ALLEN, Emly Ann	APR 01 1837
ELLIS, Henry	WILKINSON, Elizabeth	JUL 19 1839
ELLIS, Henry Charles	McINTOSH, Mary	MAY 28 1855
ELLIS, James	GRAVES, Jane	JUN 13 1839
ELLIS, James G.	FOLKNER, Susan	JUN 02 1846
ELLIS, John	MILLS, Eleanor	DEC 16 1816
ELLIS, John	NORWOOD, Sarah	OCT 12 1820
ELLIS, John	FAGAN, Ann	DEC 03 1840
ELLIS, John	MELTON, Rachel	JUL 27 1846
ELLIS, John	ROLLINS, Mary V.	OCT 17 1855
ELLIS, John B.	CUSTER, Ann Maria	JUL 04 1840
ELLIS, John B.	COCRELL, Elizabeth Ann	JUN 08 1844
ELLIS, John F.	ENNIS, Mary A.	OCT 25 1852
ELLIS, John W.	WORTHINGTON, Ruth Ann	JAN 03 1852

District of Columbia Marriage Licenses, 1811-1858

ELLIS, Leonard K.	POWERS, Elizabeth Ann	DEC 31 1846
ELLIS, Martha A.J.	KIDWELL, Hezekiah A.	DEC 23 1852
ELLIS, Martha Jane	ECKLOFF, Edward C.	SEP 02 1844
ELLIS, Mary	BEALL, William D.	NOV 12 1841
ELLIS, Mary Ann	THUCKER, James	DEC 31 1822
ELLIS, Mary E.	YATES, William A.	JUL 09 1855
ELLIS, Mary Frances	BIRCH, Randolph	APR 06 1854
ELLIS, Mary J.	NALLS, W.B.	JUN 23 1854
ELLIS, Mary M.	McINTIRE, Alexander	OCT 12 1848
ELLIS, Matilda	ROBINSON, Jefferson	SEP 01 1855
ELLIS, Minty	CLEVELAND, Caleb	JAN 01 1829
ELLIS, Miranda	BARTLE, George	OCT 11 1849
ELLIS, Mrs.	FOWLER, Thomas F.	OCT 30 1847
ELLIS, Richd. Henry	CURTIS, Ann	DEC 29 1830
ELLIS, Robert	DENNISON, Mary F.	AUG 04 1849
ELLIS, Sarah	BURCH, Jesse	JUL 15 1830
ELLIS, Susan	FALCONER, Ralph J.	MAY 05 1840
ELLIS, Susan M.M.	DREDGE, James W.	APR 24 1845
ELLIS, Virginia	THOMAS, William E.	APR 27 1858
ELLIS, William	HARPER, Ann	MAY 22 1837
ELLIS, William	WELLS, Harriet E.	FEB 24 1858
ELLISON, William H.	FISH, Elizabeth	JAN 23 1849
ELLISS, James A.	BALTZER, Eliza Jane	JAN 30 1845
ELLMORE, James	MURPHY, Mary Ann	MAR 19 1850
ELLS, Virginia M.	WOOD, George, Jr.	OCT 04 1854
ELLSWORTH, Margaret	JEFFERSON, Ferdinand	AUG 01 1838
ELLSWORTH, Mary J.	ENGLISH, James	NOV 23 1853
ELLWOOD, William D.	LONGSTON, Martha Ann	JAN 27 1857
ELLYSON, Mary J.	DRINKARD, Wm. F.	JUN 07 1850
ELMORE, Catharine	MILLER, George	SEP 15 1853
ELMORE, Elizabeth	TURNER, Charles	MAY 25 1833
ELMORE, Jerome	CONDIRCH, Barbara A.	NOV 05 1856
ELMORE, Mary Ann	PETTY, John T.	JAN 07 1856
ELMORE, Sarah	RODGERS, John	FEB 28 1857
ELMS, James	HARPER, Eliza	AUG 25 1842
ELSACURN, Maria	MAREA, Joseph	MAR 05 1813
ELSEY, Christiana	CLARKE, Charles G.	JUN 22 1820
ELVANS, Catherine	REEDER, John W.	AUG 22 1832
ELVANS, Richard	MURDOCK, Mary Ann	MAY 18 1828
ELVIN, Grace	RAMSAY, William	APR 03 1848
ELVIN, John	WRIGHT, Mary F.	MAY 27 1829
ELVINS, John	THOMPSON, Georgeana	FEB 06 1854
ELWELL, Francis H.	LOWE, Margery Ann	NOV 08 1832
ELWOOD, Isaac T.	DIGGES, Ellen M.	APR 25 1833
ELY, Albert W.	TRIPLETTE, Susannah B.	JAN 14 1856
ELY, Catherine	KUHAGEN, Frederick	APR 02 1836
ELY, Elizabeth	JACOBI, Adolph	APR 14 1847
ELY, Maria Catharine	EMERICH, Peter	MAR 11 1845
EMACK, Harriet H.	KENNEDY, Thomas R.	JUL 17 1834
EMACK, John D.	VanHORN, Mary Ann	AUG 07 1821
EMACK, Mary Ann C.	BROWN, Thomas H.	DEC 21 1819
EMBERSON, Mary	JENKINS, [blank]	NOV 20 1839
EMBRAY, Harriet	FREEMAN, Robert	FEB 25 1841
EMBREY, Esther A.	BAILEY, John P.	JAN 08 1857
EMBREY, Robert	SMITH, Jane	JUL 18 1834
EMBRY, Sarah	ANDERSON, Marshal R.	JUL 17 1852
EMBRY, Thomas M.	SPRAGUE, Ellen F.	NOV 29 1856
EMERICH, Peter	ELY, Maria Catharine	MAR 11 1845

District of Columbia Marriage Licenses, 1811-1858

EMERSON, Alethea	CLARK, John M.	JUN 11 1829
EMERSON, Charlotte (blk)	LITTEN, Benjamin	JUN 21 1848
EMERSON, Elizabeth A.	RICHARDSON, Edgar A.	JAN 05 1847
EMERSON, John P.	REEDER, Ann Thornton	MAY 24 1836
EMERSON, John S.	DUFFEY, Louisa M.	SEP 01 1847
EMERSON, Matilda	WELLS, John	APR 11 1833
EMERSON, Sarah A.	COOMBS, Wm. J.	JAN 08 1856
EMERY, Robert	JACOBS, Elizabeth	JUN 06 1831
EMMERICH, George	SMITH, Mary Ellen	FEB 26 1848
EMMERICK, Charles Frecerick L.	SANDERSON, Caroline C.	FEB 01 1848
EMMERSON, Edwin	DICKSON, Mary Louisa	JUL 02 1851
EMMERSON, Frances	FUGITT, Benjamin	DEC 11 1846
EMMERSON, Isaiah	RABBITT, Ann Delphina	APR 17 1852
EMMERSON, John P.	SPENCER, Prudence	JAN 06 1848
EMMERSON, Lemuel G.	KIDWELL, Margaret M.	MAR 29 1856
EMMERSON, Rosabella	CRISMOND, James L.	APR 02 1857
EMMERSON, Sabina	WALKER, Joseph	MAR 31 1830
EMMERSON, William	SCOTT, Rebecca	SEP 02 1844
EMMERT, Johanna Caroline Elizabeth	SCHMIDT, John Frederick	FEB 11 1850
EMMERT, Wilhelmine	FINKMANN, Conrad	MAY 27 1845
EMMERT, William	ARNEY, Caroline H. [Mrs.]	OCT 01 1833
EMMERY, Charles	MARYMAN, Elizabeth	MAY 10 1830
EMMETT, Henry	CLOAK, Caroline	NOV 26 1829
EMMIT, Caroline	ROWL, Jefferson	JAN 15 1835
EMMNER, Julius	VIETT, Eliza	APR 29 1857
EMMONS, Roberta H.	HOLMES, Silas M.	JUN 26 1857
EMMONS, William	WEEMS, Mary A.	DEC 16 1856
EMMORT, Heinrick	STROBEL, Louise	MAY 27 1845
EMMS, Sarah M.	CALLAHAN, Allen T.	AUG 28 1852
EMORE, Azeno	COLEMAN, William	APR 14 1832
EMORY, William H.	BACHE, Matilda W.	MAY 26 1838
EMRICK, Christian	HARPER, Mahala E.	DEC 22 1842
ENDRES, Adrian	HARTBRECHT, Margaret	APR 07 1855
ENGEL, Catherine	BANF, Hugh	FEB 06 1858
ENGEL, Christian	MARGGRAF, Johnana	SEP 04 1852
ENGEL, Mary	GLORIOUS, George	SEP 08 1849
ENGEL, Sophia	STEINMETZ, Jacob	MAR 24 1846
ENGEL, Thieleman	HOFFMAN, Catherine	JUN 10 1848
ENGELBRECHT, John C.	BALL, Caroline E.	FEB 19 1850
ENGELBRIGHT, Sarah A.	RENNOE, John H.	JAN 21 1854
ENGHART, Margaret	HAIRIE, John	AUG 22 1855
ENGLAND, John W.	MITCHELL, Mary Ellen	JUN 07 1855
ENGLE, John	WEIS, Mary	NOV 05 1850
ENGLE, Sophia	THOMAS, George	JUN 21 1848
ENGLEHARD, Caroline	WEST, Jacob	JUN 11 1853
ENGLISH, Adelia A.	COLE, Samuel L.	DEC 17 1845
ENGLISH, Alice	DALLAM, Josias W.	NOV 07 1844
ENGLISH, Alice	STANLEY, J.M.	MAY 01 1854
ENGLISH, David, Jr.	FECHTIE, Alcinda B.	SEP 18 1830
ENGLISH, Eliza A.B.	HENDERSON, Richardson	DEC 26 1826
ENGLISH, James	ELLSWORTH, Mary J.	NOV 23 1853
ENGLISH, Jennie	TOWNER, James L.	JUN 03 1857
ENGLISH, John C.	MORGAN, Adelia Ann	MAY 17 1831
ENGLISH, Louisa	VIOLETT, Robert G.	FEB 11 1826
ENGLISH, Mary	WILEY, Thomas	FEB 13 1816
ENGLISH, Mary Ellen	THOMPSON, Mahlon George	NOV 08 1856
ENGLISH, Mary S.	SCHOOLFIELD, Joseph N.	OCT 25 1841
ENNIS, Ann E.	MITCHELL, Henry C.	JAN 09 1848

District of Columbia Marriage Licenses, 1811-1858

ENNIS, Anna R.	O'NEALE, Timothy	NOV 04 1843
ENNIS, Gregory	LAWLER, Susan	MAY 17 1821
ENNIS, Jno.	POSTEN, Eliza	MAR 06 1856
ENNIS, John	HOUK, Mary Ann	APR 28 1835
ENNIS, Mary	HURDLE, Andrew J.	JUL 27 1858
ENNIS, Mary A.	ELLIS, John F.	OCT 25 1852
ENNIS, Mary F.	MITCHELL, Zebedee	JAN 13 1858
ENNIS, Philip	QUEENLAND, Jane	JAN 15 1823
ENNIS, Philip	RICE, Catherine	OCT 13 1849
ENNIS, Richard G.	DONNOGHUE, Mary A.	OCT 17 1848
ENO, William	LENMAN, Elizabeth	JUN 07 1841
ENRIGHT, Edward	DUNNINGAN, Hanora	OCT 19 1857
ENRIGHT, Thomas	GRANT, Mary	MAY 21 1858
ENROUGHTY, James B.	HARDAWAY, Henrietta C.	JAN 19 1854
ENROUGHTY, Thomas P.	FOULKES, Mary E.	DEC 07 1853
ENSELLOW, James	RESTON, Patty	JUL 13 1814
ENSEY, Elizabeth	EVANS, Jesse	NOV 07 1814
ENSEY, Margaret Ann	MUDD, Edward	JUL 21 1842
ENSEY, Margarett A.	SMITHY, William H.	MAR 16 1854
ENSEY, Martha	JENKINS, John	FEB 21 1821
ENST, Charles	BURKE, Margaretta	MAY 07 1853
ENTWISLE, Isaac	SANDERSON, Parthena Holbert	MAY 22 1843
ENTWISLE, James	MASON, Mary Ann [Mrs.]	JUL 06 1815
ENTWISLE, James, Jr.	RADCLIFF, Catharine A.	JAN 17 1849
ENTWISLE, Thomas	DOVE, Mary M.	SEP 26 1843
ENTWISLE, William B.	DUCKWORTH, Mary	DEC 30 1844
EPHLINE, David James	WILLIAMS, Elizabeth	JAN 02 1847
EPHLINE, James A.	MAGUIRE, Maragratee Ann	OCT 23 1848
ERB, Catharine	McCUIN, Joseph	FEB 27 1849
ERB, Henry	BEHLE, Babette	OCT 28 1856
ERB, Margt.	MIDDLETON, Richard	JUL 10 1855
ERB, Wilhelmina	TODTSCHINDER, John Adam Frederick	JUL 10 1847
ERDMANN, John Henri	LANKENAN, Johanna	SEP 21 1846
EREMANTRAUT, Barbara	KLEINDIENST, John Paul	APR 04 1842
ERETY, William G.	WHITNEY, Lucy B.	JAN 07 1826
ERICKSON, Mary Elizabeth	MANGUM, John Thomas	FEB 08 1849
ERKLINE, John	BELT, Caroline	JAN 21 1812
ERNER, Daniel	NOON, Bridget	FEB 11 1851
ERSKIN, John	BEALL, Agnes	DEC 27 1819
ERSKINE, Agnes	MARTIN, Tobias	MAR 27 1826
ERSKINE, Elizabeth	RHEA, Daniel	JUL 16 1821
ERSKINE, Elizabeth	DENNISON, William	DEC 29 1836
ERSKINE, Robert	HARPER, Elizabeth	JAN 24 1812
ERSKINE, Sarah J.	MUDD, Ignatius	SEP 16 1839
ERSKINE, Sophia Elizabeth	CROOKS, Alexr. W.	JAN 11 1837
ERSLIN, William	SLYE, Elizabeth	NOV 23 1842
ERTEL, Margaret	GLICK, John C.	AUG 03 1854
ERVIN, George H.	LYNCH, Rebecca Ellen	JUL 29 1851
ERVIN, James	BRANNAN, Sarah Ann	JUN 05 1819
ESCH, Michael	CHAFFILD, Margaret	JUL 03 1858
ESCHBACK, John	TREXLER, Margaret	OCT 02 1821
ESENBECK, Sophia	SIMS, Stephen	FEB 06 1817
ESHBACH, Elizabeth	COLLINS, George T.	AUG 23 1852
ESHUM, Ruth Ann	STANDFORD, Thomas	JAN 11 1831
ESKRIDGE, Hatley A.	COCKERILL, Harriet	NOV 10 1831
ESKRIDGE, Margaret F.	SIMS, John A.	JUL 10 1847
ESLIN, George	DOUGLASS, Anne	JUN 25 1856
ESLIN, George Ann	KIRBY, John	FEB 22 1834

District of Columbia Marriage Licenses, 1811-1858

ESLIN, James C.	LANHAM, Harriet E.	APR 19 1851
ESLIN, Mary Ann	HOLMEAD, William	MAY 10 1847
ESLIN, Peter	STREETS, Patsy	JUN 01 1837
ESLING, Georgeanna	STEWART, Daniel	MAY 15 1857
ESPERTES, Frances	PROSPERI, James	JUL 08 1848
ESPEY, Ann	GAITHER, James	SEP 09 1817
ESPEY, John	SCOTT, Ann	FEB 25 1813
ESPEY, John	TURTIN, Mary	MAY 08 1839
ESPEY, Martha	LEWIS, William S.	OCT 17 1848
ESPEY, Samuel C.	BURCH, Emily Ann	OCT 04 1845
ESPEY, Samuel C.	THOMPSON, Lydia Ann	NOV 15 1849
ESPINTA, John	WELSH, Mary	OCT 13 1853
ESPINTA, Josephine	PROSPERI, Charles	JUL 09 1853
ESPY, James	ROWE, Susan	JUN 20 1839
ESPY, Margaret	THORN, John H.	DEC 04 1849
ESPY, Mary Ann	STURGES, Handy J.	NOV 05 1845
ESSELBERNGE, Wilhelmina	FENCHT, Frederick	MAY 10 1856
ESSELBRUGGE, Hermann	RIESE, Louisa	FEB 22 1838
ESSEX, Eleanor V.	HEALD, John R.	NOV 13 1849
ESSEX, Elizabeth	FORREST, James	APR 08 1815
ESSEX, Ellen V.	TURNER, Weston B.	JAN 20 1857
ESSEX, James F.	LANG, Eliza Ann	SEP 13 1826
ESSEX, James F.	VonESSEN, Virginia S.	NOV 19 1839
ESSEX, Josiah F.	RITTER, Mary	JUN 16 1847
ESSEX, Josias	PHILIPS, Sarah	OCT 07 1823
ESSEX, Josias	FLOYD, Ruth	MAR 10 1831
ESSEX, Malvina	FORREST, Alexander F.	AUG 12 1847
ESSEX, Mary C.	WOOLS, Edward	DEC 14 1843
ESSEX, Susannah	BRYAN, Thomas	SEP 16 1815
ESSEX, William	MAZINGO, Ann	DEC 10 1823
ESTEL, Maria	RICE, Michael	JUL 24 1830
ESTEP, Alexander	MORIN, Barbara	NOV 01 1812
ESTEP, Hannah T.	GIBBONS, George F.	AUG 29 1855
ESTEP, Rebecca	SHAW, Joseph Ford	JAN 25 1834
ESTERLA, George	GASKINS, Mary E.	APR 16 1846
ESTERLEY, Daniel	GAI, Heloise	JUL 13 1842
ESTESS, Alexander	BRADY, Helen Ann	MAY 18 1839
ESTING, James	RIAND, Margaret	FEB 11 1819
ESTIS, Harriet	ESTIS, John A.	DEC 26 1853
ESTIS, John A.	ESTIS, Harriet	DEC 26 1853
ESTON, Marian	PREVAUX, John	MAR 13 1827
ESTREI, Catherine	BIGLER, John	FEB 14 1856
ETCHERN, Sarah	HUTCHINS, John	FEB 10 1821
ETCHISON, Elizabeth	HARRISON, George	AUG 23 1827
ETCHISON, Elizabeth A.	DAVIS, Thomas T.C.	DEC 30 1835
ETCHISON, L.E.	LANSDALE, Lizzie	APR 22 1858
ETHELL, Thomas	SHEID, Sarah	AUG 23 1825
ETTER, Ann	HEPBURN, Jeremiah	APR 24 1832
ETTER, Joseph	HYDE, Rachel	MAY 04 1840
ETTER, Joseph H.	CARR, Julia A.	MAY 20 1844
EUBA, Christopher	FISTER, Louisa	AUG 09 1842
EÜN, George	QUAIL, Susan	FEB 04 1858
EUSLIN, Eliza	RODBIRD, Absalom	MAR 12 1822
EUSTACE, William W.	LAUB, Martha V.	JUN 17 1851
EVAN, Ann	LEAB, Frederick	MAY 08 1822
EVANS, Abby J.	WATERS, William E.	OCT 01 1855
EVANS, Alexander	CORNWILL, Lucinda	MAR 29 1830
EVANS, Alexander H.	COXE, Maria Matilda	FEB 08 1844

District of Columbia Marriage Licenses, 1811-1858

EVANS, Amelia	MESSICK, George	MAY 10 1839
EVANS, Ann	BOONE, William	JAN 30 1851
EVANS, Ann V.	RUSSELL, Thomas	OCT 31 1857
EVANS, Benjamin	BEYER, Mary E.	JAN 16 1844
EVANS, Bernard	THOMPSON, Ann	AUG 18 1851
EVANS, Betsey	HANSON, Tobias	SEP 25 1820
EVANS, C.E.	OWENS, S.W.	JUL 31 1854
EVANS, Charlotte	DIES, Henry	FEB 18 1835
EVANS, Christianna	WOOD, Henry R.	JAN 22 1846
EVANS, Clifford	DALE, Mary Jane	FEB 07 1854
EVANS, Cora C.	CHILDS, S.D.	AUG 28 1858
EVANS, Daniel	TOOTELL, Rosana	SEP 11 1818
EVANS, David	BURNS, Lucinda (blk)	SEP 29 1830
EVANS, Deliah	EVANS, Job	MAY 17 1838
EVANS, Dolly	GRINDER, John	AUG 24 1837
EVANS, Dudley	PRINCY, Ann	APR 23 1814
EVANS, Edward, Jr.	REEDER, Rachel A.	SEP 20 1851
EVANS, Eliz.	McDOWELE, William	JUL 10 1813
EVANS, Elizabeth	O'DONNELL, John	AUG 02 1843
EVANS, Elizabeth	TALTEVAUX, Peter	FEB 04 1845
EVANS, Elizabeth	BRADLEY, Henry	AUG 25 1845
EVANS, Elizabeth	HUNTINGTEN, Thomas	SEP 02 1851
EVANS, Elizabeth	SULLIVAN, Elijah	DEC 16 1851
EVANS, Elizabeth	GESSFORD, Charles	OCT 05 1852
EVANS, Elizabeth (blk)	TAYLOR, William	APR 19 1849
EVANS, Ellen L.	DALE, George M.	JUL 07 1853
EVANS, Evan	CRUITT, Catherine E.	FEB 20 1847
EVANS, Frances L.	TREE, Jos. B.	FEB 14 1850
EVANS, French T., Rev.	O'NEALE, Georgi Ann C.	JUL 23 1829
EVANS, George	McLAIN, Nancy	JUN 06 1812
EVANS, George Anna Jackson	DOUGHERTY, Hugh	AUG 22 1846
EVANS, George W.	SCHMEDLEY, Mary Ann	SEP 05 1844
EVANS, Georgiana	LEEMAN, William E.	NOV 19 1857
EVANS, Harriott	HAYS, Charles Harrison	JUN 16 1831
EVANS, Hetely D.	PLANTT, Mary C.	JUN 04 1835
EVANS, Jacintha	GIVENS, John Henry	APR 23 1831
EVANS, James	BARNES, Mary Ann	OCT 26 1835
EVANS, James	WOODPID, Jane C.	OCT 23 1856
EVANS, James T.	EVANS, Rachel	JAN 02 1835
EVANS, Jesse	ENSEY, Elizabeth	NOV 07 1814
EVANS, Job	EVANS, Deliah	MAY 17 1838
EVANS, John	TAYLOR, Sarah	JUL 22 1826
EVANS, John	JENKINS, Susan	JAN 14 1833
EVANS, John	MILLS, Sarah Z.	MAY 16 1835
EVANS, John	PLANT, Mary Casandas	JUN 04 1835
EVANS, John	PAYNE, Cecelia	JUN 23 1840
EVANS, John D.	NESMITH, Isabella	NOV 05 1846
EVANS, John E.	LAWRENSON, Sophia S.	JAN 26 1854
EVANS, John K.	BRUSH, Mary Ann	MAY 04 1818
EVANS, John Thomas	BOWIE, Lucinda	SEP 29 1823
EVANS, John Thomas	HENDERSON, Mary Jane	JAN 13 1848
EVANS, Johnson	BRADSHAW, Elizabeth	MAY 19 1837
EVANS, Joseph	LEWIS, Nancy	AUG 21 1813
EVANS, Joseph T.	PHILLIPS, Sarah M.	OCT 28 1854
EVANS, Josephine	DAVIS, James	MAY 15 1841
EVANS, Josephine	DeVAUGHN, John T.	SEP 21 1846
EVANS, Julia A.	CANNON, William P.	NOV 06 1846
EVANS, Julian	EVINS, Francis	DEC 07 1836

District of Columbia Marriage Licenses, 1811-1858

EVANS, Lidie	BRATCHER, Litleton	JUN 01 1839
EVANS, Lotty	HART, John W.	MAY 16 1853
EVANS, Lucy M.	INGLE, Joseph	MAY 02 1818
EVANS, Margaretta L.	BENNETT, Thomas S.	MAY 19 1813
EVANS, Maria	DeKRAFT, Edward	MAY 10 1814
EVANS, Martha	BAKER, John	MAY 06 1847
EVANS, Mary	REYNOLDS, Thomas	APR 11 1812
EVANS, Mary	GRINDER, Anthony	DEC 29 1836
EVANS, Mary	LYNCH, William	NOV 20 1853
EVANS, Mary A. (blk)	PERRY, Chas. W.	NOV 07 1856
EVANS, Mary Ann	COLE, James	SEP 05 1821
EVANS, Mary Ann	HAYS, Levi	FEB 15 1830
EVANS, Mary Cath.	HENDLEY, John N.	OCT 18 1849
EVANS, Mary E.	JOHNSTON, John F.	JUN 07 1856
EVANS, Mary Virginia	LODGE, Edward	AUG 16 1851
EVANS, Paul R.	BROWN, Emma	JAN 22 1855
EVANS, Peter	JOHNSON, Betsey	JUN 01 1839
EVANS, Philip	MIDDLETON, Mary	MAR 27 1816
EVANS, Rachel	EVANS, James T.	JAN 02 1835
EVANS, Rebecca	SPALDING, James	AUG 11 1814
EVANS, Rebecca	SAYRES, James	AUG 23 1817
EVANS, Rebecca	BROWN, Christopher	MAY 09 1825
EVANS, Rebecca	ASHTON, William	JUL 21 1856
EVANS, Richard	SMITHLY, Barbara	DEC 08 1856
EVANS, Sarah	ELLIOTT, Jonathan	MAY 03 1813
EVANS, Sarah Ann	MARBURY, Thomas	FEB 02 1826
EVANS, Sarah Ann	MIDDLETON, James Henry	MAR 10 1831
EVANS, Sarah Ann	LEHMANOWSKI, Lewis F.	NOV 18 1833
EVANS, Sarah Frances	SHACKLEFORD, John	SEP 28 1854
EVANS, Susan	BENNETT, William	JUN 27 1854
EVANS, Susan Ann	BAYLYS, Pain	SEP 08 1825
EVANS, Susan Ann	BAYLISS, William P.	JUN 14 1827
EVANS, T.H.	HOWELL, Emily E.	AUG 03 1847
EVANS, Thomas [Dr.]	CHALMERS, Dorothy Ann	JAN 10 1828
EVANS, Thomas	HENDERSON, Prisila (blk)	MAR 24 1838
EVANS, Thomas	VERMILLION, Rebecca	JUL 17 1855
EVANS, Tillitha	BRADSHAW, Liton	SEP 30 1837
EVANS, Virginia	YOUNG, John T.	JUN 26 1849
EVANS, Walter	PARSONS, Maria	JUN 16 1819
EVANS, Walter	EDELIN, Matilda Jane	AUG 13 1845
EVANS, William	HUTCHINS, Tilley	AUG 01 1814
EVANS, William	KNOBLOCK, Jane	DEC 24 1827
EVANS, William T.	ANDERSON, Josephine L.	OCT 27 1853
EVELEY, Artimesa	GINGLE, James M.	JUN 23 1848
EVENS, Eliza Jane	STEURT, Samuel J.	JUN 03 1845
EVENS, Thomas F.	WALTERS, Lavenia A.	FEB 08 1849
EVERETT, Charles	KING, Sarah	JUN 10 1814
EVERETT, Charles, Jr.	DUNDAS, Harriet H.	MAR 13 1851
EVERETT, John Stanfield	FREEMAN, Ann Rebecca	JUL 02 1851
EVERETT, Rebecca	CLARKE, John F.	OCT 05 1835
EVERHART, John	McDANIEL, Ann	JUN 13 1820
EVERLY, Wm.	MAGRUDER, Ann E.V.	SEP 20 1854
EVERSON, Ann	PERRY, Stephen	FEB 01 1817
EVINS, Ann R.	NORRIS, Charles A.	SEP 18 1852
EVINS, Francis	EVANS, Julian	DEC 07 1836
EVISON, Lydia	COLE, Levi P.	SEP 30 1815
EWALD, John	SHAINING, Katharine	OCT 11 1855
EWELL, Cordelia B.	KINGMAN, Eliab	DEC 04 1828

District of Columbia Marriage Licenses, 1811-1858

EWELL, James B.	DOUGLAS, Sophia	JAN 14 1813
EWELL, Jesse [Dr.]	MacGREGOR, Ellen M.	OCT 23 1827
EWELL, John S.	McGREGOR, Helen W.	NOV 01 1852
EWELL, Martha	DAVIS, Charles W.	SEP 04 1851
EWELL, Olivia F.	MARTINDALE, Henry W.	DEC 06 1826
EWERS, Eliphalit	RODGERS, Sarah Ann	NOV 09 1837
EWING, Caroline	BRYAN, James M.	DEC 12 1848
EWING, Charles H., Rev.	PAGE, Charlotte E.	NOV 04 1845
EWING, Ellen B.	SHERMAN, William T.	MAY 01 1850
EWING, Hugh B.	YOUNG, Henrietta E.	JUL 31 1858
EWING, James	COLLINS, Mary	APR 08 1820
EWING, John	HASTINS, Elizabeth	NOV 12 1842
EWTHEY, George W.	MATTHEWS, Ann R.	NOV 09 1852
EYRE, Henry	HOLLAND, Eliza Ann	DEC 17 1856
EYRE, Lewis	SMALLWOOD, Mahala Elizabeth	JAN 01 1850
EYSBY, William	SEMMES, Elizabeth	FEB 24 1813

District of Columbia Marriage Licenses, 1811-1858

F

Name	Spouse	Date
FABRIGUE, Edward	MILLER, Eliza	AUG 11 1830
FADELEY, Jacob, Jr.	GOSSUM, Charity Ann	DEC 30 1822
FADELEY, James	GRAY, Virginia	OCT 23 1855
FADEWILKE, Wm.	DeGILSE, Louisa	AUG 19 1822
FAFF, Mary	BOSWELL, Wm. R.	JUL 19 1846
FAGAN, Ann	BROWN, John	SEP 09 1820
FAGAN, Ann	ELLIS, John	DEC 03 1840
FAGAN, Arebela	SERRIN, James H.	JAN 25 1855
FAGAN, Asa	PADGETT, Jane	OCT 16 1823
FAGAN, Bridget	McMANUS, William	AUG 27 1853
FAGAN, Catharine	BRANNAN, John	MAY 26 1853
FAGAN, Daniel	MURPHY, Ann	AUG 16 1817
FAGAN, Eliza	KINDSLEY, James	DEC 01 1821
FAGAN, Eliza A.	MURRAY, John	FEB 14 1831
FAGAN, Ellen	KELLY, Matthew	MAY 08 1852
FAGAN, Emaline (blk)	NEALE, Horatio	APR 05 1843
FAGAN, George	IRONSIDE, Mary Hellen	OCT 28 1830
FAGAN, Jane	PARKER, William	JAN 19 1833
FAGAN, Jane C.	SHYNE, Michael R.	JUN 10 1847
FAGAN, Josephine A.	McCARTY, Robert	JUL 28 1845
FAGAN, Mary	PHILLIPS, David S.	JUN 03 1840
FAGAN, Mary	BARCLAY, James	OCT 30 1849
FAGAN, Mary Jane	MOLL, John Randolph	JUL 20 1857
FAGAN, Mary M.	FLETCHER, Jas. L.	JUN 29 1837
FAGAN, Mary M.	SHYNE, Michael R.	JUN 25 1838
FAGAN, Matilda	BOTELER, Thomas	OCT 06 1818
FAGAN, Nicholas	NODDY, Mary Ann	AUG 15 1837
FAGAN, Patrick	LEE, Eliza B.	SEP 17 1853
FAHERTY, Jane E.	MATTHEWS, Edward T.	NOV 16 1857
FAHERTY, John P.	CATON, Eliza J.	JAN 20 1852
FAHERTY, William P.	TALBOT, Eliza	MAY 21 1836
FAHEY, Ann M.	RAINEY, Samuel	SEP 26 1826
FAHEY, Bridget	MALONEY, Edward	JUL 01 1852
FAHEY, Eliza	LEONARD, Michael	NOV 29 1855
FAHEY, Timothy	LALLEY, Mary	MAY 16 1857
FAHL, Ann	SCHMIDT, Jacob	JAN 05 1854
FAHRMAER, Peter	VENCISH, Mactalene	MAY 30 1857
FAIR, Elizabeth	WRIGHT, James	SEP 27 1827
FAIRALL, Joseph F.	JOHNSON, Sarah C.	AUG 16 1856
FAIRALL, Sarah J.	HICKMEN, Jeremiah	MAY 02 1856
FAIRBANKS, Francis P.	SPERRY, Warden W.	OCT 27 1857
FAIRBANKS, George M.	CLARKE, Jane	FEB 26 1852
FAIRELLY, John W., Jr.	WIDDICOMB, Gertrude	OCT 21 1856
FAIRFAX, Benjn. F.	STONE, Mary E.	DEC 13 1855
FAIRFAX, Caroline E.	SANDERS, William G.	MAR 01 1838
FAIRFAX, Emily C.	WHITTLE, Francis	MAY 12 1848
FAIRFAX, James B.	STONE, Sarah B.	AUG 13 1853
FAIRFIELD, George A.	MOORE, Fanny C.	OCT 03 1855
FAIRGRIEVE, Elizabeth	McTAGGART, Thomas	NOV 21 1843
FAISS, Damian	WEBER, Josephine	MAY 01 1841
FAITHFUL, Ann	DONIPHAN, Thornton A.	DEC 19 1844
FAITHFUL, George W.	WILLIAMS, Ann S.	JUN 08 1826
FAKEY, Catharine	PEAKS, John L.	OCT 05 1822
FALCONER, Ellen	ECKART, Henry	NOV 22 1852
FALCONER, Ralph J.	ELLIS, Susan	MAY 05 1840
FALCONER, Wm. H.	BOTELER, Mary A.J.	JAN 07 1856

District of Columbia Marriage Licenses, 1811-1858

FALCUNER, William K.	BRYAN, Mary Elizth.	MAY 04 1846
FALENSTEIN, Elizabeth	KNATZ, Conrad	AUG 11 1855
FALES, Ferolin Amelia	TREADWAY, Louis Demas	MAY 11 1852
FALES, Maria Louisa	WOOD, John	JUN 02 1856
FALES, Nathan W.	MAYO, Elizabeth [Mrs.]	JUN 03 1823
FALES, Nathan W.	SHANKS, Eliza	OCT 02 1845
FALES, William R.	BRADLEY, Mary E.	JAN 03 1856
FALION, John	HUGHES, Bridget	APR 14 1856
FALKNY, Jacob	HICKEY, Priscilla	MAY 23 1816
FALLEN, Mary M.	REED, John	NOV 23 1843
FALLON, Mary	PHILLIPS, Thomas	APR 28 1856
FALLS, Alexander J.	RITCHIE, Ella C.	JUN 15 1857
FANLAC, Adolphus	McDONALD, Mary Ann	SEP 17 1833
FANNING, Ann	DOLAN, Patrick	FEB 26 1857
FANNING, John	SEDWICK, Ann	MAR 31 1832
FANT, Hamilton G.	HELLEN, Josephine	MAY 16 1853
FANT, Henry T.	MORGAN, Louisa A.	JUL 13 1852
FAR, Thursday Ann	ROBEY, Peter	AUG 03 1836
FARBER, Mary Ann	DeRODIER, Phillebert	OCT 29 1816
FARISH, Robert O.	YATES, Mary E.	JAN 12 1854
FARISH, William F.	GOGGIN, Marcelina	MAY 19 1852
FARLAND, Harriott	BARRY, John	JUL 15 1827
FARLAND, John	FENWICK, Margaret	JUN 16 1818
FARLAND, William M.	BELL, Mary	MAR 11 1825
FARLEY, Edward W.	TURNER, Laura A.	DEC 10 1851
FARLEY, John	PEARSON, Ann Maria	MAY 15 1838
FARMER, Alfred D.	DUGAN, Susan	SEP 20 1855
FARMER, Mary	LEWIS, Joseph	NOV 20 1854
FARMER, Peter A.	LYNCH, Francis A.	NOV 14 1857
FARNAM, Elizabeth	HIGGIN, James	JUN 01 1818
FARNHAM, R. [Robert]	BLANCHARD, Jane	NOV 21 1836
FARNUM, Jane Elizabeth	RODGERS, John Wesley	MAY 31 1855
FARQUHAR, G.S. [Granville]	SMITH, Emily W.	SEP 30 1834
FARR, Abner C.	O'NEALE, Susan	SEP 04 1834
FARR, Alzira	BENSON, John	JUN 29 1840
FARR, Barbara	VERMILION, Joshua N.	OCT 20 1825
FARR, Elenora	GRAY, Basil	FEB 09 1835
FARR, Eliza	KING, Benjamin	NOV 02 1844
FARR, Eliza Ann	MOORE, Mudecai	MAY 10 1845
FARR, Elizabeth	WHITEHOUSE, Walter E.	JUL 14 1832
FARR, George	LYON, Julia E.	AUG 01 1855
FARR, James W.	BICKSLER, Jane E.	MAY 30 1856
FARR, Jane E.	BURR, John R.	OCT 26 1841
FARR, John B.	DAVIDSON, Clementia	MAY 13 1856
FARR, Julia A.	JOHNSON, Thomas T.	NOV 03 1851
FARR, Lavinia V.	COLEMAN, Charles W.	OCT 03 1853
FARR, Louisa	BRADY, Basil	MAY 09 1842
FARR, Malachi	OWENS, Amelia E.	DEC 14 1854
FARR, Malchi	HAYES, Amelia	JAN 08 1839
FARR, Margaret Ann	MOORE, James Henry	JAN 31 1854
FARR, Penelope	SKINNER, William	SEP 26 1812
FARR, Rebecca	CLARKE, Alexander	OCT 24 1814
FARR, Sarah Ann	WHITEHOUSE, Walter E.	APR 26 1834
FARR, William	CALVERT, Cidney	OCT 07 1834
FARRAGUT, James	MUNROE, Susan	AUG 17 1842
FARRAL, Mary	BARTON, James	FEB 02 1856
FARRALL, Ellen	CARRAHER, Thomas	JUL 26 1858
FARRALL, Sarah	TUCKER, William	OCT 24 1833

District of Columbia Marriage Licenses, 1811-1858

FARRAN, Terrence	DALTON, Mary	MAY 06 1846
FARRAR, John S.	HUTCHINSON, Mary Ellen	JUL 09 1836
FARREE, Lydia	BROWN, David	MAR 06 1828
FARREL, John	TURNER, Elizabeth	AUG 22 1826
FARREL, Mary	TOWSON, Joshua	JUL 29 1817
FARREL, Susanna	POWER, Thomas	APR 06 1836
FARRELL, Ann	BRONSON, Simeon D.	JAN 20 1853
FARRELL, Ann	DELACEY, John	JUN 25 1858
FARRELL, Bridgett	McNARHANY, Edward	JAN 03 1824
FARRELL, Caroline	BOYER, Frederick	AUG 01 1836
FARRELL, Catherine	MONIHAN, John	MAY 14 1857
FARRELL, Eliza	O'CALLAHAN, Cornelius	APR 27 1815
FARRELL, Harriet	WEBB, Albert J.	NOV 19 1846
FARRELL, John	RIDGWAY, Verlinda	JAN 13 1853
FARRELL, John	DUFFEY, Bridget	MAR 18 1853
FARRELL, Liddia	BUCKINGHAM, Caleb	AUG 08 1820
FARRELL, Lucinda Ann	BURCH, Thomas	MAY 12 1835
FARRELL, Maria	BYRNE, Christopher	JUL 01 1816
FARRELL, Mary	DREW, John	OCT 15 1853
FARRELL, Mary	KARR, William	DEC 22 1855
FARRELL, Mary Ann	WILDEY, Richard, Jr.	MAY 06 1820
FARRELL, Mary Ann	KEATING, Thomas P.	APR 26 1853
FARRELL, Susannah	FRENCH, Ignatius	AUG 04 1818
FARREYHOLD, Sarah S.	DEW, John W.	OCT 02 1846
FARRIS, Israel	SHEARLOCK, Nancy	JUN 19 1813
FARRIS, Julia Ann (blk)	PAYNE, Daniel A.	JAN 05 1847
FARRIS, William	CONNELLY, Margaret	APR 19 1815
FARSON, William	COLCLAZER, Mary Ann	DEC 29 1818
FASNAUGHT, George	BARNS, Mary Ellen	DEC 11 1849
FASNAUGHT, Margaret	TUDGE, William	AUG 10 1854
FASTNACHT, Sophie	COOK, Charles Jacob	MAY 01 1849
FATIO, America	PEDRICK, John C.	AUG 01 1854
FATIO, Lewis Charles Francis	BURCHE, America G.E.	JUN 26 1841
FATTREL, Jacob	TRACER, Sally	SEP 03 1822
FAUGHMAN, Dorothy	HOFFMAN, Mathias	FEB 24 1854
FAUKMAN, Margaret	RENNIKER, Henry	APR 05 1849
FAULCONER, John W.	WARING, Elizabeth	OCT 06 1845
FAULKNER, Eliza	REINTZEL, William Henry	JAN 04 1853
FAULKNER, Joseph	LANHAM, Julia A.	JAN 06 1852
FAULKNER, Michael	PIKE, Ann	DEC 19 1820
FAULKNER, Ophelia E.	DANIEL, John T.	OCT 05 1854
FAUNCE, William	STEWART, Frances	JUL 17 1858
FAUSH, Sarah Ann	McDONNELL, Thomas	APR 30 1835
FAVIER, Aezricol	BOULER, Emelie	OCT 21 1828
FAVIER, Agrigicole	MARCHAL, Albertine	SEP 05 1844
FAVIER, Honorine	JARDIN, Armand	SEP 22 1849
FAVIER, Malvina R.L.	CLEMENTS, Richard J.	JAN 31 1856
FAWCETT, David	LYDANE, Sarah Ann	FEB 14 1855
FAWCETT, Thomas	McWILLIAM, Isabella	JUN 09 1858
FAWSETT, Asbury F.	MEANS, Ann Eliza	SEP 13 1856
FAY, Ann	CHARLES, Albert	NOV 04 1851
FAY, Catharine	JOHNSON, Robert	NOV 21 1833
FAY, Mary J.	MELCHER, Andrew D.	APR 20 1831
FEAMAN, George H.	HOYE, Ann Virginia	SEP 15 1853
FEARSON, Ann Maria	SMITH, Alexander M.	AUG 30 1845
FEARSON, Christopher C.	LUCAS, Mary E.	MAY 14 1855
FEARSON, Henry	LEWIS, Mary Jane	JUN 15 1841
FEARSON, John W.	BARNES, Marietta	JUN 17 1840

District of Columbia Marriage Licenses, 1811-1858

FEARSON, Mary Lizzie	JONES, Fred W.	JAN 03 1858
FEARSON, Samuel	MECCUM, Elizabeth	NOV 23 1824
FEARSON, Samuel J.	THECKER, Mary E.	FEB 04 1850
FEATHERSTONBAUGH, James D.	CHAPMAN, Emily	JAN 17 1844
FEBREY, John E.	BALL, Mary F.	DEC 30 1854
FECHTIE, Alcinda B.	ENGLISH, David, Jr.	SEP 18 1830
FECHTIG, Louis R.	TRAVERS, Elizabeth H.	FEB 06 1849
FECHTY, Levi R.	TAYLOR, Mary L.	FEB 05 1850
FEDDON, Andrew F.	COLE, Georgiana	AUG 24 1855
FEDLINE, James A.	BARNES, Mary Ann	SEP 01 1831
FEENEY, Mary	SWEENY, Daniel	JUL 18 1856
FEENEY, Sarah	CLANSEY, Peter	SEP 14 1853
FEENY, Mary	JUDGE, John	JAN 15 1853
FEEVERS, James E.	WHITTLE, Ann R.	SEP 29 1856
FEGARRO, Antonio	KELLYS, Sarah	MAY 13 1824
FEGLER, John	HOEHN, Nette	NOV 04 1854
FEGUSON, John W.	HENRY, Sarah Ann	DEC 22 1851
FEHR, Augustin	WINDELSTAIR, Johanna	NOV 19 1832
FELAN, Elizabeth	GUTHRIE, John	JUN 21 1823
FELIUS, Frederick	SHECKELLS, Sarah	MAR 23 1835
FELIX, Michael I.	LEKAVIER, Adelade	FEB 11 1854
FELKINNIN, F.	HERNIR, Christine B.	APR 14 1856
FELLENGER, Augusta	KEPPLER, Gregory	APR 22 1858
FELSON, Alfred	JENKINS, Margaret (blk)	APR 13 1831
FELSON, Harriot (blk)	TAYLOR, Isaac	DEC 11 1833
FELVEY, Daniel	MACK, Mary	JUN 04 1852
FENCHT, Frederick	ESSELBERNGE, Wilhelmina	MAY 10 1856
FENDALL, Lucy Eleanor	MILLER, Bernard J.	JAN 31 1837
FENDLEY, Joseph J.	HOOVER, Sarah	FEB 04 1852
FENDLEY, Matilda	BOHRER, Benjamin	MAY 22 1826
FENDLEY, Sarah Ann	REEKER, Alexander	DEC 06 1832
FENDNER, Johanna	LAUBSCHER, John	SEP 29 1856
FENDNER, Louisa C.A.	SCHLEVOGT, Geo. F.J.	SEP 10 1855
FENDRICH, Xavier	CUNNINGHAM, Mary E.	JUN 14 1853
FENESEY, Sarah	DAVIS, Wesley	AUG 31 1844
FENLEY, Susan	JERVIS, Henry	DEC 02 1812
FENNEGAN, Elizabeth	NEARY, Thomas	JUN 28 1839
FENNEL, Eliza	CONROY, James	OCT 30 1852
FENNELY, Ann	MELLEDY, John	JAN 14 1852
FENNER, John P.	GARDNER, Francis D.	OCT 03 1819
FENNON, Bridget	MAHER, Dennis	OCT 07 1852
FENTON, Catharine	BUGGY, Patrick	OCT 23 1844
FENTON, Charles	MILLARD, Mary	SEP 20 1855
FENTON, Daniel	WATSON, Martha	JAN 18 1854
FENTON, Elizth. G.	DARLEY, Frank	AUG 23 1851
FENTON, James L.	ROBINSON, Martha	JUL 12 1858
FENTON, Jeremiah	CURTIN, Elizabeth	JUN 16 1824
FENTON, Robert W.	MOUNT, Sarah Ellen	FEB 19 1856
FENTON, William	RASER, Eliza	JUL 22 1850
FENTON, William H.	WALKER, Cordelia	DEC 01 1857
FENTRESS, Augustus	O'NEAL, Harriet	APR 25 1857
FENWICK, Benjamin I.	SCHWRAR, Mary E.	SEP 12 1848
FENWICK, Eleanor	KROUSE, Christian	SEP 28 1816
FENWICK, Eliza	HOWARD, George Ward	OCT 30 1833
FENWICK, Eliza A.	HILL, Richard T.	JAN 17 1854
FENWICK, Elizabeth E.	BEALL, Leven Covintgon	APR 06 1858
FENWICK, Elizabeth O.	BUCKLEY, James S.	JAN 13 1857
FENWICK, Francis	POTTER, Melvina	MAR 20 1834

District of Columbia Marriage Licenses, 1811-1858

FENWICK, Francis	MICKUM, Susan	JUN 27 1839
FENWICK, Francis X.	SWEENY, Thresa	FEB 17 1849
FENWICK, John	NEWTON, Ann	MAY 14 1814
FENWICK, John H.	SCOTT, Jane M.	JUN 19 1850
FENWICK, Margaret	FARLAND, John	JUN 16 1818
FENWICK, Margaret	SPEIDEN, Robert	JAN 22 1824
FENWICK, Mary	COX, James	OCT 20 1832
FENWICK, Mary Ann	VanRISWICK, John	JAN 04 1841
FENWICK, Mary E.	SMITH, Joseph A.	NOV 12 1856
FENWICK, Philip	STEWART, Margaret	JAN 04 1815
FENWICK, Richd. Washington	HILIARD, Eliza	OCT 05 1826
FENWICK, Robert W.	HILLYARD, Sarah E.	JAN 05 1825
FENWICK, Sarah Jane	STEWART, Walter	OCT 04 1856
FENWICK, Susan	DANT, William	APR 05 1814
FENWICK, William A.	JOHNSON, Patronilla M.	OCT 04 1856
FEPLIN, Margaret B.	KROPP, Henry	FEB 09 1857
FERGASON, Caroline	DAVIS, David	JUN 12 1821
FERGUSON, Addison	JOHNSON, Elizabeth	APR 10 1827
FERGUSON, Ann	WINGERD, John P.	OCT 24 1818
FERGUSON, Ann	PRICE, Jehu	NOV 10 1835
FERGUSON, Ann (blk)	DULANEY, Caleb	APR 10 1837
FERGUSON, Benjamin	BERLE, Rebecca	MAR 25 1851
FERGUSON, Blanche	LACEY, Robert A.	JAN 27 1847
FERGUSON, Catherine	WEBSTER, William A.	SEP 30 1850
FERGUSON, Dennis	MORGAN, Ann	MAY 10 1838
FERGUSON, Eleanor Ann	HARRISON, Columbus	OCT 29 1842
FERGUSON, Eliza J.	FERGUSON, William P.	FEB 20 1839
FERGUSON, Eliza M.	SIMMS, John W.	APR 06 1852
FERGUSON, Elizabeth	McCAHAN, Samuel	FEB 10 1812
FERGUSON, Elizabeth	IRVINS, John J.	DEC 09 1813
FERGUSON, Elizabeth R.	DAVIS, John A.	JAN 14 1839
FERGUSON, Enos D.	BERRY, Ellen	OCT 01 1842
FERGUSON, James	MASON, Martha A. (blk)	NOV 30 1852
FERGUSON, James B.	DULEY, Elizabeth C.	APR 29 1839
FERGUSON, John B.	FUGITT, Francis	FEB 26 1846
FERGUSON, John H.	BROWN, Henrietta (blk)	JUL 07 1851
FERGUSON, John W.	BURNS, Mary Ann	OCT 30 1847
FERGUSON, Joseph	MORRIS, Sarah	JUL 17 1841
FERGUSON, Joseph	SCOTT, Maria (blk)	JAN 10 1854
FERGUSON, Julia V.	McLAUGHLIN, John	OCT 23 1851
FERGUSON, Margaret	SMEDLEY, Antone	APR 21 1851
FERGUSON, Mary	BASSETT, Sydney D.	JUL 27 1850
FERGUSON, Rezin	JONES, Mary	SEP 08 1830
FERGUSON, Robert	KILBERTH, Ann	SEP 14 1848
FERGUSON, Samuel	REED, Julia	MAY 17 1837
FERGUSON, Sarah Ann	PUMPHREY, Otho	NOV 16 1841
FERGUSON, Susanna	PERRY, Elisha	DEC 17 1851
FERGUSON, William	DOIG, Elizabeth	APR 15 1844
FERGUSON, William	DIVINE, Mary F.	JAN 19 1858
FERGUSON, William B.	HUTCHINSON, Mary B.	OCT 16 1833
FERGUSON, William J.	DAVIS, Harriet Ann (blk)	JUN 24 1850
FERGUSON, William P.	FERGUSON, Eliza J.	FEB 20 1839
FERGUSON, Wm. J.	JOHNSON, Emmeline V.	JUN 11 1856
FERGUSON, Worden H.	BELT, Amanda Melvina	SEP 05 1839
FERLY, Patrick	McDERMOTT, Ann	MAY 31 1853
FERRAILLES, Pierre	MARTIN, Marie A.	DEC 20 1845
FERRALL, Anne	RANSON, Stephen	MAR 30 1824
FERRALL, Cecilia	VANRIPEN, Harman J.	NOV 21 1842

District of Columbia Marriage Licenses, 1811-1858

FERRALL, Dennis	TASKER, Ann	AUG 05 1847
FERREE, Abraham	BROWN, Esther	NOV 24 1829
FERREE, Fanny M.	McKIM, Josiah F.	JUN 23 1858
FERREE, James L.	WILEY, Catherine Ann	AUG 29 1838
FERREE, Mary Ann	PIERCE, Samuel	SEP 17 1829
FERREL, Caroline	DADLY, George William	DEC 22 1851
FERRELL, Elizabeth	THOMPSON, Geo.	SEP 27 1821
FERRELL, Frances M.D.	CHEW, Edward B.	OCT 31 1845
FERRENS, Terrence	LANAGIN, Ann	JUL 10 1844
FERRER, Margaretta	GEER, Michael	FEB 13 1857
FERRIER, Susannah	HACKETT, Peter Alex.	DEC 09 1815
FERRILL, John W.	GIBSON, Caroline (blk)	MAY 13 1841
FERRIS, Ann Maria	HUDNALL, Roach M.	OCT 03 1853
FERRIS, Christiana	GUY, William B.	FEB 27 1838
FERRIS, Elizabeth N.	CLARKE, Wilbur	APR 12 1856
FERRIS, Emma J.	THOMPSON, Minor L.	FEB 07 1857
FERRIS, Henry	EDELEN, Mary Dade	MAY 31 1838
FERRIS, Margaret	KLOPFER, Benjamin	SEP 16 1841
FERRIS, Mary	WARDEN, William	JUN 28 1832
FERRIS, Plato	BeKROFFT, Julia Ann (blk)	OCT 16 1832
FERRIS, Susan	DRUCE, Isaac W.	AUG 26 1858
FERRY, Hugh	EDWARDS, Sarah	JUL 30 1840
FERRY, James Thomas	EDWARDS, Eliza	JAN 21 1845
FERTNER, Columbus	WILLIAMS, Georgianna	AUG 17 1850
FERTNER, Elizabeth	DICKEY, Robert D.	JAN 18 1853
FERTNEY, Edwin W.	THOMAS, Mary Ann	MAR 22 1838
FETZER, Jane	KELSEY, Judson R.	MAR 01 1855
FEUTER, Nicholas	TOWMY, Mary	APR 12 1834
FEVER, Nicholas	BALL, Verlinder	JAN 25 1827
FEY, Catherine	MURPHEY, Michael	FEB 18 1854
FICKETT, Sarah A.	HINES, Abram F.	JUN 19 1851
FIEG, Jacob	DIPPLE, Agusta	JUL 05 1854
FIELD, E.M.	FOX, Maria L.	MAY 16 1853
FIELD, George	LUGLEY, Sarah Jane	JUL 16 1852
FIELD, George W.	DELPHY, Sarah Ellenor Mariana	MAY 29 1858
FIELDING, John	BRONAUGH, Mary Elizabeth	DEC 22 1841
FIELDS, Amelia	THOMPSON, James	JUL 07 1823
FIELDS, Catharine	ORISON, Arthur	SEP 17 1823
FIELDS, Edward	BRASHEARS, Amelia	APR 15 1813
FIELDS, Elizabeth (blk)	JENKINS, George	APR 04 1851
FIELDS, Elizabeth Ann	MINNIS, John T.	SEP 22 1847
FIELDS, Ellen	SMOOT, William G.	MAY 21 1856
FIELDS, Henry	JACKSON, Adelaide F.	NOV 23 1847
FIELDS, Margaret	LOWE, Joseph	APR 03 1850
FIELDS, Mary	BARRY, Joseph O.	JUL 20 1815
FIELDS, Mary Ann	MILBURN, Wm. F.M.	SEP 21 1840
FIELDY, Bridget	HAMMILL, Patrick	SEP 23 1850
FIERBRON, Frederick	BRIDGETT, Christina	JUL 01 1856
FIERMANN, John Adam	DIPPEL, Louisa	JUN 21 1849
FIFE, William	BURK, Maria	APR 05 1820
FIFE, William	EASTON, Mary	MAY 11 1821
FIGLAY, Elizabeth	FOUNTAIN, Nicholas	MAY 14 1812
FILE, Stanley	MACKALL, Catharine	OCT 09 1851
FILICE, Mary	KING, William	JAN 06 1838
FILINS, Amanda	BEELER, Louis F.	FEB 01 1851
FILL, Rebecca Jane	GLOVER, David F.	MAR 24 1855
FILLEBROWN, Henry C.	PAINE, Margaret	MAY 31 1856
FILLEBROWN, Thomas S.	POTTS, Mary Eliza	NOV 04 1856

District of Columbia Marriage Licenses, 1811-1858

FILLEY, John	EASTEN, Mary	AUG 02 1822
FILLIS, Caroline	SHECKELLS, Samuel	JUN 14 1827
FILLIUS, Catharine	HARTMAN, George	APR 14 1819
FILLIUS, Elizabeth	MEAD, John	DEC 26 1834
FILLIUS, Jacob	MEAD, Elizabeth	JAN 06 1835
FILLIUS, Samuel	RICHARDSON, Matha E.	JUL 27 1858
FILLMORE, John H.	HYATT, Sarah	JUL 03 1849
FINACUM, Stokely	FLETCHER, Mary Elizabeth	AUG 26 1846
FINAGAN, Philip	DEREAME, Eliza	JUL 29 1845
FINCH, Elvira	MOORE, John L.	JUL 02 1853
FINCH, John	McDANIEL, Jane [Mrs.]	NOV 17 1834
FINCH, John S.	RIDGWAY, Ellen Ellen	MAY 22 1849
FINCH, Margaret A.	WEAVER, Erastus C.	NOV 23 1852
FINCH, William	STARR, Eliza Ann	OCT 13 1841
FINCH, William	GIBSON, Margaret A.	AUG 01 1850
FINCKEL, Caroline A.	DAVIS, Charles E.	APR 05 1852
FINDLEY, Samuel	EASTER, Mrs. Ann	MAY 22 1828
FINESY, Sarah	BLADEN, John	JUN 22 1844
FINK, Casper	HESS, Cornelia	DEC 01 1836
FINK, Casper	KINSEY, Barbara	OCT 01 1840
FINK, John	WILLIAMS, Maria B.	JUN 23 1853
FINK, Louisa	MISCEL, George N.	OCT 01 1855
FINKMANN, Conrad	EMMERT, Wilhelmine	MAY 27 1845
FINLAY, Jonathan S.	DARSER, Henrietta C.	AUG 02 1813
FINLAY, Orilla	GIRAUD, Augustus J.T.	NOV 30 1836
FINLEY, Henry	LUXUM, Mary Ann	JUL 19 1824
FINLEY, James J.	QUIGLEY, Mary E.	APR 17 1847
FINLEY, Mary Ann	FITZSIMMONS, Philip	FEB 14 1852
FINN, Ann	WELSH, Patrick	NOV 21 1856
FINN, Mary	HOLORAN, Thomas	AUG 05 1856
FINN, Matthew	EAGAN, Jane	DEC 02 1852
FINN, Matthew	ROURKE, Mary	NOV 29 1856
FINNEGAN, Martha Jane	EDWARDS, Charles	MAY 03 1851
FINNEL, Simon	CONROY, Ann	NOV 09 1844
FINNESY, Julia	DAVIS, William	FEB 07 1846
FINNEY, Alexander	HILL, Emeline	FEB 17 1853
FINNEY, Eleanor	PALMER, James	MAR 02 1841
FINNEY, John T.	MASS, Mary E.	MAY 17 1855
FINNEY, Mary Ann	BRUCE, Robert J.	MAR 18 1856
FINNIGAN, Charles	BEACH, Jane	NOV 02 1839
FINNIGAN, Philip	KEARIN, Sarah	JAN 11 1830
FINSCEY, James	THOMPSON, Nancy	JUL 12 1824
FIROE, Ephraim A.	BAGGITT, Ann E.A.	SEP 14 1852
FISCHER, Elizabeth	WOLF, John	DEC 10 1855
FISCHER, George Andras	HASSLER, Eva	MAR 18 1846
FISCHER, Harriot Ann	ZANTZINGER, William C.	JAN 16 1844
FISCHER, Hironius	KREPPEL, Anne	JUN 13 1850
FISCHER, Margaret	NOMANN, Caspar	JAN 15 1850
FISCHER, Susanna	DREISCH, Michael	SEP 24 1842
FISH, Elizabeth	ELLISON, William H.	JAN 23 1849
FISH, Lucinda	SHERWOOD, Archibald	NOV 19 1844
FISHER, Alexander	DOWELL, Emily	SEP 12 1827
FISHER, Ann	FORMAN, Joseph	DEC 31 1819
FISHER, Ann	MERCHANT, Richard	OCT 02 1837
FISHER, Ann R.	RICKETTS, James R.	DEC 04 1855
FISHER, Anna	JONES, William	JAN 16 1851
FISHER, Anna Palmer	BRYANT, Samuel Drake	APR 10 1824
FISHER, Catherine	FORNCUP, John	JUN 25 1853

District of Columbia Marriage Licenses, 1811-1858

FISHER, Charles	PHILIPPS, Margaret	OCT 26 1820
FISHER, Charles O.	HARVEY, Elizabeth	DEC 15 1842
FISHER, David	LUCAS, Charlott F.	APR 21 1845
FISHER, E.J.	CLAXTON, A.B.	JAN 05 1854
FISHER, Eliza	BAARE, Ferdinand Rudolph	FEB 24 1847
FISHER, Eliza	TEABOWER, John	JUL 28 1856
FISHER, Elizabeth	KELLER, Michael	DEC 18 1832
FISHER, Ellen Rebecca	EDWARDS, William W.	AUG 22 1843
FISHER, Emily	FRANK, Henry	DEC 13 1830
FISHER, George	MAHONY, Ann	APR 12 1819
FISHER, Henry	BARRETT, Ellen Ann	JUL 02 1851
FISHER, Jacob	DAWSON, Sarah (blk)	AUG 11 1828
FISHER, Jacob	PATTERSON, Emma	JUN 20 1855
FISHER, James H.	CRYER, Margaret E.	SEP 07 1850
FISHER, Jane Elizth.	PATTERSON, Alexander	JAN 28 1856
FISHER, John	PEERCE, Ann	FEB 24 1813
FISHER, John	FOGLE, Mary	NOV 27 1856
FISHER, Letty	BROWN, James	AUG 16 1821
FISHER, Louisa	HOUSEMAN, Charles	APR 12 1845
FISHER, Lucretia Alice	LOUIS, John E.	MAY 30 1855
FISHER, Lydia	AGER, Jones	JUL 19 1819
FISHER, Margaret	MOORE, Thomas	DEC 25 1818
FISHER, Marvin P.	GUNNELL, Mary E.	NOV 15 1848
FISHER, Mary J.E.F.	SOWDEN, John	JAN 04 1849
FISHER, Mary Jane	LIGHTELL, John B.O.H.	FEB 06 1843
FISHER, Morris	KING, Caroline	MAY 26 1853
FISHER, Rachel Ann	CHANEY, George T.	JAN 21 1847
FISHER, Richard J.	FOWLER, Henny	JAN 02 1822
FISHER, Roselie	BROWN, Calvin	MAR 13 1848
FISHER, Sally M.	KEMPER, Hugh T.	DEC 13 1855
FISHER, Sarah A. (blk)	BROWN, John H.	DEC 23 1852
FISHER, Sarah Ann	NIXON, Robert F.	FEB 27 1838
FISHER, Thomas J.	SIOUSSA, Charlotte M.	JUN 03 1845
FISHER, Vallee	TYLER, John	JUN 06 1855
FISHER, William	GUNTON, Harriet	FEB 22 1821
FISHER, William	WOLF, Sophia	FEB 16 1858
FISHER, William C.	JACOBS, Margaret Ann	JAN 22 1850
FISHER, William T.	SUMMERS, Ann Rebecca	NOV 24 1847
FISK, C.B.	BENDER, Mary E.	OCT 25 1837
FISKE, Richard H.	COSTIN, Harriet (blk)	NOV 19 1849
FISTAR, Mary	STINZING, Frederick	JAN 10 1853
FISTER, Ann	BERRY, John	OCT 24 1842
FISTER, John	WILLIAMS, Adeline	MAY 12 1832
FISTER, Louisa	EUBA, Christopher	AUG 09 1842
FISTER, Mary	DISTAR, Aloysius Peter	OCT 08 1853
FISTER, Mary Margt.	HAUPTMAN, Philip H.	NOV 10 1853
FISTER, Sarah E.	GOOD, William T.S.	JUN 20 1853
FITCH, Chauncey W. [Rev.]	WRIGHT, Mary	JUN 09 1829
FITCH, Chauncey W., Rev., Michigan	WRIGHT, Catherine B.	SEP 08 1842
FITCH, George K.	DUVALL, Clara V.	APR 20 1857
FITNAM, Thomas, Jr.	DANT, Rosella	SEP 10 1849
FITTEN, Margaret	GATES, Thomas	SEP 21 1844
FITTEN, Thomas	CROWLEY, Julia A.	JUN 28 1820
FITTEN, William Horatio	PULLIN, Sarah Hanson	SEP 14 1844
FITTON, Mary	HALL, William J.	AUG 23 1849
FITZ, Elizabeth	BARTLETT, Isaac	OCT 17 1818
FITZGERALD, Bridget	KELLY, Michael	JUL 31 1844
FITZGERALD, Catherine	TALTY, Michael	SEP 22 1836

District of Columbia Marriage Licenses, 1811-1858

FITZGERALD, David	SINON, Margaret	FEB 20 1844
FITZGERALD, David	JACKSON, Susan	APR 10 1850
FITZGERALD, David	BARRETT, Johanna	JUN 02 1855
FITZGERALD, David	HENNESSY, Margaret	AUG 15 1856
FITZGERALD, David	KENNEDY, Margaret	AUG 07 1858
FITZGERALD, Dennis	HARGAN, Mary	FEB 19 1855
FITZGERALD, Edmund	CHRISTOPHER, Mary Ann	APR 29 1825
FITZGERALD, Edward	RAGAN, Bridget	MAY 15 1852
FITZGERALD, Edward	BUCKLEY, Johanna	MAY 07 1853
FITZGERALD, Edward	RINE, Susan	FEB 02 1856
FITZGERALD, Ellen	JACKSON, Andrew	SEP 18 1850
FITZGERALD, Ellen	MURPHEY, John	AUG 07 1852
FITZGERALD, Ellen	SHAUSNESY, Michael	JAN 09 1855
FITZGERALD, Emily E.	JOHNSON, Henry L.	FEB 07 1856
FITZGERALD, Hanora	MOORE, Michael J.	FEB 01 1854
FITZGERALD, Honora	SULLIVAN, Dennis	JUN 25 1853
FITZGERALD, James	LLOYD, Margaret	FEB 16 1833
FITZGERALD, Johanna	O'BRIAN, Daniel	SEP 19 1844
FITZGERALD, Johanna	TURNER, John	SEP 26 1854
FITZGERALD, John	LYNCH, Catharine	NOV 14 1853
FITZGERALD, John	McLAUGHLIN, Anna	JUL 11 1854
FITZGERALD, John	NORMYLE, Catharine	JUN 12 1856
FITZGERALD, Margaret	LYSETT, John	FEB 14 1851
FITZGERALD, Margaret	MURPHY, Thomas	JUL 23 1851
FITZGERALD, Margaret	LYNCH, Martin	DEC 11 1851
FITZGERALD, Margaret	RYAN, John	NOV 04 1852
FITZGERALD, Mary	NELAGAN, John	APR 25 1844
FITZGERALD, Mary	HAYS, Nicholas	APR 26 1853
FITZGERALD, Mary	DRISCOLL, Dennis	SEP 11 1855
FITZGERALD, Mary Ann	QUAIL, Charles	FEB 04 1858
FITZGERALD, Michael	COLLINS, Margaret	SEP 22 1854
FITZGERALD, Michl.	MASON, Ellen	MAY 22 1854
FITZGERALD, Patrick	COLLINS, Ellin	JAN 01 1851
FITZGERALD, Patrick	CLEARY, Bridget	JAN 29 1855
FITZGERALD, Susan	CROSSFIELD, George	DEC 12 1855
FITZGERALD, Thomas	CONNELL, Julia	NOV 13 1851
FITZGERALD, Thomas	GORDON, Bridget	JAN 31 1853
FITZGERALD, Thomas	BROSNAHAM, Julia	JAN 27 1854
FITZGERALD, Thomas	KENNEHAN, Ann	DEC 02 1854
FITZGERALD, Timothy	LOONY, Hanora	OCT 01 1853
FITZGERALD, William	FRANCES, Mary	JUN 08 1826
FITZGERALD, William B.	SEMMES, Clara	NOV 02 1850
FITZGIVENS, Edmond	HAIFY, Margaret	JUN 02 1852
FITZHUE, Elizabeth (blk)	BOSTON, George	JAN 24 1854
FITZHUE, Wm. Henry	GREENWOOD, Mary Ann	FEB 28 1828
FITZHUGH, Annie	LOCKWOOD, Joshua W.	AUG 26 1857
FITZHUGH, Clem	BOWIE, Elizabeth (blk)	JAN 06 1844
FITZHUGH, Edmund	ROBERTS, Eliza A.	MAY 29 1818
FITZHUGH, Elizabeth (blk)	BOSTON, George	AUG 08 1854
FITZHUGH, Harriet L.	SIMPSON, Wm. G.M.	OCT 06 1836
FITZHUGH, John	TAYLOR, Martha Ann	AUG 26 1847
FITZHUGH, Margaretta	CORSE, M. Percival	JAN 10 1849
FITZHUGH, Mary Ann	McGINNISS, Frederick	JUL 29 1841
FITZHUGH, Mary Anne [Mrs.]	MORSELL, James S. [Hon.]	OCT 21 1829
FITZHUGH, Mary L.	PAGE, Quincy L.	DEC 03 1850
FITZHUGH, Richd. Henry	MARBURY, Mary Ann	SEP 02 1816
FITZHUGH, Robert	CARROLL, Maria	FEB 05 1833
FITZHUGH, Robert R.	HYDE, Anna E.	MAY 03 1849

District of Columbia Marriage Licenses, 1811-1858

FITZHUGH, Thomas L.	MILLIGAN, Isabella	DEC 17 1841
FITZHUGH, William H.	RAWLINGS, Mary V.	JUL 18 1848
FITZPATRICK, Andrew	MURPHY, Margt.	AUG 10 1853
FITZPATRICK, Bernard	McWILLIAMS, Mary	JUL 29 1853
FITZPATRICK, Ellen	HUALEY, John	FEB 04 1845
FITZPATRICK, Ellen	McKEON, John	SEP 04 1852
FITZPATRICK, Emma	SULLIVAN, William	JUN 12 1851
FITZPATRICK, Henrietta R.	HAMILTON, Edward M.	MAY 22 1854
FITZPATRICK, James	HIERLEHY, Margaret	JUN 01 1836
FITZPATRICK, James	LEAHEA, Catherine	NOV 18 1856
FITZPATRICK, James	BOURNE, Mary Jane	MAY 27 1857
FITZPATRICK, John	DOUGHERTY, Mary	JUN 30 1853
FITZPATRICK, John C.	HICKEY, Mary Cecelia	JUL 17 1827
FITZPATRICK, Mary	SMITH, Michael	OCT 28 1856
FITZPATRICK, Nelly	MURPHY, Cornelius	AUG 14 1848
FITZSIMMONS, Joanna	LYLES, Enoch	OCT 12 1840
FITZSIMMONS, John	LANIGAN, Johannah	OCT 05 1832
FITZSIMMONS, John	MURPHY, Ellen	AUG 16 1834
FITZSIMMONS, Philip	FINLEY, Mary Ann	FEB 14 1852
FITZSIMMONS, Sarah	CHALMERS, Anthony	MAR 12 1818
FLACK, Constandinus	KINZLER, Barbara	JAN 08 1834
FLACK, Franz	SCHEREZ, Elizabeth C.	SEP 05 1833
FLADE, Margaret	HEIL, George	JUN 17 1848
FLAGG, Lucas	RITTER, Maria	MAR 25 1854
FLAGG, Robert S.	HUGHES, Margaret A.	JAN 25 1853
FLAHAVIN, Michael	HARRAGAN, Bridget	APR 07 1858
FLAHERTY, Ann	NARMILE, John	FEB 17 1855
FLAHERTY, Ellen	CONNELL, Dennis	FEB 07 1852
FLAHERTY, Ellen	CASEY, John	MAR 23 1852
FLAHERTY, John	MURPHY, Ellen	NOV 22 1853
FLAHERTY, John	DeVAUGHN, Mary	NOV 14 1855
FLAHERTY, Mary	DONOVAN, John	NOV 14 1850
FLAHERTY, Mary	MALONE, Michael	OCT 07 1854
FLAHERTY, Mary	McCARTEY, Thomas	JUL 26 1858
FLAHERTY, Patrick	HESHUNS, Mary	SEP 06 1852
FLAHERTY, Patrick	HENWRIGHT, Julia	OCT 07 1854
FLAHERTY, Patrick	HESSIAN, Mary	APR 06 1855
FLAHERTY, William A.	STONE, Eliza	NOV 22 1848
FLANAGAN, Francis	BELL, Mary Ann	MAY 14 1835
FLANAGAN, Garrett	SAWYER, M.	MAR 27 1856
FLANAGAN, Luke	STEELE, Elizabeth	SEP 09 1830
FLANNAGAN, Bridget	WALL, John	AUG 27 1845
FLANNAGAN, Hannora	LYNCH, James	JUN 23 1841
FLANNAGAN, Mary	LISTON, James	DEC 11 1854
FLANNIGAN, Garret	KURL, Margaret	FEB 16 1836
FLANNIGAN, Mary	CASEY, John	SEP 13 1851
FLANNIGAN, Mary Ann	O'NEALE, Christopher	JUL 07 1840
FLANNIGAN, Thomas	CLUNE, Ann	NOV 23 1853
FLANY, John	CLANSY, Catharine	OCT 04 1854
FLARITY, Mary	PHELPS, George W.	NOV 11 1833
FLAVAHAN, Catharine	SUGRUA, Timothy	FEB 01 1853
FLECHNER, William	WEIGERT, Fredricka	MAY 24 1853
FLEET, Ann	CRUSOR, Edward	SEP 25 1844
FLEET, James H.	PETERS, Hermione C. (col'd)	APR 21 1845
FLEET, Maria (blk)	JOHNSON, Robert	DEC 28 1831
FLEET, Patience (blk)	GRANT, William V.	MAY 29 1835
FLEET, Serana	CARY, Isaa N.	APR 28 1830
FLEET, Thomas	JACKSON, Susan (blk)	JUL 08 1829

District of Columbia Marriage Licenses, 1811-1858

FLEETWOOD, Louis	WISE, Maria (blk)	DEC 26 1838
FLEISHELL, Sarah J.	OBOLD, Francis S.	OCT 10 1855
FLEMING, Bridget	CLANSEY, Michael	AUG 04 1853
FLEMING, Catherine	RAGAN, Patrick	OCT 21 1853
FLEMING, John	HERRITY, Mary	AUG 13 1821
FLEMING, John	DOYLE, Ellen	JAN 26 1856
FLEMING, Margaret	McCARTY, Timothy	DEC 30 1851
FLEMING, Mary	McCORMICK, Hugh	MAY 11 1844
FLEMING, Michael	CUSHING, Johanna	JAN 21 1853
FLEMING, Michael	KEATING, Ellen	JUL 10 1858
FLEMING, Paterick	TAYLOR, Eliza	FEB 13 1843
FLEMING, Patrick	HIGGINS, Hellen	JAN 15 1856
FLEMING, Patrick	SHARK, Ann	MAR 22 1858
FLEMINGS, Catharan	CARRIGAN, John	AUG 28 1855
FLEMMING, Alice	BARTON, Richard C.	FEB 24 1849
FLEMMING, Ellen	SULLIVAN, Patrick	FEB 18 1857
FLEMMING, Laurence	MORGAN, Frances	FEB 17 1852
FLEMMING, Patrick	SHARK, Ann	APR 20 1858
FLEMMON, Francis	CRANE, Patience	JUN 27 1812
FLEMMON, Patrick	HIGGINS, Ellen	JAN 07 1857
FLENER, William	WINBERGER, Olivia	NOV 28 1833
FLENG, James	LENMAN, Deborah	DEC 21 1820
FLENINGER, Catharine	AMAN, Jos. Andrew	FEB 11 1854
FLENNER, Mary A.	GLADMON, Theophulus H.	NOV 10 1857
FLENNERY, Annie	CULLERTON, Thomas	JUN 26 1852
FLETCHER, Ann (blk)	BUTLER, Walter	NOV 29 1841
FLETCHER, Arthur W.	POOR, Elizabeth I.	DEC 29 1847
FLETCHER, Basil	SHORTER, Ann (blk)	DEC 30 1848
FLETCHER, Catherine	CONNER, Michael	DEC 27 1848
FLETCHER, Cintha	PECK, Luther C.	MAR 02 1839
FLETCHER, Cornelia	CLAY, Joseph A.	MAR 12 1835
FLETCHER, Dianna (blk)	SMITH, William M.	NOV 11 1847
FLETCHER, Eliza	PARRY, Henry	OCT 09 1856
FLETCHER, Elizabeth	BOSWELL, Wm. H.	JUL 05 1821
FLETCHER, Elizabeth	LEONARD, William	JUN 05 1843
FLETCHER, Elizabeth (blk)	LOWE, Jeremiah	JUN 15 1836
FLETCHER, Elizabeth (blk)	SCHANKS, Peter	JAN 01 1853
FLETCHER, Ellen	SMALLWOOD, Moses	DEC 09 1819
FLETCHER, Ellen (blk)	SIMMS, William	APR 17 1844
FLETCHER, Ellen (blk)	BORLAND, Thomas	DEC 23 1851
FLETCHER, Geo. [Capt.]	BRISCOE, Lucinda M.	SEP 17 1822
FLETCHER, Henrietta (blk)	BROOKS, Albert	DEC 05 1853
FLETCHER, Henry	SMALLWOOD, Elizabeth	DEC 09 1831
FLETCHER, James A.	DEMAINE, Mary A.	SEP 15 1857
FLETCHER, Jane	CAMMEL, Marlborough (blk)	MAY 21 1827
FLETCHER, Jas. L.	FAGAN, Mary M.	JUN 29 1837
FLETCHER, Joseph	INGHRAM, Mary Ann	JUN 21 1855
FLETCHER, Margaret	ALEXANDER, Sandy N.	MAY 24 1838
FLETCHER, Marion E.	MADDOX, Thomas H.	JUN 30 1857
FLETCHER, Martha	BOSWELL, George	MAY 22 1816
FLETCHER, Mary	MORAN, James	OCT 15 1842
FLETCHER, Mary (blk)	RANDOLPH, John	DEC 06 1842
FLETCHER, Mary Elizabeth	FINACUM, Stokely	AUG 26 1846
FLETCHER, Noah	PEASE, Betsey	DEC 14 1813
FLETCHER, Richard	BUSH, Mary (blk)	JUN 07 1849
FLETCHER, Sarah Ann	WHITE, Richard	FEB 12 1846
FLETCHER, Sarah Ann (blk)	MILLER, George	MAY 26 1858
FLETCHER, W.H.	CONNER, Mary Jane	SEP 22 1845

District of Columbia Marriage Licenses, 1811-1858

FLETCHER, William A.	NEWTON, Sarah Ann	FEB 07 1852
FLETCHER, William H.	WILSON, Mary	AUG 05 1833
FLETCHER, William H.	BROWN, Catharine J.	MAY 07 1852
FLEURY, John R.	KINCAID, Sarah E.	JUL 15 1825
FLEURY, Lewis Augustus	BARNARD, Caroline M.	OCT 03 1835
FLEURY, Walter A.	FREEMAN, Margaret	DEC 23 1848
FLICK, Mary	KIRBY, Thomas	AUG 10 1848
FLICK, William T.	THOMPSON, Mary Ann	APR 21 1846
FLICKER, Charlotte (blk)	RUNELS, Alexander	MAY 08 1851
FLIN, Edward	VIDLER, Ann	NOV 25 1820
FLIN, Mary	DeMYERS, John	JAN 18 1815
FLING, George W.	LENMAN, Mary B.	FEB 02 1815
FLINN, Catharine	CRONIN, Mathew	AUG 11 1851
FLINN, Daniel W.	GREEN, Amanda	DEC 27 1848
FLIN<u>N</u>, Elizabeth	BROWN, Charles	SEP 01 1842
FLINN, Margaret	MAHAR, John	JUL 27 1853
FLINN, Margaret	CARROLL, Thomas	AUG 30 1855
FLINN, Mary Adeline	FREEMAN, John Henry	OCT 09 1837
FLINN, Rebecca	PATTON, Lewis	NOV 08 1831
FLINN, Thomas	PROCTOR, Mary	JUL 03 1813
FLINN, Thomas	ROCHE, Catherine	DEC 07 1853
FLINN, Villasques H.	ROBINSON, Julia A.	SEP 13 1853
FLINN, Virginia	SEMMES, Douglass R.	NOV 30 1857
FLINN, William	ELLIOTT, Caroline	AUG 14 1848
FLOOD, John	KANE, Elizabeth	JUN 05 1857
FLOOD, Sarah	HAYWOOD, Robert	OCT 29 1836
FLOOD, Sarah	TOWERS, William	APR 21 1858
FLOOD, William H.	McWILLIAMS, Mary V.	APR 26 1858
FLORANCE, Mary	JOHNSON, Rut	OCT 11 1828
FLORIDAMAN, Caroline	GRUBB, George M.	JUN 04 1840
FLORVIN, Timothy	BARRET, Ellen	FEB 07 1853
FLOTHERON, Lewis	BROWN, Catharine	APR 12 1836
FLOWEREE, Pandora G.C.	SILCOTT, Peyton	NOV 24 1829
FLOWERS, Mary A.	WHEATLY, James	JAN 10 1824
FLOWERS, Richard	EDMONDS, Cordelia	MAR 14 1833
FLOWERS, Rosanna	GOLDSMITH, George	JUL 03 1827
FLOYD, Ann	SMITH, Abraham	FEB 09 1819
FLOYD, Elizabeth R.	STRATTON, James	APR 12 1838
FLOYD, John Brintnall	CHARLES, Mary Ann	OCT 25 1848
FLOYD, Ruth	ESSEX, Josias	MAR 10 1831
FLUHART, Margaret	CROCKET, Risdon	SEP 17 1852
FLURRY, John	GREEN, Charity	FEB 23 1830
FLURRY, Sarah	LAW, Thomas	MAY 27 1841
FLURY, Catherine E.	FREEMAN, James Y.	APR 24 1829
FLURY, Mary	FORD, John N.	OCT 24 1827
FLURY, Sarah Elizabeth	PARIO, Newell	JUL 11 1837
FLYNN, Ann	SORET, Francis	JUL 02 1825
FLYNN, Bridget	MURPHY, Patrick	JAN 28 1854
FLYNN, Bridget	BUCKLEY, John	JUN 03 1854
FLYNN, Daniel	KEYS, Sarah	DEC 30 1850
FLYNN, John	DOWNING, Mary	NOV 15 1849
FLYNN, John	GREY, Elizabeth	APR 28 1856
FLYNN, John M.	O'CONNELL, Margaret	APR 28 1853
FLYNN, Patrick	CAREY, Bridget	APR 28 1852
FLYNN, Patrick	DUFFY, Ann	JUN 26 1856
FLYNN, Patrick	DUFFEY, Ann	SEP 06 1856
FLYNN, Peter	STANTON, Eliza	JUL 27 1858
FLYNN, Thomas	PORTLEY, Catharine	SEP 21 1855

District of Columbia Marriage Licenses, 1811-1858

FOANES, Martha	REEVES, Aloysius	AUG 14 1848
FOG, Margaret	LLOYD, John	DEC 29 1828
FOGERTY, Daniel	SUGHRUE, Ellen	JUL 24 1857
FOGG, Ebenezer Wood	WILSON, Mercy Ann	JAN 11 1854
FOGG, Martin	BROWN, Harriet (blk)	MAR 18 1842
FOGG, Samuel J.	KIDWELL, Ann S.	APR 05 1849
FOGLE, Jacob	HICKS, Mahaley	NOV 17 1829
FOGLE, Mary	FISHER, John	NOV 27 1856
FOGLE, Zachariah	CARROLL, Mary Ellen	SEP 07 1837
FOILAND, Peter	WILLS, Caroline	SEP 26 1848
FOKLE, Adam	CRIMM, Margaret	MAY 12 1835
FOLAND, Valentine	JEFFERSON, Frances Ann	APR 23 1840
FOLDZ, George Jacob	HOFFMAN, Margaret	MAR 25 1848
FOLEN, Ellen	DAVIS, Patrick	JUN 13 1856
FOLEY, Ann	FOLEY, Bartholomew	DEC 23 1854
FOLEY, Ann E.	GARRETT, Joseph E.	FEB 15 1858
FOLEY, Bartholomew	FOLEY, Ann	DEC 23 1854
FOLEY, Bridget	BABBINGTON, William	MAY 08 1852
FOLEY, Caroline	BLACKWELL, Oliver C.	MAY 30 1836
FOLEY, Daniel	CONNELL, Johanna	JAN 31 1852
FOLEY, Daniel	HUTCHINSON, Elizabeth	MAY 18 1858
FOLEY, Honora	SANDS, William	JAN 16 1855
FOLEY, James	TOLLIVER, Martha	OCT 07 1828
FOLEY, John	NEVITT, Lucy	AUG 12 1815
FOLEY, John	POULY, Anna	MAR 05 1857
FOLEY, John W.	GADNER, Mary M.	JAN 13 1844
FOLEY, Margaret	KELLY, Timothy	DEC 28 1855
FOLEY, Mary	TEMPLEMAN, George	SEP 30 1835
FOLEY, Mary Jane	DeMARUEL, Henry Galway	FEB 22 1856
FOLEY, Timothy	QUINLIN, Catharine	MAY 12 1858
FOLIN, Richard	DICKEY, Ansey	JAN 26 1841
FOLKNER, Susan	ELLIS, James G.	JUN 02 1846
FOLLANSBEE, Joseph	KESSUCK, Margaret	MAR 10 1829
FOLLANSBEE, Joseph	SCHWEAR, Sarah Catherine	APR 02 1850
FOLLANSBEE, Joshua	SEWALL, Louisa A.	APR 10 1843
FOLLEN, Rachel	HARRINGTON, James	JUN 18 1857
FOLLER, Thomas	SLATMAN, Elizabeth	NOV 28 1844
FOLLIN, Adelaid	GANTT, Joseph	OCT 19 1854
FOLLIN, Catharine	PEARSON, Wm. M.	SEP 20 1823
FOLLIN, George	ANCHOES, Susan	DEC 09 1839
FOLLIN, Margaret Ann	FRIZZELL, James	JUN 26 1855
FOLLIN, Mary	HAMBLETON, Samuel	JUL 27 1833
FOLLIN, Mary Ann	PEARSON, John W.	JAN 16 1845
FOLY, Elizabeth	HARPER, John Joseph	APR 13 1843
FOLY, Fanny	REILEY, William	SEP 10 1821
FONDE, John P.	STEWART, Elizabeth	MAR 09 1820
FONES, Frances Ann	CARROLL, James J.	MAY 11 1846
FONTAINE, Felix G.	UNDERWOOD, Harriet P.	SEP 30 1856
FONTELIER, Catharine	SCHARR, John	MAR 09 1849
FONTZ, Christian	HUGHES, Julia Ann	JUN 05 1858
FONTZ, Sarah	STEWART, William	MAY 11 1858
FOOBLE, Sarah Ann	CATON, Patrick	MAY 01 1833
FOOG, Dolly	BARTLETT, John H., Jr.	APR 26 1834
FOOS, John A.	YOUNG, Martha A.	JUN 11 1855
FOOSTER, John	JOHNSON, Catharine (blk)	NOV 05 1852
FOOT, Catharine	BROWN, Peter	NOV 06 1830
FOOT, Ellen Maria	McINTOSH, John	JUL 17 1845
FOOT, Frances	BARKER, James	FEB 17 1845

District of Columbia Marriage Licenses, 1811-1858

FOOT, Fredk.	COOK, Louisa	JUN 12 1855
FOOT, Mary Ann (col'd)	YATES, William Henry	JAN 01 1857
FOOTE, Catharine	SADDLER, Jos.	DEC 18 1820
FORBES, Eleanor B.E.	BERRY, Benjamin, Jr.	MAY 15 1817
FORBES, Elizabeth A.	WALKER, George C.	JUN 05 1858
FORBES, Elizth. Jane	BEALL, Robert	JUN 02 1829
FORBES, George C.	DONALLY, Susan P.	FEB 01 1851
FORBES, Lucretia D.	BLOYES, James H.	MAR 28 1853
FORCE, Mary J.	JONES, William H.	NOV 21 1843
FORCE, William Q.	LYONS, Georgiana	OCT 19 1841
FORD, Ann	SPALDING, Bernard	MAY 22 1817
FORD, Ann	DOUGLASS, William	APR 02 1821
FORD, Ann (blk)	COGEY, Benjamin	OCT 25 1852
FORD, Anna Rosa	MORSELL, Richard A.	APR 29 1854
FORD, Benjamin	GRINDLE, Mary	DEC 12 1850
FORD, Catharine	KEATING, Thomas	NOV 09 1854
FORD, Charles	BROOKS, Gracy	AUG 29 1831
FORD, Charles F.	CARROLL, Susan	SEP 12 1854
FORD, Elizabeth	TACKETT, John E.	JUL 28 1857
FORD, Emma	HOLTZCLAW, Thomas J.	DEC 08 1856
FORD, Flora	HICKS, George	MAY 13 1816
FORD, Franklin	SIMPSON, Rebecca S.	OCT 25 1848
FORD, George	BEALL, Ann Elizabeth	DEC 31 1844
FORD, Henrietta (blk)	BELL, Henry	SEP 27 1849
FORD, Herbert	BINKS, Mary (blk)	MAY 14 1846
FORD, Ignatius	SIMPSON, Lauretta	FEB 23 1857
FORD, James	BIGGINS, Martha A.E.	JUL 20 1838
FORD, James	DOVE, Sarah	APR 19 1851
FORD, James	THOMAS, Georgeana (blk)	AUG 04 1851
FORD, James E.	SIMPSON, Harriet	OCT 18 1855
FORD, Jane (blk)	DIGGS, Mathew	JAN 08 1838
FORD, Jeanette Frances	GENTRY, Benjamin W.	OCT 01 1857
FORD, John A.	CATO, Elizabeth	JUN 06 1829
FORD, John G.	CLEMENTS, Rebecca	JAN 27 1818
FORD, John N.	FLURY, Mary	OCT 24 1827
FORD, Joseph	DAVIS, Mary Frances	APR 07 1849
FORD, Joseph S.	SHAKLEFORD, Elizabeth	JAN 06 1847
FORD, Louisa M.E.	CUNNINGHAM, James H.	JAN 01 1852
FORD, Lucinda (blk)	BROOKS, Henry	APR 28 1852
FORD, Lucinda (blk)	JACKSON, James T.	APR 24 1855
FORD, Mary (blk)	SATTERWHITE, James H.	NOV 26 1852
FORD, Mary Ann (blk)	MATHEW, Francis	NOV 28 1844
FORD, Mary Ann (blk)	JONES, Paul	APR 02 1846
FORD, Mary E.	JONES, Richard F.	JUN 23 1857
FORD, Mary Jane	HASLIP, Enoch	APR 25 1848
FORD, Mary Jane (blk)	LANCASTER, Charles	AUG 07 1848
FORD, Mary O.	GETTENER, Benj. F.	APR 20 1854
FORD, Rebecca	RIGHTSTINE, John W.	MAR 21 1854
FORD, Sally	QUEEN, Charles	JUN 09 1814
FORD, Samuel	FOX, B.A.	SEP 04 1845
FORD, Sarah	BINGUY, Thomas	MAY 03 1814
FORD, Sarah	HOLLENBACK, William	NOV 08 1815
FORD, Sarah	HAMILTON, Alexander	JUL 13 1830
FORD, Sarah	FORREST, Thomas	OCT 22 1856
FORD, Sarah F.	RUTHERFORD, Dyonicious	JUL 14 1858
FORD, Stephen C.	HOBAN, Ann R.	APR 11 1831
FORD, Stephen Calvert	CHESHIRE, Ann Louisa	SEP 03 1833
FORD, Susannah	KING, George, of Chs.	NOV 25 1816

District of Columbia Marriage Licenses, 1811-1858

FORD, Telamanchus	CANTER, Jemima	NOV 02 1853
FORD, William	HINGERTY, Pheba	AUG 31 1825
FORD, William	DOUGLASS, Elizth.	DEC 08 1829
FORD, William	THOMAS, Susan (blk)	APR 03 1834
FORD, William A.	PETTIT, Drucilla	NOV 16 1848
FOREMAN, Eliza Ellen (blk)	LEWIS, Joseph	APR 01 1858
FOREMAN, George W.	HEWIT, Mary Ann	AUG 01 1846
FOREMAN, Jos.	PAYNE, Cloe A.	MAY 04 1822
FOREMAN, William	LEMMONS, Emily (blk)	JUN 08 1853
FORESTEL, Walter	SPEIDEN, Ann	JAN 15 1836
FORKNER, Pleasent E.	YOUNG, Frances A.	MAR 14 1838
FORLORN, Michael	LIMLY, Mary	JUL 19 1814
FORMAN, Charlotte	MACE, Joseph	SEP 20 1853
FORMAN, Joseph	FISHER, Ann	DEC 31 1819
FORNANCE, Joseph	McKNIGHT, Ann	JUL 23 1840
FORNCUP, John	FISHER, Catherine	JUN 25 1853
FORNEY, Mary	RUSH, Dennis	AUG 07 1855
FORREST, Alexander F.	ESSEX, Malvina	AUG 12 1847
FORREST, Andrew	MOORE, Ann H.	DEC 31 1812
FORREST, Ann	GREEN, John	JUL 21 1814
FORREST, Bladen	KEITH, Mary Helen	AUG 05 1844
FORREST, Catharine C.	COMBS, Robert M.	OCT 08 1840
FORREST, Charles	HARTMAN, Caroline	NOV 27 1855
FORREST, Charles W.	NOURSE, Louisa P.	OCT 05 1847
FORREST, Edward	BATEMAN, Catharine Ann	APR 29 1837
FORREST, Eleanor C.	BULLEY, Michael	NOV 26 1821
FORREST, Elizabeth	REID, Upton S.	JUN 30 1814
FORREST, Emily C.	WARLEY, Alexander F.	JUN 12 1850
FORREST, French	SIMMS, Emily D.	APR 18 1831
FORREST, George P.	YATES, Eleanor M.	OCT 30 1832
FORREST, Henrietta (blk)	ROSS, Daniel	MAY 11 1826
FORREST, James	ESSEX, Elizabeth	APR 08 1815
FORREST, John	LUCKET, Julia Ann	MAY 07 1844
FORREST, Jonathan	DAVIS, Malida	FEB 24 1848
FORREST, Josephine D.	DENHAM, David B.	JUN 05 1837
FORREST, Louisa	WASHINGTON, Thomas	NOV 19 1851
FORREST, Margaret	QUEEN, John R.	APR 10 1838
FORREST, Maria	TAYLOE, John	NOV 11 1817
FORREST, Martha (blk)	HOPKINS, Joseph	FEB 04 1845
FORREST, Mary	ALTEMUS, Thomas	MAR 07 1838
FORREST, Mary Ellen	SHAFFNER, Wm. C.	NOV 26 1834
FORREST, Mary Jane (blk)	BROOKS, Basil	OCT 17 1843
FORREST, Rezin	KYLER, Sarah	JAN 15 1822
FORREST, Sarah Catherine	MURDOCK, William Charles	JUN 06 1857
FORREST, Sophia	DeBUTTS, John H.	AUG 08 1818
FORREST, Thomas	FORD, Sarah	OCT 22 1856
FORREST, Thomas J.	FORREST, Virginia	MAR 25 1850
FORREST, Virginia	FORREST, Thomas J.	MAR 25 1850
FORREST, William H.	MOORE, Sarah Jane	DEC 29 1851
FORRESTER, Isaac N.	DAVISON, Emma	JUN 16 1856
FORSTER, Annie S.	HINTON, Addison C.	OCT 03 1836
FORSYTH, Ann B.	SHILES, James W.	JUL 16 1850
FORSYTH, Clara C.	MASON, Murray	DEC 06 1837
FORSYTH, Joseph W.	CALLENDER, Rebecca	MAR 07 1846
FORSYTH, Mary	BRADY, Edwin	JUL 15 1833
FORSYTH, Mary A.	SHAAFF, Arthur	AUG 16 1825
FORTENEY, Henry	WHITE, Susanna	MAR 26 1818
FORTNER, Samuel	SIMMONS, Sarah	JUL 02 1836

District of Columbia Marriage Licenses, 1811-1858

FORTNER, Thomas	SIMMENS, Eliza	APR 12 1834
FORTUNE, James	BURNES, Elizabeth	APR 23 1830
FORTUNE, Thomas L.	BRUCE, Mary A.	APR 18 1846
FORTUNE, Wm.	McGILL, Louisa	JAN 14 1822
FOSHEE, Elizabeth	WEST, Jeremiah	OCT 13 1842
FOSKEY, Moses	SHORTER, Mary Ann	SEP 07 1853
FOSKEY, Muhala	SLINN, George	NOV 19 1857
FOSSETT, James	BROWN, Catharine N.	MAY 03 1837
FOSSETT, Margaret	HOPKINS, Richard	FEB 06 1840
FOSSETT, Mary	SIMONS, William	SEP 25 1834
FOSTER, Adams	BURCH, Sarah Jane	MAY 29 1849
FOSTER, Clara (blk)	RIDGLEY, James	JUL 20 1854
FOSTER, Edward	MITCHELL, Margaret	NOV 06 1813
FOSTER, Edward	STALLANGS, Mary Ann	MAY 02 1855
FOSTER, Eleanor	WARFIELD, Thomas	FEB 22 1816
FOSTER, Eliza Ann	SHOEMAKER, Jacob	MAY 06 1847
FOSTER, Elizabeth	ARNOLD, James	MAR 02 1852
FOSTER, Elizabeth	LUBER, Lanehart	OCT 08 1857
FOSTER, Emma	SIMMONS, William	JUL 13 1854
FOSTER, Henry K.	SLATFORD, Elizabeth	JUN 28 1839
FOSTER, James H.	POOLE, Anna Maria	MAR 17 1851
FOSTER, Jane (blk)	JOHNSON, George	DEC 08 1842
FOSTER, Jane Elizth.	LINDSAY, William	JUN 30 1836
FOSTER, John	ROLLINS, Mary E.	MAY 03 1836
FOSTER, Mary Ann	ARNOLD, James	APR 29 1840
FOSTER, Mary Ann	McCUEN, James	NOV 02 1852
FOSTER, Molinda	DOWNING, Robert	APR 02 1855
FOSTER, Rose	NORTON, Michl.	AUG 04 1854
FOSTER, Sarah L.	CULL, James	JUN 27 1831
FOSTER, Thomas	MAGRUDER, Martha (blk)	SEP 03 1857
FOSTER, William C.	BEALL, Indiana M.	MAY 18 1857
FOSTER, William J.	ANGIL, Jane E.	NOV 22 1853
FOUDRAY, Margaretta C.	JOHNSON, John R.	APR 19 1854
FOUGERES, Louis	GIBBS, Mary	MAY 30 1835
FOUKE, Jacob	McNOYE, Catherine	DEC 22 1829
FOULKE, Grafton	BROWN, Margaret	MAR 27 1835
FOULKES, Mary E.	ENROUGHTY, Thomas P.	DEC 07 1853
FOUNTAIN, Mary A.	CHAPIN, Nathan C.	SEP 28 1854
FOUNTAIN, Mary Ellen	McMANN, Michael	AUG 31 1848
FOUNTAIN, Nicholas	FIGLAY, Elizabeth	MAY 14 1812
FOUNTAINE, Louisa	WRIGHT, John	DEC 09 1850
FOUNTING, Allison	SORRELL, Sevolia A.	JAN 01 1848
FOUSHEE, Mary Ann	KELLER, John L.	MAY 14 1823
FOUSTER, Louisa	JOHNSON, Henry	SEP 29 1831
FOUWKES, John	LAMBLE, Elizabeth	JAN 24 1826
FOWBLE, William A.	CREAMER, Kate B.	JAN 13 1857
FOWKE, Eliza R.	CLIPT, James C.	JUN 18 1849
FOWLER, Abraham	PARSONS, Elizabeth	FEB 20 1816
FOWLER, Alonzo	DRAPER, Frances	NOV 05 1851
FOWLER, Ann	WOOD, William	MAY 22 1823
FOWLER, Ann	GROUSE, John G.	DEC 24 1828
FOWLER, Barbara G.	HURLEY, Henry	OCT 11 1830
FOWLER, Benjamin	PUMEROY, Mary	AUG 01 1827
FOWLER, Benjamin	DYER, Matilda	NOV 10 1827
FOWLER, Benjamin F.	HENRY, Mary A.	JUN 23 1857
FOWLER, Charles W.	MURPHEY, Martha	NOV 19 1841
FOWLER, Christiana	KING, William, Jr.	JUN 22 1813
FOWLER, Christy	EHRMANTRAUT, Joseph	FEB 02 1848

District of Columbia Marriage Licenses, 1811-1858

FOWLER, Chs. S.	POOR, Mary W.	SEP 05 1822
FOWLER, Dradey	BROWN, Francis	JAN 03 1832
FOWLER, Eleanor	SIMPSON, William	SEP 25 1826
FOWLER, Eliza	BOARMAN, Richard A.	MAR 06 1858
FOWLER, Elizabeth	THOMPSON, Benjamin	SEP 30 1839
FOWLER, Elizabeth Ann	RHODES, James	SEP 15 1849
FOWLER, Elizabeth Rebecca	STREAK, George Oliver	APR 30 1855
FOWLER, Ellen	STANDLIN, Patrick	MAR 05 1831
FOWLER, Emily A.D.	WROE, Samuel C.	SEP 20 1852
FOWLER, George	HOWARD, Brit Ann	APR 04 1820
FOWLER, Harriet	WILLIAMS, John	AUG 29 1825
FOWLER, Henderson	TEECHEM, Mary H.	DEC 10 1833
FOWLER, Henderson	TEACHEM, Susan	NOV 22 1856
FOWLER, Henny	FISHER, Richard J.	JAN 02 1822
FOWLER, James	McCAULEY, Mary	JUL 22 1823
FOWLER, James H.	APPLETON, Margaret	SEP 22 1838
FOWLER, James J.	MAGILL, Susannah	JAN 07 1845
FOWLER, James W.	HUNTER, Henrietta H.	JAN 11 1831
FOWLER, James W.	SENGSTACK, Mary E.	AUG 27 1849
FOWLER, Jesse	CRAWFORD, Caroline	JUL 28 1827
FOWLER, John	SANSBURY, Jane	SEP 28 1848
FOWLER, John H.	MURPHEY, Mary E.	DEC 18 1850
FOWLER, John L.	CREGAR, Rebecca	APR 09 1823
FOWLER, John L.	JORDAN, Eliza	MAR 11 1847
FOWLER, Joseph	McDANIEL, Lily	FEB 04 1815
FOWLER, Joseph	HOWES, Jane	DEC 21 1830
FOWLER, Joseph	WHITE, Angelica	MAY 02 1839
FOWLER, Joseph	BROWN, Mary Ann Virginia	JUL 02 1851
FOWLER, Joseph	BARNHOUSE, Alcuszera	SEP 08 1851
FOWLER, Joseph	DUNHAM, Mary W.	FEB 08 1853
FOWLER, Juliet H.	RILEY, Joshua	NOV 20 1827
FOWLER, Linney	MURPHEY, Wiley T.	AUG 19 1826
FOWLER, Margaret	DYER, Aaron	JUL 18 1812
FOWLER, Margaret E.	MONROE, Thomas T.	DEC 15 1852
FOWLER, Margt. Ann	OGDEN, William L.	FEB 06 1813
FOWLER, Maria	HEPBURN, Alexr.	APR 16 1814
FOWLER, Maria	WAINWRIGHT, William	JAN 16 1819
FOWLER, Martha A.T.	HALL, Percy Walker	DEC 11 1855
FOWLER, Mary	PRESTON, William	JUL 14 1823
FOWLER, Mary	BARKLEY, John	JUL 22 1831
FOWLER, Mary	GREEN, James	NOV 10 1834
FOWLER, Mary E.	KUHL, Henry	DEC 05 1845
FOWLER, Mary E.	SMALLWOOD, Daniel A.	MAY 19 1847
FOWLER, Mary E.	DELZELL, William	DEC 27 1848
FOWLER, Mary Harriott	HALL, Brice	AUG 17 1812
FOWLER, Mary M.	DODDS, James	APR 09 1851
FOWLER, Samuel	DUFIEF, Jane S.	JUL 23 1842
FOWLER, Samuel G.	GEASLIN, Mary E.	DEC 11 1851
FOWLER, Sarah	MACKBEE, Saml.	DEC 27 1831
FOWLER, Sarah	LEWIS, John H.	JUN 22 1852
FOWLER, Sarah D.	CASSEDY, John G.	JAN 16 1834
FOWLER, Sarah Louisa	KIRKLEY, Thomas E.	MAY 06 1856
FOWLER, Solomon L.	SERRAN, Mary Susan	NOV 27 1847
FOWLER, Thomas	O'NEALE, Eleanora	OCT 29 1838
FOWLER, Thomas F.	ELLIS, Mrs.	OCT 30 1847
FOWLER, Thomas W.	WALL, Virginia G.	JUN 04 1857
FOWLER, Virginia R.	SMITH, William B.	AUG 24 1852
FOWLER, Willey Ann	SANDSBURY, John M.	NOV 09 1824

District of Columbia Marriage Licenses, 1811-1858

FOWLER, William	SANSBURY, Christian	JAN 12 1819
FOWLER, William	SIMPSON, Priscilla	AUG 02 1824
FOWLER, William	SYMPSON, Margaret	NOV 03 1832
FOWLER, William	DRUDGE, Susan	JAN 06 1836
FOWLER, William	BOND, Mary A.	JAN 21 1845
FOWLER, William H.	DUFIEF, Mary Margaret	APR 07 1835
FOWLER, William H.	BELL, Mary Ann	NOV 11 1856
FOWLER, William R.	CRUITT, Sarah	JUL 23 1839
FOWLER, Wm. J.	KING, Anna M.	AUG 17 1857
FOWLER, Wm. W.	TALBERT, Caroline R.	OCT 14 1844
FOWLER, Wm. W.	DAY, Jane E.	OCT 08 1853
FOWLES, James	EDMONSTON, Catherine Ann	NOV 16 1831
FOWLEY, John W.	SIFFORD, Elizabeth	MAR 24 1838
FOX, Allen G.	WHALEY, Martha V.	JAN 29 1855
FOX, Ann	LANGTON, William	MAR 25 1823
FOX, Ann	THOMAS, William	JUN 30 1845
FOX, Ann	FRIEL, Michael	JUL 23 1858
FOX, B.A.	FORD, Samuel	SEP 04 1845
FOX, Benjamin	McCOY, Leanna	JUN 13 1842
FOX, Cephas	KING, Elizabeth	NOV 24 1813
FOX, Dewanna Bins	McCOY, Josiah Daniel	AUG 06 1831
FOX, Francis	HIFFLIN, Mary A.	MAR 06 1848
FOX, Henry	BRUCE, Catharine Ann	OCT 01 1840
FOX, Henry	HARRIS, Elizabeth S.	JAN 09 1855
FOX, John L.	MORRIS, Elizabeth A.	JUN 12 1847
FOX, Keziah	RIGGS, Simpson	SEP 18 1827
FOX, Maria L.	FIELD, E.M.	MAY 16 1853
FOX, Mary	COPPAGE, William	MAY 01 1854
FOX, Mary Jane	BARNES, John H.	NOV 04 1851
FOX, Michael	LYE, Ellen	SEP 03 1833
FOX, Robert C.	KENDALL, Fannie	DEC 20 1856
FOX, Samuel	LAUGHFETY, Sophia	AUG 20 1830
FOX, Sidney	HARP, Sarah Ann	JUN 15 1829
FOX, Susan	BALL, Aquilla	JUL 10 1817
FOX, Thomas	MOORE, Mary Ann (blk)	MAY 03 1841
FOX, William	THOMPSON, Virginia	AUG 09 1852
FOXALL, Mary Ann	McKENNEY, Samuel	MAR 08 1813
FOXTON, Mary	BAGE, William	DEC 05 1818
FOXVILL, Charles	BRYANT, Ann	MAR 12 1823
FOXWELL, Gabriel J.L.	DAVIS, Alice M.	NOV 29 1855
FOXWELL, Isabel A.	BOZZEL, Robert L.	JUL 14 1853
FOXWELL, Mary Ellen	STECOM, Lewis	JUL 03 1845
FOXWELL, Susan	OLIVE, Henry	DEC 28 1843
FOY, Elizabeth	BARRY, James	APR 25 1836
FOY, Ellen	FRENCH, Thomas	NOV 30 1833
FOY, Jane C.	BRUFF, Richard W.	MAY 30 1853
FOY, Mary	DEVLIN, John	AUG 25 1835
FOY, Michael	GARDNER, Mary	APR 29 1857
FOY, Patrick	DOYL, Johanna	FEB 06 1854
FOY, Rosena A.	HAWE, Edward	JUN 16 1856
FOY, Sarah N.	NEAGHER, John F.	JUN 04 1857
FOY, Thomas	MacDAVIT, Bridget	DEC 16 1830
FOYE, Barney	BURKE, Eleanor	FEB 26 1829
FOYLES, Ann	CLARK, Edward W.	JAN 26 1813
FOYLES, Caroline	OWENS, George W.	JAN 02 1855
FOYLES, Elizh.	CARLON, James	AUG 19 1814
FOYLES, Isabel	MAURY, John W.	OCT 06 1831
FOYLES, James	SEWALL, Ann T.	JUN 24 1813

District of Columbia Marriage Licenses, 1811-1858

FOYLES, James	SMITH, Caroline	FEB 19 1848
FOYLES, Margaret	LITTLE, John	JAN 25 1831
FOYLES, Sarah	MURRAY, Thomas	APR 23 1822
FOYLES, Sarah	NAYLOR, George	JUN 01 1830
FRAELER, Charles	MIDDLETON, Eleanor E.	JAN 22 1849
FRAILING, Lena	BESTOLD, Nealy	JAN 22 1855
FRAISER, Bella	POWERS, E.M.	DEC 02 1857
FRAMES, Dorah	HURLEY, George	NOV 01 1813
FRAMES, Mary	JAMEISON, S.S.	JUL 06 1821
FRANCE, John	PRATT, Maria	JAN 10 1838
FRANCE, Joseph H.	HUBBARD, Mary Elizth.	SEP 23 1843
FRANCE, Josephine A.	DORSEY, William J.H.	OCT 08 1850
FRANCE, Thomas E.	BROCKET, Annabella	APR 09 1844
FRANCE, William C.	DORMAN, Adele Albert	OCT 06 1847
FRANCES, Mary	FITZGERALD, William	JUN 08 1826
FRANCES, Richard	ROBEY, Sarah Ann	OCT 21 1848
FRANCIS, Adell	DUFF, James	OCT 29 1839
FRANCIS, Agnes	COHEN, James H.	MAY 24 1855
FRANCIS, Eliza (blk)	SHAW, Dennis	JAN 27 1842
FRANCIS, Elizabeth	SIMMONS, Shreshley	DEC 17 1845
FRANCIS, Elizabeth A.	McCARTY, Stephen W.	SEP 18 1834
FRANCIS, George W.	BAILEY, Elizabeth	APR 22 1845
FRANCIS, Henrietta	SMALLWOOD, William	JAN 15 1834
FRANCIS, Henry	ADAMS, Elizabeth (col'd)	MAY 06 1828
FRANCIS, Margaret	LOGAN, Peter	MAY 24 1852
FRANCIS, Mary Ann	DIAPER, James W.	DEC 16 1818
FRANCIS, Richard	CONNER, Mary (blk)	SEP 15 1854
FRANCIS, Sidney Virga.	WELSH, Aristides	OCT 12 1846
FRANCIS, Thomas	MOUNT, Sarah Ann	JAN 27 1831
FRANCIS, Thomas	BRYAN, Lavinia	NOV 18 1856
FRANK, Alexander	WILKINSON, Mary E.	MAR 01 1852
FRANK, Elizabeth A.	NOLAND, Samuel S.	JUN 10 1850
FRANK, Ellen	NAYLOR, Dickerson	JUL 04 1833
FRANK, Henry	FISHER, Emily	DEC 13 1830
FRANK, Jane	STEPHENS, John	DEC 14 1848
FRANK, Lewis E.	CHAPMAN, Bridget	NOV 05 1855
FRANK, Luther M.	DICKSON, Elizabeth	JUL 06 1824
FRANK, Mary	CRUTTENDEN, Harvey	APR 14 1817
FRANK, Mary Ann	HOUSTON, Robert Richards	SEP 03 1831
FRANK, Mary Ellen	EDWARDS, Levi	JUN 05 1852
FRANK, Robert	HUDSON, Ann	FEB 02 1812
FRANK, Sarah E.	COST, John M.	JAN 09 1855
FRANKINBERGER, Charles	CARL, Margaret	MAY 03 1852
FRANKLAND, George W.	GRUMMELL, Julia	DEC 01 1852
FRANKLAND, George W.	AGER, Sarah	DEC 09 1856
FRANKLAND, Sarah	HOOVER, John	JUN 28 1856
FRANKLIN, Ben	DAVIS, Mary V.	AUG 30 1855
FRANKLIN, Benjamin H.	GUY, Rebecca	AUG 21 1845
FRANKLIN, Elizabeth (blk)	CLARKE, Isaac	SEP 07 1848
FRANKLIN, Hannah	MORRISS, William	NOV 24 1831
FRANKLIN, Henry	VENNABLE, Sally	DEC 13 1820
FRANKLIN, Henry T.	BRIDWELL, Virginia	SEP 18 1851
FRANKLIN, James	WARREN, Sarah	OCT 24 1857
FRANKLIN, Jane (blk)	LOGGINS, Peter	FEB 26 1813
FRANKLIN, Mary E.	WEDDIN, James H.	OCT 25 1854
FRANKLIN, Mary E.	WEEMS, Thomas N.	MAY 17 1855
FRANKLIN, Nicholas	DUCKETT, Sophia	JUL 23 1825
FRANKLIN, Phillis	HOLLAND, Charles	DEC 25 1815

District of Columbia Marriage Licenses, 1811-1858

FRANKLIN, Stephen P.	PETTIGREW, Ann [Mrs.]	JAN 22 1827
FRANKLIN, Thomas	THOMPSON, Rachael	FEB 07 1820
FRANKLIN, William A.	SCRIVENER, Sallie W.	MAY 04 1854
FRANKS, Elizabeth	STEELE, William F.	JUL 01 1848
FRANKS, Emily	LUSKEY, Jacob	OCT 27 1840
FRANKS, Jacob	BOOTH, Ellen Jane	DEC 22 1834
FRANKS, Susan	WALKER, Francis	SEP 24 1812
FRANTUM, Mary Ann	SULLIVAN, Henry	JUL 21 1858
FRANTUM, Samuel	MORTIMORE, Louisa	JUN 25 1838
FRANZONI, Camilla	YARDELLA, Francisco	APR 07 1817
FRANZONI, Euridice	SIMMS, Elexius	MAY 25 1830
FRANZONI, Julia C.	SIMPSON, James A.	NOV 20 1850
FRANZONI, Lavinia Gertrude	ROURA, José Pabla	JUN 09 1848
FRANZONIA, Ermenia	WORRELL, William	FEB 19 1846
FRASER, James	HENNING, Priscilla	JUN 29 1821
FRASER, James	BROADLUP, Salina	DEC 09 1847
FRASER, James	LYONS, Lavinia Blake	AUG 04 1853
FRASER, Simon	DAVIS, Hanah	DEC 12 1843
FRASIER, Columbia	MORTIMER, John	APR 01 1851
FRASIER, James	MULLIKIN, Mary Elizabeth	SEP 21 1848
FRASIER, Joseph	PARKER, Rebecca W.	DEC 23 1828
FRASIER, Mary	GLOVER, Joseph	SEP 14 1843
FRASIER, Sarah A. (blk)	CHASE, Daniel	APR 28 1857
FRAYSER, Josiah	TURPIN, Sallie G.	JUN 09 1829
FRAZER, Ann	FRAZIER, James	DEC 08 1830
FRAZER, Drusey	JONES, Benjamin	FEB 22 1814
FRAZER, John	MAGEE, Ellen	JUN 22 1850
FRAZER, Lucy F.	CHANCELLOR, Melzie S.	NOV 23 1837
FRAZER, Martha A.	WALKER, John	MAR 08 1848
FRAZIER, Benjamin	MULLIKIN, Martha	MAR 24 1827
FRAZIER, Caroline	WOOD, Thomas	APR 05 1848
FRAZIER, Catherine (blk)	BROWN, John	MAY 24 1844
FRAZIER, Elizabeth	COATS, William	JUL 07 1814
FRAZIER, George	LEEK, Dolly	APR 02 1821
FRAZIER, George W.	SUTHERLAND, Isabella C.	FEB 15 1849
FRAZIER, Horace	BEACH, Nancy	DEC 07 1815
FRAZIER, James	FRAZER, Ann	DEC 08 1830
FRAZIER, Jane	BARTLETT, John	DEC 20 1816
FRAZIER, John	CARTER, Sarah	JUN 19 1819
FRAZIER, John	GRIMES, Mary	OCT 05 1820
FRAZIER, John	LANHAM, Rachel	JAN 14 1824
FRAZIER, Margaret	WHITNEY, Charles	JUN 28 1841
FRAZIER, Martha (blk)	PEIRRE, Jonathan	MAY 10 1852
FRAZIER, Mary	RIGGLES, William	AUG 29 1846
FRAZIER, Mary (blk)	HUNTER, George	JAN 11 1842
FRAZIER, Mary Eliza	HUNTT, Edwd. L.	JUL 16 1833
FRAZIER, Melinda	MULLOY, Thomas	NOV 29 1834
FRAZIER, Sarah	REINHART, Frederick	MAR 18 1844
FRAZIER, Sarah	REINHART, Frederick	JUN 20 1844
FRAZIER, Sarah L.	BICKSLER, Samuel	MAR 18 1830
FRAZIER, Sophia (blk)	SEWALL, Richard	NOV 29 1854
FRAZIER, Susannah	JOY, William	JAN 08 1835
FRAZIER, William H.	SUITER, Prudence E.	NOV 19 1849
FRECE, William W.	SWART, Margaret A.	SEP 12 1854
FRED, William	SCHWARTZ, Mary C.	APR 03 1851
FREDERICH, Florian	LIEDERER, Hellena	JAN 12 1856
FREDERICK, Lorenzo	GLANDENTZ, Preaida	JUN 24 1833
FREDERICK, Margaret	WILLIAMS, Hilleary	MAY 07 1857

District of Columbia Marriage Licenses, 1811-1858

FREDERICK, Mary	SHUMAN, John	JUN 26 1849
FREE, Ann	SYPE, Henry	JUN 09 1840
FREE, Barbara	BECKET, Walter	DEC 22 1815
FREE, Elizabeth	PINGLE, William H.M.	SEP 30 1843
FREE, Elizth.	BRYAN, Benjamin	NOV 08 1821
FREE, George W.	LOW, Catharine	OCT 28 1830
FREE, Harriot	CUMBERLAND, John	JUL 24 1823
FREE, Ignatius	TUELL, Ann	MAY 12 1827
FREE, John	JARVIS, Catharine Ann	DEC 14 1833
FREE, John B.	TUEL, Ann	DEC 25 1826
FREE, Kitty	BELL, Dory	JAN 04 1813
FREE, Lambert	BORROWS, Laura Matilda	FEB 12 1823
FREE, Louisa	THOMPSON, William	JAN 21 1845
FREE, Margaret	BEAKLEY, Kage	SEP 01 1829
FREE, Martha	BLACK, James A.	JUN 05 1855
FREE, Mary	EHARDT, Jacob	SEP 19 1822
FREE, Sarah Ann	PYLE, Lewis	JUN 22 1837
FREE, Susan	KNIGHT, Thomas	OCT 10 1833
FREE, William	TURNER, Susan	MAR 21 1845
FREEBERGER, Rachel Ann	ELIASON, James M.	JUL 18 1853
FREEDY, Christian	MADLOCK, Mary	AUG 28 1832
FREELAND, Thomas	O'DONNEL, Mary	JAN 03 1820
FREEMAN, Abalona	STALL, John	FEB 23 1850
FREEMAN, Ann Rebecca	EVERETT, John Stanfield	JUL 02 1851
FREEMAN, Barbara	SCHAFAL, Hughn	MAY 09 1856
FREEMAN, Benj.	HILL, Catherine (blk)	MAY 28 1835
FREEMAN, Benjamin C.	WRIGHT, Mary Jane (blk)	OCT 31 1849
FREEMAN, Catharine V.	DONNELLY, Bernard	FEB 19 1855
FREEMAN, Eleanor	HILLEARY, Elijah	AUG 18 1820
FREEMAN, Eleanor	CLOAKLY, Philip H.	APR 08 1824
FREEMAN, Elizabeth	MILLARD, Charles	OCT 17 1833
FREEMAN, Elizabeth	MAY, Philip	SEP 10 1845
FREEMAN, Ellen W. (blk)	THOMAS, James D.	FEB 03 1852
FREEMAN, Emily (blk)	FREEMAN, John	APR 02 1853
FREEMAN, Henrick G.	NEYMEYER, Catharine	SEP 06 1852
FREEMAN, James T.	HAVENER, Rhoda Ann	MAY 28 1855
FREEMAN, James Y.	FLURY, Catherine E.	APR 24 1829
FREEMAN, Jane (blk)	WILSON, Charles	NOV 28 1848
FREEMAN, John	COLBERT, Malind	MAR 24 1818
FREEMAN, John	THOMAS, Nancy	JAN 22 1820
FREEMAN, John	WALTER, Teresa	FEB 02 1853
FREEMAN, John	FREEMAN, Emily (blk)	APR 02 1853
FREEMAN, John D.	SIMMS, Eleanor Ann	AUG 18 1823
FREEMAN, John Henry	FLINN, Mary Adeline	OCT 09 1837
FREEMAN, John, Jr.	WALTER, Caroline	APR 28 1851
FREEMAN, John P.	MANYET, Mary M.	NOV 13 1847
FREEMAN, John W.	BROOKS, Matilda (blk)	OCT 18 1853
FREEMAN, Joseph M., Jr.	ROBINSON, Mary Augusta	DEC 27 1855
FREEMAN, Julia P. (blk)	TURLEY, John M.	SEP 26 1850
FREEMAN, Laura V.	BLAN, Joseph A.	AUG 14 1851
FREEMAN, Margaret	FLEURY, Walter A.	DEC 23 1848
FREEMAN, Mary Elizabeth	PRICE, John Thomas	MAY 03 1849
FREEMAN, Robert	EMBRAY, Harriet	FEB 25 1841
FREEMAN, William H.	SHECKELLS, Christiana	NOV 30 1853
FREEMOUNT, John Charles	BENTON, Jessie Ann	OCT 19 1841
FREER, Ann	CONNOR, Hugh	OCT 15 1850
FREESE, Mary	NEFF, Wunderlin	FEB 26 1848
FREEZER, Jacob	DUN, Mary	NOV 14 1846

District of Columbia Marriage Licenses, 1811-1858

FREIDERICK, Catherine	REINDAL, Philip	JUL 12 1853
FREIDERICK, Mary	SEIFERLAND, John	NOV 30 1846
FREIMAN, Peter	WEIMAN, Wilhelmina	MAR 10 1858
FREIRICK, Charles	HERMANN, Barbara	AUG 16 1856
FRENCH, Alexander	MILES, Ann	JAN 22 1824
FRENCH, Andrew	PETERS, Jane	AUG 06 1835
FRENCH, Ann	TENCH, Stanislaus	NOV 15 1821
FRENCH, Ann	PHILLIPS, Samuel	DEC 28 1850
FRENCH, Arianna	LONEY, Boudinot S.	FEB 06 1854
FRENCH, Benjamin F.	BROWN, Anjelica	JUN 07 1821
FRENCH, Catharine	SCRIVENER, Thomas S.	DEC 10 1855
FRENCH, Edmund [Lt.]	BEALL, Louisa	DEC 21 1831
FRENCH, Edmund F.	BRADY, Margaret A.	JUL 01 1848
FRENCH, Elizabeth	CLARKE, THomas	FEB 25 1854
FRENCH, George	VanLEAR, Sarah D.	NOV 23 1840
FRENCH, Harrison Pirobie	DUBANT, Margaret Jane	MAY 11 1839
FRENCH, Henrietta M.	SANDS, Benjamin F., U.S.N.	NOV 14 1836
FRENCH, Ignatius	FARRELL, Susannah	AUG 04 1818
FRENCH, James	CURTIS, Sarah	AUG 26 1830
FRENCH, James B.	DANT, Amanda J.	NOV 18 1851
FRENCH, James W.	DAWSON, Harriet	MAR 25 1850
FRENCH, Jane	VIELEMANN, George	OCT 07 1854
FRENCH, Jane Elizabeth	THOMAS, Charles Edward	APR 22 1851
FRENCH, John William [Rev.]	MILLER, Clara	JUL 29 1835
FRENCH, Maria B.	MEIERE, Julius	JUN 30 1855
FRENCH, Maria D.B.	COMPTON, Wm. T.	MAY 17 1847
FRENCH, Marion Blackwell	HOBAN, James, Jr.	NOV 22 1831
FRENCH, Martha	KOLTZ, Frederick	SEP 28 1849
FRENCH, Martha E.	BRADBURY, John W.	SEP 24 1857
FRENCH, Mary A.	OBER, Franklin S.	MAY 02 1854
FRENCH, Mary Ellen	CONRAD, Michael H.	FEB 03 1858
FRENCH, Mary J.	SCOTT, James G.	SEP 12 1857
FRENCH, Mary Virginia	MASON, Maynadier	NOV 18 1830
FRENCH, Matilda C.	GRAY, Franklin C.	MAR 23 1853
FRENCH, Nancy	HIGDEN, John	NOV 04 1826
FRENCH, Nathaniel	FRENCH, Zoa	JUN 01 1830
FRENCH, Samuel	LONGWELL, Peggy	OCT 09 1817
FRENCH, Sarah E.	HARVEY, Thomas M.	MAY 09 1850
FRENCH, Sarah Jane	BROOK, Robert W.	APR 09 1855
FRENCH, Thomas	FOY, Ellen	NOV 30 1833
FRENCH, Thomas	CAMPBELL, Mary	MAY 14 1835
FRENCH, William	PANCOAST, Sarah	JAN 06 1820
FRENCH, William	JOHNSON, Harriet Ann	SEP 04 1845
FRENCH, Zoa	FRENCH, Nathaniel	JUN 01 1830
FRERE, Barrow	RAWLINGS, Eliza	AUG 11 1845
FRERE, Elizabeth Eleanor	BROWN, John	MAY 28 1842
FRERE, James	DORSETT, Elizabeth	MAY 29 1822
FRERE, Mary S.	GERMAN, John H.	SEP 28 1853
FRERE, Richard	BURNETT, Elizabeth	NOV 22 1853
FRESCH, Charles	BELLIER, Mary Ann	MAR 06 1843
FREUND, Philipina	SCHUCH, George	MAY 19 1853
FREY, Mary Eleanor	VANDEMERKEN, James B.	JAN 17 1857
FREYHOLD, Edward O.	VonGLUEMER, Agnes E.C.B.	MAR 13 1855
FRICK, George P.	TURNBULL, Catharine	APR 27 1854
FRICK, Martin	LOWMEYER, Mary	OCT 18 1855
FRIDER, John	IGLEHART, Catharine	OCT 20 1851
FRIDLEY, Catherine V.	DAY, John S.	JUN 04 1850
FRIDLEY, Charles W.	MOORE, Randonia C.	JUL 05 1855

District of Columbia Marriage Licenses, 1811-1858

FRIDLEY, George	SHEPPARD, Sarah	FEB 13 1827
FRIDLEY, George	RAY, Margaret	NOV 01 1853
FRIDLEY, Jane	BURCH, Joseph	FEB 13 1850
FRIEDEL, Francis	SCHMIDT, Frederica	JUL 22 1851
FRIEDEMAN, Ernestiene	SCHUSTER, John Gotlob	SEP 25 1857
FRIEDERICH, Sophus Emil	GEBHARDT, Caroline Maria	SEP 14 1852
FRIEL, Michael	FOX, Ann	JUL 23 1858
FRIESS, Christopher F.	BITZ, Mary Dorothea	NOV 12 1852
FRINK, Oliver	PARK, Louisa	SEP 08 1840
FRISBY, Mary E.	BLAKE, Samuel	DEC 21 1855
FRISBY, William	CHASE, Elizabeth (blk)	FEB 26 1844
FRISELL, Margaret A.	ELLIOT, William P.	MAR 02 1858
FRISTOE, Milton F.	STINSON, Sarah E.	AUG 04 1856
FRITCOLE, Winny	STEPHENS, James H.	MAR 02 1842
FRITZ, Charles	GREEN, Margaret	JUN 23 1836
FRITZSCHE, Emilie	SOMMERS, Michael W.	AUG 21 1852
FRIZELL, Ann Matilda	WALKER, James H.	JUN 30 1849
FRIZELL, Robert	CHEEK, Nancy	SEP 26 1837
FRIZELLE, Charles E.	RAGAN, Sarah Ellen	JUL 28 1854
FRIZLE, Ann	LOVELACE, Philip	NOV 28 1821
FRIZZEL, Martha Jane	DELAY, Robert	MAY 13 1844
FRIZZELL, Catherine	MYERS, John	MAY 14 1857
FRIZZELL, James	FOLLIN, Margaret Ann	JUN 26 1855
FRIZZELL, Mary	GANTT, James W.	DEC 02 1850
FRIZZLE, Catherine	TUTTLE, George	MAY 27 1844
FROELIG, Hartman	SMITH, Margaret	APR 06 1858
FRONK, Catherine	McINTIRE, Robert	MAR 03 1834
FROS, Mary	WALTER, Joseph	FEB 18 1857
FROST, Elizabeth	BURGESS, Andrew	MAR 31 1849
FROST, Horace J.	WALKER, Mildred C.	SEP 30 1857
FROST, John E.	ALRICK, Ann P.	AUG 01 1820
FROST, John T.	BROOKES, Sophia	JUN 02 1829
FROUK, Mary	KNOTT, Josiah H.	JAN 02 1827
FRUCKENMILLER, Rosina B.	GOCKELER, George Jacob	JUN 14 1856
FRUSH, Catharine	THECKER, Henry	DEC 12 1833
FRY, Ann	WADE, Zephaniah	JAN 18 1815
FRY, Ann	DUVALL, Henry C.	JUN 12 1854
FRY, Chloe	RYAN, Fielder	NOV 29 1828
FRY, Edward	DUCKETT, Catherine	JAN 17 1853
FRY, Elizabeth	WHITE, Ambrose	JAN 05 1825
FRY, Henry B.	CLARKE, Lucy	APR 09 1831
FRY, James	WHITE, Ann Rebecca	JUL 17 1817
FRY, James	WILSON, Rebecca	DEC 29 1821
FRY, James H.	MILLER, Mary Ann C.	APR 23 1829
FRY, John Jacob	KNOWLES, Mary	OCT 25 1830
FRY, Maria	HURST, Ephraim H.	AUG 18 1823
FRY, Mary Ann	WALL, William R.	NOV 08 1827
FRY, Mary Jane	MARTIN, Francis	DEC 30 1850
FRY, Nancy	SMULL, Jacob	DEC 09 1816
FRY, Rebecca	MAYHEW, George	JAN 11 1842
FRY, Samuel	IRVIN, Elizabeth	FEB 11 1828
FRY, Thomas E.	SUTTON, Maria L.	FEB 13 1850
FRYE, Caroline V.B.	BOWMAN, Leonard	MAY 13 1846
FRYE, Elizabeth	BLADEN, William	JUL 21 1842
FRYE, Henry	SIMPSON, Sarah	AUG 23 1821
FRYE, Hugh W., Jr.	DAVIDSON, Mary L.	JUN 14 1852
FRYE, John H.	DUCKETT, Lucinda	OCT 23 1844
FRYE, Nathl., Jr.	BUCHANAN, Caroline V.M.	JUL 03 1817

District of Columbia Marriage Licenses, 1811-1858

FRYE, Rebecca	CARROLL, Horatio	JUN 16 1818
FRYE, Rebecca	SHAY, Michael	NOV 28 1854
FRYE, Robert	BUCKLEY, Ellen	JUL 19 1823
FRYE, Sarah M.	COX, Washington F.	DEC 23 1845
FRYER, Henrietta	GAWLER, Alfred	NOV 12 1852
FRYER, Isabella	MERCHANT, Robert	JUN 06 1848
FRYER, Susan	CATHCART, Robt.	MAR 30 1822
FRYERS, Jane E.	WHITE, Samuel	MAR 13 1850
FUCHBERGER, Ursula	SCHWEITZER, Adam	JUL 06 1845
FUCHS, Caroline	COHLMAN, Henry	OCT 11 1855
FUEND, Henrietta	COOK, John	SEP 08 1852
FUGATE, Henrietta	BERRYMAN, George	JAN 11 1828
FUGATE, Joseph	McGILTON, Susan B.	JUN 16 1838
FUGET, Ellen	SHEILDS, Connell	NOV 20 1845
FUGETT, Benjamin	CLARKE, Harriet A.	JUL 30 1855
FUGETT, Francis J.	RIGSBY, Jane	NOV 05 1846
FUGETT, Rebecca M.	DURITY, Jas. R.	SEP 28 1857
FUGETT, Sarah Jane	CHURCH, Richard	NOV 29 1833
FUGIT, Frances Ann	GALLOWAY, James	SEP 20 1844
FUGITT, Benjamin	EMMERSON, Frances	DEC 11 1846
FUGITT, Catherine	FURGISON, Alphred B.	SEP 08 1836
FUGITT, Francis	FERGUSON, John B.	FEB 26 1846
FUGITT, Gustavus	WARD, Catherine	APR 17 1817
FUGITT, Matilda	MADDOX, James M.	MAR 24 1857
FUHRER, Catharine	BICK, Fidel	APR 13 1833
FULLALOVE, Mary A.	LUTZ, Francis A.	NOV 15 1842
FULLALOVE, Susan	STAKE, John M.	FEB 28 1848
FULLER, Elizabeth (blk)	WEBSTER, James	DEC 05 1855
FULLER, Elizabeth D.	CLAGETT, Henry B.	APR 01 1845
FULLER, Enos	BRADY, Purmelia	FEB 08 1831
FULLER, Frances	KRAFFT, Philip	JAN 03 1855
FULLER, Hellen	CONNALLY, Thomas E.	FEB 13 1837
FULLER, Jeremiah	LITCHFIELD, Jane A.	DEC 16 1851
FULLER, Mary A.	VESSEY, John	OCT 09 1856
FULLER, Ruth	CLARK, Mason E.	JUN 06 1831
FULLER, William	BLACK, Susan Taylor	APR 22 1843
FULMAN, Conrod	RADCLIFF, Ann	APR 08 1834
FULMER, Christian	GERMAN, Mary	JUL 23 1845
FULMER, George H.	HOPE, Mary S. [Mrs.]	FEB 09 1827
FULREETHEN, Mary Elenora	WEISS, John C.	NOV 03 1849
FULSHER, Keziah (blk)	WILLIAMS, Barny	AUG 06 1845
FULTON, Lyle	ROBERTS, Elizabeth	FEB 03 1814
FULTON, Robert	O'BRIEN, Ann Maria	NOV 26 1817
FULTZ, Elnora	ZENKER, Francis	SEP 29 1855
FULTZ, Margaret (blk)	PECK, David	FEB 24 1853
FUNDELEHR, Mary	HAPP, Nicholas	MAY 15 1848
FUNSON, James	BEACH, Elizabeth	OCT 05 1822
FUNSTEN, Maria	BYNUM, Jesse A.	MAR 19 1835
FURGERSON, Andrew	BAILEY, Catharine	JUN 06 1849
FURGERSON, Maria	WARD, John Thomas	NOV 02 1839
FURGERSON, Mary	GREEN, John	OCT 12 1838
FURGERSON, Sarah E.	GALLION, James	NOV 19 1855
FURGISON, Alphred B.	FUGITT, Catherine	SEP 08 1836
FURGUSON, Elizth. F.	MILSTEAD, Danl. L.	SEP 18 1856
FURGUSON, Henry W.	CLARKE, Catherine C.	OCT 18 1848
FURGUSON, Mary Ann (blk)	CARTER, John H.	JAN 26 1843
FURLONG, Kitty (blk)	HOWE, Jesse	OCT 19 1848
FURNESS, James Thiring	ELIOT, Elizabeth Margaret	OCT 25 1838

District of Columbia Marriage Licenses, 1811-1858

FURR, Edward	HURST, Rachel (blk)	JAN 12 1825
FURR, Elizabeth	JONES, James R.	NOV 15 1837
FURRY, Serena	ROGERS, Nelson	FEB 11 1833
FURSE, Jane P.	PALMER, William H.	JUL 07 1856
FURTNER, Alexander	GODDARD, Eliza Ann	JUN 03 1852
FURTNER, Biddy Ann	SNYDER, Hiram M.	NOV 11 1856
FURTNEY, George H.	DOWDEN, Mary E.	DEC 28 1843
FURTNEY, Pricilla	PRETTYMAN, David G.	DEC 31 1818
FUSS, Elizabeth	BEAN, Colley W.	JAN 29 1857
FUSS, John A.	KNOBLOCK, Mary	SEP 14 1829
FUSS, John G.	JACOB, Henrietta	SEP 08 1855
FUSS, Mary Jane	RAY, Joseph B.	DEC 20 1855
FUSS, William H.	BOSOMWORTH, Mary J.	FEB 09 1853
FUTTERER, Mary	ALVEY, John	JAN 02 1838
FYE, Bridget	BATTS, Thomas	AUG 24 1851

District of Columbia Marriage Licenses, 1811-1858

G

GABLER, John C.	KNOBLOCK, Margaret	JUN 08 1830
GABRIEL, Louise	GALABRAN, Louis	FEB 17 1837
GADD, Charles	SMITH, Caroline (blk)	MAR 22 1858
GADDIS, Adam	GREEN, Julian	JAN 24 1824
GADNER, Mary M.	FOLEY, John W.	JAN 13 1844
GADSBY, Augusta	McBLAIR, John H.	OCT 20 1835
GADSBY, James	RATCLIFF, Lucinda (blk)	FEB 02 1853
GADSBY, Julia	TenEYCK, John C.	JUN 10 1845
GADSBY, William	BRUFF, Mary Augusta	JUN 28 1843
GAEER, Jane	CARROLL, Michael	DEC 20 1820
GAENSLER, Henry	WEIGAND, Margaret	OCT 04 1841
GAER, John	LLEWELLEN, Elizabeth	NOV 20 1845
GAHAN, Peter W.	TOOLE, Margaret	AUG 06 1855
GAHAN, Walter	KELLY, Mary Ann	JAN 08 1847
GAHARTY, Mary	MURDOCH, John W.	APR 26 1848
GAHMANN, Frederick	WILSON, Mary	DEC 03 1849
GAHUTZ, Cathrine	MURPHY, Patrick	JAN 24 1858
GAHUVA, William	JONSTON, Jane Ann (blk)	MAY 26 1856
GAI, Ann Jane	PATTON, William	FEB 01 1842
GAI, Heloise	ESTERLEY, Daniel	JUL 13 1842
GAILOR, Elizabeth	WARREN, Robert	JUL 08 1813
GAINER, Ellen (blk)	SCOTT, Thomas	DEC 24 1839
GAINER, John F.	McGINN, Catharine	AUG 31 1853
GAINER, Louisa	REYNOLDS, James	MAY 07 1857
GAINER, Mary	BUTLER, Jeason	JUN 26 1854
GAINES, Edward	BROWN, Caroline	JUN 14 1843
GAINES, Edwin	BOTTS, Mary V.	DEC 29 1845
GAINES, George	THOMAS, Arianna (blk)	SEP 09 1852
GAINES, George W.	HALL, Rebecca (blk)	FEB 16 1854
GAINES, Gregory	MILES, Mary D.	APR 18 1854
GAINES, John	SHRIDER, Mary	OCT 22 1833
GAINES, Louisa J.	BOWERS, Richard S.	JUN 29 1853
GAINES, Robt. H.	SAUNDERS, Sarah Ann	SEP 04 1828
GAINOR, John	WHALAN, Bridget	JAN 16 1828
GAITHER, Edward	TILLMAN, Bridget	DEC 20 1827
GAITHER, Edward	KELLY, Mary Ann	DEC 18 1839
GAITHER, Eliza McLean	SEYMOUR, Alexander R.	NOV 06 1849
GAITHER, Elizabeth	ARTHUR, James	JUN 28 1855
GAITHER, Elizabeth (blk)	DORSEY, Allen	DEC 06 1836
GAITHER, George R.	BRADLEY, Hannah	MAR 12 1822
GAITHER, Greenbury	BRUMLEY, Margaret	MAY 18 1824
GAITHER, Henry	HEUGHES, Arie Ann	DEC 24 1816
GAITHER, James	ESPEY, Ann	SEP 09 1817
GAITHER, John	SERRIN, Mary Ann	NOV 18 1824
GAITHER, John	WALKER, Sarah Ann	FEB 15 1836
GAITHER, Martha	HINKLE, Philip	DEC 18 1850
GAITHER, Matilda Riggs	RAWLINGS, James	JAN 06 1855
GAITHRIGHT, Samuel, Jr.	GEORGE, Elizabeth	JUN 23 1825
GAITOF, Catherine	THOMAS, William	SEP 13 1845
GALABRAN, Louis	GABRIEL, Louise	FEB 17 1837
GALE, Clara A.	ALLEN, William H.	JUL 13 1858
GALE, Sally	SHELTON, Moses	FEB 21 1814
GALER, Mary Louisa	BARRETT, John F.	DEC 27 1825
GALER, William Brooke	HURDLE, Francis Marion	NOV 09 1854
GALES, Ann Maria (blk)	SHELVY, Dyer	APR 14 1853
GALES, Eliza H.	RAMSAY, George D.	JUN 28 1838

District of Columbia Marriage Licenses, 1811-1858

GALES, Lucy Ann	CRAWFORD, Adam	JUL 08 1830
GALHGAM, Jane	OGLE, Richard	OCT 16 1856
GALHUGH, Mary	KNOX, John	MAY 25 1838
GALITZEN, Eliza	AGINTON, Henry	OCT 06 1813
GALLAGHAR, Hugh	WARD, Susanna	SEP 08 1835
GALLAGHER, Bridget M.	WISE, John	MAY 17 1845
GALLAGHER, Elizabeth	CHRISTOPHER, Andw.	AUG 04 1855
GALLAGHER, Hugh	BRADLEY, Julia	JUN 11 1842
GALLAGHER, John	LINKINS, Livinia E.	MAY 11 1854
GALLAGHER, Michael	CLEARY, Catherine	OCT 09 1857
GALLAHAM, Samuel	CLUB, Jane	DEC 23 1824
GALLAHAN, Thomas	PAYNE, Frances	DEC 28 1852
GALLAHER, B. Franklin	BUCKNER, Eliza A.	MAY 12 1857
GALLAHER, John S.	SHANNON, Catherine	SEP 06 1817
GALLAHER, Marcellus	BROOKS, Virginia	SEP 06 1853
GALLAHER, Mary	RAGAN, John	FEB 03 1852
GALLAHER, Mary Hellen	SENSENEY, George E.	NOV 03 1851
GALLAHER, Stephen G.R.	STEWART, Marsaline	DEC 20 1849
GALLAND, William	CROMPTON, Rebecca	JUL 15 1813
GALLANT, Edward	SPALDING, Mary Ann	JUN 19 1841
GALLANT, Peter	HOBURG, Amelia	JAN 17 1843
GALLANT, Rosine	BECKERT, Joseph	JAN 22 1850
GALLAUDET, Theodore [Rev.]	SMITH, Julia H.	FEB 08 1836
GALLAWAY, Eliza	WILLIAMS, James	MAR 17 1824
GALLAWAY, Martha	COBURN, John D.	MAR 10 1824
GALLET, Rachel	HOWLIN, Mark	JAN 02 1845
GALLIHER, Michael	SMITH, Mary Bridget	SEP 08 1823
GALLION, James	FURGERSON, Sarah E.	NOV 19 1855
GALLIVAN, Dennis	BURY, Margaret	NOV 20 1832
GALLIVIN, Mary	O'DONNELL, John	JUL 24 1858
GALLOWAN, William	DUCKET, Lucinda (blk)	AUG 30 1845
GALLOWAY, Catherine	BAGY, Michael	FEB 04 1853
GALLOWAY, James	FUGIT, Frances Ann	SEP 20 1844
GALLOWAY, Juliet	TAVENNER, George	MAR 19 1839
GALLOWAY, Mary	DITTY, Thomas R.	MAY 28 1827
GALLOWAY, Mary	WIDDICOMBE, Robert	SEP 27 1828
GALLOWAY, Mary (blk)	COKELEY, Gabriel	AUG 14 1850
GALPIN, Attilia	VELIE, George C.	APR 26 1853
GALPIN, Gracy Ann	BADGER, Alfred N.	JUN 23 1831
GALT, James	VEITCH, Elizabeth	JUL 22 1818
GALT, Richard	O'BRIEN, Bridget	AUG 05 1858
GALT, Thomas	HILL, Charlotte	NOV 04 1843
GALT, Thomas J.	HUNTER, Mary A.	DEC 07 1847
GALVIN, Caroline A.	McDOWELL, E.T.	MAR 10 1834
GALVIN, Henry	COLLINGS, Bridget	FEB 20 1854
GALVIN, Rodger	HICKS, Darcus [Mrs.]	JUL 03 1816
GALVIN, Thomas	MADIGAN, Catherine	JAN 10 1852
GAMBIER, Joseph L.	JONES, Ann	JUN 18 1831
GAMBLE, Margaret	CREAMER, James	MAY 11 1854
GAMBLE, Mary Lang	HURST, William Decatur	NOV 14 1848
GAMBLE, William	LEE, Ann	MAR 16 1817
GAMMON, Catherine	SUMMERS, Henry	DEC 02 1839
GANNON, Ann	DEVENY, Charles	OCT 19 1820
GANNON, Bridget	RAY, James	SEP 21 1854
GANNON, Bridget	O'REILY, Peter	JAN 30 1858
GANNON, Margaret	DRURY, Plummer J.	JAN 17 1814
GANNON, Martha	CUDMORE, William	APR 21 1830
GANNON, Mary	GREEN, Michael	JAN 28 1852

District of Columbia Marriage Licenses, 1811-1858

GANNON, Mary Ellen	SHAW, William P.	NOV 25 1830
GANNON, Michael	MURPHY, Sarah A.C.	JUN 01 1826
GANT, Armstead	PECK, Louisa (blk)	JUN 23 1852
GANT, Edward	GIBSON, Lucy (blk)	APR 11 1854
GANT, Sarah (blk)	BURKE, Wesley	FEB 23 1854
GANT, Thomas	MEEKES, Ann	OCT 20 1837
GANTT, Ambrose	JORDAN, Jane	MAY 14 1845
GANTT, Basil	HARRIS, Mima (blk)	OCT 16 1823
GANTT, Benjamin	CLARKE, Ann Octavia (blk)	JUL 20 1853
GANTT, Benjamin S.	SMITH, Margaret C.	OCT 25 1848
GANTT, Benjn. E.	CHANDLER, Jane	NOV 02 1826
GANTT, Eliza	HARLING, John	DEC 19 1844
GANTT, James Thomas	JOHNSON, Ann (blk)	APR 03 1844
GANTT, James W.	FRIZZELL, Mary	DEC 02 1850
GANTT, Joseph	FOLLIN, Adelaid	OCT 19 1854
GANTT, Julia (col'd)	BUTLER, Mathias	AUG 29 1851
GANTT, Lucy	PRESTON, Thomas	APR 09 1822
GANTT, Margaret Ann	DULANY, Daniel F., Jr.	OCT 20 1832
GANTT, Maria (blk)	HOWARD, William	NOV 22 1832
GANTT, Martha Ellen	HUTCHISON, Jeremiah	JUL 26 1834
GANTT, Mary Ann	HALSEY, Zachariah	FEB 01 1812
GANTT, Rosalie	JOHNSTON, Charles B.	DEC 10 1857
GANTT, Samuel	REDIN, Mary Ann (blk)	OCT 03 1848
GANTT, Thomas	DOUGLASS, Catharine (blk)	NOV 28 1839
GANTT, Thomas	JOHNSON, Ann (blk)	AUG 07 1850
GARCI, Celestin	WILSON, Henrietta	JUL 10 1856
GARDENER, John H.	HARVEY, Anna E.J.	DEC 21 1854
GARDENER, Sarah	SKIDMORE, George	SEP 23 1822
GARDINE, George W.	MOCKBEE, Eliza H.	JAN 22 1836
GARDINER, Aaron	BEILER, Elizabeth	FEB 16 1831
GARDINER, Ann	RIGAN, Patrick	JUL 09 1818
GARDINER, Ann	GODDARD, John H.	NOV 16 1820
GARDINER, Ann	DEAVER, Joshua	JAN 29 1823
GARDINER, Ann	HUTCHINSON, William	MAY 07 1833
GARDINER, Ann (blk)	JONES, Levi	MAY 17 1839
GARDINER, Caleb P.	HUDDLESTON, Mary	DEC 23 1818
GARDINER, Eliza A.	BARKER, John B.	OCT 25 1832
GARDINER, Elizabeth	WHITE, John T.	APR 01 1834
GARDINER, Henry	PARKERSON, Margaret	AUG 11 1835
GARDINER, J. Carlos	McCLERY, Indiana I.	JUN 24 1852
GARDINER, John	HUTTON, Ann	SEP 05 1820
GARDINER, John C.	SUIT, Abraella	JUL 23 1855
GARDINER, Josephine Alice	CAPLAIN, Sosthene Eugene	JAN 04 1858
GARDINER, Leonard A.	BADEN, Margaret A.	MAR 26 1838
GARDINER, Richard B.	SCANLON, Ann	APR 09 1851
GARDINER, Richard Beatty	KEENAN, Catherine	SEP 17 1855
GARDINER, William	DIDENHOOVER, Mary C.	JAN 18 1831
GARDINER, Wm. T.	BOSWELL, Phelly D.	FEB 15 1847
GARDIVAN, Honora	CORBETT, Michael	APR 19 1856
GARDNEIR, Matilda	EARP, Jno. Wm.	JUL 22 1851
GARDNER, David A.	MINCHEN, Elizabeth	APR 23 1821
GARDNER, Emma K.	MOUTON, Alexander	JAN 24 1842
GARDNER, Francis D.	FENNER, John P.	OCT 03 1819
GARDNER, George	WISE, Mary Ann	DEC 04 1827
GARDNER, Isidore	MUDD, Harriet	MAY 19 1827
GARDNER, Jacob B., Dr.	MANNING, Rosa M.	JAN 08 1852
GARDNER, Joanah	SYLVARY, Samuel	JAN 30 1818
GARDNER, John Lane [Capt.]	GOLDSBOROUGH, Caroline	OCT 05 1825

District of Columbia Marriage Licenses, 1811-1858

GARDNER, Mary	FOY, Michael	APR 29 1857
GARDNER, Sarah A. McL.	ALMY, John J.	JAN 30 1854
GARDNER, Sarah E.	GOGGIN, Robert	DEC 23 1848
GARDNER, Sarah H.	BUCKLEY, Thomas A.	JUL 11 1857
GARDNER, Susan	WEDEN, William	DEC 23 1819
GARDNER, William	ARRINGTON, Margaret	MAY 31 1827
GARDNER, William	JOHNSON, Lucy Ann	JAN 05 1828
GARDNER, William	AUSTIN, Matilda [Mrs.]	DEC 01 1829
GARDNER, William F.	YOUNG, Mary Jane	APR 30 1845
GARDNER, William F.	CLAPDORE, Amelia	MAR 16 1853
GARDNER, William H.	SELDEN, Virginia	APR 26 1853
GARDNER, Wm. H., Capt. U.S. Navy	SELDEN, Frances E.	OCT 11 1842
GARDNOR, Mary	MILLS, Lewis	DEC 29 1812
GARE, Robert	NAILON, Mary	OCT 20 1855
GARENS, Geshe Margaretha	REINING, John Conrad	APR 05 1842
GAREY, Edward E.	PETERS, Louisa (blk)	MAR 01 1848
GAREY, Mary Ann	ROCHE, Robert J.	APR 01 1841
GAREY, Owen	SULLIVAN, Catherine	OCT 21 1854
GAREY, Susan	TAYLOR, Nathaniel	FEB 23 1838
GAREY, Thomas	HUMPHREYS, Mary	JAN 16 1858
GARGES, John H.	SCOTT, Martha Ann	DEC 16 1841
GARISON, Roy A.	CROWLEY, Julia A.	NOV 30 1838
GARLAND, Ann Maria	COX, Samuel G.	DEC 23 1851
GARLAND, John S.	HOUSTON, Mary T.	AUG 24 1850
GARLEY, Joseph	HALLORAN, Mary	AUG 09 1856
GARMANN, Susanna	GOMMAN, Christian Gotlip	OCT 30 1845
GARMILLER, Francis	HEINEL, Anna Maria	JAN 04 1855
GARNAGLE, James M.	STONE, Lucretia	AUG 11 1827
GARNAR, Ann	MONKS, Isaac	JUN 12 1823
GARNER, Ann	SMITH, Charles	AUG 28 1817
GARNER, Ann	THOMAS, William	MAR 24 1832
GARNER, Ann Eliza	TAYLOR, George E.	OCT 22 1856
GARNER, Charles	THOMPSON, Ann	JUL 17 1823
GARNER, Charles N.	COOK, Lucretia A.	NOV 22 1849
GARNER, Charlotte	GARRETT, Simeon P.	AUG 02 1821
GARNER, Daniel	GRAY, Mary Ann	JUN 14 1844
GARNER, Delilah	GATES, George	JAN 11 1827
GARNER, Elizabeth F.	LENOIR, William J.	OCT 17 1842
GARNER, Harriet	WILLIAMSON, Benjamin	JUL 13 1822
GARNER, Harriet Ann	HURLEY, James W.	AUG 19 1847
GARNER, Hezekiah [Lieut.]	EDELEN, Lucy Ann	NOV 26 1827
GARNER, J.W.B.	GARNER, Susan	JUL 24 1844
GARNER, Jane	POSTON, John	AUG 29 1839
GARNER, Jefferson	WATSON, Mary	FEB 09 1848
GARNER, John	LYNCH, Mary	OCT 17 1826
GARNER, Maria	McGUIRE, John	APR 15 1853
GARNER, Mary	LYNCH, John	APR 15 1820
GARNER, Mary E.	KIDWELL, Alexander C.	APR 21 1829
GARNER, Mary Kate	CHRISTIE, Francis C.	JUN 16 1857
GARNER, Sarah	HYDE, Thos. F.	JUL 22 1822
GARNER, Susan Ann	GARNER, J.W.B.	JUL 24 1844
GARNER, Susannah	WINDSER, Henry	DEC 31 1823
GARNER, Thomas	SEBASTEN, Patty	JAN 31 1824
GARNER, Walter	JOHNSON, Martha (blk)	APR 30 1850
GARNER, William	GIPSON, Mary Ann	NOV 27 1850
GARNER, William	POSEY, Mary	MAY 11 1853
GARNER, Wm.	WHITE, Sarah	MAY 13 1856
GARNETT, George S.	POWELL, America	AUG 02 1851

District of Columbia Marriage Licenses, 1811-1858

GARRARD, Caroline M.	GRIGSBY, Alexander S.	APR 16 1827
GARRARD, George	TRAVERS, Eliza Ann	APR 19 1816
GARRET, Juliana (blk)	QUEEN, Isac	JUL 02 1831
GARRET, Powhatan J.	PHILLIPS, Nannie	SEP 23 1857
GARRETT, Ann E.	ROBERTSON, James	APR 12 1848
GARRETT, David	LOWE, Jane	APR 26 1850
GARRETT, Franklin	LATHRUM, Sarah Jane	JUN 30 1853
GARRETT, George W.	KING, Ann Jane	NOV 02 1846
GARRETT, Greenup	KIRBY, Rebecca	NOV 25 1832
GARRETT, Henry Ashton	BOSWELL, Mary Ann	APR 27 1843
GARRETT, James	BARKER, Sarah J.	DEC 23 1856
GARRETT, Joseph E.	FOLEY, Ann E.	FEB 15 1858
GARRETT, Mary A.	JOHNSON, John B.	NOV 23 1857
GARRETT, Mildred A.	STAPLE, Walter	APR 03 1852
GARRETT, Mortimer	GOODRICK, Teresa	OCT 09 1838
GARRETT, Simeon P.	GARNER, Charlotte	AUG 02 1821
GARRETT, Simon	BALL, Ann Virginia	MAY 30 1850
GARRETT, William, Junr.	WASHINGTON, Harriet Ann	JUL 07 1830
GARRETTSON, Martha Aletha	JORDAN, Robert S.	JUN 29 1858
GARRISON, Ann	PARKER, William	SEP 26 1822
GARRISON, Charity Ann	DERRIN, Charles	SEP 13 1819
GARRISON, James	SAUNDERS, Frances C.	JAN 18 1848
GARRISON, Virginia A.	COOPER, Seth R.	NOV 03 1857
GARRITT, Richard	KOONES, Caroline	MAY 14 1834
GARRITY, James	HURLEY, Honora	NOV 24 1855
GARRITY, Margaret	CURLY, John	AUG 11 1858
GARST, David	COLLISON, Susen E.	NOV 01 1855
GARSTINE, John	THUTTNER, Frances	NOV 29 1853
GARTH, Catherine Jane	HARRISON, Benjamin L.	DEC 23 1854
GARTHARD, Sarah Ann	MOUNT, James	JAN 20 1838
GARTLAND, Elizabeth F.X.	MARCERON, Peter T.	SEP 16 1851
GARTNER, Leonore	RUPPERT, Christian	JUN 01 1854
GARTRELL, William C.	ZIMMERMAN, Maria L.	SEP 10 1855
GARVAN, James	LYNCH, Bridget	JUN 18 1855
GARVEY, Ann	DORCY, Stephen	JAN 24 1857
GARVEY, Bridget	DAY, Peter	NOV 13 1851
GARVEY, Patrick	DURELL, Nancy	JAN 29 1851
GARWOOD, Margaret	LEAK, Elisha	MAR 30 1815
GASBY, John	LEE, Maria	MAY 11 1818
GASCH, Ernst	SELLE, Mary	JAN 15 1853
GASH, Julius	HAAG, Eliza	JUL 15 1852
GASH, Mary	KNOCH, John H.	NOV 17 1855
GASKINS, Alice Hester	DONOHUE, Thos. Henry	SEP 13 1853
GASKINS, Ann	NEALE, Henry	MAY 04 1829
GASKINS, Darius	SMART, Amelia	SEP 27 1827
GASKINS, Frances A.	GROVE, L. Jewitt	SEP 25 1856
GASKINS, Isaac	MESTER, Hester Ann	JUL 29 1835
GASKINS, Mary E.	ESTERLA, George	APR 16 1846
GASKINS, Priscilla S.	WOODWARD, Charles J.	APR 29 1852
GASKINS, William H.	ROACH, Susan	MAY 16 1848
GASLER, Sarah	DONALDSON, Thomas	MAR 27 1813
GASSAWAY, Emily M. (blk)	BROOKS, Daniel M.	NOV 25 1851
GASSAWAY, Joshua	JENIFER, Mary	JAN 07 1831
GASSAWAY, Madison	WHITE, Lucinda	FEB 24 1852
GASSAWAY, Margaret Ann (blk)	BELLOWS, Alfred	JUN 03 1852
GASSAWAY, Richard	DAVIS, Mary Jane	NOV 05 1846
GASSAWAY, Thomas	KEY, Mary Ann A. (blk)	JUL 26 1853
GASSEMHEIMER, Sophia	DAVID, Abram	FEB 10 1858

District of Columbia Marriage Licenses, 1811-1858

GASSENHEIMER, Leopold	LULY, Fanny	JAN 18 1856
GASTON, Eliza	GRAHAM, George W.	NOV 11 1842
GASTON, William [Hon.]	WORTHINGTON, Eliza Ann	SEP 03 1816
GASZ, Charles J.	ASHCRAFT, Louisa	SEP 20 1853
GASZ, John G.	HESSE, Louisa	FEB 23 1843
GATCHELL, John	ROSS, Mary	MAR 01 1822
GATCHELL, Mary Jane	CHARLTON, Thomas	MAR 28 1837
GATES, Ann	GATES, John N.	OCT 29 1839
GATES, Ann Catherine	WATSON, William Westley	JUL 14 1833
GATES, Caroline	GATES, Richard D.	JUN 21 1855
GATES, Charles L.	BURROWS, Mary Elizth.	AUG 29 1848
GATES, Christianna	MADDOX, Alexander	SEP 06 1836
GATES, Cornelia (blk)	WHEELER, Daniel	APR 04 1853
GATES, Dorcas Ann	HYDE, Henry	OCT 07 1852
GATES, Elias	SIMPSON, Susan	MAY 14 1815
GATES, Eliza	AVERY, Thornton	OCT 16 1854
GATES, Elizabeth	RUSTRIDGE, James	SEP 20 1837
GATES, Elizabeth	CRUMP, George W.	SEP 29 1840
GATES, Elizabeth	KIDWELL, Thomas J.	DEC 27 1842
GATES, Elizabeth E.	COX, Charles A.	OCT 23 1846
GATES, Emily Ann	ECTON, Wallace M.	AUG 04 1833
GATES, Emma Jane	PUMPHREY, John H.	DEC 01 1851
GATES, Francis	GRIFFITH, Elizabeth	JAN 01 1842
GATES, Francis	HASEL, Catherine A.	NOV 16 1850
GATES, George	LATHROME, Susannah J.	DEC 30 1826
GATES, George	GARNER, Delilah	JAN 11 1827
GATES, George L.	MULLIKIN, Martha E.	AUG 06 1850
GATES, Harriett	SHORT, Elexius	MAR 09 1841
GATES, James A.	WILLIS, Ann Eliza	DEC 14 1848
GATES, James R.	LOW, Mary Jane	FEB 03 1854
GATES, James W.	PURDY, Ann	SEP 11 1850
GATES, James W.	BURROWS, Caroline	JUL 13 1854
GATES, Jane	VICKERS, Parnell	APR 23 1858
GATES, Jane Adeline	MITCHELL, James, Jr.	MAY 31 1855
GATES, Johanna	DIXON, George	SEP 29 1857
GATES, John M.	LANGLEY, Sarah Ann	OCT 17 1837
GATES, John N.	GATES, Ann	OCT 29 1839
GATES, John T.	LEE, Elizabeth Eliza	SEP 07 1832
GATES, Lemuel A.	ROCKETT, Sarah A.	DEC 08 1853
GATES, Lydia Ann	McKENNA, William	APR 20 1844
GATES, Maria	LANGLEY, James	JAN 22 1846
GATES, Martha	HAMILTON, Edward	OCT 08 1833
GATES, Martha (blk)	BUTLER, William	MAR 15 1855
GATES, Martha E.	LIVERS, Miles P.	JAN 12 1853
GATES, Mary	POSEY, James	JUN 02 1816
GATES, Mary	WHITTLE, David	AUG 11 1837
GATES, Mary	WHITTLE, John	SEP 26 1840
GATES, Mary	BELL, Washington	SEP 24 1855
GATES, Mary N.	DUVALL, Edmund B.	OCT 28 1840
GATES, Mary R.	PHILLIPS, Thomas B.	JUL 25 1848
GATES, Nancy	OSBORN, Joseph	OCT 03 1837
GATES, Priscilla	KIDWELL, George	APR 17 1827
GATES, Rachel	TALBERT, William	JAN 06 1820
GATES, Richard D.	GATES, Caroline	JUN 21 1855
GATES, Richard L.	BEAN, Mary	MAR 07 1848
GATES, Robert O.	KING, Sarah Ann	JUN 22 1824
GATES, Sarah	BLADEN, John	AUG 08 1843
GATES, Sarah Ann	HARDY, Walter	JUN 24 1843

District of Columbia Marriage Licenses, 1811-1858

GATES, Susan	HALL, Peter	SEP 09 1830
GATES, Susan J.	MOSELY, William H.	SEP 21 1833
GATES, Sylvester F.	HOLROYD, Mary Jane	MAR 12 1851
GATES, Thomas	FITTEN, Margaret	SEP 21 1844
GATES, William	STUART, Juliann	APR 05 1836
GATES, William	HILL, Mary	DEC 09 1847
GATES, William	JENKINS, Alice	SEP 16 1852
GATES, William Henry	ROBEY, Lucinda	DEC 08 1842
GATES, Wm. O'Brien	KIDWELL, Lucretia	JUN 03 1843
GATEWOOD, Eliza T.	EDMONSTON, Franklin	DEC 23 1848
GATEWOOD, Jackson D.	BURRUSS, Amanda	DEC 28 1854
GATEWOOD, John B.	KIRK, Jane T.	MAR 03 1829
GATEWOOD, William H.	BROWN, Mary Jane	MAR 21 1850
GATRELL, Ellenora	CISSEL, George W.	NOV 23 1857
GATRELL, Frances E.	DORSEY, Augustus	NOV 18 1857
GATTIN, Mary Eliza	BRANSTON, William Henry	MAY 27 1858
GATTON, Azariah Henry	LEWIS, Mary Ann	MAY 30 1838
GATTON, Azariah Henry	LEWIS, Martha Washington	APR 15 1850
GATTON, Edward	MACKEY, Elizabeth	AUG 17 1847
GATTON, Elisha A.	BURCH, Jane H.	MAY 06 1816
GATTRELL, Aaron M.	HARTMAN, Elizabeth	AUG 28 1834
GATTRELL, Atho	ISRAEL, Ruth	OCT 01 1833
GATTSCHLICK, Ernest	DRICKSEL, Elizabeth	AUG 27 1819
GAU, Alexander	CAMPBELL, Margaret	FEB 19 1856
GAUBERT, John A.	PEAKE, Sarah Jane	NOV 03 1849
GAUBERT, John A.	PETTIS, Sarah A.	NOV 21 1853
GAUBERT, Theodore	HUNTT, Mary Ann	JAN 31 1845
GAUDEMAR, Jean Baptiste	BLOIS, Francoise	MAR 18 1819
GAULICH, Elizabeth	PILLA, John	MAY 16 1855
GAULLETT, Placedie	GREEN, Edward	APR 26 1853
GAULT, Matthew	DEALE, Laura C.	MAR 05 1845
GAUTIER, Pierre Charles	BOYLE, Alice	NOV 08 1839
GAVIN, Bridget	KEEVEN, John	JUL 09 1850
GAWLER, Alfred	FRYER, Henrietta	NOV 12 1852
GAWLER, Joseph	BENNER, Anne L.	DEC 18 1850
GAWLER, Sarah	GREEN, Edwin	APR 23 1839
GAWROUSKI, Leon Rowiez	HALL, Henrietta Maria	JUL 19 1841
GAYLE, Robert E.	NEILL, Sarah R.	JUN 27 1855
GAYLOR, John	STREET, Aglae E.	JUN 10 1838
GEANEY, Johanna	HERLIHEY, Patrick	FEB 19 1857
GEASLIN, Mary E.	FOWLER, Samuel G.	DEC 11 1851
GEASLING, Andrew	SMART, Rebecca	JAN 06 1819
GEATZ, George Jos.	LEONARD, Joanna Louisa	MAY 09 1858
GEAY, Matilda	GRAY, Cail Ellum	JAN 20 1813
GEBHARDI, Frederick	NORBECK, Maria	APR 03 1834
GEBHARDT, Caroline Maria	FRIEDERICH, Sophus Emil	SEP 14 1852
GEBHARDT, Friedericke	PANZENBINDER, Henry	FEB 27 1854
GEBHARDT, Minna	DESSAR, Leon	MAY 25 1857
GEDDIS, Rosella	OTTERBACK, Henry	NOV 19 1846
GEDNEY, Thomas R., U.S.N.	STEWART, Hebe	AUG 08 1831
GEE, Ann	DEVOLVE, Washington	MAR 30 1820
GEE, Ann Maria	PADGETT, Mason	AUG 09 1853
GEE, Frances	HUTCHINSON, James H.	OCT 27 1855
GEE, Henry	OSBORN, Ann	JUN 22 1850
GEE, Margaret	SMITH, Wilfred	AUG 11 1831
GEE, Samuel P.	BOSWELL, Mary C.	AUG 03 1858
GEE, Thomas	BREST, Lucretia	SEP 16 1818
GEEN, Louisanna A.	CORSON, Pierson	SEP 05 1857

District of Columbia Marriage Licenses, 1811-1858

GEER, Michael	FERRER, Margaretta	FEB 13 1857
GEERHAGAN, James	CLANCEY, Mary	AUG 13 1857
GEERKEN, Ann Maria	MOORE, John	MAR 14 1837
GEESTER, Rebecca	BRYON, Zechiel Orick	DEC 30 1845
GEIER, Bernard	BARBER, Ida	JUL 31 1854
GEIGER, Adolph	CRUSODOLPH, Wilhelminie	JUN 30 1855
GEIGER, Caroline	NIAGLER, Charles J.	FEB 20 1858
GEIGER, Eliza	RICKSECKER, John	MAY 28 1828
GEIGER, Frederick E.	LUTZ, Mary C.	APR 09 1849
GEIGER, Frederick E.	SHAW, Lavinia	JUN 19 1851
GEIGER, John Jacob	BARTHOLOMEW, Isabella	JUN 19 1851
GEIGER, Sophia L.	SCHERER, Jacob	JUL 19 1854
GEIR, Gertrude	LOGBALER, Joseph	APR 04 1853
GEISINDAFFER, John	KEENE, Subina	OCT 31 1839
GEISINDAFFER, William H.	SIMPSON, Mary E.	MAR 05 1842
GENAW, Daniel	COOK, Elizabeth	APR 04 1853
GENGELL, Henry	GIVEN, Jane E.	DEC 30 1843
GENGENBACH, Doratha	SHOUP, Galus	JUN 09 1842
GENGENBACH, George Frederick	DITRICH, Dorothy	DEC 18 1832
GENIGAN, Alexander B.	LEIDBURG, Sarah	JAN 19 1829
GENNELL, Charles C.	WHELAN, Julia N.M.	FEB 07 1839
GENTLE, Acquilla	DAY, Ann	SEP 26 1840
GENTLE, Elizth.	McFARLAND, William	APR 14 1834
GENTLE, Emily	BUTT, Jonathan	SEP 20 1832
GENTLE, Mary Ann	BEECH, Allen	FEB 17 1837
GENTLE, Rebecca	BATT, Thomas Henry	JUN 30 1835
GENTLE, Sarah Ann	BURROWS, Samuel	JUN 20 1850
GENTRY, Benjamin W.	FORD, Jeanette Frances	OCT 01 1857
GENTRY, Carinda A.	TYLER, Richard F.	JUN 23 1857
GENTRY, Sarah (blk)	BENTLEY, Charles	JUN 20 1857
GEORGE, Eliza (blk)	BELL, Moses	SEP 25 1856
GEORGE, Elizabeth	GAITHRIGHT, Samuel, Jr.	JUN 23 1825
GEORGE, Martha	HILL, John	FEB 25 1852
GEORGE, Mary	LEE, Alfred H.	SEP 15 1853
GEORGE, W.M.	CRECEY, Mary E. (blk)	JUN 26 1856
GEORGE, William	DIGGES, Sarah	AUG 17 1843
GERBER, Mary Ann	VANDERLEHR, George	JAN 11 1858
GERBER, Sabine	SAUER, Adam	AUG 03 1846
GERBING, Margaret	MEYER, Michl.	JUN 06 1855
GERDES, Ferdinand H.	CUMMINGS, Mary Jane	MAY 26 1842
GERECKE, August	DECKER, Juliana	APR 26 1853
GERHOLD, Charlotte	SOHL, Conrad	MAR 09 1858
GERLACK, Margaret	MILLER, Faustin	MAY 22 1836
GERMAIN, Catharine	MILLER, John	DEC 23 1836
GERMAIN, Ira V.	VANDEVENTER, Eliza	APR 03 1838
GERMAN, Fanny	HUTTON, William	OCT 23 1854
GERMAN, Francis	COLLIER, Jane	DEC 24 1851
GERMAN, George	BATT, Lavinia	MAR 02 1854
GERMAN, John H.	FRERE, Mary S.	SEP 28 1853
GERMAN, Mary	FULMER, Christian	JUL 23 1845
GERMAN, Stephen D.	JOY, Ann Elizabeth	JUL 20 1844
GERMON, Ann Emeline	ROWE, John Thomas	JUL 07 1842
GERMON, Elizabeth E.	MILLS, Armstead T.	DEC 28 1854
GERMON, Mary L.	JOHNSON, John	JAN 10 1846
GERMON, Thomas J.	LUCAS, John	OCT 29 1853
GERMON, Vincent D.	EDMONSON, Eliza	SEP 26 1821
GERNER, Patrick	CATON, Mary	FEB 01 1838
GERNHARD, Johanna	KIEFER, Philip	SEP 16 1856

District of Columbia Marriage Licenses, 1811-1858

GERRGEN, Elizabeth	LAIZ, Matthias	JUL 08 1856
GESSFORD, Charles	EVANS, Elizabeth	OCT 05 1852
GETCHENDENER, Henry	CAMPBELL, Jane	JAN 25 1845
GETTENER, Benj. F.	FORD, Mary O.	APR 20 1854
GETTINGS, Alexander	CHURCH, Catherine	DEC 13 1815
GETTINGS, James T.	WOOD, Mary Ann	FEB 26 1857
GETTINGS, Sarah Ann	COMPTON, John J.	OCT 25 1834
GETTS, William	RIVES, Mary	FEB 07 1853
GETTY, Anna Eliza	LAUB, Charles H. [Dr.]	JAN 15 1833
GETTY, Emily	BROOKE, Edmund H.	JUL 06 1840
GETTY, Gardner T.	BREWER, H. Elizabeth	OCT 27 1852
GETTY, Margaret Jane	JOHNS, Thomas H. [Lt.]	APR 20 1836
GETTYS, Elizabeth (blk)	BURRELL, John	APR 06 1839
GETZEINGER, John	HERBERT, Frances	AUG 05 1857
GEW, Anna	JOHNSON, Jefferson	JAN 08 1829
GHEEN, Frances A.	LYNN, Joseph F.	DEC 06 1856
GHEN, Anthony	LOUIS, Catherine	JUN 13 1843
GHOESLIN, Alexr.	SIMONS, Martha	NOV 26 1839
GIBBINS, Matthew	ARLETT, Mary Elizabeth	MAY 01 1843
GIBBON, Henry	JOY, Eleanor	DEC 22 1813
GIBBONS, Ann	MORRISON, Thomas	DEC 06 1832
GIBBONS, Charles H.	WATSON, Maria E.	DEC 10 1851
GIBBONS, Emeline Jane	CROOK, Joseph	SEP 20 1830
GIBBONS, George F.	ESTEP, Hannah T.	AUG 28 1855
GIBBONS, Isabella	HIGGINS, William	AUG 24 1850
GIBBONS, Jno. W.	STURGEON, Mary Ann	FEB 05 1850
GIBBONS, Mary E.	SMITH, William H.	MAY 12 1858
GIBBONS, Rebecca	CARRICO, John	MAY 03 1827
GIBBONS, Thomas	STEWART, Sarah Ann	JUN 04 1815
GIBBS, Jas. H.	MILLER, Isabella	JAN 07 1851
GIBBS, John H.	SEDWICK, Elizabeth Ann	SEP 16 1828
GIBBS, John H.	LAKIN, Frances E.	DEC 24 1840
GIBBS, Lucretia Ann	BACHELER, William Anglis	APR 10 1843
GIBBS, Margaret	UPPERMAN, Henry	NOV 12 1822
GIBBS, Margaret V.	CASEY, Francis W.	MAY 26 1855
GIBBS, Mary	FOUGERES, Louis	MAY 30 1835
GIBBS, Mary (blk)	PAYNE, Samuel	APR 25 1854
GIBBS, Mary E.	BLOGET, Lorin	DEC 11 1856
GIBBS, Nancy	McCUBBIN, Banjamin	AUG 25 1847
GIBBS, Sarah	WILLIAMS, [blank]	APR 29 1812
GIBERSON, G.L.	SPALDING, Teresa	NOV 25 1832
GIBERSON, Gilbert L.	MOULTEN, Mary G.	MAY 26 1828
GIBERSON, Gilbert L.	THOMPSON, Eliza [Mrs.]	JUN 11 1831
GIBERSON, Louisa M.	TRINE, Henry	JUL 14 1853
GIBSON, Alexander	SHAW, Mary Ann	MAY 04 1827
GIBSON, Ann S.	WARDER, Walter	OCT 20 1830
GIBSON, Caleb	HANSON, Ann	JUN 28 1856
GIBSON, Caroline (blk)	FERRILL, John W.	MAY 13 1841
GIBSON, Catherine	KIRK, Alonzo George	DEC 27 1845
GIBSON, Catherine	DOWNING, E.H.	JUL 11 1856
GIBSON, Daniel	LEWIS, Mary Jane	MAR 15 1838
GIBSON, Eleanor	HARVEY, James	JUN 23 1813
GIBSON, Eliza (blk)	WILLIAMS, Chas.	NOV 19 1856
GIBSON, Elizabeth	CARTER, William	JUL 18 1849
GIBSON, Emily (blk)	HAMPTON, Roderick	FEB 06 1834
GIBSON, Francis	HULL, Harriett (blk)	SEP 17 1844
GIBSON, Francis J.	HALL, Sarah Jane	SEP 24 1851
GIBSON, George	SIMMES, Charity	AUG 10 1826

District of Columbia Marriage Licenses, 1811-1858

GIBSON, George T.	JONES, Juliannah	JUN 24 1828
GIBSON, Hester Ellen	CLARK, Robert C.	AUG 30 1844
GIBSON, Isaac	WINGERD, Anna S.	FEB 24 1853
GIBSON, Jacob Carter	McCUTCHEN, Mary Arkansas	MAY 06 1854
GIBSON, John	THOMPSON, Elizabeth	FEB 07 1826
GIBSON, John	DEAN, Ann	DEC 27 1827
GIBSON, John	SMITH, Sarah	OCT 01 1831
GIBSON, John H.	HUNTER, Mary Catharine	APR 22 1848
GIBSON, Joseph	BRUMLEY, Hannah	APR 14 1818
GIBSON, Joshua	ALLROY, Sarah	JUL 28 1831
GIBSON, L.A.	SCOTT, Samuel	AUG 25 1847
GIBSON, Laura C. (blk)	STEWART, James	MAR 25 1847
GIBSON, Lucy (blk)	GANT, Edward	APR 11 1854
GIBSON, Margaret A.	FINCH, William	AUG 01 1850
GIBSON, Mary A.	MAKEW, William B.	JAN 11 1825
GIBSON, Mary Ann	DARNUM, George	NOV 18 1830
GIBSON, Matilda	GREEN, Wm.	FEB 03 1818
GIBSON, Rebecca	SMALLWOOD, Joseph L.	MAR 16 1836
GIBSON, Richard	CAMACK, Sarah	FEB 07 1828
GIBSON, Robert	BAKER, Lucinda	DEC 22 1857
GIBSON, Sarah	SIMPSON, James A.	JUL 09 1858
GIBSON, Sarah C.	NURSE, Michael	NOV 26 1835
GIBSON, Susanna	WARD, John	DEC 07 1829
GIBSON, Susanna	PADGETT, James	MAY 26 1853
GIBSON, Susannah	IRWIN, Thos.	DEC 20 1838
GIBSON, Walter M.	ROBINSON, Catherine G.	MAR 01 1852
GIBSON, William	LYNCH, Catherine	JAN 12 1824
GIBSON, William	HOOD, Peggy	JUL 22 1831
GIBSON, William	NEIVET, Eleanor	DEC 21 1833
GIBSON, William	HOWARD, Margaret	OCT 18 1847
GIBSON, William H.	BARKER, Martha Ann	FEB 10 1855
GIBSON, Woolman	CARTER, Catharine	SEP 17 1828
GIDDANS, Thomas	MULLIKIN, Mary	APR 19 1827
GIDDENS, Betsey	OWINGS, Joseph	FEB 12 1835
GIDDINGS, Dominick	PHELPS, Mary E.	JAN 26 1855
GIDDINGS, Eliza Ann	BROWN, James	DEC 19 1842
GIDDINGS, George	GRIFFITH, Rebecca	MAY 08 1813
GIDDINGS, James H.	LIPPARD, Elizabeth	JUL 10 1854
GIDDINGS, John	CLEMENTS, Ann	JAN 18 1819
GIDDINGS, Joseph	CHANEY, Mary Ann	JUL 27 1846
GIDDINGS, Pricilla Ann	TURNER, James	FEB 17 1846
GIDDINGS, Samuel S.	GRIFFITH, Charlotte	JUL 04 1846
GIDDINGS, William Hy.	JACKSON, Mahalable	FEB 27 1849
GIDEON, Christianna	LARNER, Michael	JAN 16 1828
GIDEON, George S.	DRAKE, Catharine C.	OCT 08 1837
GIDEON, Rebecca	ROSE, Benjamin F.	JUL 09 1832
GIDINGS, Josias Richard	CASE, Martha Ann	MAR 26 1850
GIDLOW, William	BUCKINGHAM, Eleanor	JAN 13 1826
GIEDERMACHER, Catherine	OFENSTEIN, Leopold	DEC 24 1853
GIESE, Henry	SCHOLFIELD, Sarah N.	SEP 29 1852
GIESEKING, Fred'k. W.	WHOFF, Caroline Dorothy	MAR 17 1849
GIESKING, Henry W.	HARTER, Marie	FEB 02 1856
GIGER, Margaret Ann	HOLT, George W.	JAN 25 1838
GIHON, William	RU[torn out], Mary A.	DEC 05 1857
GILBERT, Louis Momus	BEURO<u>U</u>, Sophia	SEP 25 1839
GILBERT, Thomas	BAILEY, Elizth. M. (blk)	MAY 22 1851
GILBERT, Thomas	YOUNG, Sarah A. (blk)	SEP 03 1857
GILCHRIST, George L.	SHERLOCK, Clotilda M.J.	DEC 19 1844

District of Columbia Marriage Licenses, 1811-1858

GILDEMEISTER, Eliza	HESSE, Eugene	DEC 03 1849
GILDEMEISTER, Emma	SIEBERT, Selmar	JUN 13 1851
GILDEMEISTER, Mary Louise	BECHTEL, Ernst August	JUL 18 1851
GILDEMEISTER, Shereta	SCHOTT, Charles A.	JUN 02 1854
GILDER, Caroline C.	DUDLEY, Henry, Jr.	NOV 07 1854
GILES, John A.	BRUCE, Clarissa Ann	DEC 28 1848
GILHAM, Mary Ann	COVINGTON, Harry W.	SEP 26 1828
GILL, Airry	METHENEY, Samuel	JAN 01 1817
GILL, Amelia Ellen	LEWIS, Christopher C.	JUN 12 1854
GILL, Ann	DUNN, John	NOV 03 1829
GILL, Ann	WIPPLE, Joseph	JUN 25 1838
GILL, CHristopher	LOVELISS, Ellen	MAR 25 1858
GILL, Delilah	MOXLEY, John	JAN 13 1814
GILL, Dury	PEPLES, Benjamin	AUG 22 1815
GILL, Edward	GRAHAM, Nancy	JUN 04 1822
GILL, James	PUMPHREY, Susan	JUN 19 1816
GILL, James	RICHERSON, Ann	MAY 23 1844
GILL, James	MAHUE, Margaret	MAY 30 1848
GILL, John	BROWN, Patience	MAY 03 1839
GILL, John F.	BROWN, Patience E.	MAY 22 1839
GILL, John R.	DeVAUGHN, Sarah Ann	NOV 09 1847
GILL, Joseph A.	WASHINGTON, Catherine V.	DEC 21 1850
GILL, Margaret	COOK, William	NOV 30 1852
GILL, Margaret E.	BURCH, Charles J.	JAN 12 1849
GILL, Mary A.	BROWN, James	JUN 07 1848
GILL, Mary A.	THOMPSON, Henry M.	JUL 17 1852
GILL, Mary Ann	JOY, John Washington	JUL 06 1844
GILL, Presley R.	NORRIS, Mary Ann	APR 14 1828
GILL, Prisciller	NEWMAN, Lewis	SEP 12 1826
GILL, Rebecca	RABBITT, John	AUG 26 1816
GILL, Susan Ann	JONES, William	APR 04 1826
GILL, Susannah	GOODRIDGE, Henry C.	JAN 29 1816
GILL, Theophilus Anthony	CATTON, Elizabeth	OCT 18 1820
GILL, Ursella	LEITH, William	JUL 11 1812
GILLASFY, Henry	HEARPER, Harriot	FEB 05 1822
GILLASPIE, Margaret	HARCUS, George	NOV 04 1818
GILLASPY, Mary Ann	MURDOCK, John	JUN 25 1817
GILLER, Jane	BRASCHEARS, Christopher H.	FEB 02 1843
GILLESPIE, Hannah	HOLD, James	APR 13 1822
GILLESPIE, Harriet	WALLING, William	MAY 12 1831
GILLET, L. Warrington	HOGMIRE, A. Isabella	MAY 11 1840
GILLHAM, Cornelia W.	KENNEDY, Andrew	JUL 09 1832
GILLIGAN, Mary	ROBERTS, Matthew	OCT 05 1832
GILLIN, Grace	JOHNSON, Archy	NOV 16 1818
GILLING, William	GOODRICK, Eliza	DEC 28 1836
GILLION, Margaret	SLURP, William	NOV 18 1851
GILLIS, Leah Ann	TODD, Seth J.	SEP 14 1829
GILLISPE, Hellen Mary	MALLORY, John William	MAY 13 1854
GILLISPIE, Harriet	STEWART, George W.	MAY 09 1827
GILLISPIE, Isaac	THOMPSON, Margaret	MAR 03 1813
GILLISPIE, Isaac	THOMPSON, Margaret	MAY 03 1813
GILLISS, Elizabeth J.	TODD, William B.	OCT 15 1832
GILLISS, Hannah M.	MOXLEY, Richard S.	FEB 05 1839
GILLISS, Levin I. [Rev.]	BRADLEY, Maria T.	APR 13 1819
GILLOT, Sarah	OWENS, John H.	JAN 27 1848
GILLOTT, Joseph	LOGAN, Mary Ann	MAY 30 1838
GILLUM, Ann	GRIMSLEY, Albert	NOV 25 1857
GILLUM, Cordelia (blk)	BROWN, William	APR 23 1831

District of Columbia Marriage Licenses, 1811-1858

GILLUM, Mary Ann	BRIGGS, Robert	NOV 04 1829
GILMAN, Cornelia A.	BALDWIN, William H.	MAR 09 1853
GILMAN, Elizabeth	McCLELLAND, David	NOV 15 1848
GILMAN, Imogene	POLK, Joseph G.	OCT 03 1836
GILMAN, Malvina	HAYES, Alonzo	MAY 01 1843
GILMAN, William H.	DYSON, Margaret C.	NOV 15 1848
GILMAN, Zadock D.	PARRIS, Helen	NOV 01 1842
GILMORE, James H.	DERRICK, Estelle	SEP 30 1857
GILMURRAY, Catharine	DONOVAN, Dennis	FEB 09 1852
GILP, Frederick	SHICK, Lehene	JAN 04 1855
GILPIN, Sophia	MILES, George F.	JAN 05 1833
GILSON, Catherine	MARTIN, John	JUN 10 1848
GINGELL, Henrietta	MYERS, Thomas Lycurgus	SEP 12 1854
GINGELL, James	LYNCH, Ruth Ann	FEB 29 1848
GINGELL, Joseph	GROOVER, Maria E.	AUG 02 1845
GINGELLS, Joseph	LANDON, Sarah	APR 22 1857
GINGLE, George F.	MYERS, Mary J.	JAN 01 1851
GINGLE, James M.	EVELEY, Artimesa	JUN 23 1848
GINGLEE, Lucinda	TUCKER, Henry	MAR 25 1849
GINK, Eleanor	BELL, William	JAN 24 1848
GINNET, Allice	RINEY, Philip	SEP 02 1851
GINNETY, James	BRANNAN, Mariana	OCT 09 1854
GIPSON, James V.	BROOKS, Cecelia (blk)	SEP 24 1852
GIPSON, John	MADDOX, Ann	JUL 10 1849
GIPSON, Mary Ann	GARNER, William	NOV 27 1850
GIPSON, Rosier	SPINKS, Mary Elizth.	DEC 27 1851
GIRARD, Annie	KIRK, John	APR 21 1856
GIRAUD, Augustus J.T.	FINLAY, Orrilla	NOV 30 1836
GIRD, Eudocia [Mrs.]	HILLS, Saml.	FEB 05 1823
GIRD, Joseph C.	DORSEY, Eudocia	JUL 22 1815
GIRDIN, George	BURKETT, Eliza Ann	OCT 11 1834
GISSETT, Cyrus	COOK, Sarah Ann	JUL 27 1850
GIST, B.F.	CRAIG, Margaret	FEB 13 1834
GIST, Georgia R.	STEUART, Richard S., Jr.	MAY 27 1856
GIST, Mary Ann	RESSENG, Charles	FEB 29 1848
GIST, Salena	DOWNES, Robert F.	DEC 02 1856
GITTINGS, Benjamin E.	RATCLIFF, Martha Ann	JUN 04 1829
GITTINGS, Christa Ann	STEVENS, Robert C.	NOV 05 1850
GITTINGS, Christia	CISSELL, William	DEC 21 1841
GITTINGS, Elizabeth A.	TUCKER, Charles H.	FEB 07 1856
GITTINGS, George	WILSON, Elizabeth	DEC 04 1839
GITTINGS, George	CASS, Mary	APR 10 1852
GITTINGS, Jeremiah	SCOTT, Serene O.	DEC 20 1825
GITTINGS, John S.	RITCHIE, Charlotte C.	NOV 29 1853
GITTINGS, Margaret Ann	BEAN, Silas	JUN 29 1847
GITTINGS, Martha A.	ROBERTSON, James H.	JUL 27 1858
GITTINGS, Martin Luther	THOMPSON, Mary Elizth.	SEP 26 1837
GITTINGS, William C.	OFFUTT, Ann E.	OCT 05 1841
GIVEN, George	MITCHELL, Elizabeth	JUL 22 1826
GIVEN, James E.	DUNN, Isabella	JUN 04 1840
GIVEN, Jane E.	GENGELL, Henry	DEC 30 1843
GIVEN, John T.	THOMPSON, Emily S.	FEB 24 1841
GIVEN, Mary	SHIELDS, James W.	OCT 05 1840
GIVEN, Mary Ann	CAROTHERS, Andrew	FEB 01 1827
GIVEN, Sarah Ann	DELANO, William Judah	DEC 22 1841
GIVEN, Thomas	EDMONSTON, Elizabeth B.	DEC 07 1815
GIVEN, Thomas	WILLIAMS, Elizabeth	FEB 06 1827
GIVEN, William	WILLINGFORD, Mary Ann	FEB 21 1832

District of Columbia Marriage Licenses, 1811-1858

GIVENS, John Henry	EVANS, Jacintha	APR 23 1831
GIVENY, Bernard	KIDNEY, Eleanor	JAN 05 1822
GIVENY, Joseph	TAYLOR, Eliza	JAN 15 1829
GIVIN, Elizabeth	NAYLOR, Allison	DEC 03 1831
GIVINGS, Margaret	DAVIS, Eli	JUN 20 1834
GLADDEN, Susan	HOLBROOK, John	AUG 22 1846
GLADMAN, Addison	GRIMSLEY, Amanda	JUL 12 1836
GLADMAN, Amelia	COLLINS, William	OCT 23 1851
GLADMAN, Ann	COLLINS, John	JAN 13 1819
GLADMAN, Asa	PARKER, Ann	AUG 21 1831
GLADMAN, James	NORTON, Ann	JUL 29 1835
GLADMAN, James	MOULDEN, Anna	MAY 27 1850
GLADMAN, Mary	LOWE, Nathan	JAN 29 1853
GLADMAN, Rutha R.	DAVIS, Charles W.	JUL 31 1855
GLADMEN, Emeline A.	NORTON, Robert H.	SEP 11 1855
GLADMEN, Rebecca	COLLINS, Robert	APR 04 1816
GLADMON, Theophulus H.	FLENNER, Mary A.	NOV 10 1857
GLADMOND, Ruthay	THOMAS, William M.	MAR 02 1853
GLANDENTZ, Preaida	FREDERICK, Lorenzo	JUN 24 1833
GLARSON, James	BRESSNAHAN, Margaret	JUN 12 1852
GLASCO, Elizth.	COBIE, William	OCT 10 1826
GLASCO, Rachael	SERRIN, Daniel	JAN 14 1823
GLASCOE, David	MURPHEY, Elizabeth	JUL 02 1838
GLASCOE, Elizabeth	GOLDING, Richard R.	FEB 17 1842
GLASCOE, Priscilla (blk)	BROWN, George	JUL 29 1854
GLASCOW, Augustus	GRANT, Ann E.	DEC 08 1853
GLASCOW, Beecham	McKINNY, Sarah	DEC 14 1844
GLASCOW, Eliza Jane	McCARTHY, Patrick	JUL 27 1853
GLASCOW, John	TURNER, Elizabeth (blk)	OCT 19 1857
GLASCOW, Mary M.	BOSWELL, Washington G.	JUN 28 1853
GLASGOW, Wm. James	WALLACE, Matilda	FEB 18 1827
GLASSCOCK, John H.	RECTOR, Kitty Ann	FEB 20 1834
GLASSCOW, John	GREEN, Harriet (blk)	NOV 25 1846
GLAVIN, Ellen	MURPHY, Jeremiah	APR 17 1855
GLEASON, Catharine	O'BRYAN, Timothy	FEB 22 1830
GLEASON, Charles	BEARDSLEY, Eliza	DEC 29 1829
GLEASON, Edward	KAIN, Margaret	APR 21 1855
GLEASON, James Alexander	RICHARDSON, Francis Maria	MAR 27 1856
GLEASON, Mary	GRIFFIN, John	DEC 15 1853
GLEASON, Mary	CARROLL, William	APR 14 1855
GLEASON, Patrick	O'DAY, Ellen	NOV 29 1854
GLEER, L.B.	AVERY, Susan	MAY 13 1856
GLEESON, James	HORAN, Margaret	JUL 20 1858
GLEESON, Patrick	PINDERGAST, Bridget	NOV 30 1852
GLEESON, Thomas	HICKEY, Mary	SEP 01 1854
GLENIN, Patrick	KENNEY, Catherine	JAN 15 1858
GLENN, Ann	BROWN, John	JUN 07 1828
GLENN, David	McCOSLAND, Margere	OCT 05 1835
GLENN, Elizth. Ann	ADAMS, Benedict L.	NOV 16 1824
GLENN, Mary Jane	WARD, George W.	JUN 19 1841
GLENN, Mary Jane	SMITH, William	JUL 23 1844
GLENN, Precilla	EARL, Robert	SEP 06 1825
GLICK, John C.	ERTEL, Margaret	AUG 03 1854
GLIMMON, Mary	SWOPE, John M.	FEB 12 1840
GLORIOUS, George	ENGEL, Mary	SEP 08 1849
GLOSTER, Susanna	CLEMENTS, John	AUG 30 1816
GLOVER, Charles	COCKING, Jane	AUG 19 1813
GLOVER, Charles	WETHERALL, Mary	AUG 21 1817

District of Columbia Marriage Licenses, 1811-1858

GLOVER, David F.	FILL, Rebecca Jane	MAR 24 1855
GLOVER, Eliza Jane	GRAVES, Joseph S.	AUG 19 1858
GLOVER, Elizabeth	PIERCE, John	JUL 19 1825
GLOVER, Elizabeth C.	MARCELLUS, Robert Hartley	FEB 27 1854
GLOVER, John W.	ROHAN, Eliza	MAR 12 1849
GLOVER, Joseph	FRASIER, Mary	SEP 14 1843
GLOVER, Martha Ann	TAYLOR, James	AUG 14 1834
GLOVER, Mary Jane	SHRIVER, Abram F.	AUG 01 1849
GLOVER, Matilda R.	WILLIAMSON, Robert H.	NOV 07 1837
GLOVER, Susannah	AMERICA, William	NOV 05 1844
GLOVER, Thomas	THOMPSON, Jane	JUN 26 1833
GLOVER, Thomas N.	CAUSIN, Elizabeth	JUL 09 1852
GLOVER, William	CHILES, Elizabeth	DEC 06 1816
GLOVER, William	DONALDSON, Sarah	NOV 14 1833
GLOVER, William	CLARKE, Henrietta E.	MAR 23 1846
GLOVER, William H.	ECKLOFF, Ann Elizth.	JAN 19 1856
GLOYD, Caroline	RHEA, Robert	AUG 11 1832
GLOYD, Catherine	CECILL, Thomas	AUG 12 1815
GLOYD, Elizabeth	KNOTT, Joseph	OCT 14 1834
GLOYD, Elizabeth	WAKELING, Ignatius	JUN 19 1847
GLOYD, Harriot	SIMS, Sampson	MAR 27 1817
GLOYD, Mary Elizth.	WILSON, Wm. S.	FEB 18 1845
GLOYD, Mary Jane	LOWE, John	FEB 18 1835
GLOYD, Washington	STONE, Jane	AUG 12 1817
GLYNN, Anthony Greville	BARTLETT, Elizth. B.	JUL 24 1826
GOAB, Margaret	BILD, Rudolph	DEC 23 1852
GOBRIGHT, Lawrence A.	KLIEBER, Mary Ann	OCT 27 1834
GOCHELER, Christian G.	SCHMILZ, Barbara	JUN 04 1858
GOCKELER, George Jacob	FRUCKENMILLER, Rosina B.	JUN 14 1856
GOCKELER, George Jacob	KAIBEL, Mrs. Mary	JUN 19 1858
GODDARD, Andrew	GOLDSBOROUGH, Maria C.	JAN 28 1851
GODDARD, Ann	TRUNNELL, Lawson	FEB 18 1833
GODDARD, Ann [Mrs.]	CLARKE, Isaac	OCT 07 1819
GODDARD, Benjamin	BARROTT, Eliza	MAR 28 1815
GODDARD, Benjamin	LOMAN, Ann Maria	JAN 14 1839
GODDARD, Benjamin	GORMAN, Mary	OCT 31 1849
GODDARD, Benjamin F.	SHECKELL, Rosala V.	OCT 18 1852
GODDARD, Daniel Convers	VINTON, Madeline S.	MAY 29 1846
GODDARD, Eliza Ann	FURTNER, Alexander	JUN 03 1852
GODDARD, Isaac	GOLDING, Elizabeth	JUL 02 1838
GODDARD, Isaac	SPALDING, Sarah	OCT 20 1841
GODDARD, James	RICHARDSON, Sarah Ellen	APR 06 1842
GODDARD, James G.	ECTON, Julia Ann	NOV 28 1843
GODDARD, John	LINDSAY, Harriet	FEB 12 1850
GODDARD, John	THOMPSON, Nancy	DEC 30 1851
GODDARD, John H.	GARDINER, Ann	NOV 16 1820
GODDARD, Joseph	WARRAN, Mary Jane	JAN 05 1832
GODDARD, Lawson F.	BURGESS, Sophia	APR 04 1826
GODDARD, Margaret	WINSHIP, William	OCT 09 1832
GODDARD, Margaret E.	ECKLOFF, Frederick W.	JUN 02 1842
GODDARD, Maria H.	STALLINGS, William H.	DEC 13 1832
GODDARD, Mary Ann	KING, Richard A.	FEB 11 1836
GODDARD, Mary E.	LISBY, John N.	DEC 05 1825
GODDARD, Mary Ellen	PYWELL, William W.	DEC 30 1857
GODDARD, Matilda Ann	TARMAN, Richard H.	DEC 22 1853
GODDARD, Rosaline V.	COOK, Thomas W.	JAN 08 1857
GODDARD, Ruth	REDDEN, James	DEC 14 1844
GODDARD, Samuel B.	BALLARD, Clara	JAN 18 1843

District of Columbia Marriage Licenses, 1811-1858

GODDARD, Susan	KNOTT, Richard	DEC 09 1851
GODDARD, Thomas	BELL, Matilda	JAN 09 1828
GODDARD, Thomas	LOVELACE, Harriet	MAR 19 1839
GODDARD, Thomas	MACER, Gertrude A.	SEP 04 1857
GODDARD, Virginia	VANDERLEHR, Jacob	APR 13 1858
GODDARD, William Clarke	HUNT, Nancy Ann	MAY 31 1831
GODDARD, Zachariah	ROBERTSON, Catharine	APR 17 1819
GODDARD, [torn out]	CARTER, Ann Maria A.	JUL 02 1847
GODDERD, Jane	SUIT, Horatio	JAN 07 1813
GODDIN, James E.	SUTTON, Georgiana B.	MAY 30 1853
GODEY, Edward	STAUBS, Mary Ann	NOV 27 1850
GODEY, Geo. W.	WAUGH, Cornelia V.	OCT 10 1849
GODEY, Rebecca	CARTWRIGHT, William F.	AUG 08 1844
GODEY, Walter	OYSTER, Jane A.	DEC 04 1849
GODFREY, Caroline	DAVIS, Philip	MAY 03 1838
GODFREY, Chapman	DRAKE, Maria Louisa	NOV 25 1857
GODFREY, Eliza	BAKER, Thomas E.	JUN 16 1827
GODFREY, Elizabeth	BEECH, Hidley	SEP 21 1838
GODFREY, Francis	SPEERS, Amelia	FEB 24 1827
GODFREY, Francis	HAYS, Heister	DEC 21 1833
GODFREY, Henry	ROSE, Jane	MAY 16 1850
GODFREY, John	NALLY, Lucy	JUL 24 1855
GODFREY, Martha E.	DAVIS, James	OCT 03 1854
GODFREY, Matilda	CLARK, John	AUG 27 1838
GODFREY, Roda	RATTERY, Robert	OCT 30 1850
GODFRY, Mary	MITCHELL, John	DEC 29 1841
GODFRY, William, Jr.	WILLIAMS, Patsy	MAR 12 1829
GODMAN, Elijah	BENSON, Leonora	JUN 12 1834
GODMAN, Elizabeth	TURNER, John	OCT 04 1843
GODMAN, Robert V.	GRAINGER, Mary A.	JAN 17 1855
GODRAN, William	SHARP, Cornelia A.	AUG 06 1838
GODRON, Fredericka Wilhelmina	BALSTER, John	APR 04 1846
GODRON, William H.	THOMAS, Dorthea Barbara	APR 29 1853
GODY, Eliza Ann	WOLTZ, Tobias N.	APR 22 1837
GODY, Mary A.	BERRY, Elisha D.	DEC 15 1818
GODY, Walter	CLARKE, Jane Eliza	APR 29 1840
GODY, William H.	CARTWRIGHT, Mary E.	DEC 20 1842
GOERTNER, N.W. [Rev.]	MECHLIN, Lucretia L.	DEC 24 1833
GOEZLER, Julia Ann	WALTER, James	JUL 14 1830
GOFF, Elizabeth	ANDREWS, William Henry	JUN 16 1832
GOFF, George Paul	RUD, Sarah Ellen	DEC 23 1851
GOFF, Mary	RADY, Daniel	OCT 28 1856
GOGGEN, William	SMITH, Juliet	SEP 22 1818
GOGGIN, Elizabeth E.	SAUNDERS, Thomas F.	MAR 15 1852
GOGGIN, Marcelina	FARISH, William F.	MAY 19 1852
GOGGIN, Robert	GARDNER, Sarah E.	DEC 23 1848
GOGGINS, William	ROBERTSON, Mary	APR 13 1847
GOGOT, Peter	MICHEWARD, Anthoinnet	MAY 31 1821
GOHNAN, William	HAYWOOD, Susan Elizth.	NOV 05 1853
GOING, Harmonia (blk)	TAYLOR, Dennis	AUG 08 1840
GOINGS, Benjamin	ODLEY, Elizabeth	MAY 24 1817
GOINGS, Benjamin	LEACH, Adeline	SEP 26 1838
GOINGS, Eliza	PLANTT, George H.	JUL 06 1837
GOINGS, Emily (blk)	BUTLER, Charles	JUL 31 1854
GOINGS, James	SMITH, Mary Ann	DEC 21 1830
GOINGS, Laura (blk)	BOND, Daniel	APR 21 1842
GOINGS, Mary C. (blk)	BOND, William S.	APR 30 1851
GOINGS, Wesley	HARPER, Harmony (blk)	JUL 16 1832

District of Columbia Marriage Licenses, 1811-1858

GOINS, John Thomas	STINCHCOMB, Joanna	OCT 20 1845
GOINS, Patrick	HURST, Ann (blk)	MAY 06 1830
GOLBACH, John	HARBERT, Catharine	SEP 02 1854
GOLBUCH, Constant	HESS, Margt.	DEC 01 1856
GOLD, Mary A.	GREENE, J.D.	JAN 03 1854
GOLDEN, George	DENNISON, Virginia	MAY 02 1849
GOLDEN, John Aylmer	CRANE, Margaret	JUL 02 1845
GOLDEN, Lydia (blk)	DIXON, William	MAR 23 1813
GOLDEN, M.A.	RITTER, H.G.	JAN 25 1848
GOLDEN, R.R.	MANLEY, ELizabeth	NOV 12 1822
GOLDEN, Richard	TEAL, Christeen	SEP 18 1819
GOLDEN, Singleton	THOMAS, Mary Ann	FEB 29 1848
GOLDEN, William L.	STALLINGS, Rebecca	NOV 26 1833
GOLDIE, John	RICHARDS, Sarah Ann	FEB 05 1814
GOLDIN, Eleanor Ann	WALLINGSFORD, Alfred	MAR 10 1849
GOLDIN, John	CHINGE, Lucinda	FEB 22 1842
GOLDIN, John	STEVENS, Cordelia	SEP 15 1852
GOLDIN, Matilda	DAVIS, James	DEC 22 1826
GOLDIN, R.R.	COLBY, Ann Catherine	JUL 24 1845
GOLDING, Arthur	SKINNER, Elizabeth J.	FEB 20 1841
GOLDING, Bridget	BOLLISTON, Timothy	JAN 10 1856
GOLDING, Christiana	HUNT, Charles	JAN 15 1835
GOLDING, Elizabeth	WARWICK, John	JAN 03 1829
GOLDING, Elizabeth	COAL, John	OCT 10 1829
GOLDING, Elizabeth	GODDARD, Isaac	JUL 02 1838
GOLDING, Frederick	HAIS, Elizabeth (blk)	JUN 30 1835
GOLDING, John	THOMPSON, Jane	OCT 09 1830
GOLDING, Mary	DUGLASS, James	JAN 31 1820
GOLDING, Richard R.	GLASCOE, Elizabeth	FEB 17 1842
GOLDMSITH, James W.	WELBURN, Catherine E.	APR 22 1858
GOLDSBOROUGH, Ann	DENISON, Lewis	JUN 06 1856
GOLDSBOROUGH, Caroline	GARDNER, John Lane [Capt.]	OCT 05 1825
GOLDSBOROUGH, Maria C.	GODDARD, Andrew	JAN 28 1851
GOLDSBOROUGH, Rebecca	SHEPPERD, Joseph	FEB 28 1815
GOLDSBOROUGH, Richard T.	BOWMAN, Jane	MAR 23 1829
GOLDSBORROUGH, Francis	KING, William Thomas	JUN 13 1833
GOLDSHMITH, Regine	KING, Henry	JAN 02 1858
GOLDSMITH, Ann Maria	DORSEY, William E.	AUG 23 1853
GOLDSMITH, Caroline L.	SAGE, Henry B.	JAN 08 1857
GOLDSMITH, Cordelia	MARCERON, James A.	NOV 28 1854
GOLDSMITH, Eliza	LARNER, Martin	DEC 13 1824
GOLDSMITH, Elizabeth	BALDING, William	MAR 09 1826
GOLDSMITH, Ellen Cecelia	MURPHEY, Michael	NOV 17 1841
GOLDSMITH, George	FLOWERS, Rosanna	JUL 03 1827
GOLDSMITH, Harriet A.	HURLEY, Henry	JUL 05 1854
GOLDSMITH, Henry	THOMPSON, Elizabeth	FEB 08 1842
GOLDSMITH, James	SISSEL, Julia Ann	MAR 03 1832
GOLDSMITH, James	JONES, Mary Ann	MAR 28 1848
GOLDSMITH, James	LOVELESS, Catharine	APR 29 1852
GOLDSMITH, John	KIDWELL, Ellen	OCT 11 1823
GOLDSMITH, John T.	VanTASSELL, Sarah J.	MAR 11 1854
GOLDSMITH, Lewis C.	MITCHELL, Sophinia	FEB 12 1833
GOLDSMITH, Martha Ann	ALVEY, William	JUL 12 1844
GOLDSMITH, Mary Ann	STEWART, Thomas	DEC 26 1831
GOLDSMITH, Mary E.	BEVERIDGE, Benjamin F.	AUG 22 1856
GOLDSMITH, Mary Elizabeth	TANNER, Samuel	JUL 28 1853
GOLDSMITH, Mary Jane	WALLIS, James Harrison	AUG 11 1834
GOLDSMITH, Mary Jane	PORTER, David	JUN 29 1843

District of Columbia Marriage Licenses, 1811-1858

GOLDSMITH, Rosanna	OWEN, John	AUG 08 1840
GOLDSMITH, Samuel	ROCK, Elizabeth	APR 05 1823
GOLDSMITH, Samuel	ROBERTS, Martha	OCT 24 1833
GOLDSMITH, Susannah [Mrs.]	CHANEY, Samuel	DEC 20 1827
GOLDSMITH, William	KIDWELL, Mary	JUL 08 1828
GOLDSMITH, William	CLEMENTS, Elizabeth	JUN 02 1851
GOLDSMITH, William L.	COOK, Margaret	NOV 09 1857
GOLDTHWAITE, George	WALLACK, Olivia P.	NOV 28 1835
GOLIHAR, Thomas	KING, Sarah	SEP 12 1821
GOLLOHER, Patrick	SULLIVAN, Ellen	JUN 02 1829
GOLT, Mary E.	DAVIS, Henry S.	DEC 19 1850
GOMLEY, Mary	BANGS, James C.	NOV 21 1845
GOMMAN, Christian Gotlip	GARMANN, Susanna	OCT 30 1845
GONE, Thomas	STYLES, Scilinda	DEC 16 1820
GONTER, James M.	MYERS, Lavinia	JAN 04 1847
GONTER, Samuel M.	SMITH, Hannah Ireland	DEC 30 1848
GOOCH, Catherine E.	HOWARD, Volney E.	MAR 04 1837
GOOD, Julia	SWEENEY, George	JAN 11 1830
GOOD, Sarah Jane	SWANN, Llewellyn	APR 17 1856
GOOD, Thomas G.	SPALDING, Jane	DEC 30 1825
GOOD, William H.	COOPER, Mary Elizth.	JUL 18 1843
GOOD, William T.S.	FISTER, Sarah E.	JUN 20 1853
GOODALL, George Washington	RIGDEN, Rose Ann	MAY 26 1846
GOODALL, Harriott S.	ANDERSON, Absolum A.	MAY 04 1846
GOODALL, Rebecca	GORDON, James	APR 15 1837
GOODALL, Thomas	PETER, Hannah	JUL 17 1833
GOODAN, Julia Ann	CROWLEY, Thomas	JUL 26 1825
GOODE, John	BROWN, Jerdina	MAY 08 1854
GOODE, Joseph O.	ROBINSON, Martha	DEC 28 1853
GOODELL, Hannah M.	WRIGHT, John R.	SEP 14 1853
GOODEN, John	CAVENOR, Jane	MAR 10 1828
GOODEN, Martha	TAYLOR, William	AUG 29 1850
GOODFELLER, Eleanor, Mrs.	McFARLAND, John	JAN 13 1829
GOODFRY, Lewis	RESINE, Elizabeth	APR 29 1837
GOODGER, Eliza	AVREY, George Wm.	JUN 29 1835
GOODGER, Peter	BIGGS, Chloe Ann	MAY 10 1853
GOODGER, Wm. Henry	WOOD, Sarah Elizabeth	JUL 25 1854
GOODIN, Henry	CROFTON, Ragena	OCT 07 1830
GOODIN, Juliet	SWEENY, George	JAN 24 1830
GOODIN, Martha Ellen	BARNS, James	DEC 05 1837
GOODIN, Mary Ann	JARBOE, Thomas	DEC 05 1837
GOODIN, Susannah	KENNEDY, David	NOV 15 1830
GOODLOE, Daniel R.	WARING, Mary Elizabeth	JUN 25 1851
GOODMAN, Alexander G.	ROBINSON, Lucy C.	DEC 07 1832
GOODMAN, Charles A.	BERRY, Elizabeth A.	NOV 19 1856
GOODMAN, James	KEENAN, Catherine	JUL 26 1855
GOODMAN, Jeta	HARMAN, Samuel	MAY 03 1855
GOODMAN, Sarah Ann	BRERETON, Samuel	MAY 12 1858
GOODMAN, William H.	INGRAM, Sarah Ann	AUG 03 1854
GOODRICH, Anna	BOSWELL, Robert	NOV 05 1853
GOODRICH, Archibald W. [Col.]	THAW, Eliza Jane	SEP 05 1831
GOODRICH, George M.	THOMPSON, Jane R.	JAN 21 1858
GOODRICH, Henry	BEAN, Elizabeth Olivia	JUL 08 1847
GOODRICH, James	JOHNSON, Ann Maria	SEP 16 1851
GOODRICH, Josiah	ELLIOTT, Harriet	AUG 10 1840
GOODRICH, Mary	CARROLL, Thomas	JUN 01 1816
GOODRICH, Nancy	LIGHTFOOT, William	MAR 21 1837
GOODRICK, Ann	CLARKE, John	NOV 24 1836

District of Columbia Marriage Licenses, 1811-1858

GOODRICK, Augustus	WILLIAMS, Ann	JUN 08 1824
GOODRICK, Benjamin	SEDRICKS, Marcila	JAN 14 1840
GOODRICK, Benjamin	ODEN, Elizabeth	JAN 13 1851
GOODRICK, Catherine	CHAMBERLEN, David	OCT 12 1833
GOODRICK, Dorcas	KORFHISER, Christian	APR 02 1842
GOODRICK, Eliza	KERBY, John	DEC 31 1813
GOODRICK, Eliza	KERBY, John	DEC 30 1813
GOODRICK, Eliza	GILLING, William	DEC 28 1836
GOODRICK, James	JOHNSON, Mary Ann	APR 10 1830
GOODRICK, John	JOHNSON, Ann	FEB 19 1825
GOODRICK, John F.	WILSON, Tabitha P.	JUN 08 1825
GOODRICK, Mary	REED, William	MAY 03 1827
GOODRICK, Mary Ann	MITCHELL, John	JAN 26 1854
GOODRICK, Mary Jane	VEITCH, James H.	DEC 24 1855
GOODRICK, Teresa	GARRETT, Mortimer	OCT 09 1838
GOODRICK, Thomas	CUSTARD, Isabella	JUN 19 1856
GOODRICK, Treasy Ann	MAGRUDER, William L.	AUG 02 1838
GOODRICK, William	DAVIS, Mary Ann	DEC 10 1844
GOODRICT, Mary	ARMSTRONG, Peter	JUL 10 1813
GOODRIDGE, Henry C.	GILL, Susannah	JAN 29 1816
GOODRIDGE, Jeffery	GOODRIDGE, Mary	JAN 21 1856
GOODRIDGE, Mary	GOODRIDGE, Jeffery	JAN 21 1856
GOODRIDGE, Wm. W.	LIGHTFOOT, Jane A.	DEC 09 1841
GOODS, Ellen	BARRON, Alexander	APR 30 1838
GOODS, James C.	SIMPSON, Elizabeth	OCT 25 1825
GOODS, Jane C.	MELLING, George	MAY 01 1847
GOODS, Mary Rebecca	MITCHELL, Thomas	OCT 17 1837
GOODS, William H.	STANLEY, Mary Ann B.	NOV 14 1849
GOODWIN, Agnes	HUNT, Charles	JUN 01 1843
GOODWIN, Ann Rebecca	MALONE, John	JUN 17 1856
GOODWIN, Elizabeth	TALBERT, John T.	MAR 23 1841
GOODWIN, Frances A.	HUTCHINSON, James S.	FEB 15 1842
GOODWIN, Henry E.	KING, Mary Roberta	AUG 04 1855
GOODWIN, James A.	SMALLWOOD, Elizabeth L.	JAN 29 1849
GOODWIN, James R.	BISHOP, Mary F.	MAY 03 1842
GOODWIN, Julia A.	HAMILL, Stephen	DEC 08 1852
GOODWIN, Maria	HOWARD, Saml.	APR 29 1822
GOODWIN, Mary	WRIGHT, Thomas	JUL 20 1826
GOODWIN, Mary	LYNCH, James	JUN 06 1854
GOODWIN, Nancy A.	LYNN, Andrew J.	MAR 20 1856
GOODWIN, Robert	HALL, Elizabeth	JAN 26 1825
GOODWIN, Stephen R.	HOPKINS, Mary J.	JUL 16 1853
GOODWIN, Thomas	KIDWELL, Eliza N.	SEP 05 1846
GOODWIN, Virginia	KING, Edward A.	FEB 22 1855
GOODWIN, Wm. R.	WRIGHT, Ann Eliza	DEC 11 1855
GOODWIN, Wm. R.	KING, Ann	OCT 07 1857
GOODWYN, Mary Ann	DODSON, John	JAN 11 1854
GOODY, Emily	JONES, Samuel	OCT 01 1836
GOODY, William	SOUTHARD, Mary	DEC 09 1812
GOODYEAR, Joseph	MEADE, Eleatha	AUG 04 1840
GOODYER, Peter	RAMSAY, Sarah	OCT 14 1815
GOOLDING, George	BARBER, Delilah Ann Mary	JAN 13 1848
GOOLERY, Ellen	RYAN, Michael	NOV 02 1850
GORBUTT, William H.	KEITH, Margaret R.	DEC 21 1853
GORDEN, Emily	THOMAS, John Handy	APR 08 1852
GORDEN, Richard H.	SUIT, Mary Ann	JUL 11 1842
GORDEN, Sally	LANGLEY, Charles	APR 20 1828
GORDEN, William	CLARKE, Ann	JAN 21 1828

District of Columbia Marriage Licenses, 1811-1858

GORDON, Alexander G. [Lieut.]	TAYLOR, Amanda [Wentworth]	SEP 03 1827
GORDON, Ann E.	GOTT, Richard	MAY 03 1831
GORDON, Bridget	FITZGERALD, Thomas	JAN 31 1853
GORDON, Catherine	SULLIVAN, Patrick	FEB 08 1853
GORDON, Charles	CRAWFORD, Julia	NOV 27 1827
GORDON, Charles	BROWN, Elizabeth E.	AUG 05 1839
GORDON, Charles V.	HOLMES, Julia C.	JUL 01 1850
GORDON, Charles W.	CONNER, Sarah	JAN 04 1849
GORDON, Daniel S.	BURROUGHS, Amanda E.	AUG 29 1853
GORDON, Daniel Smith	HAMMETT, Elizabeth	APR 04 1836
GORDON, Dolly (blk)	ROSS, William	APR 05 1849
GORDON, Eliza (blk)	GROSS, Wm. H.	APR 17 1855
GORDON, Eliza J.	TORREYSON, John N.	JUN 05 1855
GORDON, Elizabeth (blk)	SCHUYLER, Cornelius	AUG 17 1843
GORDON, Ellen	SLEIGHMAKER, James	MAR 05 1846
GORDON, Fannie C.	THRUSTON, Alfred B.	JUL 22 1845
GORDON, George	TAYLOR, Harriot	FEB 08 1815
GORDON, George	WHITE, Eliza A.	SEP 15 1829
GORDON, James	MAYHUE, Mariah	DEC 02 1830
GORDON, James	NELSON, Chloe	APR 06 1833
GORDON, James	GOODALL, Rebecca	APR 15 1837
GORDON, James L.	MORIN, Matilda	JUN 16 1825
GORDON, Jane	PARSONS, Samuel	MAR 03 1830
GORDON, Jennie	ELLICOTT, John, Junr.	NOV 05 1856
GORDON, John	LISBY, Sarah Jane	OCT 12 1844
GORDON, John	TAYLOR, Rachel A.	JUN 13 1849
GORDON, Juliana	SUIT, Smith	MAY 16 1832
GORDON, Letitia	JOHNSON, Benjamin	JAN 28 1836
GORDON, Manuel	REELING, Maria Elizth.	JUN 27 1851
GORDON, Maria Louisa	ADDISON, Daniel Dulany	JUL 05 1831
GORDON, Martha	MORIARTY, Daniel	JUL 08 1850
GORDON, Martha	NOLEN, Jeremiah	APR 10 1851
GORDON, Mary	NILES, Saml. V.	NOV 11 1851
GORDON, Matilda	VIDLER, Wm. Edward	JUN 01 1820
GORDON, Matilda	BETZ, William	MAR 24 1830
GORDON, Nancy (blk)	JOHNSTON, Elias	MAR 06 1850
GORDON, Obadiah	TSCHIFFELY, Eliza	JUN 18 1831
GORDON, Rebecca	TOLSON, Douglas	MAR 07 1850
GORDON, Saml. H.	LANGLEY, Isabella	NOV 13 1856
GORDON, Susan Ann	SMITH, William	JUL 24 1831
GORDON, Wm. A.	BLAKE, Glorvina	NOV 04 1830
GORDON, Worthington	BRYAN, Priscilla	APR 01 1824
GOREM, Caroline	DOVE, Wm.	MAR 13 1856
GOREM, Ellen	JACOBS, Armstead	AUG 15 1849
GORMAN, Catharine	BURKE, John	AUG 23 1856
GORMAN, James	DOVE, Liddy Ann	JAN 11 1855
GORMAN, John	MEADE, Jane	JUN 19 1820
GORMAN, Mary	GODDARD, Benjamin	OCT 31 1849
GORMAN, Mary	HOGAN, Sarah	JUL 29 1854
GORMLEY, Marcella	SPOLLAN, James	DEC 15 1855
GORMLEY, Philip	O'REILY, Margaret	JUN 28 1830
GORMLEY, Philip	POOLE, Rachel	AUG 17 1858
GORSUCH, William G.	DOUGLASS, Sarah	MAY 28 1829
GORUM, James Thos.	DEAVERS, Julia Ann	JAN 14 1858
GORUM, Mary	LINDSAY, O.P.	FEB 04 1851
GORUM, Richard	PETTITT, Mary	JAN 05 1858
GOSHELL, Mary Ann	LINNIG, F.	JUN 18 1858
GOSLAND, James	O'NEALE, Julia	OCT 14 1844

District of Columbia Marriage Licenses, 1811-1858

GOSLER, Jane	DENNEY, James M.	SEP 04 1854
GOSNEL, Richard	HARRYMAN, Ann R.	JAN 04 1853
GOSS, John	NEAD, Mary	JUN 04 1825
GOSS, Louisa	PADGET, Joseph	JAN 18 1831
GOSS, Louisa Jane	HOWE, Ignatius	APR 12 1845
GOSS, Mary	POPE, Frederick	MAY 18 1844
GOSS, Thomas	SANDERSON, Martha Ann	DEC 30 1840
GOSSER, Virginia	HUNT, Thomas F.	DEC 07 1852
GOSSLER, Catherine	GOSSLER, Henry	DEC 21 1833
GOSSLER, Henry	GOSSLER, Catherine	DEC 21 1833
GOSSON, Frances M.	MAYHEW, William H.	JAN 11 1854
GOSSUM, Charity Ann	FADELEY, Jacob, Jr.	DEC 30 1822
GOSSUM, Matilda	LYLES, James	FEB 15 1826
GOSZLER, Christianna	HOLTZMAN, Thomas	SEP 14 1824
GOSZLER, James	GOSZLER, Mary P.	JAN 13 1837
GOSZLER, Mary P.	GOSZLER, James	JAN 13 1837
GOSZLER, Thomas D.	HOLTZMAN, Eliza	MAR 17 1826
GOSZLER, Thomas D.	COLEMAN, Ann M.	DEC 03 1842
GOSZLER, William H.	WILLIAMS, Caroline	JUN 30 1838
GOTHE, Margaretha	HUD, Christian	JUN 19 1841
GOTHER, Rachel E.	LISBY, Horatio	DEC 19 1822
GOTHIER, Caroline	ARANGO, Antonio	DEC 30 1828
GOTT, Richard	GORDON, Ann E.	MAY 03 1831
GOTT, Richard	McKENSEY, Catharine	FEB 02 1835
GOTTHEIL, Louis	WOODWARD, Elizabeth	JAN 01 1840
GOUGH, Elizabeth	GREEN, John	JAN 26 1820
GOUGH, Elizabeth	GREEN, John	APR 17 1822
GOUGH, Sarah	COLEY, Henry	MAR 04 1834
GOULD, John Alfred	BLANDFORD, Mary Elizabeth Cecelia	JAN 20 1845
GOULD, Laura A.	ABBOTT, John	MAR 13 1855
GOULD, Marsallina Lavinia	EBERHART, John	FEB 19 1849
GOULD, Stephen G.	GRIGGS, Ann Maria	JUL 06 1844
GOULDING, Frederick, Jr.	WALLER, Lucinda	FEB 14 1837
GOULDING, Mary	RHODES, Edward	DEC 31 1829
GOULDING, Mary Josephine	KENNEDY, William H.	MAY 03 1838
GOULDING, Rosetta	HARTLOVE, James	AUG 16 1826
GOURLEY, Thomas	BOOTH, Ann	JAN 21 1851
GOUSHA, Napoleon B.	TOLTON, Mary E.	MAR 15 1856
GOUTIER, Caroline	PITHON, Marius Michael	JUN 30 1824
GOUVERNEUR, Elizabeth K.	HEISKELL, Henry Lee	JUN 08 1842
GOUVERNEUR, Saml. L.	CAMPBELL, Mary	MAR 02 1855
GOVER, Samuel B.	ROBINSON, Eliza	DEC 10 1857
GOVERNEUR, Samuel L.	MONROE, Maria H.	MAR 08 1820
GOWAN, Eliza Ann	LYNCH, James W.	OCT 08 1844
GOWN, Martha	CHAMBERLIN, William	JUN 10 1837
GRABILL, Mary Virginia	HAMILTON, James W.	MAY 15 1858
GRACE, Aaron B.	DANIEL, Mary E.	JUN 15 1854
GRACE, John	HUTCHISON, Ann	FEB 04 1825
GRADY, Bridget	BELT, James M.	DEC 03 1855
GRADY, Catherine	BURKE, Thomas	MAY 01 1852
GRADY, Michael	MURPHY, Catharin	AUG 02 1853
GRADY, Nancy Ann	SKINNER, Augustus P.	FEB 05 1835
GRADY, Patrick	MURPHY, Ellen	SEP 09 1854
GRAENCHER, Charles L.	MERILLET, Sophia J.	JAN 21 1858
GRAFFORD, Sally	KEHOE, William	JAN 15 1822
GRAFLY, Margaret	TRUSCOTT, John	MAY 24 1843
GRAGES, August	SAUERMANN, Maria	MAY 19 1855
GRAHAM, Adeline	HOLLIDAY, Samuel H.	MAY 03 1852

District of Columbia Marriage Licenses, 1811-1858

GRAHAM, Alexr.	CLEMENTSON, Sarah	OCT 07 1815
GRAHAM, Andrew	TSCHIFFELY, Adela	DEC 31 1832
GRAHAM, Anne (blk)	DELANY, Lewis	FEB 10 1842
GRAHAM, Eleanor	PURKS, Benjamin	APR 11 1812
GRAHAM, Eliza	THOMPSON, John	AUG 11 1856
GRAHAM, Elizabeth	AUSTIN, William G.	FEB 22 1845
GRAHAM, Ellen	HANNING, James	NOV 30 1849
GRAHAM, French	COURTNEY, Amanda	AUG 24 1858
GRAHAM, Geo. M.	SMITH, Ester B.	OCT 01 1834
GRAHAM, George	WATSON, Jane L.	JUL 07 1825
GRAHAM, George W.	GASTON, Eliza	NOV 11 1842
GRAHAM, Guy	BARRON, Catharine	FEB 25 1851
GRAHAM, Hannible	COGEE, Matilda (blk)	MAR 20 1851
GRAHAM, J. Thompson	CAMPBELL, Rebecca H.	FEB 02 1852
GRAHAM, James	JACKSON, Martha	AUG 17 1843
GRAHAM, James D.	MEADE, Charlotte	JUL 06 1828
GRAHAM, James H.	HOOE, Susan G.	FEB 10 1842
GRAHAM, Jeannie B.	DAVENPORT, Henry K.	DEC 07 1847
GRAHAM, John [Lt.]	SELDEN, Sarah E.	APR 01 1829
GRAHAM, John F.	BOONE, Priscilla A.	FEB 02 1837
GRAHAM, John W.	BRADLEY, Anne M.	JUN 01 1842
GRAHAM, Margaret	WOODWARD, Thomas E.	DEC 30 1856
GRAHAM, Mary	MAKSEY, James	JUL 14 1817
GRAHAM, Mary	ROBERTUS, Gottlieb	FEB 28 1855
GRAHAM, Nancy	GILL, Edward	JUN 04 1822
GRAHAM, Rachel (blk)	CAMPBELL, William	JUN 12 1854
GRAHAM, Richard	HEISLIP, Emilda M.	SEP 30 1839
GRAHAM, Robert H.	HILLER, Ann Sophia	APR 05 1854
GRAHAM, Virginia	SANNER, Jerome T.	JUN 26 1848
GRAHAM, William	CHAPPELL, Amelia	JAN 29 1849
GRAHAM, William S.	HUGHES, Henrietta	APR 19 1843
GRAIG, Elizabeth	PADGETT, William H.	JUN 17 1840
GRAIN, Sarah	SUTTON, William	JAN 12 1848
GRAINGER, James H.	MAGAR, Mary Elizabeth	JAN 11 1844
GRAINGER, Malinda A.	BRIGHT, Michael E.	SEP 21 1847
GRAINGER, Mary A.	GODMAN, Robert V.	JAN 17 1855
GRAIVES, Joseph	OLANT, Mary E.	JUN 12 1837
GRAMLICH, Louisa	MILLER, Philip	JUL 29 1851
GRAMMER, Andrew	HORNING, Rosena	AUG 17 1855
GRAMMER, Annie	DUNKINSON, Wm. H.	DEC 09 1852
GRAMMER, Frederick Louis	REYNOLDS, Camelia A.	FEB 05 1857
GRAMMER, Gotlieb C.	DOYNE, Eliza	APR 07 1813
GRAMMER, Rosena M.	STETTINIUS, William	JUN 17 1834
GRAMMER, Sophia	ARTES, Daniel	SEP 05 1854
GRANDERSON, Catharine	DAVENPORT, James	JUN 05 1856
GRANDISON, Alexander	JOHNSON, Maria Jane (blk)	FEB 10 1842
GRANDISON, Ann M. (blk)	THOMAS, Fras. A.	DEC 31 1855
GRANDISON, Benjamin	TRAVERS, Eliza (blk)	AUG 26 1850
GRANDISON, Benjamin	CONTEE, Mary Ann (blk)	APR 09 1853
GRANDSTAFF, Abraham	STALLARD, Molinda	SEP 26 1831
GRANEY, Michael	PRENDERBLE, Catharine	DEC 06 1852
GRANGER, Clement	BARNES, Mary	MAR 06 1821
GRANGER, James H.	YOUNG, Margaret	SEP 28 1854
GRANGER, John W.	PADGET, Elizabeth	MAY 08 1855
GRANGER, Martha A.	SERRO, John A.	APR 24 1845
GRANGER, William H.	BEACH, Margaret	FEB 14 1817
GRANT, Alexander	TAYLOR, Mary	NOV 04 1851
GRANT, Ann	BUGH, James L.	SEP 04 1820

District of Columbia Marriage Licenses, 1811-1858

GRANT, Ann E.	GLASCOW, Augustus	DEC 08 1853
GRANT, Elisha	MATTHEWS, Mary (blk)	SEP 22 1856
GRANT, Elizabeth Jane	HOLLAND, James S.	DEC 03 1839
GRANT, Jane (blk)	JOHNSON, James	MAR 07 1843
GRANT, John	BOWIE, Catherine	JAN 01 1816
GRANT, Joseph	GRIFFIN, Ann	FEB 09 1826
GRANT, Margaret	CLINCY, Patrick	SEP 09 1851
GRANT, Mary	ENRIGHT, Thomas	MAY 21 1858
GRANT, Michael	CASEY, Ellen	APR 02 1853
GRANT, Michael	CLANSEY, Margaret	JAN 02 1855
GRANT, Nora	DWYER, Edward	MAY 10 1851
GRANT, Richard	BLAKE, Margaret	NOV 24 1854
GRANT, Spencer	NUSTIC, Mary Ann	APR 11 1831
GRANT, Talburt M.	PIGGOT, Mary E.	MAY 13 1844
GRANT, Walter	O'BRIEN, Margaret	MAY 01 1857
GRANT, Westley	DINES, Eliza	JUN 14 1848
GRANT, William	ROY, Nancy	SEP 30 1815
GRANT, William M.	COLLISON, Lucinda	OCT 20 1847
GRANT, William V.	FLEET, Patience (blk)	MAY 29 1835
GRANT, William W.	WAGONNER, Louisa Ann	SEP 18 1852
GRANTAM, Peter	ALLEN, Catherine (blk)	DEC 04 1849
GRANTHAM, Henry	DOWLING, Ellen (blk)	DEC 19 1839
GRANTON, Michael	BUTLER, Rebecca	FEB 17 1845
GRANTT, Catharine	SHAW, William D.	APR 03 1823
GRANTT, George H.	VERMILLION, Margaret	JUL 20 1826
GRANTT, Josephine	STONE, James	APR 09 1849
GRANTT, Margaret	HARRISON, John	AUG 15 1833
GRASER, Adam	DENGEL, Madalena	OCT 01 1852
GRATIOT, Julia A.	CHOUTEAU, Charles P.	NOV 24 1845
GRATIOT, Mary Victoria	DeMOUTHOLON, Charles Francois	OCT 30 1837
GRAVATE, Catherine W.	ELKINS, Nathaniel	JUN 08 1852
GRAVATT, Mary V.	BAMBERGER, Henry C.	OCT 05 1857
GRAVE, Ludwig	LINDEMANN, Catherina	FEB 07 1843
GRAVES, Amanda T.	LINDSAY, James W.	MAY 05 1845
GRAVES, Ann	WATSON, John R.	APR 10 1813
GRAVES, Ann	VARNELL, George W.	SEP 17 1855
GRAVES, Austin	PURVIS, Virginia C.	NOV 02 1857
GRAVES, George	DAVIS, Eliza	DEC 23 1826
GRAVES, George W.	MACK, Mary Ann	NOV 05 1857
GRAVES, Harriet O.	MILLER, John	DEC 24 1828
GRAVES, Jane	ELLIS, James	JUN 13 1839
GRAVES, John	QUAID, Sarah	DEC 28 1813
GRAVES, John B.	JACKSON, Catharine R.	MAY 12 1858
GRAVES, Joseph S.	GLOVER, Eliza Jane	AUG 19 1858
GRAVES, Lucy A.	THOMAS, John F.	JAN 08 1857
GRAVES, Mary	BARNES, Henry	DEC 22 1814
GRAVES, Mary	McGILL, William H.	MAY 11 1844
GRAVES, Mary E.	REEVES, William L.	MAY 21 1835
GRAVES, Mary Elizabeth	LOVELESS, John	DEC 31 1849
GRAVES, Mary Elizth.	CAMMACK, Thomas	APR 29 1844
GRAVES, Sarah Ellen	SEWELL, Clement J.	FEB 06 1843
GRAVES, Susanna Eliza	BROWN, John	JUN 20 1847
GRAVES, Thomas Jefn.	READ, Elizabeth Ann	JUN 02 1855
GRAVES, William H.	NOLOON, Jane M.	OCT 14 1851
GRAVES, William L.	VARNELL, Jane A.	AUG 03 1857
GRAVIN, Norah	CRATTY, Michael	SEP 08 1853
GRAVITT, Frances A.E.	RIDDLE, William O.	DEC 20 1853
GRAW, Thomas	TILLETT, Julila	FEB 02 1839

District of Columbia Marriage Licenses, 1811-1858

GRAY, Adaline	WEDZE, James	NOV 22 1824
GRAY, Alexander	MORGAN, Mirenda	JAN 04 1821
GRAY, Anjamima	DOWNES, John	MAR 23 1840
GRAY, Ann	ARNOLD, Joseph	MAR 31 1812
GRAY, Ann Maria	MONEY, Enoah	MAR 12 1833
GRAY, Anthony	CALLAN, Alice Elizth.	MAY 06 1851
GRAY, Arenan (blk)	DAVIS, William	DEC 18 1849
GRAY, Baptist	STONE, Elizabeth	AUG 05 1838
GRAY, Basil	FARR, Elenora	FEB 09 1835
GRAY, Basil H.	SMITH, Elizabeth (blk)	DEC 28 1854
GRAY, Benjamin F.	WHITE, Almira J.	JUL 09 1857
GRAY, Cail Ellum	GEAY, Matilda	JAN 20 1813
GRAY, Caroline	CROWN, James	JAN 27 1835
GRAY, Cecelia	OWENS, Jesse	FEB 02 1844
GRAY, Charles	BUSH, Clora Ann (blk)	JUN 16 1853
GRAY, Charlotte (blk)	KENNEDY, James	JUL 21 1830
GRAY, Christy (blk)	TWINE, David	DEC 20 1848
GRAY, Ebenezer	POWERS, Elizabeth	APR 18 1843
GRAY, Edward	PARKER, Eliza Maria (blk)	MAR 16 1854
GRAY, Eleanor	BURNS, Harry	MAR 30 1820
GRAY, Eleanor (blk)	MAGRUDER, Milfred	NOV 09 1829
GRAY, Elias	MacDANIEL, Elila	JUN 28 1819
GRAY, Elizabeth	BAYN, Horatio	SEP 21 1815
GRAY, Elizabeth	BEANS, Dawson	DEC 23 1817
GRAY, Elizabeth	CARDENAS, Vincent	FEB 18 1857
GRAY, Elizabeth	BOYER, George	AUG 16 1858
GRAY, Emeline	CHURN, James	MAY 21 1840
GRAY, Francis	HARLEY, Susan	SEP 01 1831
GRAY, Franklin C.	FRENCH, Matilda C.	MAR 23 1853
GRAY, George	ATHEY, Mary Ann	APR 12 1834
GRAY, George W.	DeVAUGHN, Celia	JAN 03 1831
GRAY, Hannah Elizabeth	BUSH, John H.	MAR 25 1837
GRAY, Harriet (blk)	EDENBURR, Edward	DEC 07 1826
GRAY, Henry W.	WATERS, Mary Malvina	SEP 21 1841
GRAY, Hezekiah	WEBSTER, Ann	NOV 10 1818
GRAY, Hezekiah	BIGGS, Lottee	OCT 29 1823
GRAY, Hezekiah	BROOKES, Chloe	APR 01 1837
GRAY, Hiram	BUTLER, Caroline	MAY 31 1847
GRAY, Isaac S.	PERRIE, Elizabeth M.	NOV 08 1855
GRAY, James	HARDY, Matilda	JUL 28 1826
GRAY, James	TURNER, Ellen (blk)	SEP 07 1844
GRAY, James	THOMAS, Mary (blk)	MAY 29 1851
GRAY, James L.	CLEPHANE, Catherine	JAN 18 1858
GRAY, Jane	CONNER, William	OCT 04 1831
GRAY, Jane	RIDER, Andrew	JUN 10 1845
GRAY, Jane	WALLS, James E.	JAN 10 1853
GRAY, Jarred	WOOD, Elizabeth (blk)	OCT 20 1827
GRAY, John	MORAN, Jane	JAN 13 1842
GRAY, John	WRIGHT, Martha Ann (blk)	MAY 11 1847
GRAY, John B.	LACY, Rebecca Ann	NOV 04 1822
GRAY, John L.	MOORE, Charity Ann	FEB 07 1850
GRAY, John T.	HOOK, Virginia S.	JUN 29 1846
GRAY, John William D.	BARKER, Eliza Jane	JUL 01 1846
GRAY, Joseph B.	ANDERSON, Dorcas Ann	JAN 01 1853
GRAY, Julian	KENDRICK, Benjamin	SEP 30 1816
GRAY, Louisa	HOLLAND, Robert	JUN 04 1857
GRAY, Lucy Ann	LUSBY, A. Francis	DEC 20 1852
GRAY, Margaret	DAY, Wm.	APR 18 1814

District of Columbia Marriage Licenses, 1811-1858

GRAY, Maria	SWANY, John	JUL 28 1831
GRAY, Martha	JONES, William, of Edwd.	SEP 28 1850
GRAY, Mary	LONG, Wm.	DEC 27 1817
GRAY, Mary	ANDERSON, Frederick	OCT 03 1837
GRAY, Mary	KIER, Barney	APR 14 1842
GRAY, Mary Ann	KNOX, John	JUN 06 1822
GRAY, Mary Ann	BROWN, Edward	APR 21 1829
GRAY, Mary Ann	GARNER, Daniel	JUN 14 1844
GRAY, Mary Louisa	SELBY, Allen	DEC 04 1849
GRAY, Minia (blk)	BARKER, William H.	OCT 27 1847
GRAY, Polly	BARNES, John	NOV 27 1828
GRAY, Priscilla	McDANIEL, Allen	JUN 15 1846
GRAY, Rachel	ROBINSON, Samuel	SEP 15 1819
GRAY, Richard	DOVER, Mary (blk)	MAR 23 1846
GRAY, Robert	SIMMS, Jane Rebecca	DEC 12 1826
GRAY, Sarah Ann	THOMPSON, William	NOV 18 1824
GRAY, Sarah Jane	LUGLER, Joseph	MAY 29 1847
GRAY, Thomas	SHORTER, Nancy (blk)	JUL 08 1841
GRAY, Thomas K.	NALLY, Ellen	NOV 03 1830
GRAY, Vincent	WEAR, Matilda	JUL 03 1817
GRAY, Virginia	FADELEY, James	OCT 23 1855
GRAY, William	SANSBURY, Charlotte	NOV 14 1814
GRAY, William	STEWART, Mary	MAY 13 1850
GRAY, William H.	TARMON, Elizabeth M.	JAN 18 1843
GRAYSON, Eliza	WILLIAMS, Tobias	JAN 08 1845
GRAYSON, Eliza (blk)	REELER, Samuel	JUL 18 1840
GRAYSON, John	ORSBURN, Mary	DEC 10 1816
GRAYSON, John B.	SEARLE, Caroline	NOV 07 1828
GRAYSON, Mary C.	CHEW, Thomas R.	NOV 07 1854
GRAYSON, Nancy (blk)	TATE, Henry	MAR 28 1831
GRAYSON, Nancy (blk)	LEE, Theoderick	SEP 14 1833
GRAYSON, Thomas W.	GREEN, Mary E.	MAY 07 1851
GREAR, Martha L.	CRANDLE, Joseph H.	DEC 26 1854
GREAR, Mary Melvina	MANS, Isaac R.	AUG 28 1838
GREAVES, Eliza	MORGAN, John	MAY 28 1858
GREAVES, Matthew	ARMISTEAD, Cecelia L.	MAY 28 1855
GREEN, Aaron	PERCELL, Eliza	NOV 01 1843
GREEN, Alfred	ARMSTRONG, Susan (blk)	JUL 16 1857
GREEN, Alice	deYTURBIDE, Angel	JUN 07 1855
GREEN, Amanda	FLINN, Daniel W.	DEC 27 1848
GREEN, Ammon	LAZENBY, Ann Maria	MAY 26 1851
GREEN, Ann Laura	REED, Isaac Shelby	JUN 26 1832
GREEN, Ann Rebecca	HAUPTMAN, Jeremiah	JUN 27 1829
GREEN, Anna (blk)	LEE, Carter	JUL 23 1852
GREEN, Annie	WISHART, J. Wilson	JAN 05 1852
GREEN, Archibald R.	PETERS, Hannretta	MAY 19 1853
GREEN, Beattie T.	TINSLEY, W.T.	JAN 06 1849
GREEN, Bridget	CRAHEN, Thomas	APR 17 1851
GREEN, Catharine	KILBERTH, Henry	JUL 23 1818
GREEN, Catharine	CURRAN, Bartley	SEP 04 1856
GREEN, Catharine Ann	REILLY, George	MAY 04 1832
GREEN, Charity	FLURRY, John	FEB 23 1830
GREEN, Charity	EASTON, Robert	SEP 17 1835
GREEN, Charity	WEIZNER, Malam	NOV 19 1844
GREEN, Charles W.	HAISLIP, Jane E.	AUG 30 1830
GREEN, Christiana	SIMPSON, Thomas P.	NOV 01 1855
GREEN, Clara A.	ROSS, Charles H.	APR 25 1844
GREEN, Edward	DAVIS, Jane (blk)	NOV 11 1842

District of Columbia Marriage Licenses, 1811-1858

GREEN, Edward	GAULLETT, Placedie	APR 26 1853
GREEN, Edward E.	TAYLOR, Sarah A.	APR 10 1858
GREEN, Edwd.	DORMAN, Ann	JAN 03 1854
GREEN, Edwin	GAWLER, Sarah	APR 23 1839
GREEN, Eliza	BULLOCH, John	MAR 19 1835
GREEN, Elizabeth	SWIMLEY, Lewis	MAY 27 1829
GREEN, Elizabeth	SMITH, Geo. B.	DEC 17 1835
GREEN, Elizabeth	JENNERS, Antius	DEC 03 1835
GREEN, Elizabeth (col'd)	SPRIGG, John	AUG 31 1848
GREEN, Elizabeth R.	QUESINBURY, Nicholas	MAY 15 1849
GREEN, Ellen	SWANN, James	MAY 14 1844
GREEN, Ellen	LYNCH, Michael	NOV 01 1854
GREEN, Emily	TURNER, Abraham	MAR 12 1834
GREEN, Eveline	STEWART, William W.	MAY 17 1831
GREEN, Frances	TRIDLE, John	NOV 30 1850
GREEN, George Henry	LLOYD, Martha Ann	JAN 20 1851
GREEN, George W.	BUTLER, Eliza J. (blk)	NOV 24 1851
GREEN, Gorish	RODE, Caroline	FEB 16 1858
GREEN, Harriet (blk)	GLASSCOW, John	NOV 25 1846
GREEN, Harriet R.	McPHERSON, Henry D.	JUN 08 1857
GREEN, Henry T.	CLANCY, Mary	JAN 10 1853
GREEN, Isabella F.	WARD, William J.	DEC 04 1853
GREEN, James	KAINE, Tamor	SEP 15 1817
GREEN, James	FOWLER, Mary	NOV 10 1834
GREEN, James	ARNOLD, Eliza	JUN 02 1842
GREEN, James	MAGEE, Elizabeth	JAN 27 1847
GREEN, James	LAWRENCE, Mary Ann (blk)	FEB 10 1851
GREEN, James	McNERHANEY, Ann	FEB 18 1851
GREEN, James	DAVIS, Mary Ellen	JUL 03 1851
GREEN, Jane	CUNNINGHAM, Anthony	OCT 16 1822
GREEN, Jane	MANGUN, Zachariah	OCT 17 1834
GREEN, Jane	THOMAS, Joseph	APR 02 1855
GREEN, Joel Cephas	WHEELER, Isabella	NOV 21 1851
GREEN, John	FORREST, Ann	JUL 21 1814
GREEN, John	GOUGH, Elizabeth	JAN 26 1820
GREEN, John	GOUGH, Elizabeth	APR 17 1822
GREEN, John	WOOD, Evelina	JUL 02 1827
GREEN, John	SPEAKS, Elizabeth	AUG 28 1828
GREEN, John	FURGERSON, Mary	OCT 12 1838
GREEN, John	TINNEY, Rachel Ann	JAN 05 1843
GREEN, John	ROBB, Catharine	AUG 30 1847
GREEN, John	DAVIS, Sabina (blk)	AUG 19 1851
GREEN, John E.	NALLY, Elizabeth Ann	JUL 26 1828
GREEN, John F.	HOLT, Sarah Jane	DEC 25 1851
GREEN, Joseph	HUNT, Mary E. (blk)	JAN 28 1857
GREEN, Joseph J.	AYRES, Dorcas	MAR 06 1829
GREEN, Julia	SUMMERS, John	JUN 04 1822
GREEN, Julian	GADDIS, Adam	JAN 24 1824
GREEN, Letty (negro)	RIGGS, Warren	AUG 31 1830
GREEN, Louisa	HELMEETH, Baldin	JUN 22 1842
GREEN, Lucinda A.	ARNOLD, John H.	NOV 09 1825
GREEN, Lydia (blk)	SEAMORE, Francis	AUG 29 1849
GREEN, Mantray	BROOKS, Ann Maria (blk)	NOV 30 1837
GREEN, Margaret	FRITZ, Charles	JUN 25 1836
GREEN, Margaret M.	CALHOUN, Andrew P.	MAY 05 1836
GREEN, Maria M.	McGINNIS, Peter	NOV 12 1855
GREEN, Mary	MacKINNA, Neil	MAR 10 1818
GREEN, Mary	ASHMORE, Joseph	DEC 05 1820

District of Columbia Marriage Licenses, 1811-1858

GREEN, Mary	HAMMILL, Wesley	SEP 25 1856
GREEN, Mary Elizth.	GRAYSON, Thomas W.	MAY 07 1851
GREEN, Mary Frances	STONE, William J., Junr.	DEC 04 1849
GREEN, Mary Jane	MADDOX, Alexander	MAY 10 1852
GREEN, Mary Lou	COLLINS, William	OCT 31 1853
GREEN, Mathias	SWANN, Mary Ann (blk)	OCT 14 1822
GREEN, Matilda	BROWN, Charles	APR 02 1823
GREEN, Matilda A.	HALL, Ben H.	FEB 07 1854
GREEN, Michael	GANNON, Mary	JAN 28 1852
GREEN, Nelson	JONES, Charlotte (blk)	OCT 11 1855
GREEN, Owen	MURRAY, Susan	FEB 16 1846
GREEN, Owen	McGEE, Mary A.	JUL 29 1851
GREEN, Patrick	BOYED, Ann	JAN 22 1824
GREEN, Polly (blk)	JAMES, Aures	OCT 09 1838
GREEN, Precilla	HASWELL, James	MAY 21 1853
GREEN, Robert	DREESE, Mary	JUN 24 1840
GREEN, Robert	TARTANSON, Julia	OCT 13 1845
GREEN, Robert B.	JOHNSON, Adel (blk)	MAR 17 1853
GREEN, Sarah	DOYLE, Thomas	SEP 13 1843
GREEN, Sarah Ann	DAWSON, Aaron	SEP 05 1825
GREEN, Sarah Ann	MORTIMORE, William	DEC 24 1838
GREEN, Sarah Ann	SCOTT, William	FEB 01 1839
GREEN, Sarah Rebecca	CRAVEN, John	OCT 28 1848
GREEN, Sophia	HUNTER, Lewis J.	JAN 29 1820
GREEN, Thomas	JOHNSON, Mary (blk)	NOV 20 1833
GREEN, Thomas	LEWIS, Felton (blk)	JUN 23 1835
GREEN, Thomas	HARVEY, Lucy (blk)	AUG 25 1836
GREEN, Thomas	McCREA, Eliza (or Liddy) Ann	JUL 18 1838
GREEN, Victoria H.	TAIT, Alexander	NOV 25 1857
GREEN, William	HURDEL, Sarah Ann	NOV 09 1826
GREEN, William H.	MARSHALL, Eleanora B.	JUN 22 1854
GREEN, William H.	LOVEJOY, Harriet A.	APR 30 1855
GREEN, William P.	VENNER, Henrietta P.	AUG 14 1848
GREEN, Wm.	GIBSON, Matilda	FEB 03 1818
GREEN, Wm. L.	WINGEWROTH, Susanna J.	MAY 09 1855
GREENAICE, Mary Ann Eliza	HARTLETT, William	SEP 04 1829
GREENE, J.D.	GOLD, Mary A.	JAN 03 1854
GREENE, Maria	DEVEREUX, William	AUG 31 1848
GREENFIELD, Arianna	ATWOOD, William	NOV 23 1853
GREENFIELD, Benjamin E.	HEPBURN, Louisa V.	OCT 30 1851
GREENFIELD, Caroline	O'REILLY, John	FEB 15 1847
GREENFIELD, Henry C.	MILLER, Mary E.	MAY 16 1842
GREENFIELD, Louisa V.	DAWSON, James M.	FEB 25 1856
GREENFIELD, Neomi	HARTLY, Abraham	AUG 02 1836
GREENHALGH, Mary	BELL, Robert	DEC 08 1830
GREENHOW, Florence V.	MOORE, Seymour T.	MAR 28 1855
GREENHOW, Robert	O'NEALE, Rose Maria	MAY 23 1835
GREENLEAF, Susan	BACON, Ebenezer	JAN 24 1828
GREENLEAF, Wm. C.	BRIGHTWELL, Mary	JAN 02 1847
GREENLIEF, Thomas	BAYNE, Susan	MAY 31 1821
GREENS, Jacob	CHEROKEE, Elizabeth (blk)	SEP 14 1839
GREENTREE, Margaret	HURDLE, John	MAY 23 1818
GREENWELL, Ann	MARR, Dennis B.	JUN 29 1812
GREENWELL, Ann	WILLIAMS, Lewis	OCT 20 1834
GREENWELL, Benedict O.	McCLELLAND, Elizabeth C.	OCT 01 1844
GREENWELL, Catharine S.	JOHNSTON, James W.	MAY 08 1848
GREENWELL, Clement	SMITH, Elizabeth	JAN 02 1855
GREENWELL, Combs	RYHN, Mary	NOV 17 1842

District of Columbia Marriage Licenses, 1811-1858

GREENWELL, Eliza	LOWE, Randolph	AUG 10 1821
GREENWELL, Frances V.	McCLOSKEY, James D.	FEB 11 1858
GREENWELL, James	BOYER, Caroline	JUN 20 1839
GREENWELL, Joseph W.	COLTER, Lydia Ann	NOV 15 1825
GREENWELL, Louisa	HEFFERNAN, Patrick	JAN 29 1846
GREENWELL, Mary A.	STEWART, William E.	DEC 30 1847
GREENWELL, Mary Ann	WILKINSON, James	OCT 28 1847
GREENWELL, Mary Eliza	JEFFRIES, John B.	DEC 13 1853
GREENWELL, Monica	CESSYL, Thomas	AUG 12 1820
GREENWELL, William E.	MANNING, Margaret H.	SEP 26 1854
GREENWOOD, Benjamin	BOWMAN, Mary Ann	MAY 14 1845
GREENWOOD, Catherine	ROBEY, Horatio N.	JAN 21 1843
GREENWOOD, Elizabeth	JACOBS, Edward	DEC 24 1833
GREENWOOD, Martha A.	HENRY, George W.	JUL 23 1853
GREENWOOD, Mary Ann	FITZHUE, Wm. Henry	FEB 28 1828
GREENWOOD, Robert	SHIPLEY, Susanna	SEP 03 1824
GREENWOOD, Wm. S.	YOUNG, Mary Ann	MAY 22 1828
GREER, Chauncey F.	CARR, Mary C.	OCT 30 1848
GREER, Cornelius L.	HAGGERTY, Mary L.	JUL 02 1855
GREER, Eliza Ingham	WHEAT, Joseph H.	MAY 29 1832
GREER, Henry T.	DOWING, Martha Jane	JAN 11 1841
GREER, Isabell P.	MILBURN, Fayette T.	JUL 05 1854
GREER, James C.	IRWING, Henrietta	JAN 18 1847
GREER, Margaret B.	WILSON, Thomas K.	SEP 06 1841
GREER, Rachel	DRURY, Samuel T.	AUG 02 1848
GREEVES, John	BOYD, Amanda	FEB 11 1840
GREGG, Joseph	CROSS, Ann Matilda	MAR 30 1837
GREGG, Myron E.	WRIGHT, Mary A.	JUL 17 1858
GREGORY, Caroline M.	JOHNSON, William H.	SEP 16 1844
GREGORY, Elizabeth	UMBAUGH, George	AUG 20 1829
GREGORY, George	NALLEY, Harriet	JAN 04 1842
GREGORY, J. Alexander	STARBUCK, Maria L.	JUL 10 1856
GREGORY, John	THOMAS, Hannah A.	JUL 20 1840
GREGORY, Margaret D.	ASHBY, Francis W.	OCT 12 1854
GREINER, Joseph	PLANT, Mary E.	JUN 12 1837
GREIRHN, Frederick	BRIDON, Virginia	NOV 19 1819
GREIVEACHER, Charles	McCLELLAND, Margaret	JUL 20 1830
GREMSLEY, Elias	DANTEY, Martha A.	AUG 18 1857
GRENCHENER, Catharine	DAVIS, Henry A.	SEP 07 1836
GRENNELL, Frank	JOHNSON, Marion Gales	DEC 08 1846
GRERNIN, William	LEACH, Delila	AUG 25 1838
GRESHAM, Sterling H.	WINGERD, Catherine E.	DEC 03 1834
GRESHAM, Sterling H.R.	WINGARD, Mary Eliza	JAN 09 1821
GREY, Ann	McCARTY, Eugene	SEP 05 1851
GREY, Benjamin	SIMS, Anne	MAY 16 1815
GREY, Elizabeth	FLYNN, John	APR 28 1856
GREY, Fannie	THOMAS, George C.	JUL 14 1848
GREY, Jane (blk)	LEE, Francis	MAY 13 1857
GREY, John A.	DADE, Anna M. (blk)	MAY 04 1857
GREY, Mary	CONROY, James	NOV 18 1852
GREY, Mathew	RISEN, Jane	NOV 01 1813
GREY, Rebecca Susan	STINGER, John Frederick	FEB 16 1833
GREY, Selina A.	PETERS, John	FEB 15 1855
GREY, Stephen W.	CARTER, Frances A.	NOV 19 1829
GRIDGER, Daniel	HARTMAN, Elizabeth	OCT 22 1825
GRIDLEY, Lewis	KILBRIGHT, Rachel	SEP 11 1854
GRIEB, John	SHAEFFER, Catherine	OCT 23 1846
GRIERSON, John W.	SEELEY, Martha T.A.	MAR 20 1850

District of Columbia Marriage Licenses, 1811-1858

GRIFFEN, Ellen	PAYNE, Thomas	MAR 19 1824
GRIFFETH, Greenbury	JONES, Prudence	FEB 24 1814
GRIFFIN, Ann	GRANT, Joseph	FEB 09 1826
GRIFFIN, Ann	CISSILL, George	DEC 24 1832
GRIFFIN, Betsy	MORRIS, Francis	AUG 20 1839
GRIFFIN, Bridget	KNAUCHTEN, Martin	JAN 02 1856
GRIFFIN, Catharine	CURRAN, Daniel	APR 21 1832
GRIFFIN, Catharine	RILEY, James	MAY 30 1856
GRIFFIN, Catherine Virga.	BROWNING, George G.	NOV 07 1855
GRIFFIN, Charles	WERTZ, Elizabeth	JUL 17 1815
GRIFFIN, Charles T.	McGILL, Rebecca	SEP 30 1843
GRIFFIN, Chloe Ann	HUNTT, Benj. W.	JUN 01 1826
GRIFFIN, Clarissa Milcah	VENABLE, William Piercy	APR 24 1857
GRIFFIN, Dennis	ANDERSON, Jane	OCT 27 1853
GRIFFIN, Elizabeth	WISE, William	JUL 22 1826
GRIFFIN, Elizabeth A.	UPPERMAN, Charles E.	APR 30 1838
GRIFFIN, Ellen	JOY, Morris	OCT 21 1851
GRIFFIN, Georgianna	SWEET, Parker Hall	MAY 04 1857
GRIFFIN, Henry C.	DAW, Sarah V.	SEP 07 1857
GRIFFIN, James C.	PRATHER, Elizabeth Ann	JAN 15 1850
GRIFFIN, James L.	KIBBY, Liannah	SEP 01 1838
GRIFFIN, James L.	SOPER, Sarah Adeline	JAN 22 1858
GRIFFIN, Jesse	BRYAN, Ann J.	JUN 18 1827
GRIFFIN, Johanna	DUDLEY, William	OCT 25 1849
GRIFFIN, John	CARRICO, Mary	FEB 25 1827
GRIFFIN, John	STARK, Nancy	OCT 06 1845
GRIFFIN, John	HUMPHREYS, Mary (blk)	NOV 03 1853
GRIFFIN, John	GLEASON, Mary	DEC 15 1853
GRIFFIN, John	LANCASTER, Cassey Ann	MAY 31 1855
GRIFFIN, Julia	TAYLOR, Robert	OCT 07 1841
GRIFFIN, Lydia	JOHNSON, Edward G.	OCT 05 1840
GRIFFIN, Mary	HOWE, Ignatius	NOV 24 1831
GRIFFIN, Mary Ann	ROBERSON, Charles W.	MAY 11 1822
GRIFFIN, Mary Ann	QUILL, John	JAN 07 1856
GRIFFIN, Mary Eliza	PEAKE, James W.	MAY 07 1849
GRIFFIN, Mary Lucia	THORN, George	MAY 01 1850
GRIFFIN, Matilda J.	SOPER, Charles	APR 18 1850
GRIFFIN, Michael	WELSH, Mary	SEP 18 1855
GRIFFIN, Orlando	HALL, Amanda (blk)	DEC 22 1848
GRIFFIN, Patrick	RATLIFF, Maria	MAY 04 1852
GRIFFIN, Peter	BRISCOE, Jane Love	APR 04 1816
GRIFFIN, Peter	BRISCOE, Caroline	JUN 05 1823
GRIFFIN, Peter	DeKRAFT, Hannah	DEC 20 1827
GRIFFIN, Raphael	TUCKER, Elizabeth	MAY 30 1814
GRIFFIN, Richard	HAWKINS, Cecelia J.	SEP 26 1857
GRIFFIN, Richard B.	DONE, Sarah Ann	OCT 28 1834
GRIFFIN, Robert A.	NORRIS, Margaret A.	NOV 30 1850
GRIFFIN, Samuel	SELBY, Mary (blk)	MAY 28 1851
GRIFFIN, Thomas	HILESHIMER, Susan	DEC 26 1812
GRIFFIN, Thomas	RYAN, Bridget	JUL 26 1854
GRIFFIN, Thomas	BROWN, Bridget	OCT 31 1857
GRIFFIN, Thomas B.	PICKRELL, Rebecca	NOV 07 1849
GRIFFIN, William	CROWLEY, Cath.	NOV 22 1814
GRIFFIN, William	HAMMER, Mary Ann	NOV 29 1838
GRIFFINS, Chloe Ann	BANGS, Thomas	JUL 31 1833
GRIFFIS, Ellen	JONES, Henry	OCT 10 1842
GRIFFIS, Verlinda	BROWN, William I.	FEB 28 1844
GRIFFITH, Charles G.	KNOWLES, Frances	MAY 16 1851

District of Columbia Marriage Licenses, 1811-1858

GRIFFITH, Charlotte	EDMONSTON, Decius W.	AUG 31 1815
GRIFFITH, Charlotte	GIDDINGS, Samuel S.	JUL 04 1846
GRIFFITH, Daniel	EATON, Mary Stanly	APR 07 1853
GRIFFITH, Edward	SPALDING, Eleanor	APR 20 1819
GRIFFITH, Elizabeth	GATES, Francis	JAN 01 1842
GRIFFITH, Isabella	O'LEARY, Timothy	JUL 06 1857
GRIFFITH, James	McGEE, Mary Jane	NOV 05 1834
GRIFFITH, Kinsey	McLEOD, Elizabeth	SEP 04 1817
GRIFFITH, Kinsey	McLEOD, Mary Ann	MAR 21 1832
GRIFFITH, Maria	BROWN, Andrew	AUG 17 1850
GRIFFITH, Martin	GRIFFITH, Winfrelda	JUL 15 1854
GRIFFITH, Mary	WHITMAN, George K.	JUN 01 1850
GRIFFITH, Mary B.	PRETO, Francis	JAN 31 1828
GRIFFITH, Mary E.	TAFF, George D.	JAN 19 1847
GRIFFITH, Rebecca	GIDDINGS, George	MAY 08 1813
GRIFFITH, Richard	CAMPBELL, Ann	DEC 28 1812
GRIFFITH, Samuel C.	OULD, Pauline	FEB 15 1848
GRIFFITH, Susan	ANDERSON, Lingon	JUL 18 1850
GRIFFITH, Susan	COUNAY, John	MAY 19 1854
GRIFFITH, Thomas	PATTON, Catharine	OCT 28 1829
GRIFFITH, Thomas	COOK, Martha	JUL 24 1839
GRIFFITH, Thomas	SMITH, Eliza	DEC 24 1840
GRIFFITH, William A.	SANFORD, Frances Editha	NOV 05 1838
GRIFFITH, William T.	MATLOCK, Elizabeth G.	MAR 30 1829
GRIFFITH, William T.	TWEEDY, Margaret	SEP 30 1854
GRIFFITH, Winfrelda	GRIFFITH, Martin	JUL 15 1854
GRIFFITHS, Ritta	HENDERSON, Edward	SEP 02 1850
GRIGGES, Mary Ann	WILLIAMS, George	NOV 21 1825
GRIGGS, Abel M.	McFARLAND, Mary	JUN 01 1824
GRIGGS, Ann Maria	GOULD, Stephen G.	JUL 06 1844
GRIGGS, Frances C.	LOVELESS, Geo. Henry	JUN 02 1849
GRIGGS, Lavinia V.	STAPLES, William R.	AUG 21 1856
GRIGGS, Mary Virginia	CARLISLE, Samuel H.	JAN 12 1855
GRIGGS, William	WATERS, Rebecca	OCT 04 1853
GRIGSBY, Alexander S.	GARRARD, Caroline M.	APR 16 1827
GRIGSBY, Frances	HUMPHREVILL, Ebenezer	NOV 28 1855
GRIGSBY, James W.	PAINE, Mary	MAR 15 1855
GRIGSBY, Mary A.	LANGFITT, Israel F.	MAY 15 1832
GRIGSBY, Roxannah	PEITCHARTT, Lewis S.	OCT 06 1836
GRIMES, Alfred	BARRETT, Elizabeth	JUL 25 1836
GRIMES, Charles Wm.	COOPER, Sarah (blk)	FEB 14 1853
GRIMES, Craven F.	COSTEN, Margaret	OCT 22 1838
GRIMES, Elizabeth	HOLLAND, James	FEB 20 1841
GRIMES, Elizabeth	HALL, Thomas	NOV 24 1846
GRIMES, Elizabeth	WARD, William	MAR 01 1849
GRIMES, Geo. E.	BROWN, Susan A.	APR 03 1854
GRIMES, George	DORSEY, Elizabeth	MAR 06 1829
GRIMES, Henry	TUCKER, Sarah	AUG 20 1835
GRIMES, Henry V.	LINSEY, Catharine	OCT 03 1832
GRIMES, Hester	McCUBBIN, Nicholas	APR 28 1853
GRIMES, Ignatius	HUNT, Chloe Ann	SEP 23 1848
GRIMES, Jane	DALTON, James	FEB 26 1821
GRIMES, John	MULIKIN, Ruthy Ann	JAN 26 1848
GRIMES, John F.	MAYO, Ann Lucretia	DEC 27 1837
GRIMES, John G.	MINNIS, Martha V.	NOV 19 1855
GRIMES, Leonard	COLSTON, Ocatvia	MAY 27 1833
GRIMES, Leonia	CURTAIN, Henry	JUL 27 1839
GRIMES, Mary	DAVIS, Luke	DEC 16 1819

District of Columbia Marriage Licenses, 1811-1858

GRIMES, Mary	FRAZIER, John	OCT 05 1820
GRIMES, Mary	NEFF, Benedick	OCT 22 1840
GRIMES, Mary Ann	PURKINS, Samuel	NOV 21 1827
GRIMES, Mary S.	COHILL, Henry R.	AUG 26 1858
GRIMES, Michael	HIGDON, Mary Ann	NOV 25 1833
GRIMES, Nancy	MOORE, Joseph	AUG 13 1812
GRIMES, Robert	PETTIT, Martha	NOV 09 1849
GRIMES, Thomas	WAW, Elizabeth	NOV 27 1824
GRIMES, Thos.	McCARTY, Catharine	SEP 17 1819
GRIMES, Virginia	SCOTT, William A.	SEP 15 1857
GRIMES, William	JOHNSON, Charity	AUG 05 1838
GRIMSLEY, Albert	GILLUM, Ann	NOV 25 1857
GRIMSLEY, Amanda	GLADMAN, Addison	JUL 12 1836
GRIMSLEY, Augustus	REILY, Mary	JAN 02 1834
GRIMSLEY, Elias	HOLLEY, Catharine	AUG 07 1813
GRIMSLEY, James	HALL, Tibitha	JAN 08 1845
GRIMSLEY, Liner	OGDEN, Elias	APR 28 1831
GRINDALL, John H.	McDERMOTT, Eliza	MAY 26 1847
GRINDER, Adam	KIRBY, Maria E.	NOV 16 1854
GRINDER, Ann E.	RYDER, Clarke	OCT 26 1854
GRINDER, Anthony	EVANS, Mary	DEC 29 1836
GRINDER, John	EVANS, Dolly	AUG 24 1837
GRINDER, Joseph	KERBY, Margaret Jane	DEC 30 1848
GRINDER, Joseph	WILLIAMS, Elizabeth E.	JAN 18 1855
GRINDER, William	BOSWELL, Mary Ann	AUG 06 1842
GRINDLE, Mary	FORD, Benjamin	DEC 12 1850
GRINER, Adam	JACOBS, Mary	OCT 26 1839
GRINER, Charles E.	RYDER, Clarke	OCT 10 1854
GRINNELL, Henry	RATCLIFF, Mary (blk)	SEP 07 1854
GRINWELL, Sarah	McENDREE, James	JUL 29 1813
GRIPENSCHUTZ, Charles G.	DAVIS, Ann	JAN 04 1855
GRISLEY, John	BAYLISS, Rebecca	SEP 06 1834
GRISWOLD, George [Rev.]	COOMBE, Eliza	MAY 27 1828
GRISWOLD, Sevin	TAYLOR, Ann	JUN 21 1830
GROCE, Samuel Frederick	HENDERSON, Ann	SEP 26 1833
GROEM, John	SMITH, Margaret	DEC 16 1818
GRONARD, George Meservy	CURRAN, Bridget E.	NOV 10 1844
GROOCE, James F.	SMITT, Mary Ann	JUL 06 1837
GROOMES, Christiana	CASHELL, Samuel S.	OCT 22 1839
GROOMS, Ann Elizabeth	COOLEY, Benjamin	DEC 01 1846
GROOVER, Maria E.	GINGELL, Joseph	AUG 02 1845
GROS, Wielhilmine	ALTMANN, Charles	NOV 11 1854
GROSH, Sophia Clay	PENTZ, Samuel J.	JUL 14 1841
GROSS, Catharine	NEBLUE, Robert	AUG 12 1813
GROSS, Catherine A.	REYNOLDS, Joseph	DEC 23 1843
GROSS, Charles Philip	WESTERFELD, Fredericka L.A.	MAY 02 1857
GROSS, Francis	HULL, Mary	NOV 27 1819
GROSS, Jacob	HENDRER, Rebecca	APR 08 1848
GROSS, Jacob E.	BURROUGHS, Mary Ann	MAY 14 1851
GROSS, John	BRAN, Maria	MAY 21 1816
GROSS, John W.	MANKINS, Ann Virginia	SEP 29 1849
GROSS, Joseph H.	BAKER, Rosetta	DEC 02 1854
GROSS, Magdalena	EIGENBRODT, George	JUN 10 1850
GROSS, Margaret Ann	KIRKLAND, William	SEP 30 1847
GROSS, Mary Ann	McNEIL, Colin	MAR 30 1857
GROSS, Mary Jane	BYRNE, Patrick A.	OCT 14 1841
GROSS, Mary L. (blk)	JENIFER, Abraham	MAY 21 1857
GROSS, Matilda	DAVIS, Peter	AUG 15 1812

District of Columbia Marriage Licenses, 1811-1858

GROSS, Teresa	LAECHASE, Sebastino	FEB 03 1830
GROSS, Treasy	JENKINS, Edward	OCT 20 1825
GROSS, Wm. H.	GORDON, Eliza (blk)	APR 17 1855
GROSSENHEIN, Edward F.	PADENBERN, Henrietta Meyer	NOV 28 1856
GROTZ, Agnes M.	McGRATH, L.O.	MAY 20 1852
GROUPP, Gottlieb H.	HOFFMAN, Catharine M.	APR 15 1850
GROUSE, John G.	FOWLER, Ann	DEC 24 1828
GROVE, L. Jewitt	GASKINS, Frances A.	SEP 25 1856
GROVER, Charles	CHISM, Elizabeth	APR 01 1839
GROVES, Annis	McDANIEL, Matilda	FEB 14 1835
GROVES, Daniel	BRUMBACK, Catherine	SEP 18 1857
GROVES, Eliza	SMALL, George	JUN 12 1854
GROVES, Elizabeth	KALDENBACH, Andrew	DEC 26 1839
GROVES, Hendley	JOHNSON, Mary	DEC 10 1827
GROVES, Henley	BRAWNER, Elizabeth	NOV 25 1816
GROVES, Jacob	HARSHMAN, Harriet	OCT 24 1831
GROVES, Jacob	RISTON, Mary Jane	JUL 22 1843
GROVES, Jacob	SKIDMORE, Ann	APR 18 1850
GROVES, Jane	DELPHEY, Orlando	NOV 13 1832
GROVES, John W.	WATERS, Margaret Ann	JUN 05 1855
GROVES, Samuel	COX, Mary Jane	DEC 29 1857
GROVES, Sarah	CISSELL, William	MAY 10 1841
GROVES, Sarah A.	PETTY, Eli	JUN 27 1850
GROVES, Susan	MOCKABOY, William	JUN 07 1838
GROVES, Susan C.	O'NEAL, James	OCT 15 1852
GROVES, Thomas	TIMMONS, Julia Ann	NOV 05 1849
GROVES, William A.	JACKSON, Laura	APR 25 1857
GROVES, William A.	JACKSON, Laura	JUN 27 1857
GROVES, William G.	DONOLLE, Wille A.	NOV 04 1848
GROVES, William H.	BURCH, Mary Ann	MAY 04 1838
GRUBB, George	MANN, Mary A.E.	JUL 05 1851
GRUBB, George M.	FLORIDAMAN, Caroline	JUN 04 1840
GRUBB, Samuel	WILSON, Nelly G.	MAR 24 1826
GRUBS, Mildard A.	WUINE, Armstead L.	FEB 11 1858
GRUGLES, Harriet Ann	TUCKER, James H.	MAR 05 1844
GRUMMELL, Julia	FRANKLAND, George W.	DEC 01 1852
GRUMWELL, John H.	WARD, Catharine Virginia	MAY 05 1845
GRUPE, George Wm. Henry Louis	DELLING, Dorothie Fredericke Wilhelmine	JAN 27 1845
GRYMES, Ann B.	McDONALD, William J.	SEP 24 1841
GRYMES, Ceathy	POOL, Lewis	OCT 21 1813
GRYMES, Elizabeth	ANDERSON, Frederick	JUL 12 1845
GUARD, Lucinda	WHARTON, Thomas	APR 09 1847
GUBERNATOR, Jacob	COLLINS, Margaret	NOV 02 1857
GUEMANN, George	BARBER, Lizetta	SEP 27 1848
GUERING, Michael	KENSLOW, Eliza	MAY 09 1855
GUEST, Ellenora Nelson	SEMMES, Samuel M.	MAY 13 1840
GUEST, Francis	WHITMORE, Rachel Ann	JUN 27 1855
GUILD, James	BRENON, Ellen	DEC 12 1853
GUILDA, Eleanor	BRUNNOR, Jacob	MAR 06 1816
GUILDER, Joseph W.	ANDERSON, Margaret	DEC 10 1856
GUILLARD, Cornelia Ann	SIMONS, Robert J.	JUL 03 1830
GUINAN, Edmund	McCRADE, Honora	JUN 02 1856
GUINAND, William	ACTON, Elizabeth Jane	JAN 05 1852
GUINN, Benjamin W.	CRUMP, Susan	SEP 29 1856
GUINN, John	QUEEN, Ann	OCT 30 1821
GUIRAND, Louis	MONTRE, Eloise Melaine	APR 20 1848
GUITON, Virginia	McCAULEY, William M.	MAY 02 1855
GULD, Daniel	KENDALL, Mary Ann	AUG 11 1840

District of Columbia Marriage Licenses, 1811-1858

GULICK, Alfred	GULICK, Nancy Ann	NOV 25 1824
GULICK, George F.	DRURY, Mary A.	NOV 11 1856
GULICK, John	WILEY, Margaret Y.	JAN 31 1815
GULICK, Nancy Ann	GULICK, Alfred	NOV 25 1824
GULLYHAM, Elizabeth	McGIN, Patrick	JAN 15 1818
GUMAER, Ann Elizabeth	PEDDECORD, Eleazer	SEP 16 1844
GUMAER, Elias D.	YOUNG, Mary F.	JAN 18 1844
GUMAER, Jane	HOLSWORTH, Richard	NOV 20 1832
GUMAER, Mary	WEED, Walter H.	OCT 07 1844
GUMEAR, Martha	BOSCEDO, Lewis [Capt.]	OCT 15 1834
GUN, Mary	BIGGS, George	JUL 07 1826
GUNN, Elizabeth	STILES, Samuel	DEC 30 1815
GUNNELL, Arthur	POWELL, Mary B.	JUL 06 1858
GUNNELL, Henry	JOHNSON, Mary Eleanor	SEP 22 1827
GUNNELL, Henry D.	HINTON, Mary Ann	FEB 01 1854
GUNNELL, Ira	VERMILLION, Margaret	DEC 24 1812
GUNNELL, James S. [Dr.]	MACKALL, Hellen M.	OCT 12 1825
GUNNELL, Jemima	STROTHER, Reubin	NOV 02 1844
GUNNELL, John	SPENCER, Sarah Ann	FEB 22 1825
GUNNELL, Joshua C.	STANHOPE, Eliza J.	DEC 13 1839
GUNNELL, Leonard C.	HALL, Mary	SEP 24 1847
GUNNELL, Margaret	CLAGETT, John B.	NOV 14 1848
GUNNELL, Mary E.	FISHER, Marvin P.	NOV 15 1848
GUNNELL, Rosa H.	HALL, James D.	SEP 17 1844
GUNNELL, Virginia	SCOTT, Richard M.	SEP 09 1846
GUNNELL, Virginia A.	SKIPPEN, Charles M.	FEB 08 1855
GUNNELL, Virginia Blagden	HALL, Baruch	MAY 13 1845
GUNNELL, William H.	DUCKWORTH, Sarah	OCT 17 1822
GUNNELL, William H.	CUMMINGS, Nancy Lavenia	OCT 18 1847
GUNNELL, Wm. H.	MILLS, Mary O.	DEC 06 1853
GUNNON, Mary	KENNEDY, Thomas	JAN 11 1851
GUNTHER, Catharine	NEBHUT, John	JUN 25 1842
GUNTON, Elizabeth Livingston	BUDINGTON, William Ives	JAN 04 1841
GUNTON, Harriet	FISHER, William	FEB 22 1821
GUNZIR, Rosina	WIDMAYER, John	NOV 11 1856
GURLEY, William H.F.	RITTENHOUSE, Elizabeth S.	JAN 30 1854
GURTON, Mary	MAHUE, Clement Dent	AUG 30 1815
GUSDORF, Henrietta	LEVY, Henry	MAY 20 1858
GUSLER, Barbara	LOVEJOY, Zedekiah	FEB 27 1817
GUSTINE, Theodotia T.	RUSSELL, Frederick	MAY 03 1815
GUSTY, John	ALLEN, Betsey	DEC 11 1817
GUTHRIE, John	FELAN, Elizabeth	JUN 21 1823
GUTRICK, Ann	HAYS, Lawrence	APR 23 1812
GUTTENSOHN, John	PAULIN, Margaret	DEC 12 1814
GUTTSLICK, Elizabeth H.	BROOM, James	OCT 09 1843
GUVERNERTOR, George	MANNESMIDT, Louisa	JUN 30 1853
GUY, Benjamin F.	MORSELL, Margaret J.	DEC 13 1853
GUY, Charles	STONE, Henritta	JUN 05 1851
GUY, Frances L.	HOWELL, Elizabeth E.	JAN 18 1850
GUY, Rebecca	FRANKLIN, Benjamin H.	AUG 21 1845
GUY, Samuel C.	WYATT, Sarah A.	DEC 11 1838
GUY, Sarah E.	DAVIS, Levi	APR 28 1841
GUY, William B.	FERRIS, Christiana	FEB 27 1838
GUYTHER, John S.	HOLTON, Sarah M.	OCT 31 1854
GWINN, Susan	EATON, David	OCT 27 1834
GWYDER, Richard	POSEY, Emma Jane (blk)	APR 03 1856

District of Columbia Marriage Licenses, 1811-1858

H

HAAG, Eliza	GASH, Julius	JUL 15 1852
HAAG, Mary	BETTNER, Robert	NOV 17 1851
HAAG, Sophie	LINDNER, Nicholas	FEB 13 1851
HACHMEYER, Wilhelmine	EBERLEH, George	AUG 14 1836
HACK, Frances A.	BARNEY, Solomon P.	SEP 30 1833
HACKENIAS, Bartholomew	BANERLE, Ann M.	NOV 13 1854
HACKENJOS, John	EAKLE, Mary	OCT 10 1857
HACKER, W.T.	BROOM, Helen T.	JAN 14 1856
HACKER, William A.	HOLLAND, Angelica P.	AUG 26 1848
HACKETT, Ben	WALKER, Mary Ann (blk)	SEP 07 1815
HACKETT, Charles C.	STURGIS, Jane C.	JUL 01 1856
HACKETT, Dennis	BINKS, Eliza (blk)	OCT 11 1843
HACKETT, Helen Louisa	DeVAUGHN, Walter	OCT 02 1832
HACKETT, Peter Alex.	FERRIER, Susannah	DEC 09 1815
HACKETT, Samuel P.	WOOLFOLK, Clara W.	NOV 15 1845
HACKLETT, Eliza (blk)	DENT, Jarad	MAR 06 1838
HACKLEY, Philip	BROWN, Ann (blk)	APR 19 1823
HACKNEY, Ann	BLADEN, Charles	JAN 08 1846
HACKNEY, Barton	POSTON, Eliza A.	JUN 08 1837
HACKNEY, Geo.	NIGHT, Jane	JUN 27 1822
HACKNEY, William	BAKER, Sarah A.F.	MAY 26 1838
HADAWAY, Robert	THOMAS, Eliza	JAN 30 1823
HADEN, Henry E.	WILLIAMS, Ann M.	OCT 02 1832
HADEN, John N.	WOODSON, Eliza Ann	JUN 03 1820
HADEN, Susan	CREMANTE, John	JUL 15 1815
HADINGER, John	THOMAS, Mary	DEC 02 1826
HADLEY, Job	BARRETT, Eliza	APR 09 1818
HADLEY, Mary Jane	BURGESS, Charles	MAY 31 1856
HADT, Christina	BELZAROS, Adam	JAN 29 1844
HADUNG, Henrich	WELLMEYER, Maria Katharine	FEB 02 1855
HADY, Mary Ellen	BOLER, James	APR 23 1853
HAGAN, Ann	POWER, George	JUN 02 1849
HAGAN, Ann Maria	JOHNSON, James H.	OCT 04 1838
HAGAN, Cena R.	BARTHOLIC, Jonathan W.	DEC 08 1855
HAGAN, Henry	PATTERSON, Louisa Jane	JUL 03 1854
HAGAN, Horatio	LEE, Elizabeth	NOV 07 1834
HAGAN, James F.	HALL, Sarah	MAR 23 1855
HAGAN, John	VERMILLION, Lethe	FEB 11 1818
HAGAN, John	PAGE, Catharine	JUL 02 1827
HAGAN, John H.	McCADDEN, Julia	FEB 19 1844
HAGAN, Judson	BERRY, Ann	SEP 09 1817
HAGAN, Martha	LIPSCOMB, Jesse	APR 27 1846
HAGAN, Mary	MILLER, William	MAR 01 1842
HAGAN, Thesta	HATCHER, William	OCT 31 1850
HAGAN, William	THOMPSON, Ann Elizth.	APR 24 1851
HAGAN, Zachariah	SARGEANT, Isabella	DEC 19 1849
HAGAR, Emeline R.	HARRIS, Barton	APR 23 1827
HAGE, William H.	McELWEE, Mary C.	OCT 18 1856
HAGEN, Julia	HEART, John	FEB 27 1824
HAGER, Christopher	CLOCK, Fredericke	DEC 16 1837
HAGER, Elizabeth	HENNI, John	NOV 13 1832
HAGER, Frederick	HOWE, Teresa	NOV 13 1832
HAGER, Godfrey	HARNER, Catherine	JUL 17 1839
HAGER, Godfrey	SEITZ, Ann Catherine	MAY 28 1842
HAGER, Henrietta	BAUCHE, John Frederick	NOV 26 1853
HAGER, John F.	KRAFFT, Katherine	MAY 27 1847

District of Columbia Marriage Licenses, 1811-1858

HAGER, John F.	DEDERICH, Marietta	JUN 16 1849
HAGER, Sarah	BROWNER, Abner	AUG 24 1813
HAGER, Thos. B.	MEADE, Marianna	OCT 28 1845
HAGERMAN, Kezia A.	McCARTY, Richard C.	JAN 10 1832
HAGERMAN, Lizzetta	KUHLEMANN, Charles	AUG 24 1847
HAGERTY, Ann	CLARK, Samuel	JUN 30 1827
HAGERTY, Catharine	CANE, Daniel	FEB 08 1858
HAGERTY, John	BEALL, Elizabeth Ann	JUL 07 1831
HAGERTY, Mary E.	CALLAGHAN, Patrick	JAN 26 1856
HAGERTY, Patrick	CRYER, Mary	JUL 27 1850
HAGGARTY, Jeremiah	REARDON, Mary	APR 13 1858
HAGGERTY, Agnes Ellen	KLEISS, Daniel	SEP 30 1843
HAGGERTY, Hannah	REIDY, James	SEP 08 1856
HAGGERTY, Mary L.	GREER, Cornelius L.	JUL 02 1855
HAGNER, Charles N.	STANSBURY, Laura	APR 13 1843
HAGNER, Eliza Ann	NICHOLSON, Joseph H.	APR 09 1827
HAGNER, Mary M.	NELSON, Cleland K.	APR 19 1854
HAIFY, Margaret	FITZGIVENS, Edmond	JUN 02 1852
HAIGHT, Charles R.	STRADLING, Elvira W.	JUN 02 1858
HAIGHT, Charles W.	CONSTABLE, Anna	APR 14 1852
HAIL, John Henry	RUNLIE, Margaret	OCT 10 1857
HAILEY, Thomas	KENNEDY, Bridget	JUN 13 1856
HAIN, John G.	KRAUS, Christina	AUG 30 1856
HAINES, Anna M.	WRIGHT, Samuel N.	JUN 20 1850
HAINEY, Catherine	MUDD, James	FEB 02 1858
HAINEY, James	LACKEY, Catharine	NOV 24 1852
HAIRIE, John	ENGHART, Margaret	AUG 22 1855
HAIS, Elizabeth (blk)	GOLDING, Frederick	JUN 30 1835
HAISLIP, Jane E.	GREEN, Charles W.	AUG 30 1830
HAISLIP, Walter Alexander	THOMPSON, Lucretia	AUG 29 1836
HALBERT, Philip	BURGESS, Ann	MAY 06 1819
HALE, Bland	BROWN, Mary	OCT 05 1843
HALE, Rebecca (blk)	MEINCH, Alfred	DEC 26 1838
HALE, W.L.B.	NEILL, L.L.B.	AUG 10 1857
HALE, William B.	PORTER, Sarah Amelia	JUL 26 1851
HALE, William H.	DAVIS, Mary G.	JUN 01 1844
HALES, Mary	DAWSON, Thomas	SEP 06 1826
HALEY, Eleanor	McCARDELL, James	AUG 21 1830
HALEY, Elizabeth	CRAIG, Oliver	FEB 12 1848
HALEY, Mary Ann	MYERS, David	FEB 26 1825
HALEY, Peter	THOMAS, Elizabeth	FEB 12 1835
HALEY, Sarah Jane	BOSWELL, John W.	FEB 21 1853
HALFPENNY, Margaret	McMAHON, Patrick	MAY 09 1857
HALFPENNY, Mary Ann	MEINZERHEIRMEN, Louis	JUN 02 1849
HALFPENNY, William	ROACH, Mary Ann	JUL 21 1840
HALIDAY, Harriet E.	MARSH, Otis W.	OCT 02 1848
HALIDAY, James F.	COX, Ellen	JUL 16 1838
HALIDAY, Lydia Jane	HANLON, David H.	JUN 28 1849
HALL, Adeline	CHESSER, Ephraim	JUN 12 1850
HALL, Adolphus	PRIOR, Mary (blk)	JAN 24 1850
HALL, Alexander C.	CHILD, Mary A.	JUL 20 1857
HALL, Alfred H.	SISSON, Ann M.	JUN 28 1855
HALL, Allen F.	BELL, Sarah F.	DEC 16 1857
HALL, Amanda	SUTHERLAND, William	SEP 15 1836
HALL, Amanda (blk)	GRIFFIN, Orlando	DEC 22 1848
HALL, Andrew	HALL, Nancy	MAY 24 1849
HALL, Ann Ellenora	RANDOLPH, Samuel	MAY 09 1837
HALL, Anna M.	DONALDSON, Robert B.	FEB 13 1854

District of Columbia Marriage Licenses, 1811-1858

HALL, Baruch	GUNNELL, Virginia Blagden	MAY 13 1845
HALL, Basil D.	DAVIDSON, Margaret	SEP 07 1836
HALL, Ben H.	GREEN, Matilda A.	FEB 07 1854
HALL, Benedict	CISSELL, Catharine	JAN 04 1844
HALL, Brian	LATHAM, Rachel	MAR 18 1851
HALL, Brice	FOWLER, Mary Harriott	AUG 17 1812
HALL, Catharine	BENNETT, Joseph	MAR 05 1822
HALL, Catharine	AIRINGTON, John	FEB 20 1841
HALL, Catharine	RODIER, C. Anthony	SEP 11 1850
HALL, Charity	TILGHMAN, William	DEC 03 1823
HALL, Charles	HAMILTON, Henrietta (blk)	OCT 16 1856
HALL, Charles H., Rev.	AMES, Elizabeth M.	SEP 09 1857
HALL, Cornelia	KING, John	OCT 02 1841
HALL, Daniel	BEACH, Virginia	APR 28 1851
HALL, David A.	BULFINCH, Susan A.	SEP 27 1821
HALL, Edward	DeBUTTS, Louisa [Mrs.]	OCT 24 1820
HALL, Edward	DAVIS, Mary	JAN 28 1826
HALL, Edward	JACKSON, Susan L.	JUN 25 1851
HALL, Edward	JONES, Ann (blk)	JAN 24 1855
HALL, Edward G.W.	SCOTT, Isabel	AUG 17 1858
HALL, Elexius	CARROLL, Ann	JUL 12 1851
HALL, Eliza	DEAVERS, Launcelot	JUN 14 1838
HALL, Eliza	SWEENY, Hugh B.	NOV 11 1841
HALL, Eliza	HEMSLEY, James	DEC 27 1849
HALL, Eliza Wheat	THOMAS, John	JAN 13 1821
HALL, Elizabeth	WILBURN, John	JAN 09 1817
HALL, Elizabeth	GOODWIN, Robert	JAN 26 1825
HALL, Elizabeth	BRADY, Henry B.	DEC 23 1830
HALL, Elizabeth	HALL, Lewis J.	FEB 27 1851
HALL, Elizabeth	DISHER, Lewis	APR 10 1856
HALL, Elizabeth H.	MULLIKIN, Nathaniel	DEC 30 1823
HALL, Elizabeth J.	BEACH, William H.	AUG 16 1849
HALL, Ellen	KROUSE, John	FEB 26 1848
HALL, Emily	HANSON, Noah Chs.	AUG 09 1854
HALL, Frances A.	BROWN, Ransdale	MAY 29 1855
HALL, Frederick K.	KEATING, Catharine	MAY 26 1841
HALL, George	HALL, Martha	JAN 02 1858
HALL, George J.	HERCUS, Margaret	JAN 21 1847
HALL, George L.	BECK, Ann Maria	JUN 10 1848
HALL, George R.	BELT, Mary Ann	JUL 17 1851
HALL, Hattie A.N.	CRUX, Thomas, Jr.	NOV 13 1854
HALL, Henrietta Maria	GAWROUSKI, Leon Rowiez	JUL 19 1841
HALL, Henry	LINDSLEY, Charlotte (blk)	SEP 17 1845
HALL, Henry W.	COLLINS, Mary E. (blk)	MAR 26 1856
HALL, Hezekiah	BARROWS, Winny	FEB 01 1814
HALL, Horatio	BELL, Tracey (blk)	JUL 16 1851
HALL, Ignatius	HARP, Elizh.	MAY 15 1812
HALL, Isaac	ARRINGTON, Alcinda	OCT 22 1853
HALL, James	STINGER, Elizabeth	DEC 10 1830
HALL, James	WALKER, Cornelia S.	SEP 13 1834
HALL, James	LACEY, Elizabeth	NOV 22 1847
HALL, James	PAINE, Mary	MAR 31 1857
HALL, James A.	ROBEY, Emma	NOV 08 1854
HALL, James D.	GUNNELL, Rosa H.	SEP 17 1844
HALL, James P.	LINTHECUM, Mary	MAY 07 1858
HALL, Jane	HARRIS, Henry	JUN 28 1838
HALL, Jane Martha	McKENNEY, James H.	JUL 21 1852
HALL, John	SHAW, Maria	APR 26 1832

District of Columbia Marriage Licenses, 1811-1858

HALL, John	MITCHELL, Ellen	JUL 24 1839
HALL, John	DELANY, Jane (blk)	DEC 24 1840
HALL, John	CRANDELL, Mary	MAR 10 1842
HALL, John	BECKET, Matilda	AUG 09 1850
HALL, John	HUNTLETON, Elizabeth	APR 10 1856
HALL, John H.	RATCLIFFE, Ann	APR 04 1819
HALL, John T.	PAIRO, Sophia S.	JUN 17 1833
HALL, Joseph	WOOD, Jane F.	JAN 31 1846
HALL, Joseph	BELL, Catharine (blk)	JUL 24 1851
HALL, Laura (blk)	AMBUSH, Enoch	AUG 20 1855
HALL, Levi A.	PADGETT, Sarah Ellen	AUG 08 1846
HALL, Lewis J.	HALL, Elizabeth	FEB 27 1851
HALL, Linney	PAERS, Aquilla	APR 14 1827
HALL, Maria (blk)	CASH, Leonard	OCT 03 1855
HALL, Martha	HALL, George	JAN 02 1858
HALL, Martha E.	HORRELL, Maximillian	OCT 01 1816
HALL, Mary	SCHIMMICK, James	DEC 06 1840
HALL, Mary	JENKINS, David B.	JUN 02 1845
HALL, Mary	GUNNELL, Leonard C.	SEP 24 1847
HALL, Mary	HALL, Reuben	AUG 14 1851
HALL, Mary G.	BRADLEY, Abraham, 3rd	MAY 30 1822
HALL, Matilda	KIMBALL, Jacob	DEC 20 1842
HALL, Milly	HUNTINGTON, Haven	NOV 21 1833
HALL, Nancy	HALL, Andrew	MAY 24 1849
HALL, Percy Walker	FOWLER, Martha A.T.	DEC 11 1855
HALL, Peter	GATES, Susan	SEP 09 1830
HALL, R.B.	COLLISON, S.G.	DEC 20 1847
HALL, Rebecca (blk)	GAINES, George W.	FEB 16 1854
HALL, Reuben	HALL, Mary	AUG 14 1851
HALL, Richard	PHILLIPS, Matilda	MAY 29 1828
HALL, Richard	HOSKINS, Mary F.	MAY 11 1853
HALL, Sarah	SCOTT, Robert	JUN 22 1817
HALL, Sarah	HAGAN, James F.	MAR 23 1855
HALL, Sarah	HALL, William H.	JUN 05 1857
HALL, Sarah Ann	HAYS, Fielder	OCT 19 1837
HALL, Sarah Jane	GIBSON, Francis J.	SEP 24 1851
HALL, Sarah M.C.	DeBUTTS, Richard E.	JUL 17 1844
HALL, Sopha L.	CHEATHAM, Thomas M.	JUL 11 1855
HALL, Susan	BROOKS, John H.	OCT 21 1856
HALL, Tempel	BEACH, Jane Elizabeth	JAN 20 1848
HALL, Thomas	GRIMES, Elizabeth	NOV 24 1846
HALL, Tibitha	GRIMSLEY, James	JAN 08 1845
HALL, Walter	[torn out], Mary	JUN 03 1847
HALL, Washington	PAYNE, Julia Ann	JAN 26 1843
HALL, Wells	LEE, Rachael	DEC 18 1833
HALL, Wesley	TAYLOR, Susan M.	SEP 11 1849
HALL, William	CROSS, Mary	NOV 04 1824
HALL, William H.	HALL, Sarah	JUN 05 1857
HALL, William J.	FITTON, Mary	AUG 23 1849
HALL, Wm. C.	BAILEY, Mary	MAY 07 1853
HALLAHAN, Thomas	McGINNIS, Catherine	NOV 10 1853
HALLAR, Ellen Catherine	MAXWELL, Charles S.	MAY 24 1845
HALLARAN, Wm. E.	WILKINSON, Elizabeth	OCT 09 1854
HALLECK, John T.A.	HOWARD, Mary Jane	MAY 29 1849
HALLER, Catharine	RAGAN, Daniel	AUG 12 1819
HALLER, Eliza Jane	MOORE, Richard H.	AUG 16 1855
HALLER, Rebecca	CORNELL, Robert	DEC 10 1857
HALLEY, Margaret P.	ELKINS, Allen N.	MAR 18 1828

District of Columbia Marriage Licenses, 1811-1858

HALLEY, Martha E.	THOMAS, Thomas	APR 24 1846
HALLEY, Richard T.	CIPPERLY, Clara M.	NOV 07 1855
HALLIDAY, Ann M.	LOWRY, Charles F.	APR 10 1843
HALLON, Francis	SILAS, Rebecca	MAY 13 1822
HALLORAN, James	O'DAN, Bridget	FEB 15 1853
HALLORAN, Margaret	DONOVAN, Michael	MAY 01 1852
HALLORAN, Mary	GARLEY, Joseph	AUG 09 1856
HALLOWAY, Ranson	WARING, Eliza G.	JAN 06 1851
HALORAN, Mary	BARRETT, Dennis	AUG 19 1854
HALPEN, Nicholas	McCARTY, Ann	JAN 17 1829
HALPNER, Henry	HEIT, Louisa	SEP 05 1853
HALRAN, Thomas	HARVEY, Elizabeth	MAR 09 1814
HALSEY, Mary	JOY, Peter	JUN 08 1820
HALSEY, Tarecy	CURRY, Benjamin L.	AUG 18 1818
HALSEY, Zachariah	GANTT, Mary Ann	FEB 01 1812
HALTER, Hellen L.	MEILEY, John	JUN 02 1852
HAMACKER, Joseph	DAVIS, Eliza A.	JUN 25 1857
HAMADINGER, Mary E.	EDD, John T.	MAR 01 1855
HAMANDS, Dennis	COLBURN, Elizabeth (blk)	JUL 27 1858
HAMBLETON, Samuel	FOLLIN, Mary	JUL 27 1833
HAMBLETON, Samuel	TURNER, Elizabeth W.	SEP 02 1834
HAMBUEGER, John	SCIPES, Elizabeth	JAN 10 1843
HAMBURG, Jacob	HOWDESCHELL, Lavinia	DEC 12 1846
HAMBURGER, Hannah	SIEGEL, Saml.	AUG 26 1857
HAMDEN, Hannah	HOYE, Paul	JAN 16 1816
HAMELL, David	THOMAS, Rachel	MAY 15 1837
HAMERSLEY, Lewis R.	STEVENS, Catherine E.	MAR 18 1846
HAMERSLEY, Mary Ann	NEALE, Henry A.	OCT 05 1847
HAMES, William	WILLIAMS, Sophia (blk)	FEB 21 1855
HAMILL, Hannah Ann	WEST, Hezekiah	OCT 27 1852
HAMILL, Margaret Ann	CLARK, John	APR 22 1842
HAMILL, Stephen	GOODWIN, Julia A.	DEC 08 1852
HAMILTON, Alexander	FORD, Sarah	JUL 13 1830
HAMILTON, Catharine Ann (blk)	BUTLER, George	SEP 17 1840
HAMILTON, Charles B. [Dr.]	SHANLY, Eliza	NOV 15 1815
HAMILTON, Charles O.	McDONALD, Catherine	NOV 05 1857
HAMILTON, Christiana H.	HAMILTON, Patrick H.	JUN 04 1844
HAMILTON, Edward	GATES, Martha	OCT 08 1833
HAMILTON, Edward M.	FITZPATRICK, Henrietta R.	MAY 22 1854
HAMILTON, Eliza	MYERS, Daniel	MAY 09 1848
HAMILTON, Eliza B.	TIFFANY, Otis H.	DEC 26 1848
HAMILTON, Ellen M.	DASHIEL, Samuel K.	DEC 27 1848
HAMILTON, Francis	HURLEY, Frances Rebecca	MAY 20 1847
HAMILTON, Francis	BLACK, Mary Ann	JUN 28 1852
HAMILTON, Harriot S.	MURRAY, Stanislaus	FEB 16 1832
HAMILTON, Henrietta	LAGREE, John M.	NOV 17 1812
HAMILTON, Henrietta (blk)	HALL, Charles	OCT 16 1856
HAMILTON, James	MARS, Mary Ann	JUL 28 1830
HAMILTON, James W.	GRABILL, Mary Virginia	MAY 15 1858
HAMILTON, Jane	BEAKE, William	AUG 27 1851
HAMILTON, John	McFARLEY, Ann	FEB 15 1847
HAMILTON, Josiah	RYE, Margaret	FEB 08 1844
HAMILTON, Kitty (col'd)	BEALL, Peter	MAY 17 1832
HAMILTON, Louisa	ANDERSON, Alexander	APR 03 1815
HAMILTON, Mary	HARRIS, Angelo	AUG 12 1841
HAMILTON, Mary	MAHER, James	OCT 04 1849
HAMILTON, Mary A.V.	BROWN, John	AUG 28 1852
HAMILTON, Mary H.	MURRAY, Stanislaus	MAR 19 1839

District of Columbia Marriage Licenses, 1811-1858

HAMILTON, Patrick H.	HAMILTON, Christiana H.	JUN 04 1844
HAMILTON, Thomas	MARKS, Mary Ann	SEP 23 1857
HAMILTON, William H.	BARNES, Elizabeth	SEP 16 1845
HAMILTON, Wm. F.	STILLINGS, Sarah V.	FEB 24 1857
HAMITT, John	MARTIN, Agnes	DEC 24 1827
HAMLEY, James	EASTON, Deborah	JUL 19 1832
HAMLIN, William	ALLEN, Hannah	MAY 15 1812
HAMMACK, John D.	DODSON, Cynthia A.	OCT 29 1849
HAMMACK, Mary M.	HARE, Dennis O.	MAY 23 1843
HAMMEL, A.A. Wm.	VONDERLOEHR, Barbara	SEP 17 1851
HAMMEL, Hugh	ATHEY, Elizabeth	DEC 30 1830
HAMMELL, Catharine	CURTIS, Mason	DEC 28 1837
HAMMER, John Gutlieb	BEVANS, Elizabeth	JUN 16 1827
HAMMER, Mary Ann	GRIFFIN, William	NOV 29 1838
HAMMER, Michael	EASTERLEIN, Mary M.	DEC 26 1856
HAMMETT, Elizabeth	GORDON, Daniel Smith	APR 04 1836
HAMMILL, Bernard	McKEEVER, Elizabeth	AUG 20 1858
HAMMILL, Margaret	MADDOX, John T.	DEC 17 1835
HAMMILL, Patrick	FIELDY, Bridget	SEP 23 1850
HAMMILL, Stephen	TANNER, Susanna	MAY 22 1845
HAMMILL, Wesley	GREEN, Mary	SEP 25 1856
HAMMON, August	BROOKS, Lucinda	JAN 13 1840
HAMMOND, Caroline	WRIGHT, William R.	SEP 26 1857
HAMMOND, Ellen	EDDIE, Edward C.	OCT 16 1857
HAMMOND, Henry	STALLIONS, Rebecca	FEB 04 1854
HAMMOND, Mariann Augusta Bradley	KENNEDY, John C.	MAY 17 1853
HAMMOND, Mary	CABEL, Stephen	NOV 30 1837
HAMMOND, Nathan	TATE, Sarah Jane	DEC 18 1834
HAMMOND, Rebecca (blk)	JACKSON, Lewis	NOV 15 1856
HAMMOND, Rosetta	HANEY, Martin	FEB 09 1828
HAMMOND, Sallie H.	BURNS, George	AUG 20 1856
HAMMOND, Sarah Ann (blk)	WINKFIELD, Charles	MAY 27 1852
HAMMOND, Saralena	SIEGEL, Moses	JUL 24 1858
HAMOCK, Beryn S.	HARRINGTON, Emma	APR 26 1855
HAMORE, Wm. H.	HENNING, Sarah L.	DEC 31 1855
HAMPTMERE, Johanna	BROWN, Richard J.	NOV 16 1842
HAMPTON, Emily (blk)	VIGLE, Richard	MAY 22 1849
HAMPTON, Frances	JENKINS, Andrew	SEP 17 1836
HAMPTON, Mary	BEARD, William	DEC 09 1824
HAMPTON, Mary Ellen	WHALEN, Ledwell	NOV 15 1850
HAMPTON, Penny	CARR, Nimrod	AUG 07 1817
HAMPTON, Roderick	GIBSON, Emily (blk)	FEB 06 1834
HAMPTON, Thomas	COOPER, Eleanor	JUL 25 1815
HANASY, Margaret	O'MARA, Michael	AUG 20 1855
HANBACK, James	HEFLIN, Martha Ann	JUL 12 1853
HANCE, Rebecca	JONES, Alexr. H.	AUG 25 1853
HANCOCK, John	DUDLEY, Mary D.	AUG 24 1855
HANCOCK, Josiah H.	SOUTHORON, Mary M.	APR 21 1857
HANCOCK, Lemuel	SOTHORON, Martha A.	JAN 21 1856
HANCOCK, Margaret	TAYLOR, James W.	JAN 16 1858
HANDERSON, Elizabeth	UNDERWOOD, John	NOV 25 1836
HANDLEY, James	ALVEY, Christana	MAY 08 1827
HANDLEY, Margaret	KING, John	JAN 08 1825
HANDLEY, Margaret	SYLVESTER, Samuel R.	MAR 29 1856
HANDLEY, Martha	KIRK, Sallust	OCT 05 1853
HANDLEY, Mary J.	HODGSON, Joseph F.	SEP 19 1850
HANDRAHAN, Johnie	BROSNAHAN, Jeremiah	FEB 02 1856
HANDS, Mary	KEARSE, Patrick	MAY 22 1858

District of Columbia Marriage Licenses, 1811-1858

HANDY, Charles W.	STANFORD, Helen E.	AUG 16 1841
HANDY, Diana	WALLACE, Ezekial	SEP 16 1820
HANDY, Edward G.	BRACKENRIDGE, Attelia A.	NOV 21 1827
HANDY, Edward G.	BECK, Isabel Y.P.	APR 05 1842
HANDY, Eleanor	SMITH, Henry	DEC 28 1824
HANDY, Leah Ann	DUNHAM, Francis S.	AUG 29 1843
HANDY, Levin	BALL, Henrietta D.	SEP 06 1834
HANDY, Margaret C.	STEWART, William	APR 29 1852
HANDY, Robert J.H.	ROWAN, Virginia	MAR 24 1849
HANDY, Samuel	BURKE, Mary W.J.	JAN 27 1835
HANDY, Samuel	BRIGHT, Mary Ann	JUN 01 1849
HANDY, Samuel W.	KER, Margaret W.	DEC 20 1825
HANDY, Sarah	BUTLER, Henry	AUG 27 1838
HANDY, Sarah E.L.	HUBBARD, Joseph S.	APR 27 1848
HANDY, William	REDDALL, Ann P.	APR 29 1846
HANDY, Winifred	McCARTY, Florence	SEP 06 1821
HANEGAN, Thos.	DUVALL, Rhoda	AUG 24 1821
HANER, John	LAWLESS, Ellen	FEB 03 1853
HANERFIELD, Mary	WECHTER, Jno. G.	NOV 21 1821
HANERTY, Sarah	McGEE, Patrick	OCT 04 1831
HANES, John	HEETON, Jane	AUG 02 1849
HANES, John W.	CHAPPELL, Irene Ann E.	AUG 05 1846
HANES, Stacy	ANDREWS, Elizabeth	FEB 14 1823
HANESSY, Mary	LYNCH, John	FEB 05 1833
HANEWINKEL, Frederick W.	NICHOLLS, Bestie C.	JUN 18 1855
HANEY, Elizabeth	OGLE, Rezin H.	OCT 05 1839
HANEY, John	SMITH, Cecilia	OCT 17 1829
HANEY, Joseph	BOGLE, Julia Ann	NOV 24 1852
HANEY, Josephine (blk)	WISE, John	JAN 13 1848
HANEY, Martin	HAMMOND, Rosetta	FEB 09 1828
HANEY, Sarah Ann	CASSELL, John A.	FEB 23 1832
HANFMANN, August	REINHART, Teresa	APR 02 1853
HANGSTETTER, John	KOEHLER, Mary	FEB 25 1854
HANIGAN, John	MURPHY, Johanna	AUG 14 1858
HANLEIN, Feist	EHRLICH, Sophia	DEC 31 1851
HANLON, David H.	HALIDAY, Lydia Jane	JUN 28 1849
HANLON, Timothy	CALLAGHAN, Bridget	FEB 05 1856
HANLY, Edmund	METCALF, Jane	OCT 08 1827
HANLY, Mary Jane	DASHIELL, Robert L.	MAY 03 1854
HANNA, Ann	DOOLEY, Michael	FEB 02 1837
HANNA, Mary	SHOATS, Frederick	MAY 24 1825
HANNA, Nathaniel	KITCHEN, Kitty	OCT 02 1855
HANNAH, Ann	WIGLEY, Henry	FEB 09 1826
HANNAH, Henry	WHITE, Ann	MAY 09 1820
HANNAH, Jane	McCAUSLIND, Thomas	MAR 25 1856
HANNAH, Joana Louisa	RUSSELL, Henry	OCT 28 1851
HANNAH, Martha Ann	McKINLEY, Isaac G.	MAY 26 1834
HANNAN, Ann	NIHILL, Michael	JUL 26 1853
HANNAN, Daniel	MORRIS, Catharine	NOV 06 1856
HANNASON, Susan	LAVELY, Jesse	APR 01 1814
HANNET, Francis	WIKLE, Christianna	JAN 13 1835
HANNIFER, William	DONOHOUGH, Mary	NOV 04 1851
HANNING, James	GRAHAM, Ellen	NOV 30 1849
HANNON, Henry	WATSON, Mary A.	MAY 06 1829
HANNON, Mary	KIRBY, Samuel	AUG 23 1826
HANNON, Nathan	BRANGAN, Nancy (blk)	APR 04 1849
HANNON, Thomas	DONOHO, Catherine	JAN 14 1834
HANRAHAN, John	WELSH, Mary	JUL 21 1853

259

District of Columbia Marriage Licenses, 1811-1858

HANREHAN, James	HEARN, Margaret	JUN 06 1851
HANSBOROUGH, Eleanor	SUTER, Richard	JUL 10 1833
HANSELL, Emmerick W.	ROBINSON, Elizabeth Ann	JAN 27 1840
HANSELL, Henry	LEFFLER, Caroline	AUG 02 1858
HANSEY, John	BRIDGE, Sarah Ann	JAN 30 1826
HANSMAN, Cornelia	KIDWELL, George	OCT 14 1853
HANSON, Ann	JONES, Richard	NOV 07 1837
HANSON, Ann	NEALE, George	JUN 14 1843
HANSON, Ann	GIBSON, Caleb	JUN 28 1856
HANSON, Ann Amelia (blk)	BROWN, Charles	JUN 05 1850
HANSON, Betsy (blk)	BRISCOE, Henry	JUN 27 1850
HANSON, Caroline (blk)	BELL, Ignatius	FEB 08 1849
HANSON, Elizabeth B.	HASSLER, Ferdinand E.	SEP 15 1845
HANSON, Elizabeth Howard	PETERKIN, Joshua	SEP 25 1838
HANSON, Grafton D.	INGLE, Maria	JUN 20 1853
HANSON, Harriot McC.	KENNARD, Joel S.	MAY 23 1846
HANSON, Isaac K.	JONES, Maria H.	AUG 22 1815
HANSON, John	JOHNSON, Ann	DEC 08 1836
HANSON, Louisa Serena	WEIGHTMAN, Roger Chew	MAY 05 1814
HANSON, Maria	SHEFFEY, Daniel	JAN 30 1812
HANSON, Martha (blk)	SPRIGGS, Gabriel	NOV 07 1840
HANSON, Martha Ann	JOYCE, James	AUG 28 1856
HANSON, Mary Ann	CLEMENTS, Francis	NOV 10 1832
HANSON, Noah Chs.	HALL, Emily	AUG 09 1854
HANSON, Rebecca D.	BARKER, William N.	JUN 17 1856
HANSON, Samuel, of Ths.	BAYLY, Eleanor	MAR 13 1817
HANSON, Sarah R.	KEPPLER, Henry S.	JUN 22 1837
HANSON, Thomas	BEALL, Elizabeth	FEB 10 1820
HANSON, Thomas M.	BARRY, Mary P.	MAY 17 1853
HANSON, Thomas S.	BARNET, Mary	OCT 31 1823
HANSON, Tobias	EVANS, Betsey	SEP 25 1820
HANTZ, Washington A.	McLEWN, Eliza	AUG 28 1832
HANTZMAN, Robert	KIDWELL, Mary E.	MAY 15 1855
HANY, John	NEVITT, Mary Ann	FEB 12 1833
HANY, Margaret S.	DYER, Joseph	NOV 06 1841
HANY, Mary	MULRANY, Bernard	NOV 24 1830
HANY, William	ACHLESS, Rachel Ann	MAR 20 1829
HAPNER, William	RATCLIFF, Susan	JUL 09 1844
HAPP, Nicholas	FUNDELEHR, Mary	MAY 15 1848
HARAHAN, John	MALONY, Eliza	AUG 19 1856
HARBAUGH, Edward L.	HUTCHINS, Anne M.	OCT 04 1845
HARBAUGH, Eliza Catharine	MAYO, Robert [Dr.]	JUL 08 1831
HARBAUGH, Frances	OGLE, Columbus F.	JUN 11 1853
HARBAUGH, Leonard	PAGE, Winifred Sophia	FEB 05 1839
HARBAUGH, Theodore	WALTERS, Mary	JAN 12 1832
HARBAUGH, Valentine	PUMPHREY, Ellen	OCT 02 1838
HARBERT, Catharine	GOLBACH, John	SEP 02 1854
HARBERT, John	BUTLER, Barbara	MAY 18 1815
HARBESON, Robert	WILLIAMS, Jane Eliza	FEB 25 1833
HARBIN, James H.	BRADLEY, Jane Eliza	DEC 24 1842
HARBIN, Mary Jane	RUSSELL, John H.	DEC 17 1845
HARBIN, Philip W.	NESMITH, Sarah	NOV 14 1850
HARBIN, Thomas H.	STEWART, Mary Elizth.	OCT 02 1855
HARBOUGH, Ellen A.	BROWN, Samuel L.	NOV 19 1857
HARBOUGH, Jerome	THOMPSON, Marthan Ann	FEB 15 1830
HARCUM, Sarah C.	WALLIS, William	AUG 01 1817
HARCUS, George	GILLASPIE, Margaret	NOV 04 1818
HARDAWAY, Henrietta C.	ENROUGHTY, James B.	JAN 19 1854

District of Columbia Marriage Licenses, 1811-1858

HARDEN, Frances	LINDSAY, Hiram O.	JAN 14 1817
HARDEN, Mary	ROBERTSON, George	OCT 03 1833
HARDEN, William	SLICER, Elizabeth S.	JUN 06 1853
HARDESTER, Mary Ellen	WILSON, Marcellus	MAY 27 1848
HARDESTY, Eliza Ann	COOK, Edward	MAR 05 1820
HARDESTY, James J.	SUIT, Emily	SEP 16 1854
HARDESTY, Mary Ann	HOPKINGS, John P.	JAN 10 1854
HARDESTY, Thomas	WATERS, Mary	DEC 21 1827
HARDGROVE, Samuel	COBBS, Elizabeth M.	JUN 09 1829
HARDIG, Gustavus	KNATZ, Katherina	OCT 17 1854
HARDIN, Austin	ROBINSON, Sarah Ann	JUN 21 1831
HARDIN, Catherine Ann	SHELBY, James W.	DEC 13 1855
HARDIN, Charles H.	TARLTON, Margaret A.	NOV 04 1845
HARDIN, Mary	TRACY, John T.	SEP 15 1846
HARDIN, Sarah	SULLIVAN, John	FEB 04 1845
HARDIN, William	ADAMS, Ann Elizabeth	DEC 20 1822
HARDING, Elizabeth Ann	EDMONSTON, Grafton	MAY 23 1826
HARDING, James	DICK, Juliet A.	JUN 09 1857
HARDING, Jane	WALKER, William T.	OCT 02 1845
HARDING, Levy	ABLE, Clara	MAR 16 1832
HARDING, Maria	POOL, James	SEP 07 1852
HARDING, Mildred	MILBURN, Thomas	MAY 02 1832
HARDING, Sarah Ann	ROBINSON, Jefferson	NOV 27 1829
HARDING, Thomas	PRIEST, Catherine	MAR 30 1857
HARDING, William	DONALDSON, Eliza	JAN 07 1829
HARDISTY, Henry, Jr.	McLEAN, Eliza	JUN 27 1833
HARDISTY, Thomas J.	JONES, Mary Elizabeth	MAY 09 1854
HARDON, Susan Ann	HUTCHERSON, E.	SEP 18 1845
HARDT, Ann M.	MOULDEN, John A.	DEC 18 1849
HARDT, Juliet A.	ALLEN, James A.	DEC 24 1850
HARDY, Catharine (blk)	MANKIN, John	OCT 13 1851
HARDY, Christina	HOLLANG, John	DEC 20 1855
HARDY, Edward T.	PICKRELL, Sarah L.	JAN 17 1849
HARDY, Henry	BURCH, Mary	AUG 06 1836
HARDY, Henry M.	HELLRIGLE, Ann Maria Kent	JUL 11 1835
HARDY, Hezekiah	DICK, Adaline	MAR 26 1845
HARDY, Jane	WHITE, Robert	FEB 16 1818
HARDY, Joseph	ROLISON, Jannett	MAR 26 1829
HARDY, Mary	BYRNES, Dennis	MAY 24 1858
HARDY, Mary Ann	SMITH, John Thomas	NOV 28 1846
HARDY, Matilda	GRAY, James	JUL 28 1826
HARDY, Sarah	PAYNE, Francis	MAY 27 1818
HARDY, Walter	GATES, Sarah Ann	JUN 24 1843
HARDY, William	JONES, Mary Elizabeth	APR 26 1845
HARDY, William G.	HILL, Matilda	MAY 19 1851
HARDY, William W.	TURTON, Rebecca	AUG 10 1852
HARDY, Wm.	RAGAN, Sarah	JAN 17 1831
HARE, Dennis O.	HAMMACK, Mary M.	MAY 23 1843
HARE, Francis	BURCH, Catherine	JAN 09 1844
HARFORD, William	BRIGGES, Sarah Ann	SEP 16 1836
HARGAN, Mary	FITZGERALD, Dennis	FEB 19 1855
HARKENS, William H.	THOMAS, Alcinda (blk)	MAR 24 1858
HARKINS, Fanny	HARRY, Richard	DEC 26 1822
HARKINS, John B.	CROWN, Mary	MAY 05 1821
HARKINS, Robert	SWEICHZER, Ann	FEB 13 1823
HARKINS, William	MIDDLETON, Miranda	DEC 22 1826
HARKNESS, Daniel S.	TABLER, Martha Ellen	NOV 27 1838
HARKNESS, George W.	CLARKE, Ruth Ann	SEP 06 1836

District of Columbia Marriage Licenses, 1811-1858

HARKNESS, John C.	SMITH, Margaret	MAR 18 1828
HARKNESS, John C.	LARE, Maria	NOV 01 1855
HARKNESS, Mary S.	BARRON, Henry	NOV 28 1826
HARKNESS, Samuel, Jr.	DOVE, Elizabeth	SEP 24 1827
HARKNESS, Susan A.	HARRISON, Robert M.	APR 03 1817
HARLER, Charlotte	HEIDER, Diederick	NOV 03 1852
HARLEY, Elizabeth E.	PROCTOR, Miley	SEP 19 1853
HARLEY, James	WATSON, Elizabeth	NOV 11 1844
HARLEY, Maria	HUGHES, John	MAR 28 1821
HARLEY, Noah	HOLBROOK, Eleanor	SEP 02 1818
HARLEY, Palina	TANNER, Richard M.	OCT 16 1845
HARLEY, Pauline	DUEHAY, Alexander	OCT 18 1855
HARLEY, Sarah C.	WEAVER, William V.W.	JAN 03 1857
HARLEY, Susan	GRAY, Francis	SEP 01 1831
HARLEY, Wesley	CLARKE, Susannah	MAY 09 1833
HARLING, John	GANTT, Eliza	DEC 19 1844
HARLMAN, Conrad	NEFF, Frances	MAY 20 1840
HARLY, Briget	HENSY, Cassa Ann	AUG 13 1835
HARMAN, Augustus	ROBEY, Margaret	SEP 23 1843
HARMAN, Chas. W.	SIMMONS, Henrietta	JUN 01 1852
HARMAN, Cornelia E.	WHALEN, Henry T.	MAY 13 1852
HARMAN, Emily	SHERWOOD, Temple	JUN 25 1853
HARMAN, James	BENNETT, Betsey	NOV 11 1813
HARMAN, Lawrance	DEVAUL, Elizabeth	JAN 03 1818
HARMAN, Samuel	GOODMAN, Jeta	MAY 03 1855
HARMAN, William	BRADLEY, Ann	JAN 31 1813
HARMANN, George	BETZINGER, Margaret	OCT 31 1854
HARMON, John L.	LOVELACE, Mary Jane	MAR 31 1845
HARMON, John L.	JONES, Mary Ann	JAN 14 1858
HARMOND, Mary Ann	THOMPSON, William	JUL 13 1837
HARNER, Catherine	HAGER, Godfrey	JUL 17 1839
HARNES, John	WARD, Emily (blk)	NOV 13 1855
HAROLD, Catharine	YOUNG, John	APR 29 1842
HAROLD, Elizabeth	BELLARD, John	NOV 10 1851
HAROVER, Cassander	STEVENS, Stephen O.	JUL 05 1834
HARP, Caleb	BARBER, Mary Ann	DEC 09 1812
HARP, Elizh.	HALL, Ignatius	MAY 15 1812
HARP, Sarah Ann	FOX, Sidney	JUN 15 1829
HARPER, Andrew	ROE, Mary McDermot	NOV 15 1827
HARPER, Ann	SMITH, William	JUL 24 1821
HARPER, Ann	ELLIS, William	MAY 22 1837
HARPER, Eliza	ELMS, James	AUG 25 1842
HARPER, Elizabeth	ERSKINE, Robert	JAN 24 1812
HARPER, Fanny	ROBERTS, William	FEB 26 1820
HARPER, Francis	DONNOGHUE, Mary A.	FEB 15 1854
HARPER, Grace	BUNTHRON, John	MAR 02 1822
HARPER, Harmony (blk)	GOINGS, Wesley	JUL 16 1832
HARPER, Hester Ann	DRUMMOND, John W.	JUL 02 1840
HARPER, James	DODSON, Martha Ann	OCT 28 1837
HARPER, John Joseph	FOLY, Elizabeth	APR 13 1843
HARPER, Lucretia	NORTON, James William	FEB 07 1851
HARPER, Mahala E.	EMRICK, Christian	DEC 22 1842
HARPER, Martha A.	BIBB, Henry F.	MAR 31 1857
HARPER, Martha Maria	HOPKINS, Joseph	DEC 21 1853
HARPER, Nicholas	COLLINS, Fanney	DEC 09 1812
HARPER, William	PATTON, Sarah M.	MAR 09 1841
HARPER, William	NORTON, Mary A.	JAN 17 1853
HARPP, Nicholas	SORG, Margaretta	DEC 12 1838

District of Columbia Marriage Licenses, 1811-1858

HARR, Caroline V.	BEACH, Columbus	AUG 24 1858
HARRAD, Arra	THOMAS, George	FEB 10 1824
HARRAD, Charlotte	DICKERSON, William	APR 12 1817
HARRAGAN, Bridget	FLAHAVIN, Michael	APR 07 1858
HARRAHAN, Catherine	CORBOTT, John	JUN 12 1847
HARRAN, Charles	MARTIN, Elizabeth	NOV 07 1850
HARRAN, Thomas	RICHARDSON, Mary Jane	JUL 28 1851
HARRATY, Biddy	HUFFWIN, Patrick	JUL 01 1818
HARREN, Frederick	CROSSEN, Joanna	JUL 05 1838
HARRET, Ellen	KING, John H.	NOV 03 1825
HARRIDAN, Nathaniel	DEVERICKS, Susan	DEC 24 1812
HARRIGAN, Johanna	McGRAW, Thomas	JUN 12 1854
HARRIGAN, Margaret	COLEBURT, Edward	MAR 12 1858
HARRINGTON, Absolom T.	THOMPSON, Henrietta	AUG 21 1827
HARRINGTON, Catharine	HARRINGTON, Jeremiah	DEC 04 1852
HARRINGTON, Emma	HAMOCK, Beryn S.	APR 26 1855
HARRINGTON, George W.	CALLAGHAN, Mary M.	APR 25 1853
HARRINGTON, Honora	KELLY, Martin	APR 28 1856
HARRINGTON, Isabella	PHILLIPS, Wm. H.	APR 25 1849
HARRINGTON, James	HURLEY, Ellen	JAN 09 1851
HARRINGTON, James	FOLLEN, Rachel	JUN 18 1857
HARRINGTON, Jeremiah	HARRINGTON, Catharine	DEC 04 1852
HARRINGTON, John	COLLINS, Margaret	FEB 06 1858
HARRINGTON, Maria	QUIGLEY, William	JUN 19 1849
HARRINGTON, Martha	MEADE, William A.	SEP 21 1841
HARRINGTON, Martha R.	VENABLE, William	APR 18 1844
HARRINGTON, Patrick	BRANHAM, Elizabeth	APR 20 1821
HARRINGTON, Patrick	BETTS, Eleanor	OCT 04 1852
HARRINGTON, Patrick	REIDY, Mary	MAY 13 1854
HARRINGTON, Richd. H.	HILTON, Mary A.W.	FEB 10 1824
HARRINGTON, Selina	BREAST, George Alonzo	JUN 16 1834
HARRIS, Adelaide R.	WALKER, William T.	SEP 25 1855
HARRIS, Adelphi (blk)	JOHNSON, Henry	MAR 02 1842
HARRIS, Agnes B.	BUTLER, John	MAY 17 1853
HARRIS, Ailsey	SAMPSON, Jesse	SEP 20 1834
HARRIS, Alonzo	BROWN, Jane (blk)	DEC 13 1849
HARRIS, Angelo	HAMILTON, Mary	AUG 12 1841
HARRIS, Ann (blk)	DURAN, Francis	OCT 29 1833
HARRIS, Ann E.	TASKER, George W.	AUG 26 1834
HARRIS, Ann G.	STONESTREET, J. Harris	JUN 30 1857
HARRIS, Ann Virginia	WACHTER, Jacob	FEB 23 1846
HARRIS, Anna	HEISE, John C.	MAY 24 1854
HARRIS, Barton	HAGAR, Emeline R.	APR 23 1827
HARRIS, Benjamin D.	REED, Ann	DEC 12 1825
HARRIS, Benjamin F.	DULL, Mary E.	MAR 11 1856
HARRIS, Caroline	CLEARY, James	JUN 22 1852
HARRIS, Catharine (blk)	PAINE, Richard	OCT 18 1849
HARRIS, Charlotte	SIBLEY, John	NOV 09 1855
HARRIS, Edward S.	THORNBURY, Mary R.L.	OCT 21 1851
HARRIS, Eleanor	CLARKE, Benjamin	DEC 20 1823
HARRIS, Eleanor (blk)	HILL, Lewis	JAN 11 1831
HARRIS, Elizabeth	VERNON, Philip B.	MAY 26 1831
HARRIS, Elizabeth	PRATE_R_, William	FEB 17 1851
HARRIS, Elizabeth	HOWARD, Thomas	MAR 10 1853
HARRIS, Elizabeth	DANIEL, Peter V.	OCT 17 1853
HARRIS, Elizabeth C.	CURTIN, Thomas F.	APR 09 1857
HARRIS, Elizabeth S.	FOX, Henry	JAN 09 1855
HARRIS, Francis A.	STUART, W.D.	JUL 12 1854

District of Columbia Marriage Licenses, 1811-1858

HARRIS, George P.	BOWENS, Martha Ann	JAN 03 1856
HARRIS, Gwynn	JONES, Susan A.	OCT 20 1856
HARRIS, Henry	HALL, Jane	JUN 28 1838
HARRIS, Henry	WOODYET, Kitty (blk)	SEP 29 1842
HARRIS, Isabella	PORTER, David	MAY 15 1852
HARRIS, James	SMITH, Mary	NOV 28 1830
HARRIS, James	BURCH, Ann Virginia	JUL 06 1852
HARRIS, John	BUTLER, Chloe	JAN 23 1818
HARRIS, John	TAYLOR, Henrietta	MAR 11 1824
HARRIS, John	MAHEN, Elizabeth Ellen	JAN 22 1857
HARRIS, John	JOHNSON, Jane (blk)	JUL 29 1858
HARRIS, Joseph	LEE, Ellen (blk)	APR 09 1845
HARRIS, Joseph C.	SAFFELL, Rebecca R.	OCT 01 1852
HARRIS, Joseph Francis Wood	ABERCOMBIE, Sophia Douglass	AUG 11 1815
HARRIS, Judith J.	McKRAE, Colin	OCT 16 1818
HARRIS, Julia (blk)	LEE, Henry	MAR 17 1853
HARRIS, Marbury	SALISBURY, Susanna	MAY 11 1853
HARRIS, Margaret	STEPHENSON, John A.	NOV 19 1845
HARRIS, Martha	BRUCE, Charles	OCT 09 1851
HARRIS, Mary	WARREN, William	OCT 15 1857
HARRIS, Mary (blk)	JONES, Albert	JUN 11 1856
HARRIS, Mary Ann	WALTER, John W.	OCT 24 1834
HARRIS, Mary Ann	STEPHENSON, Joseph	MAR 03 1840
HARRIS, Mary C.	DORSEY, John T.B.	JAN 11 1849
HARRIS, Mary Elizth.	CLYNE, John W., Jr.	FEB 21 1849
HARRIS, Mary Evelyn	HUMPHRIES, Guy C.	SEP 10 1853
HARRIS, Matilda S.	CHURCH, Charles B.	MAR 04 1847
HARRIS, Matthias	SHERWOOD, Rebecca V.	OCT 18 1853
HARRIS, Michael	CALDWELL, Rosa	DEC 13 1851
HARRIS, Mima (blk)	GANTT, Basil	OCT 16 1823
HARRIS, Munroe	HENDERSON, Jane W.	MAY 25 1846
HARRIS, Nancy	WALKER, David	MAY 11 1837
HARRIS, Octavus C.	CRACKLIN, Ann E.	JUL 23 1853
HARRIS, Peyton	LIVERPOOL, Cassa (blk)	NOV 10 1845
HARRIS, Rebecca J.	ABBOTT, Richard H.	JAN 14 1852
HARRIS, Richard	LAW, Ann	JAN 30 1823
HARRIS, Richard	KELLEY, Jane	JAN 04 1831
HARRIS, Sarah	WIMSATT, Richard	SEP 03 1838
HARRIS, Sarah	ACORS, Richard	JAN 18 1849
HARRIS, Sarah Ann	BRADLEY, William	APR 07 1840
HARRIS, Virginia (blk)	DUCKET, Edward	JUL 16 1857
HARRIS, William H.	DOWNES, Mary	AUG 09 1842
HARRIS, Wm. H.	McCOY, Martha (blk)	FEB 09 1857
HARRISON, Alfred L.	BEEVERS, Catharine	AUG 23 1849
HARRISON, Ann Catharine	HUTCHINSON, William E.	JAN 25 1851
HARRISON, Ann Lucinda	MASON, George	OCT 08 1821
HARRISON, Ann Rebecca (blk)	DONALDSON, Edwin G.	APR 21 1842
HARRISON, Anne M.	MARTIN, Luther	AUG 29 1856
HARRISON, Benjamin	HIGGINS, Elizabeth	APR 27 1844
HARRISON, Benjamin L.	GARTH, Catherine Jane	DEC 23 1854
HARRISON, Columbus	FERGUSON, Eleanor Ann	OCT 29 1842
HARRISON, David	ROBINSON, Mary	MAY 22 1822
HARRISON, Eleanor	SHANKS, Charles H.	MAR 31 1834
HARRISON, Elias	BRAMELL, Sarah F.	JUN 08 1854
HARRISON, Elisha	KROUSE, Elizabeth	OCT 28 1815
HARRISON, George	ETCHISON, Elizabeth	AUG 23 1827
HARRISON, Gustavus	MAGRUDER, Elizabeth	JUN 01 1815
HARRISON, Harriet	BEECH, Garrison	JUN 11 1829

District of Columbia Marriage Licenses, 1811-1858

HARRISON, Helen A.	ASHTON, Gurden C.	JAN 20 1853
HARRISON, Henry	PUMROY, Eliza Ann	JUN 29 1830
HARRISON, Henry T.	JONES, Elizabeth Mary	NOV 28 1839
HARRISON, Horace N.	LINDENBEYER, Rebecca L.	OCT 21 1835
HARRISON, James	LEGG, Eleanor	FEB 15 1827
HARRISON, James	CROWLEY, Mary Ann	JUN 19 1827
HARRISON, James	ROWLES, Susan	JAN 03 1848
HARRISON, James F.	NOBLE, Amanda Gwynn	SEP 28 1848
HARRISON, James T.	RAWLINGS, Eliza Jane	JAN 06 1858
HARRISON, Jane	READMAN, Levi	AUG 06 1850
HARRISON, John	GRANTT, Margaret	AUG 15 1833
HARRISON, John	CHADWELL, Priscilla	JUN 27 1844
HARRISON, John B.	NELSON, Ann	OCT 13 1849
HARRISON, John T.	TARMON, Elizabeth	MAY 15 1850
HARRISON, John Thomas	BURROWS, Emeline	NOV 07 1845
HARRISON, Joseph	REDMAN, Margaret	DEC 19 1850
HARRISON, Julia Ann	SIMPSON, Benjamin	MAY 24 1824
HARRISON, Louisa	COFFIN, John H.C.	APR 09 1845
HARRISON, Martha	HARRISON, Robert	DEC 02 1851
HARRISON, Martha A.	BEAVER, John W.C.	NOV 21 1849
HARRISON, Mary Ann	BURCH, Robert	FEB 16 1833
HARRISON, Mary Ann	LYNCH, Charles	FEB 27 1854
HARRISON, Mary E.	DeGILSE, Godfrey	APR 23 1830
HARRISON, Mary E.	PRICE, John A.	OCT 04 1838
HARRISON, Mary J.	SHAW, Lloyd A.	DEC 03 1855
HARRISON, Matilda	BECK, Nicholas	JUL 12 1854
HARRISON, Matilda A.	MACKNEY, John L.	DEC 19 1850
HARRISON, Matthew	JONES, Harriotte	MAY 12 1851
HARRISON, Nancy	JONES, Daniel	JUN 09 1858
HARRISON, Napoleon B.	WELLFORD, Maria P.	MAR 19 1850
HARRISON, Peter	LUCAS, Nancy	APR 13 1829
HARRISON, Priscilla	WILBERN, James H.	JUL 20 1831
HARRISON, Ralph	SCOTT, Maria (blk)	SEP 23 1854
HARRISON, Rebecca	McGEE, John	APR 11 1831
HARRISON, Richard	TAYLOR, L.A.	JUN 15 1822
HARRISON, Robert	BURCH, Columbia	MAY 27 1833
HARRISON, Robert	HARRISON, Martha	DEC 02 1851
HARRISON, Robert M.	HARKNESS, Susan A.	APR 03 1817
HARRISON, Susan	HASLUP, Jonathan W.	JAN 21 1852
HARRISON, Susan M.	DUTTON, George W.	JUN 03 1856
HARRISON, Thomas	SCOTT, Catherine	SEP 01 1817
HARRISON, Thomas	SCOTT, Catherine	AUG 11 1817
HARRISON, Thomas	MATTINGLY, Sidney Ann	NOV 02 1835
HARRISON, Thomas	MERELL, Caroline	SEP 19 1854
HARRISON, Uriah B.	BOUVET, Sophia C.	NOV 06 1856
HARRISON, Vincent	PARKER, Mary (blk)	OCT 13 1853
HARRISON, Williamson	BRAYFIELD, Cath. Sophia	MAR 18 1852
HARRISON, Wm.	COOMBES, Margaret	NOV 04 1819
HARRISON, Wm. H.	HOLROYD, Ann R.	DEC 14 1852
HARRISS, Eleanor A.	MEANS, William A.	DEC 18 1855
HARRISS, Emily	BROWN, Rolley	NOV 17 1831
HARRISS, Geo.	DUTCHER, Jemima	MAR 31 1820
HARRISS, William	WHITE, Mary Ann	FEB 02 1831
HARRISS, William	SCOTT, Jane (blk)	JUN 14 1847
HARROCKS, George	HILL, Jane	AUG 01 1820
HARROD, Ann Rebecca (blk)	BOONE, John Lewis	AUG 11 1853
HARROD, Betsey	BEAN, Lancelot	DEC 09 1817
HARROD, Elizabeth (blk)	NEALE, Henry	JUL 19 1836

District of Columbia Marriage Licenses, 1811-1858

HARROD, Sarah Laura (blk)	SIMS, Henry	MAR 30 1849
HARRON, Columbus	NOYES, Isabella	MAY 03 1856
HARRON, Elizabeth	WATSON, Lewis Henry	MAR 31 1856
HARROT, William	McPEAKE, Mary	JUN 08 1843
HARROTT, Jane	MORFIT, Hugh	OCT 19 1847
HARROVER, Elizabeth	RICHEY, John	APR 16 1857
HARROVER, James R.	LARKER, Virginia	JUN 28 1854
HARROVER, Sarah A.	REED, Robert	FEB 27 1849
HARROVER, William H.	SMITH, Phillippe	MAY 19 1841
HARRY, Alonzo W.	COLLINS, Ann Catharine	APR 30 1853
HARRY, Alonzo W.	COLLINS, Ann C.	JAN 16 1854
HARRY, Ann C.	QUEEN, William	JUL 01 1857
HARRY, George	DAVIS, Elizabeth	DEC 11 1823
HARRY, Joseph U.	CHOPPIN, Mary E.	MAY 10 1854
HARRY, Mary Ann	CHESLEY, Nathaniel D. [Dr.]	OCT 30 1844
HARRY, Mary E.	McNEER, William W.	SEP 30 1843
HARRY, Richard	HARKINS, Fanny	DEC 26 1822
HARRY, Thomas	HARTNETT, Margaret	AUG 27 1855
HARRYMAN, Ann R.	GOSNEL, Richard	JAN 04 1853
HARRYMANN, Charity S.	RAPLEY, Wm. Washington	JAN 31 1853
HARRYMANN, Charity S.	RAPLEY, William W.	MAY 18 1853
HARSCAMP, Mary	HYDMILLER, Albert	SEP 19 1838
HARSHMAN, Harriet	GROVES, Jacob	OCT 24 1831
HARSHMAN, Henry	YOUNG, Harriot	FEB 03 1818
HARSHMAN, Jacob	WILLCOXON, Letitia	MAR 18 1824
HARSHMAN, Jesse W.	BELL, Matilda E.	JAN 24 1856
HARSHMAN, Mary S.	MOORELAND, John	DEC 24 1840
HART, Abigail	BARNHILL, Gabriel	JAN 27 1814
HART, Amy	BERRY, Washington O.	JUL 28 1851
HART, Cyrus W.	WHITELOCK, Matilda	JAN 02 1845
HART, Deborah E.	WHITMORE, John R.	OCT 30 1855
HART, Elizabeth J.	CHAMPION, William H.	SEP 11 1854
HART, Ellen	LYNCH, Michael	FEB 04 1854
HART, Hezekiah	BREAST, Rosina	JUN 05 1827
HART, John	[blank], Eliza	NOV 21 1818
HART, John	MYERS, Caroline	JAN 06 1843
HART, John W.	EVANS, Lotty	MAY 16 1853
HART, Joseph	STUDS, Lucy H.	MAY 20 1857
HART, Martha Ann	WHALEY, Bushrod D.	JAN 01 1848
HART, Michael	STUMP, Barbara	FEB 09 1833
HART, Patrick	McDONALD, Mary Ann	NOV 20 1854
HART, Richard	DUVALL, Milly	SEP 16 1813
HART, Vilette	RYAN, Theodore	JUN 24 1843
HART, William	KILHAN, Catherine	JUN 16 1857
HARTBOWER, Gottfrie	DIEDERIEN, Linner	MAR 30 1833
HARTBRECHT, Josephine	KÜBEL, Edward	NOV 12 1856
HARTBRECHT, Margaret	ENDRES, Adrian	APR 07 1855
HARTBRECHT, Stephen	ROTH, Josephine	OCT 05 1853
HARTE, Edward	HOLMEAD, Rosina M.	MAR 29 1847
HARTER, Caroline	HARTMANN, Ferdinand	FEB 01 1858
HARTER, Marie	GIESKING, Henry W.	FEB 02 1856
HARTER, Wilhelmine	MUELLER, Augustus	AUG 05 1847
HARTER, William	WELING, Maria	FEB 02 1856
HARTIGAN, Bridget	BRODEN, Patrick	APR 09 1858
HARTIGAN, Honora	McNAUGHTEN, George	APR 29 1857
HARTIGAN, Mary	MAHONEY, Daniel	AUG 08 1855
HARTIGAN, Michael	O'BRIAN, Eleanor	JUL 06 1833
HARTLETT, William	GREENAICE, Maria Ann Eliza	SEP 04 1829

District of Columbia Marriage Licenses, 1811-1858

HARTLOVE, James	GOULDING, Rosetta	AUG 16 1826
HARTLY, Abraham	GREENFIELD, Neomi S.	AUG 02 1836
HARTLY, John	ABIGINN, Sally	FEB 08 1825
HARTMAN, Calvin F.	WALKER, Ann H.	JUN 23 1851
HARTMAN, Caroline	FORREST, Charles	NOV 27 1855
HARTMAN, Charles	RITZ, Catherine	AUG 22 1812
HARTMAN, Elizabeth	GRIDGER, Daniel	OCT 22 1825
HARTMAN, Elizabeth	GATTRELL, Aaron M.	AUG 28 1834
HARTMAN, George	FILLIUS, Catharine	APR 14 1819
HARTMAN, Lucy E.	BROWN, Mandley	SEP 26 1850
HARTMAN, Torronneger	ANTREO, Albert	APR 06 1854
HARTMANN, Ferdinand	HARTER, Caroline	FEB 01 1858
HARTNETT, James	ROCHE, Ellen	MAY 08 1850
HARTNETT, Margaret	HARRY, Thomas	AUG 27 1855
HARTNETT, Margaret T.	CURRAN, Stephen M.	AUG 09 1858
HARTSHORN, George	MIDDLETON, Sarah (blk)	JAN 03 1848
HARTWELL, George	BANNERMAN, Rosina E.	OCT 27 1854
HARVEY, Ann	SMITH, Daniel	MAY 02 1816
HARVEY, Anna E.J.	GARDENER, John H.	DEC 21 1854
HARVEY, Catherine R.	SUIT, Oliver B.	MAY 08 1843
HARVEY, Eleanor	McCOLLY, Elijah G.	OCT 10 1812
HARVEY, Eleanor	AMES, Thomas	JAN 14 1822
HARVEY, Elizabeth	HALRAN, Thomas	MAR 09 1814
HARVEY, Elizabeth	LITTLEFORD, Nathan T.	DEC 22 1840
HARVEY, Elizabeth	FISHER, Charles O.	DEC 15 1842
HARVEY, Elizabeth (blk)	THOMAS, Lewis	MAR 09 1846
HARVEY, G.W.	HOLLAND, H.A.	MAR 21 1849
HARVEY, George	LIVES, Ann Sophia	NOV 20 1833
HARVEY, Harriet Eliza	ADAMS, Austin L.	DEC 25 1823
HARVEY, Henry T.	COOMBES, Mary Ann Elizabeth	MAR 24 1829
HARVEY, James	GIBSON, Eleanor	JUN 23 1813
HARVEY, James	CLARK, Catharine	FEB 11 1817
HARVEY, James F.	BORLAND, Maria E.	DEC 09 1850
HARVEY, James O.	ANDERSON, Levinia	DEC 12 1857
HARVEY, Jas. E.	MOORE, Selina	APR 22 1854
HARVEY, John	COALMAN, Charlotte [Mrs.]	JUN 05 1820
HARVEY, Jonathan	STEWART, Jane	MAR 28 1815
HARVEY, Lucy (blk)	GREEN, Thomas	AUG 25 1836
HARVEY, Margaret	BELL, George	SEP 01 1852
HARVEY, Mary Ann	BECKER, John Henry	SEP 18 1839
HARVEY, Mary E.	NICHOLSON, Jno. T.S.	APR 04 1855
HARVEY, Sarah M.	EDELIN, George T.	DEC 25 1838
HARVEY, Thomas L.	ADAMS, Julia Ann	DEC 25 1849
HARVEY, Thomas M.	FRENCH, Sarah E.	MAY 09 1850
HARVEY, Tilley	ALLEN, John	OCT 07 1813
HARVEY, William	WILLSON, Catherine T.	MAY 01 1821
HARVEY, William	JONES, Letitia R.	JAN 08 1835
HARVEY, William	NICHOLSON, Mary Ann	APR 17 1848
HARVEY, William C.	COCKRELL, Catharine	AUG 25 1853
HARVEY, William M.	MAY, Charlotte R.	OCT 29 1857
HARVIN, Jane	RUSSELL, William B.	MAR 27 1837
HARVY, John	WILLIAMS, Harriet Eliza	OCT 14 1823
HARWOOD, Andrew A.	LUCE, Margaret	DEC 11 1844
HARWOOD, Eleanor	DORNEY, Edward	JUN 18 1827
HARWOOD, Samuel	CHARLES, Mary Ann	JUN 21 1821
HARWOOD, Susan Ann	BREWER, George G.	NOV 01 1825
HARWOULD, Laura V.	WYVILL, Samuel W.	MAR 23 1854
HASEL, Catherine A.	GATES, Francis	NOV 16 1850

District of Columbia Marriage Licenses, 1811-1858

HASELBUSCH, Hermann	BERGER, Charlotte	OCT 27 1855
HASEW, William	ASHTON, Louisa	JAN 24 1828
HASKELL, Daniel H.	MacDONALD, Eliza	JUL 24 1827
HASKELL, Jos.	PEARSON, Sarah	AUG 24 1822
HASKINS, Arie (blk)	SANDERS, Lewis	FEB 23 1853
HASKINS, Basil	TAIT, Henrietta	SEP 21 1841
HASKINS, James	WILLIAMS, Margaret (blk)	MAR 30 1843
HASKINS, Margt. (blk)	BROWN, John F.	MAY 31 1856
HASKINS, Mary	MAHORNEY, Thomas	NOV 26 1838
HASKINS, Robert F.	MEDLEY, Hallie	DEC 19 1855
HASLANGER, William	HIRT, Anna	AUG 29 1857
HASLET, Martha	SUDDATH, Rezin	MAY 14 1829
HASLETINE, Charles M.	WELDEN, Margaret C.	NOV 14 1837
HASLETINE, James C.	WARNER, Eliza C.	JUL 22 1843
HASLIP, Enoch	FORD, Mary Jane	APR 25 1848
HASLIP, Lucy	CODRICK, John	JUN 23 1841
HASLUP, Elizabeth A.	IGLEHART, Charles D.	OCT 18 1853
HASLUP, Emily (blk)	BUTLER, Thomas	DEC 27 1855
HASLUP, Jonathan W.	HARRISON, Susan	JAN 21 1852
HASLUP, Susan	ALLISON, John W.	JAN 24 1839
HASLUP, Thomas M.	CROSS, Elizabeth Ann	JUN 26 1845
HASS, Powea	PEASE, Miss	JAN 29 1834
HASSELBACH, Wm. Rudolph	CEDERQUIST, Amalie Constanzie	JUL 08 1857
HASSELHOFF, Ann	BODE, George Wm.	JUN 27 1843
HASSEN, John	RUPPERT, Johanna	SEP 29 1851
HASSLER, Charles A.	NOURSE, Anna J.	OCT 04 1837
HASSLER, Eva	FISCHER, George Andras	MAR 18 1846
HASSLER, Ferdinand E.	HANSON, Elizabeth B.	SEP 15 1845
HASSLER, Fredericka	HOOD, Frederick	FEB 09 1852
HASSLER, John J.S.	HEBB, Elizabeth S.	JUN 27 1853
HASSON, Rozanna	HOWARD, Henry	APR 19 1823
HASTINGS, Eliza L.	DARNES, Richard H.	APR 04 1857
HASTINGS, James	McPHERSON, Eliza	APR 11 1834
HASTINGS, Julia	BARRETT, Erastus B.	DEC 31 1855
HASTINGS, Nicholas	CUNIC, David	NOV 18 1849
HASTINGS, William	SMITH, Margaret	APR 07 1849
HASTINS, Elizabeth	EWING, John	NOV 12 1842
HASWELL, James	GREEN, Precilla	MAY 20 1853
HATAWAY, John	NIEL, Elizabeth (blk)	JUL 05 1855
HATCH, Charles	CONLEN, Winnie	SEP 27 1852
HATCH, Ellenora	HEAD, Andrew J.	MAY 10 1849
HATCH, Loranzo	ADSIT, Clara E.	AUG 19 1846
HATCH, Rexford	MATTHEWS, Sophia M.	JAN 31 1857
HATCH, Wells	SANFORD, Hannah	JAN 16 1851
HATCHER, Sarah M.	CONWELL, Charles B.	JAN 08 1857
HATCHER, William	HAGAN, Thesta	OCT 31 1850
HATCHESON, Benjamin N.	LETTS, Sophia Matilda	JUL 09 1853
HATCHINGSON, Mary Ann	KIBEY, Alexander	OCT 01 1844
HATERWAY, Nancy	CHICHESTER, Savannah	OCT 04 1822
HATHAWAY, Susan	MILLS, John	FEB 27 1812
HATTERSLY, Rebecca	MILLS, William	APR 01 1826
HATTERWAY, James	MARTAIN, Patsey	OCT 21 1815
HATTIGAN, Catherine	MADIGAN, Patrick	APR 30 1856
HATTON, Alexander S.	SIMMONS, Margaret Ann	FEB 28 1850
HATTON, Benjamin	ALLISON, Virginia S.	APR 17 1851
HATTON, Henry D., Jr.	BROWN, Mary E.	SEP 29 1838
HATTON, Henry D.	WILSON, Sarah C.	NOV 07 1854
HATTON, Jane	BUTLER, Richard	MAR 18 1841

District of Columbia Marriage Licenses, 1811-1858

HATTON, Mary G.	BURCH, John T.	APR 18 1854
HATTON, Nathaniel H.	KIRTY, Mary E.	NOV 14 1845
HATTON, Washington	MOODY, Amelia Page	APR 14 1838
HATTON, [blank]	BULLUS, John N.	APR 06 1822
HAUCK, John G.	WEIGAND, Mary	MAY 08 1848
HAUGH, Andrew	RICE, Mary Frances	FEB 23 1841
HAUPTMAN, Elizabeth A.	DOUGLASS, Samuel E.	DEC 08 1849
HAUPTMAN, Henry	WILLIAMS, Martha	JUN 08 1837
HAUPTMAN, Jeremiah	GREEN, Ann Rebecca	JUN 27 1829
HAUPTMAN, Philip H.	FISTER, Mary Margt.	NOV 10 1853
HAUS,* Margaret Ann	BOWIE, Aquilla	JUN 11 1840
HAUSCH, Christian	PATTON, Ellenor T.	AUG 20 1850
HAUSSY, Philip	VERMILLION, Sarah	MAR 24 1815
HAVELIN, Eliza	MALONE, Lawrence	MAY 29 1846
HAVENER, Benedict	ANDERSON, Elizabeth Ann	AUG 06 1849
HAVENER, Emily Jane	SOLOMON, James W.	MAR 01 1854
HAVENER, John F.	COOPER, Ann	DEC 10 1849
HAVENER, Mary	MULLICAN, Joseph	MAY 26 1831
HAVENER, Overton	REDOWAY, Ellen R.	AUG 01 1848
HAVENER, Peter	COCHRAN, Virginia A.	NOV 11 1847
HAVENER, Rhoda Ann	FREEMAN, James T.	MAY 28 1855
HAVENNER, Charles W.	WAKE, Margaret J.	MAR 23 1853
HAVENNER, Elizabeth H.	ROWE, William N.	APR 28 1842
HAVENNER, Thomas H.	WILSON, Mary Cornelia	FEB 10 1846
HAVENNER, William H.	HAYLE, Ann	MAY 05 1845
HAVENNER, William H.	COLLINS, Catharine	NOV 25 1850
HAVERSTACK, Matthew	CATER, Ruth Ann	OCT 07 1847
HAVERSTICKS, Ruth Ann	McCLELLAND, Alfred	AUG 22 1848
HAVILAND, James C.	LACEY, Mary America	JUN 10 1843
HAVILAND, John H.	WILKINSON, Theresa B.	JUL 02 1855
HAW, Elizabeth Ann	CHEW, Henry M.	JAN 14 1833
HAW, Henry [Dr.]	BROWN, Eliza F.	OCT 27 1829
HAW, Lucinda S.	MATTHEWS, Henry C.	SEP 28 1820
HAW, Mary Ann	BERRY, Philip T.	FEB 10 1825
HAWE, Edward	FOY, Rosena A.	JUN 16 1856
HAWENSCHILL, William	POSS, Mary	OCT 19 1848
HAWIN, Ann	DONALDSON, Benjamin	AUG 08 1816
HAWKE, Laura F.	BROOKS, Joseph C.	SEP 02 1856
HAWKE, Robert	SWEENY, Mary	SEP 09 1839
HAWKE, Thomas A.	SMITH, Mary	JAN 19 1832
HAWKE, Thomas A.	SMALLWOOD, Christiann	NOV 24 1847
HAWKINS, Ann	NICHOLSON, Peter	OCT 21 1840
HAWKINS, Cecelia J.	GRIFFIN, Richard	SEP 26 1857
HAWKINS, Columbia V.	HITCHCOX, Michael M.	NOV 08 1851
HAWKINS, Diana (blk)	BETTER, Alaveqius	JUL 27 1854
HAWKINS, Edward	KELLY, Elizabeth	JUL 21 1831
HAWKINS, Edward	SWIGART, Susannah	AUG 04 1841
HAWKINS, Ellen (blk)	CLARKE, Wesley	JUN 12 1854
HAWKINS, Frances Louisa (col'd)	BARNES, James Wm.	NOV 14 1855
HAWKINS, Henry	BUTLER, Mary (blk)	JUN 22 1853
HAWKINS, Jane	SAVOY, Elijah	NOV 26 1829
HAWKINS, John	MATTHEWS, Mary J.	AUG 15 1857
HAWKINS, John Wm.	MITCHELL, Sophia (blk)	DEC 02 1852
HAWKINS, Louisa (blk)	DADE, Adam	NOV 21 1855
HAWKINS, Lucinda (blk)	SIMMS, Henry	SEP 11 1856
HAWKINS, Maria (blk)	JACKSON, James	JAN 03 1854
HAWKINS, Mary	CLEMENTS, Thomas	APR 13 1847
HAWKINS, Mary (blk)	BROWN, Jeffry	JUL 29 1857

District of Columbia Marriage Licenses, 1811-1858

HAWKINS, Phillip	DEAN, Mary Ann	FEB 20 1839
HAWKINS, Phillip	HOYLE, Ellen Ann	JAN 05 1858
HAWKINS, R. Laidler	WINEBERGER, Jane E.	OCT 13 1851
HAWKINS, Reuben A.	BURCH, Elizabeth Jane	SEP 12 1836
HAWKINS, Saullimon	CLARK, Matilda	APR 28 1819
HAWKINS, William	MILES, Ann S. (blk)	OCT 08 1844
HAWLEY, Lewis J.	MORRIS, Elizabeth A.	JUN 22 1853
HAWLEY, Phoebe	WEIR, William	MAY 04 1846
HAY, Charles	CHANDLER, Lucy	APR 20 1824
HAY, Maria Amelia	RINGGOLD, Samuel	FEB 16 1813
HAY, Mary Virginia	BALL, Charles G.	DEC 31 1851
HAY, Rebecca	ALEXANDER, Columbus	JAN 21 1840
HAYDEN, Henrietta	KERBY, George	JUN 29 1846
HAYDEN, James	McDONALD, Annie	APR 19 1853
HAYDEN, John Thomas	RUST, Elizabeth	FEB 06 1855
HAYDEN, Mary H.	BERKLEY, John T.	MAR 06 1839
HAYDEN, Mary S.	ALSOP, Samuel	APR 09 1832
HAYDEN, Sarah	TYDINGS, Thomas	DEC 07 1812
HAYDEN, William T.	STEWART, Clarissa S.	JAN 02 1849
HAYE, Henry	PLANT, Sarah Ann	SEP 28 1819
HAYES, Alonzo	GILMAN, Malvina	MAY 01 1843
HAYES, Amelia	FARR, Malchi	JAN 08 1839
HAYES, Catherine	POWERS, John	NOV 07 1832
HAYES, John	ANDERSON, Mary Ann	JAN 31 1850
HAYES, Mary	MEADER, Joseph	FEB 03 1858
HAYES, William	SULLIVAN, Abby	NOV 01 1853
HAYLE, Ann	HAVENNER, William H.	MAY 05 1845
HAYMAN, Ephraim	JAMESON, Ellen (blk)	NOV 02 1844
HAYMAN, William, Jr.	LANE, Julianna	JUN 05 1822
HAYMIRE, Mary B.	SMOOT, John W.	MAR 05 1839
HAYNE, Lewis	BOND, Elizabeth	JAN 15 1844
HAYNES, Hannah	JOHNSON, Price	MAR 29 1823
HAYNES, Mary	LYMBURN, John	JUL 05 1814
HAYNES, Mary Ann	AUSTIN, Thomas A.	JAN 01 1818
HAYNES, Robert L.	HUTCHESON, Ann M.	DEC 23 1856
HAYNIE, Hancock H.	MAGAR, Marion F.	SEP 28 1857
HAYNIE, John F.	WALKER, Sarah Catherine	AUG 12 1856
HAYRE, Ann E.	LANGLEY, William	JAN 11 1840
HAYRE, Francis	KEADLE, Mary Ann G.	JUL 23 1822
HAYRE, Francis R.	SWAIN, Jane T.	JAN 12 1850
HAYRE, Gerard	SIFFERT, Harriet	MAY 29 1816
HAYRE, John	ORME, Catharine	JAN 11 1821
HAYRE, John F.	EDWARDS, Sarah E.	DEC 26 1848
HAYS, Charles Harrison	EVANS, Harriott	JUN 16 1831
HAYS, David	KIDWELL, Ann	DEC 14 1825
HAYS, Ellen	BRADY, Stephen	FEB 08 1838
HAYS, Ellen	AHEREN, Bartholomew	JUN 01 1854
HAYS, Fanny	KIDWELL, Cortney	NOV 18 1824
HAYS, Fielder	HALL, Sarah Ann	OCT 19 1837
HAYS, Heister	GODFREY, Francis	DEC 21 1833
HAYS, Isaac N., Rev.	KING, Rebecca H.	DEC 14 1850
HAYS, James	TURNER, Christa (blk)	JUN 26 1851
HAYS, John	SULLIVAN, Ellen	AUG 29 1855
HAYS, John W.	RIDGEWAY, M.A.C.	MAR 03 1855
HAYS, Jonathan	ROBINSON, Mary E.	OCT 27 1853
HAYS, Lawrence	GUTRICK, Ann	APR 23 1812
HAYS, Levi	EVANS, Mary Ann	FEB 15 1830
HAYS, Lloyd	YOUNG, Louisa Maria	OCT 27 1841

District of Columbia Marriage Licenses, 1811-1858

HAYS, Louisa	HUFF, Levin	FEB 24 1829
HAYS, Mary	SHEEHY, John	APR 14 1855
HAYS, Mary Jane	HAZEL, Edward	AUG 15 1850
HAYS, Mary M.	RICKARD, Desire A.	JUN 17 1840
HAYS, Nicholas	FITZGERALD, Mary	APR 26 1853
HAYS, Patrick	CASSIDY, Rebecca Ann	NOV 07 1834
HAYS, Samuel	VERMILION, Carolina	JAN 22 1846
HAYS, William	UPTON, Sarah Ann	MAY 29 1827
HAYSE, John	STAFFORD, Margaret	FEB 13 1858
HAYSLUP, Mary Ann	PILES, Benjamin	SEP 24 1834
HAYWARD, Sarah R.	BERRY, Noble	JUL 07 1828
HAYWOOD, Adeline	SMITH, John H.	MAY 30 1853
HAYWOOD, John	RUSTAGE, Lucy	APR 21 1824
HAYWOOD, Robert	FLOOD, Sarah	OCT 29 1836
HAYWOOD, Sarah Ann	THOMPSON, George	MAY 15 1822
HAYWOOD, Susan Elizth.	GOHNAN, William	NOV 05 1853
HAZARD, Lucy A.	ANDERSON, Charles D.	AUG 18 1856
HAZEL, Edward	HAYS, Mary Jane	AUG 15 1850
HAZEL, Levi	LITLE, Rebecca	APR 04 1850
HAZLE, Ann Mariah	MERRYMAN, Horatio R.	FEB 26 1838
HAZLE, Charlotte	COLLINS, Joseph	DEC 31 1846
HAZLE, Ellen	WARREN, Joseph	SEP 25 1857
HAZLE, William Conway	COLLINS, Virginia Rosella	AUG 06 1846
HAZLE, Zachariah	BACON, Elizabeth	FEB 15 1817
HAZLE, Zachariah	THOMPSON, Rosetta	OCT 10 1839
HAZLEWOOD, Martin W.	ROSE, Mary A.	MAY 13 1857
HAZZARD, Caroline	TAYLOR, John F.	JUL 14 1853
HAZZARD, Elizth.	HORNBERGER, John	APR 04 1857
HAZZARD, Mary Ann	WATSON, Joshua	JAN 02 1849
HEAD, Andrew J.	HATCH, Ellenora	MAY 10 1849
HEAD, Frances	LOMAX, John	OCT 16 1852
HEAD, George M.	THOMPSON, Mary Ann Isabella	DEC 11 1833
HEAD, George M.	TILLEY, Barbara A.	JUL 10 1851
HEAD, William H.	HILL, Adaline	APR 18 1839
HEADEN, Elizabeth	NEWTON, Lewis	FEB 09 1833
HEALD, John R.	ESSEX, Eleanor V.	NOV 13 1849
HEALY, Michael	MURPHY, Mary Ann	FEB 25 1853
HEANY, John	McMAHON, Ann	OCT 24 1846
HEANY, Owen	NEENAN, Mary	OCT 27 1857
HEAP, David Porter	BOWYER, Elizabeth	SEP 28 1854
HEARD, Edmund	DANT, Teresa	OCT 10 1826
HEARD, Enoch	NORRIS, Mary	JAN 07 1813
HEARD, Enoch	LEDGICKS, Ann	JAN 28 1822
HEARD, John F.	COOK, Mary C.	AUG 31 1858
HEARD, Matthew	SHECKELLS, Mary M.	DEC 21 1852
HEARLY, [blank]	MAHONY, Battw.	MAY 05 1832
HEARN, Margaret	HANREHAN, James	JUN 06 1851
HEARN, Mary	LOUGHLIN, Michael	MAY 18 1848
HEARN, Thomas	KING, Margaret	MAY 09 1851
HEARPER, Harriot	GILLASFY, Henry	FEB 05 1822
HEART, Elizabeth	ROBERTSON, Robert	SEP 06 1817
HEART, John	HAGEN, Julia	FEB 27 1824
HEART, Margaretta	SMITH, John	JUL 25 1846
HEARTLOVE, Mary Ann	BAZELL, John	APR 20 1820
HEATH, Herman H.	SHEPPARD, Ann Rosa Semmes	NOV 28 1849
HEATH, J. Harry	SCHWARTZE, Mary V.	JUN 28 1858
HEATH, John	SLADE, Maria Catherine	NOV 28 1832
HEATH, John	WEBSTER, Ann	NOV 02 1850

District of Columbia Marriage Licenses, 1811-1858

HEATH, Josephine V.	CUMMINS, Edmund H.	NOV 14 1853
HEATH, William D.	WELLS, Catharine	AUG 03 1838
HEATHMAN, John	McCARTHY, Bridget	AUG 19 1852
HEATON, Catharine VanRanselor	AFFLEY, John Holmes	SEP 21 1825
HEBB, Elizabeth S.	HASSLER, John J.S.	JUN 27 1853
HEBB, Sallie B.	TOPPING, Evert M.	JUL 22 1850
HEBBERN, Samuel	McCULLOUCH, Lydia	JUN 11 1832
HEBBRON, Peter	SCOTT, Ann	OCT 21 1815
HECTER, Mary George	BEATTY, George W.	MAY 31 1856
HEDENDER, Nicholas	O'LEARY, Mary	FEB 01 1820
HEDENGER, John	McFARLAND, Mary Elizabeth	APR 19 1848
HEDGE, Elizabeth	MOUNTZ, Joseph	JAN 12 1826
HEDGES, Edward	RYDER, Alice	FEB 22 1855
HEDGES, John	VILLARD, Mary A.	MAY 17 1843
HEDGES, Martha	HUGHES, John E.	APR 06 1837
HEDGES, Nicholas	ATHEY, Leanor	JAN 03 1828
HEDGES, Sarah Ann	BELT, James	NOV 23 1820
HEDGES, Sarah J.W.	JOY, John	NOV 26 1850
HEDGES, Susan R.	THOMPSON, Samuel	JUN 25 1834
HEDGMAN, John G.	STUART, Cecilia A.	APR 30 1850
HEDLEY, Eliza	MEDLEY, Thomas	JUL 23 1825
HEDLEY, Wm. W.	BEECHER, Alice	FEB 03 1855
HEDRICK, Joseph	McELWEE, Susan J.	OCT 14 1850
HEELLMAN, Lawrence	WHITING, Mary Ann	NOV 18 1842
HEERE, Catharine	EGLOFF, Godfried	JUL 17 1818
HEETER, Uria	RICKETS, Mary	SEP 29 1828
HEETER, Uriah	KITCHEN, Jane	SEP 06 1849
HEETER, Uriah	YOUNG, Margaret	APR 29 1851
HEETER, Uriah	YOUNG, Annie Jane	APR 28 1855
HEETON, Jane	HANES, John	AUG 02 1849
HEFFERNAN, Patrick	GREENWELL, Louisa	JAN 29 1846
HEFFERNAN, Sarah A.	McNEIR, Wm. F.	OCT 26 1857
HEFFNER, George J.	VINSON, Francis Ann	JAN 15 1845
HEFLEY, Frederick	KORNE, Mary	FEB 11 1826
HEFLIN, Martha Ann	HANBACK, James	JUL 12 1853
HEFTLEY, Frederick	NARDEN, Harriet	DEC 01 1823
HEGELER, Johanna	LOEFFLER, Ernest	MAR 21 1853
HEGELER, Minna	SELLHAUSEN, Augustus	JUL 07 1849
HEIBSDEMAN, Geo.	RINK, Catharine	OCT 04 1843
HEICH, John R.	SCHINEN, Catharine	SEP 01 1856
HEIDER, Caroline	SCHENCK, Peter	SEP 25 1856
HEIDER, Diederick	HARLER, Charlotte	NOV 03 1852
HEIDER, William	ROCKAWAY, Sophia	JAN 17 1857
HEIDT, Wilhelmina	VOLTZ, John	MAY 13 1856
HEIGHTON, Eliza	MORGAN, John R.	AUG 22 1823
HEIL, George	FLADE, Margaret	JUN 17 1848
HEIL, Michael	MILLER, Catharine	APR 24 1854
HEILMANN, Margaret	WAGNER, John	JAN 10 1856
HEILMICK, William	RUTRING, Margaretta	DEC 27 1842
HEIN, Samuel	SIMPSON, Henrietta Sarah S.	JAN 24 1838
HEINE, Wm.	BURGER, Mary	OCT 31 1855
HEINECKE, Samuel	HINES, Joanna R.	NOV 04 1828
HEINEL, Anna Maria	GARMILLER, Francis	JAN 04 1855
HEINLINE, William D.	SIMMONS, Elizabeth	MAY 21 1838
HEINZERLING, John P.	BRAND, Dorothy	MAR 16 1858
HEINZERLING, Phillip	BAKER, Augusti	APR 29 1858
HEIRNE, David	WEBSTER, Catherine	MAY 04 1818
HEISE, John C.	HARRIS, Anna	MAY 24 1854

District of Columbia Marriage Licenses, 1811-1858

HEISE, Joseph L.	BEAGLE, Mary Frances	NOV 26 1853
HEISER, Paul	KAENER, Catherine	JAN 15 1856
HEISKELL, Henry Lee	GOUVERNEUR, Elizabeth K.	JUN 08 1842
HEISKELL, William B.	WILSON, Eliza Jane	SEP 07 1847
HEISLAND, Michael	BASAEBASE, Elizabeth	OCT 05 1846
HEISLIP, Emilda M.	GRAHAM, Richard	SEP 30 1839
HEISS, Andrew	WILSON, Margaret Ann	AUG 29 1846
HEISS, Leanna	PFEIFER, John	MAR 31 1851
HEISS, Margaretta	MULFINGER, John C.	JAN 31 1843
HEIT, Louisa	HALPNER, Henry	SEP 05 1853
HEITCH, Elizth. B.	SEITZ, Henry	MAY 21 1855
HEITMILLER, Caroline	WILLNER, Francis	NOV 23 1857
HEITMILLER, Charles	HORTSCAMP, Mary	NOV 21 1857
HEITMULLER, Anthony	HERSTHAMP, Henrietta	JUN 07 1851
HEITMULLER, Caroline	SCHWARZE, Joseph R.B.	JUN 24 1852
HEITMÜLLER, Charlotte	BERGER, William	DEC 07 1855
HEITMÜLLER, Dorethea	BÜSCHING, Henry	DEC 06 1855
HEKROTH, Anna	HYDE, William	FEB 01 1850
HELDERSCHMIDT, Mary M.	MUCK, John	MAY 19 1849
HELFINSTERY, Anna	JONES, John L.	AUG 26 1858
HELFRICK, Chatarina	WERNER, John H.T.	JUL 28 1835
HELFRIEKEN, Elizabeth	LANDNER, George	MAY 15 1845
HELLEN, Elizabeth	JARVIS, Cipriano	APR 04 1848
HELLEN, Frances (blk)	COOPER, William H.	AUG 20 1850
HELLEN, Georgeanna Adelaide	MOODEY, Theodore L.	SEP 24 1838
HELLEN, Johnson	WINNULL, Jane E.	APR 18 1829
HELLEN, Josephine	FANT, Hamilton G.	MAY 16 1853
HELLEN, Mary Catharine	ADAMS, John	FEB 19 1828
HELLEN, Walter	JOHNSON, Adelade	OCT 14 1813
HELLER, August	LISENITZNER, Ernstina F.	NOV 29 1842
HELLER, Charles	KOBELT, Wilhelmina	DEC 13 1856
HELLER, Elenora	KLEMANN, William	JUN 21 1853
HELLFREY, Catharine	ECKLOFF, Joseph W.	APR 10 1841
HELLMICH, Joseph	PELZ, Fannie	JUL 18 1857
HELLRIGLE, Ann Maria Kent	HARDY, Henry M.	JUL 11 1835
HELM, Joseph	HOLMEAD, Jane Matilda	SEP 04 1832
HELM, Margaret	ORSBORNE, Richard	APR 01 1818
HELMEETH, Baldin	GREEN, Louisa	JUN 22 1842
HELMER, Joseph W.	PETRIE, Ellen A.	APR 26 1856
HELMS, Frederick	LEACH, Angeline	AUG 04 1838
HELMS, Rebecca	PHILIPS, James	NOV 08 1827
HELRICK, Mary	NICHOLS, William	AUG 13 1850
HELTON, Thomas	SMITH, Mary Elizth.	MAY 07 1851
HEMINGTON, Martha	HENSLEY, George	JAN 20 1834
HEMLING, Rosa	HENINGHER, Matthias	AUG 24 1854
HEMSLEY, James	HALL, Eliza	DEC 27 1849
HENDERSON, Alexander	MIDDLETON, Catharine Mary	JUN 23 1858
HENDERSON, Angaline	JOSLIN, Amzy	AUG 27 1842
HENDERSON, Ann	GROCE, Samuel Frederick	SEP 26 1833
HENDERSON, Ann	WASHINGTON, John	OCT 19 1840
HENDERSON, Ann (blk)	BOND, Charles	SEP 09 1845
HENDERSON, Anne V.N.	TAYLOR, H. Allen	APR 23 1845
HENDERSON, Edward	GRIFFITHS, Ritta	SEP 02 1850
HENDERSON, Eliza	BROWN, William	OCT 07 1852
HENDERSON, Eliza G.	JONES, Edward	NOV 21 1853
HENDERSON, Elizabeth	BRIGEMAN, Zachariah	NOV 18 1826
HENDERSON, James	OWENS, Jane	MAY 27 1816
HENDERSON, James	LANE, Rosa	NOV 08 1838

District of Columbia Marriage Licenses, 1811-1858

HENDERSON, James	SHEA, Catherine	SEP 05 1853
HENDERSON, James H.	STIRLING, Mary Ann	JUL 26 1852
HENDERSON, Jane W.	HARRIS, Munroe	MAY 25 1846
HENDERSON, Janet L.	HUMPHREYS, George	DEC 26 1826
HENDERSON, Jannett	STOREY, William	DEC 03 1866
HENDERSON, John	CONNOR, Emelina	SEP 28 1833
HENDERSON, John L.	MILSTEAD, Elizabeth	OCT 25 1838
HENDERSON, Mahala Ann	WALKER, Richard A.	FEB 19 1835
HENDERSON, Mary (blk)	LEMON, Henry	MAY 27 1850
HENDERSON, Mary Jane	EVANS, John Thomas	JAN 13 1848
HENDERSON, Matilda	HOWELL, John Frederick Alexr.	JUL 18 1850
HENDERSON, Nelly (blk)	JAMISON, John	DEC 12 1832
HENDERSON, Prisila (blk)	EVANS, Thomas	MAR 24 1838
HENDERSON, Richard	ENGLISH, Eliza A.B.	DEC 26 1826
HENDERSON, Sarah	PERRY, Charles	MAR 26 1838
HENDERSON, Sarah W.	CUMMINGS, King	DEC 28 1837
HENDERSON, Tarlton T.	JACKSON, Jane J.	SEP 06 1824
HENDERSON, Thomas	MURTEN, Mrs.	APR 28 1840
HENDLEY, Ann	WHITE, George	FEB 04 1823
HENDLEY, Ann E.	RILEY, James R.	JUN 24 1856
HENDLEY, Anna E.	LANGLEY, Charles W.	MAY 12 1858
HENDLEY, John N.	EVANS, Mary Cath.	OCT 18 1849
HENDLEY, Mary V.	PAYNTER, Abraham	APR 21 1857
HENDLEY, Michael	BURROWS, Ann	AUG 16 1832
HENDLEY, Richard	DIXON, Sophia	FEB 15 1817
HENDLEY, Richd.	DIXON, Matilda	APR 12 1814
HENDLEY, Sophia	KLOFFER, Benjamin	NOV 13 1851
HENDLEY, William	DEAN, Elizabeth	OCT 30 1841
HENDLY, Elizabeth	KING, John	AUG 10 1848
HENDLY, John W.	NEALE, Mary H.	MAR 19 1853
HENDRER, Rebecca	GROSS, Jacob	APR 08 1848
HENIGER, Nancy	MAYHUE, William Thomas	DEC 07 1850
HENING, George W.	LEWIS, Sarah C.	NOV 03 1831
HENINGHER, Matthias	HEMLING, Rosa	AUG 24 1854
HENION, John	BOSTON, Julia Ann J.	JUN 25 1838
HENLEY, Catharine	HILL, Gustavus	APR 25 1834
HENLEY, Celia V.	HURLEY, Jeremiah	APR 12 1855
HENLEY, Eliza	LUCE, Stephen B.	DEC 06 1854
HENLEY, Frances L.	HIGBY, Edward T.	DEC 11 1837
HENLEY, Henrietta E.	SMITH, Bayard H.	MAR 03 1842
HENLEY, James	TUTTLE, Catharine	NOV 05 1846
HENLEY, John Perry	MUDD, Elizabeth	DEC 22 1836
HENLON, Edmund	CONNELL, Mary	NOV 13 1854
HENLY, Ann	BOND, Samuel	DEC 19 1844
HENLY, Catharine	ELLIOTT, Perry	JAN 31 1856
HENLY, Hester Ann	WILSON, Lewis C.	APR 08 1839
HENLY, Mary	PYLES, James M.	DEC 17 1853
HENN, Allerson	JEFFERS, Susanna	AUG 23 1821
HENNAND, Stephen	COOK, Milly Ann	AUG 09 1820
HENNESSEY, Ellen	CUSICK, Daniel	APR 07 1855
HENNESSY, Margaret	FITZGERALD, David	AUG 15 1856
HENNEY, Hugh	McPHEE, Mary	MAY 28 1833
HENNEY, Peter	HUGULEY, Sarah E.	OCT 23 1852
HENNI, John	HAGER, Elizabeth	NOV 13 1832
HENNIMAN, Sophia	MILLER, Jacob	MAY 21 1858
HENNING, Ann Elizabeth	WALRAVEN, James C.	MAY 06 1846
HENNING, Eliza Jane	WALRAVEN, James C.	DEC 26 1848
HENNING, George F.	WALL, Jane	OCT 30 1856

District of Columbia Marriage Licenses, 1811-1858

HENNING, Henry N.	DOWNES, Mary R.	JAN 30 1836
HENNING, John	CLARKE, Ann	DEC 02 1813
HENNING, Lucinda	HUGHES, Evan	DEC 12 1846
HENNING, Margaret Ann	BRANDSWELL, James	SEP 18 1844
HENNING, Mary Ann	STAFFAN, George	OCT 02 1847
HENNING, Mary E.	MARTIN, Tobias M.	MAR 11 1856
HENNING, Priscilla	FRASER, James	JUN 29 1821
HENNING, Sarah L.	HAMORE, Wm. H.	DEC 31 1855
HENNING, Stephen	THORN, Elizabeth	JUN 06 1833
HENNING, William	ROLLS, Elizabeth	AUG 12 1843
HENNINGER, John	McLAUGHLIN, Ann	NOV 05 1831
HENNON, Bennett	SKIPON, Mary Ann	APR 23 1840
HENNON, Cornelius	SANFORD, Lucinda	AUG 13 1833
HENNON, Eliza	MORRIS, William	NOV 13 1828
HENNON, George	McLAIN, Jane	JAN 28 1839
HENNON, Julia Ann	ARNOLD, Thomas O.	OCT 25 1847
HENNON, Nancy	RISEN, John	FEB 26 1830
HENNON, Stephen	KING, Elizabeth	MAY 14 1818
HENRICH, Eliza	LOHIDER, William	MAR 30 1835
HENRY, Ann E.	WEBB, W.L.	SEP 30 1835
HENRY, Catherine	OSTERMEIR, Bernhart	JUN 16 1840
HENRY, Christian Frederick	KROFT, Catherina	AUG 17 1841
HENRY, Eliza	MAYHEW, Francis	MAY 15 1822
HENRY, George W.	GREENWOOD, Martha A.	JUL 23 1853
HENRY, Isabella L.	MORTON, George T.	APR 03 1834
HENRY, James	CLEMENTS, Rachel Amelia	MAR 03 1852
HENRY, John	SRUCKENMEELLY, Margt.	OCT 01 1850
HENRY, Joshua	HUDSON, Ann	JUN 10 1824
HENRY, Mary A.	FOWLER, Benjamin F.	JUN 23 1857
HENRY, Mary C.	AMISS, Richard L.	DEC 27 1854
HENRY, Rebecca	MUNROE, James L.	AUG 29 1820
HENRY, Robert	NOAKES, Secelia (blk)	DEC 30 1824
HENRY, Robert	DeVAUGHN, Amanda	MAY 18 1854
HENRY, Robert V.	STANFIELD, Margaret K.	DEC 06 1854
HENRY, Sarah	PRISTON, William	MAR 21 1822
HENRY, Sarah	LEE, Samuel	APR 13 1830
HENRY, Sarah Ann	FEGUSON, John W.	DEC 22 1851
HENRY, Thomas	SAUNDERS, Elizabeth (blk)	JUN 06 1839
HENRY, William	BROWN, Sarah (blk)	DEC 18 1812
HENSEY, Henry	ABLE, Sarah M.	MAR 19 1853
HENSEY, Rodum	LEE, Sally	MAY 08 1830
HENSHAW, Frances L.	BADEN, Thomas E.	OCT 23 1856
HENSHAW, Joshua L.	NEVITT, Susanna G.	NOV 14 1826
HENSLEY, George	HEMINGTON, Martha	JAN 20 1834
HENSLEY, Mary	EDWARDS, Henry C.	MAR 03 1855
HENSLING, Elizabeth	KNIES, Louis	MAR 04 1858
HENSON, Andrew	BALLARD, Julia (blk)	JUN 17 1839
HENSON, Charles	JONES, Rebecca (blk)	OCT 05 1857
HENSON, David	WASHINGTON, Harriet (blk)	APR 16 1857
HENSON, Elizabeth (blk)	WOODLAND, George	JUL 09 1857
HENSON, George	POSEY, Mary A.	SEP 15 1856
HENSON, John	RILEY, Mary Ann (blk)	JUN 02 1828
HENSON, Julia	POSEY, Richmond	SEP 20 1832
HENSON, Mary	ALLEN, Hiram	JUL 30 1853
HENSON, Matilda	YOUNG, Richd.	MAR 18 1819
HENSON, Sarah C.	WHITE, John	AUG 30 1823
HENSY, Cassa Ann	HARLY, Binget	AUG 13 1835
HENTON, Robert	ANDERS, Elizabeth	NOV 06 1813

District of Columbia Marriage Licenses, 1811-1858

HENTZ, Joseph	LEXBIE, Ann	MAR 08 1856
HENTZELL, Casper	YEABOWER, Mary	AUG 06 1858
HENWRIGHT, Julia	FLAHERTY, Patrick	OCT 07 1854
HENYON, Elizabeth	MARLOW, Henry	DEC 15 1851
HEPBURN, Alexr.	FOWLER, Maria	APR 16 1814
HEPBURN, Ann	CLIBER, Jacob	MAY 26 1832
HEPBURN, David	OLIVER, Ann	JUL 03 1828
HEPBURN, Ellen Johnston	YARNELL, Mordecai	OCT 15 1855
HEPBURN, George S.	VanHORN, Isabella	MAY 18 1847
HEPBURN, Henry C.	COOPER, Harriet	OCT 20 1856
HEPBURN, Jane	THUMLERT, James E.	JUN 19 1841
HEPBURN, Jane J.	DALLAN, Benjamin R.	OCT 18 1849
HEPBURN, Jeremiah	RIGDEN, Louisa	OCT 17 1826
HEPBURN, Jeremiah	ETTER, Ann	APR 24 1832
HEPBURN, John	JOHNSON, Elizabeth	OCT 04 1850
HEPBURN, Juliann M.	WARRING, Arthur	APR 02 1831
HEPBURN, Louisa H.	WAITE, Matthew H.	DEC 22 1849
HEPBURN, Louisa V.	GREENFIELD, Benjamin E.	OCT 30 1851
HEPBURN, Margaret N.	NYLES, Christopher T.	JUN 28 1849
HEPBURN, Maria	JACKSON, Robert	AUG 23 1849
HEPBURN, Mary Ann	DONIPHAN, William T.	DEC 19 1839
HEPBURN, Mary Ann (blk)	MADDEN, William	OCT 05 1854
HEPBURN, Peter	YOUNG, Mary Ellen	AUG 09 1849
HEPBURN, Sarah E.	WILLARD, Edwin D.	AUG 29 1845
HEPBURNE, Annie L.	POWELL, John D.	OCT 04 1854
HEPNER, Fred	COOKSEY, Mary Ann	FEB 25 1817
HEPPARD, Louisa	MEARISS, Jacob	DEC 18 1818
HERBER, Margaretta	LONG, John	DEC 24 1857
HERBERT, Alfred	WRIGHT, Ann	DEC 06 1821
HERBERT, Alfred	WILSON, Emma (blk)	SEP 17 1857
HERBERT, Andrew	HINES, Catherine	JUL 28 1856
HERBERT, Annania	HICKS, Harriet	SEP 19 1843
HERBERT, Catharine (blk)	LANCASTER, Edward	APR 11 1843
HERBERT, Constant	MILLER, Serina	APR 07 1856
HERBERT, Elizabeth	THOMPSON, John Edward	OCT 31 1846
HERBERT, Frances	GETZEINGER, John	AUG 05 1857
HERBERT, Francis	WELLS, Sarah Ann	FEB 13 1816
HERBERT, Francis	WILLIAMS, Frances	JUN 22 1842
HERBERT, Franciska	BIGLER, Philip	NOV 17 1856
HERBERT, George	BELL, Anne	AUG 05 1815
HERBERT, Gertrude	BISHOP, Joseph	NOV 17 1851
HERBERT, Godlip	DINT, Catherine	DEC 29 1854
HERBERT, James	SCOTT, Harriet Ann	SEP 11 1845
HERBERT, James L.	LUCAS, Mary J. (blk)	JUN 25 1857
HERBERT, John	JONES, Sarah	NOV 05 1812
HERBERT, M. Josephine	BYRNE, Thomas	MAY 20 1846
HERBERT, Maria	WATSON, John	NOV 25 1837
HERBERT, Martha	WHALEY, John T.	OCT 30 1841
HERBERT, Martha (blk)	DAGGS, Monteville	MAY 28 1850
HERBERT, Martha E.	HOWARD, Thomas W.	JUN 29 1841
HERBERT, Mary A.	PERRIE, Samuel T.	APR 16 1836
HERBERT, Mary E.	KIDWELL, George F.	MAY 16 1836
HERBERT, Mary E.	JONES, James H.	JUL 10 1848
HERBERT, Nathan	BAKER, Rachael	MAY 24 1822
HERBERT, Patrick	MINNS, Mary	MAY 15 1853
HERBERT, Samuel Marshall	MATLOCK, Sarah Ellen	OCT 25 1843
HERBERT, Sarah J.	SHOEMAKER, Thomas E.	AUG 04 1857
HERBERT, Susan	BRISCOE, George	NOV 08 1855

District of Columbia Marriage Licenses, 1811-1858

HERBERT, Thomas	SANDIFORD, Martha H.	MAY 13 1815
HERBERT, Thomas	LUCAS, Margaret	NOV 09 1854
HERBERT, William	BROWN, Elizabeth	FEB 23 1838
HERBERT, William	OSBURN, Emma	FEB 27 1845
HERBERT, William	LUCAS, Sarah	NOV 07 1848
HERBET, Mary Jane	BOYER, Henry	MAR 08 1854
HERBST, Daniel	SIEVERS, Minna	JUN 19 1858
HERBST, Francis Theodore	ARNY, Caroline Christiana	JAN 25 1851
HERCUS, Christianna J.	McQUEEN, David	DEC 18 1848
HERCUS, Margaret	HALL, George J.	JAN 21 1847
HERD, Ann E.C.	CLEMENTS, Andrew J.	FEB 17 1855
HEREFORD, Caroline E.	WARING, Thomas G.	JUN 28 1842
HEREFORD, William P.	SIMPSON, Lucy	DEC 30 1851
HEREFORD, Willie Ann	NEWMAN, Horace N.	JAN 07 1835
HERFERD, Michael	PREVOTE, Martha	MAR 06 1821
HERFORD, Ann Jane	LARNED, James	JUN 01 1815
HERFORD, Caroline	ROBERTS, Francis	AUG 14 1858
HERITY, Peggy	ROSE, Thomas	APR 29 1822
HERITY, Sally	SINON, Thomas	OCT 16 1828
HERITY, Sarah	NICHOLSON, Thomas	APR 25 1822
HERLAHY, John	HUSSEY, Ellen	MAY 08 1857
HERLEHY, Michael	COCKER, Elizabeth	MAY 12 1856
HERLEY, Deborah	HERLEY, George	APR 17 1821
HERLEY, George	HERLEY, Deborah	APR 17 1821
HERLEY, John	CURTAIN, Mary	NOV 18 1845
HERLIHEY, Patrick	GEANEY, Johanna	FEB 19 1857
HERLIHY, Jane	O'NEALE, Timothy	DEC 30 1835
HERLIHY, Julia	CONNER, Bryan	OCT 27 1852
HERLIHY, Thomas	QUILL, Catherine	APR 06 1858
HERLING, Mary Ann	PETTIT, Richard	NOV 30 1826
HERLY, Cornelius	DRISTHDEN, Margaret	JUL 02 1856
HERMANN, Barbara	FREIRICK, Charles	AUG 16 1856
HERMANN, John	DINKLE, Magdalen	OCT 16 1856
HERMANN, Paul	REDLER, Sophia	OCT 23 1856
HERMITAGE, Martha	EARL, Robert	DEC 18 1832
HERN, Mariah	DISKET, Richard	JAN 22 1856
HERN, Mary	BOYD, Jacob	APR 15 1856
HERNIR, Christine B.	FELKINNIN, F.	APR 14 1856
HERO__, Mary A.	AGER, John E.	JAN 21 1847
HEROLD, Adam G.	PORTER, Mary	SEP 11 1828
HERRALD, Barney	NEAFE, Mary	OCT 29 1830
HERRELL, George M.	BURDEET, Eliza	NOV 13 1851
HERRELL, James M.	MAHONEY, Rebecca	AUG 23 1855
HERRICKS, August	STROBEL, Caroline	NOV 30 1846
HERRIN, William	PIERCE, Henrietta	NOV 05 1838
HERRINGTON, Mary Ann Lee	RILLING, John	SEP 13 1821
HERRIS, Luke	PAINE, Eleanor	DEC 15 1819
HERRITY, Bridget	WAHL, John	AUG 29 1853
HERRITY, Catherine	HUGHES, William	OCT 14 1830
HERRITY, Hannah	RYNE, Michael	JUN 01 1822
HERRITY, James	MILES, Susan	JUL 04 1833
HERRITY, James	CONINX, Julia	JAN 10 1846
HERRITY, Mary	FLEMING, John	AUG 13 1821
HERRON, Eleanor	SULLIVAN, Owen	NOV 28 1845
HERRON, Eleanor	CALLAGHAN, Francis	MAY 11 1858
HERRON, John	PRENDEBLE, Johanna	NOV 09 1852
HERRON, Michael	McCRETE, Ellen	SEP 10 1851
HERSANT, M. Esperance	THOMPSON, Mary Cecilia	APR 21 1823

District of Columbia Marriage Licenses, 1811-1858

HERSE, Ann	POWER, Monticello	JAN 18 1827
HERSEY, Caroline	LOWE, Andrew	DEC 21 1837
HERSHLEY, Clement	ANDERSON, Cinderella J.	JUN 08 1852
HERSHLEY, Conrad	BARNES, Miranda Ann	NOV 05 1851
HERSTEL, William	ABERT, Catherine M.	AUG 15 1853
HERSTHAMP, Henrietta	HEITMULLER, Anthony	JUN 07 1851
HERTELL, Amelia Ernstina	BUNGER, Charles	APR 14 1835
HERTMAN, Catharine	REATHER, Robert	JAN 12 1833
HERVEY, Sarah	DONALDSON, Lewis	OCT 30 1816
HERZBERGER, Frederick	KOCK, Elizabeth	AUG 31 1855
HESCAMP, William	SHAFER, Mary	JUN 03 1834
HESHLEY, Clement	STACKS, Elizabeth	MAY 27 1842
HESHUNS, Mary	FLAHERTY, Patrick	SEP 06 1852
HESLER, Lawrence	SCHIFFER, Elizabeth	SEP 20 1841
HESLEY, Christopher	PAINE, Artima	AUG 26 1835
HESS, Cornelia	FINK, Casper	DEC 01 1836
HESS, Harret Ann	ANCHORS, John	MAR 30 1825
HESS, Jacob	PATTERSON, Lucinda	FEB 19 1839
HESS, John	RANSCH, Catharine	NOV 11 1833
HESS, Margt.	GOLBUCH, Constant	DEC 01 1856
HESSE, Eugene	GILDEMEISTER, Eliza	DEC 03 1849
HESSE, Louisa	GASZ, John G.	FEB 23 1843
HESSELBERG, Louisa	MANKIN, William	SEP 24 1847
HESSELIUS, Rachael B.	SMITH, Sidney W.	JUL 01 1830
HESSIAN, Mary	FLAHERTY, Patrick	APR 06 1855
HEST, Jacob	COOK, Martha	DEC 24 1832
HESTER, James W.	ADDISON, Eliza R.	JUN 12 1855
HESTON, Newton, Rev.	BEEK, Elizabeth S.	JAN 06 1847
HETCHISON, John	RIFFLE, Margaret	FEB 21 1831
HETHE, Mary	SHEAR, Francis	MAR 16 1858
HEUGHES, Arie Ann	GAITHER, Henry	DEC 24 1816
HEUS, John B.	ROLLINS, Eleanor	AUG 08 1843
HEVENINGHAM, Charles S.	DUCKWORTH, S. Cornelia	DEC 31 1849
HEWES, Ann	POINDEXTER, George [Sen.]	MAY 14 1832
HEWIT, Fanny	BOURGUENOT, Ferdinand	AUG 14 1854
HEWIT, Mary Ann	FOREMAN, George W.	AUG 01 1846
HEWITT, Catherine	BURCHE, Raymond Wilson	JAN 19 1848
HEWITT, Charles	DOWLING, Mary Ann	MAR 22 1856
HEWITT, Lavenia	WALLACH, Charles S.	FEB 28 1839
HEWITT, Mary B.	DOUBLEDAY, Abner	JAN 27 1852
HEWITT, Peter	MILLS, Mary Ann	OCT 11 1825
HEWITT, Robert	COOMBE, Ruhamah	DEC 06 1831
HEWITT, Robert C.C.	CRABBS, Ann M.	JUL 26 1858
HEWITT, Wm.	BURCH, Susan L.	DEC 29 1812
HEYBOYN, John	WILSON, Mary	JUL 14 1853
HEYDER, John Frederick	BAKER, Maria	MAR 24 1845
HEYDER, Leonora	KEYSER, John	JUN 12 1858
HEYER, Louisa F.	ZANTZINGER, William P.	OCT 07 1815
HEYL, William	HUMPHREY, Mary	MAY 16 1853
HEYLIGER, Louis	SELDEN, Maria L. (blk)	NOV 29 1848
HIATT, Elizh.	ROBERTSON, Stephen	APR 26 1814
HIBBS, J. Wesley	REED, Susan	NOV 09 1857
HICKERSON, Oscar B.	McDONALD, Mary E.	MAR 16 1853
HICKERSON, Wm. M.	WRIGHT, Adelaid	JUN 14 1844
HICKEY, Ann	AUD, James	FEB 09 1822
HICKEY, Honora	KELLY, James	MAY 06 1856
HICKEY, John	TAYLOR, Cecelia	DEC 09 1837
HICKEY, John W.	CARNEY, Delphia	JAN 05 1854

District of Columbia Marriage Licenses, 1811-1858

HICKEY, Mary	GLEESON, Thomas	SEP 01 1854
HICKEY, Mary	O'DEA, John	APR 02 1858
HICKEY, Mary Cecelia	FITZPATRICK, John C.	JUL 17 1827
HICKEY, Patrick W.	McGRANN, Bridget	APR 04 1853
HICKEY, Priscilla	FALKNY, Jacob	MAY 23 1816
HICKEY, Thomas	MURPHEY, Hannah	OCT 09 1851
HICKMAN, Catharine	CHAMBLAIN, John	JAN 08 1833
HICKMAN, Emma A.	PIPER, Henley	MAR 02 1857
HICKMAN, Joseph	SIMPSON, Jane	NOV 17 1841
HICKMAN, Wm. T.	COOLY, Margaret Ann	AUG 09 1855
HICKMEN, Jeremiah R.	FAIRALL, Sarah J.	MAY 02 1856
HICKMOTT, Silas	RUMERY, Jane	JAN 24 1854
HICKS, Ann (blk)	BROOKS, Clement	MAR 04 1844
HICKS, Ann V. (blk)	KING, Isaiah	MAR 05 1844
HICKS, Darcus [Mrs.]	GALVIN, Rodger	JUL 03 1816
HICKS, Edward	McFARLAND, Mary	FEB 14 1857
HICKS, Elizabeth	LUCAS, Francis	FEB 27 1849
HICKS, Elizabeth	ADMONSON, David	JUN 26 1849
HICKS, Elizabeth Ann (blk)	COOPER, William	NOV 10 1841
HICKS, Flora (blk)	DURHAM, Clayton	DEC 10 1839
HICKS, Francis	UNDERWOOD, Eliza	APR 09 1825
HICKS, George	FORD, Flora	MAY 13 1816
HICKS, George	HILLARD, Mary	AUG 21 1819
HICKS, Harriet	HERBERT, Annania	SEP 19 1843
HICKS, Henry	BARTON, Elizabeth (blk)	AUG 13 1841
HICKS, Horace	MAHORNEY, Susan	MAY 14 1835
HICKS, James	NEWTON, Margaret Ellen	NOV 26 1833
HICKS, John	BERRY, Elizabeth	MAY 22 1844
HICKS, John T.	ARMSTRONG, Elizabeth	NOV 03 1852
HICKS, Lloyd	JACKSON, Mullady	NOV 29 1844
HICKS, Mahaley	FOGLE, Jacob	NOV 17 1829
HICKS, Patsey	THOMAS, Thomas	OCT 05 1825
HICKS, Sarah	EDELIN, Joseph	MAY 14 1845
HICKS, Thomas	BOONE, Elizabeth Emily	SEP 21 1844
HICKS, Verlinda	RICHARDSON, Mark	DEC 07 1825
HICKS, Wade H.	TOOMBS, Letha	AUG 31 1858
HICKS, William	BROOKS, Louisa (blk)	JUN 07 1855
HICKS, William G.	JARDELLA, Josephine B.	OCT 20 1838
HICKSON, Anne E.	PALMER, John M.	SEP 10 1855
HICKSON, Rusia	BRANNAN, Arther	JAN 09 1840
HICKSON, William	KIERNAN, Mary Ann	MAR 10 1828
HICKY, Cyrus	JENKINS, Priscilla	OCT 08 1847
HIDE, Ann P.R.	CHANEY, Thomas	JUL 11 1842
HIDE, George, Junr.	JAMESSON, Martha	FEB 20 1827
HIERHOLZER, Mary V.	VOEGELE, Charles L.	SEP 13 1853
HIERLEHY, Margaret	FITZPATRICK, James	JUN 01 1836
HIERT, Catherine	SHAFER, Charles	FEB 25 1851
HIET, Christiana	WOOLFET, James	JAN 12 1822
HIFFLIN, Mary A.	FOX, Francis	MAR 06 1848
HIGBY, Edward T.	HENLEY, Frances L.	DEC 11 1837
HIGBY, John W.	BLACK, Polly	APR 29 1813
HIGBY, Polly	PRITCHARD, Samuel	FEB 21 1818
HIGDEN, Ann	HILL, Giles	JUN 27 1817
HIGDEN, John	FRENCH, Nancy	NOV 04 1826
HIGDEN, Louisa	HIGDEN, Thomas	OCT 19 1826
HIGDEN, Thomas	HIGDEN, Louisa	OCT 19 1826
HIGDON, Alethy	HOLLENBACK, Enner	DEC 22 1814
HIGDON, Ann Eliza	ROBEY, John	NOV 23 1847

District of Columbia Marriage Licenses, 1811-1858

HIGDON, Eleanor	COLGLAZIER, Jacob	MAR 31 1812
HIGDON, Eleanor	BARTLY, James	OCT 25 1815
HIGDON, Ellen	CLEMENTS, Francis H.	JUN 11 1838
HIGDON, Gustavus	ROGERS, Elizabeth	MAR 28 1812
HIGDON, Harriet	DeVAUGHN, James	MAR 14 1830
HIGDON, Margaret	CALLAN, James	NOV 22 1851
HIGDON, Mary Ann	GRIMES, Michael	NOV 25 1833
HIGDON, Mary Ann	WATSON, Henry B.	APR 17 1837
HIGDON, Mary E.	SIMMES, John H.	MAR 06 1854
HIGDON, Polly	BAKER, James	OCT 21 1812
HIGDON, Rebecca	MARTIN, Richard	JAN 14 1814
HIGDON, Susan	HOWARD, James	JUL 02 1844
HIGDON, Thomas	OSBOURN, Susan	AUG 13 1828
HIGGENS, Artakerxes	WILSON, Sarah Ann Susan	APR 28 1835
HIGGIN, Catharine (blk)	CRAVEN, Philip	JUL 10 1849
HIGGIN, James	FARNAM, Elizabeth	JUN 01 1818
HIGGINS, Bridget	CROWLEY, Michael	JAN 04 1851
HIGGINS, Catherine	TINSLEY, James	MAY 01 1856
HIGGINS, David	KING, Letitia W.	OCT 01 1847
HIGGINS, Elijah H.	DUNNIN, Mary A.	MAY 08 1855
HIGGINS, Elizabeth	HARRISON, Benjamin	APR 27 1844
HIGGINS, Ellen	FLEMMON, Patrick	JAN 07 1857
HIGGINS, Eudora	VICK, Bushrod W.	SEP 14 1854
HIGGINS, Hellen	FLEMING, Patrick	JAN 15 1856
HIGGINS, John	BLANY, Mary	FEB 05 1856
HIGGINS, John Hamilton	BARNARD, Sophia Dorothy	MAY 06 1848
HIGGINS, Michael	O'DONNELL, Margaret	APR 12 1826
HIGGINS, Samuel	SOPER, Eliza Ann	MAY 26 1855
HIGGINS, William	GIBBONS, Isabella	AUG 24 1850
HIGGS, Benj. F.	ROWLES, Sarah	FEB 13 1816
HIGHLAND, Magdalina	ALBRIGHT, Leonard	JUN 14 1853
HIGHT, Joseph	SHILTON, Martha (blk)	FEB 16 1853
HIGHTAFFER, Mary L.	ROUS, John G.	FEB 06 1857
HILAND, James	DELANY, Catherine	OCT 29 1832
HILBRON, Nathan W.	O'NEALE, Mary Ann	FEB 21 1855
HILBUS, Caroline	OUSLEY, John	APR 08 1833
HILBUS, George	EARLE, Mary	MAY 26 1849
HILBUS, Sarah Ann	SCHUL, John E.	DEC 23 1841
HILDNER, Jacob	CLINE, Catharine	JUL 18 1855
HILDT, Arabella W.	WALKER, Charles E.	JAN 06 1857
HILDT, George [Rev.]	STUBS, Harriot	MAR 21 1833
HILESHIMER, Susan	GRIFFIN, Thomas	DEC 26 1812
HILGARD, Jules E.	CLEMENTS, Catherine S.	AUG 28 1848
HILIARD, Eliza	FENWICK, Richd. Washington	OCT 05 1826
HILL, Adaline	HEAD, William H.	APR 18 1839
HILL, Ann	DUNKELL, Henry	FEB 27 1812
HILL, Ann	ISAACS, George W.	JUN 20 1827
HILL, Ann	LEBO, Henry	JAN 08 1839
HILL, Ann Elizabeth	BONTZ, John	JUN 13 1849
HILL, Caroline	LARNER, Thomas	MAY 04 1848
HILL, Caroline (blk)	WILLIAMS, Jacob	FEB 10 1858
HILL, Catherine (blk)	FREEMAN, Benj.	MAY 29 1835
HILL, Cenisha	MOORE, Robert B.	APR 01 1839
HILL, Charity	BRANNAN, Wilson	MAR 25 1823
HILL, Charity (blk)	PARKER, William	FEB 03 1858
HILL, Charles	BOTELER, Mary (blk)	JUL 20 1848
HILL, Charles J.	DUNKBY, Martha Ann	OCT 13 1832
HILL, Charlotte	GALT, Thomas	NOV 04 1843

District of Columbia Marriage Licenses, 1811-1858

HILL, Edward	HOLLY, Phebe (blk)	JAN 31 1838
HILL, Edward	WOODWARD, Sophia (blk)	AUG 30 1856
HILL, Elizabeth	DAVIS, George	JUL 22 1815
HILL, Elizabeth	BAUM, Charles	JUN 12 1832
HILL, Elizabeth	CREAMER, James	APR 07 1845
HILL, Elizabeth Ann	TUCKER, Sylas	FEB 22 1849
HILL, Ellen Ann	LEE, John F.	APR 29 1845
HILL, Emeline	FINNEY, Alexander	FEB 17 1853
HILL, Francis	BENNETT, Margaret	NOV 18 1815
HILL, George W.	LEE, Mary Jane	JUL 09 1850
HILL, Georgie	BEALL, Jackson	OCT 01 1855
HILL, Gibson F.	McDANIEL, Mary Ann	OCT 22 1829
HILL, Giles	HIGDEN, Ann	JUN 27 1817
HILL, Gustavus	HENLEY, Catharine	APR 25 1834
HILL, Haley Ann	LINKINS, Francis	DEC 26 1851
HILL, Harriet	JACKSON, John Thos. Jefferson	JAN 19 1836
HILL, Henry	HILL, Sarah (blk)	MAY 07 1829
HILL, Isaac	CLEMENTS, Johanna	AUG 22 1831
HILL, James	PENNIFILL, Leander	JUN 05 1857
HILL, James N.	WATSON, Sarah Ann	SEP 02 1852
HILL, Jane	HARROCKS, George	AUG 01 1820
HILL, Jane	RICKETTS, William	APR 17 1830
HILL, Jane	BELL, Hanson	DEC 16 1847
HILL, John	KEMP, Catherine	FEB 16 1826
HILL, John	KILL, Airy	JUN 28 1828
HILL, John	PENIFIELD, Ann	MAY 24 1834
HILL, John	GEORGE, Martha	FEB 25 1852
HILL, John	ROBINSON, Mary	JUN 28 1853
HILL, Jno. Hy.	JACKSON, Lucinda	DEC 20 1844
HILL, Jonathan	SWANN, Lucinda B.	JAN 13 1829
HILL, Joseph H.	CARMODY, Avus	MAY 11 1858
HILL, Lewis	HARRIS, Eleanor (blk)	JAN 11 1831
HILL, Linny	HOUSER, William	NOV 13 1834
HILL, Margaret	BOOZE, Erasmus	MAR 01 1851
HILL, Margaret	HITAFFER, Thomas	MAR 21 1853
HILL, Margaret	CRONIN, John	MAY 21 1855
HILL, Maria	WRIGHT, F.B.	MAY 29 1833
HILL, Maria	JONES, Thomas	MAY 27 1840
HILL, Martha	TARTESON, Alexander	AUG 18 1816
HILL, Martha (blk)	SNOWDEN, Garden	SEP 19 1842
HILL, Martha A.	BERRY, John	OCT 19 1857
HILL, Mary	STALLANGS, Benjamin	MAR 02 1824
HILL, Mary	BIRD, Benjamin	DEC 13 1827
HILL, Mary	GATES, William	DEC 09 1847
HILL, Mary A.	LIGHTELLE, William E.	AUG 15 1838
HILL, Mary Ann	BURNETT, Richard	JUN 03 1844
HILL, Mary E.	CLEMENTS, Joseph E.	DEC 24 1850
HILL, Mary Jane	LYDDANE, William	JUN 11 1853
HILL, Matilda	HARDY, William G.	MAY 19 1851
HILL, Nancy	ATWOOD, James	FEB 06 1817
HILL, Nancy Ann	KERSEY, Daniel	DEC 06 1815
HILL, Phoebe (blk)	LINDSLEY, Charles	MAR 26 1842
HILL, Prudence	SPENCER, Benjamin	OCT 07 1829
HILL, Richard	BUCKINGHAM, Virginia (blk)	JAN 30 1854
HILL, Richard T.	FENWICK, Eliza A.	JAN 17 1854
HILL, Robert	McPHERSON, Jane (blk)	DEC 26 1853
HILL, Robert Park	McGARVEY, Jane	MAY 02 1850
HILL, Samuel	SHELTON, Catharine E.	MAR 07 1844

District of Columbia Marriage Licenses, 1811-1858

HILL, Sandy	LANGLY, Mary	APR 03 1825
HILL, Sarah	LUNT, Eza	FEB 20 1830
HILL, Sarah (blk)	HILL, Henry	MAY 07 1829
HILL, Silas H.	VARNUM, Mary B.	SEP 22 1835
HILL, Stephen P. [Rev.]	CORCORAN, Martha Ellen	DEC 08 1835
HILL, Washington	COOK, Adeline	MAR 28 1839
HILL, William	AMBROSE, Elizabeth	MAY 03 1831
HILL, William	DALEY, Catharine	SEP 14 1832
HILL, William	DREW, Alice	SEP 05 1835
HILL, William	CHAMBERS, Elenda	NOV 17 1838
HILL, William	MAHER, Margaret	JUN 15 1843
HILL, William B.	SMITH, Catherine B.	MAY 12 1835
HILLARD, Mary	HICKS, George	AUG 21 1819
HILLARY, Ary Ann	BEANES, Colmore	DEC 01 1815
HILLARY, John B.	WOLTZ, Susana	MAY 25 1833
HILLARY, Theodore Williams	WILSON, Malinda	MAR 22 1820
HILLARY, William H.	RAY, Ann C.	JAN 07 1858
HILLEARY, Catherine	CLAMPITT, William H.	JAN 28 1836
HILLEARY, Elijah	FREEMAN, Eleanor	AUG 18 1820
HILLEARY, John W.	WALKER, Sarah Virginia	DEC 30 1851
HILLEARY, Mary Ann	CALLENBURG, Francis	OCT 17 1837
HILLEARY, Theodore	HUTCHINS, Eliza Jane	AUG 31 1850
HILLEARY, Walter	WYMSICK, Mary	SEP 26 1843
HILLEGEIST, Frederick G.	SEITZ, Hermiae	JUL 11 1857
HILLER, Ann Sophia	GRAHAM, Robert H.	APR 05 1854
HILLER, John	BERRY, Sarah	OCT 12 1829
HILLER, Sarah	WELLS, Cornelius	NOV 08 1839
HILLERY, Charlotte	COSTIN, George	MAR 24 1834
HILLERY, Maria	McLEAN, William Hector	DEC 31 1835
HILLERY, Mary	SCHEELY, Augustus	JUL 07 1857
HILLIARD, Lucy E.	WALKER, W.E.	MAY 08 1856
HILLIARD, Mary W.	HOLMES, Philip H.	JAN 31 1852
HILLIARY, Adelia M.	ROBEY, Dorsett	DEC 08 1849
HILLORIN, Catharine	BOYLE, Thomas	FEB 05 1856
HILLS, Eudocia Gilston	MULLIN, Lewis	APR 17 1843
HILLS, Saml.	GIRD, Eudocia [Mrs.]	FEB 05 1823
HILLS, Thomas O.	SERGEANT, Helen V.	AUG 12 1857
HILLYARD, Benjamin F.	SAUTER, Mary P.	JUN 28 1858
HILLYARD, Sarah E.	FENWICK, Robert W.	JAN 05 1825
HILTON, Alphonsus L.R.	ANDERSON, Sarah Ellen	JUL 12 1850
HILTON, Amanda A.	WITHERON, James M.	JAN 20 1857
HILTON, Ann Elizabeth	THOMPSON, William J.	MAR 15 1848
HILTON, Edward	WARRENFORD, Eliza	DEC 25 1844
HILTON, Harriot E.	THOMPSON, James E.W.	JUL 16 1831
HILTON, Jno. E.S.	RANDUM, Martha Ann	MAY 24 1855
HILTON, John P.	ROUZEE, Elizabeth	APR 19 1836
HILTON, John T.	STEWART, Eliza A.	NOV 30 1855
HILTON, Joseph H.	CARR, Julia Ann	NOV 30 1843
HILTON, Joseph H.	CARR, Julia A.	MAY 14 1844
HILTON, Martha Jane	WINTHROW, Lawrence M.	NOV 07 1844
HILTON, Mary	MORROW, Francis	NOV 09 1842
HILTON, Mary A.W.	HARRINGTON, Richd. H.	FEB 10 1824
HILTON, Mary Ann	DAVIS, Samuel	SEP 08 1831
HILTON, Perry Green	SPARROW, Harriet	OCT 28 1819
HILTON, Saml. N.	ATCHISON, Mary E.	SEP 25 1855
HILTON, Sarah E.	STEWART, Leonard W.	DEC 20 1851
HILTON, Thomas	HUNT, Mary R. [Mrs.]	DEC 01 1821
HILTON, Thomas	CHURCHMAN, Elizabeth	JAN 17 1844

District of Columbia Marriage Licenses, 1811-1858

HILTON, Uriah D.	LECKRON, Caroline C.	FEB 25 1857
HILTON, William	SMITH, Ann Elizth.	MAR 09 1849
HILTON, William E.	WILLING, Mary Jane	DEC 24 1846
HILTZEL, Nicholas	KEPLEY, Mary A.	MAY 30 1836
HILYARD, John J.	KIERNAN, Christena	MAY 18 1824
HINANT, Garvy	ATTRIDGE, Elizabeth	JUL 02 1842
HINCHMAN, Adeline	POWER, Joseph	APR 07 1832
HINDMAN, Virginia H.	SOUTHARD, James W.	MAY 08 1855
HINDS, Mary Ann	CUTHBERT, James	JAN 04 1830
HINELINE, Thomas H.	SIMMONS, Julia Ann	JUL 23 1858
HINES, Abraham	BOWEN, Eleanor	DEC 19 1815
HINES, Abram F.	FICKETT, Sarah A.	JUN 19 1851
HINES, Berlinda	MORRIS, John	JUL 19 1830
HINES, Betsey (blk)	KAIN, Henry	OCT 01 1828
HINES, Catherine	HERBERT, Andrew	JUL 28 1856
HINES, Christian M.	BOHRER, Augusta M.	JUL 11 1854
HINES, David	RHEEM, Christiana	SEP 19 1846
HINES, Edward	BROWN, Louisa	AUG 16 1828
HINES, Elizabeth	BUTTNER, William G.	JUL 15 1835
HINES, Elizabeth (blk)	WILLIAMS, Daniel	JUL 09 1850
HINES, Frederick	CURAND, Christiana	JAN 04 1817
HINES, Jacob	TAYLOR, Rachel	APR 25 1837
HINES, James	CONNER, Margaret	AUG 24 1852
HINES, Joanna R.	HEINECKE, Samuel	NOV 04 1828
HINES, John B.	CUNNINGHAM, Lydia A.	JUN 15 1853
HINES, Letitia	WEAVER, William	JUL 04 1838
HINES, Mary	SHARLIN, Cornelius	JUN 20 1857
HINES, Philip	HOWARD, Julia Ann	MAY 27 1826
HINES, Rachel (blk)	BELL, John	NOV 02 1854
HINES, Samuel	WATSON, Martha	AUG 18 1827
HINES, Sarah A.N.	BARKER, James W.	AUG 22 1843
HINES, Thomas	JOYCE, Julia	JAN 16 1857
HINES, William T.	THOMPSON, Kate L.	JAN 17 1856
HINEZ, Elizabeth	CRAFT, Samuel	APR 06 1825
HINEZEL, George	BENDER, Maria	NOV 20 1838
HINGERTY, Pheba	FORD, William	AUG 31 1825
HINGETY, Elizabeth	WEBSTER, Thomas	SEP 01 1823
HINGITY, Alfred	HOWARD, Mary Jane	JUN 13 1834
HINGLE, Margaret	MAY, John	NOV 16 1854
HINKLE, John	READ, Margaret	FEB 14 1818
HINKLE, Philip	GAITHER, Martha	DEC 18 1850
HINRAHAN, Honora	DOWNEY, Patrick	JAN 26 1855
HINTEN, Chloe Ann	KUHNS, Andrew	OCT 03 1851
HINTON, Addison C.	FORSTER, Annie S.	OCT 03 1836
HINTON, Amelia	SCRIVENER, Samuel	JUL 22 1823
HINTON, Angeline	McINTOSH, Job P.	APR 10 1850
HINTON, Ann	NALLEY, Levi	JAN 17 1839
HINTON, George	PICKETT, Catherine Jane	NOV 21 1839
HINTON, John	BEAUCHAMP, Harriett	JAN 29 1829
HINTON, Mary Ann	GUNNELL, Henry D.	FEB 01 1854
HINTON, Robert	RATCLIFFE, Emeline	MAR 29 1838
HINTON, Robert William	MILBURN, Mary Ann	MAR 30 1843
HINTON, Sarah	PUMPHREY, Lewis	JUL 05 1839
HINTON, William	CALWHITE, Cassy	MAR 01 1838
HINZERLING, George	MILLER, Christiana	AUG 02 1853
HIPBURN, Moses	BRADDOCK, Amelia	MAY 26 1827
HIPKINS, Cecelia J.	DONN, Oliver P.	JUL 04 1848
HIPKINS, John L.	COMPTON, Martha	DEC 24 1849

District of Columbia Marriage Licenses, 1811-1858

HIRCH, Beattie	COUFMAN, Elias	SEP 10 1857
HIRD, Fidel	EDLE, Maria	NOV 28 1853
HIRMER, Teresa	STEGMAIER, Michael	OCT 30 1855
HIRSCH, Conrad	MOLLER, Elizabeth	APR 02 1833
HIRST, Sarah	MERCHANT, Archibald	AUG 28 1815
HIRT, Anna	HASLANGER, William	AUG 29 1857
HIRT, Sophia B.	STREP, Louis	AUG 30 1853
HIRTH, Philip	RAPP, Margaret	DEC 13 1856
HISHLEY, Cecelia	McFALL, James	NOV 18 1857
HISHLY, Clement	PAYNE, Ann	DEC 21 1854
HITAFFER, James R.	COLUMBUS, Mary L.	APR 27 1853
HITAFFER, Thomas	HILL, Margaret	MAR 21 1853
HITCHCOCK, Alfred J.	HUTCHINS, Martha E.	AUG 09 1858
HITCHCOCK, Josiah	TURNER, Catharine A.	AUG 05 1850
HITCHCOCK, Robert J.	LINDSAY, Rachel	FEB 13 1843
HITCHCOCK, Robert J.	LINDSLEY, Rachel	JUN 25 1847
HITCHCOCK, Thomas	BURCH, Sarah Ann	NOV 16 1847
HITCHCOX, Michael M.	HAWKINS, Columbia V.	NOV 08 1851
HITCHEN, John H.	CUMMINGS, Naomi	APR 08 1856
HITCHINGS, Mary Ann	VanDEUSEN, William A.	JAN 31 1854
HITCHINS, William	HOGANS, Amelia (blk)	NOV 06 1849
HITCHISON, Sarah	JOY, Thomas	APR 04 1848
HITE, Jesse	DUNLAP, Sarah Ann	MAY 07 1857
HITMAN, Elsey	BUSEY, Hezekiah	OCT 16 1822
HITZ, Anna Magdalena	CAPRETS, Jeremias	OCT 28 1846
HITZ, Christiane	HITZ, Florian	MAY 07 1838
HITZ, Christina	CASPARIS, James F.	DEC 11 1845
HITZ, Florian	HITZ, Christiane	MAY 07 1838
HITZ, Florian	DOLF, Susanna	NOV 27 1857
HITZ, George	WETZEL, Lucy	NOV 27 1857
HITZ, Madeline	KINCHEY, Paul	NOV 07 1843
HITZ, Margaret	SCHEITLIN, Jacob	MAY 18 1853
HIXON, Amanda Virginia	WALLING, Jacob W.	JUN 01 1854
HIXON, Jonathan W.	CASTEL, Mary	AUG 23 1830
HIXSON, Matilda	MOSS, Theodore	MAY 10 1832
HIZER, James	ORME, Elizabeth	SEP 06 1854
HOAG, Sheldon J.	COXEN, Ann	OCT 20 1853
HOBAN, Ann R.	FORD, Stephen C.	APR 11 1831
HOBAN, Edward	WILLIAMS, Mary Ann	DEC 31 1832
HOBAN, James, Jr.	FRENCH, Marion Blackwell	NOV 22 1831
HOBAN, Mary Ann	SCRIVENER, Charles	APR 17 1837
HOBBIE, Barbara (blk)	JOHNSON, Samuel	JUN 04 1847
HOBBIE, Elizabeth	McCLEARY, Edwin J.	DEC 10 1847
HOBBIE, Julia	JAMES, Charles A.	MAY 15 1856
HOBBIE, Mary D.	REEVE, Nathan S.	JAN 19 1854
HOBBS, Adeline T.	McGUIGGAN, Arthur J.	MAY 13 1857
HOBBS, Ann	BREWER, Thomas	SEP 06 1838
HOBBS, Edward S.	BEASLEY, Fanny A.	APR 07 1858
HOBBS, Eleanor	BENNETT, Rezin	NOV 07 1846
HOBBS, Kitty	BRISON, James	AUG 09 1821
HOBBS, Mary E.	WALL, Columbus O.	JAN 22 1852
HOBERT, Mary	ANELUG, Christian	JUN 05 1844
HOBSON, Owen H.	BADGER, Harriet M.	SEP 01 1849
HOBSON, Richard V.	BOSLEY, Laura J.	FEB 24 1857
HOBSON, Sally	BAILY, Albert	NOV 04 1817
HOBURG, Amelia	GALLANT, Peter	JAN 17 1843
HOBURG, Sophia	SOUTHERLAND, George W.	NOV 20 1838
HOCH, Anna Maria	KOEHLER, Johannes	MAR 30 1854

District of Columbia Marriage Licenses, 1811-1858

HOCKERMAN, Henry	STEVENS, Elzey	DEC 31 1850
HODEN, Thomas	WILSON, Ann	MAY 07 1816
HODGE, Anna (blk)	SIMMS, George	SEP 25 1849
HODGE, Annie	RODGERS, John, U.S.N.	NOV 25 1857
HODGE, Betsey	BROWN, Abraham	APR 13 1844
HODGE, Emma	BEEDLE, Andrew F.	FEB 06 1851
HODGE, Margaret	WOODS, John	MAY 18 1820
HODGE, Mary Ann	JONES, Elexius	JAN 26 1826
HODGE, Nancy	WHITE, Thomas	DEC 22 1813
HODGES, Ann	KELLEY, James	MAY 09 1846
HODGES, Benjamin	WALLINGSFORD, Eliza	MAR 28 1836
HODGES, Benjamin T.	RILEY, Elizabeth W.	MAY 31 1852
HODGES, Bridget	DONOVAN, John	SEP 10 1856
HODGES, Catharine Jane	CROSSFIELD, James	JUN 08 1836
HODGES, Catherine N.	BEATTY, Robert M.	FEB 07 1854
HODGES, Eliza M.	CROSSFIELD, William E.	SEP 29 1834
HODGES, George W.	CROSSFIELD, Josephine C.	DEC 24 1850
HODGES, James	TASE, Mary	FEB 07 1839
HODGES, Joseph	JETT, Elizabeth J.	AUG 28 1854
HODGKIN, Henrietta	KIDWELL, James	MAR 06 1819
HODGKIN, Lizzie S.	ALEXANDER, John R.	JUL 01 1858
HODGKIN, Malinda	TUCKER, Samuel	SEP 12 1816
HODGKIN, Samuel	THOMPSON, Ann	JUN 24 1824
HODGKINS, Elizabeth Amanda	OFFUTT, Marion	AUG 29 1851
HODGKINS, George W.	NEWTON, Mary E.	MAR 31 1849
HODGKINSON, Mary T.	DONOVAN, James	FEB 23 1855
HODGSKIN, Elizth.	ASHFERD, Thos.	JAN 25 1823
HODGSKIN, Mary Jane	OLIVER, Thomas	OCT 24 1849
HODGSON, Catharine E.	McCLELLAND, John, Jr.	JAN 07 1845
HODGSON, Franzoni	BIRCH, Thomas	NOV 05 1834
HODGSON, Harriett H.	DENNISON, John T.	JAN 01 1850
HODGSON, John	MUNROE, Margaret	SEP 03 1812
HODGSON, John W.	BARON, Ellen	DEC 14 1840
HODGSON, Joseph F.	HANDLEY, Mary J.	SEP 19 1850
HODGSON, Julia Angela	LORENTZ, Jacob Alexander	APR 19 1847
HODGSON, Mary V.	VANNATAR, Louis G.F.	DEC 31 1856
HODGSON, Susan	BIRCH, George Azariah	MAY 08 1838
HODSKIN, Nancy Ann	WESTERFIELD, David	SEP 04 1838
HODSON, Dillon	DIXON, Priscilla	NOV 10 1812
HODSON, Mary	BUTLER, Henry	NOV 01 1845
HODSON, Mary	LAWTON, Joseph	FEB 19 1848
HODSON, William	PYWELL, Jane W.	DEC 30 1846
HOEFLICH, Isaac C.	BARKER, Rebecca	DEC 30 1856
HOEHN, Nette	FEGLER, John	NOV 04 1854
HOENSTINE, Frederick	POSTON, Rahine	APR 28 1834
HOFBAUER, Mary A.	SCHEHRER, John C.	MAY 08 1851
HOFFMAN, Catharine M.	GOUPP, Gottlieb H.	APR 15 1850
HOFFMAN, Catherine	ENGEL, Thieleman	JUN 10 1848
HOFFMAN, Charles E.	MYERS, Mary E.A.	JUL 19 1855
HOFFMAN, Eliza	SCHREIBER, John W.A.	SEP 04 1852
HOFFMAN, Elizabeth	PEGNER, Peter	NOV 09 1833
HOFFMAN, Frederick	CARLIN, Anne	AUG 16 1815
HOFFMAN, George W.	REED, Jane L.	SEP 15 1849
HOFFMAN, Henry	MOORE, Mary Ann	AUG 24 1850
HOFFMAN, Henry B.	RICARD, Ann E.	MAY 05 1858
HOFFMAN, Jacob	MASSI, Ann	JUN 30 1845
HOFFMAN, Jane	SPARROW, John	DEC 23 1851
HOFFMAN, Joanna	MILLER, Jacob	AUG 27 1849

District of Columbia Marriage Licenses, 1811-1858

HOFFMAN, John D.	MITCHELL, Mary W.	FEB 21 1855
HOFFMAN, John H.	DISHER, Martha	AUG 31 1854
HOFFMAN, John P.	ALLEN, Matilda	JAN 27 1814
HOFFMAN, Magdalen Eva	BROWNING, John Henry	NOV 16 1843
HOFFMAN, Malinda B.	HULSEMAN, Bernard H.	DEC 26 1843
HOFFMAN, Margaret	FOLDZ, George Jacob	MAR 25 1848
HOFFMAN, Mathias	FAUGHMAN, Dorothy	FEB 24 1854
HOFFMAN, Matilda	BRIGGS, Andrew	JAN 09 1819
HOFFMAN, Richard	WARD, Catharine A.	SEP 03 1840
HOFFMEISTER, George	TOFFER, Elizabeth	JUN 19 1855
HOFFMEISTER, Mary	BALLMAN, John H.	MAY 17 1855
HOFHEINS, Jacob	SCHÜTTE, Caroline	JUN 10 1856
HOFMAN, Wolfgan	COX, Marion	NOV 18 1851
HOFMANN, Sarah Louisa	KURTZ, Benjamin	JUN 10 1858
HOG, Sophia	BAKER, William	JUN 20 1857
HOG, Wm.	KEMP, Mary	AUG 24 1822
HOGAN, Catharine	CAVNAUGH, John	AUG 11 1836
HOGAN, Catharine	CONNOR, Daniel	JUL 23 1853
HOGAN, Catherine	BRYNE, Patrick	MAR 07 1848
HOGAN, Edmund	SHEAHAN, Mary	MAR 07 1848
HOGAN, Eliza	BROWN, John	JUL 17 1855
HOGAN, Honora	DOOLEY, Michael	OCT 28 1850
HOGAN, Margaret	RENAHAN, Martin	AUG 12 1837
HOGAN, Margaret	BUCKLEY, Timothy	DEC 09 1844
HOGAN, Mary	BARRY, John	JUL 24 1858
HOGAN, Patrick	McCORMACK, Mary Ann	FEB 23 1852
HOGAN, Peter	JACKSON, Laura	OCT 07 1856
HOGAN, Philip	COURTNEY, Mary	MAY 02 1851
HOGAN, Sarah [Mrs.]	MOORE, James, Senr.	FEB 27 1832
HOGAN, Sarah	GORMAN, Michael	JUL 29 1854
HOGAN, Thomas	MAHONEY, Joanna	OCT 18 1849
HOGAN, William	HOLMEAD, Cornelia Virginia	SEP 09 1845
HOGANS, Amelia (blk)	HITCHINS, William	NOV 06 1849
HOGANS, John	DAWSON, Mary Ann (blk)	JAN 05 1850
HOGANS, John	DORSEY, Mary Ann (blk)	NOV 02 1850
HOGANS, Rachel (blk)	BOWEN, Fielder	APR 11 1837
HOGG, Eliza J.	BODIEN, Henry A.	MAR 22 1856
HOGG, James	WOODS, Mary Ann	OCT 23 1829
HOGG, John W.	DOW, Sarah E.	JAN 26 1852
HOGLIN, Rachael	ROBEY, Zachariah	MAY 29 1819
HOGMIRE, A. Isabella	GILLETT, L. Warrington	MAY 11 1840
HOGSETT, Josiah T.	SLAVEN, Martha J.	DEC 02 1854
HOGSKIN, John	RITCHIE, Elizabeth	JUL 08 1824
HÖHING, Mary A.	LEFLER, Philip	NOV 30 1852
HOHMANN, Carl	ARNOLD, Margretha	DEC 07 1852
HOIT, Rebecca	RISTON, Henry	SEP 19 1816
HOLAN, Ann	DEMPSEY, Moses	MAY 15 1858
HOLAND, Martha Ann	SMITH, William L.H.	SEP 07 1846
HOLAND, William E.	WILKINSON, Elizabeth	OCT 11 1850
HOLBERT, Rachael	BASSET, Assel	MAR 18 1819
HOLBROOK, Charles F.	CHANCEY, Lydia A.	AUG 01 1857
HOLBROOK, Eleanor	HARLEY, Noah	SEP 02 1818
HOLBROOK, John	GLADDEN, Susan	AUG 22 1846
HOLBROOK, John Thompson	JOHNSON, Nancy	MAY 15 1823
HOLBROOK, Susan E.	SULLIVAN, Jeremiah	JAN 29 1824
HOLBROOKS, Nancy	BUTLER, Malon	AUG 04 1835
HOLCOMB, Albert A., U.S.N.	WATTERSTON, Sara M.	JUN 06 1841
HOLD, James	GILLESPIE, Hannah	APR 13 1822

District of Columbia Marriage Licenses, 1811-1858

HOLLAN, Charles T.	QUINN, Catherine	FEB 06 1857
HOLLAND, Angelica P.	HACKER, William A.	AUG 26 1848
HOLLAND, Angelina B.	BERRY, Albert M.	JUL 20 1843
HOLLAND, Charles	FRANKLIN, Phillis	DEC 25 1815
HOLLAND, Eleanor Ann	CAROTHERS, Andrew	SEP 07 1842
HOLLAND, Elias	ELIS, Verlinda	SEP 28 1826
HOLLAND, Eliza Ann	EYRE, Henry	DEC 17 1856
HOLLAND, Elizth. R.	LAURY, Joseph S.	MAR 13 1832
HOLLAND, H.A.	HARVEY, G.W.	MAR 21 1849
HOLLAND, Isaac	DISNEY, Elizabeth	JAN 02 1838
HOLLAND, James	GRIMES, Elizabeth	FEB 20 1841
HOLLAND, James S.	GRANT, Elizabeth Jane	DEC 03 1839
HOLLAND, John E.	WATERS, Susannah	SEP 13 1836
HOLLAND, Louisa (blk)	LEVI, John	NOV 06 1828
HOLLAND, Mary Ellen	SNYDER, Albert M.	MAR 12 1855
HOLLAND, Rebecca F.	SYMINGTON, William H.	JUN 11 1844
HOLLAND, Robert	GRAY, Louisa	JUN 04 1857
HOLLAND, Thomas	DOWDY, Mary Jane	JUN 20 1838
HOLLANG, John	HARDY, Christina	DEC 20 1855
HOLLENBACK, Enner	HIGDON, Alethy	DEC 22 1814
HOLLENBACK, William	FORD, Sarah	NOV 08 1815
HOLLEY, Catharine	GRIMSLEY, Elias	AUG 07 1813
HOLLEY, Elizabeth	ROBERTSON, Saml.	MAY 29 1813
HOLLEY, James E.	HOLLISTER, Emeline L.	JAN 11 1855
HOLLEY, Leannah	JOHNSON, Charles	AUG 02 1830
HOLLEY, Margt.	VALLOR, Thomas	JAN 08 1857
HOLLEY, Mary	COLE, Elias	MAY 09 1818
HOLLEY, Mary Ann (blk)	LOWDEN, William	NOV 28 1832
HOLLEY, Reuben	DOUGLASS, Martha Ann (blk)	NOV 08 1853
HOLLIDA, Kasira	JENKINS, Charles	JAN 02 1841
HOLLIDAY, Henry	JONES, Mary	MAR 18 1841
HOLLIDAY, Samuel H.	GRAHAM, Adeline	MAY 03 1852
HOLLIDAY, William L.	PERRY, Ruth	APR 26 1833
HOLLIDGE, Annie	TALKS, Jacob	APR 12 1858
HOLLIDGE, Eliza	SENTIS, Mathew	DEC 17 1842
HOLLIDGE, Martha Eliza	LANGE, John	NOV 18 1854
HOLLINGSWORTH, Henry	O'BRIEN, Eliza	APR 29 1837
HOLLINGSWORTH, Wm. W.	DONN, Lavina D.	OCT 02 1854
HOLLINS, Mary (blk)	MUNROE, Daniel	AUG 21 1856
HOLLINSWORTH, Jepther S.	O'NEAL, Susan M.	DEC 06 1852
HOLLISTER, Emeline L.	HOLLEY, James E.	JAN 11 1855
HOLLISTY, Chas.	THROCKMORTON, Hannah (blk)	APR 03 1856
HOLLOEAN, Margaret	SHOUGHROUGH, James	MAR 23 1850
HOLLOHAN, Jno.	BRIEN, Mary	MAR 22 1856
HOLLOHAN, John T.	SMITH, Eliza	JUN 27 1850
HOLLOHAN, Mary	BROWN, Patrick	JUN 28 1856
HOLLY, Harriet	HONESTY, Daniel	SEP 17 1840
HOLLY, Phebe (blk)	HILL, Edward	JAN 31 1838
HOLLYDAY, James E.	YOUNG, Amelia	SEP 21 1837
HOLMEAD, Anthony	WEBSTER, Mary C.	MAY 06 1822
HOLMEAD, Anthony, Jr.	SMITH, Elizabeth	MAY 04 1847
HOLMEAD, Cornelia Virginia	HOGAN, William	SEP 09 1845
HOLMEAD, Emeline W.	PHILLIPS, John H.	OCT 19 1846
HOLMEAD, Emily V.	JAMES, John Dawson	NOV 01 1831
HOLMEAD, James B.	STETTINIUS, Susan	OCT 02 1817
HOLMEAD, Jane Matilda	HELM, Joseph	SEP 04 1832
HOLMEAD, John B.	PAIRO, Jane J.	OCT 12 1830
HOLMEAD, Mary Ellen	JAMES, Charles H.	JAN 09 1837

District of Columbia Marriage Licenses, 1811-1858

HOLMEAD, Rosina M.	HARTE, Edward	MAR 29 1847
HOLMEAD, Susanna J.M.	CALLAN, Christopher C.	FEB 10 1858
HOLMEAD, William	SEARS, Cordelia E.	JAN 16 1837
HOLMEAD, William	ESLIN, Mary Ann	MAY 10 1847
HOLMES, Eleanor (blk)	LIVERPOOL, John	JUL 15 1830
HOLMES, Elizabeth	KUHNIRD, John A.	NOV 10 1855
HOLMES, Fountain	TAYLOR, Alocy Ann D.	FEB 15 1830
HOLMES, Julia C.	GORDON, Charles V.	JUL 01 1850
HOLMES, Martha Jane	HONEYWELL, James	NOV 30 1841
HOLMES, Martha Jane	POWLISH, Peter	MAY 19 1847
HOLMES, Philip H.	HILLIARD, Mary W.	JAN 31 1852
HOLMES, Silas M.	EMMONS, Roberta H.	JUN 26 1857
HOLMES, William H.	WHALEN, Sarah Ann	APR 06 1853
HOLMS, John Henry	PATTIE, Jinnia	MAR 05 1853
HOLOHAN, Bridget	LOONEY, James	AUG 31 1854
HOLOHAN, Margaret	CONNELL, Timothy	JUL 11 1855
HOLOHAN, Simon	CLANSEY, Susan	JUN 15 1854
HOLORAN, Catherine	LEDWIDGE, Patrick	OCT 30 1854
HOLORAN, Thomas	FINN, Mary	AUG 05 1856
HOLROYD, Ann	MARKS, Saml.	AUG 08 1837
HOLROYD, Ann R.	HARRISON, Wm. H.	DEC 14 1852
HOLROYD, Georgiana	SANDERSON, Charles M.	SEP 25 1856
HOLROYD, John	TALBERT, Sarah	SEP 20 1832
HOLROYD, Mary	KIBBEY, Alexander	OCT 20 1836
HOLROYD, Mary Jane	GATES, Sylvester F.	MAR 12 1851
HOLSCHUH, John	CARL, Margaret	SEP 16 1852
HOLSEY, Mary	WILSON, Benjamin	DEC 18 1817
HOLSIEN, Ruth	DIXON, Jacob	JUN 27 1815
HOLSWORTH, Richard	GUMAER, Jane	NOV 20 1832
HOLT, Eleanor	TALBERT, Joshua	NOV 16 1833
HOLT, Ennals	JENKINS, Treacy	APR 17 1816
HOLT, George W.	GIGER, Margaret Ann	JAN 25 1838
HOLT, John R.	O'NEALE, Susanna	DEC 30 1824
HOLT, John R.	DAVIS, Sarah J.	APR 07 1856
HOLT, John W.	DUGAN, Julia Ann	MAY 02 1846
HOLT, Lucretia (blk)	MATTHEWS, Carr	MAR 15 1827
HOLT, Mary Margaret	LANGLY, Sylvester David	FEB 19 1853
HOLT, Sarah Jane	GREEN, John F.	DEC 25 1851
HOLT, Susan	SHERMAN, George	MAR 05 1839
HOLT, Susanna	YOUNG, Jacob	DEC 22 1851
HOLT, Thomas H.	SMITH, Adelaide L.	JUN 10 1856
HOLT, William	AUSTIN, Martha A.	FEB 02 1855
HOLT, William O.	BRASHEARS, Sarah F.	JUN 27 1853
HOLTE, Philip	MEARS, Neomy	JUL 27 1816
HOLTON, Margaret	VESSEY, John	FEB 09 1853
HOLTON, Sarah M.	GUYTHER, John S.	OCT 31 1854
HOLTSMAN, John T.	WELLS, America A.	JUN 26 1834
HOLTZCLAW, George W.	BALDWIN, Elizabeth Ann	JAN 19 1843
HOLTZCLAW, John M.	SINCLAIR, Elizabeth	SEP 30 1857
HOLTZCLAW, Thomas J.	FORD, Emma	DEC 08 1856
HOLTZMAN, Catherine	WAGLIER, Thomas	AUG 29 1839
HOLTZMAN, Celinda J. Cook	BING, Geo. W.	AUG 24 1833
HOLTZMAN, Christopher C.	CLARKE, Marsaline	AUG 18 1842
HOLTZMAN, Cordelia B.	JEWELL, William	NOV 27 1848
HOLTZMAN, Elie	BURNES, Elizabeth	OCT 10 1818
HOLTZMAN, Eliza	GOSZLER, Thomas D.	MAR 17 1826
HOLTZMAN, Eliza	HUTCHINS, John	NOV 02 1827
HOLTZMAN, Eliza Ann	CLARK, Samuel C.	SEP 18 1839

District of Columbia Marriage Licenses, 1811-1858

HOLTZMAN, Eliza G.	MORELAND, Hanson B.	MAY 11 1826
HOLTZMAN, Geo. W.	LAUB, Matilda Sophia	SEP 17 1823
HOLTZMAN, George H.	YOUNG, Susan J.	JUL 07 1842
HOLTZMAN, James Henry	SCHELL, Sophia	JUL 09 1834
HOLTZMAN, Jane J.	WILBURN, Edward	APR 16 1839
HOLTZMAN, John	NEWTON, Mary	JUN 20 1816
HOLTZMAN, John	BROME, Jane Joannah	MAY 30 1827
HOLTZMAN, John M.	POMEROY, Mary E.	NOV 13 1856
HOLTZMAN, Mary	WETZEL, William Y.	SEP 16 1817
HOLTZMAN, Mary	BEVELY, William	AUG 13 1818
HOLTZMAN, Mary E.	PHILLIPS, Charles Fenton Mercer	JAN 08 1852
HOLTZMAN, Matilda Ann	MILLS, Adam L.	DEC 16 1816
HOLTZMAN, Matilda Sophia [Mrs.]	KING, Samuel Davidson	SEP 19 1832
HOLTZMAN, Samuel	SISSEL, Mary	MAY 22 1834
HOLTZMAN, Susan	JONES, William	JUL 08 1833
HOLTZMAN, Thomas	GOSZLER, Christianna	SEP 14 1824
HOLTZMAN, Wm. F.	BARRY, Eliza G.	MAY 20 1816
HOMAN, Francis	WILSBOUGHER, Elizabeth	JUN 02 1835
HOMAN, Jane	SANDERS, Edward	MAR 09 1841
HOMANS, Benjamin	WRIGHT, Emily	JAN 14 1824
HOMANS, Daniel	BLACKSTONE, Catherine (blk)	JUL 26 1848
HOMANS, Roddy Caroline Harris	BROWN, Thomas B.	AUG 19 1846
HOMANS, Sheppard	HOUSTON, Sally L.	JUN 05 1856
HOMELLER, Lavinia	CROSS, B.J.	MAY 22 1855
HOMILLER, Charles	COLLINS, Catharine	NOV 15 1832
HOMILLER, William	DUVALL, Treacy	JAN 24 1837
HOMMOCK, Leo	KEENAN, John	OCT 19 1837
HONDIRIN, Mary	CONNALLY, John	APR 29 1854
HONEST, Martha (blk)	TRAMMELL, Washington	OCT 05 1857
HONESTY, Daniel	HOLLY, Harriet	SEP 17 1840
HONEY, Mary Ann	KENDLE, James	FEB 23 1832
HONEYWELL, James	THOMPSON, Elizth. D.	SEP 21 1819
HONEYWELL, James	HOLMES, Martha Jane	NOV 30 1841
HONTONVILLE, Harry	LANE, Mary	MAR 04 1837
HOOD, Arthur	ROCHE, Sarah Clare	OCT 17 1849
HOOD, Frederick	HASSLER, Fredericka	FEB 09 1852
HOOD, George	COONEY, Mary	APR 17 1852
HOOD, Isaac	JOHNSON, Letitia (blk)	AUG 05 1858
HOOD, James W.	NUGENT, Sophia J. (blk)	APR 22 1858
HOOD, John H.	MILLER, Harriet A.	DEC 30 1852
HOOD, Mary W.	IRONSIDE, Roger B.	AUG 02 1853
HOOD, Peggy	GIBSON, William	JUL 22 1831
HOOD, Rebecca	BRASHEARS, Thomas	SEP 01 1849
HOOE, Elizabeth T.	COOK, John F.	JUN 08 1842
HOOE, Francis F.	HOOE, Mary D.	JUL 27 1826
HOOE, Howson L.	BOYD, Eliza	OCT 06 1825
HOOE, James	WAUGH, Caroline	SEP 17 1828
HOOE, Lucinda James	DANIEL, Richard J.	SEP 16 1824
HOOE, Mary	BUTLER, John	MAY 03 1842
HOOE, Mary D.	HOOE, Francis F.	JUL 27 1826
HOOE, Susan G.	GRAHAM, James H.	FEB 10 1842
HOOF, William	SEMMES, Dorothy	FEB 23 1830
HOOK, Ellen	ROBEY, John	JUN 28 1831
HOOK, James H., Col.	BRONAUGH, Mary Ann	DEC 30 1840
HOOK, Susan	SMITH, James	AUG 07 1815
HOOK, Virginia S.	GRAY, John T.	JUN 29 1846
HOOKER, Jesse	BAKER, Eliza Ann	JUL 28 1858
HOOKER, Margaret	BAILEY, John R.	JUN 25 1858

District of Columbia Marriage Licenses, 1811-1858

HOONSWORTH, Sarah Ann	O'MEARA, William C.	MAR 19 1850
HOOPER, Ann	STEWART, Robert	MAR 15 1834
HOOPER, Charles	RICHARDSON, Catherine	SEP 17 1845
HOOPER, Dorothy	WESLEY, Joseph	APR 22 1842
HOOPER, Elizabeth	DOUGLASS, John	JAN 20 1814
HOOPER, Elizabeth Jane	DAVIS, Alexander	JAN 02 1841
HOOPER, George K.	STAPLES, Jane C.	JAN 25 1850
HOOPER, George W.	DUVALL, Elizabeth	MAY 21 1836
HOOPER, Jane	MARTIN, William	OCT 21 1851
HOOPER, Jane	WILLIAMSON, Thomas	JAN 30 1855
HOOPER, Jno. B.	COOK, Martha E.	MAR 06 1850
HOOPER, John H.	CROSS, Alethia	MAR 02 1824
HOOPER, John J.	PADGETT, S. Kate	NOV 14 1855
HOOPER, Samuel	QUEEN, Mary	NOV 20 1840
HOOPER, Sandy	CHURCH, Sally	SEP 20 1815
HOOPER, Thomas	BRADMAN, Sally	APR 21 1814
HOOPER, Thomas	BUTLER, Elizabeth	NOV 19 1856
HOOT, Mary Ann	PHILLIPS, William	OCT 09 1826
HOOTEE, Sarah Eliza	BARRON, Henry	NOV 14 1855
HOOVER, Adam M.	SIMMS, Harriet F.	APR 30 1855
HOOVER, Andrew	DOUGLASS, Elizabeth	DEC 20 1817
HOOVER, Andrew	PEARSON, Sarah	MAR 19 1822
HOOVER, Andrew	MOXLEY, Lucretia	MAR 18 1843
HOOVER, Andrew D.	MOSLEY, Mary C.	NOV 23 1855
HOOVER, Andrew P.	BARNECLOE, Julia Ann	MAY 03 1847
HOOVER, Angelica P.	HOOVER, Jonah D.	JUL 13 1844
HOOVER, Ann S.	HUMPHREY, John	APR 29 1856
HOOVER, David	POWERS, Susanna	OCT 27 1834
HOOVER, Elizabeth	BURROWS, John	DEC 03 1812
HOOVER, Hetty	MALONE, James	APR 07 1823
HOOVER, Jacob	WILAND, Eve	JUN 03 1851
HOOVER, John	MEEM, Sarah	AUG 11 1815
HOOVER, John	FRANKLAND, Sarah	JUN 28 1856
HOOVER, John T.	NAILOR, Cecelia J.	DEC 19 1855
HOOVER, John W.	BROWN, Emily S.	FEB 16 1852
HOOVER, Jonah D.	HOOVER, Angelica	JUL 13 1844
HOOVER, Julianna P.	WAUGH, William A.	FEB 25 1845
HOOVER, Michael	JOHNES, Clarissa	JAN 10 1827
HOOVER, Michael	TWEEDY, Mary	MAY 10 1831
HOOVER, Peter	HULL, Sally	SEP 19 1823
HOOVER, Samuel	HUBBARD, Lydia	SEP 03 1839
HOOVER, Sarah	WINDHAM, Charles	NOV 14 1812
HOOVER, Sarah	FENDLEY, Joseph J.	FEB 04 1852
HOOVER, Sarah E.	MAXWELL, William B.	DEC 28 1850
HOOVER, William	HUFF, Elizabeth	OCT 06 1832
HOOVER, William Henry	STRAIGHT, Eliza Ann	SEP 17 1826
HOPE, Elizabeth	HUME, Peter	NOV 01 1854
HOPE, Mary S. [Mrs.]	FULMER, George H.	FEB 09 1827
HOPHON, Jacob	SEYTON, Catherine	MAY 01 1856
HOPKINGS, John P.	HARDESTY, Mary Ann	JAN 10 1854
HOPKINS, Ann	MILES, Richard	OCT 04 1827
HOPKINS, Ann Janetta	BEARD, Wm. W.	DEC 04 1855
HOPKINS, Caroline	MARLOW, Richard	JUN 20 1855
HOPKINS, Cupid	[blank], Ruthy (negroes)	SEP 21 1824
HOPKINS, Eliza	OWENS, Samuel	APR 09 1827
HOPKINS, Elizabeth	CAMEL, George	NOV 27 1832
HOPKINS, Elizabeth A.	EARLY, Thomas R.	FEB 17 1853
HOPKINS, Emeline V.	LILBURN, Robert T.	SEP 03 1850

District of Columbia Marriage Licenses, 1811-1858

HOPKINS, George W.	BEALL, Eliza J.	OCT 06 1846
HOPKINS, George W.	BERRAMANS, Mary A.	MAY 19 1857
HOPKINS, Hannah	TINNEY, Charles	DEC 02 1817
HOPKINS, Helen	THOMPSON, James	JUL 30 1846
HOPKINS, Jas. Arthur	KENT, Mary Ann	JUL 12 1849
HOPKINS, Jason R.	BISHOP, Phebe	JUL 30 1858
HOPKINS, John S.	DASHIELL, Hester E.	AUG 13 1851
HOPKINS, Joseph	FORREST, Martha (blk)	FEB 04 1845
HOPKINS, Joseph	HARPER, Martha Maria	DEC 21 1853
HOPKINS, Major	WARD, Mary	JAN 18 1858
HOPKINS, Margaret	MERSON, Jonathan	SEP 08 1843
HOPKINS, Martha	MARLOW, John	JUN 01 1852
HOPKINS, Mary	WHITTICOMB, Benjamin F.	OCT 30 1834
HOPKINS, Mary C.	BAKER, William E.	MAY 28 1855
HOPKINS, Mary J.	GOODWIN, Stephen R.	JUL 16 1853
HOPKINS, Matilda	RUTHERFORD, William	JUN 09 1856
HOPKINS, Moore	WHEELER, Richard	FEB 01 1845
HOPKINS, Nancy	BEALE, Cyrus	APR 08 1841
HOPKINS, Philip	MARKS, Elizabeth	APR 16 1840
HOPKINS, Richard	FOSSETT, Margaret	FEB 06 1840
HOPKINS, Ruth	WILSON, Maceuny	APR 21 1835
HOPKINS, Ruth (blk)	ROSS, Rezin	OCT 04 1831
HOPKINS, Sarah A.D.	CONNELL, William F.	SEP 15 1849
HOPKINS, Solomon	MINKS, Catharine	MAY 20 1820
HOPKINS, Thomas B.	BURKE, Sarah	MAY 29 1833
HOPKINS, William	HUNTER, Catharine	NOV 26 1829
HOPKINSON, Adelaide St.M.	STELLE, Edward B.	SEP 15 1842
HOPKINSON, Anna Maria	STELLS, Thomas J.	APR 24 1844
HOPSON, Benjamin J.	WATSON, Mary Elizabeth	NOV 10 1852
HORAN, Catherine	DODEY, John	SEP 23 1854
HORAN, Margaret	CONNER, John	OCT 06 1852
HORAN, Margaret	WELSH, David	AUG 30 1856
HORAN, Margaret	GLEESON, James	JUL 20 1858
HORAN, Mary	MURPHY, Patrick	JUL 11 1853
HORAN, Richard	BIGLEY, Julia	APR 17 1858
HORBACH, Albert	SEMENS, Emilie	NOV 20 1852
HORBACH, Marcelena	LIPPITT, John	NOV 16 1855
HORLEY, Joseph	DOYES, Catharine Ann (blk)	AUG 08 1846
HORN, Barbary	PFLUGER, Ludwig	MAR 29 1853
HORN, Honora	MURPHY, Timothy	FEB 11 1854
HORN, Margaret L.	ANDERSON, George W.	APR 24 1847
HORNBACH, Valentine	BEINKERT, Barbara	MAY 12 1858
HORNBERGER, John	HAZZARD, Elizth.	APR 04 1857
HORNER, Elizabeth	CONWAY, John B.	DEC 30 1847
HORNER, John S.	WATSON, Harriet L.	OCT 30 1834
HORNER, Mary Ann	TAIT, Robert	FEB 18 1851
HORNER, William	McCUIN, Virginia M.	AUG 04 1858
HORNING, Rosena	GRAMMER, Andrew	AUG 17 1855
HORNIT, Daniel	SULLIVAN, Louisa	APR 30 1857
HORNSBURY, Ann (blk)	BOWIE, James W.	APR 28 1858
HORNUNY, Ann C.	TIEFENBACK, Philip	APR 19 1853
HORRELL, John E.	MAHORNEY, Henrietta Q.	AUG 11 1851
HORRELL, Maximillian	HALL, Martha E.	OCT 01 1816
HORSCAMP, Mary	SCHULTZE, William	NOV 22 1856
HORSEMAN, Ann M.	WRENN, Lysander	MAR 18 1856
HORSEMAN, Julian	MILLS, Bushrod	DEC 21 1839
HORSEMON, James	LEWIS, Emily	MAY 09 1844
HORSEY, Outerbridge [Sen.]	LEE, Eliza	APR 16 1812

District of Columbia Marriage Licenses, 1811-1858

HORSLEY, Saml., Doct.	DENNY, Ann	JUL 05 1815
HORSMAN, Catharine	KING, Henry	DEC 11 1827
HORSMAN, John W.	SIMMES, Ann	DEC 20 1836
HORSMAN, William H.	POOL, Sarah Jane	MAY 04 1855
HORTON, Catharine M.	WOODWARD, Daniel T.	OCT 05 1850
HORTON, Sarah Ann Frances	BROOKS, Lawson	NOV 14 1844
HORTSCAMP, Mary	HEITMILLER, Charles	NOV 21 1857
HORWELL, Edward C.	COX, Ann Maria H.	MAR 23 1829
HORWELL, Lucinda L.	HOUGH, Charles C.P.	JAN 20 1829
HOSH, August	HUNGERLING, Cehrisdin	DEC 30 1854
HOSHENLEITER, Ferdinand Artos	RUPERT, Josephine	SEP 05 1853
HOSKINS, Mary F.	HALL, Richard	MAY 11 1853
HOSKINS, Sarah	DeVAUGHN, Wm.	MAR 13 1821
HOSKINS, Susanna P.	NEWMAN, James	JAN 17 1818
HOSMER, Albert H.	ROSS, Margaret Rebecca	MAY 30 1839
HOSMONS, Mary	STEPHENSON, Alexr.	SEP 29 1832
HOSSEL, Margaret	SCHARTEL, Peter	NOV 01 1839
HOSSICKS, Mary E.A.	MONTGOMERY, James H.	APR 11 1850
HOTTA, Catherine	WENDALL, Herman	DEC 02 1854
HOUCH, Matthias	SHEDD, Elizabeth	JUL 01 1844
HOUCHENS, John F.	HOUCHENS, Sallie F.	JUL 28 1856
HOUCHENS, Sallie F.	HOUCHENS, John F.	JUL 28 1856
HOUCK, John W.	PERRIE, Catharine M.	JUL 30 1855
HOUGH, A.E.	QUEEN, Mary D.A.	NOV 27 1821
HOUGH, Charles C.P.	HORWELL, Lucinda L.	JAN 20 1829
HOUGH, Dorothy	KING, Benjamin	JUL 10 1841
HOUGH, George Campbell	DAVIS, Mary Ellen	JUN 09 1849
HOUGH, Susan	WOLTZ, Henry	MAR 22 1831
HOUGH, William W.	ROBERTSON, Sarah Jane	JUL 11 1854
HOUGHTON, Ceylon S.	BENNETT, Elizabeth E.	NOV 01 1843
HOUK, Mary Ann	ENNIS, John	APR 28 1835
HOURAN, Bridget	SHEAHAN, Patrick	OCT 16 1852
HOURST, Ann	O'ROURK, Thos. J.	SEP 23 1856
HOUSE, George E.	ELLIOTT, Ellen U.	MAR 20 1854
HOUSE, Horace H.B.	TRUNNELL, Sarah S.	FEB 23 1843
HOUSE, John	SPEAKE, Mary C.	APR 18 1850
HOUSE, Richard	DAVIS, Ann	MAR 25 1826
HOUSE, Samuel	JENNINGS, Sidney (blk)	JUN 28 1838
HOUSEMAN, Charles	FISHER, Louisa	APR 12 1845
HOUSER, Elizabeth	WHITEHOUSE, William	JAN 27 1824
HOUSER, William	HILL, Linny	NOV 13 1834
HOUSLAND, Francisco	SMITH, John G.	SEP 02 1852
HOUSON, Jane	REDMAN, Robert	MAY 30 1812
HOUSON, Rachel	MUMBY, Robert	DEC 10 1817
HOUSTON, Abraham [Dr.]	CHAMBERLAIN, Mary	JAN 13 1835
HOUSTON, Andrew	BRUCE, Agnes	SEP 12 1853
HOUSTON, Cornelia Nancrede	STRAIN, John Higgins	JAN 16 1856
HOUSTON, John Hopkins	TRUXTON, Gertrude Parker	OCT 17 1825
HOUSTON, Mary T.	GARLAND, John S.	AUG 24 1850
HOUSTON, Robert Richards	FRANK, Mary Ann	SEP 03 1831
HOUSTON, Sally L.	HOMANS, Sheppard	JUN 05 1856
HOUSTOUN, Harriot E. [Mrs.]	LIVINGSTON, Charles V.	APR 27 1820
HOUX, David F.	KLEIBER, Susan	DEC 09 1833
HOUX, Rebecca	TRETLER, John	FEB 03 1831
HOW, Edward	LEWIS, Eleanor	DEC 31 1825
HOW, John	BIGGS, Sarah	AUG 27 1834
HOW, Mary	TERRY, William	MAR 08 1820
HOW, Mary Ann	McKOME, Robert	APR 04 1820

District of Columbia Marriage Licenses, 1811-1858

HOWARD, Albert	NEVITT, Eleanor	APR 07 1828
HOWARD, Albert F.	WRIGHT, Jane E.	DEC 20 1856
HOWARD, Ann	PIERCE, John T.	FEB 14 1843
HOWARD, Ann	DAVIS, John	OCT 07 1845
HOWARD, Ann Maria	McELFRESH, James Philip	NOV 22 1847
HOWARD, Arabella	MORAN, James	JUL 13 1848
HOWARD, Benjamin S.	SCHOOLCRAFT, Jane A.	MAY 15 1855
HOWARD, Brit Ann	FOWLER, George	APR 04 1820
HOWARD, Charles	KEY, Elizth. Phebe	NOV 09 1825
HOWARD, Charles	LAWRENCE, Eliza	SEP 13 1838
HOWARD, Charles	WILLIAMS, Ann Virginia	SEP 12 1848
HOWARD, Chas. A.	DOUGLASS, Lucretia (blk)	NOV 17 1856
HOWARD, Douglass	SUTER, Maria Fletcher	MAY 18 1837
HOWARD, Eleanor	WIMSET, Lewis	OCT 20 1817
HOWARD, Eliza	DONALDSON, William	AUG 28 1827
HOWARD, Eliza (blk)	TUXON, William	JAN 15 1851
HOWARD, Eliza C.	MARTIN, George B.	JUN 05 1849
HOWARD, Elizabeth	COX, James	MAY 23 1840
HOWARD, Elizabeth	NORBECK, William	JAN 05 1841
HOWARD, Elizth.	CLAPON, John	NOV 13 1855
HOWARD, Ellen F.	TRIPPLETT, Thomas M.	NOV 16 1853
HOWARD, Emily	PICKRELL, Benjamin	AUG 23 1850
HOWARD, George T.	McCORMICK, Mary Frances	OCT 07 1848
HOWARD, George W.	COLLINS, Teresa	DEC 29 1831
HOWARD, George W.	JEFFERS, Amanda	MAY 07 1833
HOWARD, George Ward	FENWICK, Eliza	OCT 30 1833
HOWARD, Henry	PRINKMAN, Margaret	FEB 07 1816
HOWARD, Henry	HASSON, Rozanna	APR 19 1823
HOWARD, Henry	ROACH, Lucinda	NOV 25 1826
HOWARD, Henry	THEIRLOW, Elizabeth	FEB 02 1828
HOWARD, Henry	TILGHMAN, Mary Jane (blk)	AUG 09 1842
HOWARD, Hiram	EDDS, Caroline	FEB 08 1834
HOWARD, Isaiah A.	TERRIER, Annie (blk)	AUG 23 1855
HOWARD, James	HIGDON, Susan	JUL 02 1844
HOWARD, James	HURDLE, Mary Ann	OCT 04 1849
HOWARD, Jeffry	BARKER, Eleanor (blk)	SEP 07 1826
HOWARD, John	ONION, Milly	DEC 11 1812
HOWARD, John	THOMPSON, Ann	SEP 11 1821
HOWARD, John, of Philip	MITCHEL, Sarah Ann	JUN 02 1829
HOWARD, John Cornelius	CONRAD, Mary Catherine	JUL 07 1852
HOWARD, Joseph	ROBERTSON, Sarah	NOV 17 1821
HOWARD, Joseph	CROSS, Sarah Maria	JUN 30 1840
HOWARD, Julia Ann	HINES, Philip	MAY 27 1826
HOWARD, Justin H.C.	SERGEANT, S. Emma	APR 24 1852
HOWARD, Lucy Ann	BAGGOTT, James W.	SEP 25 1845
HOWARD, Lucy N.	BAGGOTT, James W.	DEC 16 1847
HOWARD, Lucy N.	BAGGOTT, James W.	DEC 16 1857
HOWARD, Margaret	GIBSON, William	OCT 18 1847
HOWARD, Maria	DANIELS, Francis	JAN 01 1830
HOWARD, Maria (blk)	PENNY, Henry	MAY 13 1851
HOWARD, Maria Jane	REPETTE, Jerome	JUN 07 1852
HOWARD, Mary	SERRY, John	JUN 10 1818
HOWARD, Mary	SHECKELLS, Thomas H.	MAY 20 1840
HOWARD, Mary	WILLIAMS, George	APR 28 1845
HOWARD, Mary	WILLIAMS, Joseph Z.	OCT 01 1852
HOWARD, Mary Ann	DONALDSON, Samuel	MAR 13 1827
HOWARD, Mary Ann	BACON, Samuel	OCT 09 1838
HOWARD, Mary Ellen	BAKER, Benajmin F.	AUG 21 1852

District of Columbia Marriage Licenses, 1811-1858

HOWARD, Mary Jane	HINGITY, Alfred	JUN 13 1834
HOWARD, Mary Jane	CRAWFORD, Adam	JAN 13 1841
HOWARD, Mary Jane	HALLECK, John T.A.	MAY 29 1849
HOWARD, Mary Jane (blk)	ANDERSON, Robert	APR 20 1854
HOWARD, Matthias	WESTERFIELD, Lucy	JUL 08 1834
HOWARD, Nelly (blk)	ODEN, Artan (blk)	JUN 04 1835
HOWARD, Oscar L.	SWETNAM, Lucy Ann	MAR 17 1856
HOWARD, Peter	RYLAND, Eliza (blk)	DEC 21 1847
HOWARD, Saml.	GOODWIN, Maria	APR 29 1822
HOWARD, Samuel	JONES, Manzilla	NOV 09 1854
HOWARD, Sarah	DONALDSON, Thomas A.	SEP 06 1851
HOWARD, Sarah Jane	MURPHEY, William H.	MAY 13 1847
HOWARD, Selre	EDDS, Ellen	DEC 10 1831
HOWARD, Sophia W.	MIDDLETON, Erasmus J.	APR 27 1826
HOWARD, Susan	MEAD, Edward	DEC 12 1844
HOWARD, Susan	DOTZLER, John	MAY 14 1845
HOWARD, Susannah	MAURICE, Elexander G.	MAY 31 1828
HOWARD, Thomas	TEDERICK, Caroline	AUG 06 1840
HOWARD, Thomas	SANDFORD, Mary	JAN 26 1849
HOWARD, Thomas	SULIVAN, Melvina	OCT 11 1851
HOWARD, Thomas	HARRIS, Elizabeth	MAR 10 1853
HOWARD, Thomas W.	HERBERT, Martha E.	JUN 29 1841
HOWARD, Volney E.	GOOCH, Catherine Elizabeth	MAR 04 1837
HOWARD, William	PEAK, Charity	AUG 25 1815
HOWARD, William	CROSS, Jane	FEB 14 1822
HOWARD, William [Dr.]	KEY, Rebecca Ann	MAY 13 1828
HOWARD, William	GANTT, Maria (blk)	NOV 22 1832
HOWARD, William E.	McCAULEY, Hannah E.	NOV 15 1838
HOWARD, William R.	MASSEY, Martha L.	AUG 23 1841
HOWARD, William T.R.	CLARKE, Anna M.	JAN 11 1858
HOWDERSHELL, G. Margaret	SHAFER, Robert M.	JUN 17 1852
HOWDERSHELL, Warner C.	DODD, Margt. A.	OCT 06 1857
HOWDESCHELL, Lavinia	HAMBURG, Jacob	DEC 12 1846
HOWE, Alexander F.	WOLTZ, Lydia Ann	JUL 07 1829
HOWE, Eliza	JOHNSON, James	SEP 22 1827
HOWE, Elizabeth	NELSON, Samuel	JAN 15 1825
HOWE, Ellen	KNOXVILLE, James	SEP 06 1832
HOWE, George	WILLARD, Mary A.	JUN 07 1850
HOWE, Hetty Jane	TURNER, William George	OCT 14 1838
HOWE, Ignatius	GRIFFIN, Mary	NOV 24 1831
HOWE, Ignatius	GOSS, Louisa Jane	APR 12 1845
HOWE, Jemima	NICHOLSON, William	JAN 07 1834
HOWE, Jesse	FURLONG, Kitty (blk)	OCT 19 1848
HOWE, Joseph	STREAKS, Lucinda	FEB 11 1850
HOWE, Margaret Ann	BRYAN, Samuel L.	JUN 26 1850
HOWE, Mary Ann	BOOTH, Edward	MAY 19 1814
HOWE, Mary Ann	RIDGEWAY, Enoch	MAR 08 1831
HOWE, Richard	JARBOE, Elizabeth A.	AUG 11 1842
HOWE, Sarah V.	BRYAN, Bernard M.	APR 16 1857
HOWE, Teresa	HAGER, Frederick	NOV 13 1832
HOWE, Thomas	DENNISON, Myrna	JUL 04 1817
HOWELL, Catherine	WINN, John C.M.	JUL 15 1850
HOWELL, Elizabeth E.	GUY, Frances L.	JAN 18 1850
HOWELL, Emily E.	EVANS, T.H.	AUG 03 1847
HOWELL, Eveline A.	OLIVER, William	APR 20 1847
HOWELL, John	BERRY, Ann	AUG 24 1822
HOWELL, John Frederick Alexr.	HENDERSON, Matilda	JUL 18 1850
HOWELL, Lucy Duncan	DUNCAN, John	OCT 16 1856

District of Columbia Marriage Licenses, 1811-1858

HOWELL, S. Harrison	WILLIAMSON, J.S.M.	JUN 14 1852
HOWELL, Sophia Augustine	BURR, David H.	AUG 03 1835
HOWELL, Thomas	HURDLE, Ann	JUL 28 1812
HOWELL, Thomas	CLEMENSON, Ellen	JAN 15 1849
HOWELL, William	LUSBY, Sarah J.	JUN 12 1856
HOWELL, William H.	PADGETT, Sarah Ann	NOV 07 1848
HOWES, Eliza	SWEENY, Thomas	JAN 14 1853
HOWES, Jane	FOWLER, Joseph	DEC 21 1830
HOWES, Sarah Ann	BAKER, William	MAY 15 1837
HOWISON, Sarah A.	THOMAS, Benjamin F.	JUN 25 1836
HOWK, Catharine	MOPS, John	DEC 29 1826
HOWKE, Sophia E.	DOUGLASS, William	DEC 22 1838
HOWLE, Eliza P.	MORRIS, Henry M.	FEB 09 1858
HOWLE, Joanna F.	YOUNG, Joseph	FEB 11 1851
HOWLE, Parke G.	CASANAVE, Joannah	MAY 07 1821
HOWLE, Rebecca	RILEY, John C.	JUN 15 1857
HOWLEY, Mary	SULLIVAN, Eugene	JUN 15 1853
HOWLIN, Mark	GALLET, Rachel	JAN 02 1845
HOWLIN, Patrick	COXING, Ruth Ann	MAY 25 1848
HOWSER, Jas.	CALLAHAN, Margaret	DEC 10 1822
HOWSER, Lucinda	METZ, Frederick	JUN 08 1837
HOWSER, Sarah	BURRIS, Nicholas	FEB 19 1822
HOY, Marthan Ann	DUEHAY, William	DEC 29 1830
HOY, Mary Ann	WELCH, George	NOV 24 1854
HOYE, Ann Virginia	FEAMAN, George H.	SEP 15 1853
HOYE, Enoch	TURNER, Susan	DEC 21 1831
HOYE, Mariam D.	JORDAN, Hanson	DEC 10 1855
HOYE, Paul	HAMDEN, Hannah	JAN 16 1816
HOYE, Thomas	TURNER, Isabella	FEB 22 1830
HOYL, William H.	McLEAN, Mary Ann	JAN 02 1857
HOYLE, Elizabeth	POOR, Frederick	APR 10 1845
HOYLE, Ellen Ann	HAWKINS, Phillip	JAN 05 1858
HOYLE, Henry J.	KURTZ, Rebecca C.	NOV 22 1849
HOYLE, Margaret	SEWALL, Thomas	JUL 17 1822
HOYT, Goold	SCOTT, Camilla	DEC 09 1851
HUALEY, John	FITZPATRICK, Ellen	FEB 04 1845
HUBBARD, Caroline Matilda	LORD, Francis B., Junr.	MAY 07 1849
HUBBARD, Catharine	JAMISON, Francis	OCT 03 1850
HUBBARD, Catharine (blk)	YOUNG, James H.	MAY 17 1850
HUBBARD, Elizabeth	DAVIS, John A.	FEB 17 1830
HUBBARD, Ellenora A.	MARR, James F.	MAY 03 1854
HUBBARD, George W.	CROSS, Clara S.	APR 07 1856
HUBBARD, Jeremiah	BENTEN, Mary Ann	SEP 29 1836
HUBBARD, John P.	McCULLOH, Adelaide S.	JUN 27 1849
HUBBARD, Joseph S.	HANDY, Sarah E.L.	APR 27 1848
HUBBARD, Lydia	HOOVER, Samuel	SEP 03 1839
HUBBARD, Mary Elizth.	FRANCE, Joseph H.	SEP 23 1843
HUBBARD, Solomon	MORIALTY, Eleanor	DEC 24 1818
HUBNER, Frederika	HURLEBAUS, Gottlieb	APR 21 1856
HUCHERSON, William	BRYAN, Elizabeth	JUN 28 1815
HUD, Christian	GOTHE, Margaretha	JUN 19 1841
HUDAL, Mary	SCHUSSLER, Charles	OCT 03 1854
HUDDLESTON, John E.	WARING, Maria L.	JAN 28 1851
HUDDLESTON, Julia	WILLIAMS, Richard	FEB 22 1844
HUDDLESTON, Mary	GARDINER, Caleb P.	DEC 23 1818
HUDDLESTON, Mary A.	RUSSELL, Lorenzo S.	MAY 05 1852
HUDDLESTON, Mathew C.	MOORE, Jane	NOV 10 1854
HUDELMANE, Charles	YOUNG, Harriet	FEB 07 1839

District of Columbia Marriage Licenses, 1811-1858

HUDGINS, Tamezene	TROUTMAN, John	MAY 22 1858
HUDGINS, William H.	SMALLWOOD, Mary V.	JUN 05 1855
HUDNALL, Roach M.	FERRIS, Ann Maria	OCT 03 1853
HUDSON, Ann	FRANK, Robert	FEB 02 1812
HUDSON, Ann	HENRY, Joshua	JUN 10 1824
HUDSON, Catherine A.S.	DAVIS, Thomas B.	SEP 29 1847
HUDSON, Eliza Ann	BINGHAM, Allen W.	NOV 23 1857
HUDSON, Elizabeth	SPILMAN, William	AUG 15 1821
HUDSON, James A.	DOGGETT, Martha A.	DEC 28 1855
HUDSON, John W.	VANRIPER, Ellen Cecelia	JAN 29 1848
HUDSON, Joseph	PARSONS, Mary Ann	OCT 29 1836
HUDSON, Lucy Ann	ROSS, John	SEP 22 1840
HUDSON, Martha	CASTEEL, John	FEB 23 1831
HUDSON, Martha F.	BUTLER, Joseph	DEC 31 1832
HUDSON, Richard	BRYAN, Hannah	SEP 25 1817
HUDSON, Samuel	COOMBS, Sarah Ann	SEP 22 1852
HUE, Catharine	LOUXMAN, Andrew	MAR 10 1840
HUFF, Elizabeth	SIMMS, James	NOV 13 1828
HUFF, Elizabeth	HOOVER, William	OCT 06 1832
HUFF, Levin	HAYS, Louisa	FEB 24 1829
HUFF, Mary E.	COLLIER, John N.	JAN 15 1849
HUFF, Powell H.	RENNER, Elizabeth	MAR 04 1816
HUFFMANN, Martha Ann	HUNTT, Benjamin F.	JAN 07 1856
HUFFWIN, Patrick	HARRATY, Biddy	JUL 01 1818
HUGGENS, Francis B.	WATSON, Sarah	DEC 22 1845
HUGGENS, Francis B.	WROE, Julia Ann	MAY 09 1853
HUGGINS, Joseph	BURCH, Sarah [Mrs.]	JUN 07 1834
HUGGINS, Mary E.	DOWNS, Steward D.	MAY 21 1855
HUGHES, Andrew	BURNS, Margaret	MAY 07 1857
HUGHES, Anna Maria	CHEEVER, Benjamin H.	SEP 08 1842
HUGHES, Ansburn	COLLINS, Ann	DEC 24 1818
HUGHES, Archibald	ROBINSON, Hipsey	MAR 24 1814
HUGHES, Arthur	O'BRIEN, Ellen	JUN 10 1858
HUGHES, Bridget	FALION, John	APR 14 1856
HUGHES, Catharine	WILSON, William	DEC 05 1833
HUGHES, Eleanor A.	ALLEN, John	FEB 19 1840
HUGHES, Elisha	NORWOOD, Rebecca	FEB 23 1841
HUGHES, Elizabeth	SUMLY, James (blk)	MAR 29 1838
HUGHES, Elizabeth	NAILOR, Washington	MAR 29 1838
HUGHES, Elizabeth (blk)	KING, Isaiah	JUL 21 1845
HUGHES, Evan	HENNING, Lucinda	DEC 12 1846
HUGHES, Fanny M.	BRONAUGH, John	DEC 27 1824
HUGHES, Frances	TAPSICO, Edmund	MAR 21 1854
HUGHES, George W.	MAXEY, Ann Sarah	DEC 16 1834
HUGHES, George W.	RAY, Mary Ann	MAY 15 1848
HUGHES, Harriot	PAYNE, William	MAY 21 1825
HUGHES, Henrietta	GRAHAM, William S.	APR 19 1843
HUGHES, Hugh	OXLEY, Emily	JAN 07 1836
HUGHES, James	SCHRY, Mahala	MAR 09 1844
HUGHES, James	DOWNEY, Mary	OCT 21 1851
HUGHES, Jane	SEWELL, John D.	APR 29 1835
HUGHES, John	HARLEY, Maria	MAR 28 1821
HUGHES, John	CLARKE, Lucy	OCT 02 1828
HUGHES, John	McCARTHY, Jane	JUL 20 1852
HUGHES, John	MOGELY, Mary Ann	OCT 07 1854
HUGHES, John	RYAN, Joanna	APR 22 1856
HUGHES, John E.	HEDGES, Martha	APR 06 1837
HUGHES, Joseph R.	LEWIS, Rachael E.	JUL 12 1853

296

District of Columbia Marriage Licenses, 1811-1858

HUGHES, Julia Ann	FONTZ, Christian	JUN 05 1858
HUGHES, Malinda	OLLIVER, Aaron P.	AUG 15 1826
HUGHES, Margaret	KING, Martin	DEC 06 1827
HUGHES, Margaret (blk)	CONNEWAY, Joseph	APR 04 1850
HUGHES, Margaret A.	FLAGG, Robert S.	JAN 25 1853
HUGHES, Maria	CAUSSEEN, Samuel	SEP 26 1820
HUGHES, Martha	JONES, Richard (blk)	MAR 24 1843
HUGHES, Martha (blk)	JONES, Richard	MAR 24 1840
HUGHES, Mary	SHOWLS, Manass	FEB 28 1815
HUGHES, Mary	BELL, George J.	JAN 17 1818
HUGHES, Mary Frances	CALDWELL, Armstead M.	OCT 10 1855
HUGHES, Nathaniel	SMITH, Ann	JUL 08 1824
HUGHES, Robert B.	SHEPPERD, Eliza Frances	JAN 16 1839
HUGHES, Rose	KEENAN, Hugh	JUL 20 1854
HUGHES, Sarah (blk)	LEE, Alexander	MAY 07 1846
HUGHES, Thomas	McCARDLE, Ann	OCT 03 1815
HUGHES, Thomas	QUEEN, Sarah	FEB 01 1818
HUGHES, Thomas	WINSATT, Julia	JUN 10 1834
HUGHES, William	HERRITY, Catherine	OCT 14 1830
HUGHES, William	JACKSON, Martha	OCT 04 1838
HUGHES, William	SWEENY, Sarah	AUG 10 1854
HUGHES, Wm.	RATCLIFF, Lucinda	OCT 02 1855
HUGHLETT, Daniel H.	MASON, Sarah C.	APR 07 1819
HUGUELY, Samuel	JENKINS, Charlotte	APR 06 1817
HUGULEY, Matilda L.	THROOP, Thomas S.	JUN 09 1823
HUGULEY, Sarah E.	HENNEY, Peter	OCT 23 1852
HUHMANN, John A.	SEITENARTEN, Margaret	NOV 15 1845
HUHN, Bernhard	REILEY, Virginia	AUG 05 1858
HUHN, Jacob Karl	BERMANN, Catherine	NOV 11 1857
HUHN, Michael	JACOB, Rosa	JUL 06 1858
HULBERT, Joseph P.	BURGESS, Mary Ann	OCT 10 1846
HULIGHAN, John	WHALAN, Bridget	OCT 14 1818
HULL, Esther	LYLES, James	MAR 09 1816
HULL, George	BACON, Alice (blk)	MAY 19 1857
HULL, Harriett (blk)	GIBSON, Francis	SEP 17 1844
HULL, Jane	BRASHEARS, Thomas	APR 20 1831
HULL, Mary	GROSS, Francis	NOV 27 1819
HULL, Rebecca	BROWN, W.H.	NOV 21 1849
HULL, Sally	HOOVER, Peter	SEP 19 1823
HULL, William B.	WISE, Sophia	NOV 18 1856
HULL, William H.	RANDOLPH, Nannie J.	JAN 14 1851
HULLS, John A.	ROBINSON, Margaret A.	MAR 11 1856
HULSE, Isaac, Jr.	JACKSON, Margaret L.	SEP 04 1850
HULSE, Rebecca	LAWSON, William	NOV 29 1854
HULSEMAN, Bernard H.	HOFFMAN, Malinda B.	DEC 26 1843
HUMBOY, Mary Ann	LANG, Israel	MAY 18 1839
HUME, E.J.	BERRY, Barbara	FEB 25 1833
HUME, Ellen A.	BERRY, Thomas C.	NOV 17 1856
HUME, Francis	DONOHOE, Ann Maria	JUN 04 1845
HUME, Peter	HOPE, Elizabeth	NOV 01 1854
HUME, Q.R.	MILLER, Virginia	JUN 01 1856
HUMES, Alexander	TIPPETT, Mary M.	OCT 12 1853
HUMES, George	DUVALL, Priscilla W.	NOV 04 1846
HUMES, Martha	BURCH, Thomas	MAY 20 1841
HUMES, Martha	BURCH, Thomas	MAY 20 1855
HUMPHREVILL, Ebenezer	GRIGSBY, Frances	NOV 28 1855
HUMPHREY, Hezekiah	WARD, Amelia (blk)	OCT 14 1826
HUMPHREY, John	HOOVER, Ann S.	APR 29 1856

District of Columbia Marriage Licenses, 1811-1858

HUMPHREY, Joshua	MITCHELL, Margaret Maria	MAR 01 1823
HUMPHREY, Mary	HEYL, William	MAY 16 1853
HUMPHREY, Susan	HUMPHREY, William	AUG 01 1853
HUMPHREY, William	HUMPHREY, Susan	AUG 01 1853
HUMPHREYS, Ann	CRAWFORD, Archibald	AUG 31 1826
HUMPHREYS, Ara A.E. (blk)	WATTS, Samuel	AUG 27 1850
HUMPHREYS, Geo. W.	ROBERTSON, Susan D.	MAR 12 1845
HUMPHREYS, George	HENDERSON, Janet L.	DEC 26 1826
HUMPHREYS, Georgianna (blk)	SPRIGG, Sandy	OCT 29 1849
HUMPHREYS, Isabella A.	COOK, H.A.	NOV 13 1856
HUMPHREYS, James	SPEEKNALL, Mary Ann	JUN 20 1831
HUMPHREYS, Jane M.	McCRABB, John W.	MAR 22 1837
HUMPHREYS, Joseph	WELLS, Ellen (blk)	OCT 16 1845
HUMPHREYS, Joshua	CHANDLER, Margaret	NOV 28 1842
HUMPHREYS, Mary	YONGE, George	AUG 29 1843
HUMPHREYS, Mary	GAREY, Thomas	JAN 16 1858
HUMPHREYS, Mary (blk)	GRIFFIN, John	NOV 03 1853
HUMPHRIES, Guy C.	PIGGOTT, Ann Rebecca	MAY 01 1849
HUMPHRIES, Guy C.	HARRIS, Mary Evelyn	SEP 10 1853
HUMPHRIES, John A.	REYNOLDS, Mary Virginia	AUG 18 1856
HUMPHRIES, John D.	COURTNEY, Sarah Ann	SEP 09 1847
HUND, John	MILLER, Margaret	FEB 06 1854
HUNGERFORD, Henrietta V.	MINIX, William H.	MAR 07 1850
HUNGERFORD, Sarah A.W.	WILSON, James O.	JUL 02 1853
HUNGERLING, Cehrisdin	HOSH, August	DEC 30 1854
HUNT, Amelia	CLARKE, William T.	MAY 07 1840
HUNT, Ann	MILLER, Isaac F.	MAR 10 1849
HUNT, Bettie M.	JEFFERS, W.R.	FEB 23 1854
HUNT, Camilla	LOWELL, Thruston	DEC 27 1853
HUNT, Caroline	ADAMS, William	MAY 10 1828
HUNT, Charles	GOLDING, Christiana	JAN 15 1835
HUNT, Charles	GOODWIN, Agnes	JUN 01 1843
HUNT, Charles	SAMPSON, Josephine (blk)	DEC 14 1857
HUNT, Chloe Ann	GRIMES, Ignatius	SEP 23 1848
HUNT, George N.	McNALLY, Catherine A.	MAR 11 1857
HUNT, Harriet	JONES, John F.	JUL 25 1844
HUNT, Harvey John	PETTICORD, Sarah Jane	DEC 16 1852
HUNT, Harvey W.	OSGOOD, Ann	NOV 09 1844
HUNT, Johanna	LEWIS, Joseph	AUG 24 1858
HUNT, Lydia Ann	JONES, William	JUL 26 1853
HUNT, Mary	HUNT, Taylor	NOV 20 1837
HUNT, Mary E. (blk)	GREEN, Joseph	JAN 28 1857
HUNT, Mary Elizabeth	COOPER, Joseph	FEB 19 1824
HUNT, Mary R. [Mrs.]	HILTON, Thomas	DEC 01 1821
HUNT, Minnie	RANSOM, R., U.S.A.	FEB 06 1856
HUNT, Nancy Ann	GODDARD, William Clarke	MAY 31 1831
HUNT, Noah	BARNES, Elizabeth	JUN 28 1838
HUNT, Robert Finley	CRANDELL, Catharine A.	NOV 25 1845
HUNT, Susan	BURGESS, William B.	DEC 13 1838
HUNT, Taylor	HUNT, Mary	NOV 20 1837
HUNT, Theodore J.	TURNER, Elizabeth J.	JUN 26 1856
HUNT, Thomas	DAVIS, Joanna	JUN 02 1848
HUNT, Thomas F. [Capt.]	LOVELL, Dorcas K. [Mrs.]	NOV 19 1829
HUNT, Thomas F.	GOSSER, Virginia	DEC 07 1852
HUNTER, Catharine	HOPKINS, William	NOV 26 1829
HUNTER, Catharine	DAUGHTON, Darius D.	MAY 22 1858
HUNTER, Ellen B.	BEVANS, David H.	AUG 15 1850
HUNTER, Emily	SELDEN, William	JUN 01 1840

District of Columbia Marriage Licenses, 1811-1858

HUNTER, George	STREAKS, Harriett A.	DEC 22 1838
HUNTER, George	FRAZIER, Mary (blk)	JAN 11 1842
HUNTER, George	TURNER, Hannah N. (blk)	SEP 25 1850
HUNTER, George	CARPENTER, Lucinda (blk)	FEB 18 1857
HUNTER, Henrietta H.	FOWLER, James W.	JAN 11 1831
HUNTER, James W.	BROWN, Mary Ann	JAN 24 1853
HUNTER, Jenne H. Raldon	LENMAN, John Thomas	OCT 28 1846
HUNTER, Lewis J.	GREEN, Sophia	JAN 29 1820
HUNTER, Marian	YOUNG, Clement	FEB 19 1852
HUNTER, Martha V.R.	LUCKETT, David W.	FEB 18 1854
HUNTER, Mary	BARNES, George	SEP 03 1828
HUNTER, Mary	BAGGETT, Samuel	JAN 05 1837
HUNTER, Mary A.	GALT, Thomas J.	DEC 07 1847
HUNTER, Mary Catharine	GIBSON, John H.	APR 22 1848
HUNTER, Mary R.	JONES, Richard H.	MAY 06 1858
HUNTER, Milbourn	WATERS, Eliza	NOV 17 1832
HUNTER, Mildred M.	MURRAY, Henry W.	MAR 20 1851
HUNTER, Robert	MERCHANT, Margaret	SEP 07 1831
HUNTER, Sarah	LOCKEY, Andrew R.	JUN 11 1827
HUNTER, Thomas	OLIVER, Jane	MAY 15 1828
HUNTER, Thomas I.	ODD, Mary E.	DEC 27 1849
HUNTER, Virginia E.	CHAUNCEY, James W.	AUG 28 1856
HUNTER, William C.	BYRN, Mary	JUL 22 1851
HUNTER, William J.	BROWN, Jane	JUL 01 1839
HUNTER, William, Jr.	SMITH, Sally Hoffman	NOV 17 1835
HUNTER, Zachariah	EDMUNDS, Julia	FEB 24 1834
HUNTINGTEN, Thomas	EVANS, Elizabeth	SEP 02 1851
HUNTINGTON, Craven	SIMMS, Emma	MAR 06 1854
HUNTINGTON, Haven	HALL, Milly	NOV 21 1833
HUNTLETON, Elizabeth	HALL, John	APR 10 1856
HUNTLETON, Matilda Ann	VALENTINE, John W.	JAN 03 1852
HUNTON, Thos. L.	MOXLEY, Ann Dent Douglass	NOV 18 1822
HUNTRE, Ann	POLETTO, Joseph	MAR 04 1826
HUNTRESS, Charles A.	WILLIAMSON, Elizabeth	NOV 23 1857
HUNTT, Amelia (blk)	NEALE, George	DEC 11 1844
HUNTT, Benj. W.	GRIFFIN, Chloe Ann	JUN 01 1826
HUNTT, Benjamin F.	HUFFMANN, Martha Ann	JAN 07 1856
HUNTT, Edwd. L.	FRAZIER, Mary Eliza	JUL 16 1833
HUNTT, Hannah	MULE, Eliot	FEB 10 1814
HUNTT, Henry [Dr.]	RINGGOLD, Anna Maria	NOV 17 1829
HUNTT, Josias	JONES, Harriet	JUN 04 1833
HUNTT, Louis	CROSS, Mary	APR 18 1835
HUNTT, Lydia Catherine	TODD, David S.	MAY 23 1843
HUNTT, Mary Ann M.	KIDWELL, Allison	AUG 13 1833
HUNTT, Mary Ann	GAUBERT, Theodore	JAN 31 1845
HUNTT, Pamelia (blk)	JOHNSON, William	JUN 26 1855
HUNTT, Susan C.	BRADT, Albert H.	OCT 01 1843
HUNTT, Teresa	SIMMONS, Thomas	SEP 12 1818
HUNTT, Thomas	MORGAN, Mary	MAR 12 1816
HUNTT, Wm.	PHETHEAN, Esther	AUG 04 1814
HUPPERT, Andrias	LORCH, Affa	JAN 16 1835
HURBERT, Ugean	CAMMELL, William	JAN 16 1837
HURD, Enoch	KILLDOVE, Elizabeth	JAN 06 1851
HURD, John	McMAGHEN, Hannah	SEP 03 1853
HURDEL, Sarah Ann	GREEN, William	NOV 09 1826
HURDLE, A.	BARREMANS, Charles	MAY 02 1829
HURDLE, Adaline	BASSETT, Isaac	DEC 26 1838
HURDLE, Andrew J.	ENNIS, Mary	JUL 27 1858

District of Columbia Marriage Licenses, 1811-1858

HURDLE, Ann	HOWELL, Thomas	JUL 28 1812
HURDLE, Ann	CHERRY, Dominick	FEB 08 1813
HURDLE, Ann Maria	KNOTT, James	AUG 05 1828
HURDLE, Caroline	PARKER, George W.	DEC 20 1837
HURDLE, Eliza	PUMPHREY, Judson	AUG 08 1834
HURDLE, Elizabeth	WALKER, James	APR 19 1843
HURDLE, Elizabeth	ROBINSON, Daniel	APR 11 1850
HURDLE, Frances E.	PRITCHETT, George A.	JAN 07 1847
HURDLE, Frances Marion	CALVERT, John James	NOV 08 1854
HURDLE, Francis Marion	GALER, William Brooke	NOV 09 1854
HURDLE, George	MASON, Susan	MAR 27 1817
HURDLE, George N.	NORRIS, Jane	JAN 15 1829
HURDLE, George W.	COLLINS, Sarah	DEC 14 1854
HURDLE, Hellen R.	MITTEREGYER, Charles H.	OCT 23 1841
HURDLE, Henry M.	BEATY, Amanda M.F.	MAR 22 1841
HURDLE, James	REEDER, Mary Ann	NOV 19 1826
HURDLE, John	GREENTREE, Margaret	MAY 23 1818
HURDLE, Margaret	EBERY, George	MAR 07 1848
HURDLE, Martha E.	DeVAUGHN, John T.	MAY 09 1842
HURDLE, Mary	BURCH, William S.	SEP 16 1846
HURDLE, Mary A.	COLLINS, Joseph	DEC 22 1851
HURDLE, Mary Ann	HOWARD, James	OCT 04 1849
HURDLE, Robert	PAYNE, Susan	MAR 16 1843
HURDLE, Robert	CARROLL, Elizabeth	AUG 15 1848
HURDLE, Samuel V.	CALVERT, Grace M.	JUN 17 1850
HURDLE, Sarah O.	BLAKE, George W.	MAY 19 1857
HURDLE, Thomas	RIDER, Ann	SEP 17 1834
HURDLE, Washington	SPINOGLE, Barbara	JAN 11 1831
HURDLE, William	ADAMS, Elizabeth	MAR 21 1826
HURLEBAUS, Gottlieb	HUBNER, Frederika	APR 21 1856
HURLEY, Ann	LYONS, John	JAN 19 1828
HURLEY, Cornelia	ATWOOD, William	FEB 19 1852
HURLEY, Cornelia	BURRISS, William A.	FEB 27 1858
HURLEY, Cornelius	MURPHY, Catharine	JUN 12 1845
HURLEY, Daniel	NALIGAN, Norah	SEP 14 1848
HURLEY, Delilah	PILES, Leonard	OCT 14 1823
HURLEY, Elizabeth	MOLAND, Geo. Air	OCT 21 1816
HURLEY, Elizabeth	POPE, John	NOV 20 1816
HURLEY, Elizabeth R.	CLEMENTS, John W.	FEB 28 1848
HURLEY, Ellen	HARRINGTON, James	JAN 09 1851
HURLEY, Ellen	DUNN, James	AUG 02 1851
HURLEY, Fendell	BAKER, Hannah	DEC 17 1822
HURLEY, Frances Rebecca	HAMILTON, Francis	MAY 20 1847
HURLEY, George	FRAMES, Dorah	NOV 01 1813
HURLEY, Henry	FOWLER, Barbara G.	OCT 11 1830
HURLEY, Henry	GOLDSMITH, Harriet A.	JUL 05 1854
HURLEY, Honora	GARRITY, James	NOV 24 1855
HURLEY, James W.	GARNER, Harriet Ann	AUG 19 1847
HURLEY, James W.	CUSICH, Mary K.	MAY 21 1857
HURLEY, Jane Rebecca	BOWEN, John Thomas	MAR 16 1850
HURLEY, Jeremiah	HENLEY, Celia V.	APR 12 1855
HURLEY, John F.	DANT, Mary Ann	OCT 05 1841
HURLEY, John P.	JOHNSON, Amanda	JUN 26 1854
HURLEY, John T.	TAYLOR, Cenia	DEC 01 1849
HURLEY, John W.	CLEMENTS, Margaret	AUG 29 1853
HURLEY, Julia	HURLEY, Timothy	MAR 09 1851
HURLEY, Lawrence	MANAHAN, Margt.	JUN 29 1855
HURLEY, Lucy	NALLY, Jno.	JUN 29 1819

District of Columbia Marriage Licenses, 1811-1858

HURLEY, Lurana R.	LOVEJOY, John T.	MAR 06 1855
HURLEY, Margaret	COLLINS, Charles	JUL 02 1836
HURLEY, Martha Ann	CATON, Thomas	NOV 20 1844
HURLEY, Mary	YOUNG, William	DEC 26 1839
HURLEY, Mary	LOONEY, Dennis	JUL 18 1851
HURLEY, Mary	MALOWNEY, John	FEB 09 1852
HURLEY, Rachael	HUTCHINSON, Benedick	FEB 04 1817
HURLEY, Roberta	THOMPSON, Wilkerson	AUG 30 1853
HURLEY, Salem	SMITH, Lawrina	DEC 23 1815
HURLEY, Sarah	DAVIS, Edward	OCT 30 1814
HURLEY, Sarah Elizth.	TUCKER, John W.	JAN 07 1856
HURLEY, Susanna M.	UMSTATTED, Richard S.	NOV 07 1847
HURLEY, Theodore	BOND, Ann	SEP 14 1852
HURLEY, Timothy	HURLEY, Julia	MAR 09 1851
HURLEY, Virginia A.	DAWSON, Edward L.	OCT 29 1850
HURLEY, William	ALDERIDGE, Alethia	FEB 01 1817
HURLEY, William	COLLINS, Mary	JAN 07 1836
HURLY, Obid	ARTIS, Jane	JAN 31 1826
HURREN, Theodore	WHITE, Issabella	JUN 05 1821
HURSE, Ann	POWERS, Montyseller	AUG 02 1826
HURSE, Mary	MYERS, C.C.	OCT 17 1854
HURSE, Thomas	HUTCHINSON, Elizabeth	NOV 15 1826
HURST, Ann (blk)	GOINS, Patrick	MAY 06 1830
HURST, Ephraim H.	FRY, Maria	AUG 18 1823
HURST, Henry [Sgt.]	CONNIX, Grace [Mrs.]	NOV 04 1828
HURST, Henry W.	LEGG, Cecelia Frances	AUG 30 1852
HURST, Jemima	WILLIAMS, William J.	FEB 27 1845
HURST, John H.	BICKSLER, Ann V.	DEC 11 1854
HURST, Mary	WHEELER, William	OCT 13 1846
HURST, Miriam E.	STEVENS, Paul	NOV 02 1844
HURST, Rachel (blk)	FURR, Edward	JAN 12 1825
HURST, Robert	MASSEY, Mary Jane	JAN 08 1852
HURST, Sarah	JONES, John L.	MAY 28 1857
HURST, Thomas	VERTZ, Ann	MAY 22 1813
HURST, Uriah	LASKEY, Elizabeth	JUN 16 1840
HURST, William B.	PERRIE, Julia Ann	DEC 09 1845
HURST, William Decatur	GAMBLE, Mary Lang	NOV 14 1848
HURT, Cyntha M.	JENKINS, John W.	SEP 03 1855
HURT, Floyd B.	CHAPPELL, Clara C.	MAY 05 1854
HUSE, Mary	RICHARDSON, Alerson	JUN 18 1818
HUSLER, Caroline	CLEMENTSON, William H.	NOV 29 1823
HUSSEY, Ellen	HERLAHY, John	MAY 08 1857
HUSSEY, Jeremiah	BAYNE, Martha	NOV 03 1856
HUSTER, Mary Ann	ASHFORD, Michael	OCT 24 1842
HUSTLER, Eleanor	BROWN, William	MAR 05 1835
HUSTON, James G.	WATSON, Elia Ann	JUL 27 1838
HUTCHENS, Charity	WHITE, Singleton	NOV 28 1831
HUTCHENSON, Sarah	O'DONNOGHUE, Timothy	OCT 25 1825
HUTCHERSON, E.	HARDON, Susan Ann	SEP 18 1845
HUTCHERSON, Thompson	SAMPSON, Martha	MAY 23 1846
HUTCHERSON, Walter	SOPER, Elizabeth	FEB 22 1816
HUTCHERSON, William	McDERMOTT, Mary	MAY 09 1848
HUTCHESON, Ambrose A.	WIRSHING, Sarah Ann	APR 28 1854
HUTCHESON, Ann M.	HAYNES, Robert L.	DEC 23 1856
HUTCHIN, Sarah (blk)	LOMIX, William	MAY 26 1823
HUTCHINGS, Mary Ann	DARNALL, James M.	MAR 23 1843
HUTCHINGSON, Thomas	BRIGHT, Apolonia	JAN 19 1853
HUTCHINS, Ann Matilda	SHAW, Nathan R.	DEC 20 1841

District of Columbia Marriage Licenses, 1811-1858

HUTCHINS, Anne M.	HARBAUGH, Edward L.	OCT 04 1845
HUTCHINS, Benedict	PAYNE, Martha E.	SEP 06 1852
HUTCHINS, Charles	RAGAN, Cecilia	SEP 27 1830
HUTCHINS, Elias	MOXLEY, Elizabeth	SEP 27 1855
HUTCHINS, Eliza Jane	HILLEARY, Theodore	AUG 31 1850
HUTCHINS, Ellen	LIPSCOMB, William	MAY 06 1830
HUTCHINS, George W.	DYER, Dianna	APR 24 1850
HUTCHINS, Hillery	BILLIPS, Eliza	OCT 06 1855
HUTCHINS, John	ETCHERN, Sarah	FEB 10 1821
HUTCHINS, John	HOLTZMAN, Eliza	NOV 02 1827
HUTCHINS, John	NOBLE, Martha	APR 14 1856
HUTCHINS, Lavinia	ELLIS, Francis	JUN 11 1851
HUTCHINS, Margaret Ann	BADGET, William B.	NOV 12 1822
HUTCHINS, Margaretta A.	COPP, Moses	DEC 11 1850
HUTCHINS, Martha E.	HITCHCOCK, Alfred J.	AUG 09 1858
HUTCHINS, Mary Ann	RABBITT, Thomas	MAR 26 1825
HUTCHINS, Mary E.	CROWN, Saml. T.	JAN 17 1856
HUTCHINS, Matilda	CUSTIS, George	AUG 21 1856
HUTCHINS, Peter A.	WOOD, Catherine Jane	OCT 22 1842
HUTCHINS, Robert	MAUL, Elizabeth	AUG 25 1842
HUTCHINS, Samuel A.	BROWN, Sarah G.	NOV 28 1829
HUTCHINS, Susan	NEWTON, Henry T.	MAR 25 1836
HUTCHINS, Susan	BARBOUR, Andrew	OCT 02 1841
HUTCHINS, Tilley	EVANS, William	AUG 01 1814
HUTCHINS, William	ROBEY, Ann	APR 21 1827
HUTCHINS, Wm. H.	CHAMLYN, Elizabeth R.	DEC 25 1850
HUTCHINS, [blank]	CROWN, Matilda	JUL 18 1826
HUTCHINSON, Amelia (blk)	DAVIS, Charles	JAN 28 1857
HUTCHINSON, Ann	SIMONTON, John W.	MAR 29 1827
HUTCHINSON, Benedick	HURLEY, Rachael	FEB 04 1817
HUTCHINSON, Betty F.	SHAPLEY, John M.	MAR 01 1852
HUTCHINSON, Caroline	MILES, John Read	SEP 09 1834
HUTCHINSON, Caroline	VENABLE, Joseph G.	DEC 31 1851
HUTCHINSON, Catharine	LITTLEFORD, Addison	FEB 25 1835
HUTCHINSON, Dory	WALKER, Miss Nancy	OCT 05 1815
HUTCHINSON, Elizabeth	HURSE, Thomas	NOV 15 1826
HUTCHINSON, Elizabeth	BUTLER, Thomas	NOV 14 1838
HUTCHINSON, Elizabeth	CODRICK, Joseph	MAY 13 1856
HUTCHINSON, Elizabeth	FOLEY, Daniel	MAY 18 1858
HUTCHINSON, Elizabeth B.	MAGRUDER, William B.	SEP 08 1835
HUTCHINSON, Hannah D.	WESTWOOD, Wm. P.	JUN 24 1858
HUTCHINSON, Hester E.	WHITEMORE, Zacha. H.	JUN 26 1855
HUTCHINSON, James	CHURCH, Elenora	JUL 30 1850
HUTCHINSON, James H.	GEE, Frances	OCT 27 1855
HUTCHINSON, James L.	LEAK, Sarah C.	JUN 10 1858
HUTCHINSON, James S.	GOODWIN, Frances A.	FEB 15 1842
HUTCHINSON, Jane	NOHS, William	DEC 06 1854
HUTCHINSON, Jemima	ASKINS, Erasmus	SEP 01 1812
HUTCHINSON, Jeremiah	CARTER, Charlotte (blk)	JUN 23 1857
HUTCHINSON, John	WOOD, Lucy	FEB 03 1818
HUTCHINSON, John	THOMPSON, Mary Ann	APR 13 1854
HUTCHINSON, John	THOMPSON, Mary Ann	JUN 06 1857
HUTCHINSON, John A.	MARTIN, Catherine M.	DEC 14 1848
HUTCHINSON, Martha B.	BARRY, John W.	OCT 01 1834
HUTCHINSON, Mary	KIDWELL, Benjamin	MAR 03 1825
HUTCHINSON, Mary	BURGESS, Washington	MAR 29 1836
HUTCHINSON, Mary A.	DEAN, George	OCT 16 1850
HUTCHINSON, Mary B.	FERGUSON, William B.	OCT 16 1833

District of Columbia Marriage Licenses, 1811-1858

HUTCHINSON, Mary Ellen	FARRAR, John S.	JUL 09 1836
HUTCHINSON, Matilda	KING, William	JAN 01 1829
HUTCHINSON, Matilda	REGAEN, Daniel	MAY 17 1832
HUTCHINSON, Matilda	CATOR, George	JAN 15 1857
HUTCHINSON, Nathan	YOUNG, Elizabeth	FEB 27 1812
HUTCHINSON, Philip	ROBINSON, Susan (blk)	MAR 17 1823
HUTCHINSON, Priscilla	WILBURN, Benj.	JAN 07 1813
HUTCHINSON, Sarah	JOHNSTON, Robert	MAR 04 1833
HUTCHINSON, Theodore	VERMILLION, Hetty Ann	FEB 09 1850
HUTCHINSON, Thomas	ALLEN, Linney	MAY 30 1839
HUTCHINSON, Thomas	MASTERS, Mary	NOV 23 1842
HUTCHINSON, Thompson	SPEAKS, Sarah	MAR 28 1821
HUTCHINSON, Valinda	PILES, Francis	JUN 09 1818
HUTCHINSON, William	GARDINER, Ann	MAY 07 1833
HUTCHINSON, William	BARBER, Catharine	JAN 29 1857
HUTCHINSON, William E.	HARRISON, Ann Catharine	JAN 25 1851
HUTCHINSON, William P.	PALMER, Frances	FEB 11 1850
HUTCHISON, Ann	GRACE, John	FEB 04 1825
HUTCHISON, Archibald	DEMARIST, Mary Ann	OCT 26 1826
HUTCHISON, Frances A.	MARTIN, John M.	MAR 13 1855
HUTCHISON, Huldah C.	CLARKE, George W.	NOV 01 1855
HUTCHISON, Jeremiah	GANTT, Martha Ellen	JUL 26 1834
HUTCHISON, John	THOMPSON, Eliza	DEC 13 1825
HUTCHISON, Joseph	WALKER, Sarah E.	MAY 25 1858
HUTCHISON, Margaret	PHILLIPS, George	JUN 18 1856
HUTCHISON, Maria	SHUMATE, Murphey C.	NOV 22 1827
HUTCHISON, Sarah J.	WHALEY, James H.	JAN 15 1855
HUTCHISON, Walter	SIMMONS, Mary	NOV 08 1825
HUTH, John Frederick	SPÜNLEIN, Christiana	AUG 07 1852
HUTSON, Mary	SIBLEY, Benjamin	FEB 24 1827
HUTSON, Samuel	WILSON, Hariot	DEC 29 1824
HUTT, Frederick	SUPPER, Eleanor	SEP 13 1853
HUTT, Mary R. (blk)	BUTLER, Samuel H.	MAR 04 1856
HUTTON, Ann	GARDINER, John	SEP 05 1820
HUTTON, Cecelia	DAFNEY, Marcus	APR 27 1821
HUTTON, George	MILLER, Sarah B.	DEC 08 1842
HUTTON, Hannah	POLKINKORN, Charles	SEP 03 1822
HUTTON, Jacob Deans	SUTTER, Catharine S.	SEP 10 1850
HUTTON, James	CATHCART, Elizth. W.	JUL 16 1821
HUTTON, James	RICH, Salome	MAY 24 1825
HUTTON, Jane (blk)	WATERS, Peter	JAN 11 1836
HUTTON, John B.	EDENBURGH, Mary Ann	APR 07 1825
HUTTON, Sarah E.	COOK, Matthew	JAN 25 1840
HUTTON, William	GERMAN, Fanny	OCT 23 1854
HYATT, Alfred	STELTINIUS, Rachael	OCT 10 1825
HYATT, Levi T.	WOLFE, Ann L.	JUL 02 1855
HYATT, Rezen	DUVAL, Orilla	NOV 20 1819
HYATT, Richard G.	LAWRENSON, Margaret A.	NOV 04 1845
HYATT, Samuel	CHURCH, Sally	MAR 24 1814
HYATT, Sarah	FILLMORE, John H.	JUL 03 1849
HYATT, Seth	SUMMERVILLE, Jane [Mrs.]	AUG 23 1813
HYATT, Virginia	WHITTLESY, Cumfort S.	SEP 30 1844
HYDE, Anna E.	FITZHUGH, Robert R.	MAY 03 1849
HYDE, Anthony	SMITH, Maria	FEB 20 1832
HYDE, Charles K.	MASON, E. Cary	APR 21 1840
HYDE, David	WALSH, Julia	SEP 09 1856
HYDE, Eleanor	ORME, Jeremiah	MAR 14 1826
HYDE, Eliza	CLEMENTS, Ben<u>nett</u>	AUG 05 1817

District of Columbia Marriage Licenses, 1811-1858

HYDE, Henry	GATES, Dorcas Ann	OCT 07 1852
HYDE, Lydia Ann	ORME, Jeremiah	JUL 15 1835
HYDE, Moses	PECHIN, Anna Maria E.	OCT 19 1836
HYDE, Rachael	ETTER, Joseph	MAY 04 1840
HYDE, Rebecca	BARBARIN, Fras. S.	APR 08 1856
HYDE, Richard A.	TUCKER, Elizabeth A.	JUL 03 1854
HYDE, Samuel Gridley	RIDGELY, Mary A. Hopkins	OCT 18 1852
HYDE, Thomas	MILLER, Ann	JAN 09 1832
HYDE, Thomas V.	BOYD, Constantine	OCT 10 1839
HYDE, Thos. F.	GARNER, Sarah	JUL 22 1822
HYDE, William	HEKROTH, Anna	FEB 01 1850
HYDMILLER, Albert	HARSCAMP, Mary	SEP 19 1838
HYER, Harriet	PEIRCE, George	APR 12 1824
HYLE, John	PEARCE, Susanna	AUG 29 1812
HYMAS, Godfrey Joseph	THOMPSON, Margaret Jane	MAR 10 1858
HYSIE, Caroline	SHEPHERD, Joseph	FEB 01 1840
HYSSETT, Joseph	PATCHETT, Amy	SEP 09 1844

District of Columbia Marriage Licenses, 1811-1858

I

IBBERTSON, Sarah	KERSEY, Edward	APR 05 1844
IDDINS, Frederick	TRUMAN, Jane	APR 29 1840
IDEAN, Catherine	BARBER, John	NOV 20 1815
IGLAND, Henry	WOODWARD, Mary Ann (blk)	FEB 17 1854
IGLEHART, Catharine	FRIDER, John	OCT 20 1851
IGLEHART, Charles D.	HASLUP, Elizabeth A.	OCT 18 1853
IGLEHART, Edward	DUVALL, Martha Ann	FEB 01 1840
IGLEHART, Isaac B.	LEWIS, Mary Amey	JUL 21 1840
ILER, Mary Jane	KRAF, Joseph	MAR 30 1857
IMERSON, Ede	DAVIS, Thomas Richard	JAN 21 1826
IMES, Elizabeth	JOHNSON, Thomas L.	MAY 01 1828
IMES, Mary	BAYER, Ferdinand	JUN 20 1817
IMHOF, Feronika	KRIEGENHOFER, George	NOV 03 1857
IMMICH, Jacob	MURRAY, Eliza	FEB 20 1851
INCH, Philip	O'NEAL, Mary	FEB 14 1830
INDERIDEN, Maria	BOLDT, August	MAY 08 1835
INDERMANER, Jeremiah	NORRIS, Margaret	JUL 24 1856
INDERMAUER, Jeremiah	BOLLINGER, Margaretta	MAY 01 1828
INGALL, Izabella	COLLINS, William	DEC 23 1845
INGERSOLL, Elizabeth Ann	BAMBERGER, George U.	JAN 06 1853
INGHRAM, Mary Ann	FLETCHER, Joseph	JUN 21 1855
INGLE, Adeline	BUTLER, George G.	JUL 03 1854
INGLE, Ann	LINDSLEY, Eleazer	APR 28 1818
INGLE, Christiana	UNDERWOOD, John	NOV 05 1822
INGLE, Henry	CHESHIRE, Rosina	MAY 02 1843
INGLE, Henry	LLOYD, Elizabeth C.	MAY 11 1852
INGLE, John	MILLER, Catharine	NOV 16 1850
INGLE, John P.	BAKER, Susan H.	AUG 29 1825
INGLE, John P.	BAKER, Mildred H.	DEC 19 1846
INGLE, John P.	BAKER, Eliza B.	AUG 06 1855
INGLE, Joseph	EVANS, Lucy M.	MAY 02 1818
INGLE, Maria	HANSON, Grafton D.	JUN 20 1853
INGLE, Mary	CAMPBELL, Wm. H.	MAR 22 1825
INGLE, Mary	CASH, John C.	NOV 23 1852
INGLE, Susan B.	CHILDS, Asaph K.	JAN 17 1856
INGMAN, William	MUDD, Julia Ann	APR 09 1831
INGRAHAM, George H.	PINDEN, Eugenia L.	NOV 27 1856
INGRAM, Elizabeth	TRAVERS, William	AUG 26 1831
INGRAM, James	MAXWELL, Susana	SEP 22 1855
INGRAM, Sarah Ann	GOODMAN, William H.	AUG 03 1854
INGRAM, Washington	SMITH, Letty (blk)	NOV 15 1827
INNEMANN, George	MILLER, Rosina	APR 12 1852
INSCOE, Toliaver	STAPLE, Ellen	JUL 17 1847
INSCOW, Uriah	CHRISMOND, Sarah J.	FEB 26 1849
IRELAND, Anna M. (blk)	BROWN, Owen W.	OCT 30 1855
IRELAND, Elizabeth	TURNER, John	NOV 18 1815
IRELAND, Mary Elizabeth	JONES, Charles J.	MAR 18 1856
IRENG, Sophia	RUHLAND, Henry	JAN 23 1858
IRETON, Michl.	RONAN, Mary	FEB 10 1855
IRONSIDE, George B.	SWIFT, Mary E.	MAR 23 1846
IRONSIDE, Mary Hellen	FAGAN, George	OCT 28 1830
IRONSIDE, Roger B.	HOOD, Mary W.	AUG 02 1853
IRONTON, Ann	WHALEN, John	OCT 28 1841
IRONTON, Martha	BELL, Littleton A.	SEP 15 1847
IRVIN, Elizabeth	FRY, Samuel	FEB 11 1828
IRVIN, Martha T.	MOONEY, Noble H.	OCT 12 1836

District of Columbia Marriage Licenses, 1811-1858

IRVIN, William W.	BACHE, Sophia A.	FEB 28 1839
IRVING, Mary E.	COLLIER, Thomas T.	AUG 03 1839
IRVINS, John J.	FERGURSON, Elizabeth	DEC 09 1813
IRWIN, Ellen Williams	BOTELER, Joseph Isaac	NOV 07 1833
IRWIN, Thos.	GIBSON, Susannah	DEC 20 1838
IRWING, Agnes V.	TOWERS, Wm. H.H.	JAN 20 1857
IRWING, Henrietta	GREER, James C.	JAN 18 1847
ISAAC, Charles A.	BUCKEY, Ann M.	AUG 28 1833
ISAACS, George W.	HILL, Ann	JUN 20 1827
ISEMANN, John Casper	WALLER, Waldburg	OCT 17 1856
ISENHOOT, Louisa	WAGNER, Philip	JUL 21 1858
ISHERWOOD, Frances Ann	DAWSON, George W., of Wm.	FEB 01 1855
ISHERWOOD, Robert	BROWN, Christiana	MAR 21 1825
ISRAEL, George W.	WOODWARD, Sarah Roszel	FEB 28 1843
ISRAEL, Martha	WILLIAMS, James	MAY 13 1851
ISRAEL, Mary E.	BOND, James L.	OCT 25 1847
ISRAEL, Robert	McNEIR, Elizabeth Guest	NOV 09 1852
ISRAEL, Ruth	GATTRELL, Atho	OCT 01 1833
IVERSON, Ellen	PAYNE, William	OCT 11 1837
IVERY, Polly	BLADEN, Joseph	AUG 24 1815
IVES, Abagail	CRUMP, Lewis A.	JAN 15 1851
IVES, Joseph C.	SEMMES, Cora M.	JAN 15 1855
IVEY, William H.	MOSS, Katherine M.	JUN 01 1839
IZENHAUSEN, Elizabeth	SIMON, Peter	AUG 09 1850

District of Columbia Marriage Licenses, 1811-1858

J

JACK, James, Junr.	EDELIN, Susannah	NOV 16 1847
JACK, Susanna	STANLEY, Joseph B.	FEB 18 1847
JACKSON, Addison	COLE, Jane	OCT 25 1842
JACKSON, Adelaide F.	NICHOLLS, William	MAR 18 1840
JACKSON, Adelaide F.	FIELDS, Henry	NOV 23 1847
JACKSON, Alexander	WALKER, Mahalia	JUN 03 1845
JACKSON, Alexander	RICKETS, Mary Elizabeth	MAY 27 1846
JACKSON, Alfred	SIMMS, Ann	NOV 02 1830
JACKSON, Alonzo	LEONARD, Catherine	APR 10 1858
JACKSON, Andrew	DUVALL, Mary Jane	AUG 19 1843
JACKSON, Andrew	JONES, Rebecca M.	MAR 29 1849
JACKSON, Andrew	FITZGERALD, Ellen	SEP 18 1850
JACKSON, Andrew M.	TUCKER, Susan J.	APR 01 1828
JACKSON, Ann (blk)	TYLER, Robert	SEP 14 1837
JACKSON, Ann M.	STEWART, Barnett	DEC 09 1844
JACKSON, Apthrope	JASPER, Jane	JUN 12 1817
JACKSON, Artridge P.	WATERS, Cyrus	JAN 19 1844
JACKSON, Catharine F.	McCLISH, George	MAR 28 1832
JACKSON, Catharine R.	GRAVES, John B.	MAY 12 1858
JACKSON, Delia (blk)	PROCTER, Isaac	FEB 05 1846
JACKSON, Edward	LICKSON, Philice	DEC 28 1815
JACKSON, Edward	O'BRIEN, Nannie B.	NOV 01 1855
JACKSON, Eleanor	RIDGELEY, Henry	JAN 12 1820
JACKSON, Eleanor	BOWLES, Charles	NOV 27 1841
JACKSON, Elethea Ann (blk)	WILLIAMS, Alfred	JUN 18 1836
JACKSON, Eli	TWINE, Eliza (blk)	AUG 02 1853
JACKSON, Eliza	McCARTY, John	FEB 24 1829
JACKSON, Eliza	NEWTON, William Thomas	FEB 07 1846
JACKSON, Eliza (col'd)	LOMAX, Dennis	AUG 31 1854
JACKSON, Eliza A.	CLARKE, James	FEB 08 1848
JACKSON, Elizabeth (blk)	JOHNS, Jacob	JUN 19 1830
JACKSON, Elizabeth (blk)	ROACH, Charles	AUG 05 1835
JACKSON, Elizabeth (blk)	MURRAY, Gilbert	JAN 21 1840
JACKSON, Elizabeth (blk)	BRANUM, John W.	OCT 26 1843
JACKSON, Elizabeth D.	PALMER, Dr. W. Gray	SEP 20 1847
JACKSON, Ellen	MINER, John	JUL 11 1837
JACKSON, Francis	BELL, Mary	FEB 13 1851
JACKSON, Francis A.	WARD, George W.	JAN 15 1846
JACKSON, George	ADAMS, Eliza (blk)	MAY 09 1848
JACKSON, George C.	CLARVOE, Mary Ann H.	SEP 30 1844
JACKSON, George W.	LOVE, Margaret A.	DEC 22 1846
JACKSON, Hannah (blk)	CHANEY, William	MAY 08 1850
JACKSON, Harriet	RUNNER, John H.	JUL 28 1858
JACKSON, Harriet L.	ST. CLAIR, Walter	OCT 07 1830
JACKSON, Henry	LYNE, Larenia [Mrs.]	JAN 02 1833
JACKSON, Henry	CALVERT, Rebecca (blk)	FEB 22 1848
JACKSON, Jacob	PERIL, Catharine	SEP 03 1818
JACKSON, Jacob	BURKE, Ellen (blk)	MAY 11 1840
JACKSON, James	WOLTZ, Mary Ann	JUN 29 1837
JACKSON, James	HAWKINS, Maria (blk)	JAN 03 1854
JACKSON, James T.	FORD, Lucinda (blk)	APR 24 1855
JACKSON, Jane (blk)	THOMPSON, Lifus	APR 04 1831
JACKSON, Jane (blk)	SHINER, Michael	SEP 08 1849
JACKSON, Jane (blk)	PROCTER, George	MAY 28 1850
JACKSON, Jane J.	HENDERSON, Tarlton T.	SEP 06 1824
JACKSON, John S. [Dr.]	EDELEN, Mary W.	MAY 04 1824

District of Columbia Marriage Licenses, 1811-1858

JACKSON, John Thos. Jefferson	HILL, Harriet	JAN 19 1836
JACKSON, John W.	TRACEY, Frances	OCT 30 1839
JACKSON, Joseph	BUTLER, Cassy	DEC 18 1817
JACKSON, Joseph	THOMSON, Jane (blk)	AUG 02 1851
JACKSON, Julia	KING, William	FEB 16 1836
JACKSON, Julia A.	ROWZEE, John	JAN 09 1837
JACKSON, Julia Ann	LANGLEY, Joseph	AUG 01 1839
JACKSON, Laura	HOGAN, Peter	OCT 07 1856
JACKSON, Laura	GROVES, William A.	APR 25 1857
JACKSON, Laura	GROVES, William A.	JUN 27 1857
JACKSON, Lethe Ann (blk)	WILLIAMS, Alfred	NOV 11 1837
JACKSON, Lewis	HAMMOND, Rebecca (blk)	NOV 15 1856
JACKSON, Lewis Thomas	POSEY, Martha Ann	MAR 25 1856
JACKSON, Louis B.	BUTLER, Harriet S. (blk)	APR 12 1852
JACKSON, Louisa	TAYLER, James	MAY 13 1826
JACKSON, Lucinda	HILL, Jno. Hy.	DEC 20 1844
JACKSON, Lucinda (blk)	MOORE, Henry	SEP 19 1855
JACKSON, Lucinda (blk)	LEWIS, Joseph	OCT 22 1857
JACKSON, Lucy Ann (blk)	PAYNE, John	MAY 29 1830
JACKSON, Mahalable	GIDDINGS, William Hy.	FEB 27 1849
JACKSON, Margaret L.	HULSE, Isaac, Jr.	SEP 04 1850
JACKSON, Marianna E. (blk)	MADELLA, John H.	JUN 13 1854
JACKSON, Martha	HUGHES, William	OCT 04 1838
JACKSON, Martha	GRAHAM, James	AUG 17 1843
JACKSON, Mary	SHORTER, Charles	SEP 17 1817
JACKSON, Mary (blk)	KING, John	JAN 08 1842
JACKSON, Mary (blk)	LEE, Overton	SEP 12 1848
JACKSON, Mary (blk)	SIMS, Thomas H.	MAR 01 1853
JACKSON, Mary Ann	MITCHELL, Isaac	JUN 28 1840
JACKSON, Mary E.	WATERS, John H.	NOV 10 1840
JACKSON, Mary Elizabeth	RINGGOLD, William H.	JUN 04 1839
JACKSON, Mary Jane (blk)	JONES, John B.	JUN 29 1848
JACKSON, Mary Virginia	DORKINS, Henry	NOV 12 1857
JACKSON, Mary W. [Mrs.]	TULEY, Joseph	APR 20 1835
JACKSON, Matilda	JACKSON, Robert R.	JUN 09 1828
JACKSON, Mullady	HICKS, Lloyd	NOV 29 1844
JACKSON, Peter	DOOLING, Sarah	JAN 16 1847
JACKSON, Philip	NEALE, Elizabeth	SEP 29 1819
JACKSON, Pompey	KEARNS, Eliza	OCT 10 1833
JACKSON, Rebecca (blk)	LARGE, John	MAR 26 1840
JACKSON, Robert	NORRIS, Sophiah (blk)	DEC 10 1827
JACKSON, Robert	SELDEN, Lucinda (blk)	MAR 15 1841
JACKSON, Robert	HEPBURN, Maria	AUG 23 1849
JACKSON, Robert R.	JACKSON, Matilda A.	JUN 09 1828
JACKSON, Rose A.	OFFUTT, Joshua W.	JUN 18 1856
JACKSON, S. (blk)	JOHNSON, Peter	MAR 30 1840
JACKSON, Serena (blk)	SELBY, Patrick	DEC 22 1842
JACKSON, Simon	SCISSELL, Sarah Ann (blk)	NOV 30 1852
JACKSON, Susan	FITZGERALD, David	APR 10 1850
JACKSON, Susan (blk)	FLEET, Thomas	JUL 08 1829
JACKSON, Susan A.R.	LEWIS, John A.	SEP 18 1841
JACKSON, Susan L.	HALL, Edward	JUN 25 1851
JACKSON, Theoffa	SAVOY, Archabald	DEC 31 1812
JACKSON, Thomas	THOMPSON, Margaret	JUN 29 1820
JACKSON, Thomas	ANDERSON, Mary (blk)	MAR 26 1840
JACKSON, Tracy	BURKE, James	NOV 07 1844
JACKSON, William	WORMLEY, Lucy (blk)	MAY 20 1839
JACKSON, William	KARNEY, Mary (blk)	JUL 22 1850

District of Columbia Marriage Licenses, 1811-1858

JACKSON, William	BRAWNER, Charlotte	MAY 01 1855
JACKSON, William W.	KNOWLES, Rebecca	APR 23 1835
JACKSON, Wilson	PROCTOR, Mary (blk)	JAN 10 1843
JACOB, Henrietta	FUSS, John G.	SEP 08 1855
JACOB, Richard F.	BRENTON, Sarah	JAN 15 1848
JACOB, Rosa	HUHN, Michael	JUL 06 1858
JACOBI, Adolph	ELY, Elizabeth	APR 14 1847
JACOBI, William	KRIMMEL, Susanna	DEC 31 1834
JACOBS, Alfred	JEFFERSON, Margaret	DEC 02 1841
JACOBS, Ann	JONES, Joseph Walker	JAN 08 1818
JACOBS, Armstead	GOREM, Ellen	AUG 16 1849
JACOBS, Augustus	WOOD, Jane Ann	JUN 21 1836
JACOBS, Catherine	SHEETS, John George	JAN 03 1843
JACOBS, Cornelius	SUTER, Ann C.	MAR 22 1838
JACOBS, Edward	GREENWOOD, Elizabeth	DEC 24 1833
JACOBS, Elizabeth	BUTLER, Ignatius	JUL 08 1818
JACOBS, Elizabeth	EMERY, Robert	JUN 06 1831
JACOBS, Francis	LYLES, Julia A.	MAY 19 1830
JACOBS, George R.	NICHOLSON, Louisa	DEC 03 1849
JACOBS, Harrison	WILLIAMS, Susan Ann	JAN 12 1844
JACOBS, Henry	BETTINGER, Margaret A.E.	JAN 21 1852
JACOBS, Jane Ann	WISE, Samuel	MAR 10 1840
JACOBS, Johnana	PARKS, William G.	FEB 18 1857
JACOBS, Margaret Ann	FISHER, William C.	JAN 22 1850
JACOBS, Mary	GRINER, Adam	OCT 26 1839
JACOBS, Mary	KILRCHAR, David	JUL 10 1857
JACOBS, Mary M.R.B.	ALLEN, George William	MAR 06 1847
JACOBS, Solomon D.	JOHNSON, Matilda N.	JUN 07 1852
JACOBS, Thomas E.	CASTEL, Julia A.	MAR 07 1837
JAMEISON, S.S.	FRAMES, Mary	JUL 06 1821
JAMES, Amelia	MURRIS, Henry	MAY 11 1846
JAMES, Aures	GREEN, Polly (blk)	OCT 09 1838
JAMES, Charles A.	HOBBIE, Julia	MAY 15 1856
JAMES, Charles H.	HOLMEAD, Mary Ellen	JAN 09 1837
JAMES, Christiana	MACLERY, James	MAR 30 1819
JAMES, David B.	WHALEY, Harriet C.	JAN 20 1853
JAMES, Dennon	PANE, Catharine	JUL 07 1831
JAMES, Elizabeth	STEPHENS, Edward	APR 06 1824
JAMES, Frances Anna	CALVERT, William Henry	JUN 08 1854
JAMES, John	RIDGEWAY, Catherine	MAY 06 1833
JAMES, John Dawson	HOLMEAD, Emily V.	NOV 01 1831
JAMES, John P.W.	MORGAN, Ann	AUG 20 1833
JAMES, John W.	SMITH, Mary K.	MAR 27 1828
JAMES, Lavinia J.	JUDD, D. Corning	JUL 03 1852
JAMES, Lucy A.	CRITTENDEN, Richard N.	OCT 11 1855
JAMES, Mary F.	BROCK, William G.	NOV 11 1851
JAMES, Mary W.	JOHNSON, Philip C.	AUG 31 1857
JAMES, Robert	JENKINS, Frances (blk)	AUG 25 1853
JAMES, Sarah Ann	CALES, Thomas	JAN 13 1825
JAMES, William	WASHINGTON, Mary W.	OCT 14 1828
JAMES, William	BALLANTYNE, Margaret	OCT 14 1854
JAMESON, Caceluy C.	JOHNSON, Ann E.M.	MAY 20 1817
JAMESON, Charlotte	CLEMENTS, Thomas	JAN 27 1812
JAMESON, Ellen (blk)	HAYMAN, Ephraim	NOV 02 1844
JAMESON, John	QUEEN, Mary Ann	JUN 16 1818
JAMESON, John	CROMWELL, Harriett	MAR 12 1835
JAMESON, John M.	THOMAS, Eliza	JAN 10 1834
JAMESON, Sarah Ellen	MUDD, Jeremiah T.	FEB 16 1857

District of Columbia Marriage Licenses, 1811-1858

JAMESON, Teresa Celestia	BARKLEY, Samuel	JUL 30 1817
JAMESON, Terese C.	CLARKE, John D.	JUN 14 1814
JAMESON, Thomas A.	BARKLEY, Mary Henrietta	AUG 07 1845
JAMESSON, Martha	HIDE, George, Junr.	FEB 20 1827
JAMESSON, Sarah Jane Triplett	LINDSLEY, Abraham Bradley	SEP 29 1827
JAMESSON, William H.	TALIAFERRO, Cornelia Lee Turberville	DEC 03 1844
JAMIESON, Adel (blk)	MARTIN, Wm. H.	OCT 22 1851
JAMIESON, Teresa	O'DONOGHUE, Dennis	MAY 12 1852
JAMISON, Ann	PEERCE, John	FEB 05 1816
JAMISON, Elias	COLSTON, Elizabeth E. (blk)	OCT 06 1842
JAMISON, Francis	HUBBARD, Catharine	OCT 03 1850
JAMISON, John	HENDERSON, Nelly (blk)	DEC 12 1832
JAMISON, Marsham	MARSTERS, Mary	MAY 18 1819
JAMISON, Mary	DORSEY, Benjamin W.	DEC 08 1835
JAMISON, Mary E.	BRIDGET, John F.	APR 15 1844
JAMISON, Peter S.	MINCHIN, Martha S.	APR 08 1819
JAMISON, Uzziel W.	SPENCER, Margaret H.	FEB 01 1855
JANISON, Mary J.	WEST, William C.	JUN 01 1857
JANNEY, Edward	LOWE, Martha Ann	JAN 02 1834
JANNEY, Lewis	BROWN, Martha A.	AUG 03 1837
JANNEY, Margaret	RENWICK, Henry B.	JUN 21 1852
JARBAUR, William	LAMBAUGH, Catharine	NOV 06 1819
JARBER, Eleanor	DEAKON, John Archy	JUN 03 1817
JARBOE, Anna E.	KESSLER, George E.	JUL 20 1855
JARBOE, Benedict	KING, Martha Ann	AUG 21 1827
JARBOE, Benedict	WILBURNE, Mary Ann	MAY 04 1854
JARBOE, Bennett	TALBERT, Elizabeth	FEB 18 1813
JARBOE, Elizabeth	SUMMERS, Anthony	FEB 21 1825
JARBOE, Elizabeth A.	HOWE, Richard	AUG 11 1842
JARBOE, Francis M.	JILTON, Harriet Mc.	DEC 06 1845
JARBOE, J.J.	SMOOT, Eliza E.	JAN 06 1838
JARBOE, John T.	SOPER, Mary H.	JUN 02 1849
JARBOE, Joshua N.	MOORE, Catharine	SEP 15 1830
JARBOE, Mary A.	RUSSELL, Chas. H.	OCT 27 1857
JARBOE, Mary J.	ROCK, Henry	JUN 24 1857
JARBOE, Mary Jane	COOMBS, Samuel	OCT 01 1845
JARBOE, Mary L.	CLARKE, Daniel D.	JAN 29 1856
JARBOE, Matthew	REYNOLDS, Mary [Mrs.]	JUL 12 1825
JARBOE, Matthew	DEVIS, Rebecca	APR 09 1853
JARBOE, Sarah J.	DENEALE, Cleland K.	MAY 06 1841
JARBOE, Thomas	GOODIN, Mary Ann	DEC 05 1837
JARBOE, William J.	BROWN, Matilda	JAN 31 1826
JARDELLA, Charles T.	WILLIAMS, Anna E.	NOV 13 1855
JARDELLA, John A.C.	BULGER, Margaret A.	DEC 31 1850
JARDELLA, Josephine B.	HICKS, William G.	OCT 20 1838
JARDELLA, Laurence	WALKER, Anna M.	JAN 25 1853
JARDIN, Armand	FAVIER, Honorine	SEP 22 1849
JARDINE, Lucy Virginia	CAMPBELL, [torn out]	JUL 02 1847
JARRETT, Eliza	BURK, William	MAR 17 1819
JARVIS, Ann Rebecca	MARKER, Jacob	FEB 14 1832
JARVIS, Catharine Ann	FREE, John	DEC 14 1833
JARVIS, Cipriana	ROBERTSON, Sarah	OCT 10 1844
JARVIS, Cipriano	HELLEN, Elizabeth	APR 04 1848
JARVIS, Eliza	SCOTT, Henry	FEB 02 1836
JARVIS, Jane E.	WALKER, Charles	MAR 03 1834
JARVIS, John	MOORE, Elizabeth	AUG 28 1844
JARVIS, John	OSBORNE, Ann	AUG 07 1848
JARVIS, John	MUNDLE, Rachel	OCT 11 1855

District of Columbia Marriage Licenses, 1811-1858

JARVIS, Miles	SIMPSON, Jane	MAR 23 1826
JASPER, Daniel S.	MAGRUDER, Adlina E.	NOV 11 1849
JASPER, Henry	CARROLL, Sarah (blk)	JAN 15 1834
JASPER, Jane	JACKSON, Apthrope	JUN 12 1817
JASPER, Julia (blk)	ROBINSON, David	JUL 31 1848
JAUDON, Samuel	ALRICKS, Marguerite P.	AUG 04 1823
JAVENS, Ann	PHILIPS, George	JUL 06 1849
JAVENS, Matilda	PENN, John	DEC 25 1829
JAVENS, Sarah	SIMMS, William	APR 16 1845
JAVINS, George	TOLBERT, Ann	APR 16 1835
JAVINS, John W.	JAVINS, Sabina	JUN 04 1846
JAVINS, Margaret	BARKMAN, George	SEP 15 1836
JAVINS, Randolph	COLE, Georgiana	JUL 17 1858
JAVINS, Sabina	JAVINS, John W.	JUN 04 1846
JAVINS, Williams	SPENCER, Sarah	JUL 05 1853
JAY, Peter Augustus	PEARSON, Josephine	JAN 12 1848
JEANTET, Marie	DUBOIS, Francois	FEB 28 1857
JEFFERS, Amanda	HOWARD, George W.	MAY 07 1833
JEFFERS, Ann	CHAMBERS, John	APR 21 1823
JEFFERS, Braxton B.	TAYLOR, Kate Cornelia	OCT 04 1855
JEFFERS, Catharine	LYON, Charles	DEC 11 1816
JEFFERS, Eliza M.	JONES, Philip R.	DEC 09 1844
JEFFERS, Hannah	O'BRIAN, Josephus	JAN 04 1814
JEFFERS, Maria	NICHOLSON, Lewis F.	FEB 09 1831
JEFFERS, Mary Ann	KAVANAUGH, John	JUL 12 1834
JEFFERS, Sarah	DOWNS, Hillary	FEB 04 1817
JEFFERS, Susan B.	STEVENS, Matthew H.	FEB 10 1847
JEFFERS, Susanna	HENN, Allerson	AUG 23 1821
JEFFERS, W.R.	HUNT, Bettie M.	FEB 23 1854
JEFFERS, William	MARTIN, Mary	MAR 27 1837
JEFFERSON, Angelina F.	STEWART, William J.	SEP 08 1842
JEFFERSON, Ann Wale	CALDWELL, Perry	JUL 05 1821
JEFFERSON, Cassa Ann (blk)	BUTLER, Charles	MAY 10 1845
JEFFERSON, Cyntha Ann	THOMAS, Manson	DEC 02 1854
JEFFERSON, Euphemia	ANDERSON, Wm.	AUG 12 1815
JEFFERSON, Fannie A.	RAIFORD, Philip H.	MAY 02 1853
JEFFERSON, Ferdinand	ELLSWORTH, Margaret	AUG 01 1838
JEFFERSON, Frances Ann	FOLAND, Valentine	APR 23 1840
JEFFERSON, Henry	MORRIS, Minervia Ann	DEC 24 1829
JEFFERSON, Henry	PYFER, Amelia (blk)	JAN 19 1841
JEFFERSON, James	McCUBBIN, Elizabeth	JUL 30 1833
JEFFERSON, Margaret	JACOBS, Alfred	DEC 02 1841
JEFFERSON, Mary E.	POSEY, James H.	SEP 19 1854
JEFFERSON, Robert	WADE, Jane	APR 28 1840
JEFFERSON, Thomas	OSBORN, Catherine	APR 26 1836
JEFFERSON, Thomas	BOSWELL, Eliza	APR 02 1840
JEFFERSON, William	TRUNNELL, Chelotte	NOV 14 1838
JEFFERSON, Winney (blk)	REDIN, Shadrach	MAY 13 1852
JEFFRIES, Jane	CAMPBELL, George	MAY 08 1839
JEFFRIES, John B.	GREENWELL, Mary Eliza	DEC 13 1853
JEFFRYS, Harrison	DARNALL, Margaret	DEC 16 1824
JENERIS, Henrietta	SOMERVILLE, Robert	DEC 26 1816
JENIFER, Abraham	GROSS, Mary L. (blk)	MAY 21 1857
JENIFER, Mary	GASSAWAY, Joshua	JAN 07 1831
JENIS, Charlotte (blk)	DAVIS, James	NOV 04 1829
JENKINS, Adelphia	BANGS, John W.	DEC 14 1850
JENKINS, Alice	GATES, William	SEP 16 1852
JENKINS, Andrew	HAMPTON, Frances	SEP 17 1836

District of Columbia Marriage Licenses, 1811-1858

JENKINS, Ann Margaret	WINFIELD, Richard S.	APR 15 1841
JENKINS, Basil	TALBERTT, Eliza	JUN 17 1822
JENKINS, Benjamin F.	MAY, Eliza Jane	NOV 08 1856
JENKINS, Bennett	LITTLEFORD, Elizabeth	FEB 17 1829
JENKINS, Catherine	BENNETT, John	MAR 28 1850
JENKINS, Catherine Ann	WARE, Spencer	JAN 03 1840
JENKINS, Cecelia	KNOTT, John B.	NOV 05 1853
JENKINS, Charles	HOLLIDA, Kasira	JAN 02 1841
JENKINS, Charlotte	HUGUELY, Samuel	APR 06 1817
JENKINS, Chloe M.	BARR, Thomas	JUN 21 1819
JENKINS, David B.	HALL, Mary	JUN 02 1845
JENKINS, Delilah	JENKINS, Harrison	MAY 16 1844
JENKINS, Edward	GROSS, Treasy	OCT 20 1825
JENKINS, Edward	BONDS, Miss Tholond	DEC 23 1825
JENKINS, Edward	SMITH, Martha Ann	DEC 21 1830
JENKINS, Eleanor	TENNISON, Charles C.	NOV 16 1818
JENKINS, Elisha	CALDWELL, Hannah	JUN 05 1837
JENKINS, Elizabeth	SOPER, Henry	FEB 07 1827
JENKINS, Ellen	ANDERSON, Charles	NOV 19 1853
JENKINS, Fanny (blk)	SMITH, William	DEC 24 1845
JENKINS, Frances (blk)	JAMES, Robert	AUG 25 1853
JENKINS, George	FIELDS, Elizabeth (blk)	APR 04 1851
JENKINS, George F.	ADAMS, Mary Jane	FEB 18 1843
JENKINS, Georgiana	McKENNEY, James E.	AUG 14 1858
JENKINS, Harrison	JENKINS, Delilah	MAY 16 1844
JENKINS, Hirum	SIMPSON, Lydia	DEC 30 1817
JENKINS, James	SANFORD, Mary E.	FEB 25 1841
JENKINS, John	ENSEY, Martha	FEB 21 1821
JENKINS, John W.	HURT, Cyntha M.	SEP 03 1855
JENKINS, Lidy	PIBSON, Samuel	NOV 30 1833
JENKINS, Lloyd	KING, Elizabeth	JAN 15 1817
JENKINS, Loline	BEELER, Rosa Louisia	DEC 08 1848
JENKINS, Lucinda (blk)	WISE, Bedy	MAY 29 1851
JENKINS, M. Elizabeth	SURRATT, John H.	AUG 04 1840
JENKINS, Margaret (blk)	FELSON, Alfred	APR 13 1831
JENKINS, Nancy	JENKINS, Samuel L.	DEC 18 1845
JENKINS, Priscella	HICKY, Cyrus	OCT 08 1847
JENKINS, Richard L.	MALONEY, Ellen	OCT 21 1856
JENKINS, Robert	LEE, Catharine	DEC 15 1847
JENKINS, Samuel L.	JENKINS, Nancy	DEC 18 1845
JENKINS, Sarah Ann	VERMILLION, Lawson	FEB 16 1848
JENKINS, Susan	EVANS, John	JAN 14 1833
JENKINS, Thomas	WILLIAMS, Catharine	JAN 12 1818
JENKINS, Thomas	MURRAY, Mary	MAY 22 1834
JENKINS, Thomas	PAYNE, Adaline	JUL 04 1857
JENKINS, Thomas Henry	SEMNEY, Elizabeth	DEC 14 1855
JENKINS, Treacy	HOLT, Ennals	APR 17 1816
JENKINS, William	WEBB, Addie E.	JAN 06 1858
JENKINS, [blank]	EMBERSON, Mary	NOV 20 1839
JENKS, Sarah E.	BAILEY, Harvey	NOV 04 1853
JENNERS, Antius	GREEN, Elizabeth	DEC 03 1835
JENNERS, James S.	DeNEALE, Ruth Ann	MAR 02 1853
JENNIFER, Mary Ann	COLLINS, Levi	NOV 06 1834
JENNINGS, Ann	DONNELLY, Charles	NOV 16 1850
JENNINGS, Horatio	WAR, Mahaly (blk)	APR 03 1827
JENNINGS, Horatio	DEAN, Leantha	SEP 21 1836
JENNINGS, John	STONE, Julia Ann	MAR 04 1852
JENNINGS, Sidney (blk)	HOUSE, Samuel	JUN 28 1838

District of Columbia Marriage Licenses, 1811-1858

JENNINGS, William G.	MARTIN, Hellen A.	MAR 16 1836
JERRIOT, Noel	CANNARD, Jaqueline Jamie	SEP 10 1825
JERVIS, Henry	FENLEY, Susan	DEC 02 1812
JESSE, Joseph	JESSE, Mary M.	FEB 18 1850
JESSE, Mary M.	JESSE, Joseph	FEB 18 1850
JESSUP, Jane Finley	NICHOLSON, Augustus S.	FEB 02 1852
JESUP, Lucy	SITGREAVES, L.	FEB 27 1854
JESUP, Mary E.	BLAIR, James	JAN 12 1846
JESURIEN, Jacob M.	JOHNSON, Anna Mariah	MAR 28 1850
JETT, Amanda	KITCHINS, Jesse W.	JUL 30 1838
JETT, Eliza	DAVIS, William	AUG 25 1831
JETT, Elizabeth J.	HODGES, Joseph	AUG 28 1854
JETT, Margaret	COZENS, George W.	SEP 07 1852
JETT, Margaret	COZZINS George	DEC 02 1852
JETT, Roberta (blk)	KENNAL, Lewis	AUG 06 1838
JETT, William Henry	BREWER, Eliza Ann	JUN 09 1858
JEWELL, Catharine	BETTY, Lewis A.	JAN 14 1826
JEWELL, Catharine	ALNUTT, William P.	OCT 23 1839
JEWELL, Elizabeth	DAWSON, Thomas B.	OCT 23 1839
JEWELL, Fanny J.	JEWELL, James Grey	JUL 05 1853
JEWELL, Fielder	BRADLEY, Sarah	NOV 13 1828
JEWELL, Flora H.	NIXON, J. Howard	APR 21 1858
JEWELL, James Grey	JEWELL, Fanny J.	JUL 05 1853
JEWELL, Presley	KELLER, Caroline P.	JUL 11 1837
JEWELL, Smallwood R.	CHICHESTER, Elizabeth	SEP 09 1834
JEWELL, William	HOLTZMAN, Cordelia B.	NOV 27 1848
JEWELL, William	MIDDLETON, Martha	JUN 27 1856
JEWELL, William	CLEMENTS, Mary E.	AUG 06 1858
JEWELL, Wilson	LYONS, Rachel	APR 22 1824
JILTON, Harriet Mc.	JARBOE, Francis M.	DEC 06 1845
JINGELL, Joseph	WILSON, Mary Ann	DEC 28 1814
JINKINS, Eliza Ellen	O'NEILL, Samuel	OCT 17 1846
JIRDINSTON, James A.N.	BRASHEARS, Mary Elizth.	SEP 26 1853
JIRDINSTON, William	ALDRIDGE, Leucresa	DEC 08 1819
JOACHIM, John	BUCK, Louisa	MAY 15 1844
JOCKEL, Margaret	LICHAN, Henry	JUN 14 1858
JOHN, Davis	MARKS, Catherine	FEB 01 1814
JOHNES, Clarissa	HOOVER, Michael	JAN 10 1827
JOHNS, Catherine	PATTERSON, William	DEC 10 1827
JOHNS, Elizabeth	KEES, John Mason	NOV 22 1841
JOHNS, Francis A.	DONALDSON, Elizabeth Jane	FEB 24 1843
JOHNS, George A.W.	MOCKEBOY, Margaret Ann	SEP 20 1841
JOHNS, Jacob	JACKSON, Elizabeth (blk)	JUN 19 1830
JOHNS, Jane (blk)	THOMAS, Alfred	DEC 02 1839
JOHNS, Jane M.	LYNN, William	FEB 08 1832
JOHNS, John	SHAAFF, Margaretta Jane	JUL 17 1838
JOHNS, L. Rebecca	CLINTON, Thomas G.	MAY 22 1854
JOHNS, Mary P.	SLYE, Thomas G.	AUG 03 1835
JOHNS, Sarah Ann	BUTLER, Henry	MAR 15 1831
JOHNS, Thomas H. [Lt.]	GETTY, Margaret Jane	APR 20 1836
JOHNS, William B.	ROCHE, Leonora de la	DEC 11 1856
JOHNSON, Abraham	CLARKE, Mary (blk)	APR 05 1850
JOHNSON, Adel (blk)	GREEN, Robert B.	MAR 17 1853
JOHNSON, Adelade	HELLEN, Walter	OCT 14 1813
JOHNSON, Adeline (blk)	WALLACE, Daniel	NOV 02 1840
JOHNSON, Albert	BRUMLEY, Sarah E.	NOV 13 1836
JOHNSON, Albert	BROOKS, Rebecca Ann	JUN 09 1856
JOHNSON, Albert E.H.	BENSON, Elizth. H.	JAN 09 1851

District of Columbia Marriage Licenses, 1811-1858

JOHNSON, Albert W.	CLARKE, Margaret	NOV 02 1857
JOHNSON, Alexander	CULLISON, Mary Ellen	DEC 05 1844
JOHNSON, Alexander	COOMES, Sarah M.	JAN 28 1850
JOHNSON, Amanda	HURLEY, John P.	JUN 26 1854
JOHNSON, Andrew	JOHNSON, Mary Elizabeth	DEC 18 1841
JOHNSON, Andrew	ROBINSON, Susan Ann	AUG 12 1845
JOHNSON, Andrew Wallace	MOORE, Elizabeth Marion	DEC 13 1855
JOHNSON, Ann	SAWYER, William	AUG 19 1816
JOHNSON, Ann	SYDNER, Richard B.	DEC 29 1818
JOHNSON, Ann	BOOTHE, Henry	JUN 26 1821
JOHNSON, Ann	GOODRICK, John	FEB 19 1825
JOHNSON, Ann	STEUSSHY, Leonard	SEP 05 1826
JOHNSON, Ann	HANSON, John	DEC 08 1836
JOHNSON, Ann (blk)	GANTT, James Thomas	APR 03 1844
JOHNSON, Ann (blk)	GANTT, Thomas	AUG 07 1850
JOHNSON, Ann E.M.	JAMESON, Caceluy C.	MAY 20 1817
JOHNSON, Ann Elizabeth	DALLAS, Stephen J.	JUN 10 1850
JOHNSON, Ann Maria	GOODRICH, James	SEP 16 1851
JOHNSON, Anna M.	YOUNG, Henry S.	MAY 05 1858
JOHNSON, Anna Maria	ANDERSON, Thomas	MAY 31 1854
JOHNSON, Anna Mariah	JESURIEN, Jacob M.	MAR 28 1850
JOHNSON, Anna T.	COX, John H.	JAN 29 1850
JOHNSON, Annie E.	DELARO, William H.	JAN 08 1857
JOHNSON, Archibald	DAVIS, Levia	MAY 05 1831
JOHNSON, Archy	GILLIN, Grace	NOV 16 1818
JOHNSON, Archy	BUTTS, Jane (blk)	JUN 06 1833
JOHNSON, Barbara Ann	CARTER, Griffin	SEP 13 1836
JOHNSON, Benedict	SHELTON, Mary Jane (blk)	OCT 05 1848
JOHNSON, Benjamin	GORDON, Letitia	JAN 28 1836
JOHNSON, Betsey	EVANS, Peter	JUN 01 1839
JOHNSON, Byran	WARNER, Ann	JUL 26 1815
JOHNSON, Caroline (blk)	BROWN, Jefferson	OCT 31 1853
JOHNSON, Cassey (blk)	DENT, Bruce	MAR 26 1840
JOHNSON, Catharine	McKEY, W.R.	DEC 08 1817
JOHNSON, Catharine	TAYLOR, John	JUN 12 1856
JOHNSON, Catharine (blk)	FOOSTER, John	NOV 05 1852
JOHNSON, Catherine	KERR, Chapman	SEP 14 1852
JOHNSON, Catherine (blk)	JOHNSON, Ulysses	JUN 24 1851
JOHNSON, Catherine Ann	PLAIN, George	JAN 30 1841
JOHNSON, Catherine Ellen	McCARTHY, William	APR 22 1844
JOHNSON, Charity	GRIMES, William	AUG 06 1838
JOHNSON, Charles	STONE, Sally	MAR 25 1820
JOHNSON, Charles	HOLLEY, Leannah	AUG 02 1830
JOHNSON, Charles E.	DYER, Martha	DEC 20 1849
JOHNSON, Chas. H.	STEWART, Georgiana (blk)	MAY 13 1856
JOHNSON, Christopher	ROWLEY, Jane	NOV 21 1818
JOHNSON, Collins	BOULDEN, Mary (blk)	JUN 04 1847
JOHNSON, Daniel T.	ANDERSON, Jane C.	AUG 17 1850
JOHNSON, David	SIMS, Eliza Jane (blk)	MAY 04 1858
JOHNSON, Dearborn	MILLS, Ann Elizabeth	NOV 27 1833
JOHNSON, Dolly	WEAVER, Jacob	AUG 17 1841
JOHNSON, Edward G.	GRIFFIN, Lydia	OCT 05 1840
JOHNSON, Eleanor	SCHUREMAN, Peter D.	JUL 13 1820
JOHNSON, Eleanor	REMELE, John C.	SEP 09 1822
JOHNSON, Eliza	THOMAS, Robert	OCT 27 1817
JOHNSON, Eliza	McDANIEL, Allerson	JAN 03 1827
JOHNSON, Eliza D.	CROWN, James F.	MAY 25 1858
JOHNSON, Elizabeth	FERGUSON, Addison	APR 10 1827

District of Columbia Marriage Licenses, 1811-1858

JOHNSON, Elizabeth	HEPBURN, John	OCT 04 1850
JOHNSON, Elizabeth (blk)	BOWSER, Thomas	DEC 02 1833
JOHNSON, Elizabeth D.	LOURY, George	JAN 29 1855
JOHNSON, Elizabeth F.	KENNER, Rodham F.	DEC 13 1815
JOHNSON, Emeline (blk)	DYER, Edward	JUN 23 1835
JOHNSON, Emmeline V.	FERGUSON, Wm. J.	JUN 11 1856
JOHNSON, Frances (blk)	PARKER, William	JAN 03 1828
JOHNSON, Francis	CRANFORD, Eliza	JUN 22 1826
JOHNSON, French T.	CROW, Emily	DEC 19 1844
JOHNSON, George	REYNOLDS, Eliz.	JAN 09 1813
JOHNSON, George	DUNAWAY, Sarah H.	NOV 22 1825
JOHNSON, George	RAWLINGS, Ester	SEP 15 1832
JOHNSON, George	LYLES, Sarah M.	JAN 19 1841
JOHNSON, George	FOSTER, Jane (blk)	DEC 08 1842
JOHNSON, George	THOMPSON, Martha	AUG 19 1846
JOHNSON, George	VODRICK, Ann M. (blk)	APR 25 1850
JOHNSON, George J.	BARRON, Annie E.	FEB 07 1856
JOHNSON, Grafton	WILSON, Mary (blk)	AUG 21 1856
JOHNSON, Harriet	BARTON, James	MAR 07 1837
JOHNSON, Harriet	STARR, William	OCT 03 1845
JOHNSON, Harriet (blk)	SAVOY, John Horatio	APR 09 1829
JOHNSON, Harriet Ann	FRENCH, William	SEP 04 1845
JOHNSON, Harriet M.	DORSEY, John	JUN 24 1854
JOHNSON, Harriett	BARNES, Elias	JAN 15 1828
JOHNSON, Henry	ARDERRY, Angelica Elizabeth	NOV 04 1820
JOHNSON, Henry [Hon.]	KEY, Elizabeth R.	OCT 01 1829
JOHNSON, Henry	O'CONNER, Catharine	DEC 01 1831
JOHNSON, Henry	FOUSTER, Louisa	SEP 29 1831
JOHNSON, Henry	WILSON, Martha Ann	NOV 29 1836
JOHNSON, Henry	HARRIS, Adelphia (blk)	MAR 02 1842
JOHNSON, Henry	COONBECK, Catherine	FEB 26 1849
JOHNSON, Henry	CALVERT, Sarah (blk)	JUL 08 1854
JOHNSON, Henry D.	ABERT, Mary	FEB 14 1854
JOHNSON, Henry L.	FITZGERALD, Emily E.	FEB 07 1856
JOHNSON, Hiram	SEBASTIAN, Eliza	JAN 18 1847
JOHNSON, James	HOWE, Eliza	SEP 22 1827
JOHNSON, James	WORMLEY, Harriet (blk)	JUN 10 1830
JOHNSON, James	LOVELESS, Cecelia	MAY 10 1831
JOHNSON, James	GRANT, Jane (blk)	MAR 07 1843
JOHNSON, James	MASON, Eliza J.	NOV 18 1845
JOHNSON, James	STRANGE, Mary D.	JAN 06 1849
JOHNSON, James	WILSON, Marcellina	APR 14 1856
JOHNSON, James	COLLINS, Mary	DEC 31 1856
JOHNSON, James A.	BANGS, Cassandra V.	JUN 25 1851
JOHNSON, James B.L.	CUTHBERT, Mary Ann	SEP 13 1856
JOHNSON, James E.	CORNWATH, Mary F.	NOV 20 1855
JOHNSON, James H.	HAGAN, Ann Maria	OCT 04 1838
JOHNSON, James H.	MARTIN, Emeline	AUG 30 1849
JOHNSON, James H.	CARPENTER, Tamandra	JUL 24 1855
JOHNSON, Jane (blk)	HARRIS, John	JUL 29 1858
JOHNSON, Jane C.	BRINKLEY, Saml.	OCT 22 1857
JOHNSON, Jane E.	WILLIAMS, Washington B.	OCT 11 1855
JOHNSON, Jefferson	GEW, Anna	JAN 08 1829
JOHNSON, Jeremiah	DAGS, Jane	AUG 05 1858
JOHNSON, John	THOMPSON, Jane	MAY 06 1814
JOHNSON, John	WHEATLY, Margaret	FEB 09 1825
JOHNSON, John	THOMPSON, Jane	DEC 24 1832
JOHNSON, John	RAY, C.A.	MAR 19 1833

District of Columbia Marriage Licenses, 1811-1858

JOHNSON, John	DIXON, Ruth	JUN 25 1835
JOHNSON, John	BOSWELL, Ellen	OCT 12 1843
JOHNSON, John	GERMON, Mary L.	JAN 10 1846
JOHNSON, John	WHEELER, Ann Eliott	FEB 09 1850
JOHNSON, John	MULLIKIN, Elizabeth Ann	JUN 03 1851
JOHNSON, John	CAREY, Mary Alice (blk)	JUN 19 1851
JOHNSON, John	ABEL, Elizabet	MAY 22 1855
JOHNSON, John	WIGHT, Priscilla	OCT 08 1856
JOHNSON, John Alexander	MURDOCK, Mary Elizabeth	AUG 07 1841
JOHNSON, John B.	GARRETT, Mary A.	NOV 23 1857
JOHNSON, John H.	BERRY, Sarah G.	JUL 01 1848
JOHNSON, John H.	MONEY, Jane E.	DEC 21 1852
JOHNSON, John R.	FOUDRAY, Margaretta C.	APR 19 1854
JOHNSON, John Richard	ORME, Maria Ann	APR 21 1855
JOHNSON, John T.	LARNER, Eliza B.	JUN 02 1856
JOHNSON, Joseph	MATTINGLY, Ann	JUN 04 1814
JOHNSON, Joseph	PARKER, Louisa (blk)	APR 18 1833
JOHNSON, Joseph	PITT, Elizabeth	JUN 04 1838
JOHNSON, Joseph	WILLIAMS, Amanda (blk)	FEB 19 1844
JOHNSON, Joseph	CHANCEY, Elizabeth	SEP 25 1851
JOHNSON, Joseph	ANDERSON, Eliza Jane (blk)	DEC 12 1855
JOHNSON, Josias	SMITH, Sarah Ann (blk)	SEP 21 1846
JOHNSON, Juliana Lee	JUMP, Thomas L.	FEB 07 1837
JOHNSON, Lemuel	YOST, Elizabeth E.	DEC 22 1854
JOHNSON, Letitia (blk)	HOOD, Isaac	AUG 05 1858
JOHNSON, Levi Brown [Dr.]	MAYNARD, Eveline	APR 14 1831
JOHNSON, Lewis	RENAGLE, Ann	DEC 02 1815
JOHNSON, Lewis	CARTWRIGHT, Susan (blk)	NOV 27 1850
JOHNSON, Littleton	LANG, Nancy	MAR 19 1822
JOHNSON, Lloyd	WALKER, Elizabeth	FEB 02 1833
JOHNSON, Lloyd	DONALDSON, Elizabeth (blk)	DEC 24 1856
JOHNSON, Lucinda	BAILEY, Wm.	NOV 21 1844
JOHNSON, Lucinda A.	LOVELESS, James A.	JUN 08 1857
JOHNSON, Lucy Ann	GARDNER, William	JAN 05 1828
JOHNSON, Marcelina (blk)	BENJAMIN, John R.	OCT 06 1857
JOHNSON, Margaret A.	READ, Richard R.	OCT 30 1838
JOHNSON, Margaret A.	MAGRUDER, Julian	APR 19 1853
JOHNSON, Maria	DUVALL, Elisha	AUG 18 1831
JOHNSON, Maria Jane (blk)	GRANDISON, Alexander	FEB 10 1842
JOHNSON, Marion Gales	GRENNELL, Frank	DEC 08 1846
JOHNSON, Martha (blk)	GARNER, Walter	APR 30 1850
JOHNSON, Martha (blk)	WILLIAMS, William	OCT 23 1856
JOHNSON, Martha Ann	JONES, William S.	JUN 01 1848
JOHNSON, Martin	WALLACE, Martha [Mrs.]	MAR 08 1827
JOHNSON, Martin H.	RANDOLPH, Mary P.	JUN 03 1852
JOHNSON, Mary	CARRICO, Peter B.	FEB 17 1813
JOHNSON, Mary	MILLER, Frederick W.	FEB 18 1817
JOHNSON, Mary	GROVES, Hendley	DEC 10 1827
JOHNSON, Mary	OFFUTT, Joseph	FEB 06 1829
JOHNSON, Mary	BEAN, Thomas	OCT 11 1830
JOHNSON, Mary	SCRIVENER, James	MAY 27 1841
JOHNSON, Mary	ELLIOTT, John Washington	SEP 08 1843
JOHNSON, Mary	ROCHE, Philip	SEP 28 1854
JOHNSON, Mary (blk)	GREEN, Thomas	NOV 20 1833
JOHNSON, Mary (blk)	SMITH, Thomas	MAY 07 1838
JOHNSON, Mary (blk)	BROWN, Thos.	SEP 11 1845
JOHNSON, Mary A. (blk)	KING, John	JUL 23 1842
JOHNSON, Mary Ann (blk)	ASHTON, Jeremiah	DEC 05 1823

District of Columbia Marriage Licenses, 1811-1858

JOHNSON, Mary Ann	GOODRICK, James	APR 10 1830
JOHNSON, Mary Ann (blk)	DETTRO, Frederick	OCT 27 1840
JOHNSON, Mary Ann	NYE, Norman Williard	DEC 02 1847
JOHNSON, Mary Ann	ALLEN, Aquilla R.	JAN 01 1848
JOHNSON, Mary E.	MILLER, Charles	JAN 02 1844
JOHNSON, Mary E. (blk)	THOMAS, William H.	JAN 01 1851
JOHNSON, Mary E.	RICHARDSON, George W.	JUL 01 1858
JOHNSON, Mary Eleanor	GUNNELL, Henry	SEP 22 1827
JOHNSON, Mary Elizabeth	JOHNSON, Andrew	DEC 18 1841
JOHNSON, Mary Ellen	BARTLETT, William	FEB 08 1848
JOHNSON, Mary J.	BURNETTE, Lewis L.	NOV 03 1857
JOHNSON, Mary Jane	WAGNER, Anthony	JUL 14 1838
JOHNSON, Matilda N.	JACOBS, Solomon D.	JUN 07 1852
JOHNSON, Melvin	SOMERS, Ann	JUL 01 1835
JOHNSON, Melvina	DIX, Thomas	JUN 18 1835
JOHNSON, Milton	CULLISON, Elizabeth	APR 02 1841
JOHNSON, Minty A.	CROSS, George	JAN 28 1823
JOHNSON, Morris	SYPHAX, Julia (blk)	JUL 26 1843
JOHNSON, Nancy	HOLBROOK, John Thompson	MAY 15 1823
JOHNSON, Neville	WINDHAM, Mary E.B.	APR 20 1835
JOHNSON, Nimrod H.	UNDERWOOD, Catherine Coyle	MAY 08 1850
JOHNSON, Pandora	LANE, Charles W.	SEP 19 1840
JOHNSON, Patronilla M.	FENWICK, William A.	OCT 04 1856
JOHNSON, Permelia	KNOWLES, William	MAR 13 1844
JOHNSON, Peter	KING, Susan	SEP 06 1832
JOHNSON, Peter	JACKSON, S. (blk)	MAR 30 1840
JOHNSON, Peter	ROSS, Harriett (blk)	MAY 19 1853
JOHNSON, Philip C.	JAMES, Mary W.	AUG 31 1857
JOHNSON, Philip P.	McCLANAHAN, Elizabeth	MAR 31 1845
JOHNSON, Price	HAYNES, Hannah	MAR 29 1823
JOHNSON, Reubin C.	ALEXANDER, Caroline	NOV 04 1851
JOHNSON, Richard	WASHINGTON, Ann Maria (blk)	OCT 10 1848
JOHNSON, Richard D.	SIMMS, Nancy Douglass	OCT 05 1841
JOHNSON, Richmond	BALMAIN, Margaret T.	JAN 04 1823
JOHNSON, Richmond [Dr.]	BALMAIN, Louisa C.	MAR 31 1819
JOHNSON, Robert	FLEET, Maria (blk)	DEC 28 1831
JOHNSON, Robert	BAILY, Margaret	NOV 08 1832
JOHNSON, Robert	FAY, Catharine	NOV 21 1833
JOHNSON, Robert	EGGLESTON, Laura R.	FEB 02 1857
JOHNSON, Robert	JOHNSON, Sarah E.	AUG 31 1858
JOHNSON, Robert G.	LOVEJOY, Mary	DEC 01 1856
JOHNSON, Roberta	PETER, Robert	FEB 01 1847
JOHNSON, Rosetta	PERMILLION, William	JUL 27 1852
JOHNSON, Rosina	MILLER, John P.	DEC 09 1850
JOHNSON, Rut	FLORANCE, Mary	OCT 11 1828
JOHNSON, Ruth	CATON, George W.	JUN 03 1854
JOHNSON, S.E.	O'DONNELL, John	OCT 06 1845
JOHNSON, Sally	WASHINGTON, Lund	APR 11 1823
JOHNSON, Samuel	ASHTON, Rosetta	SEP 21 1838
JOHNSON, Samuel	HOBBIE, Barbara (blk)	JUN 04 1847
JOHNSON, Sarah	SMITSON, John H.	JAN 12 1836
JOHNSON, Sarah	SMITH, Elijah	MAY 01 1841
JOHNSON, Sarah	LONG, Joseph	MAY 15 1858
JOHNSON, Sarah (blk)	SEMMES, Nathaniel	OCT 16 1822
JOHNSON, Sarah Ann	KING, John	APR 03 1838
JOHNSON, Sarah Ann	BARNES, Thomas J.	JAN 01 1839
JOHNSON, Sarah Ann	DeVAUGHN, William H.	JUL 11 1839
JOHNSON, Sarah C.	FAIRALL, Joseph F.	AUG 16 1856

District of Columbia Marriage Licenses, 1811-1858

JOHNSON, Sarah E.	JOHNSON, Robert	AUG 31 1858
JOHNSON, Sarah O.	NEWTON, William H.	FEB 28 1856
JOHNSON, Sianna	KIBBY, Thomas	APR 12 1827
JOHNSON, Silas	ABBEGIL, Ellen	AUG 22 1857
JOHNSON, Susan	CUMBERLAND, John	MAY 25 1848
JOHNSON, Susan (blk)	BELL, James	AUG 28 1834
JOHNSON, Susan (blk)	TINNEY, Charles	JUL 29 1840
JOHNSON, Susan Ann, Mrs.	THOMPSON, William	JUL 06 1858
JOHNSON, Susanna F.	WATSON, James R.	JAN 28 1840
JOHNSON, Sylva (blk)	NICHOLLS, John M.	NOV 25 1841
JOHNSON, Teresa	LUXAN, Horace	JUL 06 1815
JOHNSON, Thomas	SHAD<u>E</u>S, Rachel	FEB 14 1824
JOHNSON, Thomas	O'ROURKE, Mary	JUL 31 1835
JOHNSON, Thomas	KENDLE, Jane (blk)	JUN 08 1847
JOHNSON, Thomas	WORMLEY, Elexina (blk)	APR 06 1848
JOHNSON, Thomas	ROSE, Jane C.	APR 14 1855
JOHNSON, Thomas E.	THOMPSON, Elizabeth M.	JAN 08 1835
JOHNSON, Thomas L.	IMES, Elizabeth	MAY 01 1828
JOHNSON, Thomas T.	FARR, Julia A.	NOV 03 1851
JOHNSON, Thomas W.	DAVIS, Charlotte P.	DEC 13 1851
JOHNSON, Thos. W.	EARLE, Frances L.	MAR 22 1856
JOHNSON, Ulysses	JOHNSON, Catherine (blk)	JUN 24 1851
JOHNSON, Verlinda	MURRAY, James	NOV 25 1833
JOHNSON, Virginia	STOCKS, Charles	NOV 02 1848
JOHNSON, W.C.	MOORE, Catharine E.	NOV 01 1847
JOHNSON, William	MILLER, Barbara	NOV 16 1816
JOHNSON, William	TWEEDY, Sidney	APR 27 1830
JOHNSON, William	TARBLE, Susan (blk)	JAN 12 1833
JOHNSON, William	COOK, Elizabeth A.	FEB 07 1833
JOHNSON, William	COLLINS, Sarah	APR 18 1840
JOHNSON, William	WALKER, Sydney	AUG 13 1840
JOHNSON, William	SHEPPARD, Ann	OCT 21 1847
JOHNSON, William	HUNTT, Pamelia (blk)	JUN 26 1855
JOHNSON, William	POTTER, Elizabeth	DEC 30 1856
JOHNSON, William	WINDHAM, Sophia	MAY 18 1857
JOHNSON, William C.	ADAMS, Mary Louisa	JUN 27 1853
JOHNSON, William H.	GREGORY, Caroline M.	SEP 16 1844
JOHNSON, William S.	BEALL, Sarah A.B.	OCT 26 1853
JOHNSON, William T.	DIXON, Eliza	OCT 04 1844
JOHNSON, William T.	MURPHY, Eliza A.	DEC 19 1857
JOHNSON, Winey Ann	NORTON, Thomas	AUG 24 1853
JOHNSON, Wm. H.	LITTLETON, Anna E.	OCT 15 1855
JOHNSON, Wm. J.A.	BROOKBANK, Ann Maria	SEP 07 1848
JOHNSTON, Charles B.	GANTT, Rosalie	DEC 10 1857
JOHNSTON, Christopher	SMITH, Sally L.C.	SEP 25 1855
JOHNSTON, Elias	GORDON, Nancy (blk)	MAR 06 1850
JOHNSTON, Elizabeth	SULLIVAN, Marshall C.	JUL 06 1852
JOHNSTON, George W.	STILLINGS, Marian	JUL 17 1851
JOHNSTON, George W.	MISKELL, Elizabeth J.	JUL 10 1852
JOHNSTON, James	LEVEALE, Milley	JUL 27 1816
JOHNSTON, James	BLUNT, Mary Ann B.	DEC 07 1830
JOHNSTON, James W.	GREENWELL, Catharine S.	MAY 08 1848
JOHNSTON, John F.	EVANS, Mary E.	JUN 07 1856
JOHNSTON, John M.	MASI, Sarah Ann	AUG 06 1832
JOHNSTON, John R.	STONE, Ellen	DEC 27 1855
JOHNSTON, Julia	COOPER, William B.	MAR 04 1856
JOHNSTON, Julia Ann	BRUCE, William C.	FEB 05 1844
JOHNSTON, Lewis	McDONALD, Pamelia	JUL 13 1836

District of Columbia Marriage Licenses, 1811-1858

JOHNSTON, Mary	PLACE, George	APR 10 1815
JOHNSTON, Mary C.	KEATING, John	NOV 21 1851
JOHNSTON, Robert	HUTCHINSON, Sarah	MAR 04 1833
JOHNSTON, Robert	PAUL, Emeline Catherine	JUL 19 1837
JOHNSTON, Sarah	CALBERT, William	MAY 29 1844
JOHNSTON, Thomas	CHISM, Mary	FEB 11 1834
JOHNSTON, Thomas J.	WALKER, Isabella	OCT 17 1849
JOICE, Mary Ann	DAILY, John	FEB 11 1834
JOICE, Michael	RICE, Susan	JAN 19 1836
JOICE, Sarah (blk)	BROWN, George	JUN 19 1839
JOINER, James H.	DAGGS, Tamer	JUL 13 1837
JOIST, Konrad	LIPPOLD, Anna	APR 08 1857
JOLLY, Bushrod	BREWER, Lucinda J.	MAY 15 1851
JOLLY, Elizabeth	BRASHEARS, John W.	AUG 19 1819
JOLLY, John	WILSON, Elizabeth Ann	JAN 30 1849
JONES, Aaron	CLARK, Teresa (blk)	MAY 18 1857
JONES, Albert	HARRIS, Mary (blk)	JUN 11 1856
JONES, Alexander	WILLIAMS, Henrietta	OCT 20 1841
JONES, Alexander H.	HANCE, Rebecca	AUG 25 1833
JONES, Alexr. H.	HANCE, Rebecca	AUG 25 1853
JONES, Alfred	LEE, Lucy Ann	FEB 11 1856
JONES, Alfred	PAYNE, Delilah (blk)	APR 19 1858
JONES, Amelia (blk)	BICKLEY, William	MAY 23 1835
JONES, Ann	CONCKLIN, William M.	APR 11 1812
JONES, Ann	SUMMERVILLE, Walter	FEB 04 1819
JONES, Ann	GAMBIER, Joseph L.	JUN 18 1831
JONES, Ann	NALLEY, Zachariah	DEC 19 1839
JONES, Ann	MANKIN, William	SEP 23 1852
JONES, Ann (blk)	HALL, Edward	JAN 24 1855
JONES, Anna	BEOG, John	MAR 19 1857
JONES, Arabella C.	ROSS, James T.	MAY 09 1857
JONES, Augustus	COXON, Julia Ann	OCT 16 1826
JONES, Barbara	BLACK, Samuel	JUL 14 1813
JONES, Benjamin	FRAZER, Drusey	FEB 22 1814
JONES, Benjamin	UPTON, Sarah	MAR 27 1815
JONES, Benjamin H.	SIMPSON, Eliza Ann	DEC 22 1857
JONES, Betsey	WEVER, John	OCT 27 1812
JONES, Caroline Amanda	CRAIG, William H.	FEB 01 1842
JONES, Cath. Ann	CROPLEY, Washington	DEC 01 1846
JONES, Catharine	LEWIS, Thomas	JAN 23 1812
JONES, Catharine (blk)	MASON, John	OCT 09 1839
JONES, Celia	TAYLOR, William B.	JUL 30 1840
JONES, Charity Margaretta	KENT, Daniel	JAN 28 1830
JONES, Charles	LEE, Jane	MAR 14 1827
JONES, Charles	WARREN, Mary E.	AUG 02 1856
JONES, Charles J.	IRELAND, Mary Elizabeth	MAR 18 1856
JONES, Charles R.	OWENS, Elizabeth Ann	MAY 11 1858
JONES, Charles S.	STEWART, Elizabeth Rebecca	NOV 16 1841
JONES, Charlotte (blk)	MINOR, Benjamin	NOV 22 1837
JONES, Charlotte (blk)	CRUSOE, James C.	JUL 13 1849
JONES, Charlotte (blk)	GREEN, Nelson	OCT 11 1855
JONES, Chirchwill	KING, Ann	JAN 25 1854
JONES, Clara (blk)	POWELL, John	FEB 09 1833
JONES, Dangerfield	BOYD, Mary Jane	DEC 14 1847
JONES, Daniel	HARRISON, Nancy	JUN 09 1858
JONES, Edward	MOORE, Mary R.	MAR 09 1853
JONES, Edward	HENDERSON, Eliza G.	NOV 21 1853
JONES, Eleanor	SHAW, Samuel	JUN 19 1826

District of Columbia Marriage Licenses, 1811-1858

JONES, Eleanor Ann	SIMPSON, William	AUG 22 1835
JONES, Elexius	HODGE, Mary Ann	JAN 26 1826
JONES, Elexius	MORGAN, Charlotte Ann	MAR 26 1853
JONES, Eliza (blk)	CURTIS, Thomas	SEP 18 1834
JONES, Eliza C.	SEYBOLT, Daniel H.	FEB 20 1850
JONES, Elizabeth	BURGESS, Thomas	JAN 25 1816
JONES, Elizabeth	JONES, Joseph H.	DEC 17 1833
JONES, Elizabeth	SPRINGMAN, John M.	MAR 21 1838
JONES, Elizabeth	McKISITT, George	MAY 10 1839
JONES, Elizabeth	PEIRCE, Joseph M.	AUG 03 1844
JONES, Elizabeth	RAINEY, George	MAR 29 1853
JONES, Elizabeth	ADAMS, John N.	APR 29 1856
JONES, Elizabeth (blk)	TURNER, Daniel	JUN 02 1857
JONES, Elizabeth Ann	PARSONS, James H.	AUG 27 1834
JONES, Elizabeth Ann	WILSON, William H.	NOV 03 1847
JONES, Elizabeth Ann	POOLE, Lewis H.	JUN 14 1849
JONES, Elizabeth Mary	HARRISON, Henry T.	NOV 28 1839
JONES, Elizth. A.	DRANE, James W.	NOV 22 1851
JONES, Ellen	BURGESS, John T.	APR 01 1857
JONES, Eveline (blk)	LANON, John	OCT 23 1852
JONES, Flavilla	BOSWELL, James B.	JUN 10 1833
JONES, Fortune (blk)	MACKALL, Henny	OCT 05 1822
JONES, Francis	LANSDELL, Margaret A.	APR 09 1850
JONES, Fred W.	FEARSON, Mary Lizzie	JAN 03 1858
JONES, George	MEERS, Sarah	MAY 18 1821
JONES, George	ROBEY, Mahala	DEC 21 1848
JONES, Hannah Mariah	NICHOLSON, Summerville	SEP 01 1851
JONES, Harriet	HUNTT, Josias	JUN 04 1833
JONES, Harriot R. [Mrs.]	KEAN, Gilbert D.	AUG 26 1830
JONES, Harriott B.	DAVIS, Robert M.	DEC 20 1834
JONES, Harriotte	HARRISON, Matthew	MAY 12 1851
JONES, Harriotte Lee	PEYTON, Robert Eden [Dr.]	APR 18 1833
JONES, Henerietta	SOUTH, Thomas	JUL 29 1817
JONES, Henry	GRIFFIS, Ellen	OCT 10 1842
JONES, Henry	TERRELL, Ann	DEC 23 1847
JONES, Henry	BUTLER, Rebecca (blk)	APR 13 1857
JONES, Hugh	BENNETT, Elizabeth	FEB 03 1852
JONES, Indiana M.	SHOEMAKER, Edwd. I.	OCT 03 1855
JONES, Isaac	WHALEY, Anna	MAY 26 1824
JONES, Jacob	CROSS, Lydia R.	OCT 11 1847
JONES, James	BRYAN, Mary	MAY 18 1820
JONES, James	ORR, Ann	APR 04 1822
JONES, James	BOWER, Harriett	MAY 28 1845
JONES, James	RYAN, Mary Jane	NOV 13 1852
JONES, James	MARMEDUKE, Martha	DEC 30 1852
JONES, James H.	ADAMS, Eliza Peyton	NOV 26 1845
JONES, James H.	HERBERT, Mary E.	JUL 10 1848
JONES, James R.	FURR, Elizabeth	NOV 15 1837
JONES, James W.	BURDETT, Matilda J.	NOV 02 1850
JONES, James Y.	LECKIE, Hellen	APR 26 1826
JONES, Jane (blk)	WASHINGTON, Henry	OCT 04 1849
JONES, Jeremiah	TURNER, Sarah Ann	JAN 17 1839
JONES, John	NALLEY, Jamima	AUG 01 1827
JONES, John	DICKERSON, Elizabeth	APR 02 1829
JONES, John B.	JACKSON, Mary Jane (blk)	JUN 29 1848
JONES, John F.	HUNT, Harriet	JUL 25 1844
JONES, John G.	TUCKER, Mary E.	OCT 25 1816
JONES, John J.	WAHL, Sophia	APR 18 1854

District of Columbia Marriage Licenses, 1811-1858

JONES, John L.	HURST, Sarah	MAY 28 1857
JONES, John L.	HELFINSTERY, Anna	AUG 26 1858
JONES, John U.	THOMPSON, Mary E.	SEP 16 1856
JONES, John W.	WILLIAMS, Kate J.	APR 16 1856
JONES, Jonathan	STEINS, Mary M.	FEB 09 1846
JONES, Joseph	NOT, Mary	MAY 19 1830
JONES, Joseph	BROOKS, Fanny (blk)	JUN 30 1852
JONES, Joseph C.	TURNER, Harriott R.	MAR 13 1834
JONES, Joseph H.	JONES, Elizabeth	DEC 17 1833
JONES, Joseph Walker	JACOBS, Ann	JAN 08 1818
JONES, Julia	RITTER, John F.	JUL 17 1858
JONES, Juliannah	GIBSON, George T.	JUN 24 1828
JONES, Kitty (blk)	PROCTOR, Sylvester	DEC 30 1851
JONES, Letitia R.	HARVEY, William	JAN 08 1835
JONES, Levi	GARDINER, Ann (blk)	MAY 17 1839
JONES, Levi	NOWLAND, Margaret	MAY 20 1857
JONES, Louisa	BROWN, Robert	SEP 24 1845
JONES, Luther D.	DUVALL, Ellen M.	FEB 28 1855
JONES, Madison W.	MOONE, Caroline F.W.	FEB 25 1853
JONES, Malvina	BRIGHTWELL, Joshua	NOV 22 1855
JONES, Manzilla	HOWARD, Samuel	NOV 09 1854
JONES, Marcellina	MINOR, William	NOV 09 1848
JONES, Margaret	MONEY, Perrie A.	APR 08 1847
JONES, Margaret	WARRICK, Abraham	DEC 20 1850
JONES, Margaret B.	WRIGHT, Jonathan M.	SEP 26 1823
JONES, Maria E.	PAYNE, James W.	FEB 22 1858
JONES, Maria H.	HANSON, Isaac K.	AUG 22 1815
JONES, Mark	CALVERT, Susan	MAY 21 1840
JONES, Martha Ann	LAUCK, Isaac S.	NOV 23 1841
JONES, Martha Ann Ellen	PURDY, Richard Gassaway	AUG 15 1846
JONES, Mary	ALLEN, Thomas	JAN 06 1820
JONES, Mary	ANGEL, John	SEP 02 1828
JONES, Mary	BROOKS, Richard	MAR 18 1830
JONES, Mary	FERGUSON, Rezin	SEP 08 1830
JONES, Mary	SCOTT, Robert	FEB 22 1831
JONES, Mary	COFFEE, Francis	JUL 29 1835
JONES, Mary	HOLLIDAY, Henry	MAR 18 1841
JONES, Mary	TUCKER, Daniel	NOV 15 1849
JONES, Mary	SULLIVAN, Cornelius	JUN 16 1855
JONES, Mary	BROWN, John	JUL 09 1856
JONES, Mary	TENLEY, Horatio	DEC 01 1856
JONES, Mary A. (blk)	KEY, Gillip	OCT 04 1845
JONES, Mary A.	GOLDSMITH, James	MAR 28 1848
JONES, Mary A.	SCOTT, John J.	NOV 27 1855
JONES, Mary Ann	LANHAM, Elisha	APR 22 1813
JONES, Mary Ann	RUSTICK, John	AUG 01 1822
JONES, Mary Ann	THOMPSON, Harrison	OCT 29 1835
JONES, Mary Ann	BROWN, John	MAY 04 1837
JONES, Mary Ann	SMITH, William	OCT 29 1842
JONES, Mary Ann	HARMON, John L.	JAN 14 1858
JONES, Mary C.	DEBOIS, Jeremiah	FEB 26 1852
JONES, Mary E.	ROBEY, James Wilson	SEP 26 1837
JONES, Mary E.	WHYTE, Frederick	JAN 04 1844
JONES, Mary E.	MICKUM, Samuel C.	JUL 28 1853
JONES, Mary E.	MOCKABEE, Thomas C.	MAY 09 1855
JONES, Mary E.	BOSWELL, J.J.W.	MAY 27 1858
JONES, Mary E.C.	SMART, Andrew Jackson	NOV 19 1838
JONES, Mary Eleanor	ROSITHER, Thomas	JUN 05 1829

District of Columbia Marriage Licenses, 1811-1858

JONES, Mary Elizabeth	HARDY, William	APR 26 1845
JONES, Mary Elizabeth	HARDISTY, Thomas J.	MAY 09 1854
JONES, Mary Elizth.	BLUNDEN, Daniel W.	MAR 03 1849
JONES, Mary Ellen (blk)	WHEATLEY, Benjamin	NOV 04 1852
JONES, Mary F.	SMITH, Charles T.	DEC 22 1857
JONES, Mary Jane	MARLOW, Henry	JAN 14 1845
JONES, Mary Louisa	ALGER, Francis	MAY 09 1835
JONES, Nancy	MILES, Frederick	JUN 16 1831
JONES, Napoleon Bonaparte	SORRELL, Mary A.	MAY 07 1857
JONES, Nathan	BUTT, Matilda	MAY 08 1828
JONES, Nelly	VICKERS, Thomas	NOV 19 1833
JONES, Pamelia A.	BIRCH, Henry	JUL 18 1855
JONES, Patrick	STODDARTS, Nancy	SEP 15 1830
JONES, Paul	THOMAS, Diana	MAY 03 1830
JONES, Paul	YOUNG, Elizth.	MAY 07 1835
JONES, Paul	FORD, Mary Ann (blk)	APR 02 1846
JONES, Philip R.	JEFFERS, Eliza M.	DEC 09 1844
JONES, Priscilla	MAHONEY, Dominic	MAY 21 1846
JONES, Prudence	GRIFFETH, Greenbury	FEB 24 1814
JONES, Rebecca	TRAMMELL, William W.	OCT 30 1830
JONES, Rebecca	KING, Levi G.	DEC 18 1854
JONES, Rebecca	WILLIAMS, John	JUN 19 1856
JONES, Rebecca (blk)	HENSON, Charles	OCT 05 1857
JONES, Rebecca M.	JACKSON, Andrew	MAR 29 1849
JONES, Richard	HANSON, Ann	NOV 07 1837
JONES, Richard	HUGHES, Martha (blk)	MAR 24 1840
JONES, Richard	O'NEALE, Sophia	JAN 02 1843
JONES, Richard	MONEY, Catherine	JUN 01 1850
JONES, Richard F.	FORD, Mary E.	JUN 23 1857
JONES, Richard H.	HUNTER, Mary R.	MAY 06 1858
JONES, Richard J.	BURCH, Elizabeth Ann	AUG 27 1840
JONES, Robert	NOBLE, Ellen C.	AUG 12 1854
JONES, Rosina	PACKARD, Joseph	JAN 23 1838
JONES, Sally Ann	AMBROSE, Robert	FEB 13 1821
JONES, Samuel	LIPSCOMB, Sarah	MAY 02 1831
JONES, Samuel	GOODY, Emily	OCT 01 1836
JONES, Samuel W.	MORRIS, Angelina (blk)	MAR 09 1848
JONES, Sarah	HERBERT, John	NOV 05 1812
JONES, Sarah	OFFUTT, Chs.	APR 24 1821
JONES, Sarah	KING, Wilson	AUG 15 1834
JONES, Sarah	WELLS, James	DEC 11 1839
JONES, Sarah	TAYLOR, Rodiar	DEC 26 1848
JONES, Sarah	WÖVERS, George	JUL 19 1858
JONES, Sarah A.	DARMON, Albert	NOV 06 1838
JONES, Sarah Ann	SOUTH, Bradley	AUG 13 1832
JONES, Sarah Ann	CUNNINGHAM, James	JAN 11 1838
JONES, Sarah Elizabeth	MAJOR, Rev. Henry	SEP 10 1839
JONES, Sarah Elizth.	WINGATE, Henry	AUG 25 1853
JONES, Sarah M.	DUDLY, John G.	MAR 09 1854
JONES, Sophia A.	DOYLE, Patrick	OCT 16 1857
JONES, Stephen	LAWSON, Susan	MAR 21 1822
JONES, Susan	BREWER, Henry	OCT 06 1842
JONES, Susan	SCHULTZ, Karl F.	SEP 15 1849
JONES, Susan	KING, James Henry	OCT 19 1850
JONES, Susan A.	HARRIS, Gwynn	OCT 20 1856
JONES, Susannah	WHITE, John T.	JUN 05 1850
JONES, Thomas	YATES, Mary	JUN 10 1814
JONES, Thomas	MILLS, Mary	APR 15 1820

District of Columbia Marriage Licenses, 1811-1858

JONES, Thomas	MURDOCK, Margaret Elizabeth	JAN 27 1829
JONES, Thomas	PECKHAM, Martha	SEP 16 1830
JONES, Thomas	RODBURN, Eliza	JUL 09 1832
JONES, Thomas	LOVELESS, Sarah	SEP 15 1834
JONES, Thomas	ROBINSON, Elizabeth	MAR 01 1837
JONES, Thomas	THOMAS, Emeline	AUG 13 1839
JONES, Thomas	HILL, Maria	MAY 27 1840
JONES, Thomas	SWANN, Harriet E.	MAR 09 1841
JONES, Thomas	MUSTIN, Anna S.	JUL 24 1850
JONES, Thomas H.	SHECKLES, Debora R.	DEC 16 1834
JONES, Thomas W.	BEAN, Sophia W.	MAY 19 1841
JONES, Virginia	MILLER, Thomas [Dr.]	JUL 29 1833
JONES, Virginia	BROWN, David	OCT 30 1851
JONES, Warner P.	PAXTON, Rebecca L.	NOV 29 1854
JONES, Washington	BELL, Amelia (blk)	MAY 20 1841
JONES, William	UPTON, Debby	MAY 02 1816
JONES, William	LEWIS, Mary	SEP 09 1819
JONES, William	GILL, Susan Ann	APR 04 1826
JONES, William	BUTLER, Caroline	MAR 19 1832
JONES, William	HOLTZMAN, Susan	JUL 08 1833
JONES, William	NORTON, Catherine	DEC 04 1834
JONES, William	COLLINS, Eliza	MAR 06 1843
JONES, William	SHIRLEY, Nancy (blk)	MAY 04 1848
JONES, William	FISHER, Anna	JAN 16 1851
JONES, William	HUNT, Lydia Ann	JUL 26 1853
JONES, William	PARSONS, Margaret	MAR 12 1856
JONES, William Carey	BENTON, Eliza C.P.	MAR 18 1847
JONES, William H.	FORCE, Mary J.	NOV 21 1843
JONES, William H.	COLTMAN, Mary F.	AUG 21 1851
JONES, William H.	BROWN, Ann (blk)	MAY 23 1853
JONES, William, of Edwd.	GRAY, Martha	SEP 28 1850
JONES, William P.	BARSICK, Lucretia	MAR 06 1841
JONES, William S.	JOHNSON, Martha Ann	JUN 01 1848
JONES, William S.	MAY, Martha L.	SEP 29 1855
JONES, William T.	TEITJEN, Lucippia Ann	APR 08 1845
JONES, William Thomas	TEITJEN, Lucippia Ann	MAY 08 1845
JONES, William [Dr.]	CORCORAN, Sarah	DEC 18 1821
JONES, Wm. T.	REED, Mary	MAR 31 1858
JONSTON, Jane Ann (blk)	GAHUVA, William	MAY 26 1856
JORDAN, Conrad	RUPPERT, Gertrude	AUG 02 1856
JORDAN, Eliza	FOWLER, John L.	MAR 11 1847
JORDAN, Elizabeth	CLARKE, John	NOV 14 1840
JORDAN, Elizabeth (blk)	BOOTHE, John	SEP 06 1837
JORDAN, German N.	ROCHE, Mary	SEP 07 1853
JORDAN, Hanson	HOYE, Mariam D.	DEC 10 1855
JORDAN, Isham	RANDALL, Mary	DEC 06 1831
JORDAN, Jane	GANTT, Ambrose	MAY 14 1845
JORDAN, John R.	BROOKE, Henrietta T.	JUL 03 1855
JORDAN, John W.	WESTERFIELD, Mary E.	JUN 26 1851
JORDAN, Richard L.	McFARLAND, Elizabeth Ann	FEB 18 1833
JORDAN, Richard L.	BEAN, Mary Ann	OCT 21 1840
JORDAN, Robert Henry	MATTINGLY, Mary Elizth.	JUN 28 1855
JORDAN, Robert S.	GARRETTSON, Martha Aletha	JUN 29 1858
JORDAN, Wm. H.C.	TAIF, Elizabeth	MAR 28 1855
JORDEN, William	MUDD, Matilda	APR 05 1833
JORDON, John	AMANDER, Caroline	NOV 25 1828
JORDON, William	BECK, Catharine	OCT 24 1851
JOSEFF, Yetta	BLOCK, Dassiar	MAY 15 1854

District of Columbia Marriage Licenses, 1811-1858

JOSEPH, Henrietta	OPPENHEIMER, Manasset	FEB 17 1855
JOSEPH, Peter	SELBY, Mary	APR 13 1850
JOSETTY, Martin L.B.	BARRY, Anna	JUL 05 1851
JOSLIN, Amzy	HENDERSON, Angaline	AUG 27 1842
JOSTLE, Henry B.	MACKEY, Elizabeth	SEP 16 1829
JOURDAN, Daniel B.	MITCHELL, Elvira	FEB 21 1851
JOURDAN, Jane	BEGLE, William	JUL 29 1833
JOURDAN, Mrs.	THOMPSON, John	MAY 11 1818
JOURNEY, John A.	BOYER, Susan	JAN 10 1819
JOY, Ann Elizabeth	GERMAN, Stephen D.	JUL 20 1844
JOY, Christeen	MOULDER, Notley	FEB 01 1826
JOY, Eleanor	GIBBON, Henry	DEC 22 1813
JOY, John	MILLER, Ann	DEC 20 1821
JOY, John	HEDGES, Sarah J.W.	NOV 26 1850
JOY, John	PEERCE, Eleanor	JAN 29 1851
JOY, John Washington	GILL, Mary Ann	JUL 06 1844
JOY, Mary Ann	RABBITT, John E.	OCT 17 1855
JOY, Morris	GRIFFIN, Ellen	OCT 21 1851
JOY, Peter	HALSEY, Mary	JUN 08 1820
JOY, Sarah	CROSS, Andrew	JUL 21 1858
JOY, Thomas	HITCHISON, Sarah	APR 04 1848
JOY, William	FRAZIER, Susannah	JAN 08 1835
JOY, William T.	LAWRENCE, Jane	APR 30 1842
JOYCE, Andrew	NORRIS, Frances Marion	OCT 07 1843
JOYCE, James	HANSON, Martha Ann	AUG 28 1856
JOYCE, Julia	HINES, Thomas	JAN 16 1857
JOYCE, Margaret Ann	ZAPPONE, Americus	SEP 08 1853
JOYCE, Richard	ARTRIDGE, Ann	SEP 09 1824
JUCH, Charity	WILSON, George R.	OCT 17 1849
JUDD, Abraham	SHANK, Mary	JAN 24 1856
JUDD, S. Corning	JAMES, Lavinia J.	JUL 03 1852
JUDGE, John	NOWLAND, Caroline	MAR 01 1824
JUDGE, John	FEENY, Mary	JAN 15 1853
JUDINGTON, Caroline	BYRAM, John W.	JUN 17 1842
JUDSON, Elnathan [Dr.]	YOUNG, Ellen	MAY 22 1824
JULIEN, Rosa Margaretta	ROUX, Peter	DEC 02 1817
JULIUS, Julia (blk)	BROWN, Henry	JUN 27 1833
JULIUS, Rebecca (blk)	WARNER, Nicholas	MAY 19 1836
JUMP, Thomas L.	JOHNSON, Juliana Lee	FEB 07 1837
JUNKEN, Charles	MORRISON, Eliza	JUL 28 1858
JUPE, George W.	BOLYE, Susanna	APR 23 1814
JURDINSTINE, Mary L.	LOVELESS, John H.	MAY 25 1847

District of Columbia Marriage Licenses, 1811-1858

K

KABELL, Bernard	KNIPPELL, Mary	MAY 31 1849
KABLEL, Polina	ZEH, William	MAR 26 1857
KABLER, Eliza	SMITH, Joshua	MAR 17 1831
KADEY, Bridget	LAWLESS, Thomas	JUL 09 1855
KADLE, William	MAYHEW, Mary Ann	MAR 15 1836
KAENER, Catherine	HEISER, Paul	JAN 15 1856
KAHL, Elizabeth	BENTER, Henry	OCT 24 1853
KAHLER, Johanna	KIESIKAR, Adam	JAN 05 1853
KAHSE, Chloe Ann	BROOKES, Bradley	AUG 10 1827
KAIBEL, Mary, Mrs.	GOCKELER, George Jacob	JUN 19 1858
KAIL, Catharine	CAMALIER, Vincent	DEC 19 1820
KAIL, Catharine	LAUXMAN, Martin	AUG 20 1857
KAIN, Hannah C.	DIXON, William	JUN 01 1838
KAIN, Henry	HINES, Betsey (blk)	OCT 01 1828
KAIN, James	THOMPSON, Elizabeth Ann	JUL 15 1829
KAIN, Julianna	CONINX, Melchior	MAY 24 1815
KAIN, Margaret	GLEASON, Edward	APR 21 1855
KAIN, Maria (blk)	LUCAS, George	APR 20 1831
KAIN, Mary Ann D.	BERRY, George F.	APR 14 1829
KAIN, Mary Charlotte	KING, Benjamin	MAR 10 1828
KAIN, Michael	MERE, Bridget	FEB 01 1854
KAINE, Tamor	GREEN, James	SEP 15 1817
KAISER, Catherine	SIEK, William	SEP 01 1857
KAISER, George	LOFFLER, Elizth.	OCT 20 1855
KAISER, Sophia	EIGHLER, Henry	JAN 05 1847
KALAHAR, Catherine	BRUSNAR, John	JUN 10 1843
KALCLASER, John	DOUGLASS, Helen	MAY 16 1844
KALDENBACH, Andrew	GROVES, Elizabeth	DEC 26 1839
KALDENBAUGH, Elizabeth	SYMINGTON, James	MAY 26 1814
KALE, Christeen	LUSKEY, John G.	DEC 27 1820
KALE, Mary	CONKLIN, Latin	MAR 25 1820
KALEHER, Ellen	CONNOR, Daniel	MAR 29 1856
KANE, Alfred	KELLEY, Hannah	NOV 28 1834
KANE, Ann	SULLIVAN, Thomas	JUN 18 1858
KANE, Betsy	LINAHAN, Michael	OCT 08 1851
KANE, Catherine	CARBERY, John	FEB 09 1852
KANE, Chas. H.	MILBURN, Ellen E.	JUL 01 1858
KANE, Delia	LEWIS, John	APR 16 1852
KANE, Elizabeth	FLOOD, John	JUN 05 1857
KANE, Ellen	SPALLIN, John	FEB 20 1855
KANE, James	WELCH, Ann	NOV 11 1852
KANE, Jane	LYNCH, James	FEB 07 1853
KANE, Jeremiah	DOWNEY, Johanna	MAY 09 1853
KANE, Margaret	RAIDY, Morris	NOV 10 1857
KANE, Mary	RAGAN, Dennis	NOV 25 1854
KANE, Mary Ellen	SARTEN, James W.	APR 17 1856
KANE, Michael	PROSSER, Catharine	APR 02 1853
KANE, Patrick	McADAMS, Celia	APR 19 1844
KANE, Patrick	BAILEY, Hannah	OCT 16 1856
KANE, Theodore	SPERRY, Emely E.	MAY 14 1838
KANIG, John	MITZINGER, Anna	JUN 12 1858
KANKEY, Amelia Virginia	DAVIS, William	NOV 15 1834
KANKEY, Araminta M.	RIND, Saml. S.	NOV 07 1831
KANSLEY, Barbara	BONARD, Frederick	MAY 06 1834
KARLL, Mary S.	SCHAD, Francis T.	DEC 09 1840
KARNEY, Ellen	WELSH, John	MAY 06 1854

District of Columbia Marriage Licenses, 1811-1858

KARNEY, Margaret	BYRNES, James	MAY 01 1858
KARNEY, Mary (blk)	JACKSON, William	JUL 22 1850
KARNEY, Patrick	McCULLOUGH, Isabella	NOV 10 1849
KARR, John	SAUNDERS, Susan	DEC 13 1853
KARR, William	FARRELL, Mary	DEC 22 1855
KARRICK, Henrietta Maria	KILBOURN, Byron	JUN 15 1838
KARRICK, Mary	MOCHBEE, Thomas	MAR 17 1812
KARRICK, Sarah	TALBURT, Alexander	JAN 01 1812
KASPARI, Henry	WALSELS, Mary	MAY 08 1858
KASSON, John A.	ELIOT, Caroline	APR 30 1850
KASZLER, Louisa	NOLL, John Henry	MAY 09 1849
KATELAY, Richard	DESMOND, Jane	FEB 08 1853
KATZENBERGER, John	POWER, Mary	APR 14 1851
KAUFFMANN, Conrad	YOCUM, Madalena	MAR 30 1850
KAUFFMANN, Mary	WOLFE, Wolfe	MAR 17 1855
KAVANAGH, Margaret	REGAN, Hugh	JUN 30 1853
KAVANAUGH, John	JEFFERS, Mary Ann	JUL 12 1834
KAVENAUGH, Thomas	BALDWIN, Mary	SEP 03 1835
KAYSER, Alexander	BOSCHKE, Mary	FEB 21 1854
KAYSER, John Christof.	ELI, Agnes	JUN 30 1845
KEACH, Eleanor	MARCEY, William	SEP 26 1826
KEADLE, Mary Ann G.	HAYRE, Francis	JUL 23 1822
KEALEY, James	BURNETT, Sophia	SEP 24 1840
KEALEY, Jane Euphrasia	TUCKER, John F.	AUG 02 1834
KEAN, Cornelius	SHEAHAN, Maria	AUG 23 1851
KEAN, Gilbert D.	JONES, Harriot R. [Mrs.]	AUG 26 1830
KEAN, Julia [Mrs.]	THOMPSON, James	APR 15 1816
KEAN, Margaret	RILEY, Garrett	JUN 07 1853
KEANE, Stephen	BUTLER, Hannah	MAY 26 1824
KEARIN, Sarah	FINNIGAN, Philip	JAN 11 1830
KEARNAN, Edwd.	KEARNAN, Margaret	SEP 19 1821
KEARNAN, Margaret	KEARNAN, Edwd.	SEP 19 1821
KEARNEY, Frederick	AIRHART, Julia	OCT 16 1835
KEARNEY, James [Col.]	O'REILY, Louisa	NOV 03 1830
KEARNEY, Kate	PATON, John	APR 14 1855
KEARNEY, Patrick	SWEENY, Catherine	APR 18 1857
KEARNEY, Stephen	TALLENT, Pleasant	FEB 01 1855
KEARNS, Eliza	JACKSON, Pompey	OCT 10 1833
KEARNS, Eliza	THOMPSON, John	DEC 24 1850
KEARNS, Mary	O'HEARN, John	MAY 25 1852
KEARNS, Mary Ann	THAW, Joseph	DEC 30 1851
KEARRON, Robert	BRANNAN, Mary	AUG 13 1846
KEARSE, Patrick	HANDS, Mary	MAY 22 1858
KEARY, Mary	O'DONNEL, Dennis	MAY 01 1832
KEATH, James	KING, Elizabeth B.	JAN 20 1818
KEATHLEY, John	RIGSBY, Mary	MAY 24 1851
KEATHLEY, Samuel	REELAND, Martha Eliza	MAY 02 1843
KEATING, Catharine	HALL, Frederick K.	MAY 26 1841
KEATING, Ellen	FLEMING, Michael	JUL 10 1858
KEATING, John	JOHNSTON, Mary C.	NOV 21 1851
KEATING, Margaret E.	ROBY, John H.	FEB 04 1852
KEATING, Patrick M.	ROCHE, Johannah A.	APR 17 1856
KEATING, Thomas	FORD, Catharine	NOV 09 1854
KEATING, Thomas P.	FARRELL, Mary Ann	APR 26 1853
KEATLEY, Jane Eliza	MEADER, Henry	AUG 05 1856
KECK, James	NELSON, Jane	SEP 04 1834
KEDGLIE, Ann Elizabeth	KERVAND, Lazare	MAY 25 1829
KEECE, John Henry Lewis	BEVONS, Martha	OCT 12 1846

District of Columbia Marriage Licenses, 1811-1858

KEECH, Evelina	BAGBY, Robert B.	DEC 08 1856
KEECH, Jane	STARR, William	NOV 15 1856
KEECH, John E.	LANGLEY, Amanda	JAN 22 1828
KEECH, Susan H.	TOBIAS, John	JUL 22 1856
KEEF, Patrick	CROWLEY, Sally	MAY 16 1815
KEEFE, Edmund	DELAD, Margaret	JUN 13 1853
KEEFE, John	McGRATH, Catherine	JAN 14 1853
KEEFE, John	SEXTON, Ellen	JUL 13 1857
KEEFE, John P.	TRAVERS, Martha Ann	MAR 04 1848
KEEFE, Mary	ROCHE, John	JAN 07 1857
KEEFE, Patrick	MALONE, Margaret	JUL 09 1856
KEEFE, William N.	MORAN, Annina	MAY 17 1852
KEEFER, John J.	YEUBOWER, Margaret	APR 27 1857
KEEFER, Joseph A.	THOMPSON, Elizabeth L.	JAN 09 1851
KEELER, Noah B.	REEDER, Rachael	NOV 19 1823
KEELER, Rachel	TAYLER, Thomas, Jr.	OCT 18 1825
KEELING, Mary F.	CHANDLER, James T.L.	JUN 15 1839
KEELING, William H.	THOMAS, Rachael Jane (blk)	JUN 27 1840
KEELY, Catherine	McVARY, Owen	JUL 15 1853
KEEN, Nathaniel B.	DAVIS, Susan E.	NOV 27 1828
KEENAN, Bridget	MURRAY, William	FEB 19 1855
KEENAN, Bridget	KELLY, James	JAN 28 1856
KEENAN, Catherine	GOODMAN, James	JUL 26 1855
KEENAN, Catherine	GARDINER, Richard Beatty	SEP 17 1855
KEENAN, Elizabeth	DITREH, Jacob	JUL 05 1854
KEENAN, Hugh	HUGHES, Rose	JUL 20 1854
KEENAN, John	HOMMOCK, Leo	OCT 19 1837
KEENAN, John	RICHARDS, Martha Ann	MAY 21 1838
KEENAN, John	DOLOHAN, Bridget	JUN 16 1851
KEENAN, Terence	MAGUIRE, Ellen	JUN 05 1858
KEENE, Ann	DODSON, Charles T.	APR 04 1857
KEENE, Emily Jane	CHANCEY, John T.	JUL 25 1855
KEENE, Francis	SIMPSON, Thompson	OCT 19 1815
KEENE, Joseph R.	CONRAD, Sarah E.	JUL 13 1857
KEENE, Subina	GEISINDAFFER, John	OCT 31 1839
KEENE, Thomas	ROBERTSON, Frances	AUG 23 1830
KEENE, William E.G.	LOVEJOY, Ellen W.	JUN 12 1848
KEEP, Samuel	LENOX, Julia Maria	JUL 31 1830
KEES, John Mason	JOHNS, Elizabeth	NOV 22 1841
KEESE, Geo. P.	CLAY, Amanda M.	NOV 26 1822
KEESE, Georgine	REUSS, Dr. Peter J.	OCT 04 1852
KEESE, John	DUNN, Ann	JUL 03 1858
KEESIEKIN, Sophia	BOWER, George	OCT 25 1851
KEETH, Susan	THOMPSON, Samuel	DEC 19 1850
KEETLEY, Mary	KNIGHT, Caleb	JUN 27 1840
KEETON, John M.	MAZINE, Elizth.	MAY 22 1827
KEEVEN, John	GAVIN, Bridget	JUL 09 1850
KEGLY, Elizabeth	MATLOCK, William	NOV 01 1845
KEHO, Mary	O'BRIEN, Lawrence	NOV 04 1853
KEHOE, James	KELLY, Margaret O.	SEP 03 1852
KEHOE, William	GRAFFORD, Sally	JAN 15 1822
KEIFEL, Charlott	STRATTON, Robert	JUN 24 1833
KEILER, Ellen	MURRAY, Nicholas	SEP 11 1852
KEILER, John	EDWARDS, Isabella	SEP 12 1855
KEIRNAN, Sarah Ann	BECKER, George	OCT 20 1846
KEIRNES, Richard	TEMPLEMAN, Octavia C.	AUG 07 1856
KEISER, Henry	SENT, Caroline	SEP 23 1850
KEITH, Ann	McQUILLAN, John	SEP 22 1817

District of Columbia Marriage Licenses, 1811-1858

KEITH, John	TRETLIER, Margaret	MAY 17 1831
KEITH, John Henry	BECKETT, Matilda	MAR 26 1844
KEITH, Julietta	WALKER, William	JAN 31 1850
KEITH, Margaret	CROWLEY, James	JUL 05 1851
KEITH, Margaret R.	GORBUTT, William H.	DEC 21 1853
KEITH, Mary Helen	FORREST, Bladen	AUG 05 1844
KEITH, William	DENHAM, Mary	SEP 07 1827
KEITHLEY, Francis	CHAUNCEY, Jane Eliza	NOV 03 1846
KEITHLEY, John	TEACHUM, Catharine	OCT 02 1833
KEITHLEY, Sarah Ann	BOLAYER, John	MAR 30 1844
KEIZER, Henry	RYDER, Elizabeth	JUN 15 1854
KELEHER, Catherine	McCAFFRY, Hugh	JUL 08 1854
KELEHER, Julia	WILLIAMS, Alfred A.	SEP 16 1852
KELEHER, Mary	ROONEY James	MAY 10 1853
KELEHER, Thos. H.	TRUNNEL, Caroline E.	OCT 25 1855
KELL, John	EDWARDS, Catharine	MAY 03 1837
KELLEN, Robert	YOUNG, Euphemia J.	MAY 17 1851
KELLER, Andrew J.	RYAN, Margaret A.	JUN 20 1855
KELLER, Ann Margaret	LARNER, Noble D.	NOV 24 1851
KELLER, Anna Mary	STONE, John P.	AUG 16 1853
KELLER, Caroline P.	JEWELL, Presley	JUL 11 1837
KELLER, Catherine	KELLER, John	JAN 03 1851
KELLER, Charles	WALKER, Ann Rebecca	JUN 02 1854
KELLER, Cornelia M.	WILSON, Peter F.	MAY 30 1853
KELLER, Frederic	REITZ, Elizabeth	APR 30 1819
KELLER, George	REIDER, Maria	JUL 19 1831
KELLER, Henry J.	MILLER, Margaret	JUN 21 1856
KELLER, John	KELLER, Catherine	JAN 03 1851
KELLER, John L.	FOUSHEE, Mary Ann	MAY 14 1823
KELLER, Margaret	WAGGONER, Upton	APR 14 1818
KELLER, Margaretha	SAUR, George C.G.	OCT 21 1854
KELLER, Mary	VIVENS, Louis	SEP 13 1824
KELLER, Mary	WALLACE, William Rich.	SEP 22 1832
KELLER, Michael	FISHER, Elizabeth	DEC 18 1832
KELLER, Michael	SHAAFER, Barbara	APR 29 1844
KELLER, Zelena M.	McINTIRE, Arthur L.	OCT 22 1833
KELLERBY, Joseph	ANSY, Sarah Ann	SEP 19 1827
KELLEY, Bernard	SULLIVAN, Catherine	JAN 17 1856
KELLEY, Elizabeth	CLARKE, William	MAY 20 1839
KELLEY, James	RIVELL, Mary	MAR 12 1833
KELLEY, James	HODGES, Ann	MAY 09 1846
KELLEY, Jane	HARRIS, Richard	JAN 04 1831
KELLEY, Jerry	SULLIVAN, Margaret	AUG 28 1855
KELLEY, Margaret	McGILLICUDDY, Timothy	APR 30 1857
KELLEY, Maria Catharine	BOWERS, Bennionuel	SEP 30 1833
KELLEY, Martha E.	LENMAN, Charles	MAY 07 1846
KELLEY, Martin	CAMPBALL, Ann	AUG 21 1852
KELLEY, Michael	McQUEEN, Margaret	MAY 26 1852
KELLEY, Polly	WOLFENDEN, George	APR 06 1835
KELLEY, Sarah E.	CHANCELLOR, Joshua	AUG 21 1855
KELLEYS, Sarah	FEGARRO, Antonio	MAY 13 1824
KELLION, Helen Margaretta	AHMA, Frederick	SEP 19 1843
KELLMON, Elizabeth	WALLER, Edward L.	JAN 13 1846
KELLON, Susannah	OGLE, William	JAN 15 1831
KELLY, Ann	WARD, Thomas	SEP 29 1843
KELLY, Ann	CASICK, Patrick	JAN 24 1852
KELLY, Ann	WARD, Thomas	SEP 29 1854
KELLY, Arthur	BROWNING, Eliza H.	JUN 22 1854

District of Columbia Marriage Licenses, 1811-1858

KELLY, Barnard	TURNER, Mary Ann	NOV 17 1830
KELLY, Betsey	LLOYD, Thomas	APR 27 1824
KELLY, Cassa Ann	CRAIG, William T.	JUL 09 1853
KELLY, Catherine	KING, Thomas	MAY 18 1836
KELLY, Catherine	SHIELDS, John	JUN 13 1850
KELLY, Charles	TALTON, Elizabeth	SEP 19 1822
KELLY, Columbus	McCARTY, Hannah	JAN 12 1858
KELLY, Cyrus D.	YOUNG, Mary	OCT 13 1831
KELLY, Edward	CATON, Judith	MAR 30 1815
KELLY, Edward	SALLY, Ann	JAN 25 1831
KELLY, Eliza	BRANNAN, John	JUL 26 1836
KELLY, Elizabeth	HAWKINS, Edward	JUL 21 1831
KELLY, Elizabeth	BROWN, Augustus	AUG 04 1855
KELLY, Hannah	KANE, Alfred	NOV 28 1834
KELLY, Hanora	O'CARROLL, Dennis	FEB 28 1854
KELLY, Humphrey	CREED, Johanna	JUL 03 1857
KELLY, Issabella	McKLEER, John	AUG 08 1821
KELLY, James	WATSON, Margaret	FEB 14 1812
KELLY, James	SHECKLE, Ann	APR 24 1823
KELLY, James	PARADISE, Sarah Ann	AUG 10 1832
KELLY, James	KEENAN, Bridget	JAN 28 1856
KELLY, James	SHENNESEY, Mary A.	MAR 22 1856
KELLY, James	HICKEY, Honora	MAY 06 1856
KELLY, Jane	TERNAN, James	JAN 25 1812
KELLY, Jane	BOYD, Robert	FEB 28 1828
KELLY, Jane	SHIMORS, John	FEB 07 1831
KELLY, Jane	KENNEDY, Thos.	JUN 01 1857
KELLY, Jane	McCARTY, Bartholomo	FEB 17 1858
KELLY, John	MORIARTY, Elizabeth	FEB 05 1822
KELLY, John	McPHERSON, Maria C.	SEP 26 1830
KELLY, John	O'BRIEN, Mary	APR 24 1851
KELLY, John	MURPHY, Mary Ellen	JUN 13 1854
KELLY, John	McCORMICK, Elizabeth	APR 23 1855
KELLY, John F.	WHALEN, Ann	JUN 27 1854
KELLY, Josephine	SESSFORD, Andrew	JAN 14 1846
KELLY, Margaret O.	KEHOE, James	SEP 03 1852
KELLY, Margaret R.	O'REILLY, Bernard	DEC 22 1854
KELLY, Martin	HARRINGTON, Honora	APR 28 1856
KELLY, Martin	SCOTT, Honora	NOV 08 1856
KELLY, Mary	BERRY, Thomas	NOV 05 1842
KELLY, Mary	O'BRYON, Terence	JUN 08 1852
KELLY, Mary	STRINING, John	JUN 14 1853
KELLY, Mary	BURNS, Patrick	JUN 09 1858
KELLY, Mary Ann	GAITHER, Edward	DEC 18 1839
KELLY, Mary Ann	GAHAN, Walter	JAN 08 1847
KELLY, Mary Ann	MILSTEAD, William B.	JUN 06 1850
KELLY, Mary E.	SAGE, Franklin H.	APR 21 1858
KELLY, Mary E.	DUNNINGIN, John	AUG 24 1858
KELLY, Mary Jane	MURPHY, Paul	JAN 15 1838
KELLY, Mary M.	ALLEN, Thomas	JUL 24 1854
KELLY, Matthew	FAGAN, Ellen	MAY 08 1852
KELLY, Michael	FITZGERALD, Bridget	JUL 31 1844
KELLY, Michael	WILLIAMS, Mary	SEP 10 1850
KELLY, Michael	BURNES, Alice	OCT 25 1856
KELLY, Michael	McDERMOTT, Bridget	NOV 19 1856
KELLY, Miles	DUFFEY, Ellen	DEC 31 1852
KELLY, Moses	WALKER, Mary W.	JUN 05 1844
KELLY, Nathaniel	BENSON, Hester Ann	MAY 05 1835

District of Columbia Marriage Licenses, 1811-1858

KELLY, Neal	SHELLE, Bridget	OCT 22 1856
KELLY, Patrick	BUCKLY, Catherine	FEB 04 1854
KELLY, Richard	TURNER, Eliza Eleanor	OCT 02 1840
KELLY, Samuel	SESSFORD, Elizabeth	DEC 20 1844
KELLY, Sarah E.	SCHNEIDER, Gottlobe C.	NOV 14 1850
KELLY, Silas	BRADLEY, Elizabeth (blk)	JAN 09 1845
KELLY, Susan S.	WILLIAMS, James H.	DEC 27 1855
KELLY, Thomas	CLARKE, Winifred	JAN 12 1852
KELLY, Thomas	[blank], Mary	NOV 18 1852
KELLY, Thomas	MUFF, Mary Ann	JUN 24 1854
KELLY, Timothy	FOLEY, Margaret	DEC 28 1855
KELLY, Vincentia	ALLEN, Anthony	OCT 30 1856
KELLY, William	BRANNAN, Eliza	SEP 21 1850
KELLY, William H.	McCUBBIN, Margaret	DEC 27 1850
KELLY, William H.	DeVAUGHN, Mary E.	JAN 09 1854
KELLY, William M.	YOAST, Elizabeth A.R.	SEP 23 1857
KELSEY, Conklin	MULLEN, Ellenor	JAN 21 1854
KELSEY, Judson R.	FETZER, Jane	MAR 01 1855
KEMBLE, James	OGDEN, Anna E.	MAY 10 1852
KEMBLE, Mary Ann	EDWARDS, Issadore	NOV 17 1821
KEMP, Catherine	HILL, John	FEB 16 1826
KEMP, Eliza E.	THOMPSON, John W.	DEC 07 1850
KEMP, Elizabeth	WILCOXEN, Jesse T.	DEC 17 1829
KEMP, John	WILLIAMS, Mary	JUL 09 1840
KEMP, John N.	McKAY, Eleanor E.	OCT 22 1835
KEMP, Margaret	DONOHO, Joseph	FEB 08 1853
KEMP, Mary	HOG, Wm.	AUG 24 1822
KEMP, Mary A.	THOMPSON, Robert	DEC 08 1853
KEMP, Matthias	LANHAM, Permelia	JAN 16 1827
KEMP, Ragena	WESTERMAN, Andrew	APR 28 1851
KEMP, Sophia	WILCOXEN, Nathan P.	MAY 12 1831
KEMPER, Hugh T.	FISHER, Sally M.	DEC 13 1855
KEMPF, Rachel	KETTNER, Henry	NOV 11 1835
KEMPPER, Levinia	SMITH, Calvin A.	OCT 07 1857
KENAN, Michael	WISE, Julia	JUL 09 1858
KENCHEL, Antoine F.	RIDGEWAY, Augusta W.	APR 20 1858
KENCHEL, Antonie F.	RIDGEWAY, Augusta W.	AUG 20 1858
KENDALL, Adela	CULVER, Frederick Burr	NOV 20 1839
KENDALL, Elie	WALKER, M.A.	AUG 02 1822
KENDALL, Fannie	FOX, Robert C.	DEC 20 1856
KENDALL, George W.	BRIGHT, Betsey	SEP 03 1853
KENDALL, Jeannie	STICKNEY, William	JAN 13 1852
KENDALL, Mary Ann	GULD, Daniel	AUG 11 1840
KENDALL, Samuel, Junr.	VINSON, Margaret W.	SEP 12 1836
KENDLE, James	HONEY, Mary Ann	FEB 23 1832
KENDLE, Jane (blk)	JOHNSON, Thomas	JUN 08 1847
KENDRIC, Richard A.	NOLEN, Mary	JAN 07 1854
KENDRICK, Ann M.	COUMBE, John T.	FEB 18 1847
KENDRICK, Benjamin	GRAY, Julian	SEP 30 1816
KENDRICK, George	DIXON, Chloe Ann	OCT 08 1835
KENDRICK, George R.	THYSON, Emily C.	JUN 26 1857
KENDRICK, Henry H.	SHANNON, Henrietta	MAY 01 1851
KENDRICK, Jane	CAWOOD, Benjn. F.	NOV 19 1855
KENDRICK, John	EDMUNDS, Frances M.	MAR 19 1844
KENDRICK, Mary	KINGSBURY, Thomas	APR 20 1846
KENDRICK, Mary A.	KIDWELL, Thomas J.	AUG 20 1857
KENDRICK, Sarah A.	NEWELL, Alexander	MAY 07 1846
KENDRICK, William	PRENDER, Margaret H.	OCT 22 1852

District of Columbia Marriage Licenses, 1811-1858

KENEALY, Hugh	O'LEARY, Mary	MAR 27 1858
KENEMAN, Wm. T.	ROWLAND, Emily	FEB 24 1857
KENGLEY, Lewis	POOR, Susan	JUN 28 1830
KENNA, Margaret	MULLOY, Thomas	DEC 15 1857
KENNADY, Mary	NEWMAN, John	AUG 28 1851
KENNAL, Lewis	JETT, Roberta (blk)	AUG 06 1838
KENNAN, John	LONG, Ann	JUL 12 1827
KENNARD, Joel S.	HANSON, Harriot McC.	MAY 23 1846
KENNEDY, Andrew	GILLHAM, Cornelia W.	JUL 09 1832
KENNEDY, Ann	SEXTON, John	NOV 01 1856
KENNEDY, Bridget	HAILEY, Thomas	JUN 13 1856
KENNEDY, David	GOODIN, Susanah	NOV 15 1830
KENNEDY, Eliza Douglass	BARTON, Benjamin	APR 13 1846
KENNEDY, Elizabeth Hill	AGATE, Alfred T.	SEP 09 1845
KENNEDY, Fanny	DALY, William	MAR 01 1854
KENNEDY, James	GRAY, Charlotte (blk)	JUL 21 1830
KENNEDY, James	LANCASTER, Mahala	AUG 29 1838
KENNEDY, James	NELIGAN, Bridgett	JAN 01 1852
KENNEDY, James	McGEE, Mary	JUL 06 1857
KENNEDY, James A.	WILLSON, Sarah	JAN 13 1817
KENNEDY, James A.	COBB, Susan	MAY 29 1824
KENNEDY, Jane H.	CHILDS, Henry	JUN 23 1824
KENNEDY, Johanna	LISTON, James	OCT 25 1856
KENNEDY, John	KORN, Margaret	JAN 08 1822
KENNEDY, John	McCARTY, Mary	JAN 27 1852
KENNEDY, John C.	HAMMOND, Mariann Augusta Bradley	MAY 17 1853
KENNEDY, John M.	PARROTT, Mary M.	OCT 25 1820
KENNEDY, John P.	POOL, Julia E.	APR 22 1858
KENNEDY, Julia	DEMENT, William	FEB 22 1815
KENNEDY, Lewis James	DANCEY, Betsey (blk)	JUN 22 1815
KENNEDY, Lewis James	DYER, Lethy	APR 29 1841
KENNEDY, Margaret	WAYLAND, Abram C.	DEC 20 1855
KENNEDY, Margaret	FITZGERALD, David	AUG 07 1858
KENNEDY, Mary	SHANAHAN, James	DEC 06 1852
KENNEDY, Mary A.	SLINGLAND, Jacob	JAN 30 1855
KENNEDY, Mary E.	CAMPBELL, Leonidas C.	OCT 02 1856
KENNEDY, Mary H.	WILSON, Henry G.	JAN 04 1818
KENNEDY, Mary Jane	KIRKWOOD, Wallace	JUL 12 1836
KENNEDY, Mary Jane	McCAFFERY, Jos. Hugh	FEB 05 1852
KENNEDY, Michael	O'BRIEN, Mary	FEB 04 1833
KENNEDY, Michael	LYNCH, Ellen	JUL 21 1856
KENNEDY, Pater	McCARTY, Margaret	AUG 02 1851
KENNEDY, Patrick	CATON, Ellen	NOV 29 1843
KENNEDY, Samuel J.A.	AHEARN, Catherine	JUL 01 1857
KENNEDY, Thomas	GUNNON, Mary	JAN 11 1851
KENNEDY, Thomas	KANNA, Julia	JAN 23 1851
KENNEDY, Thomas R.	EMACK, Harriet H.	JUL 17 1834
KENNEDY, Thos.	KELLY, Jane	JUN 01 1857
KENNEDY, William	SIMS, Elenora (blk)	JAN 22 1839
KENNEDY, William	BUCKLEY, Margaret	MAY 14 1855
KENNEDY, William A.	DONOHO, Elizabeth T.	JAN 26 1836
KENNEDY, William H.	GOULDING, Mary Josephine	MAY 03 1838
KENNEDY, Younger	CLIFF, Ephelinda	SEP 11 1849
KENNEHAN, Ann	FITZGERALD, Thomas	DEC 02 1854
KENNER, Maria	PLUNKETT, John	OCT 18 1845
KENNER, Mary Ann	RATCLIFFE, James	MAY 13 1824
KENNER, Rodham F.	JOHNSON, Elizabeth F.	DEC 13 1815
KENNEY, Catherine	GLENIN, Patrick	JAN 15 1858

District of Columbia Marriage Licenses, 1811-1858

KENNEY, Patrick	ROGAN, Mary	OCT 02 1851
KENNON, Beverley, Capt.	PETER, Britannia W.	DEC 05 1842
KENNON, Bridget	LAURY, Michael	MAY 11 1858
KENNY, Mary	DEMSEY, Patrick	AUG 30 1852
KENRICK, Mary E.	KIDWELL, T.J.	JUN 10 1857
KENSLOW, Eliza	GUERING, Michael	MAY 09 1855
KENT, Ann	THOMPSON, James	AUG 05 1824
KENT, Daniel	JONES, Charity Margaretta	JAN 28 1830
KENT, Elijah	McCOLLISTER, Elizth.	MAY 13 1826
KENT, Ellen	LEGG, Lawson	MAR 14 1814
KENT, Mary A.	HOPKINS, Jas. Arthur	JUL 12 1849
KENT, Phillip	WELLER, Ellen Elizabeth	SEP 26 1843
KEOGH, Michael	LUPTON, Catharine	JUN 05 1819
KEPLER, John George	WILTSBURCHER, Teresa	JUL 31 1856
KEPLEY, Mary A.	HILTZEL, Nicholas	MAY 30 1836
KEPNER, Henry	DAVIS, Eliza	AUG 12 1834
KEPPLER, George	RUHL, Caroline	OCT 30 1848
KEPPLER, Gregory	FELLENGER, Augusta	APR 22 1858
KEPPLER, Henry S.	HANSON, Sarah R.	JUN 22 1837
KEPPLER, Samuel [Rev.]	WARING, Mary Jane	JUL 14 1831
KER, Jacob W.E.	WILLIAMSON, Mary	MAR 21 1838
KER, Margaret W.	HANDY, Samuel W.	DEC 20 1825
KERANS, Thomas	McNERHANY, Margaret	SEP 18 1844
KERBER, Mary M.	RUPPERT, Michael	NOV 11 1856
KERBY, George	HAYDEN, Henrietta	JUN 29 1846
KERBY, John	GOODRICK, Eliza	DEC 31 1813
KERBY, Margaret Jane	GRINDER, Joseph	DEC 30 1848
KERCHEVAL, William	BATTHROPE, Ann Maria	MAR 10 1836
KERN, Frederick S.	MILES, Mary Ann	FEB 27 1850
KERN, Xavier	LACKMAN, Catharine	APR 23 1849
KERNAN, Eliza	LINDSEY, William	SEP 07 1852
KERNAN, Mary Ann	BUSH, William	MAY 07 1851
KERNANN, Martha	KINSLEY, Henry	MAY 10 1845
KERR, Chapman	JOHNSON, Catherine	SEP 14 1852
KERR, Elizabeth	CAREY, William	JUL 07 1851
KERR, Michael	BRADY, Margaret	FEB 01 1858
KERR, Peter	DUFFEY, Mary	OCT 01 1852
KERR, Peter	DONOVAN, Catherine	JUN 22 1857
KERR, Sarah A.	MITCHELL, John T.	SEP 29 1840
KERR, William W.S.	BASSETT, Mary J.	NOV 05 1851
KERRON, John	WHITAKER, Jane C.	AUG 19 1847
KERRY, John	WOLFE, Margaret	MAY 31 1851
KERSCH, Francis	SCHRAM, Sophia	APR 17 1854
KERSEY, Catharine E.	RINE, Michael	OCT 20 1841
KERSEY, Daniel	HILL, Nancy Ann	DEC 06 1815
KERSEY, Edward	IBBERTSON, Sarah	APR 05 1844
KERSEY, James F.	THOMPSON, Mary Jane	NOV 17 1852
KERSEY, Robert	McKENNEY, Catharine	MAY 12 1821
KERSEY, Virginia A.	NALLY, William H.	MAR 14 1854
KERVAND, Lazare	KEDGLIE, Ann Elizabeth	MAY 25 1829
KERWIN, Catharine	CROGHAN, Francis	FEB 15 1836
KESH, Jacob	LISBURGHER, Henrietta	JUL 27 1852
KESLEA, Baltzer	SHAFER, Theresa	JAN 30 1856
KESLEY, Julia B.	SCHOEPH, Alvin	MAY 05 1855
KESLEY, William	BATES, Julia A.	MAR 03 1835
KESSLER, Adam	MARTELL, Mary Ann	MAY 02 1855
KESSLER, George E.	JARBOE, Anna E.	JUL 20 1855
KESSLER, John	BEAN, Elizabeth	MAY 16 1853

District of Columbia Marriage Licenses, 1811-1858

KESSLER, Peter F.	PECK, Sylvia	FEB 08 1854
KESSUCK, Eliza	TOLLANSBEE, Joseph	MAY 04 1819
KESSUCK, Margaret	FOLLANSBEE, Joseph	MAR 10 1829
KETCHEN, Lucinda A.	NEWMAN, John H.	OCT 18 1847
KETNER, Agnes	NOTT, George F.	MAY 15 1858
KETTLER, Fredeicka	KLEPPENGER, Christopher	JUL 03 1854
KETTNER, Henry	KEMPF, Rachel	NOV 11 1835
KEY, Alice	PENDLETON, George H.	JUN 01 1846
KEY, Alice	PENDLETON, George H.	JUN 01 1846
KEY, Anna	TURNER, Daniel [Hon.]	FEB 18 1829
KEY, Anna A.	THOMPSON, William E.	OCT 21 1835
KEY, Elizabeth R.	JOHNSON, Henry [Hon.]	OCT 01 1829
KEY, Elizth. Phebe	HOWARD, Charles	NOV 09 1825
KEY, Ellen L.	BLUNT, Simon F.	JAN 27 1846
KEY, Gillip	JONES, Mary A. (blk)	OCT 04 1845
KEY, John	DADE, Margaret Ann	JUN 21 1847
KEY, Lucy (blk)	DICK, Daniel	SEP 04 1850
KEY, Martha (blk)	MASON, Samuel	APR 14 1858
KEY, Mary Ann A. (blk)	GASSAWAY, Thomas	JUL 26 1853
KEY, Mary L.	NEVINS, William [Rev.]	NOV 13 1822
KEY, Rebecca Ann	HOWARD, William [Dr.]	MAY 13 1828
KEY, Wallace	DICKENSON, Sarah	AUG 20 1841
KEYES, William C.	SIMMS, Selena V.	MAY 05 1854
KEYNE, John	DONOHOE, Margaret	JUN 20 1815
KEYS, Andrew J.	ALLEN, Ann L.	JAN 05 1846
KEYS, Andrew J.	BRAWNER, Elizabeth	MAR 19 1850
KEYS, Fielding	COOMB, Catharine	NOV 15 1849
KEYS, Geo. W.	LEWIS, Mary Louisa	DEC 26 1849
KEYS, James	ELGIN, Mary J.	SEP 05 1854
KEYS, Magruder J.	McCRACKEN, Ann	JUN 15 1837
KEYS, Nancy	THOMPSON, Arthur	MAY 10 1831
KEYS, Nancy	BROWN, Richard H.	APR 30 1855
KEYS, Nicholas	DUNN, Mary	DEC 16 1851
KEYS, Peyton	COPEN, Laura H.	FEB 02 1852
KEYS, Richard B.	BARKER, Mary R.	DEC 17 1850
KEYS, Sarah	FLYNN, Daniel	DEC 30 1850
KEYS, Ujamah	LYNN, Isaac	DEC 27 1830
KEYSER, Eliza	LINDENBORN, John	AUG 13 1856
KEYSER, John	SMITH, Christina	AUG 19 1854
KEYSER, John	HEYDER, Leonora	JUN 12 1858
KEYSER, Robert	BASELER, Mary	APR 17 1857
KEYWORTH, Anna	McCLERY, Mirven J.	SEP 08 1845
KEYWORTH, Emma	TODHUNTER, Isaac E.	SEP 21 1852
KEYWORTH, Kate	PICKETT, John T.	OCT 17 1853
KEYWORTH, Robert	TAYLOR, Mary	OCT 21 1819
KEYWORTH, Robert W.	ANDERSON, Anna	OCT 30 1850
KHUNE, Adolphus	ROPHINOT, Mary Julia	JUN 04 1853
KIBBEY, Alexander	HOLROYD, Mary	OCT 20 1836
KIBBY, Eliza	SITCHER, William	FEB 14 1825
KIBBY, Liannah	GRIFFIN, James L.	SEP 01 1838
KIBBY, Penny	SEDWICK, Benj.	JAN 02 1819
KIBBY, Thomas	JOHNSON, Sianna	APR 12 1827
KIBEY, Alexander	HATCHINGSON, Mary Ann	OCT 01 1844
KIBLER, Susanah	BOWEN, Silas T.	NOV 04 1853
KICKHAM, William	DORNIN, Jane E.	JUN 05 1849
KID, William	SKIPPON, Jane	MAR 21 1844
KIDLEY, Martha Ann	SHERRY, Dominick	MAY 04 1835
KIDLOW, Ellen N.	SOPER, Basil	NOV 16 1831

District of Columbia Marriage Licenses, 1811-1858

KIDMORE, Samuel	MITCHELL, Louisa	OCT 17 1848
KIDNEY, Eleanor	GIVENY, Bernard	JAN 05 1822
KIDWELL, Addison	PRESTON, Eliza	AUG 08 1833
KIDWELL, Alexander C.	GARNER, Mary E.	APR 21 1829
KIDWELL, Allison	HUNTT, Mary Ann M.	AUG 13 1833
KIDWELL, Amanda	KING, Charles	JAN 07 1851
KIDWELL, Ann	WHITLEY, George	OCT 04 1825
KIDWELL, Ann	HAYS, David	DEC 14 1825
KIDWELL, Ann S.	FOGG, Samuel J.	APR 05 1849
KIDWELL, Benjamin	HUTCHINSON, Mary	MAR 03 1825
KIDWELL, Catharine Virginia	PETTIT, John Thomas	DEC 19 1849
KIDWELL, Cortney	HAYS, Fanny	NOV 18 1824
KIDWELL, Elijah	DUVALL, Amelia	FEB 13 1849
KIDWELL, Eliza N.	GOODWIN, Thomas	SEP 05 1846
KIDWELL, Elizabeth	SANDS, George	DEC 28 1816
KIDWELL, Elizabeth	REYNOLDS, James D.	FEB 27 1836
KIDWELL, Elizabeth M.	CROCKETT, John	DEC 21 1854
KIDWELL, Ellen	GOLDSMITH, John	OCT 11 1823
KIDWELL, Ellen S.	COOKSEY, Joshua J.	DEC 24 1850
KIDWELL, George	GATES, Priscilla	APR 17 1827
KIDWELL, George	LYNCH, Rebecca	JUN 26 1850
KIDWELL, George	HANSMAN, Cornelia	OCT 14 1853
KIDWELL, George F.	HERBERT, Mary E.	MAY 16 1836
KIDWELL, George P.	RICHARDSON, Jane	JUL 20 1839
KIDWELL, George W.	DOWELL, Sarah	FEB 10 1846
KIDWELL, Hezekiah A.	ELLIS, Martha A.J.	DEC 23 1852
KIDWELL, Isaac	OSBORN, Rosella	MAR 02 1833
KIDWELL, James	HODGKIN, Henrietta	MAR 06 1819
KIDWELL, James	WHEELER, Elizabeth	JUL 28 1823
KIDWELL, James	CLARKE, Louisa	OCT 29 1838
KIDWELL, James	LANGLEY, Martha	SEP 30 1847
KIDWELL, Jane	THOMPSON, James	JUN 10 1841
KIDWELL, Jane E.	DOWELL, Thomas M.	MAY 15 1858
KIDWELL, John H.	BRADLEY, Sarah R.	DEC 05 1848
KIDWELL, John J.	NALLY, Mary Jane	OCT 09 1848
KIDWELL, John L.	LAWRENCE, Catharine A.	NOV 16 1840
KIDWELL, Joseph F.	WATSON, Elizabeth B.	FEB 22 1849
KIDWELL, Julia Ann	THOMPSON, John Allerson	SEP 30 1830
KIDWELL, Lucretia	GATES, Wm. O'Brien	JUN 03 1843
KIDWELL, Margaret M.	EMMERSON, Lemuel G.	MAR 29 1856
KIDWELL, Martha	DAW, John	APR 02 1825
KIDWELL, Martha A.	WHEATLEY, Benedict	MAY 16 1855
KIDWELL, Martin VanBuren	BRADY, Ann	DEC 24 1857
KIDWELL, Mary	GOLDSMITH, William	JUL 08 1828
KIDWELL, Mary E.	HANTZMAN, Robert	MAY 15 1855
KIDWELL, Mary Elizth.	DAVIS, John Henry	APR 09 1855
KIDWELL, Presley	PADGETT, Harriot	JUN 19 1827
KIDWELL, Rosetta	CAMPBELL, Enoch Henry	DEC 03 1849
KIDWELL, Samuel	BOSWELL, Barbara E.	JUN 25 1850
KIDWELL, Sarah	MORELAND, John	NOV 24 1832
KIDWELL, Sarah Elizabeth	PHELPS, John T.	FEB 06 1851
KIDWELL, Susan N.	WINDSER, Elijah	SEP 24 1853
KIDWELL, T.J.	KENRICK, Mary E.	JUN 10 1857
KIDWELL, Thomas J.	GATES, Elizabeth	DEC 27 1842
KIDWELL, Thomas J.	ROBEY, Emma J.	JUN 03 1854
KIDWELL, Thomas J.	KENDRICK, Mary A.	AUG 20 1857
KIDWELL, Thompson	SIMONDS, Nancy Ann	DEC 26 1850
KIDWELL, Washington R.	WHEELER, Mary Ann	JUL 11 1834

District of Columbia Marriage Licenses, 1811-1858

KIDWELL, William	BOSWELL, Charlotte	JUL 15 1845
KIECKHOEFER, Ann	PALMER, William H.	SEP 08 1853
KIECKHOEFER, Ann	PALMER, William H.	SEP 12 1857
KIECKHOEFOR, Julia Augusta	DeMARCOLETA, J.	JUN 08 1853
KIEFER, Philip	GERNHARD, Johanna	SEP 16 1856
KIER, Barney	GRAY, Mary	APR 14 1842
KIERNAN, Catharine	DEVLIN, John	MAR 02 1824
KIERNAN, Christena	HILYARD, John J.	MAY 18 1824
KIERNAN, Honora	CONNOR, Michael	NOV 12 1855
KIERNAN, James	McKENNEDY, Catharine	OCT 04 1851
KIERNAN, Mary Ann	HICKSON, William	MAR 10 1828
KIERNAN, Nicholas	McCANN, Mary	SEP 06 1851
KIERNAN, Patrick	BROOKS, Catharine	AUG 04 1818
KIERNAN, Patrick	LYNCH, Margaret	SEP 06 1851
KIERNAN, Patrick	SCOTT, Mary Ann	FEB 02 1856
KIESIKAR, Adam	KAHLER, Johanna	JAN 05 1853
KIFF, Margaret	SMITHWICK, John	JUL 25 1820
KIGER, Alfred	THOMAS, Rachel	MAR 17 1834
KILBERTH, Ann	FERGUSON, Robert	SEP 14 1848
KILBERTH, Henry	GREEN, Catharine	JUL 23 1818
KILBOURN, Byron	KARRICK, Henrietta Maria	JUN 15 1838
KILBRIDE, Margaret	McINERNY, Dennis	SEP 13 1832
KILBRIGHT, Rachel	GRIDLEY, Lewis	SEP 11 1854
KILBY, Isaac H.	WALLER, Maria G.	DEC 26 1855
KILBY, Robert	MOTHERSHEAD, Mary	APR 12 1853
KILE, John	PUMPHREY, Sarah	APR 28 1812
KILGOUR, Mortimer	WOOTTEN, Martha W.	MAY 05 1847
KILHAN, Catherine	HART, William	JUN 16 1857
KILL, Airy	HILL, John	JUN 28 1828
KILLDEFF, Catherine	BENNETT, William T.	SEP 12 1855
KILLDOVE, Elizabeth	HURD, Enoch	JAN 06 1851
KILLEFOIL, Winifred	CRONIN, James	FEB 10 1858
KILLEGAN, James	LYNCH, Mary	MAR 10 1851
KILLIAN, Mary Margt.	TRAVERS, Nicholas	DEC 28 1846
KILLIGAN, Ellen	MEHIGAN, Daniel	OCT 17 1853
KILLIGAN, Ellen	BRYAN, John	JUL 02 1857
KILLION, Barbara M.	SCHLERP, William	DEC 12 1850
KILLMAN, Samuel	EDMONSTON, Dorothy S.	FEB 16 1820
KILLMON, John T.	SHERIFF, Mary I.	JUN 19 1845
KILLMON, Sarah A.	TUCKER, Maurice	FEB 08 1856
KILLPATRICK, Kitty	KING, James	JUN 08 1822
KILLSNAN, John	STRIFLAREN, Helen	MAY 02 1845
KILRCHAR, David	JACOBS, Mary	JUL 10 1857
KIMBALL, Jacob	HALL, Matilda	DEC 20 1842
KIMMELL, Abraham F.	LAMBELL, Mary Ann S.	JAN 08 1845
KINCAID, Sarah E.	FLEURY, John R.	JUL 15 1825
KINCHELOE, John	DAVIS, Harriet	APR 08 1830
KINCHEY, Paul	LESIARDI, Polien	AUG 08 1825
KINCHEY, Paul	HITZ, Madeline	NOV 07 1843
KINCHSLOE, Emily	MOONEY, William S.	FEB 17 1829
KINDEL, Ensey	DEANE, Nelly	SEP 25 1816
KINDEL, Mary	BRANIGAN, Henry	SEP 25 1816
KINDSLEY, James	FAGAN, Eliza	DEC 01 1821
KINEY, Patrick	SWEENY, Margaret	JUL 29 1853
KINFT, Elizabeth	SCHWIER, Henry	APR 03 1843
KING, Amasa W.	MELCHER, Annie J.	AUG 05 1858
KING, Andrew	THOMAS, Sarah	MAR 11 1824
KING, Andrew	TURNER, Betsey	NOV 13 1828

District of Columbia Marriage Licenses, 1811-1858

KING, Ann	WHETMORE, Wm.	JAN 27 1819
KING, Ann	SMITZER, Thomas	APR 17 1827
KING, Ann	SCHANER, Laurence	OCT 22 1846
KING, Ann	JONES, Chirchwill	JAN 25 1854
KING, Ann	MURRAY, Patrick	APR 17 1857
KING, Ann	GOODWIN, Wm. R.	OCT 07 1857
KING, Ann C.	McSHERRY, Richard	JAN 28 1817
KING, Ann Jane	GARRETT, George W.	NOV 02 1846
KING, Ann Maria	MADDOX, William T.	JAN 26 1819
KING, Ann Maria	LAWSON, William	OCT 13 1852
KING, Anna	DOONE, John F.	MAY 09 1857
KING, Anna M.	FOWLER, Wm. J.	AUG 17 1857
KING, Annah	LANGLEY, Francis V.	MAR 03 1829
KING, Aruthia	WHITMORE, William	MAR 23 1816
KING, Barbara Ann	BARKER, Thomas	OCT 12 1830
KING, Benjamin	KAIN, Mary Charlotte	MAR 10 1828
KING, Benjamin	KING, Elizabeth	AUG 15 1835
KING, Benjamin	HOUGH, Dorothy	JUL 10 1841
KING, Benjamin	FARR, Eliza	NOV 02 1844
KING, Bridget	McCORMICK, John B.	MAY 05 1817
KING, Caroline	BUSK, Thos. Murphy	JUL 10 1851
KING, Caroline	FISHER, Morris	MAY 26 1853
KING, Catharine	COLLIER, Frederick H.	JUL 18 1849
KING, Catharine (blk)	THOMAS, Michael	JUN 03 1827
KING, Catharine (blk)	VODRY, Robert	APR 13 1850
KING, Catherine	RECTOR, Walter	JAN 29 1846
KING, Catherine	WEAVER, Joseph	MAY 02 1853
KING, Charles	DORNEY, Sarah	JUL 12 1820
KING, Charles	ALBY, Mary M.	JUN 09 1829
KING, Charles	ANDERSON, Ann	APR 15 1847
KING, Charles	KIDWELL, Amanda	JAN 07 1851
KING, Charles	TOWNSEND, Catharine (blk)	OCT 07 1852
KING, Christine	WELCH, Leonard	SEP 26 1843
KING, Daniel	CHAMBERS, Martha Ellen	AUG 08 1839
KING, Daniel E.	KING, Sarah Ann	FEB 24 1852
KING, David	POWERS, Elizabeth	OCT 24 1837
KING, Dorcas	LOVELL, James	SEP 04 1822
KING, Edward	DUNBAR, Maria	NOV 09 1820
KING, Edward	WILLIAMS, Elvina	JUN 01 1844
KING, Edward A.	GOODWIN, Virginia	FEB 22 1855
KING, Eleanor Mary	QUEEN, Richard T.	NOV 04 1816
KING, Elijah	TURNER, Catharine	JUN 01 1820
KING, Elisha	BUTLER, Henrietta (blk)	NOV 21 1850
KING, Eliza	THOMPSON, Josias	OCT 06 1812
KING, Eliza	DEAN, Alexander	FEB 06 1840
KING, Eliza A.	STAATS, Jacob A.	FEB 24 1852
KING, Elizabeth	FOX, Cephas	NOV 24 1813
KING, Elizabeth	JENKINS, Lloyd	JAN 15 1817
KING, Elizabeth	HENNON, Stephen	MAY 14 1818
KING, Elizabeth	BURNES, Patrick	APR 25 1822
KING, Elizabeth	BROWN, James	NOV 16 1822
KING, Elizabeth	BALCH, Stephen B. [Rev.]	NOV 04 1828
KING, Elizabeth	KING, Benjamin	AUG 15 1835
KING, Elizabeth	ELLIOT, Jonathan	APR 06 1845
KING, Elizabeth	KING, John	JAN 02 1856
KING, Elizabeth (blk)	MARSHALL, Edward	JUL 08 1852
KING, Elizabeth B.	KEATH, James	JAN 20 1818
KING, Enoch	NICHOLSON, George Ann	MAR 29 1845

District of Columbia Marriage Licenses, 1811-1858

KING, Francis	THORPE, Eliza	JUN 07 1821
KING, Francis	COLUMBUS, Josephine	FEB 05 1842
KING, Genevieve A.	SLYE, Daniel W.	FEB 02 1854
KING, George	REDDIN, Mary Ann (blk)	MAY 21 1840
KING, George	BLOOD, Olympha	JAN 29 1846
KING, George G., Hon.	SEAVER, Elizabeth C.	JAN 14 1851
KING, George H.	McDONALD, Amanda	AUG 05 1852
KING, George, of Chs.	FORD, Susannah	NOV 25 1816
KING, George P.	LUSKEY, Christianna	MAY 27 1828
KING, Hannah	PHILLIPS, John	JUN 03 1830
KING, Hannah A. (blk)	PINDLE, Thomas H.	SEP 17 1855
KING, Harriet	BARNES, James T.	JAN 27 1852
KING, Henrietta (blk)	WILSON, Thomas	JUN 02 1842
KING, Henry	HORSMAN, Catharine	DEC 11 1827
KING, Henry [Dr.]	EASBY, Marian Eliza	NOV 13 1833
KING, Henry	DEAN, Martha	SEP 15 1838
KING, Henry	THOMPSON, Elizabeth Ann	FEB 07 1839
KING, Henry	CAMMACK, Catherine	AUG 17 1848
KING, Henry	GOLDSHMITH, Regine	JAN 02 1858
KING, Hiram	BLAN, Ellen	OCT 01 1838
KING, Ignatius	BROWN, Sarah	MAR 25 1826
KING, Isabella	STEER, Phineas J.	APR 18 1832
KING, Isaiah	HICKS, Ann V. (blk)	MAR 05 1844
KING, Isaiah	HUGHES, Elizabeth (blk)	JUL 21 1845
KING, Jackson	MANN, Elizabeth	SEP 22 1856
KING, James	MOCKBEE, Harriot	MAY 22 1820
KING, James	KILLPATRICK, Kitty	JUN 08 1822
KING, James	CATON, Mary	JUN 27 1828
KING, James	SMITH, Polly	DEC 20 1831
KING, James	LIBBEY, Charlotte	JUN 20 1843
KING, James Andrew	PECK, Margaret Doreas Virginia	JUN 12 1854
KING, James B.	AUSTIN, Anna	DEC 02 1856
KING, James C., Jr.	YOUNG, Margaret	JAN 02 1844
KING, James D.	SLYE, Mary A.	APR 28 1830
KING, James H.	TRUSLER, Jane	JUN 22 1854
KING, James Henry	JONES, Susan	OCT 19 1850
KING, Jennet	TAYLOR, Robert A.	JUN 17 1835
KING, Joanna M.	WILLIAMS, Thomas E.	FEB 10 1844
KING, Johanna	BROWN, Edward	AUG 04 1854
KING, John	PARKER, Susan (blk)	OCT 17 1822
KING, John	WOODWARD, Catharine	MAY 29 1824
KING, John	HANDLEY, Margaret	JAN 08 1825
KING, John	WEBSTER, Jane	MAY 28 1832
KING, John	BRANNAN, Sarah S. [Mrs.]	MAR 04 1833
KING, John	WHITE, Louisa	AUG 04 1836
KING, John	MORSON, Mary	NOV 09 1837
KING, John	JOHNSON, Sarah Ann	APR 03 1838
KING, John	HALL, Cornelia	OCT 02 1841
KING, John	JACKSON, Mary (blk)	JAN 08 1842
KING, John	JOHNSON, Mary A. (blk)	JUL 23 1842
KING, John	HENDLY, Elizabeth	AUG 10 1848
KING, John	KING, Elizabeth	JAN 02 1856
KING, John A.	BRONOUGH, Frances [Mrs.]	APR 28 1830
KING, John H.	HARRET, Ellen	NOV 03 1825
KING, John J.	COLLINS, Hester Ann	JAN 15 1852
KING, John, of Wm.	MORGAN, Amanda M.	NOV 09 1852
KING, John T.	ATWELL, Virginia	DEC 23 1845
KING, John Thomas	MALORD, Mary A.	NOV 25 1856

District of Columbia Marriage Licenses, 1811-1858

KING, John W.	McCHESNEY, Ann Maria	MAR 27 1856
KING, Joseph W.	ADAMS, Margaret A.	NOV 10 1849
KING, Josiah E.	STANGLE, Ann E.	MAY 19 1832
KING, Josias W.	WHETCROFT, Catherine	FEB 20 1817
KING, Julia	DAVIS, Ferdinand	MAR 31 1852
KING, Kitty Elizabeth	TIPPETT, Hezekiah	FEB 18 1824
KING, Laura V.	BROOKS, Samuel M.	SEP 28 1857
KING, Letitia H.	DAVIDSON, William H.	MAY 08 1828
KING, Letitia W.	HIGGINS, David	OCT 01 1847
KING, Levi G.	JONES, Rebecca	DEC 18 1854
KING, Louisa	BARTON, Thos. B. [Lieut.]	AUG 17 1819
KING, Louisa	WORMLY, William	JUL 19 1821
KING, Margaret	TOPHAM, George	DEC 11 1833
KING, Margaret	BURCH, James Albert	APR 08 1837
KING, Margaret	HEARN, Thomas	MAY 09 1851
KING, Margaret	BRADY, Silas S.	APR 17 1855
KING, Margaret	SHIELDS, John V.	JUN 30 1855
KING, Margaret A.	BIRAM, Edward J.	JAN 01 1855
KING, Margaret D.	LITTLE, Samuel J.	JAN 31 1839
KING, Margaret Elizabeth	RIDGATE, Benjamin C.	MAY 15 1845
KING, Maria	COWAN, Edward	DEC 09 1823
KING, Maria	TOWNLEY, Eugene	APR 14 1847
KING, Mariah	REED, John R.	JAN 06 1827
KING, Martha (blk)	CONWAY, William	MAY 09 1833
KING, Martha Ann	JARBOE, Benedict	AUG 21 1827
KING, Martha Ann	COLIER, Peyton	JUN 18 1845
KING, Martha E.	ANDERSON, James	NOV 30 1835
KING, Martin	OTT, Rose Anna	JAN 01 1825
KING, Martin	POLIZZI, Angelina Rosalier	NOV 20 1827
KING, Martin	HUGHES, Margaret	DEC 06 1827
KING, Martin	LEDAN, Bridget	SEP 04 1833
KING, Mary	McGLUE, Owen	NOV 06 1812
KING, Mary	ROACH, John	OCT 04 1823
KING, Mary	MOCKBEE, Carlton	MAR 09 1833
KING, Mary	MAYSE, William	JUN 24 1833
KING, Mary	SULLIVAN, John	JAN 21 1851
KING, Mary	BORLAND, Thomas	OCT 02 1852
KING, Mary	McGRATH, Peter	MAR 22 1856
KING, Mary Ann	MORRISON, Jesse	DEC 06 1823
KING, Mary Ann Maria	ANDERSON, Rezin	DEC 12 1829
KING, Mary Ann	BOSWELL, James J.	DEC 27 1853
KING, Mary Ann	MURPHY, George W.	JUL 21 1857
KING, Mary E.	McCHESNEY, John H.	JUN 12 1850
KING, Mary Frances	McKEAN, Samuel	MAY 18 1818
KING, Mary Frances Virginia	SCOTT, William T.	MAY 09 1848
KING, Mary Jane	BRUNETTE, Louis	DEC 23 1847
KING, Mary Roberta	GOODWIN, Henry E.	AUG 04 1855
KING, Miranda A.	VanNESS, George H.	AUG 06 1841
KING, Montgomery S.	MOFFETT, Mary J.	JAN 08 1857
KING, Nannie	STRAUS, Abraham	FEB 06 1857
KING, Norah	THORN, William	OCT 23 1830
KING, Patrick	LARNER, Biddy	JUN 01 1815
KING, Peter	KING, Sarah	SEP 01 1845
KING, Rebecca H.	HAYS, Rev. Isaac N.	DEC 14 1850
KING, Reke	BENSEL, George	OCT 12 1848
KING, Richard A.	GODDARD, Mary Ann	FEB 11 1836
KING, Robert	SKINNER, Ellen	OCT 14 1856
KING, Rosanna	BAYLY, Edward	MAR 26 1835

District of Columbia Marriage Licenses, 1811-1858

KING, Sally	CATON, Michael	OCT 16 1819
KING, Sally	SCOTT, William S.	OCT 02 1854
KING, Samuel	BIEGEL, Caroline	MAR 26 1857
KING, Samuel Davidson	HOLTZMAN, Matilda Sophia [Mrs.]	SEP 19 1832
KING, Sarah	EVERETT, Charles	JUN 10 1814
KING, Sarah	MURRAY, Thomas	OCT 25 1814
KING, Sarah	SIMPSON, Benjamin	APR 14 1818
KING, Sarah	GOLIHAR, Thomas	SEP 12 1821
KING, Sarah	WILSON, William A.	DEC 25 1829
KING, Sarah	KING, Peter	SEP 01 1845
KING, Sarah A.	NOLAND, John T.	OCT 14 1844
KING, Sarah A.	BENRISER, Jacob J.	AUG 24 1848
KING, Sarah Ann	GATES, Robert O.	JUN 22 1824
KING, Sarah Ann	KING, Daniel E.	FEB 24 1852
KING, Sarah Elizabeth	MANSFIELD, Thomas, Jr.	JUN 20 1856
KING, Shirley	CLIFFORD, Margaret	APR 17 1858
KING, Stephen	CROSS, Cordelia A.V.	DEC 20 1850
KING, Susan	WADE, William [Capt.]	JAN 07 1823
KING, Susan	JOHNSON, Peter	SEP 06 1832
KING, Susan Ann	BALLENGER, Henry W.	DEC 28 1852
KING, Susan Lavinia	PAXTON, Joseph	AUG 01 1848
KING, Susannah (blk)	THOMAS, Gusty	DEC 21 1826
KING, Sylvester	TALBERT, Sobrina	DEC 26 1837
KING, T. Grosvenor	McNERHANY, Kate	JUN 05 1854
KING, Thomas	McFARLIN, Mary	SEP 24 1835
KING, Thomas	KELLY, Catherine	MAY 18 1836
KING, Thomas	TAYLOR, Harriet	JUN 15 1843
KING, Thomas	WALLIS, Julia	JAN 25 1845
KING, Thomas	PARKER, Sarah (blk)	FEB 07 1849
KING, Thomas	TALBURT, Elizabeth	OCT 05 1853
KING, Thomas A.	ADAMS, Mary E.	MAY 10 1849
KING, Thomas S.	MARDIN, Hannah M.	FEB 06 1844
KING, Valinda	COLLINS, Leonard	APR 08 1834
KING, Venerando E.	BAYNE, Sallie A.	NOV 20 1849
KING, Vincent	WATERS, Sarah	APR 21 1835
KING, Violetta	SMITH, Richard T.	DEC 21 1857
KING, William	BROWN, Rachael	FEB 10 1817
KING, William	BROWN, Eleanor	MAY 13 1823
KING, William	MULLIKIN, Eleanor	OCT 13 1827
KING, William	HUTCHINSON, Matilda	JAN 01 1829
KING, William	JACKSON, Julia	FEB 16 1836
KING, William	SMART, Henrietta	OCT 07 1836
KING, William	FILICE, Mary	JAN 06 1838
KING, William	YOUNG, Hannah N. (blk)	MAR 07 1850
KING, William	MOCKABEE, Ellen	JAN 07 1851
KING, William	ANDERSON, Sarah Jane	APR 20 1853
KING, William A.	O'NEAL, Mary Elizth.	MAY 16 1853
KING, William H.	SCRIVENER, Eleanor A.	MAY 31 1851
KING, William, Jr.	FOWLER, Christiana	JUN 22 1813
KING, William N.	REALY, Mary Ellen	JAN 04 1845
KING, William Thomas	GOLDSBORROUGH, Francis	JUN 13 1833
KING, Wilson	JONES, Sarah	AUG 15 1834
KING, Wm.	DOUGHERTY, Elizabeth	FEB 28 1821
KING, Wm. H.	MABURY, Mary Ann	FEB 22 1845
KING, Wm. Samuel	McDANIEL, Ann	MAY 18 1850
KING, Zachariah	BULSEN, Mary	MAR 08 1828
KING, Zachariah	BAKER, Julia Ann	JUL 14 1830
KING, Zebulon M.P.	LANDON, Henrietta	MAR 22 1841

District of Columbia Marriage Licenses, 1811-1858

KINGMAN, Eliab	EWELL, Cordelia B.	DEC 04 1828
KINGMAN, Mary E.	BEALS, Orpheus W.	OCT 23 1855
KINGSBERRY, Mary	POSEY, William	DEC 24 1831
KINGSBURY, Johanna	WEST, James Randolph	FEB 14 1850
KINGSBURY, Mary A.	NORRIS, Henry	APR 22 1854
KINGSBURY, Sarah	BRYAN, William	JUN 23 1829
KINGSBURY, Thomas	KENDRICK, Mary	APR 20 1846
KINGSBURY, William O.	SMITH, Eleanor Ann	JAN 07 1847
KINGSTON, Charlotte	RICKETTS, Aquila	JUN 23 1830
KINGSTON, Sarah E.	CONNER, John L.	APR 22 1837
KINK, Margaret	TIBER, Albert	JUL 04 1852
KINKLE, Eliza S.	VanWYCK, Stephen M.	APR 20 1835
KINNEY, Jeremiah	PHILVORTH, Jane	SEP 05 1844
KINNEY, Mary	WATERS, Warren S.	DEC 18 1852
KINNY, Harriet	DOVE, James	JUN 03 1852
KINNY, Mary	WHELAN, William	JAN 30 1854
KINNY, Thomas	ROCHE, Margaret	NOV 04 1850
KINSBY, Eva	AIGLER, Christopher	NOV 10 1849
KINSEY, Barbara	FINK, Casper	OCT 01 1840
KINSEY, Benjamin S.	DRINKER, Elizabeth	JUL 28 1828
KINSEY, Robert E.	MASSEY, Sarah	JUL 06 1857
KINSLAR, Margaret	ELBERT, John	MAY 11 1833
KINSLEY, Henry	KERNANN, Martha	MAY 10 1845
KINSLEY, Mary Ann	SMALL, James T.	NOV 04 1843
KINSLOW, William	WARD, Catharine	NOV 15 1851
KINZEY, David	WILLIAMS, Catherine	MAR 25 1820
KINZLER, Barbara	FLACK, Constandinus	JAN 08 1834
KIRBY, Ann	BROWN, Archibald	APR 17 1824
KIRBY, Charles	SHERMAN, Mary	JAN 13 1824
KIRBY, Delia	CLARK, William	APR 14 1823
KIRBY, Edmund	BROWN, Eliza A.	FEB 12 1825
KIRBY, Eleanor	PAYNE, James	JUN 26 1815
KIRBY, Elizabeth	NICHOLSON, William	JUL 11 1854
KIRBY, Francis S.	ACTON, Jane C.	JUN 07 1853
KIRBY, Gilman	LITTLE, Virginia B.	APR 16 1853
KIRBY, Henry	CAMMACK, Martha	MAY 31 1851
KIRBY, James P.	BOAMAR, Marcellina	NOV 20 1840
KIRBY, Jno.	SULLIVAN, Joanna	APR 04 1855
KIRBY, John	ESLIN, George Ann	FEB 22 1834
KIRBY, John	BREWER, Rebecca	MAR 17 1836
KIRBY, John	WHITE, Catherine	JUL 04 1853
KIRBY, John B.	MOORE, Eleanor [Mrs.]	FEB 19 1828
KIRBY, Maria E.	GRINDER, Adam	NOV 16 1854
KIRBY, Marian E.	McKENNEY, Christopher	APR 14 1857
KIRBY, Mary	BROWN, James	SEP 03 1857
KIRBY, Mary Josephine	LESCURE, Joseph	NOV 14 1849
KIRBY, Rachel	ALLEN, James	SEP 03 1827
KIRBY, Rebecca	GARRETT, Greenup	NOV 25 1832
KIRBY, Samuel	HANNON, Mary	AUG 23 1826
KIRBY, Sarah Ann	SMITH, Thomas M.	OCT 08 1851
KIRBY, Sarah C.	DYER, Benjamin	SEP 11 1844
KIRBY, Thomas	FLICK, Mary	AUG 10 1848
KIRBY, Wallace	BEERS, Virginia	DEC 01 1852
KIRK, Alonzo George	GIBSON, Catherine	DEC 27 1845
KIRK, Andrew M.	EDELIN, Henrietta Mary	DEC 17 1818
KIRK, Eleanor	McKOY, Enos	JUL 22 1830
KIRK, Elizabeth Ann	MOORE, Douglass	NOV 07 1843
KIRK, James B.	REDIN, Emily W.	AUG 01 1843

District of Columbia Marriage Licenses, 1811-1858

KIRK, Jane T.	GATEWOOD, John B.	MAR 03 1829
KIRK, John	THURSDAY, Elizabeth	MAR 07 1817
KIRK, John	GIRARD, Annie	APR 21 1856
KIRK, Mary Ann	SIMONTON, Peter	MAR 18 1850
KIRK, Mary H.	ZELL, Enoch F.	MAR 19 1850
KIRK, Sallust	HANDLEY, Martha	OCT 05 1853
KIRK, Sarah	DOOLING, Armistead	MAY 16 1835
KIRK, Thomas A.	PELLETTI, Mary Ann	DEC 31 1847
KIRKLAND, William	GROSS, Margaret Ann	SEP 30 1847
KIRKLEY, Sarah	THURSBY, William	FEB 26 1821
KIRKLEY, Thomas C.	FOWLER, Sarah Louisa	MAY 06 1856
KIRKPATRICK, Ann	DOUGLASS, John	MAY 12 1813
KIRKPATRICK, Hannah	BREWER, Mason	JAN 08 1856
KIRKPATRICK, James A.	YOUNG, Maria E.	APR 08 1856
KIRKPATRICK, John B.	WEAVER, Margaret	JUL 03 1843
KIRKWOOD, Albert W.	YOUNG, Margaret E.	JAN 08 1845
KIRKWOOD, Jonathan	McGILL, Eleanor	APR 11 1839
KIRKWOOD, Wallace	KENNEDY, Mary Jane	JUL 12 1836
KIRSEY, Hellen P.	COLISON, Peter	FEB 21 1855
KIRTY, Mary E.	HATTON, Nathaniel H.	NOV 14 1845
KISENTUFER, Christopher	BEEKE, Jane	MAY 14 1857
KITCHEN, Jane	HEETER, Uriah	SEP 06 1849
KITCHEN, Kitty	HANNA, Nathaniel	OCT 02 1855
KITCHEN, Thompson	THOMPSON, Mahalia	DEC 22 1847
KITCHEN, Wm.	BUTLER, Elizabeth B.	MAY 11 1818
KITCHINS, Jesse W.	JETT, Amanda	JUL 30 1838
KITE, George L.	KOONTZ, Martha Ann	OCT 15 1848
KITLEN, William	BAYNE, Elizabeth	OCT 20 1825
KITSEN, Elizabeth	LACY, Richard	FEB 01 1849
KITSON, Ann	LYLES, William	AUG 20 1830
KITTLER, Babetha	SAUTIL, John Q.	FEB 08 1854
KITTNER, John Henry	LUPTON, Isabella M.	OCT 04 1851
KLAENDIEST, Varonica	RICHTER, John	OCT 26 1852
KLAPP, Harvey [Dr.]	McKNIGHT, Anna P.	APR 13 1831
KLEIBER, Adeline	SERGENT, John	DEC 24 1827
KLEIBER, Jacob	COONTES, Margaret	JUN 11 1818
KLEIBER, Laura Matilda	DELL, Thomas	MAR 06 1841
KLEIBER, Susan	HOUX, David F.	DEC 09 1833
KLEIBER, Virginia E.	LAMBORN, Samuel H.	APR 11 1850
KLEINDENST, Barbara	WEIL, John	NOV 27 1852
KLEINDENST, Mary	EIKHORN, George	APR 13 1858
KLEINDIENST, John Paul	EREMANTRAUT, Barbara	APR 04 1842
KLEINDIENST, Joseph	DELZELL, Mary E.	NOV 18 1852
KLEINE, Orsilla	SOWER, Henry	JAN 01 1844
KLEISS, Daniel	HAGGERTY, Agnes Ellen	SEP 30 1843
KLEM, George	SCHAB, Margaretta	AUG 16 1856
KLEMANN, William	HELLER, Elenora	JUN 21 1853
KLEMKE, Elizabeth	BACH, Ernst	JUL 24 1857
KLEPPENGER, Christopher	KETTLER, Fredeicka	JUL 03 1854
KLICH, Gertrude	RUPPERT, Henry	FEB 14 1857
KLICH, Gunrod	DIGGS, Mary	APR 27 1844
KLICKERMAN, Franklin W.	DICKSON, Louisa	DEC 23 1843
KLIEBER, Mary Ann	GOBRIGHT, Lawrence A.	OCT 27 1834
KLIEMAN, Anna	MEYERS, George	APR 06 1855
KLINCHANSE, George D.	MARKS, Susan C.	MAY 19 1830
KLINE, Valentine	BAECHE, Catherine	OCT 10 1857
KLINEHAUSE, George T.	MORLIN, Sarah A.F.	OCT 18 1854
KLINENCE, Catherine Jane	MOORE, William	MAY 29 1849

District of Columbia Marriage Licenses, 1811-1858

KLING, Mary Ann	WISEBAKER, Albert	SEP 28 1846
KLOFFER, Benjamin	HENDLEY, Sophia	NOV 13 1851
KLOFFER, Edwin J.	COLE, Jane F.	NOV 27 1847
KLOFFER, Henry A.	TARLTON, Rosanna	JUN 27 1848
KLONE, Margaret	McGUIRE, John	DEC 19 1851
KLOONE, Patrick	CODMORE, Bridget	FEB 12 1855
KLOPFER, Benjamin	FERRIS, Margaret	SEP 16 1841
KLOPFER, Christian G.	WARD, Ann Maria	FEB 02 1841
KLOPFER, Henry A.	TARLTON, Ellen E.G.	MAR 09 1844
KLOPFER, Martha S.	WRIGHT, Benjamin C.	AUG 03 1848
KLOTZ, Philip	PENN, Mary	MAY 12 1858
KLUG, Peter	SPIEGEL, Brigitta	APR 10 1858
KNAPP, Auren	NORFEET, Mary E.	AUG 21 1854
KNAPP, Gabriel	ORT, Elizabeth	AUG 27 1857
KNAPP, Mary Ann	MORGAN, Peter	APR 06 1835
KNATZ, Conrad	FALENSTEIN, Elizabeth	AUG 11 1855
KNATZ, Katharine	BARTZ, Lanehard	NOV 02 1855
KNATZ, Katherine	HARDIG, Gustavus	OCT 17 1854
KNAUCHTEN, Martin	GRIFFIN, Bridget	JAN 02 1856
KNELLER, Dorothy	BETTNER, Robert	NOV 27 1851
KNELLER, Mary	BELER, Lewis	OCT 10 1825
KNELLER, Samuel G.	MOUNT, Mary C.E.	DEC 18 1833
KNEPLEY, Solomon	MARL, Margt.	MAY 18 1815
KNIBB, Mary	WGILL, George	JUN 18 1834
KNIES, Louis	HENSLING, Elizabeth	MAR 04 1858
KNIGHT, Caleb	KEETLEY, Mary	JUN 27 1840
KNIGHT, Catharine	MYERS, Alexander	APR 23 1833
KNIGHT, Charlotte L.	ANDERSON, John W.	FEB 08 1858
KNIGHT, David	ROBERRY, Elizabeth	MAY 11 1854
KNIGHT, Elizabeth	PARSELL, J.F.B.	MAY 11 1853
KNIGHT, Esley	LIHAULT, Louisa M.	MAY 21 1822
KNIGHT, Frederick	PETTIT, Ann	DEC 21 1848
KNIGHT, Harriott	WONDERLY, Jacob	FEB 08 1825
KNIGHT, Jane Cunningham	KNIGHT, Lewis J.	JUN 18 1846
KNIGHT, Jane M.	CRIPPER, Miner A.	NOV 11 1852
KNIGHT, John	BURCH, Amanda	JAN 27 1849
KNIGHT, John	SCOTT, Jane	JUL 07 1853
KNIGHT, Lewis J.	CUNNINGHAM, Jane	AUG 02 1845
KNIGHT, Lewis J.	KNIGHT, Jane Cunningham	JUN 18 1846
KNIGHT, Louisa M.	McGRAW, Benjamin F.	JUL 31 1852
KNIGHT, Mary	BROWN, William	SEP 25 1817
KNIGHT, Milly	COLLIER, William	JAN 18 1819
KNIGHT, Robert T.	RIELL, Harriet	MAR 19 1850
KNIGHT, Thomas	FREE, Susan	OCT 10 1833
KNIGHT, Virginia	KROUSE, Edwin	JAN 29 1853
KNIGHT, William	BANNISTER, Caroline	JUN 26 1849
KNIGHTON, Elizabeth E.	COX, John	JUL 26 1853
KNIGHTON, John	URTHROE, Harriet	APR 07 1858
KNIGHTS, Lydia	SWAIN, Moses P.	JUL 20 1853
KNIPPELL, Mary	KABELL, Bernard	MAY 31 1849
KNIPPLE, Daniel	WIDEMAN, Mary	SEP 10 1849
KNLAHEL, Johanna	LUDICKE, Henry	MAY 01 1857
KNOAKES, Thomas	RIDGWAY, Ann	JUN 07 1831
KNOBLOCK, Elizabeth	McCOY, Alexander	JUL 23 1818
KNOBLOCK, Jane	EVANS, William	DEC 24 1827
KNOBLOCK, Margaret	GABLER, John C.	JUN 08 1830
KNOBLOCK, Martha	WHEALER, George W.	OCT 16 1844
KNOBLOCK, Mary	FUSS, John A.	SEP 14 1829

District of Columbia Marriage Licenses, 1811-1858

KNOBLOCK, Rebecca	MILLER, Robert	MAY 22 1830
KNOCH, John H.	GASH, Mary	NOV 17 1855
KNOKES, James	SANDFORD, Eliza	OCT 11 1825
KNOLLES, Emeline	SUTTON, Nicholas	APR 30 1829
KNOT, James	NELSON, Eliza	JUN 18 1822
KNOT, Rossannah	SOTHRON, John	FEB 08 1818
KNOTHE, Elizabeth	BARNS, Christian	AUG 06 1855
KNOTT, Adam	DeCLUDE, Dorathy	APR 22 1815
KNOTT, Ann	MATTINGLY, Edward	JUN 27 1812
KNOTT, Catherine	CLARK, Lawson A.	JUN 06 1815
KNOTT, Elenor	NAISSER, John Philip Machel	AUG 07 1828
KNOTT, George A.	BUERY, Catharine	OCT 20 1841
KNOTT, Harriot	DAVIS, James	JUL 24 1823
KNOTT, Ignatius M.	BEALL, Susan C.	NOV 12 1846
KNOTT, James	HURDLE, Ann Maria	AUG 05 1828
KNOTT, James	BAKER, Emily	MAY 30 1834
KNOTT, Jane	MOORE, Thomas	JUN 02 1855
KNOTT, John B.	JENKINS, Cecelia	NOV 05 1853
KNOTT, John Lewis	WATERS, Martha Ann	OCT 21 1839
KNOTT, John T.	PAYNE, Martha Ann	OCT 14 1846
KNOTT, Joseph	GLOYD, Elizabeth	OCT 14 1834
KNOTT, Josiah H.	FROUK, Mary	JAN 02 1827
KNOTT, Mary	MURRAY, William	AUG 26 1828
KNOTT, Richard	GODDARD, Susan	DEC 09 1851
KNOTT, Rosanna	BOTTOMLY, John	SEP 04 1821
KNOTT, Virginia Corrinna	WORTHINGTON, Nathan E.	JAN 03 1852
KNOTT, William	DYER, Catharine	APR 28 1836
KNOWLES, Catharine	WALKER, Henry	NOV 13 1834
KNOWLES, Ellen H.	NALLEY, William H.	MAY 23 1843
KNOWLES, Frances	GRIFFITH, Charles G.	MAY 16 1851
KNOWLES, Hamilton	BALLSEL, Margaret	FEB 06 1857
KNOWLES, James J.	DUVALL, Ann D.	JUL 24 1843
KNOWLES, John	MIDDLETON, MArtha	APR 08 1858
KNOWLES, John Thomas	AGER, Marcelia	OCT 25 1843
KNOWLES, Lethe A.	CHERY, Clayton	SEP 05 1849
KNOWLES, Lydia	LORD, Francis B.	JUN 26 1818
KNOWLES, Martha E.	McNAIR, Stephen Y.	APR 05 1854
KNOWLES, Mary	FRY, John Jacob	OCT 25 1830
KNOWLES, Mary D.	MAGRUDER, Alfred	DEC 12 1846
KNOWLES, Rebecca	OTTINGER, Charles	JAN 12 1826
KNOWLES, Rebecca	JACKSON, William W.	APR 23 1835
KNOWLES, Robert	BRAUNER, Elizabeth	JUL 19 1834
KNOWLES, Sarah	TOWNLEY, James	FEB 15 1816
KNOWLES, Thomas	OBER, Lydia	OCT 26 1818
KNOWLES, William	BARRON, Janet	APR 24 1817
KNOWLES, William	PIERCEY, Eve	JUN 20 1820
KNOWLES, William	ROBERTSON, Lucinda	APR 14 1830
KNOWLES, William	LEWIS, Charlotte Ann	OCT 03 1839
KNOWLES, William	JOHNSON, Permelia	MAR 13 1844
KNOX, Airy	McNEW, Basil	JAN 04 1825
KNOX, Alice	SULLIVAN, John W.	JAN 17 1856
KNOX, Elijah	MILLSTEAD, Martha	AUG 21 1820
KNOX, James	CURTIS, Rose	SEP 04 1850
KNOX, John	GRAY, Mary Ann	JUN 06 1822
KNOX, John	GALHUGH, Mary	MAY 25 1838
KNOX, S. Boliver	SELDEN, Mary F.	JAN 28 1852
KNOX, Susan	ALLEN, Richard	NOV 13 1832
KNOXVILLE, James	HOWE, Ellen	SEP 06 1832

District of Columbia Marriage Licenses, 1811-1858

KNOXVILLE, James	WARRING, Roberter	AUG 14 1847
KOBELT, Wilhelmina	HELLER, Charles	DEC 13 1856
KOCH, Frederick A.	KOHLER, Christine B.	MAY 19 1855
KOCH, Philip J.	KUHL, Margaretta S.	JAN 10 1853
KOCK, Elizabeth	HERZBERGER, Frederick	AUG 31 1855
KOEHLER, Charles H.	WALSH, Ellen	DEC 15 1852
KOEHLER, Christina	MURR, Gottiel	MAR 30 1854
KOEHLER, Johannes	HOCH, Anna Maria	MAR 30 1854
KOEHLER, Mary	HANGSTETTER, John	FEB 25 1854
KOFFMAN, Mary Ann	MILLER, Samuel	NOV 25 1852
KOHINE, Margaret	DONOVAN, Cornelius	JAN 12 1852
KOHLER, Christine B.	KOCH, Frederick A.	MAY 19 1855
KOLB, Gottlieb	LOKESMAN, Christina	MAR 09 1849
KOLB, Jacob	RAU, Jennie	APR 27 1853
KOLTZ, Frederick	FRENCH, Martha	SEP 28 1849
KONING, Julius	SEADLE, Mado	APR 14 1858
KONNS, Joseph	DONALDSON, Josephine	JUL 14 1857
KOOFF, John C.H.	PIETOCH, Catherine B.	MAR 09 1839
KOONES, Caroline	GARRITT, Richard	MAY 14 1834
KOONES, Catharine	DEAN, Samuel	AUG 23 1819
KOONS, Ann	SINCOX, Thomas	FEB 23 1847
KOONS, Henry	ARTH, Elizabeth	APR 16 1853
KOONS, Sylvester	NOBLE, Mary	APR 07 1855
KOONTZ, Joseph C.	THOMAS, Mary	OCT 29 1831
KOONTZ, Margaret	PLATE, Adolphus Fred.	JUL 11 1813
KOONTZ, Martha Ann	KITE, George L.	OCT 15 1848
KORFF, Harman George	ADAMS, Barbara Ellen	AUG 29 1840
KORFF, Herman George	MANTEL, Hermine Elizabeth	JAN 18 1851
KORFF, Louisa	MEMMERT, Charles	JAN 05 1856
KORFHISER, Christian	GOODRICK, Dorcas	APR 02 1842
KORN, Margaret	KENNEDY, John	JAN 08 1822
KORNE, Mary	HEFLEY, Frederick	FEB 11 1826
KOSTNER, Joseph	BORZEL, Gertrude	JAN 25 1849
KOTT, Nathaniel	WRIGHT, Elizabeth	MAY 14 1836
KOUGH, James	SHEAHAN, Bridget	DEC 11 1856
KRAF, Joseph	ILER, Mary Jane	MAR 30 1857
KRAFFT, Ava	MOORE, Philip	DEC 26 1855
KRAFFT, Christiana	THOMAS, William Henry	OCT 29 1851
KRAFFT, George	BROWER, Hannah Christiana	OCT 07 1828
KRAFFT, George	WARD, [blank]	SEP 05 1854
KRAFFT, J.	BRAUER, M.	JUN 24 1826
KRAFFT, Katherine	HAGER, John F.	MAY 27 1847
KRAFFT, Lawrinc	BROWN, Caroline	JUN 09 1834
KRAFFT, M.M.	LAUR, Louis	MAY 04 1847
KRAFFT, Philip	FULLER, Frances	JAN 03 1855
KRAFFT, Rosina	ARMBRUSTER, Ernst	NOV 14 1855
KRAFT, Christopher	BOYLE, Mary	OCT 05 1850
KRAFT, Louisa	ANDREWS, Sebastian	APR 25 1854
KRAFT, Marguretta	SCHMIDT, Ferdinand	FEB 16 1856
KRAFT, Paul	BROWN, Mary E.	JAN 19 1858
KRAMER, Elizabeth	SCHNAEBELL, Andrew	OCT 19 1833
KRAMER, William	RATZ, Elizabeth	NOV 28 1853
KRAUS, Christina	HAIN, John G.	AUG 30 1856
KRAUSE, Charles A.	PIC, Margaret Frances	AUG 02 1855
KREAMER, Charles	MARTIN, Catherine Ann	JUN 09 1847
KREAMER, Margaret	DEAN, Isaiah	APR 17 1852
KREBS, Henry H.	MECHLIN, Eliza P.	MAR 20 1834
KREEMER, Elizabeth J.	THOMAS, Edward A.	JAN 30 1844

District of Columbia Marriage Licenses, 1811-1858

KREEMER, Margaret Ann	LUGRO, John B.	JUL 11 1842
KREGELO, Jonas	ROOT, Mary Louisa	MAY 13 1846
KREI, Conrad	SCHREIBER, Scharlotte	AUG 28 1857
KREPPEL, Anne	FISCHER, Hironius	JUN 13 1850
KRESECKER, Margaretta	EBERLI, Anton	FEB 17 1849
KREY, Charles	REKENWEG, Caroline	FEB 18 1858
KRIDERMAKER, Barbara	OVERSTINE, Casper	APR 28 1846
KRIEGENHOFER, George	IMHOF, Feronika	NOV 03 1857
KRIMMEL, Susanna	JACOBI, William	DEC 31 1834
KRIMMELLY, John G.	BOWMAN, Catherine	DEC 13 1854
KROFT, Catherina	HENRY, Christian Frederick	AUG 17 1841
KROFT, Catherine	KROFT, Conrad	JUN 23 1851
KROFT, Conrad	KROFT, Catherine	JUN 23 1851
KROPP, Henry	FEPLIN, Margaret B.	FEB 09 1857
KROUSE, Ann Eliza	SLATER, David	FEB 03 1836
KROUSE, Christian	FENWICK, Eleanor	SEP 28 1816
KROUSE, Edwin	KNIGHT, Virginia	JAN 29 1853
KROUSE, Elizabeth	HARRISON, Elisha	OCT 28 1815
KROUSE, Everard	BALTZER, Catherine	MAR 24 1846
KROUSE, George	BURRIS, Rutha E.	APR 03 1856
KROUSE, John	HALL, Ellen	FEB 26 1848
KROUSE, Martha	WHELIN, John	APR 22 1839
KROUSE, Peter	SCHULER, Louisa	SEP 28 1835
KROWSE, John	DAWES, Mary	JUL 17 1814
KRUG, Lehna	ALTVETER, August	AUG 31 1857
KRULLER, Susan V.	PHILLIPS, George W.	JUN 12 1837
KRUMBHAAR, Lewis	RAMSAY, Sophia	DEC 06 1832
KRUSMANN, Rosina	PFAU, John F.	NOV 16 1855
KRUST, George	PLISH, Dorothy	JUN 29 1842
KRZYRANOWSKI, Waldimir	BURNETT, Caroline	DEC 27 1853
KÜBEL, Edward	HARTBRECHT, Josephine	NOV 12 1856
KUBLOMANN, Charles F.A.	BRASE, Sophia Elnore	OCT 14 1841
KUHAGEN, Frederick	ELY, Catherine	APR 02 1836
KUHL, Christena	EBERBACK, John H.	FEB 18 1835
KUHL, Henry	FOWLER, Mary E.	DEC 05 1845
KUHL, Margaretta S.	KOCH, Philip J.	JAN 10 1853
KUHLEMANN, Charles	HAGERMAN, Lizzetta	AUG 24 1847
KÜHLS, Theodore	SCHINZEL, Cecelia	MAY 28 1853
KUHN, Joseph	SCHMIDT, Katherine	FEB 18 1856
KUHN, Joseph L.	BEALL, Susan	AUG 07 1834
KUHN, Louisa Adelaide	WITHERSPOON, Alexander Somerville	MAY 18 1847
KUHN, Walter	LINDSAY, Rachel	JAN 01 1846
KUHNIRD, John A.	HOLMES, Elizabeth	NOV 10 1855
KUHNS, Andrew	O'REILLY, Margaret	JAN 04 1841
KUHNS, Andrew	HINTEN, Chloe Ann	OCT 03 1851
KUHNS, William	TRUXEL, Sarah	OCT 03 1831
KULP, Aaron J.	WINDSOR, Catharine	MAY 28 1855
KULP, Elizabeth (blk)	VIGAL, Richard	JUN 13 1849
KUMMER, Charles	LAMBRIGHT, Henrietta	MAY 05 1848
KUMMER, Mary	ROTH, Andrew	JUN 08 1858
KUNDELEHR, Catharine	COOMS, Michael R.	APR 05 1842
KUNKE, Christina	STINLE, Frederick	APR 14 1855
KURL, Margaret	FLANNIGAN, Garret	FEB 16 1836
KURTS, Peter	COLLINS, Sarah Ann	OCT 07 1817
KURTZ, Benjamin	HOFMANN, Sarah Louisa	JUN 10 1858
KURTZ, Daniel	LYON, Mary	JUN 04 1814
KURTZ, David	BURCH, Elizabeth	APR 17 1816
KURTZ, Elizabeth E.	CARTWRIGHT, Levin T.	JUN 03 1856

District of Columbia Marriage Licenses, 1811-1858

KURTZ, John	BROWN, Catharine W.	DEC 10 1818
KURTZ, John	BALTZER, Sarah	MAY 25 1831
KURTZ, John Daniel	WRIGHT, Jane Thompson	APR 11 1843
KURTZ, Mary Ann	DANGEL, Valentine	OCT 07 1847
KURTZ, Mary C.	ADLER, Morris	DEC 21 1854
KURTZ, Rebecca C.	HOYLE, Henry J.	NOV 22 1849
KURTZ, Sarah	ORME, Thomas	JUN 01 1816
KURTZ, William H.	CARTWRIGHT, Susan R.	NOV 28 1849
KYLE, Catharine	ROACH, John	OCT 14 1852
KYLE, Catharine E.	BULLOCK, Oscar F.	OCT 22 1857
KYLER, James W.	COOPER, Rebecca	SEP 24 1836
KYLER, Sarah	FORREST, Rezin	JAN 15 1822
KYNE, Bridget	LEONARD, John	FEB 05 1819

District of Columbia Marriage Licenses, 1811-1858

L

LaBARRE, Francis	BURKHARDT, Mary A.	AUG 20 1853
LaBILLE, Louis	BURCH, Julia	JUN 01 1857
LABILLE, Elenora	TOWNSEND, Lemuel	DEC 24 1841
LABILLE, Eliza	BRUNET, John Baptist	SEP 16 1818
LABOLD, Catharine	CONRAD, Christian	MAR 05 1846
LACEY, Agnes	CHARLTON, Henry	NOV 19 1853
LACEY, Elizabeth	HALL, James	NOV 22 1847
LACEY, Elizabeth (blk)	LEMMON, Enoch	JAN 27 1858
LACEY, Emily M.	WALKER, William H.	FEB 03 1845
LACEY, Honora	NAGLE, John	AUG 29 1851
LACEY, John	BEAGLE, Eliza	NOV 20 1851
LACEY, John E.	LYNCH, Jane R.	MAY 08 1855
LACEY, John Francis	THOMAS, Virginia	NOV 12 1857
LACEY, Julia W.	LAYTON, Almanzer W.	JUL 20 1857
LACEY, Manuel	DEEVERS, Elizabeth	JUL 03 1849
LACEY, Mary America	HAVILAND, James C.	JUN 10 1843
LACEY, Mary Ann (blk)	TURNER, Richard	SEP 16 1851
LACEY, Robert A.	FERGUSON, Blanche	JAN 27 1847
LACEY, Sarah	ROSS, William	JAN 01 1817
LACEY, Sarah C.	MILLS, John A.	JUL 31 1854
LACEY, William B.	WEEDEN, Mary	MAR 02 1852
LaCIELLE, Sophia	PECKHAM, William	APR 27 1815
LACKEY, Catharine	HAINEY, James	NOV 24 1852
LACKEY, Jane E.	CLARKE, James A.	OCT 29 1856
LACKEY, Margaret	COCHRAN, Timothy	APR 17 1857
LACKEY, Mary	COLVIN, James	OCT 23 1815
LACKMAN, Catharine	KERN, Xavier	APR 23 1849
LACOCK, Mary	WINDSOR, James	MAY 24 1853
LACOCK, William	PHILLIPS, Elizabeth	FEB 05 1853
LACY, Beverly J.	CLEVELAND, Maranda M.	AUG 17 1847
LACY, Elizabeth Ann	TRUNNELL, Henry	DEC 21 1818
LACY, Florence M.	SELBY, George	MAR 19 1856
LACY, Frances M.	SUTTON, James	NOV 05 1849
LACY, Henry	DEVERS, Penney	DEC 26 1844
LACY, Rebecca Ann	GRAY, John B.	NOV 04 1822
LACY, Richard	KITSEN, Elizabeth	FEB 01 1849
LADD, Joseph	NICOLL, Harriet V.	NOV 01 1824
LADDE, Fannie Vaulx	MANGUM, Wiley P.	OCT 23 1855
LADDE, Harriet Conway	WILSON, Hugh Bowlsby	OCT 23 1855
LADEN, Benjamin	ADAMS, Catherine	JUL 12 1838
LADEN, Nancy	McCAFFERY, Michael	SEP 03 1833
LADUCARE, Maria	STYIVER, Louis F.	JUN 02 1834
LAECHASE, Sebastino	GROSS, Teresa	FEB 03 1830
LAEK, William	MILNE, Mary	MAR 13 1838
LAFONG, Charles	DAIMOND, Catharine	FEB 07 1834
LAFONTAINE, Joseph	MAZINE, Mary	MAR 05 1832
LAGREE, John M.	HAMILTON, Henrietta	NOV 17 1812
LAGREE, Mary Ann	SESSFORD, John, Jr.	MAY 28 1846
LAHEY, Elizabeth	CARROLL, James	JUN 03 1824
LAHNAM, Horatio	STEWART, Charity	JAN 05 1819
LAIHAN, Michael	BLACKBURN, Nancy	JUL 06 1839
LAIRD, Barbara Lucinda	DUNLOP, James, Jr.	APR 07 1818
LAIZ, Matthias	GERRGEN, Elizabeth	JUL 08 1856
LAKE, Alice	SALE, Andrew	NOV 04 1822
LAKE, George	ATTWOOD, Eleanor	JUN 23 1815
LAKE, George	BEEDING, Mary	JAN 12 1818

347

District of Columbia Marriage Licenses, 1811-1858

LAKE, James	LEGG, Jane	APR 24 1839
LAKEMEYER, Frederick	ROEMMELE, Elizabeth	MAY 26 1845
LAKENAN, Ann V.	ROGERS, William W.	NOV 28 1838
LAKIN, Frances E.	GIBBS, John H.	DEC 24 1840
LAKIN, Winifred J.	THOMAS, Edward	NOV 06 1850
LALAND, Sarah	WHIPS, Wesley	NOV 15 1815
LALANNE, Caroline V.	STETTINIUS, George	JAN 17 1843
LALLEY, Ann	REARDON, Andrew	OCT 16 1856
LALLEY, Mary	FAHEY, Timothy	MAY 16 1857
LAMAR, John	MAYNIDER, Elizabeth	AUG 09 1834
LAMB, Francis	SESSFORD, Elizabeth	SEP 15 1846
LAMB, James	CARTER, Anna	DEC 24 1852
LAMB, Patrick	BRENNAN, Ellen	FEB 05 1851
LAMB, Theodore L.	WATSON, Emiline N.	MAR 14 1854
LAMB, Thomas	ELIOT, Hannah D.	OCT 25 1828
LAMBAUGH, Catharine	JARBOUR, William	NOV 06 1819
LAMBELL, Mary Ann S.	KIMMELL, Abraham F.	JAN 08 1845
LAMBERT, Edward J.	MORIN, Harriet	DEC 29 1826
LAMBERT, Eliza	CISSEL, Thomas	MAR 16 1826
LAMBERT, Francis	BRERETON, Mary Ann	OCT 15 1835
LAMBERT, Francis	SAFFER, Mary L.	MAY 20 1846
LAMBERT, Frederick	VEITCH, Sally	JUL 31 1824
LAMBERT, Isaac	CLEMENTS, Emeline	AUG 14 1855
LAMBERT, Jane	WELLS, Thomas C.	MAY 11 1836
LAMBERT, Rebecca	POWERS, Joseph	NOV 14 1826
LAMBERT, Sarah	REED, John	OCT 21 1837
LAMBERT, Thomas	COLLINS, Rosetta	APR 19 1856
LAMBERT, William H.	STEER, Laura	APR 26 1853
LAMBERTT, David	PREUSS, Fredericka Renata	JUL 19 1841
LAMBIE, James B.	TURTON, Ann B.	OCT 24 1838
LAMBIE, William	SIOUSSA, Annie	MAR 15 1841
LAMBLE, Elizabeth	FOUWKES, John	JAN 24 1826
LAMBORN, Samuel H.	KLEIBER, Virginia E.	APR 11 1850
LAMBRECHT, Reinard	BEEVES, Jane A.L.	MAY 23 1831
LAMBRIGHT, George	CRANDALL, Mary Ann	JAN 19 1832
LAMBRIGHT, Henrietta	KUMMER, Charles	MAY 05 1848
LAMER, George G.	MULLAY, Emma V.	JUN 18 1855
LAMESON, Samuel D.	LELLARD, Delia A.	JUN 09 1852
LAMKIN, Charlotte A.	REED, George A.	DEC 16 1848
LAMMOND, Peter	ROBEY, Mary C.	DEC 05 1849
LAMOND, Alexander	McINTYRE, Margaret Ann	OCT 19 1830
LAMPKIN, Jane	BOWLES, Martin	APR 04 1829
LANAGHAN, Mary	COTTER, Richard	NOV 22 1851
LANAGIN, Ann	FERRENS, Terrence	JUL 10 1844
LANAM, John H.	BATT, Catharine	JAN 10 1842
LANBINGER, John Michael	DUFFLEY, Christina	APR 29 1844
LANCASTER, Benjamin	WATTS, Malinda (blk)	JUN 05 1850
LANCASTER, Cassey Ann	GRIFFIN, John	MAY 31 1855
LANCASTER, Charles	FORD, Mary Jane (blk)	AUG 07 1848
LANCASTER, Christina (blk)	CALBERT, George	APR 12 1852
LANCASTER, Edward	HERBERT, Catharine (blk)	APR 11 1843
LANCASTER, Isaac	THOMPSON, Margaret (blk)	DEC 23 1839
LANCASTER, Isiaih	BRANUM, Rachel (blk)	NOV 28 1854
LANCASTER, Mahala	KENNEDY, James	AUG 29 1838
LANCASTER, Morris [Dr.]	PLUMMER, Rachel S.	MAR 11 1829
LANCASTER, Richard	COOPER, Sarah (blk)	APR 06 1844
LANCASTER, Stephen	BECK, Sarah	OCT 06 1817
LANCASTER, Theophilus	DALEY, Ary	JUN 12 1857

District of Columbia Marriage Licenses, 1811-1858

LAND, Helen C.	LAND, William R.	NOV 03 1848
LAND, William R.	LAND, Helen C.	NOV 03 1848
LANDAY, Lewis	DULANY, Linney (blk)	MAR 20 1837
LANDER, James	SHORTER, Margaret	NOV 11 1842
LANDERL, Louis A.	CARROLL, Martha A.	AUG 13 1850
LANDESDALE, Louisa	MILLARD, Louis	AUG 06 1840
LANDICH, Catharine	TALBERT, Abraham	OCT 14 1840
LANDICK, Betsey	TYLER, John	DEC 16 1824
LANDICK, Isaac	BUCKANAN, ELizabeth (blk)	MAY 14 1840
LANDNER, George	HELFRIEKEN, Elizabeth	MAY 15 1845
LANDON, Christina vanNess	ANDREWS, James G.	JUL 31 1838
LANDON, Henrietta	KING, Zebulon M.P.	MAR 22 1841
LANDON, James	WARD, Margaret	OCT 06 1851
LANDON, Rachel	PRATT, William D.	AUG 13 1849
LANDON, Sarah	GINGELLS, Joseph	APR 22 1857
LANDON, Sarah F.	BURCHELL, Norval B.	OCT 19 1854
LANDRAGON, Eliza	O'DONNELL, John	MAY 03 1852
LANDRICHIN, Catherine	BARRETT, Michael	SEP 16 1853
LANDRICK, Edward	CARROLL, Sarah Ann	JAN 11 1838
LANDRIE, William H.	PIPER, Sarah Ann (blk)	MAY 26 1851
LANDRITH, Sarah E.	CRAVEN, Elijah R. [Dr.]	JUN 05 1823
LANDSDELL, Asberry	WOOD, Elizabeth (blk)	DEC 16 1852
LANDSTREET, Samuel	ORME, Maria Anne	OCT 31 1837
LANDSTREET, William T.	TUCKER, M. Virginia	MAY 24 1854
LANDVOIGT, Charles Edward	THOMPSON, Elleanor Jane	JUN 22 1857
LANDVOIGT, John A.	WHEAT, Laura F.	NOV 23 1857
LANE, Charles H.	ROOKER, Ann Elizabeth	SEP 17 1838
LANE, Charles H.	DEMENT, Sue Ellen	OCT 05 1857
LANE, Charles W.	JOHNSON, Pandora	SEP 19 1840
LANE, David D.	PANE, Elizabeth T.	MAR 29 1821
LANE, Eliza	BETTON, Turbutt R.	SEP 02 1816
LANE, Elizabeth U.	SHOEMAKER, Samuel, Jr.	FEB 21 1846
LANE, Francis W.	BEACH, Mary Ann	JUN 11 1846
LANE, George A.	ALEXANDER, Rebecca	FEB 27 1852
LANE, James	O'BRIEN, Mary	FEB 26 1853
LANE, John G.	LITTLEJOHN, Ann M.	SEP 17 1839
LANE, Joseph	LUCAS, Rachel Ann	JUN 21 1845
LANE, Joseph	PRATHER, Martha Eugenia	DEC 03 1846
LANE, Julianna	HAYMAN, William, Jr.	JUN 05 1822
LANE, Margaret	ROTH, Charles	SEP 04 1855
LANE, Maria	DAVIDSON, John	OCT 06 1852
LANE, Martha Ann	CORTER, Thomas	MAY 22 1822
LANE, Mary	BARNHOUSE, Caleb	SEP 12 1819
LANE, Mary	HONTONVILLE, Harry	MAR 04 1837
LANE, Mary	DWIGHT, Harrison	APR 15 1839
LANE, Patrick	DANEHY, Hannah	OCT 19 1855
LANE, Rose	HENDERSON, James	NOV 08 1838
LANE, Sarah	BARNES, John	MAR 26 1831
LANE, Susan	BURGESS, Washington	MAR 27 1834
LANE, Willey	THOMAS, George	OCT 29 1832
LANEHART, Jacob	SPURLING, Mary	JUL 03 1849
LANEHART, John	PILCHER, Clara	MAY 13 1843
LANEHART, John	COX, Margaret	SEP 18 1845
LANG, Angeline	COBB, William D.	OCT 03 1838
LANG, Cornelia	SKIDMORE, James	JUL 31 1843
LANG, Eliza	NEWRATH, Jacob	NOV 21 1856
LANG, Eliza Ann	ESSEX, James F.	SEP 13 1826
LANG, Elizabeth	SPEAK, Geo.	JAN 28 1819

District of Columbia Marriage Licenses, 1811-1858

LANG, Elizabeth	CARTER, Libern	AUG 24 1833
LANG, Isabel	HUMBOY, Mary Ann	MAY 18 1839
LANG, John	VonESSEN, Anna	APR 24 1843
LANG, Mary	CARTER, Henry	JAN 17 1833
LANG, Mary E.	VANSKIER, John E.	MAY 09 1849
LANG, Nancy	JOHNSON, Littleton	MAR 19 1822
LANG, Robert	SCHREIVS, Emily Ann	DEC 06 1842
LANG, Robert	BUTLER, Eliza	JAN 13 1847
LANG, Sarah	COOKE, John	OCT 25 1828
LANGDEN, Charles	MAY, Martha	FEB 19 1822
LANGE, Francis	MILLHOUSE, Catherine	DEC 19 1853
LANGE, John	HOLLIDGE, Martha Eliza	NOV 18 1854
LANGENBAHN, Adolph	WILKINS, Ella	MAR 25 1857
LANGFITT, Israel F.	GRIGSBY, Mary A.	MAY 15 1832
LANGFITT, Julia F.	DRAPER, Nathan C.	JAN 06 1854
LANGFITT, Maria Louisa	DOWNING, Joseph M.	SEP 08 1846
LANGFITT, Martha	TRUEMAN, Josiah	MAR 08 1853
LANGFITT, Sibby	BAKER, Stephen M.	SEP 08 1846
LANGFITT, William J.	BUNTHRON, Mary Ann	SEP 29 1843
LANGHOR, Henry	LEHMAYER, Anna	JUN 17 1849
LANGIN, Eva	SNYDER, Leopole	NOV 08 1852
LANGLEER, Margaret	LEE, John D.	JAN 10 1821
LANGLEY, Aloysius	WILKINSON, Sarah	APR 21 1853
LANGLEY, Amanda	KEECH, John E.	JAN 22 1828
LANGLEY, Caroline	EDELIN, Joshua Thomas	APR 17 1843
LANGLEY, Catharine C.	BEAVANS, Francis W.	MAR 21 1856
LANGLEY, Catharine S.	DAVIS, James T.	AUG 21 1833
LANGLEY, Charles	GORDEN, Sally	APR 20 1828
LANGLEY, Charles W.	HENDLEY, Anna E.	MAY 12 1858
LANGLEY, Eliza Ann	SWAIN, Benjamin	JAN 16 1841
LANGLEY, Eliza Jane	McELFRESH, John Wm.	APR 17 1849
LANGLEY, Elizabeth	EDELIN, James	JUL 27 1852
LANGLEY, Emily Agnes	O'NEILL, John	JUN 08 1835
LANGLEY, Francis	BARRON, Mary	NOV 17 1849
LANGLEY, Francis H.	MacKEWON, Jane S.	APR 29 1853
LANGLEY, Francis V.	KING, Annah	MAR 03 1829
LANGLEY, Gabriel	CHEW, Mary E.	JUL 18 1846
LANGLEY, George Thos.	EDWARDS, Mary Ann	MAR 27 1843
LANGLEY, Isabella	GORDON, Saml. H.	NOV 13 1856
LANGLEY, James	MOBLEY, Rebecca	MAR 03 1829
LANGLEY, James	GATES, Maria	JAN 22 1846
LANGLEY, John	WINDSOR, Sarah Ann	MAY 10 1856
LANGLEY, John T.	RIDGEWAY, Martha Ann	JUN 16 1853
LANGLEY, Joseph	JACKSON, Julia Ann	AUG 01 1839
LANGLEY, Josephine	SULLIVAN, Washington	MAY 28 1857
LANGLEY, Margaret	SWAIN, William	DEC 15 1846
LANGLEY, Margarett E.	CROSS, Gabriel	MAY 16 1854
LANGLEY, Martha	KIDWELL, James	SEP 30 1847
LANGLEY, Martha	CLUBB, George	APR 20 1854
LANGLEY, Martha Ann	SMITH, Wm.	JUL 26 1838
LANGLEY, Martha Ann	COXEN, John Thomas	FEB 10 1848
LANGLEY, Mary A.	McFARLAND, James	NOV 09 1844
LANGLEY, Matilda	LYNCH, Trueman	JAN 01 1828
LANGLEY, Samuel	SMITH, Sarah	JUL 29 1835
LANGLEY, Sarah	COOK, Richard W.	JUL 23 1835
LANGLEY, Sarah Ann	GATES, John M.	OCT 17 1837
LANGLEY, Thomas H.	SIMPSON, Mary Ellen	NOV 09 1842
LANGLEY, William	HAYRE, Ann E.	JAN 11 1840

District of Columbia Marriage Licenses, 1811-1858

LANGLEY, William B.	STUART, Eliza	DEC 28 1835
LANGLY, Hetty	VERMILLION, James A.	JUL 01 1837
LANGLY, Mary	HILL, Sandy	APR 03 1825
LANGLY, Sylvester David	HOLT, Mary Margaret	FEB 19 1853
LANGREYHER, Robert M.	LARKIN, Amanda A.	MAR 17 1851
LANGTON, Alexander Thomas	ROSE, Rebecca Elizabeth	OCT 15 1853
LANGTON, James W.	BURCH, Mary Ann	JUL 19 1843
LANGTON, John	DOOLEY, Elizabeth	JUL 23 1813
LANGTON, William	FOX, Ann	MAR 25 1823
LANGYHER, Frances	THORNBERRY, Daniel	FEB 10 1824
LANHADY, Patrick	DANIN, Sarah	APR 26 1851
LANHAM, Benjamin	WHITE, Harriet	MAR 28 1820
LANHAM, Charlott A.	EDELEN, Raphael L.	SEP 22 1832
LANHAM, Eleanor	TUCKER, Henry	APR 26 1831
LANHAM, Elisha	JONES, Mary Ann	APR 22 1813
LANHAM, Eliza	DAVIS, Elie	NOV 15 1825
LANHAM, Eliza	PLUMSILL, Thomas P.	MAY 16 1826
LANHAM, Eliza	WALLACE, Charles	APR 09 1844
LANHAM, Elizabeth	BROWN, William T.	AUG 09 1847
LANHAM, Elizabeth A.	SONDERS, Lewis	JUN 09 1840
LANHAM, Hanson	PILES, Eliza	DEC 17 1833
LANHAM, Harriet E.	ESLIN, James C.	APR 19 1851
LANHAM, John B.	WOODS, Mary	JUL 01 1830
LANHAM, Jonathan	SIMMS, Delilah	AUG 03 1848
LANHAM, Julia A.	FAULKNER, Joseph	JAN 06 1852
LANHAM, Lloyd	METZ, Sarah V.	AUG 21 1856
LANHAM, Margaret	BEALL, Grandison	DEC 09 1852
LANHAM, Mary	SHACKELFIELD, James	APR 14 1829
LANHAM, Mary Ann	WEDDIN, Robert	APR 19 1849
LANHAM, Permilia	KEMP, Matthias	JAN 16 1827
LANHAM, Rachel	FRAZIER, John	JAN 14 1824
LANHON, Deborah	DAVIS, Gusty	SEP 18 1819
LANIGAN, Johannah	FITZSIMMONS, John	OCT 05 1832
LANKENAN, Johannah	ERDMANN, John Henri	SEP 21 1846
LANKFORD, Ann R.	ELLIOTT, John T.	MAR 05 1858
LANMAN, Charles	DODGE, Adeline	JUN 11 1849
LANMAN, Joseph	WILLIAMS, A. Cornelia	SEP 19 1842
LANOM, John	JONES, Eveline (blk)	OCT 23 1852
LANPHIER, Eliza	BAKER, Alfred	NOV 17 1827
LANPHIER, Idella Ann	WALTERS, William	JUN 26 1828
LANPHIER, Jane H.	STANTON, Frederick P.	DEC 23 1834
LANPHIER, Martha R.	DITTY, Samuel	JUL 01 1834
LANSDALE, Ann (blk)	REID, Armstead	MAY 29 1850
LANSDALE, C.W. [Christopher]	WILLS, Julia Ann	NOV 17 1830
LANSDALE, Catharine	REED, D.C.	NOV 18 1841
LANSDALE, Ellenor	MacGILL, William	JAN 21 1835
LANSDALE, Enoch	STINCHCOMB, Catherine	SEP 01 1836
LANSDALE, Henry N.	STONE, Priscilla	NOV 24 1836
LANSDALE, Lizzie	ETCHISON, L.E.	APR 22 1858
LANSDALE, Philip	LUCE, Olivia	SEP 16 1841
LANSDALE, Thomas	EDWARDS, Mary (blk)	NOV 24 1856
LANSDALE, Uriah F.	SPAITS, Anna E.	SEP 17 1855
LANSDELL, Margaret A.	JONES, Francis	APR 09 1850
LANSING, Arthur Breese	COCHRAN, Louisa	JUL 02 1849
LAPORT, Eugene	McGOWAN, Ann	MAY 24 1828
LAPORTE, Ann Elizth.	BAILEY, Josiah R.	DEC 13 1849
LAPTON, Bridget	WHEATLEY, Agnatius	AUG 06 1827
LARCOMB, Emily	BAUM, John C.	JAN 12 1847

District of Columbia Marriage Licenses, 1811-1858

LARCOMB, James M.	WINDSOR, Jane Catherine	SEP 06 1854
LARCOMBE, John, Jr.	PARKER, Catherine Smith	MAY 07 1844
LARCOMBE, Mary Ann	BOWEN, Leonidas	SEP 18 1845
LARE, John G.	ROSS, Martha M.	JAN 06 1846
LARE, Maria	HARKNESS, John C.	NOV 01 1855
LARGE, John	JACKSON, Rebecca (blk)	MAR 26 1840
LARICK, Rachel	SCAGG, Isaac	DEC 15 1842
LARKER, Virginia	HARROVER, James R.	JUN 28 1854
LARKIN, Amanda A.	LANGREYHER, Robert M.	MAR 17 1851
LARKIN, Daniel	BRODERICK, Hanora	SEP 09 1854
LARKIN, John F.	BERGAN, Vilette	JUL 18 1855
LARKIN, Julia	O'NIEL, John	JAN 29 1855
LARKIN, Lionel James	NEWTON, Mary Ann	FEB 13 1817
LARKIN, Penelope D.	RENOE, George N.B.	MAR 17 1831
LARKIN, Susan Caroline	ZEVELY, Alexr. N.	SEP 10 1839
LARNED, Benja. F.	LARNERD, Elizabeth R.	SEP 01 1851
LARNED, Charles	COLT, Sylvia	MAR 26 1816
LARNED, James	HERFORD, Ann Jane	JUN 01 1815
LARNED, James	WOODYEAR, Elizabeth R.	JUN 17 1839
LARNED, Jane	CANTER, Andrew E.	JUL 04 1853
LARNER, Biddy	KING, Patrick	JUN 01 1815
LARNER, Eliza [Mrs.]	CLEMENTS, John Thomas	JAN 08 1830
LARNER, Eliza B.	JOHNSON, John T.	JUN 02 1856
LARNER, Gideon W.	McKEAN, Laura Ann	APR 28 1853
LARNER, Martin	GOLDSMITH, Eliza	DEC 13 1824
LARNER, Mary	MURPHY, Andrew	AUG 07 1828
LARNER, Mary Ann	RUSSELL, Thomas	AUG 09 1825
LARNER, Mathew	BROOKES, Biddy	JUN 30 1815
LARNER, Michael	DONOHUGH, Mary	JUN 02 1825
LARNER, Michael	GIDEON, Christianna	JAN 16 1828
LARNER, Noble D.	KELLER, Ann Margaret	NOV 24 1851
LARNER, Thomas	HILL, Caroline	MAY 04 1848
LARNERD, Elizabeth R.	LARNED, Benja. F.	SEP 01 1851
LASHHORN, Frances J.	LETORT, James	JUL 27 1853
LASHHORN, Jno. P.	PROCTOR, Marion H.	JUN 09 1856
LASHLEY, Daniel L.	DOUGLASS, Caroline	OCT 08 1837
LASKEY, Charles	PAYNE, Ann	SEP 17 1840
LASKEY, Elizabeth	HURST, Uriah	JUN 16 1840
LASKEY, Richard	WIRT, Lucy	SEP 21 1824
LASKIE, Ann	LITTLE, Daniel	MAY 09 1829
LASKY, Robert V.	WHITE, Mary H.	FEB 14 1856
LATCHFORD, John	DREW, Margaret	JUN 12 1839
LATHAM, Ann Rebecca	TURNER, Zachariah A.	JUL 15 1858
LATHAM, Jane E.	YOUNG, Charles B.	OCT 13 1855
LATHAM, Jeremiah D.	DODSON, Ann	AUG 19 1851
LATHAM, John E.	WITHERS, Virginia	AUG 09 1853
LATHAM, Mary	BURTON, Richard	NOV 15 1849
LATHAM, Rachel	HALL, Brian	MAR 18 1851
LATHAM, Richd. P.	BACON, Ida	DEC 23 1854
LATHAM, Robert W.	DeNIEL, Susan S.	FEB 20 1855
LATHRAM, Ann	PATTERSON, James	AUG 26 1839
LATHROME, Susannah J.	GATES, George	DEC 30 1826
LATHRUM, John E.	MAHORNEY, Henrietta	OCT 19 1850
LATHRUM, Sarah Jane	GARRETT, Franklin	JUN 30 1853
LATIMER, Ann Elizabeth	SCHLIECKER, Peter Frederick	JUL 19 1848
LATIMER, Julia	TOMPKINS, Benjamin G.	OCT 01 1845
LATIMER, Marcus	McKELDEN, Clementina E.G. [Mrs.]	FEB 10 1820
LATIMER, Mary	DAY, Elijah W.	MAY 05 1851

District of Columbia Marriage Licenses, 1811-1858

LATIMER, Samuel H.	MORSELL, Rebecca R.	OCT 19 1857
LATIMORE, Rebecca Ann	BARRON, Henry A.	FEB 23 1825
LATKIN, Margaret	BUCKLEY, Thomas	JAN 23 1858
LATRUITE, John P.	ALLISON, Elizabeth Ann [Mrs.]	MAR 24 1829
LaTRUITTE, Barbara V.	WALLACE, George B.	FEB 20 1849
LAUB, Andrew M.	UPPERMAN, Eliza	JUL 10 1824
LAUB, Charles H. [Dr.]	GETTY, Anne Eliza	JAN 15 1833
LAUB, Elizabeth	BERRYMAN, Wm. B.	FEB 23 1832
LAUB, Elizabeth Ann	REDDALL, William C.	OCT 09 1854
LAUB, John Y.	RIDDALL, Cordelia V.	JUN 11 1842
LAUB, Margaret W.	DAVIDSON, John B.	JUN 30 1857
LAUB, Martha V.	EUSTACE, William W.	JUN 17 1851
LAUB, Matilda Sophia	HOLTZMAN, Geo. W.	SEP 17 1823
LAUB, Sarah Finley	PAIRO, Henry Thomas	APR 19 1836
LAUB, William B.	BROOKS, Elizth. A.	SEP 01 1834
LAUBSCHER, John	FENDNER, Johanna	SEP 29 1856
LAUCK, Isaac S.	JONES, Martha A.	NOV 23 1841
LAUCK, Robert M.	CLEMENTSON, Ann H.	OCT 13 1847
LAUDICK, Mary Jane (blk)	SEYMORE, Babel	JUN 01 1848
LAUDY, Thomas	WATTS, Kitty (blk)	APR 08 1830
LAUGHFETY, Sophia	FOX, Samuel	AUG 20 1830
LAUGHRY, Hugh	LYNCH, Jane	SEP 26 1838
LAUR, Louis	KRAFFT, M. Magdalena	MAY 04 1847
LAURENCE, Anne E.	CALCUTT, Charles	AUG 03 1850
LAURENCE, Catharine	McCREENER, James	AUG 22 1855
LAURENCE, Eliza	CUVILLIER, Joseph	JUN 02 1832
LAURENCE, Elizabeth (blk)	STUKELY, Turner	JUL 06 1858
LAURENCE, Henry	MORRIS, Hanna (blk)	OCT 27 1851
LAURENCE, Isaah	SHORTER, Elizabeth (blk)	JUN 09 1825
LAURENCE, Levi L.	UNDERWOOD, Susan J.	SEP 30 1856
LAURENSON, Eliza S.	McLAIN, Richard T.	JAN 26 1850
LAURIE, Cranston H.	McCUTCHEN, Mary A.	OCT 20 1832
LAURIE, Elizabeth W.	COLEGATE, James	JUN 13 1842
LAURIE, Isabel	RITTENHOUSE, Benjamin F.	SEP 23 1828
LAURIE, Isabel C.	MILLER, James M.	JUN 24 1856
LAURIE, Wm. S.	TARBELL, Ann Eliza	AUG 12 1828
LAURY, Joseph S.	HOLLAND, Elizth. R.	MAR 13 1832
LAURY, Michael	KENNON, Bridget	MAY 11 1858
LAURY, Sally (blk)	DORSEY, Tobias	APR 13 1825
LAUSON, Mary E.	BENIDICK, Frederick W.	AUG 25 1842
LAUVALL, Catherine	CLARKE, William	DEC 07 1815
LAUXMAN, Martin	KAIL, Catharine	AUG 20 1857
LAVALL, Jacint	VILLARD, Sophie	FEB 26 1814
LAVELLE, Miles	NELSON, Ann Eliza	JAN 22 1835
LAVELY, Jesse	HANNASON, Susan	APR 01 1814
LAVENDER, Adelaide	WOODWARD, William R.	DEC 18 1850
LAVENDER, James	LAVENDER, Mary Ellen	MAR 23 1853
LAVENDER, James	BERGES, Charlotte	APR 04 1857
LAVENDER, Mary Ellen	LAVENDER, James	MAR 23 1853
LAVEZZI, John Baptist	PIERCE, Ann	MAY 21 1846
LAVIN, Hanora	ROCHE, David	MAR 28 1853
LAVINDER, Fleming J.	O'DELL, Lizzie T.	MAY 12 1857
LAW, Ann	HARRIS, Richard	JAN 30 1823
LAW, Eliza	ROGERS, Lloyd N.	APR 03 1817
LAW, John	CARTER, Frances Ann	MAR 18 1815
LAW, Mary Frances	REID, Wesley W.	APR 20 1848
LAW, Thomas	FLURRY, Sarah	MAY 27 1841
LAWLER, Susan	GREGORY, Ennis	MAY 17 1821

District of Columbia Marriage Licenses, 1811-1858

LAWLESS, Ellen	HANER, John	FEB 03 1853
LAWLESS, Richard	CROSS, Mary	MAR 17 1855
LAWLESS, Thomas	KADEY, Bridget	JUL 09 1855
LAWN, Annie (blk)	BOSTON, Thomas	JAN 22 1852
LAWRANCE, Otho	NELSON, Catherine Murdoch	NOV 30 1815
LAWRENCE, Alexander H.	McWILLIAMS, Jane	SEP 13 1841
LAWRENCE, Caroline M.	READY, William	JUN 01 1839
LAWRENCE, Catharine A.	KIDWELL, John L.	NOV 16 1840
LAWRENCE, Eliza	HOWARD, Charles	SEP 13 1838
LAWRENCE, Eliza H.	STANT, William H.	APR 13 1849
LAWRENCE, Elizabeth	REDFERN, Samuel	DEC 15 1827
LAWRENCE, Elizabeth (blk)	RICH, Thomas	APR 06 1848
LAWRENCE, James	CAMPBELL, Ellen (blk)	JUN 26 1855
LAWRENCE, James H.	BUTLER, Cecelia (blk)	DEC 23 1852
LAWRENCE, Jane	JOY, William T.	APR 30 1842
LAWRENCE, John	COOMBS, Mary	OCT 18 1838
LAWRENCE, Joseph	BEEDING, Susan	MAY 03 1817
LAWRENCE, Joseph H.	PONS, Julia J.	MAY 17 1858
LAWRENCE, Julianna	PARSONS, Thomas H.	NOV 25 1845
LAWRENCE, Mary	WILEY, William	JUL 03 1812
LAWRENCE, Mary Ann	PERKINS, Thomas	JUN 04 1835
LAWRENCE, Mary Ann (blk)	GREEN, James	FEB 10 1851
LAWRENCE, Mary E.	LOVE, William G.	APR 19 1831
LAWRENCE, Phillipi E.W., Mrs.	BALL, Joseph P.	MAY 26 1829
LAWRENCE, Richard	WISE, Mary	MAY 24 1847
LAWRENCE, Richard J.	PRIME, Margt. R.	AUG 08 1850
LAWRENCE, Stark Robert	ROBINSON, Mary Ann	JUN 29 1839
LAWRENCE, William G.	LIVINGSTON, Catharine	AUG 05 1834
LAWRENSON, Margaret A.	HYATT, Richard G.	NOV 04 1845
LAWRENSON, Mary F.	DOVE, Milton C.	JUN 16 1857
LAWRENSON, Sophia S.	EVANS, John E.	JAN 26 1854
LAWRENSON, William S.	STONE, Elizabeth A.	APR 19 1855
LAWRIE, Elizabeth O.	BECK, Joseph W.	AUG 01 1815
LAWS, Adam J.	DUFF, Ann Rose	APR 20 1819
LAWS, Newton	CORNWELL, Ann	JAN 24 1833
LAWS, Sarah	POWELL, Burk	JUL 16 1819
LAWSON, Charles	SIMPSON, Catherine Ann	JUL 06 1848
LAWSON, Dorcas	POOLE, Marshall	AUG 05 1828
LAWSON, Henrietta A.	BUTLER, James E.	OCT 25 1855
LAWSON, Henry	LINCH, Grady Ann	JUN 06 1822
LAWSON, Jane Francis	BEAVERS, James	FEB 14 1848
LAWSON, Mary	WELSH, Edward S.	SEP 14 1854
LAWSON, Mary M.M.	MILLER, John U.A.	FEB 18 1856
LAWSON, Susan	JONES, Stephen	MAR 21 1822
LAWSON, Susanna	McNEMARA, John	JUL 19 1815
LAWSON, Thomas B.	SHUSTER, Mary E.	JUN 14 1849
LAWSON, William	PRICE, Zilla	MAY 25 1820
LAWSON, William	SIMMES, Milly Jane	JUL 08 1847
LAWSON, William	KING, Ann Maria	OCT 13 1852
LAWSON, William	HULSE, Rebecca	NOV 29 1854
LAWTON, Harriot	LOGAN, John	AUG 05 1818
LAWTON, Joseph	HODSON, Mary	FEB 19 1848
LAY, Catharine	O'DONOVAN, Timothy	JUL 16 1853
LAY, George W.	CAMPBELL, Henrietta	JUL 14 1855
LAY, Richard, Junr.	MATINGLY, Mary Susan	JAN 09 1832
LAYTON, Almanzer W.	LACEY, Julia W.	JUL 20 1857
LAYTON, George E.	WARD, Sarah C.	SEP 28 1854
LAYTON, John L.	BARBER, Almira D.	MAR 05 1857

District of Columbia Marriage Licenses, 1811-1858

LAZENBY, Amos A.	DARNES, Mary Frances	DEC 11 1849
LAZENBY, Ann	DULEY, Allen	NOV 13 1823
LAZENBY, Ann Maria	GREEN, Ammon	MAY 26 1851
LAZENBY, Benjn. C.	ORME, Isabella	JAN 10 1856
LAZENBY, Daniel L.	SMITH, Celina H.	MAY 06 1845
LAZENBY, Thomas A.	SMITH, Sarah Amanda	APR 06 1835
LAZINBY, Elisha	ADAMS, Mary Ann	DEC 09 1852
LEAB, Frederick	EVAN, Ann	MAY 08 1822
LEACH, Adeline	GOINGS, Benjamin	SEP 26 1838
LEACH, Angeline	HELMS, Frederick	AUG 04 1838
LEACH, Delila	GRERNIN, William	AUG 25 1838
LEACH, Lydia Ann	TATE, Janes	AUG 26 1834
LEACH, Martha	CRUITT, James M.	JUN 07 1845
LEACH, Mary E.	COLLINS, James A.	MAY 02 1843
LEACH, Thomas W.	McGREARY, Margaret Ann	MAR 07 1849
LEACH, Virginia	NORWOOD, Joseph S.	OCT 26 1850
LEACH, William	SCOTT, Adeline	JUL 01 1834
LEACOCK, Mary A.	McLAGAN, Wm. R.	JUN 14 1855
LEADINGHAM, Christina	RABBIT, Edward	DEC 18 1855
LEAHAN, Mary	LEHMAN, Charles	NOV 29 1855
LEAHEA, Catherine	FITZPATRICK, James	NOV 18 1856
LEAK, Elisha	GARWOOD, Martha	MAR 30 1815
LEAK, John H.	CAHO, Mary Elizabeth	OCT 15 1825
LEAK, Sarah C.	HUTCHINSON, James L.	JUN 10 1858
LEAKE, Elizabeth A.	OGDEN, Wm. L.	FEB 06 1818
LEAKE, Nathan, Jr.	McDUELL, Ann Lydia H.	JUN 20 1832
LEAKIN, George A. [Rev.]	MILLER, Anna Maria	NOV 03 1846
LEAMON, Prymus	STUART, Susan (blk)	DEC 17 1846
LEAPER, Hanson	BROWN, Eliza (blk)	JUN 25 1829
LEAR, Benjamin Lincoln	MORRIS, Maria	JUL 24 1826
LEAR, Benjamin Lincoln	BOMFORD, Louisa S.	AUG 08 1831
LEAR, John P.	THOMPSON, Delilah	JUL 30 1850
LEAR, Louisa	DERBY, Richard C.	SEP 07 1835
LEARNED, Frances C.	McCENEY, Henry C.	SEP 06 1836
LEARY, Arthur	COSTELLO, Catherine	SEP 30 1847
LEARY, Daniel	MURPHY, Bridget	APR 24 1856
LEARY, Jeremiah	CAHIL, Catherine	FEB 13 1852
LEARY, John	CALLAHAN, Mary	AUG 22 1851
LEARY, Julia	DOUGHERTY, Timothy	AUG 27 1855
LEARY, Nicholas	MURPHY, Mary	JAN 21 1857
LEATHERBERRY, Eliza	CRAMPSON, William D.	MAY 15 1845
LEATHERBURY, William	ROBERTSON, Eliza	DEC 07 1829
LEAVY, Lawrence	LEONARD, Margaret	AUG 02 1847
LEBO, Henry	HILL, Ann	JAN 08 1839
LECHALER, Charles K.	ARDIESER, Mary M.	APR 18 1857
LECKEY, Jackson	MAJORS, Emeline	OCT 09 1843
LECKEY, Mary Jane	STANSBERY, William	MAR 24 1857
LECKIE, Elizabeth	MURPHEY, Dennis	JUL 22 1852
LECKIE, Hellen	JONES, James Y.	APR 26 1826
LECKIE, James	DUFFEY, Martha	MAY 19 1834
LECKIE, Martha	MOHUN, Francis	APR 21 1856
LECKRON, Caroline C.	HILTON, Uriah D.	FEB 25 1857
LECTON, Osborn	RICHARDS, Dilia	JAN 20 1827
LECY, Thomas	O'PRADY, Mary	JUL 15 1852
LEDAN, Ann	LEDAN, Paterick	SEP 01 1840
LEDAN, Bridget	KING, Martin	SEP 04 1833
LEDAN, Paterick	LEDAN, Ann	SEP 01 1840
LEDDY, Owen	CRUPPER, Malinda	OCT 31 1842

District of Columbia Marriage Licenses, 1811-1858

LEDERER, Christian	SCHEED, Amelia	DEC 15 1846
LEDGICKS, Ann	HEARD, Enoch	JAN 28 1822
LEDMAN, Silas	REED, Cordelia	AUG 18 1842
LEDRER, Godfrey	MILLER, Eva	MAR 26 1856
LEDRER, John	BROOKMEYER, Johanna	OCT 07 1856
LEDWIDGE, Patrick	HOLORAN, Catherine	OCT 30 1854
LEE, Adeline M.	CLARKE, John	MAR 06 1849
LEE, Alexander	BARCROFT, Henrietta P.	APR 21 1840
LEE, Alexander	HUGHES, Sarah (blk)	MAY 07 1846
LEE, Alexander	PLATER, Mary	OCT 22 1856
LEE, Alfred	BEALL, Elizabeth	DEC 14 1825
LEE, Alfred	CREIK, Margaret (blk)	SEP 06 1826
LEE, Alfred H.	GEORGE, Mary	SEP 15 1853
LEE, Ann	GAMBLE, William	MAR 16 1817
LEE, Ann	MARSHALL, William	JUN 22 1826
LEE, Ann	DAVIS, Hanson	JUL 01 1833
LEE, Ann (blk)	STOKES, Thomas	APR 15 1839
LEE, Ann (blk)	DORSEY, Ephraim	DEC 29 1845
LEE, Ann Eliza	WEIGHTMAN, William	JAN 12 1830
LEE, Ann Maria (blk)	SIMMS, George	DEC 24 1857
LEE, Ann Matilda	WASHINGTON, Bailey [Dr.]	NOV 26 1829
LEE, Carter	GREEN, Anna (blk)	JUL 23 1852
LEE, Catharine	JENKINS, Robert	DEC 15 1847
LEE, Catherine Hite	MAY, George Washington [Dr.]	OCT 04 1824
LEE, Charles	LEE, Sarah (blk)	DEC 27 1855
LEE, Daniel	PILES, Delila	OCT 24 1837
LEE, Daniel C.	WAGONER, Mary E.	MAY 24 1825
LEE, Eleanor S.	WILLIAMS, George	JAN 30 1823
LEE, Eliza	HORSEY, Outerbridge [Sen.]	APR 16 1812
LEE, Eliza B.	FAGAN, Patrick	SEP 17 1853
LEE, Elizabeth	BEAN, Noble	DEC 21 1815
LEE, Elizabeth	HAGAN, Horatio	NOV 07 1834
LEE, Elizabeth	DABNEY, Clizwell	OCT 23 1838
LEE, Elizabeth (blk)	DIXON, David W.	JAN 24 1839
LEE, Elizabeth (blk)	ROUNDS, Francis	SEP 08 1853
LEE, Elizabeth Eliza	GATES, John T.	SEP 07 1832
LEE, Elizth. (blk)	MITCHELL, John	NOV 16 1855
LEE, Ellen (blk)	MITCHELL, Thomas	AUG 03 1844
LEE, Ellen (blk)	HARRIS, Joseph	APR 09 1845
LEE, Emma	BALL, Sheldon H.	APR 24 1847
LEE, Evelinia P.	MORGAN, Edwin C.	JUL 14 1853
LEE, Frances A.	MILLS, John H.	OCT 08 1857
LEE, Francis	GREY, Jane (blk)	MAY 13 1857
LEE, Gustavus	LEE, Sarah (blk)	MAR 28 1827
LEE, Henry	COLEMAN, Ann Elizth.	JAN 22 1836
LEE, Henry	BELL, Caroline (blk)	DEC 08 1846
LEE, Henry	HARRIS, Julia (blk)	MAR 17 1853
LEE, James	WISE, Mary	OCT 03 1839
LEE, Jane	JONES, Charles	MAR 14 1827
LEE, Jane	LEWIS, William	FEB 23 1832
LEE, Jesse	DUFF, Mary Ellen	MAR 07 1833
LEE, Jesse	BALL, Lucy (blk)	MAR 28 1840
LEE, John	WEFT, Rebecca	MAY 23 1816
LEE, John	WILLIAMS, Nancy	AUG 07 1818
LEE, John	LEIGHBURN, Jane	JUN 18 1820
LEE, John	SMALLWOOD, Mary Ann (blk)	MAR 22 1833
LEE, John	ASCUE, Susan	OCT 21 1835
LEE, John	SANDERS, Mary George	OCT 17 1845

District of Columbia Marriage Licenses, 1811-1858

LEE, John D.	LANGLEER, Margaret	JAN 10 1821
LEE, John F.	HILL, Ellen Ann	APR 29 1845
LEE, Joseph D.	WINDSOR, Mary A.	DEC 06 1856
LEE, Julia Ann (blk)	WRIGHT, Charles H.	MAY 13 1857
LEE, Louis	STEWART, Jane (blk)	MAR 20 1844
LEE, Louisa (blk)	LUCAS, Henry	MAR 14 1833
LEE, Louisa (blk)	RUSTIN, Osburn	NOV 17 1835
LEE, Louisa (blk)	WANZER, Louis	JUL 30 1846
LEE, Lucy Ann	JONES, Alfred	FEB 11 1856
LEE, Maria	GASBY, John	MAY 11 1818
LEE, Martha L.	LUCAS, Wm. H.	JUN 20 1855
LEE, Mary	SPEAKE, John	MAR 24 1828
LEE, Mary	DONALDSON, Thomas	JUL 30 1836
LEE, Mary	TAYLOR, Montgomery	MAY 17 1850
LEE, Mary (blk)	CARROLL, Fielder	AUG 22 1855
LEE, Mary E.	DeMALTITZ, Baron Francis de	JUN 06 1825
LEE, Mary E.D.	MILLAN, George W.	NOV 23 1840
LEE, Mary Jane	HILL, George W.	JUL 09 1850
LEE, Nelly (blk)	BARTON, William	APR 18 1843
LEE, Nelson R.	MILLS, Artimeca	JAN 11 1830
LEE, Overton	JACKSON, Mary (blk)	SEP 12 1848
LEE, Patrick	LYNCH, Ellen	JAN 21 1854
LEE, Philip	WOOD, Jane (blk)	NOV 20 1851
LEE, Priscilla (blk)	SIMS, James	NOV 16 1852
LEE, Rachael	HALL, Wells	DEC 18 1833
LEE, Rebecca	BARKER, Andrew	JUL 16 1814
LEE, S. Phillips	BLAIR, Elizabeth	APR 27 1843
LEE, Sally	HENSEY, Rodum	MAY 08 1830
LEE, Samuel	HENRY, Sarah	APR 13 1830
LEE, Samuel	BRADLEY, Catharine	JAN 03 1833
LEE, Samuel	MILLS, Catherine	APR 16 1857
LEE, Sandford	LEWIS, Serena (blk)	JAN 06 1846
LEE, Sarah	STARKS, Dyer	APR 10 1851
LEE, Sarah (blk)	LEE, Gustavus	MAR 28 1827
LEE, Sarah (blk)	LEE, Charles	DEC 27 1855
LEE, Sarah Jane	CLARKE, Thomas E.	JUN 25 1846
LEE, Sarah Jane	BENNETT, Nicholas	APR 17 1855
LEE, Sousana	MYERS, Joseph	OCT 18 1852
LEE, Susan	COLLINS, Levi	NOV 23 1837
LEE, Susanna	MILLS, John E.	NOV 15 1845
LEE, Sylvester	CEPHAS, Sophia	JUN 10 1850
LEE, Theodorick	GRAYSON, Nancy (blk)	SEP 14 1833
LEE, Thomas	BROOKS, Elizabeth (blk)	APR 19 1815
LEE, Washington	DENT, Eliza (blk)	JUL 24 1854
LEE, William	MAHONEY, Eleanor	JUN 04 1819
LEE, William	MAHORNAY, Ann	JUN 10 1833
LEE, William	DAVIS, Frances (blk)	APR 21 1840
LEE, William	SIMPSON, Matilda (blk)	DEC 05 1848
LEE, William	PINDLE, Caroline (blk)	OCT 18 1851
LEE, William W.	COSTIN, Fanny Park	MAY 08 1851
LEECH, John	DOUGLASS, Balinda	JUN 21 1821
LEECH, Margaret A.	RAYMOND, Peter	JUL 14 1858
LEECH, Moses	LODGE, Henny	DEC 01 1823
LEEDORF, Hedvig Margt.	MENZE, Hermann	OCT 02 1847
LEEDS, Isaac	THOMPSON, Mary Virginia	FEB 28 1850
LEEHY, Ellen	MURPHEY, Michael	JAN 05 1858
LEEK, Dolly	FRAZIER, George	APR 02 1821
LEEKE, Julia Ann	ARNOLD, Robert	JUL 15 1826

District of Columbia Marriage Licenses, 1811-1858

LEEMAN, William E.	EVANS, Georgiana	NOV 19 1857
LEENERS, Mary A.	MINNEKER, Deiderich George	MAY 23 1855
LEESE, Catherine	PARKER, William	DEC 06 1852
LEESON, Patrick M.	WELSH, Bridget	OCT 09 1848
LEETCH, John	WINSHIP, Victoria Emogine	JUN 22 1858
LEFEVER, Ann	BIRTH, James	MAY 02 1821
LEFEVER, Ann Maria	BURDINE, Alfred	NOV 03 1841
LEFEVOE, Ann, Mrs.	SHECKELL, Thomas H.	NOV 19 1829
LEFFLER, Caroline	HANSELL, Henry	AUG 02 1858
LEFFLER, John	VERTMILLER, Elizabeth	FEB 13 1846
LEFLER, Philip	HÖHING, Mary A.	NOV 30 1852
LEGG, Cecelia Frances	HURST, Henry W.	AUG 30 1852
LEGG, Eleanor	HARRISON, James	FEB 15 1827
LEGG, Jane	LAKE, James	APR 24 1839
LEGG, Lawson	KENT, Ellen	MAR 14 1814
LEHMAN, Charles	LEAHAN, Mary	NOV 29 1855
LEHMAN, Pauline Rosemond	SMITSON, James	JAN 14 1845
LEHMANN, Antonie	RUPERT, Barbara	OCT 03 1848
LEHMANOWSKI, Lewis F.	EVANS, Sarah Ann	NOV 18 1833
LEHMAYER, Anna	LANGHOR, Henry	JUN 17 1849
LEIB, John Michael	OTEAL, Catharine	MAY 06 1847
LEIBLEMAN, Wm. G.F.	SMITH, Sophia S.	AUG 25 1851
LEIDBURG, Sarah	GENIGAN, Alexander B.	JAN 19 1829
LEIDSBORG, Sarah	MILLS, William N.	JUL 30 1841
LEIDY, Enos	SANDERS, Isabella M.	APR 12 1852
LEIGH, Alfred	OLIVER, Mary Eshby	AUG 04 1846
LEIGH, Nancy	POWELL, Jno.	JAN 24 1828
LEIGHBURN, Jane	LEE, John	JUN 18 1820
LEIGHTFOOT, Ann E.	WALKER, William	JUL 18 1840
LEIHY, Honora	CORRIDAN, Edward	NOV 27 1850
LEIN, John	LINDEG, Charlotte	SEP 05 1853
LEISHEAR, Francis	CLEMENTS, Mary Ellen	MAY 23 1856
LEISHEAR, William W.	AGER, Laura V.	JUL 22 1857
LEISHURE, Harriet J.	LYLES, Henry	SEP 11 1845
LEITCH, Mary M.	SPARO, Thomas T.	JAN 17 1850
LEITH, William	GILL, Ursella	JUL 11 1812
LEIZEAR, Comfort W.	BURRESS, John F.	OCT 04 1838
LEIZEAR, Mary E.	TURNER, William B.	APR 01 1831
LEIZEAR, Robert	BURROWS, Elizabeth	JUL 16 1839
LEIZEAR, Robert	DUVALL, Mary Emily	FEB 21 1850
LEKAVIER, Adelade	FELIX, Michael I.	FEB 11 1854
LELAND, Mary	PALMER, John	DEC 01 1818
LELAND, Rebecca	DUNN, Samuel	FEB 10 1819
LELLARD, Delia A.	LAMESON, Samuel D.	JUN 09 1852
LEMMON, Dennis	CLARKE, Catherine (blk)	JUL 17 1845
LEMMON, Emily (blk)	BRYAN, Benjamin	AUG 21 1845
LEMMON, Enoch	LACEY, Elizabeth (blk)	JAN 27 1858
LEMMON, John	WILLIAMS, Elizabeth (blk)	MAY 18 1854
LEMMON, Martha	RIGWOOD, James	DEC 29 1821
LEMMONS, Emily (blk)	FOREMAN, William	JUN 08 1853
LeMOINE, Louisa	WILLIS, Albert S.	AUG 06 1835
LEMON, Charles, Jr.	MILES, Laurisa	MAR 02 1858
LEMON, Henry	HENDERSON, Mary (blk)	MAY 27 1850
LEMON, Lucy A.	BOSWELL, Thomas P.	NOV 22 1849
LEMON, Mary Elizth.	SOPER, William	FEB 25 1845
LEMON, Sarah A.	PRUITT, William F.	AUG 16 1855
LEMONED, Claracy Ellen	PAYNE, Thomas	DEC 06 1842
LEMP, Francis	CHAMBERLAIN, Chloe	OCT 20 1817

District of Columbia Marriage Licenses, 1811-1858

LENGARD, E. Newton	LOWE, Maggie E.	MAR 28 1856
LENIHEN, Cornelius	LOUNE, Mary	OCT 14 1852
LENK, Everard	STEERIN, Elizabeth	NOV 10 1832
LENMAN, Charles	KELLEY, Martha E.	MAY 07 1846
LENMAN, Deborah	FLENG, James	DEC 21 1820
LENMAN, Elizabeth	WAGLER, Charles K.	NOV 16 1838
LENMAN, Elizabeth	ENO, William	JUN 07 1841
LENMAN, John Thomas	HUNTER, Jenne H. Raldon	OCT 28 1846
LENMAN, Mary Ann	CHAPMAN, William	AUG 26 1839
LENMAN, Mary B.	FLING, George W.	FEB 02 1815
LENMAN, Mary E.	DRURY, William P.	SEP 16 1845
LENMAN, William	STEWART, Elizabeth	MAY 19 1817
LENOIR, William J.	GARNER, Elizabeth F.	OCT 17 1842
LENOX, Angelica	SIMPSON, Joel	APR 21 1823
LENOX, Elizabeth	POOR, Nathaniel P.	SEP 24 1822
LENOX, Julia Maria	KEEP, Samuel	JUL 31 1830
LENOX, Lucy A.	WHEELER, Theodore	MAY 25 1835
LENOX, Susan	McCAULEY, John	JUL 23 1844
LENTHALL, Elizabeth	STONE, William J.	OCT 20 1821
LENZE, Noah	AIGLER, Barbara	APR 01 1852
LEONARD, Angenline	PHILPOTT, Leonard E.	FEB 22 1834
LEONARD, Catherine	JACKSON, ALonzo	APR 10 1858
LEONARD, Deborah	MITCHELL, Judson	OCT 23 1822
LEONARD, Eve	BALL, George W.	JAN 06 1832
LEONARD, Joanna Louisa	GEATZ, George Jos.	MAY 09 1858
LEONARD, John	KYNE, Bridget	FEB 05 1819
LEONARD, John F.	O'DONOHO, Hannora	AUG 13 1825
LEONARD, Margaret	LEAVY, Lawrence	AUG 02 1847
LEONARD, Maria	NORRIS, William	APR 20 1833
LEONARD, Mary Ann	CADMAN, Walter	JAN 07 1854
LEONARD, Michael	FAHEY, Eliza	NOV 29 1855
LEONARD, Sarah	DONOHOE, Dennis	APR 25 1826
LEONARD, Susan	MASON, Stephen	FEB 09 1835
LEONARD, William	FLETCHER, Elizabeth	JUN 05 1843
LEONBACHER, John	SPEAR, Rachel	FEB 26 1852
LEPHARDT, Sophia	WILBE, Charles	MAR 18 1856
LEPPER, George A.	DOBBYN, Celestia	FEB 17 1837
LEPPOLETT, Augustus	REIDVILA, Frederika	MAR 22 1848
LEPREUX, Lewis	CAMPBELL, Jean	MAR 19 1822
LEPREUX, Louis	COOLEY, Susannah	FEB 25 1847
LERIARDI, Elizabeth	WOLF, Fremeoes Antonie	NOV 15 1817
LESCURE, Joseph	KIRBY, Mary Josephine	NOV 14 1849
LESIARDI, Polien	KINCHEY, Paul	AUG 08 1825
LESLIE, H.R.	RAY, E.L.	NOV 15 1848
LEST, Barbara	RUPERT, Edmund	JUN 21 1853
LESTER, John G.	BENNETT, Mary Ann	AUG 01 1843
LESTER, William W.	WALKER, Elizabeth J.	FEB 08 1858
LETHERBERRY, Littleton	MARSHALL, Elizabeth (blk)	SEP 07 1826
LETHERBERRY, William	ROBINSON, Elizabeth	SEP 01 1830
LETJOHN, Henry	STCHUSLER, Anna	JUN 30 1853
LETMATE, Fredericka W.	EICHLER, William	OCT 13 1855
LETNATE, Dorothy	REHM, Ferdinand	SEP 27 1852
LETORT, James	LASHHORN, Frances J.	JUL 27 1853
LETT, Martha Ellen	DORSEY, Henry J.	FEB 26 1852
LETTON, Harriot Elizabeth	McCLENAHAN, Thomas James	JUN 01 1846
LETTS, Sophia Matilda	HATCHESON, Benjamin N.	JUL 09 1853
LEVEALE, Milley	JOHNSTON, James	JUL 27 1816
LEVERING, Clinton	BURNETT, Jane R.	JUN 24 1839

District of Columbia Marriage Licenses, 1811-1858

LEVI, John	HOLLAND, Louisa (blk)	NOV 06 1828
LEVI, Sarah	McKEAN, James	JUL 08 1847
LEVY, Henry	GUSDORF, Henrietta	MAY 20 1858
LEVY, John	TASKER, Mary (blk)	APR 30 1856
LEVY, Lawrence	O'DONOGHUE, Sarah	APR 05 1850
LEVY, Louisa (blk)	LUCAS, Lewis	NOV 30 1846
LEVY, Thomas	BARRETT, Ellen	NOV 23 1852
LEVY, Wesley W.	CARR, Mary C.	FEB 14 1857
LEWELLIN, Eleanor	LEWELLIN, John B.	SEP 05 1853
LEWELLIN, John B.	LEWELLIN, Eleanor	SEP 05 1853
LEWELLYN, Frances	CURRHEY, William	JAN 22 1844
LEWELLYN, Mary	REED, James	AUG 10 1841
LEWIS, Amanda B.	WYVILL, Walter D.	MAY 12 1858
LEWIS, Ann	WELCH, Patrick	MAY 30 1853
LEWIS, Archibald	SMITH, Margaret A.V. (blk)	MAY 02 1853
LEWIS, Benjamin	MATTHEWS, Elizabeth (blk)	FEB 02 1854
LEWIS, Catharine Ann	WEBSTER, Henry	MAY 09 1829
LEWIS, Catherine E.	McFARLAND, George	JUL 08 1848
LEWIS, Charles	DAVIS, Mary A.	AUG 11 1854
LEWIS, Charlotte Ann	KNOWLES, William	OCT 03 1839
LEWIS, Christopher C.	GILL, Amelia E.	JUN 12 1854
LEWIS, Clara	YOUNG, Ezekiel, Jr.	JAN 10 1856
LEWIS, Curtis	SHAY, Sarah	OCT 02 1845
LEWIS, Daniel W.	BRIGHT, Rachel	APR 19 1848
LEWIS, David	BROWN, Rebecca (blk)	APR 05 1849
LEWIS, Edward	BROWN, Margaret	OCT 20 1841
LEWIS, Edward Simmons	WASHINGTON, Susan Jean	DEC 02 1815
LEWIS, Edward W.	BOYD, Jane C.	APR 20 1824
LEWIS, Eleanor	HOW, Edward	DEC 31 1825
LEWIS, Eliza	PUMPHREY, Dennis	NOV 02 1824
LEWIS, Eliza	WATSON, John	FEB 11 1852
LEWIS, Eliza A.	BOWEN, George W.	JUN 10 1824
LEWIS, Eliza A.	BOSS, William A.	AUG 29 1846
LEWIS, Elizabeth	SMITH, John	JUN 05 1827
LEWIS, Elizabeth	VERMILLION, Nicholas	NOV 01 1837
LEWIS, Elizabeth	BROOKE, Philip L.	JAN 29 1842
LEWIS, Elizabeth	WREN, Albert	NOV 02 1857
LEWIS, Elizabeth	STEWART, Lloyd	DEC 08 1857
LEWIS, Elizabeth C.	NALLEY, James T.	DEC 29 1846
LEWIS, Elizabeth E.	STICKNEY, Francis H.	SEP 15 1857
LEWIS, Elizabeth E.	STEWART, Lord	AUG 03 1858
LEWIS, Ellender	LUCAS, Bowen	DEC 16 1815
LEWIS, Emily	HORSEMAN, James	MAY 09 1844
LEWIS, Felton (blk)	GREEN, Thomas	JUN 23 1835
LEWIS, George W.	STEWART, Ann	MAR 05 1844
LEWIS, Henry H., U.S.N.	TAYLOE, Ann O.	NOV 30 1841
LEWIS, J.R.	PLATT, S.H.	MAR 05 1850
LEWIS, James	PUMPHREY, Airy	AUG 02 1815
LEWIS, James	BROWN, Hannah	OCT 12 1821
LEWIS, James	CUMMYKEL, Elizabeth	APR 06 1824
LEWIS, James	LUCAS, Margaret	NOV 17 1827
LEWIS, James	DUBANT, Ellen E.	JUN 11 1851
LEWIS, Jane	BRINN, William	JUN 07 1828
LEWIS, Jane	GIBSON, Daniel	MAR 15 1838
LEWIS, Jane	MOORE, Richard	JAN 03 1850
LEWIS, John	KANE, Delia	APR 16 1852
LEWIS, John A.	JACKSON, Susan A.R.	SEP 18 1841
LEWIS, John H.	FOWLER, Sarah	JUN 22 1852

District of Columbia Marriage Licenses, 1811-1858

LEWIS, John T.	LOMAX, Margaret M.	DEC 02 1852
LEWIS, John W.	DUVALL, Ann A.	JAN 12 1830
LEWIS, John W.	WATSON, Elizth. M.	MAR 08 1855
LEWIS, Joseph	FARMER, Mary	NOV 20 1854
LEWIS, Joseph	JACKSON, Lucinda (blk)	OCT 22 1857
LEWIS, Joseph	FOREMAN, Eliza Ellen (blk)	APR 01 1858
LEWIS, Joseph	HUNT, Johanna	AUG 24 1858
LEWIS, Joseph Knowles	CLARKE, Virginia	OCT 16 1854
LEWIS, Louisa Elizabeth	SEMMES, Mark Leir	JAN 06 1849
LEWIS, Lucy	OLLIVER, John	AUG 17 1829
LEWIS, Margaret	THOMAS, Lewis	NOV 28 1843
LEWIS, Margaret	ROWLES, George Wm.	JUL 27 1847
LEWIS, Martha	TRUCKSELL, Francis	JAN 24 1856
LEWIS, Martha Washington	GATTON, Azariah Henry	APR 15 1850
LEWIS, Mary	JONES, William	SEP 09 1819
LEWIS, Mary	SELBY, Joshua	APR 14 1828
LEWIS, Mary	RAY, John J.	JAN 08 1829
LEWIS, Mary Amey	IGLEHART, Isaac B.	JUL 21 1840
LEWIS, Mary Ann Elizabeth	BERNARD, William	DEC 09 1828
LEWIS, Mary Ann	PAGEOT, Joseph Ives	NOV 27 1832
LEWIS, Mary Ann	GATTON, Azariah Henry	MAY 30 1838
LEWIS, Mary Ann	ROBERTS, Levi	MAY 17 1845
LEWIS, Mary Ann	ROLLINS, J. Alexander	APR 18 1848
LEWIS, Mary Ann	CROSS, William	APR 15 1848
LEWIS, Mary Ann (blk)	TWINE, William H.	MAY 24 1854
LEWIS, Mary Jane	FEARSON, Henry	JUN 15 1841
LEWIS, Mary Louisa	KEYS, Geo. W.	DEC 26 1849
LEWIS, Matilda	McDANIEL, George	APR 20 1813
LEWIS, Nancy	EVANS, Joseph	AUG 21 1813
LEWIS, Nancy (blk)	BUTLER, John	NOV 01 1826
LEWIS, Nathan	QUIGLEY, Sarah Ann	MAY 14 1838
LEWIS, Rachael E.	HUGHES, Joseph R.	JUL 12 1853
LEWIS, Richard H.	[torn out]	DEC 07 1857
LEWIS, Saml.	DOVE, Mary Ann	JAN 20 1820
LEWIS, Sarah	MARTIN, John	OCT 06 1827
LEWIS, Sarah A.E.	LITCHFIELD, Hiram S.	JUN 27 1855
LEWIS, Sarah C.	HENING, George W.	NOV 03 1831
LEWIS, Sarah Jane	BEALL, Charles	MAY 14 1846
LEWIS, Sarah Jane	MORRIS, John T.	MAY 02 1855
LEWIS, Serena (blk)	LEE, Sandford	JAN 06 1846
LEWIS, Sinai	SMITHSON, Hezekiah	JAN 07 1818
LEWIS, Susan	SIMONDS, Stephen	MAR 26 1846
LEWIS, Susanna	PORTS, Peregrine	JUN 24 1857
LEWIS, Thomas	JONES, Catharine	JAN 23 1812
LEWIS, Thomas	DUNNING, Mary M.	FEB 01 1836
LEWIS, Thomas	PAYNE, Catherine Edney	NOV 21 1842
LEWIS, Thomas S.	ADAMS, Eliza Ann	JAN 15 1829
LEWIS, Thomas S.	ADAMS, Rachael	SEP 30 1829
LEWIS, Thomazine M.	ROWZEE, Greenbury	APR 29 1844
LEWIS, Washington	STERET, Rachel	APR 28 1824
LEWIS, William	LEE, Jane	FEB 23 1832
LEWIS, William	STEVENSON, Sophia	AUG 16 1838
LEWIS, William	WISE, Elizabeth	JUL 25 1839
LEWIS, William	MASON, Jane (blk)	SEP 18 1854
LEWIS, William S.	ESPEY, Martha	OCT 17 1848
LEWISON, Jane Frances	BEAVERS, Sampson	FEB 28 1848
LEXBIE, Ann	HENTZ, Joseph	MAR 08 1856
LEYDANE, Catharine	THOMPSON, Moses	NOV 05 1850

District of Columbia Marriage Licenses, 1811-1858

LEYDANE, Patrick	BASSETT, Marinda	FEB 26 1844
LEYNS, Bertram	ARTH, Klara	JUL 05 1853
LIBBEY, Anna M.	MOORMAN, Robert B.	JAN 07 1851
LIBBEY, C. Malvina	BETTINGER, Benjamin F.	MAY 13 1850
LIBBEY, Charlotte	KING, James	JUN 20 1843
LIBBY, Joseph	MYERS, Louisa	MAY 13 1822
LIBBY, Martha	MILLER, Benjamin	MAR 29 1855
LIBER, Sebastian	WOLTZ, Mary C.	APR 15 1840
LICET, Margaret	NESTER, Patrick	APR 28 1855
LICHAN, Henry	JOCKEL, Margaret	JUN 14 1858
LICKSON, Philice	JACKSON, Edward	DEC 28 1815
LIEDERER, Hellena	FREDERICH, Florian	JAN 12 1856
LIEPPE, Francois	COLLARD, Augustine	MAR 17 1825
LIESHER, Harriet Ann	RILEY, John	AUG 21 1852
LIGHTELL, John B.O.H.	FISHER, Mary Jane	FEB 06 1843
LIGHTELLE, William E.	HILL, Mary A.	AUG 15 1838
LIGHTELLE, William E.	STEWART, Julia A.T.	MAY 31 1845
LIGHTER, John T.	TOWNSAND, Mary	DEC 30 1851
LIGHTER, Mary E.	SKIDMORE, John	MAR 04 1847
LIGHTFOOT, Ann	VANNEMAN, James	SEP 08 1855
LIGHTFOOT, Daniel	ROBEY, Sarah Elizabeth	JAN 27 1834
LIGHTFOOT, Elizabeth	PERRY, Alexander, Jr.	DEC 02 1819
LIGHTFOOT, George	BURCH, Jane	APR 12 1827
LIGHTFOOT, George W.	BARNES, Eleanor	DEC 18 1827
LIGHTFOOT, Jane	MORTIMER, Albert	MAY 08 1834
LIGHTFOOT, Jane A.	GOODRIDGE, William W.	DEC 09 1841
LIGHTFOOT, Mary Ann	LYNCH, John	JAN 02 1856
LIGHTFOOT, William	GOODRICH, Nancy	MAR 21 1837
LIGHTFOOT, William	STEWART, Mary Ann	JAN 01 1846
LIGHTFOOT, William B.	BEVERLY, Roberta	FEB 06 1832
LIGHTFORD, Ann Matilda	VANSCIVER, William	AUG 10 1854
LIGHTFORD, Louisa	DAVIS, Edward	DEC 04 1834
LIGHTNER, John	TALBERT, Eleanor	AUG 25 1818
LIHALLENBERG, Christian	DENSEHER, Mary	JAN 13 1857
LIHAULT, Louisa M.	KNIGHT, Esley	MAY 21 1822
LIJAH, Melia Ann	MANSFIELD, Joseph	MAR 30 1843
LILBURN, Robert T.	HOPKINS, Emeline V.	SEP 03 1850
LILES, Elizabeth	BEECH, Nathaniel	MAY 10 1827
LILLARD, Andrew F.	LILLARD, Louisa W.	JAN 24 1854
LILLARD, Louisa W.	LILLARD, Andrew F.	JAN 24 1854
LILLEY, Thomas	SHADES, Ann	SEP 25 1837
LIMA, Margaret	STEWART, Samuel	OCT 01 1857
LIMLY, Mary	FORLORN, Michael	JUL 19 1814
LIMMY, William	AVEY, Margaret	APR 14 1834
LINAHAN, Michael	KANE, Betsy	OCT 08 1851
LINCH, Grady Ann	LAWSON, Henry	JUN 06 1822
LIND, Mary	MAKIBBIN, Charles L.	OCT 08 1855
LINDEG, Charlotte	LEIN, John	SEP 05 1853
LINDEMANN, Catherina	GRAVE, Ludwig	FEB 07 1843
LINDENBERGER, Anne E.	BRENT, James R.	MAR 01 1851
LINDENBEYER, Rebecca L.	HARRISON, Horace N.	OCT 21 1835
LINDENBORN, John	KEYSER, Eliza	AUG 13 1856
LINDERMANN, Philip	MILLER, Catherine Elizabeth	MAR 02 1842
LINDERWOOD, George	CRANDELL, Rachel	MAR 14 1837
LINDMAN, Philip	BROTSCAMP, Catherine Margt.	AUG 20 1838
LINDNER, Nicholas	HAAG, Sophie	FEB 13 1851
LINDSAY, Adam	ROSE, Mariah	MAY 30 1815
LINDSAY, Alfred	DYER, Willia Ann	DEC 03 1840

District of Columbia Marriage Licenses, 1811-1858

LINDSAY, Catherine	WREN, Charles B.	NOV 28 1839
LINDSAY, Harriet	GODDARD, John	FEB 12 1850
LINDSAY, Hiram O.	HARDEN, Frances	JAN 14 1817
LINDSAY, James W.	GRAVES, Amanda T.	MAY 05 1845
LINDSAY, Kiziah	SIMPSON, John	JUL 29 1817
LINDSAY, Maria A.	WATERMAN, Edwin	SEP 20 1851
LINDSAY, Mary Ann	CALLAHAN, Dennis	DEC 17 1839
LINDSAY, O.P.	GORUM, Mary	FEB 04 1851
LINDSAY, Rachel	HITCHCOCK, Robert J.	FEB 13 1843
LINDSAY, Rachel	KUHN, Walter	JAN 01 1846
LINDSAY, Richard	WILLIAMS, Rachael	APR 20 1835
LINDSAY, Robert G.	AUSTIN, Mary Anna P.	SEP 14 1841
LINDSAY, Samuel	WEBSTER, Margaret L.	NOV 15 1852
LINDSAY, Sarah L.	ATCRISON, John	JUN 30 1836
LINDSAY, William	FOSTER, Jane Elizth.	JUN 30 1836
LINDSEY, Ann M.	DAWSON, John T.	FEB 14 1850
LINDSEY, Catharine H.	CRAWFORD, John H.	MAR 20 1834
LINDSEY, Eliza (col'd)	THOMAS, Henry	MAY 27 1858
LINDSEY, William	KERNAN, Eliza	SEP 07 1852
LINDSEY, William H.	MOCKABEE, Margaret E.	JUN 13 1857
LINDSLEY, Abraham Bradley	JAMESSON, Sarah Jane Triplett	SEP 29 1827
LINDSLEY, Caroline W.	MUSSEY, William H.	MAY 04 1857
LINDSLEY, Charles	HILL, Phoebe (blk)	MAR 26 1842
LINDSLEY, Charlotte (blk)	HALL, Henry	SEP 17 1845
LINDSLEY, Christine	TAYLOR, Hudson	JAN 18 1849
LINDSLEY, Eleazer	INGLE, Ann	APR 28 1818
LINDSLEY, Glorvina Claudine	MINES, Flavel Scott [Rev.]	JUN 12 1832
LINDSLEY, Mary Ann	PORTER, Bolton S.	JAN 28 1852
LINDSLEY, Rachel	HITCHCOCK, Robert J.	JUN 25 1847
LINDSLY, Frances H.	WASHBURN, Edward A.	JUN 01 1854
LINGAN, Sarah	RANDOLPH, William B.	JUN 21 1816
LINGAN, Sarah	RANDOLPH, Wm. Beverly	MAY 21 1816
LINGEBACK, Henrietta	BUEDE, Henry	DEC 30 1843
LINGERFOOT, William	LOGY, Mahala	APR 25 1849
LINGHAM, Mary	DUNAVOUGHN, Jeremiah	JAN 06 1831
LINKIN, Anna	TINKLER, Samuel R.	SEP 11 1855
LINKIN, Henry	SWALLOW, Ellen	FEB 19 1855
LINKIN, Margaret	CORCORAN, Henry W.	JUN 21 1831
LINKINS, Catharine	NEALE, John	DEC 23 1815
LINKINS, Danl.	MAGILL, Henrietta	OCT 08 1840
LINKINS, Elizth. A.	WEBER, Henry	SEP 10 1855
LINKINS, Francis	HILL, Haley Ann	DEC 26 1851
LINKINS, George	CAMPBELL, Julia	MAR 21 1835
LINKINS, James A.	MILLER, Margaret A.	SEP 22 1856
LINKINS, John	DIATT, Betsey	JUL 17 1817
LINKINS, John	ROLLINS, Mary	MAY 26 1825
LINKINS, Joseph	COXEN, Susan	MAY 01 1849
LINKINS, Livinia E.	GALLAGHER, John	MAY 11 1854
LINKINS, Louis F.	BROWN, Margt. F.	JUN 18 1851
LINKINS, Margt. E.	CHASE, William	DEC 30 1856
LINKINS, William	MOORE, Mary	APR 29 1813
LINKINS, William	WOODWARD, Mary Ann	APR 30 1845
LINN, Samuel D.	YOUNG, Catharine W.	SEP 06 1852
LINN, Sophiah	SMITH, Frederick	JUN 26 1852
LINNEHAN, Conn	MURPHY, Elizth. Ann	MAY 24 1836
LINNIG, F.	GOSHELL, Mary Ann	JUN 18 1858
LINNINGS, Catherine Oleania	PILES, Francis B.	NOV 12 1857
LINNY, Edward	BYRNE, Mary	FEB 24 1851

District of Columbia Marriage Licenses, 1811-1858

LINSEY, Catharine	GRIMES, Henry V.	OCT 03 1832
LINTHECUM, Mary	HALL, James P.	MAY 07 1858
LINTHECUM, O.M. [Dr. Otho]	MAGRUDER, Ann E.	SEP 02 1823
LINTON, John A.	BRADLEY, Jeannette	JUL 12 1855
LINTON, Philip H.	BURCH, Martha A.	SEP 08 1857
LIPPARD, Elizabeth	GIDDINGS, James H.	JUL 10 1854
LIPPENCOTT, Adeline W.	NORTH, J. Bartram	DEC 07 1854
LIPPHARD, Adolph	BRONEL, Lorieno	JAN 21 1839
LIPPHARD, John H.	MYERS, Sophia	FEB 20 1847
LIPPINCOTT, Sarah	RICHARDS, Samuel P.	NOV 12 1856
LIPPITT, John	HORBACH, Marcelena	NOV 16 1855
LIPPITT, Mareta	STURNANAGAL, Conrad	NOV 16 1855
LIPPOLD, Anna	JOIST, Konrad	APR 08 1857
LIPPOT, John Henry	BRADLEY, Mary	MAY 03 1834
LIPSCOMB, Ann	DIXON, John	DEC 27 1824
LIPSCOMB, Conway	NALLY, Mary	JUL 18 1832
LIPSCOMB, Eleanor H.	BOOTH, Nathaniel	OCT 24 1844
LIPSCOMB, Ellen	SHERWOOD, Lewis	JUL 04 1837
LIPSCOMB, Emma E.	SPALDING, Samuel E.	FEB 07 1855
LIPSCOMB, James L.	EDWARDS, Mary E.	AUG 21 1855
LIPSCOMB, Jesse	HAGAN, Martha	APR 27 1846
LIPSCOMB, M.O.	PARKINSON, R.	MAR 24 1858
LIPSCOMB, Sarah	JONES, Samuel	MAY 02 1831
LIPSCOMB, William	HUTCHINS, Ellen	MAY 06 1830
LIPSICOMB, Overton	DILLON, Mary Ann	FEB 18 1817
LISARDE, Victoria	RITTER, John H.	MAR 12 1829
LISBURGHER, Henrietta	KESH, Jacob	JUL 27 1852
LISBY, Horatio	GOTHER, Rachel E.	DEC 19 1822
LISBY, John N.	GODDARD, Mary E.	DEC 05 1825
LISBY, Nancy Harriet	THOMPSON, Gabriel Clark	DEC 26 1844
LISBY, Samuel S.	ROLLINS, Sarah	DEC 30 1813
LISBY, Sarah Jane	GORDON, John	OCT 12 1844
LISBY, Thomas	SCOTT, Matilda	DEC 21 1816
LISENITZNER, Ernestina F.	HELLER, August	NOV 29 1842
LISSENIL, Marie L.	MARIE, Pierre Jules	AUG 26 1848
LIST, Johanna	SCHNELL, Frederick	JUL 07 1847
LISTON, James	FLANNAGAN, Mary	DEC 11 1854
LISTON, James	ALLEN, Bridget	FEB 05 1855
LISTON, James	KENNEDY, Johanna	OCT 25 1856
LISTON, Mary	CROWLEY, John	JUN 12 1858
LITCHFIELD, Hannah M.	TEACHUM, William H.	FEB 20 1856
LITCHFIELD, Hiram S.	LEWIS, Sarah A.E.	JUN 27 1855
LITCHFIELD, Jane A.	FULLER, Jeremiah	DEC 16 1851
LITLE, Mary E.	BROWNE, John M.	JAN 06 1830
LITLE, Rebecca	HAZEL, Levi	APR 04 1850
LITTELL, John DeBarth	THAW, Columbia	JUN 06 1854
LITTEN, Benjamin	EMERSON, Charlotte (blk)	JUN 21 1848
LITTLE, Ann	WELLS, Peter	FEB 17 1814
LITTLE, Catherine (blk)	BUTLER, William	MAR 18 1856
LITTLE, Daniel	LASKIE, Ann	MAY 09 1829
LITTLE, David	DOUGHERTY, Sarah E.	JUN 12 1827
LITTLE, Elizabeth	YOUNG, Adam	JUN 09 1828
LITTLE, Elizabeth E.	ELLIOT, William	DEC 30 1822
LITTLE, James	CLARE, Araminta	JUL 20 1841
LITTLE, John	[torn out]	JUL 13 1813
LITTLE, John	FOYLES, Margaret	JAN 25 1831
LITTLE, John	WASON, Caroline	OCT 02 1833
LITTLE, Joseph	ROBERTSON, Jane	JUL 31 1832

District of Columbia Marriage Licenses, 1811-1858

LITTLE, Joseph T.	AUTH, Mary M.	MAY 06 1847
LITTLE, Julia A.	BATES, John E.	JUN 04 1849
LITTLE, Mary	SIBLEY, James T.	SEP 04 1849
LITTLE, Mary E.	NEWTON, William G.	DEC 01 1852
LITTLE, Peter	WAYSON, Mary	NOV 30 1824
LITTLE, Peter, Junr.	CULLEY, Mary	JUN 16 1823
LITTLE, Samuel J.	KING, Margaret D.	JAN 31 1839
LITTLE, Virginia B.	KIRBY, Gilman	APR 16 1853
LITTLE, Warren	MILBURN, Sarah	DEC 17 1839
LITTLEFIELD, Rufus P.	McDONALD, Eugenia	JAN 15 1846
LITTLEFORD, Addison	HUTCHINSON, Catherine	FEB 25 1835
LITTLEFORD, Elizabeth	JENKINS, Bennett	FEB 17 1829
LITTLEFORD, Hanson	MINICE, Sarah	JAN 17 1824
LITTLEFORD, Mary	CLUB, Benjamin	NOV 07 1831
LITTLEFORD, Nathan T.	HARVEY, Elizabeth	DEC 22 1840
LITTLEJOHN, Alexr.	UPPERMAN, Kitty	JAN 11 1812
LITTLEJOHN, Ann M.	LANE, John G.	SEP 17 1839
LITTLEJOHN, Jane E.	MYERS, William H.	JUL 03 1843
LITTLEJOHN, Mary Ann	WARNER, Judson	DEC 24 1838
LITTLETON, Anna E.	JOHNSON, Wm. H.	OCT 15 1855
LITTON, Samuel	COSBERY, Phillis (blk)	SEP 22 1849
LIVERPOOL, Cassa (blk)	HARRIS, Peyton	NOV 10 1845
LIVERPOOL, James	MONTGOMERY, Julia (blk)	JAN 09 1854
LIVERPOOL, John	HOLMES, Eleanor (blk)	JUL 15 1830
LIVERPOOL, Moses	THOMPSON, Susan	FEB 12 1813
LIVERPOOL, Moses	DUNLAP, Patsey	SEP 03 1827
LIVERPOOL, Sylvester	BROWN, Mary (blk)	JUL 09 1853
LIVERS, Miles P.	GATES, Martha E.	JAN 12 1853
LIVES, Ann Sophia	HARVEY, George	NOV 20 1833
LIVINGSTON, Catharine	LAWRENCE, William G.	AUG 05 1834
LIVINGSTON, Charles V.	HOUSTOUN, Harriot E. [Mrs.]	APR 27 1820
LIVINGSTON, George D.	SWEENY, Mary C.	OCT 28 1850
LIVINGSTON, Henry D.	NOPER, Frances	DEC 15 1851
LIVINGSTON, Nora C.	YOUNG, Ignatius Fenwick	JAN 02 1851
LIVINGSTON, Sophie Cora	BARTON, Thomas Pennant	APR 24 1833
LIVINGTON, Sarah	DAY, James	APR 03 1823
LIZEAR, George W.	WALKER, Elizabeth Ellen	NOV 26 1850
LIZEAR, Richard	CROSS, Martha	APR 05 1855
LIZER, Cornelius	TUCKER, Ann	MAY 13 1845
LIZIER, Joseph	WHITTLE, Mary Ellen	SEP 22 1845
LIZOR, Elizabeth	BIGGS, Alfred	MAR 19 1835
LLEWELLEN, Elizabeth	GAER, John	NOV 20 1845
LLEWELLEN, Rebecca	WINDHAM, Andrew J.	MAY 27 1844
LLEWELLYN, Mary J.	ELIOT, Johnson	NOV 29 1850
LLEWLYN, Ellen Jane	ANDERSON, Richard	OCT 04 1852
LLOYD, Adam	TINCH, Sarah	APR 09 1814
LLOYD, Ann America	MILLER, George	JAN 15 1827
LLOYD, Catherin	CANNON, Patrick	JUL 01 1833
LLOYD, Charles H.	MILSTEAD, Nora	JUN 28 1855
LLOYD, Elizabeth C.	INGLE, Henry	MAY 11 1852
LLOYD, George	BLEDSOE, Susan	JAN 18 1834
LLOYD, James H.	WARNER, Mary Ann	NOV 24 1842
LLOYD, James T.	LOCKE, Louisa R.	NOV 17 1855
LLOYD, Jane	BEALL, Hezekiah	MAR 05 1833
LLOYD, Jasper S.	RANDALL, Jane	DEC 27 1854
LLOYD, John	FOG, Margaret	DEC 29 1828
LLOYD, John	McNAMEE, Margaret	MAY 29 1841
LLOYD, John	MAHORNEY, Elizabeth	JAN 29 1846

District of Columbia Marriage Licenses, 1811-1858

LLOYD, Joshua	McLAUGHLIN, Elizabeth	DEC 28 1844
LLOYD, Julia Ann	DANIEL, John	JUN 20 1846
LLOYD, Lester	WINSOR, Josephine C.	APR 19 1852
LLOYD, Lester	DARNE, Sarah Frances	JAN 14 1856
LLOYD, Margaret	FITZGERRALD, James	FEB 16 1833
LLOYD, Martha Ann	GREEN, George Henry	JAN 20 1851
LLOYD, Mary	DUNNINGTON, Jas. M.	AUG 17 1854
LLOYD, Rena C.	WALKER, Lawrence	MAR 31 1852
LLOYD, Samuel	BAILEY, Sabina	JUN 04 1846
LLOYD, Spencer	COCKREILL, Jane E.	DEC 13 1832
LLOYD, Susan A.	ADDINGTON, Wm. X.	DEC 26 1849
LLOYD, Thomas	KELLY, Betsey	APR 27 1824
LLOYD, Virginia	MILSTEAD, Thomas	MAY 04 1857
LLOYD, William	DOUGLASS, Matilda	OCT 07 1824
LOBER, Katherine	SLEIDAR, Joseph	SEP 12 1857
LOCHBOEHLER, Frank	EICHHORN, Theressa	JAN 03 1857
LOCHREY, Edward	STEVENSON, Sarah Jane	APR 25 1848
LOCKBALER, Frances	RIGGLE, Peter	MAY 17 1851
LOCKE, Catherine J.	SUTTON, James	OCT 27 1852
LOCKE, Elizabeth A.	GALDWIN, Gabriel L.	FEB 27 1851
LOCKE, John B.	BACON, Ann E.	APR 15 1820
LOCKE, John H.	MORAN, Sarah	OCT 27 1845
LOCKE, Louisa R.	LLOYD, James T.	NOV 17 1855
LOCKE, Prudence D.	BACON, Washington	NOV 21 1829
LOCKER, Anna	ROLAND, John	DEC 26 1854
LOCKER, Henley	BRYAN, Charity A.	JAN 21 1836
LOCKER, Sarah E.	WALKER, Zachariah H.T.	DEC 22 1853
LOCKEY, Andrew R.	HUNTER, Sarah	JUN 11 1827
LOCKEY, Francis	MITCHELL, Clarissa Ann	APR 01 1857
LOCKEY, Isabella	SINN, William	NOV 18 1826
LOCKWOOD, Joshua W.	FITZHUGH, Annie	AUG 26 1857
LODGE, Caroline	WEBSTER, Rezin	OCT 31 1833
LODGE, Edward	DAVIS, Mary (blk)	OCT 11 1841
LODGE, Edward	DAVIS, Mary (blk)	NOV 11 1841
LODGE, Edward	EVANS, Mary Virginia	AUG 16 1851
LODGE, Henny	LEECH, Moses	DEC 01 1823
LODGE, Henry	DAVIS, Mary (blk)	NOV 25 1841
LODGE, James	SHORE, Lavinia Ann (blk)	APR 10 1845
LODGE, Mary	PETERS, Edward	NOV 05 1840
LOEFFLER, Ernest	HEGELER, Johanna	MAR 21 1853
LOEHHAUSEN, Eleanor	SEELHORST, F.W.C.	OCT 21 1834
LOFERS, Christopher	YOUNG, Elender	DEC 27 1819
LOFFLER, Elizth.	KAISER, George	OCT 20 1855
LOFFLER, Jacob	WATZERHELDNER, Teresa	APR 17 1856
LOFTIS, John	O'HARE, Ann	DEC 01 1857
LOGAN, Elijah	ADAMS, Fanny	JUL 08 1835
LOGAN, John	LAWTON, Harriot	AUG 05 1818
LOGAN, Margaret	STEWART, George	SEP 11 1827
LOGAN, Mary Ann	GILLOTT, Joseph	MAY 30 1838
LOGAN, Mary Ann (blk)	SNOWDEN, Henry Clay	DEC 19 1851
LOGAN, Peter	FRANCIS, Margaret	MAY 21 1852
LOGAN, Richard	RATCLIFF, Malinda	APR 16 1821
LOGAN, Robt.	WHITE, Elizabeth	JUN 10 1828
LOGANS, Henry	ST. CLAIR, Mary (blk)	JUL 07 1841
LOGBALER, Joseph	GEIR, Gertrude	APR 04 1853
LOGG, Harriet Jane	WELCH, James Sylvester	JUN 18 1836
LOGGINS, Levi	CHASE, Patsy	MAY 27 1840
LOGGINS, Peter	FRANKLIN, Jane (blk)	FEB 26 1813

District of Columbia Marriage Licenses, 1811-1858

LOGY, Mahala	LINGERFOOT, William	APR 25 1849
LOHIDER, William	HENRICH, Eliza	MAR 30 1835
LOHR, Charles	DRINKHOUSE, Catherine	FEB 08 1856
LOHS, Mary	ZIMMERMANN, Anjelus	OCT 09 1854
LOKER, Mary Ann	BARNES, Trueman	JUL 27 1815
LOKESMAN, Christina	KOLB, Gottlieb	MAR 09 1849
LOKEY, Joseph	WAGNER, Ann	APR 24 1823
LOKEY, Louisa	WHITINGTON, John	MAY 30 1820
LOMACK, Dennis	BEALL, Sarah (blk)	OCT 01 1838
LOMAN, Ann Maria	GODDARD, Benjamin	JAN 14 1839
LOMAX, Alfred	LOMAX, Elizth. (blk)	JAN 20 1851
LOMAX, Caroline (blk)	RINGGOLD, Richard	DEC 16 1854
LOMAX, Dennis	JACKSON, Eliza (col'd)	AUG 31 1854
LOMAX, Elias	PARKER, Amanda (blk)	MAY 19 1858
LOMAX, Elizabeth	MOTHERSAID, Elias J.	APR 29 1851
LOMAX, Elizabeth	MOSS, William	OCT 09 1851
LOMAX, Elizth. (blk)	LOMAX, Alfred	JAN 20 1851
LOMAX, Frances	BOTTIN, James	AUG 04 1855
LOMAX, Jane T.	WORTHINGTON, Francis A.	FEB 07 1843
LOMAX, John	TURNER, Mrs. Phame	AUG 03 1850
LOMAX, John	HEAD, Frances	OCT 16 1852
LOMAX, Margaret M.	LEWIS, John T.	DEC 02 1852
LOMAX, Michael	SMITH, Sophronia A.	SEP 06 1830
LOMAX, Thomas M.	BOTELER, Eliza	JUL 06 1858
LOMAX, William	THOMAS, Nancy (blk)	MAY 19 1847
LOMBARDI, Francis	ECKLOFF, Caroline	NOV 25 1844
LOMIX, William	HUTCHIN, Sarah (blk)	MAY 26 1823
LONDON, James	AMBUSH, Rebecca	FEB 24 1857
LONEY, Bondinot S.	FRENCH, Arianna	FEB 06 1854
LONG, Ann	KENNAN, John	JUL 12 1827
LONG, Attaway	COLLINS, Joshua	OCT 20 1812
LONG, Bartholomew	CORTNEY, Margaret	AUG 25 1855
LONG, Conrad	YOUNG, Calloty	DEC 27 1819
LONG, Dennis	MAHONEY, Ellen	JUL 10 1857
LONG, Eleanor	PALMER, William	FEB 22 1840
LONG, Eliza	McINTIRE, Edward	OCT 14 1824
LONG, Elizabeth	ADAMS, Charles	AUG 17 1813
LONG, Eppy	PRICE, Robert	JUL 30 1849
LONG, Jacob F.	PATTON, Ann	JUL 31 1841
LONG, James	PAYNE, Ann J.	SEP 17 1850
LONG, James	PHELEN, Bridget	FEB 16 1853
LONG, James G.	STONE, Virginia	FEB 02 1857
LONG, Jeremiah	DONOVAN, Hanorah	FEB 17 1855
LONG, John	ALLEN, Mary Ann	JUL 11 1825
LONG, John	WALL, Bridget	JAN 13 1856
LONG, John	HERBER, Margaretta	DEC 24 1857
LONG, Joseph	CARROLL, Sarah Jane	OCT 04 1854
LONG, Joseph	JOHNSON, Sarah	MAY 15 1858
LONG, Julia	ORR, Overton L.	JAN 19 1826
LONG, Madison	BROWN, Ann	DEC 24 1829
LONG, Mary	BEALL, Thomas	SEP 23 1823
LONG, Mary	CURRAN, John	NOV 28 1837
LONG, Mary	SCHLEY, Charles	MAY 05 1840
LONG, Michael	BAIGLEY, Ellen	MAY 03 1851
LONG, Phebe	SANDERSON, Thomas	SEP 10 1812
LONG, Wm.	GRAY, Mary	DEC 27 1817
LONGDEN, Thomas	CORVIN, Julia	DEC 04 1815
LONGDON, Alice	ADAMS, James	MAR 26 1833

District of Columbia Marriage Licenses, 1811-1858

LONGDON, Charles	BROWN, Isabella C.	DEC 02 1847
LONGDON, Elizabeth	O'HARE, Richard	NOV 17 1812
LONGDON, Emily J.	MOULDER, John W.	MAR 17 1843
LONGDON, Jane Elizabeth	DIBBLE, William H.	MAY 06 1847
LONGHERY, Ardavan Scott	ROBERTSON, Eliza	MAY 07 1850
LONGLEY, Robert	PRESGRAVES, Margaret	AUG 26 1819
LONGSON, James	LUCAS, Emily A.	SEP 25 1850
LONGSTON, Martha Ann	ELLWOOD, William D.	JAN 27 1857
LONGSTON, Mary E.	BARNES, Henry L.	SEP 23 1857
LONGWELL, Peggy	FRENCH, Samuel	OCT 09 1817
LOOMIS, Erastus [Lieut.]	THOMPSON, Cecelia M.	MAY 30 1816
LOOMIS, William	NASH, Elizabeth	FEB 20 1845
LOONEY, Dennis	HURLEY, Mary	JUL 18 1851
LOONEY, James	HOLOHAN, Bridget	AUG 31 1854
LOONEY, Mary	QUILL, Dennis	JAN 28 1857
LOONEY, William	SULLIVAN, Mary	SEP 05 1853
LOONY, Hanora	FITZGERALD, Timothy	OCT 01 1853
LORCH, Affa	HUPPERT, Andrias	JAN 16 1835
LORD, Francis B.	KNOWLES, Lydia	JUN 26 1818
LORD, Francis B., Junr.	HUBBARD, Caroline Matilda	MAY 07 1849
LORD, Ruth	McINTIRE, Samuel	JAN 30 1817
LORD, W. Blair	WILLIS, Louisa L.	NOV 06 1854
LORDAN, Mary	O'BRIEN, William	MAY 20 1841
LORDEN, Cornelius	DACEY, Ellen	AUG 31 1852
LORENTZ, Jacob Alexander	HODGSON, Julia Angela	APR 19 1847
LORENZ, Louisa	RICHTER, Herrmann	APR 27 1855
LOSSER, Rosalia	BIHLER, Charles F.	NOV 04 1833
LOUDON, George	WOODLAND, Barbara	NOV 22 1831
LOUDON, George W.	THOMPSON, Betty C.	SEP 25 1855
LOUEE, Fanny	RYE, Jacob	JUL 16 1838
LOUGHBOROUGH, Jane	CARTER, John Hill, Jr.	MAY 07 1833
LOUGHLIN, Michael	HEARN, Mary	MAY 18 1848
LOUIS, Catherine	GHEN, Anthony	JUN 13 1843
LOUIS, Henry Charles	DeCARNEY, Caroline Charlotte	NOV 16 1813
LOUIS, John E.	FISHER, Lucretia Alice	MAY 30 1855
LOUNDS, Richard	BARTON, Mary Ann (blk)	OCT 09 1845
LOUNDS, William R.	TAYLOR, Serena	NOV 08 1843
LOUNE, Mary	LENIHEN, Cornelius	OCT 14 1852
LOURST, Lidian	BEARDLY, George	APR 06 1822
LOURY, Charles F.	HALLIDAY, Ann M.	APR 10 1843
LOURY, George	JOHNSON, Elizabeth D.	JAN 29 1855
LOURY, Milly	PEASE, Alfred	JAN 19 1820
LOUSEMANN, Michael	STROBLIN, Barbara	JUL 29 1833
LOUXMAN, Andrew	HUE, Catharine	MAR 10 1840
LOVE, Elie	WHITE, Sarah Ann	JAN 09 1830
LOVE, Elizabeth S.	ELLIOT, Henry	OCT 14 1847
LOVE, Leonora	DRUMMOND, Amelia	OCT 25 1849
LOVE, Margaret A.	JACKSON, George W.	DEC 22 1846
LOVE, William G.	LAWRENCE, Mary E.	APR 19 1831
LOVEGROBE, William R.	MORRISON, Anna E.	OCT 17 1853
LOVEJOY, Alexander	ROBERTSON, Elizabeth	JUL 18 1818
LOVEJOY, Amos	MONCRIEFF, Catherine V.	JUL 28 1858
LOVEJOY, Elizabeth Ann	NAYLOR, James George	JAN 16 1845
LOVEJOY, Ellen W.	KEENE, William E.G.	JUN 12 1848
LOVEJOY, Harriet	STANLEY, Thomas	APR 20 1837
LOVEJOY, Harriet A.	GREEN, William H.	APR 30 1855
LOVEJOY, John N.	BEDDO, Ann	JUL 01 1819
LOVEJOY, John T.	HURLEY, Lurana R.	MAR 06 1855

District of Columbia Marriage Licenses, 1811-1858

LOVEJOY, Mary	JOHNSON, Robert G.	DEC 01 1856
LOVEJOY, William	NALLY, Sarah	MAR 18 1829
LOVEJOY, Zedekiah	GUSLER, Barbara	FEB 27 1817
LOVELACE, Alethia	CLUBB, Levin	FEB 15 1825
LOVELACE, Harriet	GODDARD, Thomas	MAR 19 1839
LOVELACE, Jane	RAY, William	OCT 31 1842
LOVELACE, Mary Jane	HARMON, John L.	MAR 31 1845
LOVELACE, Philip	FRIZLE, Ann	NOV 28 1821
LOVELACE, Samuel	LUCAS, Barbara Ellen	FEB 07 1818
LOVELACE, William Riley	WHITMORE, Ann	MAY 16 1823
LOVELESS, Catharine	GOLDSMITH, James	APR 29 1852
LOVELESS, Cecelia	JOHNSON, James	MAY 10 1831
LOVELESS, Elijah	STEWART, Helena	NOV 21 1815
LOVELESS, Eliza	REISS, John H.	OCT 03 1846
LOVELESS, Elizabeth	MORTON, Geo. H.	JAN 28 1830
LOVELESS, Elizabeth	BRAMELL, James W.	JUN 22 1852
LOVELESS, Elizabeth Ann	STONE, John	SEP 11 1844
LOVELESS, Geo. Henry	GRIGGS, Frances C.	JUN 02 1849
LOVELESS, James	ROBEY, Elizh.	NOV 13 1815
LOVELESS, James A.	JOHNSON, Lucinda A.	JUN 08 1857
LOVELESS, John	GRAVES, Mary Elizabeth	DEC 31 1849
LOVELESS, John H.	JURDINSTINE, Mary L.	MAY 25 1847
LOVELESS, John W.	CLARK, Mary Ellen	FEB 15 1854
LOVELESS, Mary D.	WILLIAMS, Thomas G.	JUN 13 1846
LOVELESS, Mary Elizabeth	ELD, Henry Albert	NOV 30 1843
LOVELESS, Samuel H.	PAYNE, Mary	SEP 28 1846
LOVELESS, Sarah	JONES, Thomas	SEP 15 1834
LOVELESS, Sarah A.E.	LUSBY, James O.	SEP 29 1852
LOVELESS, Verlinder	SOPER, John O.	DEC 14 1815
LOVELESS, William	SPARROW, Mary	MAY 01 1813
LOVELISS, Ellen	GILL, Christopher	MAR 25 1858
LOVELISS, Rosanna	CROSS, Abraham	JUN 27 1836
LOVELL, Dorcas K. [Mrs.]	HUNT, Thomas F. [Capt.]	NOV 19 1829
LOVELL, James	KING, Dorcas	SEP 04 1822
LOVERING, Amelia	BRERETON, John A.	DEC 13 1815
LOVETT, Emma	BREESE, Saml. L.	JUN 20 1855
LOW, Abner W.	BROWN, Rosamond	JAN 16 1856
LOW, Catharine	FREE, George W.	OCT 28 1830
LOW, Martha	WARFIELD, William	SEP 25 1850
LOW, Mary	DAVIS, John	JUL 09 1839
LOW, Mary Jane	GATES, James R.	FEB 03 1854
LOWDEN, William	HOLLEY, Mary Ann (blk)	NOV 28 1832
LOWE, Andrew	HERSEY, Caroline	DEC 21 1837
LOWE, Ann Virginia	LUTRELL, John H.	NOV 17 1857
LOWE, Barbara	WOODWARD, Amon	MAR 20 1845
LOWE, Darkey	CARROLL, Daniel	DEC 28 1825
LOWE, Eckstine M.	DAVIS, Wm. M.	APR 04 1854
LOWE, Eliza H.S.	WOODWARD, John W.	JAN 10 1856
LOWE, Elizabeth	MAYO, William	JUL 14 1815
LOWE, Elizabeth	BALDING, Theopolis	DEC 24 1818
LOWE, Emily	WEBSTER, Samuel	JUL 22 1839
LOWE, Henrietta (blk)	NEWTON, Benjamin	NOV 14 1833
LOWE, Jacob	WILKERSON, Caroline V.	OCT 25 1854
LOWE, James W.	CRONION, Mary Ann	AUG 04 1858
LOWE, Jane	SMITH, John	AUG 20 1835
LOWE, Jane	GARRETT, David	APR 26 1850
LOWE, Jeremiah	FLETCHER, Elizabeth (blk)	JUN 15 1836
LOWE, John	GLOYD, Mary Jane	FEB 18 1835

District of Columbia Marriage Licenses, 1811-1858

LOWE, Joseph	FIELDS, Margaret	APR 03 1850
LOWE, Lloyd M.	BRYAN, Lucy Ann	MAY 01 1833
LOWE, Maggie E.	LENGARD, E. Newton	MAR 28 1856
LOWE, Margaret	COHICK, James	JUL 25 1812
LOWE, Margaret W.	RAWLINGS, J.W.	MAR 12 1857
LOWE, Margery A.	ELWELL, Francis H.	NOV 08 1832
LOWE, Martha	COURTANEY, John	AUG 15 1820
LOWE, Mary Ann	BALDWIN, William T.	JAN 15 1825
LOWE, Mary Ann	JANNEY, Edward	JAN 02 1834
LOWE, Mary Ann	CADLE, William	DEC 24 1842
LOWE, Mary Jane	BARRY, Francis, Jr.	FEB 03 1845
LOWE, Nathan	GLADMAN, Mary	JAN 29 1853
LOWE, Randolph	GREENWELL, Eliza	AUG 10 1821
LOWE, Teresa Ann	BLANCHARD, Constantine Andw.	AUG 12 1851
LOWE, Thomas	CROSS, Ann	DEC 26 1816
LOWE, Thomas	CLEMENTSON, Jane C.	JAN 18 1858
LOWE, Virginia	WESTCOTT, James	MAR 09 1848
LOWE, Warren	OWENS, Exy	DEC 01 1824
LOWE, Warren	ALLEN, Louisa C.	SEP 26 1854
LOWE, William M.	BAILEY, Sarah	NOV 10 1857
LOWELL, Thruston	HUNT, Camilla	DEC 27 1853
LOWMAN, Edward	BURCH, Nancy	JUL 24 1817
LOWMAN, Margaret Ann	MORELAND, Richard R.	OCT 27 1846
LOWMAN, Mary Ann	AUGUST, Samuel	JUL 23 1850
LOWMEYER, Mary	FRICK, Martin	OCT 18 1855
LOWNDES, Isaac	ROSS, Harriet Ann (blk)	OCT 26 1857
LOWNDES, Thomas	BROWN, Anne (blk)	SEP 10 1850
LOWRIE, Mary	BAIRD, Samuel	FEB 26 1834
LOWRIE, William F.	SHERIFF, Mary Elizabeth	NOV 21 1834
LOWRY, Allen	CONNELL, Eady	NOV 03 1814
LOWRY, Eliza	STEELE, James	OCT 24 1857
LOWRY, Elizabeth	RHODES, Daniel	MAY 20 1830
LOWRY, Henry M.	CALVERT, Mary Jane	JUN 04 1847
LOWRY, James H.	SAWYER, Ann [Mrs.]	APR 17 1833
LOWRY, Jane Margaret	WATERS, James T.	JUL 10 1847
LOWRY, John	DEEBLE, Ann Louisa	JAN 13 1848
LOWRY, Margaret	TAYLOR, Gillis	FEB 03 1834
LOWRY, Mary	WATERS, Elkanah	JUL 31 1832
LOWRY, Rosina M.	EASBY, John W.	JUL 29 1843
LOWRY, William	STEWART, Jane (blk)	MAY 19 1834
LOWRY, William H.	DEEBLE, Margaret Jane	MAY 16 1843
LOYD, William	PETTIT, Harriot	JUN 30 1825
LOYE, Ann	SHECKELLS, Theodore	FEB 07 1820
LOYED, Louisa A.	EDWARDS, Ogden J.	APR 22 1856
LOYUNY, William	COURTNEY, Mary	MAY 13 1852
LUBER, Lanehart	FOSTER, Elizabeth	OCT 08 1857
LUCAS, Ann	NICHOLS, William A.	APR 15 1824
LUCAS, Ann	BROADBECK, Henry	SEP 12 1832
LUCAS, Ann	BURLEY, Thomas	JAN 13 1857
LUCAS, Ann (blk)	CHAPMAN, Washington	MAY 28 1833
LUCAS, Ann Maria	SPENCER, Samuel H.	SEP 05 1843
LUCAS, Barbara Ellen	LOVELACE, Samuel	FEB 07 1818
LUCAS, Barbary	MILES, Samuel	AUG 01 1816
LUCAS, Bowen	LEWIS, Ellender	DEC 16 1815
LUCAS, Catherine	MANYAT, Anthony	DEC 10 1839
LUCAS, Charles B.	MARINER, Ellen	AUG 13 1846
LUCAS, Charlott F.	FISHER, David	APR 21 1845
LUCAS, David Henry	REED, Mary Catherine	AUG 17 1852

District of Columbia Marriage Licenses, 1811-1858

LUCAS, Eleanor	DATCHER, Francis	MAY 08 1817
LUCAS, Elizabeth Jane	TAYLOR, Edward C.	OCT 30 1849
LUCAS, Emily A.	LONGSON, James	SEP 25 1850
LUCAS, Francis	HICKS, Elizabeth	FEB 27 1849
LUCAS, George	KAIN, Maria (blk)	APR 20 1831
LUCAS, Henry	LEE, Louisa (blk)	MAR 14 1833
LUCAS, Ignatius	CUMBERLAND, Ann	SEP 28 1819
LUCAS, James	EDWARDS, Anne	JUL 05 1815
LUCAS, Jane	GERMON, Thomas J.	OCT 29 1853
LUCAS, John	COLLISON, Eliza	FEB 16 1828
LUCAS, John	MOZINGER, Ann	APR 22 1839
LUCAS, Lewis	LEVY, Louisa (blk)	NOV 30 1846
LUCAS, Maranda B.	SMITH, Thomas	FEB 25 1829
LUCAS, Margaret	LEWIS, James	NOV 17 1827
LUCAS, Margaret	HERBERT, Thomas	NOV 09 1854
LUCAS, Marian	COZENS, Gustavus	APR 04 1857
LUCAS, Martha (blk)	MUNROE, George	DEC 21 1848
LUCAS, Mary Ann	WALLER, Elijah	MAY 21 1838
LUCAS, Mary Ann	PENN, Edward	APR 25 1848
LUCAS, Mary E.	SORRELL, William T.	DEC 19 1854
LUCAS, Mary E.	FEARSON, Christopher C.	MAY 14 1855
LUCAS, Mary Eleanor	WILLETT, William H.	MAR 24 1848
LUCAS, Mary Elizabeth	LUCAS, Octavus Augustus	OCT 09 1847
LUCAS, Mary J. (blk)	HERBERT, James L.	JUN 25 1857
LUCAS, Nancy	HARRISON, Peter	APR 13 1829
LUCAS, Octavus Augustus	LUCAS, Mary Elizabeth	OCT 09 1847
LUCAS, Rachel Ann	LANE, Joseph	JUN 21 1845
LUCAS, Rezin	COOPER, Rebecca (blk)	APR 17 1857
LUCAS, Rosanna A.	RUST, Robert B.	FEB 01 1847
LUCAS, Sarah	HERBERT, William	NOV 07 1848
LUCAS, Sarah Agatha	BROWN, William	JAN 09 1844
LUCAS, Susan	DYER, Aloysius	MAY 10 1832
LUCAS, Taply	OLIVE, Mary	AUG 02 1844
LUCAS, Thomas	PULASKI, Ellen Louisa	MAY 11 1847
LUCAS, Wm. H.	LEE, Martha L.	JUN 20 1855
LUCE, Margaret	HARWOOD, Andrew A.	DEC 11 1844
LUCE, Olivia	LANSDALE, Philip	SEP 16 1841
LUCE, Stephen B.	HENLEY, Eliza	DEC 06 1854
LUCIUS, Robert	TAFFEE, Elizth.	JUL 20 1836
LUCKE, Margaret	SUTTON, James T.	DEC 09 1844
LUCKET, Amanda	TRACEY, James M.	JUL 02 1831
LUCKET, Julia Ann	FORREST, John	MAY 07 1844
LUCKET, Thomas	TAYLOR, Sarah Ann	APR 30 1844
LUCKETT, Alexander	PORTER, Mary Elizabeth	FEB 13 1851
LUCKETT, Catharine Ann	CLAXTON, Richard W.	OCT 27 1829
LUCKETT, David W.	HUNTER, Martha V.R.	FEB 18 1854
LUCKETT, Ellen	CLEMENTS, Charles	JUN 19 1851
LUCKETT, Francis	DOVE, Jane	SEP 21 1850
LUCKETT, John	MULLONEY, Margaret	JUL 24 1847
LUCKETT, Julia Ann	COX, James	JUN 05 1841
LUCKETT, LeGian J.	DOWNER, Minerva M.	OCT 22 1834
LUCKETT, Martha	BEALL, John R.	MAY 12 1831
LUCKETT, Mary E.	SPEILMAN, John	MAR 31 1845
LUCKETT, Robert P.	CLAXTON, Catharine A.	MAR 01 1858
LUCKSON, Elizabeth	RICHARDSON, Benjamin	MAY 18 1819
LUCOHESSI, Delia	MARCERON, John L.	AUG 21 1849
LUCUS, Augustus	CORIER, Abigal	JUN 07 1834
LUCUS, Carter	TINNY, Ann (blk)	JUL 21 1827

District of Columbia Marriage Licenses, 1811-1858

LUCUS, Elizabeth	WILLETT, Fielder Dorsett	JAN 17 1839
LUCUS, William	R[torn out], Sarah Ann	MAR 22 1838
LUDDY, Thomas	DUCY, Catharine	FEB 14 1833
LUDICKE, Henry	KNLAHEL, Johanna	MAY 01 1857
LUDWIG, Pierre J.	SELBY, Jinetta R.	APR 07 1858
LUEBER, Francis	SIMPSON, Hellen Marla	JUN 02 1828
LUEBER, Helen M.	ROLLÉ, Justus Albert	JAN 05 1858
LUECK, John	STORCK, Lena	DEC 25 1848
LUFBOROUGH, Barbara	OCH, George	SEP 14 1849
LUFBOROUGH, Eliza	BOHRER, Benj. S.	OCT 03 1820
LUFBOROUGH, John	BROWN, Louisa	JAN 26 1850
LUFBOROUGH, S.M.	BISSELL, S.B.	MAY 13 1840
LUFFELIN, Mary	NEWTON, Athamiss	APR 19 1816
LUGLER, Joseph	GRAY, Sarah Jane	MAY 29 1847
LUGLEY, Sarah Jane	FIELD, George	JUL 16 1852
LUGRO, John B.	KREEMER, Margaret Ann	JUL 11 1842
LULY, Fanny	GASSENHEIMER, Leopold	JAN 18 1856
LUM, A. Stewart	SHERWOOD, Helen C.	SEP 26 1853
LUNDY, Emmer K.	BATES, Mary	OCT 10 1848
LUNEY, Jane	O'HARRON, Thomas	MAR 25 1856
LUNSFORD, Mary E.	DREW, William O.	DEC 12 1850
LUNSFORD, William	PAYNE, Elizabeth Ann	NOV 08 1849
LUNT, Eza	HILL, Sarah	FEB 20 1830
LUNT, Julia	DAGGY, Peter	DEC 04 1851
LUPTON, Ann	McLAUGHLIN, John	JAN 31 1824
LUPTON, Ann	YOUNG, William	AUG 23 1849
LUPTON, Catharine	KEOGH, Michael	JUN 05 1819
LUPTON, Daniel Smith	MARLOW, Ann	SEP 19 1828
LUPTON, Isabella M.	KITTNER, John Henry	OCT 04 1851
LUPTON, Mary	DEVILLEN, Henry	MAR 01 1837
LUPTON, Mary Ann	BOTELER, Charles W.	OCT 09 1839
LUPTON, Nacey	SWEENY, James	MAR 17 1819
LURTEN, James	CROCKETT, Elizabeth	JUN 18 1847
LUSBY, A. Francis	GRAY, Lucy Ann	DEC 20 1852
LUSBY, Eliza	SHELTON, Samuel	FEB 25 1848
LUSBY, Elizabeth E.	TURNER, Thomas B.	FEB 27 1854
LUSBY, Elizabeth H.	STORM, George A.	DEC 12 1855
LUSBY, James	WILLIAMS, Adeline	NOV 16 1837
LUSBY, James	TAYLOR, Mary	JUL 11 1839
LUSBY, James H.	BERKLEY, Ann E.	FEB 20 1838
LUSBY, James H.	CHAMBERS, Ann Eliza	SEP 29 1840
LUSBY, James O.	LOVELESS, Sarah A.E.	SEP 29 1852
LUSBY, Lemuel L.	BRIGHT, Mary E.	OCT 23 1849
LUSBY, Lucretia	MARKS, Jacob	MAY 08 1844
LUSBY, Martha	TYLER, William H.	JUN 14 1845
LUSBY, Mary Ann	PRICE, John E.	NOV 14 1857
LUSBY, Noah	BURGESS, Sarah Ann	DEC 25 1820
LUSBY, Robert H.	McDERMOTT, Maria L.	DEC 22 1855
LUSBY, Sarah J.	HOWELL, William	JUN 12 1856
LUSBY, Virginia Ellen	RICHARDSON, George W.	MAY 16 1853
LUSBY, William Henry	THOMPSON, Susannah M.	DEC 27 1842
LUSE, Matthias, Jr.	DAVIS, Catherine	APR 17 1823
LUSKEY, Christianna	KING, George P.	MAY 27 1828
LUSKEY, Jacob	FRANKS, Emily	OCT 27 1840
LUSKEY, John G.	KALE, Christeen	DEC 27 1820
LUTHER, Daniel	PRICE, Mary Ann	DEC 26 1855
LUTJOHANN, Dorothea	MAIER, John	MAR 09 1857
LUTREL, Matilda	CHOPPER, William	JUL 19 1841

District of Columbia Marriage Licenses, 1811-1858

LUTRELL, James	BROWN, Matilda Ann	DEC 27 1828
LUTRELL, John H.	LOWE, Ann Virginia	NOV 17 1857
LUTT, Dorothy	SCHREKEL, Charles	OCT 23 1855
LUTTGENZ, Frances	BLAW, Herman	FEB 16 1852
LUTTLES, Pheba	BUTLER, Charles	AUG 07 1828
LUTZ, Agatha	SCHAEFFER, Ambrose	JAN 11 1856
LUTZ, Francis A.	FULLALOVE, Mary A.	NOV 15 1842
LUTZ, Jane C.	MYERS, Charles	SEP 10 1844
LUTZ, Martha D.	MARDEN, Nathaniel M.	APR 23 1856
LUTZ, Mary Ann	MARDEN, Nathaniel	JUN 09 1824
LUTZ, Mary C.	GEIGER, Frederick E.	APR 09 1849
LUTZ, Melvina	ADLER, Morris	OCT 03 1827
LUXAN, Horace	JOHNSON, Teresa	JUL 06 1815
LUXEN, Emma F.	BURNETT, William T.	APR 03 1852
LUXON, Mary Ann	BROWN, Archibald	MAR 20 1837
LUXON, Susan	TAYMAN, Benjamin J.	JUL 26 1842
LUXON, Thomas J.	WETHERALL, Ann Elizabeth	JAN 25 1843
LUXTON, Mary Ann	BEAN, William R.	JUN 23 1840
LUXTON, Sarah	STICKLE, George	MAY 30 1825
LUXUM, Mary Ann	FINLEY, Henry	JUL 19 1824
LYCETT, Bridget	MINITOR, Thomas	OCT 01 1853
LYCETT, Catharine	BURKE, John	JAN 03 1855
LYCETT, Johanna	CLEARY, Patrick	JAN 04 1856
LYDAN, Margaret	MARR, Thomas	OCT 11 1820
LYDANE, Sarah Ann	FAWCETT, David	FEB 14 1855
LYDDAN, Nancy	DERMODY, Walter W.	FEB 15 1849
LYDDANE, William	HILL, Mary Jane	JUN 11 1853
LYDICK, Francis	NEVITT, Mary	NOV 12 1816
LYDNOR, Thomas W.	CHAPIN, Sarah L.M.	OCT 15 1840
LYDON, Mary	TOOLE, Peter	JUN 28 1856
LYE, Ellen	FOX, Michael	SEP 03 1833
LYLAS, Henry	DAVIS, Rease	APR 24 1820
LYLES, Annie E.	DIXON, Frank Wood	NOV 22 1852
LYLES, Enoch	FITZSIMMONS, Joanna	OCT 12 1840
LYLES, Henrietta E.	MARSHALL, Thomas	NOV 29 1855
LYLES, Henry	LEISHURE, Harriet J.	SEP 11 1845
LYLES, James	HULL, Esther	MAR 09 1816
LYLES, James	GOSSUM, Matilda	FEB 15 1826
LYLES, John Washington	SIMMS, Rebecca	MAY 31 1841
LYLES, Julia A.	JACOBS, Francis	MAY 19 1830
LYLES, Margarett	SIMPSON, Gabriel	MAR 18 1830
LYLES, Mary A.	SHORTER, John	OCT 13 1856
LYLES, Rosanna	ST. CLAIR, George	MAR 23 1836
LYLES, Sarah M.	JOHNSON, George	JAN 19 1841
LYLES, Sarah M.	MARSHALL, Thomas	SEP 03 1846
LYLES, Susanna	WILLIAMS, Levi	JUL 14 1835
LYLES, William	KITSON, Ann	AUG 20 1830
LYLES, William H.	CRUMP, Ann E.	AUG 24 1848
LYMBURN, John	HAYNES, Mary	JUL 05 1814
LYMBURN, Nancy Pearson	TURNER, Charles William	MAY 22 1833
LYNCH, Amelia Jane	WHITE, John Thos.	MAY 28 1853
LYNCH, Ann	SULLIVAN, Edward	OCT 15 1829
LYNCH, Bartholomew	MAHONEY, Mary	NOV 30 1853
LYNCH, Bridget	LYNCH, Patrick	FEB 23 1852
LYNCH, Bridget	GARVAN, James	JUN 18 1855
LYNCH, Catharine	FITZGERALD, John	NOV 14 1853
LYNCH, Catherine	GIBSON, William	JAN 12 1824
LYNCH, Charles	HARRISON, Mary Ann	FEB 27 1854

District of Columbia Marriage Licenses, 1811-1858

LYNCH, Daniel	MILIDY, Bridget	AUG 12 1854
LYNCH, Daniel	MADDEN, Ellen	SEP 27 1856
LYNCH, Daniel	SULLIVAN, Mary	JUN 03 1857
LYNCH, Dorothy	BURKE, [blank]	JAN 30 1843
LYNCH, Elizabeth	TALLEY, Josiah	JUN 15 1812
LYNCH, Elizabeth	ECKTON, William	SEP 22 1836
LYNCH, Ellen	O'BRYAN, Timothy	MAY 06 1851
LYNCH, Ellen	LEE, Patrick	JAN 21 1854
LYNCH, Ellen	KENNEDY, Michael	JUL 21 1856
LYNCH, Ellen	CONNELL, Morris	JUL 06 1858
LYNCH, Francis A.	FARMER, Peter A.	NOV 14 1857
LYNCH, George Isaac	OSBORNE, Elizabeth Ann	OCT 06 1854
LYNCH, Henry	WALLACE, Mary	JAN 19 1825
LYNCH, James	OFFUTT, Susan	NOV 05 1839
LYNCH, James	FLANNAGAN, Hannora	JUN 23 1841
LYNCH, James	PHILIPS, Jane	JUL 24 1841
LYNCH, James	KANE, Jane	FEB 07 1853
LYNCH, James	GOODWIN, Mary	JUN 06 1854
LYNCH, James J.	THOMAS, Sarah A.	MAR 08 1856
LYNCH, James W.	GOWAN, Eliza Ann	OCT 08 1844
LYNCH, Jane	LAUGHRY, Hugh	SEP 26 1838
LYNCH, Jane	WARD, Francis	AUG 19 1844
LYNCH, Jane R.	LACEY, Jane E.	MAY 08 1855
LYNCH, Jannie F.	MEACHAM, James H.	AUG 19 1856
LYNCH, Johanna	SCANLON, Patrick	JAN 24 1853
LYNCH, Johanna	DONOVAN, Dennis	FEB 20 1855
LYNCH, John	GARNER, Mary	APR 15 1820
LYNCH, John	HANESSY, Mary	FEB 05 1833
LYNCH, John	PULIZZI, Agatha C.	NOV 04 1834
LYNCH, John	COLLINS, Alice	JUL 31 1852
LYNCH, John	BARRY, Catherine	JUN 25 1853
LYNCH, John	LIGHTFOOT, Mary Ann	JAN 02 1856
LYNCH, Julia	DOTY, Geo. W.	MAR 17 1854
LYNCH, Lorenzo	SHEETS, Mary Melvina	FEB 19 1833
LYNCH, Lucy Ann	ARMSTRONG, John T.	JUN 13 1835
LYNCH, Margaret	KIERNAN, Patrick	SEP 06 1851
LYNCH, Margaret A.	SEBASTIN, Franklin	APR 03 1854
LYNCH, Maria	DAVIS, Edward	JUL 29 1841
LYNCH, Martin	FITZGERALD, Margaret	DEC 11 1851
LYNCH, Mary	GARNER, John	OCT 17 1826
LYNCH, Mary	KILLEGAN, James	MAR 10 1851
LYNCH, Mary	DONIGAN, Thomas	MAY 18 1854
LYNCH, Mary Ann	NEWMAN, Saml.	DEC 24 1845
LYNCH, Mary Jane	SLATFORD, Robert	JUL 18 1856
LYNCH, Mary Kain	SWEENY, Edward	JAN 14 1826
LYNCH, Michael	DONOVAN, Mary	JAN 14 1854
LYNCH, Michael	HART, Ellen	FEB 04 1854
LYNCH, Michael	GREEN, Ellen	NOV 01 1854
LYNCH, Michael	SULLIVAN, Julia	FEB 21 1857
LYNCH, Michael	BARRY, Bridget	JAN 14 1858
LYNCH, Nancy	RAWLING, Benjamin	SEP 10 1832
LYNCH, Patrick	MOCKABY, Margaret Ann	FEB 13 1835
LYNCH, Patrick	LYNCH, Bridget	FEB 23 1852
LYNCH, Patrick	BLANEY, Bridget	DEC 10 1856
LYNCH, Peter	RILEY, Catharine	APR 29 1856
LYNCH, Peter A.	WOOD, Mary Ann	SEP 07 1843
LYNCH, Rebecca	KIDWELL, George	JUN 26 1850
LYNCH, Rebecca Ellen	ERVIN, George H.	JUL 29 1851

District of Columbia Marriage Licenses, 1811-1858

LYNCH, Ruth Ann	GINGELL, James	FEB 29 1848
LYNCH, Sisey Ann	McLEOD, Alexander N.	DEC 03 1855
LYNCH, Susanna	SCHAEFFER, August	FEB 03 1857
LYNCH, Thomas	TANGEY, Margaret	JUL 06 1853
LYNCH, Timothy	BLANEY, Mary	APR 20 1854
LYNCH, Trueman	LANGLEY, Matilda	JAN 01 1828
LYNCH, William	EVANS, Mary	NOV 20 1853
LYNDALL, George	TOWNSEND, Sarah	JAN 12 1837
LYNDALL, Thomas	RODGERS, Mary	NOV 02 1824
LYNE, Larenia [Mrs.]	JACKSON, Henry	JAN 02 1833
LYNE, Lavinia H.	MURPHY, Robert C.	AUG 22 1853
LYNN, Andrew J.	GOODWIN, Nancy A.	MAR 20 1856
LYNN, Isaac	KEYS, Ujamah	DEC 27 1830
LYNN, John W.	BELL, Emily M.	DEC 14 1854
LYNN, Joseph F.	GHEEN, Frances A.	DEC 06 1856
LYNN, LeRoy W.	THOMAS, Malvina	JUL 01 1844
LYNN, Luther L.	CURRELL, Mary F.J.	MAR 04 1839
LYNN, Mary C.	DAVIS, John S.	JUN 01 1852
LYNN, William	JOHNS, Jane M.	FEB 08 1832
LYON, Barbara	ROBERTS, Matthew	FEB 15 1831
LYON, Charles	JEFFERS, Catharine	DEC 11 1816
LYON, Evan	BARNES, Eveline	NOV 29 1831
LYON, Julia E.	FARR, George	AUG 01 1855
LYON, Margaret	O'BRIEN, Michael	NOV 07 1851
LYON, Mary	KURTZ, Daniel	JUN 04 1814
LYON, Mary	ELIASON, Elias A.	APR 17 1832
LYON, William H.	BRAUNER, Elizabeth	OCT 08 1849
LYONS, Amanda	CLARKE, William D.	AUG 30 1852
LYONS, Ann	MAUXLEY, Samuel	JAN 11 1820
LYONS, Ann	DERICK, William S.	AUG 08 1827
LYONS, Catharine	BRENAN, Patrick	DEC 03 1851
LYONS, Daniel R.E.	BOSWELL, Susan E.	SEP 04 1850
LYONS, Eliza	MINNIS, Thomas	DEC 21 1826
LYONS, Elizabeth	McDERMOTT, Cornelius	AUG 31 1824
LYONS, Emily Virginia	NOLAND, Theofilus	MAR 19 1849
LYONS, Emly	EDMONSON, James	AUG 26 1841
LYONS, Emma	DERRICK, Alexander Hamilton	MAY 31 1843
LYONS, Georgiana	FORCE, William O.	OCT 19 1841
LYONS, John	HURLEY, Ann	JAN 19 1828
LYONS, John	BROOKE, Ann	APR 23 1839
LYONS, Lavinia Blake	FRASER, James	AUG 04 1853
LYONS, Margaret	McNAMARA, Martin	APR 18 1857
LYONS, Mary	DAERY, John	JAN 09 1840
LYONS, Mary Jane	RILEY, James	MAY 31 1847
LYONS, Rachel	JEWELL, Wilson	APR 22 1824
LYONS, Samuel	WOOD, Elizabeth (blk)	NOV 07 1853
LYONS, Samuel	WOOD, Elizabeth (blk)	NOV 08 1853
LYONS, Treacy (blk)	PLENTY, Robert	SEP 30 1847
LYRE, Mary	SCHANATT, Adam	JAN 13 1841
LYSETT, John	FITZGERALD, Margaret	FEB 14 1851
LYSTAN, Bridget	MADIGIN, Patrick	NOV 07 1857

District of Columbia Marriage Licenses, 1811-1858

M

MAACK, Bridget	CODMORE, John	JUL 17 1855
MABURY, Mary Ann	KING, Wm. H.	FEB 22 1845
MACABEE, Emilie	OWENS, Basil	JAN 06 1848
MACABOY, James	REDIN, Mary	FEB 19 1841
MACAULEY, Charles S. [Capt.]	DICKINS, Lilia Elizth.	OCT 20 1831
MACAVOY, Peter	CONLEY, Eliza	JAN 26 1856
MacCABBIN, Thomas L.	SHOEMAKER, Elizabeth	OCT 10 1848
MacCAULY, Carlton	BALDWIN, Nelly	JAN 19 1816
MacCUBBIN, Ellen	SWEETING, Henry W.	JUL 03 1830
MacDANIEL, Albert	STORM, Julia Ann Eliza	APR 10 1829
MacDANIEL, Elila	GRAY, Elias	JUN 28 1819
MacDANIEL, George	BATT, Lavinia	JUN 18 1857
MacDANIEL, James	READ, Dolly	MAR 26 1816
MacDANIEL, Lucy C.	DAVIS, Joshua	NOV 20 1838
MacDAVIT, Bridget	FOY, James	DEC 16 1830
MacDONALD, Eliza	HASKELL, Daniel T.A.	JUL 24 1827
MACE, Ann Eliza	TWIST, Stephen	JUL 20 1827
MACE, Joseph	FORMAN, Charlotte	SEP 20 1853
MACE, Margaret	WRIGHT, Charles B.	DEC 13 1832
MACE, Thomas	BALDWIN, Frances Ann	DEC 23 1852
MACE, William	COLE, Lydia	SEP 11 1845
MacELEGET, James	TRACY, Harriot	APR 15 1830
MACER, Gertrude A.	GODDARD, Thomas	SEP 04 1857
MacETEE, Sarah	BOUTCHER, Alfred	JUN 26 1818
MacFARLAND, Caroline	RANSDALE, David D.	AUG 11 1836
MacGILL, Charles R.	WILSON, Rowanna W.H.	FEB 19 1833
MacGILL, Thomas	WILSON, Emely	FEB 15 1831
MacGILL, William	LANSDALE, Ellenor	JAN 21 1835
MacGLENON, Mary	COOK, Thomas	AUG 15 1833
MacGREGOR, Ellen M.	EWELL, Jesse [Dr.]	OCT 23 1827
MACH, Catharine	SCANLIN, Daniel	MAY 01 1852
MACHEN, Deborah	SANFORD, Whiting	MAR 07 1823
MACHEN, Lewis	WEBSTER, Caroline	DEC 03 1816
MacINTEE, Samuel	SEMMS, Eleanor	JUN 09 1818
MacINTOSH, Maria	WELCH, Hugh W.	APR 30 1818
MACK, Bridget	SHA, David	JUL 17 1852
MACK, Dennis	SHANCKNESSY, Margaret	JUL 07 1857
MACK, John	SPARROW, Rosetta	OCT 01 1816
MACK, John	MUNTS, Catharine	JUN 25 1855
MACK, Margt.	MALONE, Edward	JAN 26 1856
MACK, Martin	SMITH, Elizabeth	APR 19 1852
MACK, Mary	FELVEY, Daniel	JUN 04 1852
MACK, Mary	MORGAN, James	MAY 19 1853
MACK, Mary Ann	GRAVES, George W.	NOV 05 1857
MACKABEE, James R.	BECKETT, Elizabeth	DEC 14 1843
MACKABEE, John	NALLY, Lucy	DEC 19 1849
MACKABEE, Mary	WARD, Robert	OCT 23 1845
MACKABOY, Catharine	ROBINSON, John H.	MAY 08 1850
MACKALL, Benjamin F.	WHANN, Ann Maria	APR 06 1813
MACKALL, Brooke	SIMPSON, Jane M.E.	AUG 13 1834
MACKALL, Catharine	FILE, Stanley	OCT 09 1851
MACKALL, H. Clinton	NOYES, Mary E.	MAY 01 1841
MACKALL, Harriet M.	TAYLOR, Walter S.	JUN 16 1835
MACKALL, Harriot	BUCHLY, Christian	SEP 23 1818
MACKALL, Hellen M.	GUNNELL, James S. [Dr.]	OCT 12 1825
MACKALL, Henny	JONES, Fortune (blk)	OCT 05 1822

District of Columbia Marriage Licenses, 1811-1858

MACKALL, Richard L.	BELT, Anne C.	DEC 12 1839
MACKAY, William	CAMPBELL, Ann	NOV 30 1817
MACKBEE, Eliza V.	DAVIS, John W.	MAY 01 1856
MACKBEE, Saml.	FOWLER, Sarah	DEC 27 1831
MACKBEE, Sarah Ann	NALLEY, John	DEC 27 1831
MACKEAR, Mary	WEISNER, Thomas	OCT 31 1816
MacKEWON, Jane S.	LANGLEY, Francis H.	APR 29 1853
MACKEY, Ann Jane	CRUIKSHANK, Richard	APR 06 1830
MACKEY, Betsey	MORRISON, John	AUG 22 1832
MACKEY, Elizabeth	JOSTLE, Henry B.	SEP 16 1829
MACKEY, Elizabeth	GATTON, Edward	AUG 17 1847
MACKEY, Martha	SEAWELL, Washington [Lt.]	JUL 02 1832
MACKEY, Mary	SEAWELL, Francis T.	MAY 27 1824
MACKEY, Thomas	BARRETT, Henrietta	FEB 10 1838
MACKEY, William	NEVITT, Sarah	JUL 08 1824
MACKEY, William	ROBERSON, Rebecca	JAN 07 1845
MACKEYSEY, Mary	McCOY, Alexander	FEB 25 1819
MACKIN, Patrick	TRACY, Catherine	AUG 02 1836
MACKINNA, Neil	GREEN, Mary	MAR 10 1818
MACKNESS, Drucilla	DUDLEY, Henry	AUG 10 1827
MACKNEY, John L.	HARRISON, Matilda A.	DEC 19 1850
MACKY, Adaline	SCHANDLER, William A.	JUL 07 1831
MACLERY, James	JAMES, Christiana	MAR 30 1819
MacNAMARA, John	DWYER, Bridget	JAN 11 1851
MacNEER, Joseph E.	BIRCH, Margaret Ann	FEB 01 1843
MACNEW, Bazil	DUVALL, Caroline	SEP 28 1831
MACOMB, Alexandrine	STANTON, Henry [Maj.]	FEB 11 1834
MACOMB, Catharine	MASON, John, Jr.	APR 02 1827
MACOMB, Czarina	MACOMB, John N.	MAR 06 1838
MACOMB, Jane Octavia	MILLER, Morris Smith	JAN 11 1841
MACOMB, John N.	MACOMB, Czarina	MAR 06 1838
MACOMB, John Navarre	RODGERS, Nannie	MAR 30 1850
MACOMB, Samuel	SERRO, Ann Eliza	DEC 28 1835
MacPHERSON, Joseph S.	WASHINGTON, Mary E.	JAN 28 1819
MacPHERSON, Susan W.	EDWARDS, John S.	MAY 08 1838
MACUBBIN, Moses	DAWSON, Ann	AUG 11 1832
MADDEN, Bridget	ABBOTT, Bryan	JUL 22 1829
MADDEN, Elizabeth R.	PORTER, Daniel Parker	JUN 09 1834
MADDEN, Ellen	LYNCH, Daniel	SEP 27 1856
MADDEN, William	HEPBURN, Mary Ann (blk)	OCT 05 1854
MADDERLAGN, Helena	SCHEIDEL, Frederick	OCT 20 1834
MADDISON, Austin	ELLIS, Elizabeth	JUL 27 1848
MADDORE, Betsey	CUMSTRONG, Thomas	JUL 27 1816
MADDOX, Alexander	GATES, Christianna	SEP 06 1836
MADDOX, Alexander	GREEN, Mary Jane	MAY 10 1852
MADDOX, Ann	GIPSON, John	JUL 10 1849
MADDOX, Charlotte Ann	YERBY, Charles J.	JUN 02 1834
MADDOX, Clara	SPATES, George	AUG 24 1857
MADDOX, Eliza	NUGENT, James	NOV 30 1847
MADDOX, Elizabeth	ACTON, Aquilla	OCT 18 1825
MADDOX, Elizabeth J.	MADDOX, Wm. B.	APR 29 1856
MADDOX, Elizth. J.	WELSH, Edward S.	OCT 05 1853
MADDOX, Huriah	DUBLERVEY, Margaret	JUN 19 1828
MADDOX, James M.	FUGITT, Matilda	MAR 24 1857
MADDOX, Jane	TUCKER, James	DEC 27 1849
MADDOX, John	BARKLEY, Elizth.	FEB 09 1828
MADDOX, John T.	HAMMILL, Margaert	DEC 17 1835
MADDOX, Kate	NIXON, John W.	AUG 19 1856

District of Columbia Marriage Licenses, 1811-1858

MADDOX, Margaret	ADDAMS, William	JUL 27 1836
MADDOX, Margaret	WILLIAMS, John	NOV 17 1838
MADDOX, Martha E.	BELL, George J.	DEC 08 1855
MADDOX, Mary Ann	BOUCHER, Offert	NOV 12 1838
MADDOX, Nancy	APPLER, Jonathan	SEP 29 1812
MADDOX, Rebecca	BROOKS, Ignatius	MAY 27 1819
MADDOX, Susanah	THOMPSON, William	OCT 30 1832
MADDOX, Thomas H.	FLETCHER, Marion E.	JUN 30 1857
MADDOX, Thomas L.	DAVIS, Dorcas	JUN 01 1812
MADDOX, William C.	CARTER, Frances	SEP 28 1827
MADDOX, William T.	KING, Ann Maria	JAN 26 1819
MADDOX, Wm. B.	MADDOX, Elizabeth J.	APR 29 1856
MADELLA, John H.	JACKSON, Marianna E. (blk)	JUN 13 1854
MADELLA, Louisa (blk)	WOODWARD, John	DEC 26 1844
MADERIA, W.J.	CASSADY, Lola Montez A.	MAY 26 1853
MADES, Charles	SCHADD, Wilhelmina	MAR 30 1857
MADIGAN, Bridget	MADIGAN, Patrick	JUN 12 1858
MADIGAN, Catherine	GALVIN, Thomas	JAN 10 1852
MADIGAN, Eliza	CERRICK, John	SEP 27 1855
MADIGAN, Elizabeth	BURKE, Timothy	AUG 12 1854
MADIGAN, John	CASEY, Bridget	DEC 20 1856
MADIGAN, Luke	CONSERDINE, Eliza	JUL 21 1853
MADIGAN, Mary	McQUEEN, Patrick	NOV 20 1852
MADIGAN, Mary	BOYCE, James	DEC 27 1855
MADIGAN, Michael	MUNSTED, Ann	JUL 20 1853
MADIGAN, Patrick	HATTIGAN, Catherine	APR 30 1856
MADIGAN, Patrick	MADIGAN, Bridget	JUN 12 1858
MADIGIN, Patrick	LYSTAN, Bridget	NOV 07 1857
MADISON, Ann	McCALTY, James	OCT 03 1850
MADISON, Clarissa (blk)	WESTON, Lewis	NOV 30 1857
MADISON, Elizabeth B.	ROBINSON, William	AUG 30 1851
MADISON, Francis	MORSE, Matilda (blk)	APR 06 1835
MADISON, Luke	WARD, Grace Ann (blk)	MAR 01 1854
MADLOCK, Mary	FREEDY, Christian	AUG 28 1832
MAEGLE, Margaret	ULLE, John Abraham	JUL 25 1853
MAEGLE, Michael	MERKLE, Elizabeth	DEC 17 1832
MAFFITT, Elizabeth	MILLS, John	NOV 06 1838
MAFITT, Margaret Davidson	CARPENTER, Hamilton A.	APR 25 1839
MAGAR, Benjamin C.	ADAMS, Chloe Ann	FEB 09 1839
MAGAR, John	BELL, Winifred Connor	DEC 21 1854
MAGAR, Marion F.	HAYNIE, Hancock H.	SEP 28 1857
MAGAR, Mary Elizabeth	GAINGER, James H.	JAN 11 1844
MAGEE, Barney	WHALAN, Mary Ann	MAY 27 1845
MAGEE, Elizabeth	GREEN, James	JAN 27 1847
MAGEE, Ellen	FRAZER, John	JUN 22 1850
MAGEE, James	CURRANS, Mary Ann	JUN 05 1849
MAGEE, John	SNOWDEN, Mrs. [Arabella]	FEB 18 1831
MAGEE, Maria (blk)	SCOTT, Robert	MAR 13 1833
MAGEE, Martha Josephine	STEWART, John Adams	FEB 18 1857
MAGEE, Mary A.F.	CHENEY, Joseph Warren	JUN 14 1849
MAGEE, Robert F.	BERRY, Sarah Catharine	OCT 17 1843
MAGEE, Sarah Ann	WHITE, Gilbert	OCT 21 1824
MAGEE, Thomas	DONNELLY, Elizabeth	JAN 06 1855
MAGILL, Benedict	MILLER, Barbara	OCT 27 1842
MAGILL, Elizth. C.	BIGGS, James E.	MAY 13 1846
MAGILL, Henrietta	LINKINS, Danl.	OCT 08 1840
MAGILL, John W.	MYER, Kate C.	DEC 11 1855
MAGILL, Lucinda	WHITE, Thomas	JUN 22 1820

District of Columbia Marriage Licenses, 1811-1858

MAGILL, Saml.	MYER, Christiana Miacha	NOV 09 1816
MAGILL, Susannah	FOWLER, James J.	JAN 07 1845
MAGILL, William B.	BRONAUGH, Mary Jane	SEP 04 1850
MAGIN, Patrick	McCONNELLY, Hannah	AUG 05 1824
MAGINNIS, William H.	STEWART, Mary	JAN 09 1858
MAGLE, Elizabeth	WAGNER, John C.	NOV 07 1853
MAGNESS, Elizabeth	DARGNE, Joseph	JAN 31 1820
MAGNIER, Thomas	SHINDLE, Sarah	MAY 01 1822
MAGNIER, Thomas	CROSS, Eliza	OCT 20 1836
MAGNUS, Frederick	ATCHERSON, Eliza Ann	AUG 15 1843
MAGONEGLE, Alexander	SMITH, Mary Ann	DEC 23 1830
MAGRATH, Henrietta	BOWMAN, Henry D.	OCT 06 1844
MAGRAW, Juliana	ARMOUR, James W.	NOV 14 1820
MAGRUDER, Adlina E.	JASPER, Daniel S.	NOV 11 1849
MAGRUDER, Alfred	MINNIS, Nancy	AUG 19 1835
MAGRUDER, Alfred	KNOWLES, Mary D.	DEC 12 1846
MAGRUDER, Ann E.	LINTHICUM, O.M. [Dr. Otho]	SEP 02 1823
MAGRUDER, Ann E.V.	EVERLY, Wm.	SEP 20 1854
MAGRUDER, Ann M.L.	BRANCH, Wm. B.	JAN 12 1814
MAGRUDER, Belford	COUSINS, Harriett	FEB 06 1840
MAGRUDER, Eliza J. (blk)	CISSELL, Jackson	DEC 03 1853
MAGRUDER, Elizabeth	HARRISON, Gustavus	JUN 01 1815
MAGRUDER, Elizabeth L.	MOSHER, James	DEC 08 1819
MAGRUDER, Ellen	MAURY, Richard B.	APR 13 1831
MAGRUDER, Fielder	CARROLL, Elizabeth	MAY 01 1826
MAGRUDER, Fielder	YOUNG, [Ann]	APR 09 1835
MAGRUDER, Fielder M.	CUMMINGS, Mary Ann	FEB 15 1853
MAGRUDER, Francis	COX, Mary Jane (blk)	JAN 29 1857
MAGRUDER, Greenberry	OFFUTT, Julia L.	MAY 05 1836
MAGRUDER, Haswell	BOYD, Adaline	JUL 04 1832
MAGRUDER, Hezekiah	CRITTENDEN, Harriet Lacy	MAR 03 1830
MAGRUDER, Hezekiah	CHAPMAN, Mary	JUN 30 1841
MAGRUDER, Jesse H.	PENN, Rebecca	JUL 09 1825
MAGRUDER, Julian	JOHNSON, Margaret A.	APR 19 1853
MAGRUDER, Louisa	DIGGS, Sothern	APR 21 1845
MAGRUDER, Martha (blk)	FOSTER, Thomas	SEP 03 1857
MAGRUDER, Mary	SUIT, Nathaniel	JUL 07 1826
MAGRUDER, Mary	STAMP, John	DEC 23 1828
MAGRUDER, Mary Alice	DOWNMAN, Rawleigh Wm.	NOV 08 1854
MAGRUDER, Mary Ann (blk)	YOUNG, Henry	MAY 15 1856
MAGRUDER, Milfred	GRAY, Eleanor (blk)	NOV 09 1829
MAGRUDER, Nathaniel	RIGDEN, Louisa	MAY 07 1828
MAGRUDER, Rezin	YOUNG, Harriet (blk)	JAN 15 1852
MAGRUDER, Thomas C.	MORGAN, Elizabeth O.	FEB 05 1844
MAGRUDER, Thomas J.	BOTELER, Sarah A.P.	MAR 27 1844
MAGRUDER, Wesley L.	MULLICAN, Elizabeth V.	MAY 15 1855
MAGRUDER, William B.	HUTCHINSON, Elizabeth B.	SEP 08 1835
MAGRUDER, William B., M.D.	VanWYCK, Sarah	FEB 16 1854
MAGRUDER, William L.	GOODRICK, Treasy Ann	AUG 02 1838
MAGUIRE, Edward	DONNELLY, Ann	DEC 01 1837
MAGUIRE, Ellen	KEENAN, Terence	JUN 05 1858
MAGUIRE, James	WOOD, Mary E.A.	MAR 05 1839
MAGUIRE, Maragratee Ann	EPHLINE, James A.	OCT 23 1848
MAGUIRE, Martin	CLANSY, Margaret	APR 18 1853
MAGUIRE, Mary Ann	POOLEY, Thomas	OCT 13 1825
MAGUIRE, Patrick	CROWLEY, Catharine	DEC 31 1851
MAGUIRE, Rosanna	WOOLLS, William	AUG 19 1840
MAHAGEN, John	SPEDEN, Jannet	JAN 04 1849

District of Columbia Marriage Licenses, 1811-1858

MAHANY, Anna (blk)	BROWN, William	JUN 09 1840
MAHAR, Catherine	McMAHON, Thomas	JUL 24 1857
MAHAR, John	FLINN, Margaret	JUL 27 1853
MAHAR, Mary	SEXTON, Matthew	AUG 16 1856
MAHEN, Elizabeth Ellen	HARRIS, John	JAN 22 1857
MAHER, Dennis	FENNON, Bridget	OCT 07 1852
MAHER, James	HAMILTON, Mary	OCT 04 1849
MAHER, Johanna	RING, James	JUL 24 1852
MAHER, Margaret	HILL, William	JUN 15 1843
MAHER, Mary	BRENNAN, John	FEB 13 1852
MAHER, Mary Ann	DOLAN, Edward	SEP 28 1855
MAHER, Sarah Jane	McKIERNAN, Peter	MAY 03 1851
MAHEW, Elizabeth	ANDERSON, William	MAR 18 1815
MAHEW, Mary	BUTLER, Henry	MAY 18 1815
MAHEW, William B.	GIBSON, Mary A.	JAN 11 1825
MAHOENEY, Warren	BURROWS, Eliza (blk)	NOV 16 1847
MAHON, Alexander M.	COXE, Mary G.	MAR 28 1846
MAHON, David N., Dr.	MONTGOMERY, Julia M.	DEC 22 1851
MAHON, David W.	SMITH, Jane O.	SEP 25 1850
MAHONE, William	BUTLER, Otelia	FEB 07 1855
MAHONEY, Daniel	HARTIGAN, Mary	AUG 07 1855
MAHONEY, Dennis	CARAHAN, Sarah	AUG 23 1858
MAHONEY, Dominie	JONES, Priscilla	MAY 21 1846
MAHONEY, Eleanor	VENABLE, Joseph	FEB 25 1818
MAHONEY, Eleanor	LEE, William	JUN 04 1819
MAHONEY, Ellen	DACEY, Cornelius	MAY 16 1851
MAHONEY, Ellen	CROWLEY, Patrick	JAN 29 1856
MAHONEY, Ellen	LONG, Dennis	JUL 10 1857
MAHONEY, Joanna	HOGAN, Thomas	OCT 18 1849
MAHONEY, John	MAHONY, Mary	APR 21 1825
MAHONEY, John	NIEL, Mary	JUL 13 1855
MAHONEY, Martha A.	McDONNELL, William	JUL 06 1857
MAHONEY, Mary	LYNCH, Bartholomew	NOV 30 1853
MAHONEY, Mary (blk)	MANKINS, John C.	JUL 01 1858
MAHONEY, Mary E.	NEWMAN, W.L.	MAR 25 1856
MAHONEY, Nancy	CROWLEY, Timothy	FEB 07 1826
MAHONEY, Rebecca	HERRELL, James M.	AUG 23 1855
MAHONEY, Samuel	AGETT, Mary	JUN 12 1856
MAHONY, Ann	FISHER, George	APR 12 1819
MAHONY, Battw.	HEARLY, [blank]	MAY 05 1832
MAHONY, Catherine	BYRNE, James	JUN 17 1813
MAHONY, Cornelius	O'BRIEN, Ellen	JUL 14 1857
MAHONY, Mary	MAHONEY, John	APR 21 1825
MAHONY, Susan	DENISON, John	APR 16 1831
MAHONY, Thomas	CLUB, Elizabeth	JAN 23 1823
MAHORN, Rosa L.	MORRIS, John	DEC 18 1854
MAHORNAY, Ann	LEE, William	JUN 10 1833
MAHORNE, Sarah E.	ROSE, Charles C.	JAN 23 1855
MAHORNEY, Elizabeth	LLOYD, John	JAN 29 1846
MAHORNEY, Frances	OFFUTT, George W.	JUL 27 1848
MAHORNEY, George	O'BRIAN, Elizabeth	AUG 06 1850
MAHORNEY, Henrietta	LATHRUM, John E.	OCT 19 1850
MAHORNEY, Henrietta O.	HORRELL, John E.	AUG 11 1851
MAHORNEY, Mary	RUSSELL, Judson	OCT 24 1829
MAHORNEY, Mary E.	ROBEY, Henry	APR 22 1833
MAHORNEY, Mary E.	TUCKER, William T.	AUG 10 1850
MAHORNEY, Peyton	CALVERT, Henrietta (blk)	OCT 04 1854
MAHORNEY, Robert	BROOKS, Mary Ellen	JUL 12 1843

District of Columbia Marriage Licenses, 1811-1858

MAHORNEY, Sally (blk)	DOUGLASS, William Henry	JUN 16 1856
MAHORNEY, Susan	HICKS, Horace	MAY 14 1835
MAHORNEY, Thomas	HASKINS, Mary	NOV 26 1838
MAHORNEY, Thomas W.	SHAW, Emely B.	FEB 12 1831
MAHORNY, Elizabeth	THORN, Thomas	OCT 29 1835
MAHUE, Clement Dent	GURTON, Mary	AUG 30 1815
MAHUE, Lucinda	WEBSTER, John Wesley	AUG 27 1832
MAHUE, Margaret	GILL, James	MAY 30 1848
MAHUE, Mary	MATTINGLY, Leonard	JUN 10 1813
MAI, Peter	MILLER, Elizabeth	APR 18 1857
MAIE, Frances V.	DALLAS, Alexander J.	JAN 30 1855
MAIER, Anton	MALONEY, Hanora	MAY 31 1855
MAIER, John	LUTJOHANN, Dorothea	MAR 09 1857
MAILEY, Rosey	McCANN, Peter	FEB 20 1854
MAINE, Catherine	O'CONNELL, Jeremiah	NOV 14 1857
MAINE, R.S.	BLACKBURN, Mary E.	JUN 16 1854
MAINY, Joanna	CUSICK, John	JAN 01 1853
MAJAR, John M.	NEALE, Laura S.	JUL 21 1838
MAJOR, David B.	WARD, Elizabeth	OCT 28 1845
MAJOR, Henry, Rev.	JONES, Sarah Elizabeth	SEP 10 1839
MAJORS, Emeline	LECKEY, Jackson	OCT 09 1843
MAJORS, John	WARD, Elizabeth Ann	NOV 13 1845
MAKEL, Casper	RUPPERT, Catherine	FEB 03 1853
MAKIBBIN, Charles L.	LIND, Mary	OCT 08 1855
MAKIBBON, Charles	DELANEY, Mary	NOV 27 1855
MAKSEY, James	GRAHAM, Mary	JUL 14 1817
MALAWSON, Sarah C.	STRURER, Victor	JAN 27 1848
MALBURN, James C.	SMITH, Jane	NOV 21 1839
MALDER, Catherine	BERRY, Noble	JUN 06 1833
MALENS, Caroline	WAGNER, David	APR 29 1846
MALLARD, Susan	SPALLINGTON, Jno.	MAR 10 1818
MALLONY, James	STEPHENSON, Jane	AUG 09 1814
MALLORY, Delia	NEWELL, Thomas	FEB 13 1818
MALLORY, John William	GILLISPE, Hellen Mary	MAY 13 1854
MALOANY, Hetta	MILLER, James	MAR 29 1838
MALONE, Ann	BRUGGY, Jeremiah	MAY 11 1853
MALONE, Edward	MACK, Margt.	JAN 26 1856
MALONE, James	HOOVER, Hetty	APR 07 1823
MALONE, John	GOODWIN, Ann Rebecca	JUN 17 1856
MALONE, Lawrence	HAVELIN, Eliza	MAY 29 1846
MALONE, Margaret	KEEFE, Patrick	JUL 09 1856
MALONE, Michael	FLAHERTY, Mary	OCT 07 1854
MALONE, Sarah Elizth.	DAVIS, John T.	OCT 08 1850
MALONEY, Edward	FAHEY, Bridget	JUL 01 1852
MALONEY, Ellen	JENKINS, Richard L.	OCT 21 1856
MALONEY, Ellen	WILLIAMS, Chas. R.	AUG 31 1858
MALONEY, Hannora	WILLIAMS, James	FEB 13 1858
MALONEY, Hanora	MAIER, Anton	MAY 31 1855
MALONEY, James	STEPHENSON, Jane	MAR 08 1815
MALONEY, James	DESMOND, Ellen	SEP 17 1853
MALONEY, Margaret	O'DEAR, John	AUG 21 1854
MALONEY, Margt.	RYON, Danl.	APR 09 1855
MALONEY, Mary	CROW, Patrick	JAN 27 1852
MALONEY, Michael	McMANN, Margaret	MAR 16 1850
MALONEY, Michael	CORBIT, Bridget	JAN 27 1858
MALONY, Eliza	HARAHAN, John	AUG 19 1856
MALONY, James	STEPHENSON, Jane	JUN 09 1814
MALONY, Judy	O'DAY, Thomas	JAN 31 1853

District of Columbia Marriage Licenses, 1811-1858

MALORD, Martha M.	MARSHALL, William	MAY 13 1856
MALORD, Mary A.	KING, John Thomas	NOV 25 1856
MALOWNEY, John	HURLEY, Mary	FEB 09 1852
MALVAHILL, Mary	DUNFORD, James	JUN 14 1858
MAMBY, Margaret	VILEY, George	JUL 02 1836
MANAHAN, Margt.	HURLEY, Lawrence	JUN 29 1855
MANAHAN, Mary	DEMPSEY, Owen	JUL 23 1830
MANAY, Ann	CLARNCEY, Michael	AUG 02 1856
MANDERS, Levin H.	AKERS, Mary Ann	JAN 16 1845
MANDON, Mary Ann	POTTER, Richard M.	NOV 23 1843
MANEW, Charlotte	SANBORN, Thomas S.	MAR 13 1851
MANGAN, Maurice	SHAHAN, Margaret	SEP 10 1855
MANGUM, George T.	COLLINS, Jane	NOV 06 1855
MANGUM, James H.	NALLY, Nancy E.	SEP 17 1849
MANGUM, John G.F.	COLLINS, Susan	MAR 13 1856
MANGUM, John Thomas	ERICKSON, Mary Elizabeth	FEB 08 1849
MANGUM, Wiley P.	LADDE, Fannie Vaulx	OCT 23 1855
MANGUM, Wm. James	DULEY, Elizabeth	APR 22 1847
MANGUN, Christiana	VANSCIVER, James	JUN 08 1852
MANGUN, Francis	MULLIKIN, Elizabeth	MAY 25 1831
MANGUN, James	SANDFORD, Mary	SEP 03 1840
MANGUN, Robert H.	DEVAUN, Elizabeth A.	JUN 24 1856
MANGUN, Zachariah	GREEN, Jane	OCT 17 1834
MANIKAN, Catharine	DUGGIN, William	JUL 19 1853
MANKIN, James	MOONES, Christiana M.	JAN 15 1833
MANKIN, James	DENT, Margaretta	FEB 13 1833
MANKIN, James	DENT, Deborah	DEC 31 1838
MANKIN, Jane	NIXON, Richard	NOV 23 1837
MANKIN, John	DELAWAY, Adeline	DEC 24 1841
MANKIN, John	HARDY, Catharine (blk)	OCT 13 1851
MANKIN, John T.	WOOD, Mary E.	JAN 18 1837
MANKIN, Mathias	POSTON, Robey Harriet	FEB 12 1820
MANKIN, William	HESSELBERG, Louisa	SEP 24 1847
MANKIN, William	JONES, Ann	SEP 23 1852
MANKING, Sophia	MARSHAL, William	AUG 21 1827
MANKINS, Ann Virginia	GROSS, John W.	SEP 29 1849
MANKINS, Edward	WILSON, Melinda	AUG 29 1837
MANKINS, Ellen	CLEMENTS, William	JAN 10 1832
MANKINS, John	TYLER, Mary	APR 06 1841
MANKINS, John C.	MAHONEY, Mary (blk)	JUL 01 1858
MANKINS, John W.	RILEY, Jane S.	OCT 05 1853
MANKINS, Thomas Edwin	ALLEN, Charity A.	JAN 21 1834
MANKINS, Washington	POOLE, Susan	FEB 08 1848
MANKINS, William	DAY, Elizabeth	DEC 24 1834
MANLEY, Harirson	BOHANNER, Levenia	OCT 12 1818
MANLEY, Mary Ann	WORTHINGTON, William	DEC 10 1841
MANLEY, William A.	RYNALDO, Mary Ann	OCT 01 1842
MANLIN, Emily	PFLINGER, Jacob	OCT 16 1856
MANLY, Sarah E.	WRIGHT, Charles	NOV 03 1820
MANN, Ann Maria	SHREEVES, William O.	MAY 01 1858
MANN, Elizabeth	KING, Jackson	SEP 22 1856
MANN, Ellen	DRAKE, Robert A.	SEP 24 1847
MANN, James	SIMPSON, Mary	DEC 19 1838
MANN, Jane (blk)	COOKE, John F.	DEC 13 1832
MANN, Jesse	WINDHAM, Sarah	DEC 17 1842
MANN, Jesse F.	ANDERSON, Ann	APR 30 1846
MANN, Joseph A.	QUEEN, Mary Martha (blk)	SEP 15 1847
MANN, Lucy Amelia	VOSS, Augustus	JUN 23 1851

District of Columbia Marriage Licenses, 1811-1858

MANN, Mary A.E.	GRUBB, George	JUL 05 1851
MANN, Rachel (blk)	MASON, Henry	JUN 14 1842
MANN, Rebecca	CURTISS, Charles	DEC 12 1825
MANN, Sarah (blk)	THOMAS, William	SEP 14 1839
MANN, Virginia P.	BOYD, George K.	JUN 19 1845
MANN, Washington P.	MEREDITH, Mary	DEC 04 1837
MANNEL, Bridget	DAILEY, Peter	OCT 30 1854
MANNESMIDT, Louisa	GUVERNERTOR, George	JUN 30 1853
MANNING, Catherine A.	ROACH, Edward N.	FEB 05 1839
MANNING, Ellen	COCHRANE, John T.	OCT 31 1849
MANNING, Eveline G.	WARING, John P.	JUN 06 1843
MANNING, Frances M.	COLT, Chester A.	MAY 12 1841
MANNING, Francis A.	BURNS, Mary	JAN 29 1857
MANNING, Ignatius F.	RATCLIFFE, Mary Ann	MAY 05 1842
MANNING, Ignatius F.	COOPER, Sarah	APR 21 1857
MANNING, Margaret H.	GREENWELL, William E.	SEP 26 1854
MANNING, Martha Louise	BERRY, Horatio Edwin	OCT 20 1845
MANNING, Mary H.	CARBERY, Thomas	NOV 02 1826
MANNING, Mary T.	SEWALL, Bennett H.	MAR 23 1830
MANNING, Nathaniel W.	CRAIGHILL, Martha P.	JAN 31 1835
MANNING, Rosa M.	GARDNER, Dr. Jacob B.	JAN 08 1852
MANNING, Rosett C.	MANNING, Wilferd A.	DEC 19 1842
MANNING, Sarah Ann	BROWN, John	DEC 02 1840
MANNING, Wilferd A.	MANNING, Rosett C.	DEC 19 1842
MANNS, Rebecca (col'd)	BURKE, Richard (col.)	JUN 25 1857
MANNUX, William	WASHINGTON, Sarah	DEC 28 1847
MANS, Isaac R.	GREAR, Mary Melvina	AUG 28 1838
MANS, Mary C.A.	PARKER, John F.	JUL 16 1855
MANSFIELD, George W.	SCOTT, Mary Ann	JAN 07 1836
MANSFIELD, J.S.	NEWELL, Susan Ann	FEB 25 1843
MANSFIELD, Joseph	LIJAH, Melia Ann	MAR 30 1843
MANSFIELD, Margaret	McCARTHY, Florence	APR 08 1850
MANSFIELD, Sarah	CHURCH, Ammasa F.	OCT 07 1836
MANSFIELD, Thomas	PARRIS, Eleanor	AUG 05 1816
MANSFIELD, Thomas, Jr.	KING, Sarah Elizabeth	JUN 20 1856
MANSIL, Peter	CURTIN, Mary	JUN 21 1858
MANTEL, Hermine Elizabeth	KORFF, Herman George	JAN 18 1851
MANTZ, Frederick W.	TINGSTRON, Mary A.	APR 07 1840
MANTZ, George	WHITE, Sarah Ann	MAY 06 1847
MANTZ, Isaac	WILLIAMS, Martha	AUG 25 1825
MANTZ, Martha	THOMPSON, William	MAY 18 1833
MANUEL, John	MULLIKIN, Mary	NOV 10 1830
MANYAT, Anthony	LUCAS, Catherine	DEC 10 1839
MAPLES, Cornelius	MAPLES, Louisa M.	MAR 20 1856
MAPLES, Louisa M.	MAPLES, Cornelius	MAR 20 1856
MARBURY, Alexander H.	DODGE, Mary B.	JUL 19 1836
MARBURY, Eleanor	CARTER, John [Hon.]	FEB 06 1829
MARBURY, Eliza	RAMSAY, R.T.	OCT 11 1830
MARBURY, Francis F.	BLACKLOCK, Elizabeth C.	NOV 23 1816
MARBURY, John	CORCORAN, Harriett H.	JUN 01 1840
MARBURY, John, Junr.	MURRAY, Juliet	JUN 09 1851
MARBURY, Marbury (blk)	BALTIMORE, Thomas	MAY 08 1834
MARBURY, Martha Louisa	BEALL, William D.	NOV 01 1842
MARBURY, Mary Ann	FITZHUGH, Richd. Henry	SEP 02 1816
MARBURY, Mary Ann	NELSON, Cleland K.	JUL 10 1840
MARBURY, Matilda	BREWER, George	JUL 28 1846
MARBURY, Thomas	EVANS, Sarah Ann	FEB 02 1826
MARBURY, Wm.	BOWEN, Harriett M.	SEP 05 1822

District of Columbia Marriage Licenses, 1811-1858

MARCELLUS, Edson	AUSTIN, Mary Elizabeth	MAY 06 1846
MARCELLUS, Henry E.	AUSTIN, Mary E.	MAY 11 1846
MARCELLUS, Robert Hartley	GLOVER, Elizabeth C.	FEB 27 1854
MARCERON, James A.	GOLDSMITH, Cordelia	NOV 28 1854
MARCERON, John L.	LUCOHESSI, Delia	AUG 21 1849
MARCERON, Joseph F.	BARNES, Elizth. E.	OCT 27 1855
MARCERON, Louis	O'BRYON, Rose L.	MAR 27 1854
MARCERON, Marcellus	PARSONS, Sarah Ellen	DEC 24 1856
MARCERON, Peter T.	GARTLAND, Elizabeth F.X.	SEP 16 1851
MARCEROY, Louis	SIMPSON, Mariah	NOV 23 1824
MARCEY, Caleb	RAGAN, Lucy Ann	AUG 19 1834
MARCEY, Catherine	BALL, Horatio	OCT 10 1815
MARCEY, James	BOWLING, Mary	JUN 09 1829
MARCEY, Robert H.	THOMPSON, Sarah	SEP 28 1857
MARCEY, William	KEACH, Eleanor	SEP 26 1826
MARCEY, William	BOWLING, Ann	OCT 01 1829
MARCHAL, Albertine	FAVIER, Agrigicole	SEP 05 1846
MARCHE, Mary Jane	PRITCHETT, William Henry	APR 01 1850
MARCHE, Thomas	DAVIS, Malinda	JUN 15 1826
MARCHER, James	RILEY, Catharine	AUG 24 1858
MARCHOM, Daniel	DUGGAN, Marcella	APR 12 1856
MARCY, Louisa	NOWLAN, Thomas	DEC 17 1818
MARDEN, Nathaniel	LUTZ, Mary Ann	JUN 09 1824
MARDEN, Nathaniel M.	LUTZ, Martha D.	APR 23 1856
MARDIN, Hannah M.	KING, Thomas S.	FEB 06 1844
MAREA, Joseph	ELSACURN, Maria	MAR 05 1813
MARGGRAF, Johanna	ENGEL, Christian	SEP 04 1852
MARGRINIUS, Fredericke	REINER, Franz	JUL 01 1858
MARIE, Pierre Jules	LISSENIL, Marie L.	AUG 26 1848
MARINER, Ellen	LUCAS, Charles B.	AUG 13 1846
MARION, John	McLEOD, Mary	FEB 06 1829
MARION, Selina	COLLINS, George	JUL 15 1852
MARIOT, Charles H.	SIOUSSA, Mary	MAY 20 1838
MARKEHIN, Ellen	O'BRIEN, John	JUN 14 1853
MARKELL, Jacob	MILLER, Rebecca	FEB 23 1826
MARKER, Jacob	JARVIS, Ann Rebecca	FEB 14 1832
MARKLAND, A.H.	SIMMS, M.L.	AUG 23 1851
MARKLAND, Mary Ann	CRAWFORD, Charles	JUN 08 1844
MARKOE, Francis, Jr.	MAXCY, Mary G.	OCT 04 1834
MARKS, Arabella	BASTOW, John	DEC 08 1853
MARKS, Catherine	DAVIS, John	FEB 01 1814
MARKS, Catherine	BLAKSLEE, George	SEP 04 1824
MARKS, Drucilla	DOWLING, Patrick	OCT 02 1852
MARKS, Eleanor N.	BARBOUR, William H.	OCT 25 1855
MARKS, Elizabeth	HOPKINS, Philip	APR 16 1840
MARKS, Ellen Handy Wilson	BLACK, John M.	AUG 20 1844
MARKS, Emeline	ROACH, John	DEC 24 1839
MARKS, Harvey R.	BASSAN, Emilie	JUN 08 1849
MARKS, Hetty Maria	SHEPPARD, James H.	FEB 01 1851
MARKS, Jacob	LUSBY, Lucretia	MAY 08 1844
MARKS, Jane	NEWMAN, Peter J.	AUG 18 1849
MARKS, Julia	CROCKEN, James H.	MAR 26 1844
MARKS, Mary Ann	TOWSON, Wm. B.	DEC 21 1854
MARKS, Mary Ann	HAMILTON, Thomas	SEP 23 1857
MARKS, Saml.	HOLROYD, Ann	AUG 08 1837
MARKS, Sarah	MILLER, John	DEC 30 1821
MARKS, Sophia Maria Western	WILSON, James	MAY 25 1821
MARKS, Susan C.	KLINCHANCE, George D.	MAY 19 1830

District of Columbia Marriage Licenses, 1811-1858

MARKS, Susanna S.C.	DUNN, Edward	OCT 09 1857
MARKWARD, George W.	CLARKE, Elizabeth	SEP 01 1846
MARKWARD, Thomas	WEBSTER, Martha	JAN 14 1854
MARKWARD, William	TYLER, Sarah Ann	NOV 01 1817
MARKWELL, Mary Ann	THOMPSON, Archibald	JAN 05 1832
MARKWOOD, Charles	BALL, Siby	JAN 13 1819
MARKWOOD, Sarah Ann [Mrs.]	WILLIAMS, Philip	SEP 18 1832
MARL, Margt.	KNEPLEY, Solomon	MAY 18 1815
MARLAN, Julian	TURNER, Zachariah	DEC 06 1827
MARLBOROUGH, Mary	SKINNER, John	OCT 21 1833
MARLL, John S.	OFFUTT, Ursuler A.	NOV 11 1844
MARLL, Mary Ann	OGDEN, William J.	AUG 22 1848
MARLOW, Alfred H.	STANFORD, Margaret Eveline	SEP 14 1857
MARLOW, Ann	LUPTON, Daniel Smith	SEP 19 1828
MARLOW, Benjamin	MOODY, Harriet (blk)	JUN 16 1858
MARLOW, Henry	JONES, Mary Jane	JAN 14 1845
MARLOW, Henry	HENYON, Elizabeth	DEC 15 1851
MARLOW, John	HOPKINS, Martha	JUN 01 1852
MARLOW, John W.	WELLMORE, Mary Ann	SEP 03 1829
MARLOW, Mary Elizabeth	BALL, Andrew A.	MAY 09 1853
MARLOW, Richard	HOPKINS, Caroline	JUN 20 1855
MARLOW, Sarah Ann	BALL, George W.	MAY 11 1843
MARLOW, Thomas	WILCOX, Clarissa	NOV 28 1833
MARMAN, Washington	DEMPSEY, Ann E.	AUG 07 1850
MARMEDUKE, Martha	JONES, James	DEC 30 1852
MARNING, Edward C.	ORBISIN, Mary M.	MAY 20 1834
MARONEY, Mary	DWYRE, John	JUN 30 1851
MARONEY, Michael	CLANCEY, Margaret	NOV 22 1851
MARR, Catherine	QUIRK, James	JUN 28 1851
MARR, Dennis B.	GREENWELL, Ann	JUN 29 1812
MARR, Elizabeth A.	CRIDER, Michael	APR 14 1834
MARR, Emeline	DAY, Thomas	OCT 24 1845
MARR, James D.	BOLDEN, Rebecca	JAN 27 1844
MARR, James F.	HUBBARD, Ellenora A.	MAY 03 1854
MARR, James H.	STEWART, Sarah A.	MAY 01 1832
MARR, John T.	MITCHELL, Josephine V.	MAY 17 1855
MARR, Lucinda Ann	MURPHY, Jno. D.	MAY 05 1825
MARR, Sophia	DIX, Jonas	MAY 15 1817
MARR, Thomas	LYDAN, Margaret	OCT 11 1820
MARRETT, John	NELSON, Jane	SEP 20 1819
MARRICH, Margaret	DAVIS, George	JUL 14 1821
MARRIET, Joseph	REEDER, Catherine	APR 29 1846
MARRIOTT, Catherine W.	SAVAGE, James	JUN 27 1844
MARRIOTT, Mary	SAVAGE, James	JUN 16 1835
MARRON, Ellen	REARDON, Jeremiah	MAR 17 1856
MARRON, John	DYER, Eliza Ann	FEB 23 1832
MARS, Mary Ann	HAMILTON, James	JUL 28 1830
MARSH, Otis W.	HALIDAY, Harriet E.	OCT 02 1848
MARSH, Samuel Wilmer	MATTINGLY, Cadelia E.	JAN 08 1855
MARSHAL, Isaac	BURKE, Mary	JAN 01 1821
MARSHAL, Mary (blk)	BRUCE, Philip	MAR 12 1840
MARSHAL, William	MANKING, Sophia	AUG 21 1827
MARSHALL, Ann Jemima	OSMON, James H.	OCT 09 1817
MARSHALL, Armstead T.	DAVIS, Sarah Olivia	AUG 07 1849
MARSHALL, Caroline Grace	PAGE, Kingman F.	DEC 24 1856
MARSHALL, Edward	KING, Elizabeth (blk)	JUL 08 1852
MARSHALL, Eleanor B.	GREEN, William H.	JUN 22 1854
MARSHALL, Elizabeth	SPALDING, Lorenzo L.	NOV 26 1842

District of Columbia Marriage Licenses, 1811-1858

MARSHALL, Elizabeth (blk)	LETHERBERRY, Littleton	SEP 07 1826
MARSHALL, Elizth. A.S.	MILLER, Charles	DEC 01 1853
MARSHALL, Ellen (blk)	SHORTER, John Wesley	JAN 15 1851
MARSHALL, James	SMALLWOOD, Eliza	JUL 14 1825
MARSHALL, Jane	WILSON, Isaac	SEP 12 1845
MARSHALL, John	BRATCHER, Keziah	MAR 01 1848
MARSHALL, John	NEAL, Mary	NOV 16 1849
MARSHALL, John J.	BARRY, Lucy C.	APR 20 1858
MARSHALL, Louisa V.	BERLIN, Samuel	NOV 19 1853
MARSHALL, Mary	BARRON, Cornelius	DEC 31 1838
MARSHALL, Mary	SNOW, John	MAY 26 1855
MARSHALL, Mary Ann	WHITE, Samuel	DEC 26 1837
MARSHALL, Mary Margaret (blk)	SHORTER, John Wesley	SEP 30 1847
MARSHALL, Nancy	McCORKLE, Henry	JUL 09 1833
MARSHALL, Nancy	DAVIS, Francis	JUN 19 1856
MARSHALL, Nancy Ann	CATOR, John	AUG 20 1838
MARSHALL, P.B.	WOOD, Susa T.	FEB 02 1858
MARSHALL, Rebecca (blk)	BROWN, William	JUN 24 1845
MARSHALL, Thomas	WHETCROFT, Juliana	NOV 05 1821
MARSHALL, Thomas	LYLES, Sarah M.	SEP 03 1846
MARSHALL, Thomas	THOMPSON, Jane Eliza	FEB 06 1847
MARSHALL, Thomas	LYLES, Henrietta E.	NOV 29 1855
MARSHALL, Wellessley C.	WILKINSON, Elizabeth (blk)	NOV 25 1857
MARSHALL, William	LEE, Ann	JUN 22 1826
MARSHALL, William	MALORD, Martha M.	MAY 13 1856
MARSHALL, Wm.	REED, Emelia	DEC 29 1814
MARSHE, Esther A.	WHITE, Thomas P.	DEC 14 1854
MARSTELLER, R.L.	SMALLWOOD, Mary Cath.	NOV 22 1844
MARSTEN, Frances	WILSON, John Q.	OCT 07 1843
MARSTERS, Mary	JAMISON, Marsham	MAY 18 1819
MARSY, Elizabeth	STONE, Edward	FEB 17 1825
MARSY, Samuel	BURCH, Mary Ann	DEC 23 1854
MART, Rebecca	WILSON, William	APR 13 1846
MARTAIN, Patsey	HATTERWAY, James	OCT 21 1815
MARTELL, Ann	MULLER, Mackel	FEB 15 1825
MARTELL, Elizabeth	BOHN, John	APR 24 1851
MARTELL, Mary Ann	KESSLER, Adam	MAY 02 1855
MARTELLE, John T.	POPE, Elizabeth	JUN 08 1837
MARTHA, Ann	CHUB, Henry	FEB 01 1816
MARTIES, Sarah	MASON, John	JUN 13 1838
MARTIN, Agnes	HAMITT, John	DEC 24 1827
MARTIN, Albert W.	COOK, Mary E.	MAY 07 1849
MARTIN, Amos F.	REDMAN, Cornelia	SEP 25 1856
MARTIN, Andrew	BRIGHT, Mary Jane	MAY 01 1848
MARTIN, Ann	WARE, John	APR 01 1816
MARTIN, Ann	DENNIS, Philip	OCT 09 1828
MARTIN, Ann	DONNELL, John	APR 04 1840
MARTIN, Anthony S.	WARD, Elizabeth	APR 05 1831
MARTIN, Archibald	BRADLEY, Ann	JUN 22 1835
MARTIN, Benjamin	WILLIAMS, Ellen	DEC 14 1848
MARTIN, Benjamin M.	WILLETT, Eveline E.	MAY 19 1847
MARTIN, Betsey	PLUNT, Horatio	DEC 26 1816
MARTIN, Cassey Ann (blk)	PROCTOR, Samuel	DEC 01 1851
MARTIN, Catherine	CARPENTER, Patrick	MAR 25 1853
MARTIN, Catherine Ann	KREAMER, Charles	JUN 09 1847
MARTIN, Catherine M.	HUTCHINSON, John A.	DEC 14 1848
MARTIN, Catherine R.	ADAMS, Josiah	AUG 19 1857
MARTIN, Charlotte E. (blk)	PENNY, James	DEC 12 1853

District of Columbia Marriage Licenses, 1811-1858

MARTIN, Cinthia	MARTIN, Sampson	JUN 25 1825
MARTIN, Cosworth	SANDFORD, Ann Maria	AUG 06 1836
MARTIN, Duscilla C.	MURPHY, John	FEB 01 1855
MARTIN, Elijah	TRUNDELL, Leah	FEB 11 1812
MARTIN, Eliza	CLEMENTS, Alexander	JUN 14 1853
MARTIN, Eliza C.	CARROLL, John	MAR 26 1856
MARTIN, Elizabeth	SMITH, Francis	MAY 17 1827
MARTIN, Elizabeth	HARRAN, Charles	NOV 07 1850
MARTIN, Elizabeth	CHASE, Hamilton	NOV 04 1854
MARTIN, Elizabeth B.	McCORMICK, Wm. J.	JAN 15 1850
MARTIN, Elizabeth Jane	BUCKLY, Anthony	MAY 30 1854
MARTIN, Emeline	JOHNSON, James H.	AUG 30 1849
MARTIN, Emily Amelia	ORR, William H.	JAN 08 1853
MARTIN, Emma	PEARSON, Peter M.	SEP 25 1834
MARTIN, Eveline	McCORMICK, William J.	SEP 30 1833
MARTIN, Francis	FRY, Mary Jane	DEC 30 1850
MARTIN, George B.	HOWARD, Eliza C.	JUN 05 1849
MARTIN, George H.	NAYLOR, Joanna L.	JUN 29 1858
MARTIN, Harriet C.	WORSTER, Luther F.	AUG 24 1851
MARTIN, Hellen A.	JENNINGS, William G.	MAR 16 1836
MARTIN, Henrietta W.	TUCKER, Thomas	NOV 02 1847
MARTIN, Henry C.	CARTER, Emilie P.	NOV 06 1849
MARTIN, Hester Ann	CREWS, Joseph	FEB 17 1852
MARTIN, Isabella	McGARVEY, Patrick	JAN 08 1842
MARTIN, James	NICOLAI, Margaret	FEB 24 1853
MARTIN, James H.	SCRIVENIR, Mary	MAR 31 1834
MARTIN, Jane	DAGGETT, Aaron W.	MAR 02 1824
MARTIN, Jane	SNYDER, Matthias, Jr.	FEB 05 1828
MARTIN, John	LEWIS, Sarah	OCT 06 1827
MARTIN, John	TUCKER, Elizabeth	SEP 08 1832
MARTIN, John	PASCOR, Sarah Ann	FEB 10 1842
MARTIN, John	CULBERSON, Virginia	NOV 15 1847
MARTIN, John	GILSON, Catherine	JUN 10 1848
MARTIN, John	BOTT, Margaret	SEP 09 1851
MARTIN, John M.	HUTCHISON, Frances A.	MAR 13 1855
MARTIN, Louisa Virginia	ADAMS, Richard	DEC 22 1852
MARTIN, Luther	HARRISON, Anne M.	AUG 29 1856
MARTIN, Luther L.	DONN, Sarah L.	AUG 14 1849
MARTIN, Margaret	MASSEY, John J.	DEC 26 1816
MARTIN, Margaret A.	THOMAS, George W.	AUG 26 1858
MARTIN, Margaret Ann	MITCHELL, Joseph T.	OCT 18 1849
MARTIN, Margaret Isabella	ROBERTSON, James Wm.	SEP 29 1851
MARTIN, Maria E.	WALKER, William B.	JUL 21 1825
MARTIN, Marie A.	TERRAILLES, Pierre	DEC 20 1845
MARTIN, Mary	JEFFERS, William	MAR 27 1837
MARTIN, Mary	DAVIS, Abel G.	DEC 04 1837
MARTIN, Mary A.	MILLER, James A.	MAR 15 1852
MARTIN, Mary Ellen	MEREDITH, Moses	OCT 09 1852
MARTIN, Rebecca	RACE, Hiram	AUG 16 1838
MARTIN, Rebecca	BRICKLEY, John T.	OCT 27 1852
MARTIN, Richard	HIGDON, Rebecca	JAN 14 1814
MARTIN, Richard	TRUNNEL, Sarah	DEC 22 1818
MARTIN, Robert	DAVIS, Mary E.	JAN 18 1846
MARTIN, Robert	CLEMENTS, Ann Matilda	JUN 13 1854
MARTIN, Rosanna	SEIFFERT, Henry	APR 08 1836
MARTIN, Sally (blk)	STEWART, George	JUL 01 1839
MARTIN, Sally Maria	BOSTICK, Edward	SEP 23 1850
MARTIN, Sampson	MARTIN, Cinthia	JUN 25 1825

District of Columbia Marriage Licenses, 1811-1858

MARTIN, Samuel	SIMPSON, Elizabeth	JUN 07 1823
MARTIN, Sarah	WOODWARD, Amon	DEC 23 1817
MARTIN, Sarah	SCRIVENER, James Edward	DEC 17 1847
MARTIN, Sophiar	OLIVER, Giles	JUL 02 1839
MARTIN, Sophie	BIEWEND, Adolph	AUG 01 1844
MARTIN, Susan	COLLINS, Thomas	JUN 17 1828
MARTIN, Susan	SHRYER, Daniel	JUN 14 1837
MARTIN, Susan S.	SESSFORD, John H.	OCT 12 1846
MARTIN, Thomas	BROWN, Louisa W. (blk)	DEC 14 1857
MARTIN, Thomas J.	TAYLOR, Rebecca B.	FEB 02 1830
MARTIN, Tobias	ERSKINE, Agnes	MAR 27 1826
MARTIN, Tobias M.	HENNING, Mary E.	MAR 11 1856
MARTIN, Tyrance	CREAMER, Susan	MAY 24 1838
MARTIN, Vansonia	SMITHBY, Ann	JUN 10 1847
MARTIN, William	NESMITH, Charlotte D.	MAR 11 1826
MARTIN, William	SOUTHERLAND, Mary	MAY 21 1829
MARTIN, William	HOOPER, Jane	OCT 21 1851
MARTIN, William	COXEN, Mary C.	MAR 18 1858
MARTIN, William M.	CONNELL, Mary C.	JUN 21 1853
MARTIN, William N.	CAMPBELL, Mary Ann	MAY 18 1814
MARTIN, William S.	MURPHY, Mary E.	APR 21 1855
MARTIN, Wm. H.	JAMIESON, Adel (blk)	OCT 22 1851
MARTINDALE, Henry W.	EWELL, Olivia F.	DEC 06 1826
MARTINE, Andrew	COOLIDGE, Elizabeth A.	APR 13 1854
MARYMAN, Elizabeth	EMMERY, Charles	MAY 10 1830
MARYMAN, Horatio R.	ARTH, Mary Louisa	JAN 01 1853
MARYMAN, Josephine	CLARKE, Samuel T.	DEC 12 1850
MARZLIN, Frederick	BEECH, Martha	AUG 09 1848
MASI, Caroline A.	WADSWORTH, John	MAY 26 1829
MASI, Elizabeth	QUICKSALL, Joseph	SEP 01 1841
MASI, Kate F.	STEELE, Reginald H.	DEC 22 1855
MASI, Sarah Ann	JOHNSTON, John M.	AUG 06 1832
MASI, Seraphin	BRADFORD, Catharine A.	NOV 08 1825
MASON, Clarissa Ann	SIMPSON, Andrew Jackson	NOV 01 1856
MASON, Delia A.	COLES, Charles	NOV 07 1853
MASON, E. Cary	HYDE, Charles K.	APR 21 1840
MASON, Eliza	MASON, George	FEB 16 1813
MASON, Eliza	SULLIVAN, Thomas	OCT 19 1854
MASON, Eliza J.	JOHNSON, James	NOV 18 1845
MASON, Elizabeth (blk)	COLE, Jeremiah M.	JAN 05 1825
MASON, Ellen	FITZGERALD, Michl.	MAY 22 1854
MASON, Enoch G.	BERRY, Jane (blk)	JUL 12 1843
MASON, George	MASON, Eliza	FEB 16 1813
MASON, George	HARRISON, Ann Lucinda	OCT 08 1821
MASON, George	PEATTON, Eleanor Ann	JAN 02 1823
MASON, George	MASON, Virginia	OCT 22 1827
MASON, George	MITCHELL, Emeline (blk)	SEP 02 1840
MASON, George	MASON, Sophia (blk)	MAY 27 1852
MASON, George	BARTLES, Maria	FEB 16 1853
MASON, Henry	MANN, Rachel (blk)	JUN 14 1842
MASON, Isrial B.	WHEELER, Maria (blk)	MAY 30 1854
MASON, James	BUTLER, Catherine	APR 13 1838
MASON, Jane (blk)	LEWIS, William	SEP 18 1854
MASON, Jas. F.	BROWN, Caroline (blk)	NOV 01 1855
MASON, John	STELLINGS, Ruth	JUL 19 1819
MASON, John	MARTIES, Sarah	JUN 13 1838
MASON, John	JONES, Catharine (blk)	OCT 09 1839
MASON, John, Jr.	MACOMB, Catharine	APR 02 1827

District of Columbia Marriage Licenses, 1811-1858

MASON, Joseph T.	NICHOLS, Mary Ann	NOV 16 1847
MASON, Leeanah	BARON, William H.	APR 05 1817
MASON, Louisa Jane	MILLS, William H.	NOV 01 1855
MASON, Martha A. (blk)	FERGUSON, James	NOV 30 1852
MASON, Mary	TURNER, Peter	NOV 08 1855
MASON, Mary A.H.	BAYLY, William	SEP 21 1824
MASON, Mary Ann [Mrs.]	ENTWISLE, James	JUL 06 1815
MASON, Mary Ann (blk)	NEALE, William Henry	NOV 23 1840
MASON, Mary Eliza	MENECI, Gaetano A.	FEB 13 1843
MASON, Mary Jane (blk)	COLBERT, Lloyd	DEC 20 1855
MASON, Matilda (blk)	NUGENT, Eli	JAN 26 1841
MASON, Maynadier	FRENCH, Mary Virginia	NOV 18 1830
MASON, Michael	SULLIVAN, Fanny	FEB 10 1855
MASON, Mildred C.	DOWNEY, John	FEB 23 1854
MASON, Murray	FORSYTH, Clara C.	DEC 06 1837
MASON, Richard B.	SOMMERS, Matilda	JAN 18 1837
MASON, Saml. M.	THOMAS, Isabella	DEC 29 1856
MASON, Samuel	KEY, Martha (blk)	APR 14 1858
MASON, Sarah (blk)	BROWN, Daniel	FEB 28 1856
MASON, Sarah C.	HUGHLETT, Daniel H.	APR 07 1819
MASON, Sarah Maria	COOPER, Samuel [Lieut.]	APR 04 1827
MASON, Sophia (blk)	MASON, George	MAY 27 1852
MASON, Stephen	LEONARD, Susan	FEB 09 1835
MASON, Susan	HURDLE, George	MAR 27 1817
MASON, Thomas	COLLINS, Sarah	JUN 22 1853
MASON, Thomas	SULLIVAN, Margaret	JAN 12 1855
MASON, Virginia	MASON, George	OCT 22 1827
MASON, William H.	BURGER, Christiana	AUG 25 1853
MASS, Mary E.	FINNEY, John T.	MAY 17 1855
MASSEY, Elizabeth	BALL, Horatio	DEC 07 1831
MASSEY, Francis	SULLIVAN, Deborah J.	JAN 04 1825
MASSEY, James	BIRCH, Mary Elizabeth	FEB 08 1855
MASSEY, John J.	MARTIN, Margaret	DEC 26 1816
MASSEY, Joseph	WILKINS, Mary	MAR 19 1857
MASSEY, Leanna	ATHEY, George	OCT 07 1813
MASSEY, Martha L.	HOWARD, William R.	AUG 23 1841
MASSEY, Mary E.	OSBORNE, Seth	JUN 24 1851
MASSEY, Mary H.	WIMSATT, William H.	AUG 17 1840
MASSEY, Mary Jane	HURST, Robert	JAN 08 1852
MASSEY, Rachel A.	BUTLER, Thomas Henson	NOV 24 1857
MASSEY, Robert	DELANEY, Ann E. (blk)	MAR 27 1852
MASSEY, Sarah	KINSEY, Robert E.	JUL 06 1857
MASSEY, William D.	RHODES, Laura Ann	AUG 25 1836
MASSI, Ann	HOFFMAN, Jacob	JUN 30 1845
MASSI, Jane	PAYNE, John	NOV 01 1832
MASSI, Mary	BRIEN, Burnard	AUG 29 1846
MASSIE, Elizabeth Frankey	BIGGES, Perry	JAN 06 1848
MASSIE, John	WARREN, Caroline (blk)	JUN 20 1844
MASSIE, Mary Ann	OSBURN, William B.	DEC 17 1828
MASSOLETTI, Julietta M.	METCALF, John C.	MAY 30 1851
MASSY, Jane	DEMPSEY, Joseph	SEP 27 1848
MASTEN, Jane	ROLLINGS, James M.	JAN 26 1857
MASTERS, Mary	HUTCHINSON, Thomas	NOV 23 1842
MASTERS, Matilda	MITCHELL, Walter	JAN 09 1813
MASTERSON, Elizabeth	McGLAVEN, Thomas	SEP 29 1852
MASTERSON, Jane	WATT, John	SEP 22 1847
MASTIN, William E.	CARR, Ann R.	MAY 16 1850
MATEER, Jane R.	TRAMMELL, John	JUN 13 1840

District of Columbia Marriage Licenses, 1811-1858

MATHANEY, Harriet	ROSSE, Paton	JUL 14 1856
MATHEANEY, Jane M.	DUNKLEE, Jason	JAN 30 1830
MATHENY, William H.	ANGEL, Sarah Jane	SEP 11 1854
MATHERS, Catharine	ANDERSON, John	FEB 05 1821
MATHERS, Jane	MATTHIS, Armsted	SEP 04 1848
MATHERS, John	THOMAS, Eleanor	JAN 23 1813
MATHEW, Francis	FORD, Mary Ann (blk)	NOV 28 1844
MATHEWS, Elizabeth	PALMER, Howard	MAR 29 1822
MATHEWS, Harriet	MURPHEY, J.	NOV 13 1832
MATHEWS, Martha Ann F.	TERRETT, Colville	AUG 18 1851
MATHEWS, Mary A. (blk)	WHEELER, William H.	DEC 21 1855
MATHIAS, Petro	DALY, Julia	NOV 18 1853
MATHIEU, Joseph	DAUGHERTY, Ann T.	JUN 29 1843
MATHIS, Cornelia A.	BALDWIN, Thomas J.	MAR 05 1855
MATINGLY, Mary Susan	LAY, Richard, Junr.	JAN 09 1832
MATLACK, Armistead G.	BRANNAN, Louisa F.	AUG 03 1846
MATLEY, Elizabeth	BROWN, Addison	JUL 23 1842
MATLOCK, Eleanor	WOODY, James P.H.	MAR 25 1848
MATLOCK, Elizabeth G.	GRIFFITH, William T.	MAR 30 1829
MATLOCK, Jeremiah G.	AMES, Sarah E.	JAN 26 1843
MATLOCK, Sarah Ellen	HERBERT, Samuel Marshall	OCT 25 1843
MATLOCK, William	KEGLY, Elizabeth	NOV 01 1845
MATNEY, Maria	COLLINS, George	MAR 01 1851
MATTELY, John	WATTS, Harriet	JUN 14 1827
MATTHEWS, Ann R.	EWTHEY, George W.	NOV 09 1852
MATTHEWS, Bridget	BARRON, Michael	MAY 07 1838
MATTHEWS, Carr	HOLT, Lucretia (blk)	MAR 15 1827
MATTHEWS, Catharine	TREADWELL, Thomas	JUN 10 1812
MATTHEWS, Catherine	WOODS, Michael	DEC 02 1854
MATTHEWS, Edward T.	FAHERTY, Jane E.	NOV 16 1857
MATTHEWS, Eliza S.	SEARS, Chas. A.	FEB 23 1857
MATTHEWS, Elizabeth (blk)	COSTIN, William	JUN 06 1838
MATTHEWS, Elizabeth (blk)	LEWIS, Benjamin	FEB 02 1854
MATTHEWS, Harriet (blk)	THOMAS, Saml.	OCT 22 1857
MATTHEWS, Henry C.	HAW, Lucinda S.	SEP 28 1820
MATTHEWS, James	TUCKER, Susan	APR 12 1817
MATTHEWS, James	THOMAS, Elizabeth (blk)	DEC 05 1848
MATTHEWS, Jane Hellen	TAYLER, John	JUL 03 1854
MATTHEWS, John	THOMAS, Denzia	OCT 04 1834
MATTHEWS, John A.	BOWLIN, Mary A. (blk)	NOV 23 1853
MATTHEWS, John T.	NALLEY, Christianna A.	MAR 31 1845
MATTHEWS, Joseph	BROOK, Elizabeth W.	JAN 30 1840
MATTHEWS, Margaret	DEER, Patrick	APR 15 1856
MATTHEWS, Mary	PHILLIPS, Moses	FEB 05 1816
MATTHEWS, Mary (blk)	GRANT, Elisha	SEP 22 1856
MATTHEWS, Mary J.	HAWKINS, John	AUG 15 1857
MATTHEWS, Richard	REDIN, Elizabeth (blk)	JUL 07 1832
MATTHEWS, Robert A.	YOUNG, Matilda J.	JUN 26 1852
MATTHEWS, Samuel	WALKER, Ann (blk)	APR 21 1827
MATTHEWS, Sophia M.	HATCH, Rexford	JAN 31 1857
MATTHIS, Armsted	MATHERS, Jane	SEP 04 1848
MATTINGLY, Ann	JOHNSON, Joseph	JUN 04 1814
MATTINGLY, Anna Elizth.	BUTLER, William	APR 20 1848
MATTINGLY, Barbara Ellen	BROWN, William Edward	DEC 17 1842
MATTINGLY, C.A.	TALBURT, George W.	FEB 15 1844
MATTINGLY, Cadelia E.	MARSH, Samuel Wilmer	JAN 08 1855
MATTINGLY, Catharine	SHAW, Washington	MAY 02 1826
MATTINGLY, Catharine S.	DICKSON, Thomas	AUG 12 1843

District of Columbia Marriage Licenses, 1811-1858

MATTINGLY, Clara V.	BROWNE, Lucian C.	APR 19 1847
MATTINGLY, Edward	KNOTT, Ann	JUN 27 1812
MATTINGLY, Elizabeth	USHER, George	JUL 09 1847
MATTINGLY, Emeline W.	RANDELL, George H.	SEP 19 1842
MATTINGLY, George	SHANNAN, Mary	JUN 24 1823
MATTINGLY, Jas. E.	DUTZLER, Susan	AUG 03 1854
MATTINGLY, Jane	McLANE, William	NOV 19 1846
MATTINGLY, John	NOBLETON, Susan	SEP 26 1818
MATTINGLY, John	DONALDSON, Mary	JAN 11 1843
MATTINGLY, Joseph	VEECH, Emeline	OCT 05 1830
MATTINGLY, Joseph	REEVES, Hannah M.	NOV 19 1853
MATTINGLY, Joseph H.	McGUINEY, Kate	AUG 19 1858
MATTINGLY, Joseph W.	WILSON, Amanda J.	SEP 27 1848
MATTINGLY, Kate	CLOTWORTHY, William P.	MAY 22 1858
MATTINGLY, Leonard	MAHUE, Mary	JUN 10 1813
MATTINGLY, Leonard	POWELL, Julia A.	MAR 13 1815
MATTINGLY, Lewis	EASTON, Susanna	DEC 04 1815
MATTINGLY, Malinda J.	SIMMONS, Thomas	FEB 03 1849
MATTINGLY, Mary Ann	PAYNE, Lewis	NOV 25 1848
MATTINGLY, Mary Elizth.	JORDAN, Robert Henry	JUN 28 1855
MATTINGLY, Mary Martina	BOWLING, Edward M.	MAY 27 1858
MATTINGLY, Reubin	BALTZELL, Priscilla	APR 29 1852
MATTINGLY, Sarah	SHAFE, Jacob	OCT 08 1834
MATTINGLY, Sarah	NOLAN, Francis	FEB 14 1846
MATTINGLY, Sidney Ann	HARRISON, Thomas	NOV 02 1835
MATTINGLY, Thomas	WALKER, Jane	NOV 22 1820
MATTINGLY, Thomas	COLLINS, Maria	MAR 08 1855
MATTINGLY, William	BUTCHER, Maria	DEC 06 1816
MATTINGLY, William	BALDSWELL, Caroline	NOV 10 1849
MATTINGLY, Zachariah	BROWN, Jane Eliza	OCT 10 1843
MATTOX, Frances	YEAMAN, George	MAR 06 1819
MaTULET, Antonio	AHUMADA, Soledod Jeulet	JUL 14 1849
MAUD, Margaret	ARNOLD, Thomas B.	NOV 07 1854
MAUD, Martha A.	CONNER, John J.	NOV 11 1857
MAUD, William	McKARITHEN, Mary	AUG 21 1826
MAUGHIN, Mary	MORRISON, Richard	MAY 26 1823
MAUL, Elizabeth	HUTCHINS, Robert	AUG 25 1842
MAUL, Susan	DREWIT, James	MAR 20 1817
MAULEY, Elizabeth	GOLDEN, R.R.	NOV 12 1822
MAULEY, Thomas C.	BULER, Mary Ann	APR 13 1844
MAURICE, Elexander G.	HOWARD, Susannah	MAY 31 1828
MAURO, Charles G.	DAVIS, Charlotte E.	APR 03 1856
MAURO, William H.	WHARTON, Eliza S.	MAR 28 1831
MAURY, Charles B.	MAURY, Sallie F.	NOV 18 1850
MAURY, Elizabeth H.	MAURY, William A.	FEB 23 1857
MAURY, Ellen G.	NICHOLS, Charles H.	NOV 23 1857
MAURY, John W.	FOYLES, Isabel	OCT 06 1831
MAURY, Jourdan W.	McNEIR, Sally Maria	NOV 09 1846
MAURY, Nannie Fontaine	CORBIN, Spotswood Wellford	APR 28 1858
MAURY, Richard B.	MAGRUDER, Ellen	APR 13 1831
MAURY, Sallie F.	MAURY, Charles B.	NOV 18 1850
MAURY, Thomas F.	PARKER, Georgianna	MAY 24 1858
MAURY, William A.	MAURY, Elizabeth H.	FEB 23 1857
MAUXLEY, Samuel	LYONS, Ann	JAN 11 1820
MAUYET, Mary M.	FREEMAN, John P.	NOV 13 1847
MAXCY, Mary G.	MARKOE, Francis, Jr.	OCT 04 1834
MAXEY, Ann Sarah	HUGHES, George W.	DEC 16 1834
MAXWELL, Charles S.	HALLAR, Ellen Catherine	MAY 24 1845

District of Columbia Marriage Licenses, 1811-1858

MAXWELL, Fanny	WADE, John W.	SEP 21 1857
MAXWELL, Geo. P.	WARTHAN, Prudence	JUN 15 1822
MAXWELL, George W.	McLAUGHLIN, Mary	JUN 18 1831
MAXWELL, John S.	WILSON, Mary L.	DEC 29 1851
MAXWELL, Lucy A.	REDDICK, David	JUL 07 1832
MAXWELL, Susanna	INGRAM, James	SEP 22 1855
MAXWELL, Washington	MORAN, Elizabeth A.	SEP 07 1837
MAXWELL, William B.	HOOVER, Sarah E.	DEC 28 1850
MAY, Anna	ALISON, John H.	MAY 29 1854
MAY, Charlotte R.	HARVEY, William M.	OCT 29 1857
MAY, Columbia Ann	DARNES, Washington F.	JUL 22 1851
MAY, Edward A.	TALBOT, Solumia	JAN 29 1820
MAY, Eleanor L.	OSBURN, James M.	APR 28 1838
MAY, Eliza Jane	JENKINS, Benjamin F.	NOV 08 1856
MAY, Francis R.	STREAKS, Charlotte	MAY 05 1821
MAY, George W.	WRIGHT, Catharine	DEC 23 1830
MAY, George Washington [Dr.]	LEE, Catherine H.	OCT 04 1824
MAY, James	BOUDET, Maria	APR 15 1812
MAY, James R.	CHILDRESS, Mary A.	SEP 18 1854
MAY, John	HINGLE, Margaret	NOV 16 1854
MAY, John Thomas	RUST, Rosanna	NOV 03 1849
MAY, Julia M.	McRA, Powell	APR 30 1839
MAY, Laura	WISE, George D.	AUG 17 1843
MAY, Marcellena	DONNELLY, Robert	NOV 17 1851
MAY, Maria C.	PETTIT, William G.	DEC 28 1857
MAY, Martha	LANGDEN, Charles	FEB 19 1822
MAY, Martha Ann	EARP, James	JUN 01 1812
MAY, Martha Ann	PIERCE, John	FEB 28 1843
MAY, Martha L.	JONES, William S.	SEP 29 1855
MAY, Mary E.	PHIPPS, William C.	FEB 08 1842
MAY, Mary Elizabeth	SUIT, Fielder	NOV 20 1849
MAY, Mary Julia	McFARLAND, William H.	MAY 08 1858
MAY, Mina	STRASBURGER, Hart L.	MAR 18 1854
MAY, Philip	FREEMAN, Elizabeth	SEP 10 1845
MAYFIELD, Benj.	WRIGHT, Susanna	FEB 23 1823
MAYFIELD, Benj. R.	BROWN, Charlotte L.	SEP 01 1851
MAYFIELD, Benjamin	WALKER, Sarah	APR 27 1815
MAYFIELD, Emelia Ann	DYER, Wm. Ignatius	MAY 18 1840
MAYFIELD, Sarah Ann	COOMBS, Thomas	DEC 12 1846
MAYHEW, Ann	BALL, Thomas	JAN 09 1834
MAYHEW, Coffet	BRADLEY, Ann E.	AUG 07 1855
MAYHEW, Edward	ARUNDELL, Mary	JAN 25 1834
MAYHEW, Francis	HENRY, Eliza	MAY 15 1822
MAYHEW, George	FRY, Rebecca	JAN 11 1842
MAYHEW, John W.	MITCHELL, Martha Ann	NOV 25 1852
MAYHEW, Mary Ann	KADLE, William	MAR 15 1836
MAYHEW, Matilda	ROBERTSON, Frederick	JAN 27 1837
MAYHEW, Rebecca	ALBEY, John	JUN 15 1835
MAYHEW, Sarah	WALKER, George	DEC 02 1851
MAYHEW, William	SWANN, Lucinda	JAN 27 1831
MAYHEW, William	SOPER, Mary Ann	MAR 14 1837
MAYHEW, William Bradley	SPALDING, Catharine	DEC 17 1833
MAYHEW, William H.	GOSSON, Frances M.	JAN 11 1854
MAYHUE, Henry	WHITTLE, Mary Ann	FEB 26 1827
MAYHUE, Lewin	SPALDING, Mariah	AUG 12 1828
MAYHUE, Mariah	GORDON, James	DEC 02 1830
MAYHUE, William Thomas	HEINGER, Nancy	DEC 07 1850
MAYNADIER, Eliza	PHELPS, S. Ledyard	SEP 30 1853

District of Columbia Marriage Licenses, 1811-1858

MAYNADIER, Kate Eveleth	BROWNE, Causten	MAY 31 1852
MAYNADIER, William M.	BROWN, Catharine S.	MAR 02 1830
MAYNARD, Eveline	JOHNSON, Levi Brown [Dr.]	APR 14 1831
MAYNIDER, Elizabeth	LAMAR, John	AUG 09 1834
MAYO, Ann Lucretia	GRIMES, John F.	DEC 27 1837
MAYO, Elizabeth [Mrs.]	FALES, Nathan W.	JUN 03 1823
MAYO, Isabel C.	MITCHELL, Thomas A.	JUL 23 1851
MAYO, Margaret	THOMPSON, James M.	FEB 21 1853
MAYO, Maria E.	STEWART, William T.	AUG 19 1834
MAYO, Robert [Dr.]	HARBAUGH, Eliza Catharine	JUL 08 1831
MAYO, Ruth	BROWN, Thomas	JUN 24 1815
MAYO, William	LOWE, Elizabeth	JUL 14 1815
MAYSE, William	KING, Mary	JUN 24 1833
MAYSON, Israel	CONNOR, Mary Ann	SEP 28 1842
MAZEN, Mary	TAYLOR, James	DEC 21 1835
MAZINE, Adaline	BRASHEARS, William B.	JUN 19 1845
MAZINE, Elizth.	KEETON, John M.	MAY 22 1827
MAZINE, John	CUSLEY, Margaret	JAN 07 1852
MAZINE, Mary	LAFONTAINE, Joseph	MAR 05 1832
MAZINGO, Ann	ESSEX, William	DEC 10 1823
MAZINGO, John	RUBEY, Elizabeth	MAR 07 1837
MAZINGO, William	REDMAN, Maria	NOV 13 1816
McABEE, George	WHITMORE, Mary Jane	DEC 21 1848
McADAM, Ann	NODDY, John M.C.	AUG 12 1847
McADAMS, Celia	KANE, Patrick	APR 19 1844
McALISTER, James R.	VanCOBLE, Caroline	SEP 04 1848
McALLISTER, Catharine	TUBBAFIELD, William	DEC 05 1825
McALLISTER, Charles	McKAY, Catharine	JAN 06 1823
McALLISTER, Elizabeth	BAKER, Matthias	JUN 05 1817
McALLISTER, James	QUINN, Rose	NOV 22 1827
McALWEE, Aaron	BOOTHE, Catharine Ann	OCT 12 1829
McALWEE, Sarah A.	POMNIETYZKY, Adelbert	MAY 20 1850
McATEE, Elizabeth	BARNES, James	MAY 11 1813
McATEE, Harrison	CORCORAN, Jane	JUL 20 1815
McBAIN, Mary E.	BROWN, John P.	SEP 30 1851
McBLAIR, John H.	GADSBY, Augusta	OCT 20 1835
McBRIDE, Priestly H.	DYSON, Adeline R.L.	JUL 14 1857
McBRIDE, Susan	ROTCH, George	JAN 19 1825
McBRIDE, Thomas	CURTIS, Bridget	JAN 20 1849
McCABA, Andrew	CANNON, Jane	JAN 01 1850
McCABE, Daniel	CONNOR, Mary	NOV 10 1854
McCABE, Jane	TERETT, Nathaniel H.	NOV 29 1850
McCABE, Lorenzo D.	SEWALL, Martha E.	JUL 26 1845
McCABE, Mary E.	WATKINS, George W.	DEC 25 1848
McCADDEN, Julia	HAGAN, John H.	FEB 19 1844
McCADDEN, Thomas	McILHANEY, Bridget	NOV 14 1853
McCAFFERTY, William	WALLINGSFORD, Emily	JUN 28 1838
McCAFFERY, Jos. Hugh	KENNEDY, Mary Jane	FEB 05 1852
McCAFFERY, Margaret	BEATTY, Archibald	OCT 30 1832
McCAFFERY, Michael	LADEN, Nancy	SEP 03 1833
McCAFFREY, Mary	CONLEY, Francis	AUG 31 1822
McCAFFRY, Hugh	KELEHER, Catherine	JUL 08 1854
McCAFRY, Peter	REED, Elizabeth	SEP 06 1828
McCAHAN, Catherine	DAVIS, William	AUG 28 1812
McCAHAN, Daniel, Jr.	McDERMOTT, Mary F.	APR 10 1858
McCAHAN, Samuel	FERGUSON, Elizabeth	FEB 10 1812
McCALLA, John	COLEMAN, Mary	JUN 06 1857

District of Columbia Marriage Licenses, 1811-1858

McCALLEY, Henry	BOWIE, Mary S.	SEP 28 1842
McCALLION, James C.	WALKER, Sarah	FEB 19 1816
McCALLUM, Andrew C.	CHAPMAN, Cela	MAY 09 1814
McCALLUM, Archibald T.	BECK, Mary C.	JAN 30 1858
McCALTY, James	MADISON, Ann	OCT 03 1850
McCANDLESS, Elizabeth	CONNOLLY, Owen	MAY 05 1832
McCANN, Amanda	BANGS, John T.	APR 18 1846
McCANN, Arthur	DAUGHERTY, Rebecca	SEP 16 1812
McCANN, Edward	WELSH, Maria	APR 03 1858
McCANN, Elizabeth	BOTSFORD, William	JUN 22 1816
McCANN, Mary	KIERNAN, Nicholas	SEP 06 1851
McCANN, Mary Ann	MORRICE, Davis F.	NOV 03 1829
McCANN, Peter	MAILEY, Rosey	FEB 20 1854
McCANN, Rebecca	BANGS, Charles	JAN 06 1858
McCANNE, Jane	NUGENT, James	SEP 16 1850
McCARDELL, James	HALEY, Eleanor	AUG 21 1830
McCARDLE, Ann	HUGHES, Thomas	OCT 03 1815
McCARDLE, Rose	WATERS, Thomas	JUN 15 1850
McCARGO, William T.F.	BURWELL, Elizabeth A.	MAR 09 1850
McCARROLL, Ann	MURPHY, Thomas	JUL 10 1854
McCARROLL, Owen	TOOMEY, Ann	JUL 05 1851
McCARTER, Mary	ROBERTSON, John	JUL 17 1818
McCARTEY, Thomas	FLAHERTY, Mary	JUL 26 1858
McCARTHEY, Jane	CROGGIN, Thomas	MAY 26 1849
McCARTHEY, Mary	CRONION, John	SEP 19 1844
McCARTHY, Ann	McMAHON, Thomas	MAR 28 1853
McCARTHY, Ann Maria	RICE, Edward V.	NOV 16 1847
McCARTHY, Ann Maria	RICE, Edward V.	NOV 16 1847
McCARTHY, Bridget	HEATHMAN, John	AUG 19 1852
McCARTHY, Carahin	ATHY, Juliana	JUL 07 1825
McCARTHY, Catharine	CASEY, James	MAY 03 1856
McCARTHY, Catherine	McMANUS, Edward	JUL 10 1848
McCARTHY, Catherine	NEAL, Michael	AUG 31 1857
McCARTHY, Charles	BYRNE, Catharine	FEB 02 1856
McCARTHY, Charles	DONOVAN, Catherine	NOV 16 1857
McCARTHY, Florence	MANSFIELD, Margaret	APR 08 1850
McCARTHY, Jane	HUGHES, John	JUL 20 1852
McCARTHY, Jeremiah	DONOHAN, Bridget	MAY 07 1857
McCARTHY, John	NOLAND, Mary	FEB 07 1857
McCARTHY, Michael	SAGERSON, Ellen	JAN 16 1856
McCARTHY, Patrick	GLASCOW, Eliza Jane	JUL 27 1853
McCARTHY, William	JOHNSON, Catherine Ellen	APR 22 1844
McCARTY, Ann	HALPEN, Nicholas	JAN 17 1829
McCARTY, Bartholomo	KELLY, Jane	FEB 17 1858
McCARTY, Catharine	GRIMES, Thos.	SEP 17 1819
McCARTY, Charles	BUCKLEY, Catherine	JUN 03 1846
McCARTY, Dennis	CUSHING, Johanna	AUG 09 1854
McCARTY, Elizabeth	SULLIVAN, Dennis	SEP 16 1854
McCARTY, Eugene	GREY, Ann	SEP 05 1851
McCARTY, Florence	HANDY, Winfred	SEP 06 1821
McCARTY, Hannah	SAUNTRY, William	OCT 23 1856
McCARTY, Hannah	KELLY, Columbus	JAN 12 1858
McCARTY, Harriet Ann	DENNIS, Anderson T.	JAN 23 1835
McCARTY, James	CRONAY, Dabby	DEC 03 1853
McCARTY, Johanna	MINNEGAN, Arthur	JAN 30 1858
McCARTY, John	OLARY, Margaret	MAR 31 1821
McCARTY, John	JACKSON, Eliza	FEB 24 1829
McCARTY, John	RUSSELL, Mary	APR 12 1856

District of Columbia Marriage Licenses, 1811-1858

McCARTY, John, Rev. D.D.	STETSON, Susanna Williams	MAR 03 1856
McCARTY, Margaret	KENNEDY, Peter	AUG 02 1851
McCARTY, Maria (blk)	DORSEY, Ephraim	JUL 12 1856
McCARTY, Mary	QUIGLEY, Patrick	DEC 25 1843
McCARTY, Mary	KENNEDY, John	JAN 27 1852
McCARTY, Mary	BOYLAN, Andrew	NOV 09 1853
McCARTY, Mary	BOGAN, John	JAN 26 1858
McCARTY, Mary J.	CANNON, Daniel	FEB 03 1843
McCARTY, Michael	McKEEVER, Bridget	APR 21 1854
McCARTY, Michael	ROCHE, Mary	FEB 06 1858
McCARTY, Nancy	SMARR, James	AUG 28 1822
McCARTY, Patrick	MORIARTY, Julia	APR 13 1854
McCARTY, Richard C.	HAGERMAN, Kezia A.	JAN 10 1832
McCARTY, Robert	FAGAN, Josephine A.	JUL 28 1845
McCARTY, Stephen W.	FRANCIS, Elizabeth A.	SEP 18 1834
McCARTY, Thomas	CURRAN, Mary	APR 24 1843
McCARTY, Thomas	CURRAN, Mary	JAN 29 1844
McCARTY, Timothy	FLEMING, Margaret	DEC 30 1851
McCARTY, Timothy	NOLAND, Alice	NOV 13 1852
McCARTY, William	McKNIGHT, Lucretia	MAR 05 1831
McCARTY, Wm.	REED, Rebecca	DEC 13 1812
McCATHARIN, James	BARCLAY, Jane	JUL 11 1822
McCATHERAN, Sarah E.	DUCKETT, Augustus	SEP 29 1857
McCATHERINE, James	PEAK, Catherine	DEC 12 1848
McCATHRAN, Benjamin F.	MITCHELL, Sarah E.	MAY 27 1854
McCATHRAN, Sarah M.	BERKLEY, Enos E.	DEC 03 1855
McCATHRAN, Wm. W.	BRADLEY, Mary V.	JUN 29 1854
McCAULEY, Andrew J.	WOODS, Mary	AUG 31 1857
McCAULEY, Anna	RILEY, Francis M.	MAY 12 1857
McCAULEY, Elizabeth	RHODES, George	FEB 01 1848
McCAULEY, Ellen	BOLAND, Tobias	MAY 28 1831
McCAULEY, Frances A.	McCORMICK, Hugh	DEC 24 1850
McCAULEY, George	SHIELDS, Susan	NOV 08 1848
McCAULEY, Hannah E.	HOWARD, William E.	NOV 15 1838
McCAULEY, Isabella R.	SEARCEY, Robt. E. [Lieut.]	SEP 11 1821
McCAULEY, John	CASTEL, Elizabeth	MAR 21 1840
McCAULEY, John	LENOX, Susan	JUL 23 1844
McCAULEY, Joseph	MOTHERSAID, Jane	APR 30 1849
McCAULEY, Mary	FOWLER, James	JUL 22 1823
McCAULEY, Richard	DELANEY, Lucy	NOV 12 1856
McCAULEY, Robert	WRIGHT, Catharine	MAR 04 1856
McCAULEY, William M.	GUITON, Virginia.	MAY 02 1855
McCAULLY, Martha Jane	BULL, Daniel M.	JUN 20 1844
McCAULY, William	MOORE, Isabella	JUN 06 1850
McCAUSLAND, James	DAVIS, Mary Elizth.	JUN 21 1856
McCAUSLAND, Mary	WANNALD, William	MAR 01 1827
McCAUSLEN, William C.	BROWNING, Martha R.	JUN 07 1855
McCAUSLIND, Thomas	HANNAH, Jane	MAR 25 1856
McCENEY, George	PATTERSON, Harriet A.B.	DEC 21 1840
McCENEY, Henry C.	LEARNED, Frances C.	SEP 06 1836
McCEWING, Robert	SM[torn out], Mary J.	APR 15 1847
McCHESNEY, Ann Maria	KING, John W.	MAR 27 1856
McCHESNEY, David	WEBSTER, Ann W.	SEP 22 1815
McCHESNEY, Jane M.	ECTON, John H.	APR 17 1851
McCHESNEY, John H.	KING, Mary E.	JUN 12 1850
McCHESNEY, William R.	OWENS, Susanna	AUG 28 1856
McCLAIRING, E. Ann	BURROUGHS, Hezekiah	DEC 17 1834
McCLANAHAN, Elizabeth	JOHNSON, Philip P.	MAR 31 1845

District of Columbia Marriage Licenses, 1811-1858

McCLAREN, Duncan	SOTHORON, Rebecca	MAY 18 1812
McCLEARY, Amanda W.	DOWLING, Rev. Burr P.	NOV 20 1847
McCLEARY, Edwin J.	HOBBIE, Elizabeth	DEC 10 1847
McCLEARY, Marion J.	CLEMENTS, John F.	MAR 18 1856
McCLEES, Ellis B.	MUNROE, Jane H.	MAY 02 1851
McCLELLAN, John	WALKER, Jane Josephine	SEP 17 1842
McCLELLAN, William W.	MITCHELL, Maria	DEC 11 1837
McCLELLAND, Alfred	HAVERSTICKS, Ruth Ann	AUG 22 1848
McCLELLAND, Christiana	RALEY, Benedict J.L.	NOV 18 1841
McCLELLAND, David	GILMAN, Elizabeth	NOV 15 1848
McCLELLAND, Elizabeth	WHITTLESEY, Oliver	DEC 27 1848
McCLELLAND, Elizabeth C.	GREENWELL, Benedict O.	OCT 01 1844
McCLELLAND, Gustavus A.	RAY, Sarah	MAY 14 1830
McCLELLAND, John, Jr.	HODGSON, Catharine E.	JAN 07 1845
McCLELLAND, Margaret	GREIVEACHER, Charles	JUL 20 1830
McCLELLAND, Maria	PEGG, James	FEB 17 1825
McCLELLAND, Martha	WILSON, John	FEB 04 1829
McCLELLAND, Mary	WALLIS, Cowdin S.	JUN 26 1833
McCLELLAND, Rebecca	COLTMAN, Charles L.	DEC 27 1848
McCLELLAND, Robert	MOORE, Rosanna	SEP 11 1850
McCLELLAND, Rosina	BARR, James R.	MAY 03 1839
McCLENAHAN, Thomas James	LETTON, Harriot Elizabeth	JUN 01 1846
McCLEOD, Mary	BESTOR, Chauncey	OCT 19 1819
McCLERY, Indiana I.	GARDINER, J. Carlos	JUN 24 1852
McCLERY, Mirven J.	KEYWORTH, Anna	SEP 08 1845
McCLISH, George	JACKSON, Catharine F.	MAR 28 1832
McCLISH, James	RIGDEN, Elizabeth	FEB 08 1823
McCLISH, William	OSBOURN, Elizabeth	MAY 25 1819
McCLOERY, Mary L.	SHORTWELL, Rev. Nathan	SEP 27 1852
McCLOSKEY, Ann	DOVE, Samuel	OCT 12 1815
McCLOSKEY, Bernard	BRAITHWAIT, Caroline	JAN 06 1840
McCLOSKEY, James D.	GREENWELL, Frances V.	FEB 11 1858
McCLOSKEY, Margaret	AWKWARD, Harry	APR 20 1815
McCLOSKEY, Margaret Ann	SHEID, John T.	JUL 07 1853
McCLOSKEY, Richard	DOVE, Eleanor Jane	DEC 19 1820
McCLOSKEY, William T.	YOST, Eliza Ann	NOV 25 1850
McCLUN, A.B.	ANDERSON, Neley	OCT 20 1818
McCOLGAN, Catherine	RYAN, John	APR 10 1858
McCOLGAN, James	REINEY, Catharine	AUG 14 1852
McCOLGEN, Ellen	RYON, Thomas	SEP 24 1855
McCOLLEY, Elijah G.	HARVEY, Eleanor	OCT 10 1812
McCOLLISTER, Elizth.	KENT, Elijah	MAY 13 1826
McCOMB, Julia E.	THOMAS, Noble J.	NOV 07 1856
McCOMB, Martha E.	THORNLEY, Thomas	FEB 20 1851
McCONCHI, Jane Eliza	STAKE, Robert	APR 02 1849
McCONCHIE, John W.	BROWN, Mary V.	AUG 18 1857
McCONCHIE, Walter Alexander	SPEAKE, Mary Ellen	DEC 31 1829
McCONNELL, Esther Margaret	SCHUTTER, Hubert	JUN 08 1854
McCONNELL, George	CONNELLY, Maria	DEC 24 1836
McCONNELLY, Hannah	MAGIN, Patrick	AUG 05 1824
McCONVEY, Henry	BURCHE, Ellen M.	SEP 20 1856
McCOOMB, Alexander	WILSON, Harriett B.	MAY 26 1826
McCORD, Bernard	CRONIAN, Ann	MAY 21 1846
McCORKLE, Henry	MARSHALL, Nancy	JUL 09 1833
McCORMACK, Mary Ann	HOGAN, Patrick	FEB 23 1852
McCORMICK, Andw. Thos. [Rev.]	PLEASONTON, Hannah	JUL 20 1813
McCORMICK, Bridget	DONELEY, Thomas	AUG 31 1857
McCORMICK, Catherine	CALDWELL, James	NOV 24 1856

District of Columbia Marriage Licenses, 1811-1858

McCORMICK, Elizabeth	KELLY, John	APR 23 1855
McCORMICK, Elizth.	WRIGHT, James	OCT 01 1829
McCORMICK, Grace [Mrs.]	McKEE, William	OCT 10 1812
McCORMICK, Hannah	WARD, Horatio M.	NOV 16 1824
McCORMICK, Helen Custis	ANNIN, Roberdeau	JAN 03 1828
McCORMICK, Hugh	SEARCY, Isabella R.	JUN 09 1830
McCORMICK, Hugh	ALEXANDER, Mary	JUL 13 1842
McCORMICK, Hugh	FLEMING, Mary	MAY 11 1844
McCORMICK, Hugh	McCAULEY, Frances A.	DEC 24 1850
McCORMICK, Jane	TAYLOR, Isaac	DEC 01 1852
McCORMICK, John B.	KING, Bridget	MAY 05 1817
McCORMICK, Mary	OWENS, John	SEP 06 1838
McCORMICK, Mary	BURKE, Richard	MAY 06 1844
McCORMICK, Mary Frances	HOWARD, George T.	OCT 07 1848
McCORMICK, Patrick	BROWN, Mary	DEC 28 1852
McCORMICK, Rebecca J.	McLEAN, George W.	JUL 11 1840
McCORMICK, William	McGINN, Ann	SEP 28 1843
McCORMICK, William J.	MARTIN, Eveline	SEP 30 1833
McCORMICK, Wm. J.	MARTIN, Elizabeth B.	JAN 15 1850
McCOSKER, Hugh	DORAN, Mary	DEC 05 1826
McCOSKER, Margaret E.	McHENRY, Philip J.	AUG 14 1852
McCOSLAND, Margere	GLENN, David	OCT 05 1835
McCOSTICK, Peter	WARNER, Sophia	JUL 17 1844
McCOSTICK, Peter	WARNER, Sophia	JUL 17 1844
McCOY, Alexander	KNOBLOCK, Elizabeth	JUL 23 1818
McCOY, Alexander	MACKEYSEY, Mary	FEB 25 1819
McCOY, Andrew J.	WHITTLE, Martha	DEC 10 1850
McCOY, Ann Eliza	CHASE, Saml.	JUL 12 1854
McCOY, Benjamin M.	DUDLEY, Eliza Ann	JAN 02 1851
McCOY, Bridget	DELAHUNT, John	NOV 28 1849
McCOY, Eliza	BEAN, James	DEC 19 1844
McCOY, Elizabeth	BARNES, William	DEC 21 1844
McCOY, Hayard	THOMAS, Martha	AUG 29 1838
McCOY, Josiah Daniel	FOX, Dewanna Bins	AUG 06 1831
McCOY, Leanna	FOX, Benjamin	JUN 13 1842
McCOY, Margaret	DURLING, Jackson	APR 28 1857
McCOY, Martha (blk)	DOUGLASS, Louis	JUN 22 1850
McCOY, Martha (blk)	HARRIS, Wm. H.	FEB 09 1857
McCOY, Martin	BOND, Harriet E. (blk)	JUN 03 1851
McCOY, Mary W.	WALKER, John Westley	AUG 01 1846
McCOY, Sarah Ann	REARDEN, Michael	AUG 14 1828
McCOY, William	DODD, Mary Jane	APR 23 1845
McCRABB, John W.	HUMPHREYS, Jane M.	MAR 22 1837
McCRACKAN, John	PHILIPS, Mary	MAY 11 1816
McCRACKEN, Ann	KEYS, Magruder J.	JUN 15 1837
McCRADE, Honora	GUINAN, Edmund	JUN 02 1856
McCREA, Eliza (or Liddy) Ann	GREEN, Thomas	JUL 18 1838
McCREA, James W.F. [Dr.]	LEE, Cornelia	APR 08 1833
McCREARY, Robert G.	MOORE, Louisa A.E.	DEC 14 1848
McCREENER, James	LAURENCE, Catharine	AUG 22 1855
McCREERY, John	CRAIG, Harriott E.	AUG 18 1815
McCRETE, Ellen	HERRON, Michael	SEP 10 1851
McCREY, John	TRACY, Amanda [Mrs.]	SEP 13 1834
McCUBBIN, Benjamin	GIBBS, Nancy	AUG 25 1847
McCUBBIN, Elizabeth	JEFFERSON, James	JUL 30 1833
McCUBBIN, Margaret	KELLY, William H.	DEC 27 1850
McCUBBIN, Nicholas	CLARK, Eliza	OCT 01 1839
McCUBBIN, Nicholas	GRIMES, Hester	APR 28 1853

District of Columbia Marriage Licenses, 1811-1858

McCUBBIN, Nicholas	McDONALD, Mary Ellen	JAN 25 1854
McCUE, Bridget	McMAHON, John	AUG 13 1844
McCUE, Mathew	PRITCHET, Harriet	JUL 13 1819
McCUE, Owen	COLLINS, Mary	MAY 24 1819
McCUEN, James	FOSTER, Mary Ann	NOV 02 1852
McCUEN, John	WHEALAN, Margaret	MAY 30 1831
McCUEN, Richard	ATHEY, Eliza	MAR 14 1843
McCUIN, Joseph	ERB, Catharine	FEB 27 1849
McCUIN, Virginia M.	HORNER, William	AUG 04 1858
McCULLEN, Alsey	PITMAN, William	OCT 10 1812
McCULLOGH, Eliza	McGREGOR, James	OCT 04 1849
McCULLOGH, Isabella	CROSS, George	NOV 17 1849
McCULLOH, Adelaide S.	HUBBARD, John P.	JUN 27 1849
McCULLOH, Ann	DIGGIN, Patrick	JUN 14 1852
McCULLOH, Annie L.	BROWNE, William J.	JUN 06 1853
McCULLOUCH, Duncan	MOULSWORTH, Sarah	OCT 09 1826
McCULLOUCH, Lydia	HEBBERN, Samuel	JUN 11 1832
McCULLOUGH, Isabella	KARNEY, Patrick	NOV 10 1849
McCURDLE, John	McKAY, Rosa	SEP 02 1847
McCURDY, Dennis	MUDD, Mary S.	APR 17 1817
McCURDYS, Mary	BEALL, John	NOV 02 1848
McCUTCHEN, Elizabeth	BACON, Samuel	OCT 20 1817
McCUTCHEN, John	BACON, Ann	JUL 01 1824
McCUTCHEN, Mary A.	LAURIE, Cranston H.	OCT 20 1832
McCUTCHEN, Mary Arkansas	GIBSON, Jacob Carter	MAY 06 1854
McCUTE, Richard	CASEY, Johanna	AUG 13 1858
McDADE, Daniel	BROWN, Elizabeth	JAN 08 1824
McDADE, Elizabeth	COOPER, Edward	MAR 20 1820
McDANIEL, Allen	GRAY, Priscella	JUN 15 1846
McDANIEL, Allerson	JOHNSON, Eliza	JAN 03 1827
McDANIEL, Ann	EVERHART, John	JUN 13 1820
McDANIEL, Ann	KING, Wm. Samual	MAY 18 1850
McDANIEL, Ann Maria	OSBORNE, George W.	MAY 28 1853
McDANIEL, Calvin S.	BEACH, Sarah A.	MAR 14 1850
McDANIEL, Elaxander	MULICAN, Ann	DEC 24 1832
McDANIEL, Elizabeth	BROWN, Edmund F.	APR 29 1833
McDANIEL, Elizth. (blk)	TENNY, Pompey	MAY 05 1856
McDANIEL, Ellen	BURGESS, Mordica	NOV 05 1838
McDANIEL, Enoch T.	DUVALL, Ann Maria	FEB 22 1858
McDANIEL, George	LEWIS, Matilda	APR 20 1813
McDANIEL, James W.	ANDERSON, Ellen Ora	MAR 10 1853
McDANIEL, Jane	WILSON, Lancelot	DEC 04 1819
McDANIEL, Jane [Mrs.]	FINCH, John	NOV 17 1834
McDANIEL, John, Sr.	BEALL, Elizh. [Mrs.]	OCT 20 1812
McDANIEL, Lethe	CROSS, Jesse	MAY 18 1817
McDANIEL, Lily	FOWLER, Joseph	FEB 04 1815
McDANIEL, Martha	RIEGLE, Wm. W.	JAN 03 1816
McDANIEL, Mary Ann	HILL, Gibson F.	OCT 22 1829
McDANIEL, Mary E.	TUBMAN, George M.	JUL 10 1827
McDANIEL, Mary F.	BAYNE, Dr. Jno. H.	JAN 10 1827
McDANIEL, Matilda	GROVES, Annis	FEB 14 1835
McDANIEL, Michael	BAWLING, Emily	JAN 07 1822
McDANIEL, Rebecca	EDDS, John	JAN 01 1813
McDANIEL, Sarah	BURRE, DeVere	OCT 11 1842
McDANIEL, Thomas T.	PAYN, Jane	JAN 25 1834
McDERMOTT, Ann	FERLY, Patrick	MAY 31 1853
McDERMOTT, Bridget	KELLY, Michael	NOV 19 1856
McDERMOTT, Cornelius	LYONS, Elizabeth	AUG 31 1824

District of Columbia Marriage Licenses, 1811-1858

McDERMOTT, Eliza	CONNARY, Edward	APR 02 1839
McDERMOTT, Eliza	GRINDALL, John H.	MAY 26 1847
McDERMOTT, Elizabeth	CUMBERLAND, John	NOV 30 1854
McDERMOTT, James	DAILEY, Rose	OCT 08 1856
McDERMOTT, John	TRAIL, Elizabeth	OCT 09 1819
McDERMOTT, John	CUMBERLAND, Mary Ellen	FEB 01 1848
McDERMOTT, John	O'REILEY, Agnes	FEB 19 1849
McDERMOTT, Maria L.	LUSBY, Robert H.	DEC 22 1855
McDERMOTT, Mary	HUTCHERSON, William	MAY 09 1848
McDERMOTT, Mary F.	McCAHAN, Daniel, Jr.	APR 10 1858
McDERMOTT, William	BENDER, Josephene E.	OCT 11 1845
McDERMOTT, William	VanHORN, Frances	APR 27 1854
McDONALD, Alexander	BURGAMORE, Sophia C.	SEP 01 1848
McDONALD, Allen	WILKINSON, Patty	JAN 29 1828
McDONALD, Amanda	KING, George H.	AUG 05 1852
McDONALD, Ann	MILLIGAN, Joseph	JUN 18 1812
McDONALD, Ann	DILL, Peter	DEC 09 1852
McDONALD, Ann	CONNOR, Cornelius	NOV 27 1857
McDONALD, Annie	HAYDEN, James	APR 19 1853
McDONALD, Aurelia	BOWYER, James H.	JAN 13 1848
McDONALD, Catherine	HAMILTON, Charles O.	NOV 05 1857
McDONALD, Charles	BENSON, Mary	AUG 12 1829
McDONALD, Charles	WALLACE, Ann M.	JUL 25 1850
McDONALD, Clara Ann	PORTER, Edward Leroy	MAR 24 1852
McDONALD, Eleanor	SEARS, James	MAY 19 1824
McDONALD, Eleanor	BURTON, Joseph	FEB 14 1830
McDONALD, Elizabeth (blk)	DAVIS, Francis	JUN 01 1848
McDONALD, Eugenia	LITTLEFELD, Rufus P.	JAN 15 1846
McDONALD, James	TENNISON, Lucretia Ann	SEP 29 1825
McDONALD, James	RODDY, Ann	JAN 27 1852
McDONALD, James M.	BULGER, Mary T.R.	FEB 21 1852
McDONALD, James T.	REID, Martha Helen	APR 26 1853
McDONALD, Jane	BURN, Mathias	OCT 27 1817
McDONALD, John	RILEY, Melinda (blk)	JAN 11 1825
McDONALD, Mary Ann	FANLAC, Adolphus	SEP 17 1833
McDONALD, Mary Ann	HART, Patrick	NOV 20 1854
McDONALD, Mary E.	HICKERSON, Oscar B.	MAR 16 1853
McDONALD, Mary Ellen	McCUBBIN, Nicholas	JAN 25 1854
McDONALD, Matthew	RATCLIFF, Anne E.	MAY 07 1857
McDONALD, Michael	NILAND, Mary	OCT 03 1857
McDONALD, Pamelia	JOHNSTON, Lewis	JUL 13 1836
McDONALD, Patrick	BEALL, Susan	MAY 08 1822
McDONALD, Priscilla	CHURNE, James	SEP 18 1852
McDONALD, Rosetta	BERST, Anthony	MAY 29 1841
McDONALD, Sarah	CONVERSE, Freeman	APR 08 1833
McDONALD, Stephen	McINTIRE, Mary Eliza	NOV 19 1833
McDONALD, Thomas	BARNES, Mary Cecelia	JUN 11 1839
McDONALD, Timothy	MONTGOMERY, Rachel	MAY 20 1816
McDONALD, Walter	CANNON, Sarah	FEB 06 1817
McDONALD, William	SOPER, Priscilla	APR 25 1844
McDONALD, William J.	GRYMES, Ann B.	SEP 24 1841
McDONALD, Wm.	SKINNER, Margaret	AUG 07 1824
McDONALD, Wm. T.	SPARROW, Mary Ellen	AUG 28 1854
MCDONALD, Mary	WELSH, James	SEP 11 1854
McDONNALL, Richard	PERRY, Ann R.	FEB 08 1838
McDONNELL, Daniel	BENGURL, Alene	AUG 03 1853
McDONNELL, James	RODGERS, Elizabeth	MAY 12 1848
McDONNELL, Thomas	FAUSH, Sarah Ann	APR 30 1835

District of Columbia Marriage Licenses, 1811-1858

McDONNELL, William	MAHONEY, Martha A.	JUL 06 1857
McDONOGH, James	WESCOTT, Sarah	MAY 04 1858
McDONOUGH, James	TRUMBULL, Jannet	AUG 14 1847
McDONOUGH, John	O'BRYAN, Alice	JAN 26 1844
McDONOUGH, Juliana	STRATTAN, George	FEB 14 1851
McDONOUGH, Margaret	MUSTER, Thomas	MAY 17 1850
McDONOUGH, Mary	BURKE, John	DEC 03 1852
McDONOUGH, Mary	McGRAW, Patrick	AUG 12 1854
McDOWALL, Washington	BORELAND, Jane	MAY 16 1836
McDOWELE, William	EVANS, Eliz.	JUL 10 1813
McDOWELL, Ann	WALKER, Fielder	JUL 31 1813
McDOWELL, E.T.	GALVIN, Caroline A.	MAR 10 1834
McDOWELL, Elizabeth Jane	MILLER, James	AUG 04 1842
McDOWELL, James	McNULTY, Mary	JAN 12 1855
McDOWELL, John	MOSS, Aleana	APR 11 1812
McDOWELL, Joseph	McLEAN, Elizh.	MAR 23 1812
McDOWELL, Robert	CUMMINGS, Mary E.	OCT 11 1838
McDUE, Eliza Bartella	DORRANCE, George W.	DEC 02 1846
McDUELL, Ann Lydia H.	LEAKE, Nathan, Jr.	JUN 20 1832
McDUELL, Anna Celinder	SMALLWOOD, Richard L.	SEP 22 1852
McDUELL, George	COBB, Sarah Ann	FEB 01 1820
McDUELL, George H.	MORROW, Sarah Jane	MAR 02 1848
McDUELL, Sarah Jane	MORSELL, Benjamin F.	MAY 27 1858
McDUFFE, Daniel	MILLS, Cloey A.	NOV 22 1836
McELDERRY, John P.	COX, Ellen May	OCT 07 1852
McELEGETT, James T.	WRIGHT, Margaret	OCT 03 1850
McELFRESH, George S.	SEUFFERLE, Elizabeth M.	OCT 21 1847
McELFRESH, Henry B.	PRENAT, Virginia I.	DEC 29 1853
McELFRESH, James Philip	HOWARD, Ann Maria	NOV 22 1847
McELFRESH, John Wm.	LANGLEY, Eliza Jane	APR 17 1849
McELLGETT, James T.	WOOLFENDEN, Mary	MAY 31 1837
McELWEE, Elizabeth	BALL, Robert	SEP 18 1848
McELWEE, Mary C.	HAGE, William H.	OCT 18 1856
McELWEE, Susan J.	HEDRICK, Joseph	OCT 14 1850
McENDREE, James	GRINWELL, Sarah	JUL 29 1813
McEVOY, Sarah	DUNCAN, William	AUG 01 1816
McEWING, Levi	DAVIS, Priscilla	JAN 23 1826
McEWING, Martha	SLINGERLAND, Peter	AUG 01 1850
McEWING, Mary	CATITTON, James W.	SEP 13 1852
McFADDON, William	MORLAND, Ellen	JAN 29 1839
McFALL, James	HISHLEY, Cecelia	NOV 18 1857
McFARLAN, Daniel	MOORE, Mary Ann	JUL 16 1855
McFARLAND, Alexander B.	SARDO, Josephine M.	JAN 19 1831
McFARLAND, Ann Maria	SMART, Henry	JAN 04 1858
McFARLAND, Catharine	MYERS, George	FEB 02 1856
McFARLAND, Eliza	CARR, William E.	JUN 03 1851
McFARLAND, Eliza Jane	DUVALL, James M.	AUG 02 1842
McFARLAND, Elizabeth [Mrs.]	MILLS, John R.	MAR 19 1827
McFARLAND, Elizabeth Ann	JORDAN, Richard L.	FEB 18 1833
McFARLAND, George	LEWIS, Catherine E.	JUL 08 1848
McFARLAND, James	LANGLEY, Mary A.	NOV 09 1844
McFARLAND, John	WORK, Frances	DEC 04 1819
McFARLAND, John	GOODFELLER, Mrs. Eleanor	JAN 13 1829
McFARLAND, John B.	MORELAND, Mary Ellen	AUG 27 1841
McFARLAND, John F.	DENNIS, Alcinda L.	MAR 14 1842
McFARLAND, John M.	STEWART, Louisa M.	NOV 09 1853
McFARLAND, Mary	GRIGGS, Abel M.	JUN 01 1824
McFARLAND, Mary	HICKS, Edward	FEB 14 1857

District of Columbia Marriage Licenses, 1811-1858

McFARLAND, Mary Elizabeth	HEDENGER, John	APR 19 1848
McFARLAND, William	TRUSCOTT, Elizabeth	MAR 19 1821
McFARLAND, William	BEALL, Maria	DEC 10 1831
McFARLAND, William	GENTLE, Elizth.	APR 14 1834
McFARLAND, William H.	MAY, Mary Julia	MAY 08 1858
McFARLEY, Ann	HAMILTON, John	FEB 15 1847
McFARLIN, Mary	KING, Thomas	SEP 24 1835
McFARLIN, Nancy	BENNETT, Geo.	DEC 12 1821
McFEARSON, Mary	MORAARTY, Ambrose, Jr.	SEP 13 1827
McGAHAN, Bernard	CONNER, Catherine	JAN 31 1844
McGANN, Catherine	DESMOND, Timothy	JAN 06 1852
McGARITY, Andrew Jackson	SHRINK, Josephine	DEC 09 1856
McGARRITY, Jonathan B.	SWINK, Frances A.	JAN 20 1848
McGARVEY, Charles	RICE, Elizabeth	MAY 07 1851
McGARVEY, Jane	HILL, Robert Park	MAY 02 1850
McGARVEY, John	TINNY, Margaret	AUG 14 1858
McGARVEY, Patrick	MARTIN, Isabella	JAN 08 1842
McGEE, Jane	WELLEN, William	MAY 09 1814
McGEE, John	HARRISON, Rebecca	APR 11 1831
McGEE, Joseph	PRENDER, Mary Ann	JUL 28 1853
McGEE, Mary	KENNEDY, James	JUL 06 1857
McGEE, Mary Ann	GREEN, Owen	JUL 29 1851
McGEE, Mary Jane	GRIFFITH, James	NOV 05 1834
McGEE, Patrick	HANERTY, Sarah	OCT 04 1831
McGEE, Sarah	DUBART, M.	MAY 01 1820
McGENNELL, Alice	McLAUGHLIN, Daniel	JUL 30 1856
McGEORTY, James	DAILEY, Johanna	MAY 17 1855
McGHAN, Francis	WEAVER, Louisa	NOV 09 1857
McGILL, Agnes	BELT, Alfred C.	OCT 07 1845
McGILL, Elenor	KIRKWOOD, Jonathan	APR 11 1839
McGILL, Janet	THOMPSON, John W.	AUG 01 1850
McGILL, John B.	RATARY, Isabella R.	MAY 13 1845
McGILL, Louisa	FORTUNE, Wm.	JAN 14 1822
McGILL, Rebecca	GRIFFIN, Charles T.	SEP 30 1843
McGILL, Thomas	DOUGLAS, Mary	MAY 29 1854
McGILL, William H.	GRAVES, Mary	MAY 11 1844
McGILL, [blank]	TODD, [blank]	FEB 10 1857
McGILLICODDY, Honora	SLATTERY, James	JAN 06 1853
McGILLICUDDY, Nancy	MORGAN, Alexr. J.	SEP 11 1847
McGILLICUDDY, Timothy	KELLEY, Margaret	APR 30 1857
McGILTON, Susan B.	FUGATE, Joseph	JUN 16 1838
McGIN, Patrick	GULLYHAM, Elizabeth	JAN 15 1818
McGINLEY, Palmer C.	SEWALL, Evaline	MAY 17 1843
McGINN, Ann	McCORMICK, William	SEP 28 1843
McGINN, Catharine	GAINER, John F.	AUG 31 1853
McGINN, James	BASTABLE, Rebecca	NOV 23 1855
McGINN, Mary	BASTABLE, Charles	DEC 30 1852
McGINN, Peter	O'DANIEL, Mary	JUN 15 1831
McGINNEL, Mary Ann	PATTERSON, James	NOV 17 1853
McGINNIE, Mary E.	WALLING, John	JUL 01 1858
McGINNIS, Catherine	HALLAHAN, Thomas	NOV 10 1853
McGINNIS, Hugh	SHEA, Anna	JUN 13 1856
McGINNIS, Michael	SCANLON, Mary	JUL 13 1854
McGINNIS, Peter	GREEN, Maria M.	NOV 12 1855
McGINNISS, Frederick	FITZHUGH, Mary Ann	JUL 29 1841
McGINNITY, Thomas	OWENS, Maria	JAN 03 1851
McGLAVEN, Thomas	MASTERSON, Elizabeth	SEP 29 1852
McGLOCKLEN, Antoney	SCOTT, Margaret	JAN 23 1844

District of Columbia Marriage Licenses, 1811-1858

McGLOCKLIN, John	PURCELL, Mary	MAY 20 1857
McGLUE, Edward Skyloe	AVERETT, Elizabeth Ann	FEB 15 1832
McGLUE, Mary A.E.	SEMMES, Jesse M.	FEB 04 1823
McGLUE, Owen	KING, Mary	NOV 06 1812
McGLUE, Owen	NOWLAND, Mary Ann Eliza	NOV 23 1819
McGOLDRICK, Charles	BAYNE, Mary	JUL 07 1835
McGOLDRICK, William	WATERS, Mary Ann	OCT 04 1852
McGOVARN, Thomas	TEARGRIEFF, Ann	JUL 25 1835
McGOWAN, Ann	LAPORT, Eugene	MAY 24 1828
McGOWAN, Catharine	SHERWOOD, Samuel	FEB 10 1825
McGOWAN, James	BELL, Sarah	FEB 02 1857
McGOWAN, Patrick	DONOHOE, Bridget	NOV 16 1818
McGRANN, Bridget	HICKEY, Patrick W.	APR 04 1853
McGRANN, John	DAILEY, Ann	JUN 28 1855
McGRATH, Catherine	KEEFE, John	JAN 14 1853
McGRATH, L.O.	GROTZ, Agnes M.	MAY 20 1852
McGRATH, Michael	TOBIN, Ellen	SEP 04 1852
McGRATH, Peter	KING, Mary	MAR 22 1856
MCGRATH, Jane	CLARKE, Robert	NOV 04 1819
McGRAW, Benjamin F.	KNIGHT, Louisa M.	JUL 31 1852
McGRAW, James	WOODWARD, Esther	JAN 24 1844
McGRAW, Patrick	McDONOUGH, Mary	AUG 12 1854
McGRAW, Thomas	HARRIGAN, Johanna	JUN 12 1854
McGREADY, John	ROWE, Josephine M.	JUL 07 1857
McGREARY, Margaret Ann	LEACH, Thomas W.	MAR 07 1849
McGREEVY, Eliza Jane	DOBBS, John H.	APR 01 1857
McGREGOR, Helen W.	EWELL, John S.	NOV 01 1852
McGREGOR, James	McCULLOGH, Eliza	OCT 04 1849
McGREGOR, John R.	McGREGOR, Mary	JUN 12 1854
McGREGOR, Mary	McGREGOR, John R.	JUN 12 1854
McGRUE, Sarah A.	SHIPLEY, Joshua F.	OCT 14 1856
McGUIGGAN, Arthur J.	HOBBS, Adeline T.	MAY 13 1857
McGUINEY, Kate	MATTINGLY, Joseph H.	AUG 19 1858
McGUIRE, Ann	SMOOT, Benjamin S.	FEB 10 1831
McGUIRE, Bridget	SMITH, William	MAR 17 1855
McGUIRE, Bryan	CALLIGHAN, Nancy	AUG 16 1855
McGUIRE, George	ALLEN, Ann [Mrs.]	MAR 02 1827
McGUIRE, James	TWOOMY, Margaret	FEB 12 1852
McGUIRE, John	KLONE, Margaret	DEC 19 1851
McGUIRE, John	GARNER, Maria	APR 15 1853
McGUIRE, Michael	DIGGINS, Mary	JUL 30 1853
McGUIRE, Rose	SHEE, Henry	DEC 02 1851
McGUIRE, Rose	YOUNG, Thomas	APR 03 1858
McGUIRE, Rosetta	STAUNTON, Thomas	SEP 25 1844
McGUIRE, Terence	COLLINS, Rose	JUN 06 1838
McGUIRE, Thomas F.	REEVES, Martha	JUN 12 1854
McGURK, Owen	CROSS, Mary E.	NOV 04 1843
McHENRY, Hamilton	EDMONSTON, Mary Jane	OCT 07 1843
McHENRY, Martin D.	MOUNT, Martha E.	MAR 04 1839
McHENRY, Philip J.	McCOSKER, Margaret E.	AUG 14 1852
McHUGH, Catharine	BURGIN, John F.	MAR 25 1854
McILHANEY, Bridget	McCADDEN, Thomas	NOV 14 1853
McILHANEY, Mary L.	RENNOE, William W.	SEP 01 1848
McILLICUDDY, Ellen	O'CONNOR, James	FEB 09 1857
McILVAINE, Francis E.	SLOW, Sarah E.	SEP 09 1856
McINERNY, Dennis	KILBRIDE, Margaret	SEP 13 1832
McINTEER, Mary E.	TROTT, William T.	DEC 17 1851
McINTIRE, Alexander	MOORE, Eliza E.	SEP 04 1815

District of Columbia Marriage Licenses, 1811-1858

McINTIRE, Alexander	ELLIS, Mary M.	OCT 12 1848
McINTIRE, Anne	THORN, William G.B.	FEB 16 1858
McINTIRE, Arthur L.	KELLER, Zelena M.	OCT 22 1833
McINTIRE, Edward	LONG, Eliza	OCT 14 1824
McINTIRE, Harriet	WELSER, Ferdinand	JUL 15 1835
McINTIRE, Mary Eliza	McDONALD, Stephen	NOV 19 1833
McINTIRE, Robert	FRONK, Catharine	MAR 03 1834
McINTIRE, Samuel	LORD, Ruth	JAN 30 1817
McINTIRE, Sarah Justice	BROWN, William	JUN 13 1816
McINTIRE, Timothy C.	WILLIAMS, Sarah E.	OCT 05 1854
McINTOSH, Alexander	RAE, Margaret	AUG 28 1832
McINTOSH, Ann	WEBB, Emanuel	OCT 14 1856
McINTOSH, David	TEPPER, Ann	AUG 20 1855
McINTOSH, Edward	TYLER, Elizabeth	MAY 23 1850
McINTOSH, Elizabeth	WESTERFIELD, James	APR 13 1846
McINTOSH, James Thomas	VERNON, Lucinda	JAN 02 1840
McINTOSH, Jannet	VERNON, Henry T.	JAN 02 1838
McINTOSH, Job P.	TAYLOR, Elizabeth	JUL 19 1841
McINTOSH, Job P.	HINTON, Angeline	APR 10 1850
McINTOSH, John	DAVIS, Sarah	NOV 23 1815
McINTOSH, John	WRIGHT, Sinah	JAN 05 1826
McINTOSH, John	FOOT, Ellen Maria	JUL 17 1845
McINTOSH, John	BERRY, Nora Ann	SEP 07 1852
McINTOSH, Joseph	BRIAN, Mary A.	JUL 14 1857
McINTOSH, Maddalina S.A.	TSCHIFFELY, Charles A.G.	DEC 03 1833
McINTOSH, Mary	ELLIS, Henry Charles	MAY 28 1855
McINTOSH, Thomas	WOODWARD, Sarah Ann	AUG 06 1838
McINTOSH, Thomas	PAGE, Lucy E.	AUG 29 1854
McINTYRE, Letitia M.	DAVIDSON, Daniel D.	APR 04 1837
McINTYRE, Margaret Ann	LAMOND, Alexander	OCT 19 1830
McINTYRE, Patrick	CALLAHER, Mary	NOV 24 1857
McKAIN, James	OLIVER, Sarah	JUN 12 1828
McKAMM, Daniel K.	ROBERSON, Mary M.	MAR 30 1858
McKANNA, Julia	KENNEDY, Thomas	JAN 23 1851
McKARITHEN, Mary	MAUD, William	AUG 21 1826
McKAVICK, Thomas	DUFFY, Mary	JAN 02 1857
McKAY, Catharine	McALLISTER, Charles	JAN 06 1823
McKAY, Eleanor	KEMP, John N.	OCT 22 1835
McKAY, Rosa	McCURDLE, John	SEP 02 1847
McKEAN, James	LEVI, Sarah	JUL 08 1847
McKEAN, James P.	SHEILDS, Harriet Ann	JUL 21 1830
McKEAN, Laura Ann	LARNER, Gideon W.	APR 28 1853
McKEAN, Samuel	KING, Mary Frances	MAY 18 1818
McKECHNIE, Neil	BRUCE, Mary	SEP 08 1854
McKEE, James	WEBSTER, Mildred B.	FEB 27 1838
McKEE, Milly B.	COOK, William	DEC 07 1843
McKEE, William	McCORMICK, Grace [Mrs.]	OCT 10 1812
McKEE, William	DEMENT, Caroline	OCT 25 1856
McKEEVER, Alexander	RAINEY, Jane	APR 06 1847
McKEEVER, Bridget	McCARTY, Michael	APR 21 1854
McKEEVER, Elizabeth	HAMMILL, Bernard	AUG 20 1858
McKEEVER, Rose	MURRAY, Peter	APR 20 1857
McKEEVERS, Thomas	TROLLERS, Celeney	MAR 18 1851
McKEFFREY, Elizabeth	MILES, James H.	FEB 26 1846
McKELDEN, Andrew	RIND, Clementina	MAY 03 1814
McKELDEN, C. Jenny	YOUNG, Saml. H.	APR 22 1856
McKELDEN, Clementina E.G. [Mrs.]	LATIMER, Marcus	FEB 10 1820
McKELDEN, John C.	CHELL, Mary	APR 28 1831

District of Columbia Marriage Licenses, 1811-1858

McKELDEN, Sarah V.	WAUGH, James E.	FEB 15 1858
McKELDEN, William P.	BLAGROVE, Mary Ann	JUN 24 1834
McKELDON, Margaret	PATTERSON, Charles	MAR 26 1821
McKELGATH, Mary Ellen	ULRICK, Michael	JUL 09 1851
McKENDRY, Henry	MORRIS, Elizabeth	NOV 16 1852
McKENNA, James H.	MULLIN, Martha A.	DEC 19 1850
McKENNA, Mary M.	SMOOT, John W.	NOV 18 1856
McKENNA, Phelix	CLEARY, Catharine	AUG 13 1850
McKENNA, William	GATES, Lydia Ann	APR 20 1844
McKENNEDY, Catharine	KIERNAN, James	OCT 04 1851
McKENNERY, Sarah	BERRY, Philip T.	MAY 14 1839
McKENNEY, Catharine	KERSEY, Robert	MAY 12 1821
McKENNEY, Christopher	KIRBY, Marion E.	APR 14 1857
McKENNEY, Edward	ROBEY, Susan	AUG 03 1835
McKENNEY, Edward	OSBORNE, Anna	NOV 22 1851
McKENNEY, Elizabeth	WOODS, John	APR 27 1852
McKENNEY, Francis A.	DUFFEY, William B.	DEC 02 1852
McKENNEY, George W.	MOCKBEE, Elizabeth S.	OCT 13 1856
McKENNEY, Henrietta F.	CRAGIN, Charles H.	APR 14 1857
McKENNEY, James E.	JENKINS, Georgiana	AUG 14 1858
McKENNEY, James H.	HALL, Jane Martha	JUL 21 1852
McKENNEY, Jarrett	RELIN, Mary Ann	JUL 21 1837
McKENNEY, John	AULFEET, Elizabeth	JUL 19 1858
McKENNEY, Margaret Ann Foxall	OSBORN, William McK.	APR 26 1834
McKENNEY, Mary	CRAGIN, Charles H.	OCT 01 1845
McKENNEY, Mary F.	ALBRIGHT, Frederick	NOV 17 1857
McKENNEY, Michael	DANT, Jane	DEC 28 1831
McKENNEY, Peter	MURRAY, Mary	OCT 10 1857
McKENNEY, Samuel	FOXALL, Mary Ann	MAR 08 1813
McKENNEY, William	RAGSDALE, Anna Maria McLean	MAR 24 1852
McKENNY, Mahala Jane	ROBERTSON, Henry B.	NOV 01 1849
McKENSEY, Catharine	GOTT, Richard	FEB 02 1835
McKENSEY, Sarah	ALLEN, Ely	JAN 06 1814
McKENZIE, James W.	CAMPBELL, Jane E.	JUN 02 1858
McKENZIE, Martha Jane	SHINDOLLAR, John	NOV 03 1856
McKEON, John	FITZPATRICK, Ellen	SEP 04 1852
McKEON, Thomas	DAURACEY, Rosanna J.	JUN 30 1854
McKEOWIN, Ann	DOOLY, John	JUN 15 1857
McKEOWN, John	MILLER, Mary	MAY 01 1854
McKERVAN, Albert A.	ARRINGTON, Mary E.	AUG 03 1858
McKEWIN, Ann Maria	THUMBLERT, William H.	OCT 13 1841
McKEWIN, Mary	WOLTZ, George	MAR 10 1831
McKEWON, William	SCOTT, Rachael	NOV 22 1817
McKEY, W.R.	JOHNSON, Catharine	DEC 08 1817
McKIB, Mary	BORLAND, Alexander	JAN 12 1818
McKIERNAN, Peter	MAHER, Sarah Jane	MAY 03 1851
McKIM, Issabella	STEPHEN, Henry	JUN 25 1816
McKIM, John	PORTER, Augusta E.M.	DEC 31 1814
McKIM, Josiah F.	FERREE, Fanny M.	JUN 23 1858
McKIM, Lois	ASHWORTH, Charles S.	DEC 31 1814
McKIM, Mary	BRIDGES, James	APR 22 1817
McKIM, Sarah	CLEMENTSON, John	MAY 22 1818
McKINLEY, Isaac G.	HANNAH, Martha Ann	MAY 26 1834
McKINNEY, John W.	STATHAM, Rhoda J.	NOV 18 1842
McKINNY, Sarah	GLASGOW, Beecham	DEC 14 1844
McKINSEY, Jane	McYOUNG, Jacob	APR 26 1816
McKISITT, George	JONES, Elizabeth	MAY 10 1839
McKLEER, John	KELLY, Issabella	AUG 08 1821

District of Columbia Marriage Licenses, 1811-1858

McKNEW, Charles	ROBINSON, Maria	AUG 28 1852
McKNEW, Minerva	COOK, Elisha J.	JUL 17 1855
McKNEW, N. Clarendon	WILLSON, Miranda E.	OCT 11 1856
McKNIGHT, Ann	FORNANCE, Joseph	JUL 23 1840
McKNIGHT, Anna P.	KLAPP, Harvey [Dr.]	APR 13 1831
McKNIGHT, George B. [Dr.]	PROUT, Martha H.	SEP 16 1829
McKNIGHT, James M.	PRESTON, Anne E.	DEC 31 1846
McKNIGHT, Lucretia	McCARTY, William	MAR 05 1831
McKNIGHT, Martha	RUMNEY, John	FEB 07 1824
McKNIGHT, Samuel	UPPERMAN, Mary Ann	MAY 02 1838
McKOME, Robert	HOW, Mary Ann	APR 04 1820
McKOY, Enos	KIRK, Eleanor	JUL 22 1830
McKRAE, Colin	HARRIS, Judith J.	OCT 16 1818
McLAGAN, Wm. R.	LEACOCK, Mary A.	JUN 14 1855
McLAIN, Jane	HENNON, George	JAN 28 1839
McLAIN, Nancy	EVANS, George	JUN 06 1812
McLAIN, Richard T.	LAURENSON, Eliza S.	JAN 26 1850
McLANE, Allen	BACHE, Maria C.	DEC 17 1850
McLANE, George W.	BOYD, Rosanna	AUG 14 1849
McLANE, Mary Jane	RISTON, Thomas	FEB 01 1854
McLANE, William	MATTINGLY, Jane	NOV 19 1846
McLAUGHLIN, Ann	HENNINGER, John	NOV 05 1831
McLAUGHLIN, Anna	FITZGERALD, John	JUL 11 1854
McLAUGHLIN, Celia	CORRIGAN, Thomas M.	JUN 02 1851
McLAUGHLIN, Celia	CORRIGAN, Thomas M.	JUN 30 1851
McLAUGHLIN, Daniel	WHITNEY, Elizabeth	SEP 01 1852
McLAUGHLIN, Daniel	McGENNELL, Alice	JUL 30 1856
McLAUGHLIN, Elizabeth	COLLINS, Richard John	APR 01 1826
McLAUGHLIN, Elizabeth	LLOYD, Joshua	DEC 28 1844
McLAUGHLIN, Hugh C.	SHEEHY, Mary Ann	JUN 13 1836
McLAUGHLIN, James Alexander	CADEN, Mary Elizth.	JUN 30 1846
McLAUGHLIN, John	LUPTON, Ann	JAN 31 1824
McLAUGHLIN, John	FERGUSON, Julia V.	OCT 23 1851
McLAUGHLIN, John T., U.S.N.	MEADE, Salvadora	SEP 14 1840
McLAUGHLIN, Margaret E.	COLLINS, Reubin	APR 28 1840
McLAUGHLIN, Martha	RICHARDSON, John	JUN 20 1831
McLAUGHLIN, Mary	MAXWELL, George W.	JUN 18 1831
McLAUGHLIN, Mary	BAZIN, Alfred Auguste	OCT 31 1844
McLAUGHLIN, Salvadora	PATERSON, William	OCT 07 1852
McLAUGHLIN, Thomas	CONNOR, Mary Ann	JUL 13 1852
McLAUGHLIN, Thomas A.	MORELAND, Rachel E.	APR 28 1857
McLAY, Nathaniel	WELSH, Bridget	FEB 04 1854
McLEAN, Arabella	WEED, E.J.	MAR 26 1827
McLEAN, Bridget	MYERS, Matthew	DEC 31 1852
McLEAN, Charles [Dr.]	CAMPBELL, Margaret M.	APR 16 1832
McLEAN, Eliza	HARDISTY, Henry, Jr.	JUN 27 1833
McLEAN, Elizabeth	CRAHAN, Thomas	SEP 03 1853
McLEAN, Elizh.	McDOWELL, Joseph	MAR 23 1812
McLEAN, Evelina	TAYLOR, Joseph P. [Capt.]	NOV 20 1827
McLEAN, George W.	McCORMICK, Rebecca J.	JUL 11 1840
McLEAN, John	CRAIGHAN, Norah	JAN 08 1852
McLEAN, Mary Ann	HOYL, William H.	JAN 02 1857
McLEAN, Rebecca	RABBITT, John	JUN 03 1839
McLEAN, Rebecca E.	RICHARDS, Augustus H.	JAN 22 1829
McLEAN, Thomas	CLEMENTS, Ellen Virginia	APR 22 1852
McLEAN, William Hector	HOLERY, Maria	DEC 31 1835
McLEAR, Mary R.	WOODWARD, Richard L.	JAN 07 1852
McLELLAN, George W.	SMITH, Mary Elizabeth	OCT 19 1852

District of Columbia Marriage Licenses, 1811-1858

McLEOD, Alexander N.	LYNCH, S.Lisey Ann	DEC 03 1855
McLEOD, Ann Eliza	BOYLE, Junius J. [Lt.]	JUL 18 1832
McLEOD, Christopher Columbus	MOUNTZ, Joanna	NOV 05 1838
McLEOD, Daniel	WOOD, Mariah	AUG 07 1834
McLEOD, Elizabeth	GRIFFITH, Kinsey	SEP 04 1817
McLEOD, Jane Mary	TURNER, Janes C.	APR 13 1838
McLEOD, Mary	TILLEY, Chs.	APR 02 1821
McLEOD, Mary	MARION, John	FEB 06 1829
McLEOD, Mary	DRAINE, Charles	NOV 20 1838
McLEOD, Mary Ann	GRIFFITH, Kinsey	MAR 21 1832
McLEWN, Eliza	HANTZ, Washington A.	AUG 28 1832
McLILLEY, Samuel	ELI, Sarah	MAY 07 1850
McMAGHEN, Hannah	HURD, John	SEP 03 1853
McMAHON, Alice Mary	MURRAY, Patrick	SEP 06 1838
McMAHON, Ann	HEANY, John	OCT 24 1846
McMAHON, Bridget	O'DONOGHUE, Charles	SEP 07 1852
McMAHON, Honora	O'CONNOR, Patrick	NOV 04 1853
McMAHON, John	McCUE, Bridget	AUG 13 1844
McMAHON, John	STACKPOOL, Catherine	JUN 10 1853
McMAHON, John	SHEEDY, Bridget	JUL 11 1855
McMAHON, Mary	NUGENT, John	OCT 05 1852
McMAHON, Michael	ONLEY, Allis	AUG 28 1833
McMAHON, Patrick	HALFPENNY, Margaret	MAY 09 1857
McMAHON, Philip	BLICK, Louisa Elizabeth	AUG 19 1848
McMAHON, Thomas	McCARTHY, Ann	MAR 28 1853
McMAHON, Thomas	MAHAR, Catherine	JUL 24 1857
McMANN, Bridget	COFFY, Patrick	SEP 25 1850
McMANN, Margaret	MALONEY, Michael	MAR 16 1850
McMANN, Michael	FOUNTAIN, Mary Ellen	AUG 31 1848
McMANNUS, Rebecca	NICHOLSIN, Henry	DEC 25 1834
McMANUS, Edward	McCARTHY, Catherine	JUL 10 1848
McMANUS, Patrick	SMITH, Ellen	JAN 09 1851
McMANUS, Patrick	MOORE, Margaret	JAN 03 1853
McMANUS, William	FAGAN, Bridget	AUG 27 1853
McMARRA, Julia	McNAMEE, Patrick	NOV 28 1854
McMECHIN, Henry	MEAD, Sarah	OCT 24 1836
McMEEHEN, William G.	MORRIS, Sarah Ann	JUL 17 1836
McMILLAN, John	CLARK, Mary Ann	SEP 07 1838
McMULLIN, Lucinda	PEALE, Titian R.	AUG 12 1850
McMURRAY, Margaret	BARNES, William H.	MAR 28 1826
McMURRAY, William	TALBERT, Margaret	FEB 08 1816
McNAI, Anna C.	MYERS, John W.P.	JUN 01 1857
McNAINEE, Mary Eliza	QUIGLEY, William	MAY 13 1848
McNAIR, Eleanor	SIMS, John	DEC 27 1811
McNAIR, Stephen Y.	KNOWLES, Martha E.	APR 05 1854
McNALLY, Catherine A.	HUNT, George N.	MAR 11 1857
McNALLY, John	MURPHY, Mary Jane	JAN 05 1857
McNAMARA, Dennis	TOBIN, Ann	FEB 13 1854
McNAMARA, Margaret	DACEY, Dennis	OCT 19 1852
McNAMARA, Martin	LYONS, Margaret	APR 18 1857
McNAMARA, Michael	DONOHO, Johanna	JUL 19 1854
McNAMARA, Thomas	CONNERS, Mary	OCT 10 1854
McNAMARRAH, Ann	DUNHER, Thomas	JAN 19 1856
McNAMEE, Alice	MORRISON, Peter	MAY 15 1858
McNAMEE, Catherine T.	SANDERSON, Nicholas	OCT 28 1841
McNAMEE, Charles	TONGE, Susan Vaux	OCT 20 1841
McNAMEE, Margaret	LLOYD, John	MAY 27 1841
McNAMEE, Patrick	McMARRA, Julia	NOV 28 1854

District of Columbia Marriage Licenses, 1811-1858

McNANTZ, Patrick H.	MUDD, Louisa Jane	JUL 01 1848
McNARE, James	SPERLING, Martha	JAN 07 1814
McNARHAY, Edward	FARRELL, Bridgett	JAN 03 1824
McNAUGHTEN, George	HARTIGAN, Honora	APR 29 1857
McNAUGHTEN, Mary	DUGAN, Thomas	MAR 02 1857
McNEALE, Francis	BAXTER, Samuel	NOV 18 1857
McNEALE, Mary	WATSON, Donald	OCT 09 1823
McNEAR, Daniel	ARNOLD, Harriot	OCT 29 1825
McNEARE, Elizh.	WESNER, Matthias	DEC 02 1812
McNEER, Margarett	ROBERSON, James J.	DEC 09 1846
McNEER, Martha	TITUS, Samuel	MAR 19 1850
McNEER, William W.	HARRY, Mary E.	SEP 30 1843
McNEER, Wm.	BILLINGS, Augusta M.	FEB 28 1818
McNEIL, Colin	GROSS, Mary Ann	MAR 30 1857
McNEIR, Catherine W.	WILSON, Matthew	DEC 04 1855
McNEIR, Elizabeth Guest	ISRAEL, Robert	NOV 09 1852
McNEIR, Harriet A.	MONEY, Presley W.	DEC 20 1853
McNEIR, Mary Elizth.	STALCUP, Joshua	NOV 30 1847
McNEIR, Sally Maria	MAURY, Jourdan W.	NOV 09 1846
McNEIR, William F.	HEFFERNAN, Sarah A.	OCT 26 1857
McNEMARA, John	LAWSON, Susanna	JUL 19 1815
McNEMARA, Mary	TOBIN, William	JAN 11 1853
McNEMERA, Margaret	DYLE, William	FEB 07 1853
McNERHAN, Margaret	KERANS, Thomas	SEP 18 1844
McNERHANEY, Ann	GREEN, James	FEB 18 1851
McNERHANEY, Mary L.	TYLER, William W.	DEC 31 1856
McNERHANY, Francis	O'BRIEN, Margaret	JUL 03 1848
McNERHANY, Kate	KING, T. Grosvenor	JUN 05 1854
McNERHANY, Mary [Mrs.]	SMITH, Philip [Dr.]	MAY 31 1834
McNEVIN, Maria	McNEVIN, Michael	NOV 10 1851
McNEVIN, Michael	McNEVIN, Maria	NOV 10 1851
McNEW, Basil	KNOX, Airy	JAN 04 1825
McNEW, Basil	MOCKABEE, Elizabeth	JUN 10 1834
McNEW, Jeremiah	PICKRELL, Alethea	MAR 26 1829
McNEW, Jeremiah	TAYLOR, Rosalie B.	OCT 29 1852
McNEW, Julia	TALBOTT, Nicholas R.	JUN 13 1832
McNEW, Marietta	STEWART, Edwin R.	JUL 18 1854
McNIEL, Mark	ROBINSON, Ann	DEC 22 1848
McNOYE, Catherine	FOUKE, Jacob	DEC 22 1829
McNULTY, Ann	O'CALLAN, Francis	JUL 21 1855
McNULTY, Mary	McDOWELL, James	JAN 12 1855
McNULTY, Mary	MORTER, Thomas	MAY 25 1855
McNULTY, Philip	RILEY, Mary	DEC 05 1853
McPEAKE, Mary	HARROT, William	JUN 08 1843
McPHAIL, William	OARD, Sarah Ann	AUG 31 1835
McPHEE, Mary	HENNEY, Hugh	MAY 28 1833
McPHERSON, Ann	BOWEN, John G.	OCT 21 1813
McPHERSON, Ann	RANDALL, Benedict	APR 20 1835
McPHERSON, Edith	McPHERSON, H.M.B.	JAN 22 1855
McPHERSON, Eliza	HASTINGS, James	APR 11 1834
McPHERSON, Elizabeth	PIERCE, Thomas	MAY 27 1824
McPHERSON, H.M.B.	McPHERSON, Edith	JAN 22 1855
McPHERSON, Harriet	BRAWNER, Robert	MAY 20 1834
McPHERSON, Henrietter	SHAW, John	APR 17 1827
McPHERSON, Henry D.	GREEN, Harriet R.	JUN 08 1857
McPHERSON, Henry H.	STELLE, Elizabeth H.	SEP 17 1816
McPHERSON, Henry H., Jr.	CLARKE, Mary A.	OCT 08 1850
McPHERSON, James	SMITH, Kesiah	MAR 28 1817

District of Columbia Marriage Licenses, 1811-1858

McPHERSON, Jane (blk)	HILL, Robert	DEC 26 1853
McPHERSON, Janet	TUCKER, Enoch	OCT 03 1815
McPHERSON, John	SIMMS, Jane (blk)	MAY 02 1850
McPHERSON, Maria C.	KELLY, John	SEP 26 1830
McPHERSON, Mary Ann	PHEARSON, Jos. N.	JUL 19 1821
McPHERSON, Mary B.	PERRIE, Charles F.	FEB 19 1855
McPHERSON, Robert L.	WOODWARD, Sarah Jane	DEC 10 1836
McPHERSON, Robert M.	DAVIS, Ann Maria	MAY 10 1834
McPHERSON, Samuel	BARRETT, Rosetta	FEB 12 1831
McPHERSON, Samuel T.	STREET, Sarah Ann	MAY 25 1843
McPHERSON, Sarah Ann	TUCKER, John H.	NOV 05 1829
McPHERSON, William	QUARD, Mary	JAN 16 1815
McPHERSON, Wm.	SANDIFORD, Ann	SEP 03 1818
McQUAY, Benjamin	O'BRIEN, Emily	NOV 07 1844
McQUEEN, David	HERCUS, Christianna J.	DEC 18 1848
McQUEEN, Margaret	KELLEY, Michael	MAY 26 1852
McQUEEN, Patrick	MADIGAN, Mary	NOV 20 1852
McQUILLAN, John	KEITH, Ann	SEP 22 1817
McQUILLAN, Thomas	ROBERTSON, Mary	MAR 19 1852
McQUILLIAN, Eliza T.	O'BRIEN, William M.	DEC 15 1846
McQUILLIN, Patrick	CALLAN, Mary Ann	JUN 03 1824
McRA, Julia Matilda	OELRICHS, Henry Ferdinand	JUN 20 1849
McRA, Powell	MAY, Julia M.	APR 30 1839
McRAE, Daniel	CUNNINGHAM, Margaret	JUN 22 1854
McREA, Albert H.	RICKETTS, Mary M.	MAY 26 1856
McREA, James M.	BEALE, Elizabeth K.	SEP 01 1820
McREYNOLDS, John N.	ROADES, Lucy F.	MAR 28 1856
McSHERRY, James	CARBERY, Hellen Mary	APR 21 1852
McSHERRY, Richard	KING, Ann C.	JAN 28 1817
McSPADDIN, Robert	THOMPSON, Anne	MAR 07 1849
McTAGGART, Thomas	FAIRGRIEVE, Elizabeth	NOV 21 1843
McTILTON, Catherine	SONNENSCHMIDT, Chas. W.	MAR 07 1857
McVARRY, Bridget	BUCKLEY, Jerry	JUL 09 1852
McVARRY, Mary	McVARRY, Peter	JUL 05 1853
McVARRY, Peter	McVARRY, Mary	JUL 05 1853
McVARY, Owen	KEELY, Catherine	JUL 15 1853
McVARY, Peter	CANAVAN, Mary	SEP 12 1856
McVAY, Bridget	CAULFIELD, Bernard	JUN 06 1822
McVEAN, James	WHANN, Jane	JAN 07 1828
McWATERS, Adam	SPRIGG, Mary	AUG 28 1819
McWILLIAM, Isabella	FAWCETT, Thomas	JUN 09 1858
McWILLIAM, James	VERNON, Sarah	DEC 13 1856
McWILLIAMS, Adelaide E.	YOUNG, Noble [Dr.]	MAY 04 1836
McWILLIAMS, Elizabeth	YEATES, John	JUL 01 1846
McWILLIAMS, Jane	LAWRENCE, Alexander H.	SEP 13 1841
McWILLIAMS, Mary	FITZPATRICK, Bernard	JUL 29 1853
McWILLIAMS, Mary V.	FLOOD, William H.	APR 26 1858
McYOUNG, Jacob	McKINSEY, Jane	APR 26 1816
MEACHAM, James H.	LYNCH, Jannie F.	AUG 19 1856
MEAD, Abigal Jane	MURPHY, Samuel	OCT 07 1852
MEAD, Deborah	BOISEAU, James T.	SEP 02 1841
MEAD, Edward	HOWARD, Susan	DEC 12 1844
MEAD, Eliza	WOOD, Andrew	FEB 12 1814
MEAD, Elizabeth	WALLINGSFORD, John	DEC 04 1819
MEAD, Elizabeth	FILLIUS, Jacob	JAN 06 1835
MEAD, Franklin	WATKINS, Mary	MAY 01 1855
MEAD, John	FILLIUS, Elizabeth	DEC 26 1834

District of Columbia Marriage Licenses, 1811-1858

MEAD, Sarah	McMECHIN, Henry	OCT 24 1836
MEADE, Cecilia Ann	COX, Charles F.	JUL 10 1847
MEADE, Charlotte	GRAHAM, James D.	JUL 06 1828
MEADE, Eleatha	GOODYEAR, Joseph	AUG 04 1840
MEADE, James H.	BAILEY, Julia A.	MAY 08 1849
MEADE, Jane	GORMAN, John	JUN 19 1820
MEADE, Maria del Carmel	BACHE, Hartman	FEB 28 1829
MEADE, Marianna	HAGER, Thos. B.	OCT 28 1845
MEADE, Mary Elizabeth	TARTANSON, Francis	SEP 14 1839
MEADE, Octavia	CALLENDER, William	SEP 28 1839
MEADE, Robert H.	WEBSTER, Rosa	APR 27 1852
MEADE, Salvadora	McLAUGHLIN, John T., U.S.N.	SEP 14 1840
MEADE, William A.	HARRINGTON, Martha	SEP 21 1841
MEADER, Henry	KEATLEY, Jane E.	AUG 05 1856
MEADER, Joseph	HAYES, Mary	FEB 03 1858
MEADES, Susan	SMITH, Cyrus, Jr.	DEC 27 1839
MEADOR, Chastain C.	SHIELDS, Anna C.	JUL 29 1857
MEADS, Ann	ROLLINS, James	SEP 13 1825
MEADS, Delina	DUBANT, Peter M.	FEB 19 1850
MEAGHER, James	SHANAHAN, Catherine	JUN 06 1853
MEANEY, John	MORGAN, Margaret	SEP 19 1857
MEANS, Ann Eliza	FAWSETT, Asbury F.	SEP 13 1856
MEANS, William A.	HARRISS, Eleanor A.	DEC 18 1855
MEARISS, Jacob	HEPPARD, Louisa	DEC 18 1818
MEARS, Neomy	HOL_T_E, Philip	JUL 27 1816
MEASLEY, Mary	ALLEN, John	OCT 04 1826
MECARTNEY, John B.	PETTY, Virginia	OCT 19 1852
MECCUM, Elizabeth	FEARSON, Samuel	NOV 23 1824
MECHAM, Gaylord	BERRON, Eliza F.	FEB 14 1843
MECHLIN, A.M.	SMITH, F.A.	MAY 11 1840
MECHLIN, Bertha Maria	CLARKE, John George	OCT 03 1854
MECHLIN, Eliza P.	KREBS, Henry H.	MAR 20 1834
MECHLIN, Lucretia L.	GOERTNER, N.W. [Rev.]	DEC 24 1833
MECHLIN, Margaretta W.	SNOW, Charles B.	AUG 07 1848
MECKEL, Elizabeth	RANCK, Joseph	MAR 05 1850
MEDAIR, Joseph	WELLS, Margaret	SEP 16 1813
MEDAN, Nicholas	CROWLEY, Mary	FEB 11 1812
MEDARA, Mary A.	SMITH, Cyrus	DEC 24 1840
MEDARY, Samuel	SCOTT, Eliza	SEP 29 1823
MEDCALF, John	BUSSELL, Jane	SEP 11 1852
MEDFORD, Charles Franklin	BEACH, Amelia Maria	APR 08 1854
MEDKEFF, Rebecca	PIGGETT, Mason	NOV 27 1823
MEDLEY, Eliza	WATTS, James	JUN 04 1842
MEDLEY, Hallie	HASKINS, Robert F.	DEC 19 1855
MEDLEY, Thomas	HEDLEY, Eliza	JUL 23 1825
MEEHAN, John S.	MONINGTON, Rachel T.	OCT 27 1827
MEEHAN, Maria	BROOM, Robert H.	JAN 23 1851
MEEHAN, Susan M.	TAYLOR, Algernon S.	JUL 03 1837
MEEK, James E.	PHERSON, Sarah	DEC 23 1830
MEEK, Joseph H.	WRIGHT, Elizabeth	AUG 31 1817
MEEKES, Ann	GANT, Thomas	OCT 20 1837
MEEKS, Mary Ann	DULANEY, William Lewis	AUG 23 1852
MEEKS, William A.	EASTON, Sarah Ann	JUN 06 1821
MEEM, Ann E.	BARRETT, William D.	MAY 03 1825
MEEM, Elizabeth	DAVIS, Jonas	MAR 16 1813
MEEM, James W.	MICKUM, Elizabeth C.	MAY 10 1842
MEEM, Rebecca A.	REILY, James A.	JAN 11 1853
MEEM, Sarah	HOOVER, John	AUG 11 1815

District of Columbia Marriage Licenses, 1811-1858

MEEMS, Mary Margaret	NICHOLS, Seth H.	APR 05 1842
MEERS, Sarah	JONES, George	MAY 18 1821
MEGAN, Mary	WOODS, Joseph	MAY 17 1834
MEGARY, James W.	MYERS, Eliza	MAR 17 1849
MEGEE, William	NEWTON, Sarah Ann	APR 14 1813
MEGHEGAN, David	BARRY, Ellen	JUN 06 1857
MEGOWAN, Robert	ROTE, Rachel A.	NOV 28 1844
MEHIGAN, Daniel	KILLIGAN, Ellen	OCT 17 1853
MEHONE, Nancy	BOLEAR, John	JUL 02 1823
MEIERE, Julius	FRENCH, Maria B.	JUN 30 1855
MEIGS, Montgomery C.	RODGERS, Louisa	MAY 02 1841
MEIGS, Rhumma	WALKER, Wesley	JAN 08 1816
MEIGS, Samuel	CLARKE, Jane [Mrs.]	NOV 23 1815
MEILEY, John	HALTER, Hellen L.	JUN 02 1852
MEILLASON, Marie Magdaline	MILLIERE, Augustine D.	MAY 12 1817
MEINBERG, Amalia	WILLIAM, Michael	AUG 02 1853
MEINCH, Alfred	HALE, Rebecca (blk)	DEC 26 1838
MEINERS, Augustus	WAHL, Christina	JUL 06 1852
MEINZERHEIRMEN, Louis	HALFPENNY, Mary Ann	JUN 02 1849
MELCHER, Andrew D.	FAY, Mary J.	APR 20 1831
MELCHER, Annie J.	KING, Amasa W.	AUG 05 1858
MELINS, Conrad	BECK, Maria	NOV 15 1843
MELLEDY, John	FENNELY, Ann	JAN 14 1852
MELLER, Margaret	BRUHL, August	MAY 31 1853
MELLING, George	GOODS, Jane C.	MAY 01 1847
MELLINGTON, Jane E.	DENNIS, John P.	DEC 27 1851
MELLINGTON, Thomas	COZENS, Caroline	MAY 18 1836
MELLONTON, Margaret	PANE, Alexander	JUN 07 1823
MELSON, John, Jr.	BETKER, Emile F.	DEC 16 1856
MELSON, Regen	MULLER, Antoine	MAY 27 1854
MELSON, Teresa Elizth.	MILSTEAD, Robert A.	OCT 28 1847
MELTON, Rachel	ELLIS, John	JUL 27 1846
MELVIN, Elizabeth	PYFER, Henry	DEC 04 1813
MELVIN, James, Jr.	SWETT, Margaret C.	DEC 18 1817
MELVIN, Jannet	NOYES, Jacob	APR 07 1823
MEMMERT, Charles	KORFF, Louisa	JAN 05 1856
MEMMERT, Margaratha	WEIMERS, William	AUG 15 1857
MENABB, Selathin	PELTER, Sarah Ann Eliza	APR 10 1817
MENCH, John H.	CRAVER, Madelina	JUN 02 1849
MENECI, Gaetano A.	MASON, Mary Eliza	FEB 13 1843
MENGER, Ann [Mrs.]	THOMSON, Robert	MAY 24 1828
MENGIN, Morris	CLEARY, Mary	MAR 31 1857
MENICKHEIM, John	WINTER, Emma	OCT 21 1851
MENIFE, Catharine (blk)	BOWMAN, William	DEC 27 1824
MENKE, Meinard	EICHHORN, Elizabeth	OCT 06 1851
MENSHAMER, Mary A.	WILLIAMSON, Samuel	JAN 02 1857
MENZE, Albrecht	SHRODER, Cath. Elizabeth	JUN 06 1850
MENZE, Hermann	LEEDORF, Hedvig Margt.	OCT 02 1847
MERCER, Elizabeth	BOASMAN, John	JAN 21 1857
MERCER, James	AMBER, Julia	OCT 17 1844
MERCER, Thomas S.	CARROLL, Violetta L.	OCT 01 1856
MERCEREAN, Lewis	WILLIAMS, Margt.	JAN 02 1812
MERCHANT, Ann	WHEAT, William	DEC 27 1847
MERCHANT, Archibald	HIRST, Sarah	AUG 28 1815
MERCHANT, Elizabeth J.	BROWN, Richard	JAN 08 1838
MERCHANT, Margaret	HUNTER, Robert	SEP 07 1831
MERCHANT, Martena	DAVIS, William	AUG 28 1826
MERCHANT, Richard	FISHER, Ann	OCT 02 1837

District of Columbia Marriage Licenses, 1811-1858

MERCHANT, Robert	FRYER, Isabella	JUN 06 1848
MERCHANT, Wm. C.	SHEPPARD, Margt. A.	DEC 26 1849
MERE, Bridget	KAIN, Michael	FEB 01 1854
MEREDITH, Harriet W.	PRICHARD, Hugh F.	OCT 04 1845
MEREDITH, John F.	SMITH, Margarett D.	MAY 27 1833
MEREDITH, John Henry	WILSON, Ellen Gordon	DEC 04 1851
MEREDITH, Mary	MANN, Washington P.	DEC 04 1837
MEREDITH, Moses	MARTIN, Mary Ellen	OCT 09 1852
MEREDITH, Richard L.	THOMAS, Emily	MAY 03 1851
MEREDITH, William	COLVIN, Sarah Ann	MAR 22 1853
MERELL, Caroline	HARRISON, Thomas	SEP 19 1854
MERIGAN, Fanny	CULIGAN, Timothy	JUN 14 1852
MERILIOR, Susan	CARRICO, James	MAR 18 1833
MERILLET, Sophia J.	GRAENCHER, Charles L.	JAN 21 1858
MERIVEN, Henry B.	ALLIS, Martha Ann	NOV 29 1847
MERKLE, Elizabeth	MAEGLE, Michael	DEC 17 1832
MERLE, Harriott	WEBSTER, Isarel B.	AUG 13 1846
MERLIN, David	YOUNG, Julia Ann	JUN 16 1821
MERRICK, William M.	WICKLIFF, Mary B.	OCT 15 1844
MERRILL, Saml.	DAVIS, Mary J.	JUL 15 1858
MERRIT, Eliza	YOUNG, John M.	MAR 29 1832
MERRITT, Edward	YOUNG, Margaret [Mrs.]	NOV 17 1827
MERRITT, John	WHISTLER, Elizabeth	JUN 17 1854
MERRIWEATHER, Reubin H.	AUSTIN, Hester A.	NOV 03 1846
MERROLL, Charles H.	CAMMACK, Elizabeth E.	SEP 02 1852
MERRYMAN, Benjamin	BERRY, Francis	DEC 06 1843
MERRYMAN, Horatio R.	HAZLE, Ann Mariah	FEB 26 1838
MERSON, Jonathan	HOPKINS, Margaret	SEP 08 1843
MERTON, Mary	WILLIAMS, Zadock	NOV 15 1854
MESGER, Elizabeth	SCHROEGMAN, Henry	JUL 03 1835
MESSICK, George	EVANS, Amelia	MAY 10 1839
MESTAYER, Charles J.	PATTERSON, Margaret Ann	APR 04 1853
MESTER, Hester Ann	GASKINS, Isaac	JUL 29 1835
METCALF, Jane	HANLY, Edmund	OCT 08 1827
METCALF, John C.	MASSOLETTI, Julietta M.	MAY 30 1851
METHENEY, Samuel	GILL, Airry	JAN 01 1817
METHINA, Jane	COOK, Peter Zedick	DEC 26 1833
METTERDARL, Emily E.	ROLLINGS, Alexander	JAN 07 1856
METZ, Catharine	DILLI, George	APR 05 1856
METZ, Frederick	HOWSER, Lucinda	JUN 08 1837
METZ, Sarah V.	LANHAM, Lloyd	AUG 21 1856
METZLER, Julia Ann	RUPP, Frederick	AUG 11 1856
MEÜSELL, Mary	SELTMAN, Charles	MAR 27 1857
MEYER, Michl.	GERBING, Margaret	JUN 06 1855
MEYERS, George	KLIEMAN, Anna	APR 06 1855
MICHAEL, Susan G.	WALKER, William	APR 15 1856
MICHAELS, William S.	COURTNEY, Ann	MAR 11 1847
MICHELL, Thomas	LEE, Ellen (blk)	AUG 03 1844
MICHEWARD, Anthoinnet	GOGOT, Peter	MAY 31 1821
MICHOT, Ida	DOMONET, Charles	DEC 05 1851
MICKUM, Ann Maria	WATERS, Robert A.	APR 29 1847
MICKUM, Elizabeth C.	MEEM, James W.	MAY 10 1842
MICKUM, Mary E.	COOMBS, James W.	MAR 06 1850
MICKUM, Samuel	BROOM, Mary Ann	OCT 28 1819
MICKUM, Samuel C.	JONES, Mary E.	JUL 28 1853
MICKUM, Sarah A.H.	MURRAY, James	OCT 27 1832
MICKUM, Susan	FENWICK, Francis	JUN 27 1839
MICKUM, William B.	OGDEN, Sarah Priscilla	SEP 25 1851

District of Columbia Marriage Licenses, 1811-1858

MICKUM, William P.	EDWARDS, Sarah A.H.	JAN 11 1820
MIDDLETON, Agnes	THOMPSON, Robert E.	JUL 01 1858
MIDDLETON, Ann R.	MORAN, William P.	JUL 07 1856
MIDDLETON, Arthur	VanNESS, Ann	DEC 26 1821
MIDDLETON, Caroline	BEALL, Benjamin	FEB 13 1838
MIDDLETON, Catharine Mary	HENDERSON, Alexander	JUN 23 1858
MIDDLETON, Charles H.	THOMPSON, Margaretta H.	MAY 13 1851
MIDDLETON, Chloe Ann	BUSH, Ignatius	NOV 04 1845
MIDDLETON, Daniel Wesley	VanDYKE, Henrietta	MAY 31 1836
MIDDLETON, Eleanor	ST. CLAIR, Thomas	AUG 12 1822
MIDDLETON, Eleanor E.	FRAELER, Charles	JAN 22 1849
MIDDLETON, Eliza, Mrs.	SOPER, Jesse	FEB 24 1835
MIDDLETON, Erasmus J.	HOWARD, Sophia W.	APR 27 1826
MIDDLETON, Fanny V.	BYRNE, Christopher R.	NOV 13 1852
MIDDLETON, James Henry	EVANS, Sarah Ann	MAR 10 1831
MIDDLETON, John A.	BERRY, Annie Maria	JUN 14 1854
MIDDLETON, John H.	BRANNAN, Mary E.	SEP 29 1855
MIDDLETON, Lemuel J.	ELIOT, Catharine Mary	SEP 16 1830
MIDDLETON, Marcaline	BEALL, Thomas D.	JUN 19 1839
MIDDLETON, Martha	JEWELL, William	JUN 27 1856
MIDDLETON, Martha	KNOWLES, John	APR 08 1858
MIDDLETON, Mary	EVANS, Philip	MAR 27 1816
MIDDLETON, Miranda	HARKINS, William	DEC 22 1826
MIDDLETON, Richard	ERB, Margt.	JUL 10 1855
MIDDLETON, Robert	STALLIONS, Eliza	SEP 18 1830
MIDDLETON, Samuel	BERRY, Massaliner	APR 17 1825
MIDDLETON, Samuel C.	BRICHEAD, Mary Elizth.	APR 16 1855
MIDDLETON, Samuel S.N.	CARROLL, Virginia	MAY 16 1855
MIDDLETON, Sarah (blk)	HARTSHORN, George	JAN 03 1848
MIDDLETON, Sarah E.	COOPER, Thomas	NOV 10 1853
MIDDLETON, Theodore, Jr.	DODSON, Amelia	NOV 30 1830
MIDDLETON, Thomas	MORTON, Mary E.	DEC 18 1851
MIENDER, Jacob	EBERHART, Elizth.	APR 16 1858
MIFFLETON, Henry	ALLISON, Almey	MAY 13 1840
MIKELKAB, John	SCHNIDER, Catharine	FEB 22 1843
MILAN, Bridget	DONN, Richard	APR 12 1856
MILBOURN, John	TUCKER, Elizth.	AUG 17 1821
MILBROCK, Teresa	WENDERUTRE, Wilhelm	JUN 28 1858
MILBURN, Alice	WILLIAM, George	DEC 05 1818
MILBURN, Ann	BEAN, Alexander H.	MAY 30 1850
MILBURN, Benedict	PAGE, Martha	JAN 31 1842
MILBURN, Ellen E.	KANE, Chas. H.	JUL 01 1858
MILBURN, Fayette T.	GREER, Isabell P.	JUL 05 1854
MILBURN, George	MILBURN, Margaret	JUN 18 1836
MILBURN, Jane Lucinda	BARBER, George	MAR 30 1842
MILBURN, Joanna	DIXON, Absalom	DEC 04 1856
MILBURN, Joseph	TULL, Lucy	APR 18 1829
MILBURN, Margaret	MILBURN, George	JUN 18 1836
MILBURN, Mary Ann Elizabeth	CONNER, Martin	MAY 25 1843
MILBURN, Mary Ann	HINTON, Robert William	MAR 30 1843
MILBURN, Sarah	LITTLE, Warren	DEC 17 1839
MILBURN, Thomas	HARDING, Mildred	MAY 02 1832
MILBURN, Violet A.	WILLIAMS, William H.	FEB 08 1848
MILBURN, Wm. F.M.	FIELDS, Mary Ann	SEP 21 1840
MILES, Adeline (blk)	SMITH, William	MAR 20 1845
MILES, Ann	FRENCH, Alexander	JAN 22 1824
MILES, Ann S. (blk)	HAWKINS, William	OCT 08 1844
MILES, Benjamin	ALLEN, Mary	NOV 04 1819

District of Columbia Marriage Licenses, 1811-1858

MILES, Benjamin	TILLORE, Mary B.	JUN 19 1836
MILES, Bridget	WHYTE, John	AUG 25 1851
MILES, Catharine (blk)	BARLOW, John	JUN 06 1832
MILES, Catherine	PERRY, Josephus	NOV 20 1854
MILES, Edward	DONOHOO, Sarah	FEB 12 1828
MILES, Edward	BENSON, Elizabeth	OCT 17 1833
MILES, Elizabeth	DONOVAN, David	DEC 04 1847
MILES, Emily	BURGESS, Cornelius N.	OCT 16 1834
MILES, Francis	CONTEE, Kitty	MAR 28 1829
MILES, Frederick	JONES, Nancy	JUN 16 1831
MILES, George F.	GILPIN, Sophia	JAN 05 1833
MILES, George W.	RIDGEWAY, Eliza Ann	AUG 17 1841
MILES, Henry	DAY, Catharine	AUG 25 1836
MILES, James	SEAM, Sophia	OCT 21 1812
MILES, James	ASHTON, Eleanor E.	FEB 15 1827
MILES, James H.	McKEFFREY, Elizabeth	FEB 26 1846
MILES, James H.N.	PURSLEY, Jane	DEC 22 1852
MILES, John Read	HUTCHINSON, Caroline	SEP 09 1834
MILES, Laurisa	LEMON, Charles, Jr.	MAR 02 1858
MILES, Leathy	SHORTER, Charles	FEB 02 1832
MILES, Margaret	ANNADEL, Robert	MAY 18 1829
MILES, Margaret Ann	RATCLIFFE, Henry	JAN 26 1829
MILES, Margaret J.	DONALDSON, Henry	FEB 19 1850
MILES, Mary	WANNELL, Charles P.	AUG 01 1835
MILES, Mary Ann	DAW, William Henry	DEC 05 1837
MILES, Mary Ann	KERN, Frederick S.	FEB 27 1850
MILES, Mary D.	GAINES, Gregory	APR 18 1854
MILES, Nicholas	WOOLHOUSE, Harriet	OCT 23 1837
MILES, Richard	HOPKINS, Ann	OCT 04 1827
MILES, Rosetta	BRUMFIELD, Nathan	FEB 23 1838
MILES, Rosetta	WHITE, James A.	SEP 03 1838
MILES, Samuel	LUCAS, Barbary	AUG 01 1816
MILES, Susan	HERRITY, James	JUL 04 1833
MILES, William	TURNER, Mary Ann	DEC 16 1830
MILIDY, Bridget	LYNCH, Daniel	AUG 12 1854
MILL, George	MUDD, Rebecca	NOV 25 1817
MILLAN, George M.	SMITH, Sarah B.	JUN 24 1843
MILLAN, George W.	LEE, Mary E.D.	NOV 23 1840
MILLARD, Ann M.	ARMSTRONG, Francis W. [Col.]	APR 05 1831
MILLARD, Charles	FREEMAN, Elizabeth	OCT 17 1833
MILLARD, Louis	LANDESDALE, Louisa	AUG 06 1840
MILLARD, Mary	FENTON, Charles	SEP 20 1855
MILLARD, Patsey	BURGESS, William	DEC 30 1828
MILLARD, Robert F.	BROWN, Mary H.	FEB 07 1832
MILLER, Aaron W.	WOODWARD, Julia	MAY 03 1841
MILLER, Adam	CASTERTINE, Charlotte	MAR 15 1834
MILLER, Albright	ROLLINS, Mary	MAY 13 1819
MILLER, Ann	JOY, John	DEC 20 1821
MILLER, Ann	HYDE, Thomas	JAN 09 1832
MILLER, Ann	SPEIR, Robert	SEP 04 1844
MILLER, Ann E.	CHAPMAN, Charles L.	FEB 29 1848
MILLER, Ann Eliza	STEWART, G. Thomas	NOV 23 1852
MILLER, Anna	VERMILLION, James	MAY 26 1853
MILLER, Anna Maria	LEAKIN, George A. [Rev.]	NOV 03 1846
MILLER, Archy	CRAWFORD, Elizabeth	JUL 09 1817
MILLER, Barbara	JOHNSON, William	NOV 16 1816
MILLER, Barbara	MAGILL, Benedict	OCT 27 1842
MILLER, Barbara	ASEL, John	JUL 31 1851

District of Columbia Marriage Licenses, 1811-1858

MILLER, Benjamin	LIBBY, Martha	MAR 29 1855
MILLER, Benjamin A.	EBERLE, Caroline E.	JAN 12 1846
MILLER, Benjamin M.	WILEY, Sarah Ann	MAY 13 1823
MILLER, Bernard J.	FENDALL, Lucy Eleanor	JAN 31 1837
MILLER, Caroline	BETZ, Christian	MAY 31 1856
MILLER, Catharine	INGLE, John	NOV 16 1850
MILLER, Catharine	WEST, Wm. H.	FEB 06 1854
MILLER, Catharine	HEIL, Michael	APR 24 1854
MILLER, Catharine B.	ANDERSON, N.D.	FEB 21 1853
MILLER, Catharine Virginia	BROWNING, Horatio	MAY 20 1858
MILLER, Catherine Elizabeth	LINDERMANN, Philip	MAR 02 1842
MILLER, Charles	BRYAN, Eleanor	NOV 29 1820
MILLER, Charles	JOHNSON, Mary E.	JAN 02 1844
MILLER, Charles	DAVIS, Elizabeth (blk)	SEP 09 1852
MILLER, Charles	MARSHALL, Elizth. A.S.	DEC 01 1853
MILLER, Charles	DULEY, Anne	MAY 02 1857
MILLER, Charlotte	OTTERBACH, Benjamin L.	AUG 25 1853
MILLER, Christian	SLAGEL, Mary Eva	OCT 13 1852
MILLER, Christian	MUVERZAYS, Johnannatte	APR 02 1855
MILLER, Christiana	HINZERLING, George	AUG 02 1853
MILLER, Clara	FRENCH, John William [Rev.]	JUL 29 1835
MILLER, Edward	COUMBE, Elizth. Jane	AUG 31 1839
MILLER, Eliza	TSCHIFFELY, Louis S.	NOV 29 1825
MILLER, Eliza	FABRIGUE, Edward	AUG 11 1830
MILLER, Eliza	SHORT, Bonnafantor	OCT 03 1836
MILLER, Eliza G.	SWEENY, Louis D.	OCT 04 1855
MILLER, Eliza W.	CLARKE, George W.	SEP 16 1841
MILLER, Elizabeth	RICHTER, Peter	JUN 15 1846
MILLER, Elizabeth	DORR, Louis	DEC 11 1852
MILLER, Elizabeth	MAI, Peter	APR 18 1857
MILLER, Elizabeth Ann	STEWART, Thomas	NOV 03 1851
MILLER, Ellen	BARNES, Ephraim	APR 13 1852
MILLER, Ellen E.	CAPELL, John A.	JUL 10 1834
MILLER, Ellen S.	BORELAND, John	FEB 06 1855
MILLER, Eva	LEDRER, Godfrey	MAR 26 1856
MILLER, Faustin	GERLACK, Margaret	MAY 22 1836
MILLER, Folden	MILLER, Mary	DEC 24 1846
MILLER, Francis	STRAUB, Catharine	DEC 26 1850
MILLER, Frederick W.	JOHNSON, Mary	FEB 18 1817
MILLER, George	LLOYD, Ann America	JAN 15 1827
MILLER, George	SCHMIDT, Mary A.R.	SEP 07 1843
MILLER, George	ROGERSON, Eleanor D.	NOV 11 1852
MILLER, George	ELMORE, Catharine	SEP 15 1853
MILLER, George	CHEW, Rosina	FEB 23 1854
MILLER, George	WEINSBURG, Julia	FEB 19 1857
MILLER, George	FLETCHER, Sarah Ann (blk)	MAY 26 1858
MILLER, George W.	TULL, Sarah	APR 02 1829
MILLER, George W.	SELBY, Virginia	APR 25 1851
MILLER, George W.	BEAVEN, Julia C.	FEB 02 1856
MILLER, Hannah C.	TRIPLETT, Thos.	FEB 13 1823
MILLER, Harriet	MURPHY, Thomas	DEC 01 1852
MILLER, Harriet A.	HOOD, John H.	DEC 30 1852
MILLER, Henry	NEVITT, Catzaliner	JAN 09 1821
MILLER, Henry	WILBERT, Catharine	NOV 23 1843
MILLER, Henry V.	DUNGAN, Martha V.	OCT 07 1856
MILLER, Isaac F.	HUNT, Ann	MAR 10 1849
MILLER, Isaac F.	COX, Ellen	DEC 02 1852
MILLER, Isaac S.	SANDFORD, Jane	SEP 11 1828

District of Columbia Marriage Licenses, 1811-1858

MILLER, Isabella	GIBBS, Jas. H.	JAN 07 1851
MILLER, Jacob	TAYLOR, Sarah Ann	DEC 26 1833
MILLER, Jacob	WILSON, Elizabeth	JUL 09 1846
MILLER, Jacob	HOFFMAN, Joanna	AUG 27 1849
MILLER, Jacob	SCHOLLMEYER, Sophia W.	APR 03 1858
MILLER, Jacob	HENNIMAN, Sophia	MAY 21 1858
MILLER, Jacob B.	PARKER, Louisa	OCT 22 1835
MILLER, James	COBURN, Joannah	AUG 03 1833
MILLER, James	MALOANY, Hetta	MAR 29 1838
MILLER, James	McDOWELL, Elizabeth Jane	AUG 04 1842
MILLER, James A.	MARTIN, Mary A.	MAR 15 1852
MILLER, James M.	LAURIE, Isabel C.	JUN 24 1856
MILLER, John	MARKS, Sarah	DEC 30 1821
MILLER, John	GRAVES, Harriet O.	DEC 24 1828
MILLER, John	GERMAN, Catharine	DEC 23 1836
MILLER, John	SCHLUPP, Maria	DEC 08 1841
MILLER, John	DELMORE, Elenora	JAN 23 1854
MILLER, John C.	ELLIN, Mary Ann	JAN 27 1858
MILLER, John Francis	BARNES, Mary Jane	JUN 28 1853
MILLER, John P.	JOHNSON, Rosina	DEC 09 1850
MILLER, John Philip	WILSON, Lucinda	JAN 25 1828
MILLER, John U.A.	LAWSON, Mary M.M.	FEB 18 1856
MILLER, Joseph	SIMMONS, Louisa	JUN 27 1849
MILLER, Joseph	WILLIAMS, Henrietta	MAY 08 1858
MILLER, Lawrence	MURPHEY, Elizabeth	MAR 02 1833
MILLER, Lizzie	RIDENOUR, Upton H.	AUG 07 1854
MILLER, Lucy E.	WILDS, Darlon A.	MAR 16 1843
MILLER, M. Asinath	ELLIOTT, E.G., U.S.A.	AUG 28 1848
MILLER, Margaret	OURAND, Samuel	JAN 09 1852
MILLER, Margaret	ALTDORFER, Philip Jacob	APR 07 1853
MILLER, Margaret	HUND, John	FEB 06 1854
MILLER, Margaret	KELLER, Henry J.	JUN 21 1856
MILLER, Margaret A.	LINKINS, James A.	SEP 22 1856
MILLER, Margaret Ann	ALDRIDGE, Washington	AUG 03 1839
MILLER, Margaret S.	RICH, Thomas	SEP 03 1855
MILLER, Mariah	WASHINGTON, Burdet	MAR 16 1844
MILLER, Mary	DAVIS, Peter L.	JUN 05 1814
MILLER, Mary	BISBIN, John	AUG 09 1823
MILLER, Mary	DUFFEY, John H.	NOV 21 1826
MILLER, Mary	CASSELL, John	SEP 19 1831
MILLER, Mary	WASHINGTON, William	NOV 26 1832
MILLER, Mary	NIETZEY, George	DEC 30 1843
MILLER, Mary	MILLER, Folden	DEC 24 1846
MILLER, Mary	McKEOWN, John	MAY 01 1854
MILLER, Mary Ann C.	FRY, James H.	APR 23 1829
MILLER, Mary E.	GREENFIELD, Henry C.	MAY 16 1842
MILLER, Mary E.	SEARS, Bernard	OCT 29 1857
MILLER, Mary Rosanna	SCHMINKE, William C.	JAN 11 1855
MILLER, Morris Smith	MACOMB, Jane Octavia	JAN 11 1841
MILLER, Otelia	RUPPEL, Joseph	MAY 01 1857
MILLER, Peter	DUKEHART, Mary	MAR 25 1856
MILLER, Peter M.W.	THORPE, Martha Ann	OCT 23 1843
MILLER, Philip	GRAMLICH, Louisa	JUL 29 1851
MILLER, Rebecca	MARKELL, Jacob	FEB 23 1826
MILLER, Reid A.	MORAN, Maria	NOV 18 1848
MILLER, Richard H.	WESTERFIELD, Louisa	MAR 06 1858
MILLER, Robert	KNOBLOCK, Rebecca	MAY 22 1830
MILLER, Rosina	INNEMANN, George	APR 12 1852

District of Columbia Marriage Licenses, 1811-1858

MILLER, Royall E.	PERRIE, Susan A.	FEB 05 1851
MILLER, Samuel	REED, Hannah	APR 20 1836
MILLER, Samuel	KOFFMAN, Mary Ann	NOV 25 1852
MILLER, Sarah	MOORE, James	MAR 07 1815
MILLER, Sarah	PUMPHREY, Levi	FEB 09 1824
MILLER, Sarah	CREASER, Thomas	NOV 27 1834
MILLER, Sarah B.	HUTTON, George	DEC 08 1842
MILLER, Sarah C.	CONNER, Constantine O.	JUN 16 1858
MILLER, Sarah H.	ROTHROCK, Larkin J.	APR 28 1857
MILLER, Serina	HERBERT, Constant	APR 07 1856
MILLER, Thomas [Dr.]	JONES, Virginia	JUL 29 1833
MILLER, Thomas	TYLER, Elsey (blk)	MAY 25 1854
MILLER, Thomas J.	REED, Martha V.	MAR 01 1854
MILLER, Thomas W.	RIDGEWAY, Julia A.	JAN 20 1857
MILLER, Victoria Isabella	CROSS, Samuel	OCT 25 1854
MILLER, Virginia	HUME, Q.R.	JUN 01 1856
MILLER, William	ROBERTS, Sarah	APR 13 1816
MILLER, William	STROTHER, Jane	AUG 17 1823
MILLER, William	HAGAN, Mary	MAR 01 1842
MILLER, William	WILMAN, Catherine	MAY 04 1850
MILLETT, Saml. H.	SMALLWOOD, Teresa A.E.	MAR 12 1839
MILLHORN, Isabella	MOTHERSHEAD, John	DEC 18 1850
MILLHOUSE, Catherine	LANGE, Francis	DEC 19 1853
MILLIERE, Augustine D.	MEILLASON, Marie Magdaline	MAY 12 1817
MILLIGAN, Isabella	FITZHUGH, Thomas L.	DEC 17 1841
MILLIGAN, Joseph	McDONALD, Ann	JUN 18 1812
MILLINGTON, Mary A.	MILLS, Wm. H.	SEP 17 1855
MILLIS, Mary Jane	WINGATE, Edward	NOV 21 1853
MILLS, Adam L.	HOLTZMAN, Matilda Ann	DEC 16 1816
MILLS, Ann Elizabeth	JOHNSON, Dearborn	NOV 27 1833
MILLS, Ann Virginia	THOMAS, Noblette	JUN 04 1850
MILLS, Anna S.	COSBY, Fortinnatus	JUN 24 1854
MILLS, Armstead T.	GERMON, Elizabeth E.	DEC 28 1854
MILLS, Artimeca	LEE, Nelson R.	JAN 11 1830
MILLS, Bushrod	HORSEMAN, Julian	DEC 21 1839
MILLS, Catharine	CONNER, Valentine	JAN 28 1822
MILLS, Catherine	LEE, Samuel	APR 16 1857
MILLS, Cloey A.	McDUFFE, Daniel	NOV 22 1836
MILLS, Daniel M.	SISSON, Harriet E.	DEC 24 1853
MILLS, Eleanor	ELLIS, John	DEC 16 1816
MILLS, Eliza	BOTELER, John D.	OCT 12 1820
MILLS, Eliza	THOMPSON, Francis	AUG 21 1838
MILLS, Eliza M.	WEST, James W.	JAN 03 1850
MILLS, Elizabeth	PERPIGNON, Ferdinand	OCT 19 1850
MILLS, Elizabeth	REEL, James Leonard	MAR 20 1858
MILLS, Elizabeth Matilda	RICHARDSON, John William	APR 26 1849
MILLS, Hannah Matilda	ANGELL, Thomas	MAY 17 1827
MILLS, Jacqueline Smith	PENDLETON, Edward H.	SEP 17 1833
MILLS, John	HATHAWAY, Susan	FEB 27 1812
MILLS, John	MAFFITT, Elizabeth	NOV 06 1838
MILLS, John A.	LACEY, Sarah C.	JUL 31 1854
MILLS, John E.	LEE, Susanna	NOV 15 1845
MILLS, John F.	MORRIS, Elizabeth	SEP 09 1834
MILLS, John H.	LEE, Frances A.	OCT 08 1857
MILLS, John L.	COLE, Delila	SEP 09 1840
MILLS, John R.	McFARLAND, Elizabeth [Mrs.]	MAR 19 1827
MILLS, John S.	ADAM, Mary Ann	SEP 12 1826
MILLS, Julia Ann	REED, Duke of Wellington	APR 30 1846

District of Columbia Marriage Licenses, 1811-1858

MILLS, Lewis	GARDNOR, Mary	DEC 29 1812
MILLS, Mahlon	WEST, Eliza	APR 21 1846
MILLS, Margaret	TAYLOR, William	JAN 23 1845
MILLS, Margaret Ann	DONALDSON, John W.	JUL 01 1847
MILLS, Mary	JONES, Thomas	APR 15 1820
MILLS, Mary	ANDERSON, John	FEB 12 1822
MILLS, Mary	SMALLWOOD, John	MAR 14 1822
MILLS, Mary	RIGGS, John P.	MAR 29 1837
MILLS, Mary	RATCLIFF, John	JUL 17 1840
MILLS, Mary A.S.	TATE, Joseph B.	FEB 12 1850
MILLS, Mary Ann	HEWITT, Peter	OCT 11 1825
MILLS, Mary O.	GUNNELL, Wm. H.	DEC 06 1853
MILLS, Mary Powell	DIMITRY, Alexander	APR 03 1835
MILLS, Nancy	CROPLEY, Horatio	SEP 01 1846
MILLS, Peter	WAGGONER, Mary	MAY 13 1816
MILLS, Rebecca	DONALDSON, John	JUN 28 1814
MILLS, Rebecca	VanHORN, Jeremiah	APR 19 1824
MILLS, Robert	MOODY, Jane	SEP 08 1838
MILLS, Ruth	WOOD, Francis	MAR 19 1813
MILLS, Ruth	SCOTT, James S.	AUG 29 1842
MILLS, Sandford	DAVIS, Levinia	NOV 20 1840
MILLS, Sarah Ann	CURTIS, George	MAR 13 1824
MILLS, Sarah Ann	RITCHEN, Caleb	JAN 21 1853
MILLS, Sarah Z.	EVANS, John	MAY 16 1835
MILLS, Susan V.	SCOTT, Charles E.	MAY 12 1857
MILLS, Thomas A.	COLLINS, Eliza	NOV 11 1856
MILLS, Thomas M.	PITTS, Laura	MAR 23 1853
MILLS, William	HATTERSLY, Rebecca	APR 01 1826
MILLS, William H.	MASON, Louisa Jane	NOV 01 1855
MILLS, William M.	NALLS, Virginia C.	DEC 13 1855
MILLS, William McC.	CARTER, Catherine	NOV 10 1857
MILLS, William McCarty	STIRLING, Elizabeth Rebecca	JUN 28 1853
MILLS, William N.	LEIDSBORG, Sarah	JUL 30 1841
MILLS, Wm. H.	MILLINGTON, Mary A.	SEP 17 1855
MILLSON, Mary S.	DeVAUGHAN, John E.	JUL 03 1854
MILLSON, Susanna P.	CARROLL, Charles	MAY 16 1854
MILLSTEAD, M.E.	CLARK, W.S. (blk)	SEP 25 1855
MILLY, Catharine	CORRIGAN, Owen	JUL 05 1853
MILNE, Mary	LAEK, William	MAR 13 1838
MILSON, John	STREET, Hannah	APR 23 1831
MILSTEAD, Ann	BEAN, George	MAY 01 1842
MILSTEAD, Danl. L.	FURGUSON, Elizth. F.	SEP 18 1856
MILSTEAD, Elizabeth	TRAVERS, Levin	JUL 12 1825
MILSTEAD, Elizabeth	HENDERSON, John L.	OCT 25 1838
MILSTEAD, George E.	BALLENGER, Mary V.	DEC 18 1856
MILSTEAD, Henry	BEALL, Sally F.	MAY 24 1849
MILSTEAD, Ignatius	BLAND, Charlotte Maria	SEP 30 1826
MILSTEAD, John	VENABLE, Eliza W.	JUL 14 1832
MILSTEAD, Judson	BEAGLE, Ann	OCT 13 1824
MILSTEAD, Judson	ROBINSON, Catharine Ann	JUL 02 1826
MILSTEAD, Maria E.	CRUMP, Carlisle F.	FEB 15 1855
MILSTEAD, Martha	KNOX, Elijah	AUG 21 1820
MILSTEAD, Mary	DAVIS, Asa	DEC 18 1849
MILSTEAD, Nora	LLOYD, Charles H.	JUN 28 1855
MILSTEAD, Robert A.	MELSON, Teresa Elizth.	OCT 28 1847
MILSTEAD, Thomas	LLOYD, Virginia	MAY 04 1857
MILSTEAD, William B.	KELLY, Mary Ann	JUN 06 1850
MILSTED, Harriet	CARTER, Willoby N.	DEC 14 1848

District of Columbia Marriage Licenses, 1811-1858

MILSTON, Frances	POLLARD, Alfred	DEC 02 1833
MIM, George	NALLEY, Martha A.	FEB 28 1831
MINCHEN, Elizabeth	GARDNER, David A.	APR 23 1821
MINCHEN, Harriot	DONOHOO, John A.	MAY 13 1823
MINCHER, Ann	PENNINGTON, James	DEC 28 1814
MINCHER, Sarah	CRAVER Isaac	JUN 12 1830
MINCHIN, Martha S.	JAMISON, Peter S.	APR 08 1819
MINDENDORF, Sophia	BRIDY, George	FEB 27 1857
MINER, James	CARROLL, Mary Ann (blk)	JUL 31 1832
MINER, John	JACKSON, Ellen	JUL 11 1837
MINES, Flavel Scott [Rev.]	LINDSLEY, Glorvina Claudine	JUN 12 1832
MINICE, Sarah	LITTLEFORD, Hanson	JAN 17 1824
MINICIMA, Barbara	POWER, John	AUG 01 1846
MINITOR, Thomas	LYCETT, Bridget	OCT 01 1853
MINITREE, Andrew	STEWART, Emely R.	NOV 18 1841
MINITREE, Rosanna	STREET, John	AUG 08 1829
MINIX, John Newton	DANFORD, Catherine	MAY 01 1849
MINIX William H.	HUNGERFORD, Henrietta V.	MAR 07 1850
MINKS, Catharine	HOPKINS, Solomon	MAY 20 1820
MINNEGAN, Arthur	McCARTY, Johana	JAN 30 1858
MINNEITT, Mary	CASWELL, John A.	FEB 23 1846
MINNEKER, Deiderich George	LEENERS, Mary A.	MAY 23 1855
MINNIS, Dolly	WEBSTER, Samuel	JUL 19 1851
MINNIS, John T.	FIELDS, Elizabeth Ann	SEP 22 1847
MINNIS, Martha V.	GRIMES, John J.	NOV 19 1855
MINNIS, Nancy	MAGRUDER, Alfred	AUG 19 1835
MINNIS, Thomas	LYONS, Eliza	DEC 21 1826
MINNIX, Charlotte V.	STONE, William H.	FEB 08 1853
MINNIX, William H.	SANDIFORD, Diana	JUL 17 1845
MINNS, Mary	HERBERT, Patrick	MAY 15 1853
MINOGUE, Eliza	DULINHANTY, Patrick	APR 21 1854
MINOR, Benjamin	JONES, Charlotte (blk)	NOV 22 1837
MINOR, Benjamin	TASCOE, Margaret (blk)	NOV 19 1856
MINOR, Elizabeth	MORRIS, Henry	OCT 05 1815
MINOR, Francis	BYUS, Matilda (blk)	MAR 27 1858
MINOR, James	BOSTON, Louisa (blk)	SEP 24 1851
MINOR, John R.	SIOUSSA, Margaret	MAY 17 1849
MINOR, John West	DIGGES, Ellen Maria	AUG 26 1835
MINOR, Martha	WARING, Joseph H.	FEB 07 1839
MINOR, Martha A. (blk)	YOUNG, Henry N.	NOV 30 1852
MINOR, Mary Jane (blk)	THOMAS, Ross	NOV 03 1847
MINOR, Stephania	CHOTARD, Henry	OCT 14 1851
MINOR, William	JONES, Marcellina	NOV 09 1848
MINPLY, John P.	WAGONER, Ann	MAR 31 1831
MIRINE, Sophie George	MOLLARD, Francois	NOV 04 1857
MISCEL, George N.	FINK, Louisa	OCT 01 1855
MISKELL, Elizabeth J.	JOHNSTON, George W.	JUL 10 1852
MITCHEL, Ann H.	WATERS, George	SEP 04 1836
MITCHEL, Anne	SMOOT, George A.	JUL 13 1833
MITCHEL, Caroline	COX, William	JAN 06 1846
MITCHEL, Eliza	CHANEY, Thomas S.	APR 22 1819
MITCHEL, Elizabeth	TARMAN, Samuel	MAY 05 1819
MITCHEL, Josias	DARRITY, Hariot	OCT 20 1818
MITCHEL, Sarah Ann	HOWARD, John, of Philip	JUN 02 1829
MITCHELL, Amanda H.	BROWN, William P.	APR 09 1853
MITCHELL, Ann Maria	DUVALL, Barton	NOV 30 1831
MITCHELL, Brenda E.G.	MOCKABEE, Daniel F.	DEC 04 1854
MITCHELL, Charles	BULLY, Mary Jane	AUG 04 1840

District of Columbia Marriage Licenses, 1811-1858

MITCHELL, Charles W.	ASHTON, Sarah	OCT 17 1855
MITCHELL, Clarissa Ann	LOCKEY, Francis	APR 01 1857
MITCHELL, Daniel	SCHERRER, Sarah	MAY 14 1832
MITCHELL, Dennis	WEAVER, Ann	OCT 28 1830
MITCHELL, Dennis	BOND, Rebecca Ann	AUG 24 1840
MITCHELL, Dianna	SHAFFER, Charles	DEC 14 1844
MITCHELL, Eliza	ALLISON, John	OCT 31 1832
MITCHELL, Elizabeth	GIVEN, George	JUL 22 1826
MITCHELL, Ellen	HALL, John	JUL 24 1839
MITCHELL, Elvira	JOURDON, Daniel B.	FEB 21 1851
MITCHELL, Emeline (blk)	MASON, George	SEP 02 1840
MITCHELL, Francis	SIMONDS, Laura	SEP 07 1852
MITCHELL, George	BOONE, Eleanor	MAR 17 1831
MITCHELL, George W.	BRAFIELD, Martha A.	OCT 12 1854
MITCHELL, Harriet G.	PHELAN, A.J.F.	SEP 25 1856
MITCHELL, Harriot	ANDERSON, Joseph	AUG 03 1816
MITCHELL, Henry C.	ENNIS, Ann Elizabeth	JAN 09 1848
MITCHELL, Isaac	JACKSON, Mary Ann	JUN 29 1840
MITCHELL, James	THOMPSON, Margaret	JAN 26 1824
MITCHELL, James	MURPHEY, Ann Rebecca	JAN 21 1845
MITCHELL, James	PASSCERE, Harriet M.	MAR 02 1848
MITCHELL, James H.	ADDISON, Rebecca (blk)	AUG 14 1845
MITCHELL, James, Jr.	GATES, Jane Adeline	MAY 31 1855
MITCHELL, John	DAY, Rebecca	JAN 29 1835
MITCHELL, John	DAVIS, Caroline (blk)	MAY 12 1835
MITCHELL, John	GODFREY, Mary	DEC 29 1841
MITCHELL, John	BURNES, Lucinda	AUG 10 1848
MITCHELL, John	MULLIN, Catherine	JUL 28 1849
MITCHELL, John	GOODRICK, Mary Ann	JAN 26 1854
MITCHELL, John	LEE, Elizth. (blk)	NOV 16 1855
MITCHELL, John	DENIHER, Bridger	NOV 10 1855
MITCHELL, John F.	WARD, Mary Ann	NOV 05 1850
MITCHELL, John T.	KERR, Sarah A.	SEP 29 1840
MITCHELL, Joseph T.	MARTIN, Margaret Ann	OCT 18 1849
MITCHELL, Josephine V.	MARR, John T.	MAY 17 1855
MITCHELL, Judson	LEONARD, Deborah	OCT 23 1822
MITCHELL, Lilborn	PRATHER, Nancy	APR 30 1833
MITCHELL, Louisa	KIDMORE, Samuel	OCT 17 1848
MITCHELL, Lucy Anna	BROWNE, John Ross	NOV 13 1844
MITCHELL, Mandica	MULLICAN, Elizabeth	DEC 24 1840
MITCHELL, Marcelina (blk)	STEWART, John	NOV 02 1857
MITCHELL, Margaret	FOSTER, Edward	NOV 06 1813
MITCHELL, Margaret A. (blk)	SMITH, Emanuel	JUN 05 1856
MITCHELL, Margaret Maria	HUMPHREY, Joshua	MAR 01 1823
MITCHELL, Maria	McCLELLAN, William W.	DEC 11 1837
MITCHELL, Martha Ann	STREEKS, Francis	JUN 12 1824
MITCHELL, Martha Ann	ANDERSON, Thomas H.	OCT 25 1852
MITCHELL, Martha Ann	MAYHEW, John W.	NOV 25 1852
MITCHELL, Mary	STUITS, George	MAR 23 1845
MITCHELL, Mary	MULCARE, Morris	NOV 10 1857
MITCHELL, Mary Ann	ROWE, John	JAN 08 1833
MITCHELL, Mary Chesley	BRONAGH, William John	JAN 07 1817
MITCHELL, Mary E.	COOK, James E.	OCT 29 1857
MITCHELL, Mary Ellen	ENGLAND, John W.	JUN 07 1855
MITCHELL, Mary J.	BRANNSTEIN, Jacob	DEC 27 1856
MITCHELL, Mary W.	HOFFMANN, John D.	FEB 21 1855
MITCHELL, Matilda	ADAMS, John	FEB 12 1824
MITCHELL, Pleasant	BASHAW, Daniel	NOV 26 1828

District of Columbia Marriage Licenses, 1811-1858

MITCHELL, Rebecca	WARNER, Charles	JAN 08 1850
MITCHELL, Rector	WALLINSFORD, Sophia	MAR 28 1812
MITCHELL, Richard	BREZO, Ann	FEB 14 1822
MITCHELL, Richard T.	WILSON, Mary E.	MAY 14 1855
MITCHELL, Sarah E.	CREASY, Thomas	OCT 31 1837
MITCHELL, Sarah E.	McCATHRAN, Benjamin F.	MAY 27 1854
MITCHELL, Singleton	THURSBEY, Amy	FEB 05 1820
MITCHELL, Sophia (blk)	HAWKINS, John Wm.	DEC 02 1852
MITCHELL, Sophinia	GOLDSMITH, Lewis	FEB 12 1833
MITCHELL, Susan C.	ROCHE, James R.	DEC 15 1852
MITCHELL, Thomas	RANDALL, Matilda	FEB 16 1828
MITCHELL, Thomas	GOODS, Mary Rebecca	OCT 17 1837
MITCHELL, Thomas	COLEMAN, Catharine C.	APR 29 1848
MITCHELL, Thomas A.	MAYO, Isabel C.	JUL 23 1851
MITCHELL, Viletta S.	CHANEY, Levi	DEC 12 1839
MITCHELL, Walter	MASTERS, Matilda	JAN 09 1813
MITCHELL, William	TURNER, Cordelia	JAN 29 1845
MITCHELL, William	TRAVERS, Sydney Virginia	AUG 09 1848
MITCHELL, William	MYERS, Susan	SEP 16 1856
MITCHELL, Zebedee	ENNIS, Mary F.	JAN 13 1858
MITTEREGYER, Charles H.	HURDLE, Hellen R.	OCT 23 1841
MITZ, Catherine	AUTH, Anton	JUN 20 1854
MITZINGER, Anna	KANIG, John	JUN 12 1858
MIX, Charles E.	UPPERMAN, Catharine S.	AUG 15 1829
MIX, Grace	UPPERMAN, Charles A.	JAN 11 1848
MIX, Mary C.	TOWNSEND, Jeremiah A.	MAY 12 1825
MIX, Mary Virginia	MORRISON, William C.	DEC 15 1852
MOATON, Nancy (blk)	DOUGLASS, William H.	DEC 10 1845
MOBLEY, Linney Ann	TUCKER, Henry H.	MAY 28 1832
MOBLEY, Rebecca	LANGLEY, James	MAR 03 1829
MOBLY, Thomas	STAMP, Sarah Ann	JAN 04 1836
MOBRAY, James	COLLARD, Eliza	JUN 18 1834
MOCBEE, Carlton	KING, Mary	MAR 09 1833
MOCHBEE, Thomas	KARRICK, Mary	MAR 17 1812
MOCKABEE, Daniel F.	MITCHELL, Brenda E.G.	DEC 04 1854
MOCKABEE, Eliza Ann	WILLIAMS, James	APR 23 1846
MOCKABEE, Elizabeth	McNEW, Basil	JUN 10 1834
MOCKABEE, Ellen	KING, William	JAN 07 1851
MOCKABEE, Margaret E.	LINDSEY, William H.	JUN 13 1857
MOCKABEE, Thomas C.	JONES, Mary E.	MAY 09 1855
MOCKABOY, William	GROVES, Susan	JUN 07 1838
MOCKABY, Margaret Ann	LYNCH, Patrick	FEB 13 1835
MOCKBEE, Eliza H.	GARDINE, Geo. W.	JAN 22 1836
MOCKBEE, Elizabeth S.	McKENNEY, George W.	OCT 13 1856
MOCKBEE, Harriot	KING, James	MAY 22 1820
MOCKBEE, Joseph	DAWS, Eliza	DEC 17 1816
MOCKBEE, Richard	BENSON, Margaret E.	JUN 14 1837
MOCKBEE, William	RALY, Matilda	SEP 19 1847
MOCKEBEE, Maria	BECKET, John	DEC 02 1820
MOCKEBOY, Margaret Ann	JOHNS, George A.W.	SEP 20 1841
MOCKLER, Bridget	CAMPBELL, John	OCT 18 1852
MOCLA, Bridget	CAMPBELL, John	FEB 19 1852
MOELLER, Christine	SCHUSSLER, Charles	JAN 25 1853
MOENSTER, A.H.	RAGSDALE, Thomas S.	OCT 12 1847
MOFFETT, Joseph F.	CROPLEY, Esther	MAR 27 1847
MOFFETT, Mary J.	KING, Montgomery S.	JAN 08 1857
MOFFIT, Ann	CAMMICK, William	JAN 24 1823
MOFFITT, Alexander M.	BURMAN, Anna A.	FEB 04 1847

District of Columbia Marriage Licenses, 1811-1858

MOFFOTT, Robert	VARDEN, Elizabeth	JUL 04 1816
MOGELY, Mary Ann	HUGHES, John	OCT 07 1854
MOGGEY, Matilda	CHEW, John	MAY 17 1835
MOGLAR, George	RULING, Catherine	OCT 21 1834
MOHLDER, Elizth.	CHISOM, George	APR 13 1848
MOHLDER, Lucy	CORCORAN, John	DEC 29 1851
MOHLE, Johanna H.S.	STUTZ, John M.	OCT 20 1855
MOHLER, John W.	PADGETT, Maria E.	JUN 04 1855
MOHLOW, Margaret	SOHOENHOZ, Herman Wm.	DEC 23 1853
MOHUN, Ellen C.	WALTER, C.W.C.	MAR 10 1847
MOHUN, Francis	BARRY, Ann Margaret	JAN 29 1835
MOHUN, Francis	LECKIE, Martha	APR 21 1856
MOHUN, Rosella A.	CARRICO, William H.	OCT 25 1856
MOLAND, Geo. Air	HURLEY, Elizabeth	OCT 21 1816
MOLARE, Harriot	RENNOE, Chapman	SEP 06 1834
MOLDEN, Ann	RAGAN, George	JAN 28 1850
MOLDEN, Jane Eliza	BAILEY, William L.	SEP 25 1830
MOLDEN, Sarah Ann	NAILOR, Thompson	MAY 15 1847
MOLDEN, William	MURRAY, Mary	JAN 08 1842
MOLL, John Randolph	FAGAN, Mary Jane	JUL 20 1857
MOLLARD, Francois	MIRINE, Sophie George	NOV 04 1857
MOLLER, Elizabeth	HIRSCH, Conrad	APR 02 1833
MOLLER, Frederick	BODTBECK, Ursala	APR 13 1826
MOLLIN, Mordica	DONASON, Elizabeth	FEB 12 1835
MOLONEY, Patrick	QUINN, Margaret	JAN 27 1849
MOLQUEEN, Ellen	COLGRIFF, James	AUG 01 1853
MOLUM, Michael P.	BRAWNER, Rosella A.	DEC 31 1850
MONCRIEFF, Catherine V.	LOVEJOY, Amos	JUL 28 1858
MONDOWNEY, Thomas	CARR, Elizabeth	JUN 25 1828
MONEY, Catherine	JONES, Richard	JUN 01 1850
MONEY, Elijah	DICKEY, Elizabeth Uphema	JAN 07 1851
MONEY, Enoch	GRAY, Ann Maria	MAR 12 1833
MONEY, Jane	BYRON, James	JUL 12 1855
MONEY, Jane E.	JOHNSON, John H.	DEC 21 1852
MONEY, Perrie A.	JONES, Margaret	APR 08 1847
MONEY, Presley W.	McNEIR, Harriet A.	DEC 20 1853
MONIHAN, John	FARRELL, Catherine	MAY 14 1857
MONINGTON, Rachel T.	MEEHAN, John S.	OCT 27 1827
MONKS, Isaac	GARNAR, Ann	JUN 12 1823
MONMONIER, Francis	CONNOR, Mary A.	MAY 17 1841
MONN, Rosetta (blk)	DAY, Samuel	JUN 10 1853
MONROE, Maria H.	GOVERNEUR, Samuel L.	MAR 08 1820
MONROE, Thomas T.	FOWLER, Margaret E.	DEC 15 1852
MONROE, William R.	STALLARD, Elizabeth	OCT 29 1827
MONSERRATTE, Francis	STEWART, Elizabeth	APR 07 1830
MONTAGUE, Charles P.	DENISON, Eliza C.	JAN 16 1851
MONTAGUE, Philip H.L.	COLEMAN, Mary Susan	MAY 28 1846
MONTGOMERY, Edward A.	SMITH, Ellen M.	APR 24 1855
MONTGOMERY, Eliza	WARD, Thomas G.	MAY 06 1857
MONTGOMERY, Ellen F.	WILLETT, Warren O.	MAR 10 1857
MONTGOMERY, Gracey Louisa	RICHARDS, Alfred	OCT 30 1855
MONTGOMERY, James	SMOOT, Eliza Virginia	JUN 07 1823
MONTGOMERY, James H.	HOSSICKS, Mary E.A.	APR 11 1850
MONTGOMERY, Julia (blk)	LIVERPOOL, James	JAN 09 1854
MONTGOMERY, Julia M.	MAHON, Dr. David N.	DEC 22 1851
MONTGOMERY, Rachel	McDONALD, Timothy	MAY 20 1816
MONTGOMERY, Teresa	SMALLWOOD, James	APR 15 1816
MONTRE, Eloise Melaine	GUIRAND, Louis	APR 20 1848

District of Columbia Marriage Licenses, 1811-1858

MOODEY, Theodore L.	HELLEN, Georgeanna Adelaide	SEP 24 1838
MOODIE, John	THORN, Darie	MAR 05 1820
MOODY, Amelia Page	HATTON, Washington	APR 14 1838
MOODY, Ann	TIPPETT, John A.	SEP 01 1857
MOODY, Geo. A.	DeVAUGHN, Sinah A.	OCT 04 1849
MOODY, Georgiana	DUNNAVANT, William C.	OCT 16 1851
MOODY, Harriet (blk)	MARLOW, Benjamin	JUN 16 1858
MOODY, Henry	TURNER, Penny	NOV 04 1819
MOODY, Jane	MILLS, Robert	SEP 08 1838
MOODY, John	STEELE, Elizabeth A.	DEC 28 1848
MOODY, Mary Ann	TIPPETT, John	DEC 24 1831
MOODY, William	BLEXLEY, Catharine	DEC 23 1830
MOONE, Caroline F.W.	JONES, Madison W.	FEB 25 1853
MOONES, Christiana M.	MANKIN, James	JAN 15 1833
MOONEY, Noble H.	IRVIN, Martha T.	OCT 12 1836
MOONEY, William S.	KINCHSLOE, Emily	FEB 17 1829
MOONY, Sarah	TANNER, Jesse	FEB 23 1819
MOOR, Joseph W.	ALLEN, Mary	SEP 30 1850
MOOR, Mary	DADE, William Ball	NOV 25 1828
MOORE, Agness Maria	OVERSTREET, James	MAY 07 1822
MOORE, Alexander	CLEMENTS, Harriet	MAY 25 1815
MOORE, Alexander C.	ASHFORD, Ann	AUG 26 1824
MOORE, Alice	WILLIAM, Charles	JUL 10 1855
MOORE, Ann E.	DARNALL, Henry Washington	OCT 30 1850
MOORE, Ann H.	FORREST, Andrew	DEC 31 1812
MOORE, Ann Maria	ORME, William	JAN 05 1836
MOORE, Ann Virginia	ANDREWS, Alfred W.	SEP 21 1854
MOORE, Annah M.	CARAY, Thomas	DEC 10 1835
MOORE, Anne E.	BARBOUR, James L.	FEB 16 1857
MOORE, Barbara Ellen	PERKINS, Robert S.	JUN 25 1858
MOORE, Bridget	TAYLOR, James	MAR 07 1854
MOORE, Catharine	JARBOE, Joshua N.	SEP 15 1830
MOORE, Catharine E.	JOHNSON, W.C.	NOV 01 1847
MOORE, Catharine V.	SLUSSER, Jno. Henry	JUN 05 1856
MOORE, Charity Ann	GRAY, John L.	FEB 07 1850
MOORE, Daniel	WAGNER, Elizabeth	MAY 08 1830
MOORE, David	BROOKES, Eliza	JAN 09 1830
MOORE, Douglass	KIRK, Elizabeth A.	NOV 07 1843
MOORE, Eleanor	WOODLAND, Charles	MAY 15 1812
MOORE, Eleanor [Mrs.]	KIRBY, John B.	FEB 19 1828
MOORE, Eliza	BERRY, William	NOV 18 1823
MOORE, Eliza E.	McINTIRE, Alexander	SEP 04 1815
MOORE, Elizabeth	BEARDSLEY, George	OCT 20 1821
MOORE, Elizabeth	JARVIS, John	AUG 28 1844
MOORE, Elizabeth M.	JOHNSON, Andrew Wallace	DEC 13 1855
MOORE, Elizth.	BERNARD, William	SEP 23 1822
MOORE, Ellen M.	SAUNDERS, Addison H.	MAR 05 1835
MOORE, Emily Jane	CAMPBELL, Bernard Moore	NOV 15 1854
MOORE, Fanny C.	FAIRFIELD, George A.	OCT 03 1855
MOORE, Festus H.	BRINTNALL, Malvina	JAN 19 1853
MOORE, Fredk. L.	CAMPBELL, Christine V.	SEP 06 1855
MOORE, Grace R.	WHEELER, Thos. G.	JAN 08 1856
MOORE, Henrietta (blk)	SMALLWOOD, Ignatius	DEC 28 1843
MOORE, Henry	JACKSON, Lucinda (blk)	SEP 19 1855
MOORE, Hetty	CROMWELL, Jesse	MAR 29 1823
MOORE, Isabella	McCAULY, William	JUN 06 1850
MOORE, Jacob	SOLOMON, Margaret (blk)	MAR 08 1849
MOORE, James	MILLER, Sarah	MAR 07 1815

District of Columbia Marriage Licenses, 1811-1858

MOORE, James	DUFFEY, Mary M.	MAR 03 1831
MOORE, James A.	DEPUTY, Rachel Ella	SEP 12 1854
MOORE, James F.	WISE, Sarah C.	JAN 10 1857
MOORE, James H.	BENEZETTE, Laura Ann	APR 04 1854
MOORE, James Henry	FARR, Margaret Ann	JAN 31 1854
MOORE, James, Senr.	HOGAN, Sarah [Mrs.]	FEB 27 1832
MOORE, Jane	BEDDO, Henry	SEP 28 1841
MOORE, Jane	HUDDLESTON, Mathew C.	NOV 10 1854
MOORE, John	CROUSE, Mary	DEC 01 1821
MOORE, John	GEERKEN, Ann Maria	MAR 14 1837
MOORE, John	CONNER, Ann W.	JUN 04 1842
MOORE, John	BURCH, Rebecca	SEP 23 1850
MOORE, John	ROLLINS, Jane B.	NOV 05 1851
MOORE, John L.	BRENARD, Maria	NOV 18 1832
MOORE, John L.	FINCH, Elvira	JUL 02 1853
MOORE, Joseph	GRIMES, Nancy	AUG 13 1812
MOORE, Joseph B.	PRETTYMAN, Amelia H.	OCT 20 1852
MOORE, Leah Elizabeth Kerr	TURPIN, William	AUG 29 1848
MOORE, Lettice C.	NEVITT, Robert K.	DEC 20 1836
MOORE, Lewis	PHILLIPS, Mary A.J.	FEB 27 1847
MOORE, Louisa	CLARKE, Robert	DEC 12 1815
MOORE, Louisa A.E.	McCREARY, Robert G.	DEC 14 1848
MOORE, Lucinda (blk)	TAYLOR, Dennis	JUL 28 1845
MOORE, Margaret	DAWES, Joseph	DEC 15 1829
MOORE, Margaret	McMANUS, Patrick	JAN 03 1853
MOORE, Maria H.W.	PATRICK, John	APR 15 1823
MOORE, Mary	LINKINS, William	APR 29 1813
MOORE, Mary	ROCHFORD, William	JAN 28 1820
MOORE, Mary	TUCKER, Samuel	DEC 26 1822
MOORE, Mary	BERRYMAN, Leroy H.	SEP 13 1842
MOORE, Mary	RIDEWAY, Jesse	MAY 30 1854
MOORE, Mary	SUGRUE, Humphrey	NOV 18 1854
MOORE, Mary Ann (blk)	FOX, Thomas	MAY 03 1841
MOORE, Mary Ann	BROWN, Elias E.	DEC 25 1844
MOORE, Mary Ann	HOFFMAN, Henry	AUG 24 1850
MOORE, Mary Ann	McFARLAN, Daniel	JUL 16 1855
MOORE, Mary B.	BROWN, Ebon G.	JUL 27 1840
MOORE, Mary E.	REED, Esli D.	MAY 04 1854
MOORE, Mary E.	BERRY, Wyatt S.	OCT 31 1854
MOORE, Mary G.	MOORE, Vinson W.	FEB 04 1845
MOORE, Mary L.	BRIGHTWELL, Thomas R.	NOV 15 1852
MOORE, Mary M.	WILLIAMS, James	FEB 19 1845
MOORE, Mary M.	BROWN, William R.	JUN 21 1848
MOORE, Mary Mitchell	TOWERS, William	MAY 23 1831
MOORE, Mary R.	JONES, Edward	MAR 09 1853
MOORE, Michael J.	FITZGERALD, Hanora	FEB 01 1854
MOORE, Mudecai	FARR, Eliza Ann	MAY 10 1845
MOORE, Peter Fellers	PREANACHER, Margaretta	OCT 01 1849
MOORE, Philip	KRAFFT, Ava	DEC 26 1855
MOORE, Randonia C.	FRIDLEY, Charles W.	JUL 05 1855
MOORE, Rebecca	OGDEN, John W.	SEP 20 1841
MOORE, Richard	LEWIS, Jane	JAN 03 1850
MOORE, Richard H.	HALLER, Eliza Jane	AUG 16 1855
MOORE, Risdon A.	DUNCAN, Sarah A.	MAR 16 1848
MOORE, Robert	CLARKE, Martha	MAR 29 1855
MOORE, Robert B.	HILL, Cenisha	APR 01 1839
MOORE, Rosanna	McCLELLAND, Robert	SEP 11 1850
MOORE, Sarah Haus	CATON, George	MAY 10 1822

District of Columbia Marriage Licenses, 1811-1858

MOORE, Sarah Jane	FORREST, William H.	DEC 29 1851
MOORE, Selina	HARVEY, Jas. E.	APR 22 1854
MOORE, Seymour T.	GREENHOW, Florence V.	MAR 28 1855
MOORE, Silas	EDMONSTON, Dorithy	MAY 24 1828
MOORE, Susan	AGLETON, Richard	JUL 01 1826
MOORE, Susanna	SERRA, Augustin	JAN 01 1813
MOORE, Thomas	FISHER, Margaret	DEC 25 1818
MOORE, Thomas	ADAMS, Juliana Ann	JUN 11 1821
MOORE, Thomas	RICHARDSON, Elizabeth	OCT 08 1832
MOORE, Thomas	EATON, Margaret Ann	OCT 11 1854
MOORE, Thomas	KNOTT, Jane	JUN 02 1855
MOORE, Verlinda [Mrs.]	SMITH, John W.	JAN 26 1819
MOORE, Vinson W.	MOORE, Mary G.	FEB 04 1845
MOORE, Virginia B.	BALDWIN, Henry C.	JUN 01 1853
MOORE, William	DOUGLASS, Elizabeth	APR 28 1821
MOORE, William	KLINENCE, Catherine Jane	MAY 29 1849
MOORE, William F.	SPENCE, Catherine	JUL 13 1848
MOORE, William George	ROSE, Mary Gideon	OCT 15 1853
MOORE, Wm. Magruder	POWELL, Mary Charlotte	NOV 11 1853
MOORE, [blank]	WALL, Joseph	APR 21 1855
MOORELAND, John	HARSHMAN, Mary S.	DEC 24 1840
MOORMAN, Robert B.	LIBBEY, Anna M.	JAN 07 1851
MOPS, John	HOWK, Catharine	DEC 29 1826
MOQUEST, Sophia	O'BRIEN, John	AUG 09 1848
MORAARTY, Ambrose, Jr.	McFEARSON, Mary	SEP 13 1827
MORAN, Annina	KEEFE, William N.	MAY 17 1852
MORAN, Bridget	DEVINEY, Edmond	DEC 31 1857
MORAN, C. Angeline	MORAN, Elasah	NOV 13 1854
MORAN, Catharine	MOSELEY, William H.	JUL 09 1841
MORAN, David	CROWLEY, Ann	SEP 11 1852
MORAN, Dicen	BOWAN, Hannah	JAN 05 1846
MORAN, Dyson	EDMONSTON, Ann	MAR 20 1819
MORAN, Elasah	MORAN, C. Angeline	NOV 13 1854
MORAN, Elijah	SKINNER, Jane C.	APR 13 1848
MORAN, Elizabeth	ATRIDGE, John	OCT 01 1839
MORAN, Elizabeth A.	MAXWELL, Washington	SEP 07 1837
MORAN, Enoch V.	MURRAY, Virginia F.	JUN 30 1857
MORAN, James	FLETCHER, Mary	OCT 15 1842
MORAN, James	HOWARD, Arabella	JUL 13 1848
MORAN, Jane	GRAY, John	JAN 13 1842
MORAN, John	BEANS, Eleanor	FEB 08 1814
MORAN, John A.	UMBERFIELD, Sarah	AUG 04 1847
MORAN, John Edward	DORSEY, Charlotte H.P.	JUL 03 1843
MORAN, Joseph C.	CAHO, Susan W.	MAY 08 1848
MORAN, Lucy	COWING, Granville	APR 17 1855
MORAN, Maria	MILLER, Reid A.	NOV 18 1848
MORAN, Mary Jane	SULLIVAN, Samuel	JAN 04 1840
MORAN, Patrick	SIMMS, Ann	SEP 03 1832
MORAN, Patrick	CLANSY, Bridget	OCT 19 1854
MORAN, Perigrine	CAMPBELL, Statia	DEC 09 1812
MORAN, Samuel C.	BURNS, Mary E.	JAN 14 1829
MORAN, Sarah	SULLIVAN, William	DEC 26 1827
MORAN, Sarah	LOCKE, John H.	OCT 27 1845
MORAN, Susan M.	TIMMS, William L.	MAR 21 1850
MORAN, William	BAKER, Elizabeth	JUL 24 1816
MORAN, William M.	COX, Susannah E.	FEB 04 1850
MORAN, William P.	MIDDLETON, Ann R.	JUL 07 1856
MORAN, Wm. M.	BARNES, Mary	MAY 10 1856

District of Columbia Marriage Licenses, 1811-1858

MORANT, Eliza A.	OWENS, Robert A.	APR 09 1857
MORARTY, Ambrose	TENCH, Mary	JUN 24 1813
MORCOE, William E.	CULVERWELL, Terese Ann	MAY 26 1849
MOREHOUSE, Elizabeth	COLLINS, William	FEB 20 1830
MOREHOUSE, Isaac	BAKER, Elizabeth	OCT 30 1816
MORELAND, Amelia D.	UMBERFIELD, Albert	FEB 23 1819
MORELAND, Ann E.	DeVAUGHAN, Thomas S.	FEB 04 1858
MORELAND, Caroline	WHEATLY, Francis	SEP 24 1830
MORELAND, Eliza A.	PENN, James A.	OCT 22 1829
MORELAND, Hanson B.	HOLTZMAN, Eliza G.	MAY 11 1826
MORELAND, John	KIDWELL, Sarah	NOV 24 1832
MORELAND, Mary Ellen	McFARLAND, John B.	AUG 27 1841
MORELAND, Octavia	ROBEY, Nehemiah	JUN 21 1853
MORELAND, Paul H.	BREWER, Susan	MAR 01 1837
MORELAND, Rachel E.	McLAUGHLIN, Thomas A.	APR 28 1857
MORELAND, Richard R.	LOWMAN, Margaret Ann	OCT 27 1846
MORELAND, William A.	DASSEY, Josephine H.	JUL 07 1851
MOREMAN, John	ROACH, Margaret	FEB 05 1853
MORFIT, Hugh	HARROTT, Jane	OCT 19 1847
MORGAN, Adelia Ann	ENGLISH, John C.	MAY 17 1831
MORGAN, Adeline	THOMPSON, Allen	OCT 07 1826
MORGAN, Alexander J.	McGILLICUDDY, Nancy	AUG 11 1847
MORGAN, Alexr. J.	McGILLICUDDY, Nancy	SEP 11 1847
MORGAN, Amanda M.	KING, John, of Wm.	NOV 09 1852
MORGAN, Ann	BARNET, Charles	DEC 12 1826
MORGAN, Ann	SENDORFF, Joseph	FEB 07 1828
MORGAN, Ann	JAMES, John P.W.	AUG 20 1833
MORGAN, Ann	FERGUSON, Denis	MAY 10 1838
MORGAN, Aquilla R.	EARP, Susan	JAN 28 1826
MORGAN, Aquilla R.L.	ARP, Susan	FEB 01 1826
MORGAN, Charles	SHERRY, Ann	SEP 07 1819
MORGAN, Charlotte	TRACY, John	DEC 15 1821
MORGAN, Charlotte Ann	JONES, Elexius	MAR 26 1853
MORGAN, Edwin C.	LEE Evelinia P.	JUL 14 1853
MORGAN, Eliza	REAVER, Henry	MAY 19 1824
MORGAN, Eliza	AIKEN, William John	JUL 28 1848
MORGAN, Elizabeth	VEITCH, Thomas	MAY 16 1812
MORGAN, Elizabeth A.R.	BEALL, James H.	DEC 29 1856
MORGAN, Elizabeth O.	MAGRUDER, Thomas C.	FEB 05 1844
MORGAN, Frances	WHALING, Daniel	FEB 04 1850
MORGAN, Frances	FLEMMING, Laurence	FEB 17 1852
MORGAN, Francis	WIMSATT, Ann Eliza	OCT 14 1834
MORGAN, George	MORRIS, Mary	FEB 23 1829
MORGAN, George W.	CREAMER, Susanah	APR 06 1846
MORGAN, Harriet	VANESSEN, Peter	APR 24 1819
MORGAN, Hendley	NEWTON, May	MAY 06 1847
MORGAN, Isabella (blk)	BUTLER, Augustus	AUG 03 1840
MORGAN, James	MACK, Mary	MAY 19 1853
MORGAN, Jane	WHITE, Richard	DEC 23 1823
MORGAN, Jane R.	SIMPSON, Michael T.	MAY 31 1836
MORGAN, John	GREAVES, Eliza	MAY 28 1858
MORGAN, John Bennett	POLKINHORN, Sarah Jane	JUN 03 1837
MORGAN, John R.	HEIGHTON, Eliza	AUG 22 1823
MORGAN, John R.	WELCH, Harriet	JUN 21 1853
MORGAN, Johnsey R.	SPERLING, Elizabeth	JAN 26 1818
MORGAN, Louisa A.	FANT, Henry T.	JUL 13 1852
MORGAN, Mahalah J.	WILLIAMSON, Walter B.	DEC 13 1855
MORGAN, Margaret	MEANEY, John	SEP 19 1857

District of Columbia Marriage Licenses, 1811-1858

MORGAN, Maria L.	BOARMAN, Sylvester B.	NOV 21 1844
MORGAN, Mary	HUNTT, Thomas	MAR 12 1816
MORGAN, Mary	PENN, John	DEC 08 1821
MORGAN, Mary	PERKINS, Richard	AUG 06 1850
MORGAN, Mary Frances	THOM, Thomas	FEB 04 1856
MORGAN, Mirenda	GRAY, Alexander	JAN 04 1821
MORGAN, Neil	STONE, Amanda	NOV 08 1855
MORGAN, Peter	KNAPP, Mary Ann	APR 06 1835
MORGAN, Richard	BEEL, Mary	JAN 12 1848
MORGAN, Sarah T.	CALBERT, William S.	JUN 13 1835
MORGAN, Susan	DOYLE, Thomas	SEP 14 1840
MORGAN, Susan	BIGGINS, James	NOV 08 1855
MORGAN, Susan	DONNELLY, Patrick	FEB 24 1857
MORGAN, Thomas	DOGANS, Mary	JUL 08 1818
MORGAN, Thomas P.	WAUGH, Caroline	NOV 04 1845
MORGAN, William	DUVALL, Orella	MAY 06 1831
MORGAN, William	PADGGETT, Julia	OCT 28 1833
MORGAN, William	BURDINE, Margaret E.	JUN 30 1842
MORGAN, Winna	DALY, Michael	MAR 14 1857
MORIALTY, Eleanor	HUBBARD, Solomon	DEC 24 1818
MORIARTY, Daniel	GORDON, Martha	JUL 08 1850
MORIARTY, Daniel	WILLIAMS, Ellen	APR 30 1851
MORIARTY, Daniel	O'CONNOR, Cecilia	SEP 15 1856
MORIARTY, Elizabeth	KELLY, John	FEB 05 1822
MORIARTY, Ellen	SULLIVAN, John	OCT 13 1855
MORIARTY, Julia	McCARTY, Patrick	APR 13 1854
MORIARTY, Margaret	SULLIVAN, John	DEC 11 1854
MORIARTY, Mary	BOTELER, Charles W.	AUG 04 1818
MORIARTY, William	BARRON, Bridget	OCT 02 1851
MORIN, Barbara	ESTEP, Alexander	NOV 01 1812
MORIN, Harriet	LAMBERT, Edward J.	DEC 29 1826
MORIN, Matilda	GORDON, James L.	JUN 16 1825
MORLAND, Elizabeth	NELSON, Hendley	JAN 30 1855
MORLAND, Ellen	McFADDON, William	JAN 29 1839
MORLEN, Rubin	BURGESS, Mary (blk)	NOV 26 1839
MORLIN, Sarah A.F.	KLINEHAUSE, George T.	OCT 18 1854
MORLL, David P.	POOLE, Mary Cecelia	FEB 27 1849
MORRICE, Davis F.	McCANN, Mary Ann	NOV 03 1829
MORRILL, Wm.	STANWOOD, Mary	AUG 19 1820
MORRIS, Angelina (blk)	JONES, Samuel W.	MAR 09 1848
MORRIS, Ann	YOUNG, Joseph	JAN 04 1815
MORRIS, Benja. F.	DORSEY, Hannah N.	SEP 03 1857
MORRIS, Caroline	CARTER, Robert	APR 07 1845
MORRIS, Catharine	HANNON, Daniel	NOV 06 1856
MORRIS, Elizabeth	MILLS, John F.	SEP 09 1834
MORRIS, Elizabeth	McKENDRY, Henry	NOV 16 1852
MORRIS, Elizabeth	COWLEY, John	FEB 04 1857
MORRIS, Elizabeth A.	FOX, John L.	JUN 12 1847
MORRIS, Elizabeth A.	HAWLEY, Lewis J.	JUN 22 1853
MORRIS, Francis	GRIFFIN, Betsy	AUG 20 1839
MORRIS, George W.	ECKHARDT, Dorothy C.	APR 27 1853
MORRIS, Gerrard	CREEK, Sophia	AUG 13 1824
MORRIS, Hanna (blk)	LAURENCE, Henry	OCT 27 1851
MORRIS, Harriet B.	RINGGOLD, James S.	SEP 29 1841
MORRIS, Henry	MINOR, Elizabeth	OCT 05 1815
MORRIS, Henry M.	HOWLE, Eliza P.	FEB 09 1858
MORRIS, John	HINES, Berlinda	JUL 19 1830
MORRIS, John	MAHORN, Rosa L.	DEC 18 1854

District of Columbia Marriage Licenses, 1811-1858

MORRIS, John T.	LEWIS, Sarah Jane	MAY 02 1855
MORRIS, Lydia	PEREGOY, Thos. H.	APR 30 1836
MORRIS, Maria	LEAR, Benjamin Lincoln	JUL 24 1826
MORRIS, Maria L.	DUNCAN, Thomas	MAY 26 1857
MORRIS, Mary	NOWLAND, Wm. P.	AUG 08 1814
MORRIS, Mary	MORGAN, George	FEB 23 1829
MORRIS, Mary	MURPHEY, Thomas	NOV 17 1836
MORRIS, Mason	BUTLER, Charity (blk)	MAR 31 1818
MORRIS, Matilda (blk)	NICHOLLS, Lloyd	JUN 13 1826
MORRIS, Minervia Ann	JEFFERSON, Henry	DEC 24 1829
MORRIS, Sarah	FERGUSON, Joseph	JUL 17 1841
MORRIS, Sarah Ann	McMEEHEN, William G.	JUL 17 1836
MORRIS, Thursday	BURCH, Samuel	JUN 12 1849
MORRIS, William	HENNON, Eliza	NOV 13 1828
MORRIS, William	ROMON, Catherine	JUN 12 1843
MORRIS, William	DOOLIN, Mary Jane	SEP 05 1854
MORRISETT, Thomas	ANDERSON, Fanny	FEB 23 1853
MORRISON, A.J.	BEASLEY, F.A.	OCT 27 1852
MORRISON, Alexander	AULD, Grace	MAY 03 1838
MORRISON, Anna E.	LOVEGROBE, William R.	OCT 17 1853
MORRISON, David L.	STONE, Hettie A.	MAY 28 1855
MORRISON, David L.	STONE, Hetty A.	FEB 28 1856
MORRISON, Eliza	JUNKEN, Charles	JUL 28 1858
MORRISON, Elizabeth M.K.	BOUTZ, Henry	OCT 28 1843
MORRISON, Jesse	KING, Mary Ann	DEC 06 1823
MORRISON, John	MACKEY, Betsey	AUG 22 1832
MORRISON, Louisa E.	CULVER, Charles P.	FEB 18 1858
MORRISON, Margaret	ADAMS, Samuel	SEP 07 1842
MORRISON, Peter	McNAMEE, Alice	MAY 15 1858
MORRISON, Richard	MAUGHIN, Mary	MAY 26 1823
MORRISON, Sarah Ann	BROWN, Abraham	APR 29 1837
MORRISON, Thomas	GIBBONS, Ann	DEC 06 1832
MORRISON, William	WELLS, Miranda	DEC 28 1830
MORRISON, William C.	MIX, Mary Virginia	DEC 15 1852
MORRISON, William M.	BERRY, Louisa L.	OCT 26 1826
MORRISS, Mary	SHREVE, John	SEP 26 1815
MORRISS, William	FRANKLIN, Hannah	NOV 24 1831
MORROW, Francis	HILTON, Mary	NOV 09 1842
MORROW, Sarah Jane	McDUELL, George H.	MAR 02 1848
MORROW, William	COLLINS, Eliza S.	MAY 12 1824
MORROW, William	COONEY, Maria	AUG 31 1840
MORSE, Charles H.	WYMAN, Elizabeth	APR 10 1858
MORSE, John J.	CRUSSELL, Mary E.	OCT 19 1844
MORSE, Julius	BURKE, Catherine	DEC 31 1855
MORSE, Leonora	CARVER, B. Franklin	FEB 04 1857
MORSE, Matilda (blk)	MADISON, Francis	APR 06 1835
MORSE, Susan E.	CAMERON, John A.	JAN 16 1854
MORSELL, Benjamin F.	McDUELL, Sarah Jane	MAY 27 1858
MORSELL, Clara S.	STITH, Gerard	FEB 16 1848
MORSELL, J. William	COLLISSON, Mary E.	SEP 18 1857
MORSELL, James S. [Hon.]	FITZHUGH, Mary Anne [Mrs.]	OCT 21 1829
MORSELL, James S.	SEWALL, Jane	JUN 17 1833
MORSELL, Jane C.	SLAMM, Levi D.	DEC 15 1846
MORSELL, Jane S.	BOWIE, John E.	OCT 13 1856
MORSELL, Margaret	BOLIND, Thomas	JUL 03 1852
MORSELL, Margaret J.	GUY, Benjamin F.	DEC 13 1853
MORSELL, Mary Ann	CRAIGHILL, William P.	OCT 09 1856
MORSELL, Rebecca R.	LATIMER, Samuel H.	OCT 19 1857

District of Columbia Marriage Licenses, 1811-1858

MORSELL, Richard A.	FORD, Anna Rosa	APR 29 1854
MORSELL, Samuel	TURNER, Rebecca	APR 24 1828
MORSON, Mary	KING, John	NOV 09 1837
MORTER, Thomas	McNULTY, Mary	MAY 25 1855
MORTIMER, Albert	LIGHTFOOT, Jane	MAY 08 1834
MORTIMER, George S.	ABIGAIL, Elizabaeth	SEP 25 1854
MORTIMER, James	BROWN, Nancy	OCT 03 1812
MORTIMER, Joanna	SHAIN, Charles J.	MAR 01 1852
MORTIMER, John	FRASIER, Columbia	APR 01 1851
MORTIMER, John T.	DIX, Martha Ellen	JUL 12 1845
MORTIMER, John Thos.	BENNETT, Mary Ann	JUN 17 1856
MORTIMER, Ludwell	MORTIMORE, Mary	SEP 15 1818
MORTIMER, Mary J.	RITTER, John	APR 02 1850
MORTIMER, Susannah	CRUPSEY, James C.	MAY 05 1849
MORTIMER, William Henry	BARNES, Mary A.	AUG 27 1846
MORTIMORE, Benj.	TAYLOR, Elizabeth M.	JAN 31 1854
MORTIMORE, Louisa	FRANTUM, Samuel	JUN 25 1838
MORTIMORE, Mary	MORTIMER, Ludwell	SEP 15 1818
MORTIMORE, William	GREEN, Sarah Ann	DEC 24 1838
MORTON, Benjamin	WETHERS, Julia	OCT 04 1855
MORTON, Geo. H.	LOVELESS, Elizabeth	JAN 28 1830
MORTON, George T.	HENRY, Isabella L.	APR 03 1834
MORTON, Mary E.	MIDDLETON, Thomas	DEC 18 1851
MOSELEY, Spencer	COOMBE, Ann	APR 28 1814
MOSELEY, William H.	MORAN, Catharine	JUL 09 1841
MOSELY, William H.	GATES, Susan J.	SEP 21 1833
MOSES, Eliza	CAPERTON, Hugh	DEC 27 1842
MOSES, Simpson P.	TUCKER, Lizzie C.	JUL 05 1849
MOSHER, Imogene	TAYLOE, John	NOV 09 1841
MOSHER, James	MAGRUDER, Elizabeth L.	DEC 08 1819
MOSLEY, Mary C.	HOOVER, Andrew D.	NOV 23 1855
MOSS, Alcinda	CAMPBELL, John W.	OCT 05 1854
MOSS, Aleana	McDOWELL, John	APR 11 1812
MOSS, George W.	PARRISH, Martha J.	MAR 17 1837
MOSS, John T.	SCHOTT, Annie V.	OCT 02 1854
MOSS, Katherine M.	IVEY, William H.	JUN 01 1839
MOSS, Obadiah	ORME, Elizabeth	DEC 03 1832
MOSS, Obediah	RICKTOR, Maria	FEB 11 1830
MOSS, Sylvester	MURPHY, Susan	JUN 02 1846
MOSS, Theodore	HIXSON, Matilda	MAY 10 1832
MOSS, William	LOMAX, Elizabeath	OCT 09 1851
MOT, Mary	RUPPEL, John	NOV 03 1854
MOTHERSAID, Elias J.	LOMAX, Elizabeth	APR 29 1851
MOTHERSAID, Jane	McCAULEY, Joseph	APR 30 1849
MOTHERSHEAD, John	MILLHORN, Isabella	DEC 18 1850
MOTHERSHEAD, Margaret	CARDEN, Thomas	JAN 02 1852
MOTHERSHEAD, Mary	KILBY, Robert	APR 12 1853
MOTZER, Daniel	WASHINGTON, Fannie L.	OCT 08 1856
MOTZER, Daniel, Rev.	WILLIAMSON, Elizabeth B.	SEP 16 1848
MOULDEN, Anna	GLADMAN, James	MAY 27 1850
MOULDEN, Eliza	TRULL, John	MAR 10 1834
MOULDEN, John A.	HARDT, Ann M.	DEC 18 1849
MOULDEN, William	CROSBY, Mary E.	MAR 22 1856
MOULDER, Anna Jane	BRYANT, John Y.	DEC 24 1834
MOULDER, Eliza	WILSON, Joseph S.	SEP 01 1829
MOULDER, John W.	LONGDON, Emily J.	MAR 17 1843
MOULDER, Martha D.	DUNCANSON, John A.M.	DEC 08 1840
MOULDER, Marthalina	ROBERTS, Florian	NOV 13 1854

District of Columbia Marriage Licenses, 1811-1858

MOULDER, Mary D.	ABBOT, George D.	MAR 26 1833
MOULDER, Notley	JOY, Christeen	FEB 01 1826
MOULDER, Sarah Ann	RAY, Enos	FEB 06 1822
MOULDING, Ann Maria	RITCHE, Jno. M.	NOV 04 1829
MOULDING, Enoch	PLANTT, Henrietta	JUL 06 1837
MOULSWORTH, Sarah	McCULLOUCH, Duncan	OCT 09 1826
MOULTEN, Mary G.	GIBERSON, Gilbert L.	MAY 26 1828
MOULTON, Hannah M.	ELLIOT, James B.	JUL 18 1857
MOULTON, Thomas Henry	REEMER, Elizabeth Jane	JUN 03 1845
MOUNDZ, Margaret	DALE, John R.	FEB 12 1846
MOUNT, James	GARTHARD, Sarah Ann	JAN 20 1838
MOUNT, James W.	RATCLIFFE, Lucind	NOV 04 1845
MOUNT, Joanna	CALBERT, Mathew	JUN 15 1852
MOUNT, Martha E.	McHENRY, Martin D.	MAR 04 1839
MOUNT, Mary C.E.	KNELLER, Samuel	DEC 18 1833
MOUNT, Octavia N.	ROGERS, Johnson R.	MAR 13 1839
MOUNT, Sarah Ann	FRANCIS, Thomas	JAN 27 1831
MOUNT, Sarah Ellen	FENTON, Robert W.	FEB 19 1856
MOUNTJOY, Lemuel	ARRINGTON, Mary	JUN 13 1829
MOUNTJOY, Mary	WILSON, Charles F.	FEB 01 1854
MOUNTZ, Elizabeth C.	CRAMER, Samuel J.	SEP 15 1840
MOUNTZ, Joanna	McLEOD, Christopher Columbus	NOV 05 1838
MOUNTZ, Joseph	HEDGE, Elizabeth	JAN 12 1826
MOUNTZ, Joseph	OFFUTT, Mary Ann K.	JUN 08 1841
MOUNTZ, Maria Louisa	BISHOP, Henry	DEC 15 1847
MOUNTZER, Mary M.	BILLING, Frederick S.	NOV 11 1856
MOUTON, Alexander	GARDNER, Emma K.	JAN 24 1842
MOXLEY, Ann Dent Douglass	HUNTON, Thomas L.	NOV 18 1822
MOXLEY, Elizabeth	HUTCHINS, Elias	SEP 27 1855
MOXLEY, Henrietta B.	UNDERWOOD, George	OCT 08 1835
MOXLEY, Horatio	CURREN, Lucretia	APR 21 1826
MOXLEY, John	GILL, Delilah	JAN 13 1814
MOXLEY, Josephine	WINTER, Robert	AUG 18 1858
MOXLEY, Lucinda J.	SORREL, Francis	SEP 06 1822
MOXLEY, Lucretia	ROLLINS, James	OCT 17 1832
MOXLEY, Lucretia	HOOVER, Andrew	MAR 18 1843
MOXLEY, Matilda A.D.	SORREL, Francis	SEP 30 1829
MOXLEY, Resin	CONNOR, Mary	JUN 08 1843
MOXLEY, Richard S.	GILLISS, Hannah M.	FEB 05 1839
MOXLEY, William	CHAMBERLAIN, Eliza	AUG 25 1836
MOZINGER, Ann	LUCAS, John	APR 22 1839
MOZINGO, Jane	RICE, Cornelius B.	FEB 03 1847
MUCK, John	HELDERSCHMIDT, Mary M.	MAY 19 1849
MUCKLEARY, Richard	SOUTHERN, Maria	JUL 05 1818
MUDD, Ann Maria	TAYLOR, Samuel H.	MAY 23 1829
MUDD, Catherine	BURNHAM, Nathan	JUN 01 1858
MUDD, Edward	ENSEY, Margaret Ann	JUL 21 1842
MUDD, Elizabeth	HENLEY, John Perry	DEC 22 1836
MUDD, Emily B.	THOMPSON, Lieut. Egbert, U.S.N.	AUG 28 1854
MUDD, Harriet	GARDNER, Isidore	MAY 19 1827
MUDD, Harriott	BLENDEN, George	NOV 18 1828
MUDD, Ignatius	ERSKINE, Sarah J.	SEP 16 1839
MUDD, James	HAINEY, Catherine	FEB 02 1858
MUDD, James	THRONEY, Bridget	FEB 12 1858
MUDD, Jane	CLARKE, Jos. H.	AUG 30 1821
MUDD, Jane Elizabeth	YOUNG, William	DEC 16 1837
MUDD, Jeremiah T.	JAMESON, Sarah Ellen	FEB 16 1857
MUDD, Julia Ann	INGMAN, William	APR 09 1831

District of Columbia Marriage Licenses, 1811-1858

MUDD, Louisa Jane	McNANTZ, Patrick H.	JUL 01 1848
MUDD, Margaret Ann	REILY, John Francis	JUN 27 1842
MUDD, Marilda	JORDEN, William	APR 05 1833
MUDD, Mary	TALBURT, James	AUG 09 1844
MUDD, Mary Ellen	TAYLOR, Alfred	JUL 07 1828
MUDD, Mary Ellen	RAY, John H.	MAY 27 1852
MUDD, Mary S.	McCURDY, Dennis	APR 17 1817
MUDD, Matilda A.	CONNER, Michael	APR 13 1846
MUDD, Nancy	THOMAS, Henry	OCT 07 1815
MUDD, Rebecca	MILL, George	NOV 25 1817
MUDD, Rebecca	CONNELLY, John	DEC 27 1842
MUDD, Sylvester	PEAK, Joannah	JUL 20 1854
MUDD, William	BRYAN, Sarah	DEC 24 1844
MUDGE, Daniel C.	CARR, Emily E.	APR 12 1847
MUELLER, Augustus	HARTER, Wilhelmine	AUG 05 1847
MUELLER, Charles	WILLEY, Caroline	AUG 29 1848
MUELLER, Gustavus	SCHMIDT, Catharine	DEC 22 1856
MUFF, Mary Ann	KELLY, Thomas	JUN 24 1854
MUHLHAHER, Caroline	STOFFEL, Ignatz	FEB 13 1858
MUHLLHALM, Charlotte	SCHULTHIS, Henry	MAR 23 1857
MUIR, Robinson F.	REEVES, Mary	JUL 02 1858
MULCARE, Morris	MITCHELL, Mary	NOV 10 1857
MULE, Eliot	HUNTT, Hannah	FEB 10 1814
MULFINGER, John C.	HEISS, Margaretta	JAN 31 1843
MULHOLLEN, Mary Ann	VILLARD, Richd. H.L.	SEP 13 1815
MULHOLLOM, Sarah	CLIFFORD, James	FEB 12 1853
MULICAN, Ann	McDANIEL, Elaxander	DEC 24 1832
MULIKIN, Ruthy Ann	GRIMES, John	JAN 26 1848
MULLAN, Susan	DAUGHERTY, James	OCT 15 1822
MULLAY, Emma V.	LAMER, George G.	JUN 18 1855
MULLEN, Ellenor	KELSEY, Conklin	JAN 21 1854
MULLEN, John	REAVES, Catharine R.	JUL 16 1833
MULLEN, Margaret M.	CARROLL, Daniel	NOV 17 1851
MULLEN, Mary	ROOK, Peter	MAR 07 1831
MULLEN, Sarah	BURR, John	JUN 15 1854
MULLEN, William H.	O'DONNELL, Alice	JUN 08 1858
MULLER, Antoine	MELSON, Regen	MAY 27 1854
MULLER, Doughtery Augusta	BERGMAN, Charles William	DEC 22 1853
MULLER, Frederick	CLARK, Maria	OCT 01 1839
MULLER, James	BAKER, Harriet	MAY 22 1821
MULLER, James D.	SHUMACK, Sarah C.	AUG 03 1858
MULLER, John C.	EICHHORN, Elizabeth	MAY 01 1848
MULLER, Mackel	MARTELL, Ann	FEB 15 1825
MÜLLER, John Ferdd.	WAGNER, Christine C.	NOV 16 1855
MULLEY, William A.	SUTHERLAND, Jane F.	MAY 14 1842
MULLICAN, Elizabeth	MITCHELL, Mandica	DEC 24 1840
MULLICAN, Elizabeth V.	MAGRUDER, Wesley L.	MAY 15 1855
MULLICAN, Elizth.	RISTON, Benjamin	DEC 29 1821
MULLICAN, Jeremiah	SUIT, Polly	OCT 09 1813
MULLICAN, Joseph	HAVENER, Mary	MAY 26 1831
MULLICAN, Sarah	NORTON, Robert	MAR 04 1824
MULLICAN, Thomas W.	UPTON, Elizabeth	DEC 26 1823
MULLIGAN, Ann	CROWN, Jeremiah	JAN 01 1824
MULLIGAN, Bernard	CONROY, Mary	JUL 18 1851
MULLIKEN, Catherine	MULLIKEN, James	DEC 22 1838
MULLIKEN, James	MULLIKEN, Catherine	DEC 22 1838
MULLIKIN, Basil	BEALE, Matilda	JAN 27 1815
MULLIKIN, Caroline	ALTOERFER, Ludwig	JUL 06 1849

District of Columbia Marriage Licenses, 1811-1858

MULLIKIN, Eleanor	KING, William	OCT 13 1827
MULLIKIN, Elenora	PENN, Edward	SEP 16 1853
MULLIKIN, Elizabaeth	THOMPSON, George	OCT 15 1839
MULLIKIN, Elizabeth	MANGUN, Francis	MAY 25 1831
MULLIKIN, Elizabeth Ann	JOHNSON, John	JUN 03 1851
MULLIKIN, James	COLLINGWOOD, Elizth.	APR 20 1829
MULLIKIN, James	DOWDEN, Julia Ann	OCT 14 1851
MULLIKIN, Jeremiah	SHERLOCK, Ellenora	DEC 18 1856
MULLIKIN, John	RICKETTS, Mary Ellen	JUL 28 1857
MULLIKIN, Martha	FRAZIER, Benjamin	MAR 24 1827
MULLIKIN, Martha	MURPHY, Mila	JUN 05 1828
MULLIKIN, Martha E.	GATES, George L.	AUG 06 1850
MULLIKIN, Mary	GIDDANS, Thomas	APR 19 1827
MULLIKIN, Mary	MANUEL, John	NOV 10 1830
MULLIKIN, Mary	DUNN, Dennis	OCT 09 1852
MULLIKIN, Mary Elizabeth	FRASIER, James	SEP 21 1848
MULLIKIN, Nathaniel	HALL, Elizabeth H.	DEC 30 1823
MULLIKIN, T. McE.	RIND, Rebecca Elizabeth	JUN 09 1856
MULLIN, Basil	PIGGEE, Nancy (blk)	MAY 17 1831
MULLIN, Catherine	MITCHELL, John	JUL 28 1849
MULLIN, Lewis	HILLS, Eudocia Gilston	APR 17 1843
MULLIN, Martha A.	McKENNA, James H.	DEC 19 1850
MULLIN, Susan	COLLINS, Theodore B.	OCT 04 1855
MULLIN, William	SMALLWOOD, Permellia	SEP 05 1831
MULLIN, William S.	CODRICK, Elizabeth	MAR 23 1844
MULLIN, William S.	WARE, Ann R.	APR 17 1849
MULLING, John	YEATMAN, Mary	MAR 18 1847
MULLINS, John	PURSLEY, Laurenda	APR 18 1843
MULLINS, John H.	BROWN, Elizabeth	NOV 23 1844
MULLONE, Thomas	O'MEARA, Ann	JUL 05 1851
MULLONEY, Margaret	LUCKETT, John	JUL 24 1847
MULLOWNY, John F.	TURPIN, Amanda L.	MAY 05 1851
MULLOY, Elizabeth	CONWAY, James	JAN 27 1853
MULLOY, Frances T.	THOMPSON, James T.	FEB 12 1850
MULLOY, Mary Ann	DAVIDSON, James	JAN 16 1835
MULLOY, Thomas	FRAZIER, Melinda	NOV 29 1834
MULLOY, Thomas	KENNA, Margaret	DEC 15 1857
MULRANY, Bernard	HANY, Mary	NOV 24 1830
MULREIA, Bridget	CARROLL, John	MAY 10 1856
MULRENEY, Bernard	STEELE, Ann	DEC 02 1848
MULROY, James	DELANY, Mary	JAN 05 1857
MULVAHILL, Hanora	O'CONNELL, John	AUG 14 1858
MULVERHILL, Nancy	SULLIVAN, David O.	FEB 21 1852
MULVIHILL, Catherine	O'BRIEN, Michael	JUN 28 1853
MUMBY, Robert	HOUSON, Rachael	DEC 10 1817
MUNCH, Christian H.	WEISKITTEL, Charlotte	SEP 08 1842
MUNDENG, Mary	WALZ, George	DEC 14 1854
MUNDLE, Rachel	JARVIS, John	OCT 11 1855
MUNDOWNY, Thomas H.	DIGGES, Ellen	APR 27 1836
MUNDT, Frederick C.C.	WELSH, Hannah	AUG 27 1840
MUNFORD, Lewis	TAYLOR, Eleanor	JUN 26 1828
MUNRO, David	BAIRD, Sarah	MAR 14 1827
MUNROE, Columbus	SEATON, Julia Winston	APR 03 1839
MUNROE, Daniel	HOLLINS, Mary (blk)	AUG 21 1856
MUNROE, Eliza	BERKELEY, George N.	DEC 08 1813
MUNROE, Emily	RANDALL, Henry K.	NOV 23 1826
MUNROE, Frances W.	RAMSAY, George D.	SEP 22 1830
MUNROE, George	LUCAS, Martha (blk)	DEC 21 1848

District of Columbia Marriage Licenses, 1811-1858

MUNROE, Hannah [Mrs.]	CARLON, Robert	JUN 03 1820
MUNROE, James L.	HENRY, Rebecca	AUG 29 1820
MUNROE, James T.	CRUPPER, Frances V.	SEP 02 1845
MUNROE, Jane H.	McCLEES, Ellis B.	MAY 02 1851
MUNROE, Margaret	HODGSON, John	SEP 03 1812
MUNROE, Martha	RYE, John T.	OCT 04 1850
MUNROE, Robert M.	TYLER, Mary Ann	MAY 14 1840
MUNROE, Susan	FARRAGUT, James	AUG 17 1842
MUNROE, William	STUDER, Elizabeth	OCT 22 1833
MUNSTED, Ann	MADIGAN, Michael	JUL 20 1853
MÜNSTER, Adolph	OFENSTEIN, Lekata	APR 06 1858
MUNTS, Catharine	MACK, John	JUN 25 1855
MUNTZ, James	CARROLL, Maria	NOV 14 1850
MURDOCH, John	WETZEL, Margaret	DEC 31 1812
MURDOCH, John	VILE, Margaret	APR 03 1816
MURDOCH, John W.	GAHARTY, Mary	APR 26 1848
MURDOCK, John	GILLASPY, Mary Ann	JUN 25 1817
MURDOCK, Louise	CHILDS, Wentworth L.	NOV 12 1855
MURDOCK, Margaret	PUTNAM, Caleb	OCT 17 1820
MURDOCK, Margaret Elizabeth	JONES, Thomas	JAN 27 1829
MURDOCK, Mary Ann	ELVANS, Richard	MAY 18 1828
MURDOCK, Mary Elizabeth	JOHNSON, John Alexander	AUG 07 1841
MURDOCK, William Charles	FORREST, Sarah C.	JUN 06 1857
MURDOCK, William D.C.	BURNETT, Ellen Louisa	OCT 26 1833
MURPHEY, Ann	THOMAS, Lewis B.	JUL 05 1837
MURPHEY, Ann Rebecca	MITCHELL, James	JAN 21 1845
MURPHEY, Chloe	WARDELL, Samuel	MAY 23 1820
MURPHEY, Daniel	CAVENAUGH, Emily	JAN 02 1858
MURPHEY, David	ROACH, Mary Ann	OCT 01 1844
MURPHEY, Dennis	LECKIE, Elizabeth	JUL 22 1852
MURPHEY, Edward	PORTER, Rebecca	MAY 09 1837
MURPHEY, Elizabeth	SCOTT, Henry	DEC 23 1818
MURPHEY, Elizabeth	MILLER, Lawrence	MAR 02 1833
MURPHEY, Elizabeth	GLASCOE, David	JUL 02 1838
MURPHEY, Emily	TUCKER, Richard	DEC 23 1830
MURPHEY, Hannah	HICKEY, Thomas	OCT 09 1851
MURPHEY, J.	MATHEWS, Harriet	NOV 13 1832
MURPHEY, Johanna	CROWLEY, John	DEC 11 1857
MURPHEY, John	BLUNDER, Elizabeth	SEP 15 1819
MURPHEY, John	CAMPBELL, Julia	APR 01 1837
MURPHEY, John	RILEY, Ann	AUG 01 1840
MURPHEY, John	FITZGERALD, Ellen	AUG 07 1852
MURPHEY, Lawrence	WELLS, Jane E.	JUL 11 1844
MURPHEY, Margaret	SNEE, Michael	FEB 24 1820
MURPHEY, Martha	FOWLER, Charles W.	NOV 19 1841
MURPHEY, Mary (blk)	BATSON, Selin	AUG 12 1840
MURPHEY, Mary Ann	COLEMAN, Jeremiah	AUG 23 1823
MURPHEY, Mary E.	FOWLER, John H.	DEC 18 1850
MURPHEY, Michael	GOLDSMITH, Ellen Cecelia	NOV 17 1841
MURPHEY, Michael	FEY, Catherine	FEB 18 1854
MURPHEY, Michael	LEEHY, Ellen	JAN 05 1858
MURPHEY, Patrick	CULLAN, Margaret	APR 10 1858
MURPHEY, Rebecca A.	DIXON, James A.	JUN 12 1843
MURPHEY, Thomas	MORRIS, Mary	NOV 17 1836
MURPHEY, Thomas H.	NOTTINGHAM, Margaret	MAY 09 1846
MURPHEY, Wiley T.	FOWLER, Linney	AUG 19 1826
MURPHEY, William	BYRNE, Margaret	NOV 25 1843
MURPHEY, William H.	HOWARD, Sarah Jane	MAY 13 1847

District of Columbia Marriage Licenses, 1811-1858

MURPHY, Alexander	ALDRIDGE, Margaret	FEB 20 1821
MURPHY, Andrew	LARNER, Mary	AUG 07 1828
MURPHY, Ann	FAGAN, Daniel	AUG 16 1817
MURPHY, Ann	SULLIVAN, James	NOV 16 1850
MURPHY, Ann A.	BALL, Richard D.	NOV 28 1849
MURPHY, Benjamin	SCOTT, Elizabeth	SEP 04 1813
MURPHY, Benjamin	CARNEY, Eliza	NOV 03 1817
MURPHY, Bridget	LEARY, Daniel	APR 24 1856
MURPHY, Catharine	CRUTTENDEN, Harvey	NOV 24 1814
MURPHY, Catharine	TWYFORD, Smith	JUN 19 1821
MURPHY, Catharine	HURLEY, Cornelius	JUN 12 1845
MURPHY, Catharine	BROWN, Daniel	SEP 01 1852
MURPHY, Catharine	GRADY, Michael	AUG 02 1853
MURPHY, Cornelius	FITZPATRICK, Nelly	AUG 14 1848
MURPHY, Daniel	CAVNAGH, Emily	OCT 14 1856
MURPHY, Danl.	YOST, Mary	MAY 19 1832
MURPHY, David	CONNELL, Mary	OCT 21 1854
MURPHY, Edward	ROBINSON, Mary	DEC 19 1838
MURPHY, Eliza	DEREMEN, Jacob	FEB 21 1824
MURPHY, Eliza A.	JOHNSON, William F.	DEC 19 1857
MURPHY, Elizth. Ann	LINNEHAN, Conn	MAY 24 1836
MURPHY, Ellen	FITZSIMMONS, John	AUG 16 1834
MURPHY, Ellen	CURRY, John	AUG 08 1850
MURPHY, Ellen	WALL, Michael	JUN 10 1851
MURPHY, Ellen	WOLFE, Thomas	JAN 13 1852
MURPHY, Ellen	CRIMMIN, Patrick	APR 08 1852
MURPHY, Ellen	FLAHERTY, John	NOV 22 1853
MURPHY, Ellen	GRADY, Patrick	SEP 09 1854
MURPHY, Ellen	SHEA, Michael	JAN 06 1855
MURPHY, Ellen	SNEE, Thomas	FEB 17 1857
MURPHY, George W.	KING, Mary Ann	JUL 21 1857
MURPHY, Helena C.	SIMMONS, Samuel S.	JUN 09 1853
MURPHY, Honora	SULLIVAN, John	MAY 27 1854
MURPHY, Jeremiah	GLAVIN, Ellen	APR 17 1855
MURPHY, Johanna	HANIGAN, John	AUG 14 1858
MURPHY, John	THOMPSON, Mary	APR 18 1842
MURPHY, John	RADY, Mary	APR 22 1847
MURPHY, John	O'DONNOGHUE, Margaret E.	JUN 17 1852
MURPHY, John	DEMPSEY, Catharine	JUN 01 1853
MURPHY, John	MARTIN, Driscilla C.	FEB 01 1855
MURPHY, John	ROCHE, Mary	SEP 14 1855
MURPHY, John	SHANNAHAN, Hannorah	OCT 23 1855
MURPHY, Jno. D.	MARR, Lucinda Ann	MAY 05 1825
MURPHY, John W.	DEMPSY, Mary A.	APR 22 1858
MURPHY, Lucy D.	COGSWELL, Joseph P.	MAY 06 1856
MURPHY, Margaret	DORA, John	AUG 13 1850
MURPHY, Margt.	FITZPATRICK, Andrew	AUG 10 1853
MURPHY, Maria	ROCHE, Patrick	JUL 17 1852
MURPHY, Martha M.	UNSWORTH, John	MAY 22 1850
MURPHY, Martin	DONOVAN, Mary	APR 16 1836
MURPHY, Mary	WALLIARD, James F.	OCT 28 1840
MURPHY, Mary	WISE, William	MAY 27 1848
MURPHY, Mary	SHANAHAN, Edwd.	FEB 13 1855
MURPHY, Mary	LEARY, Nicholas	JAN 21 1857
MURPHY, Mary A.	BRINNEL, Charles H.	MAR 06 1850
MURPHY, Mary Ann	ELLMORE, James	MAR 19 1850
MURPHY, Mary Ann	HEALY, Michael	FEB 25 1853
MURPHY, Mary E.	MARTIN, William S.	APR 21 1855

District of Columbia Marriage Licenses, 1811-1858

MURPHY, Mary Ellen	KELLY, John	JUN 13 1854
MURPHY, Mary Jane	TURNBURKE, Francis	OCT 17 1854
MURPHY, Mary Jane	McNALLY, John	JAN 05 1857
MURPHY, Michael	DONOHO, Bridget	FEB 07 1857
MURPHY, Mila	MULLIKIN, Martha	JUN 05 1828
MURPHY, Morris	TOLIN, Jane	SEP 03 1855
MURPHY, Patrick	HORAN, Mary	JUL 11 1853
MURPHY, Patrick	FLYNN, Bridget	JAN 28 1854
MURPHY, Patrick	GAHUTZ, Cathrine	JAN 24 1858
MURPHY, Paul	KELLY, Mary Jane	JAN 15 1838
MURPHY, Peter	CAMMEL, Jane	MAR 26 1830
MURPHY, Peter	DEGNAN, Mary	JUL 18 1853
MURPHY, Robert C.	LYNE, Lavinia H.	AUG 22 1853
MURPHY, Samima	WHITMORE, Henry M.	JAN 03 1854
MURPHY, Samuel	MEAD, Abigal Jane	OCT 07 1852
MURPHY, Sarah A.C.	GANNON, Michael	JUN 01 1826
MURPHY, Sarah Louisa	WALKER, William H.	MAY 14 1849
MURPHY, Susan	MOSS, Sylvester	JUN 02 1846
MURPHY, Thomas	FITZGERALD, Margaret	JUL 23 1851
MURPHY, Thomas	MILLER, Harriet	DEC 01 1852
MURPHY, Thomas	McCARROLL, Ann	JUL 10 1854
MURPHY, Timothy	DONOHO, Margaret	AUG 22 1851
MURPHY, Timothy	HORN, Honora	FEB 11 1854
MURPHY, William	CARTER, Mary	NOV 18 1819
MURPHY, William	WHITTLE, Elizabeth	APR 09 1835
MURPHY, Wm.	THOMPSON, Jane	JAN 16 1849
MURPHY, Wm. C.	PIERCE, Anna L.	NOV 22 1855
MURR, Gottiel	KOEHLER, Christina	MAR 30 1854
MURRAY, Ai.	SHANKLETER, Mary L.	JUN 03 1854
MURRAY, Alexander J.	ADDISON, Mary	DEC 15 1828
MURRAY, Ann	MURRAY, Hugh	JAN 26 1853
MURRAY, Ann	CLARKE, Charles	MAY 10 1856
MURRAY, Anna	BAYLY, William Cole	MAY 28 1850
MURRAY, Araminta	PICKRELL, Samuel	AUG 30 1832
MURRAY, Catherine	TINAN, John	DEC 22 1855
MURRAY, Charles	ROBINSON, Elizabeth	APR 22 1824
MURRAY, Edward J.	NORRIS, Ann	SEP 17 1815
MURRAY, Eleanor Mary	WARREN, John O.	JUN 26 1844
MURRAY, Elijah	BROWN, Elizabeth	JUL 01 1844
MURRAY, Eliza	IMMICH, Jacob	FEB 20 1851
MURRAY, Elizabeth	BLADEN, William	SEP 26 1844
MURRAY, Elizabeth A.	ANDERSON, Elizah M.	JAN 29 1839
MURRAY, Gilbert	JACKSON, Elizabeth (blk)	JAN 21 1840
MURRAY, Henry W.	HUNTER, Mildred M.	MAR 20 1851
MURRAY, Hugh	MURRAY, Ann	JAN 26 1853
MURRAY, James	NEWTON, Julia Ann	DEC 26 1826
MURRAY, James	MICKUM, Sarah A.H.	OCT 27 1832
MURRAY, James	JOHNSON, Verlinda	NOV 25 1833
MURRAY, James	BURROUGHS, Elizth.	DEC 29 1852
MURRAY, James A.	DONLEY, Mary L.	JUL 25 1855
MURRAY, Jane	BLADEN, Willam	DEC 31 1827
MURRAY, John	PEEPLES, Drurilla	AUG 05 1818
MURRAY, John	FAGAN, Eliza A.	FEB 14 1831
MURRAY, Juliet	MARBURY, John, Junr.	JUN 09 1851
MURRAY, Levy	PHILLIPS, Catharine Ann	JUN 17 1833
MURRAY, Lucinda	BEACH, Robert	FEB 17 1852
MURRAY, Margaret C.	BROWN, Eleazer	SEP 20 1838
MURRAY, Mary	JENKINS, Thomas	MAY 22 1834

District of Columbia Marriage Licenses, 1811-1858

MURRAY, Mary	MOLDEN, William	JAN 08 1842
MURRAY, Mary	MURRAY, Owen	OCT 24 1842
MURRAY, Mary	CAVELEUX, J. Marc	DEC 22 1849
MURRAY, Mary	COGAN, Thomas	NOV 04 1850
MURRAY, Mary	RYAN, Patrick	APR 10 1857
MURRAY, Mary	McKENNEY, Peter	OCT 10 1857
MURRAY, Mary E.	SHAW, Matthias	JAN 22 1850
MURRAY, Mary J.	BROWN, Alex H.	FEB 05 1851
MURRAY, Mary M.	COOMBES, Charles	JUL 06 1858
MURRAY, Micholas	KEILER, Elen	SEP 11 1852
MURRAY, Nicholas	SMITH, Rebecca	JAN 12 1852
MURRAY, Owen	MURRAY, Mary	OCT 24 1842
MURRAY, Patrick	WRIGHT, Hester	DEC 08 1827
MURRAY, Patrick	McMAHON, Alice Mary	SEP 06 1838
MURRAY, Patrick	KING, Ann	APR 17 1857
MURRAY, Peter	McKEEVER, Rose	APR 20 1857
MURRAY, Sarah	BRIDGES, Dennis	OCT 31 1816
MURRAY, Sarah	CASSELL, Charles	MAY 22 1822
MURRAY, Stanislaus	HAMILTON, Harriot S.	FEB 16 1832
MURRAY, Stanislaus	HAMILTON, Mary H.	MAR 19 1839
MURRAY, Susan	GREEN, Owen	FEB 16 1846
MURRAY, Thomas	KING, Sarah	OCT 25 1814
MURRAY, Thomas	FOYLES, Sarah	APR 23 1822
MURRAY, Thomas	DRUMMOND, Jane	JUL 10 1839
MURRAY, Thomas I.	COMPTON, Frances Ann	JUL 26 1834
MURRAY, Thomas, Jr.	COOTE, Margaret C.	MAY 08 1832
MURRAY, Thomas S.	BUTLER, Gertrude	DEC 07 1846
MURRAY, Virginia F.	MORAN, Enoch V.	JUN 30 1857
MURRAY, William	KNOTT, Mary	AUG 26 1828
MURRAY, William	TOOMEY, Isabella	DEC 03 1846
MURRAY, William	KEENAN, Bridget	FEB 19 1855
MURRAY, William A.	WALLS, Mary E.	JAN 28 1854
MURRAY, Winefred	BEAN, Colmore	NOV 28 1812
MURRAY, Wm. A.	REDMAN, Margaret C.	MAY 10 1855
MURRIS, Henry	JAMES, Amelia	MAY 11 1846
MURRY, Bridget	SHAL<u>IM</u>, John	JUL 24 1851
MURRY, James	QUIGLEY, Biddy	OCT 05 1835
MURRY, Rebecca	NICHOLSON, George	OCT 30 1848
MURTEN, Mrs.	HENDERSON, Thomas	APR 28 1840
MURTER, Jane	DONOHO, Thomas	MAY 03 1851
MURTOCK, Patrick	QUILLAN, Ann	FEB 08 1853
MUSCHETT, James M.A.	TASTET, Virginia M.	MAY 09 1850
MUSE, John	SHREVE, Susan	AUG 01 1822
MUSE, Lindsay	BALL, Eliza M. (blk)	APR 04 1825
MUSE, Walker I.	BARTLE, Ellen Frances	OCT 27 1853
MUSGRAVE, Daniel	TAYLOR, Elizabeth	JUL 31 1827
MUSGROVE, Aaron R.	BEECH, Mariah	NOV 15 1825
MUSGROVE, Margaret	SHILES, James W.	NOV 15 1845
MUSKELL, Sarah Ann	SUTER, Richard	JAN 07 1819
MUSSEY, William H.	LINDSLEY, Caroline W.	MAY 04 1857
MUSTER, Thomas	McDONOUGH, Margaret	MAY 17 1856
MUSTIN, Anna S.	JONES, Thomas	JUL 24 1850
MUSTIN, Catharine E.	WALKER, David	OCT 14 1850
MUSTIN, Harriet M.	TASTET, Joseph M.	OCT 14 1850
MUTH, Andrew	AMANT, Theresa	FEB 20 1857
MUTH, Louisa	POWERS, Martin	OCT 20 1836
MUVERZAYS, Johnannatte	MILLER, Christian	APR 02 1855
MYER, Christiana Miach<u>a</u>	MAGILL, Saml.	NOV 09 1816

District of Columbia Marriage Licenses, 1811-1858

MYER, Franklin S.	TENNISON, Catharine C.	FEB 18 1829
MYER, Hannah Zenobia	CARVER, Hiram	OCT 19 1815
MYER, Kate C.	MAGILL, John W.	DEC 11 1855
MYER, Louisa W.	SMITH, Thomas J.	APR 08 1828
MYER, Sarah Salome	BRANNAN, John	OCT 21 1816
MYER, Susan	SIERLACH, Peter	MAR 22 1855
MYERS, Alexander	KNIGHT, Catharine	APR 23 1833
MYERS, Alexander K.	SUTER, Rebecca	JAN 04 1827
MYERS, Amelia	SCHNEIDER, Christian G.	OCT 26 1857
MYERS, Ann Maria	UPPERMAN, William H.	FEB 21 1837
MYERS, Anna	COOMBES, John	OCT 23 1834
MYERS, Benjamin B.	EDMONSTON, Mary	SEP 18 1813
MYERS, Benjamin B.	EDMONSTON, Ann Maria	JAN 26 1825
MYERS, Benjamin S.	BROWN, Emma	AUG 29 1851
MYERS, C.C.	HURSE, Mary	OCT 17 1854
MYERS, Caroline	HART, John	JAN 06 1843
MYERS, Charles	PARSONS, Susanna	APR 11 1832
MYERS, Charles	NORTON, Anna	JAN 31 1833
MYERS, Charles	LUTZ, Jane C.	SEP 10 1844
MYERS, Charlotte	WILSON, John	MAY 27 1822
MYERS, Daniel	HAMILTON, Eliza	MAY 09 1848
MYERS, David	HALEY, Mary Ann	FEB 26 1825
MYERS, Dulaney F.	ECKLOFF, William C.F.	DEC 15 1842
MYERS, Eliza	MEGARY, James W.	MAR 17 1849
MYERS, Eliza Ann C.	CASE, Shedrick B.	DEC 20 1837
MYERS, Elizabeth	BROWN, John	DEC 17 1813
MYERS, Ellen	O'CONNOR, Michael	JUN 05 1858
MYERS, Frederick	TUCKER, Elizabeth	JUN 07 1813
MYERS, George	REED, Sarah	FEB 08 1841
MYERS, George	McFARLAND, Catharine	FEB 02 1856
MYERS, Georgeanna	BURCH, Richard H.	NOV 26 1849
MYERS, Henry	THOMPSON, Margaret E.	OCT 14 1848
MYERS, John	WINEBURGER, Ann Susanna	JUN 15 1826
MYERS, John	PEARCE, Elizabeth	JUN 23 1835
MYERS, John	FRIZZELL, Catherine	MAY 14 1857
MYERS, John H.	BOTSFORD, Eliza	JUN 08 1833
MYERS, John T., Sr.	EASTON, Anne	APR 17 1819
MYERS, John W.P.	McNAI, Anna C.	JUN 01 1857
MYERS, Joseph	WILLIS, Elizabeth	OCT 10 1850
MYERS, Joseph	WELCH, Jane	FEB 13 1851
MYERS, Joseph	LEE, Sousana	OCT 18 1852
MYERS, Lavinia	GONTER, James M.	JAN 04 1847
MYERS, Louisa	LIBBY, Joseph	MAY 13 1822
MYERS, Mary E.A.	HOFFMAN, Charles E.	JUL 19 1855
MYERS, Mary J.	GINGLE, George F.	JAN 01 1851
MYERS, Matthew	McLEAN, Bridget	DEC 31 1852
MYERS, Peter	DIXON, Emilia	APR 04 1837
MYERS, Sarah (blk)	TAYLOR, George	JUL 10 1850
MYERS, Sarah Ann	BALL, George W.	FEB 22 1834
MYERS, Sarah C.	NOLAN, Thos. S.	DEC 14 1825
MYERS, Sophia	LIPPHARD, John H.	FEB 20 1847
MYERS, Susan	MITCHELL, William	SEP 16 1856
MYERS, Thomas Lycurgus	GINGELL, Henrietta	SEP 12 1854
MYERS, Victoria	BROWN, Isaac	FEB 09 1856
MYERS, Virginia A.	SIMMS, William	MAY 23 1844
MYERS, William H.	LITTLEJOHN, Jane E.	JUL 03 1843
MYRTHY, Macheol	BROWN, Bridget	JAN 13 1853

District of Columbia Marriage Licenses, 1811-1858

N

NACE, Durity	DICE, John	FEB 28 1842
NADDY, Pierce	SMITH, Mrs. Mary Ann	FEB 02 1831
NAGLE, Ann	CHAMBERS, Patrick	JAN 11 1853
NAGLE, John	LACEY, Honora	AUG 29 1851
NAILON, Mary	GARE, Robert	OCT 20 1855
NAILOR, Cecelia J.	HOOVER, John T.	DEC 19 1855
NAILOR, Thompson	MOLDEN, Sarah Ann	MAY 15 1847
NAILOR, Washington	HUGHES, Elizabeth	MAR 29 1838
NAILOR, William	EDELINE, Cecelia Jane	JUN 04 1839
NAIRN, James	WILSON, Mary	MAY 28 1821
NAIRN, John W.	NOURSE, Elizabeth R.	NOV 01 1853
NAIRY, Nancy	SMITH, Grafton	JAN 25 1838
NAISSER, John Philip Machel	KNOTT, Elenor	AUG 07 1828
NALIGAN, Norah	HURLEY, Daniel	SEP 14 1848
NALLAY, Sarah	REEVES, Alfred L.	SEP 16 1848
NALLEY, Christianna A.	MATTHEWS, John T.	MAR 31 1845
NALLEY, Elizabeth	BROWN, Richard	APR 17 1849
NALLEY, Emily	WATERS, Flavius Josephus	MAR 28 1855
NALLEY, Harriet	GREGORY, George	JAN 04 1842
NALLEY, Henry	BELL, Mary Ann	JAN 05 1831
NALLEY, James T.	LEWIS, Elizabeth C.	DEC 29 1846
NALLEY, Jamima	JONES, John	AUG 01 1827
NALLEY, Jane	VanRISWICK, John	APR 04 1815
NALLEY, John	MACKBEE, Sarah Ann	DEC 27 1831
NALLEY, Levi	HINTON, Ann	JAN 17 1839
NALLEY, Martha A.	MIM, George	FEB 28 1831
NALLEY, Matilda	SHARPE, Benjamin	SEP 08 1831
NALLEY, Matilda Ann	THOMPSON, John	JAN 27 1851
NALLEY, William	BROWN, Eleanor	DEC 13 1830
NALLEY, William H.	KNOWLES, Ellen H.	MAY 23 1843
NALLEY, Zachariah	JONES, Ann	DEC 19 1839
NALLS, Rowena A.	DAVIS, George W.	AUG 18 1856
NALLS, Thomas P.	POMERELL, Ann	JUN 18 1833
NALLS, Virginia C.	MILLS, William M.	DEC 13 1855
NALLS, W.B.	ELLIS, Mary J.	JUN 23 1854
NALLY, Ann C.	SCOTT, John	JUN 03 1856
NALLY, Elizabeth Ann	GREEN, John E.	JUL 26 1828
NALLY, Elizabeth B.	PADGETT, Joseph M.	JUL 28 1853
NALLY, Ellen	GRAY, Thomas K.	NOV 03 1830
NALLY, George	WORRELL, Nancy	SEP 21 1837
NALLY, James S.	BROWN, Hester G.	FEB 01 1858
NALLY, Jno.	HURLEY, Lucy	JUN 29 1819
NALLY, John	POWERS, Louisa	DEC 28 1824
NALLY, Lucy	MACKABEE, John	DEC 19 1849
NALLY, Lucy	GODFREY, John	JUL 24 1855
NALLY, Malinda	SHELTON, Joseph	SEP 11 1850
NALLY, Martha Ann	CHEDAL, James D.	APR 27 1836
NALLY, Mary	OWEN, Henry	AUG 05 1822
NALLY, Mary	LIPSCOMB, Conway	JUL 18 1832
NALLY, Mary Jane	KIDWELL, John J.	OCT 09 1848
NALLY, Matilda	SUSKEY, Charles	AUG 10 1854
NALLY, Nancy E.	MANGUM, James H.	SEP 17 1849
NALLY, Sarah	LOVEJOY, William	MAR 18 1829
NALLY, William	SANDERSON, Corralear V.	AUG 23 1853
NALLY, William H.	KERSEY, Virginia A.	MAR 14 1854
NALTE, Ludwig	BECK, Margaret	JAN 14 1846

District of Columbia Marriage Licenses, 1811-1858

NANCE, Mary E.	BRAY, James L.	SEP 11 1850
NAPE, Thomas W.	PIERCE, Mary A.	FEB 11 1851
NAPIER, Richard K.	BENGHN, Betty T.	DEC 23 1854
NARDEN, Harriet	BERNARD, Peter	OCT 02 1819
NARDEN, Harriet	HEFTLEY, Frederick	DEC 01 1823
NARDEN, Josephine	CONNOR, John	OCT 07 1841
NARMILE, John	FLAHERTY, Ann	FEB 17 1855
NASH, Elizabeth	LOOMIS, William	FEB 20 1845
NASH, Henry	CRATTEY, Mary	MAR 27 1849
NASH, Mary (blk)	SPRIGGS, Thos. B.	JAN 07 1836
NASH, Michael	THRETKELD, Catharine	OCT 11 1827
NASH, Michael	CLARKE, Ann M.	JUN 20 1850
NASH, Patrick F.	BARNES, Elizabeth	JUN 17 1830
NASH, Peter	ORFORD, Milly	AUG 09 1844
NASH, Robert	SLOAN, Elizabeth Throop	APR 06 1848
NASH, Robert H., Jr.	SMITH, Josephine	OCT 08 1853
NASH, Robert James	BROOKS, Catharine Ann	MAY 25 1830
NASH, Sarah (blk)	WEST, John	JAN 08 1835
NASH, Sarah A.	ANDREW, William H.	JUL 03 1854
NASH, Thomas	CARTER, Lucinda (blk)	AUG 24 1840
NASH, William	CHISIM, Jane V.	APR 26 1854
NAUGHTEN, Bridget	DELANEY, Michael	SEP 01 1851
NAUGHTON, Leonard	CISSELL, Elizabeth	NOV 30 1831
NAY, John	SPAULDING, Ann Catharine	SEP 14 1837
NAYLOR, Allison	GIVIN, Elizabeth	DEC 03 1831
NAYLOR, Ann Maria	CLARKE, Joshua	NOV 04 1856
NAYLOR, Dickerson	FRANK, Ellen	JUL 04 1833
NAYLOR, Francis Y.	BRIGHTWELL, Ann E.	DEC 04 1837
NAYLOR, George	FOYLES, Sarah	JUN 01 1830
NAYLOR, Henry	BROOKE, Susan E.	JAN 18 1853
NAYLOR, James George	LOVEJOY, Elizabeth Ann	JAN 16 1845
NAYLOR, Joanna L.	MARTIN, George H.	JUN 29 1858
NAYLOR, Lettice Ann	TOLSON, Overton Addison	OCT 10 1842
NAYLOR, Pricey Ann	SAVAGE, John	SEP 27 1826
NAYLOR, Priscilla	SHEETS, John	JUN 14 1827
NAYLOR, Virlinder E.E.	TOLSON, Watkins	JAN 17 1844
NAYLOR, William S.	THORNTON, Mary Randolph	MAR 12 1834
NEAD, Mary	GOSS, John	JUN 04 1825
NEAFE, Mary	HERRALD, Barney	OCT 29 1830
NEAGHER, John F.	FOY, Sarah N.	JUN 04 1857
NEAL, Eliza	SMITH, Laurence	DEC 04 1846
NEAL, Joseph W.	SIMPSON, Mary E.	MAY 03 1836
NEAL, Mary	MARSHALL, John	NOV 16 1849
NEAL, Mary (blk)	SMITH, William	FEB 25 1829
NEAL, Michael	McCARTHY, Catherine	AUG 31 1857
NEAL, Samuel	OLIVER, Jane	SEP 10 1832
NEAL, Sarah (blk)	POWELL, John	JUL 18 1832
NEALE, Adeline (blk)	VENEY, Jesse	DEC 02 1848
NEALE, Christopher	CHAPMAN, Virginia Clay	SEP 08 1847
NEALE, Elizabeth	JACKSON, Philip	SEP 29 1819
NEALE, George	HANSON, Ann	JUN 14 1843
NEALE, George	SCOTT, Emaline	APR 12 1844
NEALE, George	HUNTT, Amelia (blk)	DEC 11 1844
NEALE, Henry	GASKINS, Ann	MAY 04 1829
NEALE, Henry	HARROD, Elizabeth (blk)	JUL 19 1836
NEALE, Henry A.	HAMERSLEY, Mary Ann	OCT 05 1847
NEALE, Horatio	FAGAN, Emaline (blk)	APR 05 1843
NEALE, John	LINKINS, Catharine	DEC 23 1815

District of Columbia Marriage Licenses, 1811-1858

NEALE, Laura S.	MAJAR, John M.	JUL 21 1838
NEALE, Mariah (blk)	WARRING, Henry	APR 03 1837
NEALE, Mary	TALBERT, George	JAN 04 1820
NEALE, Mary H.	HENDLY, John W.	MAR 19 1853
NEALE, Rebecca	SCOTT, William A.	APR 12 1825
NEALE, Richard	TALBERT, Sarah	JUN 15 1813
NEALE, Thomas	DELANEY, Sarah Ann (blk)	MAY 27 1847
NEALE, William Henry	MASON, Mary Ann (blk)	NOV 23 1840
NEARY, Thomas	FENNEGAN, Elizabeth	JUN 28 1839
NEBHUT, John	GUNTHER, Catharine	JUN 25 1842
NEBLUE, Robert	GROSS, Catharine	AUG 12 1813
NEDAH, Parker	DOUGLASS, Jane	MAY 27 1857
NEDDY, Pierce	DRURY, Mary A.	JAN 19 1831
NEENAN, Ellen	SHEHAN, Daniel	MAR 29 1856
NEENAN, Mary	HEANY, Owen	OCT 27 1857
NEENAN, Thomas	CLANCY, Honora	AUG 30 1856
NEENIN, John	CRAVEN, Ann	SEP 22 1854
NEFF, Benedick	GRIMES, Mary	OCT 22 1840
NEFF, Frances	HARLMAN, Conrad	MAY 20 1840
NEFF, Francis	ARNOLD, Margaret	JUL 27 1839
NEFF, Frank	SHAFFER, Catherine	JUL 31 1848
NEFF, Wunderlin	FREESE, Mary	FEB 26 1848
NEIFF, Francis	SMITLEY, Margaret	SEP 10 1839
NEIL, James	DEMPSEY, Fanny	SEP 17 1839
NEILE, Louisa Ann	COOK, John Henry	OCT 12 1843
NEILL, L.L.B.	HALE, W.L.B.	AUG 10 1857
NEILL, Sarah R.	GAYLE, Robert E.	JUN 27 1855
NEILSON, Hall	PAGE, Edmonia L.	JAN 16 1832
NEIMAN, John A.	ASEL, Mary	AUG 14 1849
NEITER, Peter	BIEDINGER, Margaretha	JUL 21 1856
NEITZEY, George	SHEPHERD, Louisa	AUG 03 1847
NEIVET, Eleanor	GIBSON, William	DEC 21 1833
NELAGAN, John	FITZGERALD, Mary	APR 25 1844
NELEGAN, Mary	O'BRIEN, Patrick	JAN 25 1854
NELIGAN, Bridgett	KENNEDY, James	JAN 01 1852
NELLEGAN, Ellen	CALBERT, John	FEB 22 1851
NELLIGAN, Bridget	TANGNEY, Patrick	OCT 01 1853
NELLON, Harriet	SAUNDERS, Richard	AUG 22 1836
NELSON, Ann	HARRISON, John B.	OCT 13 1849
NELSON, Ann Eliza	LAVELLE, Miles	JAN 22 1835
NELSON, Ann V.	OGLE, Benjamin R.	JUN 09 1849
NELSON, Catherine Murdoch	LAWRANCE, Otho	NOV 30 1815
NELSON, Charles A.	WITHERS, Virginia	DEC 17 1851
NELSON, Charles E.	WITHERS, Virginia	FEB 28 1852
NELSON, Charles Edward	BRYAN, Rebecca Jane	DEC 24 1852
NELSON, Chloe	GORDON, James	APR 06 1833
NELSON, Cleland K.	MARBURY, Mary Ann	JUL 10 1840
NELSON, Cleland K.	HAGNER, Mary M.	APR 19 1854
NELSON, Edward	DOVE, Harriet	JUN 01 1837
NELSON, Eliab C.	STOCKMON, Mary M.	AUG 06 1845
NELSON, Eliza	KNOT, James	JUN 18 1822
NELSON, Elizabeth	TILLETT, William	JUN 21 1833
NELSON, Frances	PETTIT, George	JAN 13 1852
NELSON, Hendley	PRIMSLEY, Caroline	APR 04 1835
NELSON, Hendley	MORLAND, Elizabeth	JAN 30 1855
NELSON, Jane	MARRETT, John	SEP 20 1819
NELSON, Jane	KECK, James	SEP 04 1834
NELSON, John	BURROWS, Francis Harriett, Miss	NOV 18 1816

District of Columbia Marriage Licenses, 1811-1858

NELSON, John L.	WORTHINGTON, Eliza	APR 11 1849
NELSON, John S.	BELT, Martha A.C.	AUG 02 1852
NELSON, Levi	BOOTH, Jane	JAN 29 1825
NELSON, Martha	BRIDEWELL, Moses Thomas	JUL 22 1843
NELSON, Mary	TWINEY, Daniel W.	JUN 01 1837
NELSON, Mary Ann	REID, Horatio	APR 28 1829
NELSON, Samuel	HOWE, Elizabeth	JAN 15 1825
NELSON, William	PAYNE, Ann	DEC 14 1829
NELSON, William L.	DUNCAN, Ann R.	JUN 20 1854
NERY, Thomas	O'NEALE, Maria	APR 05 1842
NESBET, Elizabeth	SANDSBURY, John B.	JAN 06 1827
NESBIT, Wilson	DUVAL, Susa T.	JUL 06 1819
NESBITT, Jonathan	SANFORD, Mary E.	AUG 02 1842
NESENSOHN, Jos.	BIAR, Margaretta	AUG 31 1855
NESMITH, Charlotte D.	MARTIN, William	MAR 11 1826
NESMITH, Isabella	EVANS, John D.	NOV 05 1846
NESMITH, John	CROWN, Jane	APR 15 1828
NESMITH, Sarah	HARBIN, Philip W.	NOV 14 1850
NESTER, Patrick	LICET, Margaret	APR 28 1855
NETH, M. Elizabeth	BROWN, William	NOV 16 1844
NETTER, Sampson	THOMPSON, Milly Ann (blk)	OCT 18 1836
NEUMYER, Leopold	ECCLESTON, Margaret	MAR 18 1851
NEVERSON, Joseph	TAYLOR, Susan (blk)	NOV 14 1857
NEVINES, Patrick	WHELON, Margaret	JUL 10 1820
NEVINS, Archibald A.	ALEXANDER, Margt. M.	APR 04 1850
NEVINS, Burnett L.	REEVE, Lucy E.	JUN 05 1858
NEVINS, Mary F.	NEWTON, Aloysius	APR 07 1853
NEVINS, William [Rev.]	KEY, Mary L.	NOV 13 1822
NEVIT, Harriet	CLARKE, Thomas	JAN 04 1821
NEVITT, Amelia	WILSON, Henry	JUL 15 1834
NEVITT, Ann	SUIT, Stephen	JAN 25 1830
NEVITT, Annie	SHERWOOD, Edward	OCT 22 1855
NEVITT, Catzaliner	MILLER, Henry	JAN 09 1821
NEVITT, Eleanor	HOWARD, Albert	APR 07 1828
NEVITT, Elizabeth	SOTORON, Zachariah	APR 30 1825
NEVITT, Ellen	BLAKE, John A.	MAY 20 1834
NEVITT, Emma D.N.	SOUTHWORTH, F. Hamilton	JAN 23 1840
NEVITT, Henrietta	COLLINS, James H.	OCT 19 1839
NEVITT, Joseph	WHITE, Ann	JUN 17 1815
NEVITT, Lucy	FOLEY, John	AUG 12 1815
NEVITT, Mary	BURRIS, John	JUN 25 1812
NEVITT, Mary	LYDICK, Francis	NOV 12 1816
NEVITT, Mary Ann	HANY, John	FEB 12 1833
NEVITT, Robert K.	MOORE, Lettice C.	DEC 20 1836
NEVITT, Sarah	MACKEY, William	JUL 08 1824
NEVITT, Susanna G.	HENSHAW, Joshua L.	NOV 14 1826
NEVITT, Thomas F.	SHELTON, Ellen F.	MAY 23 1836
NEWBAULD, John	RUTHERFORD, Barbara	MAY 21 1858
NEWCOME, Henry C.	CHAPPELL, Miranda	OCT 19 1854
NEWELL, Alexander	KENDRICK, Sarah A.	MAY 07 1846
NEWELL, Harman	DUVALL, Ann M.	NOV 08 1855
NEWELL, Jane	WAGONER, Armstrong	MAR 21 1834
NEWELL, John	BROWN, Catharine J.	MAY 20 1853
NEWELL, Jonas	RUSSELL, Elizabeth	MAY 04 1830
NEWELL, Justa Mary	ANTHONY, Michael	DEC 07 1818
NEWELL, Rebecca F.	NEWELL, Thos. M.	AUG 03 1820
NEWELL, Susan Ann	MANSFIELD, J.S.	FEB 25 1843
NEWELL, Thomas	MALLORY, Delia	FEB 13 1818

District of Columbia Marriage Licenses, 1811-1858

NEWELL, Thomas M.	ADAMS, Hester R.	MAY 27 1830
NEWELL, Thos. M.	NEWELL, Rebecca F.	AUG 03 1820
NEWGENT, Bessie	CARROLL, James	MAY 02 1854
NEWHOUSE, Harvey M.	DAWSON, Sally	DEC 01 1851
NEWLAND, Artimes	ORME, Mary	NOV 15 1831
NEWLAND, Ottemus	ROBEY, Emily	DEC 31 1855
NEWMAN, Ann	DOWLING, James	DEC 16 1844
NEWMAN, Deborah	BURCH, Thomas	FEB 19 1828
NEWMAN, Eugenia E.	NEWMAN, Theron W., Jr.	AUG 05 1850
NEWMAN, Franklin	WATKINSON, Harriet	FEB 23 1838
NEWMAN, George	TUCKSON, Rachel (blk)	FEB 24 1853
NEWMAN, Horace N.	HEREFORD, Willie Ann	JAN 07 1835
NEWMAN, James	HOSKINS, Susanna P.	JAN 17 1818
NEWMAN, James R.	OWENS, Charlotte	OCT 27 1857
NEWMAN, John	PRITCHARD, Elizabeth	MAY 18 1824
NEWMAN, John	KENNADY, Mary	AUG 28 1851
NEWMAN, John	CONNOR, Johanna	JAN 18 1858
NEWMAN, John H.	PAYNE, Harrit A.	NOV 09 1835
NEWMAN, John H.	KETCHEN, Lucinda A.	OCT 18 1847
NEWMAN, Lewis	GILL, Prisciller	SEP 12 1826
NEWMAN, Mahala (blk)	CRAWFORD, John	DEC 24 1850
NEWMAN, Maria	BRADLEY, John	FEB 23 1850
NEWMAN, Matilda	TYSER, Lewis	JUN 13 1835
NEWMAN, Peter J.	MARKS, Jane	AUG 18 1849
NEWMAN, Richard M.	PARKER, Mary Brown	OCT 05 1831
NEWMAN, Saml.	LYNCH, Mary Ann	DEC 24 1845
NEWMAN, Susan Ann	BOGARDUS, Peter E.	AUG 12 1850
NEWMAN, Theron W., Jr.	NEWMAN, Eugenia E.	AUG 05 1850
NEWMAN, Thomas	BLAKEY, Mary	NOV 19 1845
NEWMAN, Thomas A.	VanRISWICK, Louisa J.	FEB 20 1844
NEWMAN, W.L.	MAHONEY, Mary E.	MAR 25 1856
NEWMEYER, Catharine	FREEMAN, Henrick G.	SEP 06 1852
NEWNAM, William	CRANSTON, Ophelia	APR 02 1829
NEWRATH, Jacob	LANG, Eliza	NOV 21 1826
NEWTON, Aloysius	NEVINS, Mary F.	APR 07 1853
NEWTON, Ann	FENWICK, John	MAY 14 1814
NEWTON, Ann Milched	CROW, John	JAN 05 1814
NEWTON, Athamiss	LUFFELIN, Mary	APR 19 1816
NEWTON, Benjamin	LOWE, Henrietta (blk)	NOV 14 1833
NEWTON, Charles A.	CROW, Sarah	SEP 12 1844
NEWTON, Clement	BURGESS, Mary Ann	AUG 23 1815
NEWTON, Francis B.	CARR, John W.	JAN 09 1854
NEWTON, Harriet	DRUDGE, James	DEC 24 1815
NEWTON, Henry T.	HUTCHINS, Susan	MAR 25 1836
NEWTON, Ignatius A.	RATCLIFF, Elizabeth	APR 06 1820
NEWTON, Isaac	PEASTER, Susan	SEP 06 1843
NEWTON, James	SMITH, Ann E.	FEB 26 1821
NEWTON, John	WALKER, Harriet	MAY 21 1825
NEWTON, John	WILLS, Ann (blk)	JUN 16 1825
NEWTON, John	REDIN, Sarah (blk)	OCT 30 1845
NEWTON, John B.	VanRISWICK, Henrietta	DEC 21 1848
NEWTON, Julia Ann	MURRAY, James	DEC 26 1826
NEWTON, Lewis	HEADEN, Elizabeth	FEB 09 1833
NEWTON, Margaret C.	WALLACH, William Douglass	SEP 08 1840
NEWTON, Margaret Ellen	HICKS, James	NOV 26 1833
NEWTON, Maria L.	RICHEY, Hiram	JUN 01 1858
NEWTON, Mary	HOLTZMAN, John	JUN 20 1816
NEWTON, Mary Ann	LARKIN, Lionel James	FEB 13 1817

District of Columbia Marriage Licenses, 1811-1858

NEWTON, Mary E.	HODGKINS, George W.	MAR 31 1849
NEWTON, Matilda	O'NEAL, Theodore	FEB 27 1829
NEWTON, May	MORGAN, Hendley	MAY 06 1847
NEWTON, Peggy	SMITH, George	JUL 06 1812
NEWTON, Sarah Ann	MEGEE, William	APR 14 1813
NEWTON, Sarah Ann	FLETCHER, William A.	FEB 07 1852
NEWTON, Susanna	COLBURN, James	SEP 22 1825
NEWTON, Virginia	BAKER, Charles T.M.	JUL 14 1851
NEWTON, William C.	DORSETT, Sarah	FEB 22 1816
NEWTON, William G.	LITTLE, Mary E.	DEC 01 1852
NEWTON, William H.	JOHNSON, Sarah O.	FEB 28 1856
NEWTON, William Thomas	JACKSON, Eliza	FEB 07 1846
NEWTON, Wm. C.	SWART, Maria Louisa	NOV 23 1834
NIAGLIER, Charles J.	GEIGER, Caroline	FEB 20 1858
NICHOLAS, Jefferson	RILEY, Sarah Ann	MAY 10 1826
NICHOLLS, Benoni S.	PUMPHREY, Eliza E.	FEB 24 1857
NICHOLLS, Bestie C.	HANEWINKEL, Frederick W.	JUN 18 1855
NICHOLLS, Drucilla	CONNELLY, Michael	MAR 30 1826
NICHOLLS, Emily	DeVOSS, Peter J.	NOV 19 1845
NICHOLLS, Isaac S.	RIND, Joanna	DEC 31 1827
NICHOLLS, John	WALKER, Martha E.	DEC 09 1845
NICHOLLS, John Mason	JOHNSON, Sylva (blk)	NOV 25 1841
NICHOLLS, Lloyd	MORRIS, Matilda (blk)	JUN 13 1826
NICHOLLS, Margaret	DOUGHTY, James W.	FEB 13 1840
NICHOLLS, Martha Smith	BOLLING, George Washington	NOV 19 1827
NICHOLLS, Mary Ami	SWINK, William	JAN 14 1829
NICHOLLS, Mary E.	REINTZEL, Henry [Dr.]	AUG 16 1832
NICHOLLS, Nicholas Y.	OSTIN, Martha Ann	MAY 09 1840
NICHOLLS, Thomas L.	WATHAN, Jane E.	JAN 23 1844
NICHOLLS, William	JACKSON, Adelaide F.	MAR 18 1840
NICHOLS, Charles H.	MAURY, Ellen G.	NOV 23 1857
NICHOLS, George M.	CHIZEM, Catharine	FEB 07 1853
NICHOLS, Isaac	RIND, Sarah	APR 13 1818
NICHOLS, Jacob	EISENRING, Mary	JUN 03 1850
NICHOLS, Mary Ann	MASON, Joseph T.	NOV 16 1847
NICHOLS, Seth H.	MEEMS, Mary Margaret	APR 05 1842
NICHOLS, William	HELRICK, Mary	AUG 13 1850
NICHOLS, William A.	LUCAS, Ann	APR 15 1824
NICHOLSEN, Rachel	VANELLET, Perry	JUL 01 1833
NICHOLSIN, Henry	McMANNUS, Rebecca	DEC 25 1834
NICHOLSON, Ann	TAVENNER, Jonah	DEC 21 1826
NICHOLSON, Annie D.	SUTHERLAND, Daniel J.	JUL 25 1850
NICHOLSON, Augustus A.	CARROLL, Sally	FEB 01 1847
NICHOLSON, Augustus S.	JESSUP, Jane Finley	FEB 02 1852
NICHOLSON, Bridget	BLAKE, John	DEC 08 1857
NICHOLSON, Eliza	DEAN, Lewis [Sergt.]	DEC 14 1827
NICHOLSON, George	CHAMBERLEN, Barbara	JAN 01 1825
NICHOLSON, George	MURRY, Rebecca	OCT 30 1848
NICHOLSON, George Ann	KING, Enoch	MAR 29 1845
NICHOLSON, Hellen L.	ROBERTS, Edmund	DEC 13 1854
NICHOLSON, Henry	ADAMS, Mary	AUG 16 1839
NICHOLSON, Henry	WALKER, Elizabeth	SEP 02 1845
NICHOLSON, John	BROOKS, Priscilla	DEC 20 1837
NICHOLSON, Jno. P.	THOMAS, Mary A.	AUG 16 1825
NICHOLSON, Jno. T.S.	HARVEY, Mary E.	APR 04 1855
NICHOLSON, Joseph	WILSON, Martha Jane	JUN 09 1841
NICHOLSON, Joseph H.	HAGNER, Eliza Ann	APR 09 1827
NICHOLSON, Lewis F.	JEFFERS, Maria	FEB 09 1831

District of Columbia Marriage Licenses, 1811-1858

NICHOLSON, Louisa	JACOBS, George R.	DEC 03 1849
NICHOLSON, Mary A.	BALLINGER, George W.	DEC 12 1839
NICHOLSON, Mary Ann	HARVEY, William	APR 17 1848
NICHOLSON, Mary E.	RICKETTS, Robert H.	JUN 11 1853
NICHOLSON, Peter	BOMAN, Susan	AUG 06 1819
NICHOLSON, Peter	HAWKINS, Ann	OCT 21 1840
NICHOLSON, Sommerville	JONES, Hannah Mariah	SEP 01 1851
NICHOLSON, Susannah	WALKER, David H.	NOV 01 1847
NICHOLSON, Thomas	HERITY, Sarah	APR 25 1822
NICHOLSON, Walter	DENNISON, Margaret	DEC 04 1834
NICHOLSON, William	HOWE, Jemima	JAN 07 1834
NICHOLSON, William	KIRBY, Elizabeth	JUL 11 1854
NICKELF, Mary	RIBNITZKY, John H.	DEC 30 1857
NICKEN, John	WIGFIELD, Ann	JUL 08 1850
NICKLIN, Ann D.	PAYNE, James	SEP 21 1850
NICOLAI, Margaret	MARTIN, James	FEB 24 1853
NICOLL, Harriet V.	LADD, Joseph	NOV 01 1824
NICOLL, William H.	CONWAY, Harriet	MAY 07 1818
NIECEY, Catharine	COLEMAN, Patrick	NOV 29 1855
NIEHAUS, Fredericka	RICK, John	SEP 07 1857
NIEL, Elizabeth (blk)	HATAWAY, John	JUL 05 1855
NIEL, Mary	MAHONEY, John	JUL 13 1855
NIETZEY, George	MILLER, Mary	DEC 30 1843
NIGHT, Jane	HACKNEY, Geo.	JUN 27 1822
NIGHT, Lucretia Ann	RODDERICK, Theodore	JUN 16 1829
NIGHTINGALE, Joseph	TODDISON, Emily	AUG 17 1839
NIHILL, Michael	HANNAN, Ann	JUL 26 1853
NILAND, Mary	McDONALD, Michael	OCT 03 1857
NILES, Jeanie Ogden	WORDEN, Ananias	JUN 09 1855
NILES, Saml. V.	GORDON, Mary	NOV 11 1851
NIXDORFF, Tobias	SCHULTZE, Julianna	OCT 28 1818
NIXON, J. Howard	JEWELL, Flora H.	APR 21 1858
NIXON, John W.	MADDOX, Kate	AUG 19 1856
NIXON, Richard	MANKIN, Jane	NOV 23 1837
NIXON, Robert F.	FISHER, Sarah Ann	FEB 27 1838
NIXTAIR, Love	CALLAN, Ann	DEC 03 1841
NOAKES, Secelia (blk)	HENRY, Robert	DEC 30 1824
NOAR, Catharine	STUTZ, Frederick	AUG 18 1845
NOBLE, Amanda Gwynn	HARRISON, James F.	SEP 28 1848
NOBLE, Ellen C.	JONES, Robert	AUG 12 1854
NOBLE, George P.	SIMMS, Mary Ellen	JUN 04 1851
NOBLE, Martha	HUTCHINS, John	APR 14 1856
NOBLE, Mary	KOONS, Sylvester	APR 07 1855
NOBLE, Mason [Rev.]	PLEASANTS, Ann Catharine	AUG 31 1836
NOBLE, Sarah	PRENDER, John	JUL 03 1850
NOBLETON, Susan	MATTINGLY, John	SEP 26 1818
NOCHTIN, Maria	DONNOGHUE, Martin	OCT 24 1856
NOCTON, John	DONOHOE, Margaret	NOV 17 1814
NODDY, John M.C.	McADAM, Ann	AUG 12 1847
NODDY, Mary Ann	FAGAN, Nicholas	AUG 15 1837
NOEL, William F.	EDDINS, Mary F.	MAY 11 1854
NOELL, William	WILKINSON, Sarah	JUL 08 1839
NOERR, Mary M.	TREDWAY, John	OCT 30 1855
NOETHLING, Eliza	DEITZ, Joseph	NOV 23 1854
NOHS, William	HUTCHINSON, Jane	DEC 06 1851
NOKES, Edward	BUMERY, Mary (blk)	MAR 02 1858
NOKES, Francis	BURGESS, Rachel	JUL 18 1827
NOKES, George W.	CASTEL, Margaret E.	APR 11 1857

District of Columbia Marriage Licenses, 1811-1858

NOKES, Margaret	SMITH, James R.	NOV 21 1853
NOKES, Mary	CLEMENTS, Robert S.	APR 27 1820
NOKES, William	CROSS, Emma I.	SEP 14 1853
NOLALIE, Anna Maria	THIELECKE, Charles W.	NOV 20 1852
NOLAN, Francis	MATTINGLY, Sarah	FEB 14 1846
NOLAN, Martin	SWEENY, Catherine	DEC 02 1854
NOLAN, Thomas	CARNEY, Mary	JUN 10 1852
NOLAN, Thos. S.	MYERS, Sarah C.	DEC 14 1825
NOLAND, Alice	McCARTY, Timothy	NOV 13 1852
NOLAND, Edward	BURTON, Eleanor	SEP 13 1827
NOLAND, Elizabeth	NORRIS, James	MAY 14 1842
NOLAND, John	BARRY, Bridget	MAY 06 1851
NOLAND, John T.	KING, Sarah A.	OCT 14 1844
NOLAND, Margaret	CAUGHLIN, Dennis	JUL 28 1853
NOLAND, Mary	McCARTHY, John	FEB 07 1857
NOLAND, Patrick	WERDERMAN, Ann	APR 26 1856
NOLAND, Samuel S.	FRANK, Elizabeth A.	JUN 10 1850
NOLAND, Theofilus	LYONS, Emily Virginia	MAR 19 1849
NOLAND, William H.	PARK, Elmira H.	JAN 02 1834
NOLAND, Winney E.	BOWERS, Samuel	APR 12 1855
NOLEAN, Jeremiah	DONAHO, Honora	JUN 08 1855
NOLEN, Jeremiah	GORDON, Martha	APR 10 1851
NOLEN, Mary	KENDRIC, Richard A.	JAN 07 1854
NOLER, William	COX, Sarah Ann	JUL 17 1834
NOLL, John Henry	KASZLER, Louisa	MAY 09 1849
NOLLAND, Sarah	BELFILS, Eugene	NOV 03 1848
NOLOON, Jane M.	GRAVES, William H.	OCT 14 1851
NOLTE, Anna	DEMPF, Anoine	MAY 15 1858
NOLTE, Tynar	VOEGLER, Elenore	AUG 25 1857
NOMANN, Caspar	FISCHER, Margaret	JAN 15 1850
NOND, Bridget	RAINEY, Charles	MAR 20 1856
NOON, Bridget	ERNER, Daniel	FEB 11 1851
NOON, Mary	SWEENY, John	JAN 21 1854
NOON, Matilda D.	PENN, William	MAR 13 1821
NOONAN, James	SHEUGHRY, Mary	OCT 14 1851
NOONE, James	EARNER, Bridget	SEP 16 1851
NOPER, Frances	LIVINGSTON, Henry D.	DEC 15 1851
NORBECK, George	RABERSOHN, Elizabeth	APR 03 1834
NORBECK, Maria	GEBHARDI, Frederick	APR 03 1834
NORBECK, William	HOWARD, Elizabeth	JAN 05 1841
NORDMANN, Wilhelm	VOLGER, Theresse	OCT 15 1853
NORFEET, Mary E.	KNAPP, Auren	AUG 21 1854
NORFLET, Thomas	WILLIAMS, Susannah	NOV 14 1848
NORFOLK, Eliza	SEARS, Douglass	APR 02 1846
NORFOLK, Elizabeth	COCKE, James H.	SEP 13 1825
NORICE, Washington J.	RALY, Sarah Jane	APR 26 1847
NORMAN, Drucilla (blk)	CROGER, Francis	NOV 22 1841
NORMAN, Elizabeth P.	SHORTER, Joseph E.	MAR 11 1856
NORMAN, M.C.	WILLIS, William L.	AUG 24 1848
NORMENT, Richard	SAMUEL, Frances Ann	OCT 02 1851
NORMENT, Richard B.	WARD, Margaret A.	OCT 05 1853
NORMENT, Samuel	WARD, Mary Ellen	JUN 25 1846
NORMYLE, Catharine	FITZGERALD, John	JUN 12 1856
NORNEY, Mary	ROACH, Morris	DEC 22 1853
NORR, Magdalene	WANDERBY, John	JUL 28 1842
NORRIS, Amanda A.	DODD, Thomas A.	FEB 13 1851
NORRIS, Ann	MURRAY, Edward J.	SEP 17 1815
NORRIS, Ann	DEAVER, Joshua	APR 11 1825

District of Columbia Marriage Licenses, 1811-1858

NORRIS, Ann B.	YATES, Zachariah	NOV 20 1833
NORRIS, Caroline	PRICE, Hezekiah	OCT 27 1828
NORRIS, Charles A.	EVINS, Ann R.	SEP 18 1852
NORRIS, Charloot (blk)	NUGENT, Eli	AUG 21 1832
NORRIS, Daniel	BEACH, Susan	JUN 17 1826
NORRIS, Edward	NORRIS, Mary	AUG 26 1854
NORRIS, Elizabeth	BOSTON, Alexander	OCT 21 1837
NORRIS, Elizabeth	WILLS, Joseph	FEB 29 1848
NORRIS, Enoch M.	WILLIAMS, Sarah	DEC 13 1854
NORRIS, Frances Marion	JOYCE, Andrew	OCT 07 1843
NORRIS, Henry	DIGGS, Ann M. (blk)	MAY 14 1834
NORRIS, Henry	KINGSBURY, Mary A.	APR 22 1854
NORRIS, James	NOLAND, Elizabeth	MAY 14 1842
NORRIS, Jane	HURDLE, George N.	JAN 15 1829
NORRIS, Jane Eliza	SOMMERVILLE, James	JAN 14 1858
NORRIS, Jas.	WILLIAMS, Elizabeth	DEC 31 1814
NORRIS, Louisa	DAVIS, James	JAN 15 1829
NORRIS, Margaret	INDERMANER, Jeremiah	JUL 24 1856
NORRIS, Margaret A.	GRIFFIN, Robert A.	NOV 30 1850
NORRIS, Margaret H.	BEATLEY, Joseph L.	FEB 03 1855
NORRIS, Martha	TURVEY, Rezin	DEC 09 1833
NORRIS, Mary	HEARD, Enoch	JAN 07 1813
NORRIS, Mary	NORRIS, Edward	AUG 26 1854
NORRIS, Mary Ann	GILL, Presley R.	APR 14 1828
NORRIS, Mary Ellen	TAYLOR, Stark B.	MAY 15 1851
NORRIS, Sarah	RAGAN, Daniel	FEB 18 1813
NORRIS, Sarah	CARTER, Richard W.	APR 21 1836
NORRIS, Sophiah (blk)	JACKSON, Robert	DEC 10 1827
NORRIS, Virginia	PARKE, William P.	NOV 06 1848
NORRIS, William	DRURY, Louisa [Mrs.]	OCT 07 1824
NORRIS, William	LEONARD, Maria	APR 20 1833
NORRIS, William	PARKER, Priscilla (blk)	NOV 27 1854
NORRISS, Margaret	BOARMAN, Joseph B.	DEC 09 1823
NORTH, Henry	TOWNSEND, Mary Ann (blk)	NOV 08 1825
NORTH, J. Bartram	LIPPENCOTT, Adeline W.	DEC 07 1854
NORTH, Mary B.	STUMP, William	SEP 01 1857
NORTON, A.S.	BROWN, Mary F.	AUG 30 1843
NORTON, Alexander	OSBORN, Eliza	JUL 18 1839
NORTON, Ann	GLADMAN, James	JUL 29 1835
NORTON, Ann M.	BEALL, Robert A.	FEB 19 1827
NORTON, Anna	MYERS, Charles	JAN 31 1833
NORTON, Catharine	BEAN, John	OCT 01 1840
NORTON, Catherine	JONES, William	DEC 04 1834
NORTON, Eliza E.	BAILEY, George K.	DEC 19 1837
NORTON, Elizabeth	SELVEY, John M.	OCT 12 1844
NORTON, James William	HARPER, Lucretia	FEB 07 1851
NORTON, Mary A.	HARPER, William	JAN 17 1853
NORTON, Michl.	FOSTER, Rose	AUG 04 1854
NORTON, Robert	MULLICAN, Sarah	MAR 04 1824
NORTON, Robert	COLLINS, Henrietta	MAY 01 1832
NORTON, Robert H.	GLADMEN, Emeline A.	SEP 11 1855
NORTON, Thomas	JOHNSON, Winey Ann	AUG 24 1853
NORTON, William	RALY, Catharine	JAN 20 1821
NORUTEN, Ellen	DONOVAN, William	APR 22 1844
NORVILL, William H.	BALLARD, Margaret R.	SEP 17 1846
NORWOOD, Eliza	WILLIAMS, William	OCT 19 1847
NORWOOD, Joseph S.	LEACH, Virginia	OCT 26 1850
NORWOOD, Mary Ann	WARD, Mitchell M.	NOV 26 1843

District of Columbia Marriage Licenses, 1811-1858

NORWOOD, Mary Ann	WARD, Mitchell M.	NOV 26 1845
NORWOOD, Rebecca	HUGHES, Elisha	FEB 23 1841
NORWOOD, Samueletta	COONEY, James	JUN 13 1853
NORWOOD, Sarah	ELLIS, John	OCT 12 1820
NOSE, Martha	AUSTIN, David	JUN 29 1816
NOT, Mary	JONES, Joseph	MAY 19 1830
NOTT, George F.	KETNER, Agnes	MAY 15 1858
NOTT, Josephine B.	CHRISTINE, Henry A.	NOV 04 1854
NOTT, William Edwin	SCOTT, Sarah	OCT 09 1852
NOTTINGHAM, Margaret	MURPHEY, Thomas H.	MAY 09 1846
NOTTINGHAM, Mary O.	TEACHEM, Robert	FEB 24 1835
NOTTINGHAM, William	SMITH, Elizabeth	DEC 07 1844
NOURSE, Anna J.	HASSLER, Charles A.	OCT 04 1837
NOURSE, Benjamin Franklin [Dr.]	STANSBURY, Josephine	JAN 03 1832
NOURSE, Caroline	DULANEY, Bladen	JAN 31 1843
NOURSE, Elizabeth R.	NAIRN, John W.	NOV 01 1853
NOURSE, Elizth. J.	SIMMS, Charles C.	NOV 13 1852
NOURSE, Emma J.	STRIBLING, Cornelius	DEC 07 1852
NOURSE, J. Harvey	RITTENHOUSE, Isobel L.	MAR 14 1853
NOURSE, John	DICKINSON, Araminta Eliza	MAR 24 1835
NOURSE, John R.	SKINNER, Elizabeth	JUN 12 1826
NOURSE, John R.	SKINNER, Lucretia C.	NOV 17 1830
NOURSE, Joseph	WRIGHT, Sarah	DEC 21 1841
NOURSE, Louisa P.	FORREST, Charles W.	OCT 05 1847
NOURSE, Mary Francis	SMITH, Rev. Mathew	SEP 25 1855
NOURSE, Sarah H.	STETTINIUS, George	JUN 11 1833
NOURSE, Susan S.	WINANS, Rev. Jacob W.	JUL 27 1853
NOWLAN, Elizabeth	BURCH, Balum	OCT 15 1822
NOWLAN, Mary	DRURY, Samuel	JUL 05 1815
NOWLAN, Thomas	MARCY, Louisa	DEC 17 1818
NOWLAND, Caroline	JUDGE, John	MAR 01 1824
NOWLAND, Margaret	JONES, Levi	MAY 20 1857
NOWLAND, Mary Ann Eliza	McGLUE, Owen	NOV 23 1819
NOWLAND, Mary Louisa	DEAN, Felix	MAR 03 1846
NOWLAND, Wm. P.	MORRIS, Mary	AUG 08 1814
NOYES, Albert	CROSS, Julia Ann	JUN 03 1852
NOYES, Emeline	PORTIAUX, Benjamin Eugene	NOV 17 1852
NOYES, George S.	CLARKE, Ellen E.	JUN 18 1833
NOYES, Henry O.	COLLISON, Emiloy L.	JAN 05 1857
NOYES, Isabella	HARRON, Columbus	MAY 03 1856
NOYES, Jacob	MELVIN, Jannet	APR 07 1823
NOYES, Joseph C.	ALLING, Hellen Maria	JUL 09 1838
NOYES, Maria V.	DeFORD, Charles De.	JUL 08 1844
NOYES, Mary E.	MACKALL, H. Clinton	MAY 01 1841
NOYES, Samuel V.	EBERBACH, Elizabeth Emilie	OCT 27 1857
NOYES, Thomas L.	BUGBEE, Jane L.	MAY 14 1834
NUCKOLS, George B.	BOXLEY, Jane E.	JUN 11 1835
NUGENT, Benjn. H.	TALBERT, Mary E. (blk)	JUN 08 1857
NUGENT, Eli	NORRIS, Charloot (blk)	AUG 21 1832
NUGENT, Eli	MASON, Matilda (blk)	JAN 26 1841
NUGENT, Esta Ann	STOTT, Charles	OCT 31 1854
NUGENT, James	MADDOX, Eliza	NOV 30 1847
NUGENT, James	McCANNE, Jane	SEP 16 1850
NUGENT, Johanna	ALLEN, Timothy	JUN 30 1855
NUGENT, John	BERGUMOT, Jane	NOV 09 1840
NUGENT, John	McMAHON, Mary	OCT 05 1852
NUGENT, Julia	WELSH, Edward	SEP 30 1857
NUGENT, Martha	WAILES, Isaac H.	MAR 10 1851

District of Columbia Marriage Licenses, 1811-1858

NUGENT, Sophia J. (blk)	HOOD, James W.	APR 22 1858
NUGENT, William	O'BRIEN, Margaret	MAR 10 1855
NUJAN, Shedrach	ASHTON, Rebecca (blk)	MAY 13 1829
NULTER, Samson	THOMPSON, Ann	MAR 06 1857
NURSE, Michael	GIBSON, Sarah C.	NOV 26 1835
NUSTIC, Mary Ann	GRANT, Spencer	APR 11 1831
NUTTER, Levin	SEDGICKS, Ellen	MAR 27 1856
NUTWELL, Levi	WATSON, Eliz.	APR 23 1814
NYE, Norman Williard	JOHNSON, Mary A.	DEC 02 1847
NYLES, Christopher T.	HEPBURN, Margaret N.	JUN 28 1849

District of Columbia Marriage Licenses, 1811-1858

O

O'BANNON, Dogobert B.	WILSON, Sarah Ann	MAR 21 1853
O'BELL, Edward	PRATLER, Termelia	DEC 01 1857
O'BRIAN, Daniel	FITZGERALD, Johanna	SEP 19 1844
O'BRIAN, Eleanor	HARTIGAN, Michael	JUL 06 1833
O'BRIAN, Elizabeth	MOHORNEY, George	AUG 06 1850
O'BRIAN, James B.	BLACKWELL, Ann	AUG 31 1835
O'BRIAN, Josephus	JEFFERS, Hannah	JAN 04 1814
O'BRIAN, Josephus	CARRICO, Dorothy	JUN 06 1822
O'BRIAN, Patrick	O'CONNEL, Hannah	FEB 20 1855
O'BRIAN, Sarah	SHANKS, John	OCT 06 1855
O'BRIEN, Ann Maria	FULTON, Robert	NOV 26 1817
O'BRIEN, Bridget	GALT, Richard	AUG 05 1858
O'BRIEN, Catharine	ROGAN, Hugh	JUL 03 1837
O'BRIEN, Catherine	AIGEN, John	JUN 17 1854
O'BRIEN, Eliza	BRIEN, Bernard	MAR 13 1821
O'BRIEN, Eliza	HOLLINGSWORTH, Henry	APR 29 1837
O'BRIEN, Ellen	MAHONY, Cornelius	JUL 14 1857
O'BRIEN, Ellen	HUGHES, Arthur	JUN 10 1858
O'BRIEN, Ellen Maria	BOWMAN, Raphael H.	SEP 15 1857
O'BRIEN, Emily	McQUAY, Benjamin	NOV 07 1844
O'BRIEN, Hanora	CONNELL, John	MAY 22 1856
O'BRIEN, Honora A.	RUNDLETT, George W.	APR 03 1858
O'BRIEN, Jane	CARRICOE, John	NOV 16 1815
O'BRIEN, John	MOQUEST, Sophia	AUG 09 1848
O'BRIEN, John	MARKEHIN, Ellen	JUN 14 1853
O'BRIEN, John	CODEY, Bridget	AUG 11 1858
O'BRIEN, Jos. H.	AMSTEAD, Sarah J.	MAR 06 1850
O'BRIEN, Julia	ALMIN, Daniel	NOV 06 1855
O'BRIEN, Lawrence	KEHO, Mary	NOV 04 1853
O'BRIEN, Margaret	McNERHANY, Francis	JUL 03 1848
O'BRIEN, Margaret	NUGENT, William	MAR 10 1855
O'BRIEN, Margaret	GRANT, Walter	MAY 01 1857
O'BRIEN, Margaret	CONNOR, Patrick	JUL 31 1858
O'BRIEN, Mary	WHITE, John	JUL 23 1830
O'BRIEN, Mary	KENNEDY, Michael	FEB 04 1833
O'BRIEN, Mary	KELLY, John	APR 24 1851
O'BRIEN, Mary	LANE, James	FEB 26 1853
O'BRIEN, Mary	COCHRAN, John	APR 20 1853
O'BRIEN, Mary Ann	CURTIS, John	AUG 12 1856
O'BRIEN, Mary Ann	CHAPMAN, John	AUG 12 1858
O'BRIEN, Michael	CARLISS, Margaret	MAR 09 1850
O'BRIEN, Michael	LYON, Margaret	NOV 07 1851
O'BRIEN, Michael	NULVIHILL, Catherine	JUN 28 1853
O'BRIEN, Nannie B.	JACKSON, Edward	NOV 01 1855
O'BRIEN, Patrick	NELEGAN, Mary	JAN 25 1854
O'BRIEN, Rosanna	WELSH, Andrew	AUG 10 1857
O'BRIEN, Sarah	TOBIN, James	JAN 03 1852
O'BRIEN, Sarah	CURTIS, Peter	NOV 23 1852
O'BRIEN, Thomas	REILY, Catherine	JAN 27 1853
O'BRIEN, Thomas M.	PORTER, Mary Elizabeth	FEB 01 1853
O'BRIEN, Timothy	ROCHE, Mary	JAN 29 1853
O'BRIEN, William	CALAHAN, Mary A.	JUL 13 1833
O'BRIEN, William	LORDAN, Mary	MAY 20 1841
O'BRIEN, William	REIDY, Mary	DEC 05 1853
O'BRIEN, William M.	McQUILLIAN, Eliza T.	DEC 15 1846
O'BRIEN, Wm.	WOLLIS, Maria	AUG 04 1818

District of Columbia Marriage Licenses, 1811-1858

O'BRYAN, Alice	McDONOUGH, John	JAN 26
O'BRYAN, Catherine	SHYNE, Michael R.	MAR 03
O'BRYAN, James	SIMPSON, Rose L.	JAN 30
O'BRYAN, John	COLLINS, Susan	OCT 14
O'BRYAN, Timothy	GLEASON, Catharine	FEB 22
O'BRYAN, Timothy	LYNCH, Ellen	MAY 06
O'BRYEN, Lucy Ann	BUELL, Martin	DEC 30
O'BRYON, Margaret Ann	BROWN, Benjamin G.	FEB 14
O'BRYON, Rosa A.	OYSTER, George M.	AUG 02
O'BRYON, Rose L.	MARCERON, Louis	MAR 27
O'BRYON, Terence	KELLY, Mary	JUN 08
O'BRYON, William	BLANCHARD, Lucy Ann	JAN 15
O'BYRNE, Dominick A.	CLEMENTS, Josephine E.	APR 16
O'CALLAGHAN, Thomas	SHIELDS, Margaret	JAN 01
O'CALLAGHEN, Patrick	O'CONNOR, Catherine	JAN 30
O'CALLAHAN, Cornelius	FARRELL, Eliza	APR 27
O'CALLAHAN, John	O'CONNOR, Mary	JUN 06
O'CALLAN, Francis	McNULTY, Ann	JUL 21
O'CARROLL, Dennis	KELLY, Hanora	FEB 28
O'CONNEL, Hannah	O'BRIAN, Patrick	FEB 20
O'CONNELL, Bridget	O'SHEY, David	JUN 11
O'CONNELL, Daniel	WRIGHT, Susan M.	FEB 13
O'CONNELL, Jeremiah	MAINE, Catherine	NOV 14
O'CONNELL, Joanna	O'REILLY, William H.	MAR 08
O'CONNELL, John	MULVAHILL, Hanora	AUG 14
O'CONNELL, Margaret	FLYNN, John M.	APR 28
O'CONNELL, Margaret	O'TOOLE, Patrick	SEP 15
O'CONNER, Catharine	JOHNSON, Henry	DEC 01
O'CONNER, Francis D.	CAHILL, Margaret	FEB 09
O'CONNER, Joanna	O'CONNER, Timothy	DEC 08
O'CONNER, Margaret	O'SULLIVAN, John	FEB 22
O'CONNER, Timothy	O'CONNER, Joanna	DEC 08
O'CONNOR, Bridget	SHANNESSY, William	JUN 17
O'CONNOR, Catherine	O'CALLAGHEN, Patrick	JAN 30
O'CONNOR, Cecilia	MORIARTY, Daniel	SEP 15
O'CONNOR, Daniel	CROWLEY, Joannah	FEB 13
O'CONNOR, Eugene	QUIGLEY, Margaret	DEC 03
O'CONNOR, Hannah	COLBERT, Thomas	JUL 21
O'CONNOR, Honora	DILLON, David	JAN 10
O'CONNOR, James	McILLICUDDY, Ellen	FEB 09
O'CONNOR, Jeremiah	DOGGON, Ellen	AUG 17
O'CONNOR, John	CORIDON, Bridget	FEB 21
O'CONNOR, Margaret	SHEAHAN, John	DEC 01
O'CONNOR, Mary	O'CONNOR, Michael	FEB 08
O'CONNOR, Mary	O'CALLAHAN, John	JUN 06
O'CONNOR, Mary	WELCH, Thomas	FEB 12
O'CONNOR, Maurice H.	PEAKE, Margaret	DEC 12
O'CONNOR, Michael	O'CONNOR, Mary	FEB 08
O'CONNOR, Michael	MYERS, Ellen	JUN 05
O'CONNOR, Patrick	McMAHON, Honora	NOV 04
O'CONNOR, Patrick P.	PAUL, Susannah Pamelia	JUL 10
O'CONNOR, Pierce	DOWNEY, Bridget	MAY 3
O'DANIEL, Mary	McGINN, Peter	JUN 15
O'DAY, Bridget	HALLORAN, James	FEB 15
O'DAY, Ellen	GLEASON, Patrick	NOV 29
O'DAY, John	CROWLEY, Anna	JAN 17
O'DAY, Mary	CONNELL, John	DEC 20
O'DAY, Mary	ROGERS, James	DEC 14

District of Columbia Marriage Licenses, 1811-1858

O'DAY, Thomas	MALONY, Judy	JAN 31 1853
O'DEA, John	HICKEY, Mary	APR 02 1858
O'DEA, Margaret	TORPEY, John	APR 02 1858
O'DEAR, John	MALONEY, Margaret	AUG 21 1854
O'DELL, Lizzie T.	LAVINDER, Fleming J.	MAY 12 1857
O'DONNEL, Dennis	KEARY, Mary	MAY 01 1832
O'DONNEL, Mary	FREELAND, Thomas	JAN 03 1820
O'DONNELL, Alice	MULLEN, William H.	JUN 08 1858
O'DONNELL, Bernard	CASSIDY, Eleanor	NOV 03 1829
O'DONNELL, Biddy	CODLIN, James	AUG 04 1818
O'DONNELL, Eleanor	DUNNINGAN, John	DEC 28 1821
O'DONNELL, John	EVANS, Elizabeth	AUG 02 1843
O'DONNELL, John	JOHNSON, S.E.	OCT 06 1845
O'DONNELL, John	LANDRAGON, Eliza	MAY 03 1852
O'DONNELL, John	GALLIVIN, Mary	JUL 24 1858
O'DONNELL, Margaret	HIGGINS, Michael	APR 12 1826
O'DONNELL, Mary	CALLAHAN, Michael	DEC 29 1821
O'DONNELL, Mary	CARROLL, Thomas	AUG 09 1851
O'DONNELL, Mary Jane	VENABLE, Thomas	OCT 29 1845
O'DONNELL, Sarah	WILLIAMS, Lemuel D.	DEC 31 1851
O'DONNELL, Susannah	COLLINS, Martin	NOV 13 1821
O'DONNELL, Thomas	CREAGH, Nancy	FEB 02 1856
O'DONNOGHUE, Kate	SMITH, Benjamin	JAN 19 1858
O'DONNOGHUE, Margaret E.	MURPHY, John	JUN 17 1852
O'DONNOGHUE, Peter, Jr.	BURKE, Rebecca	JAN 27 1852
O'DONNOGHUE, Timothy	HUTCHENSON, Sarah	OCT 25 1825
O'DONNOVAN, Mary	SHIELDS, Laurence	JUL 29 1853
O'DONNUGHUE, John	COXE, Jane	SEP 08 1837
O'DONOGHUE, Charles	McMAHON, Bridget	SEP 07 1852
O'DONOGHUE, Dennis	JAMIESON, Teresa	MAY 12 1852
O'DONOGHUE, Sarah	LEVY, Lawrence	APR 05 1850
O'DONOHO, Hannora	LEONARD, John F.	AUG 13 1825
O'DONOVAN, Timothy	LAY, Catharine	JUL 16 1853
O'FLAHERTY, Edmund	CUNNINGHAM, Hannah	DEC 13 1855
O'GRADY, Dennis	BURKE, Ellen	FEB 06 1855
O'HAGAN, Mary	BOYDE, George	AUG 15 1850
O'HAMMOND, Elizabeth	BALDWIN, Henry, Jr.	MAY 25 1858
O'HARE, Ann	LOFTIS, John	DEC 01 1857
O'HARE, Mary A.	O'SULLIVAN, William	NOV 28 1856
O'HARE, Richard	LONGDON, Elizabeth	NOV 17 1812
O'HARN, David	DUNAVAN, Catharine	APR 17 1858
O'HARRON, Thomas	LUNEY, Jane	MAR 25 1856
O'HEARN, John	KEARNS, Mary	MAY 25 1852
O'HERREN, Ellen	REARDON, John	MAY 08 1855
O'KEEFE, Daniel	WELSH, Ellen	OCT 06 1853
O'KEEFE, Patrick	WELCH, Nora	NOV 11 1852
O'KIE, Caroline	STRETCH, John	JUL 26 1820
O'LEARY, Ann	O'LEARY, Dennis	JUN 16 1852
O'LEARY, Dennis	O'LEARY, Ann	JUN 16 1852
O'LEARY, Ellen	TOOMEY, Jeremiah	JAN 11 1848
O'LEARY, Fanny M.	DARNALL, Richard B.	AUG 25 1858
O'LEARY, James	O'LEARY, Mary	JAN 03 1858
O'LEARY, John	EHERN, Margaret	MAY 24 1853
O'LEARY, John	EHRAN, Margaret	OCT 14 1854
O'LEARY, John	DOUGHERTY, Ellen	DEC 26 1855
O'LEARY, Lucy	BARNES, Samuel	OCT 15 1817
O'LEARY, Margaret	COLBERT, David	MAR 31 1853
O'LEARY, Mary	HEDENDER, Nicholas	FEB 01 1820

District of Columbia Marriage Licenses, 1811-1858

O'LEARY, Mary	READY, David	NOV 19 1852
O'LEARY, Mary	O'LEARY, James	JAN 03 1858
O'LEARY, Mary	KENEALY, Hugh	MAR 27 1858
O'LEARY, Timothy	CAHOE, Mary	JUL 10 1854
O'LEARY, Timothy	GRIFFITH, Isabella	JUL 06 1857
O'MARA, Michael	POWER, Catherine	MAY 11 1830
O'MARA, Michael	HANASY, Margaret	AUG 20 1855
O'MARA, Sarah	CALAHAN, Jeremiah	JUL 17 1847
O'MEARA, Ann	MULLONE, Thomas	JUL 05 1851
O'MEARA, William C.	HOONSWORTH, Sarah Ann	MAR 19 1850
O'NALTS, Lewis	SPARROW, Daby Ann	MAR 05 1833
O'NEAL, Araminta	BRIGHT, John	MAR 14 1854
O'NEAL, Harriet	FENTRESS, Augustus	APR 25 1857
O'NEAL, James	GROVES, Susan C.	OCT 15 1852
O'NEAL, Louisa M.	DRURY, Terence	OCT 14 1850
O'NEAL, Mary	INCH, Philip	FEB 14 1830
O'NEAL, Mary Elizth.	KING, William A.	MAY 16 1853
O'NEAL, Susan M.	HOLLINSWORTH, Jepther S.	DEC 06 1852
O'NEAL, Theodore	NEWTON, Matilda	FEB 27 1829
O'NEAL, Thomas W.	CARTER, Ann E.	NOV 01 1842
O'NEALE, Ann E.	DONALDSON, Thomas G.	SEP 29 1853
O'NEALE, Caroline M.	SPEDDEN, Edward M.	MAY 06 1841
O'NEALE, Charles	CRAWFORD, Sophia	AUG 01 1835
O'NEALE, Christi Ann	BAKER, Edmund	DEC 31 1833
O'NEALE, Christopher	FLANNIGAN, Mary A.	JUL 07 1840
O'NEALE, Eleanora	FOWLER, Thomas	OCT 29 1838
O'NEALE, Elizabeth	DAVIS, James N.	MAY 05 1840
O'NEALE, Elizabeth	CRUPPE, A.B.	JUL 09 1840
O'NEALE, Elizth.	REESE, Hugh L.	MAY 05 1853
O'NEALE, Georgi Ann C.	EVANS, Rev. French T.	JUL 23 1829
O'NEALE, Hilleary	RILEY, Elizabeth	JAN 08 1849
O'NEALE, Hugh	EASTON, Rhody	APR 17 1815
O'NEALE, Hugh	CRYER, Sarah Ann	DEC 26 1842
O'NEALE, John	CHAMILLON, Mary A.	DEC 23 1839
O'NEALE, John H.P.	VIRANS, Louisa M.	MAY 07 1845
O'NEALE, Julia	GOSLAND, James	OCT 14 1844
O'NEALE, Margaret	TIMBERLAKE, John B.	JUN 15 1816
O'NEALE, Maria	NERY, Thomas	APR 05 1842
O'NEALE, Mary	RANDOLPH, Grimes [Dr. Philip]	OCT 23 1824
O'NEALE, Mary	WILLIAMS, Peter	MAY 20 1826
O'NEALE, Mary	BOUGLEY, John	JAN 13 1830
O'NEALE, Mary A.A.	WALL, Leonard D.	JUN 20 1822
O'NEALE, Mary Ann	HILBRON, Nathan W.	FEB 21 1855
O'NEALE, Patrick	REARDON, Ann Maria	SEP 07 1812
O'NEALE, Paul	CLARKE, Mary	MAY 09 1822
O'NEALE, Rose Maria	GREENHOW, Robert	MAY 23 1835
O'NEALE, Sarah	BALLINGER, Joseph	OCT 06 1840
O'NEALE, Sophia	JONES, Richard	JAN 02 1843
O'NEALE, Susan	FARR, Abner C.	SEP 04 1834
O'NEALE, Susanna	HOLT, John R.	DEC 30 1824
O'NEALE, Thos.	CLARKE, Susan	MAR 05 1821
O'NEALE, Timothy	HERLIHY, Jane	DEC 30 1835
O'NEALE, Timothy	ENNIS, Anna R.	NOV 04 1843
O'NEIL, Hannah	WILSON, Josias D.	DEC 31 1832
O'NEILE, Mary	ROWAND, John R.	MAR 24 1838
O'NEILL, John	LANGLEY, Emily Agnes	JUN 08 1835
O'NEILL, Samuel	JINKINS, Eliza Ellen	OCT 17 1846
O'NIEL, John	LARKIN, Julia	JAN 29 1855

District of Columbia Marriage Licenses, 1811-1858

O'NIEL, Sarah B.	DONALDSON, Richard F.	MAY 29 1855
O'PRADY, Mary	LECY, Thomas	JUL 15 1852
O'REILEY, Agnes	McDERMOTT, John	FEB 19 1849
O'REILLY, Bernard	KELLY, Margaret R.	DEC 22 1854
O'REILLY, John	SIMMONS, Elizabeth	NOV 04 1837
O'REILLY, John	GREENFIELD, Caroline	FEB 15 1847
O'REILLY, Margaret	KUHNS, Andrew	JAN 04 1841
O'REILLY, Margaret	COLLINS, Maurice	JUN 07 1853
O'REILLY, William H.	O'CONNELL, Joanna	MAR 08 1852
O'REILY, Louisa	KEARNEY, James [Col.]	NOV 03 1830
O'REILY, Margaret	GORMLEY, Philip	JUN 28 1830
O'REILY, Peter	GANNON, Bridget	JAN 30 1858
O'REILY, William H.	ELLIOTT, Catharine	JUL 11 1854
O'REILY, Wm. H.	ELLETT, Catharine	JUN 18 1855
O'RILEY, Lawrence	CARTER, Alice	AUG 12 1842
O'RILEY, Rose Ann	COLLINS, Bernard	MAY 28 1828
O'ROARK, Sarah Ann	COLES, Charles	MAR 11 1858
O'ROURK, Thos. J.	HOURST, Ann	SEP 23 1856
O'ROURKE, Luke	WRIGHT, Mary R.	JUL 17 1854
O'ROURKE, Mary	JOHNSON, Thomas	JUL 31 1835
O'SHEY, David	O'CONNELL, Bridget	JUN 11 1856
O'SULLIVAN, John	O'CONNER, Margaret	FEB 22 1849
O'SULLIVAN, Michael	RYNE, Mary	JUL 19 1849
O'SULLIVAN, William	O'HARE, Mary A.	NOV 28 1856
O'TOOLE, John	CARNEY, Julia	JUL 05 1858
O'TOOLE, Patrick	O'CONNELL, Margaret	SEP 15 1857
OAKLEY, Margaret J.	CUNNINGHAM, Frederick A.	APR 03 1856
OARD, Sarah Ann	McPHAIL, William	AUG 31 1835
OATES, Thomas	SULLIVAN, Maria	OCT 09 1852
OBER, Franklin S.	FRENCH, Mary A.	MAY 02 1854
OBER, Henry N.	BURDINE, Caroline	JAN 15 1852
OBER, John	RESS, Ann	DEC 18 1822
OBER, John	CLARKE, Frances L.	JUN 19 1851
OBER, Lydia	KNOWLES, Thomas	OCT 26 1818
OBERHEIN, John	BEHERNS, Sophia	MAY 04 1858
OBOLD, Francis S.	FLEISHELL, Sarah J.	OCT 10 1855
OBRIAN, Julia	CATALANO, Antonio	MAR 27 1820
OCH, George	LUFBOROUGH, Barbara	SEP 14 1849
OCKER, George	REIGER, Catherine	FEB 25 1834
OCKERT, August Louis	PLOECHER, Louisa	JUN 24 1858
OCKERT, Emily	THOUR, Adam	APR 21 1853
OCKRSHAUSEN, Johan	SCHNEIDER, Anna Martha	JUN 25 1858
ODD, Mary E.	HUNTER, Thomas I.	DEC 27 1849
ODEN, Artan	HOWARD, Nelly (blk)	JUN 04 1835
ODEN, Elizabeth	GOODRICK, Benjamin	JAN 13 1851
ODEN, Louisa	CARLISLE, Michael H.	APR 29 1854
ODLE, Trueman	WILSON, Mary A.	APR 25 1855
ODLEY, Elizabeth	GOINGS, Benjamin	MAY 24 1817
OELRICHS, Henry Ferdinand	McRA, Julia Matilda	JUN 20 1849
OFENSTEIN, Johanna	REITH, Pius	JUL 02 1857
OFENSTEIN, Lekata	MÜNSTER, Adolph	APR 06 1858
OFENSTEIN, Leopold	GEIDERMACHER, Catherine	DEC 24 1853
OFFAIN, Dora V.	WARKENFILE, Peter	AUG 30 1853
OFFERTT, Zepheniah K.	BERRY, Matilda	APR 10 1822
OFFLEY, Hellen J.	PAULDING, Leonard	DEC 10 1851
OFFUTT, Ann E.	GITTINGS, William C.	OCT 05 1841
OFFUTT, Antaperxes F.	BAKER, Elizabeth A.	JAN 31 1837
OFFUTT, Catherine V.	CRAMPTON, John F.	FEB 09 1850

District of Columbia Marriage Licenses, 1811-1858

OFFUTT, Chs.	JONES, Sarah	APR 24 1821
OFFUTT, Cornelius A.	TRUNNEL, Laura S.	AUG 18 1857
OFFUTT, Edward T.	WILLIAMS, Ann	JAN 08 1844
OFFUTT, George W.	MAHORNEY, Frances	JUL 27 1848
OFFUTT, Henry L.	BAKER, Virginia C.	MAY 24 1847
OFFUTT, Jane Maria	CLAGETT, Thomas	MAR 11 1834
OFFUTT, John R.	ADAMS, Mary E.	DEC 15 1857
OFFUTT, Joseph	JOHNSON, Mary	FEB 06 1829
OFFUTT, Joshua W.	JACKSON, Rose A.	JUN 18 1856
OFFUTT, Julia L.	MAGRUDER, Greenberry	MAY 05 1836
OFFUTT, Lucy Beall	RAINEY, Samuel	NOV 08 1837
OFFUTT, Marion	HODGKINS, Elizabeth Amanda	AUG 29 1851
OFFUTT, Mary Ann K.	MOUNTZ, Joseph	JUN 08 1841
OFFUTT, Susan	LYNCH, James	NOV 05 1839
OFFUTT, Thomas H.	BUTT, Emeline	MAY 20 1857
OFFUTT, Ursuler A.	MARLL, John S.	NOV 11 1844
OFFUTT, Wm. R.M.	PRATHER, Emily Jane	OCT 30 1856
OFFUTT, Zachariah M.	REMINGTON, Eliza Ann	APR 07 1826
OGDEN, Ann Maria	STEVENS, Robert H.	MAY 10 1841
OGDEN, Anna E.	KEMBLE, James	MAY 10 1852
OGDEN, Elias	GRIMSLEY, Liner	APR 28 1831
OGDEN, John W.	MOORE, Rebecca	SEP 20 1841
OGDEN, John W.	ALLEN, Isabella D.	JUL 13 1848
OGDEN, Matilda	BURD, Thomas	DEC 07 1815
OGDEN, Sarah Priscilla	MICKUM, William B.	SEP 25 1851
OGDEN, Sary	THOMPSON, John	JUN 17 1830
OGDEN, William J.	MARLL, Mary Ann	AUG 22 1848
OGDEN, William L.	FOWLER, Margt. Ann	FEB 06 1813
OGDEN, Wm. L.	LEAKE, Elizabeth A.	FEB 06 1818
OGGELVIE, Walter	BROWN, Emma J.	DEC 08 1856
OGILVIE, Ann	CLEPHANE, James	OCT 10 1819
OGLE, Benjamin R.	NELSON, Anna V.	JUN 09 1849
OGLE, Columbus F.	HARBAUGH, Frances	JUN 11 1853
OGLE, Horatio	SHIPLEY, Mary	FEB 03 1812
OGLE, Louisa	CROGGAN, Isaac N.J.	JUL 02 1842
OGLE, Mary Ellen	CROUL, Peter	NOV 17 1836
OGLE, Rebecca Ann	CLEMENTS, John Francis	OCT 21 1833
OGLE, Rezin H.	HANEY, Elizabeth	OCT 05 1839
OGLE, Rezin H.	SHOEMAKER, Margaret	AUG 21 1852
OGLE, Richard	GALHGAM, Jane	OCT 16 1856
OGLE, William	KELLON, Susannah	JAN 15 1831
OGLETON, Caleb	DUCKETT, Ann Eliza	DEC 15 1842
OGLETON, Margaret	STROTHER, Frederick	MAY 27 1837
OGLEVIE, Joseph	WHITLEY, Dolly (blk)	FEB 10 1835
OHAGAN, Sarah	BENSON, Patrick	JAN 14 1823
OLARY, Margaret	McCARTY, John	MAR 31 1821
OLDFIELD, Granville S., Jr.	STEVENS, Mary Virginia	SEP 15 1852
OLDHAM, Elizabeth	ANDERSON, Joseph	MAY 21 1825
OLDHAM, James R.C.	DUNDAS, Eliza	JAN 07 1857
OLIVE, Henry	FOXWELL, Susan	DEC 28 1843
OLIVE, Mary	LUCAS, Taply	AUG 02 1844
OLIVE, Sarah Ann	BROWN, John	JUN 14 1843
OLIVER, Ann	COVER, Philomon	JUN 14 1828
OLIVER, Ann	HEPBURN, David	JUL 03 1828
OLIVER, Ann Eliza	RICH, Henry	FEB 07 1816
OLIVER, Eliza	DOOD, James	MAR 12 1818
OLIVER, Elizabeth	BROWN, John	JAN 30 1823
OLIVER, Giles	MARTIN, Sophiar	JUL 02 1839

District of Columbia Marriage Licenses, 1811-1858

OLIVER, James	THOMPSON, Nancy	DEC 12 1836
OLIVER, Jane	HUNTER, Thomas	MAY 15 1828
OLIVER, Jane	NEAL, Samuel	SEP 10 1832
OLIVER, John	DEDMORTIA, Louisa	JUN 07 1852
OLIVER, Margaret	SOPER, Charles	JUN 04 1851
OLIVER, Mary	BURGESS, Samuel	APR 29 1812
OLIVER, Mary	DECKER, James	AUG 13 1833
OLIVER, Mary Ann	COVER, Jacob	AUG 23 1823
OLIVER, Mary Eshby	LEIGH, Alfred	AUG 04 1846
OLIVER, Miranda S.	DONALDSON, Benjamin S.	DEC 04 1851
OLIVER, Rebecca	CAMDEN, William	DEC 23 1819
OLIVER, Sarah	McKAIN, James	JUN 12 1828
OLIVER, Sarah	SMITH, Temple	JAN 07 1845
OLIVER, Thomas	HODGSKIN, Mary Jane	OCT 24 1849
OLIVER, William	HOWELL, Eveline A.	APR 20 1847
OLLERMEH, Liner	SNIDER, John Adam	OCT 02 1848
OLLIFF, Robert H.	BUTLER, Mary C.	JAN 07 1854
OLLIVER, Aaron P.	HUGHES, Malinda	AUG 15 1826
OLLIVER, John	LEWIS, Lucy	AUG 17 1829
OLLIVER, Martha	SMITH, Rezin O.	JAN 31 1850
OLLIVER, Sophia	BEAN, William W.	NOV 28 1853
OLLUFF, Mary	BROWN, John	DEC 13 1849
OLZEM, John	SONENWALD, Eliza	NOV 02 1855
ONION, Milly	HOWARD, John	DEC 11 1812
ONLEY, Allis	McMAHON, Michael	AUG 28 1833
OPPENHEIMER, Manasset	JOSEPH, Henrietta	FEB 17 1855
OPPENHEIMER, Maurice	ROTHSCHILD, Hanchen	JAN 05 1856
ORBISIN, Mary M.	MARNING, Edward C.	MAY 20 1834
ORD, Catherine	WALKER, [blank]	AUG 12 1833
OREM, Alizean	PEASTOR, William	APR 07 1856
ORFORD, Milly	NASH, Peter	AUG 09 1844
ORINE, Jeremiah	HYDE, Eleanor	MAR 14 1826
ORISON, Arthur	FIELDS, Catharine	SEP 17 1823
ORKENDORF, John	RYAN, Elizabeth	JUL 27 1850
ORM, Anna	SCIOR, Otto	MAY 10 1853
ORM, Susan (blk)	BROGDEN, Jeffrey	SEP 24 1827
ORME, Ann C.	SWEET, Parker H.	SEP 06 1837
ORME, Catharine	HAYRE, John	JAN 11 1821
ORME, Elizabeth	MOSS, Obadiah	DEC 03 1832
ORME, Elizabeth	HIZER, James	SEP 06 1854
ORME, Isabella	LAZENBY, Benjn. C.	JAN 10 1856
ORME, Jane Elizabeth	BOONE, John B.	JUN 02 1829
ORME, Jeremiah	HYDE, Lydia Ann	JUL 15 1835
ORME, Lucy Ann	BARNES, Thomas T.	JAN 05 1832
ORME, Maria Ann	JOHNSON, John Richard	APR 21 1855
ORME, Maria Anne	LANDSTREET, Samuel	OCT 31 1837
ORME, Martha N.	TANNER, William	APR 02 1838
ORME, Mary	NEWLAND, Artimes	NOV 15 1831
ORME, Mary (blk)	REDER, James	JUL 01 1816
ORME, Rezin	DAVIS, Mary H.	NOV 07 1836
ORME, Thomas	KURTZ, Sarah	JUN 01 1816
ORME, William	MOORE, Ann Maria	JAN 05 1836
ORME, William C.	WARD, Jane F.	MAY 10 1831
ORMS, Emily B.	BRAWNER, William H.	SEP 13 1856
ORNTINE, Charles	ARNOLD, Sophia	SEP 23 1835
ORR, Ann	JONES, James	APR 04 1822
ORR, Henry	PENCOST, Harriet (blk)	DEC 18 1838
ORR, James	SHENNAN, Sarah Jane	JAN 31 1851

District of Columbia Marriage Licenses, 1811-1858

ORR, John	BOYD, Mary	NOV 03 1812
ORR, Overton L.	LONG, Julia	JAN 19 1826
ORR, Sarah (blk)	CLARKE, Owen	SEP 23 1840
ORR, William H.	MARTIN, Emily Amelia	JAN 08 1853
ORR, Wm. Henry	BARTON, Sarah Jane (blk)	MAY 15 1843
ORSBORNE, Richard	HELM, Margaret	APR 01 1818
ORSBURN, John	ROSS, Lucy	DEC 24 1818
ORSBURN, Mary	GRAYSON, John	DEC 10 1816
ORT, Elizabeth	KNAPP, Gabriel	AUG 27 1857
ORTLY, Bartholomew	CUNNINGHAM, Elizabeth A.	JUN 12 1854
ORTON, Charles A.	SHREEVE, Mary A.	DEC 30 1851
OSBERN, Ann	DURITY, Leonard	OCT 04 1821
OSBORN, Amanda E.	SWEENEY, Thomas	AUG 21 1857
OSBORN, Ann	GEE, Henry	JUN 22 1850
OSBORN, Catherine	WHITE, Benedict	DEC 09 1816
OSBORN, Catherine	JEFFERSON, Thomas	APR 26 1836
OSBORN, Daniel	TALBERT, Maria	MAR 19 1833
OSBORN, Eliza	NORTON, Alexander	JUL 18 1839
OSBORN, Elizabeth	RAY, Enos	NOV 23 1826
OSBORN, Francis	REED, Isabella	SEP 12 1854
OSBORN, George W.	TUTTLE, America K.	MAY 01 1858
OSBORN, Harriet Ann	STEWART, George W.	SEP 13 1827
OSBORN, Helen B.	CALVERT, George W.	NOV 29 1854
OSBORN, James	OSBURN, Drucilla	OCT 07 1815
OSBORN, Jane	CHURN, James	MAY 20 1848
OSBORN, Joseph	GATES, Nancy	OCT 03 1837
OSBORN, Rosella	KIDWELL, Isaac	MAR 02 1833
OSBORN, Sarah	BOOSE, John	JUN 01 1825
OSBORN, William McK.	McKENNEY, Margaret Ann Foxall	APR 26 1834
OSBORNE, Ann	JARVIS, John	AUG 07 1848
OSBORNE, Anna	McKENNEY, Edward	NOV 22 1851
OSBORNE, Elizabeth	BARBER, George	NOV 20 1849
OSBORNE, Elizabeth Ann	LYNCH, George Isaac	OCT 06 1854
OSBORNE, Elizabeth R.	RAY, Anthony L.	FEB 26 1855
OSBORNE, George W.	McDANIEL, Ann Maria	MAY 28 1853
OSBORNE, Harriet	WHITE, James	AUG 23 1819
OSBORNE, Lucinda	CLARKE, James	JUN 02 1818
OSBORNE, Lucinda	WILSON, John	AUG 12 1848
OSBORNE, Mary	SMITH, George H.	MAR 20 1852
OSBORNE, Mary E.	CUVILLIER, Joseph L.	JAN 02 1857
OSBORNE, Seth	MASSEY, Mary E.	JUN 24 1851
OSBORNE, Susan	WILSON, Lieut. John E.	MAY 16 1854
OSBORNE, Walter	EDELIN, Elizabeth Lucy Anna	DEC 25 1838
OSBOURN, Elizabeth	McCLISH, William	MAY 25 1819
OSBOURN, John	BALDIN, Sarah Ann	FEB 07 1831
OSBOURN, Martha	YEATMAN, William O.	APR 03 1827
OSBOURN, Susan	HIGDON, Thomas	AUG 13 1828
OSBOURN, William F.	TREE, Margaret	OCT 11 1826
OSBOURNE, Elizth. E.	ANDERSON, Hezekiah	MAY 22 1858
OSBURN, Drucilla	OSBORN, James	OCT 07 1815
OSBURN, Emma	HERBERT, William	FEB 27 1845
OSBURN, James M.	MAY, Eleanor L.	APR 28 1838
OSBURN, Levi M.	DRANE, Ann Matilda	APR 12 1838
OSBURN, Thomas H.	SCOTT, Eliza A.	APR 08 1844
OSBURN, William B.	MASSIE, Mary Ann	DEC 17 1828
OSBURNE, Thomas	SCOTT, Rachael	AUG 04 1818
OSGOOD, Ann	HUNT, Harvey W.	NOV 09 1844
OSHEA, William	CORBATT, Ann	JUL 14 1853

District of Columbia Marriage Licenses, 1811-1858

OSMON, James H.	MARSHALL, Ann Jemima	OCT 09 1817
OSTARMAYER, Sophia	SCHLEIFER, Henry	SEP 07 1857
OSTEN, Elizabeth	RABBETT, Henry	JUL 25 1814
OSTENDORFF, Henry	PULSFORT, Elizabeth	JAN 20 1853
OSTERMEIR, Bernhart	HENRY, Catherine	JUN 16 1840
OSTHAUS, Hermin	BARTHEL, Mary	AUG 07 1855
OSTIN, Martha Ann	NICHOLLS, Nicholas Y.	MAY 09 1840
OSTRANDER, George G.	PINK, Corleria Ann	OCT 05 1850
OSTRANDER, Mary Jane	COON, George G.	MAR 14 1855
OTEAL, Catharine	LEIB, John Michael	MAY 06 1847
OTRIDGE, Sarah	BUTLER, Abraham	FEB 07 1839
OTT, John	CROOKSHANK, Ann	OCT 08 1816
OTT, Mary C.	BEATTY, Robert H.	MAR 06 1826
OTT, Rose Anna	KING, Martin	JAN 01 1825
OTTERBACH, Benjamin L.	MILLER, Charlotte	AUG 25 1853
OTTERBACK, Catherine	BOHRER, George A.	APR 02 1839
OTTERBACK, Henry	GEDDIS, Rosella	NOV 19 1846
OTTERBACK, Maria	TAVENNER, Charles H.	JUN 29 1847
OTTERBACK, Philip	BURFORD, Sarah	JAN 31 1821
OTTERBACK, Sarah	WARD, William H.	MAY 02 1848
OTTINGER, Charles	KNOWLES, Rebecca	JAN 12 1826
OTTINGER, Rebecca	WALLING, William	DEC 06 1828
OTTRIDGE, Catharine	PETTIGREW, Theophilus	MAY 29 1820
OULD, Pauline	GRIFFITH, Samuel C.	FEB 15 1848
OULD, Sarah A.	TILTON, Warren	FEB 24 1851
OURAND, Alethia F.F.	POTTER, Thomas L.	JAN 03 1848
OURAND, Christiana A.T.	WADE, John K.	OCT 17 1843
OURAND, D.C.W.	TAYLOR, Julia	MAY 12 1857
OURAND, Samuel	MILLER, Margaret	JAN 09 1852
OURAND, Sophia E.F.	RIGGS, John M.	JAN 03 1848
OUSLEY, John	HILBUS, Caroline	APR 08 1833
OUTTERIDGE, Sarah	STEWART, William Hutson	AUG 16 1815
OVANSTINE, Mary	PROTD, Francis	JAN 06 1852
OVERMANN, E.L.	DRAKE, Nathan B.	DEC 15 1855
OVERSTINE, Casper	KRIDERMAKER, Barbara	APR 28 1846
OVERSTREET, James	MOORE, Agness Maria	MAY 07 1822
OVERTON, John	DAVIS, Sarah	NOV 21 1812
OWEN, Ann	BEDE, George	APR 03 1820
OWEN, Henry	NALLY, Mary	AUG 05 1822
OWEN, Isabella	BROWN, Edmund F.	OCT 03 1828
OWEN, John	GOLDSMITH, Rosanna	AUG 08 1840
OWEN, John A.	REESIDE, Caroline	JAN 31 1853
OWEN, Julia Ann	BEALL, James F.	OCT 26 1837
OWEN, Martha	TIPPETT, Joel	APR 11 1844
OWEN, Mary	SMITH, William	APR 08 1841
OWEN, Mary Elizabeth	ROSENBERRY, Joseph	APR 29 1853
OWEN, Thomas	BERRY, Ellen	MAY 16 1830
OWENS, Amelia E.	FARR, Malachi	DEC 14 1854
OWENS, Ann	THRELKIELD, James	APR 30 1817
OWENS, Ann	DORITY, John	JUL 25 1818
OWENS, Basil	TURNER, Tebitha Ann	MAR 18 1844
OWENS, Basil	MACABEE, Emilie	JAN 06 1848
OWENS, Charles	SPALDING, Winneford	APR 13 1830
OWENS, Charlotte	NEWMAN, James R.	OCT 27 1857
OWENS, David	COOK, Alice	DEC 03 1818
OWENS, Elias	CLEVELAND, Sarah E.	FEB 03 1858
OWENS, Elizabeth	OWENS, Henry	SEP 07 1847
OWENS, Elizabeth Ann	JONES, Charles R.	MAY 11 1858

District of Columbia Marriage Licenses, 1811-1858

OWENS, Exy	LOWE, Warren	DEC 01 1824
OWENS, Fieldy	PARKS, Lavina	SEP 16 1836
OWENS, Gassaway	DRURY, Ann M.	MAR 29 1853
OWENS, George W.	FOYLES, Caroline	JAN 02 1855
OWENS, Henry	OWENS, Elizabeth	SEP 07 1847
OWENS, Isaac, Jr.	BROWN, Mary Ann	APR 15 1823
OWENS, James	ALLEY, Alethea	JAN 28 1830
OWENS, James Edward	THOMPSON, Ann	AUG 12 1847
OWENS, James L.	SMART, Elizabeth	JAN 02 1834
OWENS, Jane	HENDERSON, James	MAY 27 1816
OWENS, Jane	HENDERSON, James	JUN 27 1816
OWENS, Jane	WATERS, John N.	JAN 21 1825
OWENS, Jesse	GRAY, Cecelia	FEB 02 1844
OWENS, John	McCORMICK, Mary	SEP 06 1838
OWENS, John H.	GILLOT, Sarah	JAN 27 1848
OWENS, Maria	McGINNITY, Thomas	JAN 03 1851
OWENS, Mary	CARRICO, James	MAY 17 1815
OWENS, Mary	BEALL, Thomas	DEC 08 1830
OWENS, Nancy	DREW, Daniel	NOV 30 1820
OWENS, Richard B.	CLUBB, Eliza A.M.	SEP 05 1836
OWENS, Robert A.	MORANT, Eliza A.	APR 09 1857
OWENS, S.W.	EVANS, C.E.	JUL 31 1854
OWENS, Samuel	HOPKINS, Eliza	APR 09 1827
OWENS, Susanna	McCHESNEY, William R.	AUG 28 1856
OWENS, Theodore E.	STONE, Louisa E.	JUL 07 1854
OWENS, Washington W.	WINSOR, Mary	MAY 02 1853
OWENS, William	THOMPSON, Achel Emily	JUL 16 1844
OWENS, William W.	WILKERSON, Mary S.	OCT 27 1857
OWENSTEIN, Sarah	BOMBGARDNER, George	JUL 30 1853
OWINGS, Joseph	GIDDENS, Betsy	FEB 12 1835
OWNER, Frances	COOK, John A. [Lt.]	DEC 16 1828
OWNER, Hannah	ALLEN, Henry J.	OCT 28 1813
OWNER, James	STUCK, Sarah Elizabeth	SEP 30 1848
OWNER, William	WAYNE, Catharine [Mrs.]	MAR 22 1821
OWRAN, Elijah	PICKRELL, Catharine	NOV 20 1823
OXLEY, Emily	HUGHES, Hugh	JAN 07 1836
OYSTER, George M.	O'BRYON, Rosa A.	AUG 02 1848
OYSTER, Jane A.	GODEY, Walter	DEC 04 1849

District of Columbia Marriage Licenses, 1811-1858

P

PACE, John A.	SHEPPERD, Sarah F.	DEC 24 1853
PACK, Enos	BYRNE, Catharine	DEC 30 1818
PACKARD, Joseph	JONES, Rosina	JAN 23 1838
PACKARD, Peres	YOUNG, Jemima	FEB 02 1818
PACKER, Caroline (blk)	EDWARDS, Robert	FEB 22 1838
PACO, Joshua	PRICE, Eleanor	MAR 10 1812
PADDY, John H.	BLAKE, Sarah J.	NOV 06 1854
PADENBERN, Henrietta Meyer	GROSSENHEIN, Edward F.	NOV 28 1856
PADGET, Elizabeth	GRANGER, John W.	MAY 08 1855
PADGET, James F.	ROBERTS, Elizabeth Augusta	APR 23 1856
PADGET, Joseph	GOSS, Louisa	JAN 18 1831
PADGET, Julia Amanda	COLUMBUS, William Francis	APR 30 1849
PADGET, Lewis William	DULANY, Eliza Virginia Clara	JUN 10 1845
PADGETT, Ann	BOYD, John D.	DEC 28 1843
PADGETT, Benjamin	RYON, Viletta	AUG 12 1858
PADGETT, Frances R.	SIMS, Palin Harris	MAR 29 1856
PADGETT, Harriot	KIDWELL, Presley	JUN 19 1827
PADGETT, James	GIBSON, Susanna	MAY 26 1853
PADGETT, Jane	FAGAN, Asa	OCT 16 1823
PADGETT, Jane	WILLIS, William	JUL 18 1826
PADGETT, Jane V.	ARNOLD, John W.	APR 20 1852
PADGETT, John	ROLLINS, Ann R.	NOV 27 1850
PADGETT, John	CAMPBELL, Mahaly	APR 26 1852
PADGETT, John	WHEELER, Margaret	APR 06 1857
PADGETT, John G.	BAGGETT, Susan	MAY 03 1832
PADGETT, Jonathan Turner	RICHARDS, Adelaide R.	FEB 07 1850
PADGETT, Joseph H.	SMITH, Mary A.E.	OCT 04 1853
PADGETT, Joseph M.	NALLY, Elizabeth B.	JUL 28 1853
PADGETT, Keziah	BOND, Ridgly Alex	DEC 12 1813
PADGETT, Lucretia	COXEN, James	APR 01 1853
PADGETT, Lucy	PALMER, Elisha	FEB 15 1813
PADGETT, Maria E.	MOHLER, John W.	JUN 04 1855
PADGETT, Martha A.	CRUMP, John N.	NOV 03 1847
PADGETT, Mary Ann Elizabeth	BROWN, Jerome, Jr.	JAN 03 1846
PADGETT, Mary Emily	COLLINS, James L.	OCT 04 1856
PADGETT, Mason	GEE, Ann Maria	AUG 09 1853
PADGETT, Robert T.	BERKLEY, Mary Ellen	OCT 27 1856
PADGETT, S. Kate	HOOPER, John J.	NOV 14 1855
PADGETT, Sarah Ann	BENNETT, Clark	SEP 07 1816
PADGETT, Sarah Ann	HOWELL, William H.	NOV 07 1848
PADGETT, Sarah Ellen	HALL, Levi A.	AUG 08 1846
PADGETT, Sarah L.	ROBERSON, John H.	JUN 07 1856
PADGETT, William H.	GRAIG, Elizabeth	JUN 17 1840
PADGETT, William Henry	ADAMS, Henrietta A.	JUL 24 1845
PADGETT, Wm. Henry	DROWNS, Margaret	MAY 05 1853
PADGGETT, Julia	MORGAN, William	OCT 28 1833
PAECHCOTT, Hannah	DAVIS, Richard	JUN 28 1837
PAERS, Aquilla	HALL, Linney	APR 14 1827
PAFF, Frederick	BRILL, Louisa	OCT 01 1857
PAGE, Catharine	HAGAN, John	JUL 02 1827
PAGE, Charles	CARMICHAEL, Emily	MAY 26 1852
PAGE, Charles G.	WEBSTER, Priscilla S.	SEP 23 1844
PAGE, Charlotte E.	EWING, Rev. Charles H.	NOV 04 1845
PAGE, Edmonia L.	NEILSON, Hall	JAN 16 1832
PAGE, Frederick B.	DAVIS, Ann F.	JUN 03 1846
PAGE, Kingman F.	MARSHALL, Caroline Grace	DEC 24 1856

District of Columbia Marriage Licenses, 1811-1858

PAGE, Lucy E.	McINTOSH, Thomas	AUG 29 1854
PAGE, Lura S.	PAINTER, Abraham J.	OCT 13 1849
PAGE, Martha	MILBURN, Benedict	JAN 31 1842
PAGE, Mary Elizabeth	SOUPER, Otha W.	FEB 05 1857
PAGE, Miranda	CLUBB, John Lewis	JUN 06 1833
PAGE, Quincy L.	FITZHUGH, Mary L.	DEC 03 1850
PAGE, Rebecca	BUSH, William	JAN 31 1837
PAGE, Rebecca H.	WILSON, John M.	MAY 15 1834
PAGE, Sally	SHERMAN, Charles K.	MAY 29 1852
PAGE, Sally	SHERMAN, Charles E.	OCT 09 1854
PAGE, Samuel	WAGGAMAN, Catharine	JUL 24 1834
PAGE, Thomas J.	PRICE, Benjamina	NOV 08 1838
PAGE, William A.	DUNBAR, Eliza Jane	JUN 03 1850
PAGE, Winifred Sophia	HARBAUGH, Leonard	FEB 05 1839
PAGE, Yelverton P.	ARNOLD, Martha E.	SEP 21 1847
PAGEOT, John W.	TALBOTT, Eleanor O.	JAN 04 1847
PAGEOT, Joseph Ives	LEWIS, Mary Ann	NOV 27 1832
PAGGET, George H.	DONALDSON, Mary Catherine	JAN 04 1849
PAIGE, B.P.	TATE, Mary Ann	JAN 20 1848
PAINE, Artima	HESLEY, Christopher	AUG 26 1835
PAINE, Eleanor	HERRIS, Luke	DEC 15 1819
PAINE, Elizabeth	WALKER, James	JAN 12 1818
PAINE, Ellen	BOSWELL, James H.	JUN 29 1858
PAINE, John Stone	BOMFORD, Ruth Theodora	OCT 28 1845
PAINE, Julia	WHITE, Arthur W.	JAN 28 1857
PAINE, Margaret	FILLEBROWN, Henry C.	MAY 31 1856
PAINE, Margaret A.	BARNES, Chas. W.	JUL 09 1856
PAINE, Mary	GRIGSBY, James W.	MAR 15 1855
PAINE, Mary	HALL, James	MAR 31 1857
PAINE, Mary Ellen	POOR, Francis	JAN 03 1845
PAINE, Richard	HARRIS, Catharine (blk)	OCT 18 1849
PAINE, Roberta	BARRETT, James J.	DEC 10 1850
PAINTER, Abraham J.	PAGE, Lura S.	OCT 13 1849
PAIRO, Henry Thomas	LAUB, Sarah Finley	APR 19 1836
PAIRO, Jane J.	HOLMEAD, John B.	OCT 12 1830
PAIRO, Sophia S.	HALL, John T.	JUN 17 1833
PALFREY, Jane	WEBB, Geo. W.	DEC 25 1834
PALLY, James H.	BOOTHE, Mary Matilda	APR 27 1842
PALMER, Anna Emeline	SHERWOOD, Jas. Elwood	OCT 15 1856
PALMER, Catharine	WEBSTER, George	MAR 09 1829
PALMER, Elisha	PADGETT, Lucy	FEB 15 1813
PALMER, Frances	HUTCHINSON, William P.	FEB 11 1850
PALMER, Henry	ROSS, Sarah (blk)	SEP 09 1834
PALMER, Howard	MATHEWS, Elizabeth	MAR 29 1822
PALMER, James	FINNEY, Eleanor	MAR 02 1841
PALMER, Jane V.	BRANDT, Gerard W.	MAR 23 1853
PALMER, John	LELAND, Mary	DEC 01 1818
PALMER, John	COLLINS, Frances M.	JUN 25 1838
PALMER, John M.	HICKSON, Anne E.	SEP 10 1855
PALMER, Morris	SWEENY, Ann	MAR 22 1826
PALMER, Otha	BROOKES, Elizth.	JUN 27 1822
PALMER, Thomas	TERRITT, Julia D.	MAR 13 1849
PALMER, W. Gray, Dr.	JACKSON, Elizabeth D.	SEP 20 1847
PALMER, William	LONG, Eleanor	FEB 22 1840
PALMER, William	CALVERT, Margaret	OCT 11 1850
PALMER, William H.	FURSE, Jane P.	JUL 07 1856
PALMER, William H.	KIECKHOEFER, Ann	SEP 12 1857
PALMER, Wm. Henry	CLAXTON, C.F.	JUN 25 1833

District of Columbia Marriage Licenses, 1811-1858

PALMORE, John R.	DUFFIELD, Mary A.	AUG 01 1835
PALMORE, M.E.	PALMORE, Thomas W.	APR 18 1857
PALMORE, Thomas W.	PALMORE, M.E.	APR 18 1857
PANCOAST, David	BECK, Mary	JUL 02 1823
PANCOAST, Sarah	FRENCH, William	JAN 06 1820
PANE, Alexander	MELLONTON, Margaret	JUN 07 1823
PANE, Catharine	WALKER, William	APR 16 1825
PANE, Catharine	JAMES, Dennon	JUL 07 1831
PANE, Elizabeth T.	LANE, David D.	MAR 29 1821
PANE, Matilda	THOMAS, James	MAY 02 1820
PANHAM, John	ROWAN, Margaret S.	MAR 05 1853
PANZENBINDER, Henry	GEBHARDT, Friedericke	FEB 27 1854
PAPAN, Christina	NAISA, Christian	JAN 21 1833
PARADISE, Margaret	COALE, William	JUN 20 1833
PARADISE, Mary Elizabeth	CRAIG, Harrison	SEP 17 1838
PARADISE, Sarah Ann	KELLY, James	AUG 10 1832
PARALTA, Manuel	BEALL, Ann Eliza	SEP 17 1849
PARCELLS, William	CADLE, Georgiana	DEC 18 1856
PARDINGTON, James	BOCKMAN, Eleanor	JUN 20 1816
PARDON, Henry F.B.	BARRON, Virginia C.M.	APR 30 1851
PARHAM, William I.	ROWAN, Martha	JUN 08 1846
PARIDISE, Ann	SKIDMORE, Washington	JAN 08 1835
PARIO, Newell	FLURY, Sarah Elizabeth	JUL 11 1837
PARIS, Albert Joseph	COLLINS, Anna Julia	SEP 03 1831
PARIS, Albert W.	SMOOT, Sarah E.	MAY 30 1838
PARISH, Henry A.	BLACK, Sarah C.	JAN 17 1845
PARISH, Levi H.	CRAVEN, Sarah	JUN 15 1841
PARISH, Mary Ann	CLARK, Christopher	DEC 27 1827
PARK, Alexander	READ, Harriot Gallata	JUL 19 1833
PARK, Elmira H.	NOLAND, William H.	JAN 02 1834
PARK, Josephine	SLADE, William	JUN 26 1834
PARK, Louisa	FRINK, Oliver	SEP 08 1840
PARK, Montgomery	BRUCE, Harriet E. (blk)	JUN 27 1850
PARKE, William P.	NORRIS, Virginia	NOV 06 1848
PARKER, Amanda (blk)	LOMAX, Elias	MAY 19 1858
PARKER, Amelia	VANPETT, Abraham	FEB 01 1821
PARKER, Ann	GLADMAN, Asa	AUG 21 1831
PARKER, Ann E.	DeNEALE, William Y.	DEC 10 1857
PARKER, Ann L. (blk)	THOMAS, Wm. H.	AUG 09 1855
PARKER, Ann Wright	DOVE, William Thomas	JUN 26 1838
PARKER, Atha (blk)	SEWELL, Lewis	JUN 02 1856
PARKER, Catharine	PERIOT, Noel	MAY 09 1812
PARKER, Catherine Smith	LARCOMBE, John, Jr.	MAY 07 1844
PARKER, David	WHITE, Ann Maria	DEC 19 1836
PARKER, David	COLE, Ellen (blk)	NOV 30 1848
PARKER, Eliza	CRAIG, Washington	MAR 04 1826
PARKER, Eliza Maria (blk)	GRAY, Edward	MAR 16 1854
PARKER, Elizabeth	TYLER, Edwd.	AUG 17 1819
PARKER, Elizabeth	CHISM, Lewis	DEC 27 1832
PARKER, Elizabeth (blk)	BALEY, John	FEB 18 1839
PARKER, Francis E.	DORSEY, Virginia	AUG 19 1844
PARKER, George	BOARMAN, Eleanor	DEC 21 1815
PARKER, George	WALKER, Ann Sophia [Mrs.]	JAN 21 1834
PARKER, George W.	HURDLE, Caroline	DEC 20 1837
PARKER, Georgianna	MAURY, Thomas F.	MAY 24 1858
PARKER, Hellen	PERRIE, George A.	DEC 20 1855
PARKER, James	DIGGES, Sophia (blk)	SEP 16 1841
PARKER, James	YOUNG, Mary (blk)	AUG 03 1847

District of Columbia Marriage Licenses, 1811-1858

PARKER, John	DURITY, Elizabeth	AUG 20 1816
PARKER, John	BURGESS, Eliza	OCT 25 1831
PARKER, John F.	MANS, Mary C.A.	JUL 16 1855
PARKER, John Thos.	SIBLEY, Mary Elizth.	SEP 09 1857
PARKER, Joseph	CHASE, Harriet (blk)	JUL 09 1855
PARKER, Louisa	MILLER, Jacob B.	OCT 22 1835
PARKER, Louisa (blk)	JOHNSON, Joseph	APR 18 1833
PARKER, Mary (blk)	HARRISON, Vincent	OCT 13 1853
PARKER, Mary A.	PUTNAM, Geo. M.	JUN 06 1856
PARKER, Mary Brown	NEWMAN, Richard M.	OCT 05 1831
PARKER, Mary E.	WOOD, Chas. A.	JUN 18 1858
PARKER, Moses T.	DAVIS, Virginia S.	DEC 17 1839
PARKER, Peter	WEBSTER, Harriet C.	MAR 27 1841
PARKER, Philip	CLARKE, Sarah (blk)	JAN 02 1840
PARKER, Philip	CALBOT, Margaret A. (blk)	MAY 11 1853
PARKER, Priscilla (blk)	BATEMAN, Isaiah	AUG 29 1849
PARKER, Priscilla (blk)	NORRIS, William	NOV 27 1854
PARKER, Rachel Mary	SMITH, William	NOV 28 1855
PARKER, Randolph	UNDERWOOD, Cassy Ann (blk)	SEP 27 1851
PARKER, Rebecca W.	FRASIER, Joseph	DEC 23 1828
PARKER, Robert D.	SALISBURY, Ellen	MAR 13 1849
PARKER, Sarah (blk)	KING, Thomas	FEB 07 1849
PARKER, Sarah Jane	DELANEY, Levi	SEP 20 1854
PARKER, Southey	SPALDING, Jane	JUL 26 1815
PARKER, Southey S.	WATERS, Mary Ann	MAY 04 1848
PARKER, Southey S.	WATERS, Isabella	OCT 31 1854
PARKER, Susan (blk)	KING, John	OCT 17 1822
PARKER, Teresa (blk)	SMITH, John	AUG 01 1854
PARKER, Thomas	BILL, Milley	AUG 12 1818
PARKER, Thomas	YOUNG, Caroline	MAY 17 1832
PARKER, William	COLEGATE, Nancey	APR 06 1820
PARKER, William	GARRISON, Ann	SEP 26 1822
PARKER, William	JOHNSON, Frances (blk)	JAN 03 1828
PARKER, William	FAGAN, Jane	JAN 19 1833
PARKER, William	LEESE, Catherine	DEC 06 1852
PARKER, William	HILL, Charity (blk)	FEB 03 1858
PARKERSON, Margaret	GARDINER, Henry	AUG 11 1835
PARKHURST, Laura Virginia	SULLIVAN, Roszel	SEP 19 1851
PARKINSON, R.	LIPSCOMB, M.O.	MAR 24 1858
PARKINSON, Thomas	THOMAS, Jennett	DEC 11 1837
PARKLETON, George	RABBITT, Catharine Ann	JAN 21 1850
PARKS, James	BREAST, Henrietta	OCT 09 1813
PARKS, Jane	WELSH, George	MAY 26 1854
PARKS, John A.	BLAKE, Parmelia J.	DEC 03 1853
PARKS, Lavina	OWENS, Fieldy	SEP 16 1836
PARKS, Ruebin	CHESER, Elizabeth	JAN 07 1831
PARKS, William G.	JACOBS, Johnana	FEB 18 1857
PARMER, Albert	WALLACE, Margaret	FEB 12 1840
PARMER, Chas. W.	BUTLER, Martha A. (blk)	FEB 06 1854
PARNELL, William B.	DEAVERS, Julia A.	MAY 26 1854
PAROTT, Abner	COLLINS, Eliza Ann	JUN 26 1854
PARRIS, Caroline W.	BROOKS, John C.	MAY 10 1847
PARRIS, Eleanor	MANSFIELD, Thomas	AUG 05 1816
PARRIS, Helen	GILMAN, Zadock D.	NOV 01 1842
PARRISH, Martha J.	MOSS, George W.	MAR 17 1837
PARROTT, James	DAVIS, Mary Ann	OCT 06 1855
PARROTT, Mary M.	KENNEDY, John M.	OCT 25 1820
PARROTT, Rebecca	CONNELL, John	DEC 24 1817

District of Columbia Marriage Licenses, 1811-1858

PARROTT, Sarah C.	ATKINS, Samuel G.	MAY 05 1849
PARRY, Cyrus B.	BOWIE, Lucinda	AUG 05 1822
PARRY, Elizabeth	SERRILL, James	MAR 31 1817
PARRY, Henry	FLETCHER, Eliza	OCT 09 1856
PARSELL, J.F.B.	KNIGHT, Elizabeth	MAY 11 1853
PARSON, Joseph B.	BEALL, Harriet	MAY 13 1831
PARSON, Mary Ann	BURKHART, Lewis I.	OCT 03 1846
PARSONS, Ann	RHODES, James	MAY 22 1821
PARSONS, Ann C.	BERRY, Alfred	JUL 14 1827
PARSONS, Eliza	THOMPSON, John	JAN 24 1826
PARSONS, Eliza	THOMAS, Jenkins	MAY 13 1830
PARSONS, Elizabeth	FOWLER, Abraham	FEB 20 1816
PARSONS, Elizabeth	TABLER, John	APR 23 1816
PARSONS, Elizabeth	UNGLEMAN, William	DEC 21 1826
PARSONS, Emeline	STEELE, James	JUL 07 1851
PARSONS, James H.	JONES, Elizabeth Ann	AUG 27 1834
PARSONS, Jane	BUCKEY, Mathias V.	FEB 18 1835
PARSONS, Jane Elizabeth	DENNIS, Jonathan	DEC 01 1852
PARSONS, John	CARPENTER, Betsey	DEC 03 1829
PARSONS, Lucretia	BRAWNER, Thornton	JUN 13 1826
PARSONS, Luther Osborne	SENDORFF, Mary Ann	MAR 11 1850
PARSONS, Margaret	JONES, William	MAR 12 1856
PARSONS, Maria	EVANS, Walter	JUN 16 1819
PARSONS, Martha A.	CROSS, Joseph	JAN 16 1845
PARSONS, Mary	REMINGTON, John A.	NOV 17 1829
PARSONS, Mary Ann W.	COMER, Abraham	FEB 03 1819
PARSONS, Mary Ann	HUDSON, Joseph	OCT 29 1836
PARSONS, Matilda C.	SPRATT, Thomas	NOV 11 1823
PARSONS, S. Smith	BEALL, Elijah	JAN 04 1854
PARSONS, Samuel	GORDON, Jane	MAR 03 1830
PARSONS, Samuel	SHERRY, Mary	MAY 31 1834
PARSONS, Samuel M.	WHITWELL, Virginia	MAR 02 1848
PARSONS, Sarah Ellen	MARCERON, Marcellus	DEC 24 1856
PARSONS, Susanna	MYERS, Charles	APR 11 1832
PARSONS, Thomas H.	LAWRENCE, Julianna	NOV 25 1845
PARSONS, William	RIGGLE, Ann Maria	APR 28 1840
PASCHALL, Thomas	COOMBS, Margaret L.	AUG 02 1852
PASCOR, Sarah Ann	MARTIN, John	FEB 10 1842
PASKINS, John	DeGILSE, Dorothy	JAN 20 1824
PASSCERE, Harriet M.	MITCHELL, James	MAR 02 1848
PATCHETT, Amy	HYSSETT, Joseph	SEP 09 1844
PATE, Robert W.	CHRISTIAN, Laura N.	MAY 07 1849
PATERSON, Margaret	BURGES, Cirus	APR 22 1813
PATERSON, William	McLAUGHLIN, Salvadora	OCT 07 1852
PATON, John	KEARNEY, Kate	APR 14 1855
PATRICK, John	MOORE, Maria H.W.	APR 15 1823
PATRICK, Louisa	STAUGHTON, James M.	DEC 26 1826
PATTEN, Elizabeth	CURTISS, Robert	MAR 30 1858
PATTEN, Emma M.	PATTEN, George	MAR 12 1853
PATTEN, George	PATTEN, Emma M.	MAR 12 1853
PATTEN, Larkin	CLARKE, Jane Elizabeth	OCT 25 1848
PATTEN, William	WADE, Jane Rebecca	AUG 03 1836
PATTERSON, Alexander	FISHER, Jane Elizth.	JAN 28 1856
PATTERSON, Anne M.	DYKES, George T.	AUG 23 1855
PATTERSON, Charles	McKELDON, Margaret	MAR 26 1821
PATTERSON, Charles P.	PEARSON, Eliza W.	JAN 21 1851
PATTERSON, Eliza	WARREN, Isaac	JUL 06 1835
PATTERSON, Eliza C.	BACHE, George M.	MAY 23 1837

District of Columbia Marriage Licenses, 1811-1858

PATTERSON, Emma	FISHER, Jacob	JUN 20 1855
PATTERSON, Fielder S.	AMIS, Mary S.	MAR 31 1858
PATTERSON, Georgean	PORTER, David D.	MAR 12 1839
PATTERSON, Harriet A.B.	McCENEY, George	DEC 21 1840
PATTERSON, Hellen M.	DECKER, John, Jr.	MAR 24 1852
PATTERSON, James	BRASHEARS, Eleanor	NOV 07 1822
PATTERSON, James	LATHRAM, Ann	AUG 26 1839
PATTERSON, James	McGINNEL, Mary Ann	NOV 17 1853
PATTERSON, James Orville	DeLAROCHE, Anna Jane Belt	FEB 26 1852
PATTERSON, Johannah	DRAKE, William E.	AUG 06 1828
PATTERSON, Julia	DADE, Wesley	JUN 02 1830
PATTERSON, Louisa Jane	HAGAN, Henry	JUL 03 1854
PATTERSON, Lucinda	HESS, Jacob	FEB 19 1839
PATTERSON, Margaret	WILLIAMS, Wm.	OCT 16 1830
PATTERSON, Margaret Ann	MESTAYER, Charles J.	APR 04 1853
PATTERSON, Mary	PENDER, John	NOV 20 1824
PATTERSON, Mary Jane	UPTON, William H.	SEP 30 1856
PATTERSON, Sarah A.	ALLEN, John C.	JUN 23 1854
PATTERSON, Sarah Ann	BYRNE, Patrick	OCT 29 1840
PATTERSON, T. Harman	WAINWRIGHT, Maria M.	JAN 04 1847
PATTERSON, Thomas	WILLIAMS, Elizabeth	FEB 10 1813
PATTERSON, Thomas	PRIME, Elizabeth	JUL 19 1833
PATTERSON, William	JOHNS, Catherine	DEC 10 1827
PATTERSON, William	WARNER, Amelia	JAN 31 1855
PATTERSON, William G.	CHAPMAN, Selena Ann	APR 29 1835
PATTIE, Jinnia	HOLMS, John Henry	MAR 05 1853
PATTISON, Thomas	WEBSTER, Serafina C.	JUN 28 1850
PATTON, Ann	LONG, Jacob Frederick	JUL 31 1841
PATTON, Catharine	GRIFFITH, Thomas	OCT 28 1829
PATTON, Catharine E.	PHILLIPS, John J.	AUG 09 1842
PATTON, Ellenor T.	HAUSCH, Christian	AUG 20 1850
PATTON, James A.	RUNNELLS, Jane R.	APR 27 1840
PATTON, Lewis	FLINN, Rebecca	NOV 08 1831
PATTON, Sarah M.	HARPER, William	MAR 09 1841
PATTON, Thomas H.	TAYLER, Lydia E.	JUN 16 1832
PATTON, William	GAI, Ann Jane	FEB 01 1842
PATTON, William	SINCOX, Elizabeth	MAY 21 1846
PATTY, Thomas L.	WEBSTER, Sary Ann	MAR 05 1831
PAUL, Alexander H.	DORETT, Mary Ann	AUG 20 1827
PAUL, Delilah	PAUL, Lewis	MAY 13 1816
PAUL, Delilah	POLLACK, Allen	JAN 14 1826
PAUL, Elizabeth	CARR, Benjamin	FEB 05 1840
PAUL, Ellenora	SMITH, Hamilton J.	OCT 03 1844
PAUL, Emeline Catherine	JOHNSTON, Robert	JUL 19 1837
PAUL, Lewis	PAUL, Delilah	MAY 13 1816
PAUL, Samuel B.	PICKRELL, Sophronia W.	MAR 18 1850
PAUL, Susannah Pamelia	O'CONNOR, Patrick P.	JUL 10 1851
PAULDING, Leonard	OFFLEY, Hellen J.	DEC 10 1851
PAULEY, Elizabeth M.	DEEBLE, Edward K.S.	OCT 14 1830
PAULEY, Samuel	POWAL, Ann	NOV 29 1823
PAULIN, Margaret	GUTTENSOHN, John	DEC 12 1844
PAUNAM, Ann (blk)	TILMAN, John	JUN 17 1841
PAWLEY, Andrew	ASHTON, Margaret	DEC 15 1835
PAWLEY, James	PRATHER, Ruth Ann	DEC 05 1835
PAWLEY, Mary Ann	EARTON, John W.	JUL 13 1831
PAXON, Thomas S.	RILEY, Sarah C.	MAR 22 1853
PAXTON, Altha Ann	QUEEN, Elexius	JUN 02 1831
PAXTON, Cassandria	BURROWS, Obadiah	SEP 28 1840

District of Columbia Marriage Licenses, 1811-1858

PAXTON, James	DEAN, Rebecca	FEB 28 1840
PAXTON, John	BARRON, Hannah	SEP 18 1837
PAXTON, Joseph	KING, Susan Lavinia	AUG 01 1848
PAXTON, Mary	DEVINE, Robert M.C.	NOV 18 1848
PAXTON, Rebecca L.	JONES, Warner P.	NOV 29 1854
PAXTON, Sarah McD.	WOLFORD, George W.	AUG 28 1840
PAYN, Jane	McDANIEL, Thomas T.	JAN 25 1834
PAYNE, Adaline	JENKINS, Thomas	JUL 04 1857
PAYNE, Andrew	BEAN, Eleanor	DEC 29 1825
PAYNE, Ann	NELSON, William	DEC 14 1829
PAYNE, Ann	SUMMER, Thomas	JUN 05 1834
PAYNE, Ann	LASKEY, Charles	SEP 17 1840
PAYNE, Ann	HISHLEY, Clement	DEC 21 1854
PAYNE, Ann J.	LONG, James	SEP 17 1850
PAYNE, Anna	CAUSTEN, Dr. James H.	APR 09 1850
PAYNE, Catherine Edney	LEWIS, Thomas	NOV 21 1842
PAYNE, Cecelia	EVANS, John	JUN 23 1840
PAYNE, Charity	ALLEN, Dennis	MAR 20 1817
PAYNE, Charles Henry	RIFFLE, Catharine	AUG 14 1845
PAYNE, Charles W.	DONALDSON, Elizabeth	JUL 25 1844
PAYNE, Clarissa Ellen	APPLEBY, Horatio G.	DEC 04 1855
PAYNE, Cloe A.	FOREMAN, Jos.	MAY 04 1822
PAYNE, Daniel A.	FARRIS, Julia A. (blk)	JAN 05 1847
PAYNE, Delilah (blk)	JONES, Alfred	APR 19 1858
PAYNE, Eliza	BEATTY, Charles F.	MAR 25 1845
PAYNE, Eliza (blk)	BUTLER, Benjamin	APR 10 1850
PAYNE, Elizabeth	PAYNE, Hanson	AUG 25 1846
PAYNE, Elizabeth	CARPENTER, John A.	OCT 31 1856
PAYNE, Elizabeth Ann	LUNSFORD, William	NOV 08 1849
PAYNE, Frances	GALLAHAN, Thomas	DEC 28 1852
PAYNE, Francis	HARDY, Sarah	MAY 27 1818
PAYNE, George A.	TANNAR, Sarah	SEP 17 1840
PAYNE, George W.	BIRNEY, Eliza Jane	AUG 17 1853
PAYNE, Hanson	PAYNE, Elizabeth	AUG 25 1846
PAYNE, Harriet	PAYNE, Robert	SEP 30 1833
PAYNE, Harrit A.	NEWMAN, John Henry	NOV 09 1835
PAYNE, Henry	CHAMBERLAIN, Ann	MAR 25 1837
PAYNE, Henry	SEBASTIAN, Margaret	AUG 23 1844
PAYNE, Henry Fairfax	ALLEN, Martha	DEC 27 1855
PAYNE, Hester (blk)	BROOKS, Alfred	DEC 09 1847
PAYNE, Hezekiah	RIDGEWAY, Sarah E.	SEP 08 1857
PAYNE, James	KIRBY, Eleanor	JUN 26 1815
PAYNE, James	CROWN, Lucretia	JAN 02 1843
PAYNE, James	SEBASTIAN, Emeline	AUG 23 1844
PAYNE, James	NICKLIN, Ann D.	SEP 21 1850
PAYNE, James	WEASNER, Mary C.	JUL 23 1853
PAYNE, James H.	WASHINGTON, Fairinda F.	DEC 11 1848
PAYNE, James W.	JONES, Maria E.	FEB 22 1858
PAYNE, John	SWEENEY, Cecelia	JUL 01 1828
PAYNE, John	JACKSON, Lucy Ann (blk)	MAY 29 1830
PAYNE, John	MASSI, Jane	NOV 01 1832
PAYNE, John H.	BOWMAN, Sophia N.	JAN 14 1836
PAYNE, John H.	WEPTER, Ann Virginia	MAY 15 1851
PAYNE, Joseph	COLLINS, Margaret	MAR 30 1833
PAYNE, Joseph	DORSEY, Elizabeth	DEC 22 1853
PAYNE, Judson	WILKERSON, Catharine	OCT 29 1852
PAYNE, Julia A.T.	SMITH, John F.	FEB 12 1857
PAYNE, Julia Ann	HALL, Washington	JAN 26 1843

District of Columbia Marriage Licenses, 1811-1858

PAYNE, Laura	ELD, Aquila	AUG 11 1843
PAYNE, Lewis	ATHEY, Elizabeth	OCT 09 1833
PAYNE, Lewis	MATTINGLY, Mary Ann	NOV 25 1848
PAYNE, Margaret	BOCKMAN, William	JUL 18 1827
PAYNE, Martha	CAMPBELL, Samuel	JUL 13 1858
PAYNE, Martha A.	KNOTT, John Thomas	OCT 14 1846
PAYNE, Martha E.	THOMPSON, William H.	MAR 16 1852
PAYNE, Martha E.	HUTCHINS, Benedict	SEP 06 1852
PAYNE, Mary	SHOEMAKER, George	NOV 08 1824
PAYNE, Mary	LOVELESS, Samuel H.	SEP 28 1846
PAYNE, Mary C.	COLLINS, James	DEC 12 1836
PAYNE, Oscar	BERRY, Cecelia (blk)	APR 04 1850
PAYNE, Pearson F.	ABBOTT, Mary Anna R.	DEC 23 1854
PAYNE, Rebecca (blk)	COOPER, Lewis	OCT 01 1844
PAYNE, Rice W.	SEMMES, Ann America	JAN 03 1848
PAYNE, Robert	PAYNE, Harriet	SEP 30 1833
PAYNE, Robert	BALDWIN, Martha Elizabeth	FEB 17 1854
PAYNE, Samuel	GIBBS, Mary (blk)	APR 25 1854
PAYNE, Sandford	SPITTLE, Jane	FEB 04 1847
PAYNE, Sarah	BRYANT, William	FEB 24 1858
PAYNE, Sarah Ann	SMITH, John Thomas	DEC 08 1848
PAYNE, Sarah Ann	RILEY, Andrew J.	OCT 24 1854
PAYNE, Susan	BANGS, Samuel	OCT 16 1824
PAYNE, Susan	ROGERS, Libren	MAR 24 1832
PAYNE, Susan	HURDLE, Robert	MAR 16 1843
PAYNE, Susan	ROWZEE, John	MAR 24 1852
PAYNE, Susan Britania	ALLEN, Nathan	JAN 06 1853
PAYNE, Thomas	GRIFFEN, Ellen	MAR 19 1824
PAYNE, Thomas	PORTER, Hannah	JUL 14 1832
PAYNE, Thomas	LEMONED, Claracy Ellen	DEC 06 1842
PAYNE, W.S.	BERRYMAN, C.N.	NOV 23 1857
PAYNE, William	HUGHES, Harriot	MAY 21 1825
PAYNE, William	IVERSON, Ellen	OCT 11 1837
PAYNE, William McManus	QUIGLY, Maria Ann	JUN 30 1852
PAYNE, Wm. Jefferson	THOMAS, Frances Ann (blk)	MAY 08 1851
PAYNE, Zenith	PIERSON, Daniel H.	OCT 09 1839
PAYNTER, Abraham	HENDLEY, Mary	APR 21 1857
PEABODY, John [Capt.]	CATHCART, Amelia H.	JUN 13 1828
PEABODY, Joseph L.	WARD, Ann	OCT 06 1834
PEABODY, Sophila	SMITH, Joseph L.	OCT 29 1823
PEACHEM, Catharine V.	EATON, Alexander W.	APR 26 1858
PEACO, William H.	WELSH, Ruth Ann	DEC 01 1842
PEACOCK, Elijah	ROLLES, Ann	MAR 31 1845
PEACOCK, John	BURR, Sarah B.	MAY 05 1842
PEAK, Catherine	McCATHERINE, James	DEC 12 1848
PEAK, Charity	HOWARD, William	AUG 25 1815
PEAK, Eliza	CLEMENTS, Alban	SEP 12 1823
PEAK, Joannah	MUDD, Sylvester	JUL 20 1854
PEAKE, Eliza Ann	ADAMS, John	DEC 21 1850
PEAKE, Emma L.	RICHARDSON, Marcus	NOV 04 1856
PEAKE, James	CARRICO, Lucretia	MAY 01 1841
PEAKE, James W.	GRIFFIN, Mary Eliza	MAY 07 1849
PEAKE, John	DRURY, Mary	NOV 26 1839
PEAKE, Margaret	O'CONNOR, Maurice H.	DEC 12 1850
PEAKE, Sarah Jane	GAUBERT, John A.	NOV 03 1849
PEAKS, John L.	FAKEY, Catharine	OCT 05 1822
PEALE, Lucinda (blk)	POSEY, William H.	JUN 02 1842
PEALE, Titian R.	McMULLIN, Lucinda	AUG 12 1850

District of Columbia Marriage Licenses, 1811-1858

PEARCE, Elizabeth	MYERS, John	JUN 23 1835
PEARCE, Jane L.	SHECKLES, Theodore, Jr.	JUL 23 1849
PEARCE, John	CARNES, Isabella	JUN 17 1841
PEARCE, John	PEYTON, Martha Frances Virginia	MAY 05 1847
PEARCE, Susanna	HYLE, John	AUG 29 1812
PEARCE, Valentine	BARNES, Mary	DEC 18 1832
PEARL, Martha Ann (blk)	TWINE, Andrew	MAY 14 1850
PEARL, Sarah (blk)	WOOD, Thomas	NOV 29 1842
PEARSON, Ann Maria	FARLEY, John	MAY 15 1838
PEARSON, Bernard	ARNOLD, Ann	DEC 16 1834
PEARSON, Catherine	RIECHLA, John	OCT 29 1844
PEARSON, Edward D.	TODD, Eliza Ann	FEB 21 1845
PEARSON, Eliza W.	PATTERSON, Charles P.	JAN 21 1851
PEARSON, Eliza W.	PATTERSON, Charles P.	JAN 21 1851
PEARSON, Elizabeth	AVERY, James	JUL 11 1837
PEARSON, George	SISSON, Ann	JUN 28 1821
PEARSON, George	RYNOLDS, Ann Eliza	OCT 14 1830
PEARSON, Johanna	PRICE, Thomas C.	AUG 02 1853
PEARSON, John	CARTER, Rachel	JUN 01 1835
PEARSON, John	TORP, Martha	FEB 01 1856
PEARSON, John W.	FOLLIN, Mary Ann	JAN 16 1845
PEARSON, Joseph	WERTHINGTON, Catharine	JAN 18 1821
PEARSON, Josephine	JAY, Peter Augustus	JAN 12 1848
PEARSON, Linny	CHURCH, Joseph	JUL 10 1832
PEARSON, Mary	WALSH, Joseph C.	OCT 20 1835
PEARSON, Mary Ann M.	WILLIS, Joshua	OCT 05 1824
PEARSON, Peter M.	MARTIN, Emma	SEP 25 1834
PEARSON, Sarah	HOOVER, Andrew	MAR 19 1822
PEARSON, Sarah	HASKELL, Jos.	AUG 24 1822
PEARSON, Sarah	TUCKER, Levin	OCT 14 1830
PEARSON, Sarah Ann	COCHRAN, William	AUG 18 1834
PEARSON, Verlinda	WILLIAMS, Alexander	MAY 23 1836
PEARSON, Wm. M.	FOLLIN, Catharine	SEP 20 1823
PEASE, Alfred	LOURY, Milly	JAN 19 1820
PEASE, Betsey	FLETCHER, Noah	DEC 14 1813
PEASE, Miss	HASS, Powea	JAN 29 1834
PEASE, Pamelia A.	STEEL, William C.	MAR 11 1856
PEASNER, John	ARCELL, Barbara	FEB 26 1852
PEASTER, Frederick	WALKER, Mary Jane	JUN 18 1853
PEASTER, Susan	NEWTON, Isaac	SEP 06 1843
PEASTON, Catherine Ann	REYNOLDS, James Thomas	JUL 11 1844
PEASTOR, William	OREM, Alizean	APR 07 1856
PEAT, John	DAVIS, Mary	APR 05 1819
PEATROSS, Samuel D.	SEAY, Angelina W.	OCT 10 1844
PEATTON, Eleanor Ann	MASON, George	JAN 02 1823
PECHIN, Anna Maria E.	HYDE, Moses	OCT 19 1836
PECK, David	FULTZ, Margaret (blk)	FEB 24 1853
PECK, Hellen R.	STUDER, Victor	JAN 10 1856
PECK, Joseph	WALKER, Margaret	MAR 28 1831
PECK, Louisa (blk)	GANT, Armstead	JUN 23 1852
PECK, Luther C.	FLETCHER, Cintha	MAR 02 1839
PECK, Margaret Doreas Virginia	KING, James Andrew	JUN 12 1854
PECK, Sylvia	KESSLER, Peter F.	FEB 08 1854
PECKAM, William H.	RETELLIC, Sarah	JAN 04 1833
PECKHAM, Eliza M.	WADE, Robert P.	APR 21 1845
PECKHAM, Martha	JONES, Thomas	SEP 16 1830
PECKHAM, Mary Stanton	WILSON, William A.	SEP 05 1844
PECKHAM, Sophia R.	REID, Thomas	MAY 21 1844

District of Columbia Marriage Licenses, 1811-1858

PECKHAM, William	LaCIELLE, Sophia	APR 27 1815
PECKWORTH, Margaret	ZIMMERMAN, Henry F.	MAY 11 1841
PEDDECORD, Eleazer	GUMAER, Ann Elizabeth	SEP 16 1844
PEDDICORD, Jeremiah	SPEAKS, Celindra	FEB 12 1850
PEDEGREE, Catharine	BARGELY, Joseph	APR 08 1825
PEDRICK, John C.	FATIO, America	AUG 01 1854
PEEK, Mary	DUITY, Leonard	OCT 20 1818
PEEPLES, Drurilla	MURRAY, John	AUG 05 1818
PEERCE, Ann	FISHER, John	FEB 24 1813
PEERCE, Eleanor	JOY, John	JAN 29 1851
PEERCE, Elizabeth	THOMPSON, Cyrus	DEC 26 1840
PEERCE, Helen C.	BOYD, James L.	FEB 01 1837
PEERCE, Henry	WINDELL, Martha	MAY 13 1813
PEERCE, Isabella	TAYLOE, Alexander	JUN 07 1823
PEERCE, John	JAMISON, Ann	FEB 05 1816
PEERCE, Joseph B.	ROWLS, Mary Ann	MAY 07 1833
PEERCE, Rebecca	TILGHMAN, Henry	JUL 01 1834
PEERSON, Jane	REEVES, William J.	NOV 26 1839
PEGG, Amanda	CHARLTON, Thomas	NOV 10 1842
PEGG, James	McCLELLAND, Maria	FEB 17 1825
PEGG, William	ANDERSON, Ann Maria	JUN 04 1839
PEGNER, Peter	HOFFMAN, Elizabeth	NOV 09 1833
PEIASNER, Jacob	TENLY, Mary E.	SEP 14 1847
PEIPPERT, Catherine C.	SIMONDS, George H.	MAY 22 1858
PEIRCE, Abigal Davidson	SHOEMAKER, David	DEC 29 1815
PEIRCE, George	HYER, Harriet	APR 12 1824
PEIRCE, Hannah	SPEAKMAN, Hayes	MAY 10 1836
PEIRCE, Joseph M.	JONES, Elizabeth	AUG 03 1844
PEIRRE, Jonathan	FRAZIER, Martha (blk)	MAY 10 1852
PEITCHART, Lewis S.	GRIGSLY, Roxannah	OCT 06 1836
PELKINTON, Michael	CONNOR, Sarah	FEB 05 1852
PELLETTI, Mary Ann	KIRK, Thomas A.	DEC 31 1847
PELTER, Sarah Ann Eliza	MENABB, Selathin	APR 10 1817
PELTON, Mary	PRETTYMAN, Thomas G.	OCT 10 1825
PELZ, Fannie	HELLMICH, Joseph	JUL 18 1857
PENCOST, Harriet (blk)	ORR, Henry	DEC 18 1838
PENDEL, S.F.	CLEMENTSON, Sarah A.	DEC 01 1852
PENDER, John	PATTERSON, Mary	NOV 20 1824
PENDLE, Isaac	WATERS, Mary (blk)	JUL 20 1854
PENDLETON, Edward H.	MILLS, Jacqueline Smith	SEP 17 1833
PENDLETON, Elisha Boyd	TUTT, Maria Lucinda	APR 24 1843
PENDLETON, George H.	KEY, Alice	JUN 01 1846
PENDLETON, William Armistead	COXE, Mary	FEB 07 1853
PENDLETON, William S.	WILLOUGHBY, Martha Ann	JUL 18 1856
PENDRED, Samuel	BOHANEN, Ellen	MAY 29 1815
PENDRELL, Saml.	BOHAIMAN, Ann	APR 14 1813
PENDRID, Mary E.	PETTIT, John S.	OCT 11 1833
PENIFIELD, Ann	HILL, John	MAY 24 1834
PENIFILL, Martha A.	CHAKE, Henry H.	FEB 26 1857
PENN, Alexander G.	SCOTT, Elizabeth C.	NOV 06 1852
PENN, Edward	LUCAS, Mary Ann	APR 25 1848
PENN, Edward	MULLIKIN, Elenora	SEP 16 1853
PENN, James A.	MORELAND, Eliza A.	OCT 22 1829
PENN, John	MORGAN, Mary	DEC 08 1821
PENN, John	JAVENS, Matilda	DEC 25 1829
PENN, Mary	PETTIT, William	JUN 02 1831
PENN, Mary	WEBSTER, Samuel	SEP 26 1840
PENN, Mary	KLOTZ, Philip	MAY 12 1858

District of Columbia Marriage Licenses, 1811-1858

PENN, Rachel	WILSON, George	MAY 18 1855
PENN, Rebecca	MAGRUDER, Jesse H.	JUL 09 1825
PENN, Sarah	SULLIVAN, Samuel	JAN 16 1851
PENN, Susannah	DeVAUGHN, John B.	AUG 04 1853
PENN, William	NOON, Matilda D.	MAR 13 1821
PENNIFILL, Leander	HILL, James	JUN 05 1857
PENNIFILL, Mary Jane	SHEPHARD, Harvey C.	MAY 08 1855
PENNINGTON, Alfred	SANDERSON, Elizabeth M.	JUN 02 1858
PENNINGTON, Caleb	SUTTON, Maria L.	DEC 17 1855
PENNINGTON, James	MINCHER, Ann	DEC 28 1814
PENNINGTON, James D.	SUTTON, Mary E.	MAY 14 1853
PENNINGTON, Joseph W.	BRAWNER, Eleanor	MAR 13 1837
PENNINGTON, Louisa	WALKER, William	JUN 23 1842
PENNINGTON, Mary	BURCH, John	DEC 29 1835
PENNINGTON, Saml. C.	DORSEY, Ann E.	JAN 02 1854
PENNY, Catherine	CEPHAS, Thomas	MAY 06 1835
PENNY, Henry	HOWARD, Maria (blk)	MAY 13 1851
PENNY, James	MARTIN, Charlotte E. (blk)	DEC 12 1853
PENNY, Lucinda E. (blk)	ANDERSON, Jefferson	NOV 11 1841
PENNYFIELD, John T.	RIGGLES, Sarah	JUL 14 1857
PENTZ, Samuel J.	GROSH, Sophia Clay	JUL 14 1841
PEPLES, Benjamin	GILL, Dury	AUG 22 1815
PEPPER, Ann	POWERS, Patrick	JAN 19 1856
PERCEL, Hannah	BUCKLEY, James	DEC 29 1820
PERCELL, Eliza	GREEN, Aaron	NOV 01 1843
PEREGOY, Thos. H.	MORRIS, Lydia	APR 30 1836
PERIL, Catharine	JACKSON, Jacob	SEP 03 1818
PERIOT, Noel	PARKER, Catharine	MAY 09 1812
PERKINS, Chas. A.	THOMPSON, Sarah L.	FEB 13 1855
PERKINS, Edmund T.	ADDISON, Mary E.	MAY 13 1848
PERKINS, Elizth. F.	WOOD, George W.	AUG 25 1858
PERKINS, Hector	BROWNING, Ellen	NOV 16 1823
PERKINS, Henry	TAFF, Matilda	DEC 28 1837
PERKINS, Henry	COOK, Jane (blk)	FEB 08 1849
PERKINS, Henry	WALKER, Mahala	FEB 03 1849
PERKINS, Mary Catherine	BROOKE, James C.	JAN 09 1855
PERKINS, Mary E.	ALLEN, Thomas T.	NOV 18 1856
PERKINS, Patsy J.	PIERCE, Joshua B.	JUL 09 1855
PERKINS, Richard	MORGAN, Mary	AUG 06 1850
PERKINS, Robert S.	MOORE, Barbara Ellen	JUN 25 1858
PERKINS, Samuel	WALKER, Martha	FEB 01 1817
PERKINS, Sarah	SMITH, Charles	DEC 22 1818
PERKINS, Sarah Ann	SPEIDEN, William	DEC 23 1850
PERKINS, Thomas	LAWRENCE, Mary Ann	JUN 04 1835
PERKINS, William H.	DYER, Susan	JUL 20 1830
PERMILLION, John	DUCKETT, Jane	SEP 30 1841
PERMILLION, William	JOHNSON, Rosetta	JUL 27 1852
PERPIGNON, Ferdinand	MILLS, Elizabeth	OCT 19 1850
PERREGORY, Joseph C.	BURGER, Mary A.	MAY 30 1850
PERRIE, Catharine M.	HOUCK, John W.	JUL 30 1855
PERRIE, Charles F.	McPHERSON, Mary B.	FEB 19 1855
PERRIE, Elizabeth M.	GRAY, Isaac S.	NOV 08 1855
PERRIE, George A.	PARKER, Hellen	DEC 20 1855
PERRIE, Julia Ann	HURST, William B.	DEC 09 1845
PERRIE, Samuel T.	HERBERT, Mary A.	APR 16 1836
PERRIE, Sophia A.	BAKER, John C.	JUN 15 1847
PERRIE, Susan A.	MILLER, Royall E.	FEB 05 1851
PERRY, Alexander, Jr.	LIGHTFOOT, Elizabeth	DEC 02 1819

District of Columbia Marriage Licenses, 1811-1858

PERRY, Ann R.	McDONNALL, Richard	FEB 08 1838
PERRY, Augustus E.	ROSS, Mary Jane	DEC 26 1844
PERRY, Catharine	WEBSTER, Henry A.	SEP 02 1826
PERRY, Charles	HENDERSON, Sarah	MAR 26 1838
PERRY, Chas. W.	EVANS, Mary A. (blk)	NOV 07 1856
PERRY, Cyrus Eli	SUMMERS, Sarah Ann	JUN 02 1849
PERRY, Danl.	DYSON, Isabella (col'd)	MAY 11 1852
PERRY, David	BARRETT, Rheuhama	NOV 15 1827
PERRY, Elisha	FERGUSON, Susanna	DEC 17 1851
PERRY, Elizabeth	BLACKBURN, William	MAY 19 1831
PERRY, Elizabeth	TALBERT, Tobias F.	NOV 24 1851
PERRY, Emily	ALEXANDER, John	JAN 13 1817
PERRY, James H.	STAIN, Sarah Elizabeth	APR 04 1848
PERRY, Josephus	MILES, Catherine	NOV 20 1854
PERRY, Mary A.	BROWN, Thomas B.	FEB 04 1858
PERRY, Raphael	WELLS, Ann	AUG 31 1849
PERRY, Roger	TAYLOR, Estelle Frances	APR 13 1857
PERRY, Ruth	HOLLIDAY, William L.	APR 26 1833
PERRY, Sarah	EDWARDS, Lewis	OCT 30 1816
PERRY, Stephen	EVERSON, Ann	FEB 01 1817
PERRY, Thomas	YOUNG, Elizabeth (blk)	FEB 22 1849
PERRY, Thomas J.	CRASK, Mary Ann	DEC 26 1855
PERSLEY, Doretha Ann	BUTLER, Richard C.	APR 17 1856
PESNER, Mary Ellen	WARNER, George W.	AUG 24 1848
PETER, America Pinkney	WILLIAMS, Wm. Geo.	JUN 26 1826
PETER, Ann T.	WASHINGTON, George C.	OCT 25 1821
PETER, Britannia W.	KENNON, Capt. Beverley	DEC 05 1842
PETER, Elizabeth	RAMSEY, William [Lieut.]	OCT 15 1822
PETER, George W.	BOYCE, Jane	FEB 04 1840
PETER, Hannah	GOODALL, Thomas	JUL 17 1833
PETER, Jane	BEVERLEY, James B.	MAY 04 1819
PETER, Mary	WARNER, Henry	NOV 26 1833
PETER, Robert	JOHNSON, Roberta	FEB 01 1847
PETERKIN, Joshua	HANSON, Elizabeth Howard	SEP 25 1838
PETERS, Adelaid (blk)	CARTWRIGHT, Joseph W.	FEB 03 1858
PETERS, Caroline	DRAGA, Charles	OCT 12 1857
PETERS, Cecelia Frances	BOARMAN, Francis L.	JAN 24 1854
PETERS, Charles H.	BROWN, Cora L. (blk)	DEC 26 1855
PETERS, Edward	LODGE, Mary	NOV 05 1840
PETERS, Hannretta	GREEN, Archibald R.	MAY 19 1853
PETERS, Hermione C. (col'd)	FLEET, James H.	APR 21 1845
PETERS, James	COLLINS, Elizabeth (blk)	NOV 30 1844
PETERS, Jane	FRENCH, Andrew	AUG 06 1835
PETERS, John	DORSEY, Harriet	SEP 21 1815
PETERS, John	CALVERT, Rebecca (col'd)	SEP 07 1830
PETERS, John	GREY, Selina A.	FEB 15 1855
PETERS, Louisa (blk)	GAREY, Edward E.	MAR 01 1848
PETERS, Lucy	VOSS, Hermann H.	AUG 24 1858
PETERS, Margaret	CANNEN, Boil	APR 18 1820
PETERS, Mary Elizabeth	ROBERTS, John	AUG 03 1854
PETERS, Polena	BROWN, Henry J.	DEC 02 1854
PETERS, Wilhelm	SCHONELL, Louise	DEC 07 1855
PETERS, William	ALLEN, Massa	MAR 04 1823
PETERS, William	RIX, Mary Ann	FEB 23 1830
PETERSON, August Fredk.	CARUSI, Jane D.	JAN 13 1858
PETERSON, Senith	SCHRIVER, William	JUL 10 1848
PETIT, Elizabeth	CARTER, Edward A.	AUG 18 1841
PETIT, Frances E.	SMITH, John Jeremiah M.	JAN 19 1847

District of Columbia Marriage Licenses, 1811-1858

PETIT, John	BAYERS, Mary	MAY 30 1823
PETIT, John	SEVERE, Elizth.	MAY 02 1829
PETIT, John	CARR, Artemesia	FEB 16 1837
PETIT, William F.	SPELLMAN, Elizabeth	APR 28 1853
PETITT, Sarah	BAGGETT, John	OCT 12 1852
PETRAND, F.B.	VANEL, Gertrude M.	APR 24 1837
PETRIE, Ellen A.	HELMER, Joseph W.	APR 26 1856
PETTERS, Anna (blk)	COALKEY, George W.	AUG 18 1845
PETTIBONE, Elizth. W.	SOMMERS, Henry W.	FEB 08 1851
PETTIBONE, William	DIGGS, Jane C.	MAR 21 1841
PETTICORD, Sarah Jane	HUNT, Harvey John	DEC 16 1852
PETTIGREW, Ann [Mrs.]	FRANKLIN, Stephen P.	JAN 22 1827
PETTIGREW, James	SMITH, Ann	NOV 16 1819
PETTIGREW, Theophilus	OTTRIDGE, Catharine	MAY 29 1820
PETTINGELL, Richard	PIERCE, Maria	JUL 27 1816
PETTIS, Charlott	DUDLEY, Charles E.	SEP 01 1856
PETTIS, Sarah Ann	GAUBERT, John A.	NOV 21 1853
PETTIT, Alfred	PETTIT, Verlinder	MAY 16 1845
PETTIT, Ann	KNIGHT, Frederick	DEC 21 1848
PETTIT, Caroline S.E.	BOSS, John P.	NOV 28 1848
PETTIT, Charles	BELMIRE, Eliza C.	SEP 04 1819
PETTIT, Charles W.	CROGGON, Gertrude	DEC 04 1843
PETTIT, Drucilla	FORD, William A.	NOV 16 1848
PETTIT, Edmond	THOMPSON, Julian	JUN 05 1851
PETTIT, George	ALLISON, Elizabeth	JUL 04 1836
PETTIT, George	NELSON, Frances	JAN 13 1852
PETTIT, Harriot	LOYD, William	JUN 30 1825
PETTIT, John	SAVAGE, Hortense V.	NOV 13 1856
PETTIT, John S.	PENDRID, Mary E.	OCT 11 1833
PETTIT, John S.	WOOD, Catharine Ann	JUL 02 1850
PETTIT, John Thomas	KIDWELL, Catharine Virginia	DEC 19 1849
PETTIT, Joseph	PETTIT, Sophia	OCT 13 1853
PETTIT, Kesiah	ROGERS, John Thomas	JUL 03 1843
PETTIT, Martha	GRIMES, Robert	NOV 09 1849
PETTIT, Mary C.	BEACH, Henry	FEB 18 1858
PETTIT, Richard	HERLING, Mary Ann	NOV 30 1826
PETTIT, Sallie E.	ALEXANDER, John	JAN 03 1850
PETTIT, Sarah Ann	SIPLEY, John Henry	SEP 01 1847
PETTIT, Sophia	PETTIT, Joseph	OCT 13 1853
PETTIT, Verlinder	PETTIT, Alfred	MAY 16 1845
PETTIT, William	CONNOLEY, Mary Ann	OCT 14 1819
PETTIT, William	PENN, Mary	JUN 02 1831
PETTIT, William F.	ROBINSON, Frances A.	NOV 13 1846
PETTIT, William G.	MAY, Maria C.	DEC 28 1857
PETTIT, William R.	WOOD, Sarah A.	JAN 31 1853
PETTITT, Mary	GORUM, Richard	JAN 05 1858
PETTY, Beverly	CARPENTER, Catharine	FEB 23 1832
PETTY, Eli	GROVES, Sarah A.	JUN 27 1850
PETTY, John T.	ELMORE, Mary Ann	JAN 07 1856
PETTY, Virginia	MECARTNEY, John B.	OCT 19 1852
PEUGH, Samuel A.	BLANCHARD, Caroline Sarah	DEC 27 1849
PEYTON, Ann E. [Mrs.]	WHITE, Hugh L.	NOV 29 1832
PEYTON, Ellen	STUART, Richard Henry	OCT 21 1833
PEYTON, Lucy F.	WILKINS, John Q.A.	OCT 29 1857
PEYTON, Martha Frances Virginia	PEARCE, John	MAY 05 1847
PEYTON, Mary Elizabeth	TORBERT, James McClyment	AUG 02 1836
PEYTON, Robert Eden [Dr.]	JONES, Harriotte Lee	APR 18 1833
PEYTON, Sarah (blk)	WASHINGTON, Alexander	MAR 02 1841

District of Columbia Marriage Licenses, 1811-1858

PFANZ, Adam	SCHOEDER, Sibilla	NOV 28 1853
PFAU, John F.	KRUSMANN, Rosina	NOV 16 1855
PFEIFER, John	HEISS, Leanna	MAR 31 1851
PFEIFER, John C.	STESSE, Babet	JUL 08 1857
PFERERING, Gertrud	PILLARZ, William	AUG 30 1858
PFISTER, Maria Magdalena	STEPPER, George Martin	MAR 05 1827
PFLINGER, Jacob	MANLIN, Emily	OCT 16 1856
PFLUGER, Ludwig	HORN, Barbary	MAR 29 1853
PHALAN, Julia	DRISTALL, William	NOV 22 1852
PHALEN, Patrick	CONROY, Ellen T.	JUL 11 1848
PHEARSON, Jos. N.	McPHERSON, Mary Ann	JUL 19 1821
PHEASTER, Obadiah	CHANDLER, Mary Ann	FEB 06 1845
PHEASTER, Obadiah	CHANDLER, Mary Ann	FEB 04 1845
PHEBIAN, Harriot	BENDER, Jacob A.	FEB 25 1819
PHELAN, A.J.F.	MITCHELL, Harriot G.	SEP 25 1856
PHELAN, Elizabeth	BURROWS, John	JUL 15 1843
PHELAN, Ellen T.	BRADLEY, Ambrose	MAY 02 1857
PHELAN, Margaret A.	ROSS, William L.	OCT 04 1850
PHELAN, Martin	RIGGEN, Rachel C.	SEP 24 1842
PHELAN, Nicholas	CLARKE, Martha Ann	APR 14 1853
PHELEN, Bridget	LONG, James	FEB 16 1853
PHELPS, Ezra	DOYLE, Ann	SEP 24 1828
PHELPS, George	CARROLL, Julia	MAY 17 1849
PHELPS, George W.	FLARITY, Mary	NOV 11 1833
PHELPS, James E.	SHACKELFORD, Mary C.R.	MAY 22 1854
PHELPS, John T.	KIDWELL, Sarah Elizabeth	FEB 06 1851
PHELPS, Margaret A.	BROOKS, John H.	SEP 24 1855
PHELPS, Mary E.	GIDDINGS, Dominick	JAN 26 1855
PHELPS, S. Ledyard	MAYNADIER, Eliza	SEP 30 1853
PHELPS, Sarah	SIMONDS, Stephen	AUG 13 1831
PHELPS, Thomas	WALKER, Sarah	MAY 27 1846
PHENEY, William	ROAN, Ann	APR 01 1837
PHERSON, Sarah	MEEK, James E.	DEC 23 1830
PHETHEAN, Esther	HUNTT, Wm.	AUG 04 1814
PHILIPPS, Margaret	FISHER, Charles	OCT 26 1820
PHILIPS, Betsey	CARMICHAEL, Edward	MAY 01 1817
PHILIPS, Elizabeth	ABBOTT, Joseph	APR 27 1825
PHILIPS, George	JAVENS, Ann	JUL 06 1849
PHILIPS, Isaac	BEACH, Susan	FEB 01 1818
PHILIPS, Isabella	BARTHCOLON, J. Presley	FEB 13 1856
PHILIPS, James	HELMS, Rebecca	NOV 08 1827
PHILIPS, Jane	LYNCH, James	JUL 24 1841
PHILIPS, Mary	McCRACKAN, John	MAY 11 1816
PHILIPS, Sarah	ESSEX, Josias	OCT 07 1823
PHILIPS, Susannah P.	SANDS, Saml. B.	JAN 03 1828
PHILIPS, Teresa Ann	SPENCE, James	NOV 14 1827
PHILLIPS, Ann	VERNON, Fairfax F.	MAR 22 1845
PHILLIPS, Catharine Ann	MURRAY, Levy	JUN 17 1833
PHILLIPS, Charles Fenton Mercer	HOLTZMAN, Mary E.	JAN 08 1852
PHILLIPS, David S.	FAGAN, Mary	JUN 03 1840
PHILLIPS, Edmund	CONNOR, Lucinda L.	JAN 30 1854
PHILLIPS, Eliza	APPLEGATE, John C.	NOV 22 1841
PHILLIPS, Elizabeth	DARBY, Edward	OCT 17 1833
PHILLIPS, Elizabeth	LACOCK, William	FEB 05 1853
PHILLIPS, Elizabeth Ann	CROWLEY, Patrick	JUN 06 1833
PHILLIPS, Ellen Amelia	BOTELER, B.W.	OCT 17 1846
PHILLIPS, Emiline	DEALE, Wm. G.	JUN 20 1855
PHILLIPS, George	HUTCHISON, Margaret	JUN 18 1856

District of Columbia Marriage Licenses, 1811-1858

PHILLIPS, George W.	BLAGDEN, Emily W.	MAY 07 1836
PHILLIPS, George W.	KRULLER, Susan V.	JUN 12 1837
PHILLIPS, George William	BLAGDEN, Mary Anne	JUN 12 1845
PHILLIPS, Horatio H.	TATE, Lydia Ann	AUG 14 1840
PHILLIPS, James B.	VEITCH, Mary C.	APR 15 1830
PHILLIPS, Jane Eliza	WRIGHT, George H.	JUN 24 1844
PHILLIPS, Jannett B.	SMALLWOOD, Enoch W.	JAN 04 1830
PHILLIPS, John	KING, Hannah	JUN 03 1830
PHILLIPS, John H.	HOLMEAD, Emeline W.	OCT 19 1846
PHILLIPS, John J.	PATTON, Catharine	AUG 09 1842
PHILLIPS, Johnathan	BEALL, Henrietta	APR 29 1823
PHILLIPS, Lancelot	BUMPASS, Ann N.	NOV 07 1833
PHILLIPS, Mary A.J.	MOORE, Lewis	FEB 27 1847
PHILLIPS, Mary Eliza	YERBY, George W.	AUG 26 1851
PHILLIPS, Matilda	HALL, Richard	MAY 29 1828
PHILLIPS, Moses	MATTHEWS, Mary	FEB 05 1816
PHILLIPS, Nannie	GARRET, Powhatan J.	SEP 23 1857
PHILLIPS, Roannah E.	WALKER, John H.	MAY 28 1851
PHILLIPS, Samuel	BERRY, Susan	FEB 21 1831
PHILLIPS, Samuel	BURROWS, Margaret	SEP 14 1847
PHILLIPS, Samuel	FRENCH, Ann	DEC 28 1850
PHILLIPS, Samuel H.	RITTER, Amelia A.	JUL 21 1853
PHILLIPS, Sarah	WILSON, Thomas N.	MAY 25 1815
PHILLIPS, Sarah M.	EVANS, Joseph T.	OCT 28 1854
PHILLIPS, Susannah E.	VanTYNE, Jacob S.	JAN 16 1845
PHILLIPS, Thomas	FALLON, Mary	APR 28 1856
PHILLIPS, Thomas B.	GATES, Mary R.	JUL 25 1848
PHILLIPS, William	HOOT, Mary Ann	OCT 09 1826
PHILLIPS, William	SOUTHARD, Harriet	AUG 04 1841
PHILLIPS, William Henry	COLE, Elizabeth	JUN 20 1848
PHILLIPS, Wm. H.	HARRINGTON, Isabella	APR 25 1849
PHILPOTT, Leonard E.	LEONARD, Angenline	FEB 22 1834
PHILVORTH, Jane	KINNEY, Jeremiah	SEP 05 1844
PHIPPS, John	CURSEY, Sarah	NOV 14 1843
PHIPPS, William C.	MAY, Mary E.	FEB 08 1842
PIBSON, Samuel	JENKINS, Lidy	NOV 30 1833
PIC, John	ANDREWS, Julia Ann	DEC 06 1824
PIC, Margaret Frances	KRAUSE, Charles A.	AUG 02 1855
PICKERELL, Eleanor	BURCH, Remigins	FEB 14 1816
PICKERING, John	DUCKWORTH, Elizabeth	SEP 14 1837
PICKETT, Catherine Jane	HINTON, George	NOV 21 1839
PICKETT, John T.	KEYWORTH, Kate	OCT 17 1853
PICKETT, Mary	ASHBY, John	JAN 30 1827
PICKETT, Mason	SHECKELS, Mary	DEC 26 1820
PICKFORD, Margaret Ann	SAUVAN, Robert	MAY 05 1856
PICKRELL, Alethea	McNEW, Jeremiah	MAR 26 1829
PICKRELL, Angelina	WALKER, John M.	NOV 23 1836
PICKRELL, Ann	SIMPSON, Josias	DEC 07 1816
PICKRELL, Ann W.	THORNE, John S.E.	JUN 12 1849
PICKRELL, Benjamin	HOWARD, Emily	AUG 23 1850
PICKRELL, Caroline Saloma	RISQUE, Ferdinand W.	OCT 12 1846
PICKRELL, Catharine	OWRAN, Elijah	NOV 20 1823
PICKRELL, Elizabeth	COAL, William	APR 24 1832
PICKRELL, Josias	COOMBS, Sally	NOV 10 1842
PICKRELL, Mary	WHITNEY, Jered	MAR 12 1818
PICKRELL, Rebecca	GRIFFIN, Thomas B.	NOV 07 1849
PICKRELL, Samuel	MURRAY, Araminta	AUG 30 1832
PICKRELL, Sarah L.	HARDY, Edward T.	JAN 17 1849

District of Columbia Marriage Licenses, 1811-1858

PICKRELL, Sophronia W.	PAUL, Samuel B.	MAR 18 1850
PIEARCE, Sarah Ann	WHITEMORE, H.O.	DEC 08 1823
PIENE, William	DANDRIDGE, Virginia (blk)	SEP 26 1848
PIER, Louisa (blk)	VALENTINE, William	MAR 19 1845
PIERCE, Ann	DAWES, Edward	JUL 22 1815
PIERCE, Ann	LAVEZZI, John Baptist	MAY 21 1846
PIERCE, Anna L.	MURPHY, Wm. C.	NOV 22 1855
PIERCE, Daniel	TAYLOR, Mary Ann	AUG 19 1819
PIERCE, Emeline	BISHOP, William G.	JAN 03 1851
PIERCE, Henrietta	HERRIN, William	NOV 05 1838
PIERCE, Iran	BARNES, Anne	OCT 07 1820
PIERCE, John	GLOVER, Elizabeth	JUL 19 1825
PIERCE, John	MAY, Martha Ann	FEB 28 1843
PIERCE, John	WARD, Mary E.	MAY 29 1854
PIERCE, John R.	DOWNES, Elizabeth H.	SEP 12 1848
PIERCE, John T.	HOWARD, Ann	FEB 14 1843
PIERCE, Joshua B.	PERKINS, Patsy J.	JUL 09 1855
PIERCE, Maria	PETTINGELL, Richard	JUL 27 1816
PIERCE, Martha	STREEKS, John F.	MAY 04 1854
PIERCE, Mary Ann	NAPE, Thomas William	FEB 11 1851
PIERCE, Rachel	COLLINGWOOD, Andrew	MAY 06 1822
PIERCE, Richard	CANTER, Mary	AUG 31 1841
PIERCE, Samuel	FERREE, Mary Ann	SEP 17 1829
PIERCE, Susan	WINSOR, Luke	SEP 15 1834
PIERCE, Susannah	CARMICHAEL, Alexander	MAY 02 1826
PIERCE, Susannah	WARD, Edward	FEB 01 1840
PIERCE, Thomas	McPHERSON, Elizabeth	MAY 27 1824
PIERCE, Thomas	ALLEN, Charity Ann	OCT 02 1854
PIERCE, Valinda	CLARKE, Edward	JAN 15 1839
PIERCE, William C.	VALDINAR, Louisa	APR 18 1829
PIERCEY, Eve	KNOWLES, William	JUN 20 1820
PIERCY, Catharine M.K.	VENABLE, George W.	MAR 09 1826
PIERCY, Matilda	SMOOT, John H.	OCT 07 1819
PIERRE, Jean	SEMPETZ, Marie	MAR 18 1819
PIERSON, Daniel H.	PAYNE, Zenith	OCT 09 1839
PIETOCH, Catherine B.	KOOFF, John C.	MAR 09 1839
PIEWILL, Elizabeth	BROWN, Thomas	APR 21 1836
PIFER, Joseph W.	ROLLINS, Sarah Jane	FEB 28 1849
PIGGEE, Nancy (blk)	MULLIN, Basil	MAY 17 1831
PIGGETT, Mason	MEDKEFF, Rebecca	NOV 27 1823
PIGGOTT, Ann Rebecca	HUMPHRIES, Guy C.	MAY 01 1849
PIGGOTT, Margaret E.	THORN, Owen	JUL 23 1857
PIGGOTT, Mary E.	GRANT, Talburt M.	MAY 13 1844
PIGOT, John	DENHAM, Mary Ann	AUG 15 1842
PIKE, Ann	FAULKNER, Michael	DEC 19 1820
PILCHER, Catharine	SIDEBOTTOM, William	JUL 22 1831
PILCHER, Clara	LANEHART, John	MAY 13 1843
PILCHER, Lewis	RILEY, Chloe	JUL 05 1834
PILE, Conrad	PILE, Elizabeth	SEP 24 1846
PILE, Elizabeth	PILE, Conrad	SEP 24 1846
PILES, Benjamin	HAYSLUP, Mary Ann	SEP 24 1834
PILES, Charles	CARROLL, Sarah Ann	DEC 12 1820
PILES, Charlotte M.	ALLEN, William	FEB 24 1846
PILES, Delila	LEE, Daniel	OCT 24 1837
PILES, Eleanor	BARBER, Clement	OCT 03 1816
PILES, Eliza	LANHAM, Hanson	DEC 17 1833
PILES, Francis	HUTCHINSON, Valinda	JUN 09 1818
PILES, Francis B.	LINNINGS, Catherine Oleania	NOV 12 1857

District of Columbia Marriage Licenses, 1811-1858

PILES, George W.	SWANN, Charlott Ann	DEC 30 1830
PILES, Julius H.	SANSBURY, Harriet	JUL 02 1851
PILES, Leonard	REED, Mary	APR 28 1818
PILES, Leonard	HURLEY, Delilah	OCT 14 1823
PILES, Matilda	CROSS, Newman	SEP 30 1834
PILES, Philip S.	DORSEY, Lucinda	SEP 01 1853
PILES, Sarah	WILLIAMS, Wm. F.	JAN 06 1851
PILES, Thomas E.	ALLEN, Rachel E.	JUL 28 1842
PILES, William	THORN, Milly	JAN 16 1821
PILES, William H.	DEZEL, Eliza Ann	SEP 24 1846
PILLA, John	GAULICH, Elizabeth	MAY 16 1855
PILLARZ, William	PFERERING, Gertrud	AUG 30 1858
PILLING, Caroline	BALDIN, George	JUN 30 1842
PILLING, Susanna	SHURMAN, James	FEB 01 1855
PILLINGS, James	DALTON, Mrs. D.	OCT 26 1839
PILSBURY, Elizabeth	TYLER, William	APR 20 1819
PINCH, John	SCOTT, Ann	JUN 08 1821
PINDEN, Eugenia L.	INGRAHAM, George H.	NOV 27 1856
PINDERGAST, Bridget	GLEESON, Patrick	NOV 30 1852
PINDLE, Caroline (blk)	LEE, William	OCT 18 1851
PINDLE, Thomas H.	KING, Hannah A. (blk)	SEP 17 1855
PINGLE, William H.M.	FREE, Elizabeth	SEP 30 1843
PINK, Corleria Ann	OSTRANDER, George G.	OCT 05 1850
PINKERTON, Hugh	BROWN, Mary E.	OCT 01 1857
PIOCOWSKI, Vincent	ROBERTSON, Eliza A.	SEP 07 1857
PIPER, Henley	HICKMAN, Emma A.	MAR 02 1857
PIPER, James E.	WHITING, Ann E. (blk)	SEP 30 1851
PIPER, John R., M.D.	CHESHIRE, Mary	NOV 06 1845
PIPER, Sarah Ann (blk)	LANDRIE, William H.	MAY 26 1851
PIREZYNSKI, Andrew	ROACH, Margaret	NOV 16 1857
PIRKINS, John	REILY, Ann	AUG 27 1821
PITCHER, George N.	TERRILL, Jane N.	OCT 28 1821
PITCHER, Laura V.	DOUGLASS, Albert P.	FEB 04 1858
PITHON, Marius Michael	GOUTIER, Caroline	JUN 30 1824
PITMAN, William	McCULLEN, Alsey	OCT 10 1812
PITT, Elizabeth	JOHNSON, Joseph	JUN 04 1838
PITTARD, Jabez	STORY, Deborah Ann	MAR 10 1851
PITTS, Laura	MILLS, Thomas M.	MAR 23 1853
PITTS, Mary Ann	RIGGLES, Thomas	DEC 21 1835
PITZER, Jeremiah K.	DERRICK, Lucretia H.	APR 21 1858
PLACE, George	JOHNSTON, Mary	APR 10 1815
PLAIN, George	JOHNSON, Catherine Ann	JAN 30 1841
PLANT, Gracey	BOWEN, Artemus	SEP 23 1817
PLANT, Hannah Ann	CHAPPELL, Emmert T.	MAR 13 1851
PLANT, Harriet (blk)	RHODES, Henry	SEP 21 1848
PLANT, James K.	WEST, Mary	AUG 02 1834
PLANT, James W.	COX, Julia Ann	NOV 04 1847
PLANT, John	WAY, Adeline	DEC 15 1834
PLANT, John	STRELEECK, Martha	OCT 26 1837
PLANT, Mary	SEITZ, George	JAN 29 1839
PLANT, Mary Casandas	EVANS, John	JUN 04 1835
PLANT, Mary E.	GREINER, Joseph	JUN 12 1837
PLANT, Pascal	BLISH, Mary	JUL 08 1858
PLANT, Sarah A.	SCHNIDER, Nicholas	JUN 18 1846
PLANT, Sarah Ann	HAYE, Henry	SEP 28 1819
PLANT, Susannah	TURTON, James	MAY 04 1829
PLANTT, George H.	GOINGS, Eliza	JUL 06 1837
PLANTT, Henrietta	MOULDING, Enoch	JUL 06 1837

District of Columbia Marriage Licenses, 1811-1858

PLANTT, Mary C.	EVANS, Hetely D.	JUN 04 1835
PLANTT, Sarah Ann (blk)	SMITH, James	JAN 26 1837
PLATE, Adolphus Fred.	KOONTZ, Margaret	JUL 11 1813
PLATER, James L. [Capt.]	STULL, Anna W.B.	SEP 10 1828
PLATER, Mary	LEE, Alexander	OCT 22 1856
PLATER, Rebecca	WELFORD, Horace [Dr.]	SEP 23 1822
PLATER, Sophia	PROCTOR, Joseph	DEC 17 1814
PLATT, S.H.	LEWIS, J.R.	MAR 05 1850
PLA[torn out], Mary Ann	SCREGGS, Thomas	DEC 05 1857
PLEASANTS, Ann Catharine	NOBLE, Mason [Rev.]	AUG 31 1836
PLEASANTS, Henry	POSEY, Frances	OCT 24 1843
PLEASANTS, James B.	SMOOT, Rosa S.	JUL 02 1845
PLEASANTS, Thos. L.	WHITE, Martha A.	OCT 25 1854
PLEASANTS, William H.	SMOOT, Araminta E.	NOV 02 1852
PLEASONTON, Hannah	McCORMICK, Andw. Thos. [Rev.]	JUL 20 1813
PLEASONTON, Mary M.	WATMOUGH, John G.	NOV 15 1832
PLENTY, Robert	LYONS, Treacy (blk)	SEP 30 1847
PLFAEGER, Jacob	BACH, Barbara	NOV 13 1854
PLISH, Dorothy	KRUST, George	JUN 29 1842
PLOECHER, Louisa	OCKERT, August Louis	JUN 24 1858
PLOWMAN, Catherine	BEALL, Beverly W.	JAN 18 1844
PLOWMAN, Marian Louisa	WILSON, George Gideon	DEC 31 1851
PLOWMAN, Thomas	WILSON, Margaret	OCT 15 1855
PLUGGE, Frederick	BRINKMANN, Caroline	JUN 02 1857
PLUMER, Mary G.	SEAVER, Jonathan	JUN 04 1823
PLUMMER, Adam	SANDERS, Emily (blk)	MAY 30 1841
PLUMMER, Fielder B.	COMBS, Mary L.	OCT 14 1839
PLUMMER, Henry W.	SMITH, Sarah Ann (blk)	OCT 25 1849
PLUMMER, Rachel S.	LANCASTER, Morris [Dr.]	MAR 11 1829
PLUMMER, Richard	WEDGE, Mary Eleanor	OCT 23 1830
PLUMMER, Richard	BUTLER, Anne (blk)	DEC 20 1841
PLUMMER, Richard	ANDERSON, Louisa (blk)	SEP 08 1846
PLUMMER, Robert	BELT, Stattire	JUN 11 1829
PLUMMER, Samuel	TALBOT, Lucy Dent	JUL 22 1817
PLUMSILL, Stephen B.	RODGERS, Jane H.	OCT 18 1853
PLUMSILL, Thomas P.	LANHAM, Eliza	MAY 16 1826
PLUNKETT, Jane	TAYLOR, Henry R.	NOV 17 1829
PLUNKETT, John	KENNER, Maria	OCT 18 1845
PLUNKITT, Mary J.	CULLEY, James W.	NOV 19 1846
PLUNKITT, Mary J.	CULLEY, James W.	OCT 19 1846
POARTCH, Mary Ann	WREN, Achilles A.	OCT 29 1838
POE, Caroline S.	DeBOW, J.D.B.	AUG 05 1854
POE, Maria	DENNY, William Henry	JAN 13 1854
POE, Sidney A.H.	STRATTON, Harriet N.	MAY 28 1850
POEHLMANN, Margaretha	BARTHEL, John	MAY 26 1857
POINDEXTER, George [Sen.]	HEWES, Ann	MAY 14 1832
POINDEXTER, Rufinia J.	SLATER, Melvill M.	SEP 26 1854
POITIAUX, Benjamin Eugene	NOYES, Emeline	NOV 17 1852
POLAND, Mary Ann	BUCKLEY, Alexander W.	JAN 12 1849
POLENFORD, Eveline	DOUGHERTY, Nathaniel	MAR 25 1819
POLETTI, John A.	PRINDLE, Adalade	DEC 17 1857
POLETTO, Joseph	HUNTRE, Ann	MAR 04 1826
POLINS, John	CROSS, Harriet	DEC 19 1827
POLIZZI, Angelina Rosalier	KING, Martin	NOV 20 1827
POLK, Jane (blk)	STEWART, Charles	MAY 30 1857
POLK, Joseph G.	GILMAN, Imogene	OCT 03 1836
POLK, Lucious J.	EASTON, Mary A.	APR 10 1832
POLK, Samuel C.	WARRING, Catharine	SEP 29 1849

District of Columbia Marriage Licenses, 1811-1858

POLKINHORN, Charles	HUTTON, Hannah	SEP 03 1822
POLKINHORN, Charles	CHAFFINCH, Sally	DEC 07 1826
POLKINHORN, Georgiana C.	BIRD, John H.	SEP 24 1855
POLKINHORN, Henry	BROWN, Mary Ann	JAN 27 1839
POLKINHORN, Rebecca	WOODWARD, George T.	APR 24 1856
POLKINHORN, Richard	THOMPSON, Hannah M.	OCT 29 1855
POLKINHORN, Richard W.	STEPHENSON, Jane	JUN 21 1831
POLKINHORN, Sarah Jane	MORGAN, John Bennett	JUN 03 1837
POLLACK, Allen	PAUL, Delilah	JAN 14 1826
POLLARD, Alfred	MILSTON, Frances	DEC 02 1833
POLLARD, Edward J.	DORRETT, Ellen	FEB 24 1840
POLLARD, Robert	DANDRIDGE, Sophia (blk)	OCT 02 1850
POLLEY, Bridget	BARRETT, Michael	JUN 12 1858
POLLEY, John W.	THOMAS, Eliz'th. A.	JUN 03 1858
POLLOCK, Emily M.	SMOOT, Charles B.	AUG 19 1833
POLLOCK, Mary	WALKER, William	SEP 17 1828
POLLOCK, Mary Ann	POTTER, Stephen	JUL 02 1817
POLLUCK, Orbellonia	SCHNEIDER, Joseph Lee	SEP 23 1848
POLLY, Margaret	DOYLE, Thomas	MAR 19 1844
POLTON, William	COMPTON, Rosa	JAN 01 1839
POMERELL, Ann	NALLS, Thomas P.	JUN 18 1833
POMEROY, George P.	WILSON, Mary C.	MAR 17 1842
POMEROY, Mary E.	HOLTZMAN, John M.	NOV 13 1856
POMNIETYZKY, Adelbert	McALWEE, Sarah A.	MAY 20 1850
PONS, Julia J.	LAWRENCE, Joseph H.	MAY 17 1858
POOL, Ann Jane	BROWN, Charles	JUN 22 1847
POOL, James	HARDING, Maria	SEP 07 1852
POOL, John W.	TABER, Lucy Ann	NOV 08 1853
POOL, Julia E.	KENNEDY, John P.	APR 22 1858
POOL, Levi	COLLIN, Susan	MAR 07 1823
POOL, Lewis	GRYMES, Ceathy	OCT 21 1813
POOL, Mary	RHYAN, John	FEB 11 1841
POOL, Sarah Jane	HORSMAN, William H.	MAY 04 1855
POOL, Warner	STRAWDER, Satah Ann	JAN 04 1851
POOLE, Anna Maria	FOSTER, James H.	MAR 17 1851
POOLE, Hanson	BIXTER, Julia Elizabeth	SEP 30 1836
POOLE, Jesse	ANCHERS, Nancy	OCT 09 1833
POOLE, Lewis H.	JONES, Elizabeth Ann	JUN 14 1849
POOLE, Marshall	LAWSON, Dorcas	AUG 05 1828
POOLE, Mary Cecelia	MORLL, David P.	FEB 27 1849
POOLE, Rachel	GORMLEY, Richard	AUG 17 1858
POOLE, Sarah	COLLINS, Richard	AUG 12 1858
POOLE, Susan	MANKINS, Washington	FEB 08 1848
POOLEY, Thomas	MAGUIRE, Mary Ann	OCT 13 1825
POOLEY, Thomas	CHAMBERLAIN, Margaret	JUN 21 1828
POOR, Charlotte A.	WEBB, John F.	SEP 05 1822
POOR, Elizabeth I.	FLETCHER, Arthur W.	DEC 29 1847
POOR, Ellen F.	WOODHULL, Maxwell	DEC 12 1842
POOR, Francis	PAINE, Mary Ellen	JAN 03 1845
POOR, Frederick	POOR, Mary Ann	SEP 29 1827
POOR, Frederick	HOYLE, Elizabeth	APR 10 1845
POOR, John	CLARKE, Jane	DEC 18 1817
POOR, John	BOOTHE, Sarah	FEB 10 1836
POOR, John	CAMPBELL, Rebecca	APR 24 1855
POOR, John F.	BARNES, Harriet Ann	APR 05 1853
POOR, Margaret	CROWN, John	JUN 04 1833
POOR, Mary Ann	POOR, Frederick	SEP 29 1827
POOR, Mary W.	FOWLER, Chs. S.	SEP 05 1822

District of Columbia Marriage Licenses, 1811-1858

POOR, Nathaniel P.	LENOX, Elizabeth	SEP 24 1822
POOR, Susan	KENGLEY, Lewis	JUN 28 1830
POOR, Tereser	DUVALL, Rector	DEC 19 1820
POOR, William A.	SANFORD, Amelia	DEC 31 1857
POORE, Benjamin P.	DODGE, Virginia	JUN 11 1849
POORE, Mary	COLLINS, George	FEB 01 1845
POPE, Elizabeth	MARTELLE, John T.	JUN 08 1837
POPE, Frances S.	WEST, Walter S.	JUN 25 1856
POPE, Frederick	CRAWFORD, Jane G.	APR 04 1817
POPE, Frederick	GOSS, Mary	MAY 18 1844
POPE, John	HURLEY, Elizabeth	NOV 20 1816
POPE, Mary	ARMSTEAD, Samuel	NOV 26 1842
POPER, Nathaniel	ST. CLAIR, Sarah	FEB 05 1812
POPKINS, John	ALLEN, Ann	FEB 11 1836
POPKINS, Mary Catherine	CROWN, William	APR 11 1855
PORES, Antonio	BENZETTE, Brittania	MAY 11 1858
PORTER, Augusta E.M.	McKIM, John	DEC 31 1814
PORTER, Bolton S.	LINDSLEY, Mary Ann	JAN 28 1852
PORTER, Daniel Parker	MADDEN, Elizabeth R.	JUN 09 1834
PORTER, David	GOLDSMITH, Mary Jane	JUN 29 1843
PORTER, David	HARRIS, Isabella	MAY 15 1852
PORTER, David D.	PATTERSON, Georgean	MAR 12 1839
PORTER, Edward Leroy	McDONALD, Clara Ann	MAR 24 1852
PORTER, George N.N.	SALLE, Emily	SEP 16 1836
PORTER, Grace	CONINO, Michael	AUG 25 1818
PORTER, Hannah	PAYNE, Thomas	JUL 14 1832
PORTER, Jane	TAYLOR, James	JAN 03 1856
PORTER, John	BOLLISON, Elizabeth	AUG 06 1822
PORTER, John E.	DICK, Sarah V.	JAN 07 1852
PORTER, Margaret	ARMSTRONG, Samuel	JUL 17 1817
PORTER, Mary	HEROLD, Adam G.	SEP 11 1828
PORTER, Mary Elizabeth	LUCKETT, Alexander	FEB 13 1851
PORTER, Mary Elizabeth	O'BRIEN, Thomas M.	FEB 01 1853
PORTER, Normand M.	CLARK, Priscilla	OCT 24 1840
PORTER, Rebecca	MURPHEY, Edward	MAY 09 1837
PORTER, Richard M.	BURDITT, Mary A.	AUG 10 1857
PORTER, Roberta V.	BRADDOCK, William	FEB 28 1843
PORTER, Sarah Amelia	HALE, William B.	JUL 26 1851
PORTER, William D.	BEALE, Elizabeth	FEB 27 1839
PORTLEY, Catharine	FLYNN, Thomas	SEP 21 1855
PORTS, Anne E.	COOMBS, John M.	MAY 24 1856
PORTS, Peregrine	LEWIS, Susanna	JUN 24 1857
PORTTES, Elizabeth M.	SHOEMAKER, Charles E.	MAY 05 1857
POSEY, Benjamin	POSEY, Mary	JUL 17 1838
POSEY, Elizabeth	POSEY, Roger, Jr.	DEC 31 1842
POSEY, Emma Jane (blk)	GWYDER, Richard	APR 03 1856
POSEY, Frances	PLEASANTS, Henry	OCT 24 1843
POSEY, Francis	BRANSUM, Mary Frances	JUN 26 1850
POSEY, George	PULLIN, Sarah	MAY 24 1855
POSEY, James	GATES, Mary	JUN 02 1816
POSEY, James H.	JEFFERSON, Mary E.	SEP 19 1854
POSEY, Lawrence	CORRY, Ann	NOV 24 1856
POSEY, Martha Ann	JACKSON, Lewis Thomas	MAR 25 1856
POSEY, Mary	QUEEN, William	MAY 11 1837
POSEY, Mary	POSEY, Benjamin	JUL 17 1838
POSEY, Mary	GARNER, William	MAY 11 1853
POSEY, Mary A.	HENSON, George	SEP 15 1856
POSEY, Middleton	TRIPLETT, Rebecca	MAY 05 1851

District of Columbia Marriage Licenses, 1811-1858

POSEY, Minty	WOOD, William	SEP 03 1816
POSEY, Richard	STEWART, Sarah	MAY 27 1851
POSEY, Richmond	HENSON, Julia	SEP 20 1832
POSEY, Roger, Jr.	POSEY, Elizabeth	DEC 31 1842
POSEY, William	KINGSBERRY, Mary	DEC 24 1831
POSEY, William H.	PEALE, Lucinda (blk)	JUN 02 1842
POSS, Margaret	WILLNER, George	FEB 03 1841
POSS, Mary	HAWENSCHILL, William	OCT 19 1848
POST, Christian	DISE, George	DEC 12 1832
POSTEN, Eliza	ENNIS, Jno.	MAR 06 1856
POSTON, Eliza	DAVIDSON, John	FEB 23 1858
POSTON, Eliza A.	HACKNEY, Barton	JUN 08 1837
POSTON, Fielder B.	CRAGER, Eliza	APR 17 1817
POSTON, Jane	BUTLER, William Judson	OCT 12 1833
POSTON, John	GARNER, Jane	AUG 29 1839
POSTON, Rahine	HOENSTINE, Frederick	APR 28 1834
POSTON, Robey Harriet	MANKIN, Mathias	FEB 12 1820
POSTON, William	WHALING, Sarah Ann	APR 05 1842
POSY, Thomas	ROLSEY, Mandy Ann	AUG 13 1840
POTE, William	STONEHAM, Elizabeth [Mrs.]	JUL 07 1831
POTTER, Anne Margaretta	STOCKTON, Robert F., Jr.	SEP 07 1852
POTTER, Delilah	ROBINSON, William	SEP 08 1851
POTTER, Eliza	ALEXANDER, Walter B.	FEB 07 1844
POTTER, Elizabeth	JOHNSON, William	DEC 30 1856
POTTER, James	ALLISON, Elizabeth	MAY 20 1824
POTTER, John	CAMPBELL, Ann	SEP 07 1815
POTTER, John	THOMPSON, Sarah Ann	DEC 26 1833
POTTER, John	CRUMP, Susan	MAR 01 1849
POTTER, Mary	POTTS, John	SEP 27 1819
POTTER, Mary E.	ROBINSON, James R.	APR 17 1852
POTTER, Melvina	FENWICK, Francis	MAR 20 1834
POTTER, Richard M.	MANDON, Mary Ann	NOV 23 1843
POTTER, Stephen	POLLOCK, Mary Ann	JUL 02 1817
POTTER, Susan	BAYLY, George N.	JAN 26 1818
POTTER, Thomas L.	OURAND, Alethia F.F.	JAN 03 1848
POTTERS, Mary	BIGLEY, Lawrence	MAY 06 1830
POTTS, Caroline C.	CARTER, Samuel P.	JUL 16 1851
POTTS, David	ADDISON, Mrs. Ann Elizabeth	AUG 27 1858
POTTS, John	POTTER, Mary	SEP 27 1819
POTTS, Mary Eliza	FILLEBROWN, Thomas S.	NOV 04 1856
POTTS, Samuel J.	ROSS, Mary Ann	JAN 28 1817
POULY, Anna	FOLEY, John	MAR 05 1857
POWAL, Ann	PAULEY, Samuel	NOV 29 1823
POWEL, Granvill	BRONOUGH, Jane (blk)	JAN 04 1854
POWELL, Albert	TAYLOR, Mary E. (blk)	SEP 08 1857
POWELL, Alcinda J.	DRISCOLL, Charles M.	MAY 16 1853
POWELL, Amanda P.	TURNLEY, John F.	JAN 12 1858
POWELL, America	GARNETT, George S.	AUG 02 1851
POWELL, Burk	LAWS, Sarah	JUL 16 1819
POWELL, Catharine A.	SNEDEKER, Samuel M.	AUG 11 1853
POWELL, Edward B.	ARMSTRONG, Cordelia S.	NOV 04 1850
POWELL, Granville	EDWARDS, Rosina (blk)	APR 15 1840
POWELL, Hyrum	THOMPSON, Nancy	MAY 06 1817
POWELL, Jackson T.	YOWELL, Mandanna	MAY 14 1832
POWELL, James	DELIHINTIY, Ann Maria	MAY 31 1852
POWELL, Jno.	LEIGH, Nancy	JAN 24 1828
POWELL, John	NEAL, Sarah (blk)	JUL 18 1832
POWELL, John	JONES, Clara (blk)	FEB 09 1833

District of Columbia Marriage Licenses, 1811-1858

POWELL, John	CHASE, Anna (blk)	AUG 24 1840
POWELL, John	WALL, Ellen	JAN 16 1855
POWELL, John D.	HEPBURNE, Annie L.	OCT 04 1854
POWELL, Julia A.	MATTINGLY, Leonard	MAR 13 1815
POWELL, Levin M.	THRUSTON, Jeannette C.	JAN 24 1842
POWELL, Marie	DOWNS, James	JUL 20 1839
POWELL, Mary A.V.	SHAFER, John C.	DEC 01 1849
POWELL, Mary B.	GUNNELL, Arthur	JUL 06 1858
POWELL, Mary Charlotte	MOORE, Wm. Magruder	NOV 11 1853
POWELL, Mary D.	DOWLING, John	FEB 11 1834
POWELL, Mary Elizabeth	VAUGHN, Richard W.	DEC 25 1852
POWELL, Robert J.	WOOD, Almira	APR 13 1841
POWELL, Ruth Armer	BONTZ, William C.	MAY 17 1858
POWELL, Ruthe	SPALDING, Basil	OCT 08 1812
POWELL, Sarah J.	CONRAD, Daniel	APR 05 1848
POWELL, William	RATLIFF, Rebecca	DEC 12 1813
POWELLS, Mary J.	COLCLAZIER, John	OCT 31 1850
POWER, Catherine	O'MARA, Michael	MAY 11 1830
POWER, Elizabeth	COLLINGWOOD, John	MAY 30 1822
POWER, George	HAGAN, Ann	JUN 02 1849
POWER, Jane	CLEMENTSTON, Edward	JUN 17 1844
POWER, John	MINICIMA, Barbara	AUG 01 1846
POWER, John	CUDIHAY, Julia	DEC 02 1854
POWER, John F.	CALHOUN, Amanda M.	FEB 22 1855
POWER, John T.	CALHOUN, Amanda M.	MAR 07 1855
POWER, Joseph	HINCHMAN, Adeline	APR 07 1832
POWER, Mary	KATZENBERGER, John	APR 14 1851
POWER, Monticello	HERSE, Ann	JAN 18 1827
POWER, Sarah	COOK, Martin	NOV 30 1830
POWER, Thomas	FARREL, Susanna	APR 06 1836
POWERS, Amelia (blk)	WILLIAMS, John	OCT 05 1853
POWERS, E.M.	FRAISER, Bella	DEC 02 1857
POWERS, Elizabeth	REEDER, William A.	AUG 19 1830
POWERS, Elizabeth	KING, David	OCT 24 1837
POWERS, Elizabeth	DICKERSON, James	JUL 16 1839
POWERS, Elizabeth	GRAY, Ebenezer	APR 18 1843
POWERS, Elizabeth Ann	ELLIS, Leonard K.	DEC 31 1846
POWERS, Ellen	SALISBURY, John	JUN 03 1833
POWERS, Hester L.	COLCUER, Joseph J.	MAY 20 1856
POWERS, Jacob	DEACANS, Ellen	MAR 19 1844
POWERS, James E.	DAVIS, Elizabeth S.	FEB 24 1840
POWERS, John	HAYES, Catharine	NOV 07 1832
POWERS, Joseph	LAMBERT, Rebecca	NOV 14 1826
POWERS, Louisa	NALLY, John	DEC 28 1824
POWERS, Martin	MUTH, Louisa	OCT 20 1836
POWERS, Matilda	CROOK, Richard	NOV 01 1825
POWERS, Montyseller	HURSE, Ann	AUG 02 1826
POWERS, Patrick	PEPPER, Ann	JAN 19 1856
POWERS, Sophia	TUCKER, William H.	JAN 17 1843
POWERS, Susanna	HOOVER, David	OCT 27 1834
POWERS, Thomas	BADEN, Mary	SEP 08 1840
POWERS, Thomas F.	STEATER, Mary M.	NOV 12 1855
POWERS, William	QUAIDE, Jane	FEB 22 1827
POWERS, William	TRUCKSON, Margaret	APR 29 1829
POWHORN, Ann	RYE, William	JUN 22 1815
POWLISH, Peter	HOLMES, Martha Jane	MAY 19 1847
PRAKER, Bennart	COOK, Mary	MAR 28 1853
PRALL, Wm. Livingston	BUCKNER, Mary F.	JUN 12 1828

District of Columbia Marriage Licenses, 1811-1858

PRATER, William	HARRIS, Elizabeth	FEB 17 1851
PRATHER, Ann Rebecca	CONNER, William	OCT 28 1845
PRATHER, Benjamin A.	PUMPHREY, Mary A.V.	FEB 24 1855
PRATHER, Elizabeth Ann	GRIFFIN, James C.	JAN 15 1850
PRATHER, Emily Jane	OFFUTT, Wm. R.M.	OCT 30 1856
PRATHER, Flavilla	TURNER, Thomas P.	MAY 08 1834
PRATHER, Henry A.	BOTELER, Mary Ann	APR 27 1826
PRATHER, James E.	STINER, Henrietta	JUL 09 1834
PRATHER, Joseph	BELT, Martha	FEB 01 1848
PRATHER, Martha Eugenia	LANE, Joseph	DEC 03 1846
PRATHER, Nancy	MITCHELL, Lilborn	APR 30 1833
PRATHER, Overton J.	CARRICO, Ann E.	FEB 05 1830
PRATHER, Overton J.	BERRY, Mary M.	OCT 24 1834
PRATHER, Ruth Ann	PAWLEY, James	DEC 05 1835
PRATHER, Sarah E.	CHINK, Jesse	JAN 16 1856
PRATLER, Termelia	O'BELL, Edward	DEC 01 1857
PRATT, Cary, Capt.	WILKINSON, Nancy	AUG 11 1827
PRATT, Eliza	SIMS, George	MAY 18 1837
PRATT, Elmira	CANNIGAN, Daniel	SEP 10 1818
PRATT, Henry D.J.	ADDISON, Maria L.	SEP 23 1857
PRATT, Maria	FRANCE, John	JAN 10 1838
PRATT, William D.	LANDON, Rachel	AUG 13 1849
PREANACHER, Margaretta	MOORE, Peter Fellers	OCT 01 1849
PREAVOS, Elizabeth	WILBER, Joel	MAR 20 1821
PRECISE, Logan	SMITH, Catherine	JAN 27 1857
PREINKERT, Conrad	TAVERSCHMIDT, Barbara	DEC 02 1847
PREINKERT, John	SCHULMEN, Charlotte	MAY 16 1857
PRENAT, Virginia I.	McELFRESH, Henry B.	DEC 29 1853
PRENDEBLE, Johanna	HERRON, John	NOV 09 1852
PRENDER, John	NOBLE, Sarah	JUL 03 1850
PRENDER, Margaret H.	KENDRICK, William	OCT 22 1852
PRENDER, Mary Ann	McGEE, Joseph	JUL 28 1853
PRENDERBLE, Catherine	GRANEY, Michael	DEC 06 1852
PRENOT, Charles	BLAIR, Louisa	SEP 21 1840
PRENTISS, Margaret I.	CAMFIELD, Charles	OCT 10 1844
PRENTISS, William	BROWN, Maria	JUN 18 1829
PRENTISS, Wm. H.	STOCKWELL, Sarah	JUL 06 1818
PRENTISS, Wm. H.	COOPER, Sarah Ann	SEP 29 1831
PRESGRAVE, Rebecca	PRESGRAVE, William W.	FEB 15 1838
PRESGRAVE, William W.	PRESGRAVE, Rebecca	FEB 15 1838
PRESGRAVES, Margaret	LONGLEY, Robert	AUG 26 1819
PRESSEY, William	PUMPHREY, Sophia	JAN 08 1824
PRESTON, Adaline	BOYCE, Abraham	JUL 27 1829
PRESTON, Anne E.	McKNIGHT, James M.	DEC 31 1846
PRESTON, Anthony	SIMPSON, Mary	JUN 14 1824
PRESTON, Edward	WAGONER, Christiana	JAN 01 1846
PRESTON, Eliza	KIDWELL, Addison	AUG 08 1833
PRESTON, Julia Ann	WOODSIDE, James D. [Capt.]	JUL 10 1819
PRESTON, Mary	SCHAEFFER, Charles A.	AUG 28 1856
PRESTON, Thomas	GANTT, Lucy	APR 09 1822
PRESTON, Wainwright	CAUGHMAN, Amelia	NOV 20 1846
PRESTON, William	FOWLER, Mary	JUL 14 1823
PRETO, Francis	GRIFFITH, Mary B.	JAN 31 1828
PRETTYMAN, Amelia H.	MOORE, Joseph B.	OCT 20 1852
PRETTYMAN, David G.	FURTNEY, Pricilla	DEC 31 1818
PRETTYMAN, Sarah E.	VEDDER, Isaac D.	FEB 14 1849
PRETTYMAN, Thomas G.	PELTON, Mary	OCT 10 1825
PREUSS, Constantia	REEVE, Samuel	AUG 06 1846

District of Columbia Marriage Licenses, 1811-1858

PREUSS, Frederica Renata	LAMBERTT, David	JUL 19 1841
PREVAUX, John	ESTON, Marian	MAR 13 1827
PREVOTE, Martha	HERFERD, Michael	MAR 06 1821
PRIBRAM, Amilie	WANBERG, Henry	JAN 06 1858
PRIBRAM, Augusta	SAMSTAG, Samuel	AUG 07 1858
PRICE, Augustus	CARROLL, Sarah Ann	APR 08 1837
PRICE, Benjamin F.	UMPHREYS, Mary	SEP 05 1846
PRICE, Benjamina	PAGE, Thomas J.	NOV 08 1838
PRICE, Eleanor	PACO, Joshua	MAR 10 1812
PRICE, Elizabeth	BEACH, Zachariah	JUL 10 1851
PRICE, Geo. E.	BAGGOTT, Hester A.	JUL 06 1858
PRICE, George	ROBINSON, Mary Ann	SEP 01 1831
PRICE, George C.	BASFORD, Mary Jane	JUN 04 1842
PRICE, Hezekiah	NORRIS, Caroline	OCT 27 1828
PRICE, Jehu	FERGUSON, Ann	NOV 10 1835
PRICE, John	STANDISH, Lucy [Mrs.]	DEC 21 1822
PRICE, John A.	HARRISON, Mary E.	OCT 04 1838
PRICE, John E.	LUSBY, Mary Ann	NOV 14 1857
PRICE, John Thomas	FREEMAN, Mary Elizabeth	MAY 03 1849
PRICE, Julianna J.	CHAMBERLAIN, Edward	SEP 22 1828
PRICE, Mary Ann	BEACH, William	JUL 13 1815
PRICE, Mary Ann	BROWN, James	AUG 08 1846
PRICE, Mary Ann	LUTHER, Daniel	DEC 26 1855
PRICE, Mary Elizth. H.	BOUDINOT, Henry Clay	FEB 28 1854
PRICE, Robert	LONG, Eppy	JUL 30 1849
PRICE, Samuel	BULLER, Mary	AUG 24 1847
PRICE, Thomas C.	PEARSON, Johanna	AUG 02 1853
PRICE, Zilla	LAWSON, William	MAY 25 1820
PRICHARD, Hugh F.	MEREDITH, Harriet W.	OCT 04 1845
PRIEST, Catherine	HARDING, Thomas	MAR 30 1857
PRIEST, John	ANDERSON, Ellen Jane	OCT 15 1855
PRIME, Elizabeth	PATTERSON, Thomas	JUL 19 1833
PRIME, Margt. R.	LAWRENCE, Richard J.	AUG 08 1850
PRIME, Mary	DURHAM, Aaron	JAN 19 1837
PRIME, Mary Jane	SOPER, John A.	JAN 24 1846
PRIME, Mary R. (blk)	THOMAS, Thomas F.	DEC 04 1856
PRIME, William J.	BAULWIN, Rebecca	FEB 23 1826
PRIMSLEY, Caroline	NELSON, Hendley	APR 04 1835
PRINCE, Ann	WATSON, James W.	OCT 26 1826
PRINCE, Henry	RICKETTS, Agnes H.	NOV 17 1857
PRINCE, Thomas	TALTY, Mary Ellen	NOV 09 1855
PRINCY, Ann	EVANS, Dudley	APR 23 1814
PRINDEVILL, Mary	BARRET, Michael	FEB 20 1855
PRINDLE, Adalade	POLETTI, John A.	DEC 17 1857
PRINGLE, Ann Rebecca	DELPHEY, Orlando R.	JAN 12 1847
PRINGLE, Ellen F.	THORNTON, Thomas	MAY 05 1858
PRINGLE, Wm. P.	BECK, Ann R.	AUG 17 1839
PRINKMAN, Margaret	HOWARD, Henry	FEB 07 1816
PRINZHORN, Henry	BINNE, Charlott	MAR 09 1855
PRIOR, George	CHANDLER, Fanny	JUN 26 1819
PRIOR, Mary (blk)	HALL, Adolphus	JAN 24 1850
PRIOR, Mary Jane (blk)	ANDERSON, James Francis	MAY 02 1849
PRIOR, Sarah Ann (blk)	BUTLER, Henry	DEC 13 1839
PRIOR, Thomas O.	BARRETT, Emily A.	DEC 11 1851
PRISTON, William	HENRY, Sarah	MAR 21 1822
PRITCHARD, Arthur	WOOTTON, Mary	JUN 28 1823
PRITCHARD, Edward	THOMAS, Lettice E.	DEC 24 1838
PRITCHARD, Elizabeth	NEWMAN, John	MAY 18 1824

District of Columbia Marriage Licenses, 1811-1858

PRITCHARD, Levin	WISE, Eliza	NOV 02 1826
PRITCHARD, Samuel	HIGBY, Polly	FEB 21 1818
PRITCHARD, Virginia	CONNOR, Samuel W.	MAY 25 1848
PRITCHET, Benjamin	ROBERSON, Elizabeth	NOV 11 1817
PRITCHET, Ellen	DENHAM, A.W.	SEP 19 1835
PRITCHET, Harriet	McCUE, Mathew	JUL 13 1819
PRITCHET, Susan	ALLEN, William T.	JAN 03 1828
PRITCHETT, George A.	HURDLE, Frances E.	JAN 07 1847
PRITCHETT, Mary	CONNOR, John	SEP 07 1837
PRITCHETT, William Henry	MARCHE, Mary Jane	APR 01 1850
PROBY, Thomas	BRYAN, Mary	FEB 19 1831
PROCTER, George	JACKSON, Jane (blk)	MAY 28 1850
PROCTER, Gustavus	SAVOY, Susan	JAN 28 1817
PROCTER, Isaac	JACKSON, Delia (blk)	FEB 05 1846
PROCTER, John	DOVER, Sarah (blk)	OCT 24 1850
PROCTER, John B.	SMITH, Catharine J.	NOV 19 1832
PROCTER, Milo	SAVOY, Mary	JAN 25 1853
PROCTOR, Elizabeth (blk)	SAVOY, James	DEC 12 1850
PROCTOR, John	SAVOY, Lucretia (blk)	NOV 09 1854
PROCTOR, John C.	DAVISON, Mary Ann	OCT 08 1856
PROCTOR, John H.	BARTON, Levi Ann (blk)	JAN 08 1852
PROCTOR, Joseph	PLATER, Sophia	DEC 17 1814
PROCTOR, Marion H.	LASHHORN, Jno. P.	JUN 09 1856
PROCTOR, Mary	FLINN, Thomas	JUL 03 1813
PROCTOR, Mary (blk)	JACKSON, Wilson	JAN 10 1843
PROCTOR, Mary J. (blk)	BROOME, John	APR 27 1857
PROCTOR, Matilda	SIMPSON, Tobias	DEC 28 1824
PROCTOR, Miley	HARLEY, Elizabeth E.	SEP 19 1853
PROCTOR, Samuel	MARTIN, Cassey Ann (blk)	DEC 01 1851
PROCTOR, Sylvester	JONES, Kitty (blk)	DEC 30 1851
PROSISE, Benjamin	TANNER, Virginia	DEC 07 1857
PROSPER, Julia Ann	TERRY, William W.	OCT 29 1857
PROSPERI, Aspasia	EDWARDS, James	APR 15 1850
PROSPERI, Charles	ESPINTA, Josephine	JUL 09 1853
PROSPERI, Frederick	COOK, Mary Ellen	MAY 09 1853
PROSPERI, James	ESPERTES, Frances	JUL 08 1848
PROSSER, Catharine	KANE, Michael	APR 02 1853
PROTD, Francis	OVANSTINE, Mary	JAN 06 1852
PROTZMAN, Henry	STEMPLE, Eliza	FEB 27 1822
PROUT, Jonathan	SMALLWOOD, Eliza B.	SEP 11 1827
PROUT, Martha H.	McKNIGHT, George B. [Dr.]	SEP 16 1829
PROUT, Mary	BRADLEY, Henry	OCT 12 1837
PROVEST, Alexander	VERMILLION, Matilda	DEC 23 1828
PRUIT, Mary	TYLER, Ephraim	JUL 21 1847
PRUITT, William F.	LEMON, Sarah A.	AUG 16 1855
PRYOR, Ralph	BROWN, Sally	FEB 15 1838
PRYSE, Elizabeth	BUGH, Richard	OCT 29 1818
PUDDONAR, Henry	SHOEMAKER, Eliza	FEB 08 1854
PUDROUSKY, Theodore	TREIGLER, Elizabeth	FEB 12 1849
PULASKI, Ellen Louisa	LUCAS, Thomas	MAY 11 1847
PULEM, Francis	TRUSSLER, Sarah	DEC 04 1844
PULIZZI, Agatha C.	LYNCH, John	NOV 04 1834
PULIZZI, Mary A.	DEVLIN, John S.	NOV 20 1826
PULIZZI, Vernerando	TALBERT, Elizabeth M.A.	JAN 15 1827
PULLIN, Ann	ROLEY, William	OCT 05 1848
PULLIN, Hanson	ADAMS, Sarah Shaw	MAY 24 1849
PULLIN, John	CARDEN, Susanna G.	JAN 12 1854
PULLIN, Sarah	POSEY, George	MAY 24 1855

District of Columbia Marriage Licenses, 1811-1858

PULLIN, Sarah Hanson	FITTEN, William Horatio	SEP 14 1844
PULSFORT, Elizabeth	OSTENDORFF, Henry	JAN 20 1853
PUMEROY, Mary	FOWLER, Benjamin	AUG 01 1827
PUMPHREY, Airy	LEWIS, James	AUG 02 1815
PUMPHREY, Ann Eliza	SMITHSON, George	OCT 23 1856
PUMPHREY, Arthur G.	CHIDRESS, Lavenia F.	MAY 11 1854
PUMPHREY, Benjamin F.	CLINE, Mary Elizabeth	JUL 28 1858
PUMPHREY, Catherine L.	THOMAS, William H.	JUN 21 1848
PUMPHREY, Dennis	LEWIS, Eliza	NOV 02 1824
PUMPHREY, Dennis	BEALL, Tobertha	SEP 28 1835
PUMPHREY, Eliza E.	NICHOLLS, Benoni S.	FEB 24 1857
PUMPHREY, Ellen	HARBAUGH, Valentine	OCT 02 1838
PUMPHREY, James B.	CLIENT, Agnes	MAR 08 1856
PUMPHREY, John H.	GATES, Emma Jane	DEC 01 1851
PUMPHREY, Judson	HURDLE, Eliza	AUG 08 1834
PUMPHREY, Levi	MILLER, Sarah	FEB 09 1824
PUMPHREY, Levi	SWEETING, Ellen	JAN 21 1854
PUMPHREY, Lewis	HINTON, Sarah	JUL 05 1839
PUMPHREY, Mary A.V.	PRATHER, Benjamin A.	FEB 24 1855
PUMPHREY, Otho	FERGUSON, Sarah Ann	NOV 16 1841
PUMPHREY, Rachel A.	BEALL, Charles	JUL 31 1856
PUMPHREY, Rezin	SIMPSON, Harriot	JAN 17 1824
PUMPHREY, Samuel	WAKE, Elizabeth A.	JUN 05 1845
PUMPHREY, Sarah	KILE, John	APR 28 1812
PUMPHREY, Sarah	CLEMENTS, Thomas	NOV 25 1857
PUMPHREY, Sarah Ann	TALBOT, William W.	APR 14 1846
PUMPHREY, Sophia	PRESSEY, William	JAN 08 1824
PUMPHREY, Susan	GILL, James	JUN 19 1816
PUMPHREY, Susanna	TUCKER, Enoch G.	AUG 23 1843
PUMPHREY, Walter M.	REED, Ann E.	DEC 13 1853
PUMROY, Eliza Ann	HARRISON, Henry	JUN 29 1830
PUNNELL, Levi	SMITH, Tamer (blk)	DEC 31 1832
PUPO, Harriet	BURRISS, Obadiah	JUL 18 1853
PURCELL, Emma	STONE, Josiah	NOV 26 1855
PURCELL, Mary	McGLOCKLIN, John	MAY 20 1857
PURCELL, Samuel	STEPTOE, Elizabeth	APR 25 1843
PURCELL, Sophia W.	COX, Geo. C.	DEC 29 1849
PURCELL, Thomas Francis	COX, Matilda	NOV 05 1829
PURDEU, John	BEARDSLEY, Catharine	SEP 07 1839
PURDY, Ann	GATES, James W.	SEP 11 1850
PURDY, Elizabeth	WHEAT, Jesse	FEB 26 1824
PURDY, Ellen R.	WALLACE, William F.	AUG 31 1847
PURDY, Richard Gassaway	JONES, Martha Ann Ellen	AUG 15 1846
PURDY, Virginia	THOMPSON, James E.	JAN 25 1858
PURKINS, Samuel	GRIMES, Mary Ann	NOV 21 1827
PURKS, Benjamin	GRAHAM, Eleanor	APR 11 1812
PURRINGTON, Tobias	ARCHER, Amelia J.	JAN 20 1848
PURSELL, Ann	PURSELL, Thomas T.	JAN 19 1854
PURSELL, Thomas T.	PURSELL, Ann	JAN 19 1854
PURSELY, Frances	WEAVER, William	MAY 28 1849
PURSILL, George Ann	BENNETT, Andrew	JUN 20 1849
PURSLEY, Felin	BOLER, Alice	MAY 21 1855
PURSLEY, Jane	MILES, James H.N.	DEC 22 1852
PURSLEY, John	SHACKLEFORD, Clarissa A.	MAY 08 1851
PURSLEY, Laurenda	MULLINS, John	APR 18 1843
PURSLEY, Vincent	ROSE, Nancy	DEC 20 1842
PURVIS, Virginia C.	GRAVES, Austin	NOV 02 1857
PURVIS, William	SAUNDERS, Mary J.	FEB 28 1851

District of Columbia Marriage Licenses, 1811-1858

PUTNAM, Caleb	MURDOCK, Margaret	OCT 17 1820
PUTNAM, George M.	PARKER, Mary A.	JUN 06 1856
PUTNEY, Livia J.	SLIGHT, James P.	DEC 17 1857
PUTTS, Mary M.	CLANTICE, William R.	MAR 28 1855
PYFER, Amelia (blk)	JEFFERSON, Henry	JAN 19 1841
PYFER, Henry	MELVIN, Elizabeth	DEC 04 1813
PYLE, Lewis	FREE, Sarah Ann	JUN 22 1837
PYLE, Mifflin	SPATES, Elizabeth S.	MAR 15 1837
PYLES, James M.	HENLY, Mary	DEC 17 1853
PYNE, Samuel	SWEENY, Virginia	OCT 09 1855
PYWELL, James W.	HODSON, William	DEC 30 1846
PYWELL, William W.	GODDARD, Mary Ellen	DEC 30 1857

District of Columbia Marriage Licenses, 1811-1858

Q

QEINHARDT, Karl	TAUBERSCHMIDT, Katharina	MAR 02 1855
QUACKENBUSH, Nicholas	WORTHINGTON, Juliet A.	AUG 31 1846
QUADE, Ruthia	BALTZER, Jacob	MAY 06 1816
QUAID, Daniel	DOWNEY, Mary	JUL 30 1858
QUAID, Malinda J.	WINDSOR, Francis H.	DEC 29 1853
QUAID, Sarah	GRAVES, John	DEC 28 1813
QUAIDE, Jane	POWERS, William	FEB 22 1827
QUAIL, Charles	FITZGERALD, Mary Ann	FEB 04 1858
QUAIL, Margaret R.	WALLIS, Overton	NOV 25 1825
QUAIL, Susan	EUN, George	FEB 04 1858
QUAIL, Susan	EÜN, George	FEB 04 1858
QUALLS, Benjamin	BUTLER, Louisa (blk)	JUL 13 1854
QUANTRILL, Cornelia J.	EARNSHAW, Thomas T.	FEB 22 1847
QUARD, Mary	McPHERSON, William	JAN 16 1815
QUEEN, Ann	GUINN, John	OCT 30 1821
QUEEN, Ann	CALVERT, Thomas	DEC 27 1821
QUEEN, Ann (blk)	BELL, Joseph	OCT 05 1848
QUEEN, Ann Edwardina	SLYE, Edwin D.	SEP 09 1842
QUEEN, Ann Margaret	BROOKS, Jehiel	MAY 19 1830
QUEEN, Catharine J.	BOONE, Robert	APR 14 1817
QUEEN, Charles	FORD, Sally	JUN 09 1814
QUEEN, Elexius	PAXTON, Altha Ann	JUN 02 1831
QUEEN, Eugenea	BROOKE, Edmund	APR 09 1844
QUEEN, Isac	GARRET, Juliana (blk)	JUL 02 1831
QUEEN, James A.	RITCHIE, Mary R.	OCT 10 1844
QUEEN, Johanna	COLBERT, Michael	APR 19 1852
QUEEN, John R.	FORREST, Margaret	APR 10 1838
QUEEN, John W.	WELLS, Mary G.	DEC 09 1823
QUEEN, Joseph	WOODWARD, Maria	FEB 09 1839
QUEEN, Julius B.A.	CARSON, Sarah Ann	JAN 18 1856
QUEEN, Maria (blk)	COGER, John	JUN 14 1848
QUEEN, Maria Regina	CAMPBELL, Saml. [Hon.]	FEB 11 1823
QUEEN, Mary	HOOPER, Samuel	NOV 20 1840
QUEEN, Mary	WHIPPLE, Samuel	JUN 19 1842
QUEEN, Mary Ann	JAMESON, John	JUN 16 1818
QUEEN, Mary D.A.	HOUGH, A.E.	NOV 27 1821
QUEEN, Mary Emily	BURROUGHS, P.B.	JUN 29 1852
QUEEN, Mary H.	DAVIS, John B.	JUL 02 1831
QUEEN, Mary Martha (blk)	MANN, Joseph A.	SEP 15 1847
QUEEN, Michael	RILEY, Ann	MAR 19 1844
QUEEN, Oscar B.	SCOTT, Sarah A.	NOV 03 1847
QUEEN, Richard T.	KING, Eleanor Mary	NOV 04 1816
QUEEN, Sarah	HUGHES, Thomas	FEB 01 1818
QUEEN, Thomas H.	DINES, Martha (blk)	DEC 23 1848
QUEEN, William	POSEY, Mary	MAY 11 1837
QUEEN, William	HARRY, Ann C.	JUL 01 1857
QUEENLAND, Jane	ENNIS, Philip	JAN 15 1823
QUEGAN, Maria	[blank], Charles	JAN 01 1826
QUENDLAN, Bridget	SULLIVAN, Danl.	MAY 31 1856
QUESINBURY, Nicholas	GREEN, Elizabeth R.	MAY 15 1849
QUEST, Jane	ADAMSON, Roger	MAR 19 1844
QUEWELLE, P. Felicia	BROWN, Albertius E.	MAY 20 1852
QUICK, Patrick	DALTON, Margaret	FEB 17 1857
QUICKSALL, Joseph	MASI, Elizabeth	SEP 01 1841
QUIG, Elizabeth	ROACH, John	APR 11 1828
QUIGLEY, Biddy	MURRY, James	OCT 05 1835

District of Columbia Marriage Licenses, 1811-1858

QUIGLEY, John	DUFFEY, Bridget	NOV 23 1857
QUIGLEY, Margaret	O'CONNOR, Eugene	DEC 03 1839
QUIGLEY, Mary Ann	WHALEY, John L.	DEC 03 1833
QUIGLEY, Mary E.	FINLEY, James J.	APR 17 1847
QUIGLEY, Patrick	McCARTY, Mary	DEC 25 1843
QUIGLEY, Sarah Ann	LEWIS, Nathan	MAY 14 1838
QUIGLEY, William	McNAINEE, Mary Eliza	MAY 13 1848
QUIGLEY, William	HARRINGTON, Mary	JUN 19 1849
QUIGLY, Bliss Elizabeth	WILKINSON, John	APR 28 1836
QUIGLY, Daniel	BOOTH, Mary Elizabeth	FEB 12 1839
QUIGLY, Maria Ann	PAYNE, William McManus	JUN 30 1852
QUILL, Catherine	HERLIHY, Thomas	APR 06 1858
QUILL, Dennis	LOONEY, Mary	JAN 28 1857
QUILL, Dennis	SULLIVAN, Ann	JUL 01 1858
QUILL, John	GRIFFIN, Mary Ann	JAN 07 1856
QUILLAN, Ann	MURTOCK, Patrick	FEB 08 1853
QUILLAN, Timothy	SULLIVAN, Mary	JUN 24 1854
QUIN, Michael	WALLIS, Ann	AUG 27 1817
QUINCHE, Alexander J.	WILCOX, Mary J.	SEP 12 1857
QUINLAN, Lawrence	BURKE, Mary	JUN 15 1854
QUINLIN, Catharine	FOLEY, Timothy	MAY 12 1858
QUINLIN, Julian	BURK, Redmond	SEP 01 1852
QUINN, Bernard	CARTER, Mary Ann	AUG 18 1845
QUINN, Bridget	RAGAN, Rick	JUL 17 1852
QUINN, Catharine	TASISTRO, Louis Fitzgerald	APR 15 1853
QUINN, Catherine	RAGAN, Jeremiah	SEP 22 1849
QUINN, Catherine	HOLLAN, Charles T.	FEB 06 1857
QUINN, Christopher	TRACEY, Catharine	SEP 23 1853
QUINN, Edward	COFFEE, Mary	AUG 07 1856
QUINN, Margaret	MOLONEY, Patrick	JAN 27 1849
QUINN, Patrick	BURNS, Mary Ann	JAN 11 1856
QUINN, Rose	McALLISTER, James	NOV 22 1827
QUINN, William	DOWNS, Johanna	NOV 03 1856
QUIRK, Edward	WELSH, Mary	APR 21 1854
QUIRK, James	MARR, Catherine	JUN 28 1851
QUIRK, John B.	SKIRVING, Mary Ann	DEC 29 1851

District of Columbia Marriage Licenses, 1811-1858

R

RAAB, Michael	BOHN, Mary	MAR 04 1848
RABBETT, Henry	OSTEN, Elizabeth	JUL 25 1814
RABBIT, Ann Delphina	EMMERSON, Isaiah	APR 17 1852
RABBIT, Catharine Ann	PARKLETON, George	JAN 21 1850
RABBIT, Edward	LEADINGHAM, Christina	DEC 18 1855
RABBIT, Eliza Ellen	THRIFT, Colmore	FEB 06 1827
RABBIT, Mary	BUCKEYE, John	AUG 14 1851
RABBIT, Mary E.	SHOEMAKER, George W.	AUG 19 1851
RABBIT, Rebecca	ROBINSON, Francis	JAN 03 1854
RABBITT, James A.	WHITE, Mary C.	AUG 25 1851
RABBITT, John	GILL, Rebecca	AUG 26 1816
RABBITT, John	McLEAN, Rebecca	JUN 03 1839
RABBITT, John E.	JOY, Mary Ann	OCT 17 1855
RABBITT, Mary C.	WINDHAM, Willm. C.	SEP 16 1851
RABBITT, Mary Jane	CUNNINGHAM, Charles W.	OCT 15 1855
RABBITT, Rebecca J.	DUFFY, James	JUL 02 1856
RABBITT, Ruthe E.	SHOEMAKER, William H.	APR 26 1858
RABBITT, Samuel E.	THORNE, Mary J.	SEP 21 1850
RABBITT, Thomas	HUTCHINS, Mary Ann	MAR 26 1825
RABERSOHN, Elizabeth	NORBECK, George	APR 03 1834
RABITT, James	SEMMES, Eleanor	DEC 11 1830
RABITT, Martha Ellen	THOMAS, Richard Franklin	MAY 17 1842
RACE, Andrew J.	ACRES, Lucy Ann	FEB 25 1853
RACE, Hiram	MARTIN, Rebecca	AUG 16 1838
RACHEL, Mary Ann	WHITE, Callender	JAN 03 1826
RADCLIFF, Ann	FULMAN, Conrad	APR 08 1834
RADCLIFF, Ann M.	CRAIG, Charles E.	SEP 05 1843
RADCLIFF, Catharine A.	ENTWISLE, James, Jr.	JAN 17 1849
RADCLIFF, Margt. Ann	ADAMS, Sylvester	OCT 19 1853
RADCLIFF, Mary A.	SPEAKE, Wm. F.	OCT 29 1855
RADCLIFF, William, Junr.	ARNOLD, Matilda	AUG 04 1831
RADCLIFF, Wm. S.	BURNES, Rebecca A.W.	OCT 05 1816
RADCLIFFE, Alexander	SMITH, Catharine A.	FEB 17 1849
RADCLIFFE, Fannie A.	YERBY, Albert F.	FEB 19 1849
RADCLIFFE, Mary S.	YERBY, Adonis L.	APR 05 1851
RADLIFF, Sarah Amanda	WOOD, Charles Temple	OCT 25 1854
RADY, Daniel	GOFF, Mary	OCT 28 1856
RADY, James	BLOY, Rosanna	APR 10 1857
RADY, Johanna	RILEY, Charles	MAY 23 1856
RADY, John	DAVIS, Mary	OCT 11 1855
RADY, Mary	MURPHY, John	APR 22 1847
RADY, Thomas	DORIN, Mary	JAN 07 1857
RADY, William	CRAWLEY, Margaret	JUN 06 1817
RAE, Margaret	McINTOSH, Alexander	AUG 28 1832
RAFFERTY, Mary	RYON, John	APR 25 1857
RAFFERTY, Mary	DWYRE, Edward	APR 13 1858
RAFFIGNON, Alphonse	DONOHO, Bridget	JAN 22 1858
RAGAN, Andrew Jackson	THOMPSON, Alice Elizabeth	DEC 20 1849
RAGAN, Bridget	FITZGERALD, Edward	MAY 15 1852
RAGAN, Cecilia	HUTCHINS, Charles	SEP 27 1830
RAGAN, Daniel	NORRIS, Sarah	FEB 18 1813
RAGAN, Daniel	TRUNNELL, Sarah Ann Eliza	DEC 12 1833
RAGAN, Daniel	WRIGHT, Julia V.	JUN 25 1858
RAGAN, Dennis	KANE, Mary	NOV 25 1854
RAGAN, Elizabeth	SILENCE, John	APR 08 1813
RAGAN, George	MOLDEN, Ann	JAN 28 1850

District of Columbia Marriage Licenses, 1811-1858

RAGAN, Jeremiah	QUINN, Catherine	SEP 22 1849
RAGAN, John	CARPENTER, Mary	JUL 02 1844
RAGAN, John	GALLAHER, Mary	FEB 03 1852
RAGAN, Lucy Ann	MARCEY, Caleb	AUG 19 1834
RAGAN, Maria	DOWNES, Patrick	SEP 28 1854
RAGAN, Mary	SHANNEHAN, Daniel	JUN 02 1849
RAGAN, Mary	COLLINS, Patrick	JUN 07 1856
RAGAN, Mary M.	SILENCE, Walter	SEP 17 1847
RAGAN, Michael	ELDER, Mary Agnes	SEP 16 1851
RAGAN, Patrick	FLEMING, Catherine	OCT 21 1853
RAGAN, Rick	QUINN, Bridget	JUL 17 1852
RAGAN, Sarah	HARDY, Wm.	JAN 17 1831
RAGAN, Sarah E.	FRIZELLE, Charles E.	JUL 28 1854
RAGAN, William	BEACH, Mary Eliza	DEC 26 1850
RAGLAND, Jane (blk)	WALKER, William A.	MAY 06 1835
RAGON, Catharine	SENGSTICK, Charles P.	MAY 10 1821
RAGON, Daniel	HALLER, Catharine	AUG 12 1819
RAGON, Louisa	ADAMS, John Q.	MAR 13 1856
RAGON, Richard	SULLIVAN, Ann	JAN 03 1825
RAGSDALE, Anna Maria McLean	McKENNEY, William	MAR 24 1852
RAGSDALE, Thomas S.	MOENSTER, A.H.	OCT 12 1847
RAIDY, Maurice	CAUCHLIN, Mary	APR 19 1851
RAIDY, Morris	KANE, Margaret	NOV 10 1857
RAIDY, Thomas	SHANSSNEY, Margaret	JAN 18 1855
RAIFORD, Philip H.	JEFFERSON, Fannie A.	MAY 02 1853
RAILEY, James	STORY, Margaret	FEB 07 1839
RAILEY, Mary C.	WILLETT, Alexander	MAY 04 1846
RAINBOW, Mary Ann	DENHAM, Thomas S.	SEP 15 1835
RAINCISER, Lorenz	BECK, Salome	NOV 17 1832
RAINEY, Charles	NOND, Bridget	MAR 20 1856
RAINEY, Eliza	BRANTNER, Francis	JUL 24 1855
RAINEY, George	JONES, Elizabeth	MAR 29 1853
RAINEY, Jane	McKEEVER, Alexander	APR 06 1847
RAINEY, Samuel	FAHEY, Ann M.	SEP 26 1826
RAINEY, Samuel	OFFUTT, Lucy Beall	NOV 08 1837
RAINSFORD, Ann	BRADY, Peter	NOV 20 1821
RALEB, Adam	RAPP, Gertrutha	AUG 16 1848
RALEY, Benedict J.L.	McCLELLAND, Christiana	NOV 18 1841
RALEY, Elizabeth	WILSON, Charles	APR 17 1847
RALY, Catharine	NORTON, William	JAN 20 1821
RALY, Maria	BEALL, Edmund	NOV 30 1825
RALY, Matilda	MOCKBEE, William	SEP 19 1847
RALY, Sarah Jane	NORICE, Washington J.	APR 26 1847
RALY, Thomas	SUIT, Harriot	MAR 09 1815
RAMBER, David	ZEPFEN, Elizabeth	NOV 23 1842
RAMSAY, Anna	REDFIELD, Chandler [Dr.]	APR 22 1824
RAMSAY, Caroline H.	WATKINS, George S.	JUN 01 1841
RAMSAY, Charles R.	ASHTON, Caroline H.	MAY 30 1833
RAMSAY, Eliza	EDWARDS, James	SEP 18 1824
RAMSAY, Elizabeth B.	WILSON, Offa E.	DEC 11 1849
RAMSAY, Ezra J.	COMBS, Ann	APR 04 1820
RAMSAY, George D.	MUNROE, Frances W.	SEP 22 1830
RAMSAY, George D.	GALES, Eliza H.	JUN 28 1838
RAMSAY, Jane G.	TURNBULL, William [Lieut.]	JAN 05 1827
RAMSAY, R.T.	MARBURY, Eliza	OCT 11 1830
RAMSAY, Sarah	GOODYER, Peter	OCT 14 1815
RAMSAY, Sophia	KRUMBHAAR, Lewis	DEC 06 1832
RAMSAY, William	ELVIN, Grace	APR 03 1848

District of Columbia Marriage Licenses, 1811-1858

RAMSDELL, Caroline	ANDREW, Charles	SEP 29 1846
RAMSDILL, Martha	DICKINSON, Townsend	NOV 10 1845
RAMSEY, Sarah C.	TURPIN, William T.	JUL 26 1854
RAMSEY, William	DICINS, Caroline	MAY 25 1831
RAMSEY, William [Lieut.]	PETER, Elizabeth	OCT 15 1822
RANCK, Joseph	MECKEL, Elizabeth	MAR 05 1850
RANDALL, Augustus	AMOS, Caroline	SEP 09 1836
RANDALL, Benedict	McPHERSON, Ann	APR 20 1835
RANDALL, Edward	CATOR, Nancy	DEC 29 1812
RANDALL, Eleanor	ROSWELL, George	MAY 26 1828
RANDALL, Emily M.	WEBB, William B.	OCT 30 1856
RANDALL, Henry K.	MUNROE, Emily	NOV 23 1826
RANDALL, Jane	LLOYD, Jasper S.	DEC 27 1854
RANDALL, Joseph	BLADEN, Julian	JAN 18 1838
RANDALL, Juliana M.	ELLIOTT, Samuel B.	NOV 23 1847
RANDALL, Mary	JORDAN, Isham	DEC 06 1831
RANDALL, Matilda	MITCHELL, Thomas	FEB 16 1828
RANDALL, Saml.	RICHARDS, Matilda	JAN 30 1815
RANDALL, Thomas	WIRT, Laura	AUG 20 1827
RANDELL, George H.	MATTINGLY, Emeline W.	SEP 19 1842
RANDOLPH, Emma Beverley	STARK, Henry	JUL 03 1855
RANDOLPH, Francis	BUTLER, Louisa (col'd)	MAY 30 1844
RANDOLPH, Grimes [Dr. Philip]	O'NEALE, Mary	OCT 23 1824
RANDOLPH, John	FLETCHER, Mary (blk)	DEC 06 1842
RANDOLPH, John B.	TIMBERLAKE, Margaret R.	JAN 16 1843
RANDOLPH, Martha Jane	CODWISE, Charles Ferdinand	JUN 23 1840
RANDOLPH, Mary Ann	YOUNG, Abner Humphrey	OCT 02 1826
RANDOLPH, Mary M.	TURNER, Wm. W.	SEP 13 1855
RANDOLPH, Mary P.	JOHNSON, Martin H.	JUN 03 1852
RANDOLPH, Nannie I.	HULL, William H.	JAN 14 1851
RANDOLPH, Samuel	HALL, Ann Ellenora	MAY 09 1837
RANDOLPH, Wm. Beverly	LINGAN, Sarah	MAY 21 1816
RANDOM, James M.	COOPER, Hannah	MAY 10 1832
RANDUM, Martha Ann	HILTON, Jno. E.S.	MAY 24 1855
RANKEN, John W.	ANDERSON, Gertrude	MAY 31 1852
RANKIN, Jeames	BIRGE, Mary H.	NOV 29 1854
RANKIN, Nancy	WHITE, Robert	NOV 24 1853
RANSCH, Catharine	HESS, John	NOV 11 1833
RANSDALE, David D.	MacFARLAND, Caroline	AUG 11 1836
RANSOM, R., U.S.A.	HUNT, Minnie	FEB 06 1856
RANSOM, Stephen	FERRALL, Anne	MAR 30 1824
RAPETTI, Gaetano	CALVI, Maria	APR 28 1847
RAPETTI, Teresa	SANTUCCI, Isadore	FEB 16 1858
RAPINE, Anna E.	WHITTLESEY, Wm. C. [Dr.]	NOV 20 1822
RAPINE, Martha M.	BOWIE, Richard C.	NOV 24 1829
RAPINE, Mary	BOWIE, George Washington	MAY 22 1828
RAPLEY, William W.	HARRYMAN, Charity S.	MAY 18 1853
RAPLEY, Wm. Washington	HARRYMAN, Charity S.	JAN 31 1853
RAPP, Gertrutha	RALEB, Adam	AUG 16 1848
RAPP, Margaret	HIRTH, Philip	DEC 13 1856
RAPP, Mary	DECKER, Philip	JUN 20 1857
RAPPETTY, Jerom	UMBROOK, Elizabeth	FEB 12 1849
RARGIN, Margaret	SULLIVAN, Patrick	SEP 25 1852
RARIDON, John	RODGER, Margaret	OCT 18 1853
RASER, Eliza	FENTON, William	JUL 22 1850
RATARY, Isabella R.	McGILL, John B.	MAY 13 1845
RATCLIFF, Alexander	DELOZIER, Mary	SEP 16 1837
RATCLIFF, Alexander	COLLINS, Ann C.	JUL 12 1855

District of Columbia Marriage Licenses, 1811-1858

RATCLIFF, Anne E.	McDONALD, Matthew	MAY 07 1857
RATCLIFF, Catherine	BARRETT, Thomas J.	FEB 28 1854
RATCLIFF, Elizabeth	NEWTON, Ignatius A.	APR 06 1820
RATCLIFF, Fanny A.	BURR, Richard W.	JUN 01 1852
RATCLIFF, George	SIMS, Susan	MAY 31 1830
RATCLIFF, Gracy Ann	BLAGROVE, Henry B.	JUN 04 1817
RATCLIFF, James A.	ROBINSON, Sarah Ann	APR 25 1835
RATCLIFF, John	MILLS, Mary	JUL 17 1840
RATCLIFF, John	WEASNER, Sarah Jane	FEB 06 1847
RATCLIFF, John U.	BARRETT, Mary Ann	JAN 15 1853
RATCLIFF, Joseph	SHEPHERD, Ann	SEP 24 1814
RATCLIFF, Laura E.	RAY, Nicholas B.	SEP 25 1855
RATCLIFF, Lucinda	HUGHES, Wm.	OCT 02 1855
RATCLIFF, Lucinda (blk)	GADSBY, James	FEB 02 1853
RATCLIFF, Malinda	LOGAN, Richard	APR 16 1821
RATCLIFF, Margaret R.	BASHELBRIDGE, Joseph	MAY 21 1853
RATCLIFF, Martha	EDES, William H.	OCT 20 1829
RATCLIFF, Martha Ann	GITTINGS, Benjamin E.	JUN 04 1829
RATCLIFF, Mary	CHILES, Samuel A.	APR 23 1818
RATCLIFF, Mary (blk)	GRINNELL, Henry	SEP 07 1854
RATCLIFF, Mary E.	COLLINS, Owen J.	NOV 26 1851
RATCLIFF, Susan	HAPNER, William	JUL 09 1844
RATCLIFFE, Ann	HALL, John H.	APR 04 1819
RATCLIFFE, Catherine	TRUNALE, Lawson	JAN 09 1826
RATCLIFFE, Charles	TRUCKSON, Eliza	JAN 01 1828
RATCLIFFE, Eliza	DUNN, James C.	AUG 14 1822
RATCLIFFE, Elizabeth H.	CULL, John	FEB 19 1834
RATCLIFFE, Emeline	HINTON, Robert	MAR 29 1838
RATCLIFFE, Henry	MILES, Margaret Ann	JAN 26 1829
RATCLIFFE, James	KENNER, Mary Ann	MAY 13 1824
RATCLIFFE, Lewis	BARRETT, Margaret	JUN 15 1830
RATCLIFFE, Lucind	MOUNT, James W.	NOV 04 1845
RATCLIFFE, Margaret J.	THOMPSON, Charles W.	SEP 05 1854
RATCLIFFE, Mary Ann	MANNING, Ignatius F.	MAY 05 1842
RATCLIFFE, Richard	DANIEL, Jane P.	JUN 10 1827
RATCLIFFE, Thomas H.	DISMOND, Margaret	OCT 15 1850
RATELLICK, Mary Ann	SYLVESTER, Thomas	DEC 23 1823
RATLIFF, Maria	GRIFFIN, Patrick	MAY 04 1852
RATLIFF, Rebecca	POWELL, William	DEC 12 1813
RATRIE, William	CREAGOR, Susan	DEC 23 1812
RATTERY, Robert	GODFREY, Roda	OCT 30 1850
RATZ, Elizabeth	KRAMER, William	NOV 28 1853
RAU, Jennie	KOLB, Jacob	APR 27 1853
RAUB, Elizabeth	WILD, Robert	NOV 08 1848
RAUB, Geo. T.	RILEY, Ann E.	SEP 16 1843
RAULINGS, Wm. A.	BROWN, Anne E.	MAY 24 1847
RAWLING, Benjamin	LYNCH, Nancy	SEP 10 1832
RAWLING, Mary	COOPER, Edward	JAN 04 1826
RAWLINGS, Ann	WHEAT, Noah	JAN 07 1813
RAWLINGS, Benjamin	CAUFIN, Mary Ann	APR 03 1843
RAWLINGS, David	BERKLEY, Rebecca	SEP 19 1833
RAWLINGS, David	CARROLL, Fanny K.	OCT 01 1855
RAWLINGS, Eleanor	CROSS, William	APR 13 1825
RAWLINGS, Eliza	FRERE, Barrow	AUG 11 1845
RAWLINGS, Eliza A.	RUSSK, Robert F.	MAY 05 1852
RAWLINGS, Eliza Jane	HARRISON, James T.	JAN 06 1858
RAWLINGS, Ester	JOHNSON, George	SEP 15 1832
RAWLINGS, J.W.	LOWE, Margaret W.	MAR 12 1857

District of Columbia Marriage Licenses, 1811-1858

RAWLINGS, James	GAITHER, Matilda Riggs	JAN 06 1855
RAWLINGS, Mary	SMALLWOOD, Aquilla W.	FEB 03 1815
RAWLINGS, Mary V.	FITZHUGH, William H.	JUL 18 1848
RAWLINGS, Octavia	CROSS, Nimrod J.	MAR 30 1846
RAWLINGS, Susana	BELL, William	JUL 18 1837
RAWLINGS, Thomas H.	WILLIAMS, Mary Jane	DEC 16 1847
RAWLINGS, Williams	BELL, Sarah	JAN 08 1846
RAWLINS, George M.	DOUGLASS, John V.	AUG 02 1855
RAWLINS, William C.	BADDEN, Mary	MAY 29 1830
RAY, Albert	CLARY, Amanda J.	APR 21 1851
RAY, Alexander	ROSS, Hannaett	OCT 24 1822
RAY, Alfred	WHITE, Lydia A.	AUG 17 1853
RAY, Ann	TURNER, Zachariah	DEC 28 1825
RAY, Ann C.	HILLARY, William H.	JAN 07 1858
RAY, Anthony L.	OSBORNE, Elizabeth R.	FEB 26 1855
RAY, C.A.	JOHNSON, John	MAR 19 1833
RAY, Carrie E.	SHREVE, James H., Jr.	DEC 08 1857
RAY, E.L.	LESLIE, H.R.	NOV 15 1848
RAY, Elila	BRADLEY, Alexander	FEB 04 1822
RAY, Enos	MOULDER, Sarah Ann	FEB 06 1822
RAY, Enos	OSBORN, Elizabeth	NOV 23 1826
RAY, James	GANNON, Bridget	SEP 21 1854
RAY, John	SCHMIDT, Elizabeth	DEC 02 1848
RAY, John H.	MUDD, Mary Ellen	MAY 27 1852
RAY, John J.	LEWIS, Mary	JAN 08 1829
RAY, Joseph B.	FUSS, Mary Jane	DEC 20 1855
RAY, Josiah	CLARKE, Eleanor	MAY 12 1831
RAY, Margaret	FRIDLEY, George	NOV 01 1853
RAY, Mariah	CARNES, John	FEB 09 1814
RAY, Mary	STEEL, Horatio N.	MAY 14 1827
RAY, Mary Ann	HUGHES, George W.	MAY 15 1848
RAY, Mary Ellen	BECK, S. Zebulon	NOV 16 1854
RAY, Nicholas B.	RATCLIFF, Laura E.	SEP 25 1855
RAY, Paul	BAILY, Mary	FEB 22 1836
RAY, Sarah	McCLELLAND, Gustavus A.	MAY 14 1830
RAY, Sarah J.	EAGAN, Peter	NOV 13 1856
RAY, William	LOVELACE, Jane	OCT 31 1842
RAY, William A.	CAVENAUGH, Mary A.	JAN 19 1858
RAYHILL, Dominick	COLEMAN, Martha Ann	JUN 10 1837
RAYMOND, Charles H.	UNDERWOOD, Mary Jane	NOV 05 1844
RAYMOND, Peter	LEECH, Margaret A.	JUL 14 1858
RAYMOND, Sarah	SCHNEIDER, Charles A.	JAN 03 1848
REA, Martha	BOOSE, John	JUL 29 1822
READ, Alexander	SHUMATE, Mary Elizabeth	NOV 19 1856
READ, Dianna	WALKER, David	AUG 21 1819
READ, Dolly	MacDANIEL, James	MAR 26 1816
READ, Elizabeth Ann	GRAVES, Thomas Jefn.	JUN 02 1855
READ, George	BURGES, Delpha Ann	JUL 07 1836
READ, Harriot Gallata	PARK, Alexander	JUL 19 1833
READ, Henry F.	ROBINSON, Martha M.M.	DEC 02 1845
READ, Jane (blk)	DAGGES, Jacob	SEP 21 1850
READ, Joshua	BREWER, Mary Ann	JUL 22 1858
READ, Margaret	HINKLE, John	FEB 14 1818
READ, Richard R.	JOHNSON, Margaret A.	OCT 30 1838
READ, Sraah Ann C.	WELCH, Lewis	DEC 05 1836
READDING, Henry	WEDDING, Ann	NOV 01 1853
READING, Peirson Barton	WASHINGTON, Fannie Wallace	MAR 12 1856
READMAN, Levi	HARRISON, Jane	AUG 06 1850

District of Columbia Marriage Licenses, 1811-1858

READY, David	O'LEARY, Mary	NOV 19 1852
READY, John	SCANLAN, Mary	APR 23 1832
READY, Margaret	CULHAN, Michael	JAN 25 1855
READY, William	LAWRENCE, Caroline M.	JUN 01 1839
REALY, Mary Ellen	KING, William N.	JAN 04 1845
REARDAN, John	CRONIN, Johanna	SEP 18 1851
REARDEN, Dennis	ROACH, Catharine	JUL 31 1854
REARDEN, Michael	McCOY, Sarah Ann	AUG 14 1828
REARDON, Andrew	LALLEY, Ann	OCT 16 1856
REARDON, Ann Maria	O'NEALE, Patrick	SEP 07 1852
REARDON, Catherine	TOOMEY, Michael	SEP 30 1851
REARDON, Daniel	CHAMBERLAIN, Barbara	JUN 02 1831
REARDON, Hannah	WOLF, Richard	AUG 17 1858
REARDON, Jeremiah	MARRON, Ellen	MAR 17 1856
REARDON, John	O'HERREN, Ellen	MAY 08 1855
REARDON, Mary	HAGGARTY, Jeremiah	APR 13 1858
REATHER, Robert	HERTMAN, Catharine	JAN 12 1833
REAVER, Emaline	SIMPSON, Archd. N.	NOV 12 1846
REAVER, Henry	MORGAN, Eliza	MAY 19 1824
REAVES, Catharine R.	MULLEN, John	JUL 16 1833
RECARD, John Edward	TALBERT, Eliza	SEP 30 1843
RECKTER, Ludwell L.	WIGS, Jane	SEP 14 1835
RECTOR, Kitty Ann	GLASSCOCK, John H.	FEB 20 1834
RECTOR, Thompson	CAYNOR, Nancy	JUN 06 1834
RECTOR, Walter	KING, Catherine	JAN 29 1846
REDD, Edmonia B.	CARTER, Gustavus Q.	JUN 02 1857
REDDALL, Ann P.	HANDY, William	APR 29 1846
REDDALL, William C.	LAUB, Elizabeth Ann	OCT 09 1854
REDDEN, Ann Mariah	SELBY, John E.	OCT 04 1827
REDDEN, Fielder	WILDERSON, Mary (blk)	NOV 13 1848
REDDEN, James	GODDARD, Ruth	DEC 14 1844
REDDEN, Thomas	TURNER, Mary Elizabeth	AUG 21 1845
REDDICK, David	MAXWELL, Lucy A.	JUL 07 1832
REDDIN, Mary Ann (blk)	KING, George	MAY 21 1840
REDDIN, Shedrick	DODSON, Ann (blk)	JAN 30 1856
REDDING, Joseph	BOYL, Mary	APR 28 1853
REDER, James	ORMES, Mary (blk)	JUL 01 1816
REDFERN, Joseph	VIVANS, Josephine	OCT 29 1851
REDFERN, Mary M.	BURNETT, Wm.	SEP 22 1838
REDFERN, Richard	EDDUS, Sarah L.	SEP 22 1838
REDFERN, Samuel	LAWRENCE, Elizabeth	DEC 15 1827
REDFIELD, Chandler [Dr.]	RAMSAY, Anna	APR 22 1824
REDIN, Catharine	STEPHENSON, John	FEB 13 1836
REDIN, David	WOODLAND, Catharine (blk)	JUL 05 1849
REDIN, Elizabeth (blk)	MATTHEWS, Richard	JUL 07 1832
REDIN, Emily W.	KIRK, James B.	AUG 01 1843
REDIN, Frances	SOUTHERN, Richard	JAN 05 1826
REDIN, Mary	MACABOY, James	FEB 19 1841
REDIN, Mary A.	WOODWARD, William R.	APR 08 1852
REDIN, Mary Ann (blk)	GANTT, Samuel	OCT 03 1848
REDIN, Sarah (blk)	NEWTON, John	OCT 30 1845
REDIN, Selby	WILLIAMS, Charlotte (blk)	NOV 11 1847
REDIN, Shadrach	JEFFERSON, Winney (blk)	MAY 13 1852
REDIN, Susan	UPTON, William	MAY 08 1850
REDIN, William	VanPELT, Kesiah	AUG 12 1848
REDING, Jane	BEAUGRAND, Peter	JUL 06 1827
REDLER, Sophia	HERMANN, Paul	OCT 23 1856
REDMAN, Cornelia	MARTIN, Amos F.	SEP 25 1856

District of Columbia Marriage Licenses, 1811-1858

REDMAN, J.R.	SPENCER, Sophia F.	MAR 04 1837
REDMAN, Joseph	TARLTON, Sarah	SEP 13 1834
REDMAN, Margaret	HARRISON, Joseph	DEC 19 1850
REDMAN, Margaret C.	MURRAY, Wm. A.	MAY 10 1855
REDMAN, Maria	MAZINGO, William	NOV 13 1816
REDMAN, Robert	HOUSON, Jane	MAY 30 1812
REDMAN, Virginia	BIRCH, William	SEP 04 1856
REDMOND, Benjamin P.	BOONE, Henrietta	MAY 09 1833
REDMOND, Maria C.H.	CREGG, Nathaniel	NOV 04 1820
REDMOND, Mary	SCALLAND, James	FEB 08 1820
REDOWAY, Ellen R.	HAVENER, Overton	AUG 01 1848
REDSTRAKE, William J.	ALBINGER, Emily	NOV 19 1849
REED, Alexander	TAYLOR, Charlotte (blk)	NOV 07 1854
REED, Allen	ROBINSON, Louisa	SEP 02 1830
REED, Ann	HARRIS, Benjamin D.	DEC 12 1825
REED, Ann E.	PUMPHREY, Walter M.	DEC 13 1853
REED, Bushrod M.	WILSON, Anna M.	MAY 31 1855
REED, Catharine	BLAKENEY, John	MAY 29 1827
REED, Cordelia	LEDMAN, Silas	AUG 18 1842
REED, D.C.	LANSDALE, Catharine	NOV 18 1841
REED, Duke of Wellington	MILLS, Julia Ann	APR 30 1846
REED, Elizabeth	McCAFRY, Peter	SEP 06 1828
REED, Elizabeth	BOWEN, Joseph O.D.	JUN 28 1836
REED, Elizabeth	BYRAM, James H.	MAY 26 1858
REED, Emelia	MARSHALL, Wm.	DEC 29 1814
REED, Emeline	CAVANAUGH, Michael	JUN 06 1839
REED, Eslie D.	MOORE, Mary E.	MAY 04 1854
REED, Filitia	WODDEY, John	DEC 03 1828
REED, Francis A.	ELDRIDGE, Marinda	AUG 11 1857
REED, George A.	LAMPKIN, Charlotte A.	DEC 16 1848
REED, George F.	THORP, Jane C.	FEB 06 1847
REED, George W.	SIMMONS, Mary Ellen	AUG 18 1851
REED, Hannah	MILLER, Samuel	APR 20 1836
REED, Hester A.	DAVIS, Charles M.	OCT 22 1856
REED, Isaac	WIMSATT, Caroline	MAY 13 1831
REED, Isaac Shelby	GREEN, Ann Laura	JUN 26 1832
REED, Isabella	OSBORN, Francis	SEP 12 1854
REED, James	LEWELLYN, Mary	AUG 10 1841
REED, James	SPIGGS, Mary (blk)	DEC 17 1850
REED, Jane L.	HOFFMAN, George W.	SEP 15 1849
REED, John	LAMBERT, Sarah	OCT 21 1837
REED, John	FALLEN, Mary M.	NOV 23 1843
REED, John	TUXON, Margaret (blk)	MAY 03 1858
REED, John R.	KING, Mariah	JAN 06 1827
REED, John Thomas	WILLIAMS, Ellen	JUL 03 1850
REED, John W.	WILLIAMSON, Sarah A.	APR 15 1857
REED, Joseph H.	DADE, Susan Ann (blk)	JAN 25 1849
REED, Josiah F.	BELLING, Caroline C.	DEC 28 1826
REED, Julia	FERGUSON, Samuel	MAY 17 1837
REED, Lucinda	SANFORD, William	MAY 26 1840
REED, Margaret	BYRNE, Wm.	NOV 09 1821
REED, Margaret	BUSH, Frederick	AUG 03 1841
REED, Margaret Ann	RICARD, Caleb B.	NOV 13 1854
REED, Martha V.	MILLER, Thomas J.	MAR 01 1854
REED, Mary	PILES, Leonard	APR 28 1818
REED, Mary	JONES, Wm. T.	MAR 31 1858
REED, Mary Catherine	LUCAS, David Henry	AUG 17 1852
REED, Polly	SPEERLING, Hanson	AUG 23 1813

District of Columbia Marriage Licenses, 1811-1858

REED, Rebecca	McCARTY, Wm.	DEC 13 1812
REED, Richard S.	BALL, Mary M.	MAR 13 1833
REED, Robert	HARROVER, Sarah A.	FEB 27 1849
REED, Sarah	CHRONYAN, Philip	JAN 09 1819
REED, Sarah	MYERS, George	FEB 08 1841
REED, Sarah	BUCHANAN, John	NOV 18 1850
REED, Sarah E.	SULLIVAN, John H.	APR 11 1850
REED, Shadey (blk)	CRAIG, Henry	JAN 23 1845
REED, Susan	HIBBS, J. Wesley	NOV 09 1857
REED, Susan (blk)	CALVERT, John	FEB 20 1850
REED, Susan (blk)	CALVERT, John	JAN 23 1850
REED, Thomas E.	CUNNINGHAM, Margt. E.	NOV 03 1851
REED, William	GOODRICK, Mary	MAY __ 1827
REED, William	BEAN, Margarett	FEB 05 1848
REED, William	BEALL, Mary Eliza	MAY 27 1848
REED, William H.	UPTON, Josephine P.	APR 24 1858
REEDE, Jacob	BROWN, Phillis (blk)	DEC 14 1848
REEDER, Ann Thornton	EMERSON, John P.	MAY 24 1836
REEDER, Cadah	COATS, Albin	DEC 26 1817
REEDER, Catherine	MARRIET, Joseph	APR 29 1846
REEDER, Eliza	DOWLING, William	APR 17 1841
REEDER, Elizabeth J.	SHEATZ, Henry	APR 18 1831
REEDER, John T.	REEVES, Elizabeth	NOV 02 1841
REEDER, John W.	ELVANS, Catherine	AUG 22 1832
REEDER, Mary Ann	HURDLE, James	NOV 19 1826
REEDER, Rachael	KEELER, Noah B.	NOV 19 1823
REEDER, Rachel A.	EVANS, Edward, Jr.	SEP 20 1851
REEDER, Richard	SMITH, Mrs. Ann	JUN 19 1858
REEDER, Sarah	LUTHER, Daniel	AUG 27 1833
REEDER, William	BOSWELL, Elizabeth	SEP 18 1816
REEDER, William A.	POWERS, Elizabeth	AUG 19 1830
REEKER, Alexander	FENDLEY, Sarah Ann	DEC 06 1832
REEL, James Leonard	MILLS, Elizabeth	MAR 20 1858
REELAND, Martha Eliza	KEATHLEY, Samuel	MAY 02 1843
REELER, John	RICHARDSON, Mary F. (blk)	OCT 19 1854
REELER, Samuel	GRAYSON, Eliza (blk)	JUL 18 1840
REELING, Maria Elizth.	GORDON, Manuel	JUN 27 1851
REEM, John	SNYDER, Catherine G.	SEP 26 1853
REEMER, Elizabeth Jane	MOULTON, Thomas Henry	JUN 03 1845
REESE, Hugh L.	O'NEALE, Elizth.	MAY 05 1853
REESE, John	BOWEN, Virginia	JUN 26 1854
REESE, William L.	SKIDMORE, Jane E.	OCT 22 1839
REESIDE, Caroline	OWEN, John A.	JAN 31 1853
REEVE, Lucy E.	NEVINS, Burnett L.	JUN 05 1858
REEVE, Nathan S.	HOBBIE, Mary D.	JAN 19 1854
REEVE, Samuel	PREUSS, Constantia	AUG 06 1846
REEVES, Alfred L.	NALLAY, Sarah	SEP 16 1848
REEVES, Aloysius	FOANES, Martha	AUG 14 1848
REEVES, Catharine E.	ATHEY, George W.	FEB 18 1845
REEVES, Elizabeth	REEDER, John T.	NOV 02 1841
REEVES, Hannah M.	MATTINGLY, Joseph	NOV 19 1853
REEVES, Hezekiah James	BOSS, Matilda	OCT 11 1815
REEVES, James	WESTERFIELD, Julian	FEB 21 1837
REEVES, Jas. W.	CRAWFORD, Mary	MAY 15 1855
REEVES, Jno. U.	CONNOR, Jane	JUL 17 1855
REEVES, John C.	WALLER, Mary E.A.	AUG 19 1846
REEVES, Julia A.	SWANN, Elkanah S.	NOV 08 1836
REEVES, Martha	McGUIRE, Thomas F.	JUN 12 1854

District of Columbia Marriage Licenses, 1811-1858

REEVES, Mary	MUIR, Robinson F.	JUL 02 1858
REEVES, Mary Ann	DUVALL, William H.	SEP 26 1844
REEVES, Randolph C.	ELLIOT, Ellen	NOV 17 1829
REEVES, Ryland	SYPHAX, Bertha Ellen (blk)	DEC 18 1850
REEVES, Samuel S.	STEWART, Eliza	AUG 22 1839
REEVES, Sarah	DELPHEY, Bartholomew	NOV 07 1832
REEVES, William J.	WARREN, Kitty	MAY 22 1832
REEVES, William J.	PEERSON, Jane	NOV 26 1839
REEVES, William L.	GRAVES, Mary E.	MAY 21 1835
REGAEN, Daniel	HUTCHINSON, Matilda	MAY 17 1832
REGAN, Elen A.	DUNAWIN, James E.F.	APR 06 1848
REGAN, Ellen	COX, Clement	FEB 17 1849
REGAN, Hugh	KAVANAGH, Margaret	JUN 30 1853
REGLIEN, Frederic	TRUXELL, Catharine	APR 08 1823
REHM, Ferdinand	LETMATE, Dorathy	SEP 27 1852
REICHERT, Francis L.	BROTT, Mary A.	AUG 04 1857
REID, Armstead	LANSDALE, Ann (blk)	MAY 29 1850
REID, Benjamin	BLANFORD, Mary	JUL 07 1824
REID, Cerucia E.	VAURTERS, William N.	AUG 07 1858
REID, Horatio	NELSON, Mary Ann	APR 28 1829
REID, James	ARNOLD, Elizth. Ann	AUG 30 1845
REID, John	CONNER, Mary Ann	JUL 25 1825
REID, Martha Helen	McDONALD, James T.	APR 26 1853
REID, Thomas	PECKHAM, Sophia R.	MAY 21 1844
REID, Upton S.	FORREST, Elizabeth	JUN 30 1814
REID, Wesley W.	LAW, Mary Frances	APR 20 1848
REIDER, Eliza Jane	SULLIVAN, Patrick	APR 10 1846
REIDER, Maria	KELLER, George	JUL 19 1831
REIDMULLER, Christina	BECK, John	NOV 26 1855
REIDVILA, Frederika	LEPPOLETT, Augustus	MAR 22 1848
REIDY, Hannora	DALEY, Michael	FEB 01 1851
REIDY, James	HAGGERTY, Hannah	SEP 08 1856
REIDY, Mary	O'BRIEN, William	DEC 05 1853
REIDY, Mary	HARRINGTON, Patrick	MAY 13 1854
REIFENBACH, Frederick	RIGGS, Sophie	JUL 06 1855
REIGER, Catherine	OCKER, George	FEB 25 1834
REILEY, Ellen	CONLAN, Maurice	NOV 12 1857
REILEY, Virginia	HUHN, Bernhard	AUG 05 1858
REILEY, William	SELBY, Martha	OCT 25 1816
REILEY, William	FOLY, Fanny	SEP 10 1821
REILLY, Ellen	SAVAGE, James	FEB 05 1856
REILLY, George	GREEN, Catharine Ann	MAY 04 1832
REILLY, George	THOMPSON, Alila	DEC 03 1836
REILY, Ann	PIRKINS, John	AUG 27 1821
REILY, Catherine	O'BRIEN, Thomas	JAN 27 1853
REILY, Eliza	SMITH, Fielder	DEC 23 1811
REILY, Farrell	TENLEY, Elizabeth	JAN 25 1812
REILY, James A.	MEEM, Rebecca A.	JAN 11 1853
REILY, John	CANN, Catherine	FEB 23 1846
REILY, John Francis	MUDD, Margaret Ann	JUN 27 1842
REILY, John M.	BRODERS, Jane Eliza	OCT 22 1849
REILY, Mary	GRIMSLEY, Augustus	JAN 02 1834
REINAGLE, Georgianna	DAVIS, George M.	JAN 25 1831
REINDAL, Philip	FREIDERICK, Catherine	JUL 12 1853
REINDEL, Barbara	RUEHL, John W.	JUN 21 1853
REINER, Franz	MARGRINIUS, Fredericke	JUL 01 1858
REINEY, Catharine	McCOLGAN, James	AUG 14 1852
REINHARD, Carl	BRIENER, Catharine	SEP 21 1853

District of Columbia Marriage Licenses, 1811-1858

REINHART, Frederick	DORSEY, Matilda	MAY 03 1844
REINHART, Frederick	FRAZIER, Sarah	MAR 18 1844
REINHART, Frederick	FRAZIER, Sarah	JUN 20 1844
REINHART, Teresa	HAUFMANN, August	APR 02 1853
REINING, John Conrad	GARENS, Geshe Margaretha	APR 05 1842
REINTZEL, Henry [Dr.]	NICHOLLS, Mary E.	AUG 16 1832
REINTZEL, Samuel	BALL, Amelia	DEC 25 1813
REINTZEL, William Henry	FAULKNER, Eliza	JAN 04 1853
REINTZELL, John	CHICK, Eliza	OCT 05 1837
REISER, Adam	WILLIAMS, Hannah	NOV 21 1846
REISS, Benjamin	SIMPSON, Maria Elizabeth	DEC 14 1837
REISS, Caroline	COHEN, Abram	JUN 03 1856
REISS, John H.	LOVELESS, Eliza	OCT 03 1846
REITH, Pius	OFENSTEIN, Johanna	JUL 02 1857
REITZ, Elizabeth	KELLER, Frederic	APR 30 1819
REKENWEG, Caroline	KREY, Charles	FEB 18 1858
RELIN, Mary Ann	McKENNEY, Jarrett	JUL 21 1837
REMELE, John C.	JOHNSON, Eleanor	SEP 09 1822
REMELE, Sopha	SOUTHALL, Tyler	SEP 02 1856
REMICK, Mark	SEWELL, Amelia	JUL 06 1815
REMICK, Timothy	BEALL, Mary Ann	APR 20 1843
REMINGTON, Eliza Ann	OFFUTT, Zachariah M.	APR 07 1826
REMINGTON, James	CLARKE, Mary Matilda	MAY 05 1834
REMINGTON, Jane Roberta	TRUNNEL, John H.	DEC 06 1842
REMINGTON, John A.	PARSONS, Mary	NOV 17 1829
REMINGTON, Mary Ann	BROCKWAY, Charles	OCT 06 1832
REMINGTON, Ruth A.	CHISM, William L.	SEP 13 1853
REMMINGTON, Catherine	RIKER, Alfred	SEP 16 1852
REN, Sabret	BALLINGER, Milly Maria	FEB 18 1836
RENAGLE, Ann	JOHNSON, Lewis	DEC 02 1815
RENAHAN, Martin	HOGAN, Margaret	AUG 12 1837
RENNER, Deitrich	ZENTEL, Maria	JUN 22 1833
RENNER, Elizabeth	HUFF, Powell H.	MAR 04 1816
RENNER, John	AUSTIN, Eliza	JAN 14 1817
RENNER, William G.	RIND, Jane A.	SEP 11 1832
RENNEY, Patrick	CRONIN, Elizabeth	OCT 17 1818
RENNIKER, George R.	DICE, Caroline M.	MAR 26 1857
RENNIKER, Henry	FAUKMAN, Margaret	APR 05 1849
RENNOE, Chapman	MOLARE, Harriot	SEP 06 1834
RENNOE, John H.	SLEIGH, Catharine	MAY 05 1849
RENNOE, John H.	ENGLEBRIGHT, Sarah A.	JAN 21 1854
RENNOE, William W.	McILHANEY, Mary L.	SEP 01 1848
RENNOLDS, Abert	BERRYMAN, Eliza R.	MAY 20 1823
RENNOLDS, Gassaway	TRUCK, Elizabeth	FEB 07 1850
RENNOLDS, Mary	SEMMES, William N.	JUL 25 1839
RENO, Jesse L.	CROSS, Mary	OCT 25 1853
RENOE, George N.B.	LARKIN, Penelope D.	MAR 17 1831
RENTER, Henry	WOLF, Margaretta	DEC 01 1849
RENWICK, Henry B.	JANNEY, Margaret	JUN 21 1852
REPETTE, Jerome	HOWARD, Maria Jane	JUN 07 1852
REPETTE, Joseph	RODER, Dorothy	APR 17 1843
REPP, Sophia	ROPFER, Herman	OCT 11 1855
REPROGLE, Catharine	BRADLEY, Robert	FEB 08 1812
RESINE, Elizabeth	GOODFRY, Lewis	APR 29 1837
RESS, Ann	OBER, John	DEC 18 1822
RESSENG, Charles	GIST, Mary Ann	FEB 29 1848
RESTON, Patty	ENSELLOW, James	JUL 13 1814
RESWICK, Catharine	VanRESWICK, Wilferd	NOV 09 1819

District of Columbia Marriage Licenses, 1811-1858

RETELLIC, Sarah	PECKHAM, William H.	JAN 04 1833
RETTER, Elizabeth A.	WARREN, Thomas G.	MAY 23 1836
REUSS, Peter J., Dr.	KEESE, Georgine	OCT 04 1852
REVES, Ann Maria	COLTER, Thomas	JUL 29 1851
REYNOLDS, Camelia A.	GRAMMER, Frederick Louis	FEB 05 1857
REYNOLDS, Cornelia	CARR, Caldwell	JAN 13 1829
REYNOLDS, E.K.	COCHRAN, Kate Pleasants	JUN 18 1856
REYNOLDS, Eliz.	JOHNSON, George	JAN 09 1813
REYNOLDS, Eliza A.	VERMILLION, Dennis	JUN 01 1826
REYNOLDS, Elizabeth	BLADEN, Westley	DEC 19 1839
REYNOLDS, Emily	WILLIAMS, Wm. C.	NOV 25 1856
REYNOLDS, Enos	CARMAN, Margaret	JUN 15 1839
REYNOLDS, Harriet	CORCORAN, James	FEB 19 1819
REYNOLDS, James	GAINER, Louisa	MAY 07 1857
REYNOLDS, James D.	KIDWELL, Elizabeth	FEB 27 1836
REYNOLDS, James Thomas	PEASTON, Catherine Ann	JUL 11 1844
REYNOLDS, John	WILSON, Sarah Evaline	JUL 09 1836
REYNOLDS, John	DRUMMONDS, Annetta	OCT 04 1849
REYNOLDS, John	BYRNES, Margaret	SEP 19 1857
REYNOLDS, John Henry	ROBINSON, Julia Ann	AUG 08 1854
REYNOLDS, Joseph	BELT, Mary Levina	DEC 19 1837
REYNOLDS, Joseph	GROSS, Catherine A.	DEC 23 1843
REYNOLDS, Letitia	EASTON, James B.	JUN 25 1839
REYNOLDS, Margaret Ann (blk)	TILLMAN, Henry H.	SEP 30 1840
REYNOLDS, Maria	COLLIN, Henry	AUG 04 1855
REYNOLDS, Mary	CAMBELL, John	SEP 16 1813
REYNOLDS, Mary [Mrs.]	JARBOE, Matthew	JUL 12 1825
REYNOLDS, Mary Ann	BEATTY, Robert M.	MAY 27 1839
REYNOLDS, Mary, Mrs.	SULLY, Robert	FEB 24 1835
REYNOLDS, Mary Virginia	HUMPHRIES, John A.	AUG 18 1856
REYNOLDS, Michael	CARROLL, Ann	JUN 07 1851
REYNOLDS, Richard	CHESTER, Emeline M.	AUG 29 1829
REYNOLDS, Samuel	AIRS, Anna (blk)	JUN 09 1848
REYNOLDS, Samuel L.	BARRETT, Louisa	OCT 07 1829
REYNOLDS, Thomas	EVANS, Mary	APR 11 1812
REYNOLDSON, Catherine E.	DENT, Zachariah	SEP 27 1848
REYNOLDSON, Robert	DUMPHEY, Catharine E.	SEP 04 1832
RHAY, Sarah Ann	CHISM, Lewis	APR 01 1830
RHEA, Daniel	ERSKINE, Elizabeth	JUL 16 1821
RHEA, Robert	GLOYD, Caroline	AUG 11 1832
RHEEM, Christiana	HINES, David	SEP 19 1846
RHEES, William J.	CLARKE, Laura O.	NOV 12 1856
RHINE, Margaret	BARKER, John H.	AUG 21 1852
RHODES, Cassindra	CROSAN, Samuel	SEP 08 1817
RHODES, Daniel	LOWRY, Elizabeth	MAY 20 1830
RHODES, Edward	GOULDING, Mary	DEC 31 1829
RHODES, George	CUNNINGHAM, Eliza	MAR 06 1838
RHODES, George	McCAULEY, Elizabeth	FEB 01 1848
RHODES, Henry	PLANT, Harriet (blk)	SEP 21 1848
RHODES, Hilry H. [Lt.]	CARTER, Marion Stewart	MAY 21 1834
RHODES, James	PARSONS, Ann	MAY 22 1821
RHODES, James	FOWLER, Elizabeth Ann	SEP 15 1849
RHODES, Laura Ann	MASSEY, William D.	AUG 25 1836
RHODES, Peter	STROUD, Drusilla	MAR 31 1812
RHODES, Varnell	TREAKLE, Mary	AUG 05 1812
RHODES, William	BURCH, Melinda	OCT 19 1814
RHODES, William	DUFF, Susan C.	DEC 22 1856
RHODIER, Mary Ann	SETTLE, Alexander L.	APR 27 1836

District of Columbia Marriage Licenses, 1811-1858

RHYAN, John	POOL, Mary	FEB 11 1841
RHYN, Mary	GREENWELL, Combs	NOV 17 1842
RIAND, Margaret	ESTING, James	FEB 11 1819
RIBAS, Antonio L.	THORP, Emma R.	FEB 06 1840
RIBNITZKY, John H.	NICKELF, Mary	DEC 30 1857
RICAR, Anna	SANDERS, James A.	AUG 21 1844
RICARD, Ann E.	HOFFMAN, Henry B.	MAY 05 1858
RICARD, Caleb B.	REED, Margaret Ann	NOV 13 1854
RICARD, Edward	COOK, Ann	FEB 02 1824
RICAUD, John	CARMINE, Mary	APR 03 1816
RICE, Catherine	ENNIS, Philip	OCT 13 1849
RICE, Cornelius B.	MOZINGO, Jane	FEB 03 1847
RICE, Edward V.	McCARTHY, Ann Maria	NOV 16 1847
RICE, Eleanor	SAUNDERS, Daniel	AUG 03 1820
RICE, Elizabeth	McGARVEY, Charles	MAY 07 1851
RICE, Ellen	BROWN, Edward H.	DEC 17 1851
RICE, John	DUFFEY, Margaret	JUL 26 1851
RICE, Mary	BURNES, Charles	FEB 23 1819
RICE, Mary E.	EDWARD, Rowles	OCT 19 1838
RICE, Mary Frances	HAUGH, Andrew	FEB 23 1841
RICE, Michael	ESTEL, Maria	JUL 24 1830
RICE, Nancy	BROWN, James	MAR 25 1819
RICE, Susan	JOICE, Michael	JAN 19 1836
RICE, Thomas	DICKEY, Catharine	OCT 20 1818
RICE, Thomas	COLLAMER, Ellen	JUL 29 1850
RICH, Ann Eliza	CROSSFIELD, Jehiel	JUL 10 1830
RICH, Henry	OLIVER, Ann Eliza	FEB 07 1816
RICH, Josiah W.	ROACH, Mary	NOV 26 1833
RICH, Salome	HUTTON, James	MAY 24 1825
RICH, Thomas	LAWRENCE, Elizabeth (blk)	APR 06 1848
RICH, Thomas	MILLER, Margaret S.	SEP 03 1855
RICHARD, Almarin Cooley	ROTHWELL, Mary Ann	DEC 31 1855
RICHARDS, Adelaide R.	PADGETT, Jonathan Turner	FEB 07 1850
RICHARDS, Alfred	MONTGOMERY, Gracey Louisa	OCT 30 1855
RICHARDS, Ann	BOGLE, James	JUL 14 1812
RICHARDS, Ann (blk)	THOMAS, John	AUG 01 1840
RICHARDS, Anne E.	WELLS, Elijah	OCT 21 1851
RICHARDS, Augustus H.	McLEAN, Rebecca E.	JAN 22 1829
RICHARDS, Dilia	LECTON, Osborn	JAN 20 1827
RICHARDS, Elizabeth	TUCKER, Samuel	JUL 20 1825
RICHARDS, Isaac	BROWN, Eliza (blk)	MAY 23 1831
RICHARDS, John H.D.	BRENNER, Cathaerine	APR 11 1850
RICHARDS, Jonathan	CURKWOOD, Elizabeth	OCT 02 1816
RICHARDS, Martha Ann	KEENAN, John	MAY 21 1838
RICHARDS, Martha J.	ROBERTS, Waller	NOV 02 1855
RICHARDS, Mary	DUSAN, William	OCT 13 1838
RICHARDS, Matilda	RANDALL, Saml.	JAN 30 1815
RICHARDS, Matilda Catherine	ROCKETT, Edmund	JUL 02 1842
RICHARDS, Samuel P.	LIPPINCOTT, Sarah	NOV 12 1856
RICHARDS, Sarah Ann	GOLDIE, John	FEB 05 1814
RICHARDS, Sarah Ann	BEVIN, James C.	SEP 07 1847
RICHARDS, Thomas	BUNTON, Eleanor	JUL 21 1823
RICHARDS, William	ECKTON, Harriet	JAN 12 1830
RICHARDS, William B., Junr.	URIE, Maria Louisa	MAY 24 1851
RICHARDS, William E.	WEEDEN, Mary J.	MAY 13 1858
RICHARDS, William G.	ADAMS, Mary R.	APR 16 1853
RICHARDSON, Alerson	HUSE, Mary	JUN 18 1818
RICHARDSON, Alfred	STONE, Malinda	MAR 09 1852

District of Columbia Marriage Licenses, 1811-1858

RICHARDSON, Anne	SLATER, Richard	JUL 29 1815
RICHARDSON, Benjamin	LUCKSON, Elizabeth	MAY 18 1819
RICHARDSON, Betty	RUTHERFORD, Thomas J.	SEP 18 1854
RICHARDSON, Catherine	HOOPER, Charles	SEP 17 1845
RICHARDSON, Charles F.E.	WILLIAMSON, Charlotte A.	MAY 17 1848
RICHARDSON, Edgar A.	EMERSON, Elizabeth A.	JAN 05 1847
RICHARDSON, Eleanor	CONNELLY, Charles	DEC 02 1816
RICHARDSON, Eliza	SIMMONS, William	NOV 15 1849
RICHARDSON, Elizabeth	MOORE, Thomas	OCT 08 1832
RICHARDSON, Frances (blk)	AMBUSH, Edward	JUL 29 1858
RICHARDSON, Francis Maria	GLEASON, James Alexander	MAR 27 1856
RICHARDSON, George W.	LUSBY, Virginia Ellen	MAY 16 1853
RICHARDSON, George W.	JOHNSON, Mary E.	JUL 01 1858
RICHARDSON, Jane	KIDWELL, George P.	JUL 20 1839
RICHARDSON, John	McLAUGHLIN, Martha	JUN 20 1831
RICHARDSON, John	CLARKE, Henrietta	APR 29 1837
RICHARDSON, John William	MILLS, Elizabeth Matilda	APR 26 1849
RICHARDSON, Judson, Junr.	BOARMAN, Ellen	JUN 14 1842
RICHARDSON, Marcus	PEAKE, Emma L.	NOV 04 1856
RICHARDSON, Mark	HICKS, Verlinda	DEC 07 1825
RICHARDSON, Martha E.	FILLIUS, Samuel	JUL 27 1858
RICHARDSON, Martha L.	CROSON, Armsted A.	AUG 03 1846
RICHARDSON, Mary	ROBY, Edward	JUL 25 1815
RICHARDSON, Mary	WOOD, Robert	MAR 07 1822
RICHARDSON, Mary Ann	WILLIAMSON, Joseph	JAN 31 1839
RICHARDSON, Mary F. (blk)	REELER, John	OCT 19 1854
RICHARDSON, Mary Jane	HARRAN, Thomas	JUL 28 1851
RICHARDSON, Matilda (blk)	WRAX, Benjamin	JUN 16 1845
RICHARDSON, Peterson T.	ROSE, Elizabeth A.	SEP 18 1827
RICHARDSON, Rebecca J.	BIDDLE, William	OCT 13 1857
RICHARDSON, Sarah A.	DAVIS, John W.	JUN 28 1858
RICHARDSON, Sarah Ellen	GODDARD, James	APR 06 1842
RICHARDSON, Thomas S.	BAUFRE, Anna M.	APR 14 1857
RICHARDSON, William	SMITH, Lucinda	MAR 21 1856
RICHERSON, Ann	GILL, James	MAY 23 1844
RICHEY, Hiram	NEWTON, Maria L.	JUN 01 1858
RICHEY, John	HARROVER, Elizabeth	APR 16 1857
RICHEY, Margaret	CARROLL, John	JUL 05 1833
RICHMOND, Maria	STACKER, Marinus	MAR 21 1846
RICHTER, Herrmann	LORENZ, Louisa	APR 27 1855
RICHTER, John	KLAENDIEST, Varonica	OCT 26 1852
RICHTER, Peter	MILLER, Elizabeth	JUN 15 1846
RICK, John	BURCKHARTT, Lenne	OCT 18 1855
RICK, John	NIEHAUS, Fredericka	SEP 07 1857
RICKABY, Alfred	ROGERS, Jane Teresa.	NOV 08 1851
RICKARD, Desire A.	HAYS, Mary M.	JUN 17 1840
RICKETS, Catharine	ROSE, Samuel	FEB 26 1827
RICKETS, Edward	TRAIL, Catharine	JAN 13 1829
RICKETS, Mary	HEETER, Uria	SEP 29 1828
RICKETS, Mary Elizabeth	JACKSON, Alexander	MAY 27 1846
RICKETS, Mary Jane	BALL, Horatio	APR 14 1853
RICKETTS, Abraham	EASTON, Sarah	JUL 05 1812
RICKETTS, Agnes H.	PRINCE, Henry	NOV 17 1857
RICKETTS, Anthony	BEAN, Mary Ann	MAR 23 1852
RICKETTS, Aquila	KINGSTON, Charlotte	JUN 23 1830
RICKETTS, James R.	FISHER, Ann R.	DEC 04 1855
RICKETTS, Mary Ellen	MULLIKIN, John	JUL 28 1857
RICKETTS, Mary M.	McREA, Albert H.	MAY 26 1856

District of Columbia Marriage Licenses, 1811-1858

RICKETTS, Robert H.	NICHOLSON, Mary E.	JUN 11 1853
RICKETTS, William	HILL, Jane	APR 17 1830
RICKSECKER, John	GEIGER, Eliza	MAY 28 1828
RICKTOR, Maria	MOSS, Obediah	FEB 11 1830
RIDDALL, Cordelia V.	LAUB, John Y.	JUN 11 1842
RIDDLE, Charles J.	DAY, Louisa	JUN 23 1852
RIDDLE, James	SENOLON, Ellen	MAR 18 1848
RIDDLE, William O.	GRAVITT, Frances A.E.	DEC 20 1853
RIDDLEMOSER, Geo. W.	BARNACLO, Virginia	NOV 09 1857
RIDDLEMOSER, J.D.	BEVERIDGE, H.M.	OCT 14 1851
RIDENOUR, Upton H.	MILLER, Lizzie	AUG 07 1854
RIDER, Andrew	GRAY, Jane	JUN 10 1845
RIDER, Ann	HURDLE, Thomas	SEP 17 1834
RIDER, Jane Maria	WHITE, Charles	OCT 13 1849
RIDEWAY, Jesse	MOORE, Mary	MAY 30 1854
RIDGATE, Benjamin C.	KING, Margaret Elizabeth	MAY 15 1845
RIDGELEY, Henry	JACKSON, Eleanor	JAN 12 1820
RIDGELEY, Nicholas	THOMAS, Ann	DEC 10 1856
RIDGELY, Greenbury	WISE, Margaret E.	JUN 26 1848
RIDGELY, Henry	ROBINSON, Ann (blk)	AUG 14 1851
RIDGELY, Hester Frances	RIDGELY, John [Dr.]	MAR 25 1835
RIDGELY, John [Dr.]	RIDGELY, Hester Frances	MAR 25 1835
RIDGELY, Mary A. Hopkins	HYDE, Samuel Gridley	OCT 18 1852
RIDGELY, Samuel	ROBB, Ann Eliza	MAR 20 1854
RIDGELY, William R.	STONE, Sally R.	SEP 26 1853
RIDGEWAY, Augusta W.	KENCHEL, Antoine F.	APR 20 1858
RIDGEWAY, Catherine	JAMES, John	MAY 06 1833
RIDGEWAY, Eden	BRADEN, Elizabeth	APR 10 1813
RIDGEWAY, Eden	BRADEN, Elizabeth	AUG 10 1813
RIDGEWAY, Eliza Ann	MILES, George W.	AUG 17 1841
RIDGEWAY, Enoch	HOWE, Mary Ann	MAR 08 1831
RIDGEWAY, Enoch	ECKLOFF, Henrietta F.	JUN 04 1850
RIDGEWAY, Geo. W.W.	WEAVER, Mary	FEB 10 1835
RIDGEWAY, James	WILLIAMS, Eliza	DEC 28 1812
RIDGEWAY, James F.	BURCH, Elizabeth V.	NOV 01 1853
RIDGEWAY, John	CLEMENTS, Elizabeth	NOV 30 1820
RIDGEWAY, John	CURRAN, Jane	DEC 20 1824
RIDGEWAY, Julia A.	MILLER, Thomas W.	JAN 20 1857
RIDGEWAY, M.A.C.	HAYS, John W.	MAR 03 1855
RIDGEWAY, Martha Ann	LANGLEY, John T.	JUN 16 1853
RIDGEWAY, Sarah E.	ECKLOFF, Adolphus	JUN 14 1849
RIDGEWAY, Sarah E.	PAYNE, Hezekiah	SEP 08 1857
RIDGEWAY, Susan	DAWSON, William	FEB 26 1829
RIDGEWAY, William	WALLICE, Harriet	JUN 18 1823
RIDGLEY, Charles	SHAW, Eliza (blk)	MAR 06 1855
RIDGLEY, Elizabeth (blk)	BRADLEY, Isaac	DEC 11 1850
RIDGLEY, James	FOSTER, Clara (blk)	JUL 20 1854
RIDGLEY, Martha (blk)	BELT, Ignatius	AUG 06 1856
RIDGWAY, Ann	KNOAKES, Thomas	JUN 07 1831
RIDGWAY, Barbara Ann	CUNNINGHAM, David	JAN 22 1828
RIDGWAY, Christiana E.	COOKE, James L.	DEC 19 1857
RIDGWAY, Ellen Eliza	FINCH, John S.	MAY 22 1849
RIDGWAY, Harriet	BEALL, Alfred	SEP 17 1826
RIDGWAY, Mordica	SOPER, Margaret	FEB 09 1826
RIDGWAY, Sarah Ann	DANSKIN, Washington A.	OCT 02 1839
RIDGWAY, Verlinda	FARRELL, John	JAN 13 1853
RIECHLA, John	PEARSON, Catherine	OCT 29 1844
RIEDEMANN, Heinrich	SIECK, Sophia Lisette	JUL 21 1858

District of Columbia Marriage Licenses, 1811-1858

RIEGLE, Wm. W.	McDANIEL, Martha	JAN 03 1856
RIEHTMÜLLER, Eknaz	ALBACH, Mary	OCT 13 1853
RIELL, Harriet	KNIGHT, Robert T.	MAR 19 1850
RIELY, William	COLLINS, Julia	MAY 22 1843
RIESE, Louisa	ESSELBRUGGE, Hermann	FEB 22 1838
RIFFEL, Mary	CUSTARD, Jacob	APR 13 1816
RIFFLE, Catharine	PAYNE, Charles Henry	AUG 14 1845
RIFFLE, Margaret	HETCHISON, John	FEB 21 1831
RIGAN, Patrick	GARDINER, Ann	JUL 09 1818
RIGBEY, Edward	WALLECE, Grace Ann	DEC 24 1821
RIGDEN, Elizabeth	McCLISH, James	FEB 08 1823
RIGDEN, Henry	SPALDING, Catherine	JUL 18 1815
RIGDEN, Louisa	HEPBURN, Jeremiah	OCT 17 1826
RIGDEN, Louisa	MAGRUDER, Nathaniel	MAY 07 1828
RIGDEN, Rose Ann	GOODALL, George Washington	MAY 26 1846
RIGG, Sarah W.	SMITH, James W.	MAR 28 1837
RIGGEN, Rachel C.	PHELAN, Martin	SEP 24 1842
RIGGLE, Ann Maria	PARSONS, William	APR 28 1840
RIGGLE, Evelina	SPENCER, Amos	OCT 05 1854
RIGGLE, Peter	LOCKBALER, Frances	MAY 17 1851
RIGGLES, Eliza	EDWARDS, James	SEP 15 1854
RIGGLES, James	TINKLER, Eliza	AUG 20 1855
RIGGLES, John	BARRETT, Catherine	NOV 06 1834
RIGGLES, Joseph	ECKARD, Rebecca	FEB 24 1858
RIGGLES, Mary Ann	ELLIN, Benjamin	OCT 27 1841
RIGGLES, Mary Ann	TILDEN, William Chas.	JUN 12 1851
RIGGLES, Sarah	PENNYFIELD, John T.	JUL 14 1857
RIGGLES, Sarah Ann	TURTON, John B.	NOV 19 1846
RIGGLES, Thomas	PITTS, Mary Ann	DEC 21 1835
RIGGLES, Thomas	BORLAND, Catherine	MAY 10 1842
RIGGLES, William	FRAZIER, Mary	AUG 29 1846
RIGGS, John M.	OURAND, Sophia E.F.	JAN 03 1848
RIGGS, John P.	MILLS, Mary	MAR 29 1837
RIGGS, Lawrenson	CRUTTENDEN, Sophia T.	FEB 03 1840
RIGGS, Simpson	FOX, Keziah	SEP 18 1827
RIGGS, Sophie	REIFENBACH, Frederick	JUL 06 1855
RIGGS, Warren	GREEN, Letty (negro)	AUG 31 1830
RIGHT, Kitty	DAVIS, Asa	JUL 10 1819
RIGHTER, Anthony	BALDIN, Elizabeth	MAY 24 1836
RIGHTER, Jacob	STEWARD, Ann	AUG 23 1815
RIGHTER, James	BUTLER, Henny	MAY 12 1812
RIGHTSTINE, John W.	FORD, Rebecca	MAR 21 1854
RIGNEY, Bridget	TRAVERS, John	JUN 12 1858
RIGSBY, Charlotte E.	SPEAKES, Edward	NOV 20 1823
RIGSBY, Cynthia	THOMAS, George	OCT 27 1841
RIGSBY, James	BEECHEM, Mary	JUN 23 1836
RIGSBY, Jane	FUGETT, Francis J.	NOV 05 1846
RIGSBY, Mary	KEATHLEY, John	MAY 24 1851
RIGSBY, Rachael	BERRY, William	JUN 19 1845
RIGWOOD, James	LEMMON, Martha	DEC 29 1821
RIKER, Alfred	REMMINGTON, Catherine	SEP 16 1852
RILAY, Selina	SCHIVER, John	JUL 20 1835
RILES, Sally	DAVIS, Thomas	JUL 18 1814
RILEY, Alexander	SUTHERLAND, Julia Ann	MAR 31 1851
RILEY, Andrew J.	PAYNE, Sarah Ann	OCT 24 1854
RILEY, Ann	DALEY, Edward	JUL 07 1830
RILEY, Ann	MURPHEY, John	AUG 01 1840
RILEY, Ann	QUEEN, Michael	MAR 19 1844

District of Columbia Marriage Licenses, 1811-1858

RILEY, Ann E.	RAUB, Geo. T.	SEP 16 1843
RILEY, Benjamin T.	THOMPSON, Jane	FEB 04 1842
RILEY, Catharine	LYNCH, Peter	APR 29 1856
RILEY, Catharine	MARCHER, James	AUG 24 1858
RILEY, Charles	SEWALL, Susana	MAR 21 1818
RILEY, Charles	RADY, Johanna	MAY 23 1856
RILEY, Chloe	PILCHER, Lewis	JUL 05 1834
RILEY, Elizabeth	O'NEALE, Hilleary	JAN 08 1849
RILEY, Elizabeth W.	HODGES, Benjamin T.	MAY 31 1852
RILEY, Ellen	THOMAS, William H.	MAY 13 1856
RILEY, Ellen	TOBIN, Patrick	AUG 21 1858
RILEY, Francis M.	McCAULEY, Anna	MAY 12 1857
RILEY, Garrett	KEAN, Margaret	JUN 07 1853
RILEY, James	LYONS, Mary Jane	MAY 31 1847
RILEY, James	GRIFFIN, Catharine	MAY 30 1856
RILEY, James R.	HENDLEY, Ann E.	JUN 24 1856
RILEY, Jane	BREAST, James A.	DEC 08 1853
RILEY, Jane S.	MANKINS, John W.	OCT 05 1853
RILEY, John	LIESHER, Harriet Ann	AUG 21 1852
RILEY, John C.	HOWLE, Rebecca	JUN 15 1857
RILEY, Joseph	SUMMERS, Sidney	FEB 05 1852
RILEY, Joshua	FOWLER, Juliet H.	NOV 20 1827
RILEY, Julia	ARMAR, David	JUN 20 1855
RILEY, Margaret	DEAVERS, John	APR 03 1826
RILEY, Margaret	CAMPBELL, James	SEP 26 1853
RILEY, Margaret	CARBERY, Christopher	NOV 14 1853
RILEY, Mariah	AULD, James	DEC 16 1830
RILEY, Mary	SMITH, James	OCT 04 1849
RILEY, Mary	McNULTY, Philip	DEC 05 1853
RILEY, Mary	CAVENER, Thomas	MAY 19 1854
RILEY, Mary Ann (blk)	HENSON, John	JUN 02 1828
RILEY, Melinda (blk)	McDONALD, John	JAN 11 1825
RILEY, Peter	WALLACE, Mary	AUG 11 1851
RILEY, Sarah Ann	NICHOLAS, Jefferson	MAY 10 1826
RILEY, Sarah C.	PAXON, Thomas S.	MAR 22 1853
RILEY, Thomas	TUCKER, Harriot	APR 29 1812
RILEY, Thomas W.	YOUNG, Mary	MAY 14 1846
RILEY, William, U.S.N.	ROCHE, Ellen T.	MAR 02 1853
RILLEN, Mary	CHEW, John	DEC 06 1842
RILLING, John	HERRINGTON, Mary Ann Lee	SEP 13 1821
RIND, Clementina	McKELDEN, Andrew	MAY 03 1814
RIND, Henry G.	ROWZEE, Rebecca Ann	JAN 17 1835
RIND, Jane A.	RENNER, William G.	SEP 11 1832
RIND, Joanna	NICHOLLS, Isaac S.	DEC 31 1827
RIND, Rebecca Elizabeth	MULLIKIN, T. McE.	JUN 09 1856
RIND, Saml. S.	KANKEY, Araminta M.	NOV 07 1831
RIND, Sarah	NICHOLS, Isaac	APR 13 1818
RIND, William A.	BRUFF, Susan M.	NOV 16 1818
RINE, Michael	KERSEY, Catharine E.	OCT 20 1841
RINE, Susan	FITZGERALD, Edward	FEB 02 1856
RINEY, Philip	GINNET, Allice	SEP 02 1851
RING, James	SIMPSON, Ann	OCT 18 1851
RING, James	MAHER, Johanna	JUL 24 1852
RING, Johanna	COLLINS, Patrick	JAN 31 1853
RING, Margaret	BURNS, Thomas	JAN 26 1854
RING, Mary	BUCKLEY, Timothy	JUN 07 1856
RING, Norah	COLLINS, Daniel	SEP 05 1857
RING, Rebecca	DUCKWORTH, George	MAR 22 1826

District of Columbia Marriage Licenses, 1811-1858

RING, William	BRIGHT, Catharine	JUL 17 1837
RINGGOLD, Anna Maria	HUNTT, Henry [Dr.]	NOV 17 1829
RINGGOLD, Harriet Bowen	COOLIDGE, Richard Hoffman	FEB 22 1854
RINGGOLD, James S.	MORRIS, Harriet B.	SEP 29 1841
RINGGOLD, Mary	COX, Clement	NOV 10 1825
RINGGOLD, Richard	LOMAX, Caroline (blk)	DEC 16 1854
RINGGOLD, Samuel	HAY, Maria Amelia	FEB 16 1813
RINGGOLD, William H.	JACKSON, Mary Elizabeth	JUN 04 1839
RINK, Catharine	HEIBSDEMAN, Geo.	OCT 04 1843
RIORDAN, Andrew	DENAHY, Mary	JUL 01 1852
RIORDAN, John	CUNNINGHAM, Margaret	JUL 30 1853
RIORDAN, Mary L.	THOMPSON, Joseph B.	SEP 05 1853
RIORDAN, Patrick	CONNOLLY, Bridget	DEC 30 1854
RIPLEY, Charles	DRAKE, Margaret B.	AUG 12 1858
RISEN, Jane	GREY, Mathew	NOV 01 1813
RISEN, John	HENNON, Nancy	FEB 26 1830
RISEN, Louisa	ALLEN, Thomas	NOV 07 1844
RISON, Elizabeth	WESTON, Jerard	MAY 21 1825
RISON, Margaret R.	CARNEY, Valentine P.	AUG 20 1824
RISQUE, Ferdinand W.	PICKRELL, Caroline Saloma	OCT 12 1846
RISTON, Benjamin	MULLICAN, Elizth.	DEC 29 1821
RISTON, Benjamin	CALLENDER, Catherine O.	NOV 25 1844
RISTON, Benjamin	SWALLOW, Delilah A.	DEC 08 1853
RISTON, Fielder	YOUNG, Sarah	MAY 15 1823
RISTON, Henry	HOIT, Rebecca	SEP 19 1816
RISTON, Mary Ann	ROBERSON, William	MAY 28 1855
RISTON, Mary Jane	GROVES, Jacob	JUL 22 1843
RISTON, Thomas	McLANE, Mary Jane	FEB 01 1854
RITAN, Patrick	WELSH, Winifred	JUL 23 1853
RITCHE, Jno. H.	MOULDING, Ann Maria	NOV 04 1829
RITCHEN, Caleb	MILLS, Sarah Ann	JAN 21 1853
RITCHIE, Ann Eliza	CROSS, William B.B.	OCT 25 1849
RITCHIE, Ann H. [Mrs.]	TIAR, William A.	OCT 21 1829
RITCHIE, Charlotte C.	GITTINGS, John S.	NOV 29 1853
RITCHIE, Elizabeth	HOGSKIN, John	JUL 08 1824
RITCHIE, Ella C.	FALLS, Alexander J.	JUN 15 1857
RITCHIE, John T. [Lieut.]	BEATTY, Rosannah A.	AUG 23 1820
RITCHIE, Joshua A.	CARBERY, Mary S.	DEC 16 1839
RITCHIE, Margaret Fouche	STONE, Robert King	APR 17 1849
RITCHIE, Mary R.	QUEEN, James A.	OCT 10 1844
RITCHIE, Roseannah A., Mrs.	DeKRAFFT, Frederick W.	DEC 05 1833
RITER, Eve	VINEE, John	JUN 11 1832
RITER, Peter	ALLHOUSEN, Dorothy	FEB 02 1825
RITTENHOUSE, Benj. F.	DAVIDSON, Henrietta Waring	OCT 15 1835
RITTENHOUSE, Benjamin F.	LAURIE, Isabel	SEP 23 1828
RITTENHOUSE, Charles Edwin	WHITALL, Sarah Matilda	SEP 10 1841
RITTENHOUSE, Elizabeth S.	GURLEY, William H.F.	JAN 30 1854
RITTENHOUSE, Henrietta W.	WILSON, Thomas	MAY 01 1858
RITTENHOUSE, Isobel L.	NOURSE, J. Harvey	MAR 14 1853
RITTER, Amelia A.	PHILLIPS, Samuel H.	JUL 21 1853
RITTER, Catharine	ALBER, William	OCT 23 1852
RITTER, Francis D.	TUEL, Mary I.	JUL 19 1834
RITTER, H.G.	GOLDEN, M.A.	JAN 25 1848
RITTER, John	MORTIMER, Mary J.	APR 02 1850
RITTER, John E.	ELLIOT, Elizabeth	DEC 04 1855
RITTER, John F.	WELSH, Alice	FEB 15 1854
RITTER, John F.	JONES, Julia	JUL 17 1858
RITTER, John H.	LISARDE, Victoria	MAR 12 1829

District of Columbia Marriage Licenses, 1811-1858

RITTER, Maria	FLAGG, Lucas	MAR 25 1854
RITTER, Mary	ESSEX, Josiah F.	JUN 16 1847
RITTER, Obadiah D.	UPPERMAN, Cordelia	JUL 24 1851
RITTUE, Andrew J.	TODD, Eliza Jane	OCT 12 1852
RITZ, Catherine	HARTMAN, Charles	AUG 22 1812
RIVELL, Mary	KELLEY, James	MAR 12 1833
RIVES, James T.	RIVES, Lucinda	AUG 30 1849
RIVES, John C.	ELLIOTT, Mary Ann	JAN 11 1836
RIVES, Lucinda	RIVES, James T.	AUG 30 1849
RIVES, Mary	GETTS, William	FEB 07 1853
RIX, Mary Ann	PETERS, William	FEB 23 1830
RIXGLEY, Ellen (blk)	BUTLER, Thomas	JAN 07 1858
ROACH, Andrew J.	COOK, Angelina	FEB 10 1847
ROACH, Catharine	REARDEN, Dennis	JUL 31 1854
ROACH, Charles	JACKSON, Elizabeth (blk)	AUG 05 1835
ROACH, Edward N.	MANNING, Catherine A.	FEB 05 1839
ROACH, Gustavus	BEAN, Ann	OCT 29 1815
ROACH, James	ROACH, Mary	SEP 20 1851
ROACH, John	KING, Mary	OCT 04 1823
ROACH, John	QUIG, Elizabeth	APR 11 1828
ROACH, John	MARKS, Emeline	DEC 24 1839
ROACH, John	KYLE, Catharine	OCT 14 1852
ROACH, Lucinda	HOWARD, Henry	NOV 25 1826
ROACH, Margaret	MOREMAN, John	FEB 05 1853
ROACH, Margaret	PIREZYNSKI, Andrew	NOV 16 1857
ROACH, Mary	RICH, Josiah W.	NOV 26 1833
ROACH, Mary	ROACH, James	SEP 20 1851
ROACH, Mary Ann	HALFPENNY, William	JUL 21 1840
ROACH, Mary Ann	MURPHEY, David	OCT 01 1844
ROACH, Morris	NORNEY, Mary	DEC 22 1853
ROACH, Susan	GASKINS, William H.	MAY 16 1848
ROADES, Lucy F.	McREYNOLDS, John N.	MAR 28 1856
ROAN, Ann	PHENEY, William	APR 01 1837
ROAN, Mary M.B.	ACKER, John F.	MAR 12 1856
ROANE, Archibald	ALLEN, Ruth	JAN 09 1851
ROBACK, C.W., Dr.	SINNICKSON, Mary H.	MAY 24 1858
ROBB, Ann Eliza	RIDGELY, Samuel	MAR 20 1854
ROBB, Catharine	GREEN, John	AUG 30 1847
ROBB, Michael A.	WHITE, Margaret	OCT 03 1839
ROBBINS, Elizabeth	TRUNNELL, Silas	NOV 16 1855
ROBBINS, Isaac H.	BOYD, Mary Ann	JUL 07 1827
ROBBINS, Patrick	ELKY, Elizabeth	JUN 29 1835
ROBBINS, Thomas	WROE, Margaret	MAY 15 1832
ROBBINS, William	ZIMMERMAN, Eliza	MAR 11 1829
ROBBINS, William	ROBINSON, Jane	AUG 31 1837
ROBBINSON, Sarah	STUBBLEFIELD, Samuel	OCT 08 1838
ROBERRY, Elizabeth	KNIGHT, David	MAY 11 1854
ROBERSON, Charles W.	GRIFFIN, Mary Ann	MAY 11 1822
ROBERSON, Eleanor	BALIS, Geo.	OCT 18 1823
ROBERSON, Elizabeth	PRITCHET, Benjamin	NOV 11 1817
ROBERSON, James J.	McNEER, Margarett	DEC 09 1846
ROBERSON, John H.	PADGETT, Sarah L.	JUN 07 1856
ROBERSON, Mary M.	McKAMM, Daniel K.	MAR 30 1858
ROBERSON, Rebecca	MACKEY, William	JAN 07 1845
ROBERSON, William	RISTON, Mary Ann	MAY 28 1855
ROBERTS, Edmund	NICHOLSON, Hellen L.	DEC 13 1854
ROBERTS, Eliza A.	FITZHUGH, Edmund	MAY 29 1818
ROBERTS, Elizabeth	FULTON, Lyle	FEB 03 1814

District of Columbia Marriage Licenses, 1811-1858

ROBERTS, Elizabeth Augusta	PADGET, James F.	APR 23 1856
ROBERTS, Florian	MOULDER, Marthalina	NOV 13 1854
ROBERTS, Francis	HERFORD, Caroline	AUG 14 1858
ROBERTS, John	PETERS, Mary Elizabeth	AUG 03 1854
ROBERTS, John H.	ELDER, Matilda C.	OCT 16 1838
ROBERTS, John S.	WELSH, Matilda	NOV 20 1834
ROBERTS, Jonathan [Hon.]	BUSHBY, Elizabeth H.	APR 21 1814
ROBERTS, Levi	LEWIS, Mary Ann	MAY 17 1845
ROBERTS, Margaret	DWYER, Thomas R.	MAR 13 1856
ROBERTS, Margaret H.	THOMAS, Harrison M.	APR 24 1844
ROBERTS, Martha	GOLDSMITH, Samuel	OCT 24 1833
ROBERTS, Martha E.	SWINK, William	AUG 29 1843
ROBERTS, Matthew	LYON, Barbara	FEB 15 1831
ROBERTS, Matthew	GILLIGAN, Mary	OCT 05 1832
ROBERTS, Robert	WALKER, Catherine	DEC 13 1834
ROBERTS, Robert E.	WARD, Eliza Jane	JUL 18 1836
ROBERTS, Sarah	MILLER, William	APR 13 1816
ROBERTS, Sarah	WOODWARD, Charles	JUN 03 1828
ROBERTS, Waller	RICHARDS, Martha J.	NOV 02 1855
ROBERTS, William	HARPER, Fanny	FEB 26 1820
ROBERTSON, Catharine	GODDARD, Zachariah	APR 17 1819
ROBERTSON, Catharine	BELL, William	DEC 03 1850
ROBERTSON, Chas. F.	CALVERT, Lydia	JUN 19 1856
ROBERTSON, Daniel	SCOTT, Elizabeth R.	SEP 26 1844
ROBERTSON, Eliza	LEATHERBURY, William	DEC 07 1829
ROBERTSON, Eliza	LONGHERY, Ardavan Scott	MAY 07 1850
ROBERTSON, Eliza A.	PIOCOWSKI, Vincent	SEP 07 1857
ROBERTSON, Eliza C.	BYRAN, John W.	JAN 13 1857
ROBERTSON, Eliza W.	SEMMES, John H.	JUN 19 1850
ROBERTSON, Elizabeth	LOVEJOY, Alexander	JUL 18 1818
ROBERTSON, Elizabeth Maria	CADLE, James Gibson	NOV 23 1835
ROBERTSON, Elizth. H.	WRIGHT, Robt. [Hon.]	MAR 18 1822
ROBERTSON, Fortune	DAWSY, Susannah (blk)	SEP 22 1815
ROBERTSON, Frances	KEENE, Thomas	AUG 23 1830
ROBERTSON, Frederick	MAYHEW, Matilda	JAN 27 1837
ROBERTSON, George	HARDEN, Mary	OCT 03 1833
ROBERTSON, Grandison	WILLIAMS, Frances	JUL 13 1857
ROBERTSON, Henry B.	McKENNY, Mahala Jane	NOV 01 1849
ROBERTSON, Holdsworth	WILLIAMS, Mary	DEC 30 1830
ROBERTSON, James	ROWLANDS, Susanna	MAY 12 1814
ROBERTSON, James	BOSTIC, Jane	FEB 01 1816
ROBERTSON, James	GARRETT, Ann E.	APR 12 1848
ROBERTSON, James	ELLIS, Frances	MAY 17 1851
ROBERTSON, James H.	GITTINGS, Martha A.	JUL 27 1858
ROBERTSON, James Wm.	MARTIN, Margaret Isabella	SEP 29 1851
ROBERTSON, Jane	LITTLE, Joseph	JUL 31 1832
ROBERTSON, Jane	BARN, Wm. Thomas	DEC 22 1842
ROBERTSON, Jane M.	BUNNEL, Eliab	NOV 09 1812
ROBERTSON, Jessie	CALLOW, William	APR 09 1858
ROBERTSON, John	McCARTER, Mary	JUL 17 1818
ROBERTSON, John	DAVIS, Maria	MAY 12 1825
ROBERTSON, John	CONNELL, Elizabeth	APR 05 1827
ROBERTSON, John	WALKER, Elizabeth	NOV 26 1845
ROBERTSON, Lampkin	TURVEY, Elizabeth	DEC 20 1826
ROBERTSON, Leanna	BEEDLE, Alexander B.	AUG 16 1825
ROBERTSON, Lucinda	KNOWLES, William	APR 14 1830
ROBERTSON, Marietta H.	DREW, Columbus	NOV 26 1840
ROBERTSON, Martha	BENSLEY, John	AUG 28 1841

District of Columbia Marriage Licenses, 1811-1858

ROBERTSON, Mary	GOGGINS, William	APR 13 1847
ROBERTSON, Mary	McQUILLAN, Thomas	MAR 19 1852
ROBERTSON, Mary E. (blk)	WINTERS, William	NOV 05 1856
ROBERTSON, Minty	CUMMINS, Nathaniel	OCT 10 1815
ROBERTSON, Nicholas	CONNER, Ann	FEB 07 1853
ROBERTSON, Robert	HEART, Elizabeth	SEP 06 1817
ROBERTSON, Saml.	HOLLEY, Elizabeth	MAY 29 1813
ROBERTSON, Sarah	HOWARD, Joseph	NOV 17 1821
ROBERTSON, Sarah	CAMFIELD, Cipriana	OCT 10 1844
ROBERTSON, Sarah Jane	HOUGH, William W.	JUL 11 1854
ROBERTSON, Seth	WILSON, Elizabeth	FEB 11 1813
ROBERTSON, Stephen	HIATT, Elizh.	APR 26 1814
ROBERTSON, Susan D.	HUMPHREYS, Geo. W.	MAR 12 1845
ROBERTSON, Thomas	CHRISTIA, Agness	JUL 21 1817
ROBERTSON, Wm. B.	EASTERDAY, Ann	MAY 01 1820
ROBERTUS, Gottlieb	GRAHAM, Mary	FEB 28 1855
ROBEY, Ann	ARNOLD, Thomas	APR 01 1820
ROBEY, Ann	HUTCHINS, William	APR 21 1827
ROBEY, Benjamin	WARD, Rebecca	APR 17 1812
ROBEY, Chloe	CHICK, Joseph	MAR 10 1812
ROBEY, Delila	THOMPSON, William H.	JAN 10 1833
ROBEY, Dorsett	HILLIARY, Adelia M.	DEC 08 1849
ROBEY, Edgar	ALDRIDGE, Martha	DEC 24 1840
ROBEY, Eliza Ann	WATERS, William	JUL 29 1857
ROBEY, Elizabeth A.	TOWNSEND, Mathias B.	NOV 29 1853
ROBEY, Elizh.	LOVELESS, James	NOV 13 1815
ROBEY, Emily	NEWLAND, Ottemus	DEC 31 1855
ROBEY, Emma	HALL, James A.	NOV 08 1854
ROBEY, Emma J.	KIDWELL, Thomas J.	JUN 03 1854
ROBEY, Harriett	ROBEY, Joshia	SEP 08 1838
ROBEY, Henry	BERON, Jeroma	DEC 26 1843
ROBEY, Hezekiah	TAYLOR, Hannah	JUL 17 1813
ROBEY, Horatio N.	GREENWOOD, Catherine	JAN 21 1843
ROBEY, James Wilson	JONES, Mary Ellen	SEP 26 1837
ROBEY, Jane	SMITH, John W.	OCT 18 1816
ROBEY, Jenry	MAHORNEY, Mary E.	APR 22 1833
ROBEY, John	BERDINE, Hannah	NOV 23 1816
ROBEY, John	COOK, Ellen	JUN 28 1831
ROBEY, John	HIGDON, Ann Eliza	NOV 23 1847
ROBEY, John E.	SCOTT, Mary E.	SEP 06 1838
ROBEY, John H.	BEDE, Georgea Emma	APR 02 1857
ROBEY, John Thomas	THOMAS, Amanda Ellen	JUN 09 1855
ROBEY, Joshia	ROBEY, Harriett	SEP 08 1838
ROBEY, Lucinda	GATES, William Henry	DEC 08 1842
ROBEY, Mahala	JONES, George	DEC 21 1848
ROBEY, Margaret	HARMAN, Augustus	SEP 23 1843
ROBEY, Martha A.	WHEELER, Alfred	MAY 21 1850
ROBEY, Mary Ann	SMITH, William	JUL 28 1838
ROBEY, Mary C.	LAMMOND, Peter	DEC 05 1849
ROBEY, Matilda	BROWN, Richard	OCT 20 1827
ROBEY, Nancy	UNDERWOOD, John	MAY 28 1823
ROBEY, Nehemiah	MORELAND, Octavia	JUN 21 1853
ROBEY, Peter	FAR, Thursday Ann	AUG 03 1836
ROBEY, Richard T.	SCOTT, Sarah E.	JAN 26 1853
ROBEY, Sarah	TALBERT, Robert	JAN 09 1840
ROBEY, Sarah Ann	FRANCES, Richard	OCT 21 1848
ROBEY, Sarah B.	BEAVERS, Andrew	SEP 09 1818
ROBEY, Sarah Elizabeth	LIGHTFOOT, Daniel	JAN 27 1834

District of Columbia Marriage Licenses, 1811-1858

ROBEY, Sarah Ellen	COATRIGHT, William	JUL 16 1856
ROBEY, Susan	McKENNEY, Edward	AUG 03 1835
ROBEY, Susannah	STONE, David	JAN 19 1826
ROBEY, Theodore	SILAS, Mary Ann	MAY 24 1842
ROBEY, Thomas	ACTON, Elizabeth	JAN 26 1826
ROBEY, Tobias	CLOCK, Frances Ann	MAY 06 1858
ROBEY, Washington	TALBOTT, Sarah	AUG 14 1823
ROBEY, William	SUIT, Matilda Ann	JUL 16 1846
ROBEY, Winn Ann	WILKINSON, John H.	JUL 15 1843
ROBEY, Zachariah	HOGLIN, Rachael	MAY 29 1819
ROBINS, Joseph H.	ASHTON, Louisa A.	APR 10 1847
ROBINS, Philip	STEVENSON, Louisa (blk)	SEP 18 1828
ROBINSON, Ann	SESFORD, John, Jr.	FEB 28 1837
ROBINSON, Ann	McNIEL, Mark	DEC 22 1848
ROBINSON, Ann (blk)	RIDGELY, Henry	AUG 14 1851
ROBINSON, Ann Eliza	WALLIS, Thomas	DEC 30 1837
ROBINSON, Benjamin J.F.	WRIGHT, Mary Octavia	SEP 17 1856
ROBINSON, Caroline Virginia	WILLIAMS, Lemuel	MAR 31 1835
ROBINSON, Catharine	SHECKLES, Samuel	MAY 09 1831
ROBINSON, Catharine Ann	MILSTEAD, Judson	JUL 02 1826
ROBINSON, Catherine G.	GIBSON, Walter M.	MAR 01 1852
ROBINSON, Charles	SMITH, Eleanor (blk)	FEB 12 1835
ROBINSON, Charles	BELL, Susan Clarinda	NOV 13 1856
ROBINSON, Daniel	HURDLE, Elizabeth	APR 11 1850
ROBINSON, David	JASPER, Julia (blk)	JUL 31 1848
ROBINSON, David	ELLIS, Amelia (col'd)	AUG 17 1853
ROBINSON, Edward B.	WROT, Sarah Ann	JUL 17 1827
ROBINSON, Eleanor (blk)	DETTRE, Thomas	SEP 01 1836
ROBINSON, Eliza	WOODWARD, Clement	MAR 29 1825
ROBINSON, Eliza	WATSON, John C.	NOV 17 1829
ROBINSON, Eliza	GOVER, Samuel S.	DEC 10 1857
ROBINSON, Eliza A.	SMITH, G.A.C.	FEB 28 1857
ROBINSON, Elizabeth	MURRAY, Charles	APR 22 1824
ROBINSON, Elizabeth	LETHERBERRY, William	SEP 01 1830
ROBINSON, Elizabeth	JONES, Thomas	MAR 01 1837
ROBINSON, Elizabeth	BURR, Thomas S.	SEP 07 1847
ROBINSON, Elizabeth Ann	HANSELL, Emmerick W.	JAN 27 1840
ROBINSON, Ellen	BYERS, James F.	AUG 28 1852
ROBINSON, Ellen Ann	ATZ, Christopher	JAN 10 1843
ROBINSON, Ellen J.	BROWN, William W.	FEB 14 1849
ROBINSON, Fielding	BOYD, Ann (blk)	NOV 07 1839
ROBINSON, Frances A.	PETTIT, William F.	NOV 13 1846
ROBINSON, Francis	RABBIT, Rebecca	JAN 03 1854
ROBINSON, Hipsey	HUGHES, Archibald	MAR 24 1814
ROBINSON, Isabella M.	DULEY, Jonathan	OCT 11 1841
ROBINSON, James	SALES, Harriet	SEP 28 1829
ROBINSON, James R.	POTTER, Mary E.	APR 17 1852
ROBINSON, Jane	ROBBINS, William	AUG 31 1837
ROBINSON, Jane (blk)	DOUGLASS, Louis	NOV 22 1851
ROBINSON, Jean	TODD, John	FEB 19 1829
ROBINSON, Jefferson	HARDING, Sarah Ann	NOV 27 1829
ROBINSON, Jefferson	ELLIS, Matilda	SEP 01 1855
ROBINSON, John	SIMMONS, Rebecca	MAR 24 1828
ROBINSON, John	ALEXANDER, Clarrissa (blk)	NOV 12 1850
ROBINSON, John G.	CHARLES, Eliza	OCT 15 1822
ROBINSON, John H.	MACKABOY, Catharine	MAY 08 1850
ROBINSON, John M.	BIGGS, Eliza	NOV 15 1851
ROBINSON, John P.	DAVIS, Alethea Ann	OCT 11 1832

District of Columbia Marriage Licenses, 1811-1858

Name	Spouse	Date
ROBINSON, Joseph	CRAWFORD, Eleanor	MAY 20 1813
ROBINSON, Julia A.	FLINN, Villasques H.	SEP 13 1853
ROBINSON, Julia Ann	REYNOLDS, John Henry	AUG 08 1854
ROBINSON, Louisa	REED, Allen	SEP 02 1830
ROBINSON, Lucy C.	GOODMAN, Alexander G.	DEC 07 1832
ROBINSON, Margaret	THOMPSON, William	JUL 06 1848
ROBINSON, Margaret	SINER, John	NOV 23 1857
ROBINSON, Margaret A.	HULLS, John A.	MAR 11 1856
ROBINSON, Maria	McKNEW, Charles	AUG 28 1852
ROBINSON, Maria P.	SPALDING, William E.	MAY 23 1848
ROBINSON, Martha	COOPER, Edward	JAN 21 1835
ROBINSON, Martha	GOODE, Joseph O.	DEC 28 1853
ROBINSON, Martha	FENTON, James L.	JUL 12 1858
ROBINSON, Martha (blk)	SUMBY, Dennis	DEC 11 1851
ROBINSON, Martha M.	COLLINS, William T.	MAY 16 1850
ROBINSON, Martha M.M.	READ, Henry F.	DEC 02 1845
ROBINSON, Mary	HARRISON, David	MAY 22 1822
ROBINSON, Mary	ARNOLD, Thomas	JUN 28 1831
ROBINSON, Mary	MURPHY, Edward	DEC 19 1838
ROBINSON, Mary	HILL, John	JUN 28 1853
ROBINSON, Mary Ann	PRICE, George	SEP 01 1831
ROBINSON, Mary Ann	LAWRENCE, Stark Robert	JUN 29 1839
ROBINSON, Mary Ann	STREEKS, Richard W.	NOV 01 1845
ROBINSON, Mary Augusta	FREEMAN, Joseph M., Jr.	DEC 27 1855
ROBINSON, Mary E.	HAYS, Jonathan	OCT 27 1853
ROBINSON, Mary Spence (blk)	SUMBY, James	MAR 18 1846
ROBINSON, Olivia A.	SINCLAIR, John W.	SEP 23 1857
ROBINSON, Peggy	ALLEN, Thomas	JUN 27 1815
ROBINSON, Polly	SHERWOOD, Lewellin	JUN 01 1815
ROBINSON, Robert Emmet, Dr.	STAINBACK, Virginia E.	MAR 31 1843
ROBINSON, S. Lizzie	SPALDING, James W.	JUN 18 1856
ROBINSON, Samuel	GRAY, Rachel	SEP 15 1819
ROBINSON, Samuel	BRADFORD, Caroline A.	OCT 13 1836
ROBINSON, Sarah Ann	HARDIN, Austin	JUN 21 1831
ROBINSON, Sarah Ann	RATCLIFF, James A.	APR 25 1835
ROBINSON, Solomon	WALKER, Maria (blk)	OCT 26 1854
ROBINSON, Susan (blk)	HUTCHINSON, Philip	MAR 17 1823
ROBINSON, Susan Ann	JOHNSON, Andrew	AUG 12 1845
ROBINSON, Thomas H.	BROOKS, Christiana	JAN 21 1852
ROBINSON, William	TURNER, Frances H.P.	AUG 04 1829
ROBINSON, William	POTTER, Delilah	SEP 08 1851
ROBINSON, William	MADISON, Elizabeth B.	AUG 30 1851
ROBINSON, William	BUTLER, Cecelia (blk)	NOV 10 1853
ROBINSON, William M.	BONNYCASTLE, Anna M.	OCT 22 1849
ROBINSON, William T.	WAYSON, Matilda F.	FEB 09 1854
ROBISON, Eliza (blk)	SUMBE, William H.	FEB 03 1852
ROBY, Edward	RICHARDSON, Mary	JUL 25 1815
ROBY, John H.	KEATING, Margaret E.	FEB 04 1852
ROBY, Luther S.	BLOYES, Annie	AUG 11 1853
ROBY, Nancy	WILKINSON, John H.	AUG 28 1851
ROBY, Thomas	STEWART, Rosina	FEB 13 1849
ROCHE, Catherine	FLINN, Thomas	DEC 07 1853
ROCHE, Catherine	TOBIN, Patrick	JAN 09 1855
ROCHE, David	LAVIN, Hanora	MAR 28 1853
ROCHE, Ellen	HARTNETT, James	MAY 08 1850
ROCHE, Ellen T.	RILEY, William, U.S.N.	MAR 02 1853
ROCHE, Francis N.	BUTLER, Hellen M.	NOV 22 1854
ROCHE, James R.	MITCHELL, Susan E.	DEC 15 1852

District of Columbia Marriage Licenses, 1811-1858

ROCHE, Johanna A.	KEATING, Patrick M.	APR 17 1856
ROCHE, John	KEEFE, Mary	JAN 07 1857
ROCHE, Leonora de la	JOHNS, William B.	DEC 11 1856
ROCHE, Margaret	KINNY, Thomas	NOV 04 1850
ROCHE, Margaret	CONNERS, William	JUL 13 1852
ROCHE, Margaret	BRESNEN, Hugh	NOV 25 1857
ROCHE, Mary	O'BRIEN, Timothy	JAN 29 1853
ROCHE, Mary	JORDAN, German N.	SEP 07 1853
ROCHE, Mary	MURPHY, John	SEP 14 1855
ROCHE, Mary	McCARTY, Michael	FEB 06 1858
ROCHE, Patrick	MURPHY, Maria	JUL 17 1852
ROCHE, Philip	JOHNSON, Mary	SEP 28 1854
ROCHE, Robert J.	GAREY, Mary Ann	APR 01 1841
ROCHE, Sarah Clare	HOOD, Arthur	OCT 17 1849
ROCHFORD, John	SHANAHAN, Johanna	JUN 15 1858
ROCHFORD, William	MOORE, Mary	JAN 28 1820
ROCK, Elizabeth	GOLDSMITH, Samuel	APR 05 1823
ROCK, Henry	JARBOE, Mary J.	JUN 24 1857
ROCK, Theophilus	WEAVER, Mary	APR 28 1853
ROCKAWAY, Sophia	HEIDER, William	JAN 17 1857
ROCKET, Mary C.	CALDWELL, John H.	AUG 14 1855
ROCKETT, Edmund	RICHARDS, Matilda Catherine	JUL 02 1842
ROCKETT, Sarah A.	GATES, Lemuel A.	DEC 08 1853
ROCKETT, Thomas E.	STAPLES, Margaret	JAN 02 1850
ROCKWELL, Seth	ATWELL, Ann Julia	OCT 29 1828
RODBIRD, Absolom	EUSLIN, Eliza	MAR 12 1822
RODBIRD, Eliza	ELLIS, Edmund	SEP 05 1856
RODBIRD, Elizabeth	SELBY, Wm. Thomas	DEC 05 1844
RODBIRD, Ephraim B.	SLOANE, Mary Welby	MAY 20 1843
RODBURD, Jane	CAMPBELL, Daniel	OCT 25 1831
RODBURN, Eliza	JONES, Thomas	JUL 09 1832
RODDERICK, Theodore	NIGHT, Lucretia Ann	JUN 16 1829
RODDY, Ann	McDONNALD, James	JAN 27 1852
RODE, Caroline	GREEN, Gorish	FEB 16 1858
RODEN, Jane (blk)	CALVERT, John	AUG 22 1839
RODER, Dorothy	REPETTE, Joseph	APR 17 1843
RODGERS, Augustus F.	CROGHAN, Serena L.	JUN 09 1858
RODGERS, Benjamin	SPENCER, Mary Ann	MAY 04 1854
RODGERS, Bridget	RUTHERDALE, John S.	MAY 07 1851
RODGERS, Elizabeth	McDONNELL, James	MAY 12 1848
RODGERS, Jane	SPENCER, Daniel	SEP 03 1856
RODGERS, Jane H.	PLUMSILL, Stephen B.	OCT 18 1853
RODGERS, John	ELMORE, Sarah	FEB 28 1857
RODGERS, John, U.S.N.	HODGE, Annie	NOV 25 1857
RODGERS, Louisa	MEIGS, Montgomery C.	MAY 02 1841
RODGERS, Louisa	RODIER, Philibert Louis	JUL 02 1847
RODGERS, Margaret	RARIDON, John	OCT 18 1853
RODGERS, Mary	LYNDALL, Thomas	NOV 02 1824
RODGERS, Nannie	MACOMB, John Navarre	MAR 30 1850
RODGERS, Sarah Ann	EWERS, Eliphalit	NOV 09 1837
RODGERS, Thomas Robinson	CALDWELL, Margaret	JUL 11 1855
RODGERS, William	SEATON, Mary Ann (blk)	OCT 18 1832
RODGERS, William	SCOTT, Jane (blk)	NOV 28 1854
RODIER, C. Anthony	HALL, Catharine	SEP 11 1850
RODIER, Charles H.	SMART, Elizabeth C.	FEB 03 1842
RODIER, Charles H.	CLEMENTS, Elizabeth	NOV 17 1853
RODIER, James	CLEMENTS, Susanna	NOV 10 1842
RODIER, John	SUTTLE, Maria Elizabeth	MAY 14 1838

District of Columbia Marriage Licenses, 1811-1858

RODIER, Mary Jane	BROWN, John P.	JUL 08 1840
RODIER, Philibert Louis	RODGERS, Louisa	JUL 02 1847
RODSTEIN, Daniel	DIBBELL, Marian	MAY 21 1857
ROE, Mary McDermot	HARPER, Andrew	NOV 15 1827
ROE, Norah McDermott	CASTLEMAN, Thomas	NOV 03 1814
ROE, Sally McDermot	CANNA, John	OCT 18 1814
ROEMMELE, Elizabeth	LAKEMEYER, Frederick	MAY 26 1845
ROEMMELÉ, Mary Ellen	BURL, John McLane	SEP 16 1851
ROGAN, Hugh	O'BRIEN, Catharine	JUL 03 1837
ROGAN, Hugh	BROWN, Julia	FEB 05 1855
ROGAN, Mary	KENNEY, Patrick	OCT 02 1851
ROGAN, Mary Ann	CARR, John	SEP 18 1852
ROGERS, Amelia	DRYDEN, Robert R.	SEP 28 1839
ROGERS, Beverly	COOK, Sarah Ann	FEB 11 1826
ROGERS, Elizabeth	HIGDON, Gustavus	MAR 28 1812
ROGERS, Esther A. (blk)	WEBSTER, Daniel C.	JUL 06 1857
ROGERS, Eugene	STEELE, Fannie	OCT 01 1856
ROGERS, Gilbert, Jr.	BLACK, Delie M.	OCT 06 1845
ROGERS, James	O'DAY, Mary	DEC 14 1855
ROGERS, Jane Teresa.	RICKABY, Alfred	NOV 08 1851
ROGERS, John	BARRINGER, Mary	APR 04 1826
ROGERS, John	DEVOIN, Margaret	JAN 14 1854
ROGERS, John T.	CHILDS, Theresa A.	AUG 12 1851
ROGERS, John Thomas	PETTIT, Kesiah	JUL 03 1843
ROGERS, John Wesley	FARNUM, Jane Elizabeth	MAY 31 1855
ROGERS, Johnson R.	MOUNT, Octavia N.	MAR 13 1839
ROGERS, Joseph	VATERS, Mary Jane	JUL 27 1857
ROGERS, Libren	PAYNE, Susan	MAR 24 1832
ROGERS, Lloyd N.	LAW, Eliza	APR 03 1817
ROGERS, Mary E.	DAVIDSON, Christopher P.	OCT 09 1846
ROGERS, Nelson	FURRY, Serena	FEB 11 1833
ROGERS, Rachel	ANTHONY, Joseph	NOV 21 1820
ROGERS, Sabina	THOMPSON, Jno.	DEC 26 1814
ROGERS, William W.	LAKENAN, Ann V.	NOV 28 1838
ROGERSON, Eleanor D.	MILLER, George	NOV 11 1852
ROGERSON, George T.	DAVISON, Sarah T.	SEP 30 1854
ROHAN, Eliza	GLOVER, John W.	MAR 12 1849
ROHRER, Margaret B.A.	WANDLING, David	APR 30 1851
ROI, Seraphine	BELT, Paul	AUG 06 1850
ROLAND, Elizabeth	CUMBERLAND, Charles	OCT 05 1830
ROLAND, John	LOCKER, Anna	DEC 26 1854
ROLES, John	WALTERS, Mary Jane	SEP 06 1842
ROLES, William W.	SHEPPERLY, Deliphia	MAR 24 1852
ROLEY, William	PULLIN, Ann	OCT 05 1848
ROLISON, Jannett	HARDY, Joseph	MAR 26 1829
ROLLAN, George W.	DERGAN, Mary A.C.	OCT 30 1827
ROLLÉ, Justus Albert	LUEBER, Helen M.	JAN 05 1858
ROLLIN, Caroline	CORSON, Hiram	SEP 12 1854
ROLLIN, Daniel G.	ADAMS, Sarah E.	MAR 05 1849
ROLLINGS, Alexander	METTERDARL, Emily E.	JAN 07 1856
ROLLINGS, James M.	MASTEN, Jane	JAN 26 1857
ROLLINGS, Mary Ann	CROGGEN, Henry B.	OCT 20 1834
ROLLINGS, Mary E.	DIVINE, Hugh G.	AUG 03 1841
ROLLINS, Ann R.	PADGETT, John	NOV 27 1850
ROLLINS, Barbara	SLATER, Abraham	MAY 15 1818
ROLLINS, Eleanor	HEUS, John B.	AUG 08 1843
ROLLINS, Eliza	CHAMBERS, John	NOV 04 1819
ROLLINS, Elizabeth	THOMAS, Benjamin	NOV 13 1815

District of Columbia Marriage Licenses, 1811-1858

ROLLINS, Emeline	TAYLOR, Franklin	APR 03 1855
ROLLINS, George	SMITH, Pricilla	DEC 22 1834
ROLLINS, J. Alexander	LEWIS, Mary Ann	APR 18 1848
ROLLINS, James	MEADS, Ann	SEP 13 1825
ROLLINS, James	MOXLEY, Lucretia	OCT 17 1832
ROLLINS, Jane B.	MOORE, John	NOV 05 1851
ROLLINS, John	WILSON, Gady Ann (blk)	NOV 28 1846
ROLLINS, John A.	DAY, Susan Ellen	FEB 01 1844
ROLLINS, John W.	BALL, Sarah Ann	JAN 17 1824
ROLLINS, Joseph	SMITH, Henrietta (blk)	SEP 18 1854
ROLLINS, Joshua	WHITE, Rachael	DEC 18 1818
ROLLINS, Joshua	DUGGINS, Eliza	JAN 12 1824
ROLLINS, Martha	CUMBERLAND, Thomas	MAY 14 1850
ROLLINS, Mary	MILLER, Albright	MAY 13 1819
ROLLINS, Mary	LINKINS, John	MAY 26 1825
ROLLINS, Mary	BROWN, Eli	DEC 29 1853
ROLLINS, Mary E.	FOSTER, John	MAY 03 1836
ROLLINS, Mary Jane	STODDARD, John H.	NOV 12 1849
ROLLINS, Mary V.	ELLIS, John	OCT 17 1855
ROLLINS, Robert	ADAMS, Susannah	DEC 04 1824
ROLLINS, Sally	TRIDLE, William	DEC 31 1824
ROLLINS, Sarah	LISBY, Samuel S.	DEC 30 1813
ROLLINS, Sarah Ann	BUTLER, James	OCT 15 1829
ROLLINS, Sarah Jane	PIFER, Joseph W.	FEB 28 1849
ROLLINS, Susan	WYERS, Charles	OCT 20 1838
ROLLINS, William R.	TRAMMILL, Martha Ann	MAR 10 1857
ROLLIS, Ann	PEACOCK, Elijah	MAR 31 1845
ROLLS, Elizabeth	HENNING, William	AUG 12 1843
ROLLS, Gustavus	BLAND, Susan	JUL 02 1846
ROLOSON, William H.	DUVALL, Rosella L.	OCT 05 1836
ROLSEY, Mandy A.	POSY, Thomas	AUG 13 1840
ROMINE, Thomas	AYLOR, Sarah F.	JUL 13 1857
ROMNEY, Cloe Ann	STEPHENSON, Henry	JUN 26 1827
ROMON, Catherine	MORRIS, William	JUN 12 1843
RONAN, Catherine	CASEY, Patrick	JAN 18 1853
RONAN, Mary	IRETON, Michl.	FEB 10 1855
RONEN, Sarah	THORNTON, Dennis	OCT 13 1852
RONEY, Patrick	WHILAN, Bridget	OCT 25 1836
ROOD, Oliver P.	WANS, Sarah Jane	SEP 20 1838
ROOK, Peter	MULLEN, Mary	MAR 07 1831
ROOKER, Ann Elizabeth	LANE, Charles H.	SEP 17 1838
ROONEY, Francis	CONNOR, Elizabeth	NOV 22 1851
ROONEY, James	KELEHER, Mary	MAY 10 1853
ROOT, Mary Louisa	KREGELO, Jonas	MAY 13 1846
ROPES, Archer	TUCKER, Emilie W.	JAN 07 1852
ROPHINOT, Mary Julia	KHUNE, Adolphus	JUN 04 1853
RORICK, Michael	WELLS, Jane E.	DEC 27 1855
ROSE, Ailsa	EDMONDS, Thornton	SEP 13 1824
ROSE, Ann Elizabeth	YOUNG, John G.	APR 30 1833
ROSE, Benjamin F.	GIDEON, Rebecca	JUL 09 1832
ROSE, Charles C.	MAHORNE, Sarah E.	JAN 23 1855
ROSE, Charles S.	COX, Ann [Mrs.]	APR 24 1835
ROSE, Elizabeth A.	RICHARDSON, Peterson T.	SEP 18 1827
ROSE, George W.	BODINE, Malvina	OCT 04 1854
ROSE, H. Adelaide	SPINDLE, Benjamin T.	MAY 14 1856
ROSE, Jane	GODFREY, Henry	MAY 16 1850
ROSE, Jane C.	JOHNSON, Thomas	APR 14 1855
ROSE, John R.	SELBY, Minerva A.	NOV 07 1853

District of Columbia Marriage Licenses, 1811-1858

ROSE, Juliet Ann	SPOONER, George W.	SEP 26 1844
ROSE, Mariah	LINDSAY, Adam	MAY 30 1815
ROSE, Martha Ann	BRANGEL, George	OCT 09 1845
ROSE, Mary A.	HAZLEWOOD, Martin W.	MAY 13 1857
ROSE, Mary Gideon	MOORE, William George	OCT 15 1853
ROSE, Nancy	PURSLEY, Vincent	DEC 20 1842
ROSE, Rebecca Elizabeth	LANGTON, Alexander Thomas	OCT 15 1853
ROSE, Samuel	RICKETS, Catharine	FEB 26 1827
ROSE, Samuel	CRAIG, Caroline	DEC 15 1829
ROSE, Sarah Eliza	DIXON, Daniel	MAY 15 1852
ROSE, Thomas	HERITY, Peggy	APR 29 1822
ROSEBERRY, John M.	CONWAY, Mary Ann	JUL 25 1855
ROSEMOIN, Elizabeth	ZEIGLER, Adam	SEP 18 1838
ROSENBERRY, Joseph	OWEN, Mary Elizabeth	APR 29 1853
ROSEWAG, Godfrey	DORSEY, Anne Priscilla	AUG 07 1851
ROSIER, Susan	COLE, Charles	DEC 24 1817
ROSITHER, Thomas	JONES, Mary Eleanor	JUN 05 1829
ROSS, Benjamin	BELT, Henrietta (blk)	SEP 10 1850
ROSS, Charles	GREEN, Clara A.	APR 25 1844
ROSS, Charles A.	CANNON, Alice M.	SEP 28 1853
ROSS, Daniel	FORREST, Henrietta (blk)	MAY 11 1826
ROSS, Elizabeth	BUCKHER, Joseph	DEC 28 1824
ROSS, Elizabeth (blk)	COLE, Samuel	OCT 28 1841
ROSS, Hannaett	RAY, Alexander	OCT 24 1822
ROSS, Harriet (blk)	JOHNSON, Peter	MAY 19 1853
ROSS, Harriet Ann (blk)	LOWNDES, Isaac	OCT 26 1857
ROSS, Henry	SHORTER, Moses	AUG 16 1817
ROSS, Herbert	STOODLEY, Matilda (blk)	SEP 05 1850
ROSS, Isaac W.	WALLINGSFORD, Mary Ann	SEP 09 1830
ROSS, James T.	JONES, Arabella C.	MAY 09 1857
ROSS, John	HUDSON, Lucy Ann	SEP 22 1840
ROSS, John W.	WAUGH, Emeline A.	APR 16 1847
ROSS, Lucy	ORSBURN, John	DEC 24 1818
ROSS, Margaret Rebecca	HOSMER, Albert H.	MAY 30 1839
ROSS, Martha M.	LARE, John G.	JAN 06 1846
ROSS, Mary	GATCHELL, John	MAR 01 1822
ROSS, Mary Ann	POTTS, Samuel J.	JAN 28 1817
ROSS, Mary Jane	PERRY, Augustus E.	DEC 26 1844
ROSS, Matilda Eveline	WEISTLING, Benj. J. [Dr.]	JUN 21 1831
ROSS, Rezin	HOPKINS, Ruth (blk)	OCT 04 1831
ROSS, Richard	TAYLOR, Annie (blk)	JAN 10 1849
ROSS, Richard Lorman	TAYLOR, Louisa	MAR 06 1844
ROSS, Salina	DIXON, John A.J.	FEB 02 1843
ROSS, Sarah	CARROLL, John B.	NOV 19 1833
ROSS, Sarah (blk)	PALMER, Henry	SEP 09 1834
ROSS, Sarah Rebecca	SIEBEL, John C.	JUN 21 1851
ROSS, Trueman	SHEPHARD, Jane	JAN 03 1849
ROSS, William	LACEY, Sarah	JAN 01 1817
ROSS, William	GORDON, Dolly (blk)	APR 05 1849
ROSS, William L.	PHELAN, Margaret A.	OCT 04 1850
ROSSE, Paton	MATHANEY, Harriet	JUL 14 1856
ROSSER, John K.	WETHERALL, Mildred Ann	OCT 14 1854
ROSSITER, John	COURTNEY, Mary	APR 16 1852
ROSWELL, George	RANDALL, Eleanor	MAY 26 1828
ROSZEL, Stephen C.	CHALMERS, Mary Jane	JUL 09 1830
ROTCH, George	McBRIDE, Susan	JAN 19 1825
ROTE, Rachel A.	MEGOWAN, Robert	NOV 28 1844
ROTH, Andrew	KUMMER, Mary	JUN 08 1858

District of Columbia Marriage Licenses, 1811-1858

ROTH, Charles	LANE, Margaret	SEP 04 1855
ROTH, Josephine	HARTBRECHT, Stephen	OCT 05 1853
ROTH, Julius	BREIGENSEE, Maria T.	FEB 21 1852
ROTH, Mary	BURNETT, Richard	AUG 01 1844
ROTHROCK, Larkin J.	MILLER, Sarah H.	APR 28 1857
ROTHSCHILD, Hanchen	OPPENHEIMER, Maurice	JAN 05 1856
ROTHWELL, Andrew	BORROWS, Mary Ann	APR 17 1824
ROTHWELL, Andrew	DEWEES, Ann	FEB 03 1831
ROTHWELL, Andrew	DEWEES, Ann	FEB 03 1831
ROTHWELL, Laura E.	BROWN, Thomas B.	OCT 02 1845
ROTHWELL, Mary Ann	RICHARD, Almarin Cooley	DEC 31 1855
ROTHWELL, Susan B.	SHERIFF, George L.	APR 30 1856
ROUCKENDORFF, Maria	BROWN, William	OCT 26 1826
ROUNDS, Francis	LEE, Elizabeth (blk)	SEP 08 1853
ROURA, José Pabla	FRANZOM, Lavinia Gertrude	JUN 09 1848
ROURK, Mary	DONOHOO, Daniel	JUN 06 1857
ROURKE, Mary	FINN, Matthew	NOV 29 1856
ROUS, John G.	HIGHTAFFER, Mary L.	FEB 06 1857
ROUSE, Thomas	BRADLEY, Rosetta	JUN 07 1855
ROUSSEAU, Charles J.	RUPPERT, Elizabeth Catherine	NOV 24 1857
ROUSSEAU, Charles Joseph	RUPPERT, Elizabeth C.	APR 26 1856
ROUSTAGE, James	WARFIELD, Margaret	AUG 10 1828
ROUT, Caroline	WEAVER, Joseph	DEC 15 1846
ROUX, Peter	JULIEN, Rosa Margaretta	DEC 02 1817
ROUZEE, Elizabeth	HILTON, John P.	APR 19 1836
ROW, Margaret	STANSBURY, John	JUN 19 1857
ROWAN, James	STOCKARD, Margaret	APR 02 1819
ROWAN, Margaret S.	PANHAM, John	MAR 05 1853
ROWAN, Martha	PARHAM, William I.	JUN 08 1846
ROWAN, Stephen C.	STARKE, Mary B.	JUN 06 1839
ROWAN, Virginia	HANDY, Robert J.H.	MAR 24 1849
ROWAND, John R.	O'NEILE, Mary	MAR 24 1838
ROWAND, Virginia	WHAILLING, Daniel	JUL 28 1857
ROWARK, Ann	CALLAHAN, Thomas	JUN 23 1830
ROWE, Adeline R.L.	DYSON, Geo. E.	OCT 24 1826
ROWE, Charlotte Creusa	BURNS, Kennedy	MAR 22 1813
ROWE, John	MITCHELL, Mary Ann	JAN 08 1833
ROWE, John Thomas	GERMON, Ann Emiline	JUL 07 1842
ROWE, Josephine M.	McGEADY, John	JUL 07 1857
ROWE, Mary Ann	SPEAKE, Thomas L.	AUG 06 1833
ROWE, Susan	ESPY, James	JUN 20 1839
ROWE, William N.	HAVENNER, Elizabeth H.	APR 28 1842
ROWL, Jefferson	EMMIT, Caroline	JAN 15 1835
ROWL, Sophia M.	DIETERICH, Christian P.	APR 10 1856
ROWLAND, Elizabeth	CROUSE, Evered	APR 22 1823
ROWLAND, Emily	KENEMAN, Wm. T.	FEB 24 1857
ROWLAND, William	ROWLES, Kesia	FEB 25 1837
ROWLANDS, Susanna	ROBERTSON, James	MAY 12 1814
ROWLES, Charlotte	WILLIAMS, George	JUN 29 1813
ROWLES, George Wm.	LEWIS, Margaret	JUL 27 1847
ROWLES, Kesia	ROWLAND, William	FEB 25 1837
ROWLES, Sarah	HIGGS, Benj. F.	FEB 13 1816
ROWLES, Sarah	DOVE, Hezekiah	MAY 31 1843
ROWLES, Susan	HARRISON, James	JAN 03 1848
ROWLES, Thomas	BEAVERS, Delilah	AUG 07 1844
ROWLES, William H.	DAWSON, Margaret A.	NOV 05 1857
ROWLEY, James	VERMILLION, Eliza	NOV 23 1819
ROWLEY, Jane	JOHNSON, Christopher	NOV 21 1818

District of Columbia Marriage Licenses, 1811-1858

ROWLEY, John	COOK, Martha	MAY 21 1830
ROWLEY, Mary Jane	SIMS, John M.	AUG 29 1848
ROWLEY, Sarah	DUMBLETON, John	DEC 24 1819
ROWLINGS, Ann	DAWSON, Hugh	JUN 04 1818
ROWLINGS, Maria M.	SMITH, Henry C.	OCT 15 1853
ROWLINS, Jonathan	TREACY, Nancy	JAN 10 1816
ROWLS, Julia	UPTON, William	JAN 01 1846
ROWLS, Mary Ann	PEERCE, Joseph B.	MAY 07 1833
ROWZEE, Greenbury	LEWIS, Thomazine M.	APR 29 1844
ROWZEE, John	JACKSON, Julia A.	JAN 09 1837
ROWZEE, John	PAYNE, Susan	MAR 24 1852
ROWZEE, Rebecca Ann	RIND, Henry G.	JAN 17 1835
ROY, Mary M.	COX, Philip Lansdale	MAY 18 1843
ROY, Nancy	GRANT, William	SEP 30 1815
ROYALL, Mary (blk)	DAVIS, George	MAR 14 1855
ROYED, Maria (blk)	BROWN, Robert	JUL 21 1829
ROYER, Lewis August Francois	ALBUS, Marie Anne	MAY 28 1839
ROZELL, William	SETTLES, Julia Ann F.	SEP 06 1825
ROZIER, John W.	BRUCE, Hannah A. (blk)	NOV 15 1848
RUBEY, Elizabeth	MAZINGO, John	MAR 07 1837
RUBY, James	VERMILLION, Maria	APR 23 1814
RUCKER, James S.	SCOTT, Nannie S.	OCT 21 1857
RUD, Sarah Ellen	GOFF, George Paul	DEC 23 1851
RUDD, Almira	BROWN, Francis C.	APR 20 1858
RUDD, John W.	DAVIS, Harriet M.	MAY 11 1850
RUDD, Joseph	SHEPHERD, Elizabeth	APR 02 1838
RUDD, Martha E.	WHITING, William B.	MAY 04 1841
RUDOLPH, Catherine	SAUER, Charles H.	SEP 15 1856
RUEHL, John W.	REINDEL, Barbara	JUN 21 1853
RUFF, George Ryland	CRANDELL, Sarah Jane	AUG 31 1846
RUFF, John A.	BRYAN, Dorothy Ann	OCT 10 1848
RUFFEL, Jacob	BECKWORTH, Ann	APR 09 1825
RUGER, Jennie	BLOODGOOD, Delavan	MAY 05 1857
RUHL, Caroline	KEPPLER, George	OCT 30 1848
RUHL, Elizabeth	RUPP, William	APR 17 1847
RUHLAND, Henry	IRENG, Sophia	JAN 23 1858
RULE, Mary Elizth.	BAESCHLIN, Fredk.	JUN 21 1855
RULING, Catherine	MOGLAR, George	OCT 21 1834
RUMAGE, Linny Ann	SEARS, Hector	NOV 08 1842
RUMERY, Jane	HICKMOTT, Silas	JAN 24 1854
RUMLERLER, Peter	SHRIVER, Lena	DEC 30 1835
RUMMAGE, Mary	ELD, Henry A.	DEC 02 1847
RUMNEY, John	McKNIGHT, Martha	FEB 07 1824
RUMNEY, Margaret	WARNER, Leander A.	AUG 15 1823
RUMPFF, Henry	WIMSET, Sophia	SEP 17 1822
RUMPFF, Mary Emily	CLARKE, Henry A.	NOV 20 1845
RUNDELL, Addison	BARNES, Elizabeth	JUL 07 1841
RUNDLE, Patsey	DONALDSON, William	JUL 05 1834
RUNDLETT, George W.	O'BRIEN, Honora A.	APR 03 1858
RUNELS, Alexander	FLICKER, Charlotte (blk)	MAY 08 1851
RUNLIE, Margaret	HAIL, John Henry	OCT 10 1857
RUNNELLS, Jane R.	PATTON, James A.	APR 27 1840
RUNNELS, Leathia Ann	DAVIS, George	DEC 21 1816
RUNNER, John H.	JACKSON, Harriet	JUL 28 1858
RUNNER, John Henry	SUCKETT, Penelope C.	AUG 24 1852
RUNTZEL, Elizabeth	CROWN, William	NOV 10 1843
RUPERT, Barbara	LEHMANN, Antonie	OCT 03 1848
RUPERT, Edmund	LEST, Barbara	JUN 21 1853

District of Columbia Marriage Licenses, 1811-1858

RUPERT, Josephine	HOSHENLEITER, Ferdinand Artos	SEP 05 1853
RUPHERT, Joseph	BEAVERS, Elizabeth	JAN 04 1858
RUPLEY, Charles J.	DURR, Mary C.	JUL 17 1858
RUPLY, Anna Barbara	BRECK, John	MAR 24 1856
RUPP, Frederick	METZLER, Julia Ann	AUG 11 1856
RUPP, William	RUHL, Elizabeth	APR 17 1847
RUPPEL, John	MOT, Mary	NOV 03 1854
RUPPEL, Joseph	MILLER, Otelia	MAY 01 1857
RUPPEL, Michael	WILD, Elizabeth	AUG 29 1856
RUPPERD, Casper	ARNOLD, Drasey	JUN 17 1852
RUPPERT, Anton	SHWING, Anna	NOV 03 1857
RUPPERT, Catherine	MAKEL, Casper	FEB 03 1853
RUPPERT, Christian	GARTNER, Leonore	JUN 01 1854
RUPPERT, Elizabeth C.	ROUSSEAU, Charles Joseph	APR 26 1856
RUPPERT, Elizabeth Catherine	ROUSSEAU, Charles J.	NOV 24 1857
RUPPERT, Gertrude	JORDAN, Conrad	AUG 02 1856
RUPPERT, Henry	KLICH, Gertrude	FEB 14 1857
RUPPERT, Ignatius	SORG, Catherine	OCT 19 1844
RUPPERT, Johanna	HASSEN, John	SEP 29 1851
RUPPERT, Michael	KERBER, Mary M.	NOV 11 1856
RUPPERT, Walburg	SORG, John P.	AUG 02 1856
RUSH, Dennis	FORNEY, Mary	AUG 07 1855
RUSH, Mary J.	COLEMAN, George G.	JUL 18 1854
RUSS, Frances	CRONER, Michael	NOV 16 1848
RUSSELL, A.W.	CAMPBELL, Julia A.	APR 26 1855
RUSSELL, Benjamin B.	SMITH, Mary Ann	OCT 08 1835
RUSSELL, Chas. H.	JARBOE, Mary A.	OCT 27 1857
RUSSELL, Elizabeth	SHEPHERD, Abraham	MAY 27 1817
RUSSELL, Elizabeth	NEWELL, Jonas	MAY 04 1830
RUSSELL, Francis (blk)	TURNER, James	FEB 01 1844
RUSSELL, Frederick A.	GUSTINE, Theodotia T.	MAY 03 1815
RUSSELL, Geniza E.	BRYANT, William	FEB 27 1850
RUSSELL, George	SOMERS, Sarah	SEP 02 1813
RUSSELL, Henry	HANNAH, Joana Louisa	OCT 28 1851
RUSSELL, John H.	HARBIN, Mary Jane	DEC 17 1845
RUSSELL, John Henry	WILLIAMS, Lydia Ann	SEP 04 1845
RUSSELL, Judson	MAHORNEY, Mary	OCT 24 1829
RUSSELL, Lorenzo S.	HUDDLESTON, Mary A.	MAY 05 1852
RUSSELL, Mary	McCARTY, John	APR 12 1856
RUSSELL, Mary	TOBIN, James	MAY 22 1858
RUSSELL, Rebecca	BOSWELL, Jacob	APR 26 1817
RUSSELL, Sarah	WINDER, Samuel	APR 23 1812
RUSSELL, Thomas	LARNER, Mary Ann	AUG 09 1825
RUSSELL, Thomas	EVANS, Ann V.	OCT 31 1857
RUSSELL, William B.	HARVIN, Jane	MAR 27 1837
RUSSK, Robert F.	RAWLINGS, Eliza A.	MAY 05 1852
RUST, Elizabeth	HAYDEN, John Thomas	FEB 06 1855
RUST, George	WADE, Ann	AUG 04 1812
RUST, Robert B.	LUCAS, Rosanna A.	FEB 01 1847
RUST, Rosanna	MAY, John Thomas	NOV 03 1849
RUSTAGE, Elizabeth	AUKWARD, Francis	APR 10 1824
RUSTAGE, Lucy	HAYWOOD, John	APR 21 1824
RUSTICK, John	JONES, Mary Ann	AUG 01 1822
RUSTIN, Basil	BULL, Ann Maria (blk)	OCT 11 1823
RUSTIN, Osburn	LEE, Louisa (blk)	NOV 17 1835
RUSTREGE, Susan Ann	BARRET, Thomas J.	DEC 18 1832
RUSTRIDGE, James	CAMPBELL, Elizabeth	MAY 19 1836
RUSTRIDGE, James	GATES, Elizabeth	SEP 20 1837

District of Columbia Marriage Licenses, 1811-1858

RUTH, Enoch Fenwick	DIMITRY, Eliza Virginia	JAN 02 1857
RUTHERDALE, John S.	RODGERS, Bridget	MAY 07 1851
RUTHERFORD, Alexander	ATRIDGE, Mary	SEP 20 1838
RUTHERFORD, Barbara	NEWBAULD, John	MAY 21 1858
RUTHERFORD, Dyonicious	FORD, Sarah F.	JUL 14 1858
RUTHERFORD, Susan A.	CONANT, James E.	JUL 08 1854
RUTHERFORD, Thomas J.	RICHARDSON, Betty	SEP 18 1854
RUTHERFORD, William	HOPKINS, Matilda	JUN 09 1856
RUTMOND, Ellen	CUMMING, Robert	DEC 31 1855
RUTRING, Margaretta	HEILMICK, William	DEC 27 1842
RU[torn out], Mary A.	GIHON, William	DEC 05 1857
RYALE, George C.	BROWN, Mary	FEB 03 1841
RYAN, Ann	CANFIELD, James	OCT 18 1856
RYAN, Bridget	RYAN, Patrick	FEB 18 1854
RYAN, Bridget	GRIFFIN, Thomas	JUL 26 1854
RYAN, Bridget	DANAHY, Dennis	MAY 18 1855
RYAN, Elizabeth	ORKENDORF, John	JUL 27 1850
RYAN, Fielder	FRY, Chloe	NOV 29 1828
RYAN, Joanna	HUGHES, John	APR 22 1856
RYAN, John	BORGESS, Susannah	DEC 20 1814
RYAN, John	FITZGERALD, Margaret	NOV 04 1852
RYAN, John	McCOLGAN, Catherine	APR 10 1858
RYAN, John W.	DUCKETT, Ellen E.	DEC 11 1844
RYAN, Margaret A.	KELLER, Andrew J.	JUN 20 1855
RYAN, Margaret Ann	DORSEY, William B.	NOV 21 1831
RYAN, Mary E.	COOPER, Francis A.	JUL 25 1850
RYAN, Mary Jane	JONES, James	NOV 13 1852
RYAN, Michael	GOOLERY, Ellen	NOV 02 1850
RYAN, Patrick	RYAN, Bridget	FEB 18 1854
RYAN, Patrick	MURRAY, Mary	APR 10 1857
RYAN, Theodore	HART, Vilette	JUN 24 1843
RYAN, Thomas	WHEELER, Jane	NOV 16 1815
RYAN, Thomas	BENNET, Johanna	JUL 20 1850
RYDER, Alice	HEDGES, Edward	FEB 22 1855
RYDER, Clarke	GRINER, Charles E.	OCT 10 1854
RYDER, Clarke	GRINDER, Ann E.	OCT 26 1854
RYDER, Elizabeth	KEIZER, Henry	JUN 15 1854
RYE, Jacob	LOUEE, Fanny	JUL 16 1838
RYE, John T.	MUNROE, Martha	OCT 04 1850
RYE, Margaret	HAMILTON, Josiah	FEB 08 1844
RYE, Mary Frances	WHITE, Robert B.	SEP 03 1850
RYE, William	POWHORN, Ann	JUN 22 1815
RYLAND, Eliza (blk)	HOWARD, Peter	DEC 21 1847
RYLEY, Alice	BOYLE, James	APR 18 1857
RYNALDO, Mary Ann	MANLEY, William A.	OCT 01 1842
RYNE, Mary	O'SULLIVAN, Michael	JUL 19 1849
RYNE, Michael	HERRITY, Hannah	JUN 01 1822
RYNOLDS, Ann Eliza	PEARSON, George	OCT 14 1830
RYON, Alfred	ADAMS, Frances Catherine	AUG 19 1853
RYON, Danl.	MALONEY, Margt.	APR 09 1855
RYON, John	SOLOMON, Susan Ann	JAN 29 1845
RYON, John	RAFFERTY, Mary	APR 25 1857
RYON, Richard J.	WHEELER, Julia M.	OCT 01 1849
RYON, Thomas	McCOLGEN, Ellen	SEP 24 1855
RYON, Viletta	PADGETT, Benjamin	AUG 12 1858
RYTHER, Edwin A.	SPICER, Margt. R.	NOV 15 1856
R[torn out], Sarah Ann	LUCUS, William	MAR 22 1838

District of Columbia Marriage Licenses, 1811-1858

S

S___ENER, Margaret	DIDENHOVER, William	DEC 22 1832
SACHS, Margaret	TEGELER, Henry	NOV 03 1857
SACREY, Elizabeth C.	BERRY, John K.	SEP 21 1853
SADDLER, Jos.	FOOTE, Catharine	DEC 18 1820
SAFFELL, Anna M.	YOUNG, Wm. H.	MAY 13 1856
SAFFELL, Charles	COLUMBUS, Anna M.	JUN 08 1857
SAFFELL, Chas. H.	COLUMBUS, Anna N.	JAN 21 1858
SAFFELL, Rebecca R.	HARRIS, Joseph C.	OCT 01 1852
SAFFER, John W.	TAYLOR, Lucy Jane	FEB 25 1851
SAFFER, Mary L.	LAMBERT, Francis	MAY 20 1846
SAFFER, William	CUNNINGHAM, Susan	MAR 26 1812
SAGE, Franklin H.	KELLY, Mary E.	APR 21 1858
SAGE, Henry B.	GOLDSMITH, Caroline L.	JAN 08 1857
SAGE, Louisa E.	SIMPSON, Josiah	JUL 01 1858
SAGERSON, Ellen	McCARTHY, Michael	JAN 16 1856
SAKER, Elizabeth A.	BOUNDS, Joseph	MAY 10 1856
SALE, Andrew	LAKE, Alice	NOV 04 1822
SALE, Jane F.	TRENT, Thomas H.	DEC 15 1846
SALES, Harriet	ROBINSON, James	SEP 28 1829
SALISBURY, Ellen	PARKER, Robert D.	MAR 13 1849
SALISBURY, John	POWERS, Ellen	JUN 03 1833
SALISBURY, Susanna	HARRIS, Marbury	MAY 11 1853
SALLE, Emily	PORTER, George N.N.	SEP 16 1836
SALLSBERRY, Mary Frances	WILSON, James H.	OCT 09 1855
SALLY, Ann	KELLY, Edward	JAN 25 1831
SALMOND, Francis	CALBERT, Georgeanna (blk)	MAY 04 1840
SALOMON, Kenner	SMITH, Lucinda (blk)	MAY 02 1853
SALOON, Daniel	BRICKLEY, Mary	APR 19 1853
SALZER, David	SMITH, Eliza	APR 22 1847
SAMMONS, Stephen	CALDWELL, Harriet Maria	JUL 18 1844
SAMONTON, Mary	STROUD, James	AUG 26 1820
SAMPLE, Margaret	BARTON, Thomas [Rev.]	NOV 04 1824
SAMPSON, Eliza (blk)	SPRIGG, John	NOV 25 1851
SAMPSON, Jesse	HARRIS, Ailsey	SEP 20 1834
SAMPSON, Josephine (blk)	HUNT, Charles	DEC 14 1857
SAMPSON, Martha	HUTCHERSON, Thompson	MAY 23 1846
SAMSON, Thos. Hamilton	BAYLEY, Elizabeth (blk)	OCT 07 1856
SAMSTAG, Samuel	PRIBRAM, Augusta	AUG 07 1858
SAMUEL, Frances Ann	NORMENT, Richard	OCT 02 1851
SAMUEL, William	ALBY, Henrietta	MAR 29 1823
SANBORN, Thomas S.	MANEW, Charlotte	MAR 13 1851
SANDERS, Catherine	SEWELL, Clement	MAR 14 1814
SANDERS, Daniel N.	TOWNSEND, Mary A.	MAR 13 1856
SANDERS, Edward	HOMAN, Jane	MAR 09 1841
SANDERS, Emily (blk)	PLUMMER, Adam	MAY 30 1841
SANDERS, Henrietta (blk)	THOMAS, John	MAY 25 1854
SANDERS, Isabella M.	LEIDY, Enos	APR 12 1852
SANDERS, James A.	RICAR, Anna	AUG 21 1844
SANDERS, Joseph	CLUBB, Sarah	APR 14 1812
SANDERS, Lewis	HASKINS, Arie (blk)	FEB 23 1853
SANDERS, Mahala Ann	BEALE, Andrew	FEB 02 1843
SANDERS, Mary George	LEE, John	OCT 17 1845
SANDERS, Richard	SMITH, Margaret	JAN 03 1855
SANDERS, William G.	FAIRFAX, Caroline E.	MAR 01 1838
SANDERSON, Caroline C.	EMMERICK, Charles Frederick L.	FEB 01 1848
SANDERSON, Charles M.	HOLROYD, Georgiana	SEP 25 1856

District of Columbia Marriage Licenses, 1811-1858

SANDERSON, Corralear V.	NALLY, William	AUG 23 1853
SANDERSON, Elizabeth M.	PENNINGTON, Alfred	JUN 02 1858
SANDERSON, Henrietta	SHELTON, John	NOV 20 1848
SANDERSON, James Overton	BARNES, Ellen C.	JUL 24 1855
SANDERSON, Martha A.	GOSS, Thomas	DEC 30 1840
SANDERSON, Nicholas	McNAMEE, Catherine T.	OCT 28 1841
SANDERSON, Parthena Holbert	ENTWISLE, Isaac	MAY 22 1843
SANDERSON, Thomas	LONG, Phebe	SEP 10 1812
SANDERSON, William	WATKINS, Martha Ann	JUN 11 1812
SANDFORD, Ann Maria	MARTIN, Cosworth	AUG 06 1836
SANDFORD, Eliza	KNOKES, James	OCT 11 1825
SANDFORD, George W.	WHEATLEY, Mary C.	NOV 21 1854
SANDFORD, Jane	MILLER, Isaac S.	SEP 11 1828
SANDFORD, Joseph	THOMPSON, Mary	JUL 03 1834
SANDFORD, Maria	DOLEMAN, James	DEC 07 1854
SANDFORD, Mary	MANGUN, James	SEP 03 1840
SANDFORD, Mary	HOWARD, Thomas	JAN 26 1849
SANDFORD, Thomas E.	DEVON, Elizabeth	APR 04 1816
SANDIFORD, Ann	McPHERSON, Wm.	SEP 03 1818
SANDIFORD, Diana	MINNIX, William H.	JUL 17 1845
SANDIFORD, Elizabeth	EDWARDS, James	JUN 29 1842
SANDIFORD, Martha H.	HERBERT, Thomas	MAY 13 1815
SANDIFORD, Phebe Ann [Mrs.]	COOPER, Joseph	JAN 03 1833
SANDIFORD, Samuel	SERRINS, Phebe Ann	SEP 07 1815
SANDISON, Eliza	ANDERSON, Charles A.	DEC 24 1846
SANDON, Mary	CROWN, Samuel	APR 02 1857
SANDS, Benjamin F., U.S.N.	FRENCH, Henrietta M.	NOV 14 1836
SANDS, Frances R.	COWLING, Atwell	NOV 27 1855
SANDS, George	KIDWELL, Elizabeth	DEC 28 1816
SANDS, Saml. B.	PHILIPS, Susannah P.	JAN 03 1828
SANDS, Thomas F.	DAVIS, Ann E.	DEC 20 1855
SANDS, William	FOLEY, Honora	JAN 16 1855
SANDSBARY, Thomas	WINKLER, Margt.	DEC 26 1816
SANDSBURY, Benjamin Harrard	SANDSBURY, Harriot	FEB 03 1814
SANDSBURY, Harriot	SANDSBURY, Benjamin Harrard	FEB 03 1814
SANDSBURY, John B.	NESBET, Elizabeth	JAN 06 1827
SANDSBURY, John M.	FOWLER, Willey Ann	NOV 09 1824
SANFORD, Amelia	POOR, William A.	DEC 31 1857
SANFORD, Bushrod	CLARKE, Mary Ann	MAY 04 1849
SANFORD, Caroline	WILSON, John M.	NOV 18 1823
SANFORD, Frances Editha	GRIFFITH, William A.	NOV 05 1838
SANFORD, Hannah	HATCH, Wells	JAN 16 1851
SANFORD, Jane	SANFORD, William T.	NOV 23 1820
SANFORD, Jemima	COLLINS, L.B.	JUL 08 1845
SANFORD, Julia	COALE, Charles B.	JUL 13 1831
SANFORD, Linas	BELL, Elizth. Rebecca	SEP 12 1848
SANFORD, Lucinda	HENNON, Cornelius	AUG 13 1833
SANFORD, Margaret R.	CROSS, Robert R.	DEC 18 1852
SANFORD, Mary E.	JENKINS, James	FEB 25 1841
SANFORD, Mary E.	NESBITT, Jonathan	AUG 02 1842
SANFORD, Robert	CLUB, Drury Ann	JAN 14 1813
SANFORD, Whiting	MACHEN, Deborah	MAR 07 1823
SANFORD, William	REED, Lucinda	MAY 26 1840
SANFORD, William T.	SANFORD, Jane	NOV 23 1820
SANGER, George David	DOUGLASS, Elizabeth Ann	JUN 29 1858
SANNER, Ann Elizabeth	BRIDGET, James A.	APR 27 1843
SANNER, Jerome T.	GRAHAM, Virginia	JUN 26 1848
SANNER, Rebecca	CLEMENTS, Benjamin	APR 15 1843

District of Columbia Marriage Licenses, 1811-1858

SANS, Elizabeth Jane	DONOLSON, William	DEC 29 1848
SANSBERRY, James	TILLION, Juliet	MAR 29 1842
SANSBERY, Eliza	ALLEN, Benjamin	MAR 05 1849
SANSBURY, Charlotte	GRAY, William	NOV 14 1814
SANSBURY, Christian	FOWLER, William	JAN 12 1819
SANSBURY, Harriet	PILES, Julius H.	JUL 02 1851
SANSBURY, James T.	DULY, Sarah Jane	FEB 17 1852
SANSBURY, Jane	FOWLER, John	SEP 28 1848
SANSBURY, Rebecca	BRIGHT, Jacob	MAY 07 1822
SANSBURY, Sarah Ann R.	BALL, John W.	FEB 20 1849
SANSBURY, Susan	DULEY, Wm. W.	MAY 08 1854
SANSFORD, Ann R.	STONER, Frederick A.	MAR 27 1856
SANTUCCI, Isadore	RAPETTI, Teresa	FEB 16 1858
SARCEVES, Rhodey	COOKE, William	SEP 15 1831
SARDO, Fortunate Mary	BROWN, Robert	FEB 08 1825
SARDO, Joseph	EARHART, Ann Eliza	MAR 01 1826
SARDO, Josephine M.	McFARLAND, Alexander B.	JAN 19 1831
SARGEANT, Isabella	HAGAN, Zachariah	DEC 19 1849
SARGENT, James	BORTLE, Mary E.	JUL 27 1852
SARTAIN, John	SHEPHERD, Ann	MAY 24 1849
SARTEN, James W.	KANE, Mary Ellen	APR 17 1856
SASSCER, Elizth. A.	BRISCOE, G.B.	FEB 18 1857
SASSCER, James G.	SOUTHORON, Henrietta M.	FEB 12 1855
SASSCER, William B.	DIXON, Elizabeth J.	SEP 04 1841
SATTERWHITE, George	THOMAS, Elizabeth (blk)	MAR 07 1848
SATTERWHITE, James H.	FORD, Mary (blk)	NOV 26 1852
SATTERWHITE, Margaret T.	VALENTINE, John	JUN 04 1819
SAUER, Adam	GERBER, Sabine	AUG 03 1846
SAUER, Charles H.	RUDOLPH, Catherine	SEP 15 1856
SAUER, George Henry	DOOLEY, Louisa Virginia	MAY 25 1853
SAUERMANN, Maria	GRAGES, August	MAY 19 1855
SAULS, Edward	BAYLISS, Nancy	SEP 14 1848
SAUNDERS, Addison H.	MOORE, Ellen M.	MAR 05 1835
SAUNDERS, Alexander	SMITH, Frances	OCT 23 1847
SAUNDERS, Alvin	BARLOW, Marthena	MAR 11 1856
SAUNDERS, Anne	WALKER, Samuel	JAN 31 1837
SAUNDERS, B.J.	BARRETT, Nancy	FEB 04 1851
SAUNDERS, Beverly C.	WEBSTER, Charlotte	NOV 01 1830
SAUNDERS, Daniel	RICE, Eleanor	AUG 03 1820
SAUNDERS, Elizabeth (blk)	HENRY, Thomas	JUN 06 1839
SAUNDERS, Ellis G.	SAUNDERS, Sarah A.	JUN 07 1852
SAUNDERS, Frances C.	GARRISON, James	JAN 18 1848
SAUNDERS, John C.	SMITH, Rebecca J.	OCT 06 1851
SAUNDERS, Mary J.	PURVIS, William	FEB 28 1851
SAUNDERS, Richard	NELLON, Harriet	AUG 22 1836
SAUNDERS, Sarah A.	SAUNDERS, Ellis G.	JUN 07 1852
SAUNDERS, Sarah Ann	GAINES, Robt. H.	SEP 04 1828
SAUNDERS, Sarah P.	EDSON, Silas D.	NOV 27 1833
SAUNDERS, Susan	KARR, John	DEC 13 1853
SAUNDERS, Thomas C.	DOUGERTY, Sarah	AUG 26 1820
SAUNDERS, Thomas F.	GOGGIN, Elizabeth E.	MAR 15 1852
SAUNDERS, Thompson H.	DAVIS, Ann C.	AUG 10 1840
SAUNDERS, William H.	BRADLEY, Hannah S.	DEC 24 1851
SAUNER, Mary M.	COLISON, James R.	NOV 21 1843
SAUNTRY, Ellen	BENNETT, John	MAY 30 1856
SAUNTRY, Kennedy	DONOVAN, Margaret	JUN 16 1855
SAUNTRY, William	McCARTY, Hannah	OCT 23 1856
SAUR, George C.G.	KELLER, Margaretha	OCT 21 1854

District of Columbia Marriage Licenses, 1811-1858

SAUTER, Henry S.	SHERY, Mary E.	DEC 02 1856
SAUTER, Mary P.	HILLYARD, Benjamin F.	JUN 28 1858
SAUTER, Wendelin	COOLIN, Catharine	OCT 21 1833
SAUTIL, John Q.	KITTLER, Babetha	FEB 08 1854
SAUVAN, Robert	PICKFORD, Margaret Ann	MAY 05 1856
SAVAGE, Ann	BEALL, Richd. B.W.	APR 11 1834
SAVAGE, Hortense V.	PETTIT, John	NOV 13 1856
SAVAGE, James	BLINKHORN, Mary	NOV 22 1818
SAVAGE, James	MARRIOTT, Mary	JUN 16 1835
SAVAGE, James	MARRIOTT, Catherine W.	JUN 27 1844
SAVAGE, James	REILLY, Ellen	FEB 05 1856
SAVAGE, James W.	WHITEMAN, Elizabeth E.	DEC 22 1857
SAVAGE, John	NAYLOR, Pricey Ann	SEP 27 1826
SAVAGE, Mary Elizabeth	BATES, John	OCT 09 1847
SAVOY, Archabald	JACKSON, Theoffa	DEC 31 1812
SAVOY, Elijah	HAWKINS, Jane	NOV 26 1829
SAVOY, Elizabeth (blk)	BENNETT, Eli	JUN 13 1849
SAVOY, Elizabeth A. (blk)	CLARK, Stephen	MAY 04 1850
SAVOY, James	PROCTOR, Elizabeth (blk)	DEC 12 1850
SAVOY, Jane (blk)	BUTLER, George	MAR 13 1834
SAVOY, John H.	JOHNSON, Harriet (blk)	APR 09 1829
SAVOY, Laura (blk)	WARD, Charles	JUN 04 1855
SAVOY, Lucretia (blk)	PROCTOR, John	NOV 09 1854
SAVOY, Mary	PROCTER, Milo	JAN 25 1853
SAVOY, Mary (blk)	SEMMES, Judson	JAN 25 1848
SAVOY, Samuel W.	BAILEY, Anna E.	JUN 11 1856
SAVOY, Susan	PROCTER, Gustavus	JAN 28 1817
SAWKINS, Eliza	ANDERSON, Garret	DEC 21 1833
SAWKINS, Penelope Gay	TEST, John	MAR 17 1841
SAWYER, Ann [Mrs.]	LOWRY, James H.	APR 17 1833
SAWYER, Lemuel	WORTH, Camilla	DEC 23 1820
SAWYER, Lemuel	WERTZ, Mary	MAR 23 1826
SAWYER, M.	FLANAGAN, Garrett	MAR 27 1856
SAWYER, William	JOHNSON, Ann	AUG 19 1816
SAXTON, Joseph	ABERCROMBIE, Mary H.	APR 15 1850
SAYERS, Elizabeth	BROWN, Alexander	MAY 23 1855
SAYRES, James	EVANS, Rebecca	AUG 23 1817
SCAGG, Isaac	LARICK, Rachel	DEC 15 1842
SCAGGS, George B.	CLARK, Ruth	NOV 09 1857
SCALA, Francis	WOOD, Mary Ann	MAR 20 1844
SCALLAND, James	REDMOND, Mary	FEB 08 1820
SCANDALIER, Thomas	SHANEHAN, Catherine	FEB 04 1854
SCANLAN, Mary	READY, John	APR 23 1832
SCANLIN, Daniel	MACH, Catharine	MAY 01 1852
SCANLON, Ann	GARDINER, Richard B.	APR 09 1851
SCANLON, Honora	COLLINS, Dennis	JUL 29 1852
SCANLON, Jane	CHRISMOND, Oscar B.	OCT 12 1857
SCANLON, Johanna	SHUGHRUE, Daniel	NOV 22 1851
SCANLON, Mary	McGINNIS, Michael	JUL 13 1854
SCANLON, Patrick	LYNCH, Johanna	JAN 24 1853
SCARCE, Eleanor A.	CHURCH, William E.	JAN 01 1840
SCARCE, Harriet	BONTZ, Henry	JUN 01 1840
SCELLER, Rosa	SCHELL, Alvin	FEB 11 1856
SCHAB, Margaretta	KLEM, George	AUG 16 1856
SCHAD, Francis T.	KARLL, Mary S.	DEC 09 1840
SCHAD, John	WEIMER, Rosena Justena	JAN 14 1834
SCHAD, Justina	SIEGERT, Joseph	APR 12 1855
SCHADD, Henrietta	CLEMENSON, William Henry	FEB 07 1854

District of Columbia Marriage Licenses, 1811-1858

SCHADD, Wilhelmina	MADES, Charles	MAR 30 1857
SCHAEFER, Ann	WOODS, John	JUL 08 1852
SCHAEFFER, Ambrose	LUTZ, Agatha	JAN 11 1856
SCHAEFFER, August	LYNCH, Ausanna	FEB 03 1857
SCHAEFFER, Charles A.	PRESTON, Mary	AUG 28 1856
SCHAEFFER, Jinnie	SCHAEFFER, Martin	SEP 15 1852
SCHAEFFER, Martin	SCHAEFFER, Jinnie	SEP 15 1852
SCHAEFFER, Peter	SCHLOTTMANN, Mary Catherine	NOV 25 1850
SCHAENHERE, Carolina	DEITER, Francis Joseph	MAR 12 1857
SCHAEPLER, Charles	SCHICKEN, Rosina	JAN 31 1857
SCHAFAL, Hughn	FREEMAN, Barbara	MAY 09 1856
SCHAFER, Conrad	SUPPERS, Katharina	DEC 17 1852
SCHAFER, Frederick	DAVIS, Mary	JUN 19 1851
SCHAHAN, Johanna	DEVLIN, John	JAN 31 1856
SCHALLENBERESS, Frederick	WEHRMEIEN, Fredericke	JUL 27 1854
SCHALLENBERG, Henry R.	STOHLMANN, Anna C.	DEC 09 1851
SCHAMDTS, Jane	BURGAMAL, Joseph	DEC 03 1834
SCHANATT, Adam	LYRE, Mary	JAN 13 1841
SCHANDLER, William A.	MACKY, Adaline	JUL 07 1831
SCHANER, Lawrence	KING, Ann	OCT 22 1846
SCHANKS, Peter	FLETCHER, Elizabeth (blk)	JAN 01 1853
SCHARR, John	FONTELIER, Catharine	MAR 09 1849
SCHARTEL, Peter	HOSSEL, Margaret	NOV 01 1839
SCHAUMBURY, Frederick	SCHUTZ, Caroline	AUG 04 1845
SCHEDD, Margaret	WEISS, Joseph	SEP 15 1855
SCHEED, Amelia	LEDERER, CHristian	DEC 15 1846
SCHEELY, Augustus	HILLERY, Mary	JUL 07 1857
SCHEEP, Maria	AMAN, Frederick	OCT 05 1854
SCHEERER, Katherine Marie	DIETRICH, Franc Lewis	MAR 24 1854
SCHEFFIELD, John Joseph	WAGGONER, Elizabeth	FEB 03 1855
SCHEHRER, John C.	HOFBAUER, Mary Ann	MAY 08 1851
SCHEIDA, Henry	ASTHMUS, Mary	JUN 02 1848
SCHEIDEL, Frederick	MADDERLAGN, Helena	OCT 20 1834
SCHEITLIN, Jacob	HITZ, Margaret	MAY 18 1853
SCHELL, Alvin	SCELLER, Rosa	FEB 11 1856
SCHELL, Ann Maria	EDDS, James	JAN 05 1843
SCHELL, Sophia	HOLTZMAN, James Henry	JUL 09 1834
SCHENCK, John	STROH, Mary	OCT 08 1857
SCHENCK, Peter	HEIDER, Caroline	SEP 25 1856
SCHERER, Jacob	GEIGER, Sophia L.	JUL 19 1854
SCHERER, John F.	TRIPP, Mary Virginia	JUN 25 1853
SCHEREZ, Elizabetha C.	FLACK, Franz	SEP 05 1833
SCHERRER, Sarah	MITCHELL, Daniel	MAY 14 1832
SCHEWOOD, Charles W.	DIGGES, Margaret Malvina	JUN 07 1854
SCHICKEN, Rosina	SCHAEPLER, Charles	JAN 31 1857
SCHIDMORE, Mahala	ANDERSON, Thomas	JAN 07 1847
SCHIEBLER, Maria S.O.	BEARDSLEY, William H.	SEP 18 1855
SCHIFFER, Elizabeth	HESTER, Lawrence	SEP 20 1841
SCHIHOLM, Frederick	ALLBUS, Elizabeth	JAN 30 1841
SCHIMMICK, James	HALL, Mary	DEC 06 1840
SCHINEN, Catharine	HEICH, John R.	SEP 01 1856
SCHINZEL, Cecelia	KÜHLS, Theodore	MAY 28 1853
SCHIO, Peter	CUNIO, Joanna	APR 16 1855
SCHIVER, John	RILAY, Selina	JUL 20 1835
SCHLAB, Christian	CALERN, Mary	JUN 26 1845
SCHLASSER, George	SCHORNBERGER, Anna	DEC 02 1856
SCHLAYER, Wilhelmina	EDELMANN, Charles	MAR 19 1857
SCHLECHT, Regina	WAGNER, John	DEC 17 1832

District of Columbia Marriage Licenses, 1811-1858

SCHLEGEL, Ferdinand John	DILLER, Louise	FEB 20 1843
SCHLEIFER, Henry	OSTARMAYER, Sophia	SEP 07 1857
SCHLERP, William	KILLION, Barbara M.	DEC 12 1850
SCHLETMAN, Mary T.	CORD, William	JUL 21 1851
SCHLETTMANN, Maria Louise	BERGLING, Henrich	FEB 12 1855
SCHLEVOGT, Geo. F.J.	FENDNER, Louisa C.	SEP 10 1855
SCHLEY, Charles	LONG, Mary	MAY 05 1840
SCHLEY, Emeline	BIDDLEMAN, Daniel	AUG 31 1835
SCHLIECKER, Peter Frederick	LATIMER, Ann Elizabeth	JUL 19 1848
SCHLIEVER, Wilhelmina L.C.P.	BERGMAN, William	NOV 07 1854
SCHLOE, Mary	SKEY, George Smith	MAR 01 1851
SCHLOTTMANN, Mary Catherine	SCHAEFFER, Peter	NOV 25 1850
SCHLUPP, Maria	MILLER, John	DEC 08 1841
SCHMEDLEY, Mary Ann	EVANS, George W.	SEP 05 1844
SCHMEHL, Joanna A.	SPINDLER, Frederick	AUG 09 1852
SCHMIDT, Catharine	MUELLER, Gustavus	DEC 22 1856
SCHMIDT, Doris	VonSCHEELE, H.C.	DEC 30 1856
SCHMIDT, Elizabeth	RAY, John	DEC 02 1848
SCHMIDT, Elizabeth	SHWAB, George	JUN 26 1855
SCHMIDT, Ferdinand	KRAFT, Margueretta	FEB 16 1856
SCHMIDT, Frederica	FRIEDEL, Francis	JUL 22 1851
SCHMIDT, Jacob	FAHL, Ann	JAN 05 1854
SCHMIDT, John Frederick	EMMERT, Johanna Caroline Elizabeth	FEB 11 1850
SCHMIDT, Katherine	KUHN, Joseph	FEB 18 1856
SCHMIDT, Mary A.R.	MILLER, George	SEP 07 1843
SCHMILZ, Barbara	GOCHELER, Christian G.	JUN 04 1858
SCHMINKE, William C.	MILLER, Mary Rosanna	JAN 11 1855
SCHNABEN, Leopold J.	BLISCH, Mary Elizth.	SEP 05 1854
SCHNAEBELL, Andrew	KRAMER, Elizabeth	OCT 19 1833
SCHNAPPAUF, Kanigunda	DAWM, John Andon	DEC 22 1851
SCHNEIDER, Anna Martha	OCKRSHAUSEN, Johan	JUN 25 1858
SCHNEIDER, Caroline	ACKER, Jacob	APR 10 1840
SCHNEIDER, Catharine	SHRINER, Lawrence	SEP 28 1841
SCHNEIDER, Catherine	BEIGLER, Philip	DEC 28 1844
SCHNEIDER, Charles A.	RAYMOND, Sarah	JAN 03 1848
SCHNEIDER, Christian G.	MYERS, Amelia	OCT 26 1857
SCHNEIDER, Christiana	SHERER, Philip	JAN 21 1841
SCHNEIDER, Gottlobe C.	KELLY, Sarah E.	NOV 14 1850
SCHNEIDER, Joseph Lee	POLLUCH, Orbellonia	SEP 23 1848
SCHNEIDER, Leopold	SCHNIER, Catharine M.	JUL 21 1849
SCHNEIDER, Rosina	BREUN, Michael	JAN 21 1841
SCHNEIDER, William	BODEMAN, Sophia	JUN 02 1855
SCHNEITHER, Joseph Levi	WEBER, Mary Jane	DEC 29 1848
SCHNEKT, Karl	WILLS, Anna Katterina	JUN 29 1858
SCHNELL, Frederick	LIST, Johanna	JUL 07 1847
SCHNIDER, Catharine	MIKELKAB, John	FEB 22 1843
SCHNIDER, Nicholas	PLANT, Sarah A.	JUN 18 1846
SCHNIER, Catharine M.	SCHNEIDER, Leopold	JUL 21 1849
SCHOEDER, Sibilla	PFANZ, Adam	NOV 28 1853
SCHOENEBERGER, George	BLEDNER, Wilhelmie	JAN 02 1857
SCHOEPH, Albin	KESLEY, Julia B.	MAY 05 1855
SCHOFFIELD, John	CROWN, Rebecca	MAY 16 1830
SCHOLFIELD, John D.	CROUN, Ann Rebecca	SEP 09 1857
SCHOLFIELD, Sarah N.	GIESE, Henry	SEP 29 1852
SCHOLLMEYER, Sophia W.	MILLER, Jacob	APR 03 1858
SCHONELL, Louise	PETERS, Wilhelm	DEC 07 1855
SCHOOLCRAFT, Jane A.	HOWARD, Benjamin S.	MAY 15 1855
SCHOOLFIELD, Joseph N.	ENGLISH, Mary S.	OCT 25 1841

District of Columbia Marriage Licenses, 1811-1858

SCHORNBERGER, Anna	SCHLASSER, George	DEC 02 1856
SCHOTT, Annie V.	MOSS, John T.	OCT 02 1854
SCHOTT, Charles A.	GILDENMEISTER, Shereta	JUN 02 1854
SCHRAB, Maria	SIOUSA, John	JUN 29 1847
SCHRAM, Sophia	KERSCH, Francis	APR 17 1854
SCHRAMM, Lene	COLDERSTROTH, George	APR 06 1853
SCHREIBER, Emilie A.	BURKENNE, George	JUN 18 1853
SCHREIBER, John W.A.	HOFFMAN, Eliza	SEP 04 1852
SCHREIBER, Scharlotte	KREI, Conrad	AUG 28 1857
SCHREIVER, George	SMITH, Mary Ann	OCT 19 1852
SCHREKEL, Charles	LUTT, Dorothy	OCT 23 1855
SCHREPLE, Caspus	WESEL, Agnes	JAN 15 1844
SCHRIBER, Elizabeth	WAGNER, John	AUG 12 1853
SCHRINKEL, Teresa	BLISCH, George	JAN 15 1846
SCHRIVER, William	PETERSON, Senith	JUL 10 1848
SCHROEDER, Francis	SEATON, Caroline	FEB 10 1847
SCHROEGMAN, Henry	MESGER, Elizabeth	JUL 03 1835
SCHRY, Mahala	HUGHES, James	MAR 09 1844
SCHUCH, George	FREUND, Philipina	MAY 19 1853
SCHUL, John E.	HILBUS, Sarah Ann	DEC 23 1841
SCHULDIES, Nicholas	[blank], Theodora	JUN 13 1854
SCHULER, Louisa	KROUSE, Peter	SEP 28 1835
SCHULMEN, Charlotte	PREINKERT, John	MAY 16 1857
SCHULTHIS, Henry	MUHLLHAHM, Charlotte	MAR 23 1857
SCHULTZ, George	WINKLER, Mary	JUL 09 1853
SCHULTZ, John	WOLFE, Elizabeth	MAR 06 1846
SCHULTZ, Karl F.	JONES, Susan	SEP 15 1849
SCHULTZE, Julianna	NIXDORFF, Tobias	OCT 28 1818
SCHULTZE, William	HORSCAMP, Mary	NOV 22 1856
SCHUREMAN, Ann M. (blk)	THOMAS, John F.	JUL 30 1844
SCHUREMAN, Peter D.	JOHNSON, Eleanor	JUL 13 1820
SCHUREMAN, Peter D.	BRAGDON, Sarah Ann	JUL 29 1823
SCHUREMAN, William	AMBUSH, Elizabeth	MAY 23 1844
SCHUSSLER, Charles	MOELLER, Christine	JAN 25 1853
SCHUSSLER, Charles	HUDAL, Mary	OCT 03 1854
SCHUSTLER, John Gotlob	FRIEDEMAN, Ernestiene	SEP 25 1857
SCHÜTTE, Caroline	HOFHEINS, Jacob	JUN 10 1856
SCHUTTER, Hubert	McCONNELL, Esther Margaret	JUN 08 1854
SCHUTZ, Caroline	SCHAUMBURY, Frederick	AUG 04 1845
SCHUTZ, Malvina	BLUAHER, John T.	APR 13 1857
SCHUYLER, Cornelius	GORDON, Elizabeth (blk)	AUG 17 1843
SCHUYSSLER, Mary	SUTTON, Thomas	MAY 29 1846
SCHWAB, Dorothea	WAGNER, James Henry	APR 19 1856
SCHWARTZ, Henry	TAGGART, Eliza	SEP 18 1851
SCHWARTZ, Margaret	STUMP, Jacob	APR 05 1853
SCHWARTZ, Mary C.	FRED, William	APR 03 1851
SCHWARTZE, Augusta M.	BEATTY, Charles U.	JAN 03 1854
SCHWARTZE, Mary V.	HEATH, J. Harry	JUN 28 1858
SCHWARZE, Joseph R.B.	HEITMULLER, Caroline	JUN 24 1852
SCHWARZKOPF, Charles	VOSS, Dorette Antonie	NOV 07 1850
SCHWARZKOPF, Metta	EIGHSTADT, Adolph	JUL 25 1853
SCHWEAR, Sarah Catherine	FOLLANSBEE, Joseph	APR 02 1850
SCHWEITZER, Adam	FUCHBERGER, Ursula	JUL 06 1845
SCHWERAS, Sophia	STELLO, Henry	OCT 04 1855
SCHWERING, John Ernst Frederick	THIELE, Eliza Auguste	MAR 09 1849
SCHWIER, Henry	KINFT, Elizabeth	APR 03 1843
SCHWITZER, Peter	BREW, Elizabeth	NOV 11 1850
SCHWRAR, Mary E.	FENWICK, Benjamin I.	SEP 12 1848

District of Columbia Marriage Licenses, 1811-1858

SCIOR, Otto	ORM, Anna	MAY 10 1853
SCIPES, Elizabeth	HAMBUEGER, John	JAN 10 1843
SCISSELL, Sarah Ann (blk)	JACKSON, Simon	NOV 30 1852
SCOTT, Adeline	LEACH, William	JUL 01 1834
SCOTT, Airy	WILLSON, John	OCT 06 1836
SCOTT, Albert	SHEARWOOD, Matilda Jane	DEC 30 1846
SCOTT, Alexr. B.	DIXON, Mary Jane	DEC 29 1821
SCOTT, Ann	ESPEY, John	FEB 25 1813
SCOTT, Ann	HEBBRON, Peter	OCT 21 1815
SCOTT, Ann	PINCH, John	JUN 08 1821
SCOTT, Ann Rebecca	SCOTT, William A.	SEP 07 1854
SCOTT, Anna R.	WALKER, Nathan	MAY 17 1854
SCOTT, Anna W.	YOUNG, James M.	DEC 06 1854
SCOTT, Arabella	SUIT, Fielder, Jr.	MAY 15 1855
SCOTT, Camilla	HOYT, Gould	DEC 09 1851
SCOTT, Catherine	HARRISON, Thomas	SEP 01 1817
SCOTT, Catherine	HARRISON, Thomas	AUG 11 1817
SCOTT, Charles E.	MILLS, Susan V.	MAY 12 1857
SCOTT, Charles Emanuel	TILLETT, Nancy Ann	DEC 16 1848
SCOTT, Chas.	DOUGHERTY, Mrs.	DEC 22 1825
SCOTT, Deilah	THOMPSON, James	OCT 05 1822
SCOTT, Dory	SCOTT, Rebecca	DEC 17 1818
SCOTT, E. Adalade	SWEENY, William H.	JUN 25 1857
SCOTT, Edward P.	SULLIVAN, Mary Elizabeth	JUN 06 1842
SCOTT, Eliza	MEDARY, Samuel	SEP 29 1823
SCOTT, Eliza A.	OSBURN, Thomas H.	APR 08 1844
SCOTT, Elizabeth	MURPHY, Benjamin	SEP 04 1813
SCOTT, Elizabeth	TINSCEY, James	APR 28 1815
SCOTT, Elizabeth	WILSON, James	JUL 17 1828
SCOTT, Elizabeth (blk)	TALBURT, Andrew	MAR 15 1853
SCOTT, Elizabeth A.	WORCESTER, Samuel H.	OCT 09 1855
SCOTT, Elizabeth C.	PENN, Alexander G.	NOV 06 1852
SCOTT, Elizabeth R.	ROBERTSON, Daniel	SEP 26 1844
SCOTT, Ellen	BRYON, John	NOV 06 1840
SCOTT, Emaline	NEALE, George	APR 12 1844
SCOTT, Frances Ann	SHEELA, Frederick	JAN 11 1854
SCOTT, George A.	DAVIS, Ann S.	AUG 04 1853
SCOTT, George B.	TALBERT, Rachel	DEC 29 1832
SCOTT, George W.	SKINNER, Juliana	MAY 19 1836
SCOTT, Harriet Ann	HERBERT, James	SEP 11 1845
SCOTT, Henry	MURPHEY, Elizabeth	DEC 23 1818
SCOTT, Henry	JARVIS, Eliza	FEB 02 1836
SCOTT, Henry	DINES, Jane	NOV 19 1842
SCOTT, Henry	BIAS, Matilda (blk)	AUG 20 1845
SCOTT, Henry	BUSH, Frances (blk)	OCT 05 1846
SCOTT, Hezekiah	DEAN, Elizabeth	MAR 22 1815
SCOTT, Honora	KELLY, Martin	NOV 08 1856
SCOTT, Isaac	WILLIAMS, Mary (blk)	JUL 01 1846
SCOTT, Isabel	HALL, Edward G.W.	AUG 17 1858
SCOTT, Isabel A.	WYATT, William B.	AUG 22 1848
SCOTT, James	CHARLTON, Secelem	JUL 23 1829
SCOTT, James	BROWN, Mary	NOV 21 1839
SCOTT, James G.	FRENCH, Mary J.	SEP 12 1857
SCOTT, James S.	MILLS, Ruth	AUG 29 1842
SCOTT, Jane	CARTWRIGHT, Alfred G.	OCT 23 1839
SCOTT, Jane	KNIGHT, John	JUL 07 1853
SCOTT, Jane (blk)	HARRIS, William	JUN 14 1847
SCOTT, Jane (blk)	RODGERS, William	NOV 28 1854

District of Columbia Marriage Licenses, 1811-1858

SCOTT, Jane M.	FENWICK, John H.	JUN 19 1850
SCOTT, John	SUMMERS, Priscilla	APR 15 1828
SCOTT, John	BINGY, Catherine	OCT 29 1850
SCOTT, John	WHITTLE, Maria	OCT 10 1850
SCOTT, John	NALLY, Ann C.	JUN 03 1856
SCOTT, John D.	BEATTY, Jane Court F. Harrison	MAR 14 1820
SCOTT, John J.	THOMAS, Dorcas	JUL 03 1830
SCOTT, John J.	WARD, Mary Jane	FEB 03 1834
SCOTT, John J.	JONES, Mary A.	NOV 27 1855
SCOTT, Juliet	VONESSEN, Peter	JAN 07 1833
SCOTT, Kate B.	DRURY, Samuel T.	MAR 06 1855
SCOTT, Leonidas	THOMAS, Martha Ann (blk)	MAY 29 1851
SCOTT, Levi	DAVIS, Mary (blk)	AUG 06 1840
SCOTT, Louisa	WARREN, Joseph	OCT 08 1817
SCOTT, Margaret	McGLOCKLEN, Antoney	JAN 23 1844
SCOTT, Margaret A.	STOCKETT, Wesley A.	JAN 29 1846
SCOTT, Margaret A.	WILSON, Chas. H.	APR 13 1858
SCOTT, Maria (blk)	FERGUSON, Joseph	JAN 10 1854
SCOTT, Maria (blk)	HARRISON, Ralph	SEP 23 1854
SCOTT, Maria A.	SCOTT, Samuel E.	SEP 18 1850
SCOTT, Maria E.	COX, Fleet	JUL 12 1831
SCOTT, Martha Ann	GARGES, John H.	DEC 16 1841
SCOTT, Mary	BOOTHE, George	AUG 13 1812
SCOTT, Mary	DEMING, Jacob	OCT 28 1830
SCOTT, Mary	TRUDER, Samuel	JAN 12 1856
SCOTT, Mary (blk)	BROWN, Lloyd	MAY 29 1834
SCOTT, Mary Ann	MANSFIELD, George W.	JAN 07 1836
SCOTT, Mary Ann	BLAKE, William J.	DEC 18 1852
SCOTT, Mary Ann	KIERNAN, Patrick	FEB 02 1856
SCOTT, Mary Ann (blk)	ANDERSON, William	DEC 15 1857
SCOTT, Mary C.	CHEW, Walter B.	APR 28 1828
SCOTT, Mary C.	SUTER, Thomas R.	JUN 23 1841
SCOTT, Mary C.	WARRINGTON, Lewis, Jr.	FEB 03 1845
SCOTT, Mary E.	ROBEY, John E.	SEP 06 1838
SCOTT, Mary E.A.	STEPHENS, William A.k	JUN 16 1843
SCOTT, Mary L.	BLUNDEN, Owen Thomas	JAN 03 1852
SCOTT, Matilda	LISBY, Thomas	DEC 21 1816
SCOTT, Nannie S.	RUCKER, James S.	OCT 21 1857
SCOTT, Rachael	McKEWON, William	NOV 22 1817
SCOTT, Rachael	OSBURNE, Thomas	AUG 04 1818
SCOTT, Rebecca	SCOTT, Dory	DEC 17 1818
SCOTT, Rebecca	EMMERSON, William	SEP 02 1844
SCOTT, Richard K.	TUCKER, Emma Virginia	MAR 14 1850
SCOTT, Richard M.	GUNNELL, Virginia	SEP 09 1846
SCOTT, Robert	HALL, Sarah	JUN 22 1817
SCOTT, Robert	JONES, Mary	FEB 22 1831
SCOTT, Robert	MAGEE, Maria (blk)	MAR 13 1833
SCOTT, Russia	WISE, Eliza	MAY 09 1816
SCOTT, Samuel	GIBSON, L.A.	AUG 25 1847
SCOTT, Samuel E.	SCOTT, Maria A.	SEP 18 1850
SCOTT, Sarah	SIMS, Joseph	OCT 09 1814
SCOTT, Sarah	NOTT, William Edwin	OCT 09 1852
SCOTT, Sarah A.	STRETCH, John	MAY 14 1836
SCOTT, Sarah A.	QUEEN, Oscar B.	NOV 03 1847
SCOTT, Sarah E.	ROBEY, Richard T.	JAN 26 1853
SCOTT, Sarah Ellen	TURNER, William H.F.	NOV 08 1853
SCOTT, Sarah V.	TAYLOR, Marion M.	MAY 26 1853
SCOTT, Serene O.	GITTINGS, Jeremiah	DEC 20 1825

District of Columbia Marriage Licenses, 1811-1858

SCOTT, Thomas	SELVY, Adaline	JAN 12 1830
SCOTT, Thomas	BOSWELL, Martha Ann	JAN 21 1833
SCOTT, Thomas	GAINER, Ellen (blk)	DEC 24 1839
SCOTT, Thomas Edwin	CRUMP, Lydia	JUL 08 1844
SCOTT, William	GREEN, Sarah Ann	FEB 01 1839
SCOTT, William	SOPER, Martha	FEB 04 1841
SCOTT, William	WILLIAMS, Catherine V.	OCT 07 1854
SCOTT, William A.	NEALE, Rebecca	APR 12 1825
SCOTT, William A.	SCOTT, Ann Rebecca	SEP 07 1854
SCOTT, William A.	GRIMES, Virginia	SEP 15 1857
SCOTT, William H.	STRUDER, Elizabeth	AUG 30 1850
SCOTT, William H.	DAVIS, Matilda E.	DEC 01 1851
SCOTT, William S.	KING, Sally	OCT 02 1854
SCOTT, William T.	KING, Mary Frances Virginia	MAY 09 1848
SCREGGS, Thomas	PLA[torn out], Mary Ann	DEC 05 1857
SCREWS, Emily Ann	LANG, Robert	DEC 06 1842
SCRIVENER, Ann A.	WILSON, Jesse B.	SEP 25 1849
SCRIVENER, Charles	HOBAN, Mary Ann	APR 17 1837
SCRIVENER, Eleanor A.	KING, William H.	MAY 31 1851
SCRIVENER, James	JOHNSON, Mary	MAY 27 1841
SCRIVENER, James Edward	MARTIN, Sarah	DEC 17 1847
SCRIVENER, Lewis H.	DEREMER, Amanda M.F.	APR 06 1841
SCRIVENER, Sallie W.	FRANKLIN, William A.	MAY 04 1854
SCRIVENER, Samuel	HINTON, Amelia	JUL 22 1823
SCRIVENER, Thomas	WALLER, Elizabeth Ann	APR 14 1830
SCRIVENER, Thomas S.	FRENCH, Catharine	DEC 10 1855
SCRIVENGER, Rebecca	WOOD, John	JAN 13 1831
SCRIVENIR, Mary	MARTIN, James H.	MAR 31 1834
SCRIVNER, John	CISSELL, Maria	JUL 31 1823
SCRIVNER, Susan Sophia	WALSH, Francis S.	NOV 11 1839
SCRIVNER, William	CRAVEN, Eleanor	JUL 21 1836
SCUFFARLAIN, John	BUCK, Sophia	NOV 19 1847
SEABORN, Susan I.	CARROLL, George W.	JAN 03 1854
SEADENBERG, Deiderick	SHARZ, Barbara	DEC 31 1856
SEADLE, Mado	KONING, Julius	APR 14 1858
SEALOCK, Elizabeth P.	SMITH, Ransdle	SEP 20 1825
SEAM, Ann	THOMAS, Orrel T.	DEC 24 1825
SEAM, Sophia	MILES, James	OCT 21 1812
SEAMORE, Francis	GREEN, Lydia (blk)	AUG 29 1849
SEARCEY, Robt. E. [Lieut.]	McCAULEY, Isabella R.	SEP 11 1821
SEARCY, Isabella R.	McCORMICK, Hugh	JUN 09 1830
SEARLE, Caroline	GRAYSON, John B.	NOV 07 1828
SEARLES, Isaac	BATES, Eliza	JUL 15 1854
SEARS, Bernard	MILLER, Mary E.	OCT 29 1857
SEARS, Charlotte	CLARKE, Arthur T.	NOV 09 1847
SEARS, Chas. A.	MATTHEWS, Eliza S.	FEB 23 1857
SEARS, Cordelia E.	HOLMEAD, William	JAN 16 1837
SEARS, Douglass	NORFOLK, Eliza	APR 02 1846
SEARS, Hector	RUMAGE, Linny Ann	NOV 08 1842
SEARS, James	McDONALD, Eleanor	MAY 19 1824
SEARS, Virginia H.	CROZIER, Robert H.	MAR 01 1847
SEATON, Caroline	SCHROEDER, Francis	FEB 10 1847
SEATON, George	SMITH, Matilda	SEP 23 1815
SEATON, Julia Winston	MUNROE, Columbus	APR 03 1839
SEATON, Malcolm	SPRIGG, Jane E.	NOV 18 1857
SEATON, Mary Ann (blk)	RODGERS, William	OCT 18 1832
SEAVER, Elizabeth C.	KING, George G., Hon.	JAN 14 1851
SEAVER, Jonathan	PLUMER, Mary G.	JUN 04 1823

District of Columbia Marriage Licenses, 1811-1858

SEAVER, Martha, Mrs.	BOWEN, Benjamin	SEP 20 1825
SEAWELL, Francis T.	MACKEY, Mary	MAY 27 1824
SEAWELL, Washington [Lt.]	MACKEY, Martha	JUL 02 1832
SEAY, Angelina W.	PEATROSS, Samuel D.	OCT 10 1844
SEAY, William P.	DRAKE, Martha Jane	SEP 02 1837
SEBASTEN, Patty	GARNER, Thomas	JAN 31 1824
SEBASTIAN, Ann	BURCH, George H.	NOV 07 1837
SEBASTIAN, Eliza	JOHNSON, Hiram	JAN 18 1847
SEBASTIAN, Emeline	PAYNE, James	AUG 23 1844
SEBASTIAN, Jane Elizabeth	DEAN, James William	DEC 20 1845
SEBASTIAN, Leanna	ALLEN, William	APR 20 1850
SEBASTIAN, Margaret	PAYNE, Henry	AUG 23 1844
SEBASTIAN, Mary	BORMAN, Charles	AUG 16 1842
SEBASTIAN, Mary Virginia	BALLENDER, George William	MAY 13 1858
SEBASTIAN, Nicholas	DEAN, Catherine Ellen	DEC 09 1845
SEBASTIAN, Richard	DONALDSON, Anna Maria	JUN 14 1836
SEBASTIAN, Sarah F.	CAMERON, Charles E.	MAR 19 1856
SEBASTIN, Franklin	LYNCH, Margaret A.	APR 03 1854
SEBER, Monika	TEHER, Adam	JUL 11 1854
SEDDON, Joanah	BOGGESS, Thomas	MAR 07 1838
SEDGICKS, Ellen	NUTTER, Levin	MAR 27 1856
SEDGWICK, R.H.	SILENCE, Mary A.	FEB 22 1841
SEDRICKS, Marcila	GOODRICK, Benjamin	JAN 14 1840
SEDWICK, Ann	FANNING, John	MAR 31 1832
SEDWICK, Benjamin	KIBBY, Penny	JAN 02 1819
SEDWICK, Elizabeth Ann	GIBBS, John H.	SEP 16 1828
SEDWICK, Susan	CALBURT, John	SEP 17 1831
SEELEY, Martha T.A.	GRIERSON, John W.	MAR 20 1850
SEELHORST, F.W.C.	LOEHHAUSEN, Eleanor	OCT 21 1834
SEGAR, Francis	WHARTON, Nancy	JUN 04 1830
SEGIUN, Jacqous	BIGLE, Serile	JUN 01 1846
SEIFEL, Henry	DEISCHER, Barbara	DEC 26 1854
SEIFERLAND, John	FREIDERICK, Mary	NOV 30 1846
SEIFERT, Caroline	CLARKSON, Robert	JUL 28 1853
SEIFFERT, Henry	MARTIN, Rosanna	APR 08 1836
SEILER, Francis W.	WOLFROMM, Christina	DEC 21 1849
SEISS, Samuel	DOVE, Margaret	JAN 10 1851
SEITENARTEN, Margaret	HUHMANN, John Adam	NOV 15 1845
SEITZ, Ann Catherine	HAGER, Godfrey	MAY 28 1842
SEITZ, George	PLANT, Mary	JAN 29 1839
SEITZ, Henry	BEHLEN, Elizabeth	DEC 24 1853
SEITZ, Henry	HEITCH, Elizth. B.	MAY 21 1855
SEITZ, Hermiae	HILLEGEIST, Frederick G.	JUL 11 1857
SEITZ, John	ALTER, Amelia	NOV 25 1846
SELBEY, James	CREAMER, Mary	DEC 13 1841
SELBEY, Nancy	WRIGHT, James	JAN 17 1822
SELBY, Allen	GRAY, Mary Louisa	DEC 04 1849
SELBY, Amelia	EDMONSTON, Thomas	NOV 09 1816
SELBY, Catherine P.	DeVEAU, Andrew	SEP 25 1856
SELBY, Eleanor	BEALL, Elijah	NOV 26 1818
SELBY, Frances	SHEAHAN, John	APR 16 1846
SELBY, Frances	BUTLER, David	NOV 15 1849
SELBY, George	LACY, Florence M.	MAR 19 1856
SELBY, Jinetta R.	LUDWIG, Pierre J.	APR 07 1858
SELBY, John E.	REDDEN, Ann Mariah	OCT 04 1827
SELBY, Joshua	LEWIS, Mary	APR 14 1828
SELBY, Joshua	SUIT, Susan	FEB 22 1843
SELBY, Lucinda (blk)	TYLER, Washington	NOV 27 1849

District of Columbia Marriage Licenses, 1811-1858

SELBY, Martha	REILEY, William	OCT 25 1816
SELBY, Mary	JOSEPH, Peter	APR 13 1850
SELBY, Mary (blk)	GRIFFIN, Samuel	MAY 28 1851
SELBY, Mary Ann	EATON, Richard	NOV 29 1838
SELBY, Minerva A.	ROSE, John R.	NOV 07 1853
SELBY, Patrick	JACKSON, Serena (blk)	DEC 22 1842
SELBY, Sarah	BURFORD, John A.	SEP 23 1813
SELBY, Virginia	MILLER, George W.	APR 25 1851
SELBY, Wm. Thomas	RODBIRD, Elizabeth	DEC 05 1844
SELDEN, Bettie	BRANDT, Logan	MAY 23 1853
SELDEN, Emma (blk)	THOMAS, Thomas W.	MAY 25 1844
SELDEN, Frances E.	GARDNER, Wm. H., Capt. U.S. Navy	OCT 11 1842
SELDEN, James	WALKER, Margaret	APR 08 1846
SELDEN, Lucinda (blk)	JACKSON, Robert	MAR 15 1841
SELDEN, Maria L. (blk)	HEYLIGER, Louis	NOV 29 1848
SELDEN, Mary F.	KNOX, S. Boliver	JAN 28 1852
SELDEN, Sarah E.	GRAHAM, John [Lt.]	APR 01 1829
SELDEN, Virginia	GARDNER, William H.	APR 26 1853
SELDEN, William	HUNTER, Emily	JUN 01 1840
SELDNER, Pinchas	WOOG, Amelia	SEP 07 1854
SELECMAN, Thomas L.	ALLEN, Caroline F.	SEP 02 1841
SELF, Bradley	CARROLL, Julia Ann	MAY 02 1849
SELLE, Mary	GASCH, Ernst	JAN 15 1853
SELLHAUSEN, Augustus	HEGELER, Minna	JUL 07 1849
SELTMAN, Charles	MEÜSELL, Mary	MAR 27 1857
SELVEY, Henry E.	BALDWIN, Caroline	SEP 15 1831
SELVEY, John M.	NORTON, Elizabeth	OCT 12 1844
SELVEY, Patrick	COOPER, Louisa (blk)	MAY 11 1848
SELVY, Adaline	SCOTT, Thomas	JAN 12 1830
SELVY, Arthur	SHELTON, Margaret	NOV 27 1857
SEMENS, Emilie	HORBACH, Albert	NOV 20 1852
SEMMES, Alexander	BEATTY, Eleanor	SEP 26 1820
SEMMES, Alphonso Thos.	SEMMES, Mary Sabina	SEP 20 1856
SEMMES, Ann	BLACKWELL, William	SEP 30 1826
SEMMES, Ann America	PAYNE, Rice W.	JAN 03 1848
SEMMES, Clara	FITZGERALD, William B.	NOV 02 1850
SEMMES, Cora M.	IVES, Joseph C.	JAN 15 1855
SEMMES, Dorothy	HOOF, William	FEB 23 1830
SEMMES, Douglass R.	FLINN, Virginia	NOV 30 1857
SEMMES, Eleanor	RABITT, James	DEC 11 1830
SEMMES, Eleanor H.	BRAWNER, Basil	JUN 17 1830
SEMMES, Elizabeth	EYSBY, William	FEB 24 1813
SEMMES, Jesse M.	McGLUE, Mary A.E.	FEB 04 1823
SEMMES, John H.	ROBERTSON, Eliza W.	JUN 19 1850
SEMMES, Joseph	BEATTY, Ann	SEP 10 1816
SEMMES, Josephine (blk)	DULANEY, Thomas	DEC 19 1844
SEMMES, Judson	SAVOY, Mary (blk)	JAN 25 1848
SEMMES, Marcelina Virginia	WILSON, John Henry	JAN 09 1850
SEMMES, Mark Leir	LEWIS, Louisa Elizabeth	JAN 06 1849
SEMMES, Mary Ann	TOMPKINS, William	JAN 13 1829
SEMMES, Mary Ann E.	WOOD, Ferdinand F.	JUN 23 1831
SEMMES, Mary Sabina	SEMMES, Alphonso Thos.	SEP 20 1856
SEMMES, Nathaniel	JOHNSON, Sarah (blk)	OCT 16 1822
SEMMES, Samuel M.	GUEST, Ellenora Nelson	MAY 13 1840
SEMMES, Susanna	CROWN, John	OCT 01 1845
SEMMES, Thomas	WINTER, Catherine	NOV 08 1837
SEMMES, William N.	RENNOLDS, Mary	JUL 25 1839
SEMMS, Eleanor	MacINTEE, Samuel	JUN 09 1818

District of Columbia Marriage Licenses, 1811-1858

SEMNEY, Elizabeth	JENKINS, Thomas Henry	DEC 14 1855
SEMON, Charles	TAYLOR, Amelia	MAY 11 1842
SEMPET, Mary Ann	BIZET, Charlet	SEP 25 1824
SEMPETZ, Marie	PIERRE, Jean	MAR 18 1819
SENDORFF, Joseph	MORGAN, Ann	FEB 07 1828
SENDORFF, Mary Ann	PARSONS, Luther Osborne	MAR 11 1850
SENGEND, Sophia	TAUBERSCHMID, Lanehard	MAY 20 1858
SENGSTICK, Charles P.	RAGON, Catharine	MAY 10 1821
SENOLON, Ellen	RIDDLE, James	MAR 18 1848
SENSENEY, George E.	GALLAHER, Mary Hellen	NOV 03 1851
SENT, Caroline	KEISER, Henry	SEP 23 1850
SENTIS, Mathew	HOLLIDGE, Eliza	DEC 17 1842
SERGEANT, Helen V.	HILLS, Thomas O.	AUG 12 1857
SERGEANT, Henry	WAUGH, Sarah (blk)	JUL 10 1829
SERGEANT, S. Emma	HOWARD, Justin H.C.	APR 24 1852
SERGENT, John	KLEIBER, Adeline	DEC 24 1827
SERGSTACK, Margaret E.	CLARK, Wm. H.	DEC 19 1843
SERGSTACK, Mary E.	FOWLER, James W.	AUG 27 1849
SERPELL, Richard	DEAKINS, Jane P.	MAR 09 1836
SERPENTINE, Margaret	STONE, Henry	NOV 14 1833
SERRA, Augustin	MOORE, Susanna	JAN 01 1813
SERRA, Mary Ann	ADAMS, William	APR 21 1831
SERRAN, Mary Susan	FOWLER, Solomon	NOV 27 1847
SERRATT, Sarah	BANKS, Richard	MAR 30 1812
SERREN, Thomas	CUMBERLAND, Elizabeth E.	DEC 17 1857
SERRILL, James	PARRY, Elizabeth	MAR 31 1817
SERRIN, Daniel	GLASCO, Rachael	JAN 14 1823
SERRIN, Hetty Jane	DOWLING, Thomas	MAR 08 1827
SERRIN, James H.	FAGAN, Arabela	JAN 25 1855
SERRIN, Mary Ann	GAITHER, John	NOV 18 1824
SERRIN, William	DURR, Christianna	JAN 25 1825
SERRIN, William D.	CUMBERLAND, Sarah A.	NOV 06 1851
SERRINS, Phebe Ann	SANDIFORD, Samuel	SEP 07 1815
SERRO, Ann Eliza	MACOMB, Samuel	DEC 28 1835
SERRO, John A.	GRANGER, Martha A.	APR 24 1845
SERRY, John	HOWARD, Mary	JUN 10 1818
SES, John	WILLECLIST, Elizabeth	JUN 22 1839
SESFORD, Ann J.	STANLEY, Thos.	JAN 27 1819
SESFORD, John, Jr.	ROBINSON, Ann	FEB 28 1837
SESSFORD, Andrew	KELLY, Josephine	JAN 14 1846
SESSFORD, Elizabeth	KELLY, Samuel	DEC 20 1844
SESSFORD, Elizabeth	LAMB, Francis	SEP 15 1846
SESSFORD, Jane	STINGER, George	AUG 26 1824
SESSFORD, Jefferson	SHEPPARD, Mary Ann	MAY 26 1821
SESSFORD, John H.	MARTIN, Susan S.	OCT 12 1846
SESSFORD, John, Jr.	LAGREE, Mary Ann	MAY 28 1846
SESSFORD, Joseph	CREAMER, Sarah	JUL 05 1837
SESSFORD, Joseph	STEWART, Sarah Elizth.	APR 23 1850
SESSFORD, Joseph S.	WEEDEN, Sallie E.	NOV 25 1856
SESSFORD, Martha	BERNEY, Auguste	JUN 11 1825
SETTLE, Alexander L.	RHODIER, Mary Ann	APR 27 1836
SETTLES, Julia Ann F.	ROZELL, William	SEP 06 1825
SEUFFERLE, Elizabeth M.	McELFRESH, George S.	OCT 21 1847
SEUFFERLE, George J.	WARDER, Helen C.	NOV 15 1853
SEUFFERLE, Harriet	DAVIS, James	JAN 19 1841
SEVERE, Elizth.	PETIT, John	MAY 02 1829
SEVERE, Frs.	CONNER, Elizabeth	MAR 08 1821
SEVERMAN, John C.	WHITE, Mary	APR 05 1813

District of Columbia Marriage Licenses, 1811-1858

SEWALL, Ann D.	STONE, Henry	OCT 10 1825
SEWALL, Ann Eliza	WELLS, George R.	APR 19 1854
SEWALL, Ann T.	FOYLES, James	JUN 24 1813
SEWALL, Bennett H.	MANNING, Mary T.	MAR 23 1830
SEWALL, Charles Fenton	DOVE, Mary Elizabeth	AUG 29 1853
SEWALL, Christopher	SMITH, Elizth. (blk)	FEB 14 1855
SEWALL, Evaline	McGINLEY, Palmer C.	MAY 17 1843
SEWALL, Jane	MORSELL, James S.	JUN 17 1833
SEWALL, John	THOMPSON, Susannah	OCT 11 1813
SEWALL, Louisa A.	FALLANSBEE, Joshua	APR 10 1843
SEWALL, Maria (blk)	BAILEY, John Richard	MAY 25 1847
SEWALL, Martha E.	McCABE, Lorenzo D.	JUL 26 1845
SEWALL, Mary	BALL, James T.	FEB 11 1835
SEWALL, Mary	DANT, Francis X.	OCT 16 1838
SEWALL, Richard	FRAZIER, Sophia (blk)	NOV 29 1854
SEWALL, Sarah (blk)	BELT, Thomas	MAR 28 1848
SEWALL, Susan J.B.	DAINGERFIELD, Henry	OCT 20 1823
SEWALL, Susana	RILEY, Charles	MAR 21 1818
SEWALL, Thomas	HOYLE, Margaret	JUL 17 1822
SEWALL, William	ADAMS, Elizabeth A.	AUG 09 1821
SEWELL, Amelia	REMICK, Mark	JUL 06 1815
SEWELL, Clement	SANDERS, Catherine	MAR 14 1814
SEWELL, Clement J.	GRAVES, Sarah Ellen	FEB 06 1843
SEWELL, Frances Ann	SHREVE, James H.	FEB 14 1854
SEWELL, John D.	HUGHES, Jane	APR 29 1835
SEWELL, Lewis	PARKER, Atha (blk)	JUN 02 1856
SEWELL, Lewis H.	SHREVE, Susannah	JUN 17 1858
SEWELL, Martha E.	DAVIS, James N.W.	MAY 29 1855
SEXSMITH, Harriet	BALDWIN, Isaac P.	JAN 31 1848
SEXSMITH, Martha	WOODWARD, Clement	NOV 22 1827
SEXSMITH, William	TOWNSEND, Lucinda Ann	AUG 21 1837
SEXTON, Ellen	KEEFE, John	JUL 13 1857
SEXTON, John	COCKERILLE, Mary Ellen	NOV 01 1849
SEXTON, John	KENNEDY, Ann	NOV 01 1856
SEXTON, Matthew	MAHAR, Mary	AUG 16 1856
SEXTON, Patrick	DOODEY, Catherine	JAN 01 1857
SEYBOLT, Daniel H.	JONES, Eliza C.	FEB 20 1850
SEYMORE, Babel	LANDICK, Mary Jane (blk)	JUN 01 1848
SEYMORE, Carolin	THOMPSON, Vincent	OCT 15 1852
SEYMORE, Mary [Mrs.]	BLOXTON, Thomas	AUG 10 1816
SEYMOUR, Alexander R.	GAITHER, Eliza McLean	NOV 06 1849
SEYMOUR, Francis	WALLACE, Harriet Ann (blk)	MAY 31 1853
SEYMOUR, William F.	SMITH, Mary Catherine	NOV 14 1840
SEYTON, Catherine	HOPHON, Jacob	MAY 01 1856
SGRAN, Henrietta	BURR, Cinrod	OCT 26 1835
SHA, David	MACK, Bridget	JUL 17 1852
SHAAD, Catherine	ZEIGENHAIN, John	APR 20 1843
SHAAFER, Barbara	KELLER, Michael	APR 29 1844
SHAAFF, Arthur	FORSYTH, Mary A.	AUG 16 1825
SHAAFF, Margaretta Jane	JOHNS, John	JUL 17 1838
SHAAHY, James	CALLAHAN, Bridget	DEC 30 1854
SHAAHY, John	CASICK, Catharine	JAN 10 1852
SHACKELFIELD, James	LANHAM, Mary	APR 14 1829
SHACKELFORD, John	EVANS, Sarah Frances	SEP 28 1854
SHACKELFORD, Mary C.R.	PHELPS, James E.	MAY 22 1854
SHACKLEFORD, Clarissa A.	PURSLEY, John	MAY 08 1851
SHACKLEFORD, Eliza	ANDERSON, Elijah	DEC 19 1829
SHACKLEFORD, James	DUNCAN, Elizabeth C.	AUG 20 1831

District of Columbia Marriage Licenses, 1811-1858

SHACKLETT, Ann	CARTER, Wormly	MAR 06 1832
SHACKLETT, Robert	BERKLEY, Susan H.	DEC 02 1828
SHACKLETT, Sally T.	CARTER, John W.	OCT 02 1834
SHADD, Absalom	BROCKET, Eliza (blk)	MAR 28 1843
SHADDOWS, Louisa	BUTLER, John	APR 10 1833
SHADE, Thompson	BOSWELL, Mary Ann	APR 09 1818
SHADES, Ann	LILLEY, Thomas	SEP 25 1837
SHAD<u>E</u>S, Rachel	JOHNSON, Thomas	FEB 14 1824
SHADRACH, Catharine	ANDERSON, William H.	NOV 23 1852
SHADRACK, Jame F.	WHITE, Jeremiah T.	JAN 22 1848
SHAEFER, Henry	SHUMAN, Christiana	JAN 05 1854
SHAEFF, Mary	STEVENSON, Andrew, Hon.	JUN 27 1849
SHAEFFER, Catherine	GRIEB, John	OCT 23 1846
SHAEFFER, Ellen	BLANK, John	APR 03 1851
SHAFE, Jacob	MATTINGLY, Sarah	OCT 08 1834
SHAFER, Charles	HIERT, Catherine	FEB 25 1851
SHAFER, Christian	BALLANGER, Susan	MAY 01 1834
SHAFER, George F.	STROHMEYER, Minna	MAY 03 1851
SHAFER, John	COPF, Minna	APR 10 1851
SHAFER, John C.	POWELL, Mary A.V.	DEC 01 1849
SHAFER, Mary	HESCAMP, William	JUN 03 1834
SHAFER, Robert M.	HOWDERSHELL, G. Margaret	JUN 17 1852
SHAFER, Theresa	KESLEA, Baltzer	JAN 30 1856
SHAFFER, Catherine	NEFF, Frank	JUL 31 1848
SHAFFER, Charles	MITCHELL, Dianna	DEC 14 1844
SHAFFER, Jacob Frederick	WALLIS, Mary M.	JUN 18 1840
SHAFFER, John	CLEMENTS, Mary Elizabeth	AUG 06 1845
SHAFFNER, Wm. C.	FORREST, Mary E.	NOV 26 1834
SHAHAN, Margaret	MANGAN, Maurice	SEP 10 1855
SHAIN, Charles J.	MORTIMER, Joanna	MAR 01 1852
SHAINING, Katharine	EWALD, John	OCT 11 1855
SHAKES, Selestia Maria Veronici	CAMPBELL, James Washington	SEP 04 1832
SHAKLEFORD, Elizabeth	FORD, Joseph S.	JAN 06 1847
SHALI<u>M</u>, John	MURRY, Bridget	JUL 24 1851
SHALLOO, Eliza	DOUGHERTY, Thomas	FEB 24 1852
SHAMBLING, Mary E.	SMALLWOOD, James W.	SEP 16 1841
SHANAHAN, Catherine	MEAGHER, James	JUN 06 1853
SHANAHAN, Edwd.	MURPHY, Mary	FEB 13 1855
SHANAHAN, James	KENNEDY, Mary	DEC 06 1852
SHANAHAN, Johanna	ROCHFORD, John	JUN 15 1858
SHANAHAN, Margaret	CANTWELL, Michael	APR 19 1856
SHANAHAN, Mary	SULLIVAN, Owen	NOV 03 1855
SHANAHAN, Timothy	CONNAL, Joanna	MAY 28 1853
SHANCKNESSY, Margaret	MACK, Dennis	JUL 07 1857
SHANCKNESSY, Michael	CORBITT, Ann	AUG 07 1858
SHANE, Ann	COLLIER, Joseph	SEP 01 1825
SHANEHAN, Catherine	SCANDALIER, Thomas	FEB 04 1854
SHANK, Mary	JUDD, Abraham	JAN 24 1856
SHANKLAND, Robert H.	BRONAUGH, Elizabeth H.	FEB 07 1856
SHANKLAND, Thomas	DEGEN, Laura Louisa	APR 11 1835
SHANKLETER, Mary L.	MURRAY, Ai.	JUN 03 1854
SHANKS, Charles H.	HARRISON, Eleanor	MAR 31 1834
SHANKS, Eliza	FALES, Nathan W.	OCT 02 1845
SHANKS, Elizabeth T.	THAW, Joseph	DEC 25 1830
SHANKS, John	O'BRIAN, Sarah	OCT 06 1855
SHANKS, Michael	WATERS, Catherine N.	MAY 18 1836
SHANKS, Rosanna	CHESHIRE, Archibald	MAY 11 1813
SHANLY, Eliza	HAMILTON, Charles B. [Dr.]	NOV 15 1815

District of Columbia Marriage Licenses, 1811-1858

SHANNAHAN, Hannorah	MURPHY, John	OCT 23 1855
SHANNAN, Mary	MATTINGLY, George	JUN 24 1823
SHANNEHAN, Daniel	RAGAN, Mary	JUN 02 1849
SHANNESSY, William	O'CONNOR, Bridget	JUN 17 1854
SHANNESY, James	SHEAHAN, Ellen	JUL 29 1853
SHANNON, Catherine	GALLAHER, John S.	SEP 06 1817
SHANNON, Catherine Ann	DEMENTSION, Francis	SEP 18 1841
SHANNON, Henrietta	KENDRICK, Henry H.	MAY 01 1851
SHANNON, Timothy	WELSH, Maria	APR 10 1852
SHANSSNEY, Margaret	RAIDY, Thomas	JAN 18 1855
SHAPLEY, John M.	HUTCHINSON, Betty F.	MAR 01 1852
SHARK, Ann	FLEMING, Patrick	MAR 22 1858
SHARK, Ann	FLEMMING, Patrick	APR 20 1858
SHARKEY, Michl.	CROSGROVE, Cridget	JUN 21 1852
SHARLIN, Cornelius	HINES, Mary	JUN 20 1857
SHARP, Cornelia A.	GODRAN, William	AUG 06 1838
SHARPE, Benjamin	NALLEY, Matilda	SEP 08 1831
SHARPE, Joseph	WHITMORE, Elizabeth	JUL 12 1816
SHARPER, Samuel	CARTER, Laura Ann (blk)	FEB 09 1854
SHARPLESS, Sarah D.	CORNOG, John	JAN 07 1846
SHARPLESS, Wm.	AVIS, Mary	JUN 26 1813
SHARRETTS, John F.	BRERETON, Martha A.E.	NOV 30 1841
SHARZ, Barbara	SEADENBERG, Deiderick	DEC 31 1856
SHAUSNESY, John	BURKE, Bridget	DEC 02 1854
SHAUSNESY, Michael	FITZGERALD, Ellen	JAN 09 1855
SHAW, Alfred C.	WALSH, Julia E.	JAN 31 1852
SHAW, Archibald	SHAW, Sophia	FEB 28 1854
SHAW, Dennis	FRANCIS, Eliza (blk)	JAN 27 1842
SHAW, Edward	WARD, Eliza	FEB 29 1840
SHAW, Eliza (blk)	RIDGLEY, Charles	MAR 06 1855
SHAW, Elizabeth	SIMMONS, William	JUN 25 1817
SHAW, Emely B.	MAHORNEY, Thomas W.	FEB 12 1831
SHAW, Emily Virginia	DEVINE, Lewis McKendrie	MAY 16 1848
SHAW, Henrietta	TAYLOR, Geo. W.	DEC 28 1835
SHAW, James B.	BONNYCASTLE, Mary	JAN 15 1857
SHAW, Jerusha Ann	WATERS, Richard R.	DEC 15 1817
SHAW, John	McPHERSON, Henrietter	APR 17 1827
SHAW, Joseph Ford	ESTEP, Rebecca	JAN 25 1834
SHAW, Lavinia	GEIGER, Frederick E.	JUN 19 1851
SHAW, Lemuel D.	CLOXTON, Ann B.	APR 17 1829
SHAW, Lloyd A.	HARRISON, Mary J.	DEC 03 1855
SHAW, Maria	HALL, John	APR 26 1832
SHAW, Mary	TOWSON, Charles	AUG 27 1831
SHAW, Mary Ann	GIBSON, Alexander	MAY 04 1827
SHAW, Mary Ann (blk)	THOMAS, William	SEP 17 1833
SHAW, Matthias	MURRAY, Mary E.	JAN 22 1850
SHAW, Nathan R.	HUTCHINS, Ann Matilda	DEC 20 1841
SHAW, Richard	BURCH, Mary Ann	DEC 13 1838
SHAW, Samuel	JONES, Eleanor	JUN 19 1826
SHAW, Sandy	WILSON, Mary (blk)	NOV 13 1856
SHAW, Sophia	SHAW, Archibald	FEB 28 1854
SHAW, Stephen	BRANNER, Margt.	OCT 01 1855
SHAW, Susana	THOMPSON, Barnett Henry	FEB 02 1847
SHAW, Thomas	WHEAT, Sarah Ann	JUL 24 1815
SHAW, Washington	MATTINGLY, Catharine	MAY 02 1826
SHAW, William B.	BURKE, Belle	AUG 30 1856
SHAW, William D.	GRANTT, Catharine	APR 03 1823
SHAW, William P.	GANNON, Mary Ellen	NOV 25 1830

District of Columbia Marriage Licenses, 1811-1858

SHAY, Bridget	BROSNAHAN, Jeremiah	FEB 16 1858
SHAY, Catharine	BOYLE, John	FEB 08 1853
SHAY, Elijah	TRETTER, Sarah	MAY 02 1816
SHAY, Michael	FRYE, Rebecca	NOV 28 1854
SHAY, Sarah	LEWIS, Curtis	OCT 02 1845
SHEA, Anna	McGINNIS, Hugh	JUN 13 1856
SHEA, Catherine	HENDERSON, James	SEP 05 1853
SHEA, Dennis	CONNOR, Mary	MAY 31 1856
SHEA, Ellen	SULLIVAN, Jeremiah	NOV 15 1856
SHEA, Ellen	DINNIGAN, Michael	JUL 15 1857
SHEA, Julia	DONOVAN, Corns.	JUN 27 1857
SHEA, Julia	SULLIVAN, John	JUL 22 1857
SHEA, Julia	SULLIVAN, John	MAY 20 1858
SHEA, Mary	CORCORAN, Patrick	JAN 11 1858
SHEA, Michael	MURPHY, Ellen	JAN 06 1855
SHEA, Michael	BRIEN, Maria	MAR 30 1858
SHEA, Patrick	CONNER, Margaret	JAN 19 1858
SHEA, Richard	WHITE, Catherine	JUL 21 1853
SHEAHAN, Ann	BREGAN, James	FEB 25 1856
SHEAHAN, Bridget	KOUGH, James	DEC 11 1856
SHEAHAN, Bridget	[blank]	AUG 07 1858
SHEAHAN, Catherine	CONNER, Patrick	JUL 30 1852
SHEAHAN, Ellen	SHANNESY, James	JUL 29 1853
SHEAHAN, James W.	DRURY, Mary Elizth.	MAY 25 1848
SHEAHAN, John	SELBY, Frances	APR 16 1846
SHEAHAN, John	DALEY, Mary	JUL 14 1855
SHEAHAN, John	O'CONNOR, Margaret	DEC 01 1855
SHEAHAN, John	DRISCOLL, Catherine	MAY 03 1858
SHEAHAN, Margaret	SHEAHAN, Patrick	FEB 03 1855
SHEAHAN, Maria	KEAN, Cornelius	AUG 23 1851
SHEAHAN, Mary	HOGAN, Edmund	MAR 07 1848
SHEAHAN, Patrick	HOURAN, Bridget	OCT 16 1852
SHEAHAN, Patrick	SHEAHAN, Margaret	FEB 03 1855
SHEAR, Francis	HETHE, Mary	MAR 16 1858
SHEARLOCK, Nancy	FARRIS, Israel	JUN 19 1813
SHEARWOOD, Matilda Jane	SCOTT, Albert	DEC 30 1846
SHEARWOOD, William	BLUNDEN, Jane	JAN 12 1818
SHEATZ, Henry	REEDER, Elizabeth J.	APR 18 1831
SHECKELL, George A.	BUCKLEY, Ann Louisa	SEP 20 1856
SHECKELL, Merrit A.	CONNOR, Harriet L.	MAR 07 1855
SHECKELL, Rosala V.	GODDARD, Benj. F.	OCT 18 1852
SHECKELL, Thomas H.	LEFEVOE, Mrs. Ann	NOV 19 1829
SHECKELLS, Christiana	FREEMAN, William H.	NOV 30 1853
SHECKELLS, Elizabeth	BARRETT, Isaac	NOV 15 1831
SHECKELLS, Emma Frances	BURDINE, James	MAR 04 1846
SHECKELLS, Harriet A.	BURNS, Samuel F.	JUN 11 1850
SHECKELLS, Julia Ann	DODSON, Robert Middleton	MAY 21 1831
SHECKELLS, Mary Ann	BYER, James	AUG 30 1852
SHECKELLS, Mary M.	HEARD, Matthew	DEC 21 1852
SHECKELLS, Samuel	VERMILLIONS, Sahah	DEC 21 1816
SHECKELLS, Samuel	FILLIS, Caroline	JUN 14 1827
SHECKELLS, Sarah	FELIUS, Frederick	MAR 23 1835
SHECKELLS, Sarah	BUCKLEY, James W.	AUG 09 1855
SHECKELLS, Theodore	LOYE, Ann	FEB 07 1820
SHECKELLS, Thomas	EATOR, Catharine	APR 18 1853
SHECKELLS, Thomas H.	HOWARD, Mary	MAY 20 1840
SHECKELS, Airy	STUIED, George B.	OCT 31 1814
SHECKELS, Charles	SMITH, Julia	DEC 03 1835

District of Columbia Marriage Licenses, 1811-1858

SHECKELS, Levi	TUCKER, Margaret	OCT 17 1826
SHECKELS, Mary	PICKETT, Mason	DEC 26 1820
SHECKELS, Theodore, Jr.	PEARCE, Jane L.	JUL 23 1849
SHECKLE, Ann	KELLY, James	APR 24 1823
SHECKLE, Susan	TALTON, Merrit	JUL 20 1812
SHECKLES, Debora R.	JONES, Thomas H.	DEC 16 1834
SHECKLES, Emily	CAHILL, John	SEP 17 1825
SHECKLES, Merrit	TARLTON, Mary Ann	NOV 25 1847
SHECKLES, Samuel	ROBINSON, Catharine	MAY 09 1831
SHEDD, Elizabeth	HOUCH, Matthias	JUL 01 1844
SHEDDEN, Jane Agnes	COOPER, Grenville C.	JUN 13 1829
SHEE, Ann	STEIGAUFF, Philip	FEB 21 1852
SHEE, Henry	McGUIRE, Rose	DEC 02 1851
SHEEDY, Bridget	McMAHON, John	JUL 11 1855
SHEEHY, John	HAYS, Mary	APR 14 1855
SHEEHY, Mary Ann	McLAUGHLIN, Hugh C.	JUN 13 1836
SHEELA, Frederick	SCOTT, Francis A.	JAN 11 1854
SHEELE, Augustus Danl.	COLTER, Margaret	MAY 01 1828
SHEEN, Henrietta	WEHN, Henry	MAY 22 1858
SHEENWOOD, Hezekiah	ALLIN, Jemima	JUN 11 1821
SHEETER, Mary	STOOKEY, George	MAY 09 1850
SHEETING, Cordelia	ZEIGLER, Christian	APR 19 1852
SHEETS, John	NAYLOR, Priscilla	JUN 14 1827
SHEETS, John George	JACOBS, Catherine	JAN 03 1843
SHEETS, Mary Melvina	LYNCH, Lorenzo	FEB 19 1833
SHEFFEY, Daniel	HANSON, Maria	JAN 30 1812
SHEFFNER, Peter R.	SOLOMON, Ann C.	DEC 20 1851
SHEHAN, Daniel	NEENAN, Ellen	MAR 29 1856
SHEID, John T.	McCLOSKEY, Margaret Ann	JUL 07 1853
SHEID, Martha R.	COLUMBUS, Chas. J.	DEC 29 1847
SHEID, Sarah	ETHELL, Thomas	AUG 23 1825
SHEIRBURN, William L.	DARNALL, Eliza A.	JUN 16 1856
SHEKELL, B.O.	DOWNES, Sarah	SEP 04 1828
SHEKELL, Richd. R.	BOHRER, Harriet A.	OCT 28 1823
SHELDON, Henry B.	SMITH, Mary	JUN 28 1858
SHELL, Jacob	CURRAN, Eliz.	JUN 24 1815
SHELLE, Bridget	KELLY, Neal	OCT 22 1856
SHELLY, Caroline	STEWART, Charles	MAR 04 1825
SHELLY, James W.	HARDIN, Catherine Ann	DEC 13 1855
SHELTON, Catharine E.	HILL, Samuel O.	MAR 07 1844
SHELTON, Eliza	BURGESS, Joseph	AUG 05 1837
SHELTON, Elizabeth (blk)	BOWMAN, James	SEP 16 1857
SHELTON, Ellen F.	NEVITT, Thomas F.	MAY 23 1836
SHELTON, James	BAILEY, Rebecca	JUL 21 1856
SHELTON, John	SANDERSON, Henrietta	NOV 20 1848
SHELTON, Joseph	NALLY, Malinda	SEP 11 1850
SHELTON, Margaret	SELVY, Arthur	NOV 27 1857
SHELTON, Mary Jane (blk)	JOHNSON, Benedict	OCT 05 1848
SHELTON, Moses	GALE, Sally	FEB 21 1814
SHELTON, Pamelia	CROUTHERS, Thomas	FEB 17 1844
SHELTON, Samuel	ADAMS, Susan	SEP 17 1835
SHELTON, Samuel	LUSBY, Eliza	FEB 25 1848
SHELTON, Sarah	BERKELEY, [blank]	FEB 19 1837
SHELVY, Dyer	GALES, Ann Maria (blk)	APR 14 1853
SHENALT, Sarah	THORNBERRY, John	DEC 11 1824
SHENNESEY, Mary A.	KELLY, James	MAR 22 1856
SHENSLER, Doratha	SHWITZER, Adam	JUL 02 1847
SHEPHARD, Eliza	CREHEN, Eugene	JAN 23 1854

District of Columbia Marriage Licenses, 1811-1858

SHEPHARD, Elizabeth	YEATES, Bartholomew LaCount	DEC 13 1820
SHEPHARD, Harvey C.	PENNIFILL, Mary Jane	MAY 08 1855
SHEPHARD, Henry	WHITE, Elizabeth	MAY 26 1840
SHEPHARD, Jane	ROSS, Trueman	JAN 03 1849
SHEPHARD, Samuel	DAINTY, Eliza	JUL 31 1849
SHEPHARD, William J.	CANNON, Mary	AUG 22 1843
SHEPHEARD, Henny	TYLER, William	OCT 09 1824
SHEPHERD, Abraham	RUSSELL, Elizabeth	MAY 27 1817
SHEPHERD, Ann	RATCLIFF, Joseph	SEP 24 1814
SHEPHERD, Ann	SARTAIN, John	MAY 24 1849
SHEPHERD, Elias	BONDS, Columbia (blk)	DEC 29 1856
SHEPHERD, Elizabeth	RUDD, Joseph	APR 02 1838
SHEPHERD, Francis	CONWAY, Michael	JAN 02 1839
SHEPHERD, Henrietta F.	TYLER, Edward James	MAY 24 1845
SHEPHERD, Henry	DOOLY, Mary Ann	SEP 21 1833
SHEPHERD, Joseph	HYSIE, Caroline	FEB 01 1840
SHEPHERD, Louisa	NEITZEY, George	AUG 03 1847
SHEPHERD, Rebecca M.	SMITH, John L.	APR 13 1836
SHEPHERD, Sarah Ann	WILKINSON, Richard	AUG 31 1833
SHEPPARD, Ann	JOHNSON, William	OCT 21 1847
SHEPPARD, Ann Rosa Semmes	HEATH, Herman H.	NOV 28 1849
SHEPPARD, Charlotte	SUMMERS, Owen	FEB 13 1827
SHEPPARD, James H.	MARKS, Hetty Maria	FEB 01 1851
SHEPPARD, John M.	YOUNG, Virginia Anne	AUG 13 1846
SHEPPARD, Margt. A.	MERCHANT, William C.	DEC 26 1849
SHEPPARD, Mary Ann	SESSFORD, Jefferson	MAY 26 1821
SHEPPARD, Sarah	FRIDLEY, George	FEB 13 1827
SHEPPARD, Sarah Jane	DAVIS, George Augustus	FEB 05 1828
SHEPPERD, A.H. [Hon. Augustine]	TURNER, Martha P.T.	FEB 24 1830
SHEPPERD, Eliza Frances	HUGHES, Robert B.	JAN 16 1839
SHEPPERD, James	WHEELER, Mary Ann	APR 23 1812
SHEPPERD, Joseph	GOLDSBOROUGH, Rebecca	FEB 28 1815
SHEPPERD, Sarah F.	PACE, John A.	DEC 24 1853
SHEPPERD, William	SOUTHALE, Mary Ann	SEP 06 1830
SHEPPERLY, Deliphia	ROLES, William W.	MAR 24 1852
SHERBERTT, Martha	COLE, Robert	SEP 12 1854
SHERER, Philip	SCHNEIDER, Christiana	JAN 21 1841
SHERHEN, Margaret	CLEARY, Maurice	OCT 18 1856
SHERIDAN, Bridget	COTTER, James	NOV 29 1852
SHERIDAN, Catharine	CLAHERTY, Anthony	JAN 25 1858
SHERIFF, Cornelia M.	WARDER, Wm.	JUN 21 1848
SHERIFF, Dionysius	DOVE, Margaret Ann	SEP 25 1845
SHERIFF, Edwin	WEAVER, Adaline	OCT 25 1827
SHERIFF, Edwin	WALKER, Amelia H.	JUN 21 1831
SHERIFF, George L.	ROTHWELL, Susan B.	APR 30 1856
SHERIFF, John	ARNOLD, Eleanor	APR 18 1820
SHERIFF, Levi	WILSON, Matilda	MAY 31 1813
SHERIFF, Mary Cornelia	DEAN, John T.W.	SEP 04 1845
SHERIFF, Mary Elizabeth	LOWRIE, William Frederick	NOV 21 1834
SHERIFF, Mary I.	KILLMON, John T.	JUN 19 1845
SHERIFF, Samuel	YOUNG, Susan B.	SEP 04 1836
SHERLEY, Ann	DAVIDSON, Thomas	JUN 01 1830
SHERLOCK, Clotilda M.J.	GILCHRIST, George L.	DEC 19 1844
SHERLOCK, Ellenora	MULLIKIN, Jeremiah	DEC 18 1856
SHERLOCK, Victoria A.	EDMONSTON, Thomas J.	MAY 13 1852
SHERMAN, Charles A.	BRADLEY, Sarah D.	NOV 21 1855
SHERMAN, Charles E.	PAGE, Sally	OCT 09 1854
SHERMAN, Charles K.	PAGE, Sally	MAY 29 1852

District of Columbia Marriage Licenses, 1811-1858

SHERMAN, Daniel	BALL, Sarah Ann	JUL 01 1831
SHERMAN, George	HOLT, Susan	MAR 05 1839
SHERMAN, Mary	KIRBY, Charles	JAN 13 1824
SHERMAN, Mary	CANNON, John	NOV 12 1843
SHERMAN, Sarah	BURCH, Caleb	NOV 24 1845
SHERMAN, Sarah Jane	ORR, James	JAN 31 1851
SHERMAN, William D.	WALLINGSFORD, Ellen	SEP 05 1834
SHERMAN, William T.	EWING, Ellen B.	MAY 01 1850
SHERMINTINE, Ann	ARMSWAY, Wm.	SEP 09 1826
SHERMINTINE, John	WOOTTEN, Ann	SEP 09 1826
SHERPF, Eberhard	DRIER, Mary	NOV 06 1843
SHERRY, Ann	MORGAN, Charles	SEP 07 1819
SHERRY, Dominick	KIDLEY, Martha Ann	MAY 04 1835
SHERRY, Mary	PARSONS, Samuel	MAY 31 1834
SHERTER, Betsey (blk)	ADAMS, Henry	NOV 07 1814
SHERWOOD, Archibald	FISH, Lucinda	NOV 19 1844
SHERWOOD, Edward	NEVITT, Annie	OCT 22 1855
SHERWOOD, Helen C.	LUM, A. Stewart	SEP 26 1853
SHERWOOD, James	ALLEN, Mary	OCT 06 1851
SHERWOOD, Jane	DAVIS, Josiah	NOV 16 1852
SHERWOOD, Jas. Elwood	PALMER, Anna Emeline	OCT 15 1856
SHERWOOD, John	BROOKS, Elizabeth	NOV 12 1845
SHERWOOD, Lewellin	ROBINSON, Polly	JUN 01 1815
SHERWOOD, Lewis	LIPSCOMB, Ellen	JUL 04 1837
SHERWOOD, Mary Ellen	BREWER, Zachariah J.	JAN 10 1849
SHERWOOD, Mary Virginia	EDMONSTON, Ethan A.	AUG 05 1850
SHERWOOD, Perry	TINES, Mary	SEP 10 1851
SHERWOOD, Rebecca V.	HARRIS, Matthias	OCT 18 1853
SHERWOOD, Samuel	McGOWAN, Catharine	FEB 10 1825
SHERWOOD, Samuel	WALKER, Caroline	DEC 24 1836
SHERWOOD, Temple	HARMAN, Emily	JUN 25 1853
SHERWOOD, William	CROWLEY, Sarah	MAR 22 1838
SHERWOOD, Zachariah	COLE, Elizabeth	SEP 01 1856
SHERY, Mary E.	SAUTER, Henry S.	DEC 02 1856
SHETHER, Sophia	WOLFF, William	APR 10 1844
SHEUGHRY, Mary	NOONAN, James	OCT 14 1851
SHICK, Lehene	GILP, Frederick	JAN 04 1855
SHIEDS, Ann Ophelia	SHRYOCK, Henry S.	APR 02 1833
SHIELDS, Ann Selena	BAKER, Charles	MAY 12 1841
SHIELDS, Anna C.	MEADOR, Chastain C.	JUL 29 1857
SHIELDS, Connell	FUGET, Ellen	NOV 20 1845
SHIELDS, Harriet Ann	McKEAN, James P.	JUL 21 1830
SHIELDS, James	VARDEN, Sarah	APR 13 1817
SHIELDS, James W.	GIVEN, Mary	OCT 05 1840
SHIELDS, John	KELLY, Catherine	JUN 13 1850
SHIELDS, John V.	KING, Margaret	JUN 30 1855
SHIELDS, Laurence	O'DONNOVAN, Mary	JUL 29 1853
SHIELDS, Margaret	O'CALLAGHAN, Thomas	JAN 01 1852
SHIELDS, Rebecca	USTICK, John S.	SEP 06 1824
SHIELDS, Sarah	BURKE, James	APR 15 1828
SHIELDS, Sarah	SOURBERGER, Rgoerge	NOV 22 1839
SHIELDS, Susan	McCAULEY, George	NOV 08 1848
SHIELDS, William	STALLINGS, Louisa	OCT 18 1845
SHIELLS, Elizabeth D.	WARREN, James, Jr.	SEP 19 1844
SHILES, James W.	MUSGROVE, Margaret	NOV 15 1845
SHILES, James W.	FORSYTH, Ann B.	JUL 16 1850
SHILLING, Alexander	DICE, Margaret	AUG 09 1856
SHILTON, Martha (blk)	HIGHT, Joseph	FEB 16 1853

District of Columbia Marriage Licenses, 1811-1858

SHIMORS, John	KELLY, Jane	FEB 07 1831
SHINCO, John	DUBANT, Margaret	SEP 21 1844
SHINDLE, Sarah	MAGNIER, Thomas	MAY 01 1822
SHINDOLLAR, John	McKENZIE, Martha Jane	NOV 03 1856
SHINER, Michael	JACKSON, Jane (blk)	SEP 08 1849
SHINN, John R.	BARKMAN, Martha	OCT 29 1855
SHINN, Mary V.	CLARKE, John P.	AUG 14 1851
SHINNERS, Mary Jane	WELLS, John W.	SEP 24 1851
SHIP, Ann T.	WEIR, James V.	JUN 21 1838
SHIPLEY, Catharine	CLEMMONS, John	JAN 06 1823
SHIPLEY, Joshua F.	McGRUE, Sarah A.	OCT 14 1856
SHIPLEY, Mary	OGLE, Horatio	FEB 03 1812
SHIPLEY, Susanna	BOYER, Peter D.	JAN 04 1813
SHIPLEY, Susanna	GREENWOOD, Robert	SEP 03 1824
SHIPMAN, John	COVER, Mary A.	JAN 22 1842
SHIPMAN, John	WELLS, Margaret	JUL 18 1857
SHIPMAN, John James	CARROLL, Procilla J.	DEC 22 1856
SHIRLEY, Nancy (blk)	JONES, William	MAY 04 1848
SHIRLOCK, Catharine M.	CHAMBERS, William	APR 14 1846
SHIRMAN, James W.	THORN, Ellen F.	DEC 31 1857
SHIRNEY, Eliza	WEIGHTMAN, William	FEB 07 1816
SHITPOEL, Daniel	DUESENBURY, Laura	AUG 31 1858
SHIVELY, John M.	ELLIOTT, Susan L.	MAR 27 1847
SHIVERIN, Mary (blk)	BOND, David	MAY 08 1856
SHLWIERING, Frederika	VINEER, Lewis	JUN 20 1846
SHOATS, Frederick	HANNA, Mary	MAY 24 1825
SHOBER, W.A.	WITHERS, Margaret A.	SEP 05 1855
SHOEMAKER, Charles	COLLINS, Mary Elizabeth	SEP 02 1843
SHOEMAKER, Charles E.	PORTTES, Elizabeth M.	MAY 05 1857
SHOEMAKER, David	PEIRCE, Abigal Davidson	DEC 29 1815
SHOEMAKER, David	BURSON, Tacy	OCT 09 1817
SHOEMAKER, David L.	THOMPSON, Estelle E.	FEB 09 1853
SHOEMAKER, Edwd. I.	JONES, Indiana M.	OCT 03 1855
SHOEMAKER, Eliza	PUDDONAR, Henry	FEB 08 1854
SHOEMAKER, Elizabeth	MacCABBIN, Thomas L.	OCT 10 1848
SHOEMAKER, Elizabeth L.	BUCKEY, Chas. A.	NOV 19 1856
SHOEMAKER, George	PAYNE, Mary	NOV 08 1824
SHOEMAKER, George W.	RABBIT, Mary E.	AUG 19 1851
SHOEMAKER, Iziah	DEANN, Harriet Ann	AUG 27 1844
SHOEMAKER, Jacob	FOSTER, Eliza Ann	MAY 06 1847
SHOEMAKER, Margaret	OGLE, Resin H.	AUG 21 1852
SHOEMAKER, Mary	BURROWS, Hezekiah	JUN 30 1846
SHOEMAKER, Mary Ann	BURDETT, Hilleary	MAY 05 1853
SHOEMAKER, Mary R.	WALTON, Coates	FEB 09 1853
SHOEMAKER, Pierce	CARBERY, Martha L.	JUL 17 1855
SHOEMAKER, Samuel	WELLS, Margaret	MAY 06 1847
SHOEMAKER, Samuel, Jr.	LANE, Elizabeth U.	FEB 21 1846
SHOEMAKER, Thomas E.	HERBERT, Sarah J.	AUG 04 1857
SHOEMAKER, William H.	RABBITT, Ruthe E.	APR 26 1858
SHONNARD, Catharine	ARNOLD, Lemuel H.	JUN 21 1847
SHOPE, Laura	CHANEY, Christopher C.	AUG 25 1851
SHORE, Lavinia Ann (blk)	LODGE, James	APR 10 1845
SHORT, Bonnafantor	MILLER, Eliza	OCT 03 1836
SHORT, Elexius	GATES, Harriet	MAR 09 1841
SHORT, William E.	BRIGHT, Elizabeth Ann	SEP 27 1848
SHORTER, Ann (blk)	FLETCHER, Basil	DEC 30 1848
SHORTER, Catharine E. (blk)	BROWN, Jno. T.	OCT 23 1855
SHORTER, Charity	BUTLER, Alectius	JAN 31 1818

District of Columbia Marriage Licenses, 1811-1858

SHORTER, Charles	JACKSON, Mary	SEP 17 1817
SHORTER, Charles	MILES, Leathy	FEB 02 1832
SHORTER, Charles	BOOTH, Mary (blk)	AUG 16 1832
SHORTER, Charles	BROOKES, Elizabeth (blk)	NOV 24 1835
SHORTER, Charles	WILLIAMS, Laura	APR 06 1857
SHORTER, Elizabeth (blk)	LAURENCE, Isaah	JUN 09 1825
SHORTER, Henry	THOMAS, Hannah (blk)	FEB 12 1840
SHORTER, Isaac	BELL, Caroline (blk)	MAR 17 1832
SHORTER, James A.	CARTER, Maria (blk)	NOV 04 1851
SHORTER, John	LYLES, Mary A.	OCT 13 1856
SHORTER, John Wesley	MARSHALL, Mary Margaret (blk)	SEP 30 1847
SHORTER, John Wesley	MARSHALL, Ellen (blk)	JAN 15 1851
SHORTER, Joseph E.	NORMAN, Elizabeth P.	MAR 11 1856
SHORTER, Louisa (blk)	WRIGHT, James Henry	NOV 29 1841
SHORTER, Margaret	LANDER, James	NOV 11 1842
SHORTER, Maria	WILKINSON, William	AUG 05 1846
SHORTER, Martha (blk)	SIMMS, John	MAY 07 1849
SHORTER, Mary Ann (blk)	BINS, Charles	NOV 23 1826
SHORTER, Mary Ann	FOSKEY, Moses	SEP 07 1853
SHORTER, Moses	ROSS, Henry	AUG 18 1817
SHORTER, Nancy (blk)	GRAY, Thomas	JUL 08 1841
SHORTER, Priscilla	BROOKES, Nathaniel	AUG 20 1840
SHORTER, Susan (blk)	SNOW, Jerry	SEP 22 1836
SHORTER, Tresy	COLSON, Joseph	NOV 04 1819
SHORTER, Verlinda	ADAMS, William	OCT 08 1818
SHORTER, William H.	BARBER, Catherine (blk)	SEP 10 1849
SHORTER, [blank] (blk)	COOPER, Charles	NOV 14 1844
SHORTWELL, Nathan, Rev.	McCLOERY, Mary L.	SEP 27 1852
SHOUGHROUGH, James	HOLLORAN, Margaret	MAR 23 1850
SHOUP, Galus	GENGENBACH, Doratha	JUN 09 1842
SHOWARD, Samuel	THOMPSON, Elizabeth	DEC 22 1845
SHOWLS, Manass	HUGHES, Mary	FEB 28 1815
SHRAKE, Julia A.	WARING, Basil	DEC 05 1846
SHREAVE, Ann	ALLISON, Thomas	DEC 28 1820
SHREEVE, John	CROGGIN, Mary	AUG 07 1855
SHREEVE, Margaret N.	DORSEY, Allen S.	JUN 04 1851
SHREEVE, Mary A.	ORTON, Charles A.	DEC 30 1851
SHREEVE, Samuel	THOMAS, Eliz.	JAN 19 1812
SHREEVES, William O.	MANN, Ann Maria	MAY 01 1858
SHREVE, James H.	SEWELL, Frances Ann	FEB 14 1854
SHREVE, James H., Jr.	RAY, Carrie E.	DEC 08 1857
SHREVE, John	MORRISS, Mary	SEP 26 1815
SHREVE, Julia Ann	WATERS, William	JAN 31 1833
SHREVE, Margaret Ann	BALL, John	OCT 01 1834
SHREVE, Susan	MUSE, John	AUG 01 1822
SHREVE, Susanah	SEWELL, Lewis H.	JUN 17 1858
SHREVE, William H.	SOTHORON, Mary	NOV 10 1838
SHRIDER, Mary	GAINES, John	OCT 22 1833
SHRIEVE, Elizabeth	ARNOLD, Samuel	DEC 29 1814
SHRIEVE, Julia Ann	BURCH, William	DEC 28 1838
SHRINER, Lawrence	SCHNEIDER, Catharine	SEP 28 1841
SHRINK, Josephine	McGARITY, Andrew Jackson	DEC 09 1856
SHRIVER, Abram F.	GLOVER, Mary Jane	AUG 01 1849
SHRIVER, Joseph	CAUSTEN, Henrietta J.	DEC 03 1834
SHRIVER, Lena	RUMLERLER, Peter	DEC 30 1835
SHRODER, Cath. Elizabeth	MENZE, Albrecht	JUN 06 1850
SHROPSHIRE, Eliza	VENABLE, Charles	FEB 01 1816
SHRUMAN, James	PILLING, Susanna	FEB 01 1855

District of Columbia Marriage Licenses, 1811-1858

SHRYER, Daniel	MARTIN, Susan	JUN 14 1837
SHRYOCK, Henry S.	SHIEDS, Ann Ophelia	APR 02 1833
SHUBIRCK, Mary	CLYMER, George	MAY 08 1845
SHUE, George E.	ADAMS, Ann	MAY 09 1853
SHUEKHART, George	DONOHUE, Jane	OCT 04 1856
SHUGHRUE, Daniel	SCANLON, Johanna	NOV 22 1851
SHUMACK, Sarah C.	MULLER, James D.	AUG 03 1858
SHUMAN, Christiana	SHAEFER, Henry	JAN 05 1854
SHUMAN, John	FREDERICK, Mary	JUN 26 1849
SHUMATE, Cornelia F.	SHUMATE, Thomas S.	MAY 25 1857
SHUMATE, Mary Elizabeth	READ, Alexander	NOV 19 1856
SHUMATE, Murphey C.	HUTCHISON, Maria	NOV 22 1827
SHUMATE, Thomas S.	SHUMATE, Cornelia F.	MAY 25 1857
SHUMATE, Walker D.	WILLIAMS, Sarah	JUL 29 1830
SHUNK, James F.	BLACK, Rebecca	MAR 10 1858
SHURTS, Sarah	CATON, Patrick	JUN 08 1857
SHUSTER, Christopher	BOSSERT, Christina	JUL 25 1842
SHUSTER, Frederick	SWANN, Mary	SEP 02 1851
SHUSTER, Mary E.	LAWSON, Thomas B.	JUN 14 1849
SHWAB, George	SCHMIDT, Elizabeth	JUN 26 1855
SHWING, Anna	RUPPERT, Anton	NOV 03 1857
SHWITZER, Adam	SHEUSLER, Doratha	JUL 02 1847
SHYNE, Michael R.	FAGAN, Mary M.	JUN 25 1838
SHYNE, Michael R.	FAGAN, Jane C.	JUN 10 1847
SHYNE, Michael R.	O'BRYAN, Catheine	MAR 03 1851
SIBLEY, Amelia	APPLETON, Thomas	APR 29 1812
SIBLEY, Benjamin	HUTSON, Mary	FEB 24 1827
SIBLEY, Henrietta	THOMPSON, Garland	AUG 24 1837
SIBLEY, James T.	LITTLE, Mary	SEP 04 1849
SIBLEY, John	HARRIS, Charlotte	NOV 09 1855
SIBLEY, Mary	BALDWIN, William	SEP 14 1840
SIBLEY, Mary Ann	COOLAN, Nicholas	JUN 22 1838
SIBLEY, Mary Elizth.	PARKER, John Thos.	SEP 09 1857
SIDEBOTTAM, Elizabeth	WHATON, Lewis	SEP 14 1837
SIDEBOTTOM, Sarah	DICKENSON, John	MAY 28 1839
SIDEBOTTOM, William	PILCHER, Catharine	JUL 22 1831
SIDES, Margaret	WELL, John	NOV 29 1834
SIEBEL, John C.	ROSS, Sarah Rebecca	JUN 21 1851
SIEBERT, Selmar	GILDEMIESTER, Emma	JUN 13 1851
SIEBERT, Thora M.	CUMMING, Charles F.P.	JUN 24 1857
SIECK, Sophia Lisette	RIEDEMANN, Heinrich	JUL 21 1858
SIEGEL, Moses	HAMMOND, Saralena	JUL 24 1858
SIEGEL, Saml.	HAMBURGER, Hannah	AUG 26 1857
SIEGERT, Joseph	SCHAD, Justina	APR 12 1855
SIEK, William	KAISER, Catherine	SEP 01 1857
SIERLACH, Peter	MYER, Susan	MAR 22 1855
SIEVERS, Minna	HERBST, Daniel	JUN 19 1858
SIFFERT, Harriet	HAYRE, Gerard	MAY 29 1816
SIFFORD, Elizabeth	FOWLEY, John W.	MAR 24 1838
SILAS, Mary Ann	ROBEY, Theodore	MAY 24 1842
SILAS, Rebecca	HALLON, Francis	MAY 13 1822
SILCOTT, Peyton	FLOWERREE, Pandora G.C.	NOV 24 1829
SILENCE, Chloe Ann	BELL, Benjamin	DEC 22 1823
SILENCE, John	RAGAN, Elizabeth	APR 08 1813
SILENCE, Margaret Catherine	ADAMS, John	NOV 14 1835
SILENCE, Mary A.	SEDGWICK, R.H.	FEB 22 1841
SILENCE, Mary L.	BROWN, Alfred	DEC 30 1857
SILENCE, Walter	RAGAN, Mary M.	SEP 17 1847

District of Columbia Marriage Licenses, 1811-1858

SILLIVAN, Mary	WHEELER, Frederick	OCT 24 1820
SIMARKER, Leonard	CROSS, Indiana	FEB 15 1858
SIMES, Joseph	BURGESS, Cecelia Ann (blk)	APR 20 1840
SIMINGTON, Peter	BRUMNER, Catharine	JUL 14 1821
SIMKINS, Maria E.	CALHOUN, J. Edward	FEB 03 1839
SIMLY, Samuel	DIGGES, Henrietta (blk)	DEC 12 1834
SIMMENS, Eliza	FORTNER, Thomas	APR 12 1834
SIMMES, Ann	HORSMAN, John W.	DEC 20 1836
SIMMES, Augustus	WHITTER, Louisa	JAN 23 1834
SIMMES, Charity	GIBSON, George	AUG 10 1826
SIMMES, George	CASH, Stacia	MAY 29 1834
SIMMES, John	CALLIGAN, Rose	AUG 22 1857
SIMMES, John H.	HIGDON, Mary E.	MAR 06 1854
SIMMES, John Thomas	BEAMS, Mary Jane (blk)	JUN 16 1851
SIMMES, Milly Jane	LAWSON, William	JUL 08 1847
SIMMES, Rebecca	CAMPBELL, James	AUG 20 1833
SIMMONS, Benjamin	WILLIAMS, Sarah	DEC 23 1815
SIMMONS, Catherine	BARKER, George	JAN 09 1850
SIMMONS, Elizabeth	WARTHAM, Thomas	OCT 12 1812
SIMMONS, Elizabeth	O'REILLY, John	NOV 04 1837
SIMMONS, Elizabeth	HEINLINE, William D.	MAY 21 1838
SIMMONS, Henrietta	HARMAN, Chas. W.	JUN 01 1852
SIMMONS, James	BARCLAY, Mary M.	MAY 20 1813
SIMMONS, Jane	DUVALL, George W.	NOV 14 1843
SIMMONS, John	BINGY, Rutha Ann	JAN 15 1834
SIMMONS, Julia Ann	HINELINE, Thomas H.	JUL 23 1858
SIMMONS, Louisa	MILLER, Joseph	JUN 27 1849
SIMMONS, Margaret	DOWLING, Patrick	MAY 09 1839
SIMMONS, Margaret Ann	HATTON, Alexander S.	FEB 28 1850
SIMMONS, Mary	HUTCHISON, Walter	NOV 08 1825
SIMMONS, Mary Ellen	WEIZER, Edward	DEC 05 1848
SIMMONS, Mary Ellen	REED, George W.	AUG 18 1851
SIMMONS, Matilda	WILLIAMS, James	OCT 25 1825
SIMMONS, Rachael	BURCH, Samuel	FEB 05 1834
SIMMONS, Rebecca	ROBINSON, John	MAR 24 1828
SIMMONS, Robert	DAVIS, Catherine	JUL 07 1836
SIMMONS, Ruth Ann	BEATLEY, Kadget B.	OCT 08 1851
SIMMONS, Samuel S.	MURPHY, Helena C.	JUN 09 1853
SIMMONS, Sarah	FORTNER, Samuel	JUL 02 1836
SIMMONS, Sarah	BRADLEY, Wm. W.	JAN 12 1854
SIMMONS, Sarah E.	EASTON, John T.	SEP 23 1856
SIMMONS, Scelia	WALKER, Edward	OCT 25 1825
SIMMONS, Sthreshley	FRANCIS, Elizabeth	DEC 17 1845
SIMMONS, Susan (blk)	WILLIAMS, Walter	MAR 11 1846
SIMMONS, Thomas	HUNTT, Teresa	SEP 12 1818
SIMMONS, Thomas	MATTINGLY, Malinda J.	FEB 03 1849
SIMMONS, Thomas J.	ARMSTRONG, Virginia	SEP 14 1847
SIMMONS, Washington	BROWN, Louise G.	OCT 15 1840
SIMMONS, William	SHAW, Elizabeth	JUN 25 1817
SIMMONS, William	RICHARDSON, Eliza	NOV 15 1849
SIMMONS, William	FOSTER, Emma	JUL 13 1854
SIMMS, Ann	JACKSON, Alfred	NOV 02 1830
SIMMS, Ann	MORAN, Patrick	SEP 03 1832
SIMMS, Ann Eliza (blk)	STOKES, Thomas	MAR 20 1844
SIMMS, Basil	BEALL, Elizabeth	OCT 10 1822
SIMMS, Betsey (blk)	CLOAKLEY, Richard	JUL 12 1828
SIMMS, Camilla	WHIPPLE, Edward A.	MAY 13 1853
SIMMS, Charles C.	NOURSE, Elizth. J.	NOV 13 1852

District of Columbia Marriage Licenses, 1811-1858

SIMMS, Delilah	LANHAM, Jonathan	AUG 03 1848
SIMMS, Eleanor Ann	FREEMAN, John D.	AUG 18 1823
SIMMS, Elexius	FRANZONI, Euridice	MAY 25 1830
SIMMS, Elizabeth (blk)	SIMMS, George	NOV 03 1840
SIMMS, Elizabeth (blk)	STEVENSON, Robert	APR 11 1850
SIMMS, Elizabeth T.	AUSTIN, Francis L.	NOV 20 1849
SIMMS, Emily D.	FORREST, French	APR 18 1831
SIMMS, Emma	HUNTINGTON, Craven	MAR 06 1854
SIMMS, George	SIMMS, Elizabeth (blk)	NOV 03 1840
SIMMS, George	BELL, Charlotte (blk)	NOV 28 1844
SIMMS, George	HODGE, Anna (blk)	SEP 25 1849
SIMMS, George	LEE, Ann Maria (blk)	DEC 24 1857
SIMMS, George Washington	DAVIS, Margaret	OCT 09 1856
SIMMS, Harriet F.	HOOVER, Adam M.	APR 30 1855
SIMMS, Henry	DORSEY, Harriet Ann	SEP 22 1852
SIMMS, Henry	HAWKINS, Lucinda (blk)	SEP 11 1856
SIMMS, James	THOMPSON, Dolly	OCT 28 1819
SIMMS, James	HUFF, Elizabeth	NOV 13 1828
SIMMS, Jane	TYLER, Washington	NOV 15 1832
SIMMS, Jane (blk)	McPHERSON, John	MAY 02 1850
SIMMS, Jane E.	DUNSCOMB, Daniel E.	OCT 16 1848
SIMMS, Jane Rebecca	GRAY, Robert	DEC 12 1826
SIMMS, John	SHORTER, Martha (blk)	MAY 07 1849
SIMMS, John W.	FERGUSON, Eliza M.	APR 06 1852
SIMMS, Josiah	TURNER, Eliza (blk)	OCT 12 1848
SIMMS, Julia (blk)	BEALL, Joseph	NOV 22 1849
SIMMS, Julian	WASHINGTON, John	JAN 15 1857
SIMMS, M.L.	MARKLAND, A.H.	AUG 23 1851
SIMMS, Margt.	ADAMS, William	DEC 22 1825
SIMMS, Mary Ann	COX, James	AUG 07 1845
SIMMS, Mary Ann	ADAMS, John Quincy	JAN 27 1846
SIMMS, Mary E.	CARROLL, Joseph G.	NOV 09 1854
SIMMS, Mary Ellen	NOBLE, George P.	JUN 04 1851
SIMMS, Nancy Douglass	JOHNSON, Richard D.	OCT 05 1841
SIMMS, Noble T.	WRIGHT, Jane E.	MAY 24 1856
SIMMS, Pheby M.	WEIGHTMAN, Henry T.	MAY 07 1822
SIMMS, Rebecca	LYLES, John Washington	MAY 31 1841
SIMMS, Richard	BROCKETT, Nancy (negro)	JUL 07 1834
SIMMS, Selena V.	KEYES, William C.	MAY 05 1854
SIMMS, Virginia (blk)	BROWN, Paul	FEB 23 1852
SIMMS, Virginia W.	TAYLOR, Frank	SEP 14 1835
SIMMS, Washington	DAY, Elizabeth (blk)	FEB 03 1836
SIMMS, William	BANKS, Delia	APR 08 1822
SIMMS, William	FLETCHER, Ellen (blk)	APR 17 1844
SIMMS, William	MYERS, Virginia A.	MAY 23 1844
SIMMS, William	JAVENS, Sarah	APR 16 1845
SIMMS, [blank]	BOWIE, Charles	FEB 15 1848
SIMON, Peter	IZENHAUSEN, Elizabeth	AUG 09 1850
SIMONDS, E. Lewis	CROSS, Rosanna	DEC 10 1855
SIMONDS, George H.	PEIPPERT, Catherine C.	MAY 22 1858
SIMONDS, Jane	WILCOX, Richard	FEB 11 1845
SIMONDS, Laura	MITCHELL, Francis	SEP 07 1852
SIMONDS, Nancy Ann	KIDWELL, Thompson	DEC 26 1850
SIMONDS, Stephen	PHELPS, Sarah	AUG 13 1831
SIMONDS, Stephen	LEWIS, Susan	MAR 26 1846
SIMONS, Daniel	CART, Sarah	OCT 02 1817
SIMONS, John	STORY, Martha	NOV 23 1837
SIMONS, John	STEWART, Elizabeth	DEC 08 1857

District of Columbia Marriage Licenses, 1811-1858

SIMONS, Louisa	BUCKLEY, James	JUN 21 1831
SIMONS, Martha	GHOESLIN, Alexr.	NOV 26 1839
SIMONS, Robert J.	GUILLARD, Cornelia Ann	JUL 03 1830
SIMONS, William	FOSSETT, Mary	SEP 25 1834
SIMONS, William H.	THOMPSON, Eliza Jane (blk)	MAY 23 1850
SIMONTON, John W.	HUTCHINSON, Ann	MAR 29 1827
SIMONTON, Peter	KIRK, Mary Ann	MAR 18 1850
SIMPKINS, Mary Jane	CHESHIRE, Shadrach	MAY 11 1844
SIMPSON, Adaline	COSTIN, James A.	DEC 24 1845
SIMPSON, Andrew Jackson	MASON, Clarissa Ann	NOV 01 1856
SIMPSON, Ann	RING, James	OCT 18 1851
SIMPSON, Ann Sophia	BOLAND, Daniel	APR 05 1842
SIMPSON, Archd. N.	REAVER, Emaline	NOV 12 1846
SIMPSON, Benjamin	KING, Sarah	APR 14 1818
SIMPSON, Benjamin	HARRISON, Julia Ann	MAY 24 1824
SIMPSON, Bernard	BEACH, Catharine	SEP 15 1831
SIMPSON, Betsey	YOUNG, Thomas	APR 26 1814
SIMPSON, Catherine Ann	LAWSON, Charles	JUL 06 1848
SIMPSON, Charles R.	WATERS, Sally Ann	SEP 11 1852
SIMPSON, Chloe	BARTLEY, Fielder	OCT 16 1823
SIMPSON, Eleanor	STEWART, John C.	AUG 25 1827
SIMPSON, Eliza Ann	JONES, Benjamin H.	DEC 22 1857
SIMPSON, Elizabeth	SINGOR, James	MAY 11 1814
SIMPSON, Elizabeth	MARTIN, Samuel	JUN 07 1823
SIMPSON, Elizabeth	GOODS, James C.	OCT 25 1825
SIMPSON, Elizabeth	THOMPSON, Andrew E.	APR 18 1826
SIMPSON, Elizabeth	CROSS, Richard	APR 19 1831
SIMPSON, Elizabeth	BARRY, Richard N.	DEC 14 1833
SIMPSON, Elizabeth (blk)	COKE, Rev. William	APR 08 1856
SIMPSON, Ezekiel Green	SWEENEY, Mary Ann	JUN 18 1850
SIMPSON, Gabriel	LYLES, Margarett	MAR 18 1830
SIMPSON, Harriet	FORD, James E.	OCT 18 1855
SIMPSON, Harriot	PUMPHREY, Rezin	JAN 17 1824
SIMPSON, Hellen Maria	LUEBER, Francis	JUN 02 1828
SIMPSON, Henrietta Sarah S.	HEIN, Samuel	JAN 24 1838
SIMPSON, James	CRAWFORD, Sophia	APR 18 1835
SIMPSON, James A.	FRANZONI, Julia C.	NOV 20 1850
SIMPSON, James A.	GIBSON, Sarah	JUL 09 1858
SIMPSON, James E.	BEACH, Annette R.	MAY 20 1856
SIMPSON, Jane	JARVIS, Miles	MAR 23 1826
SIMPSON, Jane	HICKMAN, Joseph	NOV 17 1841
SIMPSON, Jane M.E.	MACKALL, Brooke	AUG 13 1834
SIMPSON, Joel	LENOX, Angelica	APR 21 1823
SIMPSON, John	LINDSAY, Kiziah	JUL 29 1817
SIMPSON, John	DULANY, Sarah (blk)	MAR 12 1840
SIMPSON, John	BROWN, Teresa (blk)	DEC 23 1854
SIMPSON, John Wesley	WHITMORE, Sarah Ellen	AUG 14 1841
SIMPSON, Joseph	WHEAT, Sarah	JAN 07 1817
SIMPSON, Josiah	SAGE, Louisa E.	JUL 01 1858
SIMPSON, Josias	PICKRELL, Ann	DEC 07 1816
SIMPSON, Lauretta	FORD, Ignatius	FEB 23 1857
SIMPSON, Lewis F.	BLADEN, Matilda E.	SEP 15 1857
SIMPSON, Lucinda C.	ATWELL, John	NOV 29 1855
SIMPSON, Lucy	HEREFORD, William P.	DEC 30 1851
SIMPSON, Lydia	JENKINS, Hirum	DEC 30 1817
SIMPSON, Maria Elizabeth	REISS, Benjamin	DEC 14 1837
SIMPSON, Mariah	MARCEROY, Louis	NOV 23 1824
SIMPSON, Martha Ellen	STORY, Robert	OCT 11 1850

District of Columbia Marriage Licenses, 1811-1858

SIMPSON, Mary	DUCKETT, Richard	MAR 21 1816
SIMPSON, Mary	PRESTON, Anthony	JUN 14 1824
SIMPSON, Mary	MANN, James	DEC 19 1838
SIMPSON, Mary E.	NEAL, Joseph W.	MAY 03 1836
SIMPSON, Mary E.	GEISINDAFFER, William H.	MAR 05 1842
SIMPSON, Mary E.	BROWN, Dr. Bedford, Jr.	JUN 30 1852
SIMPSON, Mary Ellen	LANGLEY, Thomas H.	NOV 09 1842
SIMPSON, Matilda (blk)	LEE, William	DEC 05 1848
SIMPSON, Michael T.	MORGAN, Jane R.	MAY 31 1836
SIMPSON, Nathan	BROWN, Clarissa	AUG 22 1820
SIMPSON, Patsey	SWEENY, Dennis	APR 14 1818
SIMPSON, Priscilla	FOWLER, William	AUG 02 1824
SIMPSON, Rebecca S.	FORD, Franklin	OCT 25 1848
SIMPSON, Rose L.	O'BRYAN, James	JAN 30 1827
SIMPSON, Sarah	FRYE, Henry	AUG 23 1821
SIMPSON, Sarah Ann	ARMSTEAD, Wm. C.	NOV 05 1852
SIMPSON, Susan	GATES, Elias	MAY 14 1815
SIMPSON, Thomas P.	GREEN, Christiana	NOV 01 1855
SIMPSON, Thompson	KEENE, Francis	OCT 19 1815
SIMPSON, Tobias	PROCTOR, Matilda	DEC 28 1824
SIMPSON, Tobias	BEANS, Harrietta (blk)	JUN 19 1851
SIMPSON, William	FOWLER, Eleanor	SEP 25 1826
SIMPSON, William	JONES, Eleanor Ann	AUG 22 1835
SIMPSON, William G.	CARSON, Emma F.	AUG 23 1856
SIMPSON, Wm. G.M.	FITZHUGH, Harriet L.	OCT 06 1836
SIMS, Ann Amelia (blk)	WILLIAMS, James	SEP 15 1857
SIMS, Anne	GREY, Benjamin	MAY 16 1815
SIMS, Benjamin	DUELL, Susan Ann	OCT 22 1855
SIMS, Catharine	DRURY, William	JUL 03 1841
SIMS, Catharine (blk)	BANKS, John	MAY 10 1856
SIMS, Eleanor (blk)	KENNEDY, William	JAN 22 1839
SIMS, Eliza Jane (blk)	JOHNSON, David	MAY 04 1858
SIMS, Elizabeth Ann	BEALL, Horatio	DEC 02 1843
SIMS, Enoch	THOMAS, Harriet A.	DEC 14 1852
SIMS, George	PRATT, Eliza	MAY 18 1837
SIMS, George	ATKINS, Margaret (blk)	NOV 26 1851
SIMS, Henry	HARROD, Sarah Laura (blk)	MAR 30 1849
SIMS, James	LEE, Priscilla (blk)	NOV 16 1852
SIMS, Jane	CREAGER, Michael	APR 25 1820
SIMS, John	McNAIR, Eleanor	DEC 27 1811
SIMS, John A.	ESKRIDGE, Margaret F.	JUL 10 1847
SIMS, John M.	ROWLEY, Mary Jane	AUG 29 1848
SIMS, Joseph	SCOTT, Sarah	OCT 09 1814
SIMS, Josephine	ECKLOFF, R.G.	AUG 03 1857
SIMS, Martha S.	BRANDENBERG, F. Wm.	NOV 04 1853
SIMS, Nancy (blk)	ADAMS, Benjamin	FEB 24 1827
SIMS, Palin Harris	PADGETT, Frances R.	MAR 29 1856
SIMS, Rachael Ann	BERKLEY, John D.	OCT 20 1823
SIMS, Sampson	GLOYD, Harriot	MAR 27 1817
SIMS, Sarah (blk)	YOUNG, Thomas H.	OCT 28 1851
SIMS, Stephen	ESENBECK, Sophia	FEB 06 1817
SIMS, Susan	RATCLIFF, George	MAY 31 1830
SIMS, Thomas	CHINN, Georgiana (blk)	JAN 26 1858
SIMS, Thomas H.	JACKSON, Mary (blk)	MAR 01 1853
SIMS, Verlinda (blk)	BUTLER, James	JAN 16 1839
SINCLAIR, Eleanor Ann	SURRATT, George D.	APR 07 1849
SINCLAIR, Elizabeth	HOLTZCLAW, John M.	SEP 30 1857
SINCLAIR, John	CLAMPIT, Maria	MAR 29 1832

District of Columbia Marriage Licenses, 1811-1858

SINCLAIR, John W.	ROBINSON, Olivia A.	SEP 23 1857
SINCLAIR, Margaret	BIXBY, Nathaniel B.	SEP 22 1813
SINCLAIR, Robert	COOPER, Margaret	APR 18 1815
SINCLAIR, Sarah	CARTWRIGHT, Seth	AUG 23 1830
SINCLAIR, Thomas B.	BUCKLEY, Posey	MAR 29 1823
SINCOX, Alexander	BOSWELL, Sarah	JUN 09 1821
SINCOX, Elizabeth	PATTON, William	MAY 21 1846
SINCOX, Thomas	KOONS, Ann	FEB 23 1847
SINER, John	ROBINSON, Margaret	NOV 23 1857
SINGER, Ellen	WILDE, George Andrew	JAN 14 1835
SINGOR, James	SIMPSON, Elizabeth	MAY 11 1814
SINN, William	LOCKEY, Isabella	NOV 18 1826
SINNICKSON, Mary H.	ROBACK, Dr. C.W.	MAY 24 1858
SINON, John	DRAIN, Mary	OCT 19 1827
SINON, Margaret	FITZGERALD, David	FEB 20 1844
SINON, Thomas	HERITY, Sally	OCT 16 1828
SIOUSA, John	SCHRAB, Maria	JUN 29 1847
SIOUSSA, Annie	LAMBIE, William	MAR 15 1841
SIOUSSA, Augustus	BERRY, Catherine	NOV 30 1852
SIOUSSA, Charlotte M.	FISHER, Thomas J.	JUN 03 1845
SIOUSSA, Edward P.	SLOAN, Harriet L.	DEC 02 1843
SIOUSSA, John	DERMOT, Charlotte Julia [Mrs.]	MAR 02 1820
SIOUSSA, Margaret	MINOR, John P.	MAY 17 1849
SIOUSSA, Mary	MARIOT, Charles H.	MAY 20 1838
SIPE, Hezekiah	COLEMAN, Louisa	OCT 18 1832
SIPES, Mary	DOVE, George W.	JUN 16 1857
SIPLEY, John Henry	PETTIT, Sarah Ann	SEP 01 1847
SIPPLE, Margaret	DACEY, Roger	MAR 14 1853
SISSEL, Julia Ann	GOLDSMITH, James	MAR 03 1832
SISSEL, Mary	HOLTZMAN, Samuel	MAY 22 1834
SISSON, Ann	PEARSON, George	JUN 28 1821
SISSON, Ann M.	HALL, Alfred H.	JUN 28 1855
SISSON, George	BURCHELL, Elizabeth	DEC 21 1846
SISSON, Harriet E.	MILLS, Daniel M.	DEC 24 1853
SISSON, John B.	DAWSON, Dianna	AUG 25 1836
SITCHER, William	KIBBY, Eliza	FEB 14 1825
SITGREAVES, L.	JESUP, Lucy	FEB 27 1854
SKAHAN, John	COLBAT, Eliza	FEB 09 1858
SKAM, Thomas	WHITE, Mary	SEP 16 1840
SKEAHAN, Bridget	CONLAN, Michael	JUL 10 1855
SKELLY, William E.	BEAN, Margaret E.	MAR 29 1847
SKEY, George Smith	SCHLOE, Mary	MAR 01 1851
SKIDMORE, Ann	GROVES, Jacob	APR 18 1850
SKIDMORE, Catharine	CROFT, Arhot	AUG 29 1839
SKIDMORE, Columbia	BERRY, Washington	DEC 07 1854
SKIDMORE, George	GARDENER, Sarah	SEP 23 1822
SKIDMORE, Henry	SMITH, Matilda	APR 17 1840
SKIDMORE, James	LANG, Cornelia	JUL 31 1843
SKIDMORE, Jane E.	REESE, William L.	OCT 22 1839
SKIDMORE, John	LIGHTER, Mary E.	MAR 04 1847
SKIDMORE, John W.	WIMSATT, Mary A.	FEB 04 1845
SKIDMORE, Margaretta	BOUCHER, Oxford	JUL 26 1851
SKIDMORE, Mary D.	ALLEN, William H.	OCT 01 1850
SKIDMORE, Nancy	TAYLOR, Rezin P.	JUN 03 1851
SKIDMORE, Octaver	BOSWELL, Amanuel H.	JUL 02 1858
SKIDMORE, Raymond	CAULK, Mary Ann	MAR 22 1855
SKIDMORE, Rebecca	DAVIS, Henry	APR 08 1815
SKIDMORE, Rebecca	BAYLISS, Sanford	FEB 23 1830

District of Columbia Marriage Licenses, 1811-1858

SKIDMORE, Samuel	CAUSIN, Julia Ann	AUG 14 1822
SKIDMORE, Samuel	SOPER, Mary Ann	DEC 20 1849
SKIDMORE, Sarah	BAILISS, Collin	AUG 06 1833
SKIDMORE, Washington	PARIDISE, Ann	JAN 08 1835
SKINNER, Augustus P.	GRADY, Nancy Ann	FEB 05 1835
SKINNER, Caroline	COWLING, Thomas	AUG 11 1853
SKINNER, Elizabeth	NOURSE, John R.	JUN 12 1826
SKINNER, Elizabeth J.	GOLDING, Arthur	FEB 20 1841
SKINNER, Ellen	KING, Robert	OCT 14 1856
SKINNER, Jane C.	MORAN, Elijah	APR 13 1848
SKINNER, Jane Charotte	BATHAN, John	DEC 09 1837
SKINNER, John	MARLBOROUGH, Mary	OCT 21 1833
SKINNER, Julianna	SCOTT, George W.	MAY 19 1836
SKINNER, Lucretia C.	NOURSE, Jno. R.	NOV 17 1830
SKINNER, Margaret	McDONALD, Wm.	AUG 07 1824
SKINNER, Mary	COWLING, James	FEB 22 1855
SKINNER, Penelope	CRUPPER, Benjamin	NOV 16 1820
SKINNER, Virginia F.	BURKE, John T.	DEC 16 1856
SKINNER, William	FARR, Penelope	SEP 26 1812
SKIPON, Mary Ann	HENNON, Bennett	APR 23 1840
SKIPPEN, Charles M.	GUNNELL, Virginia A.	FEB 08 1855
SKIPPEN, John	CAMMACK, Elizabeth	FEB 09 1818
SKIPPON, Jane	KID, William	MAR 21 1844
SKIRVING, Mary Ann	QUIRK, John B.	DEC 29 1851
SLACK, James	BLADEN, Mary Jane	MAY 27 1858
SLACK, Lydia L.	CARPER, Thomas J.	OCT 10 1856
SLACUM, Emmeline	THOMPSON, Samuel	OCT 29 1821
SLADE, Maria Catherine	HEATH, John	NOV 28 1832
SLADE, Martha Morgan	CULBRETH, Thomas	DEC 04 1827
SLADE, William	PARK, Josephine	JUN 26 1834
SLAGEL, Mary Eva	MILLER, Christian	OCT 13 1852
SLAMM, Levi D.	MORSELL, Jane E.	DEC 15 1846
SLATER, Abraham	ROLLINS, Barbara	MAY 15 1818
SLATER, Ann (blk)	WILSON, Henry	AUG 07 1823
SLATER, Betsey	TARMAN, Philip	APR 02 1815
SLATER, Caroline (blk)	BECKETT, William	DEC 08 1846
SLATER, David	KROUSE, Ann Eliza	FEB 03 1836
SLATER, Ellen (blk)	CHURCH, Alfred	OCT 20 1845
SLATER, James	BROWN, Rebecca (blk)	FEB 27 1838
SLATER, James T.	TILGHMAN, Margaret	DEC 30 1856
SLATER, Lucy	WHITE, John B.	DEC 04 1817
SLATER, Melvill M.	POINDEXTER, Rufinia J.	SEP 26 1854
SLATER, Richard	RICHARDSON, Anne	JUL 29 1815
SLATER, William	COOPER, Margaret	APR 02 1829
SLATFIRD, James	TRUXON, Sarah	JUN 20 1853
SLATFORD, Elizabeth	FOSTER, Henry K.	JUN 28 1839
SLATFORD, Louisa	COLLINS, William	DEC 22 1825
SLATFORD, Louisa	COOKE, Thomas	JUN 11 1849
SLATFORD, Robert	LYNCH, Mary Jane	JUL 18 1856
SLATMAN, Elizabeth	FOLLER, Thomas	NOV 28 1844
SLATTERY, James	McGILLYCODDY, Honora	JAN 06 1853
SLATTERY, James	BROWN, Mary	APR 09 1855
SLATTERY, James	BROWN, Mary	APR 07 1855
SLAVEN, Martha J.	HOGSETT, Josiah T.	DEC 02 1854
SLEIDAR, Joseph	LOBER, Katherine	SEP 12 1857
SLEIGH, Catharine	RENNOE, John H.	MAY 05 1849
SLEIGH, Charles	BATEMAN, Jemima C.	NOV 11 1857
SLEIGHMAKER, James	GORDON, Ellen	MAR 05 1846

District of Columbia Marriage Licenses, 1811-1858

SLICER, Elizabeth S.	HARDEN, William	JUN 06 1853
SLIGHT, James P.	PUTNEY, Lina J.	DEC 17 1857
SLINGERLAND, Peter	McEWING, Martha	AUG 01 1850
SLINGLAND, Jacob	KENNEDY, Mary A.	JAN 30 1855
SLINN, George	FOSKEY, Mulala	NOV 19 1857
SLOAN, Anna Rebecca	BOWEN, John	DEC 22 1832
SLOAN, Elizabeth Throop	NASH, Robert	APR 06 1848
SLOAN, Harriet L.	SIOUSSA, Edward P.	DEC 02 1843
SLOAN, Mary	WALLIS, John H.	JUN 14 1856
SLOANE, Mary Welby	RODBIRD, Ephraim B.	MAY 20 1843
SLOTT, Catharine	DENIS, L. Felix	JUL 19 1853
SLOW, Sarah E.	McILVAINE, Francis E.	SEP 09 1856
SLURP, William	GILLION, Margaret	NOV 18 1851
SLUSSER, Jno. Henry	MOORE, Catharine V.	JUN 05 1856
SLY, Eliza Jane	ALLEN, Edwin O.	NOV 06 1855
SLY, Mary	ASHTON, James	MAY 15 1817
SLYE, Daniel W.	KING, Geneveve A.	FEB 02 1854
SLYE, Edwin D.	QUEEN, Ann Edwardina	SEP 09 1842
SLYE, Elizabeth	ERSLIN, William	NOV 23 1842
SLYE, Henry	DEVAN, Elizabeth A.	FEB 09 1827
SLYE, Mary A.	KING, James D.	APR 28 1830
SLYE, Thomas G.	JOHNS, Mary P.	AUG 03 1835
SMALL, George	GROVES, Elizabeth	JUN 12 1854
SMALL, James T.	KINSLEY, Mary Ann	NOV 04 1843
SMALL, John H.	CUNNINGHAM, Mary A.	MAR 26 1850
SMALLWOOD, Abraham	AMBUSH, Patsey (blk)	OCT 05 1825
SMALLWOOD, Ann Rebecca	WILKERSON, William	DEC 30 1847
SMALLWOOD, Aquilla W.	RAWLINGS, Mary	FEB 03 1815
SMALLWOOD, Catharine	WINKLER, Thomas	JAN 11 1835
SMALLWOOD, Catherine	WILLIAMS, James	JUL 01 1816
SMALLWOOD, Christiann	HAWKE, Thomas A.	NOV 24 1847
SMALLWOOD, Cloah Ann	SPENCER, William	JAN 03 1851
SMALLWOOD, Daniel A.	FOWLER, Mary E.	MAY 19 1847
SMALLWOOD, Eliza	MARSHALL, James	JUL 14 1825
SMALLWOOD, Eliza B.	PROUT, Jonathan	SEP 11 1827
SMALLWOOD, Elizabeth	FLETCHER, Henry	DEC 09 1831
SMALLWOOD, Elizabeth L.	GOODWIN, James A.	JAN 29 1849
SMALLWOOD, Emma of Newt. Cor. MA	SMOOT, Samuel C. of Washington DC	APR 29 1846
SMALLWOOD, Enoch W.	PHILLIPS, Jannett B.	JAN 04 1830
SMALLWOOD, George	COLLINS, Mary	AUG 01 1817
SMALLWOOD, George F.	BAILEY, Sarah Jane	AUG 02 1855
SMALLWOOD, Harriet E.	BROOKES, Richard	APR 13 1857
SMALLWOOD, Ignatius	MOORE, Henrietta (blk)	DEC 28 1843
SMALLWOOD, James	MONTGOMERY, Teresa	APR 15 1816
SMALLWOOD, James W.	SHAMBLING, Mary E.	SEP 16 1841
SMALLWOOD, Jane	DOBBYN, John F.	SEP 25 1854
SMALLWOOD, Jane K.	CHARLES, Wm. B.	APR 18 1822
SMALLWOOD, John	MILLS, Mary	MAR 14 1822
SMALLWOOD, John	THOMAS, Eliza	JUL 31 1828
SMALLWOOD, John	WOOD, Mary	JUL 25 1848
SMALLWOOD, John	WILKINS, Julia	JUL 17 1856
SMALLWOOD, Joseph L.	GIBSON, Rebecca	MAR 16 1836
SMALLWOOD, Mahala Elizabeth	EYRE, Lewis	JAN 01 1850
SMALLWOOD, Maria	BIGGS, Levy	AUG 30 1821
SMALLWOOD, Mary	SMITH, Henry W.	SEP 27 1821
SMALLWOOD, Mary	WOOD, John	NOV 13 1823
SMALLWOOD, Mary (blk)	THOMAS, Edward	NOV 07 1844
SMALLWOOD, Mary Ann (blk)	BROWN, Thomas	JUL 27 1831

District of Columbia Marriage Licenses, 1811-1858

SMALLWOOD, Mary Ann (blk)	LEE, John	MAR 22 1833
SMALLWOOD, Mary Ann	CARTER, John (blk)	JUL 29 1835
SMALLWOOD, Mary Cath.	MARSTELLER, R.L.	NOV 22 1844
SMALLWOOD, Mary E.	ADDISON, John, Jr.	OCT 15 1834
SMALLWOOD, Mary Jane (blk)	BARNES, Overton	NOV 30 1852
SMALLWOOD, Mary V.	HUDGINS, William H.	JUN 05 1855
SMALLWOOD, Moses	FLETCHER, Ellen	DEC 09 1819
SMALLWOOD, Moses	YOUNG, Ann	FEB 03 1836
SMALLWOOD, Permellia	MULLIN, William	SEP 05 1831
SMALLWOOD, Rachel	TAYLOR, John B.	JUL 06 1840
SMALLWOOD, Richard L.	McDUELL, Anna Celinder	SEP 22 1852
SMALLWOOD, Richard T.	BOSWELL, Sarah Ellen	FEB 21 1850
SMALLWOOD, Teresa A.E.	MILLETT, Saml. H.	MAR 12 1839
SMALLWOOD, Thomas	ANDERSON, Elizabeth	FEB 24 1836
SMALLWOOD, William	FRANCIS, Henrietta	JAN 15 1834
SMALLWOOD, William	SMITH, Elizabeth	AUG 13 1853
SMALLWOOD, William A.	BREARLEY, Mary Bernard	MAR 29 1825
SMARR, Elizabeth	COCHRAN, James	SEP 08 1829
SMARR, James	McCARTY, Nancy	AUG 28 1822
SMART, Amelia	GASKINGS, Darius	SEP 27 1827
SMART, Andrew Jackson	JONES, Mary E.C.	NOV 19 1838
SMART, Elizabeth	OWENS, James L.	JAN 02 1834
SMART, Elizabeth C.	RODIER, Charles H.	FEB 03 1842
SMART, Henrietta	KING, William	OCT 07 1836
SMART, Henry	McFARLAND, Ann Maria	JAN 04 1858
SMART, John P.	WILLING, Sarah	MAR 29 1827
SMART, Mary Ann	BERRY, Peter	MAR 10 1832
SMART, Rebecca	GEASLING, Andrew	JAN 06 1819
SMART, Samuel	STREEKS, Martha A.	MAR 29 1842
SMEDLEY, Antone	FERGUSON, Margaret	APR 21 1851
SMETHER, Robert	BAGGS, Elizabeth	FEB 28 1826
SMETHEY, Lewis	TENCH, Matilda	APR 03 1829
SMILER, Henry	DAVIS, Maria (blk)	FEB 06 1834
SMILEY, Edward	TENNY, Ann	MAY 23 1837
SMITH, Abbie B.	SPANGLER, William H.	JUN 09 1849
SMITH, Abijah	CARRICO, Winny Ann	AUG 13 1816
SMITH, Abner C.	BUCLE, Elizabeth D.	APR 23 1839
SMITH, Abraham	FLOYD, Ann	FEB 09 1819
SMITH, Adelaide L.	HOLT, Thomas H.	JUN 10 1856
SMITH, Alexander M.	FEARSON, Ann Maria	AUG 30 1845
SMITH, America M.	BEASLEY, George	MAY 24 1849
SMITH, Amos	BOWEN, Janie (blk)	MAY 16 1833
SMITH, Anderson	DREW, Jane	AUG 29 1826
SMITH, Andrew	BROWN, Matilda	FEB 21 1843
SMITH, Andrew J.	WHEELER, Christina E.	JUL 07 1857
SMITH, Ann	PETTIGREW, James	NOV 16 1819
SMITH, Ann	HUGHES, Nathaniel	JUL 08 1824
SMITH, Ann	CONNOR, John	JUL 29 1824
SMITH, Ann	BEANS, Francis	SEP 21 1824
SMITH, Ann	WOOD, [blank] (blk)	OCT 24 1833
SMITH, Ann	THOMAS, Maponilla	JUN 25 1846
SMITH, Ann E.	NEWTON, James	FEB 26 1821
SMITH, Ann Elizth.	HILTON, William	MAR 09 1849
SMITH, Ann, Mrs.	REEDER, Richard	JUN 19 1858
SMITH, Ann Sophia	COX, John W.	JUL 05 1842
SMITH, Anthony	SMITH, Middleton	DEC 16 1813
SMITH, Archar B. [Rev.]	DEWERS, Mary	OCT 06 1829
SMITH, Bayard H.	HENLEY, Henrietta E.	MAR 03 1842

547

District of Columbia Marriage Licenses, 1811-1858

SMITH, Benjamin	O'DONNOGHUE, Kate	JAN 19 1858
SMITH, Bernard	ALLEN, Priscilla H.	APR 29 1812
SMITH, Britania A.	BUCKLEY, Albert	NOV 27 1850
SMITH, Calvin A.	KEMPPER, Levinia	OCT 07 1857
SMITH, Caroline	BACON, Samuel P.	MAY 18 1836
SMITH, Caroline	FOYLES, James	FEB 19 1848
SMITH, Caroline	ZEIGLER, Christian	MAR 28 1855
SMITH, Caroline (blk)	YATES, Francis	FEB 16 1848
SMITH, Caroline (blk)	GADD, Charles	MAR 22 1858
SMITH, Caroline S.	DeVAUGHAN, Thomas S.	AUG 12 1842
SMITH, Catharine A.	RADCLIFFE, Alexander	FEB 17 1849
SMITH, Catharine J.	PROCTER, John B.	NOV 19 1832
SMITH, Catherine	PRECISE, Logan	JAN 27 1857
SMITH, Catherine B.	HILL, William B.	MAY 12 1835
SMITH, Cecilia	HANEY, John	OCT 17 1829
SMITH, Celina H.	LAZENBY, Daniel L.	MAY 06 1845
SMITH, Charles	GARNER, Ann	AUG 28 1817
SMITH, Charles	PERKINS, Sarah	DEC 22 1818
SMITH, Charles B.	COFFER, Jane M.	AUG 18 1846
SMITH, Charles T.	JONES, Mary F.	DEC 22 1857
SMITH, Charlotte (blk)	BROWN, Marshal	APR 22 1846
SMITH, Christian	WINEBERG, Elizabeth	DEC 04 1856
SMITH, Christina	KEYSER, John	AUG 19 1854
SMITH, Christina	BENTZ, Charles	JAN 26 1856
SMITH, Clara (col'd)	BUTLER, William	NOV 07 1837
SMITH, Clara E.	BUTLER, Rev. Jno. George	OCT 15 1851
SMITH, Cyrus	MEDARA, Mary A.	DEC 24 1840
SMITH, Cyrus, Jr.	MEADES, Susan	DEC 27 1839
SMITH, Daniel	HARVEY, Ann	MAY 02 1816
SMITH, Daniel	CROGGON, Matilda B.	SEP 14 1840
SMITH, Dolly	CLARKE, Thompson	DEC 26 1833
SMITH, Edward	SMITH, Lucy	APR 20 1835
SMITH, Edward A.	DAVIS, Elizabeth A.	JUN 19 1851
SMITH, Edward Jaquelin	BUCKNER, Ella Alice	OCT 23 1848
SMITH, Eleanor (blk)	ROBINSON, Charles	FEB 12 1835
SMITH, Eleanor Ann	KINGSBURY, William O.	JAN 07 1847
SMITH, Elijah	JOHNSON, Sarah	MAY 01 1841
SMITH, Eliza	GRIFFITH, Thomas	DEC 24 1840
SMITH, Eliza	SALZER, David	APR 22 1847
SMITH, Eliza	HOLLOHAN, John T.	JUN 27 1850
SMITH, Eliza (blk)	CARTER, Robert	MAY 07 1850
SMITH, Elizabeth	COCHRAN, John	JAN 12 1818
SMITH, Elizabeth [Caldwell]	DUNCAN, Joseph [Hon.]	MAY 13 1828
SMITH, Elizabeth	BOOTES, Samuel Massey	SEP 29 1828
SMITH, Elizabeth	STONE, James Edward	OCT 13 1828
SMITH, Elizabeth	DISCHER, Henry	AUG 17 1833
SMITH, Elizabeth	WALCH, Joseph	SEP 05 1843
SMITH, Elizabeth	COLLINS, George	DEC 23 1843
SMITH, Elizabeth	NOTTINGHAM, William	DEC 07 1844
SMITH, Elizabeth	HOLMEAD, Anthony, Jr.	MAY 04 1847
SMITH, Elizabeth	MACK, Martin	APR 19 1852
SMITH, Elizabeth	CAMPBELL, Patrick	OCT 07 1852
SMITH, Elizabeth	SMALLWOOD, William	AUG 13 1853
SMITH, Elizabeth	GREENWELL, Clement	JAN 02 1855
SMITH, Elizabeth (blk)	SWANN, John	NOV 07 1849
SMITH, Elizabeth (blk)	GRAY, Basil H.	DEC 28 1854
SMITH, Elizabeth Ann	DARNES, Simon	OCT 03 1837
SMITH, Elizabeth Ann	BENTLEY, Thomas	FEB 23 1850

District of Columbia Marriage Licenses, 1811-1858

SMITH, Elizabeth B.	SMITH, Mordecai James	MAR 01 1851
SMITH, Elizabeth C.	SWEENY, Patrick	OCT 30 1838
SMITH, Elizabeth C.	DEARING, George T.	APR 09 1852
SMITH, Elizabeth R.	CHEW, Robert Smith	JAN 26 1842
SMITH, Elizth. (blk)	SEWALL, Christopher	FEB 14 1855
SMITH, Ellen	McMANUS, Patrick	JAN 09 1851
SMITH, Ellen M.	MONTGOMERY, Edward A.	APR 24 1855
SMITH, Ellen V.	ARCHER, Andrew J.	JUL 05 1854
SMITH, Emanuel	MITCHELL, Margaret A. (blk)	JUN 05 1856
SMITH, Emily	COOK, Benoni	JUL 16 1846
SMITH, Emily W.	FARQUHAR, G.S. [Granville]	SEP 30 1834
SMITH, Ester B.	GRAHAM, Geo. M.	OCT 01 1834
SMITH, Fielder	REILY, Eliza	DEC 23 1811
SMITH, Fielder	SMITH, Lucy	SEP 21 1824
SMITH, Frances	SAUNDERS, Alexander	OCT 23 1847
SMITH, Frances S.	BOWEN, Abram O.	AUG 05 1841
SMITH, Francis	MARTIN, Elizabeth	MAY 17 1827
SMITH, Francis C.	BAILEY, Sampson P.	DEC 09 1846
SMITH, Francis H.	BIRGE, Annie E.	APR 12 1858
SMITH, Frank A.	MECHLIN, A.M.	MAY 11 1840
SMITH, Frederick	LIMP, Sophiah	JUN 26 1852
SMITH, G.A.C.	ROBINSON, Eliza A.	FEB 28 1857
SMITH, Geo. B.	GREEN, Elizabeth	DEC 17 1835
SMITH, Geo. R.	BUTLER, Catharine A. (blk)	JAN 03 1853
SMITH, George	NEWTON, Peggy	JUL 06 1812
SMITH, George	BRUCE, Rutha (blk)	MAY 08 1834
SMITH, George	DALTY, Ann	JUN 25 1858
SMITH, George H.	OSBORNE, Mary	MAR 20 1852
SMITH, Grafton	NAIRY, Nancy	JAN 25 1838
SMITH, Hamilton J.	PAUL, Ellenora	OCT 03 1844
SMITH, Hannah	STEPHENS, Saml.	JUL 25 1812
SMITH, Hannah Ireland	GONTER, Samuel M.	DEC 30 1848
SMITH, Harriet (blk)	TAYLOR, Thomas	JUL 19 1834
SMITH, Harriet Ann	DeVAUGHN, Samuel H.	MAY 07 1838
SMITH, Henrietta	BEULTO, William	OCT 04 1842
SMITH, Henrietta (blk)	ROLLINS, Joseph	SEP 18 1854
SMITH, Henry	BLANSDELL, Harriot	JUL 05 1820
SMITH, Henry	HANDY, Eleanor	DEC 28 1824
SMITH, Henry C.	ROWLINGS, Maria M.	OCT 15 1853
SMITH, Henry T.	BOATMAN, Ann B.	OCT 03 1839
SMITH, Henry W.	SMALLWOOD, Mary	SEP 27 1821
SMITH, Hilleary M.	CHAPPULL, Seraphina E.	APR 03 1848
SMITH, Hugh	CARRIGAN, Mary	APR 25 1856
SMITH, Isaac C.	VanZANDT, Rosalie M.	NOV 04 1837
SMITH, Isabella Graham	WEAVER, Jacob Mott	JUN 25 1828
SMITH, Jacob	BAKER, Flora [Mrs.]	APR 06 1827
SMITH, Jacob A.	CAMPBELL, Julia Ann	DEC 19 1835
SMITH, James	HOOK, Susan	AUG 07 1815
SMITH, James	PLANTT, Sarah Ann (blk)	JAN 26 1837
SMITH, James	BARRY, Teresa	JUN 02 1849
SMITH, James	RILEY, Mary	OCT 04 1849
SMITH, James	DONNEL, Ann	SEP 01 1852
SMITH, James F.	CARRICO, Jane R.	AUG 28 1847
SMITH, James G.	STILLINS, Ann E.	FEB 19 1847
SMITH, James H.	BROWN, Ann E.	JAN 08 1852
SMITH, James M.	BOUTWELL, Martha S.	MAY 22 1845
SMITH, James M.	SMITH, Rosalie M.	MAR 12 1855
SMITH, James R.	WHITE, Mary Catherine	JUL 01 1845

District of Columbia Marriage Licenses, 1811-1858

SMITH, James R.	NOKES, Margaret	NOV 21 1853
SMITH, James R.	WHITE, Georgia A.	JAN 10 1854
SMITH, James R.	SOPER, Eliza Ann	MAY 10 1858
SMITH, James W.	RIGG, Sarah W.	MAR 28 1837
SMITH, Jane	EMBREY, Robert	JUL 18 1834
SMITH, Jane	WROE, Jerome R.	DEC 27 1838
SMITH, Jane	MALBURN, James C.	NOV 21 1839
SMITH, Jane (blk)	BROOKS, Charles	JUL 05 1836
SMITH, Jane Eliza	CROGGON, William	MAR 08 1833
SMITH, Jane O.	MAHON, David W.	SEP 25 1850
SMITH, Jane Owen	THOMPSON, Harvey M.	MAY 11 1843
SMITH, Jared	WALKER, Dolly	APR 22 1824
SMITH, Joanna (blk)	TURLEY, George	JUN 15 1852
SMITH, John	BOWEN, Harriot	JAN 01 1818
SMITH, John	BRIDGE, Margaret	SEP 29 1825
SMITH, John	LEWIS, Elizabeth	JUN 05 1827
SMITH, John	WATERS, Eliza	SEP 02 1830
SMITH, John	LOWE, Jane	AUG 20 1835
SMITH, John	HEART, Margaretta	JUL 25 1846
SMITH, John	PARKER, Teresa (blk)	AUG 01 1854
SMITH, John	VIBBER, Phebe Ann	SEP 27 1854
SMITH, John	ALLEN, Martha L.	NOV 14 1855
SMITH, John A.	BROWN, Clary (blk)	AUG 10 1826
SMITH, John A.	WINDSOR, Rosanna N.	JUN 09 1827
SMITH, John A.	WESSEL, Rosina	APR 02 1850
SMITH, John Addison	COX, Sally	NOV 22 1825
SMITH, John C.	WACHTEN, Matilda	JUN 27 1837
SMITH, John C.	WACHTEN, Matilda	MAY 27 1837
SMITH, John F.	PAYNE, Julia A.T.	FEB 12 1857
SMITH, John F.	CATING, Catherine T.	AUG 03 1857
SMITH, John G.	HOUSLAND, Francisco	SEP 02 1852
SMITH, John G.	COOK, Christiana S.	SEP 08 1853
SMITH, John H.	HAYWOOD, Adeline	MAY 30 1853
SMITH, John Jeremiah M.	PETIT, Frances E.	JAN 19 1847
SMITH, John Johnson	CASSIN, Virginia Jane	NOV 04 1857
SMITH, John L.	SHEPHERD, Rebecca M.	APR 13 1836
SMITH, John M.	DRURY, Elizabeth	AUG 24 1851
SMITH, John P.	CLARK, Frances M.	JUN 22 1853
SMITH, John T.	HARDY, Mary Ann	NOV 28 1846
SMITH, John T.	BROWN, Susan (blk)	MAR 08 1852
SMITH, John T.	DAMMON, Anna	JUN 02 1857
SMITH, John Thomas	PAYNE, Sarah Ann	DEC 08 1848
SMITH, John Thomas	WHITE, Mary	JUN 02 1851
SMITH, John Thomas	WATKINS, Mary T. Catherine	JUL 21 1856
SMITH, John V.	THOMPSON, Maria E.	MAR 23 1858
SMITH, John W.	ROBEY, Jane	OCT 18 1816
SMITH, John W.	MOORE, Verlinda [Mrs.]	JAN 26 1819
SMITH, John W.	COAD, Jane	DEC 11 1826
SMITH, John W.	CAMPBELL, Rebecca W.	NOV 23 1829
SMITH, John W.	COLLINS, Dorcas E.	MAY 21 1850
SMITH, John W., Jr.	DEVALL, Louisa M.	JUN 23 1857
SMITH, John [Lieut.]	BAYLY, Mary R.	NOV 14 1821
SMITH, Joseph	BAKER, Elizabeth	MAY 31 1837
SMITH, Joseph A.	FENWICK, Mary E.	NOV 12 1856
SMITH, Joseph C.	DUNLOP, Harriet (blk)	SEP 29 1857
SMITH, Joseph L.	PEABODY, Sophila	OCT 29 1823
SMITH, Joseph M.	COOPER, Amanda V.	NOV 16 1852
SMITH, Joseph S.	CRAMPSTIN, Caroline E.	JUN 30 1831

District of Columbia Marriage Licenses, 1811-1858

SMITH, Joseph W.	WIGGINS, Eliza	MAY 13 1833
SMITH, Josephine	NASH, Robert H., Jr.	OCT 08 1853
SMITH, Josephine Elizth	STONE, Thomas	DEC 08 1855
SMITH, Joshua	KABLER, Eliza	MAR 17 1831
SMITH, Julia	SHECKELS, Charles	DEC 03 1835
SMITH, Julia H.	GALLUDET, Theodore [Rev.]	FEB 08 1836
SMITH, Juliet	GOGGEN, William	SEP 22 1818
SMITH, Justine	DAVIS, Benjamin	JAN 22 1852
SMITH, Kate	ALBERT, Rudolph	AUG 05 1856
SMITH, Kesiah	McPHERSON, James	MAR 28 1817
SMITH, Kitty	BRYANT, Enoch	FEB 06 1828
SMITH, Laurena (blk)	BROWN, William	OCT 26 1843
SMITH, Laurence	NEAL, Eliza	DEC 04 1846
SMITH, Lawrina	HURLEY, Salem	DEC 23 1815
SMITH, Lethe	ALLEN, George	JAN 04 1858
SMITH, Letty (blk)	INGRAM, Washington	NOV 15 1827
SMITH, Louise	BURGDORFF, Louis	DEC 30 1851
SMITH, Lucinda	RICHARDSON, William	MAR 21 1856
SMITH, Lucinda (blk)	SALOMON, Kenner	MAY 02 1853
SMITH, Lucy	SMITH, Fielder	SEP 21 1824
SMITH, Lucy	SMITH, Edward	APR 20 1835
SMITH, Margaret	GROEM, John	DEC 16 1818
SMITH, Margaret	HARKNESS, John C.	MAR 18 1828
SMITH, Margaret	WACHTER, Jacob	NOV 07 1837
SMITH, Margaret	AVERY, William B.	APR 22 1848
SMITH, Margaret	HASTINGS, William	APR 07 1849
SMITH, Margaret	SANDERS, Richard	JAN 03 1855
SMITH, Margaret	YATES, William	JUN 15 1857
SMITH, Margaret	FROELIG, Hartman	APR 06 1858
SMITH, Margaret A.V. (blk)	LEWIS, Archibald	MAY 02 1853
SMITH, Margaret C.	GANTT, Benjamin S.	OCT 25 1848
SMITH, Margarett D.	MEREDITH, John F.	MAY 27 1833
SMITH, Margt. P.	BALL, James P.	NOV 14 1831
SMITH, Maria	HYDE, Anthony	FEB 20 1832
SMITH, Mariah A.	CARTER, Jacob, Jr.	OCT 03 1827
SMITH, Martha Ann	JENKINS, Edward	DEC 21 1830
SMITH, Martha Ellen	TAYLOR, William Henry	JUL 07 1831
SMITH, Mary	HARRIS, James	NOV 28 1830
SMITH, Mary	HAWKE, Thomas A.	JAN 19 1832
SMITH, Mary	TRUMAN, Henry	OCT 03 1843
SMITH, Mary	STEWART, James	APR 17 1849
SMITH, Mary	SHELDON, Henry B.	JUN 28 1858
SMITH, Mary (blk)	COLE, Martin	NOV 13 1828
SMITH, Mary A.E.	PADGETT, Joseph H.	OCT 04 1853
SMITH, Mary Ann	MAGONEGLE, Alexander	DEC 23 1830
SMITH, Mary Ann	GOINGS, James	DEC 21 1830
SMITH, Mary Ann, Mrs.	NADDY, Pierce	FEB 02 1831
SMITH, Mary Ann	TALBOT, Edmond	DEC 16 1834
SMITH, Mary Ann	RUSSELL, Benjamin B.	OCT 08 1835
SMITH, Mary Ann	STURGEON, James G.	DEC 08 1841
SMITH, Mary Ann	WILLIAMS, Jesse	FEB 27 1852
SMITH, Mary Ann	SCHREIVER, George	OCT 19 1852
SMITH, Mary Ann (blk)	YOUNG, William	DEC 13 1853
SMITH, Mary Bridget	GALLIHER, Michael	SEP 08 1823
SMITH, Mary C.	THOMPSON, William B.	FEB 15 1834
SMITH, Mary C.	BROWNELL, Charles H.	NOV 03 1851
SMITH, Mary Catherine	SEYMOUR, William F.	NOV 14 1840
SMITH, Mary Elizabeth	McLELLAN, George W.	OCT 19 1852

District of Columbia Marriage Licenses, 1811-1858

Bride/Groom	Spouse	Date
SMITH, Mary Elizth.	HELTON, Thomas	MAY 07 1851
SMITH, Mary Ellen	EMMERICH, George	FEB 26 1848
SMITH, Mary Ellen	BRIGGS, James Marion	MAY 25 1853
SMITH, Mary Isabell	VESSEY, Leonard	NOV 10 1853
SMITH, Mary Jane (blk)	WORMLEY, Andrew	JUL 11 1848
SMITH, Mary K.	JAMES, John W.	MAR 27 1828
SMITH, Mary L.	VENABLE, George W.	DEC 24 1856
SMITH, Mary M.	CROUSE, John Walter	AUG 25 1825
SMITH, Mathew, Rev.	NOURSE, Mary Francis	SEP 25 1855
SMITH, Matilda	SEATON, George	SEP 23 1815
SMITH, Matilda	SKIDMORE, Henry	APR 17 1840
SMITH, Matilda E.	ALLEN, James W.	JAN 27 1848
SMITH, Michael	WHITTLE, Adelia	NOV 27 1852
SMITH, Michael	FITZPATRICK, Mary	OCT 28 1856
SMITH, Middleton	SMITH, Anthony	DEC 16 1813
SMITH, Mordecai James	SMITH, Elizabeth B.	MAR 01 1851
SMITH, Nelly	DYNES, Peter	FEB 23 1819
SMITH, Oliver James	TOPPING, Barbara A. (blk)	FEB 06 1847
SMITH, Patsey	CROSBY, Sylvanus	MAY 14 1832
SMITH, Philip [Dr.]	McNERHANY, Mary [Mrs.]	MAY 31 1834
SMITH, Phillippe	HARROVER, William H.	MAY 19 1841
SMITH, Polly	KING, James	DEC 20 1831
SMITH, Pricilla	ROLLINS, George	DEC 22 1834
SMITH, Rachel A.	BRYDON, John	MAR 20 1841
SMITH, Ransdle	SEALOCK, Elizabeth P.	SEP 20 1825
SMITH, Rebecca	MURRAY, Nicholas	JAN 12 1852
SMITH, Rebecca J.	SAUNDERS, John C.	OCT 06 1851
SMITH, Reubin	WILSON, Hannah (blk)	MAY 08 1846
SMITH, Reubin	WILSON, Harriet Elizabeth (blk)	SEP 08 1851
SMITH, Rezin O.	OLLIVER, Martha	JAN 31 1850
SMITH, Richard	SPALDING, Catharine	MAR 01 1821
SMITH, Richard	SMITH, Sarah	NOV 07 1838
SMITH, Richard	COLE, Vanilla (blk)	APR 14 1852
SMITH, Richard H.	DeNEALE, Jannet S.W.	OCT 26 1853
SMITH, Richard S.	CLARKE, Ellen Marian	FEB 02 1837
SMITH, Richard T.	KING, Violetta	DEC 21 1857
SMITH, Robert	BOYD, Elizabeth R. (blk)	JAN 06 1858
SMITH, Robert E.	CARBERY, Catharine	OCT 02 1850
SMITH, Rosalie M.	SMITH, James M.	MAR 12 1855
SMITH, Sally Hoffman	HUNTER, William, Jr.	NOV 17 1835
SMITH, Sally L.C.	JOHNSTON, Christopher	SEP 25 1855
SMITH, Saml. Owen	BOWLING, Ann W.	OCT 22 1816
SMITH, Samuel	ADAMS, Milly	OCT 12 1812
SMITH, Samuel	TALBERT, Ann	AUG 31 1815
SMITH, Samuel	CROSS, Rutha	JAN 26 1847
SMITH, Samuel	BUSTLE, Maria	SEP 22 1854
SMITH, Samuel E.	ST. CLAIR, Miss	JUN 05 1845
SMITH, Sarah	TALBERT, Thomas	JAN 03 1827
SMITH, Sarah	SMITH, Thomas	MAY 24 1831
SMITH, Sarah	GIBSON, John	OCT 01 1831
SMITH, Sarah	LANGLEY, Samuel	JUL 29 1835
SMITH, Sarah	SMITH, Richard	NOV 07 1838
SMITH, Sarah (blk)	DAVIS, Richard	NOV 07 1838
SMITH, Sarah (blk)	CARTER, James	AUG 16 1848
SMITH, Sarah Amanda	LAZENBY, Thomas A.	APR 06 1835
SMITH, Sarah Ann (blk)	JOHNSON, Josias	SEP 21 1846
SMITH, Sarah Ann (blk)	PLUMMER, Henry W.	OCT 25 1849
SMITH, Sarah B.	MILLAN, George M.	JUN 24 1843

District of Columbia Marriage Licenses, 1811-1858

SMITH, Sidney W.	HESSELIUS, Rachael B.	JUL 01 1830
SMITH, Silas	WELLS, Frances	AUG 30 1850
SMITH, Sophia	DAVIS, James	SEP 23 1834
SMITH, Sophia S.	LEIBLEMAN, William G.F.	AUG 25 1851
SMITH, Sophronia A.	LOMAX, Michael	SEP 06 1830
SMITH, Susan	CROWLEY, Thomas	SEP 06 1830
SMITH, Susan	CROWLEY, Thomas	NOV 14 1837
SMITH, Susan E.	THOMPSON, Oscar D.	OCT 06 1847
SMITH, Susannah B.	TARLTON, Henry	MAY 11 1829
SMITH, Tamer (blk)	PUNNELL, Levi	DEC 31 1832
SMITH, Temple	OLIVER, Sarah	JAN 07 1845
SMITH, Thomas	CARMAN, Sarah Ann	FEB 23 1819
SMITH, Thomas	LUCAS, Maranda B.	FEB 25 1829
SMITH, Thomas	SMITH, Sarah	MAY 24 1831
SMITH, Thomas	JOHNSON, Mary (blk)	MAY 07 1838
SMITH, Thomas	DAVIS, Henrietta	SEP 04 1838
SMITH, Thomas	TRIGER, Lavina	JAN 09 1840
SMITH, Thomas	CARBERY, Mrs.	MAY 27 1856
SMITH, Thomas A.	BURGESS, Sarah	FEB 15 1847
SMITH, Thomas J.	MYER, Louisa W.	APR 08 1828
SMITH, Thomas M.	KIRBY, Sarah Ann	OCT 08 1851
SMITH, Washington	BLAKE, Julia Ann	AUG 24 1835
SMITH, Wesley A.	TAYLOR, Emily W.	FEB 28 1856
SMITH, Wilfred	GEE, Margaret	AUG 11 1831
SMITH, William	COOK, Annetty	OCT 16 1820
SMITH, William	HARPER, Ann	JUL 24 1821
SMITH, William	THORNTON, Mary	JUN 13 1822
SMITH, William	WEGLIE, Anne	FEB 21 1823
SMITH, William	NEAL, Mary (blk)	FEB 25 1829
SMITH, William	GORDON, Susan Ann	JUL 24 1831
SMITH, William	CHARLES, Maria	MAR 24 1835
SMITH, William	ROBEY, Mary Ann	JUL 28 1838
SMITH, William	OWEN, Mary	APR 08 1841
SMITH, William	JONES, Mary Ann	OCT 29 1842
SMITH, William	GLENN, Mary Jane	JUL 23 1844
SMITH, William	MILES, Adeline (blk)	MAR 20 1845
SMITH, William	JENKINS, Fanny (blk)	DEC 24 1845
SMITH, William	McGUIRE, Bridget	MAR 17 1855
SMITH, William	PARKER, Rachel Mary	NOV 28 1855
SMITH, William B.	FOWLER, Virginia R.	AUG 24 1852
SMITH, William B.	FOWLER, Virginia R.	NOV 28 1855
SMITH, William H.	WELSH, Elizabeth	NOV 24 1857
SMITH, William H.	GIBBONS, Mary E.	MAY 12 1858
SMITH, William L.H.	HOLAND, Martha Ann	SEP 07 1846
SMITH, William M.	FLETCHER, Dianna (blk)	NOV 11 1847
SMITH, William R.	EASBY, Wilhelmine M.	JUN 13 1854
SMITH, William S.	BROWNE, Ann Eilbeck	FEB 25 1858
SMITH, Wm.	TENCH, Balinda	APR 05 1823
SMITH, Wm.	LANGLEY, Martha Ann	JUL 26 1838
SMITH, Wm. H.	DASHIELD, Sally	APR 08 1817
SMITH, Zachariah	COOK, Elizabeth	JAN 04 1832
SMITH, [blank]	BARRETT, [blank]	OCT 04 1834
SMITHBY, Ann	MARTIN, Vansonia	JUN 10 1847
SMITHIA, William	COOK, Mary Drucilla	JUL 23 1845
SMITHLY, Barbara	EVANS, Richard	DEC 08 1856
SMITHLY, Theodore	BETTS, Elizabeth	APR 15 1839
SMITHSON, George	PUMPHREY, Ann Eliza	OCT 23 1856
SMITHSON, Hezekiah	LEWIS, Sinai	JAN 07 1818

District of Columbia Marriage Licenses, 1811-1858

SMITHSON, Mary Jane	SMITHSON, Thomas E.	FEB 13 1858
SMITHSON, Thomas E.	SMITHSON, Mary Jane	FEB 13 1858
SMITHWICK, John	KIFF, Margaret	JUL 25 1820
SMITHY, William H.	ENSEY, Margarett A.	MAR 16 1854
SMITLEY, Margaret	NEIFF, Francis	SEP 10 1839
SMITSON, Alcana	BURGESS, Mary Ann	NOV 03 1835
SMITSON, James	LEHMAN, Pauline Rosemond	JAN 14 1845
SMITSON, John H.	JOHNSON, Sarah	JAN 12 1836
SMITSON, Mary	SMITSON, William	MAY 21 1832
SMITSON, Mary Jane	STARSTONE, Charles Francis	MAY 31 1855
SMITSON, William	SMITSON, Mary	MAY 21 1832
SMITT, Mary Ann	GROOCE, James F.	JUL 06 1837
SMITZER, Thomas	KING, Ann	APR 17 1827
SMOOT, Araminta E.	PLEASANTS, William H.	NOV 02 1852
SMOOT, Benjamin S.	McGUIRE, Ann	FEB 10 1831
SMOOT, Catharine Adaline	TURNER, William B.	JUL 13 1829
SMOOT, Charles B.	POLLOCK, Emily M.	AUG 19 1833
SMOOT, Eliza E.	JARBOE, J.J.	JAN 06 1838
SMOOT, Eliza Virginia	MONTGOMERY, James	JUN 07 1823
SMOOT, George A.	MITCHEL, Anne	JUL 13 1833
SMOOT, George C.	EDELIN, Mary	JAN 15 1828
SMOOT, George H.	WESTERN, Mary	NOV 01 1825
SMOOT, J.G.	CALDER, Hellen M.	JAN 20 1841
SMOOT, John H.	PIERCY, Matilda	OCT 07 1819
SMOOT, John H.	SPEIDEN, Elizabeth	MAR 13 1827
SMOOT, John H.	CAMPBELL, Charlotte Q.	MAY 07 1856
SMOOT, John W.	HAYMIRE, Mary B.	MAR 05 1839
SMOOT, John W.	McKENNA, Mary M.	NOV 18 1856
SMOOT, Laura V.	STERN, John W.	MAY 12 1856
SMOOT, Lydia K.	WAGGAMAN, John H.	SEP 28 1837
SMOOT, Mary	DAVIS, William	OCT 07 1845
SMOOT, Mary Jane	DEMENT, John D.	OCT 29 1853
SMOOT, Rosa S.	PLEASANTS, James B.	JUL 02 1845
SMOOT, Samuel C. of Washington DC	SMALLWOOD, Emma of Newt. Cor. MA	APR 29 1846
SMOOT, Sarah	TRICE, Richard	JUN 21 1832
SMOOT, Sarah E.	PARIS, Albert W.	MAY 30 1838
SMOOT, Thomas	WATERS, Elizabeth	JAN 20 1831
SMOOT, Thomas Walter	DAUSEY, Lucretia Ann	JAN 11 1845
SMOOT, William G.	FIELDS, Ellen	MAY 21 1856
SMULL, Jacob	FRY, Nancy	DEC 09 1816
SMYTH, Elizabeth	BAHM, Valintine	FEB 17 1846
SM[blank], Mary Jane	McCEWING, Robert	APR 15 1847
SNAPE, Mary A.	UPPERMAN, James H.	SEP 03 1855
SNAUBER, Catherine	BELL, Solomon	SEP 10 1846
SNEAD, Martha	SPALDING, Richard	JUL 06 1839
SNEDEKER, Samuel M.	POWELL, Catharine A.	AUG 11 1853
SNEE, Michael	MURPHEY, Margaret	FEB 24 1820
SNEE, Thomas	MURPHY, Ellen	FEB 17 1857
SNEED, Sarah	WINEBERGER, Cyrus	JUL 10 1841
SNIDER, John Adam	OLLERMEH, Liner	OCT 02 1848
SNIFFEN, Theodore	BOHLAYER, Mary C.	JUN 07 1852
SNIFFIN, Thodore	DENNISON, Susan A.	APR 26 1847
SNOW, Charles B.	MECHLIN, Margaretta W.	AUG 07 1848
SNOW, Jerry	SHORTER, Susan (blk)	SEP 22 1836
SNOW, John	MARSHALL, Mary	MAY 26 1855
SNOWDEN, Caroline (blk)	BAILEY, Adam	SEP 30 1839
SNOWDEN, Eliza (blk)	EDENBOROUGH, Henry	APR 17 1827
SNOWDEN, Gerrard H.	STEWART, Arrabella Orr	APR 28 1824

District of Columbia Marriage Licenses, 1811-1858

SNOWDEN, Gurden	HILL, Martha (blk)	SEP 19 1842
SNOWDEN, Henry Clay	LOGAN, Mary Ann (blk)	DEC 19 1851
SNOWDEN, Mrs. [Arabella]	MAGEE, John	FEB 18 1831
SNYDER, Albert Martin	HOLLAND, Mary Ellen	MAR 12 1855
SNYDER, Armedia	CLARK, Bainbridge S.	DEC 17 1855
SNYDER, Benjamin	WAPLES, Louisa E.	OCT 14 1846
SNYDER, Caroline	DUCKETT, Arthur	OCT 17 1854
SNYDER, Catherine G.	REEM, John	SEP 26 1853
SNYDER, Dorothy A.J.	ST. JOHN, John	JUN 15 1850
SNYDER, Hiram M.	FURTNER, Biddy Ann	NOV 11 1856
SNYDER, John Adam	BELL, Mary Jane	JAN 16 1855
SNYDER, Leopole	LANGIN, Eva	NOV 08 1852
SNYDER, Lewis H.	TURTON, Jane	MAR 08 1852
SNYDER, Luther L.	BURCH, Eugenia E.	SEP 03 1857
SNYDER, Matthias, Jr.	MARTIN, Jane	FEB 05 1828
SNYDER, William	TALBOT, Mary	DEC 15 1852
SOHL, Conrad	GERHOLD, Charlotte	MAR 09 1858
SOHOENHOZ, Herman Wm.	MOHLOW, Margaret	DEC 23 1853
SOLLERS, William	CLARKE, Jane Elizabeth	SEP 30 1837
SOLOMON, Ann C.	SHEFFNER, Peter R.	DEC 20 1851
SOLOMON, Daniel	VINSON, Mary E. (blk)	NOV 27 1856
SOLOMON, James W.	HAVENER, Emily Jane	MAR 01 1854
SOLOMON, Margaret (blk)	MOORE, Jacob	MAR 08 1849
SOLOMON, Sarah Ann (blk)	BURKE, Albert	MAR 20 1850
SOLOMON, Susan Ann	RYON, John	JAN 28 1845
SOMERS, Ann	JOHNSON, Melvin	JUL 01 1835
SOMERS, Judson	VERMILLION, Priscilla	NOV 03 1815
SOMERS, Sarah	RUSSELL, George	SEP 02 1813
SOMERS, Sarah A.	TALBURT, Thomas	JAN 09 1843
SOMERVILLE, Arnold	CURTIS, Eliza	DEC 22 1818
SOMERVILLE, Jane	TERRILL, James W.	APR 20 1852
SOMERVILLE, Robert	JENERIS, Henrietta	DEC 26 1816
SOMERVILLE, Thomas	TILMAN, Mary	JAN 31 1843
SOMMER, John	WEIMAN, Helena	JUL 19 1838
SOMMERS, Henry W.	PETTIBONE, Elizth. W.	FEB 08 1851
SOMMERS, John A.	WOOD, Ellen	OCT 09 1845
SOMMERS, Judson	ARNOLD, Elizabeth	DEC 21 1816
SOMMERS, Mary Elizabeth	CLARVOE, John H.	JUN 19 1844
SOMMERS, Matilda	MASON, Richard B.	JAN 18 1837
SOMMERS, Michael W.	FRITZSEHE, Emilie	AUG 21 1852
SOMMERVILLE, James	NORRIS, Jane Eliza	JAN 14 1858
SONDERS, Lewis	LANHAM, Elizabeth A.	JUN 09 1840
SONENWALD, Eliza	OLZEM, John	NOV 02 1855
SONNENSCHMIDT, Chas. W.	McTILTON, Catherine	MAR 07 1857
SOPER, Basil	KIDLOW, Ellen N.	NOV 16 1831
SOPER, Basil	COOK, Mary Ann P.	JUN 15 1833
SOPER, Bazil	EDWARDS, Frances	FEB 04 1817
SOPER, Charles	GRIFFIN, Matilda J.	APR 18 1850
SOPER, Charles	OLIVER, Margaret	JUN 04 1851
SOPER, Eliza Ann	HIGGINS, Samuel	MAY 26 1855
SOPER, Eliza Ann	SMITH, James R.	MAY 10 1858
SOPER, Elizabeth	HUTCHERSON, Walter	FEB 22 1816
SOPER, George F.D.	CARROLL, Jane	FEB 22 1853
SOPER, Henry	JENKINS, Elizabeth	FEB 07 1827
SOPER, Jesse	MIDDLETON, Mrs. Eliza	FEB 24 1835
SOPER, John A.	PRIME, Mary Jane	JAN 24 1846
SOPER, John O.	LOVELESS, Verlinder	DEC 14 1815
SOPER, Maranda E.	CROSEN, Thomas	FEB 03 1839

District of Columbia Marriage Licenses, 1811-1858

SOPER, Margaret	RIDGWAY, Mordica	FEB 09 1826
SOPER, Maria	COLLINGS, George	JUN 10 1815
SOPER, Martha	SCOTT, William	FEB 04 1841
SOPER, Mary Ann	MAYHEW, William	MAR 14 1837
SOPER, Mary Ann	SKIDMORE, Samuel	DEC 20 1849
SOPER, Mary H.	JARBOE, John T.	JUN 02 1849
SOPER, Priscilla	McDONALD, William	APR 25 1844
SOPER, Robert	COOK, Abitha	FEB 17 1823
SOPER, Sarah Adeline	GRIFFIN, James L.	JAN 22 1858
SOPER, William	LEMON, Mary Elizth.	FEB 24 1845
SORAN, Ellen C.	BELKNAP, Edward	OCT 19 1857
SORET, Francis	FLYNN, Ann	JUL 02 1825
SORG, Catherine	RUPPERT, Ignatius	OCT 19 1844
SORG, John P.	RUPPERT, Walburg	AUG 02 1856
SORG, Margaretta	HARPP, Nicholas	DEC 12 1838
SORREL, Francis	MOXLEY, Lucinda J.	SEP 06 1822
SORREL, Francis	MOXLEY, Matilda A.D.	SEP 30 1829
SORRELL, Mary A.	JONES, Napoleon Bonaparte	MAY 07 1857
SORRELL, Mary Lucinda	USHER, John P.	DEC 13 1849
SORRELL, Sevolia A.	FOUNTING, Allison	JAN 01 1848
SORRELL, William T.	LUCAS, Mary E.	DEC 19 1854
SOTER, John	STOCK, Mary	JAN 11 1845
SOTHOREN, Elizabeth	CONROY, Humphrey	APR 21 1837
SOTHORON, John	BURROUGH, Mary	APR 05 1856
SOTHORON, John	ADAMS, Virginia	MAR 30 1858
SOTHORON, Martha A.	HANCOCK, Lemuel	JAN 21 1856
SOTHORON, Mary	SHREVE, William H.	NOV 10 1838
SOTHORON, Rebecca	McCLAREN, Duncan	MAY 18 1812
SOTHORON, Zachariah	NEVITT, Elizabeth	APR 30 1825
SOTHRON, John	KNOT, Rossannah	FEB 08 1818
SOUISSA, John, Junr.	CAMMACK, Mary	MAY 22 1848
SOUNDERS, Elizabeth F.	CROSS, Benjamin	MAY 19 1840
SOUPER, Otha W.	PAGE, Mary Elizabeth	FEB 05 1857
SOURBERGER, George	SHIELDS, Sarah	NOV 22 1839
SOUTH, Bradley	JONES, Sarah Ann	AUG 13 1832
SOUTH, Thomas	JONES, Henerietta	JUL 29 1817
SOUTHALE, Mary Ann	SHEPERD, William	SEP 06 1830
SOUTHALL, Tyler	REMELE, Sopha	SEP 02 1856
SOUTHARD, Harriet	PHILLIPS, William	AUG 04 1841
SOUTHARD, James W.	HINDMAN, Virginia H.	MAY 08 1855
SOUTHARD, Mary	GOODY, William	DEC 09 1812
SOUTHERLAND, George W.	HOBURG, Sophia	NOV 20 1838
SOUTHERLAND, Mary	MARTIN, William	MAY 21 1829
SOUTHERN, Elizabeth	CARTWRIGHT, Levin	DEC 30 1826
SOUTHERN, Maria	MUCKLEARY, Richard	JUL 05 1818
SOUTHERN, Richard	REDIN, Frances	JAN 05 1826
SOUTHGATE, James, Jr.	WINNE, Delia H.	AUG 03 1858
SOUTHORON, Henrietta M.	SASSCER, James G.	FEB 12 1855
SOUTHORON, Mary M.	HANCOCK, Josiah H.	APR 21 1857
SOUTHWORTH, F. Hamilton	NEVITT, Emma D.N.	JAN 23 1840
SOWDEN, John	FISHER, Mary J.E.F.	JAN 04 1849
SOWER, Henry	KLEINE, Orsilla	JAN 01 1844
SPAITS, Anna E.	LANSDALE, Uriah F.	SEP 17 1855
SPALDING, Ann	COTES, John	JUL 02 1857
SPALDING, Basil	POWELL, Ruthe	OCT 08 1812
SPALDING, Bernard	FORD, Ann	MAY 22 1817
SPALDING, Catharine	SMITH, Richard	MAR 01 1821
SPALDING, Catharine	MAYHEW, William Bradley	DEC 17 1833

District of Columbia Marriage Licenses, 1811-1858

SPALDING, Catherine	RIGDEN, Henry	JUL 18 1815
SPALDING, Daniel J.	SYMPSON, Margaret L.	MAY 18 1857
SPALDING, Eleanor	GRIFFITH, Edward	APR 20 1819
SPALDING, Elexis	WALKER, Mary	JAN 26 1819
SPALDING, Francis A.	STEWART, Sarah	FEB 20 1830
SPALDING, George S.	DeVAUGHN, Catharine E.	JAN 06 1852
SPALDING, Hilleary C.	CASSIN, Margaret A.	NOV 07 1842
SPALDING, James	EVANS, Rebecca	AUG 11 1814
SPALDING, James W.	ROBINSON, S. Lizzie	JUN 18 1856
SPALDING, Jane	PARKER, Southey	JUL 26 1815
SPALDING, Jane	GOOD, Thomas G.	DEC 30 1825
SPALDING, Jane E.	WELSH, William	FEB 04 1845
SPALDING, Kate V.	BOUCHER, Joseph W.	JAN 16 1852
SPALDING, Lorenzo L.	MARSHALL, Elizabeth	NOV 26 1842
SPALDING, Maria	SPENCE, Christopher	MAR 01 1833
SPALDING, Mariah	MAYHUE, Lewin	AUG 12 1828
SPALDING, Martha Ann	WILSON, John	DEC 27 1827
SPALDING, Mary	BURKE, John	JUL 19 1856
SPALDING, Mary Ann	GALLANT, Edward	JUN 19 1841
SPALDING, Mary Ann	DEGGES, Robert Hamilton	JAN 09 1844
SPALDING, Mary Ellen	CRIPPS, William M.L.	SEP 14 1824
SPALDING, Richard	SNEAD, Martha	JUL 06 1839
SPALDING, Richard T.	THOMPSON, Sarah	NOV 16 1815
SPALDING, Samuel E.	LIPSCOMB, Emma E.	FEB 07 1855
SPALDING, Sarah	GODDARD, Isaac	OCT 20 1841
SPALDING, Teresa	GIBERSON, G.L.	NOV 25 1832
SPALDING, Thomas F.P.	BRYAN, Sally	NOV 17 1835
SPALDING, William E.	ROBINSON, Maria P.	MAY 23 1848
SPALDING, Winneford	OWENS, Charles	APR 13 1830
SPALLIN, John	KANE, Ellen	FEB 20 1855
SPALLINGTON, Jno.	MALLARD, Susan	MAR 10 1818
SPANGLER, William H.	SMITH, Abbie B.	JUN 09 1849
SPARKS, John W.	THOMAS, Rachel E.	MAY 01 1851
SPARKS, William	AUSPIN, Chloe Ann	AUG 09 1853
SPARO, Thomas T.	LEITCH, Mary M.	JAN 17 1850
SPARROW, Daby Ann	O'NALTS, Lewis	MAR 05 1833
SPARROW, Harriet	HILTON, Perry Green	OCT 28 1819
SPARROW, Jacob	SPARROW, Julia Ann	NOV 12 1851
SPARROW, John	HOFFMAN, Jane	DEC 23 1851
SPARROW, Joseph	STEWART, Mary	JAN 21 1857
SPARROW, Juia Ann	SPARROW, Jacob	NOV 12 1851
SPARROW, Kinsey	SPARROW, Mary	NOV 28 1825
SPARROW, Mary	LOVELESS, William	MAY 01 1813
SPARROW, Mary	SPARROW, Kinsey	NOV 28 1825
SPARROW, Mary	ATKINS, William	JUL 15 1837
SPARROW, Mary Ellen	McDONALD, Wm. T.	AUG 28 1854
SPARROW, Rosetta	MACK, John	OCT 01 1816
SPATES, Elizabeth S.	PYLE, Mifflin	MAR 15 1837
SPATES, George	MADDOX, Clara	AUG 24 1857
SPAULDING, Ann Catharine	NAY, John	SEP 14 1837
SPEAK, Geo.	LANG, Elizabeth	JAN 28 1819
SPEAKE, Henrietta Maria	BAINBRIDGE, John	JUL 12 1838
SPEAKE, John	LEE, Mary	MAR 24 1828
SPEAKE, Josias M.	VALDENARE, Mary Margaret	JAN 31 1814
SPEAKE, Mary C.	HOUSE, John	APR 18 1850
SPEAKE, Mary Ellen	McCONCHIE, Walter Alexander	DEC 31 1829
SPEAKE, Thomas L.	ROWE, Mary Ann	AUG 06 1833
SPEAKE, Wm. F.	RADCLIFF, Mary A.	OCT 29 1855

District of Columbia Marriage Licenses, 1811-1858

SPEAKES, Edward	RIGSBY, Charlotte E.	NOV 20 1823
SPEAKES, Eliza	WARDER, James	SEP 15 1842
SPEAKMAN, Hayes	PEIRCE, Hannah	MAY 10 1836
SPEAKS, Celindra	PEDDICORD, Jeremiah	FEB 12 1850
SPEAKS, Elizabeth	GREEN, John	AUG 28 1828
SPEAKS, John	BACON, Jane	APR 06 1822
SPEAKS, John	WILSON, Sarah Catherine	DEC 19 1851
SPEAKS, Sarah	HUTCHINSON, Thompson	MAR 28 1821
SPEAKS, Sarah Susan	DeSAULES, Julius	FEB 19 1852
SPEAR, Mary E.	BIRCH, Joseph E.	APR 28 1855
SPEAR, Rachel	LEONBACHER, John	FEB 26 1852
SPECHT, Jenivefer	CREAMER, Charles	MAR 19 1855
SPEDDEN, Edward M.	O'NEALE, Caroline M.	MAY 06 1841
SPEDEN, Jannet	MAHAGEN, John	JAN 04 1849
SPEEDEN, Ann Maria	WHITE, Joshua E.	AUG 23 1831
SPEEDIN, Marion E.	BAYNE, George H.	NOV 02 1853
SPEEKNALL, Mary Ann	HUMPHREYS, James	JUN 20 1831
SPEER, Alexander	COYLE, Maria H.	AUG 25 1846
SPEER, George	DAVIS, Mary J.	JAN 31 1856
SPEERLING, Hanson	REED, Polly	AUG 23 1813
SPEERS, Amelia	GODFREY, Francis	FEB 24 1827
SPEIDEN, Ann	FORESTEL, Walter	JAN 15 1836
SPEIDEN, Elizabeth	SMOOT, John H.	MAR 13 1827
SPEIDEN, Robert	FENWICK, Margaret	JAN 22 1824
SPEIDEN, William	COOTE, Marain	OCT 07 1828
SPEIDEN, William	PERKINS, Sarah Ann	DEC 23 1850
SPEILMAN, John	LUCKETT, Mary E.	MAR 31 1845
SPEIR, Robert	MILLER, Ann	SEP 04 1844
SPELAUN, John	COSGROVE, Alice	JUN 13 1854
SPELLING, Margaret	DEMPSEY, Rodey	JUN 25 1858
SPELLMAN, Catharine	THOMPSON, Benjamin	NOV 15 1833
SPELLMAN, Elizabeth	PETIT, William F.	APR 28 1853
SPELLMAN, George	TAYLOR, Louisa	AUG 28 1829
SPENCE, Catherine	MOORE, William F.	JUL 13 1848
SPENCE, Christopher	SPALDING, Maria	MAR 01 1833
SPENCE, Edward B.	ANDREW, Margaret	SEP 07 1850
SPENCE, Elizabeth	WILLIS, John	JUL 31 1841
SPENCE, James	PHILIPS, Teresa Ann	NOV 14 1827
SPENCER, Amos	RIGGLE, Evelina	OCT 05 1854
SPENCER, Benjamin	HILL, Prudence	OCT 07 1829
SPENCER, Daniel	RODGERS, Jane	SEP 03 1856
SPENCER, George D.	BACON, Caroline	AUG 10 1830
SPENCER, George W.	WALKER, Virginia	JAN 23 1849
SPENCER, Margaret H.	JAMISON, Uzziel W.	FEB 01 1855
SPENCER, Mary Ann	RODGERS, Benjamin	MAY 04 1854
SPENCER, Prudence	EMMERSON, John P.	JAN 06 1848
SPENCER, Richard D.	TURNBALL, Jane A.	MAR 11 1837
SPENCER, Samuel H.	LUCAS, Ann Maria	SEP 05 1843
SPENCER, Sarah	JAVINS, William	JUL 05 1853
SPENCER, Sarah Ann	GUNNELL, John	FEB 22 1825
SPENCER, Sophia F.	REDMAN, J.R.	MAR 04 1837
SPENCER, Thomas H.	ATWELL, Ann Amanda	JAN 31 1856
SPENCER, William	SMALLWOOD, Cloah Ann	JAN 03 1851
SPERLING, Elizabeth	MORGAN, Johnsey R.	JAN 26 1818
SPERLING, Martha	McNARE, James	JAN 07 1814
SPERRY, Emely E.	KANE, Theodore	MAY 14 1838
SPERRY, Warden W.	FAIRBANKS, Frances P.	OCT 27 1857
SPICER, Frederick	BURFORD, Maria	JUL 03 1830

District of Columbia Marriage Licenses, 1811-1858

SPICER, John Frederick	BRYAN, Mary Ellen	FEB 07 1850
SPICER, Margt. R.	RYTHER, Edwin A.	NOV 15 1856
SPICER, Samuel	WALKER, Amanda Elizth.	MAR 13 1844
SPIEGEL, Brigitta	KLUG, Peter	APR 10 1858
SPIES, James P.	CORLEY, Catherine	APR 08 1858
SPILLMAN, Edward M.	DAY, Eliza C.	SEP 04 1849
SPILLMAN, Thomas	WARD, Rachael	MAY 28 1835
SPILMAN, Elizabeth	ANDERSON, John Wm.	JUL 25 1835
SPILMAN, Nancy	COLLINS, William	SEP 02 1844
SPILMAN, Thomas K.	BARNHISEL, Elizabeth	SEP 22 1831
SPILMAN, William	HUDSON, Elizabeth	AUG 15 1821
SPINDLE, Benjamin T.	ROSE, H. Adelaide	MAY 14 1856
SPINDLER, Frederick	SCHMEHL, Joanna A.	AUG 09 1852
SPINKS, Mary Elizth.	GIPSON, Rosier	DEC 27 1851
SPINKS, William	WELLS, Ann	MAY 25 1820
SPINKS, William	ALLEN, Elizabeth	NOV 23 1826
SPINOGLE, Barbara	HURDLE, Washington	JAN 11 1831
SPITTLE, Jane	PAYNE, Sandford	FEB 04 1847
SPLANN, David	WORK, Mary One-days	AUG 26 1834
SPOLLAN, James	GORMLEY, Marcella	DEC 15 1855
SPOONER, George W.	ROSE, Juliet Ann	SEP 26 1844
SPRAGUE, Ellen F.	EMBRY, Thomas M.	NOV 29 1856
SPRAGUE, William	BECKET, Mary Ann	OCT 04 1854
SPRATT, James	BRYSON, Sarah	AUG 05 1816
SPRATT, Thomas	PARSONS, Matilda C.	NOV 11 1823
SPRIGG, Benjamin	THORNTON, Ann G.	NOV 05 1818
SPRIGG, Eliza B.	BAKER, John H.	NOV 21 1826
SPRIGG, Fanny (blk)	BARNES, Peter	NOV 03 1842
SPRIGG, James C.	ADDISON, Lucy E.	JUL 15 1850
SPRIGG, Jane E.	SEATON, Malcolm	NOV 18 1857
SPRIGG, John	GREEN, Elizabeth (col'd)	AUG 31 1848
SPRIGG, John	SAMPSON, Eliza (blk)	NOV 25 1851
SPRIGG, John B.	STANSBURY, Martha R.	JAN 08 1851
SPRIGG, Mary	McWATERS, Adam	AUG 28 1819
SPRIGG, Mary	BROOKE, Walter B.	SEP 07 1824
SPRIGG, Sandy	HUMPHREYS, Georgianna (blk)	OCT 29 1849
SPRIGG, Thomas B.	ADAMS, Jane	JUN 08 1820
SPRIGGS, Gabriel	HANSON, Martha (blk)	NOV 07 1840
SPRIGGS, Horace	BUTLER, Matilda (blk)	JUL 13 1847
SPRIGGS, Mary (blk)	REED, James	DEC 17 1850
SPRIGGS, Thos. B.	NASH, Mary (blk)	JAN 07 1836
SPRINGER, Jacobina	WETZELL, Frederick	APR 15 1833
SPRINGER, John	DOWLER, Annie J.	APR 14 1858
SPRINGMAN, John M.	JONES, Elizabeth	MAR 21 1838
SPÜNLEIN, Christiana	HUTH, John Frederick	AUG 07 1852
SPUNOGLE, Catherine	ADAMS, Leonard	JUN 26 1812
SPURLENS, James	COX, Mary	DEC 10 1841
SPURLING, Mary	LANEHART, Jacob	JUL 03 1849
SPURLING, Matilda	SPURLING, William	JUL 05 1816
SPURLING, William	SPURLING, Matilda	JUL 05 1816
SRUCKENNEELLY, Margt.	HENRY, John	OCT 01 1850
SRYOCK, Virginia L.	BRUCE, George N.	MAR 28 1848
ST. CLAIR, Alcinda	WILLIAMS, James A.	JUN 16 1842
ST. CLAIR, Eleanor	WATERS, Sewall D.	MAR 12 1829
ST. CLAIR, George	LYLES, Rosanna	MAR 23 1836
ST. CLAIR, James W.	BURCHE, Mary E.	DEC 04 1854
ST. CLAIR, Julia A.E.	WARD, George W.	DEC 06 1856
ST. CLAIR, Mary (blk)	LOGANS, Henry	JUL 07 1841

District of Columbia Marriage Licenses, 1811-1858

ST. CLAIR, Miss	SMITH, Samuel E.	JUN 05 1845
ST. CLAIR, Sarah	POPER, Nathaniel	FEB 05 1812
ST. CLAIR, Thomas	MIDDLETON, Eleanor	AUG 12 1822
ST. CLAIR, Walter	JACKSON, Harriet L.	OCT 07 1830
ST. JOHN, John	SNYDER, Dorothy A.J.	JUN 15 1850
ST. JOHNS, Margarett	TRUNNELL, Henry	MAY 12 1855
STAATS, Jacob A.	KING, Eliza A.	FEB 24 1852
STACKER, Marinus	RICHMOND, Maria	MAR 21 1846
STACKPOOL, Catherine	McMAHON, John	JUN 10 1853
STACKS, Elizabeth	HESHLEY, Clement	MAY 27 1842
STACKS, Joseph	CHAMBERLAIN, Elizabeth	AUG 19 1830
STACKS, Joseph E.	BOOTH, Sarah E.	OCT 31 1854
STACOM, Mary E.	SWAIN, George W.	APR 01 1852
STAFFAN, Christian	BEETSTONE, Mary	JAN 13 1836
STAFFAN, George	HENNING, Mary Ann	OCT 02 1847
STAFFORD, Margaret	HAYSE, John	FEB 13 1858
STAHL, Jacob	VanRESWICK, Ellen	OCT 18 1825
STAIN, Sarah Elizabeth	PERRY, James H.	APR 04 1848
STAINBACK, Virginia E.	ROBINSON, Dr. Robert Emmet	MAR 31 1843
STAKE, John M.	FULLALOVE, Susan	FEB 28 1848
STAKE, Robert	McCOUCHI, Jane Eliza	APR 02 1849
STALCUP, Joshua	McNEIR, Mary Elizth.	NOV 30 1847
STALIN, Ann S.	WILSON, Joseph H.	AUG 16 1855
STALL, John	FREEMAN, Abalona	FEB 23 1850
STALLANGS, Benjamin	HILL, Mary	MAR 02 1824
STALLANGS, Mary Ann	FOSTER, Edward	MAY 02 1855
STALLARD, Elizabeth	MONROE, William R.	OCT 29 1827
STALLARD, Molinda	GRANDSTAFF, Abraham	SEP 26 1831
STALLINGS, Geneva A.	SUIT, Benj. B.	MAR 06 1856
STALLINGS, Louisa	SHIELDS, William	OCT 18 1845
STALLINGS, Rebecca	GOLDEN, William L.	NOV 26 1833
STALLINGS, Theodore P.	DAY, Hanora Ann	MAY 11 1849
STALLINGS, William H.	GODDARD, Maria H.	DEC 13 1832
STALLIONS, Eliza	MIDDLETON, Robert	SEP 18 1830
STALLIONS, Rebecca	HAMMOND, Henry	FEB 04 1854
STAMP, John	MAGRUDER, Mary	DEC 23 1828
STAMP, John	WHITE, Martha	JAN 14 1854
STAMP, Matilda	ELDER, William	NOV 26 1818
STAMP, Sarah Ann	MOBLY, Thomas	JAN 04 1836
STANDAGE, Marcia	CLOAKEY, John	NOV 08 1830
STANDFORD, Henry	TOWNSEND, Elizabeth	NOV 05 1828
STANDFORD, Thomas	ESHUM, Ruth Ann	JAN 11 1831
STANDISH, Lucy [Mrs.]	PRICE, John	DEC 21 1822
STANDLIN, Patrick	FOWLER, Ellen	MAR 05 1831
STANFIELD, George	[blank], Hester A.	DEC 27 1830
STANFIELD, Margaret K.	HENRY, Robert V.	DEC 06 1854
STANFORD, Charles E.	WEBSTER, Louisa	MAY 27 1857
STANFORD, Helen E.	HANDY, Charles W.	AUG 16 1841
STANFORD, James	BELL, Elizabeth (blk)	APR 18 1827
STANFORD, Margaret Eveline	MARLOW, Alfred H.	SEP 14 1857
STANFORD, William S.H.	WOOD, Sarah Eliza	OCT 17 1833
STANGLE, Ann E.	KING, Josiah E.	MAY 19 1832
STANHOPE, Eliza J.	GUNNELL, Joshua C.	DEC 13 1839
STANLEY, Ann	DONOVAN, John	AUG 27 1847
STANLEY, Elizabeth	DONOVAN, Dennis	FEB 02 1850
STANLEY, Hellen	TURPIN, Henry	APR 08 1857
STANLEY, Henry E.	BERRY, Louisa E.	JUN 25 1846
STANLEY, J.M.	ENGLISH, Alice	MAY 01 1854

District of Columbia Marriage Licenses, 1811-1858

STANLEY, John T.	DeVAUGHN, Sarah E.	AUG 09 1847
STANLEY, Joseph B.	JACK, Susannah	FEB 18 1847
STANLEY, Louisa E.	DULIN, Edward L.	APR 09 1849
STANLEY, Mary	DAVIS, Augustus	SEP 29 1850
STANLEY, Mary Ann B.	GOODS, William H.	NOV 14 1849
STANLEY, Thomas	LOVEJOY, Harriet	APR 20 1837
STANLEY, Thos.	SESFORD, Ann J.	JAN 27 1819
STANSBERRY, Ann	CREIG, Robert	JAN 09 1858
STANSBERRY, William	LECKEY, Mary Jane	MAR 24 1857
STANSBURY, Augusta	DUNN, John O.	JUN 25 1828
STANSBURY, Delila	STANSBURY, Elisha	SEP 11 1825
STANSBURY, Elisha	STANSBURY, Delila	SEP 11 1825
STANSBURY, Emerson	WEAVER, Catherine Mary	OCT 06 1836
STANSBURY, Emma	WINES, E.C.	JUN 14 1832
STANSBURY, John	ROW, Margaret	JUN 19 1857
STANSBURY, Josephine	NOURSE, Benjamin Franklin [Dr.]	JAN 03 1832
STANSBURY, Laura	HAGNER, Charles N.	APR 13 1843
STANSBURY, Martha R.	SPRIGG, John B.	JAN 08 1851
STANT, William H.	LAWRENCE, Eliza H.	APR 13 1849
STANT, Wm. H.	WALKER, Mary Ann	MAY 01 1849
STANTON, Eliza	FLYNN, Peter	JUL 27 1858
STANTON, Frederick P.	LANPHIER, Jane H.	DEC 23 1834
STANTON, Henry [Maj.]	MACOMB, Alexandrine	FEB 11 1834
STANTON, Mary	BROCCHUS, Thomas W.	JUL 09 1831
STANWOOD, Mary	MORRILL, Wm.	AUG 19 1820
STAPLE, Ellen	INSCOE, Toliaver	JUL 17 1847
STAPLE, Walter	GARRETT, Mildred A.	APR 03 1852
STAPLES, Elizabeth	SUMMERS, Albert	JAN 26 1853
STAPLES, Jane C.	HOOPER, George K.	JAN 25 1850
STAPLES, Margaret	ROCKETT, Thomas E.	JAN 02 1850
STAPLES, William R.	GRIGGS, Lavinia V.	AUG 21 1856
STAPLETON, John	CONNERS, Mary	FEB 02 1833
STARBUCK, Maria L.	GREGORY, Alexander J.	JUL 10 1856
STARK, Henry	RANDOLPH, Emma Beverley	JUL 03 1855
STARK, Nancy	GRIFFIN, John	OCT 06 1845
STARKE, Mary B.	ROWAN, Stephen C.	JUN 06 1839
STARKES, Daniel	TALBOT, Martha (blk)	OCT 10 1848
STARKS, Dyer	LEE, Sarah	APR 10 1851
STARLING, Jane G.	WARE, Henry A.	OCT 04 1854
STARLING, Thomas	ANDERSON, Mary	AUG 20 1833
STARR, Eliza Ann	FINCH, William	OCT 13 1841
STARR, George	EHMORE, Hulkey	FEB 23 1836
STARR, William	JOHNSON, Harriet	OCT 03 1845
STARR, William	KEECH, Jane	NOV 15 1856
STARSTONE, Charles Francis	SMITSON, Mary Jane	MAY 31 1855
STATFORD, Robert	AUDREY, Elizabeth	MAY 09 1817
STATFORD, Susan	AVERY, John	MAY 14 1815
STATHAM, Rhoda J.	McKINNEY, John W.	NOV 18 1842
STATINIUS, Mary	CANA, Frederick	DEC 07 1816
STATON, Benjamin S.	CONNOR, Sarah C.	DEC 31 1857
STAUBS, Mary Ann	GODEY, Edward	NOV 27 1850
STAUGHTON, Elizabeth A.	TEMPLE, John T.	APR 06 1824
STAUGHTON, James M.	PATRICK, Louisa	DEC 26 1826
STAUM, Christian	CROWDER, Elizth. C.	NOV 29 1842
STAUNTON, Thomas	McGUIRE, Rosetta	SEP 25 1844
STCHUSLER, Anna	LETJOHN, Henry	JUN 30 1853
STEAD, Samuel	DAVISON, Martha	JAN 31 1853
STEADMAN, Marshall B.	BERRY, Mary E.	JUL 02 1852

District of Columbia Marriage Licenses, 1811-1858

STEATER, Mary M.	POWERS, Thomas F.	NOV 12 1855
STECK, John	DORRETT, Sarah	DEC 17 1824
STECOM, Lewis	FOXWELL, Mary Ellen	JUL 03 1845
STEDMAN, Mary	AMERIGE, George	NOV 20 1839
STEEL, Horatio N.	RAY, Mary	MAY 14 1827
STEEL, John	DUFFEY, Mary	JAN 04 1820
STEEL, Martin	TOLLIVER, Harriet	MAY 27 1826
STEEL, Mary A.R.	DAVIS, John S.	SEP 12 1832
STEEL, Peter	CAPRON, Rachael	JUL 20 1814
STEEL, Sarah Jane	BEECH, Ephraim Mc.	MAR 10 1840
STEEL, Tapley	DAVIS, Mary	SEP 08 1829
STEEL, Thomas	TALHEM, Nancy	MAR 30 1817
STEEL, William C.	PEASE, Pamelia A.	MAR 11 1856
STEELE, Ann	MULRENEY, Bernard	DEC 02 1848
STEELE, Ann Rebecca	COOK, John H.	JAN 27 1853
STEELE, Elizabeth	WELCH, Patrick	APR 14 1828
STEELE, Elizabeth	FLANAGAN, Luke	SEP 09 1830
STEELE, Elizabeth	CONTNOR, Isaac	FEB 27 1838
STEELE, Elizabeth A.	MOODY, John	DEC 28 1848
STEELE, Fannie	ROGERS, Eugene	OCT 01 1856
STEELE, James	PARSONS, Emeline	JUL 07 1851
STEELE, James	LOWRY, Eliza	OCT 24 1857
STEELE, James R.	BELT, Mary E.	JUL 16 1849
STEELE, John A.	COZENS, Charlotte	AUG 07 1847
STEELE, Reginald H.	MASI, Kate F.	DEC 22 1855
STEELE, William F.	FRANKS, Elizabeth	JUL 01 1848
STEER, Laura	LAMBERT, William H.	APR 26 1853
STEER, Phineas J.	KING, Isabella	APR 18 1832
STEERIN, Elizabeth	LENK, Everard	NOV 10 1832
STEFFIN, Margaret	TEILICH, Frederick	JUL 03 1852
STEFFNER, Carl	BODENMÜLLER, Eliese	AUG 22 1854
STEGMAIER, Michael	HIRMER, Teresa	OCT 30 1855
STEIGAUFF, Philip	SHEE, Ann	FEB 21 1852
STEIGER, Kate Brengle	WILSON, Ephraim King	JUL 14 1856
STEIGER, Lavinia	COOPER, Franklin	MAY 10 1841
STEINER, Mary Elizabeth	BECKER, William	FEB 21 1843
STEINMETZ, Jacob	ENGEL, Sophia	MAR 24 1846
STEINS, Mary M.	JONES, Jonathan	FEB 09 1846
STELLE, Edward B.	HOPKINSON, Adelaide St.M.	SEP 15 1842
STELLE, Elizabeth H.	McPHERSON, Henry H.	SEP 17 1816
STELLINGS, Ruth	MASON, John	JUL 19 1819
STELLO, Henry	SCHWERAS, Sophia	OCT 04 1855
STELLS, Thomas J.	HOPKINSON, Anna Maria	APR 24 1844
STELLWAGEN, Charles K.	TUCKER, Eliza S.	DEC 31 1842
STELTINIUS, Rachael	HYATT, Alfred	OCT 10 1825
STEM, John W.	SMOOT, Laura V.	MAY 12 1856
STEMPLE, Eliza	PROTZMAN, Henry	FEB 27 1822
STEPHEN, Henry	McKIM, Isabella	JUN 25 1816
STEPHENS, Edward	JAMES, Elizabeth	APR 06 1824
STEPHENS, Hazelwood	TALBOTT, Elizth.	MAR 23 1822
STEPHENS, James	BAKER, Jane	APR 28 1819
STEPHENS, James H.	FRITCOLE, Winny	MAR 02 1842
STEPHENS, John	FRANK, Jane	DEC 14 1848
STEPHENS, Mary Leah	WALKER, Joseph T.	FEB 22 1856
STEPHENS, Saml.	SMITH, Hannah	JUL 25 1812
STEPHENS, Susan (blk)	VASSON, Mordaza	DEC 21 1825
STEPHENS, William A.	SCOTT, Mary E.A.	JUN 16 1843
STEPHENS, William H.	WATSON, Mary	SEP 25 1845

District of Columbia Marriage Licenses, 1811-1858

STEPHENSON, Alexr.	HOSMONS, Mary	SEP 29 1832
STEPHENSON, Alfred	BOWEN, Sarah	OCT 29 1835
STEPHENSON, Amelia	CHURCH, Samuel	MAY 15 1827
STEPHENSON, Ann	ADAMS, Isaac	NOV 26 1816
STEPHENSON, Barbara	WOOD, Joseph	MAY __ 1827
STEPHENSON, Catharine	COLLINS, Owen J.	JUN 10 1843
STEPHENSON, Hannah	BANBERGER, William C.	JUL 14 1840
STEPHENSON, Henry	ROMNEY, Cloe Ann	JUN 26 1827
STEPHENSON, Jane	MALONY, James	JUN 09 1814
STEPHENSON, Jane	MALLONY, James	AUG 09 1814
STEPHENSON, Jane	MALONEY, James	MAR 08 1815
STEPHENSON, Jane	POLKINHORN, Richard W.	JUN 21 1831
STEPHENSON, John	BURCH, Catharine	SEP 24 1822
STEPHENSON, John	REDIN, Catharine	FEB 13 1836
STEPHENSON, John A.	HARRIS, Margaret	NOV 19 1845
STEPHENSON, Joseph	HARRIS, Mary Ann	MAR 03 1840
STEPHENSON, Sophia	TURNER, Jasper	NOV 28 1822
STEPPER, Anthony	EAPOWER, Margaret	JUN 15 1833
STEPPER, Barbara Gaitrut	BRODHEAD, John George	SEP 01 1837
STEPPER, George Martin	PFISTER, Maria Magdalena	MAR 05 1827
STEPPER, Mary	CYER, Bennet	DEC 23 1843
STEPTOE, Elizabeth	PURCELL, Samuel	APR 25 1843
STER, Parmelia M.	TAYLOR, Robert B.	APR 06 1845
STERET, Rachel	LEWIS, Washington	APR 28 1824
STERLING, Mary	ATHEY, Elijah L.	MAY 16 1839
STESSE, Babet	PFEIFER, John C.	JUL 08 1857
STETSON, John	DeNIROTH, Charlotte	JUL 13 1813
STETSON, Mary A.	WAITE, Edward	SEP 02 1851
STETSON, Susanna Williams	McCARTY, Rev. John, D.D.	MAR 03 1856
STETTINIUS, George	NOURSE, Sarah H.	JUN 11 1833
STETTINIUS, George	LALANNE, Caroline V.	JAN 17 1843
STETTINIUS, Julia	CLARK, John F.	JUN 07 1831
STETTINIUS, Susan	HOLMEAD, James B.	OCT 02 1817
STETTINIUS, William	GRAMMER, Rosena M.	JUN 17 1834
STEUART, Adam D.	ATKINSON, Mary B.	MAR 04 1844
STEUART, H. Clay	BARKER, Elizabeth S.	MAY 17 1858
STEUART, Margaret M.	ASHTON, John N.	NOV 01 1847
STEUART, Richard S., Jr.	GIST, Georgia R.	MAY 27 1856
STEUART, William	CRAWFORD, Eleanor	JUL 03 1812
STEURT, Samuel J.	EVENS, Eliza Jane	JUN 03 1845
STEUSSHY, Leonard	JOHNSON, Ann	SEP 05 1826
STEVENS, Amanda W.	DORSEY, John Warfield	JAN 14 1854
STEVENS, Augt. R.	STONE, Maria H.	OCT 25 1853
STEVENS, Catharine	STONE, James H.	JAN 25 1853
STEVENS, Catharine E.	HAMERSLY, Lewis R.	MAR 18 1846
STEVENS, Cordelia	GOLDIN, John	SEP 15 1852
STEVENS, Elizabeth (blk)	BUTLER, John Lewis	DEC 27 1849
STEVENS, Elzey	HOCKERMAN, Henry	DEC 31 1850
STEVENS, Emma Maria	WIGG, William Hazzard	JUL 20 1853
STEVENS, Ezra L.	DURHAM, Catherine S.	AUG 02 1848
STEVENS, Henry	EDWARDS, Louisa	FEB 13 1821
STEVENS, Henry	CLEMENTS, Rebecca	SEP 22 1857
STEVENS, Isabella	THOMPSON, William H.	SEP 13 1852
STEVENS, John B.	STEVENSON, Elizabeth I.	JUL 03 1848
STEVENS, Leonard L.	TAYLOR, Elizabeth Ann	NOV 06 1835
STEVENS, Lewis G.	WALL, Caroline M.	JAN 23 1857
STEVENS, Mary Virginia	OLDFIELD, Granville S., Jr.	SEP 15 1852
STEVENS, Matilda	EDMONSTON, William A.	NOV 25 1850

District of Columbia Marriage Licenses, 1811-1858

STEVENS, Matthew H.	JEFFERS, Susan B.	FEB 10 1847
STEVENS, Paul	HURST, Miriam E.	NOV 02 1844
STEVENS, Robert C.	GITTINGS, Christa Ann	NOV 05 1850
STEVENS, Robert H.	OGDEN, Ann Maria	MAY 10 1841
STEVENS, Sarah	VERMILLION, Samuel	JUL 16 1814
STEVENS, Stephen	WHITE, Ann	MAY 08 1845
STEVENS, Stephen O.	HAROVER, Cassander	JUL 05 1834
STEVENSON, Abgail	BAKER, Troless	AUG 24 1826
STEVENSON, Andrew, Hon.	SHAEFF, Mary	JUN 27 1849
STEVENSON, Elizabeth I.	STEVENS, John B.	JUL 03 1848
STEVENSON, George W.	THOMPSON, Phoebe R.	APR 24 1834
STEVENSON, Jacob Wesley	BRASHEARS, Mary Ann	MAR 06 1849
STEVENSON, Louisa (blk)	ROBINS, Philip	SEP 18 1828
STEVENSON, Robert	CAREY, Verlinda	SEP 07 1819
STEVENSON, Robert	SIMMS, Elizabeth (blk)	APR 11 1850
STEVENSON, Sarah Jane	LOCHREY, Edward	APR 25 1848
STEVENSON, Sophia	LEWIS, William	AUG 16 1838
STEWARD, Ann	RIGHTER, Jacob	AUG 23 1815
STEWARD, Ann Elizabeth	BOYSE, John	MAY 29 1834
STEWARD, Catherine	VINSON, Isaac	NOV 28 1833
STEWARD, Charles J.	STEWARD, Ruth	AUG 04 1849
STEWARD, Charles W.	WHITE, Mary Rebecca	JAN 21 1839
STEWARD, Magdelina	BROWN, Robert	JUL 13 1821
STEWARD, Ruth	STEWARD, Charles J.	AUG 04 1849
STEWART, Adeline F.	THORNTON, Stewart G.	JAN 31 1817
STEWART, Ann	WILSON, Thomas	MAR 02 1820
STEWART, Ann	LEWIS, George W.	MAR 05 1844
STEWART, Arrabella Orr	SNOWDEN, Gerrard H.	APR 28 1824
STEWART, Barnett	JACKSON, Ann M.	DEC 09 1844
STEWART, Caleb	CAVILIER, Josephine	MAY 26 1853
STEWART, Catherine	BROWN, Charles	MAY 11 1848
STEWART, Charity	LAHNAM, Horatio	JAN 05 1819
STEWART, Charles	WILLIAMS, Nancy (blk)	MAR 12 1823
STEWART, Charles	SHELLY, Caroline	MAR 04 1825
STEWART, Charles	BLOICE, Mary	MAR 02 1841
STEWART, Charles	CREAMER, Elizabeth	NOV 30 1841
STEWART, Charles	POLK, Jane (blk)	MAY 30 1857
STEWART, Clarissa S.	HAYDEN, William T.	JAN 02 1849
STEWART, Daniel	ESLING, Georgeanna	MAY 15 1857
STEWART, David	BURNS, Eliza	MAR 12 1816
STEWART, Donald	TAIT, Mary M.	MAR 17 1841
STEWART, Edwin R.	McNEW, Marietta	JUL 18 1854
STEWART, Eliza	REEVES, Samuel S.	AUG 22 1839
STEWART, Eliza A.	HILTON, John T.	NOV 30 1855
STEWART, Eliza Ann	BRERETON, John	APR 28 1842
STEWART, Elizabeth	LENMAN, William	MAY 19 1817
STEWART, Elizabeth	FONDE, John P.	MAR 09 1820
STEWART, Elizabeth	BARRON, James	OCT 17 1826
STEWART, Elizabeth	MONSERRATTE, Francis	APR 07 1830
STEWART, Elizabeth	WEST, Henry	JUL 14 1836
STEWART, Elizabeth	VERMILLION, Charles A.	APR 17 1848
STEWART, Elizabeth	SIMONS, John	DEC 08 1857
STEWART, Elizabeth Rebecca	JONES, Charles S.	NOV 16 1841
STEWART, Emely R.	MINITREE, Andrew	NOV 18 1841
STEWART, Frances	FAUNCE, William	JUL 17 1858
STEWART, G. Thomas	MILLER, Ann Eliza	NOV 23 1852
STEWART, George	LOGAN, Margaret	SEP 11 1827
STEWART, George	MARTIN, Sally (blk)	JUL 01 1839

District of Columbia Marriage Licenses, 1811-1858

STEWART, George	BOWEN, Mary E.	JUN 05 1840
STEWART, George W.	GILLISPIE, Harriet	MAY 09 1827
STEWART, George W.	OSBORN, Harriet Ann	SEP 13 1827
STEWART, Georgiana (blk)	JOHNSON, Chas. H.	MAY 13 1856
STEWART, Hebe	GEDNEY, Thomas R., U.S.N.	AUG 08 1831
STEWART, Helena	LOVELESS, Elijah	NOV 21 1815
STEWART, Israel	WASON, Eliza	NOV 04 1830
STEWART, James	HARVEY, Jonathan	MAR 28 1815
STEWART, James	GIBSON, Laura C. (blk)	MAR 25 1847
STEWART, James	SMITH, Mary	APR 17 1849
STEWART, Jane (blk)	LOWRY, William	MAY 19 1834
STEWART, Jane (blk)	LEE, Louis	MAR 20 1844
STEWART, John	BARNES, Charlotte	AUG 13 1812
STEWART, John	ELLIS, Eliza	OCT 23 1852
STEWART, John	BULLIT, Martha A.	DEC 03 1856
STEWART, John	MITCHELL, Marcelina (blk)	NOV 02 1857
STEWART, John Adams	MAGEE, Martha Josephine	FEB 18 1857
STEWART, John C.	SIMPSON, Eleanor	AUG 25 1827
STEWART, Joseph N. [Dr.]	ASHTON, Mary D.	MAR 31 1829
STEWART, Julia A.T.	LIGHTELLE, William E.	MAY 31 1845
STEWART, Leo P.	CLAMPITT, Annie	SEP 01 1857
STEWART, Leonard W.	HILTON, Sarah E.	DEC 20 1851
STEWART, Lloyd	LEWIS, Elizabeth	DEC 08 1857
STEWART, Lord	LEWIS, Elizabeth E.	AUG 03 1858
STEWART, Louisa M.	McFARLAND, John M.	NOV 09 1853
STEWART, Margaret	FENWICK, Philip	JAN 04 1815
STEWART, Margaret Ann	BECKENBAUGH, William W.	NOV 12 1846
STEWART, Marsaline	GALLAHER, Stephen G.R.	DEC 20 1849
STEWART, Mary	GRAY, William	MAY 13 1850
STEWART, Mary	SPARROW, Joseph	JAN 21 1857
STEWART, Mary	MAGINNIS, WIlliam H.	JAN 09 1858
STEWART, Mary Ann	TURNER, Daniel	SEP 23 1817
STEWART, Mary Ann	THRIFFT, Stephen	FEB 19 1822
STEWART, Mary Ann	LIGHTFOOT, William	JAN 01 1846
STEWART, Mary E.	WILLIAMS, Frederic B.	AUG 21 1855
STEWART, Mary Elizth.	HARBIN, Thomas H.	OCT 02 1855
STEWART, Rebecca M.	BUTT, Solomon	APR 06 1844
STEWART, Richard H.	BROWNING, Mary Ellen	MAY 15 1838
STEWART, Robert	HOOPER, Ann	MAR 15 1834
STEWART, Robert	TOLDBRIDGE, Elizabeth	DEC 19 1838
STEWART, Rosina	ROBY, Thomas	FEB 13 1849
STEWART, Samuel	LIMA, Margaret	OCT 01 1857
STEWART, Sarah	SPALDING, Francis A.	FEB 20 1830
STEWART, Sarah	POSEY, Richard	MAY 27 1851
STEWART, Sarah A.	MARR, James H.	MAY 01 1832
STEWART, Sarah Ann	GIBBONS, Thomas	JUN 04 1815
STEWART, Sarah Elizth.	SESSFORD, Joseph	APR 23 1850
STEWART, Stephen C.	SUTTON, Susanna	MAY 08 1823
STEWART, Thomas	GOLDSMITH, Mary Ann	DEC 26 1831
STEWART, Thomas	MILLER, Elizabeth Ann	NOV 03 1851
STEWART, Townshend	CARTER, Sarah Maria	OCT 06 1836
STEWART, W.H.	WHALEY, Ann	SEP 29 1842
STEWART, Walter	COMPTON, Frances	NOV 27 1817
STEWART, Walter	FENWICK, Sarah Jane	OCT 04 1856
STEWART, William	ALBEY, Elizabeth	SEP 16 1848
STEWART, William	HANDY, Margaret C.	APR 29 1852
STEWART, William	BELL, Letty	OCT 17 1853
STEWART, William	FONTZ, Sarah	MAY 11 1858

District of Columbia Marriage Licenses, 1811-1858

STEWART, William E.	GREENWELL, Mary E.	DEC 30 1847
STEWART, William Hutson	OUTTERIDGE, Sarah	AUG 16 1815
STEWART, William I.	SUPPLE, Maria	MAR 02 1848
STEWART, William J.	JEFFERSON, Angelina F.	SEP 08 1842
STEWART, William T.	MAYO, Maria E.	AUG 19 1834
STEWART, William W.	GREEN, Eveline	MAY 17 1831
STEWART, Wm. Edward	BANKS, Mary Elizth.	MAY 31 1853
STICK, David Henry	DAVIS, Laura Victoria	FEB 21 1857
STICKELL, Joseph	COOLEY, Mary Ann	MAY 31 1853
STICKLE, George	LUXTON, Sarah	MAY 30 1825
STICKLE, Mary Ann	CHICK, Richard T.	OCT 21 1845
STICKNEY, Francis H.	LEWIS, Elizabeth E.	SEP 15 1857
STICKNEY, William	KENDALL, Jeannie	JAN 13 1852
STIDHAM, George W.	THORNBERRY, Sarah C.	AUG 27 1856
STIFFLER, Eliza	CROCKETT, Hugh G.	JUL 10 1850
STIFLE, Nancy	COINER, William	SEP 08 1819
STIGER, Benjamin	WISDOM, Mary H.	JAN 11 1827
STILES, Elizabeth	DULEY, Aquilla	FEB 23 1826
STILES, Samuel	GUNN, Elizabeth	DEC 30 1815
STILES, Thomas	TARMAN, Sally	SEP 28 1816
STILLINGS, Elizabeth E.	ANGEL, John T.	JUL 12 1851
STILLINGS, Marian	JOHNSTON, George W.	JUL 17 1851
STILLINGS, Sarah V.	HAMILTON, Wm. F.	FEB 24 1857
STILLINS, Ann E.	SMITH, James G.	FEB 19 1847
STILLWELL, Tobias H.	BURGESS, Eliza A.	SEP 19 1855
STIMMEL, Sophia	COGSWELL, Aaron	OCT 08 1831
STIMMELL, Anna Maria	COOVER, George	JUN 17 1814
STIMMELL, Lydia	COGSWELL, Joseph	JAN 04 1825
STINCHCOMB, Catherine	LANSDALE, Enoch	SEP 01 1836
STINCHCOMB, Joanna	GOINS, John Thomas	OCT 20 1845
STINCHCOMB, John Henry	WRIGHT, Emma Elizabeth	MAY 25 1854
STINCHCOMB, Noah	BOYD, Sarah	OCT 13 1832
STINCHINCOE, Noah	CROWN, Mary Ann	JAN 06 1816
STINEMETZ, Benj. H.	WARDELL, Arene V.	JAN 03 1853
STINER, Henrietta	PRATHER, James E.	JUL 09 1834
STINGER, Andrew	STINGER, Mary Magdalene	FEB 18 1835
STINGER, Ann Elizabeth	WELTNER, Jacob R.	APR 24 1833
STINGER, Elizabeth	HALL, James	DEC 10 1830
STINGER, George	SESSFORD, Jane	AUG 26 1824
STINGER, John Frederick	GREY, Rebecca Susan	FEB 16 1833
STINGER, Mary Magdalene	STINGER, Andrew	FEB 18 1835
STINGER, Sarah Jane [Mrs.]	BROWN, James	NOV 23 1835
STINLE, Frederick	KUNKE, Christina	APR 14 1855
STINSON, Sarah E.	FRISTOE, Milton F.	AUG 04 1856
STINZING, Frederick	FISTAR, Mary	JAN 10 1853
STIRLING, Elizabeth Rebecca	MILLS, William McCarty	JUN 28 1853
STIRLING, Mary Ann	HENDERSON, James H.	JUL 26 1852
STITH, Gerard	MORSELL, Clara S.	FEB 16 1848
STITH, Louisa Stuart	BROWN, Marshall	NOV 16 1837
STIVER, Henry	COULTER, Sarah	MAR 31 1821
STOCK, Mary	SOTER, John	JAN 11 1845
STOCK, Mary Ann	WOOD, Joseph H.	JUL 14 1841
STOCKARD, Margaret	ROWAN, James	APR 02 1819
STOCKETT, Charles	CHANEY, Annie Maria	SEP 09 1854
STOCKETT, Wesley A.	SCOTT, Margaret A.	JAN 29 1846
STOCKMON, Mary M.	NELSON, Eliab C.	AUG 06 1845
STOCKS, Charles	JOHNSON, Virginia	NOV 02 1848
STOCKS, Elizabeth	STROBEL, George	JUN 21 1843

District of Columbia Marriage Licenses, 1811-1858

STOCKTON, Robert F., Jr.	POTTER, Anne Margaretta	SEP 07 1852
STOCKWELL, Sarah	PRENTISS, Wm. H.	JUL 06 1818
STODDARD, Isaac	SWIGERT, Elizabeth	AUG 18 1836
STODDARD, John H.	ROLLINS, Mary Jane	NOV 12 1849
STODDARD, John M.	DONALDSON, Ann	FEB 24 1852
STODDARD, Mary Ann	CLEMENTS, Ignatius N.	SEP 14 1844
STODDARD, Samuel	WINDSOR, Maria	FEB 19 1851
STODDART, James	DEVENY, Catharine	JUN 27 1853
STODDART, John	DREWRY, Ann	APR 21 1825
STODDARTS, Nancy	JONES, Patrick	SEP 15 1830
STOFFEL, Ignatz	MUHLHAHER, Caroline	FEB 13 1858
STOHL, Thos. H.	UPPERMAN, Heryetta	FEB 04 1858
STOHLMANN, Anna C.	SCHALLENBERG, Henry R.	DEC 09 1851
STOKES, Cordelia	TAYLOR, William	NOV 17 1847
STOKES, Thomas	LEE, Ann (blk)	APR 15 1839
STOKES, Thomas	SIMMS, Ann Eliza (blk)	MAR 20 1844
STONE, Amanda	MORGAN, Neil	NOV 08 1855
STONE, Ann	CREIG, Lewis	AUG 14 1813
STONE, David	ROBEY, Susannah	JAN 19 1826
STONE, Edward	STONE, Hannah	MAY 31 1815
STONE, Edward	MARSY, Elizabeth	FEB 17 1825
STONE, Eliza	THOMPSON, Caleb	FEB 03 1814
STONE, Eliza	FLAHERTY, William A.	NOV 22 1848
STONE, Elizabeth	GRAY, Baptist	AUG 05 1838
STONE, Elizabeth A.	COLE, John T.	NOV 22 1848
STONE, Elizabeth A.	LAWRENSON, William S.	APR 19 1855
STONE, Elizabeth E.	TRAIL, Richard F.	JUN 18 1850
STONE, Ellen	JOHNSTON, John R.	DEC 27 1855
STONE, Frances H.	BALL, Henry M., Jr.	JAN 06 1844
STONE, George B.	SWEENY, Harriet V.	NOV 03 1838
STONE, Hannah	STONE, Edward	MAY 31 1815
STONE, Harriet A.	ALLEN, Edmund M.	JUN 09 1856
STONE, Henrietta	GUY, Charles	JUN 05 1851
STONE, Henry	SEWALL, Ann D.	OCT 10 1825
STONE, Henry	SERPENTINE, Margaret	NOV 14 1833
STONE, Hettie A.	MORRISON, David L.	MAY 28 1855
STONE, Hetty A.	MORRISON, David L.	FEB 28 1856
STONE, James	GRANTT, Josephine	APR 09 1849
STONE, James Edward	SMITH, Elizabeth	OCT 13 1828
STONE, James H.	STEVENS, Catharine	JAN 25 1853
STONE, Jane	GLOYD, Washington	AUG 12 1817
STONE, Jane	COADY, Michael	JUN 21 1855
STONE, Jane L.	ABERT, James M.	OCT 21 1844
STONE, John	BALDWIN, Verlinda	AUG 07 1813
STONE, John	LOVELESS, Elizabeth Ann	SEP 11 1844
STONE, John P.	KELLER, Anna Mary	AUG 16 1853
STONE, Josiah	PURCELL, Emma	NOV 26 1855
STONE, Julia Ann	JENNINGS, John	MAR 04 1852
STONE, Louisa E.	OWENS, Theodore E.	JUL 07 1854
STONE, Lucretia	GARNAGLE, James M.	AUG 11 1827
STONE, Lucy Alvira	WINTERS, Francis B.	MAY 03 1858
STONE, Malinda	RICHARDSON, Alfred	MAR 09 1852
STONE, Maria H.	STEVENS, Augt. R.	OCT 25 1853
STONE, Mary	CHALMERS, John	DEC 09 1815
STONE, Mary Ann	BICKSLER, John	MAR 30 1840
STONE, Mary Ann	WELCH, Patrick	JUL 04 1853
STONE, Mary E.	FAIRFAX, Benjn. F.	DEC 13 1855
STONE, Mary Jane	WINDSOR, Zachariah L.	MAY 08 1854

District of Columbia Marriage Licenses, 1811-1858

STONE, Nancy	TALBERT, Overton	MAR 03 1840
STONE, Nehemiah	TENELY, Rachael	SEP 03 1835
STONE, Priscilla	LANSDALE, Henry N.	NOV 24 1836
STONE, Robert King	RITCHIE, Margaret Fouche	APR 17 1849
STONE, Sally	JOHNSON, Charles	MAR 25 1820
STONE, Sally R.	RIDGELY, William R.	SEP 26 1853
STONE, Sarah B.	FAIRFAX, James B.	AUG 13 1853
STONE, Thomas	SMITH, Josephine Elizth.	DEC 08 1855
STONE, Virginia	WHITE, Alexander	FEB 04 1853
STONE, Virginia	LONG, James G.	FEB 02 1857
STONE, William H.	MINNIX, Charlotte V.	FEB 08 1853
STONE, William J.	LENTHALL, Elizabeth	OCT 20 1821
STONE, William J., Junr.	GREEN, Mary Frances	DEC 04 1849
STONEHAM, Elizabeth [Mrs.]	POTE, William	JUL 07 1831
STONEHAM, Thomas	THOMPSON, Elizabeth	JUL 12 1824
STONELL, Jno. Worton	ELLIOTT, Sarah E.	JUL 14 1855
STONER, Frederick A.	SANSFORD, Ann R.	MAR 27 1856
STONESTREET, J. Harris	HARRIS, Ann G.	JUN 30 1857
STONESTREET, Patsey	TAYLER, Thomas	FEB 10 1841
STONNELL, John A.	ANNIS, Mary V.	FEB 14 1855
STOODLEY, Matilda (blk)	ROSS, Herbert	SEP 05 1850
STOOKEY, George	SHEETER, Mary	MAY 09 1850
STOOPS, Margaret Ellen	WHITE, Benjamin F.	AUG 30 1853
STOOPS, Walter	BROOKE, Margaret Ellen	APR 25 1842
STORCK, Lena	LUECK, John	DEC 25 1848
STORES, Amariah	BLOUNT, Annie Isabella	NOV 26 1853
STOREY, William	HENDERSON, Jannett	DEC 03 1855
STORM, George A.	LUSBY, Elizabeth H.	DEC 12 1855
STORM, Julia Ann Eliza	MacDANIEL, Albert	APR 10 1829
STORY, Deborah Ann	PITTARD, Jabez	MAR 10 1851
STORY, John T.	WOODALL, Laura A.	JAN 03 1853
STORY, Margaret	RAILEY, James	FEB 07 1839
STORY, Martha	SIMONS, John	NOV 23 1837
STORY, Robert	SIMPSON, Martha Ellen	OCT 11 1850
STOTT, Charles	NUGENT, Esta Ann	OCT 31 1854
STOTT, Samuel	THOMPSON, Mary E.	OCT 29 1856
STOTT, Sarah R.	WESTCOTT, Rev. William A.	MAR 10 1847
STOUT, Edward C.	AULICK, Julia	FEB 01 1847
STOVALL, Bolling A.	WILSON, Martha S.	SEP 19 1856
STOVER, Solomon	TRAVERS, Hester Ann	JUN 04 1851
STRACHAN, Ann J.	STRACHAN, Richard F.	NOV 14 1849
STRACHAN, Richard F.	STRACHAN, Ann J.	NOV 14 1849
STRADLING, Elvira W.	HAIGHT, Charles R.	JUN 02 1858
STRAHN, Charles	SWEENY, Susan C.H.	NOV 10 1830
STRAIGHT, Eliza Ann	HOOVER, William Henry	SEP 17 1826
STRAIGHT, Mary A.	CASSELL, William	NOV 04 1839
STRAIN, John Higgins	HOUSTON, Cornelia Nancrede	JAN 16 1856
STRANGE, Mary D.	JOHNSON, James	JAN 06 1849
STRASBURGER, Hart L.	MAY, Mina	MAR 18 1854
STRASBURGER, Isaac	BRAUMAN, Hanche	MAY 03 1855
STRATTAN, George	McDONOUGH, Juliana	FEB 14 1851
STRATTIN, Sarah E.	WHITE, Robert B.	JAN 07 1852
STRATTON, Benjamin W. [Dr.]	WHITALL, Emeline N.	MAY 11 1830
STRATTON, Harriet N.	POE, Sidney A.H.	MAY 28 1850
STRATTON, James	FLOYD, Elizabeth R.	APR 12 1838
STRATTON, Robert	KEIFEL, Charlott	JUN 24 1833
STRAUB, Catharine	MILLER, Francis	DEC 26 1850
STRAUB, Catherine	WIEL, Frederick	OCT 06 1851

District of Columbia Marriage Licenses, 1811-1858

STRAUB, John L.	WALKER, Amanda M.	SEP 27 1856
STRAUS, Abraham	KING, Nannie	FEB 06 1857
STRAUSZ, Alexander	YOUNG, Annie	FEB 16 1856
STRAWDER, Sarah Ann	POOL, Warner	JAN 04 1851
STREAK, George Oliver	FOWLER, Elizabeth Rebecca	APR 30 1855
STREAKES, Richard W.J.T.	BYRNES, Eliza Ann	OCT 08 1835
STREAKS, Ann	CONLEY, Patrick	JAN 13 1824
STREAKS, Charlotte	MAY, Francis R.	MAY 05 1821
STREAKS, Harriett A.	HUNTER, George	DEC 22 1838
STREAKS, Lucinda	HOWE, Joseph	FEB 11 1850
STREEKS, Francis	MITCHELL, Martha Ann	JUN 12 1824
STREEKS, John F.	PIERCE, Martha	MAY 04 1854
STREEKS, Martha Ann	SMART, Samuel	MAR 29 1842
STREEKS, Richard W.	ROBINSON, Mary Ann	NOV 01 1845
STREET, Aglae E.	GAYLOR, John	JUN 10 1838
STREET, Catharine E.	ALLSOP, Samuel	MAY 06 1852
STREET, Hannah	MILSON, John	APR 23 1831
STREET, John	MINITREE, Rosanna	AUG 08 1829
STREET, Sarah Ann	McPHERSON, Samuel T.	MAY 25 1843
STREETS, Patsy	ESLIN, Peter	JUN 01 1837
STREIDENBERGER, Catherine	BAKER, Lawrence	SEP 05 1854
STRELEECK, Martha	PLANT, John	OCT 26 1837
STREP, Louis	HIRT, Sophia B.	AUG 30 1853
STRETCH, Ellen	ABERT, John J.	JAN 24 1812
STRETCH, John	O'KIE, Caroline	JUL 26 1820
STRETCH, John	SCOTT, Susan A.	MAY 14 1836
STRETCH, Mary E.	WINDSOR, George B.	APR 04 1838
STRETCH, Susan Ann	BROWN, James W.	FEB 15 1844
STRIBLING, Cornelius	NOURSE, Emma J.	DEC 07 1852
STRIDER, John L.	WEBSTER, Catherine	SEP 20 1844
STRIDER, Samuel	CARRICO, Eliza J.	MAR 17 1858
STRIFLAREN, Helen	KILLSNAN, John	MAY 02 1845
STRIFLER, Margaretta	VOLK, John Frederick	SEP 29 1847
STRIKE, Wm.	VERMILLION, Rachel	JUN 17 1813
STRINGASSER, Joseph	BURTON, Caroline	OCT 30 1825
STRINING, John	KELLY, Mary	JUN 14 1853
STROAM, Margaret	TUCKER, Thomas	MAY 28 1849
STROBEL, Caroline	HERRICKS, August	NOV 30 1846
STROBEL, George	STOCKS, Elizabeth	JUN 21 1843
STROBEL, Louise	EMMORT, Heinrick	MAY 27 1845
STROBLIN, Barbara	LOUSEMANN, Michael	JUL 29 1833
STROH, Mary	SCHENCK, John	OCT 08 1857
STROHMEYER, Minna	SHAFER, George F.	MAY 03 1851
STRONG, Julia Ann	CROSS, Henry	AUG 13 1828
STRONG, Mary	DAVISON, Samuel	MAY 28 1832
STROTHER, Francis	CUSICK, Jane	MAY 29 1845
STROTHER, Frederick	OGLETON, Margaret	MAY 27 1837
STROTHER, Geo. W.	THOMAS, Ann	JUL 08 1854
STROTHER, Jane	MILLER, William	AUG 17 1823
STROTHER, Reubin	GUNNELL, Jemima	NOV 02 1844
STROTHER, Sarah E.	WILLIAMS, George	MAR 14 1854
STROTHERD, Anne Elizth. (blk)	CISSELL, John Granison	AUG 23 1856
STROUD, Drusilla	RHODES, Peter	MAR 31 1812
STROUD, George W.	DUGAN, Julia Ann	JUL 07 1842
STROUD, George W.	TIPPETT, Matilda Jane	JUN 09 1843
STROUD, James	SAMONTON, Mary	AUG 26 1820
STROUT, Caroline	BRUMER, Theodore	MAY 08 1855
STRUDER, Elizabeth	SCOTT, William H.	AUG 30 1850

District of Columbia Marriage Licenses, 1811-1858

STRURER, Victor	MALAWSON, Sarah C.	JAN 27 1848
STUART, Cecilia A.	HEDGMAN, John G.	APR 30 1850
STUART, Charles	EDMONSTON, Catharine	OCT 18 1849
STUART, Eliza	LANGLEY, William B.	DEC 28 1835
STUART, Juliann	GATES, William	APR 05 1836
STUART, Mary W.	TERRETT, Frederick A.C.	NOV 07 1851
STUART, Richard Henry	PEYTON, Ellen C.	OCT 21 1833
STUART, Sarah Ann	CLEMENS, William	MAY 12 1851
STUART, Susan (blk)	LEAMON, Prymus	DEC 17 1846
STUART, W.D.	HARRIS, Francis A.	JUL 12 1854
STUART, William	WILLIAMS, Mary Ann (blk)	FEB 29 1848
STUBBLEFIELD, Samuel	ROBBINSON, Sarah	OCT 08 1838
STUBBS, Harriot	HILDT, George [Rev.]	MAR 21 1833
STUBBS, John O.	WHITLOCK, Mary J.	SEP 21 1855
STUBBS, William E.	BOYLE, Catharine Ann	APR 18 1843
STUCK, Ferdinand F.	COOPER, Jane	DEC 31 1822
STUCK, Sarah Elizabeth	OWNER, James	SEP 30 1848
STUCKERT, Margaret	SWARTZ, William	JUL 23 1851
STUDDS, George	TRUE, Mary Jane	JUN 21 1854
STUDER, Elizabeth	MUNROE, William	OCT 22 1833
STUDER, Victer	PECK, Hellen R.	JAN 10 1856
STUDS, Lucy H.	HART, Joseph	MAY 20 1857
STUIED, George B.	SHECKELS, Airy	OCT 31 1814
STUITS, George	MITCHELL, Mary	MAR 23 1845
STUKELY, Turner	LAURENCE, Elizabeth (blk)	JUL 06 1858
STULL, Anna W.B.	PLATER, James L. [Capt.]	SEP 10 1828
STUMP, Barbara	HART, Michael	FEB 09 1833
STUMP, Celia	BRUNNER, Laurence	SEP 17 1855
STUMP, Jacob	SCHWARTZ, Margaret	APR 05 1853
STUMP, William	NORTH, Mary B.	SEP 01 1857
STURGEON, James G.	SMITH, Mary Ann	DEC 08 1841
STURGEON, Mary Ann	GIBBONS, Jno. W.	FEB 05 1850
STURGES, Handy J.	ESPY, Mary Ann	NOV 05 1845
STURGIS, Jane C.	HACKETT, Charles C.	JUL 01 1856
STURNANAGAL, Conrad	LIPPITT, Mareta	NOV 16 1855
STUTZ, Frederick	NOAR, Catherine	AUG 18 1845
STUTZ, John M.	MOHLEY, Johanna H.S.	OCT 20 1855
STYIVER, Louis F.	LADUCARE, Maria	JUN 02 1834
STYLES, Ann	ALKARD, A.B.	FEB 03 1842
STYLES, Scilinda	GONE, Thomas	DEC 16 1820
SUCKETT, Penelope C.	RUNNER, John Henry	AUG 24 1852
SUDDATH, Rezin	HASLET, Martha	MAY 14 1829
SUGHRUE, Ellen	FOGERTY, Daniel	JUL 24 1857
SUGHRUE, John	SUGHRUE, Mary	AUG 16 1858
SUGHRUE, Mary	SUGHRUE, John	AUG 16 1858
SUGRUA, Hannora	CONNER, Daniel	FEB 01 1853
SUGRUA, Timothy	FLAVAHAN, Catharine	FEB 01 1853
SUGRUE, Humphrey	MOORE, Mary	NOV 18 1854
SUGRUE, John	CONNOR, Mary	APR 28 1853
SUIT, Abraella	GARDINER, John E.	JUL 23 1855
SUIT, Benj. B.	STALLINGS, Geneva A.	MAR 06 1856
SUIT, Edward, Jr.	BROWN, Margaret A.	MAY 11 1852
SUIT, Emily	HARDESTY, James J.	SEP 16 1854
SUIT, Emily	DOZIER, Cader W.	MAR 15 1855
SUIT, Fielder	MAY, Mary Elizabeth	NOV 20 1849
SUIT, Fielder, Jr.	SCOTT, Arabella	MAY 15 1855
SUIT, Harriot	RALY, Thomas	MAR 09 1815
SUIT, Horatio	GODDERD, Jane	JAN 07 1813

District of Columbia Marriage Licenses, 1811-1858

SUIT, James H.	CREAMER, Mary	SEP 26 1848
SUIT, John L.	BALLER, Mary E.	APR 02 1821
SUIT, Josiah S.W.	CRAWFORD, Mary Ann	NOV 04 1823
SUIT, Mary Ann	BAYLISS, Thomas	OCT 27 1840
SUIT, Mary Ann	GORDEN, Richard H.	JUL 11 1842
SUIT, Mary F.	CHAMBERS, Benjamin B.	MAY 26 1849
SUIT, Matilda Ann	ROBEY, William	JUL 16 1846
SUIT, Nathaniel	MAGRUDER, Mary	JUL 07 1826
SUIT, Newman	YOUNG, Elizabeth	MAY 19 1828
SUIT, Oliver B.	HARVEY, Catherine R.	MAY 08 1843
SUIT, Polly	MULLICAN, Jeremiah	OCT 09 1813
SUIT, Samuel S.	WEDDLER, Matilda [Mrs.]	SEP 23 1830
SUIT, Smith	GORDON, Juliana	MAY 16 1832
SUIT, Stephen	NEVITT, Ann	JAN 25 1830
SUIT, Susan	SELBY, Joshua	FEB 22 1843
SUIT, Susannah	BAWLDING, Thomas	OCT 23 1818
SUITER, Prudence E.	FRAZIER, William H.	NOV 19 1849
SUITER, Sarah Maria	BOWIE, Charles	FEB 14 1838
SUITT, Samuel	COLLINS, Rebecca	NOV 05 1844
SULLIVAN, Abbie	DUGAN, John E.	MAR 16 1857
SULLIVAN, Abby	HAYES, William	NOV 01 1853
SULLIVAN, Ann	RAGON, Richard	JAN 03 1825
SULLIVAN, Ann	BOYLE, Robert	FEB 02 1853
SULLIVAN, Ann	BARRY, Michael	NOV 11 1854
SULLIVAN, Ann	QUILL, Dennis	JUL 01 1858
SULLIVAN, Ann Maria	BROWN, William H.	DEC 26 1857
SULLIVAN, Barbara	DOYLE, Philip	DEC 30 1826
SULLIVAN, Bridgett	SULLIVAN, John	FEB 24 1852
SULLIVAN, Cath.	GAREY, Owen	OCT 21 1854
SULLIVAN, Catharine	BURKE, John	APR 02 1853
SULLIVAN, Catharine	BARR, John	FEB 04 1854
SULLIVAN, Catharine	CULLOTAN, Patrick	JAN 10 1857
SULLIVAN, Catherine	CASEY, John	NOV 15 1852
SULLIVAN, Catherine	KELLEY, Bernard	JAN 17 1856
SULLIVAN, Charles O.	DRUMMER, Mary	JUN 20 1854
SULLIVAN, Charlotte	BOARMAN, Richard A.	AUG 21 1847
SULLIVAN, Cornelius	JONES, Mary	JUN 16 1855
SULLIVAN, Daniel	COFFEE, Mary	MAY 01 1854
SULLIVAN, Daniel Eugene	CRAIHEN, Maria	NOV 19 1853
SULLIVAN, Danl.	QUENDLAN, Bridget	MAY 31 1856
SULLIVAN, David O.	MULVERHILL, Nancy	FEB 21 1852
SULLIVAN, Deborah J.	MASSEY, Francis	JAN 04 1825
SULLIVAN, Dennis	FITZGERALD, Honora	JUN 25 1853
SULLIVAN, Dennis	McCARTY, Elizabeth	SEP 16 1854
SULLIVAN, Dennis	DONOHOO, Bridget	AUG 17 1858
SULLIVAN, Edward	LYNCH, Ann	OCT 15 1829
SULLIVAN, Edward	CRISSMAN, Mary	DEC 31 1857
SULLIVAN, Eleanor	WALLACE, James	JUN 05 1843
SULLIVAN, Elijah	EVANS, Elizabeth	DEC 16 1851
SULLIVAN, Elizabeth	ANDERSON, George	MAR 05 1817
SULLIVAN, Elizabeth	BRANNEN, William	AUG 26 1819
SULLIVAN, Elizabeth	WHITING, George C.	MAR 17 1840
SULLIVAN, Elizabeth F.	BAKER, Charles M.	JAN 10 1833
SULLIVAN, Ellen	GOLLOHER, Patrick	JUN 02 1829
SULLIVAN, Ellen	HAYS, John	AUG 29 1855
SULLIVAN, Ellen	DOYE, Garret	JUL 31 1858
SULLIVAN, Eugene	HOWLEY, Mary	JUN 15 1853
SULLIVAN, Fanny	MASON, Michael	FEB 10 1855

District of Columbia Marriage Licenses, 1811-1858

SULLIVAN, Fanny	DUNNOGHUE, Cornelius	JAN 28 1856
SULLIVAN, Hanora	CROWLEY, Jeremiah	JAN 05 1853
SULLIVAN, Henry	FRANTUM, Mary Ann	JUL 21 1858
SULLIVAN, Honora	DENAHY, Jeremiah	MAY 13 1852
SULLIVAN, J. [Edward]	BRISCOE, Charlotte	JUL 04 1836
SULLIVAN, James	MURPHY, Ann	NOV 16 1850
SULLIVAN, Jeremiah	HOLBROOK, Susan E.	JAN 29 1824
SULLIVAN, Jeremiah	COX, Anne	MAY 17 1848
SULLIVAN, Jeremiah	DACY, Catharine	FEB 14 1852
SULLIVAN, Jeremiah	SHEA, Ellen	NOV 15 1856
SULLIVAN, Joanna	DONNELLY, James	JUL 03 1851
SULLIVAN, Joanna	KIRBY, Jno.	APR 04 1855
SULLIVAN, Johanna	CULHANEY, Patrick	JAN 31 1857
SULLIVAN, John	SULLIVAN, Margaret	JUN 10 1826
SULLIVAN, John	HARDIN, Sarah	FEB 04 1845
SULLIVAN, John	DEMPHY, Julia	JUN 22 1850
SULLIVAN, John	CUNNINGHAM, Catharine	JUL 08 1850
SULLIVAN, John	SULLIVAN, Bridgett	FEB 24 1852
SULLIVAN, John	DRISCOLL, Catharine	MAY 04 1852
SULLIVAN, John	WHITTINGTON, Sarah	APR 22 1854
SULLIVAN, John	MURPHY, Honora	MAY 27 1854
SULLIVAN, John	MORIARTY, Margaret	DEC 11 1854
SULLIVAN, John	MORIARTY, Ellen	OCT 13 1855
SULLIVAN, John	CURTEN, Kate	JAN 05 1857
SULLIVAN, John	SHEA, Julia	JUL 22 1857
SULLIVAN, John	SHEA, Julia	MAY 20 1858
SULLIVAN, John H.	REED, Sarah E.	APR 11 1850
SULLIVAN, John W.	KNOX, Alice	JAN 17 1856
SULLIVAN, Joseph	DELAHUNT, Eliza	MAY 03 1855
SULLIVAN, Julia	LYNCH, Michael	FEB 21 1857
SULLIVAN, Louisa	HORNIT, Daniel	APR 30 1857
SULLIVAN, Margaret	SULLIVAN, John	JUN 10 1826
SULLIVAN, Margaret	MASON, Thomas	JAN 12 1855
SULLIVAN, Margaret	KELLEY, Jerry	AUG 28 1855
SULLIVAN, Margaret L.	BOHRER, Benjamin R.	JAN 03 1848
SULLIVAN, Margaret Virginia	BIRD, William	NOV 20 1829
SULLIVAN, Maria	OATES, Thomas	OCT 09 1852
SULLIVAN, Marshall C.	JOHNSTON, Elizabeth	JUL 06 1852
SULLIVAN, Mary	WREN, Michael	FEB 08 1853
SULLIVAN, Mary	LOONEY, William	SEP 05 1853
SULLIVAN, Mary	QUILLAN, Timothy	JUN 24 1854
SULLIVAN, Mary	SUMMERSCALE, Thomas	APR 10 1855
SULLIVAN, Mary	LYNCH, Daniel	JUN 03 1857
SULLIVAN, Mary Ann	BOYLE, John	SEP 03 1849
SULLIVAN, Mary Elizabeth	SCOTT, Edward P.	JUN 06 1842
SULLIVAN, Melvina	HOWARD, Thomas	OCT 11 1851
SULLIVAN, Michael	WELCH, Johanna	FEB 06 1856
SULLIVAN, Owen	HERRON, Eleanor	NOV 28 1845
SULLIVAN, Owen	SHANAHAN, Mary	NOV 03 1855
SULLIVAN, Patrick	REIDER, Eliza Jane	APR 10 1846
SULLIVAN, Patrick	DONOVAN, Mary	JUL 31 1852
SULLIVAN, Patrick	RARGIN, Margaret	SEP 25 1852
SULLIVAN, Patrick	GORDON, Catherine	FEB 08 1853
SULLIVAN, Patrick	AHERN, Julia	APR 11 1853
SULLIVAN, Patrick	FLEMMING, Ellen	FEB 18 1857
SULLIVAN, Robert W.	THOMAS, Marcella E.	FEB 04 1850
SULLIVAN, Roszel	PARKHURST, Laura Virginia	SEP 19 1851
SULLIVAN, Samuel	MORAN, Mary Jane	JAN 04 1840

District of Columbia Marriage Licenses, 1811-1858

SULLIVAN, Samuel	PENN, Sarah	JAN 16 1851
SULLIVAN, Thomas	CAREY, Mary	APR 09 1853
SULLIVAN, Thomas	MASON, Eliza	OCT 19 1854
SULLIVAN, Thomas	KANE, Ann	JUN 18 1858
SULLIVAN, Washington	LANGLEY, Josephine	MAY 28 1857
SULLIVAN, William	MORAN, Sarah	DEC 26 1827
SULLIVAN, William	FITZPATRICK, Emma	JUN 12 1851
SULLIVAN, William J.	CHILDS, Elizabeth A.	SEP 29 1849
SULLIVIN, Jeremiah	BARNISH, Barbarah	MAR 13 1822
SULLY, Robert	REYNOLDS, Mrs. Mary	FEB 24 1835
SUMBE, William H.	ROBISON, Eliza (blk)	FEB 03 1852
SUMBY, Dennis	ROBISON, Martha (blk)	DEC 11 1851
SUMBY, James	ROBINSON, Mary Spence (blk)	MAR 18 1846
SUMBY, Lucy Ann (blk)	BOWEN, George	MAR 19 1852
SUMBY, Mary (blk)	[blank]	JUN 25 1850
SUMLY, James	HUGHES, Elizabeth (blk)	MAR 29 1838
SUMMELL, Lucinda (blk)	ALLEN, James	MAY 08 1837
SUMMER, Thomas	PAYNE, Ann	JUN 05 1834
SUMMERS, Albert	STAPLES, Elizabeth	JAN 26 1853
SUMMERS, Ann Rebecca	FISHER, William T.	NOV 24 1847
SUMMERS, Anthony	JARBOE, Elizabeth	FEB 21 1825
SUMMERS, Aquila T.	CROSS, Rebecca	OCT 27 1842
SUMMERS, Dorcas	CLEMENTS, Thomas	JUL 26 1821
SUMMERS, Edward	BOSSEL, Mary	DEC 29 1851
SUMMERS, Henry	GAMMON, Catherine	DEC 02 1839
SUMMERS, James H.	ALLEN, Josephine	NOV 01 1853
SUMMERS, John	GREEN, Julia	JUN 04 1822
SUMMERS, John	WAHL, Catherine	MAY 12 1845
SUMMERS, John H.	WALKER, Sarah Ann	AUG 04 1849
SUMMERS, Judson	BOONE, Mary Matilda	JUL 04 1827
SUMMERS, Martha Ann (blk)	YOUNG, James	AUG 30 1849
SUMMERS, Nathan	BOSWELL, A.V.	JAN 26 1858
SUMMERS, Owen	SHEPPARD, Charlotte	FEB 13 1827
SUMMERS, Priscilla	SCOTT, John	APR 15 1828
SUMMERS, Sarah Ann	PERRY, Cyrus Eli	JUN 02 1849
SUMMERS, Sarah Phelps	ARNOLD, Thomas	MAY 13 1817
SUMMERS, Sidney	RILEY, Joseph	FEB 05 1852
SUMMERS, Sophia	ADAMSON, Washington	NOV 10 1835
SUMMERS, Warren	DARCEY, Eliza Jane	JUN 22 1844
SUMMERS, William	CASH, Mary	MAY 06 1819
SUMMERSCALE, Thomas	SULLIVAN, Mary	APR 10 1855
SUMMERVILLE, Adeline (blk)	COOPER, John	APR 28 1842
SUMMERVILLE, Elizth. (blk)	THOMAS, Charles G.	NOV 19 1855
SUMMERVILLE, Jane [Mrs.]	HYATT, Seth	AUG 23 1813
SUMMERVILLE, Walter	JONES, Ann	FEB 04 1819
SUPPER, Eleanor	HUTT, Frederick	SEP 13 1853
SUPPERS, Katharina	SCHAFER, Conrad	DEC 17 1852
SUPPLE, Maria	STEWART, William I.	MAR 02 1848
SURRATT, George D.	SINCLAIR, Eleanor Ann	APR 07 1849
SURRATT, John H.	JENKINS, M. Elizabeth	AUG 04 1840
SURRY, Margaret	BUHLER, John	JAN 21 1836
SUSKEY, Charles	NALLY, Matilda	AUG 10 1854
SUTER, Ann C.	JACOBS, Cornelius	MAR 22 1838
SUTER, George G.	DAVIS, Mary Elizabeth	FEB 10 1854
SUTER, Henderson	DAVIDSON, Minerva	JUN 06 1854
SUTER, James Z.	ZEBOLD, Ann Maria	APR 19 1834
SUTER, John T.	WEYBOURNE, Louisa	SEP 22 1853
SUTER, Maria Fletcher	HOWARD, Douglass	MAY 18 1837

District of Columbia Marriage Licenses, 1811-1858

SUTER, Mary A.	WALTER, Rev. L.D.	JUN 18 1857
SUTER, Nicholas	COEN, Margaret	JUN 30 1827
SUTER, Rebecca	MYERS, Alexander K.	JAN 04 1827
SUTER, Richad	HANSBOROUGH, Eleanor	JUL 10 1833
SUTER, Richard	MUSKELL, Sarah Ann	JAN 07 1819
SUTER, Richard	ADAMS, Catherine	SEP 02 1834
SUTER, Richard S.	WHELER, Mary Ann	NOV 27 1846
SUTER, Sarah	THOMAS, James	JUL 29 1835
SUTER, Sarah E.	YATEMAN, Auther H.	MAY 29 1837
SUTER, Sarah E.	WATKINS, Robert H.	APR 08 1850
SUTER, Thomas R.	SCOTT, Mary C.	JUN 23 1841
SUTER, William	BROWN, Sarah	DEC 07 1837
SUTHERLAND, Daniel J.	NICHOLSON, Annie D.	JUL 25 1850
SUTHERLAND, Isabella C.	FRAZIER, George W.	FEB 15 1849
SUTHERLAND, Jane F.	MULLEY, William A.	MAY 14 1842
SUTHERLAND, Julia Ann	RILEY, Alexander	MAR 31 1851
SUTHERLAND, William	HALL, Amanda	SEP 15 1836
SUTTER, Catharine S.	HUTTON, Jacob Deans	SEP 10 1850
SUTTLE, Maria Elizabeth	RODIER, John	MAY 14 1838
SUTTLE, Mary	WARFORD, David	MAR 02 1817
SUTTON, Catherine Cecilia	DIGGES, Samuel J.	APR 08 1837
SUTTON, Emily J.	ANDRE, William E.	APR 15 1852
SUTTON, Felix K.	WRIGHT, Lucy J.	JUL 25 1855
SUTTON, Georgiana B.	GODDIN, James E.	MAY 30 1853
SUTTON, James	LACY, Frances M.	NOV 05 1849
SUTTON, James	LOCKE, Catherine J.	OCT 27 1852
SUTTON, James T.	LUCKE, Margaret	DEC 09 1844
SUTTON, Juliet	BERNHARD, John	MAY 28 1849
SUTTON, Maria L.	FRY, Thomas E.	FEB 13 1850
SUTTON, Maria L.	PENNINGTON, Caleb	DEC 17 1855
SUTTON, Maria Terese	BURKE, William	JUN 30 1855
SUTTON, Mary Ann	BLACKMON, William	NOV 15 1847
SUTTON, Mary E.	PENNINGTON, James D.	MAY 14 1853
SUTTON, Nicholas	KNOLLES, Emeline	APR 30 1829
SUTTON, Robert M.	DEGGES, Laura V.	DEC 13 1852
SUTTON, Susanna	STEWART, Stephen C.	MAY 08 1823
SUTTON, Thomas	SCHUYSSLER, Mary	MAY 29 1846
SUTTON, Washington	TRUSSLER, Catherine	OCT 04 1853
SUTTON, William	GRAIN, Sarah	JAN 12 1848
SUTTON, William	DENON, Mary	JUL 22 1848
SWAIN, Benjamin	LANGLEY, Eliza Ann	JAN 16 1841
SWAIN, Catharine	WILLIAMS, Jackson	OCT 06 1851
SWAIN, Dorcas Ann	BALL, Isaac, Jr.	SEP 02 1834
SWAIN, Elizabeth Ann	BECKETT, Alfred	NOV 28 1848
SWAIN, Elizabeth Mahaley	SWAIN, James Alexr.	MAR 23 1830
SWAIN, George W.	STACOM, Mary E.	APR 01 1852
SWAIN, Harriet S.	TURNBURK, George	SEP 11 1856
SWAIN, James Alexr.	SWAIN, Elizabeth Mahaley	MAR 23 1830
SWAIN, Jane T.	HAYRE, Francis R.	JAN 12 1850
SWAIN, John	ANDERSON, Elizabeth Ellen	AUG 01 1847
SWAIN, Julius Gabriael	DEMAINE, Jane	SEP 10 1833
SWAIN, Moses P.	KNIGHTS, Lydia	JUL 20 1853
SWAIN, Stephen	DAY, Elizabeth Martha	MAY 04 1842
SWAIN, Thomas	BALL, Nancy	JAN 28 1826
SWAIN, William	WILSON, Milly	JAN 05 1814
SWAIN, William	LANGLEY, Margaret	DEC 15 1846
SWAINE, Jane	WADE, John H.	JAN 16 1819
SWALLER, Margaret	BALISS, Thomas	FEB 07 1828

District of Columbia Marriage Licenses, 1811-1858

SWALLOW, Delilah A.	RISTON, Benjamin	DEC 08 1853
SWALLOW, Ellen	LINKIN, Henry	FEB 19 1855
SWAN, Maria H.	BRYAN, William	MAY 21 1812
SWANN, Charlott Ann	PILES, George W.	DEC 30 1830
SWANN, Elizabeth	DAVIS, John	JUN 29 1837
SWANN, Elkanah S.	REEVES, Julia A.	NOV 08 1836
SWANN, Elzina	WHALING, John	APR 14 1858
SWANN, Harriet E.	JONES, Thomas	MAR 09 1841
SWANN, James	GREEN, Ellen	MAY 14 1844
SWANN, James	DAVIS, Martha A.	APR 19 1855
SWANN, Jane Ann	BARKER, Edward	SEP 10 1832
SWANN, John	SMITH, Elizabeth (blk)	NOV 07 1849
SWANN, Llewellyn	GOOD, Sarah Jane	APR 17 1856
SWANN, Lucinda	MAYHEW, William	JAN 27 1831
SWANN, Lucinda B.	HILL, Jonathan	JAN 13 1829
SWANN, Mary	ATCHERSON, John F.	DEC 20 1838
SWANN, Mary	SHUSTER, Frederick	SEP 02 1851
SWANN, Mary Ann (blk)	GREEN, Mathias	OCT 14 1822
SWANN, Nathaniel	DIAL, Jane	FEB 21 1831
SWANN, Thomas T.	WARD, Mildred S.	MAR 10 1836
SWANN, Zachariah	BROWN, Frances	NOV 22 1855
SWANY, John	GRAY, Maria	JUL 28 1831
SWART, Bernard T.	BRYAN, Sallie Ann	MAY 01 1855
SWART, Margaret A.	FREECE, William W.	SEP 12 1854
SWART, Maria Louisa	NEWTON, Wm. C.	NOV 23 1834
SWARTZ, Augusta	TAYLOR, Marcellus K.	MAY 03 1849
SWARTZ, William	STUCKERT, Margaret	JUL 23 1851
SWEENEY, Jane	BLAKE, Royal	APR 21 1831
SWEENEY, Mary Ann	SIMPSON, Ezekiel Green	JUN 18 1850
SWEENEY, Thomas	OSBORN, Amanda E.	AUG 21 1857
SWEENY, Ann	PALMER, Morris	MAR 22 1826
SWEENY, Ann	COOMBS, Samuel	JUN 28 1828
SWEENY, Anna R.	VAUGHN, Thomas	NOV 04 1813
SWEENY, Arthur W.	YOUNG, Camilla	FEB 01 1854
SWEENY, Bridget	COSWAY, John	OCT 23 1854
SWEENY, Catherine	NOLAN, Martin	DEC 02 1854
SWEENY, Catherine	KEARNEY, Patrick	APR 18 1857
SWEENY, Cecelia	PAYNE, John	JUL 01 1828
SWEENY, Daniel	FEENEY, Mary	JUL 18 1856
SWEENY, Dennis	SIMPSON, Patsey	APR 14 1818
SWEENY, Edward	LYNCH, Mary Kain	JAN 14 1826
SWEENY, George	BURGESS, Harriet	FEB 03 1830
SWEENY, George	GOODIN, Juliet	JAN 24 1830
SWEENY, George	GOOD, Julia	JAN 11 1830
SWEENY, George	BRENT, Jane	DEC 28 1835
SWEENY, Harriet V.	STONE, George B.	NOV 03 1838
SWEENY, Henry M.	WOODWARD, Mary S.	MAR 28 1832
SWEENY, Hugh B.	HALL, Eliza	NOV 11 1841
SWEENY, James	LUPTON, Nacey	MAR 17 1819
SWEENY, Joanna K.	TRACEY, Joseph	MAY 28 1853
SWEENY, John	NOON, Mary	JAN 21 1854
SWEENY, Julia	WOOLLARD, Samuel	SEP 10 1844
SWEENY, Louis D.	MILLER, Eliza G.	OCT 04 1855
SWEENY, Margaret	KINEY, Patrick	JUL 29 1853
SWEENY, Margaret	CONNELL, Jeremiah	OCT 24 1854
SWEENY, Maria E.	ALLEN, Philip H.	OCT 02 1851
SWEENY, Mary	HAWKE, Robert	SEP 09 1839
SWEENY, Mary C.	LIVINGSTON, George D.	OCT 28 1850

District of Columbia Marriage Licenses, 1811-1858

SWEENY, Mary E.	TITTROW, David A.	MAY 03 1858
SWEENY, Mary Ellen	TITLOO, David Arthur	DEC 28 1857
SWEENY, Matilda Jane	WATKINS, William	OCT 07 1856
SWEENY, Patrick	SMITH, Elizabeth C.	OCT 30 1838
SWEENY, Robert	CHAMNEY, Virginia	MAY 26 1849
SWEENY, Sarah	HUGHES, William	AUG 10 1854
SWEENY, Susan C.H.	STRAHN, Charles	NOV 10 1830
SWEENY, Thomas	CROCKER, Mary Ann	APR 14 1834
SWEENY, Thomas	VENABLE, Jane	SEP 30 1847
SWEENY, Thomas	HOWES, Eliza	JAN 14 1853
SWEENY, Thresa	FENWICK, Francis X.	FEB 17 1849
SWEENY, Virginia	PYNE, Samuel	OCT 09 1855
SWEENY, William	WILLIAMS, Sarah	JUL 19 1838
SWEENY, William H.	SCOTT, E. Adalade	JUN 25 1857
SWEET, Parker H.	ORMER, Ann C.	SEP 06 1837
SWEET, Parker Hall	GRIFFIN, Georgianna	MAY 04 1857
SWEET, Sarah M.	APPLEBY, Franklin E.	JUN 24 1858
SWEETING, Ellen	PUMPHREY, Levi	JAN 21 1854
SWEETING, Henry W.	MacCUBBIN, Ellen	JUL 03 1830
SWEICHZER, Ann	HARKINS, Robert	FEB 13 1823
SWETNAM, Lucy Ann	HOWARD, Oscar L.	MAR 17 1856
SWETT, Margaret C.	MELVIN, James, Jr.	DEC 18 1817
SWIFT, Mary E.	IRONSIDE, George B.	MAR 23 1846
SWIGART, Hannah	DICKEY, Benjamin	DEC 14 1837
SWIGART, Susannah	HAWKINS, Edward	AUG 04 1841
SWIGERT, Elizabeth	STODDARD, Isaac	AUG 18 1836
SWIMLEY, Lewis	GREEN, Elizabeth	MAY 27 1829
SWINK, Frances A.	McGARRITY, Jonathan B.	JAN 20 1848
SWINK, Michael	WHITMORE, Mary Ann	FEB 19 1814
SWINK, Sarah Ann	WALKER, Edward	JUL 19 1823
SWINK, William	NICHOLLS, Mary Ami	JAN 14 1829
SWINK, William	ROBERTS, Martha E.	AUG 29 1843
SWOPE, John M.	GLIMMON, Mary	FEB 12 1840
SWORD, Charles	BEVIES, Catherine	MAR 28 1853
SYDNER, Richard B.	JOHNSON, Ann	DEC 29 1818
SYLVARY, Samuel	GARDNER, Joanah	JAN 30 1818
SYLVESTER, Caroline	WILSON, Robert	FEB 09 1822
SYLVESTER, Samuel R.	HANDLEY, Margaret	MAR 29 1856
SYLVESTER, Thomas	RATELLICK, Mary Ann	DEC 23 1823
SYMINGTON, Elizabeth	WISE, Charles S.	JUN 15 1844
SYMINGTON, Elizabeth Ann	WRIGHT, Charles J.	MAR 11 1845
SYMINGTON, James	KALDENBAUGH, Elizabeth	MAY 26 1814
SYMINGTON, Mary Ann	WROE, Charles	JUN 06 1843
SYMINGTON, William H.	HOLLAND, Rebecca F.	JUN 11 1844
SYMPSON, Margaret	FOWLER, William	NOV 03 1832
SYMPSON, Margaret L.	SPALDING, Daniel J.	MAY 18 1857
SYNGE, William Webb Follett	WAINWRIGHT, Henrietta Mary	JAN 27 1853
SYPE, Henry	FREE, Ann	JUN 09 1840
SYPE, John	DEMENT, Ellen	JUN 09 1840
SYPHAX, Bertha Ellen (blk)	REEVES, Ryland	DEC 18 1850
SYPHAX, Charles, Jr.	CRITTENDEN, Mary V.	NOV 10 1857
SYPHAX, Julia (blk)	JOHNSON, Morris	JUL 26 1843

District of Columbia Marriage Licenses, 1811-1858

T

TABER, Lucy Ann	POOL, John W.	NOV 08 1853
TABLER, Ann	DANIEL, Joseph H.	NOV 09 1837
TABLER, John	PARSONS, Elizabeth	APR 23 1816
TABLER, Margaret E.	DENHAM, Columbus	AUG 21 1843
TABLER, Martha Ellen	HARKNESS, Daniel S.	NOV 27 1838
TACK, Mary Ann	WILLISS, George	DEC 08 1836
TACKETT, John E.	FORD, Elizabeth	JUL 28 1857
TAFF, George D.	GRIFFITH, Mary E.	JAN 19 1847
TAFF, Matilda	PERKINS, Henry	DEC 28 1837
TAFFEE, Elizth.	LUCIUS, Robert	JUL 20 1836
TAGGART, Eliza	SCHWARTZ, Henry	SEP 18 1851
TAGGART, Saml. [Hon.]	AYRES, Mary	MAR 14 1816
TAIF, Elizabeth	JORDAN, Wm. H.C.	MAR 28 1855
TAIT, Alexander	GREEN, Victoria H.	NOV 25 1857
TAIT, Henrietta	HASKINS, Basil	SEP 21 1841
TAIT, Jane	DOUGLASS, John	JUN 29 1839
TAIT, Mary M.	STEWART, Donald	MAR 17 1841
TAIT, Robert	HORNER, Mary Ann	FEB 18 1851
TAIT, Robert C.	BRAWZELL, Mary Ann	JUN 09 1849
TALBERT, Abraham	LANDICH, Catharine	OCT 14 1840
TALBERT, Adam	CRANDLE, Elizabeth	DEC 10 1844
TALBERT, Amelia	ARNOLD, Rezin	JAN 02 1835
TALBERT, Ann	SMITH, Samuel	AUG 31 1815
TALBERT, Area	TWEEDY, Robert	APR 17 1819
TALBERT, Caroline R.	FOWLER, Wm. W.	OCT 14 1844
TALBERT, Eleanor	WILSON, Aquilla	JAN 29 1818
TALBERT, Eleanor	LIGHTNER, John	AUG 25 1818
TALBERT, Eliza	RECARD, John Edward	SEP 30 1843
TALBERT, Elizabeth	JARBOE, Bennett	FEB 18 1813
TALBERT, Elizabeth M.A.	PULIZZI, Venerando	JAN 15 1827
TALBERT, George	NEALE, Mary	JAN 04 1821
TALBERT, Isaac	DUNBAR, George Anna	MAY 26 1857
TALBERT, John	COLLARD, Ellen	JUN 08 1835
TALBERT, John T.	GOODWIN, Elizabeth	MAR 23 1841
TALBERT, Joshua	HOLT, Eleanor	NOV 16 1833
TALBERT, Mackenzie	CROW, Elizabeth	OCT 06 1815
TALBERT, Margaret	McMURRAY, William	FEB 08 1816
TALBERT, Margaret	COOK, Richard Henry	JAN 16 1847
TALBERT, Maria	CHESLEY, Robert	OCT 28 1828
TALBERT, Maria	OSBORN, Daniel	MAR 19 1833
TALBERT, Maria E.	CARROLL, Daniel	JAN 14 1823
TALBERT, Mary	BROWN, Richard	JAN 13 1831
TALBERT, Mary Ann	BENSON, Jonathan B.	FEB 20 1816
TALBERT, Mary E. (blk)	NUGENT, Benjn. H.	JUN 08 1857
TALBERT, Mary Frances	THOMPSON, John A.	NOV 13 1850
TALBERT, Overton	ANDERSON, Maria	MAY 12 1832
TALBERT, Overton	STONE, Nancy	MAR 03 1840
TALBERT, Rachael	BROWN, Adam Crawford	MAR 07 1820
TALBERT, Rachel	SCOTT, George B.	DEC 29 1832
TALBERT, Robert	ROBEY, Sarah	JAN 09 1840
TALBERT, Sarah	McBEE, Walter	NOV 12 1812
TALBERT, Sarah	NEALE, Richard	JUN 15 1813
TALBERT, Sarah	HOLROYD, John	SEP 20 1832
TALBERT, Sobrina	KING, Sylvester	DEC 26 1837
TALBERT, Sydny G.	COX, Ann	FEB 07 1831
TALBERT, Thomas	SMITH, Sarah	JAN 03 1827

District of Columbia Marriage Licenses, 1811-1858

TALBERT, Tobias F.	PERRY, Elizabeth	NOV 24 1851
TALBERT, William	GATES, Rachel	JAN 06 1820
TALBERT, William	WILBURN, Eleanor	JUL 08 1834
TALBERTT, Eliza	JENKINS, Basil	JUN 17 1822
TALBOT, Ann	CUNNINGHAM, Patk.	OCT 03 1854
TALBOT, Edmond	SMITH, Mary Ann	DEC 16 1834
TALBOT, Eliza	FAHERTY, William P.	MAY 21 1836
TALBOT, Frances	ALOISI, Salvatore	JUN 10 1853
TALBOT, Isham [Hon.]	THOMASON, Adelaide	MAR 27 1817
TALBOT, Jane	CRISS, Henry	DEC 29 1836
TALBOT, Lucinda	CLARKE, William T.	JAN 29 1835
TALBOT, Lucy Dent	PLUMMER, Samuel	JUL 22 1817
TALBOT, Martha (blk)	STARKES, Daniel	OCT 10 1848
TALBOT, Mary	SNYDER, William	DEC 15 1852
TALBOT, Solumia	MAY, Edward A.	JAN 29 1820
TALBOT, Thomas	WALL, Rebecca L.	DEC 12 1853
TALBOT, William W.	PUMPHREY, Sarah Ann	APR 14 1846
TALBOTT, Ann	WOOD, Benjamin C.	MAY 30 1815
TALBOTT, Eleanor O.	PAGEOT, John W.	JAN 04 1847
TALBOTT, Elizabeth (blk)	BELL, David	MAR 06 1858
TALBOTT, Elizth.	STEPHENS, Hazelwood	MAR 23 1822
TALBOTT, J.B.	BARNETT, Lucy	APR 01 1845
TALBOTT, Nicholas R.	McNEW, Julia	JUN 13 1832
TALBOTT, Sarah	ROBEY, Washington	AUG 14 1823
TALBURT, Alexander	KARRICK, Sarah	JAN 01 1812
TALBURT, Alfred	DeRIDGES, Ellen	FEB 06 1845
TALBURT, Andrew	SCOTT, Elizabeth (blk)	MAR 15 1853
TALBURT, Elizabeth	KING, Thomas	OCT 05 1853
TALBURT, George M.	ARNOLD, Elizabeth	JUL 15 1845
TALBURT, George W.	MATTINGLEY, C.A.	FEB 15 1844
TALBURT, James	MUDD, Mary	AUG 09 1844
TALBURT, Jane	WOODRUFF, Hezekiah	MAY 26 1836
TALBURT, Martha A.	CLARKE, Robert	APR 11 1837
TALBURT, McKinsey	DAVIDSON, Nancy	SEP 01 1826
TALBURT, Thomas	SOMERS, Sarah Ann	JAN 09 1843
TALBURT, William Henry	ARNOLD, Margaret Ann	OCT 15 1842
TALBURTT, Elizabeth A.	ARNOLD, Charles W.	MAR 27 1844
TALBUT, Sidney	WELLING, Rebecca	APR 13 1833
TALHEM, Nancy	STEEL, Thomas	MAR 30 1817
TALIAFERO, Evelina O.	DAVIS, William B.	MAY 19 1848
TALIAFERRO, Cornelia Lee Turberville	JAMESSON, William H.	DEC 03 1844
TALIAFERRO, Helen B.	TOLSON, Alexander H.	DEC 06 1842
TALIFFERO, Jane E.	CHICHESTER, William S.	NOV 06 1834
TALKS, Jacob	HOLLIDGE, Annie	APR 12 1858
TALLENT, Pleasant	KEARNEY, Stephen	FEB 01 1855
TALLEY, Josiah	LYNCH, Elizabeth	JUN 15 1812
TALLIAFERRO, Wm. W.	COLEMAN, V.A.	SEP 27 1847
TALMIE, Margaret	BEVEREDGE, Francis	SEP 21 1812
TALTEVOUX, Peter	EVANS, Elizabeth	FEB 04 1845
TALTON, Elizabeth	WEBB, Robert	JUN 22 1812
TALTON, Elizabeth	KELLY, Charles	SEP 19 1822
TALTON, James	BERRY, Elizabeth	MAY 08 1817
TALTON, Merrit	SHECKLE, Susan	JUL 20 1812
TALTY, Mary Ellen	PRINCE, Thomas	NOV 09 1855
TALTY, Michael	FITZGERALD, Catherine	SEP 22 1836
TALTY, Stephen	COLLINS, Mary	APR 04 1850
TANER, Jesse	DUITY, Ann	MAY 01 1824
TANEY, Anne Arnold	CAMPBELL, James Mason	MAY 27 1834

District of Columbia Marriage Licenses, 1811-1858

TANEY, Augustus	YOUNG, Mary	SEP 09 1816
TANEY, Sarah (blk)	COXEN, John	APR 10 1851
TANGEY, Margaret	LYNCH, Thomas	JUL 06 1853
TANGNEY, Patrick	NELLIGAN, Bridget	OCT 01 1853
TANNAR, Sarah	PAYNE, George A.	SEP 17 1840
TANNER, Ann	CROCKING, James	FEB 19 1816
TANNER, Hester Jane	DENNISON, Harvey A.	JUN 05 1843
TANNER, Jesse	MOONY, Sarah	FEB 23 1819
TANNER, Mary Ann	YEAMAN, George	FEB 21 1823
TANNER, Rebecca	WINDER, John H.	DEC 24 1825
TANNER, Richard M.	HARLEY, Palina	OCT 16 1845
TANNER, Samuel	GOLDSMITH, Mary Elizabeth	JUL 28 1853
TANNER, Sarah A.	EDMONSON, John	MAY 22 1834
TANNER, Susanna	HAMMILL, Stephen	MAY 22 1845
TANNER, Thomas	EARSLING, Sarah	FEB 24 1820
TANNER, Virginia	PROSISE, Benjamin	DEC 07 1857
TANNER, William	ORME, Martha N.	APR 02 1838
TANSILL, Robert	BENDER, Anna Lucinda	OCT 17 1849
TANSLEY, Thomas	CAPLES, Sarah E.	MAY 03 1851
TAPSICO, Edmund	HUGHES, Frances	MAR 21 1854
TARBELL, Ann Eliza	LAURIE, Wm. S.	AUG 12 1828
TARBELL, Henrietta	DYER, Edward	FEB 09 1833
TARBLE, Susan (blk)	JOHNSON, William	JAN 12 1833
TARE, Mary	HODGES, James	FEB 07 1839
TARLTON, Eleanor	DOVE, Zachariah	APR 28 1832
TARLTON, Ellen E.G.	KLOPFER, Henry A.	MAR 09 1844
TARLTON, Henry	SMITH, Susannah B.	MAY 11 1829
TARLTON, Jane E.	DETWEILER, Frederick M.	FEB 16 1852
TARLTON, Lewis A.	WEST, Julia	MAR 15 1845
TARLTON, Margaret A.	HARDIN, Charles H.	NOV 04 1845
TARLTON, Mary Ann	SHECKELS, Merrit	NOV 25 1847
TARLTON, N.	BLANEY, James	APR 08 1826
TARLTON, Rosanna	KLOFFER, Henry A.	JUN 27 1848
TARLTON, Sarah	REDMAN, Joseph	SEP 13 1834
TARMAN, Ann	BARRETT, Levi G.	AUG 31 1835
TARMAN, Philip	SLATER, Betsey	APR 02 1815
TARMAN, Richard H.	GODDARD, Matilda Ann	DEC 22 1853
TARMAN, Sally	STILES, Thomas	SEP 28 1816
TARMAN, Samuel	DYER, Elizabeth	JAN 16 1812
TARMAN, Samuel	MITCHEL, Elizabeth	MAY 05 1819
TARMON, Elizabeth	HARRISON, John T.	MAY 15 1850
TARMON, Elizabeth M.	GRAY, William H.	JAN 18 1843
TARMON, Rebecca	TRAMMEL, John L.	APR 21 1849
TARR, Levi	WINSETT, Ann	DEC 08 1814
TARTANSON, Francis	MEADE, Mary Elizabeth	SEP 14 1839
TARTANSON, Julia	GREEN, Robert	OCT 13 1845
TARTESON, Alexander	HILL, Martha	AUG 18 1816
TASCOE, Margaret (blk)	MINOR, Benjamin	NOV 19 1856
TASCOE, Maria (blk)	WILKINSON, John	NOV 28 1854
TASCOL, Thomas	EASLY, Admonia (blk)	NOV 19 1847
TASCOR, Wm. James	TWINE, Margaret (blk)	JAN 17 1849
TASISTRO, Louis Fitzgerald	QUINN, Catharine	APR 15 1853
TASKER, Ann	FERRALL, Dennis	AUG 05 1847
TASKER, George W.	HARRIS, Anne E.	AUG 26 1834
TASKER, Mary (blk)	LEVY, John	APR 30 1856
TASTET, Joseph M.	MUSTIN, Harriet M.	OCT 14 1850
TASTET, Nicholas	BOWLING, Sarah P.	NOV 28 1825
TASTET, Virginia M.	MUSCHETT, James M.A.	MAY 09 1850

District of Columbia Marriage Licenses, 1811-1858

TATE, Andrew	BURROWS, Sarah	JUN 07 1813
TATE, Eliza (blk)	DORSEY, John Henry	JAN 12 1852
TATE, Elizabeth	TAYLOR, George	OCT 19 1848
TATE, Francis	TRANIVER, Meredith	AUG 22 1835
TATE, Henry	GRAYSON, Nancy (blk)	MAR 28 1831
TATE, James	LEACH, Lydia Ann	AUG 26 1834
TATE, James A.	BECK, Marian L.	SEP 19 1838
TATE, Joseph B.	MILLS, Mary A.S.	FEB 12 1850
TATE, Lydia Ann	PHILLIPS, Horatio H.	AUG 14 1840
TATE, Mary Ann	PAIGE, B.P.	JAN 20 1848
TATE, Peter	THOMPSON, Phebe	FEB 05 1818
TATE, Sarah Jane	HAMMOND, Nathan	DEC 18 1834
TATE, William R.	ATWOOD, Mary S.	MAY 23 1839
TATHAM, William	VILLARD, Sophia	AUG 30 1813
TATSPAUGH, Mary Ann	COX, George S.	APR 14 1841
TATTERSON, Martha E.	CHAMBERLAIN, Luther	SEP 24 1849
TATTERSON, Sarah	BROADBECK, Henry	OCT 11 1838
TAUBERSCHMID, Lanehard	SENGEND, Sophia	MAY 20 1858
TAUBERSCHMIDT, Katharina	QEINHARDT, Karl	MAR 02 1855
TAUBERSCHMIDT, Margaretha	ZANGE, Nicholaus	OCT 01 1853
TAUNSAND, James	COALE, Mary Ann	OCT 26 1818
TAVENER, James M.	CAMMACK, Jane	OCT 06 1852
TAVENNER, Charles H.	OTTERBACK, Maria	JUN 29 1847
TAVENNER, George	GALLOWAY, Juliet	MAR 19 1839
TAVENNER, Jonah	NICHOLSON, Ann	DEC 21 1826
TAVERSCHMIDT, Barbara	PREINKERT, Conrad	DEC 02 1847
TAYLER, James	JACKSON, Louisa	MAY 13 1826
TAYLER, John	BECKETT, Eliza	JUN 21 1820
TAYLER, John	MATTHEWS, Jane Hellen	JUL 03 1854
TAYLER, Lydia E.	PATTON, Thomas H.	JUN 16 1832
TAYLER, Mary Ann	DYE, Denry	APR 13 1835
TAYLER, Thomas	STONESTREET, Patsey	FEB 10 1841
TAYLER, Thomas, Jr.	KEELER, Rachel	OCT 18 1825
TAYLOE, Alexander	PEERCE, Isabella	JUN 07 1823
TAYLOE, Ann O.	LEWIS, Henry H., U.S.N.	NOV 30 1841
TAYLOE, Catherine C.	BAKER, James	MAY 20 1824
TAYLOE, E. Poinsett	CARR, Louisa C.	APR 23 1857
TAYLOE, Elizabeth M.	CARTER, Robert W.	MAY 11 1829
TAYLOE, Eugenia P.W.	WARREN, George B., Jr.	APR 29 1856
TAYLOE, John	FORREST, Maria	NOV 11 1817
TAYLOE, John	MOSHER, Imogene	NOV 09 1841
TAYLOE, Maria [Mrs.]	BOHRER, Benjamin S. [Dr.]	JUN 09 1834
TAYLOR, Alfred	MUDD, Mary Ellen	JUL 07 1828
TAYLOR, Alfred	BRONAUGH, Nancy M.	JUL 18 1842
TAYLOR, Algernon S.	MEEHAN, Susan M.	JUL 03 1837
TAYLOR, Allender	CRAWLEY, Eliza	MAY 05 1837
TAYLOR, Alocy Ann D.	HOLMES, Fountain	FEB 15 1830
TAYLOR, Amanda [Wentworth]	GORDON, Alexander G. [Lieut.]	SEP 03 1827
TAYLOR, Amelia	SEMON, Charles	MAY 11 1842
TAYLOR, Ann	GRISWOLD, Sevin	JUN 21 1830
TAYLOR, Ann L.	BOPP, James	JUL 26 1856
TAYLOR, Ann V.	CLAPDORE, Jacob H.	APR 26 1855
TAYLOR, Annie (blk)	ROSS, Richard	JAN 10 1849
TAYLOR, Catharine	BUTLER, John	MAR 22 1815
TAYLOR, Catharine	WHEAT, John F.	NOV 08 1832
TAYLOR, Cecelia	HICKEY, John	DEC 09 1837
TAYLOR, Cenia	HURLEY, John T.	DEC 01 1849
TAYLOR, Charles H.	TUCKER, Anna E.	AUG 30 1854

District of Columbia Marriage Licenses, 1811-1858

TAYLOR, Charlotte (blk)	REED, Alexander	NOV 07 1854
TAYLOR, Daniel	CROSEN, Mary	MAR 17 1832
TAYLOR, Dennis	GOING, Harmonia (blk)	AUG 08 1840
TAYLOR, Dennis	MOORE, Lucinda (blk)	JUL 28 1845
TAYLOR, Edward	TAYLOR, Laura	MAY 17 1854
TAYLOR, Edward C.	LUCAS, Elizabeth Jane	OCT 30 1849
TAYLOR, Edward, Jr.	BURGESS, Mary	JUN 09 1852
TAYLOR, Eleanor	CAMPBELL, James	JAN 19 1825
TAYLOR, Eleanor	MUNFORD, Lewis	JUN 26 1828
TAYLOR, Eliza	DAILEY, James	MAY 01 1821
TAYLOR, Eliza	GIVENY, Joseph	JAN 15 1829
TAYLOR, Eliza	THOMAS, John	AUG 27 1840
TAYLOR, Eliza	FLEMING, Paterick	FEB 13 1843
TAYLOR, Eliza Ann	BUTLER, Abraham (blk)	JUL 19 1837
TAYLOR, Elizabeth	MUSGRAVE, Daniel	JUL 31 1827
TAYLOR, Elizabeth	BIRTH, William W.	MAY 05 1834
TAYLOR, Elizabeth	McINTOSH, Job P.	JUL 19 1841
TAYLOR, Elizabeth A.	STEVENS, Leonard L.	NOV 06 1835
TAYLOR, Elizabeth A.	BAYNE, William H.	JUL 17 1838
TAYLOR, Elizabeth M.	MORTIMORE, Benj.	JAN 31 1854
TAYLOR, Ellen	DYER, Amos	DEC 23 1834
TAYLOR, Emily W.	SMITH, Wesley A.	FEB 28 1856
TAYLOR, Estelle Frances	PERRY, Roger	APR 13 1857
TAYLOR, Fanny	CARTER, Joseph	FEB 09 1815
TAYLOR, Frank	SIMMS, Virginia W.	SEP 14 1835
TAYLOR, Franklin	ROLLINS, Emeline	APR 03 1855
TAYLOR, G.W.	CLOUD, Elizabeth	JAN 27 1857
TAYLOR, Garrett	CLARK, Caroline [Mrs.]	JUN 11 1829
TAYLOR, Geo. W.	SHAW, Henrietta	DEC 28 1835
TAYLOR, George	COX, Mary	FEB 11 1823
TAYLOR, George	ASHTON, Mary B.	AUG 05 1847
TAYLOR, George	TATE, Elizabeth	OCT 19 1848
TAYLOR, George	MYERS, Sarah (blk)	JUL 10 1850
TAYLOR, George E.	GARNER, Ann Eliza	OCT 22 1856
TAYLOR, Georgiana	BRERETON, Wm. Henry	SEP 06 1848
TAYLOR, Gillis	LOWRY, Margaret	FEB 03 1834
TAYLOR, H. Allen	HENDERSON, Anne V.N.	APR 23 1845
TAYLOR, Hannah	ROBEY, Hezekiah	JUL 17 1813
TAYLOR, Harriet	KING, Thomas	JUN 15 1843
TAYLOR, Harriott	GORDON, George	FEB 08 1815
TAYLOR, Harriott	GORDON, George	FEB 09 1815
TAYLOR, Henrietta	HARRIS, John	MAR 11 1824
TAYLOR, Henry	DANIEL, Levinia	JAN 31 1812
TAYLOR, Henry R.	PLUNKETT, Jane	NOV 17 1829
TAYLOR, Hudson	LINDSLEY, Christine	JAN 18 1849
TAYLOR, Isaac	FELSON, Harriot (blk)	DEC 11 1833
TAYLOR, Isaac	McCORMICK, Jane	DEC 01 1852
TAYLOR, James	GLOVER, Martha Ann	AUG 14 1834
TAYLOR, James	MAZEN, Mary	DEC 21 1835
TAYLOR, James	MOORE, Bridget	MAR 07 1854
TAYLOR, James	PORTER, Jane	JAN 03 1856
TAYLOR, James H.C.	WRIGHT, Martha A.	AUG 12 1852
TAYLOR, James W.	HANCOCK, Margaret	JAN 16 1858
TAYLOR, John	DENNISON, Ann	JAN 14 1818
TAYLOR, John	JOHNSON, Catharine	JUN 12 1856
TAYLOR, John B.	SMALLWOOD, Rachel	JUL 06 1840
TAYLOR, John F.	HAZZARD, Caroline	JUL 14 1853
TAYLOR, John F.	CADDINGTON, Sophia	JUN 23 1857

District of Columbia Marriage Licenses, 1811-1858

TAYLOR, John H.	USHER, Jane	OCT 21 1846
TAYLOR, Joseph P. [Capt.]	McLEAN, Evelina	NOV 20 1827
TAYLOR, Joshua	CORNWALL, Artemesia Griffin	OCT 30 1817
TAYLOR, Julia	OURAND, D.C.W.	MAY 12 1857
TAYLOR, Julia Ann	ANDERSON, John	MAY 04 1818
TAYLOR, Julia Ann	THORNTON, Bennitt W.	JAN 31 1837
TAYLOR, Kate Cornelia	JEFFERS, Braxton B.	OCT 04 1855
TAYLOR, L.A.	HARRISON, Richard	JUN 15 1822
TAYLOR, Laura	TAYLOR, Edward	MAY 17 1854
TAYLOR, Louisa	SPELLMAN, George	AUG 28 1829
TAYLOR, Louisa	ROSS, Richard Lorman	MAR 06 1844
TAYLOR, Lucy Jane	SAFFER, John W.	FEB 25 1851
TAYLOR, Marcellus K.	SWARTZ, Augusta	MAY 03 1849
TAYLOR, Margaret E.	CAMMACK, William	JAN 13 1851
TAYLOR, Marion M.	SCOTT, Sarah V.	MAY 26 1853
TAYLOR, Martha Ann	FITZHUGH, John	AUG 26 1847
TAYLOR, Martha E.	WEBSTER, Philip L.	DEC 26 1846
TAYLOR, Mary	KEYWORTH, Robert	OCT 21 1819
TAYLOR, Mary	LUSBY, James	JUL 11 1839
TAYLOR, Mary	BLAIDEN, Augustus	NOV 18 1840
TAYLOR, Mary	GRANT, Alexander	NOV 04 1851
TAYLOR, Mary Ann	PIERCE, Daniel	AUG 19 1819
TAYLOR, Mary E. (blk)	POWELL, Albert	SEP 08 1857
TAYLOR, Mary Jane	WATSON, William A.	JUL 23 1846
TAYLOR, Mary L.	FECHTY, Levi R.	FEB 05 1850
TAYLOR, Mildred L.	BEACH, Headley	DEC 04 1856
TAYLOR, Montgomery	LEE, Mary	MAY 17 1850
TAYLOR, Moses	WHITE, Nancy	FEB 06 1815
TAYLOR, Nathaniel	GAREY, Susan	FEB 23 1838
TAYLOR, Patrick	WILLIAMS, Ann (blk)	MAY 30 1854
TAYLOR, Phema	TURNER, William	JUN 11 1845
TAYLOR, Punnell	WHITMORE, Ruth	JUL 17 1823
TAYLOR, Rachel	HINES, Jacob	APR 25 1837
TAYLOR, Rachel A.	GORDON, John	JUN 13 1849
TAYLOR, Rebecca B.	MARTIN, Thomas J.	FEB 02 1830
TAYLOR, Rezin P.	SKIDMORE, Nancy	JUN 03 1851
TAYLOR, Robert	GRIFFIN, Julia	OCT 07 1841
TAYLOR, Robert A.	KING, Jennet	JUN 17 1835
TAYLOR, Robert B.	STER, Parmelia M.	APR 06 1845
TAYLOR, Rodiar	JONES, Sarah	DEC 26 1848
TAYLOR, Rosalie B.	McNEW, Jeremiah	OCT 29 1852
TAYLOR, Rufus	COCKE, Sarah E.	DEC 23 1856
TAYLOR, Samuel H.	MUDD, Ann Maria	MAY 23 1829
TAYLOR, Sanford	BURKLEY, Catharine	MAR 20 1832
TAYLOR, Sarah	EVANS, John	JUL 22 1826
TAYLOR, Sarah A.	GREEN, Edward E.	APR 10 1858
TAYLOR, Sarah Ann	MILLER, Jacob	DEC 26 1833
TAYLOR, Sarah Ann	LUCKET, Thomas	APR 30 1844
TAYLOR, Serena	LOUNDS, William R.	NOV 08 1843
TAYLOR, Stark B.	NORRIS, Mary Ellen	MAY 15 1851
TAYLOR, Susan (blk)	NEVERSON, Joseph	NOV 14 1857
TAYLOR, Susan M.	HALL, Wesley	SEP 11 1849
TAYLOR, Susan P.McD.	WELLER, John B.	MAR 05 1845
TAYLOR, Thomas	SMITH, Harriet (blk)	JUL 19 1834
TAYLOR, Thomas	CISSEL, Sarah Ann	DEC 09 1847
TAYLOR, Virginia W.	COOK, James	FEB 22 1849
TAYLOR, Walter S.	MACKALL, Harriet M.	JUN 16 1835
TAYLOR, Walter W.	WHITNEY, Harriet	JAN 14 1830

District of Columbia Marriage Licenses, 1811-1858

TAYLOR, Washington	WILLIAMS, Caroline (blk)	OCT 25 1852
TAYLOR, William	TRAVERS, Elizabeth	JUN 05 1839
TAYLOR, William	MILLS, Margaret	JAN 23 1845
TAYLOR, William	STOKES, Cordelia	NOV 17 1847
TAYLOR, William	CALLAHAN, Julia	JUL 12 1848
TAYLOR, William	EVANS, Elizabeth (blk)	APR 19 1849
TAYLOR, William	GOODEN, Martha	AUG 29 1850
TAYLOR, William B.	JONES, Celia	JUL 30 1840
TAYLOR, William H.	WILLIAMS, Amelia (blk)	OCT 18 1836
TAYLOR, William H.	BURCH, Emily	JAN 03 1854
TAYLOR, William Harrison	WHITE, Mary Jane	JAN 08 1846
TAYLOR, William Henry	SMITH, Martha Ellen	JUL 07 1831
TAYLOR, Wm. H.	WHEATLEY, Martha A.	OCT 12 1857
TAYMAN, Benjamin J.	LUXON, Susan	JUL 26 1842
TEABOWER, John	FISHER, Eliza	JUL 28 1856
TEACHEM, Elizabeth	WALKER, William S.	SEP 14 1835
TEACHEM, Susan	FOWLER, Henderson	NOV 22 1856
TEACHEN, James H.	WALKER, Ann Elizabeth	DEC 02 1843
TEACHUM, Catharine	KEITHLEY, John	OCT 02 1833
TEACHUM, Wm. H.	LITCHFIELD, Hannah M.	FEB 20 1856
TEAL, Christeen	GOLDEN, Richard	SEP 18 1819
TEALLE, Cesecitia	WARNER, James	DEC 28 1815
TEARGRIEFF, Ann	McGOVARN, Thomas	JUL 25 1835
TEARNEY, Polly	BRADY, Terance	JAN 24 1822
TEASDALE, Emma H.	CHURCH, William J.	JAN 22 1857
TEATCHEM, Robert	NOTTINGHAM, Mary O.	FEB 24 1835
TEDERICK, Caroline	HOWARD, Thomas	AUG 06 1840
TEECHEM, Mary H.	FOWLER, Henderson	DEC 10 1833
TEELIN, Charles	BAILEY, Rebecca	MAR 02 1857
TEGELER, Henry	SACHS, Margaret	NOV 03 1857
TEHER, Adam	SEBER, Monika	JUL 11 1854
TEILICH, Frederick	STEFFIN, Margaret	JUL 03 1852
TEITJEN, Lucippia Ann	JONES, William Thomas	MAY 08 1845
TELFORD, Charles L.	TOTTEN, Susan M.	NOV 15 1842
TELLEY, Mary	WEBB, John	JAN 02 1845
TEMMS, Armenia	BARTLETT, Burgiss D.	MAR 23 1846
TEMPLE, John T.	STAUGHTON, Elizabeth A.	APR 06 1824
TEMPLE, William Greenville	TOTTEN, Catlyna Tillman	OCT 06 1851
TEMPLEMAN, George	FOLEY, Mary	SEP 30 1835
TEMPLEMAN, Hetty B.	COMLY, Charles A.	APR 12 1838
TEMPLEMAN, Octavia C.	KEIRNES, Richard	AUG 07 1856
TEMPS, William H.	CARROLL, Virginia Elizth.	NOV 08 1851
TENCH, Balinda	SMITH, Wm.	APR 05 1823
TENCH, Julia	BURT, Edmund B.	FEB 21 1852
TENCH, Mary	MORARTY, Ambrose	JUN 24 1813
TENCH, Matilda	SMETHEY, Lewis	APR 03 1829
TENCH, Stanislaus	FRENCH, Ann	NOV 15 1821
TENELY, Rachael	STONE, Nehemiah	SEP 03 1835
TenEYCK, John C.	GADSBY, Julia	JUN 10 1845
TENLEY, Elizabeth	REILY, Farrell	JAN 25 1812
TENLEY, Henry	TENLEY, Telly	FEB 13 1812
TENLEY, Horatio	JONES, Mary	DEC 01 1856
TENLEY, Mary	ANNANDEL, William	SEP 29 1827
TENLEY, Mary L.	WALMSLEY, Theodore	MAR 16 1858
TENLEY, Telly	TENLEY, Henry	FEB 13 1812
TENLEY, Theodore	BASSETT, Rachael	NOV 06 1828
TENLY, George B.	WEBSTER, Mary Jane	DEC 30 1845
TENLY, John T.	WALKER, Lucretia	SEP 14 1847

District of Columbia Marriage Licenses, 1811-1858

TENLY, John T.	BAKER, Eliza Jane	OCT 21 1851
TENLY, Mary E.	PEIASNER, Jacob	SEP 14 1847
TENNANT, John	CASSADY, Margaret	FEB 15 1833
TENNISON, Catharine C.	MYER, Franklin S.	FEB 18 1829
TENNISON, Charles	VERMILLION, Mahala	NOV 14 1822
TENNISON, Charles C.	JENKINS, Eleanor	NOV 16 1818
TENNISON, Charlotte E.	BALLENGER, John T.	OCT 10 1835
TENNISON, John	TURBY, Martha	JUN 28 1850
TENNISON, Lucretia Ann	McDONALD, James	SEP 29 1825
TENNISON, William A.	BROOKE, Mary Virginia	FEB 09 1847
TENNY, Andrew	BUTLER, Marian (blk)	OCT 15 1844
TENNY, Ann	SMILEY, Edward	MAY 23 1837
TENNY, Elizabeth Ann	BROWN, Joseph	FEB 14 1835
TENNY, Matilda (blk)	TENNY, Pompy	OCT 17 1840
TENNY, Pompey	McDANIEL, Elizth. (blk)	MAY 05 1856
TENNY, Pompy	TENNY, Matilda (blk)	OCT 17 1840
TENNY, William H.	CROPLEY, Eliza	APR 16 1842
TEPPER, Ann	McINTOSH, David	AUG 20 1855
TERETT, Nathaniel H.	McCABE, Jane	NOV 29 1850
TERLY, George L.	BARRETT, Henrietta	SEP 04 1856
TERNAN, James	KELLY, Jane	JAN 25 1812
TERRELL, Ann	JONES, Henry	DEC 23 1847
TERRETT, Colville	MATHEWS, Martha Ann F.	AUG 18 1851
TERRETT, Frederick A.C.	STUART, Mary W.	NOV 07 1851
TERRIER, Annie (blk)	HOWARD, Isaiah A.	AUG 23 1855
TERRILL, James W.	SOMERVILLE, Jane	APR 20 1852
TERRILL, Jane N.	PITCHER, George N.	OCT 28 1821
TERRITT, Julia D.	PALMER, Thomas	MAR 13 1849
TERRON, Victor	DEVERAUX, Catharine	FEB 06 1826
TERRY, Brooklin	DELPHY, Matilda	AUG 19 1819
TERRY, William	HOW, Mary	MAR 08 1820
TERRY, William W.	PROSPER, Julia Ann	OCT 29 1857
TERVIS, Juliet N.	WRIGHT, Wm. C.	APR 08 1845
TEST, John	SAWKINS, Penelope Gay	MAR 17 1841
TEST, Penelope G.	WHARTON, Robert S.	FEB 17 1857
TEWELL, Rebecca	BROWN, John	JUN 21 1819
THAW, Columbia	LITTELL, John DeBarth	JUN 06 1854
THAW, Eliza Jane	GOODRICH, Archibald W. [Col.]	SEP 05 1831
THAW, Hannah M.	WALKER, John	OCT 06 1831
THAW, Joseph	SHANKS, Elizabeth T.	DEC 25 1830
THAW, Joseph	KEARNS, Mary Ann	DEC 30 1851
THAYER, Maria T.	WARD, John P.	JAN 02 1845
THECKER, Henry	FRUSH, Catharine	DEC 12 1833
THECKER, James A.	BRADY, Abigail I.	JAN 03 1848
THECKER, Mary E.	FEARSON, Samuel J.	FEB 04 1850
THECKER, William H.	ELLIS, Elizabeth Jane	OCT 17 1848
THEIRLOW, Elizabeth	HOWARD, Henry	FEB 02 1828
THIELE, Eliza Auguste	SCHWERING, John Ernst Frederick	MAR 09 1849
THIELECKE, Charles W.	NOLALIE, Anna Maria	NOV 20 1852
THOM, Christopher N.	CORCORAN, Sarah C.	AUG 05 1856
THOM, George	GRIFFIN, Mary Lucia	MAY 01 1850
THOM, Thomas	MORGAN, Mary Frances	FEB 04 1856
THOMAS, Addison Newton	BARNES, Elizabeth L.	SEP 20 1823
THOMAS, Alcinda (blk)	HARKENS, William H.	MAR 24 1858
THOMAS, Alfred	JOHNS, Jane (blk)	DEC 02 1839
THOMAS, Amanda Ellen	ROBEY, John Thomas	JUN 09 1855
THOMAS, Andreas	WIESSMANN, Rosine	JAN 20 1845
THOMAS, Andrew Merecin	WEBB, Elizabeth Gibbs	MAY 18 1847

District of Columbia Marriage Licenses, 1811-1858

THOMAS, Ann	ALFORD, Henry	SEP 22 1826
THOMAS, Ann	STROTHER, Geo. W.	JUL 08 1854
THOMAS, Ann	RIDGELEY, Nicholas	DEC 10 1856
THOMAS, Ann (blk)	BOWIE, Richard	APR 21 1838
THOMAS, Arianna (blk)	GAINES, George	SEP 09 1852
THOMAS, Augustus	WATTS, Sarah (blk)	MAY 21 1833
THOMAS, Benjamin	ROLLINS, Elizabeth	NOV 13 1815
THOMAS, Benjamin F.	HOWISON, Sarah A.	JUN 25 1836
THOMAS, Caroline (blk)	DICK, Robert	MAY 26 1831
THOMAS, Charles	CALLAN, Elizabeth	MAY 10 1845
THOMAS, Charles Edward	FRENCH, Jane Elizabeth	APR 22 1851
THOMAS, Charles G.	SUMMERVILLE, Elizth. (blk)	NOV 19 1855
THOMAS, Columbus	CHAMBERLIN, Mary L.	APR 07 1858
THOMAS, Cornelia P.	CALHOUN, Wm. H.	JAN 30 1847
THOMAS, Denzie	MATTHEWS, John	OCT 04 1834
THOMAS, Diana	JONES, Paul	MAY 03 1830
THOMAS, Dorcas	SCOTT, John J.	JUL 03 1830
THOMAS, Dorthea Barbara	GODRON, William H.	APR 29 1853
THOMAS, Edward	SMALLWOOD, Mary (blk)	NOV 07 1844
THOMAS, Edward	LAKIN, Winifred J.	NOV 06 1850
THOMAS, Edward	BLAGBURN, Emeline (blk)	JUN 09 1852
THOMAS, Edward A.	KREEMER, Elizabeth J.	JAN 30 1844
THOMAS, Edwd. M.	BRENT, Clarissa (blk)	OCT 23 1846
THOMAS, Eleanor	MATHERS, John	JAN 23 1813
THOMAS, Eliz.	SHREEVE, Samuel	JAN 19 1812
THOMAS, Eliz'th. A.	POLLEY, John W.	JUN 03 1858
THOMAS, Eliza	HADAWAY, Robert	JAN 30 1823
THOMAS, Eliza	SMALLWOOD, John	JUL 31 1828
THOMAS, Eliza	THOMAS, Samuel	NOV 25 1830
THOMAS, Eliza	JAMESON, John M.	JAN 10 1834
THOMAS, Eliza	CONWAY, James	JUN 18 1842
THOMAS, Eliza Jane	ZERLAUT, Frederick Ernst	SEP 09 1839
THOMAS, Elizabeth	HALEY, Peter	FEB 12 1835
THOMAS, Elizabeth	ATES, C.	JUN 29 1843
THOMAS, Elizabeth (blk)	SATTERWHITE, George	MAR 07 1848
THOMAS, Elizabeth (blk)	MATTHEWS, James	DEC 05 1848
THOMAS, Elizth. (blk)	BROWN, Charles	AUG 17 1829
THOMAS, Emeline	JONES, Thomas	AUG 13 1839
THOMAS, Emily	BARKER, William	APR 26 1834
THOMAS, Emily	COCKRILL, Benjamin D.	DEC 09 1839
THOMAS, Emily	MEREDITH, Richard L.	MAY 03 1851
THOMAS, Frances Ann (blk)	PAYNE, Wm. Jefferson	MAY 08 1851
THOMAS, Frances E.	WINE, Jacob T.	MAY 13 1858
THOMAS, Fras. A.	GRANDISON, Ann M. (blk)	DEC 31 1855
THOMAS, Frederick [Lt.]	BEANES, Mary B.	MAY 01 1828
THOMAS, George	BUTTLER, Lydia	NOV 07 1818
THOMAS, George	HARRAD, Alla	FEB 10 1824
THOMAS, George	LANE, Willey	OCT 29 1832
THOMAS, George	RIGSBY, Cynthia	OCT 27 1841
THOMAS, George	ENGLE, Sophia	JUN 21 1848
THOMAS, George C.	GREY, Fannie	JUL 14 1848
THOMAS, George W.	THOMAS, Lucy Ann	MAY 28 1829
THOMAS, George W.	MARTIN, Margaret A.	AUG 26 1858
THOMAS, Georgeana (blk)	FORD, James	AUG 04 1851
THOMAS, Gusty	KING, Susannah (blk)	DEC 21 1826
THOMAS, Gwynneir	BATTER, Mary M.	DEC 16 1850
THOMAS, Hannah (blk)	SHORTER, Henry	FEB 12 1840
THOMAS, Hannah A.	GREGORY, John	JUL 20 1840

District of Columbia Marriage Licenses, 1811-1858

THOMAS, Harriet A.	SIMS, Enoch	DEC 14 1852
THOMAS, Harrison M.	ROBERTS, Margaret H.	APR 24 1844
THOMAS, Henrietta (blk)	WALLACE, Benjamin S.	SEP 08 1856
THOMAS, Henry	DINES, Charity (blk)	SEP 27 1814
THOMAS, Henry	MUDD, Nancy	OCT 07 1815
THOMAS, Henry	DOOLING, Ann Sally	JUN 10 1826
THOMAS, Henry	THOMPSON, Mary	JUN 10 1826
THOMAS, Henry	THOMPSON, Mary	AUG 18 1828
THOMAS, Henry	WARRINGSFORD, Sarah	APR 01 1830
THOMAS, Henry	WIGLE, Johanna	OCT 13 1848
THOMAS, Henry	BARTON, Adeline (col'd)	JUN 28 1852
THOMAS, Henry	LINDSEY, Eliza (col'd)	MAY 27 1858
THOMAS, Henry L.	THOMAS, Jane E.	JUL 29 1847
THOMAS, Isabella	TIRPEN, James H.	OCT 25 1838
THOMAS, Isabella	MASON, Saml. M.	DEC 29 1856
THOMAS, James	WHITE, Ann	DEC 25 1817
THOMAS, James	PANE, Matilda	MAY 02 1820
THOMAS, James	BALTZER, Margaret	FEB 01 1825
THOMAS, James	SU_T_ER, Sarah	JUL 29 1835
THOMAS, James D.	WILKERSON, Manerva	APR 24 1833
THOMAS, James D.	BAKER, Sarah Catharine	APR 15 1847
THOMAS, James D.	FREEMAN, Ellen W. (blk)	FEB 03 1852
THOMAS, James H.	BUTLER, Susan (blk)	JUL 15 1829
THOMAS, James H.	BELT, Eliza (blk)	SEP 21 1857
THOMAS, James [Col.]	DAVIS, Ann	NOV 07 1818
THOMAS, Jane	TUHEY, Jeremiah	AUG 14 1852
THOMAS, Jane (blk)	DUTCH, Hillery	FEB 03 1858
THOMAS, Jane E.	THOMAS, Henry L.	JUL 29 1847
THOMAS, Jenkin	BARRITT, Ann E.	JUN 17 1848
THOMAS, Jenkins	PARSONS, Eliza	MAY 13 1830
THOMAS, Jennett	PARKINSON, Thomas	DEC 11 1837
THOMAS, John	HALL, Eliza Wheat	JAN 13 1821
THOMAS, John	CLARKE, Rachel	APR 08 1829
THOMAS, John	DAVIS, Mary	AUG 03 1833
THOMAS, John	RICHARDS, Ann (blk)	AUG 01 1840
THOMAS, John	TAYLOR, Eliza	AUG 27 1840
THOMAS, John	WIENDHOLTZ, Louisa	MAR 24 1853
THOMAS, John	SANDERS, Henrietta (blk)	MAY 25 1854
THOMAS, John Dill	CRANDELL, Harriet Ann	JUL 02 1853
THOMAS, John F.	SCHUREMAN, Ann M. (blk)	JUL 30 1844
THOMAS, John F.	WILLIAMS, Lucy (blk)	NOV 13 1851
THOMAS, John F.	PRIME, Mary R. (blk)	DEC 04 1856
THOMAS, John F.	GRAVES, Lucy A.	JAN 08 1857
THOMAS, John Handy	GORDEN, Emily	APR 08 1852
THOMAS, Jno. M.	TURNER, Catherine C.	MAY 12 1823
THOMAS, Joseph	GREEN, Jane	APR 02 1855
THOMAS, Julia	BRONSON, Simeon D.	FEB 11 1843
THOMAS, Lettice E.	PRITCHARD, Edward	DEC 24 1838
THOMAS, Lewis	LEWIS, Margaret	NOV 28 1843
THOMAS, Lewis	HARVEY, Elizabeth (blk)	MAR 09 1846
THOMAS, Lewis B.	MURPHEY, Ann	JUL 05 1837
THOMAS, Lucy Ann	THOMAS, George W.	MAY 28 1829
THOMAS, Malvina	LYNN, LeRoy W.	JUL 01 1844
THOMAS, Manson	JEFFERSON, Cyntha Ann	DEC 02 1854
THOMAS, Maponilla	SMITH, Ann	JUN 25 1846
THOMAS, Marcella E.	SULLIVAN, Robert W.	FEB 04 1850
THOMAS, Margaret	THOMAS, William	OCT 20 1847
THOMAS, Margaret E.	CLARKE, Reubin B.	DEC 26 1848

District of Columbia Marriage Licenses, 1811-1858

THOMAS, Martha	McCOY, Hayard	AUG 29 1838
THOMAS, Martha	THOMPSON, Wm.	JAN 13 1846
THOMAS, Martha Ann (blk)	SCOTT, Leonidas	MAY 29 1851
THOMAS, Martha Virginia	CAHO, Joseph M.	MAY 20 1843
THOMAS, Mary	HADINGER, John	DEC 02 1826
THOMAS, Mary	CUMMINS, James	MAR 15 1828
THOMAS, Mary	KOONTZ, Joseph C.	OCT 29 1831
THOMAS, Mary	COOPER, George	MAR 06 1843
THOMAS, Mary (blk)	GRAY, James	MAY 29 1851
THOMAS, Mary (blk)	WHEADLOCK, George	MAR 22 1858
THOMAS, Mary A.	NICHOLSON, Jno. P.	AUG 16 1825
THOMAS, Mary A.	BUTLER, William H.B.	MAY 24 1854
THOMAS, Mary Ann	FERTNEY, Edwin W.	MAR 22 1838
THOMAS, Mary Ann	CRAWFORD, James	DEC 27 1845
THOMAS, Mary Ann	GOLDEN, Singleton	FEB 29 1848
THOMAS, Mary Elizabeth	EDGCOMB, William	NOV 10 1828
THOMAS, Mary Elizth. (blk)	COLE, William	NOV 30 1848
THOMAS, Matilda	BUTLER, Joseph	JUL 19 1813
THOMAS, Michael	KING, Catharine (blk)	JUN 03 1827
THOMAS, Moses W.	BOSWELL, Sophronia	SEP 07 1853
THOMAS, Nancy	FREEMAN, John	JAN 22 1820
THOMAS, Nancy	THOMAS, Sandy	MAR 04 1823
THOMAS, Nancy (blk)	LOMAX, William	MAY 19 1847
THOMAS, Nathan	CREAGER, Mary	MAR 11 1816
THOMAS, Noble J.	McCOMB, Julia E.	NOV 07 1856
THOMAS, Noblette J.	MILLS, Ann Virginia	JUN 04 1850
THOMAS, Orrel T.	SEAM, Ann	DEC 24 1825
THOMAS, Rachael Jane (blk)	KEELING, William H.	JUN 27 1840
THOMAS, Rachel	KIGER, Alfred	MAR 17 1834
THOMAS, Rachel	HAMELL, David	MAY 15 1837
THOMAS, Rachel E.	SPARKS, John W.	MAY 01 1851
THOMAS, Richard F.	RABITT, Martha Ellen	MAY 17 1842
THOMAS, Robert	JOHNSON, Miss Eliza	OCT 27 1817
THOMAS, Robert	CRAWFORD, Frances (blk)	DEC 03 1855
THOMAS, Ross	MINOR, Mary J.	NOV 03 1847
THOMAS, Saml.	MATTHEWS, Harriet (blk)	OCT 22 1857
THOMAS, Samuel	THOMAS, Eliza (blk)	NOV 25 1830
THOMAS, Samuel	WEBSTER, Hannah (blk)	FEB 05 1835
THOMAS, Samuel M.	TILGHMAN, Mary Ann Caroline (blk)	MAR 09 1848
THOMAS, Sandy	THOMAS, Nancy	MAR 04 1823
THOMAS, Sarah	KING, Andrew	MAR 11 1824
THOMAS, Sarah (col'd)	WALKER, William	OCT 25 1854
THOMAS, Sarah A.	WALLACE, Samuel	DEC 18 1828
THOMAS, Sarah A.	LYNCH, James J.	MAR 08 1856
THOMAS, Sarah C.	WILKINSON, Samuel C.	MAY 28 1855
THOMAS, Sidney	ALLOWAY, John	MAY 16 1844
THOMAS, Sophia (blk)	CARROLL, Andrew	JUL 31 1851
THOMAS, Susan (blk)	FORD, William	APR 03 1834
THOMAS, Thomas	HICKS, Patsey	OCT 05 1825
THOMAS, Thomas	HALLEY, Martha E.	APR 24 1846
THOMAS, Thomas J.	WARREN, Mary R.	OCT 17 1856
THOMAS, Thomas W.	SELDEN, Emma (blk)	MAY 25 1844
THOMAS, Virginia	LACEY, John Francis	NOV 12 1857
THOMAS, William	GARNER, Ann	MAR 24 1832
THOMAS, William	SHAW, Mary Ann (blk)	SEP 17 1833
THOMAS, William	MANN, Sarah (blk)	SEP 14 1839
THOMAS, William	WASHINGTON, Caroline (blk)	FEB 04 1843
THOMAS, William	BATTON, Priscilla	APR 13 1843

District of Columbia Marriage Licenses, 1811-1858

THOMAS, William	TUCKER, Jane M.	OCT 17 1843
THOMAS, William	FOX, Ann	JUN 30 1845
THOMAS, William	THOMAS, Margaret	OCT 20 1847
THOMAS, William	VODRA, Isabella (blk)	DEC 11 1855
THOMAS, William	WILLIAMS, Catherine A. (blk)	APR 15 1857
THOMAS, William	TILGHMAN, Ann (blk)	OCT 19 1857
THOMAS, William E.	ELLIS, Virginia	APR 27 1858
THOMAS, William H.	PUMPHREY, Catherine L.	JUN 21 1848
THOMAS, William H.	JOHNSON, Mary E. (blk)	JAN 01 1851
THOMAS, William Henry	KRAFFT, Christiana	OCT 29 1851
THOMAS, WIlliam	GAITOF, Catherine	SEP 13 1845
THOMAS, Wm. H.	PARKER, Ann L. (blk)	AUG 09 1855
THOMAS, Wm. H.	RILEY, Ellen	MAY 13 1856
THOMAS, Wm. M.	GLADMOND, Ruthay	MAR 02 1853
THOMASON, Adelaide	TALBOT, Isham [Hon.]	MAR 27 1817
THOMPSON, Achel Emily	OWENS, William	JUL 16 1844
THOMPSON, Aira	DRURY, William	DEC 06 1821
THOMPSON, Alice	BARKER, Adolphus	JUL 01 1857
THOMPSON, Alice Elizabeth	RAGAN, Andrew Jackson	DEC 20 1849
THOMPSON, Alila	REILLY, George	DEC 03 1836
THOMPSON, Allen	MORGAN, Adeline	OCT 07 1826
THOMPSON, Andrew E.	SIMPSON, Elizabeth	APR 18 1826
THOMPSON, Andrew J.	WRIGHT, Jane Eliza	AUG 17 1850
THOMPSON, Ann	HOWARD, John	SEP 11 1821
THOMPSON, Ann	GARNER, Charles	JUL 17 1823
THOMPSON, Ann	HODGKIN, Samuel	JUN 24 1824
THOMPSON, Ann	ANDERSON, John	JUL 07 1829
THOMPSON, Ann	OWENS, James Edward	AUG 12 1847
THOMPSON, Ann	EVANS, Bernard	AUG 18 1851
THOMPSON, Ann	NULTER, Samson	MAR 06 1857
THOMPSON, Ann Elizth.	HAGAN, William	APR 24 1851
THOMPSON, Ann Grezela	ANDERSON, Joshua	JUN 27 1853
THOMPSON, Anna E. (blk)	WORMLEY, James	JAN 30 1841
THOMPSON, Anne	McSPADDIN, Robert	MAR 07 1849
THOMPSON, Anthony	BUTLER, Geneva	JUL 08 1858
THOMPSON, Archibald	MARKWELL, Mary Ann	JAN 05 1832
THOMPSON, Arthur	KEYS, Nancy	MAY 10 1831
THOMPSON, Augusta M.	DICKINS, James J.	OCT 05 1846
THOMPSON, Barnett Henry	SHAW, Susana	FEB 02 1847
THOMPSON, Benjamin	SPELLMAN, Catharine	NOV 15 1833
THOMPSON, Benjamin	FOWLER, Elizabeth	SEP 30 1839
THOMPSON, Betty C.	LOUDON, George W.	SEP 25 1855
THOMPSON, Caleb	STONE, Eliza	FEB 03 1814
THOMPSON, Cassandray	DONALDSON, John A.	OCT 22 1850
THOMPSON, Catharine L.	DeBRISSON, Charles	JAN 23 1823
THOMPSON, Cecelia M.	LOOMIS, Erastus [Lieut.]	MAY 30 1816
THOMPSON, Charles	ASKINS, Catharine Ann	APR 03 1828
THOMPSON, Charles B.	BALDWIN, Elizabeth L.	JUN 29 1842
THOMPSON, Charles G.	WADSWORTH, E.W.	JUN 10 1841
THOMPSON, Charles W.	RATCLIFFE, Margaret J.	SEP 05 1854
THOMPSON, Charlotte	THOMPSON, John	NOV 08 1827
THOMPSON, Cyrus	PEERCE, Elizabeth	DEC 26 1840
THOMPSON, David H.	THOMPSON, Delilah Ann	DEC 14 1852
THOMPSON, Delilah	LEAR, John P.	JUL 30 1850
THOMPSON, Delilah Ann	THOMPSON, David H.	DEC 14 1852
THOMPSON, Dolly	SIMMS, James	OCT 28 1819
THOMPSON, Dolly	COONES, Fredk.	FEB 07 1820
THOMPSON, Egbert, Lt., U.S.N.	MUDD, Emily B.	AUG 28 1854

District of Columbia Marriage Licenses, 1811-1858

THOMPSON, Eleanor	BOSWELL, Benjn.	NOV 18 1822
THOMPSON, Eleanor	VINCENT, Isaac	APR 07 1825
THOMPSON, Eleanor	DONALDSON, Robert H.	FEB 07 1831
THOMPSON, Eleanor	EDWARDS, Edward	DEC 24 1844
THOMPSON, Eliza	HUTCHISON, John	DEC 13 1825
THOMPSON, Eliza [Mrs.]	GIBERSON, Gilbert L.	JUN 11 1831
THOMPSON, Eliza Ann	BROWN, Absolam	DEC 30 1845
THOMPSON, Eliza Jane (blk)	SIMONS, William H.	MAY 23 1850
THOMPSON, Elizabeth	WHEELER, Bennedict	OCT 16 1815
THOMPSON, Elizabeth	STONEHAM, Thomas	JUL 12 1824
THOMPSON, Elizabeth	GIBSON, John	FEB 07 1826
THOMPSON, Elizabeth	GOLDSMITH, Henry	FEB 08 1842
THOMPSON, Elizabeth	SHOWARD, Samuel	DEC 22 1845
THOMPSON, Elizabeth	ANTHONY, Joseph	MAY 20 1848
THOMPSON, Elizabeth	WOOD, Henry S.	MAY 16 1855
THOMPSON, Elizabeth A.	BURFORD, William B.	JAN 10 1854
THOMPSON, Elizabeth Ann	KAIN, James	JUL 15 1829
THOMPSON, Elizabeth Ann	KING, Henry	FEB 07 1839
THOMPSON, Elizabeth D.	VAIL, Morris	FEB 16 1833
THOMPSON, Elizabeth L.	KEEFER, Joseph A.	JAN 09 1851
THOMPSON, Elizabeth M.	JOHNSON, Thomas E.	JAN 08 1835
THOMPSON, Elizth. D.	HONEYWELL, James	SEP 21 1819
THOMPSON, Elleanor Jane	LANDVOIGT, Charles Edward	JUN 22 1857
THOMPSON, Elzey	DAVIS, Eliza	AUG 01 1815
THOMPSON, Emily S.	GIVEN, John T.	FEB 24 1841
THOMPSON, Estelle E.	SHOEMAKER, David L.	FEB 09 1853
THOMPSON, Frances	BLANCHARD, Valentine	MAR 23 1841
THOMPSON, Francis	MILLS, Eliza	AUG 21 1838
THOMPSON, Gabriel Clark	LISBY, Nancy Harriet	DEC 26 1844
THOMPSON, Garland	SIBLEY, Henrietta	AUG 24 1837
THOMPSON, Geo.	FERRELL, Elizabeth	SEP 27 1821
THOMPSON, Geo.	THOMPSON, Mary	JUL 18 1837
THOMPSON, Geo. C.	WHEATLEY, Elizabeth A.	JUL 14 1830
THOMPSON, George	HAYWOOD, Sarah Ann	MAY 15 1822
THOMPSON, George	TOUCHEREZ, Estelle M.	JUL 24 1832
THOMPSON, George	DUNKLER, Joanna Maria	FEB 21 1835
THOMPSON, George	DONALDSON, Margaret	NOV 23 1836
THOMPSON, George	MULLIKIN, Elizabeth	OCT 15 1839
THOMPSON, George C.	TURPIN, Ellen	SEP 28 1852
THOMPSON, Georgeana	ELVINS, John	FEB 06 1854
THOMPSON, Gilbertine L.	VanZANDT, Joseph A.	JUL 19 1847
THOMPSON, Gillies	CARTER, Mary L.	JUN 01 1816
THOMPSON, Hannah M.	POLKINHORN, Richard O.	OCT 29 1855
THOMPSON, Harrison	JONES, Mary Ann	OCT 29 1835
THOMPSON, Harvey M.	SMITH, Jane Owen	MAY 11 1843
THOMPSON, Henrietta	HARRINGTON, Absolom T.	AUG 21 1827
THOMPSON, Henry M.	GILL, Mary A.	JUL 17 1852
THOMPSON, James	WELSH, Mary	APR 04 1816
THOMPSON, James	KEAN, Julia [Mrs.]	APR 15 1816
THOMPSON, James	SCOTT, Deilah	OCT 05 1822
THOMPSON, James	FIELDS, Amelia	JUL 07 1823
THOMPSON, James	KENT, Ann	AUG 05 1824
THOMPSON, James	KIDWELL, Jane	JUN 10 1841
THOMPSON, James	HOPKINS, Helen	JUL 30 1846
THOMPSON, James E.	PURDY, Virginia	JAN 25 1858
THOMPSON, James E.W.	HILTON, Harriot E.	JUL 16 1831
THOMPSON, James M.	MAYO, Margaret	FEB 21 1853
THOMPSON, James R.	COLLIER, Mary A.	DEC 18 1852

District of Columbia Marriage Licenses, 1811-1858

THOMPSON, James T.	MULLOY, Frances T.	FEB 12 1850
THOMPSON, Jane	JOHNSON, John	MAY 06 1814
THOMPSON, Jane	GOLDING, John	OCT 09 1830
THOMPSON, Jane	JOHNSON, John	DEC 24 1832
THOMPSON, Jane	GLOVER, Thomas	JUN 26 1833
THOMPSON, Jane	BARRON, Augustin	SEP 23 1837
THOMPSON, Jane	RILEY, Benjamin T.	FEB 04 1842
THOMPSON, Jane	DIMSEY, John	SEP 02 1847
THOMPSON, Jane	MURPHY, Wm.	JAN 16 1849
THOMPSON, Jane Eliza	MARSHALL, Thomas	FEB 06 1847
THOMPSON, Jane R.	THOMPSON, John J.	SEP 28 1855
THOMPSON, Jane R.	GOODRICH, George M.	JAN 21 1858
THOMPSON, Jno.	ROGERS, Sabina	DEC 26 1814
THOMPSON, John	CURRAN, Eleanor [Mrs.]	MAY 15 1812
THOMPSON, John	JOURDAN, Mrs.	MAY 11 1818
THOMPSON, John	CHANDLER, Kitty	JUN 26 1824
THOMPSON, John	PARSONS, Eliza	JAN 24 1826
THOMPSON, John	THOMPSON, Charlotte	NOV 08 1827
THOMPSON, John	OGDEN, Sary	JUN 17 1830
THOMPSON, John	BOSWELL, Margaret H.	AUG 26 1846
THOMPSON, John	KEARNS, Eliza	DEC 24 1850
THOMPSON, John	NALLEY, Matilda Ann	JAN 27 1851
THOMPSON, John	GRAHAM, Eliza	AUG 11 1856
THOMPSON, John A.	THOMPSON, Sarah, Mrs.	JAN 07 1836
THOMPSON, John A.	TALBERT, Mary Frances	NOV 13 1850
THOMPSON, John A.	TURTIN, Elizth. M.	FEB 15 1854
THOMPSON, John Allerson	KIDWELL, Julia Ann	SEP 30 1830
THOMPSON, John Edward	HERBERT, Elizabeth	OCT 31 1846
THOMPSON, John H.	WATERS, Harriet I.	NOV 01 1848
THOMPSON, John J.	THOMPSON, Jane R.	SEP 28 1855
THOMPSON, John T.	CHISLEDINE, Elizabeth	MAY 16 1845
THOMPSON, John W.	CLEMENTS, Martha	JAN 09 1821
THOMPSON, John W.	McGILL, Janet	AUG 01 1850
THOMPSON, John W.	KEMP, Eliza E.	DEC 07 1850
THOMPSON, Joseph	TSCHIFFELY, Charlotte L.	JAN 17 1839
THOMPSON, Joseph	DAY, Margaret Eleanor (blk)	MAY 29 1858
THOMPSON, Joseph B.	RIORDAN, Mary L.	SEP 05 1853
THOMPSON, Josias	KING, Eliza	OCT 06 1812
THOMPSON, Julian	PETTIT, Edmond	JUN 05 1851
THOMPSON, Kate L.	HINES, William T.	JAN 17 1856
THOMPSON, Landon	TILLEY, Elizabeth	MAY 19 1840
THOMPSON, Lewis	BROCKETT, Ann	DEC 05 1839
THOMPSON, Lifus	JACKSON, Jane (blk)	APR 04 1831
THOMPSON, Lucretia	HAISLIP, Walter Alexander	AUG 29 1836
THOMPSON, Lydia Ann	ESPEY, Samuel C.	NOV 15 1849
THOMPSON, Mahalia	KITCHEN, Thompson	DEC 22 1847
THOMPSON, Mahlon George	ENGLISH, Mary Ellen	NOV 08 1856
THOMPSON, Margaret	GILLISPIE, Isaac	MAR 03 1813
THOMPSON, Margaret	JACKSON, Thomas	JUN 29 1820
THOMPSON, Margaret	MITCHELL, James	JAN 26 1824
THOMPSON, Margaret	CRUMP, Daniel F.	MAR 14 1842
THOMPSON, Margaret (blk)	LANCASTER, Isaac	DEC 23 1839
THOMPSON, Margaret E.	MYERS, Henry	OCT 14 1848
THOMPSON, Margaret Jane	HYMAS, Godfrey Joseph	MAR 10 1858
THOMPSON, Margaretta H.	MIDDLETON, Charles H.	MAY 13 1851
THOMPSON, Maria	CARBERRY, Henry	APR 15 1817
THOMPSON, Maria	ANDERSON, Thomas	DEC 20 1853
THOMPSON, Maria E.	SMITH, John V.	MAR 23 1858

District of Columbia Marriage Licenses, 1811-1858

THOMPSON, Martha	JOHNSON, George	AUG 19 1846
THOMPSON, Marthan Ann	HARBOUGH, Jerome	FEB 15 1830
THOMPSON, Mary	BURR, Rd. R.	MAR 14 1823
THOMPSON, Mary	THOMAS, Henry	AUG 18 1828
THOMPSON, Mary	SANDFORD, Joseph	JUL 03 1834
THOMPSON, Mary	THOMPSON, Geo.	JUL 18 1837
THOMPSON, Mary	MURPHY, John	APR 18 1842
THOMPSON, Mary	BRIDGMAN, Samuel	AUG 29 1848
THOMPSON, Mary	DEAN, John E.	DEC 10 1849
THOMPSON, Mary	BONINI, John	APR 27 1853
THOMPSON, Mary A.	HUTCHINSON, John	JUN 06 1847
THOMPSON, Mary Ann E.	BROWN, Charles B.	JUN 01 1826
THOMPSON, Mary Ann Isabella	HEAD, George M.	DEC 11 1833
THOMPSON, Mary Ann	FLICK, William T.	APR 21 1846
THOMPSON, Mary Ann	COOPER, Samuel	JUN 11 1846
THOMPSON, Mary Ann	HUTCHINSON, John	APR 13 1854
THOMPSON, Mary Ann	HUTCHINSON, John	JUN 06 1857
THOMPSON, Mary Cecelia	HERSANT, M. Esperance	APR 21 1823
THOMPSON, Mary E.	JONES, John U.	SEP 16 1856
THOMPSON, Mary E.	STOTT, Samuel	OCT 29 1856
THOMPSON, Mary Elizth.	GITTINGS, Martin Luther	SEP 26 1837
THOMPSON, Mary Jane	KERSEY, James F.	NOV 17 1852
THOMPSON, Mary Virginia	LEEDS, Isaac	FEB 28 1850
THOMPSON, Michael	DOUGLASS, Mary G.	NOV 08 1855
THOMPSON, Milly Ann (blk)	NETTER, Sampson	OCT 18 1836
THOMPSON, Minor L.	FERRIS, Emma J.	FEB 06 1857
THOMPSON, Moses	LEYDANE, Catharine	NOV 05 1850
THOMPSON, Nancy	POWELL, Hyrum	MAY 06 1817
THOMPSON, Nancy	FINSCEY, James	JUL 12 1824
THOMPSON, Nancy	OLIVER, James	DEC 12 1836
THOMPSON, Nancy	CADY, William A.	SEP 15 1849
THOMPSON, Nancy	GODDARD, John	DEC 30 1851
THOMPSON, Nancy V.	BIRCH, Joseph	JUN 10 1856
THOMPSON, Nicholas	BALLARD, Ann	SEP 19 1850
THOMPSON, Noemi	BOGAN, Martin V.B.	JUN 29 1853
THOMPSON, Oscar D.	SMITH, Susan E.	OCT 06 1847
THOMPSON, Phebe	TATE, Peter	FEB 05 1818
THOMPSON, Phoebe R.	STEVENSON, George W.	APR 24 1834
THOMPSON, Rachael	FRANKLIN, Thomas	FEB 07 1820
THOMPSON, Rachael	COUMBE, William	APR 06 1822
THOMPSON, Richard H.	BROWN, Hellen	FEB 05 1850
THOMPSON, Robert	WEBSTER, Harriet	JAN 28 1847
THOMPSON, Robert	KEMP, Mary A.	DEC 08 1853
THOMPSON, Robert E.	MIDDLETON, Agnes	JUL 01 1858
THOMPSON, Rosetta	HAZLE, Zachariah	OCT 10 1839
THOMPSON, Ruth	BENJAMIN, John	NOV 08 1841
THOMPSON, Samnes H.	COX, Mary J.	JAN 05 1857
THOMPSON, Samuel	SLACUM, Emmeline	OCT 29 1821
THOMPSON, Samuel	HEDGES, Susan R.	JUN 25 1834
THOMPSON, Samuel	KEETH, Susan	DEC 19 1850
THOMPSON, Sarah	SPALDING, Richard T.	NOV 16 1815
THOMPSON, Sarah	DUVALL, Perry	SEP 15 1834
THOMPSON, Sarah	CONNELLY, Thomas	AUG 14 1845
THOMPSON, Sarah	MARCEY, Robert H.	SEP 28 1857
THOMPSON, Sarah A.	POTTER, John	DEC 26 1833
THOMPSON, Sarah A.M.	DORAN, James	JUN 03 1858
THOMPSON, Sarah Catharine	DYER, Peter	SEP 24 1840
THOMPSON, Sarah Eleanor	WETHERELL, John	MAR 04 1823

District of Columbia Marriage Licenses, 1811-1858

THOMPSON, Sarah L.	PERKINS, Chas. A.	FEB 13 1855
THOMPSON, Sarah, Mrs.	THOMPSON, John A.	JAN 07 1836
THOMPSON, Smith	CLAGETT, Mary Ann	APR 23 1846
THOMPSON, Susan	LIVERPOOL, Moses	FEB 12 1813
THOMPSON, Susan Amelia	YEATMAN, Henry	MAY 14 1851
THOMPSON, Susanna E.	DUNN, George	JUN 13 1853
THOMPSON, Susannah	SEWALL, John	OCT 11 1813
THOMPSON, Susannah	BURCH, John	JAN 14 1836
THOMPSON, Susannah	ALLEN, Samuel E.	APR 21 1849
THOMPSON, Susannah M.	LUSBY, William Henry	DEC 27 1842
THOMPSON, Thomas W.	CORBIN, Frances C.	JAN 24 1854
THOMPSON, Thomas W.	WHELAN, Mahala C.	MAR 30 1857
THOMPSON, Vincent	SEYMORE, Carolin	OCT 15 1852
THOMPSON, Virginia	FOX, William	AUG 09 1852
THOMPSON, Wilkerson	HURLEY, Roberta	AUG 30 1853
THOMPSON, William	MADDOX, Susannah	OCT 30 1832
THOMPSON, William	MANTZ, Martha	MAY 18 1833
THOMPSON, William	DUNN, Amanda	MAY 10 1834
THOMPSON, William	HARMOND, Mary Ann	JUL 13 1837
THOMPSON, William	DELANO, Mary Elizabeth	APR 29 1843
THOMPSON, William	BAYLEY, Elizabeth	NOV 16 1844
THOMPSON, William	FREE, Louisa	JAN 21 1845
THOMPSON, William	ROBINSON, Margaret	JUL 06 1848
THOMPSON, William	JOHNSON, Mrs. Susan Ann	JUL 06 1858
THOMPSON, William B.	SMITH, Mary C.	FEB 15 1834
THOMPSON, William E.	KEY, Anna A.	OCT 21 1835
THOMPSON, William H.	ROBEY, Delila	JAN 10 1833
THOMPSON, William H.	PAYNE, Martha E.	MAR 16 1852
THOMPSON, William H.	DELANEY, Margaret	AUG 17 1852
THOMPSON, William H.	STEVENS, Isabella	SEP 13 1852
THOMPSON, William J.	HILTON, Ann Elizabeth	MAR 15 1848
THOMPSON, William, Jr.	BALTZER, Elizabeth	MAY 19 1814
THOMPSON, WIlliam	GRAY, Sarah Ann	NOV 18 1824
THOMPSON, Winney	DYER, Elias	SEP 17 1840
THOMPSON, Wm.	DURR, Elizabeth	OCT 21 1820
THOMPSON, Wm.	THOMAS, Martha	JAN 13 1846
THOMPSON, Wm. J.A.	DELOZIER, Ann	NOV 13 1838
THOMSON, Jane (blk)	JACKSON, Joseph	AUG 02 1851
THOMSON, Robert	MENGER, Ann [Mrs.]	MAY 24 1828
THORM, Darie	MOODIE, John	MAR 05 1820
THORN, Catharine A.B.	COX, Samuel A.	MAY 26 1841
THORN, Elizabeth	HENNING, Stephen	JUN 06 1833
THORN, Elizabeth	BELL, William	JAN 03 1855
THORN, Ellen	SHIRMAN, James W.	DEC 31 1857
THORN, Honora	TREATLOR, John	JUN 16 1840
THORN, John H.	ESPY, Margaret	DEC 04 1849
THORN, Joseph O.	DAVIS, Elizabeth H. [Mrs.]	JUN 02 1834
THORN, Judson H.	BOUCHER, Sarah E.	SEP 27 1850
THORN, Milly	PILES, William	JAN 16 1821
THORN, Owen	PIGGOTT, Margaret E.	JUL 23 1857
THORN, Thomas	MAHORNY, Elizabeth	OCT 29 1835
THORN, Victoria	WARREN, Robert	NOV 08 1856
THORN, William	KING, Norah	OCT 23 1830
THORN, William G.B.	McINTIRE, Anne	FEB 16 1858
THORN, William T.	WATSON, Agnes	OCT 29 1857
THORNBERRY, Daniel	LANGYHER, Frances	FEB 10 1824
THORNBERRY, John	SHENALT, Sarah	DEC 11 1824
THORNBERRY, Sarah C.	STIDHAM, George W.	AUG 27 1856

District of Columbia Marriage Licenses, 1811-1858

THORNBURY, Mary R.L.	HARRIS, Edward S.	OCT 21 1851
THORNE, John S.E.	PICKRELL, Ann W.	JUN 12 1849
THORNE, Mary J.	RABBITT, Samuel E.	SEP 21 1850
THORNLEY, Mary Smith	THORNTON, Henry F.	AUG 16 1847
THORNLEY, Thomas	McCOMB, Martha E.	FEB 20 1851
THORNTON, Ann G.	SPRIGG, Benjamin	NOV 05 1818
THORNTON, Bennitt W.	TAYLOR, Julia Ann	JAN 31 1837
THORNTON, Dennis	THORNTON, Mary Ann	FEB 13 1850
THORNTON, Dennis	ROWEN, Sarah	OCT 13 1852
THORNTON, Henry F.	THORNLEY, Mary Smith	AUG 16 1847
THORNTON, Jane E.B.	CHESLEY, Zadock C.	OCT 30 1817
THORNTON, Margaret E. [Mrs.]	CLARK, James [Hon.]	MAR 03 1829
THORNTON, Mary	SMITH, William	JUN 13 1822
THORNTON, Mary Ann	THORNTON, Dennis	FEB 13 1850
THORNTON, Mary Randolph	NAYLOR, William S.	MAR 12 1834
THORNTON, Owen	WELBY, Margaret	JUL 24 1857
THORNTON, Sarah J. (blk)	BECKETT, Theofolas	FEB 01 1853
THORNTON, Stewart	WILLIAMS, Elizabeth	SEP 30 1850
THORNTON, Stewart G.	STEWART, Adeline F.	JAN 31 1817
THORNTON, Thomas	CRONIN, Margaret	MAY 12 1857
THORNTON, Thomas	PRINGLE, Ellen F.	MAY 05 1858
THORNTON, Thomas C.	WHEAT, Elizabeth D.	JUL 04 1815
THORP, Emma R.	RIBAS, Antonio L.	FEB 06 1840
THORP, Evelina B.	BEACH, Albert H.	NOV 24 1847
THORP, Jane C.	REED, George F.	FEB 06 1847
THORPE, C.J.R.	DUNN, S.J.	OCT 20 1840
THORPE, Eliza	KING, Francis	JUN 07 1821
THORPE, Martha Ann	MILLER, Peter M.W.	OCT 23 1843
THOUR, Adam	OCKERT, Emily	APR 21 1853
THRALL, James	THRALL, Judith S.	OCT 10 1817
THRALL, Judith S.	THRALL, James	OCT 10 1817
THRELKELD, Jane	COX, John [Col.]	JAN 14 1818
THRELKIELD, James	OWENS, Ann	APR 30 1817
THRETKELD, Catharine	NASH, Michael	OCT 11 1827
THRIFFT, Stephen	STEWART, Mary Ann	FEB 19 1822
THRIFT, Ann A.	WATERS, Richard H.	JUN 16 1857
THRIFT, Colmore	RABBIT, Eliza Ellen	FEB 06 1827
THRIFT, James	BALL, Linah	MAY 22 1813
THROCKMORTON, Hannah (blk)	HOLLISTY, Chas.	APR 03 1856
THROLS, Elizabeth	DOWRY, Alonzo	MAR 11 1820
THRONEY, Bridget	MUDD, James	FEB 12 1858
THROOP, Kanarias	COVER, Daniel P.	DEC 22 1848
THROOP, Thomas S.	HUGULEY, Matilda L.	JUN 09 1823
THRUSTON, Alfred B.	GORDON, Fannie C.	JUL 22 1845
THRUSTON, Caroline (blk)	BONN, Ignatius	APR 30 1842
THRUSTON, Jeannette C.	POWELL, Levin M.	JAN 24 1842
THRUSTON, Sidney Ann	BRADLEY, William A.	AUG 03 1820
THUCKER, James	ELLIS, Mary Ann	DEC 31 1822
THUMBLERT, William H.	McKEWIN, Ann Maria	OCT 13 1841
THUMLERT, James E.	HEPBURN, Jane	JUN 19 1841
THUMLERT, William	YOUNG, Esther	DEC 30 1841
THURSBEY, Amy	MITCHELL, Singleton	FEB 05 1820
THURSBY, William	KIRKLEY, Sarah	FEB 26 1821
THURSDAY, Elizabeth	KIRK, John	MAR 07 1817
THUTTNER, Frances	GARSTINE, John	NOV 29 1853
THYSON, Emily C.	KENDRICK, George R.	JUN 26 1857
TIAR, William A.	RITCHIE, Ann H. [Mrs.]	OCT 21 1829
TIBER, Albert	KINK, Margaret	JUL 04 1852

District of Columbia Marriage Licenses, 1811-1858

TIDINGS, Sophia	CUDMORE, Paul	SEP 11 1813
TIE, Julia	COLDEN, James	AUG 07 1855
TIEFENBACK, Philip	HORNUNY, Ann C.	APR 19 1853
TIERNEY, Catherine	CASEY, John	SEP 06 1848
TIERNEY, Michael	CAHIL, Honora	NOV 11 1850
TIFFANY, Otis H.	HAMILTON, Eliza B.	DEC 26 1848
TILDEN, William Chas.	RIGGLES, Mary Ann	JUN 12 1851
TILGHMAN, Ann (blk)	THOMAS, William	OCT 19 1857
TILGHMAN, Henry	PEERCE, Rebecca	JUL 01 1834
TILGHMAN, Margaret	SLATER, James F.	DEC 30 1856
TILGHMAN, Mary Ann Caroline (blk)	THOMAS, Samuel M.	MAR 09 1848
TILGHMAN, Mary Jane (blk)	HOWARD, Henry	AUG 09 1842
TILGHMAN, Sharlotte (blk)	COLLINS, Frederick	DEC 21 1826
TILGHMAN, William	HALL, Charity	DEC 03 1823
TILLETT, Julila	GRAW, Thomas	FEB 02 1839
TILLETT, Margarett	BODINE, John	MAR 15 1815
TILLETT, Nancy Ann	SCOTT, Charles Emanuel	DEC 16 1848
TILLETT, Samuel	CURTAIN, Kitty	MAY 30 1812
TILLETT, William	NELSON, ELizabeth	JUN 21 1833
TILLEY, Barbara A.	HEAD, George M.	JUL 10 1851
TILLEY, Chs.	McLEOD, Mary	APR 02 1821
TILLEY, Eliza	BEALL, Richard M.	FEB 19 1827
TILLEY, Elizabeth	THOMPSON, Landon	MAY 19 1840
TILLEY, Elizabeth M.	ARNOLD, George	MAY 09 1854
TILLEY, Henry	WARENSFORD, Debby	JUN 21 1813
TILLEY, Henry	BROWN, Mary Ellen	MAY 02 1838
TILLEY, John	CLARKE, Ann	JUN 17 1835
TILLEY, Mary	WATKINS, William W.	OCT 04 1821
TILLINGHAST, Rebecca	WILLING, Charles	MAR 24 1840
TILLION, Juliet	SANSBERRY, James	MAR 29 1842
TILLMAN, Henry H.	REYNOLDS, Margaret Ann (blk)	SEP 30 1840
TILLMAN, Rachael	GAITHER, Edward	DEC 20 1827
TILLORE, Mary B.	MILES, Benjamin	JUN 19 1836
TILLY, Nancy	CULVER, William	JAN 09 1819
TILMAN, John	PAUNAM, Ann (blk)	JUN 17 1841
TILMAN, Mary	SOMERVILLE, Thomas	JAN 31 1843
TILSON, Jonathan, Rev.	ANDERSON, Martha D.	DEC 23 1851
TILTON, Warren	OULD, Sarah A.	FEB 24 1851
TIMBERLAKE, John	ANDERSON, Joeanas	APR 04 1839
TIMBERLAKE, John B.	O'NEALE, Margaret	JUN 15 1816
TIMBERLAKE, Margaret	EATON, John H.	JAN 01 1829
TIMBERLAKE, Margaret R.	RANDOLPH, John B.	JAN 16 1843
TIMBERLAKE, Sarah J.F.	BLACKLEY, John W.	MAR 26 1856
TIMMONS, Julia Ann	GROVES, Thomas	NOV 05 1849
TIMMS, Catherine	COUROD, Godfred	MAY 22 1822
TIMMS, Wm. L.	MORAN, Susan M.	MAR 21 1850
TIMON, Margaret	CAMPBELL, Peter	FEB 05 1856
TIMS, Ann	BARROTT, Sabriet Cissel	DEC 13 1814
TIMS, Sarah	ARNOLD, James	JUL 17 1830
TINAN, John	MURRAY, Catherine	DEC 22 1855
TINCH, Sarah	LLOYD, Adam	APR 09 1814
TINCY, Donotius	BOWIE, Matilda	SEP 09 1820
TINES, Mary	SHERWOOD, Perry	SEP 10 1851
TINGEY, Thomas [Capt.]	DELANY, Ann B.	DEC 09 1812
TINGSTRON, Mary A.	MANTZ, Frederick W.	APR 07 1840
TINKLER, Eliza	RIGGLES, James	AUG 20 1855
TINKLER, Samuel R.	LINKIN, Anna	SEP 11 1855
TINNEY, Charles	HOPKINS, Hannah	DEC 02 1817

District of Columbia Marriage Licenses, 1811-1858

TINNEY, Charles	JOHNSON, Susan (blk)	JUL 29 1840
TINNEY, Eliza Ann	WARNER, Nicholas	AUG 05 1847
TINNEY, Rachel Ann	GREEN, John	JAN 05 1843
TINNY, Ann (blk)	LUCUS, Carter	JUL 21 1827
TINNY, Margaret	McGARVEY, John	AUG 14 1858
TINSCEY, James	SCOTT, Elizabeth	APR 28 1815
TINSEY, William	ADAMS, Nancy	MAR 12 1816
TINSLEY, James	HIGGINS, Catherine	MAY 01 1856
TINSLEY, Sallie A.E.	COLEMAN, Hawes N.	OCT 20 1856
TINSLEY, W.T.	GREEN, Beattie T.	JAN 06 1849
TIPIT, John T.	BAYLISS, Margaret J.	APR 14 1857
TIPPETT, Caroline	COSTIGAN, James	SEP 27 1828
TIPPETT, Edward D.	TUCHEN, Gracy Ann	MAY 09 1827
TIPPETT, Ella A.	WHITTE, Chas. T.	FEB 13 1855
TIPPETT, Hezekiah	KING, Kitty Elizabeth	FEB 18 1824
TIPPETT, Joel	OWEN, Martha	APR 11 1844
TIPPETT, John	MOODY, Mary Ann	DEC 24 1831
TIPPETT, John A.	MOODY, Ann	SEP 01 1857
TIPPETT, Julia Ann	BARTON, Henry	OCT 11 1832
TIPPETT, Mary	BAWLDING, Judson	OCT 02 1823
TIPPETT, Mary Ann	BURR, Charles	MAR 26 1814
TIPPETT, Mary Ellen	BROWN, William M.	OCT 20 1853
TIPPETT, Mary M.	HUMES, Alexander	OCT 12 1853
TIPPETT, Matilda Jane	STROUD, George W.	JUN 09 1843
TIPPETT, Maxwell	BALDWIN, Jamima	AUG 21 1823
TIPPETT, Thomas J.N.	CHAMBERLAIN, Ann	AUG 09 1830
TIPPETT, William H.	BRANSON, Mary L.	DEC 03 1857
TIRPEN, James H.	THOMAS, Isabella	OCT 25 1838
TITLOO, David Arthur	SWEENY, Mary Ellen	DEC 28 1857
TITTROW, David A.	SWEENY, Mary E.	MAY 03 1858
TITUS, Samuel	McNEER, Martha	MAR 19 1850
TOBIAS, John	KEECH, Susan H.	JUL 22 1856
TOBIN, Ann	McNAMARA, Dennis	FEB 13 1854
TOBIN, Ellen	McGRATH, Michael	SEP 04 1852
TOBIN, James	O'BRIEN, Sarah	JAN 03 1852
TOBIN, James	RUSSELL, Mary	MAY 22 1858
TOBIN, John	WHELAN, Catharine E.	FEB 03 1824
TOBIN, Patrick	ROCHE, Catherine	JAN 09 1855
TOBIN, Patrick	RILEY, Ellen	AUG 21 1858
TOBIN, William	McNEMARA, Mary	JAN 11 1853
TODD, David S.	HUNTT, Lydia Catherine	MAY 23 1843
TODD, Eliza Ann	PEARSON, Edward D.	FEB 21 1845
TODD, Eliza Jane	RITTUE, Andrew J.	OCT 12 1852
TODD, Ellen G.	ASHBY, John R.	OCT 04 1848
TODD, John	ROBINSON, Jean	FEB 19 1829
TODD, John	CRAIG, Josephine S.	APR 19 1852
TODD, Mary	BRATCHER, Severn	MAR 02 1830
TODD, Samuel	WINDSOR, Mary	APR 20 1854
TODD, Samuel P.	DAWSON, Rebecca A.	JUN 24 1812
TODD, Seth J.	GILLISS, Leah Ann	SEP 14 1829
TODD, Thomas	WASHINGTON, Lucy	MAR 28 1812
TODD, William B.	GILLISS, Elizabeth J.	OCT 15 1832
TODD, [blank]	McGILL, [blank]	FEB 10 1857
TODDISON, Emily	NIGHTINGALE, Joseph	AUG 17 1839
TODHUNTER, Isaac C.	KEYWORTH, Emma	SEP 21 1852
TODTSCHINDER, John Adam Frederick	ERB, Wilhelmina	JUL 10 1847
TOFFER, Elizabeth	HOFFMEISTER, George	JUN 19 1855
TOLBERT, Ann	JAVINS, George	APR 16 1835

District of Columbia Marriage Licenses, 1811-1858

TOLBERT, Charles	TOLBERT, Margaret	DEC 20 1814
TOLBERT, Elizabeth	COOK, Samuel	SEP 28 1813
TOLBERT, Margaret	TOLBERT, Charles	DEC 20 1814
TOLBURT, Mary Ann A.	WALTER, John H.	SEP 13 1831
TOLDBRIDGE, Elizabeth	STEWART, Robert	DEC 19 1838
TOLES, Ann Maria	BROWN, Lewis S.	MAR 26 1832
TOLGLASE, Benjamin	CROWN, Martha E.	FEB 26 1853
TOLIN, Jane	MURPHY, Morris	SEP 03 1855
TOLLANSBEE, Joseph	KESSUCK, Eliza	MAY 04 1819
TOLLE, Susan	TOLLE, Thomas N.	MAR 13 1828
TOLLE, Thomas N.	TOLLE, Susan	MAR 13 1828
TOLLIVER, Harriet	STEEL, Martin	MAY 27 1826
TOLLIVER, Martha	FOLEY, James	OCT 07 1828
TOLSON, Alexander H.	TALIAFERRO, Helen B.	DEC 06 1842
TOLSON, Alexr.	[blank], Ellen	JUL 04 1816
TOLSON, Douglas	GORDON, Rebecca	MAR 07 1850
TOLSON, Maria	COLE, Charles	SEP 18 1832
TOLSON, Overton Addison	NAYLOR, Lettice Ann	OCT 10 1842
TOLSON, Watkins	NAYLOR, Virlinder E.E.	JAN 17 1844
TOLTON, Mary E.	GOUSHA, Napoleon B.	MAR 15 1856
TOLTY, Thomas H.	COLLIER, Mary	MAY 12 1855
TOMBS, Henry M.	CULLISS, Jane M.	NOV 29 1822
TOMILTY, Hugh	DORN, Mary	NOV 10 1851
TOMKINS, Lucinda	YATES, John L.	JUL 25 1826
TOMPKINS, Benjamin G.	LATIMER, Julia	OCT 01 1845
TOMPKINS, Caleb	DAVIS, Elizabeth	JAN 01 1821
TOMPKINS, William	SEMMES, Mary Ann	JAN 13 1829
TONE, Jeannete	WATERHOLDNER, Frederick W.	NOV 17 1856
TONGE, John	BUTLER, Margt. Ellen	SEP 17 1846
TONGE, Mary	BATES, William	MAY 11 1843
TONGE, Richard	CLARKE, Ellen	MAR 04 1851
TONGE, Susan Vaux	McNAMEE, Charles	OCT 20 1841
TONGE, Thomas	DORRETT, Elizabeth	DEC 31 1844
TOOKER, Lansing	WILSON, Susan	AUG 24 1835
TOOLE, Margaret	GAHAN, Peter W.	AUG 06 1855
TOOLE, Peter	LYDON, Mary	JUN 28 1856
TOOMBS, Letha	HICKS, Wade H.	AUG 31 1858
TOOMBS, Sallie	DeBOSE, Dudley McJ.	APR 15 1858
TOOMEY, Ann	WILLIAMSON, Joseph	FEB 19 1846
TOOMEY, Ann	McCARROLL, Owen	JUL 05 1851
TOOMEY, Isabella	MURRAY, William	DEC 03 1846
TOOMEY, Jeremiah	O'LEARY, Ellen	JAN 11 1848
TOOMEY, Michael	REARDON, Catherine	SEP 30 1851
TOOTELL, Rosana	EVANS, Daniel	SEP 11 1818
TOPFER, Herman	REPP, Sophia	OCT 11 1855
TOPHAM, George	KING, Margaret	DEC 11 1833
TOPHAM, James S.	WHITE, Ann M.M.	APR 06 1858
TOPHAN, Phobe E.	BROWN, Cumberland G.	JAN 16 1856
TOPMAN, Alfred	BURLEY, Clarisa (blk)	DEC 12 1839
TOPPING, Barbara Ann (blk)	SMITH, Oliver James	FEB 06 1847
TOPPING, Elisha	DAVIS, Emely (blk)	FEB 22 1844
TOPPING, Evert M.	HEBB, Sallie B.	JUL 22 1850
TOPPING, Nathan H.	CULVERWELL, Mary E.	JUN 10 1848
TORBERT, James McClyment	PEYTON, Mary Elizabeth	AUG 02 1836
TORP, Martha	PEARSON, John	FEB 01 1856
TORPEY, John	O'DEA, Margaret	APR 02 1858
TORRENCE, James	DIDENHOVER, Ann	DEC 05 1822
TORRENS, Manuel	BUTLER, Flavillar	JUL 07 1827

District of Columbia Marriage Licenses, 1811-1858

TORREYSON, John N.	GORDON, Eliza J.	JUN 05 1855
TOTTEN, Catlyna Tillman	TEMPLE, William Greenville	OCT 06 1851
TOTTEN, Susan M.	TELFORD, Charles L.	NOV 15 1842
TOTTEN, Vianna	WEEKS, Joseph	MAY 17 1854
TOUCHEREZ, Estelle M.	THOMPSON, George	JUL 24 1832
TOUHY, Hugh	DOWNEY, Bridget	FEB 09 1848
TOUPET, Francis	BARNETT, Rebecca	MAR 31 1812
TOWERS, John	BAILEY, Susan Burrows	DEC 11 1834
TOWERS, William	MOORE, Mary Mitchell	MAY 23 1831
TOWERS, William	FLOOD, Sarah	APR 21 1858
TOWERS, Wm. H.H.	IRWING, Agnes V.	JAN 20 1857
TOWMY, Mary	FEUTER, Nicholas	APR 12 1834
TOWNER, James L.	ENGLISH, Jennie	JUN 03 1857
TOWNLEY, Eugene	KING, Maria	APR 14 1847
TOWNLEY, James	KNOWLES, Sarah	FEB 15 1816
TOWNLEY, Maria Virginia Antoinetta	AHRENS, Adolph F.	AUG 05 1846
TOWNSAND, Heneretta	CALHOUND, William	FEB 10 1820
TOWNSAND, Mary	LIGHTNER, John T.	DEC 30 1851
TOWNSEND, Bridgett Ann	COFFER, Joseph	NOV 29 1838
TOWNSEND, Catharine (blk)	KING, Charles	OCT 07 1852
TOWNSEND, Edward Davis	WAINWRIGHT, Ann Overing	MAY 08 1848
TOWNSEND, Eliza	BARRY, Richard	SEP 06 1828
TOWNSEND, Elizabeth	STANDFORD, Henry	NOV 05 1828
TOWNSEND, Jeremiah A.	MIX, Mary C.	MAY 12 1825
TOWNSEND, Lemuel	LABILLE, Elenora	DEC 24 1841
TOWNSEND, Lucinda Ann	SEXSMITH, William	AUG 21 1837
TOWNSEND, Mary A.	SANDERS, Daniel N.	MAR 13 1856
TOWNSEND, Mary Ann (blk)	NORTH, Henry	NOV 08 1825
TOWNSEND, Mathias B.	ROBEY, Elizabeth A.	NOV 29 1853
TOWNSEND, Sarah	LYNDALL, George	JAN 12 1837
TOWNSON, Sophia (blk)	CRAWFORD, William	OCT 14 1852
TOWSON, Caroline Evaline Archer	CALDWELL, William Mackey	NOV 21 1846
TOWSON, Charles	SHAW, Mary	AUG 27 1831
TOWSON, Joshua	FARREL, Mary	JUL 29 1817
TOWSON, Wm. B.	MARKS, Mary Ann	DEC 21 1854
TOY, Reuben	BOYD, Maria (blk)	NOV 25 1845
TRACER, Sally	FATTREL, Jacob	SEP 03 1822
TRACEY, Catharine	QUINN, Christopher	SEP 23 1853
TRACEY, Frances	JACKSON, John W.	OCT 30 1839
TRACEY, James M.	LUCKET, Amanda	JUL 02 1831
TRACEY, Jane	EASTON, Hezekiah	JUL 05 1815
TRACEY, Joseph	SWEENY, Joanna K.	MAY 28 1853
TRACEY, Noland	BLUNDEN, Jane	NOV 10 1843
TRACY, Amanda [Mrs.]	McCREY, John	SEP 13 1834
TRACY, Catherine	MACKIN, Patrick	AUG 02 1836
TRACY, Elizabeth	CRANDE, William	MAY 06 1818
TRACY, Harriot	MacELEGET, James	APR 15 1830
TRACY, Jane	BROOKS, Samuel D.	JUN 25 1850
TRACY, John	MORGAN, Charlotte	DEC 15 1821
TRACY, John T.	HARDIN, Mary	SEP 15 1846
TRACY, William	WHALING, Sarah Ann	JUN 21 1847
TRAHEAN, Priscilla	TRAHEAN, Thomas	JUL 25 1839
TRAHEAN, Thomas	TRAHEAN, Priscilla	JUL 25 1839
TRAIL, Catharine	RICKETS, Edward	JAN 13 1829
TRAIL, Elizabeth	McDERMOTT, John	OCT 09 1819
TRAIL, Richard F.	STONE, Elizabeth E.	JUN 18 1850
TRAINER, William W.	CLAYTON, Elizabeth A.	NOV 24 1850
TRAMMEL, Margaret	ADAMS, West	MAR 14 1816

District of Columbia Marriage Licenses, 1811-1858

TRAMMELL, George W.	CARLISLE, Rachel N.	APR 23 1857
TRAMMELL, Jarrett B.	DAILY, Bytha	APR 13 1837
TRAMMELL, John L.	TARMON, Rebecca	APR 21 1849
TRAMMELL, Washington	HONEST, Martha (blk)	OCT 05 1857
TRAMMELL, William W.	JONES, Rebecca	OCT 30 1830
TRAMMILL, Martha Ann	ROLLINS, William R.	MAR 10 1857
TRANIVER, Meredith	TATE, Francis	AUG 22 1835
TRANNELL, John	MATEER, Jane R.	JUN 13 1840
TRAVASS, Mile	DORSET, Ann	DEC 21 1827
TRAVERS, Drusilla	WHETCROFT, William W.	JAN 01 1828
TRAVERS, Elias	WARNER, Mary E.	JAN 20 1855
TRAVERS, Eliza (blk)	GRANDISON, Benjamin	AUG 26 1850
TRAVERS, Eliza (blk)	CARPENTER, William	MAY 24 1853
TRAVERS, Eliza Ann	GARRARD, George	APR 19 1816
TRAVERS, Elizabeth	TAYLOR, William	JUN 05 1839
TRAVERS, Elizabeth H.	FECHTIG, Louis R.	FEB 06 1849
TRAVERS, Hester Ann	STOVER, Solomon	JUN 04 1851
TRAVERS, John	CAUSIN, Elizabeth	APR 22 1824
TRAVERS, John	BARKER, Mary	NOV 22 1849
TRAVERS, John	RIGNEY, Bridget	JUN 12 1858
TRAVERS, John Clinton	WISE, Mary Ellen	JUN 25 1856
TRAVERS, John W.	DYER, Rachel	FEB 26 1851
TRAVERS, Levin	MILSTEAD, Elizabeth	JUL 12 1825
TRAVERS, Martha Ann	KEEFE, John P.	MAR 04 1848
TRAVERS, Mary	DANEOLD, Francis Henry	JUN 01 1836
TRAVERS, Mary	WINNE, James	FEB 27 1838
TRAVERS, Nicholas	KILLIAM, Mary Margt.	DEC 28 1846
TRAVERS, Rebecca	DYER, Robert	OCT 08 1851
TRAVERS, Sydney Virginia	MITCHELL, William	AUG 09 1848
TRAVERS, William	INGRAM, Elizabeth	AUG 26 1831
TRAVERSE, John C.	WISE, Martha E.	SEP 19 1857
TRAYLOR, Richard	BRIGGS, Virginia P.	NOV 08 1836
TREACY, Nancy	ROWLINS, Jonathan	JAN 10 1816
TREADWAY, Louis Demas	FALES, Ferolin Amelia	MAY 11 1852
TREADWELL, Thomas	MATTHEWS, Catharine	JUN 10 1812
TREAKLE, Elizabeth	DELLA, Andrew	AUG 10 1852
TREAKLE, Mary	RHODES, Varnell	AUG 05 1812
TREDWAY, John	NOERR, Mary M.	OCT 30 1855
TREE, Jos. B.	EVANS, Frances L.	FEB 14 1850
TREE, Margaret	OSBOURN, William F.	OCT 11 1826
TREIGLER, Elizabeth	PUDROUSKY, Theodore	FEB 12 1849
TRENHOLM, John Howard	BELT, Ann Rosina	SEP 21 1842
TRENNELL, Julia	CROSS, Alexander	APR 22 1837
TRENT, Robert W.	DAVIS, Mary E.	AUG 13 1858
TRENT, Thomas H.	SALE, Jane F.	DEC 15 1846
TRETLER, John	HOUX, Rebecca	FEB 03 1831
TRETLER, John H.	DOUGHRITY, Fanny	JUL 10 1856
TRETLIER, Margaret	KEITH, John	MAY 17 1831
TRETLOR, John	THORN, Honora	JUN 16 1840
TRETTER, Sarah	SHAY, Rlijah	MAY 02 1816
TREXLER, Margaret	ESCHBACK, John	OCT 02 1821
TREXLER, Peter	BALL, Martha	MAR 05 1853
TREXLER, Samuel P.	DODD, Sabra Ann	FEB 03 1851
TRICE, Delelah	BEARDS, John	JUN 01 1826
TRICE, Richard	SMOOT, Sarah	JUN 21 1832
TRIDLE, John	GREEN, Frances	NOV 30 1850
TRIDLE, William	ROLLINS, Sally	DEC 31 1824
TRIGER, Lavina	SMITH, Thomas	JAN 09 1840

District of Columbia Marriage Licenses, 1811-1858

TRIMBLE, Jacob B.	BARRY, Mary	JUN 22 1848
TRIMMILL, Elizabeth	DOVE, Joseph	NOV 04 1824
TRINE, Henry	GIBERSON, Louisa M.	JUL 14 1853
TRIPLETT, Rebecca	POSEY, Middleton	MAY 05 1851
TRIPLETT, Ross	COE, Willie Ann (blk)	MAY 16 1856
TRIPLETT, Thos.	MILLER, Hannah C.	FEB 13 1823
TRIPLETTE, Susannah B.	ELY, Albert W.	JAN 14 1856
TRIPP, Mary Virginia	SCHERER, John F.	JUN 25 1853
TRIPPLETT, Thomas M.	HOWARD, Ellen F.	NOV 16 1853
TRITTLE, Walter A.	WALKER, Dorcas Ann	MAR 06 1832
TRIVIS, Augustus	BALTIMORE, Elizth. (blk)	MAY 20 1852
TROLLERS, Celeney	McKEEVERS, Thomas	MAR 18 1851
TROOK, John N.	CONN, Susan C.	SEP 26 1833
TROTER, Charlotte Maria	CLARKE, George W.	APR 29 1858
TROTT, William T.	McINTEER, Mary E.	DEC 17 1851
TROUP, Margaret Ann	ANDISON, Sanford	JUN 28 1821
TROUTMAN, John	HUDGINS, Tamezene	MAY 22 1858
TROUTMANN, Anna Barbara	BIHLER, Gottlieb	OCT 26 1846
TRUCK, Elizabeth	RENNOLDS, Gassaway	FEB 07 1850
TRUCKSELL, Francis	LEWIS, Martha	JAN 24 1856
TRUCKSON, Eliza	RATCLIFFE, Charles	JAN 01 1828
TRUCKSON, Margaret	POWERS, William	APR 29 1829
TRUDER, Samuel	SCOTT, Mary	JAN 12 1856
TRUE, Edwin E.	ANGEL, Mary Ellen	OCT 01 1851
TRUE, Mary Jane	STUDDS, George	JUN 21 1854
TRUEMAN, Josiah	LANGFITT, Martha	MAR 08 1853
TRUEMAN, William	ELLIOTT, Martha Ann	APR 02 1856
TRUITTE, Mary DeLa	BASTEANELLI, Titus	NOV 13 1846
TRULL, John	MOULDEN, Eliza	MAR 10 1834
TRUMAN, Henry	SMITH, Mary	OCT 03 1843
TRUMAN, Jane	IDDINS, Frederick	APR 29 1840
TRUMBULL, Jannet	McDONOUGH, James	AUG 14 1847
TRUMMINS, Mary	ZIER, Charles	OCT 26 1853
TRUMP, Mary	ATKINSON, Guy C.	MAY 18 1844
TRUNALE, Lawson	RATCLIFFE, Catherine	JAN 09 1826
TRUNDELL, Leah	MARTIN, Elijah	FEB 11 1812
TRUNNEL, Caroline E.	KELEHER, Thos. H.	OCT 25 1855
TRUNNEL, John H.	REMINGTON, Jane Roberta	DEC 06 1842
TRUNNEL, Laura S.	OFFUTT, Cornelius A.	AUG 18 1857
TRUNNEL, Sarah	MARTIN, Richard	DEC 22 1818
TRUNNELL, Ann C.	BROWN, Addison	DEC 11 1850
TRUNNELL, Chelotte	JEFFERSON, William	NOV 14 1838
TRUNNELL, Henrietta	CALLAHER, James	AUG 19 1837
TRUNNELL, Henry	LACY, Elizabeth Ann	DEC 21 1818
TRUNNELL, Henry	ST. JOHNS, Margarett	MAY 12 1855
TRUNNELL, Lawson	GODDARD, Ann	FEB 18 1833
TRUNNELL, Mary Ann	EDMONSTON, Chas. T.	FEB 27 1850
TRUNNELL, Mary Elizabeth	VANCE, Samuel	FEB 16 1846
TRUNNELL, Rezin	ADAMS, Ann Maria	OCT 19 1833
TRUNNELL, Richard H.	CUNNINGHAM, Margaret P.	FEB 19 1852
TRUNNELL, Sarah Ann Eliza	RAGAN, Daniel	DEC 12 1833
TRUNNELL, Sarah S.	HOUSE, Horace H.B.	FEB 23 1843
TRUNNELL, Silas	ROBBINS, Elizabeth	NOV 16 1855
TRUNNELL, Thomas	CONOWAY, Mary	FEB 06 1851
TRUNNELL, William D.	WEBB, Elizabeth C.	MAY 28 1850
TRUNNELL, William J.	DEAN, Julia Ann	AUG 05 1847
TRUSCOTT, Elizabeth	McFARLAND, William	MAR 19 1821
TRUSCOTT, John	GRAFLY, Margaret	MAY 24 1843

District of Columbia Marriage Licenses, 1811-1858

TRUSLER, Jane	KING, James H.	JUN 22 1854
TRUSSLER, Catherine	SUTTON, Washington	OCT 04 1853
TRUSSLER, Sarah	PULEM, Francis	DEC 04 1844
TRUX, Ann	ANDERSON, William	DEC 24 1823
TRUXEL, Sarah	KUHNS, William	OCT 03 1831
TRUXEL, William	CLARKE, Ann	JUN 08 1830
TRUXELL, Catharine	REGLIEN, Frederic	APR 08 1823
TRUXON, Sarah	SLATFIRD, James	JUN 20 1853
TRUXTON, William	WILBURN, Matilda	FEB 26 1829
TRUXTUN, Gertrude Parker	HOUSTON, John Hopkins	OCT 17 1825
TSCHEFFELLY, Charles	TSCHEFFELLY, Rosetta	MAR 28 1844
TSCHEFFELLY, Rosetta	TSCHEFFELLY, Charles	MAR 28 1844
TSCHIFFELY, Adela	GRAHAM, Andrew	DEC 31 1832
TSCHIFFELY, Catharine Emily	WILSON, John	JUN 06 1833
TSCHIFFELY, Charles A.G.	McINTOSH, Maddalina S.A.	DEC 03 1833
TSCHIFFELY, Charlotte L.	THOMPSON, Joseph	JAN 17 1839
TSCHIFFELY, Eliza	GORDON, Obadiah	JUN 18 1831
TSCHIFFELY, Elizabeth G.	DEEBLE, Joseph A.	AUG 15 1844
TSCHIFFELY, Louis S.	MILLER, Eliza	NOV 29 1825
TSCHIFFILY, Frederick A.	BERRY, Elizabeth A.W.	JUL 20 1840
TSCHISFFELY, Elizabeth A.	BROOKS, John T.	AUG 25 1852
TUBBAFIELD, William	McALLISTER, Catharine	DEC 05 1825
TUBMAN, George M.	McDANIEL, Mary E.	JUL 10 1827
TUBMAN, George W.	DEMENT, Laura	DEC 08 1857
TUCHEN, Gracy Ann	TIPPETT, Edward D.	MAY 09 1827
TUCKER, Ann	CURTIS, Thomas	NOV 10 1829
TUCKER, Ann	LIZER, Cornelius	MAY 13 1845
TUCKER, Anna E.	TAYLOR, Charles H.	AUG 30 1854
TUCKER, Charles C.	CROSS, Mary Virginia	APR 20 1853
TUCKER, Charles H.	GITTINGS, Elizabeth A.	FEB 07 1856
TUCKER, Charlott	CROWN, Samuel	JUN 04 1829
TUCKER, Christiana	DORSEY, Francis	JUN 03 1850
TUCKER, Daniel	JONES, Mary	NOV 15 1849
TUCKER, Durbin	DOVE, Sarah Ann	SEP 04 1854
TUCKER, Eliza S.	STELLWAGEN, Charles K.	DEC 31 1842
TUCKER, Elizabeth	MYERS, Frederick	JUN 07 1813
TUCKER, Elizabeth	GRIFFIN, Raphael	MAY 30 1814
TUCKER, Elizabeth	MARTIN, John	SEP 08 1832
TUCKER, Elizabeth	WILLIAMSON, Edward	AUG 14 1856
TUCKER, Elizabeth A.	HYDE, Richard A.	JUL 03 1854
TUCKER, Elizth.	MILBOURN, John	AUG 17 1821
TUCKER, Emilie W.	ROPES, Archer	JAN 07 1852
TUCKER, Emma Virginia	SCOTT, Richard K.	MAR 14 1850
TUCKER, Enoch	McPHERSON, Janet	OCT 03 1815
TUCKER, Enoch G.	PUMPHREY, Susanna	AUG 23 1843
TUCKER, Enoch G.	PUMPHREY, Susanna	OCT 23 1843
TUCKER, Frances	BURNES, Samuel	AUG 22 1854
TUCKER, Francis Asbury	CARTER, Elizabeth	SEP 27 1837
TUCKER, Geo. H.	DUNNING, Margaret	APR 12 1831
TUCKER, Harriot	RILEY, Thomas	APR 29 1812
TUCKER, Henry	LANHAM, Eleanor	APR 26 1831
TUCKER, Henry	GINGLEE, Lucinda	MAR 25 1849
TUCKER, Henry H.	MOBLEY, Linney Ann	MAY 28 1832
TUCKER, James	TUCKER, Mary	APR 26 1833
TUCKER, James	MADDOX, Jane	DEC 27 1849
TUCKER, James F.	BOSWELL, Susan E.	AUG 08 1849
TUCKER, James H.	GRUGLES, Harriet Ann	MAR 05 1844
TUCKER, James M.	THOMAS, William	OCT 17 1843

District of Columbia Marriage Licenses, 1811-1858

TUCKER, James M.	ALDEN, Mary L.	MAR 09 1858
TUCKER, Jeannette	BARKER, Irwin S.	MAY 08 1851
TUCKER, John A.	CROSS, Sarah C.	OCT 21 1856
TUCKER, John F.	KEALEY, Jane Euphrasia	AUG 02 1834
TUCKER, John H.	McPHERSON, Sarah Ann	NOV 05 1829
TUCKER, John W.	HURLEY, Sarah Elizth.	JAN 07 1856
TUCKER, Josephine	CURNEY, Alexander	AUG 14 1855
TUCKER, Levi	BENNET, Margaret	MAR 08 1831
TUCKER, Levin	PEARSON, Sarah	OCT 14 1830
TUCKER, Lizzie C.	MOSES, Simpson P.	JUL 05 1849
TUCKER, M. Virginia	LANDSTREET, William T.	MAY 24 1854
TUCKER, Margaret	SHECKLES, Levi	OCT 17 1826
TUCKER, Margaret	BARTLEY, Walter	JUN 12 1838
TUCKER, Maria S.	WILLIAMS, Samuel L.	MAY 20 1847
TUCKER, Mary	BARNES, Robert	JUN 05 1817
TUCKER, Mary	TUCKER, James	APR 26 1833
TUCKER, Mary	BROWN, James	OCT 05 1850
TUCKER, Mary E.	JONES, John G.	OCT 25 1816
TUCKER, Mary J.	BRAXTON, John T.	OCT 25 1854
TUCKER, Maurice	KILLMON, Sarah A.	FEB 08 1856
TUCKER, Melinda	TUCKER, Nathan	JUN 10 1830
TUCKER, Nathan	TUCKER, Melinda	JUN 10 1830
TUCKER, Patsey	COOKE, Zadack	SEP 13 1836
TUCKER, Richard	MURPHEY, Emily	DEC 23 1830
TUCKER, Samuel	HODGKIN, Malinda	SEP 12 1816
TUCKER, Samuel	MOORE, Mary	DEC 26 1822
TUCKER, Samuel	RICHARDS, Elizabeth	JUL 20 1825
TUCKER, Samuel W.	COLLINS, Martha E.	JUN 28 1839
TUCKER, Sarah	ANDERSON, Jesse	FEB 22 1827
TUCKER, Sarah	GRIMES, Henry	AUG 20 1835
TUCKER, Sarah C.	WALKER, Thomas H.	NOV 19 1856
TUCKER, Susan	MATTHEWS, James	APR 12 1817
TUCKER, Susan J.	JACKSON, Andrew M.	APR 01 1828
TUCKER, Sylas	HILL, Elizabeth Ann	FEB 22 1849
TUCKER, Thomas	MARTIN, Henrietta W.	NOV 02 1847
TUCKER, Thomas	STROAM, Margaret	MAY 28 1849
TUCKER, William	FARRALL, Sarah	OCT 24 1833
TUCKER, William	YOUNG, Elizabeth Margaret	JAN 07 1836
TUCKER, William H.	POWERS, Sophia	JAN 17 1843
TUCKER, William Henry	TURTON, Ann E.	DEC 13 1838
TUCKER, William N.	BEACHUM, Fenton Sarah	AUG 04 1858
TUCKER, William T.	MAHORNEY, Mary E.	AUG 10 1850
TUCKSON, Francis (blk)	DYSON, Robert H.	JAN 31 1853
TUCKSON, Rachel (blk)	NEWMAN, George	FEB 24 1853
TUDGE, William	FASNAUGHT, Margaret	AUG 10 1854
TUEL, Ann	FREE, John B.	DEC 25 1826
TUEL, Erasmus	TUEL, Sarah	JUL 10 1813
TUEL, Mary I.	RITTER, Francis D.	JUL 19 1834
TUEL, Sarah	TUEL, Erasmus	JUL 10 1813
TUELL, Ann	FREE, Ignatius	MAY 12 1827
TUELL, Laurence A.	DOUGLASS, Ann E.	SEP 30 1841
TUELL, Rebecca	WILLIAMS, David	APR 14 1834
TUFTS, Almanza	WEEMS, Mary S.	JUL 02 1855
TUHEY, Jeremiah	THOMAS, Jane	AUG 14 1852
TULEY, Joseph	JACKSON, Mary W. [Mrs.]	APR 20 1835
TULL, Lucy	MILBURN, Joseph	APR 18 1829
TULL, Sarah	MILLER, George W.	APR 02 1829
TUNE, Steptoe T.	CLARKE, Mary A.	SEP 29 1846

District of Columbia Marriage Licenses, 1811-1858

TUNEY, William	CHURCH, Comfort	JUL 17 1844
TUNGEL, Ernst	WITHAFT, Louisa	JUN 19 1852
TUNION, Robert	WILLIAMS, Elizth. (blk)	JUN 11 1846
TUNSTILL, George N.	CRUMP, Margaret S.	FEB 11 1853
TURBY, Martha	TENNISON, John	JUN 28 1850
TURLEY, George	SMITH, Joanna (blk)	JUN 15 1852
TURLEY, John M.	FREEMAN, Julia P. (blk)	SEP 26 1850
TURNBALL, Jane A.	SPELCER, Richard D.	MAR 11 1837
TURNBULL, Catharine	FRICK, George P.	APR 27 1854
TURNBULL, William [Lieut.]	RAMSAY, Jane G.	JAN 05 1827
TURNBURK, George	SWAIN, Harriet S.	SEP 11 1856
TURNBURKE, Francis	MURPHY, Mary Jane	OCT 17 1854
TURNER, Abraham	GREEN, Emily	MAR 12 1834
TURNER, Ann A. (blk)	WILLIAMS, Robt.	AUG 02 1855
TURNER, Ann P.	CONNELL, James	JAN 26 1833
TURNER, Aquila	TURNER, Kitty S.	FEB 22 1841
TURNER, Betsey	KING, Andrew	NOV 13 1828
TURNER, Catharine	KING, Elijah	JUN 01 1820
TURNER, Catharine A.	HITCHCOCK, Josiah	AUG 05 1850
TURNER, Catherine C.	THOMAS, Jno. M.	MAY 12 1823
TURNER, Catherine P.	BARNACLO, Richard W.	FEB 21 1854
TURNER, Charles	ELMORE, Elizabeth	MAY 25 1833
TURNER, Charles William	LYMBURN, Nancy Pearson	MAY 22 1833
TURNER, Christa (blk)	HAYS, James	JUN 26 1851
TURNER, Chs.	BRIGHT, Maria	FEB 27 1821
TURNER, Cordelia	MITCHELL, William	JAN 29 1845
TURNER, Daniel	STEWART, Mary Ann	SEP 23 1817
TURNER, Daniel [Hon.]	KEY, Anna	FEB 18 1829
TURNER, Daniel	JONES, Elizabeth (blk)	JUN 02 1857
TURNER, Elbert	EDMUNSTON, Ann	JAN 30 1839
TURNER, Eliza	DAVIS, Thomas	NOV 24 1819
TURNER, Eliza	SIMMS, Josiah (blk)	OCT 12 1848
TURNER, Eliza Eleanor	KELLY, Richard	OCT 02 1840
TURNER, Eliza K.	WOOD, Frederick	JUL 18 1820
TURNER, Elizabeth	FARREL, John	AUG 22 1826
TURNER, Elizabeth	BARTLEY, James T.	FEB 22 1842
TURNER, Elizabeth	BOWEN, James A.	JUL 19 1843
TURNER, Elizabeth (blk)	GLASCOW, John	OCT 19 1857
TURNER, Elizabeth J.	HUNT, Theodore J.	JUN 26 1856
TURNER, Elizabeth W.	HAMBLETON, Samuel	SEP 02 1834
TURNER, Ellen (blk)	GRAY, James	SEP 07 1844
TURNER, Frances H.P.	ROBINSON, William	AUG 04 1829
TURNER, George	WHITE, Caroline	AUG 02 1838
TURNER, Goalin	BOWEN, Martha	JAN 19 1847
TURNER, Hannah N. (blk)	HUNTER, George	SEP 25 1850
TURNER, Harriott R.	JONES, Joseph C.	MAR 13 1834
TURNER, Henry	BELL, Sarah	DEC 21 1824
TURNER, Isabella	HOYE, Thomas	FEB 22 1830
TURNER, Isabella S.	YANCEY, Joel	OCT 01 1840
TURNER, James	McLEOD, Jane Mary	APR 13 1838
TURNER, James	RUSSELL, Francis (blk)	FEB 01 1844
TURNER, James	GIDDINGS, Pricilla Ann	FEB 17 1846
TURNER, Jane	DUVALL, Alexander	JUN 06 1834
TURNER, Jane (blk)	BUDD, William	JUN 03 1851
TURNER, Jasper	STEPHENSON, Sophia	NOV 28 1822
TURNER, John	IRELAND, Elizabeth	NOV 18 1815
TURNER, John	GODMAN, Elizabeth	OCT 04 1843
TURNER, John	FITZGERALD, Johanna	SEP 26 1854

District of Columbia Marriage Licenses, 1811-1858

TURNER, John W.	UNDERWOOD, Rachel	JAN 20 1812
TURNER, John W.	BEALL, Ann	DEC 08 1831
TURNER, Kitty S.	TURNER, Aquila	FEB 22 1841
TURNER, Laura A.	FARLEY, Edward W.	DEC 10 1851
TURNER, Letetia	ALLEN, William	APR 08 1839
TURNER, Louisa	BURNS, Laurence	DEC 12 1857
TURNER, Margaret	AIRY, Samuel	AUG 06 1846
TURNER, Mariam	CLARK, Samuel	FEB 04 1845
TURNER, Martha Jane	DORNOLD, Parkerson	APR 03 1837
TURNER, Martha P.T.	SHEPPERD, A.H. [Hon. Augustine]	FEB 24 1830
TURNER, Mary	BEALL, Andrew	OCT 18 1817
TURNER, Mary A.	WALLINGSFORD, Washington	FEB 20 1840
TURNER, Mary Ann	ARGILL, Lewis	JUN 19 1826
TURNER, Mary Ann Davis	BURRISS, Thomas	JUL 07 1828
TURNER, Mary Ann	MILES, William	DEC 16 1830
TURNER, Mary Ann	KELLY, Barnard	NOV 17 1830
TURNER, Mary Ann Amanda	CRAWFORD, James	MAR 10 1855
TURNER, Mary Elizabeth	REDDEN, Thomas	AUG 21 1845
TURNER, Penny	MOODY, Henry	NOV 04 1819
TURNER, Peter	MASON, Mary	NOV 08 1855
TURNER, Phame, Mrs.	LOMAX, John	AUG 03 1850
TURNER, Rebecca	WEBB, Aquilla	JAN 19 1826
TURNER, Rebecca	MORSELL, Samuel	APR 24 1828
TURNER, Richard	BEALL, Sarah	MAR 28 1833
TURNER, Richard	LACEY, Mary Ann (blk)	SEP 16 1851
TURNER, Samuel	WINGERD, Mary E.	MAR 17 1858
TURNER, Sarah Ann	JONES, Jeremiah	JAN 17 1839
TURNER, Susan	HOYE, Enoch	DEC 21 1831
TURNER, Susan	COYLE, James	DEC 14 1839
TURNER, Susan	FREE, William	MAR 21 1845
TURNER, Tebitha Ann	OWENS, Basil	MAR 18 1844
TURNER, Thomas B.	LUSBY, Elizabeth E.	FEB 27 1854
TURNER, Thomas P.	PRATHER, Flavilla	MAY 08 1834
TURNER, Virginia	WEBSTER, Hiram	APR 28 1851
TURNER, Weston B.	ESSEX, Ellen V.	JAN 20 1857
TURNER, William	WALKER, Mary E.	SEP 05 1818
TURNER, William	CLARKE, Christine	JAN 15 1833
TURNER, William	TAYLOR, Phema	JUN 11 1845
TURNER, William	BAR, Mary	FEB 10 1848
TURNER, William B.	SMOOT, Catharine Adaline	JUL 13 1829
TURNER, William B.	LEIZEAR, Mary E.	APR 01 1831
TURNER, William George	HOWE, Hetty Jane	OCT 14 1838
TURNER, William H.F.	SCOTT, Sarah Ellen	NOV 08 1853
TURNER, Wm. W.	RANDOLPH, Mary M.	SEP 13 1855
TURNER, Zachariah	RAY, Ann	DEC 28 1825
TURNER, Zachariah	MARLAN, Julian	DEC 06 1827
TURNER, Zachariah A.	LATHAM, Ann Rebecca	JUL 15 1858
TURNEY, William	WALKER, Elizabeth	JUN 06 1826
TURNLEY, John F.	POWELL, Amanda P.	JAN 12 1858
TURPIN, Amanda L.	MULLOWNY, John F.	MAY 05 1851
TURPIN, Ann Jane	DELAHAY, Mark W.	JUL 16 1838
TURPIN, Ellen	THOMPSON, George C.	SEP 28 1852
TURPIN, Henry	STANLEY, Hellen	APR 08 1857
TURPIN, Sally G.	FRAYSER, Josiah	JUN 09 1829
TURPIN, William	MOORE, Leah Elizabeth Kerr	AUG 29 1848
TURPIN, William T.	RAMSEY, Sarah C.	JUL 26 1854
TURRELL, David	ARRINGTON, Sarah	OCT 30 1856
TURTIN, Elizth. M.	THOMPSON, John A.	FEB 15 1854

District of Columbia Marriage Licenses, 1811-1858

TURTIN, Mary	ESPEY, John	MAY 08 1839
TURTON, Ann B.	LAMBIE, James B.	OCT 24 1838
TURTON, Ann E.	TUCKER, William Henry	DEC 13 1838
TURTON, James	PLANT, Susannah	MAY 04 1829
TURTON, Jane	SNYDER, Lewis H.	MAR 08 1852
TURTON, John B.	RIGGLES, Sarah Ann	NOV 19 1840
TURTON, Rebecca	HARDY, William W.	AUG 10 1852
TURTON, William H.	ARNOLD, Rachel M.A.	FEB 04 1850
TURVEY, Elizabeth	ROBERTSON, Lampkin	DEC 20 1826
TURVEY, Rezin	NORRIS, Martha	DEC 09 1833
TURVEY, Thomas	VOLEN, Fanney Frances	MAY 25 1844
TUSH, Catherine	BROSNEHAN, John	JUN 16 1857
TUSTON, Septimus	BALCH, Eliza M.	JAN 31 1825
TUT, Eliza (blk)	BOSTON, Edward	OCT 19 1854
TUTOR, Elizabeth	CLAGETT, William	DEC 26 1855
TUTT, Maria Lucinda	PENDLETON, Elisha Boyd	APR 24 1843
TUTTLE, America K.	OSBORN, George W.	MAY 01 1858
TUTTLE, Catharine	HENLEY, James	NOV 05 1846
TUTTLE, Delia Ann	ALLEN, William	MAY 03 1852
TUTTLE, George	FRIZZLE, Catherine	MAY 27 1844
TUTTLE, Jannette	BROWN, Edward	DEC 31 1849
TUTTLE, John Thomas	BARRY, Mrs. Kurdelin	DEC 21 1839
TUTTLE, Thomas	WEBSTER, Mary Lynn	FEB 02 1817
TUTTON, Sarah E.	VERNON, Charles K.	MAY 17 1837
TUXON, Margaret (blk)	REED, John	MAY 03 1858
TUXON, William	HOWARD, Eliza (blk)	JAN 15 1851
TWEDY, Umphemy	BASSET, Simian	MAR 06 1819
TWEEDY, Julia E.	WATERS, John	JUN 08 1852
TWEEDY, Margaret	GRIFFITH, William T.	SEP 30 1854
TWEEDY, Mary	HOOVER, Michael	MAY 10 1831
TWEEDY, Robert	TALBERT, Area	APR 17 1819
TWEEDY, Sidney	JOHNSON, William	APR 27 1830
TWINE, Andrew	PEARL, Martha Ann (blk)	MAY 14 1850
TWINE, David	GRAY, Christy (blk)	DEC 20 1848
TWINE, Eliza (blk)	JACKSON, Eli	AUG 02 1853
TWINE, Margaret (blk)	TASCOR, Wm. James	JAN 17 1849
TWINE, William H.	LEWIS, Mary Ann (blk)	MAY 24 1854
TWINEY, Daniel W.	NELSON, Mary	JUN 01 1837
TWIST, Stephen	MACE, Ann Eliza	JUL 20 1827
TWOMEY, Elizabeth	ECKLOFF, Charles G.	OCT 04 1850
TWOMY, Catharine	WARD, James	OCT 31 1855
TWOOMEY, Cornelius	BUCKLEY, Bridget	SEP 05 1857
TWOOMY, Margaret	McGUIRE, James	FEB 12 1853
TWYFORD, Smith	MURPHY, Catharine	JUN 19 1821
TYDINGS, Thomas	HAYDEN, Sarah	DEC 07 1812
TYLER, Augusta	CALDWELL, John M.	NOV 01 1853
TYLER, Dennis	BERRY, Jane (blk)	JUL 31 1852
TYLER, Edward James	SHEPHERD, Henrietta F.	MAY 24 1845
TYLER, Edwd.	PARKER, Elizabeth	AUG 17 1819
TYLER, Eliza Ann	BRATCHER, Thomas	MAY 31 1839
TYLER, Elizabeth	WILKINSON, Edward P. (blk)	DEC 04 1837
TYLER, Elizabeth	BEIGLER, Philip	JUL 10 1841
TYLER, Elizabeth	WALLER, William	JAN 31 1842
TYLER, Elizabeth	McINTOSH, Edward	MAY 23 1850
TYLER, Elsey (blk)	MILLER, Thomas	MAY 25 1854
TYLER, Ephraim	PRUIT, Mary	JUL 21 1847
TYLER, Henrietta (blk)	CLARKE, Bernard	JUL 10 1856
TYLER, Jane Eliza	YOUNG, Ichabod	SEP 02 1828

District of Columbia Marriage Licenses, 1811-1858

TYLER, John	LANDICK, Betsey	DEC 16 1824
TYLER, John	COOPER, Ellen	MAY 14 1842
TYLER, John	FISHER, Vallee	JUN 06 1855
TYLER, Josiah	BRADSHAW, Britania	DEC 05 1836
TYLER, Mary	MANKINS, John	APR 06 1841
TYLER, Mary Ann	MUNROE, Robert M.	MAY 14 1840
TYLER, Mary Maria	CASH, Levoy	AUG 13 1816
TYLER, Mary Scott	BALL, John T.	JAN 23 1834
TYLER, Matilda	CRUMP, William	APR 01 1833
TYLER, Richard F.	GENTRY, Carinda A.	JUN 23 1857
TYLER, Robert	JACKSON, Ann (blk)	SEP 14 1837
TYLER, Sarah Ann	MARKWARD, William	NOV 01 1817
TYLER, Serina (blk)	BUTLER, Sanford	AUG 14 1851
TYLER, Washington	SIMMS, Jane	NOV 15 1832
TYLER, Washington	SELBY, Lucinda (blk)	NOV 27 1849
TYLER, William	PILSBURY, Elizabeth	APR 20 1819
TYLER, William	SHEPHEARD, Henny	OCT 09 1824
TYLER, William	DICKERSON, Mary E.	SEP 09 1857
TYLER, William W.	NERHANEY, Mary L.	DEC 31 1856
TYLER, Wm. H.	LUSBY, Martha	JUN 14 1845
TYREL, Mary A.E.	CLARKSON, Joseph	JUN 15 1844
TYSER, Lewis	NEWMAN, Matilda	JUN 13 1835
TYSER, Susannah	BEARDSLEY, Joseph	DEC 18 1832

District of Columbia Marriage Licenses, 1811-1858

U

UBEL, Helena	ZIMMERMAN, William	FEB 10 1855
ULLE, John Abraham	MEAGLE, Margaret	JUL 25 1853
ULMER, Mary E.	CORNWALL, John D.	AUG 23 1858
ULRICK, Michael	McKELGATH, Mary Ellen	JUL 09 1851
UMBAUGH, George	GREGORY, Elizabeth	AUG 20 1829
UMBERFIELD, Albert	MORELAND, Amelia D.	FEB 23 1819
UMBERFIELD, Elizabeth C.	COGSWELL, Albert G.	OCT 05 1846
UMBERFIELD, Marian	WILSON, George Claibourn	FEB 03 1857
UMBERFIELD, Mary A.	DREW, George W.	AUG 01 1843
UMBERFIELD, Sarah	MORAN, John A.	AUG 04 1847
UMBROOK, Elizabeth	RAPPETTY, Jerom	FEB 12 1849
UMHAN, Christian	WOHLFART, Christina	JUL 10 1852
UMPHREYS, Mary	PRICE, Benjamin F.	SEP 05 1846
UMSTATTED, Richard S.	HURLEY, Susanna M.	NOV 07 1847
UNCLEMAN, Elizabeth	ADAMS, Samuel	JUL 09 1832
UNDERHILL, Halbert	DUNHAM, Freelove	DEC 03 1853
UNDERWOOD, Cassy Ann (blk)	PARKER, Randolph	SEP 27 1851
UNDERWOOD, Catherine Coyle	JOHNSON, Nimrod H.	MAY 08 1850
UNDERWOOD, Eliza	HICKS, Francis	APR 09 1825
UNDERWOOD, George	MOXLEY, Henrietta B.	OCT 08 1835
UNDERWOOD, Harriet P.	FONTAINE, Felix G.	SEP 30 1856
UNDERWOOD, Isaac N.	WORSTER, Julia A.	JUN 19 1856
UNDERWOOD, John	INGLE, Christiana	NOV 05 1822
UNDERWOOD, John	ROBEY, Nancy	MAY 28 1823
UNDERWOOD, John	HANDERSON, Elizabeth	NOV 25 1836
UNDERWOOD, Joseph R.	COX, Elizabeth	FEB 25 1839
UNDERWOOD, Mary Jane	RAYMOND, Charles H.	NOV 05 1844
UNDERWOOD, Rachel	TURNER, John W.	JAN 20 1812
UNDERWOOD, Rebecca	BUCKLEE, Benedict	MAY 22 1826
UNDERWOOD, Susan J.	LAURENCE, Levi L.	SEP 30 1856
UNDERWOOD, William	BRAWNER, Susan V.	MAR 26 1846
UNGERA, Lydia H.	BEATON, Farquharson	SEP 10 1856
UNGLEMAN, William	PARSONS, Elizabeth	DEC 21 1826
UNIACK, John	WHEELAN, Catharine	MAY 16 1840
UNIACK, Julia	WOLFGRAN, Adolph	FEB 11 1852
UNSWORTH, John	MURPHY, Martha M.	MAY 22 1850
UPPERMAN, Catherine S.	MIX, Charles E.	AUG 15 1829
UPPERMAN, Charles A.	MIX, Grace	JAN 11 1848
UPPERMAN, Charles E.	GRIFFIN, Elizabeth A.	APR 30 1838
UPPERMAN, Cordelia	RITTER, Obadiah D.	JUL 24 1851
UPPERMAN, Eliza	LAUB, Andrew M.	JUL 10 1824
UPPERMAN, Henry	GIBBS, Margaret	NOV 12 1822
UPPERMAN, Heryetta	STOHL, Thos. H.	FEB 04 1858
UPPERMAN, James H.	SNAPE, Mary A.	SEP 03 1855
UPPERMAN, Kitty	LITTLEJOHN, Alexr.	JAN 11 1812
UPPERMAN, Mary Ann	DAVIDSON, John	SEP 04 1821
UPPERMAN, Mary Ann	McKNIGHT, Samuel	MAY 02 1838
UPPERMAN, William H.	MYERS, Ann Maria	FEB 21 1837
UPSHUR, John H.	WILLIAMS, Catherine A.	FEB 05 1851
UPTON, Debby	JONES, William	MAY 02 1816
UPTON, Edward P.	BURR, Elizabeth C.	JAN 22 1838
UPTON, Elizabeth	MULLICAN, Thomas W.	DEC 26 1823
UPTON, Josephine P.	REED, William H.	APR 24 1858
UPTON, Rebecca P.	ALLYN, Rufus B.	OCT 17 1840
UPTON, Sarah	JONES, Benjamin	MAR 27 1815
UPTON, Sarah Ann	HAYS, William	MAY 29 1827

District of Columbia Marriage Licenses, 1811-1858

UPTON, William	ROWLS, Julia	JAN 01 1846
UPTON, William	REDIN, Susan	MAY 08 1850
UPTON, William H.	PATTERSON, Mary Jane	SEP 30 1856
URIE, Maria Louisa	RICHARDS, William B., Junr.	MAY 24 1851
URTHROE, Harriet	KNIGHTON, John	APR 07 1858
USHER, George	MATTINGLY, Elizabeth	JUL 09 1847
USHER, Jane	TAYLOR, John H.	OCT 21 1846
USHER, John	COLLINS, Jane	DEC 21 1825
USHER, John P.	SORRELL, Mary Lucinda	DEC 13 1849
USHER, Martha	COGSWELL, William	MAY 19 1858
USHER, Mary	WORSTER, Giles	MAR 01 1847
USTICK, John S.	SHIELDS, Rebecca	SEP 06 1824
UTTERBACK, Olivia	BURGESS, Addison	AUG 08 1853
UTTERBACK, Westward	BAILEY, Juliet	AUG 14 1838
UTTERMUHLE, Augusta	DIPPEL, William	DEC 01 1840
UTTERMULE, Meney	CYPHER, Mary	MAY 08 1847

District of Columbia Marriage Licenses, 1811-1858

V

VAIL, Morris	THOMPSON, Elizabeth D.	FEB 16 1833
VAINE, Eleanora	BREAST, Walter W.	DEC 04 1854
VALDENARE, Mary Margaret	SPEAKE, Josias M.	JAN 31 1814
VALDENIER, James	ALLDRIDGE, Darcus	FEB 08 1812
VALDINAR, Louisa	PIERCE, William C.	APR 18 1829
VALENTINE, Jane	DENTON, William	APR 29 1819
VALENTINE, John	SATTERWHITE, Margaret T.	JUN 04 1819
VALENTINE, John W.	HUNTLETON, Matilda Ann	JAN 03 1852
VALENTINE, William	PIER, Louisa (blk)	MAR 19 1845
VALLOR, Thomas	HOLLEY, Margt.	JAN 08 1857
VanALLEN, Douglass	DICKSON, Margaret	AUG 13 1827
VANCE, Samuel	TRUNNELL, Mary Elizabeth	FEB 16 1846
VanCOBLE, Aaron	BURKHEAD, Ann	DEC 30 1821
VanCOBLE, Caroline	McALISTER, James R.	SEP 04 1848
VANDELEHR, Jacob	GODDARD, Virginia	APR 13 1858
VANDEMERKEN, James B.	FREY, Mary Eleanor	JAN 17 1857
VANDERLEHR, George	GERBER, Mary Ann	JAN 11 1858
VanDEUSEN, William A.	HITCHINGS, Mary A.	JAN 31 1854
VANDEVENTER, Eliza	GERMAIN, Ira V.	APR 03 1838
VanDYKE, Henrietta	MIDDLETON, Daniel Wesley	MAY 31 1836
VANE, Samuel	BROWN, Mary Ann	DEC 21 1849
VANEL, Gertrude M.	PETRAND, F.B.	APR 24 1837
VANELLET, Perry	NICHOLSEN, Rachel	JUL 01 1833
VANESSEN, Peter	MORGAN, Harriet	APR 24 1819
VanHORN, Adda E.	BRUEST, Robert	NOV 17 1829
VanHORN, Alethia	ALLEN, Robert	MAR 03 1825
VanHORN, Benjamin	DEBELL, Nancy Ann	MAR 23 1841
VanHORN, Frances	McDERMOTT, William	APR 27 1854
VanHORN, Isabella	HEPBURN, George S.	MAY 18 1847
VanHORN, Jeremiah	MILLS, Rebecca	APR 19 1824
VanHORN, Mary Ann	EMACK, John D.	AUG 07 1821
VanKLEECK, Adeline V.	WOOD, J.M.	MAY 14 1832
VanKLEECK, Margt.	CROSS, Trueman [Maj.]	OCT 01 1835
VanLEAR, Mary A.	BREWER, John M.	JAN 17 1849
VanLEAR, Sarah D.	FRENCH, George	NOV 23 1840
VANNATAR, Louis G.F.	HODGSON, Mary V.	DEC 31 1856
VANNEMAN, James	LIGHTFOOT, Ann	SEP 08 1855
VanNESS, Ann	MIDDLETON, Arthur	DEC 26 1821
VanNESS, George H.	KING, Miranda A.	AUG 06 1841
VanPELT, Kesiah	REDIN, William	AUG 12 1848
VANPETT, Abraham	PARKER, Amelia	FEB 01 1821
VanRESWICK, Ellen	STAHL, Jacob	OCT 18 1825
VanRESWICK, Thompson	WILBURN, Henrietta	OCT 20 1835
VanRESWICK, Wilferd	RESWICK, Catharine	NOV 09 1819
VanRESWICK, Wilford	CHURCH, Sally	MAY 18 1826
VanRESWICK, William	BEAN, Ann Olivia	MAY 05 1846
VANRIPEN, Harman J.	FERRALL, Cecilia	NOV 20 1842
VANRIPER, Ellen C.	HUDSON, John W.	JAN 29 1848
VanRISWICK, Henrietta	NEWTON, John B.	DEC 21 1848
VanRISWICK, John	NALLEY, Jane	APR 04 1815
VanRISWICK, John	FENWICK, Mary Ann	JAN 04 1841
VanRISWICK, Louisa J.	NEWMAN, Thomas A.	FEB 20 1844
VanRISWICK, Phebe E.	ELLIOTT, William A.S.	AUG 05 1844
VANSCIVER, James	MANGUN, Christiana	JUN 08 1852
VANSCIVER, William	WILLIAMS, Ann	AUG 02 1823
VANSCIVER, William	WARDELL, Laurene	JUN 08 1846

District of Columbia Marriage Licenses, 1811-1858

VANSCIVER, William	LIGHTFORD, Ann Matilda	AUG 10 1854
VANSKIER, John E.	LANG, Mary E.	MAY 09 1849
VanTASSELL, Sarah J.	GOLDSMITH, John T.	MAR 11 1854
VanTYNE, Jacob S.	PHILLIPS, Susannah E.	JAN 16 1845
VanWYCK, Juliet C.	ANDERSON, Adna	OCT 15 1856
VanWYCK, Sarah	MAGRUDER, William B., M.D.	FEB 16 1854
VanWYCK, Stephen M.	KINKLE, Eliza S.	APR 20 1835
VanZANDT, Dolley Payne	DeKRAFFT, John W.	JAN 17 1835
VanZANDT, Joseph A.	THOMPSON, Gilbertine L.	JUL 19 1847
VanZANDT, Nicholas H.	CABEL, James H.M.	OCT 17 1853
VanZANDT, Rosalie M.	SMITH, Isaac C.	NOV 04 1837
VARDEN, Edmund	BOTELER, Elizabeth	JAN 21 1841
VARDEN, Elizabeth	MOFFOTT, Robert	JUL 04 1816
VARDEN, Sarah	SHIELDS, James	APR 13 1817
VARDIN, Joseph	BAGGOT, Susan	MAY 25 1839
VARMAN, John	WHELAN, Mary	AUG 07 1837
VARNALL, Thomas L.	BARNES, Georgiana	DEC 01 1856
VARNELL, George H.	BOGAN, Susan S.	NOV 18 1852
VARNELL, George W.	GRAVES, Ann	SEP 17 1855
VARNELL, Jane A.	GRAVES, William L.	AUG 03 1857
VARNEY, William	CRISTOFF, Margaret	MAY 01 1813
VARNUM, John	VARNUM, Mary P.	MAY 19 1826
VARNUM, Mary B.	HILL, Silas H.	SEP 22 1835
VARNUM, Mary P.	VARNUM, John	MAY 19 1826
VASSEY, Elizabeth C.	CROSS, Leo George	OCT 23 1856
VASSON, Mordaza	STEPHENS, Susan (blk)	DEC 21 1825
VATERS, Mary Jane	ROGERS, Joseph	JUL 27 1857
VAUGHN, Martin	BROWN, Mary	AUG 28 1819
VAUGHN, Richard W.	POWELL, Mary Elizabeth	DEC 25 1852
VAUGHN, Thomas	SWEENY, Anna R.	NOV 04 1813
VAURTERS, William N.	REID, Cerucia E.	AUG 07 1858
VEDDER, Isaac D.	PRETTYMAN, Sarah E.	FEB 14 1849
VEECH, Emeline	MATTINGLY, Joseph	OCT 05 1830
VEITCH, Eliza	GALT, James	JUL 22 1818
VEITCH, James H.	GOODRICK, Mary Jane	DEC 24 1855
VEITCH, John W.	DYE, Mary A.	DEC 03 1856
VEITCH, Mary C.	PHILLIPS, James B.	APR 15 1830
VEITCH, Sally	LAMBERT, Frederick	JUL 31 1824
VEITCH, Thomas	MORGAN, Elizabeth	MAY 16 1812
VELIE, George C.	GALPIN, Attilia	APR 26 1853
VEN__, Ann Sophia	BOSS, James H.	JUN 15 1840
VENABLE, Ann	BATES, David	FEB 13 1817
VENABLE, Ann	BROWN, William	DEC 17 1829
VENABLE, Anne V.	BARKER, James	MAY 17 1855
VENABLE, Charles	SHROPSHIRE, Eliza	FEB 01 1816
VENABLE, Eliza W.	MILSTEAD, John	JUL 14 1832
VENABLE, Ellen R.	VENABLE, William S.	FEB 04 1839
VENABLE, George W.	PIERCY, Catharine M.K.	MAR 09 1826
VENABLE, George W.	SMITH, Mary L.	DEC 24 1856
VENABLE, Jane	SWEENY, Thomas	SEP 30 1847
VENABLE, Joseph	COYLE, Terresa	AUG 22 1812
VENABLE, Joseph	MAHONEY, Eleanor	FEB 25 1818
VENABLE, Joseph G.	HUTCHINSON, Caroline	DEC 31 1851
VENABLE, Sarah E.	BRIGHTWELL, Thomas	SEP 13 1841
VENABLE, Teresa Ann	BRADY, James S.	NOV 27 1846
VENABLE, Thomas	O'DONNELL, Mary Jane	OCT 29 1845
VENABLE, William	BERNASON, Sarah	FEB 19 1833
VENABLE, William	HARRINGTON, Martha R.	APR 18 1844

District of Columbia Marriage Licenses, 1811-1858

VENABLE, William	EDELIN, Mary	FEB 08 1851
VENABLE, William Piercy	GRIFFIN, Clarissa Milcah	APR 24 1857
VENABLE, William S.	VENABLE, Ellen R.	FEB 04 1839
VENCISH, Mactalene	FAHRMAER, Peter	MAY 30 1857
VENEBLE, Patrick	CUNNINGHAM, Margaret	NOV 04 1847
VENEY, Jesse	NEALE, Adeline (blk)	DEC 02 1848
VENNABLE, Sally	FRANKLIN, Henry	DEC 13 1820
VENNER, Henrietta P.	GREEN, William P.	AUG 14 1848
VERMILION, Carolina	HAYS, Samuel	JAN 22 1846
VERMILION, Eliza	DANFORD, James H.	FEB 09 1848
VERMILION, John	CLEMENTS, Ann	AUG 17 1815
VERMILION, Joshua N.	FARR, Barbara	OCT 20 1825
VERMILLION, Barshala	WILSON, Francis	JUL 18 1818
VERMILLION, Charles A.	STEWART, Elizabeth	APR 17 1848
VERMILLION, Christina	BELL, Richard	MAY 06 1856
VERMILLION, Dennis	REYNOLDS, Eliza A.	JUN 01 1826
VERMILLION, Eliza	ROWLEY, James	NOV 23 1819
VERMILLION, Fendall	DUVALL, Ellen	NOV 10 1831
VERMILLION, Hetty Ann	HUTCHINSON, Theodore	FEB 09 1850
VERMILLION, James	MILLER, Anna	MAY 26 1853
VERMILLION, James A.	LANGLY, Hetty	JUL 01 1837
VERMILLION, Julia Ann	ANDERSON, George W.	SEP 20 1855
VERMILLION, Lawson	JENKINS, Sarah Ann	FEB 16 1848
VERMILLION, Lethe	HAGAN, John	FEB 11 1818
VERMILLION, Lewin	BLACK, Barbara	FEB 25 1836
VERMILLION, Lucinda	ANDREWS, William	SEP 29 1818
VERMILLION, Mahala	TENNISON, Charles	NOV 14 1822
VERMILLION, Margaret	GUNNELL, Ira	DEC 24 1812
VERMILLION, Margaret	WILSON, Euias	JUL 09 1818
VERMILLION, Margaret	GRANTT, George H.	JUL 20 1826
VERMILLION, Maria	RUBY, James	APR 23 1814
VERMILLION, Martha M.	CROSS, Jeremiah	NOV 19 1845
VERMILLION, Mary	ARNOLD, Thomas	FEB 01 1815
VERMILLION, Matilda	PROVEST, Alexander	DEC 23 1828
VERMILLION, Nicholas	LEWIS, Elizabeth	NOV 01 1837
VERMILLION, Otha F.	BERKLEY, Deby	DEC 17 1822
VERMILLION, Priscilla	SOMERS, Judson	NOV 03 1815
VERMILLION, Rachel	STRIKE, Wm.	JUN 17 1813
VERMILLION, Rebecca	EVANS, Thomas	JUL 17 1855
VERMILLION, Samuel	STEVENS, Sarah	JUL 16 1814
VERMILLION, Sarah	HAUSSY, Philip	MAR 24 1815
VERMILLION, Sarah	ARNOLD, James	FEB 21 1816
VERMILLION, Susan	CARROLL, Charles H.	APR 17 1827
VERMILLION, William	WARD, Harriet	FEB 20 1844
VERMILLIONS, Sahah	SHECKELLS, Samuel	DEC 21 1816
VERNON, Charles K.	TUTTON, Sarah E.	MAY 17 1837
VERNON, Fairfax F.	PHILLIPS, Ann	MAR 22 1845
VERNON, Henry T.	McINTOSH, Jennet	JAN 02 1838
VERNON, Lucinda	McINTOSH, James Thomas	JAN 02 1840
VERNON, Philip B.	HARRIS, Elizabeth	MAY 26 1831
VERNON, Sarah	McWILLIAM, James	DEC 13 1856
VERTMILLER, Elizabeth	LEFFLER, John	FEB 13 1846
VERTZ, Ann	HURST, Thomas	MAY 22 1813
VESSEY, John	HOLTON, Margaret	FEB 09 1853
VESSEY, John	FULLER, Mary A.	OCT 09 1856
VESSEY, Leonard	SMITH, Mary Isabell	NOV 10 1853
VESSEY, Mary A.	BOWEN, B.F.	AUG 14 1855
VIBBER, Phebe Ann	SMITH, John	SEP 27 1854

District of Columbia Marriage Licenses, 1811-1858

VICK, Bushrod W.	HIGGINS, Eudora	SEP 14 1854
VICKERS, Parnell	GATES, Jane	APR 23 1858
VICKERS, Thomas	JONES, Nelly	NOV 19 1833
VIDLER, Ann	FLIN, Edward	NOV 25 1820
VIDLER, Wm. Edward	GORDON, Matilda	JUN 01 1820
VIEBUCHEN, John Peter	BOTHE, William	MAY 15 1857
VIEL, Victor Just	BRIDON, Pauline	NOV 14 1825
VIELEMANN, George	FRENCH, Jane	OCT 07 1854
VIERS, William A.	BRAYS, Rebecca T.	MAY 02 1853
VIETT, Eliza	EMMNER, Julius	APR 29 1857
VIGAL, Ann	ADAMS, George	FEB 19 1857
VIGAL, Richard	KULP, Elizabeth (blk)	JUN 13 1849
VIGLE, Richard	HAMPTON, Emily (blk)	MAY 22 1849
VILE, Margaret	MURDOCH, John	APR 03 1816
VILEY, George	MAMBY, Margaret	JUL 02 1836
VILLARD, Mary A.	HEDGES, John	MAY 17 1843
VILLARD, Richd. H.L.	MULHOLLEN, Mary Ann	SEP 13 1815
VILLARD, Sophia	TATHAM, William	AUG 30 1813
VILLARD, Sophia Louisa	DELANY, Michael	DEC 28 1841
VILLARD, Sophi<u>e</u>	LAVALL, Jacint	FEB 26 1814
VILLARD, Thomas J.	BRYAN, Caroline C.	OCT 25 1848
VILLENEUVE, Julius Constantius	CAVALCANTI, Anna Maria Francisca deP.	MAY 23 1857
VINCENT, William D.	DELAY, Martha	JAN 06 1857
VINCE<u>NT</u>, Isaac	THOMPSON, Eleanor	APR 07 1825
VINCE<u>NT</u>, Mary Ann	DUNLOP, Nathan	NOV 17 1824
VINEE, John	RITER, Eve	JUN 11 1832
VINEER, Lewis	SCHWIERING, Fredericka	JUN 20 1846
VINSON, Charles	CAPRON, Harriet F.R.	JUN 03 1851
VINSON, Frances Ann	HEFFNER, George J.	JAN 15 1845
VINSON, Isaac	STEWARD, Catherine	NOV 28 1833
VINSON, John J.	DADISMAN, Harriet E.	MAR 01 1842
VINSON, Julia Grace	BALCH, George Beall	DEC 24 1844
VINSON, Margaret W.	RANDALL, Samuel, Junr.	SEP 12 1836
VINSON, Mary E. (blk)	SOLOMON, Daniel	NOV 27 1856
VINSOR, William	CURTIN, Julia Ann	JUN 26 1854
VINTON, Madeline S.	GODDARD, Daniel Convers	MAY 29 1846
VIOLETT, Robert G.	ENGLISH, Louisa	FEB 11 1826
VIOLETT, Robert G.	ANDERSON, Amanda	AUG 23 1849
VIRANS, Louisa M.	O'NEALE, John H.P.	MAY 07 1845
VIVANS, Josephine	REDFERN, Joseph	OCT 29 1851
VIVANS, Marie C.	WAITE, Samuel B.	SEP 26 1849
VIV<u>EN</u>S, Louis	KELLER, Mary	SEP 13 1824
VODERY, Robert	CONNER, Cordelia (blk)	SEP 10 1857
VODRA, Isabella (blk)	THOMAS, William	DEC 11 1855
VODRICK, Ann M. (blk)	JOHNSON, George	APR 25 1850
VODRY, Robert	KING, Catharine (blk)	APR 13 1850
VOEGELE, Charles L.	HIERHOLZER, Mary V.	SEP 13 1853
VOEGLER, Elenore	NOLTE, Tynar	AUG 25 1857
VOEKER, Margaret	WILTZ, Adam	FEB 14 1835
VOGEL, Jacob	BAUER, Fanny	MAY 16 1854
VOIGT, Fredk.	BEHRENS, Caroline	OCT 02 1855
VOLEN, Fanney Frances	TURVEY, Thomas	MAY 25 1844
VOLGER, Theresse	NORDMANN, Wilhelm	OCT 15 1853
VOLK, John Frederick	STRIFLER, Margaretta	SEP 29 1847
VOLTZ, John	HEIDT, Wilhelmina	MAY 13 1856
VonBEHREN, Marie	BERGMANN, Heinrich	JUL 24 1845
VONDALIER, Elizabeth	CLEMENTS, Aloysius N.	NOV 09 1843
VONDERLOEHR, Barbara	HAMMEL, A.A. Wm.	SEP 17 1851

District of Columbia Marriage Licenses, 1811-1858

VonESSEN, Anna	LANG, John	APR 24 1843
VonESSEN, Virginia S.	ESSEX, James F.	NOV 19 1839
VONESSEN, Peter	SCOTT, Juliet	JAN 07 1833
VonGLUEMER, Agnes E.C.B.	FREYHOLD, Edward O.	MAR 13 1855
VonSCHEELE, H.C.	SCHMIDT, Doris	DEC 30 1856
VonSCIIMIDT, August A.	YOUNG, Sarah Virginia Ann	FEB 02 1847
VOSS, Augustus	MANN, Lucy Amelia	JUN 23 1851
VOSS, Dorette Antonie	SCHWARZKOPF, Charles	NOV 07 1850
VOSS, Hermann H.	PETERS, Lucy	AUG 24 1858
VOSS, Paulina	WALDECKER, Louis	OCT 03 1857
VYER, Bernard A.	BARXTALL, Ann E.	MAY 21 1853

District of Columbia Marriage Licenses, 1811-1858

W

WACHTEN, Matilda	SMITH, John C.	JUN 27 1837
WACHTER, Jacob	SMITH, Margaret	NOV 07 1837
WACHTER, Jacob	HARRIS, Ann Virginia	FEB 23 1846
WADDEY, Benjamin F.	ABBY, Henrietta	SEP 01 1849
WADDEY, James E.	CORE, Mary L.	SEP 03 1856
WADDLES, Mary	DOWELL, Oliver W.	OCT 20 1857
WADDY, Sarah C.	WADDY, William	JUN 14 1855
WADDY, William	WADDY, Sarah C.	JUN 14 1855
WADE, Ann	RUST, George	AUG 04 1812
WADE, Ann Maria	BALLINGER, Spencer	FEB 19 1857
WADE, Arabella	DONALDSON, Wm. B.	MAY 13 1856
WADE, Jane	JEFFERSON, Robert	APR 28 1840
WADE, Jane Rebecca	PATTEN, William	AUG 03 1836
WADE, John H.	SWAINE, Jane	JAN 16 1819
WADE, John K.	OURAND, Christiana A.T.	OCT 17 1843
WADE, John W.	ATHEY, Georginna	MAR 05 1842
WADE, Mary Ann	BURNETT, Richard	FEB 10 1830
WADE, Mary Ann	MAXWELL, Fanny	SEP 21 1857
WADE, Robert P.	PECKHAM, Eliza M.	APR 21 1845
WADE, William [Capt.]	KING, Susan	JAN 07 1823
WADE, Zephaniah	FRY, Ann	JAN 18 1815
WADSWORTH, Alexander L. [Capt.]	DENISON, Louisa I.	NOV 08 1824
WADSWORTH, E.W.	THOMPSON, Charles G.	JUN 10 1841
WADSWORTH, Hiram N.	WHITNEY, Sophia	JUL 03 1849
WADSWORTH, John	MASI, Caroline A.	MAY 26 1829
WADSWORTH, Louisa D.	BAYLOR, Chas. G.	JAN 05 1853
WAGGAMAN, Catharine	PAGE, Samuel	JUL 24 1834
WAGGAMAN, John H.	SMOOT, Lydia K.	SEP 28 1837
WAGGAMAN, Sallie	CANTATORE, John B.	SEP 02 1857
WAGGONER, Elizabeth	SCHEFFIELD, John Josephe	FEB 03 1855
WAGGONER, John David	COOPER, Rosanna	SEP 30 1853
WAGGONER, Mary	MILLS, Peter	MAY 13 1816
WAGGONER, Upton	KELLER, Margaret	APR 14 1818
WAGLER, Charles K.	LENMAN, Elizabeth	NOV 16 1838
WAGLIER, Thomas	HOLTZMAN, Catherine	AUG 29 1839
WAGNER, Ann	LOKEY, Joseph	APR 24 1823
WAGNER, Ann	MINPLY, John P.	MAR 31 1831
WAGNER, Anthony	JOHNSON, Mary Jane	JUL 14 1838
WAGNER, Christine C.	MÜLLER, John Ferdd.	NOV 16 1855
WAGNER, David	MALENS, Caroline	APR 29 1846
WAGNER, Elizabeth	MOORE, Daniel	MAY 08 1830
WAGNER, George	BELDRECH, Mary	FEB 17 1849
WAGNER, Henry C.H.	CLEMENTS, Dorothy	FEB 05 1851
WAGNER, James Henry	SCHWAB, Dorathea	APR 19 1856
WAGNER, John	SCHLECHT, Regina	DEC 17 1832
WAGNER, John	CROSS, Ann Elizabeth	APR 01 1846
WAGNER, John	SCHRIBER, Elizabeth	AUG 12 1853
WAGNER, John	HEILMANN, Margaret	JAN 10 1856
WAGNER, John C.	MAGLE, Elizabeth	NOV 07 1853
WAGNER, Philip	ISENHOOT, Louisa	JUL 21 1858
WAGNER, Rebecca R.	WILLIAMS, Charles D.	OCT 02 1854
WAGONER, Armstrong	NEWELL, Jane	MAR 21 1834
WAGONER, Christiana	PRESTON, Edward	JAN 01 1846
WAGONER, Mary E.	LEE, Daniel C.	MAY 24 1825
WAGONNER, Louisa Ann	GRANT, William W.	SEP 18 1852
WAHL, Catherine	SUMMERS, John	MAY 12 1845

District of Columbia Marriage Licenses, 1811-1858

WAHL, Christina	MEINERS, Augustus	JUL 06 1852
WAHL, John	HERRITY, Bridget	AUG 29 1853
WAHL, Sophia	JONES, John J.	APR 18 1854
WAIDER, Barney	BERRY, Mary	OCT 31 1853
WAILES, Isaac H.	NUGENT, Martha	MAR 10 1851
WAILES, Mary N.H.	BUTTERFIELD, Franklin	MAR 15 1853
WAINWRIGHT, Ann Overing	TOWNSEND, Edward Davis	MAY 08 1848
WAINWRIGHT, Henrietta Mary	SYNGE, William Webb Follett	JAN 27 1853
WAINWRIGHT, Maria M.	PATTERSON, T. Harman	JAN 04 1847
WAINWRIGHT, Richard	BACHE, Sally Franklin	FEB 28 1849
WAINWRIGHT, William	FOWLER, Maria	JAN 16 1819
WAITE, Edward	STETSON, Mary A.	SEP 02 1851
WAITE, Matthew H.	HEPBURN, Louisa H.	DEC 22 1849
WAITE, Samuel B.	VIVANS, Marie C.	SEP 26 1849
WAIZENEGGER, Norbert	BEUR, Josephine	APR 17 1855
WAKE, Elizabeth A.	PUMPHREY, Samuel	JUN 05 1845
WAKE, Margaret J.	HAVENNER, Charles W.	MAR 23 1853
WAKELING, Ignatius	GLOYD, Elizabeth	JUN 19 1847
WAKINS, George W.	McCABE, Mary E.	DEC 25 1848
WALBRIDGE, Hiram	BLAKE, Jenny M.	AUG 31 1857
WALCH, Bridget Ann	COX, William	JUL 24 1830
WALCH, Joseph	SMITH, Elizabeth	SEP 05 1843
WALDECKER, Louis	VOSS, Paulina	OCT 03 1857
WALDSCHMIDT, Elizabeth	BALLAUFF, William	MAY 25 1853
WALES, John	WOOLHOUSE, Eliza	FEB 02 1829
WALFENDEN, Charlotte	WIMSATT, Joseph	AUG 29 1838
WALKER, Almea V.	DAVIS, James V.	NOV 04 1852
WALKER, Amanda Elizth.	SPICER, Samuel	MAR 13 1844
WALKER, Amanda M.	STRAUB, John L.	SEP 27 1856
WALKER, Amelia H.	SHERIFF, Edwin	JUN 21 1831
WALKER, Ann	DONALL, William	JAN 10 1816
WALKER, Ann (blk)	MATTHEWS, Samuel	APR 21 1827
WALKER, Ann Elizabeth	TEACHEN, James H.	DEC 02 1843
WALKER, Ann H.	HARTMAN, Calvin F.	JUN 23 1851
WALKER, Ann Rebecca	KELLER, Charles	JUN 02 1854
WALKER, Ann Sophia [Mrs.]	PARKER, George	JAN 21 1834
WALKER, Anna M.	JARDELLA, Laurence	JAN 25 1853
WALKER, Caroline	SHERWOOD, Samuel	DEC 24 1836
WALKER, Catharine	WATKINS, Stephen	JUL 13 1818
WALKER, Catharine	BEALL, John	JUL 29 1834
WALKER, Catharine	BORELAND, Samuel	SEP 21 1835
WALKER, Catherine	ROBERTS, Robert	DEC 13 1834
WALKER, Charles	JARVIS, Jane E.	MAR 03 1834
WALKER, Charles E.	HILDT, Arabella W.	JAN 06 1857
WALKER, Cordelia	FENTON, William H.	DEC 01 1857
WALKER, Cornelia S.	HALL, James	SEP 13 1834
WALKER, David	READ, Dianna	AUG 21 1819
WALKER, David	HARRIS, Nancy	MAY 11 1837
WALKER, David	MUSTIN, Catharine E.	OCT 14 1850
WALKER, David H.	NICHOLSON, Susannah	NOV 01 1847
WALKER, David T.	ALLEN, Julia	MAR 06 1855
WALKER, Dolly	SMITH, Jared	APR 22 1824
WALKER, Dorcas Ann	TRITTLE, Walter A.	MAR 06 1832
WALKER, Dudley	ASHTON, Jane C.	JAN 16 1832
WALKER, Edward	SWINK, Sarah Ann	JUL 19 1823
WALKER, Edward	SIMMONS, Secelia	OCT 25 1825
WALKER, Elizabeth	COOK, John	OCT 28 1824
WALKER, Elizabeth	TURNEY, William	JUN 06 1826

District of Columbia Marriage Licenses, 1811-1858

WALKER, Elizabeth	JOHNSON, Lloyd	FEB 02 1833
WALKER, Elizabeth	NICHOLSON, Henry	SEP 02 1845
WALKER, Elizabeth	ROBERTSON, John	NOV 26 1845
WALKER, Elizabeth Ellen	LIZEAR, George W.	NOV 26 1850
WALKER, Elizabeth J.	LESTER, William W.	FEB 08 1858
WALKER, Emily M.	BRICELAND, Isaac N.	OCT 22 1856
WALKER, Emma	BROWN, Thomas	MAR 25 1856
WALKER, Fanney	CLARK, Thomas	JUN 19 1822
WALKER, Fielder	McDOWELL, Ann	JUL 31 1813
WALKER, Francis	FRANKS, Susan	SEP 24 1812
WALKER, Geo. C.	WALLINGSFORD, Mary E.	JUN 22 1850
WALKER, George	WEBSTER, Elizabeth	DEC 28 1844
WALKER, George	MAYHEW, Sarah	DEC 02 1851
WALKER, George C.	FORBES, Elizabeth A.	JUN 05 1858
WALKER, George H.	ANDERSON, Mary O.	NOV 30 1854
WALKER, Harriet	NEWTON, John	MAY 21 1825
WALKER, Harriet	DANT, Thomas E., Jr.	MAR 11 1858
WALKER, Henry	KNOWLES, Catharine	NOV 13 1834
WALKER, Henry T.	WHEELER, Sarah A.	SEP 21 1855
WALKER, Isabella	JOHNSTON, Thomas J.	OCT 17 1849
WALKER, James	PAINE, Elizabeth	JAN 12 1818
WALKER, James	COVER, Ann Sophia	JUL 22 1830
WALKER, James	HURDLE, Elizabeth	APR 19 1843
WALKER, James C.	CHRISTIAN, Caroline C.	APR 15 1851
WALKER, James H.	FRIZELL, Ann Matilda	JUN 30 1849
WALKER, Jane	MATTINGLY, Thomas	NOV 22 1820
WALKER, Jane Josephine	McCLELLAN, John	SEP 17 1842
WALKER, John	THAW, Hannah M.	OCT 06 1831
WALKER, John	BROOM, Susana	JUN 15 1837
WALKER, John	FRAZER, Martha A.	MAR 08 1848
WALKER, John H.	PHILLIPS, Roannah E.	MAY 28 1851
WALKER, John M.	PICKRELL, Angelina	NOV 23 1836
WALKER, John Westley	McCOY, Mary W.	AUG 01 1846
WALKER, Jonathan Thomas	BENSON, Amelia Jane	OCT 12 1833
WALKER, Joseph	EMMERSON, Sabrina	MAR 31 1830
WALKER, Joseph T.	STEPHENS, Mary Leah	FEB 22 1856
WALKER, Joseph W.	LEE, Sarah F.	FEB 06 1840
WALKER, Lawrence	LLOYD, Rena C.	MAR 31 1852
WALKER, Lemuel	ARRINGTON, Matilda	JUL 04 1846
WALKER, Louisa	BALLARD, Richard	DEC 10 1822
WALKER, Lucretia	TENLY, John T.	SEP 14 1847
WALKER, Luther M.	CURTIS, Mildred M.	OCT 13 1853
WALKER, M.A.	KENDALL, Elie	AUG 02 1822
WALKER, Mahala	PERKINS, Henry	FEB 03 1849
WALKER, Mahalia	JACKSON, Alexander	JUN 03 1845
WALKER, Malinda	BOYLE, Uys	AUG 01 1844
WALKER, Margaret	PECK, Joseph	MAR 28 1831
WALKER, Margaret	SELDEN, James	APR 08 1846
WALKER, Maria (blk)	ROBINSON, Solomon	OCT 26 1854
WALKER, Maria C.	CARROLL, John T.	OCT 12 1853
WALKER, Martha	PERKINS, Samuel	FEB 01 1817
WALKER, Martha E.	NICHOLLS, John	DEC 09 1845
WALKER, Mary	SPALDING, Elexis	JAN 26 1819
WALKER, Mary	BEALL, George Ingham	NOV 24 1831
WALKER, Mary	COLE, James	NOV 19 1835
WALKER, Mary	DESLONDE, Adrien	MAY 24 1858
WALKER, Mary Ann (blk)	HACKETT, Ben	SEP 07 1815
WALKER, Mary Ann	STAUT, Wm. H.	MAY 01 1849

District of Columbia Marriage Licenses, 1811-1858

WALKER, Mary E.	TURNER, William	SEP 05 1818
WALKER, Mary E.	WEBSTER, Charles P.	FEB 02 1857
WALKER, Mary Elizabeth	WILLIAMS, David	JUL 22 1843
WALKER, Mary Jane	PEASTER, Frederick	JUN 18 1853
WALKER, Mary W.	KELLY, Moses	JUN 05 1844
WALKER, Matilda A.	ANNERSON, Ratio	JAN 12 1837
WALKER, Mildred C.	FROST, Horace J.	SEP 30 1857
WALKER, Nancy	CLEVELAND, John	APR 02 1839
WALKER, Nancy, Miss	HUTCHINSON, Dory	OCT 05 1815
WALKER, Nathan	SCOTT, Anna R.	MAY 17 1854
WALKER, Peyton B.	BOSWELL, Amanda M.	DEC 22 1845
WALKER, Philly	WHITE, Thomas	JAN 02 1822
WALKER, Rebecca K.	BILLING, William W.	MAR 07 1827
WALKER, Richard A.	HENDERSON, Mahala Ann	FEB 19 1835
WALKER, Richard H.	BOHRER, Elizabeth	NOV 10 1849
WALKER, Rosa Lee	WIPPERMANN, Frederic	OCT 29 1856
WALKER, Samuel	CANTER, Priscilla	MAY 07 1814
WALKER, Samuel	ANDERSON, Elizabeth	AUG 05 1817
WALKER, Samuel	SAUNDERS, Anne	JAN 31 1837
WALKER, Samuel T.	ALLEN, Margaretta	JAN 16 1846
WALKER, Sandford	ANDERSON, Patsey	SEP 14 1818
WALKER, Sarah	MAYFIELD, Benjamin	APR 27 1815
WALKER, Sarah	McCALLION, James C.	FEB 19 1816
WALKER, Sarah	YOUNG, John	SEP 17 1816
WALKER, Sarah	PHELPS, Thomas	MAY 27 1846
WALKER, Sarah	DIGGS, George A.	OCT 29 1856
WALKER, Sarah Ann	GAITHER, John	FEB 15 1836
WALKER, Sarah Ann	SUMMERS, John H.	AUG 04 1849
WALKER, Sarah Catherine	HAYNIE, John F.	AUG 12 1856
WALKER, Sarah E.	HUTCHISON, Joseph	MAY 25 1858
WALKER, Sarah Virginia	HILLEARY, John W.	DEC 30 1851
WALKER, Singleton S.	CAREW, Rosanna Eliza	OCT 11 1825
WALKER, Sydney	JOHNSON, William	AUG 13 1840
WALKER, Thomas Douglass	WARWICK, Ellen Virginia	MAY 30 1854
WALKER, Thomas H.	TUCKER, Sarah C.	NOV 19 1856
WALKER, Virginia	SPENCER, George W.	JAN 23 1849
WALKER, W.E.	HILLIARD, Lucy E.	MAY 08 1856
WALKER, Wesley	MEIGS, Rhumma	JAN 08 1816
WALKER, William	PANE, Catharine	APR 16 1825
WALKER, William	POLLOCK, Mary	SEP 17 1828
WALKER, William	LEIGHTFOOT, Ann E.	JUL 18 1840
WALKER, William	PENNINGTON, Louisa	JUN 23 1842
WALKER, William	ALFRED, Elizabeth	MAR 22 1843
WALKER, William	DICKENS, Mary	APR 20 1846
WALKER, William	KEITH, Julietta	JAN 31 1850
WALKER, William	THOMAS, Sarah (col'd)	OCT 25 1854
WALKER, William	MICHAEL, Susan G.	APR 15 1856
WALKER, William A.	RAGLAND, Jane (blk)	MAY 06 1835
WALKER, William B.	MARTIN, Maria E.	JUL 21 1825
WALKER, William H.	LACEY, Emily M.	FEB 03 1845
WALKER, William H.	MURPHY, Sarah Louisa	MAY 14 1849
WALKER, William S.	TEACHEM, Elizabeth	SEP 14 1835
WALKER, William T.	HARDING, Jane	OCT 02 1845
WALKER, Wm. T.	HARRIS, Adelaide	SEP 25 1855
WALKER, Zachariah	COX, Lucy B.	JAN 27 1825
WALKER, Zachariah	WILES, Ann Eliza	FEB 27 1827
WALKER, Zachariah H.T.	LOCKER, Sarah E.	DEC 22 1853
WALKER, [blank]	ORD, Catherine	AUG 12 1833

District of Columbia Marriage Licenses, 1811-1858

WALL, Benjamin M.	DELEWARE, Julia Ann	MAR 10 1842
WALL, Bridget	LONG, John	JAN 13 1856
WALL, Caroline M.	STEVENS, Lewis G.	JAN 23 1857
WALL, Catharine E.	CHURCH, George C.	OCT 16 1852
WALL, Catherine	CARROLL, Jas.	APR 18 1855
WALL, Columbus O.	HOBBS, Mary E.	JAN 22 1852
WALL, Ellen	POWELL, John	JAN 16 1855
WALL, Honnorah	DOYLE, Michael	APR 25 1856
WALL, Jane	HENNING, George F.	OCT 30 1856
WALL, Jesse D.	WALL, Mary	APR 12 1841
WALL, John	FLANNAGAN, Bridget	AUG 27 1845
WALL, Joseph	MOORE, [blank]	APR 21 1855
WALL, Leonard D.	O'NEALE, Mary A.A.	JUN 20 1822
WALL, Mary	WALL, Jesse D.	APR 12 1841
WALL, Mary Elizth.	BURDETT, Wm. Thomas	AUG 16 1852
WALL, Michael	MURPHY, Ellen	JUN 10 1851
WALL, Michael	DAILEY, Eliza	JUL 28 1856
WALL, Racel M.	BARNACLOE, John M.	JUN 03 1840
WALL, Rebecca L.	TALBOT, Thomas	DEC 12 1853
WALL, Robert	BROWN, Ann	APR 27 1830
WALL, Thomas	BOGUE, Charlotte E.	DEC 09 1844
WALL, Thomas	WHELAN, Catherine	NOV 02 1847
WALL, Virginia G.	FOWLER, Thomas W.	JUN 04 1857
WALL, William R.	FRY, Mary Ann	NOV 08 1827
WALLACE, Ann M.	McDONALD, Charles	JUL 25 1850
WALLACE, Benjamin S.	THOMAS, Henrietta (blk)	SEP 08 1856
WALLACE, Charles	LANHAM, Eliza	APR 09 1844
WALLACE, Clarinda	BURRISS, Benjamin	MAY 05 1828
WALLACE, Daniel	JOHNSON, Adeline (blk)	NOV 02 1840
WALLACE, Eliza (blk)	BRISCOE, Henry	APR 21 1858
WALLACE, Emily Ann	DAUSON, Robert G.	DEC 01 1828
WALLACE, Ezekiel	HANDY, Diana	SEP 16 1820
WALLACE, George B.	LaTRUITTE, Barbara B.	FEB 20 1849
WALLACE, Hanson	BRADY, Susan	JAN 23 1827
WALLACE, Harriet Ann (blk)	SEYMOUR, Francis	MAY 31 1853
WALLACE, Israel	BLACK, Betsey (blk)	AUG 15 1828
WALLACE, James	SULLIVAN, Eleanor	JUN 05 1843
WALLACE, Linda (blk)	BRISCOE, Henry	OCT 02 1837
WALLACE, Margaret	PARMER, Albert	FEB 12 1840
WALLACE, Martha [Mrs.]	JOHNSON, Martin	MAR 08 1827
WALLACE, Mary	LYNCH, Henry	JAN 19 1825
WALLACE, Mary	RILEY, Peter	AUG 11 1851
WALLACE, Mary Ann K.	BADEN, John W.	MAR 03 1851
WALLACE, Mary Jane (blk)	BOND, John	DEC 05 1855
WALLACE, Matilda	GLASGOW, Wm. James	FEB 18 1827
WALLACE, Richard D.	WILLIAMS, Harriot	MAR 19 1816
WALLACE, Samuel	THOMAS, Sarah A.	DEC 18 1828
WALLACE, Susan	BUTLER, Elijah	FEB 01 1827
WALLACE, William F.	PURDY, Ellen R.	AUG 31 1847
WALLACE, William Rich.	KELLER, Mary	SEP 22 1832
WALLACE, WIlliam H.	DUNLAP, Sarah S.	APR 22 1850
WALLACH, Charles S.	HEWITT, Lavenia	FEB 28 1839
WALLACH, Cuthbert P.	BEALL, Annie E.T.	OCT 21 1847
WALLACH, Richard	BROWN, Rosa	APR 03 1856
WALLACH, Rosa	BACHENHEIMER, Herz	MAY 30 1856
WALLACH, William Douglass	NEWTON, Margaret C.	SEP 08 1840
WALLACK, Olivia P.	GOLDTHWAITE, George	DEC 24 1821
WALLACK, Olivia P.	GOLDTHWAITE, George	NOV 28 1835

District of Columbia Marriage Licenses, 1811-1858

WALLECE, Grace Ann	RIGBEY, Edward	DEC 24 1821
WALLER, Ann	WHITE, James [Capt.]	MAY 24 1823
WALLER, Edward	BIBB, Virginia	JUL 07 1853
WALLER, Edward L.	KELLMON, Elizabeth	JAN 13 1846
WALLER, Elijah	LUCAS, Mary Ann	MAY 21 1838
WALLER, Elijah	LUCAS, Mary Ann	JUL 21 1838
WALLER, Elizabeth Ann	SCRIVENER, Thomas	APR 14 1830
WALLER, Frances E.	CAMP, Eben	SEP 15 1852
WALLER, James D.	CHAILLE, Maria	DEC 29 1830
WALLER, Louisa M.	COSNAHAN, J.B.H.	AUG 05 1843
WALLER, Lucinda	GOULDING, Frederick, Jr.	FEB 14 1837
WALLER, Maria G.	KILBY, Isaac H.	DEC 26 1855
WALLER, Mary E.A.	REEVES, John C.	AUG 19 1846
WALLER, Waldburg	ISEMANN, John Casper	OCT 17 1856
WALLER, William	TYLER, Elizabeth	JAN 31 1842
WALLICE, Harriet	RIDGEWAY, William	JUN 18 1823
WALLING, Jacob W.	HIXON, Amanda Virginia	JUN 01 1854
WALLING, John	McGINNIE, Mary E.	JUL 01 1858
WALLING, William	OTTINGER, Rebecca	DEC 06 1828
WALLING, William	GILLESPIE, Harriet	MAY 12 1831
WALLINGSFORD, Alfred	GOLDIN, Eleanor Ann	MAR 10 1849
WALLINGSFORD, Ann	WALLINGSFORD, George N.	JUN 30 1825
WALLINGSFORD, Eliza	HODGES, Benjamin	MAR 28 1836
WALLINGSFORD, Ellen	SHERMAN, William D.	SEP 05 1834
WALLINGSFORD, Emily	McCAFFERTY, William	JUN 28 1838
WALLINGSFORD, George N.	WALLINGSFORD, Ann	JUN 30 1825
WALLINGSFORD, John	MEAD, Elizabeth	DEC 04 1819
WALLINGSFORD, Mary Ann	ROSS, Isaac W.	SEP 09 1830
WALLINGSFORD, Mary E.	WALKER, Geo. C.	JUN 22 1850
WALLINGSFORD, Washington	TURNER, Mary A.	FEB 20 1840
WALLINSFORD, Sophia	MITCHELL, Rector	MAR 28 1812
WALLIS, Ann	QUIN, Michael	AUG 27 1817
WALLIS, Cowdin S.	McCLELLAND, Mary	JUN 26 1833
WALLIS, Henry	CONNOR, Catherine	DEC 30 1850
WALLIS, James Harrison	GOLDSMITH, Mary Jane	AUG 11 1834
WALLIS, John Henry	SLOAN, Mary	JUN 14 1856
WALLIS, Julia	KING, Thomas	JAN 25 1845
WALLIS, Mary M.	SHAFFER, Jacob Frederick	JUN 18 1840
WALLIS, Overton	QUAIL, Margaret R.	NOV 25 1825
WALLIS, Thomas	ROBINSON, Ann Eliza	DEC 30 1837
WALLIS, William	HARCUM, Sarah C.	AUG 01 1817
WALLS, James E.	GRAY, Jane	JAN 10 1853
WALLS, James F.	ALLISON, Mary	MAY 17 1856
WALLS, John N.	BOSWELL, Johanna	MAY 11 1857
WALLS, Maria E.	BOWMANN, Charles	JAN 01 1855
WALLS, Mary Ann	CATON, Patrick	NOV 07 1855
WALLS, Mary E.	MURRAY, William A.	JAN 28 1854
WALLS, William	CROSS, Elizabeth	DEC 26 1850
WALMSLEY, Theodore	TENLEY, Mary L.	MAR 16 1858
WALRAVEN, James C.	HENNING, Ann Elizabeth	MAY 06 1846
WALRAVEN, James C.	HENNING, Eliza Jane	DEC 26 1848
WALSELS, Mary	KASPARI, Henry	MAY 08 1858
WALSH, Ellen	KOEHLER, Charles H.	DEC 15 1852
WALSH, Francis S.	SCRIVNER, Susan Sophia	NOV 11 1839
WALSH, Joseph C.	PEARSON, Mary	OCT 20 1835
WALSH, Julia	HYDE, David	SEP 09 1856
WALSH, Julia E.	SHAW, Alfred C.	JAN 31 1852
WALTER, C.W.C.	MOHUN, Ellen C.	MAR 10 1847

District of Columbia Marriage Licenses, 1811-1858

WALTER, Caroline	FREEMAN, John, Jr.	APR 28 1851
WALTER, Herman	WOLFURT, Hester Ann	JUL 13 1857
WALTER, James	GOEZLER, Julia Ann	JUL 14 1830
WALTER, John	DENGLER, Ablona	JUL 15 1842
WALTER, John	AUSTINGS, Elizabeth	APR 05 1843
WALTER, John H.	TOLBURT, Mary Ann A.	SEP 13 1831
WALTER, John W.	HARRIS, Mary Ann	OCT 24 1834
WALTER, Joseph	FROS, Mary	FEB 18 1857
WALTER, L.D., Rev.	SUTER, Mary A.	JUN 18 1857
WALTER, Robert	WHITE, Biddy	JAN 26 1842
WALTER, Teresa	FREEMAN, John	FEB 02 1853
WALTER, Thomas	WEIGGMANN, Elizabeth	OCT 11 1853
WALTERS, Lavenia A.	EVENS, Thomas F.	FEB 08 1849
WALTERS, Maria (blk)	BELL, Nace	AUG 02 1858
WALTERS, Mary	HARBAUGH, Theodore	JAN 12 1832
WALTERS, Mary	WHITE, Richard	APR 21 1835
WALTERS, Mary Jane	ROLES, John	SEP 06 1842
WALTERS, William	LANPHIER, Ann Idella	JUN 26 1828
WALTON, Coates	SHOEMAKER, Mary R.	FEB 09 1853
WALTON, Cornelia H.	DAVIS, Almond W.	JUL 17 1854
WALTON, James H.	ANDERSON, Eliza	JAN 03 1852
WALZ, George	MUNDENG, Mary	DEC 14 1854
WANBERG, Henry	PRIBRAM, Amilie	JAN 06 1858
WANDERBY, John	NORR, Magdalene	JUL 28 1842
WANDLING, David	ROHRER, Margaret B.A.	APR 30 1851
WANNALD, William	McCAUSLAND, Mary	MAR 01 1827
WANNELL, Charles P.	MILES, Mary	AUG 01 1835
WANNELL, Joseph F.	COLLEY, Jannett E.	JAN 10 1846
WANS, Sarah Jane	ROOD, Oliver P.	SEP 20 1838
WANSFOOT, Eliza	BELL, John Thomas	DEC 10 1846
WAPLES, Louisa E.	SNYDER, Benjamin	OCT 14 1846
WAR, Mahaly (blk)	HORATIO, Jennings	APR 03 1827
WARD, Amelia (blk)	HUMPHREYS, Hezekiah	OCT 14 1826
WARD, Ann	PEABODY, Joseph L.	OCT 06 1834
WARD, Ann Maria	KLOPFER, Christian G.	FEB 02 1841
WARD, Caroline	BREVITT, Edwin W.	JUL 13 1842
WARD, Catharine	KINSLOW, William	NOV 15 1851
WARD, Catharine A.	HOFFMAN, Richard	SEP 03 1840
WARD, Catharine Virginia	GRUMWELL, John H.	MAY 05 1845
WARD, Catherine	FUGITT, Gustavus	APR 17 1817
WARD, Charles	AGNUE, Martha	OCT 07 1827
WARD, Charles	SAVOY, Laura (blk)	JUN 04 1855
WARD, Christiana (blk)	BELL, Thomas	APR 01 1840
WARD, Christiana (blk)	WILLIAMS, George	AUG 18 1851
WARD, Edward	PIERCE, Susannah	FEB 01 1840
WARD, Eliza	BROWN, William	APR 16 1822
WARD, Eliza	SHAW, Edward	FEB 29 1840
WARD, Eliza Jane	ROBERTS, Robert E.	JUL 18 1836
WARD, Elizabeth	MARTIN, Anthony S.	APR 05 1831
WARD, Elizabeth	MAJOR, David B.	OCT 28 1845
WARD, Elizabeth Ann	MAJORS, John	NOV 13 1845
WARD, Emily (blk)	HARNES, John	NOV 13 1855
WARD, Francis	LYNCH, Jane	AUG 19 1844
WARD, George W.	GLENN, Mary Jane	JUN 19 1841
WARD, George W.	JACKSON, Francis A.	JAN 15 1846
WARD, George W.	ST. CLAIR, Julia A.E.	DEC 06 1856
WARD, Grace Ann (blk)	MADISON, Luke	MAR 01 1854
WARD, Harriet	VERMILLION, William	FEB 20 1844

District of Columbia Marriage Licenses, 1811-1858

WARD, Henry	BENSTON, Kesiah (blk)	JUL 01 1829
WARD, Horatio M.	McCORMICK, Hannah	NOV 16 1824
WARD, James	TWOMY, Catharine	OCT 31 1855
WARD, Jane F.	ORME, William C.	MAY 10 1831
WARD, John	YOUNG, Hellen (blk)	AUG 10 1826
WARD, John	GIBSON, Susanna	DEC 07 1829
WARD, John P.	THAYER, Maria T.	JAN 02 1845
WARD, John Thomas	FURGERSON, Maria	NOV 02 1839
WARD, Joseph D.	DUNNINGTON, Anna E.	AUG 22 1849
WARD, Julia Ann	BRANNER, Peter	NOV 17 1825
WARD, Lucinda (blk)	WATERS, John	APR 27 1854
WARD, Margaret	LANDON, James	OCT 06 1851
WARD, Margaret A.	NORMENT, Richard B.	OCT 05 1853
WARD, Martha W.	BRADLY, Jos. S.	JUN 20 1855
WARD, Mary	HOPKINS, Major	JAN 18 1858
WARD, Mary Ann (blk)	BROWN, William	FEB 21 1850
WARD, Mary Ann	MITCHELL, John F.	NOV 05 1850
WARD, Mary E.	PIERCE, John	MAY 29 1854
WARD, Mary Ellen	NORMENT, Samuel	JUN 25 1846
WARD, Mary Jane	SCOTT, John J.	FEB 03 1834
WARD, May A.	CRANSTON, Robert S.	JUN 16 1837
WARD, Mildred S.	SWANN, Thomas T.	MAR 10 1836
WARD, Mitchell M.	NORWOOD, Mary Ann	NOV 26 1845
WARD, Rachael	SPILLMAN, Thomas	MAY 28 1835
WARD, Rebecca	ROBEY, Benjamin	APR 17 1812
WARD, Robert	MACKABEE, Mary	OCT 23 1845
WARD, Rosena	DRAIN, Henry	DEC 30 1820
WARD, Sarah	BURNES, Henry	APR 06 1858
WARD, Sarah C.	LAYTON, George E.	SEP 28 1854
WARD, Susanna	GALLAGHAR, Hugh	SEP 08 1835
WARD, Thomas	BURROWS, Mary A.E.	APR 04 1844
WARD, Thomas	KELLY, Ann	SEP 29 1854
WARD, Thomas G.	MONTGOMERY, Eliza	MAY 06 1857
WARD, Ulysses B.	WATERS, Ann E.	OCT 26 1855
WARD, Ulyssus	BEALL, Susan Virlinda	SEP 26 1816
WARD, William	GRIMES, Elizabeth	MAR 01 1849
WARD, William H.	OTTERBACK, Sarah	MAY 02 1848
WARD, William J.	GREEN, Isabella F.	DEC 04 1853
WARD, [blank]	KRAFFT, George	SEP 05 1854
WARDELL, Arene V.	STINEMETZ, Benj. H.	JAN 03 1853
WARDELL, Laurene	VANSCIVER, William	JUN 08 1846
WARDELL, Maria	DIXON, William T.D.	JAN 08 1852
WARDELL, Samuel	MURPHEY, Chloe	MAY 23 1820
WARDELL, Samuel P.	DIXON, Mary J.	NOV 22 1847
WARDEN, William	FERRIS, Mary	JUN 28 1832
WARDER, Helen C.	SEUFFERLE, George J.	NOV 15 1853
WARDER, James	SPEAKES, Eliza	SEP 15 1842
WARDER, Mary	WHEELER, Alexander	JUL 18 1849
WARDER, Mary V.	BOWIE, William F.	JAN 21 1851
WARDER, Walter	GIBSON, Ann S.	OCT 20 1830
WARDER, Walter	DAVIS, Mary Jane	DEC 02 1853
WARDER, Wm.	SHERIFF, Cornelia M.	JUN 21 1848
WARE, Ann R.	MULLIN, William S.	APR 17 1849
WARE, George	BUTLER, Betsey (blk)	JUL 28 1831
WARE, Henry A.	STARLING, Jane G.	OCT 04 1854
WARE, John	MARTIN, Ann	APR 01 1816
WARE, Martha E.	BEAN, James W.	DEC 22 1855
WARE, McKimsey	BUTLER, Mary	JUN 17 1813

District of Columbia Marriage Licenses, 1811-1858

WARE, Samuel	WEAVER, Margaret	APR 02 1818
WARE, Spencer	JENKINS, Catherine Ann	JAN 03 1840
WARE, Thomas	BURNETT, Barbar	SEP 30 1839
WARENSFORD, Debby	TILLEY, Henry	JUN 21 1813
WARFIELD, Able	ADAMS, Sarah Ann	JUN 28 1838
WARFIELD, Flavilla (blk)	WORMLEY, John	JAN 04 1833
WARFIELD, Margaret	ROUSTAGE, James	AUG 10 1828
WARFIELD, Mary Elizabeth	ARLETT, Constantine	JAN 31 1839
WARFIELD, Sarah	BROMELL, John	FEB 09 1822
WARFIELD, Thomas	FOSTER, Eleanor	FEB 22 1816
WARFIELD, William	LOW, Martha	SEP 25 1850
WARFORD, David	SUTTLE, Mary	MAR 02 1817
WARFORD, Jane	DAVIS, John	JUL 27 1826
WARING, Basil	SHRAKE, Julia A.	DEC 05 1846
WARING, Basil H.	BENNETT, Sarah B.	OCT 27 1829
WARING, Eleanor	BRENT, James R.	MAY 17 1831
WARING, Eliza G.	HALLOWAY, Ranson	JAN 06 1851
WARING, Elizabeth	FAULCONER, John W.	OCT 06 1845
WARING, John P.	MANNING, Eveline G.	JUN 06 1843
WARING, Joseph H.	MINOR, Martha	FEB 07 1839
WARING, Maria L.	HUDDLESTON, John E.	JAN 28 1851
WARING, Mary	BROOKE, Nicholas	JAN 12 1836
WARING, Mary Elizabeth	GOODLOE, Daniel R.	JUN 25 1851
WARING, Mary Jane	KEPPLER, Samuel [Rev.]	JUL 14 1831
WARING, Rachel E.	BARTON, Green H.	MAY 12 1847
WARING, Thomas B.	CLARK, Elizabeth A.	FEB 27 1855
WARING, Thomas G.	HEREFORD, Caroline E.	JUN 28 1842
WARK, Frances	McFARLAND, John	DEC 04 1819
WARKENFILE, Peter	OFFAIN, Dora V.	AUG 30 1853
WARLEY, Alexander F.	FORREST, Emily C.	JUN 12 1850
WARNER, Amelia	PATTERSON, William	JAN 31 1855
WARNER, Ann	JOHNSON, Byran	JUL 26 1815
WARNER, Charles	MITCHELL, Rebecca	JAN 08 1850
WARNER, Edward	DASHIELL, Sarah Ellen	MAY 09 1842
WARNER, Eliza C.	HASLETINE, James C.	JUL 22 1843
WARNER, Elizth. (blk)	WARNER, Henry	NOV 22 1856
WARNER, George, Jr.	CHUBB, Mary Virginia	OCT 27 1856
WARNER, George W.	PESNER, Mary Ellen	AUG 24 1848
WARNER, Henry	PETER, Mary	NOV 26 1833
WARNER, Henry	WARNER, Elizth. (blk)	NOV 22 1856
WARNER, James	TEALLE, Cesecitia	DEC 28 1815
WARNER, James	WILSON, Maria (blk)	MAY 23 1849
WARNER, Judson	LITTLEJOHN, Mary Ann	DEC 24 1838
WARNER, Leander A.	RUMNEY, Margaret	AUG 15 1823
WARNER, Maria (blk)	BELL, Thomas	NOV 07 1854
WARNER, Mary Ann	LLOYD, James H.	NOV 24 1842
WARNER, Mary E.	TRAVERS, Elias	JAN 20 1855
WARNER, Nicholas	CONNER, Ann (blk)	FEB 25 1826
WARNER, Nicholas	JULIUS, Rebecca (blk)	MAY 19 1836
WARNER, Nicholas	TINNEY, Eliza Ann	AUG 05 1847
WARNER, Sophia	McCOSTICK, Peter	JUL 17 1844
WARRAN, Mary Jane	GODDARD, Joseph	JAN 05 1832
WARREN, Caroline (blk)	MASSIE, John	JUN 20 1844
WARREN, George B., Jr.	TAYLOE, Eugenia P.W.	APR 29 1856
WARREN, George H.	BUTLER, Ann Maria T.	MAR 23 1847
WARREN, Harriet L.	COSLEY, Howard W.	JUN 02 1856
WARREN, Isaac	PATTERSON, Eliza	JUL 06 1835
WARREN, James, Jr.	SHIELLS, Elizabeth D.	SEP 19 1844

District of Columbia Marriage Licenses, 1811-1858

WARREN, John O.	MURRAY, Eleanor Mary	JUN 26 1844
WARREN, Joseph	SCOTT, Louisa	OCT 08 1817
WARREN, Joseph	HAZLE, Ellen	SEP 25 1857
WARREN, Kitty	REEVES, William J.	MAY 22 1832
WARREN, Lucinda (blk)	WARREN, Augustus	JUN 20 1844
WARREN, Martha Jane (blk)	BINNS, Frederick E.	FEB 15 1849
WARREN, Mary E.	JONES, Charles	AUG 02 1856
WARREN, Mary R.	THOMAS, Thomas J.	OCT 17 1856
WARREN, Robert	GAILOR, Elizabeth	JUL 08 1813
WARREN, Robert	BLAUIS, Rebecca	MAY 07 1829
WARREN, Robert	THORN, Victoria	NOV 08 1856
WARREN, Sarah	FRANKLIN, James	OCT 24 1857
WARREN, Thomas G.	RETTER, Elizabeth A.	MAY 23 1836
WARREN, William	HARRIS, Mary	OCT 15 1857
WARRENFORD, Eliza	HILTON, Edward	DEC 25 1844
WARRENSFORD, Matilda	AUSTIN, William	DEC 26 1818
WARRICK, Abraham	JONES, Margaret	DEC 20 1850
WARRING, Arthur	HEPBURN, Juliann M.	APR 02 1831
WARRING, Catharine	POLK, Samuel C.	SEP 29 1849
WARRING, Erasmus G.	BRASHEARS, Mary	DEC 28 1833
WARRING, Henrietta M.S.	YOUNG, Edward D.	JAN 10 1826
WARRING, Henry	NEALE, Mariah (blk)	APR 03 1837
WARRING, Roberter	KNOXVILLE, James	AUG 14 1847
WARRINGSFORD, Sarah	THOMAS, Henry	APR 01 1830
WARRINGTON, Eliza Crane	CHUBB, Charles St. John	APR 03 1850
WARRINGTON, Lewis, Jr.	SCOTT, Mary C.	FEB 03 1845
WARTHAM, Thomas	SIMMONS, Elizabeth	OCT 12 1812
WARTHAN, Prudence	MAXWELL, Geo. P.	JUN 15 1822
WARTHEN, Charles	COLLINS, Henrietta	JUL 02 1816
WARTHEN, Henrietta	WETZELL, Lazarus	MAY 24 1825
WARWICK, Ellen Virginia	WALKER, Thomas Douglass	MAY 30 1854
WARWICK, John	GOLDING, Elizabeth	JAN 03 1829
WARWICK, William D.	CARROLL, Mary	NOV 04 1856
WARWICK, William F.	WHEELE, Susanna	JUL 07 1812
WASHBURN, Edward A.	LINDSLY, Frances H.	JUN 01 1854
WASHBURN, Sylvanus N.	BELL, Mary Jane	MAY 08 1843
WASHINGTON, Alexander	PEYTON, Sarah (blk)	MAR 02 1841
WASHINGTON, Ann Maria (blk)	JOHNSON, Richard	OCT 10 1848
WASHINGTON, Bailey [Dr.]	LEE, Ann Matilda	NOV 26 1829
WASHINGTON, Burdet	MILLER, Mariah	MAR 16 1844
WASHINGTON, Caroline (blk)	THOMAS, William	FEB 04 1843
WASHINGTON, Cassilla	BUSH, Thomas	JUN 21 1854
WASHINGTON, Catherine V.	GILL, Joseph A.	DEC 21 1850
WASHINGTON, Fairinda F.	PAYNE, James H.	DEC 11 1848
WASHINGTON, Fannie L.	MOTZER, Daniel	OCT 08 1856
WASHINGTON, Fannie Wallace	READING, Pierson Barton	MAR 12 1856
WASHINGTON, George	WILLIAMS, Christy (blk)	JUL 05 1856
WASHINGTON, George C.	PETER, Ann T.	OCT 25 1821
WASHINGTON, Hariet A. (blk)	HENSON, David	APR 16 1857
WASHINGTON, Harriet Ann	GARRETT, William, Junr.	JUL 07 1830
WASHINGTON, Henry	JONES, Jane	OCT 04 1849
WASHINGTON, James	COLE, Harriet	SEP 15 1847
WASHINGTON, Jane (col'd)	CATLETT, George	SEP 18 1830
WASHINGTON, John	HENDERSON, Ann	OCT 19 1840
WASHINGTON, John	SIMMS, Juilan	JAN 15 1857
WASHINGTON, John Tayloe	ASHTON, Mary D.	JUN 10 1850
WASHINGTON, Lucy	TODD, Thomas	MAR 28 1812
WASHINGTON, Lund	BIGGS, Sarah	JUN 11 1819

District of Columbia Marriage Licenses, 1811-1858

WASHINGTON, Lund	JOHNSON, Sally	APR 11 1823
WASHINGTON, Marcelena	COOK, George	OCT 25 1837
WASHINGTON, Margaret (blk)	WATERS, Richard	OCT 09 1851
WASHINGTON, Mary E.	MacPHERSON, Joseph S.	JAN 28 1819
WASHINGTON, Mary J. (blk)	BROWN, Francis	APR 16 1850
WASHINGTON, Mary V.	DAY, Thomas	APR 21 1858
WASHINGTON, Mary W.	JAMES, William	OCT 14 1828
WASHINGTON, Sarah	MANNUX, William	DEC 28 1847
WASHINGTON, Susan Jean	LEWIS, Edward Simmons	DEC 02 1815
WASHINGTON, Thomas	FORREST, Louisa (blk)	NOV 19 1851
WASHINGTON, Virginia M.	WELLS, Benjamin F.	DEC 06 1849
WASHINGTON, William	MILLER, Mary	NOV 26 1832
WASON, Caroline	LITTLE, John	OCT 02 1833
WASON, Eliza	STEWART, Isreal	NOV 04 1830
WASON, Israel	BOOTH, Mary	AUG 06 1836
WATERHELDNER, Teresa	LOFFLER, Jacob	APR 17 1856
WATERHOLDNER, Frederick W.	TONE, Jeannete	NOV 17 1856
WATERMAN, Edwin	LINDSAY, Maria A.	SEP 20 1851
WATERMAN, Edwin	YOUNG, Elizabeth O.	OCT 14 1854
WATERS, Ann E.	WARD, Ulysses B.	OCT 26 1855
WATERS, Ann Eliza	CARR, Edmund	MAY 16 1848
WATERS, Catharine (blk)	BUDD, Daniel	AUG 28 1849
WATERS, Catherine N.	SHANKS, Michael	MAY 18 1836
WATERS, Cyrus	JACKSON, Artridge P.	JAN 19 1844
WATERS, Deborah	ADAMS, George A.	MAY 19 1825
WATERS, Dwight R.	EDMONSTON, Marcelia	APR 05 1852
WATERS, Eliza	SMITH, John	SEP 02 1830
WATERS, Eliza	HUNTER, Milbourn	NOV 17 1832
WATERS, Elizabeth	SMOOT, Thomas	JAN 20 1831
WATERS, Elizabeth (blk)	BROWN, Thomas	JUN 21 1832
WATERS, Elkanah	LOWRY, Mary	JUL 31 1832
WATERS, Emily	BROWN, Arch	JUL 07 1857
WATERS, Flavius Josephus	NALLEY, Emily	MAR 28 1855
WATERS, Franklin	BROOKE, Mary Ann	JUN 05 1855
WATERS, George	MITCHEL, Ann H.	SEP 04 1836
WATERS, Harriet I.	THOMPSON, John H.	NOV 01 1848
WATERS, Isabella	PARKER, Southey S.	OCT 31 1854
WATERS, James T.	LOWRY, Jane Margaret	JUL 10 1847
WATERS, Jane	CUNNINGHAM, William	SEP 13 1845
WATERS, John	DAVIS, Catherine S.	MAY 02 1848
WATERS, John	TWEEDY, Julia E.	JUN 08 1852
WATERS, John	WARD, Lucinda (blk)	APR 27 1854
WATERS, John C.D.	WELLS, Eliza	MAR 08 1827
WATERS, John H.	JACKSON, Mary E.	NOV 10 1840
WATERS, John N.	OWENS, Jane	JAN 21 1825
WATERS, Kavia M.	BECK, William	JAN 11 1819
WATERS, Mahala Ann	DREW, Edward M.	JAN 12 1832
WATERS, Margaret Ann	GROVES, John W.	JUN 05 1855
WATERS, Martha (blk)	ADAMS, Caleb	DEC 27 1843
WATERS, Martha Ann	KNOTT, John Lewis	OCT 21 1839
WATERS, Mary	HARDESTY, Thomas	DEC 21 1827
WATERS, Mary (blk)	PENDLE, Isaac	JUL 20 1854
WATERS, Mary Ann	PARKER, Southey S.	MAY 04 1848
WATERS, Mary Ann	McGOLDRICK, William	OCT 04 1852
WATERS, Mary Malvina	GRAY, Henry M.	SEP 21 1841
WATERS, Mary V.	BAILEY, Ignatius	AUG 02 1858
WATERS, Peter	HUTTON, Jane (blk)	JAN 11 1836
WATERS, Priscilla Ann	CROWN, Joseph F.	JUL 29 1850

District of Columbia Marriage Licenses, 1811-1858

WATERS, Rebecca	GRIGGS, William	OCT 04 1853
WATERS, Richard	WASHINGTON, Margaret (blk)	OCT 09 1851
WATERS, Richard H.	THRIFT, Ann A.	JUN 16 1857
WATERS, Richard R.	SHAW, Jerusha Ann	DEC 15 1817
WATERS, Robert	DORRELL, Anna Louisa	JUN 17 1849
WATERS, Robert A.	MICKUM, Ann Maria	APR 29 1847
WATERS, Sally Ann	SIMPSON, Charles R.	SEP 11 1852
WATERS, Samuel	BROWN, Catherine	JUN 03 1845
WATERS, Sarah	KING, Vincent	APR 21 1835
WATERS, Sewall D.	ST. CLAIR, Eleanor	MAR 12 1829
WATERS, Susannah	HOLLAND, John E.	SEP 13 1836
WATERS, Thomas	McCARDLE, Rose	JUN 16 1850
WATERS, Thomas R.	WINTERS, Mary	OCT 15 1816
WATERS, Warren S.	KINNEY, Mary	DEC 18 1852
WATERS, William	SHREVE, Julia Ann	JAN 31 1833
WATERS, William	ROBEY, Eliza Ann	JUL 29 1857
WATERS, William E.	EVANS, Abby J.	OCT 01 1855
WATHAN, Jane E.	NICHOLLS, Thomas L.	JAN 23 1844
WATHEN, Catherine	ALWINE, Jacob	OCT 06 1857
WATHEN, Elias	COLEMAN, Sarah J.	NOV 23 1818
WATHEN, Jane	BAKER, John	FEB 23 1816
WATKINS, Adam	DAVID, Clarissa (blk)	SEP 22 1847
WATKINS, Ann E.	BELT, Thomas J.	SEP 29 1820
WATKINS, Anna	CHALMERS, Charles [Lt.]	JUL 01 1834
WATKINS, Caroline L.	WATKINS, Julius	JUL 05 1825
WATKINS, Catherine	BURNS, James	APR 29 1823
WATKINS, Eliada	WRIGHT, Emily	MAR 14 1853
WATKINS, George S.	RAMSAY, Caroline H.	JUN 01 1841
WATKINS, Julius	WATKINS, Caroline L.	JUL 05 1825
WATKINS, Martha Ann	SANDERSON, William	JUN 11 1812
WATKINS, Mary	CARLTON, Henry L.	JAN 29 1833
WATKINS, Mary	MEAD, Franklin	MAY 01 1855
WATKINS, Mary Agnes	BLACKFAN, Ogden W.	SEP 16 1854
WATKINS, Mary T. Catherine	SMITH, John Thomas	JUL 21 1856
WATKINS, Octavus	CHALMERS, Laura Rebecca Isadore	DEC 11 1833
WATKINS, Peyton	BELL, Harriett (blk)	DEC 10 1834
WATKINS, Robert H.	SUTER, Sarah E.	APR 08 1850
WATKINS, Stephen	WALKER, Catharine	JUL 13 1818
WATKINS, William	SWEENY, Matilda Jane	OCT 07 1856
WATKINS, William W.	TILLEY, Mary	OCT 04 1821
WATKINSON, Harriet	NEWMAN, Franklin	FEB 23 1838
WATMOUGH, John G.	PLEASONTON, Mary M.	NOV 15 1832
WATSON, Agnes	THORN, William T.	OCT 29 1857
WATSON, Alexander R.	CLARKE, Charlotte	APR 20 1822
WATSON, Allison	ADAMS, Mariah R.	OCT 06 1832
WATSON, Ann	WATSON, James	APR 13 1820
WATSON, Benjamin	BUTLER, Jane	APR 08 1833
WATSON, David L.	DeANGLAS, Belinda	APR 06 1857
WATSON, Donald	McNEALE, Mary	OCT 09 1823
WATSON, Edward B.	BROWN, Rhoda S.	APR 01 1824
WATSON, Elia Ann	HUSTON, James G.	JUL 27 1838
WATSON, Eliz.	NUTWELL, Levi	APR 23 1814
WATSON, Elizabeth	ANDREWS, William W.	JAN 06 1821
WATSON, Elizabeth	HARLEY, James	NOV 11 1844
WATSON, Elizabeth B.	KIDWELL, Joseph F.	FEB 22 1849
WATSON, Elizth. M.	LEWIS, John W.	MAR 08 1855
WATSON, Emiline N.	LAMB, Theodore L.	MAR 14 1854
WATSON, Harriet L.	HORNER, John S.	OCT 30 1834

District of Columbia Marriage Licenses, 1811-1858

WATSON, Henry B.	HIGDON, Mary Ann	APR 17 1837
WATSON, Isaac	BEALL, Emily Orman	MAY 27 1830
WATSON, James	WATSON, Ann	APR 13 1820
WATSON, James M.	CROSBY, Therese N.	JAN 23 1850
WATSON, James R.	JOHNSON, Susanna F.	JAN 28 1840
WATSON, James W.	PRINCE, Ann	OCT 26 1826
WATSON, Jane L.	GRAHAM, George	JUL 07 1825
WATSON, John	BANSWELL, Sarah	FEB 11 1819
WATSON, John	HERBERT, Maria	NOV 25 1837
WATSON, John	LEWIS, Eliza	FEB 11 1852
WATSON, John C.	ROBINSON, Eliza	NOV 17 1829
WATSON, John R.	GRAVES, Ann	APR 10 1813
WATSON, John R.	BURNETT, Sarah	APR 13 1820
WATSON, Joshua	HAZZARD, Mary Ann	JAN 02 1849
WATSON, Laura	WATSON, Robt. D.	MAY 20 1848
WATSON, Lewis Henry	HARRON, Elizabeth	MAR 31 1856
WATSON, Margaret	KELLY, James	FEB 14 1812
WATSON, Maria E.	GIBBONS, Charles H.	DEC 10 1851
WATSON, Martha	HINES, Samuel	AUG 18 1827
WATSON, Martha	FENTON, Daniel	JAN 18 1854
WATSON, Mary	STEPHENS, William H.	SEP 25 1845
WATSON, Mary	GARNER, Jefferson	FEB 09 1848
WATSON, Mary	DEEVERS, Henry	OCT 20 1852
WATSON, Mary A.	HANNON, Henry	MAY 06 1829
WATSON, Mary E.	WILLIAMS, Raymond W.	MAY 11 1854
WATSON, Mary Elizabeth	HOPSON, Benjamin J.	NOV 10 1852
WATSON, Mary Jane	CURTIN, Richard	AUG 19 1852
WATSON, Peter	WHITEFORD, Marthy	DEC 09 1816
WATSON, Robert	CARTER, Elizabeth	OCT 23 1851
WATSON, Robert D.	WATSON, Laura	MAY 20 1848
WATSON, Sarah	HUGGENS, Francis	DEC 22 1845
WATSON, Sarah Ann	HILL, James N.	SEP 02 1852
WATSON, Sarah E.	EATON, Edward H.	JUL 13 1848
WATSON, Sarah E.	DANT, William T.	MAR 13 1849
WATSON, Sophia E.	CARRINGTON, William	SEP 26 1854
WATSON, Thomas P.	BARGEVIN, Mary A.	MAY 19 1854
WATSON, William	CURTIN, Eliza	JUL 11 1853
WATSON, William A.	TAYLOR, Mary Jane	JUL 23 1846
WATSON, William Westley	GATES, Ann Catherine	JUL 14 1833
WATT, James	ANDREA, Christina	AUG 12 1845
WATT, John	MASTERSON, Jane	SEP 22 1847
WATTERSTON, Sara M.	HOLCOMB, Albert A., U.S.N.	JUN 06 1841
WATTS, Augustus	BARNES, Ellen (blk)	OCT 14 1839
WATTS, Harriet	MATTELY, John	JUN 14 1827
WATTS, Harriet Ann (blk)	DAY, Roda	DEC 05 1850
WATTS, James	MEDLEY, Eliza	JUN 04 1842
WATTS, Kitty (blk)	LAUDY, Thomas	APR 08 1830
WATTS, Lewis	CHASE, Maria (blk)	MAY 06 1858
WATTS, Malinda (blk)	LANCASTER, Benjamin	JUN 05 1850
WATTS, Martha B.	ELBERT, John L.	APR 26 1815
WATTS, Rebecca (blk)	BUTLER, David	DEC 05 1850
WATTS, Samuel	HUMPHREYS, Ara A.E. (blk)	AUG 27 1850
WATTS, Sarah (blk)	THOMAS, Augustus	MAY 21 1833
WATTS, William	BROOKS, Susan (blk)	MAY 05 1831
WAUGH, Beverly	BUSHLEY, Cathn. B.	APR 21 1812
WAUGH, Caroline	HOOE, James	SEP 17 1828
WAUGH, Caroline	MORGAN, Thomas P.	NOV 04 1845
WAUGH, Cornelia V.	GODEY, George W.	OCT 10 1849

District of Columbia Marriage Licenses, 1811-1858

WAUGH, Emeline A.	ROSS, John W.	APR 16 1847
WAUGH, Henrietta	DODSON, James B.	SEP 28 1841
WAUGH, James E.	McKELDEN, Sarah V.	FEB 15 1858
WAUGH, Samuel	YOUNG, Eliza	APR 21 1852
WAUGH, Sarah (blk)	SERGEANT, Henry	JUL 10 1829
WAUGH, Susan J.	BROWN, Benjamin Franklin	OCT 19 1839
WAUGH, William	BALL, Nancy	JUN 16 1834
WAUGH, William A.	HOOVER, Julianna P.	FEB 25 1845
WAUZER, Louis	LEE, Louisa (blk)	JUL 30 1846
WAW, Elizabeth	GRIMES, Thomas	NOV 27 1824
WAY, Adeline	PLANT, John	DEC 15 1834
WAY, Thomas	CURRY, Mary	NOV 30 1820
WAYBORN, Horace	DARLEY, Susan	MAY 02 1830
WAYLAND, Abram C.	KENNEDY, Margaret	DEC 20 1855
WAYLAND, Benjamin C.	BUCKNER, Elizabeth M.	SEP 27 1847
WAYNE, Catharine [Mrs.]	OWNER, William	MAR 22 1821
WAYSON, Mary	LITTLE, Peter	NOV 30 1824
WAYSON, Matilda F.	ROBINSON, William T.	FEB 09 1854
WAYSON, Nicholas	BATEMAN, Hannah J.	FEB 11 1858
WEADON, Richard W.	COLE, Matilda	MAR 14 1821
WEAR, Matilda	GRAY, Vincent	JUL 03 1817
WEASNER, Mary Ann	CUMBERLAND, John	OCT 12 1835
WEASNER, Mary C.	PAYNE, James	JUL 23 1853
WEASNER, Sarah Jane	RATCLIFF, John	FEB 06 1847
WEAST, Eleanor	BUCKINGHAM, William	NOV 25 1817
WEATHERALL, Ann	CONNOR, John	JUL 15 1817
WEAVER, Adaline	SHERIFF, Edwin	OCT 25 1827
WEAVER, Ann	MITCHELL, Dennis	OCT 28 1830
WEAVER, Ann	ANDERSON, Noble	AUG 25 1853
WEAVER, Ann E.	BANKS, Saml. N.	FEB 26 1857
WEAVER, Ann M.	ARMSTRONG, James	NOV 05 1835
WEAVER, Catharine	BAKER, Henry	JUL 08 1845
WEAVER, Catharine Mary	STANSBURY, Emerson	OCT 06 1836
WEAVER, Catherine	DOUTSCH, Peter	MAY 14 1840
WEAVER, Charity	BURGESS, William F.	APR 05 1849
WEAVER, David	WURTON, Ellen	JAN 30 1844
WEAVER, Elizabeth	COOK, William	FEB 03 1825
WEAVER, Elizabeth	CHAMBERLAIN, John U.	SEP 20 1856
WEAVER, Erastus C.	FINCH, Margaret A.	NOV 23 1852
WEAVER, Helen M.	CHAPIN, Erastus M.	MAR 28 1854
WEAVER, Henry	BARNES, Mary Ann	JAN 01 1848
WEAVER, Jacob	JOHNSON, Dolly	AUG 17 1841
WEAVER, Jacob Mott	SMITH, Isabella Graham	JUN 25 1828
WEAVER, James	WINDHAM, Ann Delia	SEP 07 1839
WEAVER, Joseph	ROUT, Caroline	DEC 15 1846
WEAVER, Joseph	KING, Catherine	MAY 02 1853
WEAVER, Louisa	McGHAN, Francis	NOV 09 1857
WEAVER, Margaret	WARE, Samuel	APR 02 1818
WEAVER, Margaret	KIRKPATRICK, John B.	JUL 03 1843
WEAVER, Mary	ROCK, Theophilus	APR 28 1853
WEAVER, Rachael Ann	BOONE, Robert	AUG 23 1831
WEAVER, Samuel	CUNNINGHAM, Agness Ann	NOV 09 1844
WEAVER, William	HINES, Letitia	JUL 04 1838
WEAVER, William	PURSELY, Frances	MAY 28 1849
WEAVER, William V.W.	HARLEY, Sarah C.	JAN 03 1857
WEBB, Addie E.	JENKINS, William	JAN 06 1858
WEBB, Albert J.	FARRELL, Harriet	NOV 19 1846
WEBB, Aquilla	TURNER, Rebecca	JAN 19 1826

District of Columbia Marriage Licenses, 1811-1858

WEBB, Edward	BURGEE, Emma R.	OCT 11 1853
WEBB, Elizabeth C.	TRUNNELL, William D.	MAY 28 1850
WEBB, Elizabeth Gibbs	THOMAS, Andrew Merecin	MAY 18 1847
WEBB, Emanuel	McINTOSH, Ann	OCT 14 1856
WEBB, Fanny	WHITMORE, Francis	FEB 08 1821
WEBB, Geo. W.	PALFREY, Jane	DEC 25 1834
WEBB, John	TELLEY, Mary	JAN 02 1845
WEBB, John F.	POOR, Charlotte A.	SEP 05 1822
WEBB, Rachel	BEALL, Lawson	JUL 12 1823
WEBB, Robert	TALTON, Elizabeth	JUN 22 1812
WEBB, W.L.	HENRY, Ann E.	SEP 30 1835
WEBB, William B.	RANDALL, Emily M.	OCT 30 1856
WEBER, Henry	LINKINS, Elizth. A.	SEP 10 1855
WEBER, John	BOWER, Mary	OCT 25 1851
WEBER, Josephine	FAISS, Damian	MAY 01 1841
WEBER, Margaret	BOMBAUGH, Harman	OCT 28 1845
WEBER, Mary Jane	SCHNEITHER, Joseph Levi	DEC 29 1848
WEBSTER, Alexander	CRUSOE, Charlotte (blk)	APR 17 1832
WEBSTER, Ann	GRAY, Hezekiah	NOV 10 1818
WEBSTER, Ann	DEAN, Samuel	JUL 10 1824
WEBSTER, Ann	HEATH, John	NOV 02 1850
WEBSTER, Ann Maria	CLEMENTS, William	JUN 24 1847
WEBSTER, Ann W.	McCHESNEY, David	SEP 22 1815
WEBSTER, Caroline	MACHEN, Lewis	DEC 03 1816
WEBSTER, Caroline	EDELIN, Charles	FEB 22 1830
WEBSTER, Cassy Ann (blk)	BUTLER, William	DEC 07 1843
WEBSTER, Catherine	HEIRNE, David	MAY 04 1818
WEBSTER, Catherine	STRIDER, John L.	SEP 20 1844
WEBSTER, Catherine E.	DEWDNEY, William T.	FEB 16 1858
WEBSTER, Charles P.	WALKER, Mary E.	FEB 02 1857
WEBSTER, Charlotte	SAUNDERS, Beverly C.	NOV 01 1830
WEBSTER, Daniel C.	ROGERS, Esther A. (blk)	JUL 06 1857
WEBSTER, Daniel L.	CROSS, Lydia B.	MAY 02 1854
WEBSTER, Elizabeth	WINDSOR, John	JAN 10 1825
WEBSTER, Elizabeth	WALKER, George	DEC 28 1844
WEBSTER, Elizth. Eleanor	DUBANT, Mark	MAY 14 1821
WEBSTER, Emeline	CARTER, John E.	AUG 18 1847
WEBSTER, George	PALMER, Catharine	MAR 09 1829
WEBSTER, Hannah (blk)	THOMAS, Samuel	FEB 05 1835
WEBSTER, Harriet	THOMPSON, Robert	JAN 28 1847
WEBSTER, Harriet C.	PARKER, Peter	MAR 27 1841
WEBSTER, Henry	LEWIS, Catharine Ann	MAY 09 1829
WEBSTER, Henry A.	PERRY, Catharine	SEP 02 1826
WEBSTER, Hiram	TURNER, Virginia	APR 28 1851
WEBSTER, Israel B.	MERLE, Harriott	AUG 13 1846
WEBSTER, James [Dr.]	CRUTTENDEN, Mary Jane	APR 28 1829
WEBSTER, James	WELLING, Harriet	APR 16 1833
WEBSTER, James	FULLER, Elizabeth (blk)	DEC 05 1855
WEBSTER, Jane	KING, John	MAY 28 1832
WEBSTER, John Wesley	MAHUE, Lucinda	AUG 27 1832
WEBSTER, Linda	DAVIS, John	DEC 25 1826
WEBSTER, Louisa	STANFORD, Charles E.	MAY 27 1857
WEBSTER, Lucinda	BEERS, James	AUG 25 1846
WEBSTER, Margaret L.	LINDSAY, Samuel	NOV 15 1852
WEBSTER, Martha	MARKWARD, Thomas	JAN 14 1854
WEBSTER, Martha Ann (blk)	COKLEY, George W.	JUL 10 1832
WEBSTER, Mary Ann	BUTLER, William Alexander	SEP 11 1852
WEBSTER, Mary C.	HOLMEAD, Anthony	MAY 06 1822

District of Columbia Marriage Licenses, 1811-1858

WEBSTER, Mary Jane	TENLY, George B.	DEC 30 1845
WEBSTER, Mary Lynn	TUTTLE, Thomas	FEB 02 1817
WEBSTER, Mildred B.	McKEE, James	FEB 27 1838
WEBSTER, Philip L.	TAYLOR, Martha E.	DEC 26 1846
WEBSTER, Priscilla S.	PAGE, Charles G.	SEP 23 1844
WEBSTER, Rebecca	CROSS, Thomas	APR 09 1831
WEBSTER, Rezin	LODGE, Caroline	OCT 31 1833
WEBSTER, Rosa	MEADE, Robert H.	APR 27 1852
WEBSTER, Samuel	LOWE, Emily	JUL 22 1839
WEBSTER, Samuel	PENN, Mary	SEP 26 1840
WEBSTER, Samuel	MINNIS, Dolly	JUL 19 1851
WEBSTER, Sary Ann	PATTY, Thomas L.	MAR 05 1831
WEBSTER, Serafina C.	PATTISON, Thomas	JUN 28 1850
WEBSTER, Sophia	WICKS, Washington	OCT 09 1837
WEBSTER, Stephen	BATES, Fanny	MAY 24 1832
WEBSTER, Susan	ALPHIN, Walter	JUN 18 1822
WEBSTER, Thomas	HINGETY, Elizabeth	SEP 01 1823
WEBSTER, William	WOOTTEN, Mary	SEP 20 1834
WEBSTER, William	CONNER, Mary	JUL 30 1840
WEBSTER, William	CONTEE, Jane (blk)	JUN 17 1858
WEBSTER, William A.	FERGUSON, Catherine	SEP 30 1850
WEBSTER, William H.	DILE, Margaret	JAN 23 1854
WEBSTER, Zachariah	ANDERSON, Caroline	DEC 30 1845
WECHTER, Jno. G.	HANNERFIELD, Mary	NOV 21 1821
WEDDIN, James H.	FRANKLIN, Mary E.	OCT 25 1854
WEDDIN, Robert	LANHAM, Mary Ann	APR 19 1849
WEDDING, Ann	READDING, Henry	NOV 01 1853
WEDDLER, Matilda [Mrs.]	SUIT, Samuel S.	SEP 23 1830
WEDEN, William	GARDNER, Susan	DEC 23 1819
WEDGE, Mary Eleanor	PLUMMER, Richard	OCT 23 1830
WEDZE, James	GRAY, Adaline	NOV 22 1824
WEEB, Samuel	AVERSON, Catherine (blk)	MAY 14 1833
WEED, E.J.	McLEAN, Arabella E.	MAR 26 1827
WEED, Elijah J.	WHITNEY, Julia L.	FEB 09 1837
WEED, Walter H.	GRUMAER, Mary	OCT 07 1844
WEEDEN, Benjamin F.	CAUSIN, Mary Jane	APR 13 1843
WEEDEN, Henry A.	CAUSIN, Ann M.	MAR 10 1836
WEEDEN, Mary	LACEY, William B.	MAR 02 1852
WEEDEN, Mary J.	RICHARDS, William E.	MAY 13 1858
WEEDEN, Sallie E.	SESSFORD, Joseph S.	NOV 25 1856
WEEDON, William C.	CHAMPION, Martha	JUL 21 1856
WEEKES, Joseph	COX, Eliza Jane	AUG 14 1855
WEEKS, Joseph	TOTTEN, Vianna	MAY 17 1854
WEEMS, Franklin	BOWIE, Mary M.	JUN 06 1854
WEEMS, Mary A.	EMMONS, William	DEC 16 1856
WEEMS, Mary S.	TUFTS, Almanza	JUL 02 1855
WEEMS, Thomas N.	FRANKLIN, Mary E.	MAY 17 1855
WEEMS, William M.	BLACKMAN, Mary J.	JUN 29 1855
WEEVER, Mary	RIDGEWAY, Geo. W.W.	FEB 10 1835
WEFT, Rebecca	LEE, John	MAY 23 1816
WEGLIE, Anne	SMITH, William	FEB 21 1823
WEHN, Henry	SHEEN, Henrietta	MAY 22 1858
WEHRMEIEN, Fredericke	SCHALLENBERESS, Frederick	JUL 27 1854
WEICHAND, Matilda	BUSCHER, Henry	OCT 27 1857
WEIGAND, Margaret	GAENSLER, Henry	OCT 04 1841
WEIGAND, Mary	HAUCK, John G.	MAY 08 1848
WEIGERT, Fredericka	FLECHNER, William	MAY 24 1853
WEIGGMANN, Elizabeth	WALTER, Thomas	OCT 11 1853

District of Columbia Marriage Licenses, 1811-1858

WEIGHORN, Amalia	BAUER, Andon	NOV 12 1855
WEIGHTMAN, Henry T.	SIMMS, Pheby M.	MAY 07 1822
WEIGHTMAN, Richard Hanson	COXE, Susan B.	MAR 29 1842
WEIGHTMAN, Roger Chew	HANSON, Louisa Serena	MAY 05 1814
WEIGHTMAN, William	SHIRNEY, Eliza	FEB 07 1816
WEIGHTMAN, William	LEE, Ann Eliza	JAN 12 1830
WEIGLE, John	ARVENGINE, Caroline	JUL 19 1854
WEIKER, Casper	BOMKER, Catherine	MAY 14 1835
WEIL, John	KLEINDENST, Barbara	NOV 27 1852
WEIMAN, Helena	SOMMER, John	JUL 19 1838
WEIMAN, Wilhelmina	FREIMAN, Peter	MAR 10 1858
WEIMER, Rosena Justena	SCHAD, John	JAN 14 1834
WEIMERS, William	MEMMERT, Margaratha	AUG 15 1857
WEINSBURG, Julia	MILLER, George	FEB 19 1857
WEIR, James V.	SHIP, Ann T.	JUN 21 1838
WEIR, William	HAWLEY, Phoebe	MAY 04 1846
WEIS, Mary	ENGLE, John	NOV 05 1850
WEISKITTEL, Charlotte	MUNCH, Christian H.	SEP 08 1842
WEISNER, Thomas	MACKEAR, Mary	OCT 31 1816
WEISS, John C.	FULREETHEN, Mary Elenora	NOV 03 1849
WEISS, Joseph	SCHEDD, Margaret	SEP 15 1855
WEISTLING, Benj. J.	ROSS, Matilda Eveline	JUN 21 1831
WEITZEL, John W.	WHALEN, Sarah Jane	JUN 29 1847
WEIZER, Edward	SIMMONS, Mary Ellen	DEC 05 1848
WEIZNER, Malam	GREEN, Charity	NOV 19 1844
WELBURN, Catherine E.	GOLDSMITH, James W.	APR 22 1858
WELBY, Margaret	THORNTON, Owen	JUL 24 1857
WELCH, Ann	KANE, James	NOV 11 1852
WELCH, Aristides	ARMSTRONG, Henrietta R.	MAR 01 1856
WELCH, Catharine	BLUNDEN, Andrew	MAR 30 1847
WELCH, Dennis	CRAINER, Ellen	NOV 13 1851
WELCH, George	HOY, Mary Ann	NOV 24 1854
WELCH, Harriet	MORGAN, John R.	JUN 21 1853
WELCH, Hugh W.	MacINTOSH, Maria	APR 30 1818
WELCH, James Sylvester	LOGG, Harriet Jane	JUN 18 1836
WELCH, Jane	MYERS, Joseph	FEB 13 1851
WELCH, Johanna	SULLIVAN, Michael	FEB 06 1856
WELCH, John	CONGROSE, Eliza	JAN 01 1826
WELCH, John	COLVERT, Ellen	JAN 02 1847
WELCH, Leonard	KING, Christine	SEP 26 1843
WELCH, Lewis	READ, Sarah A.C.	DEC 05 1836
WELCH, Maria J.	DAVIS, Robert T.	FEB 09 1852
WELCH, Nora	O'KEEFE, Patrick	NOV 11 1852
WELCH, Patrick	STEELE, Elizabeth	APR 14 1828
WELCH, Patrick	LEWIS, Ann	MAY 30 1853
WELCH, Patrick	STONE, Mary Ann	JUL 04 1853
WELCH, Sarah E.	BAILEY, Hanson	MAR 23 1857
WELCH, Stephen	WHITE, Mary	OCT 07 1812
WELCH, Theresa	DUFFY, Patrick	SEP 01 1851
WELCH, Thomas	O'CONNOR, Mary	FEB 12 1858
WELCH, William	DONAHY, Margaret	JUL 30 1853
WELDEN, Margaret C.	HASLETINE, Charles M.	NOV 14 1837
WELFORD, Horace [Dr.]	PLATER, Rebecca	SEP 23 1822
WELING, Maria	HARTER, William	FEB 02 1856
WELL, John	SIDES, Margaret	NOV 29 1834
WELLEN, William	McGEE, Jane	MAY 09 1814
WELLER, Ellen Elizabeth	KENT, Phillip	SEP 26 1843
WELLER, John B.	TAYLOR, Susan P. McD.	MAR 05 1845

District of Columbia Marriage Licenses, 1811-1858

WELLFORD, Maria P.	HARRISON, Napoleon B.	MAR 19 1850
WELLING, Harriet	WEBSTER, James	APR 16 1833
WELLING, Rebecca	TALBUT, Sidney	APR 13 1833
WELLMEYER, Maria Katharine	HADUNG, Henrich	FEB 02 1855
WELLMORE, Mary Ann	MARLOW, John W.	SEP 03 1829
WELLS, Amanda M.	DONALDSON, William H.	SEP 23 1843
WELLS, America A.	HOLTSMAN, John T.	JUN 25 1834
WELLS, Ann	SPINKS, William	MAY 25 1820
WELLS, Ann	PERRY, Raphael	AUG 31 1849
WELLS, Anne	BALLANGER, John	DEC 22 1814
WELLS, Benjamin F.	WASHINGTON, Virginia M.	DEC 06 1849
WELLS, Catharine	HEATH, William D.	AUG 03 1838
WELLS, Catharine E.	DUMPHY, John	JUN 04 1823
WELLS, Cornelius	HILLER, Sarah	NOV 08 1839
WELLS, Elijah	RICHARDS, Anne E.	OCT 22 1851
WELLS, Eliza	WATERS, John C.D.	MAR 08 1827
WELLS, Elizabeth	EDMONSTON, Leonidas A.	JAN 16 1849
WELLS, Ellen (blk)	HUMPHREYS, Joseph	OCT 16 1845
WELLS, Frances	SMITH, Silas	AUG 30 1850
WELLS, George Anthony	BAKER, Harriet Jane	JUL 26 1858
WELLS, George R.	SEWALL, Ann Eliza	APR 19 1854
WELLS, Geraldine	CURTIS, Armistead B.	FEB 03 1857
WELLS, Harriet E.	BREWER, Albert	SEP 17 1857
WELLS, Harriet E.	ELLIS, William	FEB 24 1858
WELLS, Henry	COXEN, Martha	DEC 10 1850
WELLS, James	JONES, Sarah	DEC 11 1839
WELLS, Jane E.	MURPHY, Lawrence	JUL 11 1844
WELLS, Jane E.	RORICK, Michael	DEC 27 1855
WELLS, Jemima	CONNER, William	MAY 09 1827
WELLS, John	EMERSON, Matilda	APR 11 1833
WELLS, Julia Ann	LANSDALE, C.W. [Christopher]	NOV 17 1830
WELLS, John W.	SHINNERS, Mary Jane	SEP 24 1851
WELLS, Malvinia	DOWNS, Cornelius	JUN 08 1858
WELLS, Margaret	MEDAIR, Joseph	SEP 16 1813
WELLS, Margaret	SHOEMAKER, Samuel	MAY 06 1847
WELLS, Margaret	SHIPMAN, John	JUL 18 1857
WELLS, Maria Louisa	WILLIAMS, John	DEC 13 1831
WELLS, Mary E.	BUTTS, Laffayette W.	DEC 18 1843
WELLS, Mary E.	WILLIAMS, Moses	APR 13 1854
WELLS, Mary G.	QUEEN, John W.	DEC 09 1823
WELLS, Miranda	MORRISON, William	DEC 28 1830
WELLS, Nathaniel	ADAMSON, Mary Ellen	MAR 14 1850
WELLS, Nathaniel	BURNS, Mary C.	JAN 23 1856
WELLS, Peter	LITTLE, Ann	FEB 17 1814
WELLS, Richard	BAILEY, Elizabeth	NOV 22 1814
WELLS, Sarah	YOUNG, John	OCT 05 1853
WELLS, Sarah Ann	HERBERT, Francis	FEB 13 1816
WELLS, Thomas C.	LAMBERT, Jane	MAY 11 1836
WELSER, Ferdinand	McINTIRE, Harriet	JUL 15 1835
WELSH, Alice	RITTER, John F.	FEB 15 1854
WELSH, Andrew	O'BRIEN, Rosanna	AUG 10 1857
WELSH, Ann	CRONAN, James	JUN 04 1853
WELSH, Annora	WRIGHT, Michael	OCT 31 1853
WELSH, Aristides	FRANCIS, Sidney Virga.	OCT 12 1846
WELSH, Bartholomew	CONROY, Bridget	JAN 29 1856
WELSH, Bridget	LEESON, Patrick M.	OCT 09 1848
WELSH, Bridget	DWHEY, Timothy	MAY 13 1853
WELSH, Bridget	McLAY, Nathaniel	FEB 04 1854

District of Columbia Marriage Licenses, 1811-1858

WELSH, Catharine	CAVANAGH, Arthur	JUN 29 1857
WELSH, Daniel	CASHMAN, Catharine	DEC 20 1856
WELSH, David	HORAN, Margaret	AUG 30 1856
WELSH, Edmund	WRENN, Bridget	MAY 18 1858
WELSH, Edward	NUGENT, Julia	SEP 30 1857
WELSH, Edward S.	MADDOX, Elizth. J.	OCT 05 1853
WELSH, Edward S.	LAWSON, Mary	SEP 14 1854
WELSH, Elizabeth	SMITH, William H.	NOV 24 1857
WELSH, Ellen	O'KEEFE, Daniel	OCT 06 1853
WELSH, George	PARKS, Jane	MAY 26 1854
WELSH, Hannah	MUNDT, Frederick C.C.	AUG 27 1840
WELSH, James	CLOONAN, Ann	JUN 08 1854
WELSH, James	McDONALD, Mary	SEP 11 1854
WELSH, Johanna	DEELY, Patrick	JUN 23 1852
WELSH, John	KARNEY, Ellen	MAY 06 1854
WELSH, Joseph	ANDERSON, Ann	OCT 28 1817
WELSH, Maria	SHANNON, Timothy	APR 10 1852
WELSH, Maria	McCANN, Edward	APR 03 1858
WELSH, Mary	THOMPSON, James	APR 04 1816
WELSH, Mary	HANRAHAN, John	JUL 21 1853
WELSH, Mary	ESPINTA, John	OCT 13 1853
WELSH, Mary	QUIRK, Edward	APR 21 1854
WELSH, Mary	GRIFFIN, Michael	SEP 18 1855
WELSH, Matilda	ROBERTS, John S.	NOV 20 1834
WELSH, Patrick	FINN, Ann	NOV 21 1856
WELSH, Ruth Ann	PEACO, William H.	DEC 01 1842
WELSH, Sarah	DONAVAN, David	OCT 19 1825
WELSH, William	SPALDING, Jane E.	FEB 04 1845
WELSH, Winifred	RITAN, Patrick	JUL 23 1853
WELTNER, Jacob R.	STINGER, Ann Elizabeth	APR 24 1833
WENDALL, Herman	HOTTA, Catherine	DEC 02 1854
WENDERUTRE, Wilhelm	MILBROCK, Teresa	JUN 28 1858
WENTHAL, George	BRIGHT, Margaret	OCT 05 1854
WENZEL, John	WOLF, Barbara	AUG 20 1844
WENZELL, Adam	BRIGHT, Anna B.	MAR 26 1856
WEPTER, Ann Virginia	PAYNE, John H.	MAY 15 1851
WERDERMAN, Ann	NOLAND, Patrick	APR 26 1856
WERNER, Charles	BOGUSCH, Sophia Mary	MAY 10 1854
WERNER, Dorathy	BETZOLD, David	JUL 02 1818
WERNER, John H.T.	HELFRICK, Chatarina	JUL 28 1835
WERTHINGTON, Catharine	PEARSON, Joseph	JAN 18 1821
WERTZ, Elizabeth	GRIFFIN, Charles	JUL 17 1815
WERTZ, Mary	SAWYER, Lemuel	MAR 23 1826
WESCOTT, Sarah	McDONOGH, James	MAY 04 1858
WESEL, Agnes	SCHREPLE, Caspus	JAN 15 1844
WESLEY, Joseph	HOOPER, Dorothy	APR 22 1842
WESNER, Matthias	McNEARE, Elizh.	DEC 02 1812
WESSEL, Rosina	SMITH, John A.	APR 02 1850
WEST, Catharine	CLAIR, Peter	DEC 31 1833
WEST, Covington O.	BARKER, Atheriah	JAN 02 1851
WEST, Douglass	DELANEY, Catherine	SEP 11 1850
WEST, Eleanor	CLARKE, Timothy	SEP 30 1848
WEST, Eliza	MILLS, Mahlon	APR 21 1846
WEST, Frances	BLOXOM, Levi	AUG 07 1852
WEST, Guslie	BIAS, Mary	DEC 16 1851
WEST, Henry	STEWART, Elizabeth	JUL 14 1836
WEST, Hezekiah	HAMILL, Hannah Ann	OCT 27 1852
WEST, Jacob	ENGELHARD, Caroline	JUN 11 1853

District of Columbia Marriage Licenses, 1811-1858

WEST, James Randolph	KINGSBURY, Johanna	FEB 14 1850
WEST, James W.	MILLS, Eliza M.	JAN 03 1850
WEST, Jeremiah	FOSHEE, Elizabeth	OCT 13 1842
WEST, John	NASH, Sarah (blk)	JAN 08 1835
WEST, John	BIGGS, Jane	AUG 09 1855
WEST, John P.	BIRD, Ann E.	SEP 24 1835
WEST, Julia	TARLTON, Lewis A.	MAR 15 1845
WEST, Mary	PLANT, James K.	AUG 02 1834
WEST, Mary	ALLISON, Robert	MAY 07 1836
WEST, Matilda	ABBOTT, Benjamin	APR 25 1848
WEST, Sarah	CLEAVER, William Evans	JAN 17 1852
WEST, Thomas	ANDERSON, Fanny	DEC 03 1829
WEST, Walter S.	POPE, Frances S.	JUN 25 1856
WEST, William	CRONIN, Francis	NOV 26 1850
WEST, William C.	JANISON, Mary J.	JUN 01 1857
WEST, Wm. H.	MILLER, Catharine	FEB 06 1854
WESTCOAT, Ann Maria	CROSS, Washington	DEC 21 1833
WESTCOTT, James	CALVERT, Harriet A.	FEB 13 1845
WESTCOTT, James	LOWE, Virginia	MAR 09 1848
WESTCOTT, John	BRIGHTMAN, Mary	MAY 29 1813
WESTCOTT, William A., Rev.	STOTT, Sarah R.	MAR 10 1847
WESTERFELD, Fredericka L.A.	GROSS, Charles Philip	MAY 02 1857
WESTERFIELD, David	HODSKIN, Nancy Ann	SEP 04 1838
WESTERFIELD, David	WILSON, Elizabeth E.	AUG 13 1846
WESTERFIELD, James	McINTOSH, Elizabeth	APR 13 1846
WESTERFIELD, Julian	REEVES, James	FEB 21 1837
WESTERFIELD, Louisa	MILLER, Richard H.	MAR 06 1858
WESTERFIELD, Lucy	HOWARD, Matthias	JUL 08 1834
WESTERFIELD, Mary E.	JORDAN, John W.	JUN 26 1851
WESTERFIELD, Rebecca	ANDERSON, Anthony L.	MAY 27 1852
WESTERMAN, Andrew	KEMP, Ragena	APR 28 1851
WESTERMAN, Faederick	WETMEYER, Anna M.	MAR 27 1857
WESTERN, Mary	SMOOT, George H.	NOV 01 1825
WESTIRMAN, Andrew	ALLEN, Martin	SEP 27 1837
WESTON, Jerard	RISON, Elizabeth	MAY 21 1825
WESTON, John	BROWN, Ann	APR 06 1825
WESTON, Lewis	ALLISON, Sarah	FEB 23 1832
WESTON, Lewis	MADISON, Clarissa (blk)	NOV 30 1857
WESTWOOD, Wm. P.	HUTCHINSON, Hannah D.	JUN 24 1858
WETHEFT, William	BOSSE, Dora	JUL 17 1851
WETHERALL, Ann Elizabeth	LUXON, Thomas J.	JAN 25 1843
WETHERALL, James M.	DIXON, Rebecca A.	DEC 10 1833
WETHERALL, Mary	GLOVER, Charles	AUG 21 1817
WETHERALL, Mildred Ann	ROSSER, John K.	OCT 14 1854
WETHERELL, John	THOMPSON, Sarah Eleanor	MAR 04 1823
WETHERILL, Martha	YOUNG, William W.	NOV 13 1852
WETHERS, Julia	MORTON, Benjamin	OCT 04 1855
WETMEYER, Anna M.	WESTERMEYER, Faederick	MAR 27 1857
WETZEL, Lucy	HITZ, George	NOV 27 1857
WETZEL, Margaret	MURDOCH, John	DEC 31 1812
WETZEL, William Y.	HOLTZMAN, Mary	SEP 16 1817
WETZELL, Frederick	SPRINGER, Jaccobina	APR 15 1833
WETZELL, Lazarus	WARTHEN, Henrietta	MAY 24 1825
WETZLEBON, L. Arthurvon	CUDLIPP, Isabel	JAN 02 1858
WEVER, John	JONES, Betsey	OCT 27 1812
WEYBOURNE, Louisa	SUTER, John T.	SEP 22 1853
WGILL, George	KNIBB, Mary	JUN 18 1834
WHAILLING, Daniel	ROWAND, Virginia	JUL 28 1857

District of Columbia Marriage Licenses, 1811-1858

WHALAN, Bridget	HULIGHAN, John	OCT 14 1818
WHALAN, Bridget	GAINOR, John	JAN 16 1828
WHALAND, William	CASSADAY, Susan	JUN 09 1852
WHALEN, Ann	KELLY, John F.	JUN 27 1854
WHALEN, Biddy	CULBERTSON, James F.	JUN 12 1828
WHALEN, Henry T.	HARMAN, Cornelia E.	MAY 13 1852
WHALEN, John	IRONTON, Ann	OCT 28 1841
WHALEN, John W.	BELL, Martha	JAN 26 1854
WHALEN, Ledwell	HAMPTON, Mary Ellen	NOV 15 1850
WHALEN, Mary Ann	MAGEE, Barney	MAY 27 1845
WHALEN, Sarah Ann	HOLMES, William H.	APR 06 1853
WHALEN, Sarah Jane	WEITZEL, John W.	JUN 29 1847
WHALEN, Stephen P.	CHARLES, Catharine	DEC 23 1834
WHALEN, Thomas R.	DOYLE, Mary	JUN 10 1854
WHALEY, Ann	STEWART, W.H.	SEP 29 1842
WHALEY, Anna	JONES, Isaac	MAY 26 1824
WHALEY, Bushrod D.	HART, Martha Ann	JAN 01 1848
WHALEY, Harriet C.	JAMES, David B.	JAN 20 1853
WHALEY, James H.	HUTCHISON, Sarah J.	JAN 15 1855
WHALEY, John L.	QUIGLEY, Mary Ann	DEC 03 1833
WHALEY, John T.	HERBERT, Martha	OCT 30 1841
WHALEY, John Thomas	DOVE, Elizabeth	OCT 09 1845
WHALEY, Martha	COXEN, Henry	OCT 22 1853
WHALEY, Martha V.	FOX, Allen G.	JAN 29 1855
WHALEY, Robert M.	CONNOR, Mary A.	DEC 16 1841
WHALEY, William H.	BLOCKSON, Jane Eliza	DEC 14 1837
WHALIN, Joseph H.	WOODWARD, Martha E.	NOV 19 1851
WHALING, Daniel	MORGAN, Frances	FEB 04 1850
WHALING, John	SWANN, Elzina	APR 14 1858
WHALING, Sarah Ann	POSTON, William	APR 05 1842
WHALING, Sarah Ann	TRACY, William	JUN 21 1847
WHALING, William	WHURE, Eliza	MAR 31 1851
WHANN, Ann Maria	MACKALL, Benjamin F.	APR 06 1813
WHANN, Jane	McVEAN, James	JAN 07 1828
WHARTON, Augustus	COKELY, Jane	JUL 10 1856
WHARTON, Charles	BRIDGET, Mary Ann	DEC 24 1839
WHARTON, Eliza S.	MAURO, William H.	MAR 28 1831
WHARTON, James	WILEY, Elizabeth Bennett	AUG 27 1812
WHARTON, Nancy	SEGAR, Francis	JUN 04 1830
WHARTON, Robert S.	TEST, Penelope G.	FEB 17 1857
WHARTON, Thomas	GUARD, Lucinda	APR 09 1847
WHATON, Lewis	SIDEBOTTAM, Elizabeth	SEP 14 1837
WHE, Martha Rebecca	BAINE, Andrew	DEC 23 1856
WHEADLOCK, George	THOMAS, Mary (blk)	MAR 22 1858
WHEALAN, Margaret	McCUEN, John	MAY 30 1831
WHEALAN, William	CONNELLEN, Bridget	NOV 28 1834
WHEALER, George W.	KNOWBLOCK, Martha	OCT 16 1844
WHEAT, Eleanor C.	DAVIS, William, Jr.	JUN 26 1834
WHEAT, Elizabeth	WHITE, Warren	MAR 03 1832
WHEAT, Elizabeth D.	THORNTON, Thomas C.	JUL 04 1815
WHEAT, Jesse	PURDY, Elizabeth	FEB 26 1824
WHEAT, John F.	TAYLOR, Catharine	NOV 08 1832
WHEAT, Joseph Henry	GREER, Eliza Ingham	MAY 29 1832
WHEAT, Laura F.	LANDVOIGT, John A.	NOV 23 1857
WHEAT, Lemuel C.	ADAMS, Anne H.	JAN 27 1847
WHEAT, Noah	RAWLINGS, Ann	JAN 07 1813
WHEAT, Rebecca	BEALL, Wm.	DEC 13 1814
WHEAT, Sarah	SIMPSON, Joseph	JAN 07 1817

District of Columbia Marriage Licenses, 1811-1858

WHEAT, Sarah Ann	SHAW, Thomas	JUL 24 1815
WHEAT, William	MERCHANT, Ann	DEC 27 1847
WHEATLEY, Andrew J.	BAILESS, Sarah Ann	JUN 28 1852
WHEATLEY, Benedict	BENTON, Juliet	MAY 11 1826
WHEATLEY, Benedict	KIDWELL, Martha A.	MAY 16 1855
WHEATLEY, Benjamin	JONES, Mary Ellen (blk)	NOV 04 1852
WHEATLEY, Elizabeth A.	THOMPSON, Geo. C.	JUL 14 1830
WHEATLEY, Martha A.	TAYLOR, Wm. H.	OCT 12 1857
WHEATLEY, Mary	WILLIAMSON, James	MAR 13 1833
WHEATLEY, Mary C.	SANDFORD, George W.	NOV 21 1854
WHEATLY, Agnatius	LAPTON, Bridget	AUG 06 1827
WHEATLY, Francis	MORELAND, Caroline	SEP 24 1830
WHEATLY, James	FLOWERS, Mary A.	JAN 10 1824
WHEATLY, Margaret	JOHNSON, John	FEB 09 1825
WHEATLY, Wm. J.	DONOHO, Hannah	MAR 10 1835
WHEATON, Frank	COOPER, Maria Mason	FEB 04 1857
WHEATON, Mary W.P.	BURKE, John	JAN 04 1812
WHEATON, Susan D.	ANDERSON, Saml.	MAY 13 1817
WHEELAN, Catharine	UNIACK, John	MAY 16 1840
WHEELE, Susana	WARWICK, William F.	JUL 07 1812
WHEELER, Alexander	WARDER, Mary	JUL 18 1849
WHEELER, Alfred	ROBEY, Martha A.	MAY 21 1850
WHEELER, Ann Eliott	JOHNSON, John	FEB 09 1850
WHEELER, Bennedict	THOMPSON, Elizabeth	OCT 16 1815
WHEELER, Caroline C.	BEAN, George	NOV 24 1852
WHEELER, Christina E.	SMITH, Andrew J.	JUL 07 1857
WHEELER, Daniel	GATES, Cornelia (blk)	APR 04 1853
WHEELER, Elizabeth	KIDWELL, James	JUL 28 1823
WHEELER, Elizth. B.	BEALE, George N.	JUN 02 1851
WHEELER, Frederick	SILLIVAN, Mary	OCT 24 1820
WHEELER, George	BUTLER, Eliza	JUN 26 1845
WHEELER, George W.	DOUGLASS, Adaly	FEB 27 1838
WHEELER, Grafton	DOWNS, Elizabeth Ellen	APR 20 1857
WHEELER, Isabella	GREEN, Joel Cephas	NOV 21 1851
WHEELER, Jane	RYAN, Thomas	NOV 16 1815
WHEELER, John H.	BROWN, Mary	APR 19 1830
WHEELER, Julia M.	RYON, Richard J.	OCT 01 1849
WHEELER, Juvius B.	BEALE, Emily T.	SEP 18 1855
WHEELER, Margaret	PADGETT, John	APR 06 1857
WHEELER, Maria (blk)	MASON, Israel B.	MAY 30 1854
WHEELER, Mary Ann	SHEPPERD, James	APR 23 1812
WHEELER, Mary Ann	KIDWELL, Washington R.	JUL 11 1834
WHEELER, Mary L.	DANIEL, Joseph H.	MAY 21 1855
WHEELER, Richard	HOPKINS, Moore	FEB 01 1845
WHEELER, Robert	WILLIAMS, Mary Ann (blk)	MAY 06 1851
WHEELER, Sarah A.	WALKER, Henry T.	SEP 21 1855
WHEELER, Simeon	COCKE, Anna	MAY 17 1814
WHEELER, Theodore	LENOX, Lucy A.	MAY 25 1835
WHEELER, Thos. G.	MOORE, Grace R.	JAN 08 1856
WHEELER, William	HURST, Mary	OCT 13 1846
WHEELER, William	EASBY, Ellen	OCT 27 1852
WHEELER, William H.	MATHEWS, Mary A. (blk)	DEC 21 1855
WHEELOCK, Edward W.	CLACK, Mary L.	DEC 19 1854
WHELAN, Catherine	WALL, Thomas	NOV 02 1847
WHELAN, Catherine	CARROLL, Laurence	NOV 11 1856
WHELAN, Catherine E.	TOBIN, John	FEB 03 1824
WHELAN, John	BAILY, Lydia	FEB 09 1839
WHELAN, Julia N.M.	GRENNELL, Charles C.	FEB 07 1839

District of Columbia Marriage Licenses, 1811-1858

WHELAN, Mahala C.	THOMPSON, Thomas W.	MAR 30 1857
WHELAN, Mary	VARMAN, John	AUG 07 1837
WHELAN, Mary	DEVIS, Craven	JUN 29 1852
WHELAN, William	KINNY, Mary	JAN 30 1854
WHELAND, Ann Elizabeth	DONNOGHUE, Patrick	MAY 28 1823
WHELER, John	CROWLEY, Mary	DEC 13 1815
WHELER, Mary Ann	SUTER, Richard S.	NOV 27 1846
WHELIN, John	DROUSE, Martha	APR 22 1839
WHELON, Margaret	NEVINES, Patrick	JUL 10 1820
WHETCROFT, Catherine	KING, Josias W.	FEB 20 1817
WHETCROFT, Juliana	MARSHALL, Thomas	NOV 05 1821
WHETCROFT, Mary Frances	CHASE, Samuel [Hon.]	JUN 24 1828
WHETCROFT, William W.	TRAVERS, Drusilla	JAN 01 1828
WHETMORE, Wm.	KING, Ann	JAN 27 1819
WHETZELL, Ann	DAWSON, William	JUN 30 1825
WHILAN, Bridget	RONEY, Patrick	OCT 25 1836
WHIPPLE, Ann	DAVIS, William L.	JUN 29 1848
WHIPPLE, Edward A.	SIMMS, Camilla	MAY 13 1853
WHIPPLE, Joseph	WILLIAMS, Orellar	OCT 20 1837
WHIPPLE, Mary J.	ELIOT, Frank Andrew	SEP 11 1854
WHIPPLE, Samuel	QUEEN, Mary	JUN 19 1842
WHIPS, Wesley	LALAND, Sarah	NOV 15 1815
WHISTLER, Elizabeth	MERRITT, John	JUN 17 1854
WHITACRE, Robert	WOOD, Elizabeth W.	MAY 02 1839
WHITAKER, John C.	KERRON, John	AUG 19 1847
WHITAKER, John T.	CRAIG, Sarah Jane	AUG 06 1855
WHITAKER, Maria C.	CLARKE, Christopher C.	DEC 19 1850
WHITALL, Emeline N.	STRATTON, Benjamin W. [Dr.]	MAY 11 1830
WHITALL, Sarah Matilda	RITTENHOUSE, Charles Edwin	SEP 10 1841
WHITE, Alexander	STONE, Virginia	FEB 04 1853
WHITE, Almira J.	GRAY, Benjamin F.	JUL 09 1857
WHITE, Ambrose	FRY, Elizabeth	JAN 05 1825
WHITE, Amelia J.	DAY, Bradley	MAR 28 1850
WHITE, Angelica	FOWLER, Joseph	MAY 02 1839
WHITE, Ann	NEVITT, Joseph	JUN 17 1815
WHITE, Ann	THOMAS, James	DEC 25 1817
WHITE, Ann	HANNAH, Henry	MAY 09 1820
WHITE, Ann	STEVENS, Stephen	MAY 08 1845
WHITE, Ann M.M.	TOPHAM, James S.	APR 06 1858
WHITE, Ann Maria	DIGGS, James	OCT 03 1815
WHITE, Ann Maria	PARKER, David	DEC 19 1836
WHITE, Ann Rebecca	FRY, James	JUL 17 1817
WHITE, Arthur W.	PAINE, Julia	JAN 28 1857
WHITE, Ashton S.H.	BRADLEY, Abrahamie	OCT 16 1843
WHITE, Benedict	OSBORN, Catherine	DEC 09 1816
WHITE, Benjamin F.	STOOPS, Margaret Ellen	AUG 30 1853
WHITE, Biddy	WALTER, Robert	JAN 26 1842
WHITE, Callender	RACHEL, Mary Ann	JAN 03 1826
WHITE, Caroline	BEALL, Rufus	NOV 08 1837
WHITE, Caroline	TURNER, George	AUG 02 1838
WHITE, Cary W.	CARROLL, Julia A.	NOV 30 1846
WHITE, Catharine	COLLINS, Lemuel Everett	JAN 10 1846
WHITE, Catherine	SHEA, Richard	JUL 21 1853
WHITE, Catherine	KIRBY, John	JUL 04 1853
WHITE, Charles	RIDER, Jane Maria	OCT 13 1849
WHITE, Edward	BROWN, Elizabeth (blk)	MAY 26 1858
WHITE, Eleanor	CLARK, Isaac	OCT 13 1831
WHITE, Eliza	COME, Stephen	OCT 20 1824

District of Columbia Marriage Licenses, 1811-1858

WHITE, Eliza A.	GORDON, George	SEP 15 1829
WHITE, Eliza Jane	WHITE, Nathan	JAN 16 1843
WHITE, Elizabeth	WHITE, Fielder	MAY 09 1818
WHITE, Elizabeth	LOGAN, Robt.	JUN 10 1828
WHITE, Elizabeth	SHEPHARD, Henry	MAY 26 1840
WHITE, Elizabeth A.	BEATTY, Theophelus	FEB 23 1842
WHITE, Ellen	BROWN, Daniel	JUN 16 1855
WHITE, Ellen M.	CONNEL, Robert A.	OCT 15 1846
WHITE, Enoch	BARRON, Eliza	DEC 27 1827
WHITE, Fielder	WHITE, Elizabeth	MAY 09 1818
WHITE, Fielder L.	ELLIOTT, Ellender	JUL 30 1825
WHITE, George	HENDLEY, Ann	FEB 04 1823
WHITE, George B.	WINN, Nouraly A.	JUL 08 1836
WHITE, Georgia A.	SMITH, James R.	JAN 10 1854
WHITE, Gilbert	MAGEE, Sarah Ann	OCT 21 1824
WHITE, Harriet	LANHAM, Benjamin	MAR 28 1820
WHITE, Harriet A.	WOLCOTT, Liman B.	MAY 30 1831
WHITE, Henrietta	BROWN, John	FEB 28 1831
WHITE, Hester Ann	DUNCAN, Francis	NOV 20 1841
WHITE, Horace	WILSON, Hannah	MAY 31 1844
WHITE, Hugh L.	PEYTON, Ann E. [Mrs.]	NOV 29 1832
WHITE, Issabella	HURREN, Theodore	JUN 05 1821
WHITE, James	OSBORNE, Harriet	AUG 23 1819
WHITE, James A.	MILES, Rosetta	SEP 03 1838
WHITE, James [Capt.]	WALLER, Ann	MAY 24 1823
WHITE, Jeremiah T.	SHADRACK, Jane F.	JAN 22 1848
WHITE, John	HENSON, Sarah C.	AUG 30 1823
WHITE, John	O'BRIEN, Mary	JUL 23 1830
WHITE, John	WHITE, Mary	MAR 21 1848
WHITE, John B.	SLATER, Lucy	DEC 04 1817
WHITE, John T.	GARDINER, Elizabeth	APR 01 1834
WHITE, John T.	JONES, Susannah	JUN 05 1850
WHITE, John Thos.	LYNCH, Amelia Jane	MAY 28 1853
WHITE, John W.	BELL, Ann	JUN 15 1844
WHITE, Joshua E.	SPEEDEN, Ann Maria	AUG 23 1831
WHITE, Levi	ARMSTRONG, Sarah	MAY 31 1825
WHITE, Lloyd	BURGESS, Eliza	MAR 06 1821
WHITE, Louisa	KING, John	AUG 04 1836
WHITE, Lucinda	GASSAWAY, Madison	FEB 24 1852
WHITE, Lydia A.	RAY, Alfred	AUG 17 1853
WHITE, Margaret	ROBB, Michael A.	OCT 03 1839
WHITE, Martha	STAMP, John	JAN 14 1854
WHITE, Martha A.	PLEASANTS, Thos. L.	OCT 25 1854
WHITE, Martha Ann	BRITTON, James H.	NOV 17 1855
WHITE, Mary	WELCH, Stephen	OCT 07 1812
WHITE, Mary	SEVERMAN, John C.	APR 05 1813
WHITE, Mary	SKAM, Thomas	SEP 16 1840
WHITE, Mary	WHITE, John	MAR 21 1848
WHITE, Mary	SMITH, John Thomas	JUN 02 1851
WHITE, Mary	COLLINS, James	FEB 19 1855
WHITE, Mary	DAVIS, Thomas	MAY 12 1845
WHITE, Mary Ann	HARRISS, William	FEB 02 1831
WHITE, Mary C.	RABBITT, James A.	AUG 25 1851
WHITE, Mary Catherine	SMITH, James R.	JUL 01 1845
WHITE, Mary F.	DAWSON, William P.	FEB 20 1851
WHITE, Mary H.	LASKY, Robert V.	FEB 14 1856
WHITE, Mary J.	CAMERON, John	NOV 06 1856
WHITE, Mary Jane	TAYLOR, William Harrison	JAN 08 1846

District of Columbia Marriage Licenses, 1811-1858

WHITE, Mary Rebecca	STEWARD, Charles W.	JAN 21 1839
WHITE, Nancy	TAYLOR, Moses	FEB 06 1815
WHITE, Nathan	WHITE, Eliza Jane	JAN 16 1843
WHITE, Olivia	CISSELL, Ricard	JAN 07 1858
WHITE, Rachel	ROLLINS, Joshua	DEC 18 1818
WHITE, Rezen	DUFF, Priscilla	OCT 14 1813
WHITE, Richard	MORGAN, Jane	DEC 17 1823
WHITE, Richard	WALTERS, Mary	APR 21 1835
WHITE, Richard	FLETCHER, Sarah Ann	FEB 12 1846
WHITE, Richard H.	deSHIELDS, Maria	AUG 19 1841
WHITE, Robert	HARDY, Jane	FEB 16 1818
WHITE, Robert	RANKIN, Nancy	NOV 24 1853
WHITE, Robert B.	RYE, Mary Frances	SEP 03 1850
WHITE, Robert B.	STRATTIN, Sarah E.	JAN 07 1852
WHITE, Sallie E.	BENHAM, Spencer C.	FEB 14 1855
WHITE, Samuel	MARSHALL, Mary Ann	DEC 26 1837
WHITE, Samuel	FRYERS, Jane E.	MAR 13 1850
WHITE, Sarah	GARNER, Wm.	MAY 13 1856
WHITE, Sarah Ann	LOVE, Elie	JAN 09 1830
WHITE, Sarah Ann	DAY, Loyd	SEP 10 1840
WHITE, Sarah Ann	MANTZ, George	MAY 06 1847
WHITE, Sarah E.	DONALDSON, George W.	NOV 05 1846
WHITE, Sarah F.	DONAHO, Thomas	DEC 23 1818
WHITE, Singleton	HUTCHENS, Charity	NOV 28 1831
WHITE, Susan	BURGES, John	JAN 30 1812
WHITE, Susanna	FORTENEY, Henry	MAR 26 1818
WHITE, Susannah	WILLIAMS, Peter	SEP 25 1832
WHITE, Terese Ann	BALLARD, Richard	SEP 17 1814
WHITE, Thomas	HODGE, Nancy	DEC 22 1813
WHITE, Thomas	MAGILL, Lucinda	JUN 22 1820
WHITE, Thomas	WALKER, Philly	JAN 02 1822
WHITE, Thomas	DONOGAN, Mary	JUN 10 1852
WHITE, Thomas P.	MARSHE, Esther A.	DEC 14 1854
WHITE, Thomas P.	COLLINS, Mary A.	MAY 17 1855
WHITE, Violetta	DANDERSON, Thomas	OCT 09 1832
WHITE, Warren	WHEAT, Elizabeth	MAR 03 1832
WHITE, William G.W.	CARTER, Susan Sophia	JUL 02 1835
WHITE, William H.	DYER, Ruth	JUL 10 1848
WHITE, William W.	CARTER, Sarah Ann	SEP 27 1825
WHITE, William W.	COLE, Mary Ann	SEP 24 1839
WHITEFORD, Marthy	WATSON, Peter	DEC 09 1816
WHITEFORD, Sarah	BROWN, Henry	DEC 27 1819
WHITEHEAD, Bazella	WHITEHEAD, Mary Ann	AUG 15 1844
WHITEHEAD, Hezekiah	WHITEHEAD, Louisa	AUG 15 1844
WHITEHEAD, Louisa	WHITEHEAD, Hezekiah	AUG 15 1844
WHITEHEAD, Mary Ann	WHITEHEAD, Bazella	AUG 15 1844
WHITEHEAD, Richard	COOK, Heny	JUL 17 1813
WHITEHOUSE, Walter E.	FARR, Elizabeth	JUL 14 1832
WHITEHOUSE, Walter E.	FARR, Sarah Ann	APR 26 1834
WHITEHOUSE, William	HOUSER, Elizabeth	JAN 27 1824
WHITELOCK, Matilda	HART, Cyrus W.	JAN 02 1845
WHITEMAN, Elizabeth Ann	DAVIS, John Truman	NOV 07 1850
WHITEMAN, Elizabeth E.	SAVAGE, James W.	DEC 22 1857
WHITEMORE, H.O.	PIEARCE, Sarah Ann	DEC 08 1823
WHITEMORE, Mary Ellen	BELT, Alfred	MAY 22 1854
WHITEMORE, Zacha. H.	HUTCHINSON, Hester E.	JUN 26 1855
WHITING, Ann E. (blk)	PIPER, James E.	SEP 30 1851
WHITING, Artridge	CARROLL, Washington	JUN 04 1829

District of Columbia Marriage Licenses, 1811-1858

WHITING, Eliza (blk)	BROWN, William	DEC 21 1830
WHITING, Elizabeth	BRYAN, James D.	MAY 29 1816
WHITING, George C.	SULLIVAN, Elizabeth	MAR 17 1840
WHITING, Mary Ann	HEELLMAN, Lawrence	NOV 18 1842
WHITING, William B.	RUDD, Martha E.	MAY 04 1841
WHITINGTON, John	LOKEY, Louisa	MAY 30 1820
WHITLEY, Dolly (blk)	OGLEVIE, Joseph	FEB 10 1835
WHITLEY, George	KIDWELL, Ann	OCT 04 1825
WHITLOCK, Mary J.	STUBBS, John O.	SEP 21 1855
WHITMAN, George K.	GRIFFITH, Mary	JUN 01 1850
WHITMORE, Ann	LOVELACE, William Riley	MAY 16 1823
WHITMORE, Betsey	CAMPBELL, Robert	FEB 20 1814
WHITMORE, Edward	BEAGLE, Ann	JUL 02 1825
WHITMORE, Elizabeth	SHARPE, Joseph	JUL 12 1816
WHITMORE, Francis	WEBB, Fanny	FEB 08 1821
WHITMORE, George	CLUB, Rodey A.D.	DEC 27 1825
WHITMORE, Henry M.	MURPHY, Samima	JAN 03 1854
WHITMORE, James S.	ADAMS, Eliza	NOV 02 1848
WHITMORE, Jno. F.W.	CHIPLEY, Sarah E.	JUN 11 1851
WHITMORE, John P.	DAVIS, Jane	MAR 20 1830
WHITMORE, John R.	HART, Deborah E.	OCT 30 1855
WHITMORE, Mary Ann	SWINK, Michael	FEB 19 1814
WHITMORE, Mary Jane	McABEE, George	DEC 21 1848
WHITMORE, Rachel Ann	GUEST, Francis	JUN 27 1855
WHITMORE, Ruth	TAYLOR, Punnell	JUL 17 1823
WHITMORE, Sarah Ellen	SIMPSON, John W.	AUG 14 1841
WHITMORE, William	KING, Aruthia	MAR 23 1816
WHITMORE, William	COLLISON, Catharine C.	DEC 12 1844
WHITMORE, William	EDWARDS, Catherine	DEC 08 1855
WHITMORE, Zachariah H.	DAVIDSON, Elizabeth	JUL 08 1833
WHITNEY, Asa	CAMPBELL, C.M.	OCT 01 1852
WHITNEY, Charles	FRAZIER, Margaret	JUN 28 1841
WHITNEY, Ebenezer	BRADLEY, Catharine	NOV 21 1847
WHITNEY, Elizabeth	McLAUGHLIN, Daniel	SEP 01 1852
WHITNEY, Harriet	TAYLOR, Walter W.	JAN 14 1830
WHITNEY, Jered	PICKRELL, Mary	MAR 12 1818
WHITNEY, Joseph	BALL, Margaret	DEC 02 1824
WHITNEY, Julia L.	WEED, Elijah J.	FEB 09 1837
WHITNEY, Lucy B.	ERETY, William G.	JAN 07 1826
WHITNEY, Phineas S.	COLLARD, Eliza S.	DEC 31 1836
WHITNEY, Sophia	WADSWORTH, Hiram N.	JUL 03 1849
WHITNEY, William	COGSWELL, Eveline	AUG 30 1842
WHITTAKER, Margaret	ANDERSON, Alexander	DEC 31 1852
WHITTE, Chas. T.	TIPPETT, Ella A.	FEB 13 1855
WHITTER, Louisa	SIMMONS, Augustus	JAN 23 1834
WHITTICOMB, Benjamin F.	HOPKINS, Mary	OCT 30 1834
WHITTINGTON, Sarah	SULLIVAN, John	APR 22 1854
WHITTLE, Adelia	SMITH, Michael	NOV 27 1852
WHITTLE, Ann R.	FEEVERS, James E.	SEP 29 1856
WHITTLE, David	GATES, Mary	AUG 11 1837
WHITTLE, Elizabeth	MURPHY, William	APR 09 1835
WHITTLE, Francis A.	FAIRFAX, Emily C.	MAY 12 1848
WHITTLE, John	CAMPBELL, Adelia	MAR 10 1827
WHITTLE, John	GATES, Mary	SEP 26 1840
WHITTLE, Maria	CAMPBELL, George	DEC 27 1828
WHITTLE, Maria	SCOTT, John	OCT 10 1850
WHITTLE, Martha	McCOY, Andrew J.	DEC 10 1850
WHITTLE, Mary Ann	MAYHUE, Henry	FEB 26 1827

District of Columbia Marriage Licenses, 1811-1858

WHITTLE, Mary Ellen	LIZIER, Joseph	SEP 22 1845
WHITTLE, Rachel	BROWN, Addison	SEP 06 1826
WHITTLESEY, E.M.	DeZEYK, Albert J.	MAR 10 1857
WHITTLESEY, Oliver	McCLELLAND, Elizabeth	DEC 27 1848
WHITTLESEY, Wm. C. [Dr.]	RAPINE, Anna E.	NOV 20 1822
WHITTLESY, Cumfort S.	HYATT, Virginia	SEP 30 1844
WHITWELL, John Geo.	COYLE, Ann W.	OCT 31 1822
WHITWELL, Virginia	PARSONS, Samuel M.	MAR 02 1848
WHOFF, Caroline Dorothy	GIESEKING, Fred'k. W.	MAR 17 1849
WHURE, Eliza	WHALING, William	MAR 31 1851
WHYCOF, Margaret E.	DAVIS, Isaac F.	MAR 13 1838
WHYTE, Frederick	JONES, Mary E.	JAN 04 1844
WHYTE, John	MILES, Bridget	AUG 25 1851
WICHAND, Louisa	DIPPLE, Charles	JAN 22 1847
WICKERS, Eliza	WIGGINS, Ths.	JUL 20 1821
WICKLE, Mary	CULLINS, John	MAY 13 1822
WICKLIFF, Mary B.	MERRICK, William M.	OCT 15 1844
WICKLIFFE, Robert C.	DAWSON, Ann R.	FEB 28 1843
WICKS, Washington	WEBSTER, Sohpia	OCT 09 1837
WIDDICOMB, Gertrude	FAIRELLY, John W., Jr.	OCT 21 1856
WIDDICOMBE, Harriet	BODMAN, George W.	AUG 08 1854
WIDDICOMBE, Robert	GALLOWAY, Mary	SEP 27 1828
WIDEMAN, Mary	KNIPPLE, Daniel	SEP 10 1849
WIDMAYER, John	GUNZIR, Rosina	NOV 11 1856
WIEDERMAN, Augustus	BORDING, Mrs.	JUL 02 1845
WIEL, Frederick	STRAUB, Catherine	OCT 06 1851
WIENAND, George	BECKER, Helena A.	DEC 03 1851
WIENDHOLTZ, Louisa	THOMAS, John	MAR 24 1853
WIESSMANN, Rosine	THOMAS, Andreas	JAN 20 1845
WIESSNER, Christianna	BRANN, Frederick	NOV 21 1854
WIGFIELD, Ann	NICKEN, John	JUL 08 1850
WIGFIELD, James	CLOAKEY, Jane	MAY 09 1814
WIGG, William Hazzard	STEVENS, Emma Maria	JUL 20 1853
WIGGIN, Benjamin F.	BENJAMIN, Mary E.	DEC 28 1854
WIGGINS, Eliza	SMITH, Joseph W.	MAY 13 1833
WIGGINS, Ths.	WICKERS, Eliza	JUL 20 1821
WIGGINTON, Emily	WITHERS, Picket	SEP 08 1821
WIGHT, Priscilla	JOHNSON, John	OCT 08 1856
WIGLE, Johanna	THOMAS, Henry	OCT 13 1848
WIGLEY, Ann	YEBOWER, John	JUN 14 1836
WIGLEY, Henry	HANNAH, Ann	FEB 09 1826
WIGS, Jane	RECKTER, Ludwell L.	SEP 14 1835
WIKLE, Christianna	HANNET, Francis	JAN 13 1835
WILAND, Eve	HOOVER, Jacob	JUN 03 1851
WILBE, Charles	LEPHARDT, Sophia	MAR 18 1856
WILBER, Joel	PREAVOS, Elizabeth	MAR 20 1821
WILBERN, Elizabeth	CAMBELL, James	NOV 11 1829
WILBERN, James H.	HARRISON, Priscilla	JUL 20 1831
WILBERN, Mary	CARROLL, Bennett	MAY 01 1826
WILBERT, Catharine	MILLER, Henry	NOV 23 1843
WILBOURNE, Elizabeth	WILLIS, Benjamin Littlefield	DEC 01 1827
WILBURN, Benj.	HUTCHINSON, Priscilla	JAN 07 1813
WILBURN, Edward	HOLTZMAN, Jane J.	APR 16 1839
WILBURN, Eleanor	TALBERT, William	JUL 08 1834
WILBURN, Henrietta	VanRESWICK, Thompson	OCT 20 1835
WILBURN, John	HALL, Elizabeth	JAN 09 1817
WILBURN, Matilda	TRUXTON, William	FEB 26 1829
WILBURNE, Mary Ann	JARBOE, Benedict	MAY 04 1854

District of Columbia Marriage Licenses, 1811-1858

WILCOX, Clarissa	MARLOW, Thomas	NOV 28 1833
WILCOX, Elizabeth C.	BRONAUGH, Jeremiah W.	DEC 09 1839
WILCOX, John A.	DONELSON, Mary E.	MAY 25 1852
WILCOX, Mary J.	QUINCHE, Alexander J.	SEP 12 1857
WILCOX, Richard	SIMONDS, Jane	FEB 11 1845
WILCOXEN, Nathan P.	WILSON, Mary Emeline	DEC 18 1828
WILCOXEN, Nathan P.	KEMP, Sophia	MAY 12 1831
WILCOXEN, Washington	DAY, Trecinder	OCT 25 1824
WILCOXIN, Nathan	DOVE, Serena	OCT 19 1837
WILCOXON, Jesse T.	KEMP, Elizabeth	DEC 17 1829
WILCOXON, Margaret	BEAN, Benjamin	MAR 04 1822
WILCOXON, Rezin	DeBELL, Fanny	JUN 18 1851
WILD, Elizabeth	RUPPEL, Michael	AUG 29 1856
WILD, Robert	RAUB, ELizabeth	NOV 08 1848
WILDE, George Andrew	SINGER, Ellen	JAN 14 1835
WILDEY, Richard, Jr.	FARRELL, Mary Ann	MAY 06 1820
WILDMAN, Nathan G.	WILSON, Sarah F.	DEC 13 1845
WILDS, Darlon A.	MILLER, Lucy E.	MAR 16 1843
WILES, Ann Eliza	WALKER, Zachariah	FEB 27 1827
WILEY, Catharine Ann	FERREE, James L.	AUG 29 1838
WILEY, Elizabeth Bennett	WHARTON, James	AUG 27 1812
WILEY, Jeremiah	CURTIS, Lina	APR 15 1851
WILEY, John	CLAGETT, Sarah Ann	JUN 20 1816
WILEY, John	BROWERS, Maria	MAY 18 1833
WILEY, John	BROWN, Frances	APR 24 1851
WILEY, Lewis B.	COINER, Susanna M.	FEB 14 1855
WILEY, Margaret Y.	GULICK, John	JAN 31 1815
WILEY, Parkerson R.	DEARBORN, Christiana	AUG 27 1849
WILEY, Sarah Ann	MILLER, Benjamin M.	MAY 13 1823
WILEY, Thomas	ENGLISH, Mary	FEB 13 1816
WILEY, William	LAWRENCE, Mary	JUL 03 1812
WILHELM, Maria	DURN, John	NOV 30 1857
WILKERSON, Caroline V.	LOWE, Jacob	OCT 25 1854
WILKERSON, Catharine	PAYNE, Judson	OCT 29 1852
WILKERSON, John N.	WILLIAMS, Mima (blk)	DEC 23 1828
WILKERSON, Manerva	THOMAS, James D.	APR 24 1833
WILKERSON, Mary (blk)	REDDEN, Fielder	NOV 13 1848
WILKERSON, Mary S.	OWENS, William W.	OCT 27 1857
WILKERSON, Sarah	BEAVERS, James S.	SEP 08 1851
WILKERSON, William	SMALLWOOD, Ann Rebecca	DEC 30 1847
WILKINS, Ella	LANGENBAHN, Adolph	MAR 25 1857
WILKINS, Henrietta	BURROWS, Wiliam	JAN 17 1846
WILKINS, John Q.A.	PEYTON, Lucy F.	OCT 29 1857
WILKINS, Julia	SMALLWOOD, John	JUL 17 1856
WILKINS, Mary	MASSEY, Joseph	MAR 19 1857
WILKINSON, A. George	DORMAN, Julia A.	JUL 31 1857
WILKINSON, Alfred Berry	COBY, Mary Amelia	OCT 09 1852
WILKINSON, Edward P.	TYLER, Elizabeth (blk)	DEC 04 1837
WILKINSON, Elizabeth	ELLIS, Henry	JUL 19 1839
WILKINSON, Elizabeth	HOLAND, William E.	OCT 11 1850
WILKINSON, Elizabeth	HALLARAN, William E.	OCT 09 1854
WILKINSON, Elizabeth (blk)	MARSHALL, Wellessley C.	NOV 25 1857
WILKINSON, Elizth. J.	WILSON, Jacob H.	MAY 08 1855
WILKINSON, George	BATEMAN, Ellen	NOV 22 1855
WILKINSON, James	BROWN, Rebecca (blk)	NOV 23 1843
WILKINSON, James	GREENWELL, Mary Ann	OCT 28 1847
WILKINSON, James	AIKIN, Jane	MAR 10 1853
WILKINSON, John	QUIGLY, Bliss Elizabeth	APR 28 1836

District of Columbia Marriage Licenses, 1811-1858

WILKINSON, John	BARRY, Jane	NOV 05 1840
WILKINSON, John	TASCOE, Maria (blk)	NOV 28 1854
WILKINSON, John H.	ROBEY, Winn Ann	JUL 15 1843
WILKINSON, John H.	ROBY, Nancy	AUG 28 1851
WILKINSON, Mary	AIKEN, Mathew	OCT 04 1852
WILKINSON, Mary E.	FRANK, Alexander	MAR 01 1852
WILKINSON, Nancy	PRATT, Capt. Cary	AUG 11 1827
WILKINSON, Newman B.	WILLETT, Susan Ann	DEC 21 1826
WILKINSON, Newman B.	BEAN, Sarah	MAY 02 1844
WILKINSON, Patty	McDONALD, Allen	JAN 29 1828
WILKINSON, Richard	SHEPHERD, Sarah Ann	AUG 31 1833
WILKINSON, Samuel C.	THOMAS, Sarah C.	MAY 28 1855
WILKINSON, Sarah	NOELL, William	JUL 08 1839
WILKINSON, Sarah	LANGLEY, Aloysius	APR 21 1853
WILKINSON, Theresa B.	HAVILAND, John H.	JUL 02 1855
WILKINSON, Walter	COX, Jane Elizabeth	DEC 18 1849
WILKINSON, William	SHORTER, Maria	AUG 05 1846
WILKISON, Ann	DUNCAN, James	JAN 22 1855
WILKISON, Emeline	BEAN, Colley Williams	MAY 24 1845
WILLARD, Mary A.	HOWE, George	JUN 07 1850
WILLCOXON, Letitia	HARSHMAN, Jacob	MAR 18 1824
WILLECLIST, Elizabeth	SES, John	JUN 22 1839
WILLET, Daniel	COX, Mary Ann	AUG 20 1829
WILLET, John F.	DUCKET, Margaret	NOV 01 1851
WILLET, Marinus	BOHRER, Saah	OCT 02 1838
WILLET, Susan Ann	WILKINSON, Newman B.	DEC 21 1826
WILLETT, Alexander	RAILEY, Mary C.	MAY 04 1846
WILLETT, Eveline E.	MARTIN, Benjamin M.	MAY 19 1847
WILLETT, Fielder Dorsett	LUCUS, Elizabeth	JAN 17 1839
WILLETT, Warren O.	MONTGOMERY, Ellen F.	MAR 10 1857
WILLETT, William H.	LUCAS, Mary Eleanor	MAR 24 1848
WILLEY, Caroline	MUELLER, Charles	AUG 29 1848
WILLEY, John	ADAMS, Frances A.	JUN 30 1841
WILLIAM, Charles	MOORE, Alice	JUL 10 1855
WILLIAM, George	MILBURN, Alice	DEC 05 1818
WILLIAM, Mary E.	ALLEN, Thomas D.	MAY 06 1857
WILLIAM, Michael	MEINBERG, Amalia	AUG 02 1853
WILLIAMS, A. Cornelia	LANMAN, Joseph	SEP 19 1842
WILLIAMS, Adeline	FISTER, John	MAY 12 1832
WILLIAMS, Adeline	LUSBY, James	NOV 16 1837
WILLIAMS, Alexander	PEARSON, Verlinda	MAY 23 1836
WILLIAMS, Alfred	JACKSON, Elethea Ann (blk)	JUN 18 1836
WILLIAMS, Alfred	JACKSON, Lethe Ann (blk)	NOV 11 1837
WILLIAMS, Alfred A.	KELEHER, Julia	SEP 16 1852
WILLIAMS, Amanda (blk)	JOHNSON, Joseph	FEB 19 1844
WILLIAMS, Amelia (blk)	TAYLOR, William H.	OCT 18 1836
WILLIAMS, Ann	CORCORAN, Walter Joseph	MAY 23 1818
WILLIAMS, Ann	VANSCIVER, William	AUG 02 1823
WILLIAMS, Ann	GOODRICK, Augustus	JUN 08 1824
WILLIAMS, Ann	ASHFORD, Henry	APR 27 1829
WILLIAMS, Ann	EDWARDS, James A.	OCT 19 1829
WILLIAMS, Ann	OFFUTT, Edward T.	JAN 08 1844
WILLIAMS, Ann (blk)	TAYLOR, Patrick	MAY 30 1854
WILLIAMS, Ann (blk)	BOONE, David	OCT 04 1855
WILLIAMS, Ann M.	HADEN, Henry E.	OCT 02 1832
WILLIAMS, Ann Matilda (blk)	WILLIAMS, Charles	NOV 22 1839
WILLIAMS, Ann S.	FAITHFUL, George W.	JUN 08 1826
WILLIAMS, Ann Virginia	HOWARD, Charles	SEP 12 1848

District of Columbia Marriage Licenses, 1811-1858

WILLIAMS, Anna (blk)	CROSS, Thomas	JAN 20 1853
WILLIAMS, Anna E.	JARDELLA, Charles T.	NOV 13 1855
WILLIAMS, Barny	FULSHER, Kaziah (blk)	AUG 06 1845
WILLIAMS, Benjamin	BUTT, Easther Ann	MAY 01 1834
WILLIAMS, Betsey	BELL, James	JUL 08 1813
WILLIAMS, Brooke	BECK, Rebecca	SEP 04 1822
WILLIAMS, Brooke B.	DeBODISCO, Caroline	JAN 11 1848
WILLIAMS, Caesar	BUTLER, Margaret	JUN 09 1835
WILLIAMS, Caroline	GOSZLER, William H.	JUN 30 1838
WILLIAMS, Caroline (blk)	TAYLOR, Washington	OCT 25 1852
WILLIAMS, Catharine	JENKINS, Thomas	JAN 12 1818
WILLIAMS, Catharine	KINZEY, David	MAR 25 1820
WILLIAMS, Catharine	BRYAN, Samuel	FEB 11 1820
WILLIAMS, Catharine	EDWARDS, Washington	APR 17 1828
WILLIAMS, Catharine Ann	CHISM, John	NOV 03 1836
WILLIAMS, Catherine A.	UPSHUR, John H.	FEB 05 1851
WILLIAMS, Catherine A. (blk)	THOMAS, William	APR 15 1857
WILLIAMS, Catherine V.	SCOTT, William	OCT 07 1854
WILLIAMS, Charles	WILLIAMS, Ann Matilda (blk)	NOV 22 1839
WILLIAMS, Charles	WILLIAMS, Maria (blk)	JUN 08 1853
WILLIAMS, Charles D.	WAGNER, Rebecca R.	OCT 02 1854
WILLIAMS, Charlotte	DAVIS, Charles Atkerson	MAY 27 1824
WILLIAMS, Charlotte (blk)	REDIN, Selby	NOV 11 1847
WILLIAMS, Charlotte J.	BATES, John E.	JAN 06 1852
WILLIAMS, Chas.	GIBSON, Eliza (blk)	NOV 19 1856
WILLIAMS, Chas. R.	MALONEY, Ellen	AUG 31 1858
WILLIAMS, Christy (blk)	WASHINGTON, George	JUL 05 1856
WILLIAMS, Clorinda M.	BASSETT, George A.	NOV 05 1856
WILLIAMS, Daniel	HINES, Elizabeth (blk)	JUL 09 1850
WILLIAMS, David	TUELL, Rebecca	APR 14 1834
WILLIAMS, David	WALKER, Mary Elizabeth	JUL 22 1843
WILLIAMS, Elie	COOK, Sarah	JUL 25 1829
WILLIAMS, Eliza	RIDGEWAY, James	DEC 28 1812
WILLIAMS, Eliza	ELLIS, Alexander	JAN 01 1842
WILLIAMS, Eliza	COX, Richard S.	JAN 31 1849
WILLIAMS, Elizabeth	PATTERSON, Thomas	FEB 10 1813
WILLIAMS, Elizabeth	NORRIS, Jas.	DEC 31 1814
WILLIAMS, Elizabeth	CARTER, Luke	FEB 15 1821
WILLIAMS, Elizabeth	GIVEN, Thomas	FEB 06 1827
WILLIAMS, Elizabeth	EPHLINE, David James	JAN 02 1847
WILLIAMS, Elizabeth	THORNTON, Stewart	SEP 30 1850
WILLIAMS, Elizabeth (blk)	LEMMON, John	MAY 18 1854
WILLIAMS, Elizabeth Ann Sabrina	BEAN, John	DEC 23 1820
WILLIAMS, Elizabeth E.	GRINDER, Joseph	JAN 18 1855
WILLIAMS, Elizth. (blk)	TUNION, Robert	JUN 11 1846
WILLIAMS, Ellen	MARTIN, Benjamin	DEC 14 1848
WILLIAMS, Ellen	REED, John Thomas	JUL 03 1850
WILLIAMS, Ellen	MORIARTY, Daniel	APR 30 1851
WILLIAMS, Elvina	KING, Edward	JUN 01 1844
WILLIAMS, Frances	HERBERT, Francis	JUN 22 1842
WILLIAMS, Frances	ROBERTSON, Grandison	JUL 13 1857
WILLIAMS, Frederic B.	STEWART, Mary E.	AUG 21 1855
WILLIAMS, George	ROWLES, Charlotte	JUN 29 1813
WILLIAMS, George	LEE, Eleanor S.	JAN 30 1823
WILLIAMS, George	GRIGGES, Mary Ann	NOV 21 1825
WILLIAMS, George	HOWARD, Mary	APR 28 1845
WILLIAMS, George	WARD, Christiana (blk)	AUG 18 1851
WILLIAMS, George	STROTHER, Sarah E.	MAR 14 1854

District of Columbia Marriage Licenses, 1811-1858

WILLIAMS, George W.	YOUNG, Janett Ann	JUN 29 1826
WILLIAMS, Georgianna	FERTNER, Columbus	AUG 17 1850
WILLIAMS, Hannah	REISER, Adam	NOV 21 1846
WILLIAMS, Harriet	BODISCO, Alexander	APR 07 1840
WILLIAMS, Harriet Eliza	HARVY, John	OCT 14 1823
WILLIAMS, Harriot	WALLACE, Richard D.	MAR 19 1816
WILLIAMS, Henrietta	JONES, Alexander	OCT 20 1841
WILLIAMS, Henrietta	MILLER, Joseph	MAY 08 1858
WILLIAMS, Henry	BROOKS, Adaline (blk)	OCT 12 1830
WILLIAMS, Henry	DONNELL, Jane	JUL 15 1833
WILLIAMS, Hilleary	FREDERICK, Margaret	MAY 07 1857
WILLIAMS, Jackson	SWAIN, Catharine	OCT 06 1851
WILLIAMS, Jacob	HILL, Caroline (blk)	JAN 20 1858
WILLIAMS, Jacob	HILL, Caroline (blk)	FEB 10 1858
WILLIAMS, James	SMALLWOOD, Catherine	JUL 01 1816
WILLIAMS, James	BAYLISS, May	DEC 05 1821
WILLIAMS, James	GALLAWAY, Eliza	MAR 17 1824
WILLIAMS, James	ARNOLD, Susan	JUN 18 1824
WILLIAMS, James	SIMMONS, Matilda	OCT 25 1825
WILLIAMS, James	MOORE, Mary M.	FEB 19 1845
WILLIAMS, James	MOCKABEE, Eliza Ann	APR 23 1846
WILLIAMS, James	ISRAEL, Martha	MAY 13 1851
WILLIAMS, James	SIMS, Ann Amelia (blk)	SEP 15 1857
WILLIAMS, James	MALONEY, Hannora	FEB 13 1858
WILLIAMS, James A.	ST. CLAIR, Alcinda	JUN 16 1842
WILLIAMS, James H.	KELLY, Susan S.	DEC 27 1855
WILLIAMS, Jane	BOSWELL, George	APR 13 1816
WILLIAMS, Jane E.	CONNELL, Theophilus	APR 07 1858
WILLIAMS, Jane Eliza	HARBESON, Robert	FEB 25 1833
WILLIAMS, Jesse	SMITH, Mary Ann	FEB 27 1852
WILLIAMS, Joanna	BROSNAN, John	JUL 27 1852
WILLIAMS, John	FOWLER, Harriet	AUG 29 1825
WILLIAMS, John	BALLINGER, Lydia	AUG 13 1827
WILLIAMS, John	WELLS, Maria Louisa	DEC 13 1831
WILLIAMS, John	CHAPMAN, Ann	JUL 01 1833
WILLIAMS, John	BOYD, Lucy	MAY 25 1836
WILLIAMS, John	MADDOX, Margaret	NOV 17 1838
WILLIAMS, John	ALFRED, Ann	JUL 10 1841
WILLIAMS, John	POWERS, Amelia (blk)	OCT 05 1853
WILLIAMS, John	COWPER, Virginia (blk)	DEC 18 1855
WILLIAMS, John	JONES, Rebecca	JUN 19 1856
WILLIAMS, John	COOLIDGE, Leonora M.	MAR 18 1857
WILLIAMS, John A.	BEATLEY, Eliza J.	OCT 15 1857
WILLIAMS, John E.	WOODWARD, Laura E.	AUG 26 1847
WILLIAMS, John H.	BLOSSOM, Electa J.	JUN 12 1856
WILLIAMS, John James	COBURN, Eliza Maria	JUN 19 1845
WILLIAMS, John W.	WROE, Georgiana	JAN 22 1839
WILLIAMS, John W.	CAMMACK, Mary	NOV 14 1846
WILLIAMS, Joseph Z.	HOWARD, Mary	OCT 01 1852
WILLIAMS, Josephine	BRYAN, Lee (blk)	JUN 25 1846
WILLIAMS, Julia	WILLIAMS, Lloyd	FEB 25 1834
WILLIAMS, Kate J.	JONES, John W.	APR 16 1856
WILLIAMS, Laura	SHORTER, Charles	APR 06 1857
WILLIAMS, Lawrence	DACY, Elizabeth	JUL 02 1849
WILLIAMS, Lemuel	BATES, Lydia	OCT 06 1830
WILLIAMS, Lemuel	ROBINSON, Caroline Virginia	MAR 31 1835
WILLIAMS, Lemuel D.	O'DONNELL, Sarah	DEC 31 1851
WILLIAMS, Levi	LYLES, Susanna	JUL 14 1835

District of Columbia Marriage Licenses, 1811-1858

WILLIAMS, Lewis	GREENWELL, Ann	OCT 20 1834
WILLIAMS, Lewis	BRUDEROFKI, Elizabeth	MAY 08 1854
WILLIAMS, Lewis Western	DOWDEN, Sarah Emily	NOV 06 1838
WILLIAMS, Lloyd	WILLIAMS, Julia	FEB 25 1834
WILLIAMS, Lucy (blk)	THOMAS, John F.	NOV 13 1851
WILLIAMS, Lydia Ann	RUSSELL, John Henry	SEP 04 1845
WILLIAMS, Margaret (blk)	HASKINS, James	MAR 30 1843
WILLIAMS, Margt.	MERCEREAN, Lewis	JAN 02 1812
WILLIAMS, Maria (blk)	WILLIAMS, Charles	JUN 08 1853
WILLIAMS, Maria B.	FINK, John	JUN 23 1853
WILLIAMS, Martha	MANTZ, Isaac	AUG 25 1825
WILLIAMS, Martha	HAUPTMAN, Henry	JUN 08 1837
WILLIAMS, Mary	ROBERTSON, Holdsworth	DEC 30 1830
WILLIAMS, Mary	KEMP, John	JUL 09 1840
WILLIAMS, Mary	KELLY, Michael	SEP 10 1850
WILLIAMS, Mary (blk)	SCOTT, Isaac	JUL 01 1846
WILLIAMS, Mary Ann	HOBAN, Edward	DEC 31 1832
WILLIAMS, Mary Ann (blk)	STUART, William	FEB 29 1848
WILLIAMS, Mary Ann (blk)	WHEELER, Robert	MAY 06 1851
WILLIAMS, Mary Ann	COOPER, Tego	JAN 14 1852
WILLIAMS, Mary Elizth.	DAVIS, John H.	NOV 27 1832
WILLIAMS, Mary Jane	RAWLINGS, Thomas H.	DEC 16 1847
WILLIAMS, Mima (blk)	WILKERSON, John N. (blk)	DEC 23 1828
WILLIAMS, Moses	WELLS, Mary E.	APR 13 1854
WILLIAMS, Nancy	LEE, John	AUG 07 1818
WILLIAMS, Nancy (blk)	STEWART, Charles	MAR 12 1823
WILLIAMS, Orellar	WHIPPLE, Joseph	OCT 20 1837
WILLIAMS, Orellar	BELL, Benjamin H.	OCT 21 1837
WILLIAMS, Patsy	GODFRY, William, Jr.	MAR 12 1829
WILLIAMS, Peter	O'NEALE, Mary	MAY 20 1826
WILLIAMS, Peter	WHITE, Susannah	SEP 25 1832
WILLIAMS, Philip	MARKWOOD, Sarah Ann [Mrs.]	SEP 18 1832
WILLIAMS, Pius	BREST, Henrietta	NOV 03 1851
WILLIAMS, Rachael	BROWN, John B.	MAY 29 1830
WILLIAMS, Rachael	LINDSAY, Richard	APR 20 1835
WILLIAMS, Raymond W.	WATSON, Mary E.	MAY 11 1854
WILLIAMS, Richard	HUDDLESTON, Julia	FEB 22 1844
WILLIAMS, Richard	DRUMMOND, Elicia C.	SEP 04 1856
WILLIAMS, Robert	BURROWS, Rebecca	MAR 08 1852
WILLIAMS, Robert W. [Col.]	BRANCH, Rebecca B.	APR 19 1831
WILLIAMS, Robt.	TURNER, Ann A. (blk)	AUG 02 1855
WILLIAMS, Samuel	CARPENTER, Mary Jane	SEP 21 1852
WILLIAMS, Samuel L.	TUCKER, Maria S.	MAY 20 1847
WILLIAMS, Sarah	SIMMONS, Benjamin	DEC 23 1815
WILLIAMS, Sarah	SHUMATE, Walker D.	JUL 29 1830
WILLIAMS, Sarah	SWEENY, William	JUL 19 1838
WILLIAMS, Sarah	NORRIS, Enoch M.	DEC 13 1854
WILLIAMS, Sarah Ann	CROGGINGS, James H.	APR 28 1846
WILLIAMS, Sarah D.	COOK, George T.	NOV 18 1852
WILLIAMS, Sarah E.	McINTIRE, Timothy C.	OCT 05 1854
WILLIAMS, Sophia (blk)	HAMES, William	FEB 21 1855
WILLIAMS, Susan	BANISTER, Aquila	APR 28 1829
WILLIAMS, Susan	CAMERON, William H.	OCT 02 1854
WILLIAMS, Susan Ann	JACOBS, Harrison	JAN 12 1844
WILLIAMS, Susanna J.	WILLIAMS, William A.	SEP 27 1856
WILLIAMS, Susannah	NORFLET, Thomas	NOV 14 1848
WILLIAMS, Thomas	WOODFIELD, Mary	JUL 22 1815
WILLIAMS, Thomas E.	KING, Joanna M.	FEB 10 1844

District of Columbia Marriage Licenses, 1811-1858

WILLIAMS, Thomas G.	LOVELESS, Mary D.	JUN 13 1846
WILLIAMS, Thomas W.	CLARKE, Lucinda J.	JUN 23 1858
WILLIAMS, Tobias	GRAYSON, Eliza	JAN 08 1845
WILLIAMS, Tobias	BELT, Elizabeth (blk)	DEC 31 1852
WILLIAMS, Virginia J.	COLDWELL, Joseph T.	JUL 31 1854
WILLIAMS, Walter	SIMMONS, Susan (blk)	MAR 11 1846
WILLIAMS, Washington B.	JOHNSON, Jane E.	OCT 11 1855
WILLIAMS, William	WILSON, Susan	JUL 10 1817
WILLIAMS, William	WINEBERGER, Adeline	JUL 05 1827
WILLIAMS, William	ADAMS, Mary	JUL 01 1830
WILLIAMS, William	BLAKE, Jane	OCT 15 1835
WILLIAMS, William	NORWOOD, Eliza	OCT 19 1847
WILLIAMS, William	JOHNSON, Martha (blk)	OCT 23 1856
WILLIAMS, William	COLE, Barbara A. (blk)	NOV 17 1856
WILLIAMS, William A.	WILLIAMS, Susanna J.	SEP 27 1856
WILLIAMS, William H.	CUSINS, Sarah	DEC 03 1845
WILLIAMS, William H.	MILBURN, Violet A.	FEB 08 1848
WILLIAMS, William Hy.	BURNES, Marcia E.	APR 25 1844
WILLIAMS, William J.	HURST, Jemima	FEB 27 1845
WILLIAMS, William P.	DOYLE, Mary A.	SEP 25 1839
WILLIAMS, William P.	DOYLE, Mary A.	FEB 26 1840
WILLIAMS, William W.	ANDREWS, Susan	NOV 25 1824
WILLIAMS, Wm.	PATTERSON, Margaret	OCT 16 1830
WILLIAMS, Wm. C.	REYNOLDS, Emily	NOV 25 1856
WILLIAMS, Wm. F.	PILES, Sarah	JAN 06 1851
WILLIAMS, Wm. Geo.	PETER, America Pinkney	JUN 26 1826
WILLIAMS, Zadock	BAILY, Elizabeth	NOV 17 1823
WILLIAMS, Zadock	DENOU, Edney Ann	NOV 14 1828
WILLIAMS, Zadock	MERTON, Mary	NOV 15 1854
WILLIAMS, [blank]	GIBBS, Sarah	APR 29 1812
WILLIAMSON, Benjamin	GARNER, Harriet	JUL 13 1822
WILLIAMSON, Charlotte A.	RICHARDSON, Charles F.E.	MAY 17 1848
WILLIAMSON, Dinah	ABBOT, Richard	FEB 25 1843
WILLIAMSON, Edward	TUCKER, Elizabeth	AUG 14 1856
WILLIAMSON, Elizabeth	HUNTRESS, Charles A.	NOV 23 1857
WILLIAMSON, Elizabeth B.	MOTZER, Rev. Daniel	SEP 16 1848
WILLIAMSON, Harriet	BARRON, George O.	MAY 08 1845
WILLIAMSON, J.S.M.	HOWELL, S. Harrison	JUN 14 1852
WILLIAMSON, James	WHEATLEY, Mary	MAR 13 1833
WILLIAMSON, James B.	EBERLE, A.W.	AUG 13 1850
WILLIAMSON, Joseph	RICHARDSON, Mary Ann	JAN 31 1839
WILLIAMSON, Joseph	TOOMEY Ann	FEB 19 1846
WILLIAMSON, Martha	DENTY, Thomas	APR 29 1856
WILLIAMSON, Mary	KER, Jacob W.E.	MAR 21 1838
WILLIAMSON, Mary Ann	BARRON, Samuel	JAN 29 1850
WILLIAMSON, Mary E.	DOVE, Andrew	AUG 13 1846
WILLIAMSON, Robert H.	GLOVER, Matilda R.	NOV 07 1837
WILLIAMSON, Samuel	MENSHAMER, Mary A.	JAN 02 1857
WILLIAMSON, Sarah A.	REED, John W.	APR 15 1857
WILLIAMSON, Thomas	HOOPER, Jane	JAN 30 1855
WILLIAMSON, Virginia E.	CLAYTON, James R.	APR 12 1852
WILLIAMSON, Walter B.	MORGAN, Mahalah Jane	DEC 13 1855
WILLIAMSON, Wm.	BALCH, Jane Whann	SEP 23 1823
WILLIARD, Edwin D.	HEPBURN, Sarah E.	AUG 29 1845
WILLIARD, James F.	MURPHY, Mary	OCT 28 1840
WILLING, Charles	TILLINGHAST, Rebecca	MAR 24 1840
WILLING, Mary Jane	HILTON, William E.	DEC 24 1846
WILLING, Sarah	SMART, John P.	MAR 29 1827

District of Columbia Marriage Licenses, 1811-1858

WILLINGFORD, Mary Ann	GIVEN, WIlliam	FEB 21 1832
WILLIS, A. Murat	AMBLER, F.E.	DEC 20 1847
WILLIS, Albert S.	LeMOINE, Louisa D.	AUG 06 1835
WILLIS, Ann Eliza	GATES, James A.	DEC 14 1848
WILLIS, Benjamin Littlefield	WILBOURNE, Elizabeth	DEC 01 1827
WILLIS, Elizabeth	MYERS, Joseph	OCT 10 1850
WILLIS, Elizabeth (blk)	BLACK, Tobias	MAY 10 1822
WILLIS, Henry	BROOKS, Mary Ann	MAR 30 1847
WILLIS, John	SPENCE, Elizabeth	JUL 31 1841
WILLIS, Joshua	PEARSON, Mary Ann M.	OCT 05 1824
WILLIS, Louisa L.	LORD, W. Blair	NOV 06 1854
WILLIS, Louisa L.	LORD, W. Blair	NOV 06 1854
WILLIS, Martha Ann	EDMONDSON, B.B.	DEC 12 1848
WILLIS, William	PADGETT, Jane	JUL 18 1826
WILLIS, William L.	NORMAN, M.C.	AUG 24 1848
WILLISS, George	TACK, Mary Ann	DEC 08 1836
WILLNER, Francis	HEITMILLER, Caroline	NOV 23 1857
WILLNER, George	POSS, Margaret	FEB 03 1841
WILLOUGHBY, Martha Ann	PENDLETON, William S.	JUL 18 1856
WILLS, Ann (blk)	NEWTON, John	JUN 16 1825
WILLS, Anna Katterina	SCHNEKT, Karl	JUN 29 1858
WILLS, Caroline	FOILAND, Peter	SEP 26 1848
WILLS, John	COX, Ann Lauretta	MAY 21 1845
WILLS, Joseph	NORRIS, Elizabeth	FEB 29 1848
WILLSON, Catherine T.	HARVEY, William	MAY 01 1821
WILLSON, Janet	CUNNINGHAM, Archibald	MAR 02 1825
WILLSON, John	SCOTT, Airy	OCT 06 1836
WILLSON, Miranda E.	McKNEW, N. Clarendon	OCT 11 1856
WILLSON, Richard B.	YOUNG, Ann Martha	OCT 03 1842
WILLSON, Sarah	KENNEDY, James A.	JAN 13 1817
WILMAN, Catherine	MILLER, William	MAY 04 1850
WILMS, Elizabeth, Mrs.	BOHRER, Jacob	AUG 12 1815
WILSBOUGHER, Elizabeth	HOMAN, Francis	JUN 02 1835
WILSON, Amanda J.	MATTINGLY, Joseph W.	SEP 27 1848
WILSON, Ann	CHALMERS, John, Senr.	JUN 18 1812
WILSON, Ann	HODEN, Thomas	MAY 07 1816
WILSON, Ann	BUTLER, Philip	JUL 12 1828
WILSON, Ann	BLUNDER, James A.	NOV 27 1854
WILSON, Anna M.	REED, Bushrod M.	MAY 31 1855
WILSON, Aquilla	TALBERT, Eleanor	JAN 29 1818
WILSON, Barbara E. (blk)	COLE, Robert	JUN 28 1856
WILSON, Barbary	ANDERSON, Librun	AUG 13 1857
WILSON, Benjamin	HOLSEY, Mary	DEC 18 1817
WILSON, Benoni	CRAWFORD, Ariana	FEB 01 1813
WILSON, Caroline	COLEMAN, Edmond W.	MAR 19 1828
WILSON, Catharine [Mrs.]	COOKE, Thomas	OCT 18 1821
WILSON, Charles	RALEY, Elizabeth	APR 17 1847
WILSON, Charles	FREEMAN, Jane (blk)	NOV 28 1848
WILSON, Charles	BLOXHAM, Mary T.	APR 10 1850
WILSON, Charles E.	BUTLER, Mary V.	JUN 30 1858
WILSON, Charles F.	MOUNTJOY, Mary	FEB 01 1854
WILSON, Chas. H.	SCOTT, Margaret A.	APR 13 1858
WILSON, David	BLACK, Mary Ann	MAR 18 1829
WILSON, Eliza	ARCHER, William	SEP 14 1826
WILSON, Eliza	CARRO, Barny	AUG 11 1841
WILSON, Eliza	BARNES, Richard	APR 15 1845
WILSON, Eliza Jane	HEISKELL, William B.	SEP 07 1847
WILSON, Elizabeth	ROBERTSON, Seth	FEB 11 1813

District of Columbia Marriage Licenses, 1811-1858

WILSON, Elizabeth	CURRY, Robert	AUG 10 1820
WILSON, Elizabeth	GITTINGS, George	DEC 04 1839
WILSON, Elizabeth	MILLER, Jacob	JUL 09 1846
WILSON, Elizabeth Ann	JOLLY, John	JAN 30 1849
WILSON, Elizabeth E.	WESTERFIELD, David	AUG 13 1846
WILSON, Ellen Gordon	MEREDITH, John Henry	DEC 04 1851
WILSON, Emely	MacGILL, Thomas	FEB 15 1831
WILSON, Emma (blk)	HERBERT, Alfred	SEP 17 1857
WILSON, Ephraim King	STEIGER, Kate Brengle	JUL 14 1856
WILSON, Euias	VERMILLION, Margaret	JUL 09 1818
WILSON, Francis	VERMILLION, Barshala	JUL 18 1818
WILSON, Frederick T.	BORLAND, Mary E.	DEC 24 1853
WILSON, Gady Ann (blk)	ROLLINS, John	NOV 28 1846
WILSON, Geo. H.	ADAMS, Ellen V.	SEP 25 1850
WILSON, George	PENN, Rachel	MAY 18 1855
WILSON, George Claibourn	UMBERFIELD, Marian	FEB 03 1857
WILSON, George Gideon	PLOWMAN, Marian Louisa	DEC 31 1851
WILSON, George R.	JUCH, Charity	OCT 17 1849
WILSON, George W.	BROWN, Signet A.	OCT 20 1856
WILSON, George Washington	WRIGHT, Mary Ann Elizabeth [Mrs.]	DEC 20 1827
WILSON, Hannah	WHITE, Horace	MAY 31 1844
WILSON, Hannah (blk)	SMITH, Reubin	MAY 08 1846
WILSON, Hariot	HUTSON, Samuel	DEC 29 1824
WILSON, Harriet Elizabeth (blk)	SMITH, Reubin	SEP 08 1851
WILSON, Harriett B.	McCOOMB, Alexander	MAY 26 1826
WILSON, Harriot	ASKINS, Jos.	FEB 13 1823
WILSON, Henrietta	GARCI, Celestin	JUL 10 1856
WILSON, Henry	SLATER, Ann (blk)	AUG 07 1823
WILSON, Henry	NEVITT, Amelia	JUL 15 1834
WILSON, Henry G.	KENNEDY, Mary H.	JAN 04 1818
WILSON, Hester A.	BOGS, John W.	MAY 02 1854
WILSON, Hugh Bowlsby	LADDE, Harriet C.	OCT 23 1855
WILSON, Isaac	MARSHALL, Jane	SEP 12 1845
WILSON, Isaac	CAMPBELL, Catharine	NOV 13 1856
WILSON, Jacob H.	WILKINSON, Elizth. J.	MAY 08 1855
WILSON, James	MARKS, Sophia Maria Western	MAY 25 1821
WILSON, James	SCOTT, Elizabeth	JUL 17 1828
WILSON, James Campbell	BALCH, Anna Emma Beall	JAN 18 1816
WILSON, James H.	SALLSBERRY, Mary Frances	OCT 09 1855
WILSON, James O.	HUNGERFORD, Sarah A.W.	JUL 02 1853
WILSON, James S.	BEALL, Eleanor L.	JAN 23 1834
WILSON, James W.	BURGESS, Sarah A.	AUG 09 1843
WILSON, Jane	BOYD, William	APR 18 1850
WILSON, Jesse B.	SCRIVENER, Ann A.	SEP 25 1849
WILSON, John	MYERS, Charlotte	MAY 27 1822
WILSON, John	SPALDING, Martha Ann	DEC 27 1827
WILSON, John	McCLELLAND, Martha	FEB 04 1829
WILSON, John	TSCHIFFELY, Catharine Emily	JUN 06 1833
WILSON, John	COLLINS, Mary	NOV 16 1833
WILSON, John	DeVAUGHN, Columbia	MAR 19 1845
WILSON, John	OSBORNE, Lucinda	AUG 12 1848
WILSON, John	OSBORNE, Lucinda	AUG 12 1848
WILSON, John E., Lieut.	OSBORNE, Susan	MAY 16 1854
WILSON, John F.	CUSTARD, Mary E.	DEC 12 1857
WILSON, John H.	BALDWIN, Sarah Jane	AUG 03 1843
WILSON, John H.A.	BURY, Adelaide	DEC 12 1846
WILSON, John Henry	SEMMES, Marcelina Virginia	JAN 09 1850
WILSON, John M.	SANFORD, Caroline	NOV 18 1823

District of Columbia Marriage Licenses, 1811-1858

WILSON, John M.	PAGE, Rebecca H.	MAY 15 1834
WILSON, John Q.	BOTELER, Ellen	APR 29 1847
WILSON, John Q.	MARSTEN, Frances	OCT 07 1848
WILSON, Joseph	DIVINE, Mary Ann	DEC 05 1842
WILSON, Joseph H.	STALIN, Ann S.	AUG 16 1855
WILSON, Joseph S.	MOULDER, Eliza	SEP 01 1829
WILSON, Josias D.	O'NEIL, Hannah	DEC 31 1832
WILSON, Lancelot	McDANIEL, Jane	DEC 04 1819
WILSON, Laura V.	DELLZELL, Alexander W.	NOV 20 1854
WILSON, Levi E.	DAWES, Sarah	JUN 05 1850
WILSON, Lewis C.	COX, Mary	DEC 14 1835
WILSON, Lewis C.	HENLY, Hester Ann	APR 08 1839
WILSON, Lucinda	MILLER, John Philip	JAN 25 1828
WILSON, Malinda	HILLARY, Theodore Williams	MAR 22 1820
WILSON, Marcellina	JOHNSON, James	APR 14 1856
WILSON, Marcellus	HARDESTER, Mary Ellen	MAY 27 1848
WILSON, Marceuny	HOPKINS, Ruth	APR 21 1835
WILSON, Margaret	DULANY, George	JAN 09 1812
WILSON, Margaret	DRAKE, Wallard	OCT 10 1815
WILSON, Margaret	DONOVAN, James	SEP 09 1850
WILSON, Margaret	PLOWMAN, Thomas	OCT 15 1855
WILSON, Margaret Ann	HEISS, Andrew	AUG 29 1846
WILSON, Maria (blk)	WARNER, James	MAY 23 1849
WILSON, Martha Ann	JOHNSON, Henry	NOV 29 1836
WILSON, Martha C.	CONNOLLY, Robert J.J.	JUN 22 1857
WILSON, Martha Jane	NICHOLSON, Joseph	JUN 09 1841
WILSON, Martha S.	STOVALL, Bolling A.	SEP 19 1856
WILSON, Mary	NAIRN, James	MAY 28 1821
WILSON, Mary	FLETCHER, William H.	AUG 05 1833
WILSON, Mary	GAHMANN, Frederick	DEC 03 1849
WILSON, Mary	HEYBOYN, John	JUL 14 1853
WILSON, Mary	COWLING, Edward	SEP 04 1855
WILSON, Mary (blk)	JOHNSON, Grafton	AUG 21 1856
WILSON, Mary (blk)	SHAW, Sandy	NOV 13 1856
WILSON, Mary A.	ODLE, Trueman	APR 25 1855
WILSON, Mary Ann	JINGELL, Joseph	DEC 28 1814
WILSON, Mary Ann	BERCKMANN, John H.	OCT 09 1850
WILSON, Mary C.	POMEROY, George P.	MAR 17 1842
WILSON, Mary Cornelia	HAVENNER, Thomas H.	FEB 10 1846
WILSON, Mary E.	MITCHELL, Richard T.	MAY 14 1855
WILSON, Mary Elizth.	CROSS, James	NOV 14 1848
WILSON, Mary Ellen [Mrs.]	ARNOLD, Rezin	DEC 21 1827
WILSON, Mary Emeline	WILCOXEN, Nathan P.	DEC 18 1828
WILSON, Mary L.	MAXWELL, John S.	DEC 29 1851
WILSON, Mary L.	CISSELL, Thos.	OCT 22 1857
WILSON, Mary S.	DUNCAN, Thomas	AUG 25 1852
WILSON, Matilda	SHERIFF, Levi	MAY 31 1813
WILSON, Matthew	McNEIR, Catherine W.	DEC 04 1855
WILSON, Melinda	MANKINS, Edward	AUG 29 1837
WILSON, Mercy Ann	FOGG, Ebenezer W.	JAN 11 1854
WILSON, Milly	SWAIN, William	JAN 05 1814
WILSON, Narcissa	BEALL, John A.	JUL 26 1825
WILSON, Nelly G.	GRUBB, Samuel	MAR 24 1826
WILSON, Offa	CHALMERS, Ann [Mrs.]	SEP 22 1825
WILSON, Offa E.	RAMSAY, Elizabeth B.	DEC 11 1849
WILSON, Peter F.	KELLER, Cornelia M.	MAY 30 1853
WILSON, Priscilla	DOUGHERTY, James	JUN 28 1832
WILSON, Rebecca	FRY, James	DEC 29 1821

District of Columbia Marriage Licenses, 1811-1858

WILSON, Rebecca	CUSTARD, William H.	DEC 02 1843
WILSON, Robert	SYLVESTER, Caroline	FEB 09 1822
WILSON, Robert	BRADLEY, Mary (blk)	FEB 19 1840
WILSON, Rowanna W.H.	MacGILL, Charles	FEB 19 1833
WILSON, Sarah (blk)	BALTIMORE, Joseph	OCT 31 1833
WILSON, Sarah Ann Susan	HIGGENS, Artakerxes	APR 29 1835
WILSON, Sarah Ann	OBANNON, Dogobert B.	MAR 21 1853
WILSON, Sarah Ann	COLE, Thomas W.	MAY 06 1853
WILSON, Sarah C.	HATTON, Henry D.	NOV 07 1854
WILSON, Sarah Catherine	SPEAKS, John	DEC 19 1851
WILSON, Sarah Evaline	REYNOLDS, John	JUL 09 1836
WILSON, Sarah F.	WILDMAN, Nathan G.	DEC 13 1845
WILSON, Susan	WILLIAMS, William	JUL 10 1817
WILSON, Susan	TOOKER, Lansing	AUG 24 1835
WILSON, Susanah M.	BRYAN, Enoch	JUN 15 1819
WILSON, Tabitha P.	GOODRICK, John F.	JUN 08 1825
WILSON, Thomas	STEWART, Ann	MAR 02 1820
WILSON, Thomas	CAVENAUGH, Margaret	SEP 09 1840
WILSON, Thomas	KING, Henrietta (blk)	JUN 02 1842
WILSON, Thomas	RITTENHOUSE, Henrietta W.	MAY 01 1858
WILSON, Thomas C.	CAMPBELL, Margaret	DEC 16 1835
WILSON, Thomas C.	DAILEY, Mary	JAN 19 1847
WILSON, Thomas K.	GREER, Margaret B.	SEP 06 1841
WILSON, Thomas L.	BENDER, Julianna M.	MAY 06 1824
WILSON, Thomas N.	PHILLIPS, Sarah	MAY 25 1815
WILSON, Virginia Hills	DUSENBERY, Constantine	SEP 17 1856
WILSON, William	CUNNINGHAM, Catharine	DEC 05 1827
WILSON, William	ARMSTRONG, Hulday	MAR 31 1832
WILSON, William	HUGHES, Catharine	DEC 05 1833
WILSON, William	MART, Rebecca	APR 13 1846
WILSON, William	CARROLL, Agatha (blk)	JUN 06 1850
WILSON, William A.	KING, Sarah	DEC 25 1829
WILSON, William A.	PECKHAM, Mary Stanton	SEP 05 1844
WILSON, William F.	CLINTON, Mary Ann	MAY 29 1846
WILSON, William H.	JONES, Elizabeth Ann	NOV 03 1847
WILSON, William S.	GLOYD, Mary Elizth.	FEB 18 1845
WILSON, William T.	BENVANIDA, Louisa C.	JUL 01 1844
WILSON, Zachariah	BIND, Sarah	SEP 18 1818
WILT, William H.	WOODYARD, Elizabeth	DEC 24 1835
WILTBERGER, Charles H.	BURCH, Verlinda Mary	JUL 09 1821
WILTSBURCHER, Teresa	KEPLER, John George	JUL 31 1856
WILTZ, Adam	VOEKER, Margaret	JAN 14 1835
WILTZ, Adam	VOEKER, Margaret	FEB 14 1835
WIMER, James	COLLISON, Elizth. J.	MAY 09 1844
WIMSATT, Ann Eliza	MORGAN, Francis	OCT 14 1834
WIMSATT, Caroline	REED, Isaac	MAY 13 1831
WIMSATT, Joseph	WALFENDEN, Charlotte	AUG 29 1838
WIMSATT, Mary A.	SKIDMORE, John W.	FEB 04 1845
WIMSATT, Richard	HARRIS, Sarah	SEP 03 1838
WIMSATT, William H.	MASSEY, Mary H.	AUG 17 1840
WIMSET, Lewis	HOWARD, Eleanor	OCT 20 1817
WIMSET, Sophia	RUMPFF, Henry	SEP 17 1822
WINANS, Jacob W., Rev.	NOURSE, Susan S.	JUL 27 1853
WINBERGER, Olivia	FLENER, William	NOV 28 1833
WINCHELL, William R.	COOPER, Emma A.	APR 06 1854
WINDELL, Martha	PEERCE, Henry	MAY 13 1813
WINDELSTAIR, Johanna	FEHR, Augustin	NOV 19 1832
WINDER, John H.	TANNER, Rebecca	DEC 24 1825

District of Columbia Marriage Licenses, 1811-1858

WINDER, Samuel	RUSSELL, Sarah	APR 23 1812
WINDER, Sarah	DANFORD, James	DEC 02 1813
WINDHAM, Andrew J.	LLEWELLEN, Rebecca	MAY 27 1844
WINDHAM, Caroline	BENNETT, Hiram	DEC 27 1827
WINDHAM, Charles	HOOVER, Sarah	NOV 14 1812
WINDHAM, Mary E.B.	JOHNSON, Neville	APR 20 1835
WINDHAM, Sarah	MANN, Jesse	DEC 17 1842
WINDHAM, Sophia	JOHNSON, William	MAY 18 1857
WINDHAM, Willm. C.	RABBITT, Mary C.	SEP 16 1851
WINDHAN, Ann Delia	WEAVER, James	SEP 07 1839
WINDSER, Elijah	KIDWELL, Susan N.	SEP 24 1853
WINDSER, Henry	GARNER, Susannah	DEC 31 1823
WINDSOR, A. Rina Elizabeth	ZIMMERMAN, John H.	SEP 17 1836
WINDSOR, Benjamin	ARVIN, Mary Ann	JUN 09 1840
WINDSOR, Catharine	KULP, Aaron J.	MAY 28 1855
WINDSOR, Francis H.	QUAID, Malinda J.	DEC 29 1853
WINDSOR, George B.	STRETCH, Mary E.	APR 04 1838
WINDSOR, Henry	ASKEW, Eleanor	AUG 12 1817
WINDSOR, Henry C.	BAKER, Hattie R.	JUN 27 1856
WINDSOR, Henry J.	BENSON, Susan H.	APR 16 1851
WINDSOR, James	LACOCK, Mary	MAY 24 1853
WINDSOR, Jane Catherine	LARCOMB, James M.	SEP 06 1854
WINDSOR, John	WEBSTER, Elizabeth	JAN 10 1825
WINDSOR, John A[lexan]der	BUCKLEY, Susan	FEB 27 1812
WINDSOR, Lemuel H.	BELT, Catherine P.	DEC 29 1853
WINDSOR, Maria	STODDARD, Samuel	FEB 19 1851
WINDSOR, Martha	BELL, Henry	JUN 10 1847
WINDSOR, Mary	TODD, Samuel	APR 20 1854
WINDSOR, Mary A.	LEE, Joseph D.	DEC 06 1856
WINDSOR, Rosanna N.	SMITH, John A.	JUN 09 1827
WINDSOR, Sarah Ann	LANGLEY, John	MAY 10 1856
WINDSOR, Sukey	EAGLIN, Lila Susan	DEC 13 1838
WINDSOR, Wm. L.	ADAMS, Catharine R.	SEP 08 1853
WINDSOR, Zachariah L.	STONE, Mary Jane	MAY 08 1854
WINE, Jacob T.	THOMAS, Frances E.	MAY 13 1858
WINE, William T.	COCKRELL, Patsey	NOV 03 1835
WINEBERBER, Cyrus	SNEED, Sarah	JUL 10 1841
WINEBERG, Elizabeth	SMITH, Christian	DEC 04 1856
WINEBERGER, Adeline	WILLIAMS, William	JUL 05 1827
WINEBERGER, Jane E.	HAWKINS, R. Laidler	OCT 13 1851
WINEBURGER, Ann Susanna	MYERS, John	JUN 15 1826
WINEKLER, Benjamin	BALL, Sarah	NOV 26 1835
WINES, E.C.	STANSBURY, Emma	JUN 14 1832
WINFIELD, Richard	CARTER, Elizabeth	SEP 16 1854
WINFIELD, Richard S.	JENKINS, Ann Margaret	APR 15 1841
WINFIELD, Susan	BROWN, Charles E.	APR 04 1848
WINGARD, Jacob B.	ANDERSON, Jane I.	APR 06 1835
WINGARD, Marcaline A.	CAMPBELL, George W.	MAR 24 1835
WINGARD, Mary Eliza	GRESHAM, Sterling H.R.	JAN 09 1821
WINGATE, Edward	MILLIS, Mary Jane	NOV 21 1853
WINGATE, Henry	JONES, Sarah Elizth.	AUG 25 1853
WINGENROTH, Frederick F.	BECKER, Johanna S.	NOV 20 1849
WINGENROTH, Susanna J.	GREEN, Wm. L.	MAY 09 1855
WINGERD, Anna S.	GIBSON, Isaac	FEB 24 1853
WINGERD, Catherine E.	GRESHAM, Sterling H.	DEC 03 1834
WINGERD, John P.	FERGUSON, Ann	OCT 24 1818
WINGERD, Mary E.	TURNER, Samuel	MAR 17 1858
WINGETT, Mary Ann	BURNETT, Henry	DEC 11 1821

District of Columbia Marriage Licenses, 1811-1858

WINGFIELD, Josephine	COAKLEY, John	SEP 26 1857
WINGLERIN, Mary Barbara	ALTDORFER, Philip Jacob	SEP 04 1852
WINKFIELD, Charles	HAMMOND, Sarah Ann (blk)	MAY 27 1852
WINKFIELD, Mary	CURLEY, Warner	SEP 14 1843
WINKLER, Benjamin	DAY, Julia Ann	FEB 23 1832
WINKLER, Eleanor	CATER, Benjamin	MAY 06 1819
WINKLER, Margt.	SANDSBARY, Thomas	DEC 26 1816
WINKLER, Mary	SCHULTZ, George	JUL 09 1853
WINKLER, Thomas	SMALLWOOD, Catharine	JAN 11 1835
WINKLER, William	COXON, Rutha	JUN 14 1831
WINKLEY, Harriett	WISSINGER, George	SEP 30 1845
WINN, James T.	BAUM, Elizabeth V.	MAR 10 1842
WINN, John C.M.	HOWELL, Catherine	JUL 15 1850
WINN, Mary Louisa	DUNLOP, Richard G.	MAY 22 1840
WINN, Nouraly A.	WHITE, George B.	JUL 08 1836
WINNE, Delia H.	SOUTHGATE, James, Jr.	AUG 03 1858
WINNE, James	TRAVERS, Mary	FEB 27 1838
WINNULL, Jane E.	JOHNSON, Hellen	APR 18 1829
WINSATT, Julia	HUGHES, Thomas	JUN 10 1834
WINSETT, Ann	TARR, Levi	DEC 08 1814
WINSETT, Clinton	CROWN, Mary Ann	JUL 31 1834
WINSHIP, Victoria Emogine	LEETCH, John	JUN 22 1858
WINSHIP, William	GODDARD, Margaret	OCT 09 1832
WINSOR, Josephine C.	LLOYD, Lester	APR 19 1852
WINSOR, Luke	PIERCE, Susan	SEP 15 1834
WINSOR, Mary	OWENS, Washington W.	MAY 02 1853
WINSTON, Louisa	DRINKARD, John Bragg	JUN 19 1855
WINTER, Catherine	SEMMES, Thomas	NOV 08 1837
WINTER, Emma	MENICKHEIM, John	OCT 21 1851
WINTER, Robert	MOXLEY, Josephine	AUG 18 1858
WINTER, Wilhelmina C.	BECK, Frederick	JUL 16 1855
WINTERS, Charles	BUTLER, Letty	OCT 21 1822
WINTERS, Francis B.	STONE, Lucy Alvira	MAY 03 1858
WINTERS, Henry	WOODLAND, Ann	DEC 24 1822
WINTERS, Margaret (blk)	CARROLL, Henry	AUG 24 1826
WINTERS, Mary	WATERS, Thomas R.	OCT 15 1816
WINTERS, Richard	DADE, Sarah Ann (blk)	JAN 18 1845
WINTERS, William	CLARKE, Alice	FEB 12 1813
WINTERS, William	ROBERTSON, Mary E. (blk)	NOV 05 1856
WINTERS, William H.	DOWNER, Martha A.	JUL 02 1840
WINTHROW, Lawrence M.	HILTON, Martha Jane	NOV 07 1844
WIPPERMANN, Frederic	WALKER, Rosa Lee	OCT 29 1856
WIPPLE, Joseph	GILL, Ann	JUN 25 1838
WIRSHING, Sarah Ann	HUTCHESON, Ambrose A.	APR 28 1854
WIRT, Hannah Sophia	BASHAW, Rawleigh	APR 01 1834
WIRT, John L.	DULEY, Margaret R.	JUL 06 1837
WIRT, Laura	RANDALL, Thomas	AUG 20 1827
WIRT, Lucy	LASKEY, Richard	SEP 21 1824
WISDOM, Mary H.	STIGER, Benjamin	JAN 11 1827
WISE, Arthur	CARTER, Letitia (blk)	JUN 23 1849
WISE, Bedy	JENKINS, Lucinda (blk)	MAY 29 1851
WISE, Charles S.	SYMINGTON, Elizabeth	JUN 15 1844
WISE, Elisha	BOSWELL, Elizabeth	OCT 13 1836
WISE, Eliza	SCOTT, Russia	MAY 09 1816
WISE, Eliza	PRITCHARD, Levin	NOV 02 1826
WISE, Elizabeth	LEWIS, William	JUL 25 1839
WISE, Elizth.	BAYLISS, William	MAY 13 1837
WISE, George D.	MAY, Laura	AUG 17 1843

District of Columbia Marriage Licenses, 1811-1858

WISE, Jane Elizth.	DUNTY, George W.	JAN 19 1854
WISE, John	BRADSHAW, Ann	SEP 16 1819
WISE, John	GALLAGHER, Bridget M.	MAY 17 1845
WISE, John	HANEY, Josephine (blk)	JAN 13 1848
WISE, John H.	CHA__, Elizabeth Jane	MAY 23 1845
WISE, Julia	KENAN, Michael	JUL 09 1858
WISE, Margaret E.	RIDGELY, Greenbury	JUN 26 1848
WISE, Maria (blk)	FLEETWOOD, Louis	DEC 26 1838
WISE, Martha E.	TRAVERSE, John C.	SEP 19 1857
WISE, Mary	LEE, James	OCT 03 1839
WISE, Mary	LAWRENCE, Richard	MAY 24 1847
WISE, Mary Ann	GARDNER, George	DEC 04 1827
WISE, Mary Ellen	TRAVERS, John Clinton	JUN 25 1856
WISE, Samuel	JACOBS, Jane Ann	MAR 10 1840
WISE, Sarah C.	MOORE, James F.	JAN 10 1857
WISE, Sophia	HULL, William B.	NOV 18 1856
WISE, Uriah	BOZELL, Jane	FEB 27 1850
WISE, William	GRIFFIN, Elizabeth	JUL 22 1826
WISE, William	MURPHY, Mary	MAY 27 1848
WISEBAKER, Albert	KLING, Mary Ann	SEP 28 1846
WISEMAN, Ann Elizabeth	COOK, John A.	MAR 14 1820
WISEMAN, John	COOKE, Mary	DEC 24 1817
WISHART, Ann S.	BROWNE, William H.	JUL 15 1842
WISHART, J. Wilson	GREEN, Annie	JAN 05 1852
WISHART, Letitia S.	BROWNE, William Henry	SEP 23 1837
WISSINGER, George	WINKLEY, Harriett	SEP 30 1845
WISTER, Isaac	DIXON, Prisey Ann	MAY 31 1845
WITHAFT, Louisa	TUNGEL, Ernst	JUN 19 1852
WITHERON, James M.	HILTON, Amanda A.	JAN 20 1857
WITHERS, Margaret A.	SHOBER, W.A.	SEP 05 1855
WITHERS, Picket	WIGGINTON, Emily	SEP 08 1821
WITHERS, Virginia	NELSON, Charles A.	DEC 17 1851
WITHERS, Virginia	NELSON, Charles E.	FEB 28 1852
WITHERS, Virginia	LATHAM, John E.	AUG 09 1853
WITHERSPOON, Alexander Somerville	KUHN, Louisa Adelaide	MAY 18 1847
WODDEY, John	REED, Filitia	DEC 03 1828
WOGAN, John	CALLIN, Monica	APR 27 1853
WOHLFART, Christina	UMHAN, Christian	JUL 10 1852
WOHLFERTH, George	BRIDGEMAN, Mary	OCT 14 1857
WOLCOTT, Liman B.	WHITE, Harriet Ann	MAY 30 1831
WOLF, Barbara	WENZEL, John	AUG 20 1844
WOLF, Caroline	COUFMAN, Nehm	JUN 09 1854
WOLF, Fremeoes Antonie	LERIARDI, Elizabeth	NOV 15 1817
WOLF, John	FISCHER, Elizabeth	DEC 10 1855
WOLF, Margaretta	RENTER, Henry	DEC 01 1849
WOLF, Richard	REARDON, Hannah	AUG 17 1857
WOLF, Sophia	FISHER, William	FEB 16 1858
WOLFE, Andrew	ZIMMERMAN, Amanda	DEC 28 1841
WOLFE, Ann L.	HYATT, Levi T.	JUL 02 1855
WOLFE, Elizabeth	SCHULTZ, John	MAR 06 1846
WOLFE, Margaret	KERRY, John	MAY 31 1851
WOLFE, Thomas	MURPHY, Ellen	JAN 13 1852
WOLFE, Wolfe	KAUFFMANN, Mary	MAR 17 1855
WOLFENDEN, George	KELLEY, Polly	APR 06 1835
WOLFENDEN, James T.	BROWN, Eliza E.	SEP 04 1846
WOLFF, William	SHETHER, Sophia	APR 10 1844
WOLFGRAN, Adolph	UNIACK, Julia	FEB 11 1852
WOLFORD, George W.	PAXTON, Sarah McD.	AUG 28 1840

District of Columbia Marriage Licenses, 1811-1858

WOLFORD, Sara	CHAPPEL, John E.	OCT 30 1849
WOLFORD, Susan E.	BERRY, Charles M.	APR 03 1852
WOLFROMM, Christina	SEILER, Francis W.	DEC 21 1849
WOLFURT, Hester Ann	WALTER, Herman	JUL 13 1857
WOLLIS, Maria	O'BRIEN, Wm.	AUG 04 1818
WOLSEY, Mary Jane	DEVITT, Edward	AUG 15 1850
WOLTZ, George	McKEWIN, Mary	MAR 10 1831
WOLTZ, Henry	HOUGH, Susan	MAR 22 1831
WOLTZ, Lydia	HOWE, Alexander F.	JUL 07 1829
WOLTZ, Mary Ann	JACKSON, Jackson	JUN 29 1837
WOLTZ, Mary C.	LIBER, Sebastian	APR 15 1840
WOLTZ, Susana	HILLARY, John B.	MAY 25 1833
WOLTZ, Tobias N.	GODY, Eliza Ann	APR 22 1837
WONDERLY, Jacob	KNIGHT, Harriott	FEB 08 1825
WOOD, Alfred	DULANY, Rachel Ann (blk)	MAY 06 1831
WOOD, Almira	POWELL, Robert J.	APR 13 1841
WOOD, Andrew	MEAD, Eliza	FEB 12 1814
WOOD, Andrew Jackson	BURRISS, Margaret Ann	AUG 05 1847
WOOD, Anne (blk)	BRISCOE, Henry	NOV 28 1833
WOOD, Benja. P.B.	CISSELL, Sarah C.	JUN 30 1855
WOOD, Benjamin C.	TALBOTT, Ann	MAY 30 1815
WOOD, Catharine Ann	PETTIT, John S.	JUL 02 1850
WOOD, Catherine Jane	HUTCHINS, Peter A.	OCT 22 1842
WOOD, Charles	ELLIS, Ariann	AUG 03 1829
WOOD, Charles F.	COMPTON, Sarah Catharine	OCT 30 1843
WOOD, Charles Temple	RADCLIFF, Sarah Amanda	OCT 25 1854
WOOD, Chas. A.	PARKER, Mary E.	JUN 18 1858
WOOD, Elexius A.	BLOOMER, Mary A.	FEB 15 1855
WOOD, Elizabeth (blk)	GRAY, Jarred	OCT 20 1827
WOOD, Elizabeth (blk)	LANDSDELL, Asberry	DEC 16 1852
WOOD, Elizabeth (blk)	LYONS, Samuel	NOV 07 1853
WOOD, Elizabeth (blk)	LYONS, Samuel	NOV 08 1853
WOOD, Elizabeth W.	WHITACRE, Robert	MAY 02 1839
WOOD, Ellen	SOMMERS, John A.	OCT 09 1845
WOOD, Evelina	GREEN, John	JUL 02 1827
WOOD, Ferdinand F.	SEMMES, Mary Ann E.	JUN 23 1831
WOOD, Francis	MILLS, Ruth	MAR 19 1813
WOOD, Frederick	TURNER, Eliza K.	JUL 18 1820
WOOD, George E.	COLE, Sarah B.	OCT 12 1848
WOOD, George, Jr.	ELLS, Virginia M.	OCT 04 1854
WOOD, George K.	ALLEN, Louisa M.	MAY 19 1857
WOOD, George W.	PERKINS, Elizth. F.	AUG 25 1858
WOOD, Henry	BAILEY, Harriet	JAN 08 1853
WOOD, Henry R.	EVANS, Christianna	JAN 22 1846
WOOD, Henry S.	THOMPSON, Elizabeth	MAY 16 1855
WOOD, J.M.	VanKLEECK, Adeline V.	MAY 14 1832
WOOD, Jane (blk)	LEE, Philip	NOV 20 1851
WOOD, Jane Ann	JACOBS, Augustus	JUN 21 1836
WOOD, Jane F.	HALL, Joseph	JAN 31 1846
WOOD, John	SMALLWOOD, Mary	NOV 13 1823
WOOD, John	SCRIVENGER, Rebecca	JAN 13 1831
WOOD, John	FALES, Maria Louisa	JUN 02 1856
WOOD, John W.	DAY, Ann	MAR 17 1837
WOOD, Joseph	STEPHENSON, Barbara	MAY 03 1827
WOOD, Joseph	DONLAY, Mary	OCT 04 1832
WOOD, Joseph	BRANE, Jane	MAY 13 1833
WOOD, Joseph H.	STOCK, Mary Ann	JUL 14 1841
WOOD, Lucy	HUTCHINSON, John	FEB 03 1818

District of Columbia Marriage Licenses, 1811-1858

WOOD, Lydia Amanda	DUNN, Francia A.	MAY 16 1842
WOOD, Lydia Ann	CHAFEE, William E.	AUG 03 1850
WOOD, Margaret Ann	BROWNING, Peregrine Warfield	JAN 17 1833
WOOD, Maria	COLLINS, Geo.	DEC 23 1823
WOOD, Mariah	McLEOD, Daniel	AUG 07 1834
WOOD, Mary	DEAN, Hiram	MAY 28 1844
WOOD, Mary	SMALLWOOD, John	JUL 25 1848
WOOD, Mary Ann	LYNCH, Peter A.	SEP 07 1843
WOOD, Mary Ann	SCALA, Francis	MAR 20 1844
WOOD, Mary Ann	GETTINGS, James T.	FEB 26 1857
WOOD, Mary E.	CATON, George W.	JUL 24 1827
WOOD, Mary E.	MANKIN, John T.	JAN 18 1837
WOOD, Mary E.A.	MAGUIRE, James	MAR 05 1839
WOOD, Nancy	DOVER, George	MAR 28 1818
WOOD, Oscar F.	YARDLEY, Martha Jane	JUL 24 1848
WOOD, Owen	CURRY, Elizabeth	DEC 10 1825
WOOD, Pliny	DOVE, Elizabeth	JUN 17 1845
WOOD, Richard J.	EDELIN, Mary E.	DEC 23 1848
WOOD, Robert	RICHARDSON, Mary	MAR 07 1822
WOOD, Robert	BROWN, Martha Ann	DEC 24 1846
WOOD, Samuel M.	CLEMENTS, Caroline Virginia	MAY 19 1856
WOOD, Sarah A.	PETTIT, William R.	JAN 31 1853
WOOD, Sarah Ann	DEVERS, Alexander	MAY 05 1849
WOOD, Sarah Eliza	STANFORD, William S.H.	OCT 17 1833
WOOD, Sarah Elizabeth	GOODGER, Wm. Henry	JUL 25 1854
WOOD, Susan T.	MARSHALL, P.B.	FEB 02 1858
WOOD, Thomas	DIXON, Maria	JUN 23 1823
WOOD, Thomas	YOUNG, Rachael A. (blk)	MAR 25 1833
WOOD, Thomas	PEARL, Sarah (blk)	NOV 29 1842
WOOD, Thomas	FRAZIER, Caroline	APR 05 1848
WOOD, Thomas	ALLAN, Kesiah L.	JUL 23 1855
WOOD, Thomas W.	YEATMAN, Mary	JAN 31 1850
WOOD, William	POSEY, Minty	SEP 03 1816
WOOD, William	FOWLER, Ann	MAY 22 1823
WOOD, William W.	BARRETT, Mary A.	NOV 23 1857
WOOD, [blank]	SMITH, Ann (blk)	OCT 24 1833
WOODALL, Laura A.	STORY, John T.	JAN 03 1853
WOODFIELD, Mary	WILLIAMS, Thomas	JUL 22 1815
WOODHULL, Maxwell	POOR, Ellen F.	DEC 12 1842
WOODLAND, Ann	WINTERS, Henry	DEC 24 1822
WOODLAND, Barbara	LANDON, George	NOV 22 1831
WOODLAND, Catharine (blk)	REDIN, David	JUL 05 1849
WOODLAND, Charles	MOORE, Eleanor	MAY 15 1812
WOODLAND, Eleanor	BUTLER, Henry	MAY 30 1817
WOODLAND, George	HENSON, Elizabeth (blk)	JUL 09 1857
WOODLAND, Joseph	BOTLER, Margaret (blk)	NOV 10 1840
WOODLEY, Jane (blk)	BROOKES, Theodore	JAN 03 1839
WOODPID, Jane C.	EVANS, James	OCT 23 1856
WOODRUFF, A.D.	DAVIDSON, Anna	JUL 03 1845
WOODRUFF, Hezekiah	TALBURT, Jane	MAY 26 1836
WOODS, Charles P.	DILLEN, Mary Ann	OCT 11 1849
WOODS, James S.	CLAGETT, Mary F.	DEC 08 1852
WOODS, John	HODGE, Margaret	MAY 18 1820
WOODS, John	McKENNEY, Elizabeth	APR 27 1852
WOODS, John	SCHAEFER, Ann	JUL 08 1852
WOODS, Joseph	MEGAN, Mary	MAY 17 1834
WOODS, Mary	LANHAM, John B.	JUL 01 1830
WOODS, Mary	CONNER, Michael	MAY 31 1839

District of Columbia Marriage Licenses, 1811-1858

WOODS, Mary	McCAULEY, Andrew J.	AUG 31 1857
WOODS, Mary Ann	HOGG, James	OCT 23 1829
WOODS, Michael	MATTHEWS, Catherine	DEC 02 1854
WOODS, Sarah	BYRNS, Michael	DEC 17 1845
WOODSIDE, Ann A.	BARCLAY, John D.	NOV 08 1814
WOODSIDE, James D. [Capt.]	PRESTON, Julia Ann	JUL 10 1819
WOODSIDE, Maria	COZENS, Lewis A.	MAR 04 1817
WOODSON, Eliza Ann	HADEN, John N.	JUN 03 1820
WOODWARD, Amon	MARTIN, Sarah	DEC 23 1817
WOODWARD, Amon	LOWE, Barbara	MAR 20 1845
WOODWARD, Catharine	KING, John	MAY 29 1824
WOODWARD, Charles	ROBERTS, Sarah	JUN 03 1828
WOODWARD, Charles J.	GASKINS, Priscilla S.	APR 29 1852
WOODWARD, Clement	ROBINSON, Eliza	MAR 29 1825
WOODWARD, Clement	SEXSMITH, Martha	NOV 22 1827
WOODWARD, Clement	WOOLLS, Sarah P.	SEP 25 1832
WOODWARD, Daniel T.	HORTON, Catharine M.	OCT 05 1850
WOODWARD, Elizabeth	GOTTHEIL, Louis	JAN 01 1840
WOODWARD, Esther	McGRAW, James	JAN 24 1844
WOODWARD, George T.	POLKINHORN, Rebecca	APR 24 1856
WOODWARD, James M.	BATES, Mary Elizabeth	AUG 24 1854
WOODWARD, John	MADELLA, Louisa (blk)	DEC 26 1844
WOODWARD, John W.	LOWE, Eliza H.S.	JAN 10 1856
WOODWARD, Julia	MILLER, Aaron W.	MAY 03 1841
WOODWARD, Laura E.	WILLIAMS, John E.	AUG 26 1847
WOODWARD, Lizzie A.	CLARK, Shelby	JUN 20 1855
WOODWARD, Maria	QUEEN, Joseph	FEB 09 1839
WOODWARD, Martha E.	WHALIN, Joseph H.	NOV 19 1851
WOODWARD, Mary	BALL, Stephen	JUL 26 1815
WOODWARD, Mary	COMBES, George	OCT 28 1824
WOODWARD, Mary (blk)	BARTON, James	MAY 13 1848
WOODWARD, Mary Ann	LINKINS, William	APR 30 1845
WOODWARD, Mary Ann (blk)	IGLAND, Henry	FEB 17 1854
WOODWARD, Mary S.	SWEENY, Henry S.	MAR 28 1832
WOODWARD, Nancy	BANGS, William H.	APR 09 1833
WOODWARD, Richard L.	McLEAR, Mary R.	JAN 07 1852
WOODWARD, Sarah Ann	McINTOSH, Thomas	AUG 06 1838
WOODWARD, Sarah Jane	McPHERSON, Robert L.	DEC 10 1836
WOODWARD, Sarah Roszel	ISRAEL, George W.	FEB 28 1843
WOODWARD, Sophia (blk)	HILL, Edward	AUG 30 1856
WOODWARD, Susannah	COLLINS, Joseph	APR 18 1846
WOODWARD, Thomas E.	GRAHAM, Margaret	DEC 30 1856
WOODWARD, Virginia C.	CORNELIUS, Samuel	DEC 24 1851
WOODWARD, William	BRADLEY, Susan	MAY 22 1833
WOODWARD, William R.	LAVENDER, Adelaide	DEC 18 1850
WOODWARD, William R.	REDIN, Mary A.	APR 08 1852
WOODWORTH, H.E.	BURCHARD, J.	MAR 18 1830
WOODY, James P.H.	MATLOCK, Eleanor	MAR 25 1848
WOODYARD, Elizabeth	WILT, William H.	DEC 24 1835
WOODYARD, George	ATHEY, Elizabeth	SEP 03 1836
WOODYARD, Moses	DAVIS, Sarah	JUL 14 1829
WOODYEAR, Elizabeth R.	LARNED, James	JUN 17 1839
WOODYET, Kitty (blk)	HARRIS, Henry	SEP 29 1842
WOOG, Amelia	SELDNER, Pinchas	SEP 07 1854
WOOLARD, Julia	DENNISON, Thomas	DEC 23 1854
WOOLFENDEN, Mary	McELLGETT, James T.	MAY 31 1837
WOOLFET, James	HIET, Christiana	JAN 12 1822
WOOLFOLK, Clara W.	HACKETT, Samuel P.	NOV 15 1845

District of Columbia Marriage Licenses, 1811-1858

WOOLHOUSE, Eliza	WALES, John	FEB 02 1829
WOOLHOUSE, Harriet	MILES, Nicholas	OCT 23 1837
WOOLLARD, Samuel	SWEENY, Julia	SEP 10 1844
WOOLLS, Sarah P.	WOODWARD, Clement	SEP 25 1832
WOOLLS, William	MAGUIRE, Rosanna	AUG 19 1840
WOOLS, Edward	ESSEX, Mary C.	DEC 14 1843
WOOTTEN, Ann	SHERMINTINE, John	SEP 09 1826
WOOTTEN, Martha W.	KILGOUR, Mortimer	MAY 05 1847
WOOTTEN, Mary	WEBSTER, William	SEP 20 1834
WOOTTON, Mary	PRITCHARD, Arthur	JUN 28 1823
WORCESTER, Samuel	SCOTT, Elizabeth A.	OCT 09 1855
WORCESTER, Sarah B.	BOUCK, Nicholas	MAY 20 1839
WORDEN, Ananias	NILES, Jeanie Ogden	JUN 09 1855
WORK, Mary One-days	SPLANN, David	AUG 26 1834
WORMLEY, Andrew	SMITH, Mary Jane (blk)	JUL 11 1848
WORMLEY, Elexina (blk)	JOHNSON, Thomas	APR 06 1848
WORMLEY, Elizabeth	BROWN, John	JAN 05 1831
WORMLEY, Harriet (blk)	JOHNSON, James	JUN 10 1830
WORMLEY, James	THOMPSON, Anna E. (blk)	JAN 30 1841
WORMLEY, John	WARFIELD, Flavilla (blk)	JAN 04 1833
WORMLEY, Lucy (blk)	JACKSON, William	MAY 20 1839
WORMLEY, Ralph	DOVE, Dorcas (blk)	JUN 09 1829
WORMLY, William	KING, Louisa	JUL 19 1821
WORRELL, Nancy	NALLY, George	SEP 21 1837
WORRELL, William	FRANZONIA, Ermenia	FEB 19 1846
WORSTER, Giles	USHER, Mary	MAR 01 1847
WORSTER, Julia A.	UNDERWOOD, Isaac N.	JUN 19 1856
WORSTER, Luther F.	MARTIN, Harriet C.	AUG 24 1851
WORTH, Camilla	SAWYER, Lemuel	DEC 23 1820
WORTH, Wm.	DRAPER, Mary Ann	SEP 20 1836
WORTHINGTON, Catharine L.	DAVIS, William W.	FEB 17 1842
WORTHINGTON, Eliza	NELSON, John L.	APR 11 1849
WORTHINGTON, Eliza Ann	GASTON, William [Hon.]	SEP 03 1816
WORTHINGTON, Francis A.	LOMAX, Jane T.	FEB 07 1843
WORTHINGTON, Juliet A.	QUACKENBUSH, Nicholas	AUG 31 1846
WORTHINGTON, Nathan E.	KNOTT, Virginia Corrinna	JAN 03 1852
WORTHINGTON, Ruth Ann	ELLIS, John W.	JAN 03 1852
WORTHINGTON, Susan	COX, Henry N.	APR 30 1845
WORTHINGTON, William	MANLEY, Mary Ann	DEC 10 1841
WORTHMILLER, John	AUSTIN, Anna	JUL 31 1855
WÖVERS, George	JONES, Sarah	JUL 19 1858
WRAX, Benjamin	RICHARDSON, Matilda (blk)	JUN 16 1845
WREN, Achilles A.	POARTCH, Mary Ann	OCT 29 1838
WREN, Albert	LEWIS, Elizabeth	NOV 02 1857
WREN, Charles B.	LINDSAY, Catherine	NOV 28 1839
WREN, John R.	CHILDS, Mary Y.	SEP 01 1827
WREN, Julia Ann	WREN, Thomas	DEC 05 1833
WREN, Michael	SULLIVAN, Mary	FEB 08 1853
WREN, Thomas	WREN, Julia Ann	DEC 05 1833
WRENN, Bridget	WELSH, Edmund	MAY 18 1858
WRENN, Lysander	HORSEMAN, Ann M.	MAR 18 1856
WRIGHT, Addison	CHANEY, Sarah	DEC 28 1812
WRIGHT, Adelaide	HICKERSON, William M.	JUN 14 1844
WRIGHT, Ann	HERBERT, Alfred	DEC 06 1821
WRIGHT, Ann Eliza	GOODWIN, Wm. R.	DEC 11 1855
WRIGHT, Annie	ADAMS, Thomas J.	NOV 30 1854
WRIGHT, Benjamin	BROWNING, Harriet	JUL 03 1858
WRIGHT, Benjamin C.	KLOPFER, Martha S.	AUG 03 1848

District of Columbia Marriage Licenses, 1811-1858

WRIGHT, Catharine	MAY, George W.	DEC 23 1830
WRIGHT, Catharine	McCAULEY, Robert	MAR 04 1856
WRIGHT, Catherine B.	FITCH, Chauncey W., Rev., Michigan	SEP 08 1842
WRIGHT, Charles	MANLY, Sarah E.	NOV 03 1820
WRIGHT, Charles B.	MACE, Margaret	DEC 13 1832
WRIGHT, Charles H.	LEE, Julia Ann (blk)	MAY 13 1857
WRIGHT, Charles J.	SYMINGTON, Elizabeth Ann	MAR 11 1845
WRIGHT, Elizabeth	MEEK, Joseph H.	AUG 31 1817
WRIGHT, Elizabeth	KOTT, Nathaniel	MAY 14 1836
WRIGHT, Elizabeth	BADEN, John H.	AUG 26 1857
WRIGHT, Emily	HOMANS, Benjamin	JAN 14 1824
WRIGHT, Emily	WATKINS, Eliada	MAR 14 1853
WRIGHT, Emma Elizabeth	STINCHCOMB, John Henry	MAY 25 1854
WRIGHT, F.B.	HILL, Maria	MAY 29 1833
WRIGHT, George	CUNNINGHAM, Sarah Ann	MAY 29 1843
WRIGHT, George H.	PHILLIPS, Jane Eliza	JUN 24 1844
WRIGHT, Henry S.	WRIGHT, Margaret	SEP 26 1850
WRIGHT, Hester	MURRAY, Patrick	DEC 08 1827
WRIGHT, James	SELBEY, Nancy	JAN 17 1822
WRIGHT, James	FAIR, Elizabeth	SEP 27 1827
WRIGHT, James	McCORMICK, Elizth.	OCT 01 1829
WRIGHT, James Henry	SHORTER, Louisa (blk)	NOV 29 1841
WRIGHT, Jane E.	SIMMS, Noble T.	MAY 24 1856
WRIGHT, Jane E.	HOWARD, Albert F.	DEC 20 1856
WRIGHT, Jane Eliza	THOMPSON, Andrew J.	AUG 17 1850
WRIGHT, Jane Eliza	BROWERS, John	FEB 11 1854
WRIGHT, Jane Thompson	KURTZ, John Daniel	APR 11 1843
WRIGHT, John	FOUNTAINE, Louisa	DEC 09 1850
WRIGHT, John R.	GOODELL, Hannah M.	SEP 14 1853
WRIGHT, John Thomas	YOUNG, Sarah	SEP 15 1834
WRIGHT, Jonathan M.	JONES, Margaret B.	SEP 26 1823
WRIGHT, Joseph H.	WRIGHTENHOUSE, Henrietta	JAN 05 1854
WRIGHT, Joseph S.	BRYANT, Deborah F.	SEP 30 1857
WRIGHT, Julia V.	RAGAN, Daniel	JUN 25 1858
WRIGHT, Lucy J.	SUTTON, Felix K.	JUL 25 1855
WRIGHT, Margaret	WRIGHT, Henry S.	SEP 26 1850
WRIGHT, Margaret	McELEGETT, James T.	OCT 03 1850
WRIGHT, Martha A.	TAYLOR, James H.C.	AUG 12 1852
WRIGHT, MArtha Ann (blk)	GRAY, John	MAY 11 1847
WRIGHT, Mary	YOUNG, David	OCT 22 1814
WRIGHT, Mary	FITCH, Chauncey W. [Rev.]	JUN 09 1829
WRIGHT, Mary A.	DAVIS, George S.	AUG 15 1834
WRIGHT, Mary A.	BROWN, James A.	JAN 19 1854
WRIGHT, Mary A.	GREGG, Myron E.	JUL 17 1858
WRIGHT, Mary Ann Elizabeth [Mrs.]	WILSON, George Washington	DEC 20 1827
WRIGHT, Mary F.	ELVIN, John	MAY 27 1829
WRIGHT, Mary Jane (blk)	FREEMAN, Benjamin C.	OCT 31 1849
WRIGHT, Mary Octavia	ROBINSON, Benjamin J.F.	SEP 17 1856
WRIGHT, Mary R.	O'ROURKE, Luke	JUL 17 1854
WRIGHT, Michael	WELSH, Annora	OCT 31 1853
WRIGHT, Robt. [Hon.]	ROBERTSON, Elizth. H.	MAR 18 1822
WRIGHT, Samuel N.	HAINES, Anna M.	JUN 20 1850
WRIGHT, Sarah	NOURSE, Joseph	DEC 21 1841
WRIGHT, Sinah	McINTOSH, John	JAN 05 1826
WRIGHT, Susan M.	O'CONNELL, Daniel	FEB 13 1849
WRIGHT, Susanna	MAYFIELD, Benj.	FEB 23 1823
WRIGHT, Thomas	GOODWIN, Mary	JUL 20 1826
WRIGHT, William	BURCH, Elizabeth	JUN 26 1822

District of Columbia Marriage Licenses, 1811-1858

WRIGHT, William R.	HAMMOND, Caroline	SEP 26 1857
WRIGHT, Wm. C.	TERVIS, Juliet N.	APR 08 1845
WRIGHTENHOUSE, Henrietta	WRIGHT, Joseph H.	JAN 05 1854
WROE, Charles	SYMINGTON, Mary Ann	JUN 06 1843
WROE, Everett	DUVALL, Margaret E.	FEB 27 1851
WROE, Georgiana	WILLIAMS, John W.	JAN 22 1839
WROE, Jane	BALLENGER, Peyton	OCT 24 1833
WROE, Jerome R.	SMITH, Jane	DEC 27 1838
WROE, John	DAVIS, Lucy Ann	NOV 13 1844
WROE, Julia Ann	HUGGENS, Francis B.	MAY 09 1853
WROE, Margaret	ROBBINS, Thomas	MAY 15 1832
WROE, Mary Ann	DUNKLEY, Joseph	MAR 02 1835
WROE, Saml. C.	DODSON, Vanduden	APR 11 1844
WROE, Samuel C.	FOWLER, Emily A.D.	SEP 20 1852
WROE, William A.	DODSON, Margaret V.	OCT 21 1847
WROT, Sarah Ann	ROBINSON, Edward B.	JUL 17 1827
WUINE, Armstead L.	GRUBS, Mildard A.	FEB 11 1858
WURDEMAN, Herman	BALLAUFF, Mary	DEC 21 1852
WURTON, Ellen	WEAVER, David	JAN 30 1844
WYATT, Sarah A.	GUY, Samuel C.	DEC 11 1838
WYATT, Wm. B.	SCOTT, Isabel A.	AUG 22 1848
WYERS, Charles	ROLLINS, Sysan	OCT 20 1838
WYERS, Susan	DALTON, John	APR 08 1842
WYERS, Susan	DALTON, John	NOV 02 1843
WYMAN, Elizabeth	MORSE, Charles H.	APR 10 1858
WYMAN, Nancy	BROWN, Thomas	SEP 26 1854
WYMSICK, Mary	HILLEARY, Walter	SEP 26 1843
WYNN, James Henry	DAVIS, Caroline P.	APR 05 1855
WYVILL, Samuel W.	HARWOULD, Laura V.	MAR 23 1854
WYVILL, Walter D.	LEWIS, Amanda B.	MAY 12 1858

District of Columbia Marriage Licenses, 1811-1858

Y

YANCEY, Joel	TURNER, Isabella S.	OCT 01 1840
YARDELLA, Francisco	FRANZONI, Camilla	APR 07 1817
YARDLEY, Martha Jane	WOOD, Oscar F.	JUL 24 1848
YARNELL, Mordecai	HEPBURN, Ellen Johnston	OCT 15 1855
YATEMAN, Auther H.	SUTER, Sarah E.	MAY 29 1837
YATES, Alexander	BOLDER, Matilda	SEP 19 1825
YATES, Anna Catharine	BORREMANS, Louis	AUG 18 1831
YATES, Eleanor M.	FORREST, George P.	OCT 30 1832
YATES, Elizabeth (blk)	CLARK, Wesley	APR 22 1858
YATES, Francis	SMITH, Caroline (blk)	FEB 16 1848
YATES, John	CHAPMAN, Eleanor	JUL 04 1819
YATES, John L.	TOMKINS, Lucinda	JUL 25 1826
YATES, Mary	JONES, Thomas	JUN 10 1814
YATES, Mary E.	FARISH, Robert O.	JAN 12 1854
YATES, William	SMITH, Margaret	JUN 15 1857
YATES, William A.	ELLIS, Mary E.	JUL 09 1855
YATES, William Henry	FOOT, Mary Ann (col'd)	JAN 01 1857
YATES, Zachariah	NORRIS, Ann B.	NOV 20 1833
YEABOWER, Mary	HENTZELL, Casper	AUG 06 1858
YEAGER, Christian F.	DOUGHTY, Mary Ann	MAY 08 1839
YEAMAN, George	MATTOX, Frances	MAR 06 1819
YEAMAN, George	TANNER, Mary Ann	FEB 21 1823
YEARLEY, Alexander	YOUNG, Elizabeth	JAN 08 1857
YEATES, Bartholomew LaCount	SHEPHARD, Elizabeth	DEC 13 1820
YEATES, John	McWILLIAMS, Elizabeth	JUL 01 1846
YEATMAN, Henry	THOMPSON, Susan Amelia	MAY 14 1851
YEATMAN, Mary	MULLING, John	MAR 18 1847
YEATMAN, Mary	WOOD, Thomas W.	JAN 31 1850
YEATMAN, William O.	OSBOURN, Martha	APR 03 1827
YEATS, Mary E.	BERRY, Samuel	APR 04 1850
YEBOWER, John	WIGLEY, Ann	JUN 14 1836
YEOCUM, Louisa	CARR, George	JUL 17 1856
YERBY, Adonis L.	RADCLIFFE, Mary S.	APR 05 1851
YERBY, Albert F.	RADCLIFFE, Fannie A.	FEB 19 1849
YERBY, Charles J.	MADDOX, Charlotte Ann	JUN 02 1834
YERBY, Eugenia	YOUNG, Samuel C.	FEB 11 1852
YERBY, George W.	PHILLIPS, Mary Eliza	AUG 26 1851
YERBY, Lucretia V.	BEALL, George A.	MAY 07 1856
YERKEAS, Harman	CROSS, Elizabeth	NOV 11 1817
YEUBOWER, Margaret	KEEFER, John J.	APR 27 1857
YOAST, Benedict	BENSON, Elizabeth	OCT 09 1834
YOAST, Elizabeth A.R.	KELLY, William M.	SEP 23 1857
YOASTE, Ann Elizth.	BRITTNER, Daniel	DEC 09 1852
YOCUM, Madalena	KAUFFMAN, Conrad	MAR 30 1850
YOKUM, Josephine C.	CLICK, John H.	DEC 31 1849
YONGE, George	HUMPHREYS, Mary	AUG 29 1843
YONGE, Wm. P.	EASTON, Sarah A.	JUN 07 1820
YOOLL, Juliana	EAKEN, William D.	MAR 09 1814
YORK, John	DERRICK, Julia (blk)	MAY 22 1851
YOST, Eliza Ann	McCLOSKEY, William T.	NOV 25 1850
YOST, Elizabeth E.	JOHNSON, Lemuel	DEC 22 1854
YOST, Mary	MURPHY, Danl.	MAY 19 1832
YOUNG, Abner Humphrey	RANDOLPH, Mary Ann	OCT 02 1826
YOUNG, Adam	LITTLE, Elizabeth	JUN 09 1828
YOUNG, Alfred P.	YOUNG, Sarah E.	APR 18 1837
YOUNG, Amelia	HOLLYDAY, James E.	SEP 21 1837

District of Columbia Marriage Licenses, 1811-1858

YOUNG, Ann	BAILEY, John	NOV 14 1822
YOUNG, Ann	SMALLWOOD, Moses	FEB 03 1836
YOUNG, [Ann]	MAGRUDER, Fielder	APR 09 1835
YOUNG, Ann Maria	BUCKMINSTER, Jacob	SEP 18 1851
YOUNG, Ann Martha	WILLSON, Richard B.	OCT 03 1842
YOUNG, Annie	STRAUSZ, Alexander	FEB 16 1856
YOUNG, Annie Jane	HEETER, Uriah	APR 28 1855
YOUNG, Calloty	LONG, Conrad	DEC 27 1819
YOUNG, Camilla	SWEENY, Arthur W.	FEB 01 1854
YOUNG, Caroline	ADAMS, Hugh	DEC 13 1825
YOUNG, Caroline	PARKER, Thomas	MAY 17 1832
YOUNG, Catharine	ADAMS, John	DEC 21 1829
YOUNG, Catharine W.	LINN, Samuel D.	SEP 06 1852
YOUNG, Charles B.	LATHAM, Jane E.	OCT 13 1855
YOUNG, Charlot	BARRESFORD, John	MAY 30 1820
YOUNG, Charlot	BARRESFORD, John	MAY 03 1820
YOUNG, Clement	HUNTER, Marian	FEB 19 1852
YOUNG, David	WRIGHT, Mary	OCT 22 1814
YOUNG, Edmund	BEALL, Rachel A. (blk)	JUN 23 1831
YOUNG, Edward D.	WARRING, Henrietta M.S.	JAN 10 1826
YOUNG, Eleanor	BEAN, Richard	OCT 09 1817
YOUNG, Elender	LOFERS, Christopher	DEC 27 1819
YOUNG, Eliza	WAUGH, Samuel B.	APR 21 1852
YOUNG, Elizabeth	HUTCHINSON, Nathan	FEB 27 1812
YOUNG, Elizabeth	SUIT, Newman	MAY 19 1828
YOUNG, Elizabeth	CLAREY, Roger	SEP 12 1843
YOUNG, Elizabeth	YEARLEY, Alexander	JAN 08 1857
YOUNG, Elizabeth	BURGESS, Francis B.F.	MAY 31 1858
YOUNG, Elizabeth (blk)	PERRY, Thomas	FEB 22 1849
YOUNG, Elizabeth Margaret	TUCKER, William	JAN 07 1836
YOUNG, Elizabeth O.	WATTERMAN, Edwin	OCT 14 1854
YOUNG, Elizabeth W.	CLARKE, James B.	NOV 22 1844
YOUNG, Elizth.	JONES, Paul	MAY 07 1835
YOUNG, Ellen	JUDSON, Elnathan [Dr.]	MAY 22 1824
YOUNG, Esther	THUMLERT, William	DEC 30 1841
YOUNG, Euphemia J.	KELLEN, Robert	MAY 17 1851
YOUNG, Ezekiel, Jr.	LEWIS, Clara	JAN 10 1856
YOUNG, Forrester	EDMONSTON, Martha Ellen (blk)	APR 26 1841
YOUNG, Frances A.	FORKNER, Pleasent E.	MAR 14 1838
YOUNG, George A.	ANDERSON, Martha R.	MAR 19 1853
YOUNG, Hannah N. (blk)	KING, William	MAR 07 1850
YOUNG, Harriet	HUDELMANE, Charles	FEB 07 1839
YOUNG, Harriet (blk)	MAGRUDER, Rezin	JAN 15 1852
YOUNG, Harriot	HARSHMAN, Henry	FEB 03 1818
YOUNG, Harriot	HARSHMAN, Henry	FEB 03 1818
YOUNG, Hellen (blk)	WARD, John	AUG 10 1826
YOUNG, Henrietta E.	EWING, Hugh B.	JUL 31 1858
YOUNG, Henry	MAGRUDER, Mary Ann (blk)	MAY 15 1856
YOUNG, Henry N.	MINOR, Martha A. (blk)	NOV 30 1852
YOUNG, Henry S.	JOHNSON, Anna M.	MAY 05 1858
YOUNG, Ichabod	TYLER, Jane Eliza	SEP 02 1828
YOUNG, Ignatius Fenwick	LIVINGSTON, Nora C.	JAN 02 1851
YOUNG, Jacob	HOLT, Susanna	DEC 22 1851
YOUNG, James	SUMMERS, Martha Ann (blk)	AUG 30 1849
YOUNG, James H.	HUBBARD, Catharine (blk)	MAY 17 1850
YOUNG, James M.	SCOTT, Anna W.	DEC 06 1854
YOUNG, Janett Ann	WILLIAMS, George W.	JUN 29 1826
YOUNG, Jemima	PACKARD, Peres	FEB 02 1818

District of Columbia Marriage Licenses, 1811-1858

YOUNG, John	WALKER, Sarah	SEP 17 1816
YOUNG, John	BROKER, Margaret	JUN 16 1830
YOUNG, John	CRANSTON, Julia	JUN 22 1839
YOUNG, John	HAROLD, Catharine	APR 29 1842
YOUNG, John	WELLS, Sarah	OCT 05 1853
YOUNG, John G.	ROSE, Ann Elizabeth	APR 30 1833
YOUNG, John M.	MERRIT, Eliza	MAR 29 1832
YOUNG, John T.	EVANS, Virginia	JUN 26 1849
YOUNG, Joseph	MORRIS, Ann	JAN 04 1815
YOUNG, Joseph	HOWLE, Joanna F.	FEB 11 1851
YOUNG, Joshua	DICKEY, Julia Ann	JAN 20 1848
YOUNG, Julia Ann	MERLIN, David	JUN 16 1821
YOUNG, Kate	CLARKE, John W.	NOV 07 1853
YOUNG, Louisa Maria	HAYS, Lloyd	OCT 27 1841
YOUNG, Manduit	BEALL, Elizabeth T.	DEC 09 1813
YOUNG, Margaret [Mrs.]	MERRITT, Edward	NOV 17 1827
YOUNG, Margaret	KING, James C., Jr.	JAN 02 1844
YOUNG, Margaret	HEETER, Uriah	APR 29 1851
YOUNG, Margaret	GRANGER, James H.	SEP 28 1854
YOUNG, Margaret (blk)	BURNS, Robert	MAY 27 1852
YOUNG, Margaret E.	KIRKWOOD, Albert W.	JAN 08 1845
YOUNG, Maria E.	KIRKPATRICK, James A.	APR 08 1856
YOUNG, Marion	BEVANS, John	FEB 03 1834
YOUNG, Martha A.	FOOS, John A.	JUN 11 1855
YOUNG, Mary	TANEY, Augustus	SEP 09 1816
YOUNG, Mary	KELLY, Cyrus D.	OCT 13 1831
YOUNG, Mary	RILEY, Thomas W.	MAY 14 1846
YOUNG, Mary (blk)	PARKER, James	AUG 03 1847
YOUNG, Mary Ann	GREENWOOD, Wm. S.	MAY 22 1828
YOUNG, Mary Ellen	HEPBURN, Peter	AUG 09 1849
YOUNG, Mary F.	GUMAER, Elias D.	JAN 18 1844
YOUNG, Mary Jane	GARDNER, William F.	APR 30 1845
YOUNG, Mary L.	DANT, George W.	OCT 25 1856
YOUNG, Matilda J.	MATTHEWS, Robert A.	JUN 26 1852
YOUNG, McClintock	CAUSTEN, Josephine C.	NOV 09 1841
YOUNG, Noble [Dr.]	McWILLIAMS, Adelaide E.	MAY 04 1836
YOUNG, Owen	CLARKSTON, Harriet	JAN 30 1827
YOUNG, Rachael	BEEK, William	SEP 08 1831
YOUNG, Rachael A. (blk)	WOOD, Thomas	MAR 25 1833
YOUNG, Rebecca	BAILEY, John E.	OCT 17 1844
YOUNG, Richard J.	YOUNG, Sarah E.	SEP 28 1843
YOUNG, Richd.	HENSON, Matilda	MAR 18 1819
YOUNG, Robert	CLEMENTSON, Eleanor	NOV 07 1827
YOUNG, Roberta E.	BROWN, A.G.	JAN 09 1841
YOUNG, Saml. H.	McKELDEN, C. Jenny	APR 22 1856
YOUNG, Samuel C.	YERBY, Eugenia	FEB 11 1852
YOUNG, Sarah	CLAGETT, William D.	APR 20 1819
YOUNG, Sarah	RISTON, Fielder	MAY 15 1823
YOUNG, Sarah	WRIGHT, John Thomas	SEP 15 1834
YOUNG, Sarah	BRENT, John Carroll	NOV 11 1851
YOUNG, Sarah A. (blk)	GILBERT, Thomas	SEP 03 1857
YOUNG, Sarah E.	YOUNG, Alfred P.	APR 18 1837
YOUNG, Sarah E.	YOUNG, Richard J.	SEP 28 1843
YOUNG, Sarah Virginia Ann	VonSCHMIDT, August A.	FEB 02 1847
YOUNG, Susan B.	SHERIFF, Samuel	SEP 04 1836
YOUNG, Susan J.	HOLTZMAN, George H.	JUL 07 1842
YOUNG, Thomas	SIMPSON, Betsey	APR 26 1814
YOUNG, Thomas	McGUIRE, Rose	APR 03 1858

District of Columbia Marriage Licenses, 1811-1858

YOUNG, Thomas H.	SIMS, Sarah (blk)	OCT 28 1851
YOUNG, Thomas S.	BRIGHT, Amelia	FEB 15 1812
YOUNG, Virginia Anne	SHEPPARD, John M.	AUG 13 1846
YOUNG, Wilfred	BOARMAN, Elizabeth A.	FEB 02 1847
YOUNG, William	MUDD, Jane Elizabeth	DEC 16 1837
YOUNG, William	HURLEY, Mary	DEC 26 1839
YOUNG, William	CHASE, Chloe Ann (blk)	AUG 18 1840
YOUNG, William	LUPTON, Ann	AUG 23 1849
YOUNG, William	BUDE, Christina	FEB 21 1851
YOUNG, William	SMITH, Mary Ann (blk)	DEC 13 1853
YOUNG, William L.	DOVE, Ann E.	AUG 10 1840
YOUNG, William P.	[blank], Permelia A.	JUN 25 1847
YOUNG, William W.	COOK, Eliza	NOV 27 1844
YOUNG, William W.	WETHERILL, Martha	NOV 13 1852
YOUNG, Wm. H.	SAFFELL, Anna M.	MAY 13 1856
YOUNGER, Edward C.	ADAMS, Delilah (blk)	NOV 05 1844
YOUNGER, John	BRANDSELL, Mary	OCT 07 1839
YOUNGER, Richard	AMBUSH, Sally	AUG 24 1820
YOUNGER, Sarah (blk)	DUGINS, Wesley	NOV 28 1849
YOUNK, Elizabeth	BUTTCHER, Frederick	NOV 12 1853
YOWELL, Mandanna	POWELL, Jackson T.	MAY 14 1832

District of Columbia Marriage Licenses, 1811-1858

Z

ZANGE, Nicholaus	TAUBERSCHMIDT, Margaretha	OCT 01 1853
ZANTZINGER, William C.	FISCHER, Harriot Ann	JAN 16 1844
ZANTZINGER, William P.	HEYER, Louisa F.	OCT 07 1815
ZAPPONE, Americus	JOYCE, Margaret Ann	SEP 08 1853
ZEBOLD, Ann Maria	SUTER, James Z.	APR 19 1834
ZEBOULD, Robert	DUNNING, Ann	NOV 20 1830
ZEH, William	KABLEL, Polina	MAR 26 1857
ZEIGENHAIN, John	SHAAD, Catherine	APR 20 1843
ZEIGLER, Adam	ROSEMOIN, Elizabeth	SEP 18 1838
ZEIGLER, Christian	SHEETING, Cordelia	APR 19 1852
ZEIGLER, Christian	SMITH, Caroline	MAR 28 1855
ZEIGLER, Harriet V.	DEAN, Henry C.	JUL 02 1851
ZELL, Bernard A.	BYRNE, Julia M.	MAY 22 1849
ZELL, Enoch F.	KIRK, Mary H.	MAR 19 1850
ZELLER, Francisca	EBERT, Isidor	JAN 25 1857
ZENKER, Francis	FULTZ, Elnora	SEP 29 1855
ZENTEL, Maria	RENNER, Deitrich	JUN 22 1833
ZEPFEN, Elizabeth	RAMBLER, David	NOV 23 1842
ZERLAUT, Frederick Ernst	THOMAS, Eliza Jane	SEP 09 1839
ZEVELY, Alexr. N.	LARLIN, Susan Caroline	SEP 10 1839
ZIER, Charles	TRUMMINS, Mary	OCT 26 1853
ZIMMERMAN, Amanda	WOLFE, Andrew	DEC 28 1841
ZIMMERMAN, Eliza	ROBBINS, William	MAR 11 1829
ZIMMERMAN, Helena	BOUS, Frederick	NOV 13 1855
ZIMMERMAN, Henry F.	PECKWORTH, Margaret	MAY 11 1841
ZIMMERMAN, Henry F.	CALDWELL, Sarah V.	AUG 06 1844
ZIMMERMAN, Henry F.	CALDWELL, Sarah V.	AUG 06 1855
ZIMMERMAN, John H.	WINDSOR, A. Rina Elizabeth	SEP 17 1836
ZIMMERMAN, Maria L.	GARTRELL, William C.	SEP 10 1855
ZIMMERMAN, William	UBEL, Helena	FEB 10 1855
ZIMMERMANN, Anjelus	LOHS, Mary	OCT 09 1854

INCOMPLETE RECORDS

[blank]	BAKER, Zachariah	JUL 15 1817
[blank]	SUMBY, Mary (blk)	JUN 25 1850
[blank]	SHEAHAN, Bridget	AUG 07 1858
[blank], Casander	BUTLER, Jacob	JUN 01 1819
[blank], Charles	QUEGAN, Maria	JAN 01 1826
[blank], Eliza	HART, John	NOV 21 1818
[blank], Ellen	TOLSON, Alexr.	JUL 04 1816
[blank], Hester A.	STANFIELD, George	DEC 27 1830
[blank], Johanna	BLANEY, Dennis	FEB 08 1853
[blank], Mary	KELLY, Thomas	NOV 18 1852
[blank], Permelia A.	YOUNG, William P.	JUN 25 1847
[blank], Ruthy	HOPKINS, Cupid (negroes)	SEP 21 1824
[blank], Theodora	SCHULDIES, Nicholas	JUN 13 1854
[blank], William	DUNS__, Julia M.	JAN 14 1846
[torn out]	LITTLE, John	JUL 13 1813
[torn out]	CURTIN, William A.	JUN 03 1847
[torn out]	CLARKE, Robert C.	JUN 03 1847
[torn out]	LEWIS, Richard H.	DEC 07 1857
[torn out]UTHALL, Lucy Henry	CUTTS, Charles	JUL 07 1812
[torn out], Caroline	DAVIS, John	JUN 03 1847
[torn out], Mary	HALL, Walter	JUN 03 1847

Other Books by Wesley E. Pippenger:

Alexandria (Arlington) County, Virginia Death Records, 1853-1896

Alexandria City and Arlington County, Virginia Records Index: Vol. 1

Alexandria City and Arlington County, Virginia Records Index: Vol. 2

Alexandria County, Virginia Marriage Records, 1853-1895

Alexandria Virginia Marriage Index, January 10, 1893 to August 31, 1905

Alexandria, Virginia Marriages, 1870-1892

Alexandria, Virginia Town Lots, 1749-1801
Together with the Proceedings of the Board of Trustees, 1749-1780

Alexandria, Virginia Wills, Administrations and Guardianships, 1786-1800

Alexandria, Virginia 1808 Census (Wards 1, 2, 3, and 4)

Alexandria, Virginia Death Records, 1863-1896

Alexandria, Virginia Hustings Court Orders, Volume 1, 1780-1787

Connections and Separations: Divorce, Name Change and Other Genealogical Tidbits from the Acts of the Virginia General Assembly

Daily National Intelligencer *Index to Deaths, 1855-1870*

Daily National Intelligencer, *Washington, District of Columbia Marriages and Deaths Notices (January 1, 1851 to December 30, 1854)*

Dead People on the Move: Reconstruction of the Georgetown Presbyterian Burying Ground, Holmead's (Western) Burying Ground, and other Removals in the District of Columbia

Death Notices from Richmond, Virginia Newspapers, 1841-1853

District of Columbia Ancestors, A Guide to Records of the District of Columbia

District of Columbia Death Records: August 1, 1874-July 31, 1879

District of Columbia Foreign Deaths, 1888-1923

District of Columbia Guardianship Index, 1802-1928

District of Columbia Interments (Index to Deaths)
January 1, 1855 to July 31, 1874

District of Columbia Marriage Licenses, Register 1: 1811-1858

District of Columbia Marriage Licenses, Register 2: 1858-1870

District of Columbia Marriage Records Index, 1877-1885

District of Columbia Marriage Records Index
October 20, 1885 to January 20, 1892: Marriage Record Books 21 to 30

District of Columbia Probate Records, 1801-1852

District of Columbia: Original Land Owners, 1791-1800

Early Church Records of Alexandria City and Fairfax County, Virginia

Georgetown, District of Columbia 1850 Federal Population Census (Schedule I) and 1853 Directory of Residents of Georgetown

Georgetown, District of Columbia Marriage and Death Notices, 1801-1838

Husbands and Wives Associated with Early Alexandria, Virginia (and the Surrounding Area), 3rd Edition, Revised

Index to Virginia Estates, 1800-1865
Volumes 4, 5 and 6

John Alexander, a Northern Neck Proprietor, His Family, Friends and Kin

Legislative Petitions of Alexandria, 1778-1861

Pippenger and Pittenger Families

Proceedings of the Orphan's Court, Washington County, District of Columbia, 1801-1808

The Georgetown Courier *Marriage and Death Notices: Georgetown, District of Columbia, November 18, 1865 to May 6, 1876*

The Georgetown Directory for the Year 1830: to which is appended, a Short Description of the Churches, Public Institutions, and the Original Charter of Georgetown, and Extracts of the Laws Pertaining to the Chesapeake and Ohio Canal Company

The Virginia Gazette and Alexandria Advertiser:
Volume 1, September 3, 1789 to November 11, 1790

The Virginia Journal and Alexandria Advertiser:
Volume I (February 5, 1784 to January 27, 1785)

Volume II (February 3, 1785 to January 26, 1786)

Volume III (March 2, 1786 to January 25, 1787)

Volume IV (February 8, 1787 to May 21, 1789)

The Washington and Georgetown Directory of 1853

Tombstone Inscriptions of Alexandria, Volumes 1-4

www.ingramcontent.com/pod-product-compliance
Lightning Source LLC
Chambersburg PA
CBHW070904300426
44113CB00008B/929